"This is a bold project, some might say foolhardy, but Mark Dever has brilliantly succeeded. This is no mere textbook; it is powerful preaching. We are not only introduced to the sweep and message of each book of the Bible but, above all, confronted by our great God and called to obey his living word."
>   —VAUGHN ROBERTS
>   Rector, St. Ebbe's Church, Oxford, England, Author of *God's Big Picture*

"In these distinctive overview sermons, Mark Dever manages to bring together around the core issues of each biblical book three concerns that ought to occupy every faithful preacher of God's Word: theological content, exegetical wisdom, and pastoral application. Here is a walk through the Bible that is well worth taking!"
>   —TIMOTHY GEORGE
>   Dean, Beeson Divinity School
>   Executive Editor, *Christianity Today*

"Mark Dever has done the Christian community a great service in publishing these sermons. The material is academically informed but presented in a very accessible way with relevant application. With its Christological focus and careful Christian application of the Old Testament, this book enables readers to get into the theological heart of the message of each biblical book."
>   —DAVID PETERSON
>   Principal, Oak Hill College

"Mark Dever has written a needed book and written it well. With a pastor's heart, a scholar's mind, and the intimacy of a friend, Dever introduces the reader clearly and creatively to a book that has changed the world but to which contemporary culture remains largely unexposed. This book is warm, engaging, straightforward, and profound. It will be a valuable resource for individuals, study groups, churches, unbelievers and believers alike. Dever takes the reader on an unforgettable journey into the most remarkable and moving book ever written."
>   —JOHN SHOUSE
>   Professor of Christian Theology, Golden Gate Baptist Theological Seminary

"This is a good book, written by a pastor/scholar for people in the pew. Clear, concise, thoroughly readable. Buy two and give one to a friend."
>   —ALISTAIR BEGG
>   Senior Pastor, Parkside Church, Chagrin Falls, Ohio

"For many Christians the Old Testament is daunting and confusing. The books are long and speak about a culture dramatically different from ours. Mark Dever's sermons do not substitute for reading the Old Testament, but they do provide a wonderful help in understanding it. Dever unpacks the major themes of each book with remarkable clarity, and the book also shines in conveying the message of the Old Testament for today. Here is a survey to the Old Testament that is accessible and spiritually edifying."
>   —THOMAS R. SCHREINER
>   Professor of New Testament, Associate Dean of Scripture and Interpretation,
>   The Southern Baptist Theological Seminary

"The modern Church is biblically illiterate. Her members do not know the basic content of the Bible or the great themes that weave its beautiful tapestry together. This series of sermons by Mark Dever, a superb and faithful expositor, provides a helpful strategy in healing a major malady of the twenty-first-century church. I am delighted to commend this excellent volume to all who love the Word of God and the great truths contained therein."
>   —DANIEL L. AKIN
>   President, Southeastern Baptist Theological Seminary

"This book is a landmark in the history of Bible exposition—a homiletical *tour de force*. At the rate of one long sermon per book, Mark Dever has preached his way through the entire Bible. Reading this collection of his messages is an ideal way to get a sweeping overview of the Old Testament, or else to begin preparing to teach or preach any one of its individual books."
　　—PHILIP GRAHAM RYKEN
　　　　Senior Minister, Tenth Presbyterian Church, Philadelphia
　　　　Bible Teacher, "Every Last Word"

"In a day of worrisome biblical illiteracy, even among Christians, there is a pressing need for books that give the big picture and provide surefooted guides for negotiating the Bible's vast and subtle territory. To produce such a book is no easy task, yet that is what Dr. Dever has done. Forged in the furnace of weekly expository preaching and pastoral ministry, this book is a wonderful gift to the church that will, I am sure, be of great help in promoting deeper understanding of the message of the whole Bible, not just those parts with which readers are most familiar or comfortable. Buy two copies: one to keep, one to give to your pastor."
　　—CARL R. TRUEMAN
　　　　Professor of Historical Theology and Church History,
　　　　Westminster Theological Seminary

"Mark Dever does here what all pastors should do—preach the *whole Bible* patiently and thoroughly. These sermons will help readers see the Bible as a unity inspired by a God who is a unified and coherent person. They focus on God; therefore, they drive readers to worship and obedience."
　　—PAUL R. HOUSE
　　　　Associate Dean and Professor of Divinity, Beeson Divinity School

"I have long desired a book that would unlock the richness of the Old Testament—assisting both the pastor in the pulpit and Christians in their devotions. This is that book."
　　—C. J. MAHANEY
　　　　Sovereign Grace Ministries, Author of *The Cross Centered Life*

"To hear the Bible tell its own story in its own way—this is the obvious but all-too-rare strategy for reading the Book of books. I thank Dr. Mark Dever for showing us how. We are immeasurably enriched."
　　—RAY ORTLUND, JR.
　　　　Senior Pastor, Christ Presbyterian Church, Nashville

"Mark Dever's one-sermon whole-Bible-book overviews are a treasure trove for preachers, Bible teachers, and growing Christians. Dr. Dever has already given us a comprehensive overview of the New Testament, and here he covers the Old. Preachers will recognize these expositions as Greidanus and Goldsworthy applied. That is, Dever preaches the person and work of Christ, from all of Scripture, naturally and exegetically, in a way that does justice to redemptive history. Christians hungry for a spiritual feast in the Word will find here faithful, biblical, rich, meaty, challenging pastoral overviews of Scripture from the heart of a preacher who wants his people to know, love, and live the truth. Dever gives us a model for how to preach didactically, practically, apologetically and evangelistically all at once."
　　—J. LIGON DUNCAN III
　　　　Senior Minister, First Presbyterian Church, Jackson, Mississippi
　　　　President, Alliance of Confessing Evangelicals

THE MESSAGE OF
THE OLD TESTAMENT

THE MESSAGE OF THE OLD TESTAMENT

PROMISES MADE

MARK DEVER

FOREWORD BY
GRAEME GOLDSWORTHY

CROSSWAY BOOKS
WHEATON, ILLINOIS

Library of Congress Cataloging-in-Publication Data
Dever, Mark.
  The message of the Old Testament : promises made / Mark Dever ;
foreword by Graeme Goldsworthy.
    p. cm.
  Includes bibliographical references and index.
  ISBN 13: 978-1-58134-717-3 (HC : alk. paper)
  ISBN 10: 1-58134-717-0
  1. Bible. O.T.—Criticism, interpretation, etc. 2. Bible. O.T.—Sermons.
3. Baptists—Sermons. 4. Sermons, American—21st century. I. Title.
BS1171.3.D43   2006
221'.06—dc22   2005031730

Crossway is a publishing ministry of Good News Publishers.

SH		20	19	18	17	16	15	14	13	
17	16	15	14	13	12	11	10	9	8	7

To

Ligon Duncan,
C. J. Mahaney,
and R. Albert Mohler, Jr.,

*friends and colaborers,
together for the gospel*

CONTENTS

ANCIENT WISDOM

BIG HOPES

ETERNAL QUESTIONS

FOREWORD

THE UNDENIABLE EMPHASIS that Jesus placed upon the Old Testament Scriptures is that they testify to him. Of course they testify to all sorts of other things as well: godliness, faithfulness, the progress and regress of God's people, sinfulness, judgment, and so on. But Jesus, along with the apostles and the other authors of the New Testament, emphasized that the Old Testament, above all, is about him.

Why then is the first question we often ask about a passage in the Old Testament, "What does this tell us about ourselves?" Surely, the first and main question we should ask is, "How does this passage testify to Christ?"

We must always begin with the latter question because Jesus Christ, the fulfiller of the Old Testament, is the one who alone defines the life of the Christian. If the Old Testament does not point to Christ, it does not point to the Christian either. For a sermon to be authentically and Christianly people-centered it must first be Christ-centered. We can learn much from the lives and experiences of the men and women, both good and bad, who come before us in the pages of the Old Testament. But, in the final analysis, only Christ can define how those individuals are good or bad. Furthermore, our Christian growth comes from becoming more like Christ, not more like Abraham or David or Daniel. These heroes of the Old Testament are examples for us only insofar as they foreshadow and point to Christ.

In this book, Mark Dever has undertaken a difficult and important task. He has set out to crystallize the message of each Old Testament book, and he has endeavored to show something of the Christian value of each book. These sermons should not be regarded as models for routine preaching from the Old Testament, for rarely would the preacher try to cover a whole book in one sermon. But they do provide broad perspectives on the way the books point to Christ and are fulfilled by him. The preacher will need to extrapolate the principles of preaching Christ from the Old Testament and apply them to the textual units that are more appropriate for expository sermons.

There are three main ways that Dever traces the relationship of the Old

Testament to the message of our redemption in Christ. These three ways are not mutually exclusive but rather different perspectives on the unity of Scripture. At the heart of all of them is the principle that the Old Testament records many promises made by the Lord concerning the redemption of his people. These promises are not given their ultimate answer in the Old Testament, which concludes leaving us in suspense. It remains for the New Testament to record how the promises are fulfilled perfectly in and through the life, death, and resurrection of Jesus of Nazareth.

The first approach the author uses is to isolate the main themes in the specific book being preached. These themes are then picked up through direct references in the New Testament or through the same theological themes as they are found in Christ. That is, we start with the theological themes in the Old Testament and work forward to the explication of those themes by the gospel of Christ.

The second type of connection explored is one that follows the lead given by New Testament allusions to and quotations from the Old. One estimate is that there are about 1,600 such references in the New Testament. Every book of the New Testament, with the possible exception of 2 and 3 John, makes these overt connections, which are mostly theological and not merely analogical.

The third method is a broadly typological one. Typology is based on the fact that the God of Scripture has revealed himself and his saving purposes in a progressive way by stages. After all, why was the Old Testament the only Bible of Jesus and the apostles? And why did the Christian Church from the beginning recognize the Old Testament as Christian Scripture? It was because the people of the New Testament understood that what God said and did throughout the history of Israel prepared the way for the coming of the Messiah, who is Jesus Christ the Lord. This preparation was specifically achieved by foreshadowing the truth as it was to be fully revealed in Jesus.

When the Jews claimed to have the pedigree of Moses, Jesus responded: "If you believed Moses, you would believe me; for he wrote of me" (John 5:46, ESV). When they claimed Abraham as their father, Jesus' response was: "Your father Abraham rejoiced that he would see my day. He saw it and was glad" (John 8:56, ESV). Clearly the day of Christ somehow extends back into the Old Testament. The promises to Abraham are fulfilled in Christ. When the risen Jesus appeared to his demoralized disciples, he reminded them of the necessity for the suffering of the Christ. Then, "beginning with Moses and all the Prophets, he interpreted to them in all the Scriptures the things concerning himself" (Luke 24:27, ESV). Jesus' final words on the interpretation of the Scriptures of the Old Testament were: "Thus it is written, that the Christ should suffer and on the third day rise from the dead, and that repentance and forgiveness of sins should be proclaimed in his name to all nations, beginning from Jerusalem" (Luke 24:46-47, ESV). This can only mean that the Old Testament is about the gospel of Christ.

Many preachers neglect the Old Testament because—it has to be admitted—it is a lot harder to preach than the New Testament. Some who find it easier than I have suggested, do so, I believe, because they find it congenial to reduce the Old Testament to a source book for moralizing homilies. The role of the Old Testament characters is accepted as purely exemplary. Then there are the narrative preachers, who are satisfied with retelling the stories and leaving the hearers to draw their own conclusions. But the story of the Bible is one. It has great variety and diversity, but it is still one story. From a Christian point of view it begins with Christ the Creator (John 1:1-3), it climaxes with Christ the Savior, and is consummated with the return of Christ in glory. We can no more make sense of an Old Testament narrative isolated from the Christ who provides its meaning than we could make sense of one scene from a drama isolated from the climax and denouement. Mark Dever's book reminds us of the unity within the diversity of the many scenes of the one great divine drama of Scripture.

—Graeme Goldsworthy
Visiting lecturer in Hermeneutics
Moore Theological College
Sydney

ACKNOWLEDGMENTS

ONCE AGAIN, I AM indebted to many others who have aided and assisted, without whom you would not be reading this book.

A number of friends have been especially encouraging to me. C. J. Mahaney has been unfailing in this regard. On one occasion, I was preaching to a group of Sovereign Grace pastors and had finished one overview sermon when he told me to preach another—even though a Duke/Maryland basketball game was being broadcast!

The scholars who have taught me the Old Testament—either in person or through their books—are Gordon Hugenberger, Graeme Goldsworthy, Alec Motyer, Christopher Wright, Ray Ortlund, Jr., William Dumbrell, and Doug Stuart. And, of course, I cannot omit the grandfather of them all, Geerhardus Vos. God has used these men to shape my understanding of the great sweep of redemption history.

Editors are a race of people who, if they are converted, must have special virtues. Bill Deckard at Crossway has been kind and quick to respond to questions and to shepherd this manuscript through the publication process. Jonathan Leeman gave a year of his life to read and edit my overview sermons from the New and the Old Testaments. I can only begin to perceive the virtues that must have grown in him through working with me for a year in this task. Certainly what you now read has been clarified by Jonathan's careful and thoughtful questions, suggestions, and edits. He has given his time generously and has been a joy to work with.

Preaching is a wonderful and demanding calling. It is a joyful work that helps a preacher both to understand himself and to attempt to teach others in a way that will hold interest. Our congregation in Washington, D.C., has been blessed with many who love this work and are good at it. All of them have been an encouragement to me. Michael Lawrence particularly has been a colaborer in the gospel in our congregation, and he has more than once been an example, a questioner, and a corrector in helping me to think through and preach the Old Testament. He loves God's Word and has been gifted to understand

and communicate it well for God's glory. Conversations with him have sharpened and improved these sermons.

The preacher's family always stands in a special place of difficulty and of blessing. The difficulties come, in part, through the expectations of others and of themselves, as people who are redeemed sinners like other Christians. The blessings are sometimes less obvious. These sermons were prepared in the hope that those blessings will be realized in the life of each member of my family—Connie, Annie, and Nathan. I praise God for how much I can see that now, and look forward to even more of God's marvelous plan.

And now, reader, to the book at hand! May God help you to see even more of his marvelous plan throughout history and in your own life as you peruse these sermons.

—Mark Dever
Capitol Hill Baptist Church
Washington, D.C.
August 2005

INTRODUCTION:
FLY FIRST, WALK LATER

THE HIGHEST I HAVE ever been above the surface of the earth has been in an airplane. A commercial airline cruises at around 34,000 feet, which is about 5,000 feet higher than the tallest mountain on earth. Only military pilots, astronauts, and a few daredevils have been higher than I! Of course, countless people—millions?—have been just as high, sitting comfortably in pressurized cabins, munching away on peanuts or pretzels.

Every year more and more people travel to faraway destinations by flying. When we fly, we routinely get higher above sea level than anyone had ever been just one hundred years ago! For all of history, the record for how high a human ascended into the atmosphere would have rested with some adventurous, hardworking climber. Now, all we have to do is get to the airport an hour ahead of time, stand in a couple of lines, and then sit in a well-padded chair for several hours.

My favorite moment is takeoff. The airplane rolls along slowly. A pause comes, then it lurches into a higher gear. Seconds later you look out the window and see that you are racing faster than any car on the highway. Then the wheels lift off the ground, first the front, then the back. Before you know it, you're looking down at the tops of the buildings around the airport, the highways that feed into it, the layout of the city, the hills and rivers and coastline!

I've just looked away from the computer because I'm writing this introduction on a train, and we've just crossed a high bridge over a wide river. Looking out, I can see for a great distance. Such sights—from an airplane or a train—give you a whole new perspective on where you are. You can locate yourself, and better understand where you are going and how you are getting there.

In all of life, of course, we need to better understand where we are going, and this requires locating where we are in the first place.

The collection of sermons contained in this volume—first preached at

Capitol Hill Baptist Church in Washington, D.C.—tries to help us do just that by flying higher than sermons often go. Each sermon in this book presents an overview of an entire book of the Old Testament (I have also thrown in a sermon on the entire Old Testament and one on the whole Bible). I have hoped that these "Bible overviews" would help my congregation better learn both where we are and where we are going. I hope they will do the same for you. They certainly have for me.

I was already familiar with some of the Old Testament books when the week came to preach them—Genesis, Deuteronomy, the Psalms, Jonah, Malachi. But turning to other books felt more like my first trip into a new country! In both categories, however, I found far more than what I expected: a richness, a newness, a healthy strangeness, and, simultaneously, a familiar quality that let me know I was simply seeing more of the same God I have come to know and love through Jesus Christ.

I remember preaching through the Major Prophets in a series entitled "Big Hopes." As I worked through Isaiah one Sunday, Jeremiah the next, then Ezekiel, and finally Daniel, it seemed as if I were hearing the four movements of a great symphony. Isaiah begins the symphony with grand and brooding premonitions of destruction, the terrible love of atonement, and then the triumphant joy of eschatological hope. Jeremiah takes over the second movement with the horrifying siege of Jerusalem, minor in its key, yet not without sweet themes of a promised deliverance and justice. Then we turn our ears to Babylon, where we hear Ezekiel's variations on Jeremiah. His tune is familiar, but it is less particularized, more abstracted. It gives us new and riveting perspectives on God's love for his people and his people's rejection of him. Finally, Daniel, taking the great themes of the previous books, recasts them in several beautiful vignettes of individuals who trust and hope in God, who oppose and are opposed by God, and of some who experience his judgment and restoration. The themes carry forward into Daniel's visions of a mystifying and marvelous future, as the "music" of the Major Prophets fades out.

Understanding each book on its own is one thing. Seeing them next to one another—how each one complements, counterbalances, and expands on the others—brings a new luster to each and to the whole.

In this volume, we turn particularly to the Old Testament. For some Christians, the New Testament can feel like the densely populated states on America's East Coast. The New Testament books are generally smaller, more traveled, more familiar. The books of the Old Testament, on the other hand, can feel like the unknown and storied lands of the American West probably felt to nineteenth-century pioneers. The great open plains of Patriarchal history, the impenetrable Rockies of Levitical law, and the thick forests and deep canyons of prophets frighten off many would-be travelers. Everyone knows a favorite story or two brought back by the brave souls who have ventured into the unknown, but many Christians are content to spend their quiet times among the more well-known, seemingly habitable landscapes of the Gospels or the epistles. The books of the Old Testament are large. We don't know them very well. They require us to know all sorts of history we have either forgotten or never learned. And all those unpronounceable names! The whole idea of journeying into the Old Testament begins to sound overwhelming, time-consuming, unprofitable, maybe even dangerous.

For reasons like these, most of us have abandoned the Old Testament for the New. Let the scholars, the archaeologists, the prophecy-hounds, and the children's Sunday school teachers deal with it!

Yet, by abandoning these books, we abandon the revelation of God. More than that, we hinder our ability to understand the New Testament's revelation of Jesus Christ. If Christ is the key to human history, the Old Testament carefully describes the lock.

If Christ is the climax of the story, the Old Testament sets the stage and begins the plot. Do you read just the endings of books?

If the New Testament presents God's promises kept, the Old Testament tells us about God's promises made.

In other words, if you don't *get* what the Old Testament teaches, you'll never *get* Christ. Our God does not waste words. Each Testament needs the other. You will best be able to comprehend Christ's cross if you first understand the question left unanswered by the Old Testament. The cross is the answer. How well do you know the question?

In order to acquire a sense of the grandiosity of God's work, the majesty of his plan, the tenacity of his love, there is no replacement for the Old Testament. Deprive yourself of this part of God's revelation, and your God will seem smaller, less holy, and less loving than God really is.

Yet in view of the fears people have concerning the Old Testament, I have attempted in these overview sermons to display God's amazing work in the Old Testament not by walking step-by-step across the plains, over the mountains, and through the canyons but by flying at 34,000 feet. That way, we can all begin by seeing the great sweep of the whole continent. My hope is that you will be inspired to return later and explore the Old Testament's many trails more minutely.[1]

---

[1] If you want to know more about this kind of preaching, you may read the introduction to the companion volume for this book, *The Message of the New Testament: Promises Kept* (Wheaton, Ill.: Crossway, 2005). Or you may read the articles on preaching on the Internet at http://www.9marks.org/mark1. The original versions of these sermons are also available in audio format at www.capitolhillbaptist.org.

As I have mentioned in the introduction to the companion volume *The Message of the New Testament: Promises Kept,* we have included at the beginning of every chapter the date on which each sermon was first preached, in part because of occasional references to *then*-current events. Yet in recognition of the continuing relevance of God's Word, we are delighted to present these sermons for print.

These sermons go out with my prayer that God will magnify himself in the life of you, the reader, as you learn more of the ways he has chosen to reveal himself in his Word. If you do, then I will have been more than repaid for the comparatively small price of the effort that has gone into preparing them.

—Mark Dever
Capitol Hill Baptist Church
Washington, D.C.
August 2005

THE WHOLE BIBLE: WHAT DOES GOD WANT OF US?

THE BIG PICTURE

PROMISES MADE: THE MESSAGE OF THE OLD TESTAMENT
A Particular History
A Passion for Holiness
A Promise of Hope

PROMISES KEPT: THE MESSAGE OF THE NEW TESTAMENT
The Promised Redeemer: Christ
The Promised Relationship: A New Covenant People
The Promised Renewal: A New Creation

CONCLUSION

THE WHOLE BIBLE:
WHAT DOES GOD WANT OF US?

THE BIG PICTURE[1]

The Bible has been the subject of numerous and varying opinions.

Many people have not liked it. The great French philosopher Voltaire predicted the Bible would vanish within a hundred years. He said that more than two hundred years ago—in the eighteenth century. His kind of skepticism may have been rare when he lived, but it became more commonplace in the following century. One historian writes, "By the nineteenth century Westerners were already more certain that atoms exist than they were confident of any of the distinctive things the Bible speaks of."[2] By the twentieth century, great sections of the formerly "Christian" parts of the world had fallen into official skepticism about the Bible. A Dictionary of Foreign Words, published by the Soviet government about fifty years ago, defined the Bible as, "A collection of different legends, mutually contradictory and written at different times and full of historical errors, issued by churches as a 'holy' book."

At the same time, many people have had a very high opinion of the Bible. Ambrose, bishop of Milan in the fourth century, described the Bible beautifully when he said, "As in paradise, God walks in the Holy Scriptures seeking man." Immanuel Kant once stated, "A single line in the Bible has consoled me more than all the books I have ever read." Daniel Webster said of it, "I pity the man who cannot find in it a rich supply of thought and of rules for conduct." Abraham Lincoln called it, "the best gift God has given to man." He also claimed, "But for it we could not know right from wrong." Theodore Roosevelt said, "A thorough knowledge of the Bible is worth more than a college education." Certainly one of the most profound understandings of the Bible comes from the great Greek scholar A. T. Robertson, who attested, "Give a man an open Bible, an open mind, a conscience in good working order, and he will have a hard time to keep from being a Baptist."[3]

---

[1] This sermon was originally preached on January 9, 2000, at Capitol Hill Baptist Church in Washington, D.C.
[2] Huston Smith, "Postmodernism and the World's Religion," in Walter Truett Anderson, ed., The Truth About the Truth: De-Confusing and Re-Constructing the Postmodern World (New York: G. P. Putnam's Sons, 1995), 205.
[3] Everett Gill, A. T. Robertson: A Biography (New York: Macmillan, 1943), 181.

Some people believe they have great faith in the Bible, yet their sincerity is no guarantee of understanding. King Menelik II, the emperor of Ethiopia a hundred years ago, had great faith in the Bible. Whenever he felt sick, he ripped a few pages from the holy book and ate them! This was his regular practice, and it never did seem to harm him. He was recovering from a stroke in December 1913, when he began to feel particularly sick. He asked an aide to tear out the complete books of 1 and 2 Kings and feed them to him page by page. He died before he could eat both books.

Whether you like the Bible or not, it has certainly been popular. It is an all-time best-seller. Polls show that Americans generally say they believe the Bible.

Yet the book is probably more purchased than read. Most Americans may not have the gastronomic fervor of King Menelik, which is just fine; but they may also have less knowledge of the Bible than he did. Pollster George Gallup reports, "Americans revere the Bible, but they don't read it. And because they don't read it, they have become a nation of biblical illiterates. Four Americans in five believe the Bible is the literal or inspired Word of God, and yet only 4 in 10 could tell you that it was Jesus who gave the Sermon on the Mount and fewer than half can name the Four Gospels. . . . The cycle of biblical illiteracy seems likely to continue—today's teenagers know even less about the Bible than do adults. The celebration of Easter . . . is central to the faith, yet 3 teenagers in 10—20% of regular churchgoing teens—do not even know why Easter is celebrated. The decline in Bible reading is due in part to the widely held conviction that the Bible is inaccessible and less emphasis on religious training in the churches."[4]

It is exactly such ignorance we hope to help remove with this study. You or I may not be able to learn everything about Christianity in one fell swoop. In fact, I am certain we cannot. But I do hope to bring your attention to the overarching theme of the Bible as well as the basic message of Christianity, or what is called "the gospel."

Many people are surprised to hear that the Bible has any sort of overarching theme. It is well-known as a collection of books. As one Bible scholar put it,

No less than sixty-six separate books, one of which consists itself of one hundred and fifty separate compositions, immediately stare us in the face. These treatises come from the hands of at least thirty distinct writers, scattered over a period of some fifteen hundred years, and embrace specimens of nearly every

---

[4] Cited by Michael S. Horton, "Recovering the Plumb Line," in John H. Armstrong, ed., *The Coming Evangelical Crisis: Current Challenges to the Authority of Scripture and the Gospel* (Chicago: Moody, 1996), 259.

kind of writing known among men. Histories, codes of law, ethical maxims, philosophical treatises, discourses, dramas, songs, hymns, epics, biographies, letters both official and personal, vaticinations . . .

Their writers, too, were of like diverse kinds. The time of their labors stretches from the hoary past of Egypt to and beyond the bright splendor of Rome under Augustus. . . .

We may look, however, on a still greater wonder. Let us once penetrate beneath all this primal diversity and observe the internal character of the volume, and a most striking unity is found to pervade the whole. . . . The parts are so linked together that the absence of any one book would introduce confusion and disorder. The same doctrine is taught from beginning to end. . . . Each book, indeed, adds something in clearness, definition, or even increment, to what the others proclaim. . . . [5]

Clearly, the Bible is made up of many parts. Yet this book is one whole: "utter diversity in origin of these books, and yet utter nicety of combination of one with all."[6]

Have you heard of the *Above* series of large coffee-table photography books? There is *Above Washington* and *Above London* and *Above Europe* and many others. I enjoy the series because of the sweeping panoramas it provides. The plans of the original city planners, hidden when walking down the streets with building tops high overhead, suddenly become visible as the pictures let us rise up and look down on the whole. The aerial photographs provide a sense of perspective and interrelatedness, and we see what the planners envisioned in their minds and blueprints. Clearly, the sense of the whole is important for understanding and for planning. Some people suggest the ecology movement did not begin until the first pictures of the whole earth, taken from space, were published around 1970. Wasn't it on the cover of the old *Whole Earth Catalog*? Seeing a photograph of the earth, I think, jelled our understanding of the world as a whole and galvanized certain individuals to action. In the same way, we want in this sermon to pull up and get an "Above the Bible" or "Whole Bible" view all at once.

Or we might consider the concept of time-lapse photography. In time-lapse photography, the photographer positions the camera to take a shot of the same location multiple times over the course of a day. That allows him to see the changes that occur in one place over a long period of time in just a few moments of flipping through pictures. Reading through the Bible has the same effect. The Bible is of course much briefer than what it records. I know it would take you

---

[5] B. B. Warfield, "The Divine Origin of the Bible," in *Revelation and Inspiration,* vol. 1 of *The Works of Benjamin B. Warfield* (Grand Rapids, Mich.: Baker, 1981), 436, 437.
[6] Ibid., 437.

a long time to read it, but it would take you much less time to read it than it took to write it; and it took less time to write it than it took for the events to happen. So the text of Scripture itself is already like a time-lapsed series of photographs, and in the course of this study we will try to flip through an even more condensed series of pictures that present the message of the whole.

The story line we will follow, and the outline of this study, is the story of *promises made* and *promises kept*. God makes promises to his people in the Old Testament, and he keeps his promises in the New Testament. This message of promises made and promises kept is the most important message in all the world, including for you. Maybe you will "get it" in this study. Or maybe it will get you. As Martin Luther said, "The Bible is alive, it speaks to me; it has feet, it runs after me; it has hands, it lays hold on me." I pray that happens to you.

Before we continue, let me mention several good resources for helping you understand the Bible further. First, J. I. Packer's *God Has Spoken*[7] will help you understand why you should study and read the Bible as a Christian. Second, whether you are a Christian or a non-Christian, Chris Wright has written a great little book called *User's Guide to the Bible*[8] that will help you know what the Bible contains. It has pictures and timelines and bright colors, and it is so very thin! It is a wonderful resource. Finally, Graeme Goldsworthy's little *Gospel and Kingdom,* which comprises the first of three works in his *Goldsworthy Trilogy,*[9] is one of the best treatments of the story line of the whole Bible. In all of Scripture, Goldsworthy contends, God is bringing *his* people into *his* place under *his* rule.

PROMISES MADE: THE MESSAGE OF THE OLD TESTAMENT

Not everyone who reads the Bible regards it as one whole. Some ignore the Old Testament. Toward the close of the second century, the followers of a man named Marcion rejected the Old Testament, even though the Old Testament was the Bible of Jesus and the apostles. Marcion and his followers also cut everything out of the New Testament except Luke and ten of Paul's epistles. Though Christians quickly and universally rejected this radical surgery, the Old Testament too often suffers a similar fate in evangelical circles today. No one says what Marcion said, but the effect is the same: the Old Testament is ignored. We may mine it for good stories about Joseph, David, or Moses. Perhaps we look for good examples of bravery or devotion for our children to

[7] J. I. Packer, *God Has Spoken* (Downers Grove, Ill.: InterVarsity, 1979).
[8] Chris Wright, *User's Guide to the Bible* (Belleville, Mich.: Lion, 1984).
[9] Graeme Goldsworthy, *Gospel and Kingdom: A Christian Interpretation of the Old Testament* (Exeter, UK: Paternoster, 1981); *The Goldsworthy Trilogy* (Exeter, UK: Paternoster, 2000).

emulate. Maybe we sentimentalize a few of our favorite psalms and proverbs. But on the whole, we ignore it. Is it just laziness?

If you are a Christian, you surely know of God's wonderful revelation of himself in Christ as recorded in the New Testament. Yet if you ignore the Old Testament, you ignore the basis and foundation of the New. The context for understanding the person and work of Christ is the Old Testament. God's work of creation, humanity's rebellion against him, sin's consequence in death, God's election of a particular people, his revelation of sin through the law, the history of his people, his work among other peoples—I could go on and on—all these form the setting for Christ's coming. Christ came in history at a particular point in the story line. So the parables taught by Jesus often refer back to the story line begun in Genesis. His verbal battles with the Pharisees are rooted in differences over the meaning of the law. And the epistles build upon the Old Testament again and again. Understanding God's purpose in history, understanding the story line, requires us to begin at the beginning. If we can better understand the Old Testament, we will have gone a long way toward better understanding the New Testament and, therefore, better understanding Jesus Christ, Christianity, God, and ourselves. Within the Old Testament, we will first consider a *particular history*. Second, we will consider God's *passion for holiness*. Third, we will observe the Old Testament's *promise of hope*.

A Particular History

Our text begins, not surprisingly, on page 1 of your Bible: "In the beginning God created the heavens and the earth" (Gen. 1:1). That is where the story line of a particular history begins. The Bible is not only a book of wise religious counsel and theological propositions, though it has both. It is a story, a real story set in real history. It is a historical saga—an epic. And the story in the Old Testament is amazing!

In this very first verse, the story begins with the greatest event in world history. You have nothing, and then all of a sudden you have something.

But keep reading; there is more! You have inanimate creation, and then all of a sudden you have life.

You have creatures, and then you have man made in God's image.

You have the Garden of Eden, and then you have the Fall.

And all this occurs in the first three chapters of the Bible. Some people have called the third chapter of Genesis, where Adam and Eve sin in the Garden, the most important chapter for understanding the whole Bible. Cut out Genesis 3, and the rest of the Bible would be meaningless.

After Adam and Eve's sin, Cain kills his brother Abel. Humankind further degenerates for a number of generations. And God finally judges the world with a flood, saving just one righteous man—Noah—and his family. The generations following Noah fare no better. Humankind rebels at the Tower of Babel; this time God disperses everyone over the face of the earth. A new beginning is then promised as God shows his faithfulness to another particular person, Abraham, and his family. After a brief period of prosperity, Abraham's descendents, now called Israel, fall into slavery in Egypt. Then the Exodus occurs, in which Moses leads the people out of Egypt. God gives Israel the law. The people enter the Promised Land. They are ruled by a series of judges for a short time. A kingdom is established, with kings David and David's son Solomon representing the pinnacle. Solomon builds the temple, which houses the ark of the covenant and functions as the center of Israel's worship of Yahweh. Shortly after Solomon's death, the kingdom divides between Israel and Judah—the northern and southern kingdoms. Idolatry grows in Israel until the Assyrians destroy the northern kingdom. Judah then deteriorates until it is destroyed by Babylon. Survivors are carried off to exile in Babylon, where they remain for seventy years. A remnant then returns to Jerusalem and rebuilds the temple, yet Israel never regains the glory it knew under David and Solomon. And that is the whole history of the Old Testament!

If you turn to the table of contents in your Bible, you can see that this story line is not recounted in just one book but in thirty-nine smaller books. These books, which together make up the Old Testament, are quite different from one another. Genesis through Deuteronomy, the first five books, is called the Pentateuch or the five books of the Law. Following these five are twelve books called the histories—Joshua through Esther. Taken together, these seventeen books chronicle the narrative from Creation to the exiles' return, and they conclude about four hundred years before Christ. All seventeen books, one after the other, are fairly chronological.

The five books that follow the historical narrative books in your table of contents—Job, Psalms, Proverbs, Ecclesiastes, and Song of Songs—focus on some of the more personal experiences of the people of God. These books are largely collections taken from throughout this Old Testament period of wisdom literature, devotional poems, and ceremonial literature from the Temple.

Following Song of Songs, you will see in the table of contents a series of seventeen books, beginning with Isaiah and ending with Malachi, the last book of the Old Testament. These are the prophets. If the first seventeen books follow Israel's history, and the middle group describes individual experiences within that history, this last group provides God's own commentary on the history. The books of prophecy are, as it were, God's authoritative editorials.

So the Old Testament as a whole provides one very clear and concrete revelation of God to his people, given through a variety of authors and genres over a long stretch of time. And what a tremendous way God has chosen to reveal himself to us. If you have ever been in a position to hire someone, you know what it is like to get a one-page résumé that attempts to sum up an individual. And you know how unsatisfying a one-page summary is for knowing an individual and making an important decision. Meeting and interacting with someone in person is much more revealing. Well, in the Old Testament, God provides us far more than a flat résumé. He gives us an account of how he worked with his people over the ages. We see how he treated them. We see how they responded to him. We see what he is like. And that brings us to the second thing for us to notice about the Old Testament if we want to understand the message of the Bible.

A Passion for Holiness

The Old Testament presents us not only with the *particular history* of Israel; it introduces us to God's *passion for holiness.*

A lot of people associate the Old Testament with an angry God. They even think of this Old Testament God as unjust. But nothing could be further from the truth! When God becomes angry in the Old Testament, you can be sure it is not whimsical tyranny. He is committed to his own holy and glorious character, and he is committed to his covenant with his people. Sin, the culprit that stirs up God's anger, robs God of glory and breaks his covenant with his people.[10]

What is meant by this language of "covenant"? Christians refer to a "covenant" when they gather at the Lord's Supper and recall Jesus' words, "this cup is the new covenant in my blood" (Luke 22:20). Jesus' language of covenant is not cold or legal, as some might think; he takes it from the Old Testament language for relationship-making. A covenant is a relational commitment of trust, love, and care, and God makes a number of covenants with his people in the Old Testament—with Abraham, Moses, and others. God's passion for holiness becomes most evident when his people break the terms of their covenantal relationship with him, terms that are defined by the Mosaic Law and that accord with his own holy character. So we can define sin as law-breaking, but we also know that law-breaking means covenant-breaking, relationship-breaking, and—at the deepest level—"God's holiness–defying." So does the Old Testament present us with an angry God? Yes, but it is a God who is angry exactly because he is not indifferent to sin and the incredible pain and suffering it causes.

Like the New Testament, the Old Testament teaches that every man and

---

[10] Hab. 1:13; Isa. 59:2; Prov. 15:29; also Col. 1:21; Heb. 10:27.

woman is a sinner, and that no one can deal with this by himself or herself.[11] Sin requires some kind of reparation. But how can reparation occur? God is holy, and justice can be restored only, it would seem, when God justly condemns the person who has wickedly broken his law (the terms of his covenant with Moses). So the sinner must be condemned! Or—and here is our only hope—some type of atonement must be made.

What is atonement? Our English word "atonement," Anglo-Saxon in origin, is a great picture of what the word means—*at-one*-ment. An offering of atonement enables two warring parties to be *at one*, or reconciled. The people of Israel were not the only people in the ancient Near Eastern world who knew they needed atonement before God; the idea of placating a deity was common, yet only the Old Testament places the idea of atonement within the context of a genuine covenantal relationship between God and man.

Atonement in the Old Testament is unique in another way. As in many cultures, it is linked with sacrifice. But in the Bible, a sacrifice of atonement does not depend on human initiative, such as some pitiful attempt to propitiate a volcano god by dropping a beloved object into the fire. In the Old Testament, the living God speaks, and he tells his people how to approach him. He takes the initiative in providing the way of reconciliation.

Sacrifice is not the only image the Old Testament uses to describe atonement,[12] but it does play a central role from the beginning. Immediately after the Fall, Cain and Abel offer sacrifices (Gen. 4:3-4). Before leaving Egypt, the Israelites are commanded to slaughter a Passover Lamb without defect and paint its blood on the doors of their houses (Exodus 12). The lamb's blood causes the Spirit of God to *pass over* a house, sparing the life of a family's firstborn (who represents the whole family) from God's just punishment of sin. In all of this, God very clearly is the object of the sacrificial event. Sacrifices are done to satisfy him and his just requirements. So God says to Moses, "when *I* see the blood . . ." (Ex. 12:13).

The book of Leviticus played a large role in teaching the Israelite people that their relationship with God needed to be restored through a sacrifice. Every sacrifice was to be voluntary, costly, accompanied by a confession of sin, and according to God's prescriptions. The life of the animal victim, symbolized by its blood, was given in exchange for the life of the guilty human worshiper. What does some animal have to do with an individual's guilt? In one sense, nothing. In fact, the animal was supposed to be unblemished.[13] Yet

---

[11] 1 Kings 8:46; Ps. 14:3; Prov. 20:9; Eccles. 7:20; also Mark 10:18; Rom. 3:23.
[12] For instance, Isaiah uses the images of a hot coal that purges unclean lips (Isa. 6:6-7); Hosea describes the purchase of an offender (Hos. 3:2-3); Zechariah refers to the removing of filthy clothes (Zech. 3:4).
[13] E.g., Lev. 1:3, 10; 3:1, 6; 4:3, 23, 28.

atonement had to be made through blood.[14] God tells the people that "the life of a creature is in the blood, and I have given it to you to make atonement for yourselves on the altar; it is the blood that makes atonement for one's life" (Lev. 17:11). God used the sacrificial act to implant in his people's minds the image of an innocent life being given in exchange for guilty lives. The shed blood plainly revealed that sin causes death. Sin is costly. Salvation and forgiveness are costly. Now, I know the whole idea of sacrifices and all that blood is unpopular—to say the least!—among many people today. Still, this is how the Old Testament shows God's holiness and his wrath against sin. Unlike other ancient sacrifices, biblical sacrifices were not made by the grateful so much as by the guilty; they were not made by the ignorant so much as by the instructed.

The design of the Old Testament temple was also used to teach the people that their sin separated them from God. In the back of your Bible you might find a diagram of the temple, which shows that it was designed as a series of concentric squares and rectangles. The worshipers on the outside were separated from God in the innermost square, called the Most Holy Place. The temple's design physically demonstrated that sin hinders access to God. It was a visual picture of how sin separates humans from their Creator. Aside from the sacrifices that occurred throughout the year in the outer court, the high priest entered the Most Holy Place once a year to offer a sacrifice for all the people (Leviticus 16). This was the Day of Atonement.

Yet the mere fact that the sacrifices had to be repeated annually showed that the sacrifices, in and of themselves, were never the point.[15] Their repetition showed instead that the people were in a state of sin, and that no perfect and complete sacrifice could take away sin entirely. Sacrifices were most efficacious, ironically, when they were made with the understanding that they were *not* efficacious and that only God's grace saves. But notice the problem here. If the sacrifices were not finally effective for the removing of sin, how could God's grace justly save?

Here we come to the riddle of the Old Testament. In Exodus 34, God refers to himself by saying, "The LORD, the LORD, the compassionate and gracious God, slow to anger, abounding in love and faithfulness, maintaining love to thousands, and forgiving wickedness, rebellion and sin. Yet he does not leave the guilty unpunished" (34:6-7). Now how can that be? How can God "forgive wickedness, rebellion and sin" and yet "not leave the guilty unpunished"?

---

[14] E.g., Gen. 9:5; Lev. 1:4; 4:4; 14:51; 16:21.
[15] As you can tell if you read Jeremiah's denunciations of them in Jeremiah 7.

That brings us to the last thing we need to understand about the Old Testament and the God it reveals.

A Promise of Hope

The Old Testament does not portray God as an uncaring dispenser of grim condemnation. Yes, he is holy, just, and unwavering in his commitment to punish sin, as he is in the New Testament. But the God of the Old Testament is also a God of love, even toward his enemies. He is the "compassionate and gracious God, slow to anger, abounding in love and faithfulness" (Ex. 34:6). Love is not a uniquely Christian thing; it is a biblical thing.

The Old Testament enjoins love in many places. For instance, what Jesus will eventually call the greatest command is first given to Israel: "Love the LORD your God with all your heart and with all your soul and with all your strength" (Deut. 6:5). The second command that follows from the first comes from the Old Testament as well: "Love him [a foreigner living among you] as yourself" (Lev. 19:34). And the pattern for how Israel should love is how God himself loves: "He defends the cause of the fatherless and the widow, and loves the alien, giving him food and clothing. And you are to love those who are aliens, for you yourselves were aliens in Egypt" (Deut. 10:18-19). Since God loves his enemies, his people must do the same. Proverbs 24 commands, "Do not gloat when your enemy falls; when he stumbles, do not let your heart rejoice" (24:17). And Proverbs 25 teaches, "If your enemy is hungry, give him food to eat; if he is thirsty, give him water to drink" (25:21). The God of the Old Testament is a God of love.

When we consider the whole sweep of Old Testament history, and observe God's patience toward those who have declared themselves his enemies through disobedience, we see a God of unspeakable love and forbearance. He did not have to let human history continue after the Fall in the Garden. He did not have to persevere with the wayward nation of Israel. Yet we watch his grace, love, mercy, and patience on an epic scale—stretched out across the history of a people. It almost looks as if God planned to use history to reveal his glory to his people. And in fact, he did.

Understanding the Old Testament, as I said, requires understanding its promise of hope. What hope? We have talked plenty about God's commitment to holiness and the failure of his people to live up to the requirements of holiness. And we have considered God's promise to punish the wicked (in Exodus 34). So what hope could sinners have? Their hope was not in their history. The history of the Old Testament proved them (and us) to be moral and spiritual failures. Nor was their hope finally in the sacrificial system. As the psalmist said, "Sacrifice and offering you did not desire,"[16] at least not without something even more basic. How then could the hope held out in Exodus 34:6-7 be true? How could God "forgive wickedness" and still "not leave the guilty unpunished"? If the answer was not in the Old Testament people themselves or in their own history, it was in God and his promise, particularly in God's *promised person.* As we have seen, blood must be shed in order to assuage the righteous wrath of God against sin. Justice demands that sin be paid for either by the guilty party himself or herself *or* by an innocent substitute who bears the suffering and death on behalf of the guilty party. Furthermore, the punishment of a substitute requires some sort of relation between the guilty one and the one being offered as the sacrifice. But where would a perfect substitute be found?

Sources from the first century suggest that Messianic hope and expectation were prominent at the time of Jesus' birth. People did not wonder if the Messiah would come. They took it for granted that their only hope lay with a specially anointed one of God—the Messiah. Why? The Old Testament is filled with the promise of a coming person. God's people waited for the prophet God promised to Moses (Deut. 18:15-19). They waited for the king and, perhaps, the suffering servant (Isa. 9:6; 11:1-5; 53). They waited for the son of man coming on the clouds seen by Daniel (Dan. 7:13).

These promises point toward the answer to the Old Testament riddle. And these promises are the hope of the Old Testament. More than anything else, in fact, the Old Testament teaches us that these promises offer us our only hope.

PROMISES KEPT: THE MESSAGE OF THE NEW TESTAMENT

I wonder what you have your hopes set on. This is a crucial question for both you and me to answer. Many, even most, of our problems come from attaching our hopes to things that were not made to bear them—things that will sink like stones in water and pull us down with them. Some things even hold out great promise in the beginning but eventually prove to be passing fancies, or worse. In this old world, it is not only in politics where promises made are not necessarily promises kept.

So we must turn to God. He made us and knows us. He knows where our hopes should be placed. He has set before us in the Old Testament the very

---

[16] Ps. 40:6. The psalmist, among other Old Testament writers, seemed to share the insight of the New Testament writer to the Hebrews, who wrote, "The Law . . . can never, by the same sacrifices repeated endlessly year after year, make perfect those who draw near to worship. If it could, would they not have stopped being offered? For the worshipers would have been cleansed once for all, and would no longer have felt guilty for their sins. But those sacrifices are an annual reminder of sins, because it is impossible for the blood of bulls and goats to take away sins" (Heb. 10:1-4).

promises upon which we should set our hope. And we look to the New Testament to find the fulfillment of those promises.

The nation of Israel had waxed and waned for almost two millennia until their hopes almost vanished. Even after their release from Babylonian exile, only several hundred years passed before another alien invader crushed them— the mighty Roman Empire. Feelings of disappointment verged on despair. What about all their old hopes? Would their deliverer never come? Would fellowship with God never be restored? Would the world never be put right? God had promised his people all these things.

And God delivered on his promises. The New Testament is the story of how all the promises God made in the Old Testament, God kept.

In order to understand the New Testament, we will look first at Christ, then at God's covenant people, and finally at the renewal of all creation. You might be helped by thinking of these three themes as three concentric circles. We begin with the heart of the matter and move outward. In all of this, we find that God has penetrated human history and has worked for his own purposes.

The Promised Redeemer: Christ

First, would Israel's deliverer ever come? The New Testament answers this Old Testament promise with a resounding yes! In fact, the one who fulfills this promise is the very center of the New Testament: Jesus Christ.

The New Testament teaches that God planned before history began to send Christ. Adam and Eve rebelled against God's rightful rule in the Garden, and God's people rebelled continuously over millennia. Yet God's plan remained in place through everything. An anointed deliverer would come—a Messiah (Hebrew) or a Christ (Greek). And he would come from a tattered remnant of Israel living amid Roman occupation.

The collection of twenty-seven books that comprise the New Testament begins by directly addressing this promise with four accounts of the life of the Messiah. The four documentaries of Matthew, Mark, Luke, and John all argue that Jesus of Nazareth is the Messiah. He is the promised one for whom God's people have been waiting. Where Adam and Israel failed, Jesus was faithful. As did his predecessors, he faced Satan's temptations. Yet he survived them without sin. He is the prophet promised by Moses, the king prefigured by David, and the divine Son of Man promised by Daniel. In fact, Jesus is the very Word of God made flesh (John 1:1, 14).

Following these first four, the next book in the New Testament, Acts, shows how Jesus continues to be active in the world as his church expands to all nations. Acts begins with Jesus' ascending to heaven and then giving out his Spirit at Pentecost. Over the ensuing chapters, his Spirit establishes the church as God's new society and empowers it to grow and to do Christ's work. The book concludes with Paul's imprisonment in Rome.

We see the fulfillment of God's Old Testament promises to his people frequently in the book of Acts (e.g., 15:13-18), and this pattern is typical of the whole New Testament. Jesus is the new Adam (1 Cor. 15:45-47). Jesus is the righteous one (1 Pet. 3:18; Acts 3:14; 1 John 2:1). Jesus is greater than Moses (John 1:17; 5:45-46; Heb. 3:1-6) and greater than David (Matt. 22:41-45; Acts 2:29-36). Abraham, Jesus said, rejoiced to see his day (John 8:56-58). According to the New Testament, promises made in the Old Testament are promises kept in Jesus.

Indeed, Jesus Christ *is* the point of the Bible. It is all about him. If you wanted to sum up the Bible in one word, you could do so by pointing to Christ. The Old Testament makes promises about Christ, and the New Testament keeps promises in Christ.

We read the Bible because we love Christ, and we want to know more about his love for us. John Stott writes, "A man who loves his wife will love her letters and her photographs because they speak to him of her. So if we love the Lord Jesus we shall love the Bible because it speaks to us of him. The husband is not so stupid as to prefer his wife's letters to her voice, or her photographs to herself. He simply loves them because of her. So, too, we love the Bible because of Christ. It is his portrait. It is his love-letter."[17] There are cold religious legalists who fight for the Bible but who do not love the Lord described in its pages. The Bible shows us Christ so that we can look to him as the focus of our hopes and the center of our satisfaction. In him we find all the answers we need about God and his call on our lives. Christ is the promised deliverer not just for God's Old Testament people but for you and me as well.

The Promised Relationship: A New Covenant People

This brings us to our second concentric circle for understanding the message of the New Testament: Christ came for a people. Because of sin, mankind, though created in the image of God, lost the ability to perfectly image God. Christ came and displayed that image once more. But not only that! He came to make a people for God, a special covenant people particularly called to reflect God's image to all creation. We have seen that the "covenant" language in the Bible is not cold, legal language, but relational language. We have also

---

[17] John Stott, *Fundamentalism and Evangelism* (Grand Rapids, Mich.: Eerdmans, 1959), 41.

seen that Jesus Christ uses this sort of language of Christians when he offers us the "new covenant in my blood"—words we recall when we partake of the Lord's Supper. This new covenant signifies the new relationship that we Christians, God's people, have with God.

How did Christ accomplish this? At one point, Jesus says to his followers, "Destroy this temple, and I will raise it again in three days" (John 2:19). He was standing in the temple at the time, but he did not mean the building; he meant himself. In the New Testament, Jesus himself *is* the new temple. He *is* the new meeting place for God and his people. He *is* the mediator. You see, Christ came not only to fulfill the Old Testament hope for Messiah as Prophet and King; he came to fulfill the hope for a Priest. Jesus our mediating priest grants us a new relationship with God by solving the riddle of the Old Testament: how can the Lord "forgive wickedness" and yet "not leave the guilty unpunished"? When Jesus was nailed to the cross, the guilt of all who would ever repent and put their trust in him *was* punished. He received that punishment! He stood in for the guilty, so that the guilty might be forgiven. After his resurrection, Jesus used the Old Testament to teach these lessons:

> beginning with Moses and all the Prophets, he explained to them what was said in all the Scriptures concerning himself. . . .
>
> Then he opened their minds so they could understand the Scriptures. He told them, "This is what is written: The Christ will suffer and rise from the dead on the third day, and repentance and forgiveness of sins will be preached in his name to all nations, beginning at Jerusalem" (Luke 24:27, 45-47).

Christ's suffering provides a way for us his people to be forgiven, which is exactly what the LORD had promised through the prophet Isaiah:

> Surely he took up our infirmities
>> and carried our sorrows,
> yet we considered him stricken by God,
>> smitten by him, and afflicted.
> But he was pierced for our transgressions,
>> he was crushed for our iniquities;
> the punishment that brought us peace was upon him,
>> and by his wounds we are healed.
> We all, like sheep, have gone astray,
>> each of us has turned to his own way;
> and the LORD has laid on him the iniquity of us all (Isa. 53:4-6).

This is what Christ did! He was pierced. He was crushed. And he had our iniquities laid upon him. His own body provides the priestly sacrifice we need to stand in between God and us, so that we might be God's own people. As Jesus taught his disciples, "the Son of Man did not come to be served, but to serve, and to give his life as a ransom for many" (Mark 10:45; cf. Gal. 4:4-5; Philippians 2).

In giving himself, Christ combined an amazing strength and humility. One of the best portrayals of this occurs in Revelation 5. The apostle John is told to look and see the Lion of the tribe of Judah. He turns to see the Lion, but what does he behold? A Lamb. The message is not that there are two gods; the message is that the Lion is the Lamb. The Lion of Judah has become the Lamb slain for our sins. This is the story of our great God. He has become our sacrificial lamb—our substitute. And by acting as our substitute, he has purchased us, his church, with his own blood (Acts 20:28).

So Christ is the answer to the Old Testament's riddle. And in Christ, the people are made holy. The very thing that God wanted of his people in the Old Testament, that he planned toward, that they never achieved on their own, God now has through Christ: a remnant, a nation, a people to praise him with lips and lives of holiness. He has a *new* covenant people who are genuinely holy in Christ.

When we open the New Testament, we find throughout its pages this all-important emphasis on salvation from sin to holiness. Paul tells the Ephesian Christians they have been saved (Eph. 2:8-9). He tells the Corinthian Christians they are being saved (1 Cor. 1:18). And he tells the Christians in Rome they shall be saved (Rom. 5:9). Christians are already counted as holy in Christ; we are being made holy even now; and someday, thanks to God, we will be holy in ourselves. The work of the kingdom of God has begun in us, and we look forward to its completion.

The New Testament paints the contrast between the world and the kingdom of God starkly. The world is marked by unbelief; the kingdom of God is marked by faith. The world is characterized by bondage and darkness; the covenant people of God enjoy freedom and light. The world knows only death; those belonging to the kingdom are promised eternal life. Hate and fear typify the first; love typifies the second. Apart from the covenant in Christ, our lives are marked by lawlessness. In Christ, we abide in God. The Scriptures have been given to the people of God so that they will perceive these contrasts, discover where salvation is found, and know what God's judgment will entail. So our own church's statement of faith (taken from the 1833 New Hampshire Confession) begins with the words,

Of The Scriptures: We believe that the Holy Bible was written by men divinely inspired, and is a perfect treasure of heavenly instruction; that it has God for its author, salvation for its end, and truth without any mixture of error for its matter; that it reveals the principles by which God will judge us; and therefore is, and shall remain to the end of the world, the true centre of Christian union, and the supreme standard by which all human conduct, creeds, and opinions should be tried.

Following after the Gospels, which focus on the identity of Jesus Christ, the rest of the New Testament helps define and fill out what it means for us to be the special covenant people of Christ. If you look back to the table of contents for the New Testament, you see the four Gospels. Then you see the book of Acts, which is really the transition from these Gospels to the books about living as God's people. In Acts, the gospel expands outward from Jerusalem, to Judea, to Samaria, and, beginning with the three missionary journeys of Paul, to the ends of the world. After Acts you see a number of books that are letters, and these letters describe what it means to live as God's specially covenanted people.

Paul wrote the first thirteen of these letters. Originally a noted rabbi of the stricter sort of Jews, Paul was remarkably converted by God as he was traveling, in his words, to persecute some Christians "to their death" (Acts 22:4).

Following Paul's letters are eight more, written by James, Peter, John, Jude, and one unknown author (Hebrews). As we read through all of these letters, we find that the promises made by God in the Old Testament have been kept in God's new covenant people. You see, God has desired to show himself not merely in Christ but in a community of people who live and love one another in a manner that displays God's character to the world. If we are Christians, that is happening this very day in our churches!

As Christians, we often pray, "Thy kingdom come. Thy will be done in earth, as it is in heaven" (Matt. 6:10, KJV). Have you ever wondered what that means? Some people limit their hopes to those things they can achieve in their own strength. But Christianity has never been like that. As Christians, we have always put our hope in something that goes beyond what we can bring about by our own power. Peter writes in his second letter, "we are looking forward to a new heaven and a new earth, the home of righteousness" (2 Pet. 3:13). This *kingdom come,* this *new heaven* and *new earth,* this *home of righteousness,* points us to the fulfillment of our final and first hope: the whole world being put right. This is the third movement of God's plan in the New Testament as it extends from Christ to his covenant people to the outermost circle—his whole creation.

The Promised Renewal: A New Creation

What is the point of history? Why do life and the universe and you and I exist at all? All history and all creation exist ultimately for God's glory. This is what we find at the conclusion of the New Testament. In the book of Revelation, written by the apostle John, all creation is taken up into God's glory.

I know the book of Revelation is sometimes the subject of sensationalistic documentaries with ominous music. But Revelation is actually a book of wonderful hope and encouragement for God's people. It presents the consummation of our salvation. We are finally in God's place, under his rule, and in a perfectly right relationship to him. The heavens and the earth are re-created, and the struggling *church militant* becomes the resting *church triumphant* (see Rev. 21:1-4; 21:22–22:5).

Some people get to Revelation and say, "This is just idealistic Greek Platonism." Or, "This is just another world-denying Gnosticism, as if only the invisible matters." But that is not what John presents us at all. In Revelation, creation is re-finished, refurbished, and re-presented in a new heaven and a new earth, all of which tends toward the great end of the Bible and world history—the glory of God himself. That is no Platonism or Gnosticism! As Christians, we do not merely believe in an eternal soul that ascends and lives with God in the clouds. We believe in a doctrine that was offensive to the ancient Greeks: the resurrection of the body. In a manner beyond our comprehension, God will one day reconstitute these presently rotting bodies of ours. Jesus' own resurrection was only the "firstfruits." It was the beginning of the great harvest to follow (1 Cor. 15:20). And his remaking of our bodies is a picture of what he will do with all creation.

The holiness of God's people will finally be complete, and we will dwell together with him. Really, Revelation presents the Garden of Eden restored, only better. Now it is a heavenly and perfect city, a city that works not because the sewers are good and the taxes are low but because God abides with his people. John describes the measurements of this heavenly city as a great cube. Any Christian who knows the Old Testament knows that John's vision harks back to the Most Holy Place. This special place within Israel's temple was itself a perfect cube and the most manifest location of God's presence on earth. Now, in this cube-shaped heavenly city, God's full, unmediated presence is given to all his people. The whole world becomes the temple. John writes, "And I heard a loud voice from the throne saying, 'Now the dwelling of God is with men, and he will live with them. They will be his people, and God himself will be with them and be their God. He will wipe every tear from their eyes. There will be no more death or mourning or crying or pain, for the old order of things has passed away" (Rev. 21:3-4).

Since we know what this world is all about, we Christians have great news to offer. I remember sitting cross-legged one day in an undergraduate philosophy class at Duke University in a room with purple shag carpet on the floor, walls, and ceiling, lit by one dangling light bulb (I am dating myself quite clearly). The professor began the hour by asking the question, "What's the purpose of life?" Well, nobody would say anything, because these days answering that kind of question sounds prideful. But I was a young Christian, and the silence was killing me. I remember thinking to myself that here were all these people made in the image of God, and I was not saying anything. So I finally blurted out, "The purpose of life is to glorify God and to enjoy him forever!" Christian friend, that is the purpose of life! We are not clueless about that fact. You may not know why you are in the job you are in. You may not know why you have the disease that you have. You may not know a lot of very significant things. But right now, you know the most significant thing in all the world: the purpose of life is to know God so that you may glorify him and enjoy him forever.

Presently, we live in a time of waiting, and for that reason the book of Revelation appropriately concludes the New Testament. It was written by an old man who had been left alone and deserted in exile. Everything this world values had been taken from him, and he was utterly desperate. Still, he was full of hope! And that is Christianity. We are to live filled with such hope. God has promised that the earth will be filled with the knowledge of his glory, and he will keep this promise in his new creation. Every promise made by God will be kept by God.

CONCLUSION

We all know that some disappointments have their uses. The ruins of cherished plans are often the first steps to the true good that God has in store for us. The apostle Paul learned this when he asked God to remove the thorn in his flesh (2 Cor. 12:7-9). God, in his great and strange mercy, said no. Nationalistic Israelites also learned this in how they were waiting for the Messiah. God had something better in his plans than the immediate political supremacy of Israel over her enemies.

And that is true in your life and mine. Neither you nor I have a life perfectly attuned to the will, desires, and hopes of God. So we will inevitably face disappointment. We will watch the things we fix our hopes upon sink like stones in water. And it is God's grace to us that they do. As strange as it may seem, if we really believe the Bible, we must learn to trust that he knows what he is doing, and that his plans for us are better than whatever we have planned for ourselves. So often we cling with all our might to what we have in this world. But God has something even better prepared for his children.

If you are a child of God through new birth in Christ, the conclusion God has in mind for you is unimaginably good! As John writes in one of his letters, "Dear friends, now we are children of God, and what we will be has not yet been made known. But we know that when he appears, we shall be like him, for we shall see him as he is" (1 John 3:2). And Paul dissolves into doxology when he thinks of what God has done and will do: "Oh, the depth of the riches of the wisdom and knowledge of God! How unsearchable his judgments, and his paths beyond tracing out!" (Rom. 11:33).

Of course, our minds are not always fixed on such lofty things. We are not always sitting in church or reading sermons about the whole Bible. Very often, our lives are consumed with other hopes, and we look for contentment amid smaller things. William Wilberforce was such a man. He thought he possessed everything a man could want. He was born into an old family in Yorkshire, England, in 1759. He grew up in great privilege, was given to ease, and had a wonderful wit. He did well in his undergraduate studies at Cambridge University, where he also befriended William Pitt, who very soon became the prime minister of England. Almost immediately upon his graduation from Cambridge in 1781, Wilberforce was elected to Parliament. He was very fashionable and quickly became prominent in London because of his close friendships with many important society and political leaders. He soon defined the "in" crowd and even in his early twenties held a position of considerable power and eminence. In the winter of 1784–1785, Wilberforce toured the south of France with several friends, among them Isaac Milner. On the trip, Wilberforce made frequent jibes at what he thought was the overheated piety of evangelical Christians. Unbeknownst to the witty Wilberforce, his traveling companion Milner was such a Christian. At one point, Wilberforce referred to one prominent evangelical leader by saying he was a good man but that he "carried things a bit too far." Milner, who had not yet remonstrated his young friend, responded, "Not a bit too far." He suggested that carefully perusing the whole New Testament might cause Wilberforce to form a different estimate of this man. Wilberforce, a little surprised at his friend's forwardness, said he would. And he did! Over the next few weeks on that trip, God used the Bible to make William Wilberforce a new man. As he later told it, the Bible's message about God and man, sin and Christ's sacrifice, the forgiveness and new birth that can be ours through repentance and faith in Christ—all those things we have been talking about in this study—came alive to Wilberforce. He was born again. He changed from just another nameless wit haunting the environs of London, always on the lookout for what benefited himself, to Wilberforce the Great Liberator, a man who committed his life to ending slavery in Britain. It took him decades of work, but he eventually managed to push bills through Parliament abolishing first the slave trade and then slavery itself. His life had been transformed. Wilberforce became the champion of liberty only after God had freed his own soul with the message of the Bible—with the good news of Jesus Christ.

The Bible is God's revelation of himself to us. In the Old Testament and New, he reveals himself to us through the promises he makes and keeps. And then he calls us to respond to him in trust. In the 1813 Baptist Catechism, a variation of the Westminster Shorter Catechism, question 6 reads,

> Q. What things are chiefly contained in the holy scriptures?
> A. The holy scriptures chiefly contain what man ought to believe concerning
> God, and what duty God requireth of man (2 Tim. 1:13; 3:15-16).

Paul points to the same duty to believe when he writes, "I am not ashamed of the gospel, because it is the power of God for the salvation of everyone who believes: first for the Jew, then for the Gentile" (Rom. 1:16).

The question for you is, will you believe? Will you turn your life over to him? Will you trust him for what he says? We need that time-lapse camera sometimes to show us that God is faithful, because sometimes—if we are honest—it feels as if our prayers are not answered. So step back and look at what God does through the pages of Scripture. You will begin to see that he is faithful, just as he was to Abraham when he called him to an unfamiliar land. Abraham did not understand everything God was doing; yet he believed God and followed his instructions. And God blessed him. He gave Abraham the gift of faith so that Abraham could come to know him.

God gives us the promises in his Word as well, and we are called to respond in trust to them. Unlike Adam and Eve in the Garden of Eden, and much like Jesus in the Garden of Gethsemane, we must hear and believe God's Word. When we do, we will be restored to the relationship with God for which we were made.

This is the hope in which we can trust, because this is the hope that will not disappoint. And this is the chief concern of the whole Bible, Old Testament and New: God's restored relationship with his people for his own glory and his own pleasure.

Let us pray:

Lord God, we invariably come into your presence with lesser aims than you have for us. Yet we pray that you would take the great story of your revelation of yourself in your Word and speak it into our hearts. We pray that you would give your Word a tongue that we can hear, as well as hands that hold us and feet that pursue us. Lord, be tenacious in your love for us, as you have been throughout your history of dealing with your people. We pray for Jesus' sake. Amen.

Questions for Reflection

1. As we considered at the beginning, the Bible has been the subject of numerous and varying opinions. What are several of the most prominent opinions of the Bible that people have today?

2. If the Bible is comprised of 66 different books and has more than 30 different human authors, how could it possibly have one overarching story line and one message?

3. What are some of the advantages of examining the whole Bible and its message in one fell swoop?

4. We have observed that the Bible is not only a book of wise religious counsel and theological propositions, though it has both. It is a story, a real story set in real history. Why do you think God might have revealed himself within a historical narrative? What advantages does that give us as readers?

5. What is atonement? How does the Old Testament link atonement and sacrifice? Were the sacrifices of the Old Testament *effective* in reconciling man to God?

6. What is the "riddle" of the Old Testament?

7. Suppose a Christian friend told you that he struggles with the God of the Old Testament because he just seems so angry and wrathful. How would you respond?

8. How does Christ solve the riddle of the Old Testament? What do we mean when we refer to Christ as our "priest"?

9. What is the Christian gospel?

10. What do Christians have awaiting them at the consummation of all creation? What will Christians fully enjoy that was last enjoyed by Adam in the Garden and partially by the high priest in the Most Holy Place? What do you think that will be like? Do you think you will grow tired of it? Can you imagine anything so beautiful and wonderful and marvelous that you would never grow tired of it?

11. If you were sitting in an undergraduate philosophy class—or wherever you happen to sit among non-Christians these days—and someone asked what the point of life was, what would you say? Could you defend your answer?

12. William Wilberforce seemed to take seriously Paul's own dilemma: "I desire to depart and be with Christ, which is better by far; but it is more necessary for you that I remain in the body" (Phil. 1:23-24). Wilberforce knew his prize awaited him in heaven, and so he was free to spend himself entirely on earth for God's work. Where is your ultimate prize? You prize *something* the most. You can figure out what it is by asking what you spend all your physical, financial, social, and mental resources trying to build, protect, or accomplish. What is it? Is your life increasingly lining up with the great promise of the Scriptures—or with something else?

THE OLD TESTAMENT: PROMISES MADE

IS THE OLD TESTAMENT REALLY WORTH READING?[1]

I confess that I spend a good deal of time in bookstores. One of the trends I have noticed in secular bookstores over the last few years is to stock more and more religious books. Of course, the stores often classify them under "spirituality." Still, in this growing section you can browse through offerings on angels, warm thoughts, Ancient Eastern texts, the maxims of management gurus, and on and on in endless variety. Many of these books sell surprisingly well, too.

What do you think people are looking for in this blossoming spiritual book market? Guidance? Hope? Whatever the answer is, my guess is that comparatively few people would turn to the Old Testament.

You remember the Old Testament: "In the beginning" and all that! These words not only open the Bible, they are probably the most famous words in the Old Testament, and perhaps one of the most well-known phrases in the English language.

Yet it must be said that the majesty of this opening line has not endeared the Old Testament to many people. Many Christians and non-Christians alike consider the Old Testament too long and tedious, too obscure and cryptic. Besides, wasn't the Old Testament superseded by the New Testament? Studying the Old Testament compared to studying the New, some might think, would be like eating a fish with bones when you could have the boneless fillet, or like watching the big game from bad seats with a blocked view when you could be standing on the field.

Other people's problems with the Old Testament run a bit deeper. They will point to its frenzied prophets, its animal sacrifices, and its seemingly archaic laws and pejoratively label the whole thing as "primitive" or "crude." And, given that multiculturalism is the preeminent virtue of our own day, one could hardly find a book more out-of-step with the times than the Old

---

[1] This sermon was originally preached on September 1, 1996, at Capitol Hill Baptist Church in Washington, D.C.

Testament. One might say that it represents one of the worst displays of ethnocentrism in history.

Isn't this the book of the angry God who kills a man for trying to steady a decorated box, who sends bears to kill children for being disrespectful to their elders, who silences grumblers with deadly serpents simply for their grumbling?[2] Isn't this the book with divinely ordained threats and floods and hailstorms and fire and brimstone?

The wrath ascribed to God in this book does not make him seem grand or powerful to many people today. In fact, such wrath can tempt the most pious among us to regard him as arbitrary and cruel: a god who causes us not to worship, but to worry; an object not for admiration, but for abhorrence; the supreme embodiment not of beauty, but of ugliness. Well, now, we have gone and said it. And in a sermon! I have heard people say such things in other places. So we might as well be honest in a sermon that this is what many people think of the Old Testament.

Such ideas are not new, of course. People have been embarrassed by the Old Testament throughout the history of the church. Toward the close of the second century, a man named Marcion and his followers broke off relations with other Christians. They rejected the entire Old Testament because its God seemed too cruel, wrathful, and inconsistent with the God revealed in Jesus of Nazareth. Of course, the Old Testament *was* the Bible of Jesus of Nazareth! (Marcion also accepted only the Gospel of Luke and ten of Paul's epistles from the New Testament.)

Though the church quickly and universally rejected Marcion's radical surgery of the Bible, the Old Testament has too often suffered a similar fate in our own circles of evangelical Christians. We don't make theological statements about it, but the effect is the same. Maybe we mine it for some good stories about Joseph, David, Moses, and Elijah. We may quote a couple of psalms, memorize several of the proverbs, and commend most of the Ten Commandments. But on the whole, we simply ignore it.

Well, before we make the sweeping decision to omit such a large part of the Bible, I suggest that we should increase our understanding of what the Old Testament contains. And I would like to summarize it for you under three headings:

> first, a particular history,
> second, a passion for holiness, and
> third, a promise of hope.

---

[2] 2 Sam. 6:6-9; 2 Kings 2:23-25; Num. 21:4-9.

I cannot deal with all the questions you might have about the Old Testament, but I can help with the framework. Some people have summed up the message of the Old Testament as "God's people in God's place under God's rule." In a sense, that's similar to what I am suggesting. I would sum up the message of the Old Testament with the phrase *promises made*. The promises God *made* in the Old Testament have been *kept* in the New, particularly in Jesus Christ.

I am convinced, in other words, that if we can better understand the Old Testament, it will go a long way toward helping us understand the New Testament, which means we will better understand Christ, Christianity, God, and ourselves.

A PARTICULAR HISTORY

We will understand nothing about the Old Testament—or the God it reveals—if we do not understand that it is about a particular history. I know that I only have to say the word "history" and every other person will fall asleep. I know that history has a bad reputation as being quite boring. Perhaps in school you were taught to memorize long lists of dates and names. I am sorry about that. Not all of this sermon will be long lists of dates and names! Really, the story of the Old Testament is quite amazing.

Our text for this sermon begins, not surprisingly, on page 1 of your Bible: "In the beginning, God created the heavens and the earth" (Gen. 1:1). Notice, this amazing story begins with *nothing*. And then the most extraordinary thing happens: from nothing we get *something*.

In that something, we see God's marvelous creative work. First, there is inanimate creation—water, earth, sun. Then God brings life—vegetation, fish, birds, animals. Perhaps you read in the newspapers about how excited scientists became when they thought they might have found water on the planet Mars, because where water exists, life exists. That might be exciting for secular people, but for Christians the most amazing thing is what God did next: he made people in his image, to reflect his character. All of this happens in the first two chapters of the Bible.

In the third chapter, God's first humans disobey him, and the whole cosmos falls into ruin as a consequence.

From chapters 4 to 6, we read a story of disintegration, beginning with the first son, Cain, who murders his brother, to the people of Noah's day, who are so bad that God decides to wipe out all the earth. You may think, "Maybe if we start over with just one righteous man and his family, human history will fare better." Of course, humanity did not fare better.

Beginning in chapter 10, the world is repopulated and then disintegrates again, epitomized by chapter 11's story of the Tower of Babel. At Babel, proud man tries to strike out independently from God, to which God responds with more judgment.

God then calls Abraham, in chapter 12, which marks yet another new beginning.

Before we get any further, we should note the vast scale of history contained in the Bible. I personally think that most of the history of the world may have happened before the days of Noah as recorded in Genesis 6. In the apostle Peter's second letter, he refers to the world before the Flood as the "ancient world" or "the age that then was" (2 Pet. 2:5, author's translation). It's possible that whole empires that we have not even dreamed of rose and fell in the time before Noah. Also, the time from Abraham to Jesus was as long as the time from Jesus to us today.

Anyway, God calls Abraham to be the first of God's new people. He gives Abraham descendants. Through Abraham's grandson, Jacob (also called Israel), God's people begin to experience prosperity. After a series of providential twists, these people end up as slaves in Egypt, yet they also quickly reproduce to become a vast nation.

Moses then brings the nation of Israel (named after Abraham's grandson) out of Egypt. God first gives Israel the law, which marks them off as his very special people. Second, he gives them the land he has promised, where this marked-off people are to live and display God's character to the nations. But instead of their displaying God's character, moral and political confusion follows during the rule of leaders called judges.

After some centuries, the people of Israel ask for and receive a king in the person of Saul, and then David follows Saul. David's reign best represents the archetype of a kingdom in which God's chosen man and God's Word rule over his people. The kingdom then arguably reaches its peak in the time of prosperity and the building of the temple by David's son, Solomon. Yet Solomon becomes ungodly in many ways; and under Solomon's son Rehoboam, the kingdom divides in two. Both parts of the now-divided nation fall into idolatry, until God finally destroys the northern half through the Assyrian empire. A little over a century later, he exiles the southern half to Babylon. Several generations pass in exile, and then the people return and rebuild the temple and Jerusalem's wall. This is where Old Testament history ends, with the people reduced to a position of utter desperation and dependence on God.

This is the history recounted through the thirty-nine books of the Old Testament. The Old Testament is not just one book, you know, but thirty-nine smaller ones which, together, make up the whole.

And these thirty-nine books are quite different. If you look at the table of contents in your Bible, you can distinguish the main categories. The first five books (Genesis to Deuteronomy) make up the Pentateuch, or the Law. The next twelve books (Joshua to Esther) are referred to as the Histories. Taken together, these first seventeen books form the narrative from Creation to the return of the exiles from Babylon about four hundred years before Christ. The next five books (Job to Song of Songs) are called the Writings. Then the last seventeen books are the Prophecies (Isaiah to Malachi). One way to divide the Christian canon of the Old Testament, then, would be to say there are seventeen books in the first group, five in the middle group, and seventeen in the last group. We will follow that division here.

Historical Narrative

The first seventeen books of historical narrative (from Genesis to Esther) are fairly chronological. Yet the history of these books is not the dry history scholars write today that purports to be objective and balanced. No, it is confessional history. It is history written by people who know who God is and that they are his people.

- *Genesis,* as we have already said, describes how the world and the first humans were made. The Garden of Eden presents the model of God and man living in perfect peace, which we will not see again until the final heavenly city in the New Testament book of Revelation. This peace is devastated by the Fall, of course. God then initiates his plan of salvation through Abraham and his descendants. At the end of Genesis, God's people—the nation of Israel—are bound in slavery in Egypt.

- *Exodus* follows the history of God's people from the death of Joseph in Egypt through the Exodus to the construction of the tabernacle in the wilderness, a building that symbolizes God's presence with his people. God uses Moses both to deliver the law and to deliver his people in the Exodus.

- *Leviticus* presents a digest of God's laws given to his people in the wilderness. These laws highlight the problem of how sinful humans can approach a holy God. Holiness is the theme of the book of Leviticus.

- *Numbers* mostly tells the story of the people of Israel traveling to the Promised Land. It describes several dramatic instances of the people's unfaithfulness, together with God's persevering faithfulness.

- *Deuteronomy* is called Deuteronomy because it presents the second giving of the law (*deutero* = second; *nomos* = law). The people have reached the end of their forty-year wandering. The older generation has died off. So now God repeats the law for this new generation as they prepare to enter the Promised Land.

- *Joshua* describes the conquest of the Promised Land, and its apportionment among the twelve tribes. The people were ruled by Moses' successor, Joshua.

- *Judges* comes next with the story of fourteen judges who ruled over Israel (or regions of Israel) after Joshua. The people continually reverted to lawlessness, and the times were well summed up by the phrase, "In those days Israel had no king; everyone did as he saw fit" (Judg. 21:25).
- *Ruth* is a little story set during the days of the judges. It functions as an Old Testament annunciation story, preparing the way for the birth of David.
- *1 and 2 Samuel* are about the last judge, Samuel; a "false-start" king, Saul; and the first real king, David.
- *1 and 2 Kings* turn the focus to the reign of David's son, Solomon, followed by the fall of both Solomon and his line. The kingdom divides into two parts during the time of Solomon's son Rehoboam, and it's mostly downhill from there. Apart from several noteworthy revivals, both the northern and the southern kingdom gradually dissolve amid immorality and idolatry.
- *1 and 2 Chronicles* present a kind of interesting summation of everything from Adam through the beginning of the exile. Their focus is on David, Solomon, the role of the temple, and then the kings of the southern kingdom leading up to the exile.

The last three books of history are about the exile and the return from exile:

- *Ezra* describes the return of the Jews from their captivity in Babylon and the rebuilding of the temple.
- *Nehemiah* continues the story by describing the rebuilding of Jerusalem's walls, a partial fulfillment of God's promises of restoration to his people.
- *Esther* is the last book of history. It is a story of God's providential deliverance of the Jewish community inside the Persian Empire late in the exile.

The Writings

The Old Testament's middle five books are known as the Writings, and they focus on some of the more personal experiences of the people of God. They are largely collections of wisdom literature, devotional poems, and ceremonial literature from the temple.

- *Job* is a story about a righteous man who is tried by God. We don't know when Job was written.
- The *Psalms* are poetic prayers of praise, confession, and lament to God. Almost half of them appear to have been written by David. The collection was written over a wide span of time.
- *Proverbs* presents the wisdom of Solomon and others concerning the practical issues of life.

- *Ecclesiastes,* again probably by Solomon, recounts one man's search for the path to happiness and meaning in this world. It reads like the account of a man walking down the street at night, shining his flashlight down a number of dead-end alleys and saying, "this is no good; this is no good; this is no good . . ."
- *Song of Songs* is the collection of love songs between a bridegroom and his bride. It emphasizes the importance of loving relationships.

The Prophets

The final collection of books in the Old Testament is the Prophets. If the first seventeen books present historical narrative, while the middle five books present the reflections of various individuals, this last group of seventeen presents God's commentary on Israel's history, particularly Israel's disobedience.

The first five books are called the Major Prophets because of their size; some of them are very long.

- *Isaiah* was a prophet in the southern kingdom, called "Judah." The first thirty-nine chapters are composed of prophecies leading up to the captivity. Chapters 40 to 66 then point to a future restoration and redemption.
- *Jeremiah* uttered his prophecies in Jerusalem during the years the city was besieged, a siege that ended in the city's fall in 586 B.C. He then continued to prophesy for seven years after the city's fall.
- *Lamentations* is the prophet Jeremiah's lament over Jerusalem's siege and destruction.
- *Ezekiel* prophesied in Babylon during this same time. He had actually been carried off from Jerusalem and taken to Babylon by Nebuchadnezzar in 597 B.C., along with a number of other Jews. Trained as a priest, Ezekiel prophesied against Judah up to the fall of Jerusalem, and then he turned to promising God's judgment on the nations and the restoration of God's people.
- *Daniel,* part prophecy and part history, chronicles the story of a Jewish captive in Babylon and how God used him in that place.

Following the five books of the Major Prophets are the twelve books of the Minor Prophets. They are called the Minor Prophets not because they lack importance but merely because they lack length.

- *Hosea* prophesied to the northern kingdom (generally called "Israel") at the same time that Isaiah prophesied to the southern kingdom. Hosea spoke of Israel's unfaithfulness, while God used Hosea's adulterous wife as a living example of how Israel had been unfaithful to God.
- *Joel* preached about the coming judgment of God on the southern kingdom. Then he promised that God's blessing would follow their repentance. (That's really the main theme for most of these prophets.)

- *Amos* predicted the judgment and restoration of Israel, the northern kingdom, while Isaiah was prophesying in the south.
- *Obadiah* uttered his very short prophecy of judgment against one of Judah's neighbors, Edom. He also promised restoration to the shattered Israelites.
- *Jonah,* when called to prophesy to the Assyrian city of Nineveh, fled and was swallowed by a great fish. In the belly of the fish, he prayed, repented, was delivered, and obeyed.
- *Micah* prophesied at the same time as Isaiah and Hosea. He spoke to both Israel and Judah concerning judgment and deliverance.
- *Nahum,* who lived about a century after Jonah, spoke out against Nineveh concerning the coming judgment of God. He also promised a future deliverance for Judah.
- *Habakkuk* reminded God's people living in a time of evil that God's judgment is certain, and that they can put their trust in his promise of restoration and ultimate protection.
- *Zephaniah* promised that judgment would come upon Judah. He also called them to repent, and he promised future blessing.

The last three prophets prophesied during the time of the rebuilding of Jerusalem under Ezra and Nehemiah.

- *Haggai* was a contemporary of Zechariah. He may have been born in captivity in Babylon, but he returned to Jerusalem and prodded the people to get on with rebuilding the temple.
- *Zechariah,* a contemporary of Haggai, prophesied two months after Haggai and presented a series of wild dreams that attacked the religious lethargy of the people and foresaw the messianic age.
- *Malachi,* perhaps a contemporary of Nehemiah in post-exilic Jerusalem, also attacked the religious apathy of the people and promised a coming Messiah. He was the last Old Testament prophet.

All this history teaches that God picked a very specific people for himself. Some people feel that it is unfair for God to pick whom he wants. But let me remind you, God made the world. He can do as he pleases. He picked a people specifically to teach them who he is as God, what it means for him to be holy, and what it means for his people to be sinful and therefore dependent upon him and his mercy.

As we step back and look at the whole broad sweep, we find that we do not have some disembodied theology about the Lord; we have a very clear and specific earthy revelation of him. You know what it's like to look at a person's résumé; in comparison, you know what it's like to work with someone in person. In the Old Testament, we get the résumé *and* we observe God actually working with his people. We see what God is like, how people respond to him, and how he deals with them in turn.

A PASSION FOR HOLINESS

That brings us to the second thing to observe in the Old Testament. We must understand not only the particular history of Israel, we must also consider God's passion for holiness.

As we have already considered, many people associate the Old Testament with an angry God, and they condemn him as unjust. But nothing could be further from the truth! I think that we will better understand God if we better understand his character.

When we Christians celebrate the Lord's Supper together, we often recite Jesus' words from the Gospels, "this cup is the new covenant in my blood." Jesus took this language of "covenant" straight out of the Old Testament, where the concept of a covenant is crucial. Now, maybe such covenant language sounds cold and legal to you, but in the Bible it isn't like that at all. It's the language of relationship! God's covenants were used to draw his people into a committed relationship with himself. And it is in the context of God's committed covenantal relationships that we find God's *passion for holiness* expressed. In short, he was passionate for his covenanted people to be set apart unto him and to have characters and lives that were like his own. This is why sin is such a problem in the Bible, because sin is not like God. There is not the least trace of sin in God, and so it causes big problems for humans in relating to him. It separates God from us.

So does the Old Testament present a God who can be angry? Yes, but his expressions of anger are not whimsical tyranny. His anger expresses his commitment to his own holy character and his implacable opposition to human sin. Sin (the breaking of divine commandments) separates God's people from God and shows clearly their need to be reconciled to him.[3] God can be angry, in short, because he is not indifferent to sin and he is angry at the destruction of his creation.

The Old Testament explicitly teaches that all people are sinners,[4] and the story line as a whole quickly leads to the conclusion that people are not able to deal with sin themselves (see Rom. 3:20; Gal. 2:16). Instead, the relationships that sin breaks require some sort of divinely initiated reparation. But how can this happen? Given God's holiness, how can peace with God be restored?

This is where the biblical references to atonement become significant. The

---

[3] Prov. 15:29; Isa. 59:2; Hab. 1:13; Col. 1:21; Heb. 10:27.
[4] 1 Kings 8:46; Ps. 14:3; Prov. 20:9; Eccles. 7:20; cf. Mark 10:18; Rom. 3:23.

Anglo-Saxon word we use—"atonement"—means, quite literally, at-one-ment. Atonement must occur for two warring parties to be made *at one*.

The idea of offering an atoning act or ritual to placate an offended deity was not unique to ancient Israel; in fact, it was common among ancient religions. But the Old Testament authors uniquely placed the idea of atonement within the context of a relationship, and so they refer to the need for reconciliation in a way that *was* utterly unique in the ancient world.

A number of images are used to describe atonement in the Old Testament. But the most prominent image God used to teach the people about atonement was sacrifice. Sinners could seek to restore their relationship with God through sacrifice. Now, the picture of sacrifice given is not of a moody tribal deity who required the people to throw a young virgin into the volcano in order to be pacified. You will find this picture if you read about other ancient cultures—blind attempts to get some god to calm down by hurting yourself. But you won't find that idea in the Bible. In the Old Testament, God *himself* speaks and provides a way for propitiation—a way to turn his wrath aside and restore a rebellious people to himself.

In some ways, the idea of sacrifice almost seems innate. Shortly after Adam and Eve's eviction from the Garden of Eden, their sons Cain and Abel offered sacrifices, even though God had not yet revealed the law. Abraham and his descendants offered sacrifices as well. Perhaps this innate compulsion to offer sacrifices, along with the ordinary habit of human mimicry, explains why sacrifices were so common among ancient religions.

Yet what's interesting about the Old Testament sacrifices, as we have already been suggesting, is how they differed from the sacrificial practices of the nations around them. Biblical sacrifices were not only for the grateful (to thank God for a wonderful harvest); and they certainly were not for the manipulative (to persuade God to send a good harvest). Instead, they were for the guilty—people who personally understood that they had violated God's commandments. Not only that, biblical sacrifices were not only for the ignorant person who thinks, "Maybe doing this will make things better." No, they were performed according to God's own instructions.

Specifically, God required the animals used as offerings to be without defect, to be costly, and to be voluntary by the person bringing the sacrifice.[5] The life of the unblemished animal victim, symbolized by its blood, would then be given in exchange for the life of the guilty human worshiper. In Exodus 12, for instance, the blood of the Passover lamb was given in exchange for a family's firstborn, who in turn represented the whole family. In Leviticus, God told

---

[5] E.g., Gen. 9:5; Lev. 1:4; 4:4; 14:51; 16:21.

the people, "the life of a creature is in the blood, and I have given it to you to make atonement for yourselves on the altar; it is the blood that makes atonement for one's life" (Lev. 17:11). Furthermore, the guilty human party in a Levitical sacrifice was required to place his or her hand on the head of the animal being sacrificed in order to indicate the transfer of guilt.

I know that the whole idea of such sacrifices is unpopular with many people—maybe they sound primitive and cruel. But can you see what God was teaching the people? First, he was teaching about his holiness and his passion for holiness. Second, he was teaching that sin is serious—deathly serious!—because it's such an aberration from his holiness. And third, he was teaching that atonement could be accomplished when an innocent one dies in place of the guilty. In and of themselves, Levitical sacrifices were never the point (as you can tell by Jeremiah's denunciations of what the people's sacrifices were leaving out; see Jer. 7:21f.). Ironically, sacrifices were most appropriate when the person offering the sacrifice realized that the offering was *not* sufficient to atone for sins. So you have the psalmist saying "Against thee, thee only, have I sinned" (Ps. 51:4, KJV). Sacrifices were not efficacious except by God's grace. They taught that sin defiles. They taught that sin physically hinders access to God. They taught that purification was needed. And they taught that sin is so serious that only death can make atonement. Salvation and forgiveness would be costly.

Both God's passion for holiness and the ultimately ineffective nature of sacrifices can be seen in the Old Testament through the Jewish Day of Atonement, a day on which a special sin offering was made for the whole nation. You can read about it in Leviticus 16. Representing the people, the high priest entered the temple's Most Holy Place on one day of the year in order to offer a sacrifice in the very presence of God. First, he would make atonement for himself, since he too was a sinner. Then, he would make atonement for all the people. Who could see that blood offering that the high priest brought? No one but God! The high priest then confessed the sins of Israel over a second goat, which would be released outside of the city in order to symbolize the total removal of sin by the penalty of being alienated, cast out, estranged from God's people.

It is particularly interesting that this ritual had to be repeated annually. Other nations would tend to offer sacrifices only when the nation was not prospering. But the Israelites were commanded to make sacrifice once a year regardless of the nation's situation. Why? God was teaching them that they were needy and separated from God, regardless of what had occurred in the nation's life. They regularly needed to make amends. They regularly needed to make atonement. They were in a *state* of sin, and no animal sacrifice could ultimately remove their guilt. There was no perfect sacrifice. If there had been, the people could have stopped offering them (Heb. 10:1-3). Instead, these imperfect sacrifices emphasized the fact that God is holy, that sin separates us from God, and that he provides a way for the forgiveness of sins and access to him.

This brings up a question that I would call the riddle of the Old Testament. In Exodus 34, the Lord describes himself to Moses, saying "The LORD, the LORD, the compassionate and gracious God, slow to anger, abounding in love and faithfulness, maintaining love to thousands, and forgiving wickedness, rebellion and sin. Yet he does not leave the guilty unpunished" (Ex. 34:6-7a). Think about what God said: how can God both "forgive wickedness" and "not leave the guilty unpunished"?

A PROMISE OF HOPE

That brings me, in conclusion, to the last thing we need to observe if we want to understand the Old Testament and its God: the Old Testament's promise of hope.

The Old Testament's picture of God is not one of grim condemnation. He is the same God we find in the New Testament. He is holy, just, and unwavering in his commitment to punish sin, but he is also a God of love, even toward his enemies.

Does that surprise you? Many people are surprised when they hear that love is enjoined in the Old Testament. For instance,

- *The* great commandment given to Israel is, "Love the LORD your God with all your heart and with all your soul and with all your strength" (Deut. 6:5).
- The Lord commands the people to love their neighbors as themselves (Lev. 19:34). Jesus was quoting the Old Testament when he said this!
- God commands the Israelites to love foreigners because he does (Deut. 10:18-19).
- God even told the Israelites to return lost property to their enemies: "Do not gloat when your enemy falls; when he stumbles, do not let your heart rejoice" (Prov 24:17). And, "If your enemy is hungry, give him food to eat; if he is thirsty, give him water to drink" (Prov. 25:21).

All of this is from the Old Testament, and I could go on and on! I don't know which Old Testament you have been reading, but the real one is about love.

Now, this is one way we could try to demonstrate that the God of the Old Testament is the same God as the God of the New Testament—going through the text piece by piece and pointing to all the individual injunctions and examples of love. But even more convincing, I believe, is considering the whole sweep of history presented in the Old Testament, where we witness God's patience and loving forbearance toward creatures made in his image who nevertheless reject him. Why is Old Testament history so long? "He is patient with you, not wanting anyone to perish, but everyone to come to repentance," said the apostle Peter (2 Pet. 3:9). God's forbearance can be seen in the fact that he did not end human history right at the Fall, when he would have been just to do so. Then throughout centuries and centuries of Israel's history, God patiently forbore with the wayward nation. Ultimately, the Old Testament presents God's grace, love, mercy, and patience on an epic scale.

God has always planned and promised to reveal his glory to his people. And so he did, throughout the Old Testament.

What then is the promise of hope God's people can look to in the Old Testament? Clearly, their hope could not be in their own history. It was a history of repeated failure! Nor, finally, could their hope be in the sacrificial system. As the psalmist said, "Sacrifice and offering you did not desire, but my ears you have pierced" (Ps. 40:6), meaning God made the psalmist his own. The authors of the Old Testament even seemed to understand what the author of Hebrews meant when he wrote,

> The law is only a shadow of the good things that are coming—not the realities themselves. For this reason it can never, by the same sacrifices repeated endlessly year after year, make perfect those who draw near to worship. If it could, would they not have stopped being offered? For the worshipers would have been cleansed once for all, and would no longer have felt guilty for their sins. But those sacrifices are an annual reminder of sins, because it is impossible for the blood of bulls and goats to take away sins (Heb. 10:1-4).

So where is the hope? To find the answer, we have to return to Exodus 34 where we saw the riddle of the Old Testament. Remember, we asked, how can God both "forgive wickedness" and still "not leave the guilty unpunished"? After all, you and I both deserve God's punishment, no matter how virtuous you might think you are for persevering through a sermon on the entire Old Testament! We all stand guilty before God. And Exodus 34 promises that God will not leave our sin unpunished. So what hope is there?

Atonement requires, we said, a substitution of suffering and death by an innocent party on behalf of the guilty party. But, we have also suggested, it takes more than the death of an animal to accomplish this. Some relationship between the victim and the guilty is required, a relationship far closer than what's possible between us and an animal who is not made in God's image.

The answer to the Old Testament riddle for the Israelites and for us could never be in ourselves or in a lamb. Their hope and ours has to be in the Old Testament's *promised person.*

People in Jesus' day did not wonder whether a Messiah would come. They took it for granted that their only hope was in the specially "anointed one" of God. But when this anointed one came, his manner of coming took everyone by surprise. He—Jesus—presented himself as fulfilling not just the Old Testament promises of a kingly Messiah but also another set of promises—the promise of the Lord's servant who would come to suffer for his people in their stead. Jesus brought together the Old Testament prophecies of the Messiah-King *and* the prophecies of the Lord's servant who would suffer for his people. Obviously, Jesus had meditated on the Old Testament deeply and knew these words from Isaiah:

> Surely he took up our infirmities
>   and carried our sorrows,
> yet we considered him stricken by God,
>   smitten by him, and afflicted.
> But he was pierced for our transgressions,
>   he was crushed for our iniquities;
> the punishment that brought us peace was upon him,
>   and by his wounds we are healed.
> We all, like sheep, have gone astray,
>   each of us has turned to his own way;
> and the LORD has laid on him
>   the iniquity of us all (Isa. 53:4-6).

This promise points to the answer to the riddle of the Old Testament. This promise is the hope of the Old Testament. In fact, what the Old Testament teaches us more than anything is that this promise is our only hope at all!

Let us pray:

Lord, when we are inattentive, history can seem irrelevant. And when we are attentive, we are not entirely sure what history means. But when we look in your Word and see your character, your passion for holiness, and your promise to judge all unrighteousness and wickedness, we are fearful. Yet, Lord, we also see that you have made a way for us to be reconciled to you, and we find hope in that offer. You reassure us in your Word that when we do not have the resources to trust in ourselves, we can trust in you. Lord, we know today that our only hope is in you. Forgive us for the ways we trust in our own devices and our own plans. Teach us what it means to trust in you alone for our salvation. We pray for Jesus' sake. Amen.

Questions for Reflection

1. How would you describe the Old Testament compared to the New? How much time have you spent studying the Old Testament? What essential lessons about the Christian life have you learned from it?

2. Why is reading, studying, and understanding the history of God's work with his people in the Old Testament helpful, even essential, for understanding who God is? What dangers do we risk by failing to understand how God has worked in history?

3. Is the God of the Old Testament an angry God? More angry than the God of the New Testament?

4. Is there any sense in which a Christian should be grateful for and find comfort in the fact that God becomes angry over sin? Why?

5. Did the Old Testament sacrifices remove the guilt of the person bringing the sacrifice? What purpose did the Passover sacrifice and the Levitical sacrifices serve?

6. Why would it benefit a Christian to spend time studying and meditating upon Old Testament sacrifices such as the Passover, or even the entire book of Leviticus?

7. What's the riddle of the Old Testament? What's the answer to the riddle?

8. Why was the manner in which Jesus came and presented himself as the Messiah surprising? Why is it hope-giving?

9. Why should the average Christian spend more time reading, studying, and meditating on the Old Testament?

PART ONE

THE GREAT STORY

THE MESSAGE OF GENESIS: ". . . WHICH IN THEIR SEEDS AND WEAK BEGINNING LIE INTREASURED"

THE IMPORTANCE OF BEGINNINGS

INTRODUCING GENESIS

GOD DISPLAYS HIS CHARACTER THROUGH THE WORLD HE HAS CREATED (CHAPTERS 1–11)

God's Holiness and Judgment Against Sin
God's Mercy
God's Sovereignty
Our Response: Obedience and Faith

GOD DISPLAYS HIS CHARACTER THROUGH HIS SPECIAL PEOPLE (CHAPTERS 12–50)

God's Holiness and Judgment Against Sin
God's Mercy
God's Sovereignty
Our Response: Obedience and Faith

CONCLUSION

1

THE MESSAGE OF GENESIS: ". . . WHICH IN THEIR SEEDS AND WEAK BEGINNING LIE INTREASURED"

THE IMPORTANCE OF BEGINNINGS[1]

Britain's Prince Harry is in trouble. He apparently has been drunk in public. They say it is the influence of his friends. "Bad company spoils good manners." Some are concerned this could mean he is unfit to succeed to the throne of England. No one who begins like this can be royal material, right?

This is also what everyone was saying of another young Prince Harry, or Hal Bolingbroke, son of Henry IV and the future Henry V. William Shakespeare wrote a whole cycle of plays that centered on the accession of this young prince to the throne. Have you heard of the comedic character "Falstaff"? He comes from this series. Falstaff was the wayward companion accused of leading prince Harry into the public drunkenness and debauchery that shamed his father the king.

In Shakespeare's play, *The Second Part of Henry IV,* an ailing King Henry recalls a dark prophecy once spoken to him, and he wonders if it is true. In his response, the Earl of Warwick (not an entirely historical figure) utters the words you will find as this sermon's title: "There is a history in all men's lives, / Figuring the nature of the times deceas'd; / The which observed, a man may prophesy, / With a near aim, of the main chance of things / As yet not come to life, which in their seeds / And weak beginning lie intreasured" (III.i.80-85). In other words, carefully studying the history of something, particularly its beginnings, allows you to know its ultimate outcome before it happens.

---

[1] This sermon was originally preached January 20, 2002, at Capitol Hill Baptist Church in Washington, D.C.

What do you think? Is that your experience?

Certainly beginnings are important. For many people, they are the favorite part of a journey. Plato said they are the most important part of a work. Get the foundations wrong, and nothing else in the building will matter. The Bible tells us that fearing God is always a good beginning point. Surely beginnings often tell us about the whole. They are portentous, carrying in them the seeds of the outcome. You show me how you begin your day, and I can probably tell you something about what the day will be like. So we give the advice, "Begin as you mean to go on." And all this is why I am so careful about how I begin sermons. I will put a disproportionate amount of time into how I begin a sermon. Beginnings are *very* significant. They can reveal everything from trajectory to purpose, from methods to motives.

INTRODUCING GENESIS

In this series of five studies, we will look at the beginning of the Bible. You can see in the table of contents of your Bible that the first five books are Genesis, Exodus, Leviticus, Numbers, and Deuteronomy. In this study we look particularly at the book of Genesis. The story of the book of Genesis is the story of beginnings. There is much in the book, but the basic line is simple: God, Creation, Adam and Eve, and the Fall take up the first three chapters. Chapters 4–11 cover the time from Adam to Abraham, including the Flood and the Tower of Babel. And chapters 12–50 focus on Abraham and his family (12–25 focus on Abraham; 26–36 largely on his grandson Jacob; and 37–50 mainly on Jacob's son Joseph).

The story is beautifully and captivatingly told. It contains parts so majestic and grand that no translation can hide it: "In the beginning God created the heavens and the earth" (Gen. 1:1). Yet it also contains small and precious details: "Jacob served seven years to get Rachel, but they seemed like only a few days to him because of his love for her" (29:20). Oh, friend, if you have not read this book, read it. Let me encourage you to read it in one sitting. It will take you three or four hours, but reading Genesis is a Sunday afternoon or a Saturday evening well spent; perhaps better spent than your last Saturday evening?

As you progress through the book, you will find that time slows down. In the early chapters we swoop through the centuries at the speed of the wind. Yet when we draw near the time in which these first five books were composed—probably when the children of Israel were getting ready to enter the Promised Land—time slows down. If the first five books of the Bible together form the beginning of the whole Bible, the book of Genesis provides the prologue to this beginning. It gets us from Creation to the starting point of the Exodus, and it is the Exodus that will finally launch God's people into God's land. In this series of five studies, we will look at one book per study. If this is the first sermon of mine you have read, let me say that this is not one of my normal sermons. But I do believe these types of sermons are useful. I do these Bible book overview sermons occasionally in order for our congregation to become more knowledgeable about what the Bible teaches. Sometimes you can see things from a great height, where you can take in the whole, that you cannot see down below. It can be difficult to get to such a position and it might take a little more work, but it bears great fruit.

For many people, Genesis is simply a jumble of famous Bible characters. Someone this week asked me to name the five most important characters in the book of Genesis. They were surprised when I did not mention Moses, but he does not come up until our next study, in Exodus. In order, I said the five most important characters would be—well, who do *you* think? God? Okay, that's not fair. The most important character would have to be Adam. And then it has to be Abraham. After that it gets a little dicey. But I would think Joseph, then Jacob, and finally Noah. Take it up with me later if you want to talk more about this.

If you take a copy of the Bible and open it, you will find the very first book is Genesis. We will not have any one main text in this study. Instead, we will look around the whole book, which is basically divided into two parts. The first part runs through the first 11 chapters. This section is about God creating the world and the whole human race. The main characters here are Adam and Noah. The second section takes up the rest of the book, running from chapter 12 through the end. In this section, the camera zooms in. It stops looking at the whole human race and instead looks at one particular family through whom God intends to accomplish his special purposes: God chooses a special people for himself to redeem out of the world for his own glory. The main characters here are Abraham, Abraham's son Isaac, Isaac's son Jacob, and Jacob's son Joseph. And that completes the book.

We do not have time to look through all this wonderful book—it inspires more questions than I could ever answer!—but we want to look at the key lessons I think we are intended to learn about God and about ourselves. In both parts of this book, we want to consider the display of God's holiness and judgment on sin, his mercy, and his sovereignty, followed by a consideration of what our response should be. As I have read and reread the book of Genesis over the past couple of weeks, these seem to be the four themes that emerge throughout the stories. The author of Genesis, Moses, could have written down a lot of other things. Genesis does not include everything that happened over the span of time it covers. Moses might have told the children of Israel a number of other things as they prepared to enter the Promised Land. But in God's sovereignty, these are the stories included for teaching, I think, what God intends us to learn. These themes emerge in the first part; and then, in the way God often reveals himself, they emerge even more clearly in the second part. God's revelation often becomes clearer over time.

GOD DISPLAYS HIS CHARACTER THROUGH THE WORLD HE HAS CREATED (CHAPTERS 1–11)

The first part of Genesis, chapters 1–11, provides everything the Bible says about a large chunk of human history. Some scholars suggest most of human history occurred before the Flood, based on the apostle Peter's comment about the "ancient world" (2 Pet. 2:5). Whether it did or not, the Bible clearly does not have a lot to say about the years between Adam and Abraham, who shows up at the end of chapter 11. Assuming that Abraham lived about four thousand years ago, everything we know about the years from Creation until Abraham are contained in these few chapters. In them are the stories of Creation and the Fall, Cain and Abel, Noah and the Flood, and the Tower of Babel. Also, some fundamental matters about God become evident in these earliest chapters of the Bible.

First among these must certainly be that God is self-existent. That is how the theologians would put it. In other words, nobody made him. In the beginning, *God* created the heavens and the earth. He is not dependent on anyone; not on you, not on me. He is not dependent on the weekly church offering. We do not have to pay him a salary. Indeed, all that we have is his. He is the one who made us. The Bible does not spend a lot of time talking about God's self-existence except in this first famous chapter about Creation.[2] The magnificence of God's Creation is not even the focus of Genesis. Still, his self-existence is the background for everything else. The rest of the biblical writers assume it. So Genesis tells the story of Creation very briefly and clearly in the first two chapters, and then it turns to focus on the fact that this God who created the world is holy. Our Creator will be our Judge. He has given us our lives, and we will give him an account for them.

God's Holiness and Judgment Against Sin

We first clearly observe God's holiness and his commitment to condemn those who sin again him in the great sequence of events running from the Creation

---

[2] See also Job 36–39; Psalm 50; Proverbs 8; Isaiah 40; Acts 17:24-25.

to the Fall to the Flood. In chapter 3, we encounter the story of the first sin in the Garden, when Adam and Eve take the fruit from the one tree that was forbidden them. We read about Eve foolishly looking at the fruit, debating with Satan about what God has said, and contemplating the fruit in its appearance and its effects. She even observes that the fruit is good to look at. She then takes it, holds it (God didn't say not to hold it, did he?), and finally eats it. Adam defaults on his responsibility to protect and lead his wife, before taking the sin as his own. God, of course, is as good as his word. We read, "So the LORD God banished him from the Garden of Eden to work the ground from which he had been taken" (Gen. 3:23).

God's commitment to good and right continues through to the famous climax in the Flood in chapter 7. Now, most everyone knows the story of the Flood. We have told and retold it; we have sentimentalized it with our pictures and our toys. I remember once, when our children were little, my wife and I bought them a plastic ark with Noah, Mrs. Noah, and all the animals. Yet the more I have reflected on it, the more I see how poorly our little bathtub could represent the horror of this story. Surely, the Flood represents one of the four great judgments in the Bible, along with the fall of Adam, the cross of Christ, and the final judgment. Surely, the Flood was a horrible calamity in which God wiped out almost the entire human race. Noah's ark was not a plaything, and the rising waters were not a warm bath! The waters covered the earth as the expression of God's death-dealing wrath against men whom the Lord describes with the chilling phrase "every inclination of his heart is evil from childhood" (8:21). Has anyone ever told you that total depravity is never taught in the Old Testament? The Lord's words here suggest otherwise.

Friend, if you are not a Christian, I implore you to take the time to read through the book of Genesis. You may find some details that confuse you. You may have some unanswered questions. But you cannot fail to find the message loudly and clearly proclaimed: there *is* a God, he made you with meaning and purpose, and you have failed to live and love as you were made to do.

Is it any wonder that the first chapters of the Bible have been under so much attack over the last two centuries? If we think we came into existence simply by an accidental process, then we may feel accountable to no one. Yet such freedom is lonely. It is purposeless. And it is false. It is the freedom that ignores evidence of design in the world, that rejects the idea that people are special to God, and that clones human beings only to grow spare parts with them and then discard them. This is what we call naturalism. Naturalism is the philosophy that says, since God did not make us, we are only as special as we want to think of ourselves as being. So we kill babies in the womb and old people in the nursing homes for our own convenience. Some say we do it for the betterment of society! May God deliver us in our day from such lies. And they are lies. Whether taught by a neighbor across the street or a professor at Princeton, they are lies. We need to call them such.

God is holy, and he will come in Christ to judge our sins. As the apostle Peter said, the Lord Jesus "commanded us to preach to the people and to testify that he is the one whom God appointed as judge of the living and the dead."[3] We should praise God for the majesty and beauty of his creation, which matches the majesty and beauty of his own character. And we should prepare ourselves for his scrutinizing judgment. We are called to both praise him and prepare for him. I pray that God will enable our church to do both. We need to be able to see the goodness of God's creation. Continually talking about the cross and our need for salvation does not mean we should not be able to perceive any good in this world. We can see many good things in our family, friends, and society at large. But we must also be able to perceive our sins. Let us *as a church* cultivate a readiness to see all of God's goodness in creation— whether coming naturally or through people; whether through Christians or non-Christians—but let us also cultivate a readiness to see our own sins in order to reverently confess and turn away from them. God is good in his creation, yet creation is fallen. He is holy, and he will judge us for our sins.

God's Mercy

But thank God that we not only find his holiness displayed in these early chapters of the Bible; we also find his mercy displayed. While pronouncing the curse itself, his judgment on the first sin, God offers a glimmer of hope that he will provide for us in our sins. In what Christians call the "proto-gospel," he promises that the woman's offspring "will crush your [the serpent's] head" (3:15). Does that not sound like the God of the Bible we read about again and again? Even in his first judgment, our great and holy Creator shows mercy. And he speaks so tenderly. In these early chapters, the expression "God remembered" is used a number of times. So in 8:1, God mercifully "remembered Noah" and the animals and livestock that were with him in the ark. After the judgment of the Flood, God promises to "remember" the covenant he is making with Noah and his offspring (9:15-16). In the midst of wrath, God remembers mercy.

Friend, it is important for you to see God's mercy as part of the Bible's basic picture of him. We cannot just speak of his holiness and perfection and not also speak of his mercy. Here in these first chapters of the Bible, where God

---

[3] Acts 10:42; cf. 17:31; John 5:27.

judges sinful humans for marring his creation and themselves—who were made specially in his image!—he remembers mercy.

Interestingly, the early church presented Noah's ark as a symbol of Christ. Some of the earliest drawings of Christ are representations of an ark affixed to a cross, indicating that Christ is our ark. He is the vessel of mercy that we, once inside, can safely ride through the floods of God's judgment. God has always been merciful, and never more so than by giving himself in Christ. Our only hope is God's mercy. As Christians, we have no ground for pride. We have sinned against God and are morally bankrupt. We have completely spent our small resources and now cannot provide for our most basic spiritual needs. We are entirely dependent upon God's mercy and grace for salvation.

This is why the cross of Christ must always be at the center of our worship, whether public or private. I don't mean a physical cross for us to stare at, but an understanding and a pronouncement of what God has done in the cross of Christ. These first chapters of Genesis present no hope for the human race apart from God's mercy! We know today with clarity what the characters in Genesis only dimly perceived: how God would specifically accomplish our salvation by giving himself in Christ. So we should praise God as Creator *and* Redeemer. We should sing of his truth *and* his mercies. We should praise the Lamb who was slain for us. As we sing in the hymn "God, All Nature Sings Thy Glory": "Our sins have spoiled Thine image; Nature, conscience only serve as unceasing, grim reminders of the wrath which we deserve. Yet Thy grace and saving mercy in Thy Word of truth revealed claim the praise of all who know Thee, in the blood of Jesus sealed."[4] Isn't that a marvelous truth about God? The holy one is the merciful one!

Yet this leaves us with another question: How can he do that? How can God act with such holiness *and* mercy?

God's Sovereignty

Here in these early chapters of Genesis, we also find that God is a sovereign God. He is, we must remember, the Creator of everything that is; so we should not be surprised to find him sovereign over what he has made. The author of all has authority over all. So in the first couple of chapters we learn that he made all that is, and in the third chapter we see that he can judge what he has made, even the creature that bears his image. If any doubt remains concerning his power and authority, chapter 7 should end it: "Every living thing that moved on the earth perished. . . . Everything on dry land that had the breath

[4] "God, All Nature Sings Thy Glory," from *Hymns II*. Words: copyright © David Clowney, assigned to InterVarsity Christian Fellowship/USA. Used with permission of InterVarsity Press, P.O. Box 1400, Downers Grove, Illinois 60515.

of life in its nostrils died. . . . Every living thing on the face of the earth was wiped out . . ." (7:21-23).

Do not arrogantly ignore God and his claims. He is holy and he is committed to vindicating his name. He will judge sin in those made in his image, and *you* bear the image of God. At the same time, you need not ignorantly despair. God is *able* to show mercy; he has power to do it, however difficult or complicated you may think your situation is. "Oh, there is no way God can make sense of my messed-up life." Yes, he can. He is powerful and he is gracious.

If you have any doubt about this, consider the life and death of our Lord Jesus Christ. Peter puts it so well in his prayer in Acts 4, when he prays, "Sovereign Lord, you made the heaven and the earth and the sea, and everything in them. . . . Herod and Pontius Pilate met together with the Gentiles and the people of Israel in this city to conspire against your holy servant Jesus, whom you anointed. They did what your power and will had decided beforehand should happen." Herod and Pilate *did* what God's power and God's will decided beforehand would happen. Did you ever notice that? Of course, Jesus had told the confident Pilate as much. When Pilate had asserted to Jesus, "Don't you realize I have power either to free you or to crucify you?" Jesus answered, "You would have no power over me if it were not given to you from above" (John 19:10-11). Or as Jesus had said earlier to a group of Pharisees, "I lay down my life—only to take it up again. No one takes it from me, but I lay it down of my own accord. I have authority to lay it down and authority to take it up again" (John 10:17-18). Wow! These are not the words of one more advocate of passive, nonviolent resistance. This is not Mahatma Gandhi or Martin Luther King, Jr. This is leagues beyond those people. Jesus is saying, "not only am I willing to expose myself to risk, but I *will* lay down my life. I have the authority to do it." How does he have authority to do it? Through the instrumentality of the Jews and the Gentiles, the Israelite and Roman authorities. Not only does he have control over when he will die, he controls how he will die, and what characters will be involved. No one has authority like that but God himself, and that is who Jesus is. So Peter asserts in his prayer that God is the sovereign Lord who arranged all those who conspired in Jesus' death. And the proof of all this? Not only does Jesus have the authority to lay down his life, he has authority to take it up again. Now that is authority!

If God has made promises to us, as he made to Adam and Eve and Noah, we can be certain he has the power and authority to keep his promises. God is able to do what he says, and he is committed to doing it! One of the reasons our church is careful to teach honestly about the power and sovereignty of God is so that we can love and trust him as we should. Please tune in if you thought the sovereignty of God is just something to argue about. The God we pray to is the same God who made this world and everything in it. The God whose praises we sing is the God who made us. The God whose Word we are now considering is the God who both righteously and terribly judged the world in the Flood. He is able to fulfill all the promises he makes quite well, and as his people we must remind one another about that. Sometimes, less mature Christians will bat ideas of God's sovereignty around like it's a game for young seminarians. But nothing could be less helpful! Of course there are difficult questions about how God's sovereignty and our responsibility fit together, but we get no more light in the matter by denying either of those great truths. You should not deny human responsibility in an effort to better understand the balance between the two. And you certainly should not deny God's sovereignty in order to better understand the balance. We desperately need to know the truth of God's greatness if we as individuals and as a church expect to rely on him wholly. God is sovereign, and he displays himself as sovereign in these earliest chapters of the Bible.

Our Response: Obedience and Faith

These early chapters of Genesis also teach us how we must respond to God in obedience and faith. We should believe God's words. If he says it, we should believe it, and we should obey him. Early on, Adam and Eve fail to believe and obey, as does Cain, as do the people of Noah's day. When Jesus wanted to express how morally bankrupt the future days of his return would be, he reached all the way back behind his own days on earth, behind Israel's decline and fall into idolatry, behind the confusion of the judges' era, behind the rebellion in the wilderness, behind the Tower of Babel, all the way back to the days of Noah. Only there could he find a time sufficiently wicked. He said,

> "As it was in the days of Noah, so it will be at the coming of the Son of Man. For in the days before the flood, people were eating and drinking, marrying and giving in marriage, up to the day Noah entered the ark; and they knew nothing about what would happen until the flood came and took them all away. That is how it will be at the coming of the Son of Man" (Matt. 24:37-39).

Now with all that in mind, consider Noah. Maybe you'll grow in respect for him a bit. Noah, by God's grace, stood as a counterexample. He stuck out. In Genesis 6 and 7, Noah's righteousness is prominent: "Noah was a righteous man" (6:9). And again a few verses later: "Noah did everything just as God commanded him" (6:22). And again in the next chapter, "Noah did all that the LORD commanded him" (7:5). Did Noah not share our depraved human nature? Was he completely sinless? Of course not. Speaking of all men, including Noah, the Lord says in chapter 8, "his heart is evil" (8:21). In chapter 9, Noah gets drunk. And that is just what the Bible mentions. I wonder how he treated his wife on the thirtieth day in the ark. Clearly, in chapter 6 God is speaking in a summary fashion about Noah's comparative obedience, while in chapter 7 he is referring to Noah's obedience in matters pertaining to the building of the ark. Noah is called righteous in the same way it should be said that your life, as a Christian, stands out as comparatively blameless from the world around you. I don't mean in an obnoxious way that makes people run from you. I mean your life should look different—if you call yourself a Christian—because you bear Christ's name. Your life bears a testimony to him, whether it is a true or false testimony. Incidentally, that is why our church encourages you to stop being a member if you stop living in a manner worthy of your calling as a Christian.

Well, how could Noah live in a comparatively righteous way? Was he just better than other people? Not at all. Noah simply believed the promises God had made him. He responded to God's words by having faith in them—by trusting that God's words were true and should be obeyed. Noah got to work building the ark, because when God spoke, Noah assumed that God was telling the truth. This is what the writer to the Hebrews tells us in Hebrews 11: "By faith Noah, when warned about things not yet seen, in holy fear built an ark to save his family. By his faith he condemned the world and became heir of the righteousness that comes by faith" (Heb. 11:7). No, Noah was not somehow exempted from the Fall. Noah, by God's grace, had God's life-giving word spoken to him. And Noah had faith. He believed what God said.

If you have never considered the truth of God's Word, but are feeling moved by it, let me urge you to heed his Word. Turn from your sins and to him. The times in which we live are marked by the kinds of sin and unrighteousness that seemed to mark Noah's days. Our own days have almost reached the point where fewer people object to divorce than to marriage, to abortion than to birth, to homosexuality than to one-man, one-woman covenants. God made us in his image, and we are called to trust and obey him as fully as Jesus Christ did. Do you remember what happened in that other garden in the Bible? Not the Garden of Eden, but the Garden of Gethsemane? How different the story that transpired in Gethsemane! In the first garden, the first Adam chose his own way—sin. In the second garden, the second Adam chose God's way—obedience. May we do the same, even if we end up as lonely as Noah, or as rejected as Christ.

To live like this, we need churches that work, don't we? God has always intended for Christians to gather in churches that are not deceived by a fair show of words about what they believe, but in churches that are committed to seeing those words backed up by actions of repentance, holiness, and discipline. May our church so obediently and faithfully respond to God's Word.

GOD DISPLAYS HIS CHARACTER THROUGH HIS SPECIAL PEOPLE (CHAPTERS 12–50)

The story of Genesis continues on past Noah and the Flood. In chapter 10 we read about the nations that descend from Noah. In chapter 11 we read about the Tower of Babel and God's judgment there. And then, the most crucial event in the Bible between the fall of Adam and the birth of Christ happens. Yes, I am making grand statements today, but this is the book of Genesis, not Titus! So I will say it again: the most crucial event in the Bible between the fall of Adam and the birth of Christ occurs in Genesis 12. Do you know what it is? The Lord calls Abram (12:1-3). This call sets off the story of the rest of the Bible. Here, the camera zooms in on this one family line, the line of Abraham, Isaac, and Jacob. And just as we found that God displays his character through all of creation, so we find in the latter part of Genesis that God means to display his character through the special people he calls out from the world. The same themes introduced in chapters 1–11 are worked out more fully in the lives of God's specially called people in chapters 12–50.

God's Holiness and Judgment Against Sin

To begin with, God's holiness is clearly taught in these chapters. His commitment to purity and righteousness is emphasized, and his judgment on sin is displayed. We see this in many ways: Abraham appeals to God's holiness (18:25); Jacob confesses his unworthiness (32:10); he also forbids idolatry (35:2-4); and God strikes down Judah's wicked sons (38:7, 10). God's special people must be holy, as God is holy.

Nowhere do God's holiness and condemnation of sin appear more vividly in the second part of Genesis than in the destruction of Sodom and Gomorrah. Certainly the invention of weapons of mass destruction in the modern era has not made this account any less chilling. God's destruction is total:

> The LORD rained down burning sulfur on Sodom and Gomorrah—from the LORD out of the heavens. . . .
>
> Early the next morning Abraham got up. . . . He looked down toward Sodom and Gomorrah, toward all the land of the plain, and he saw dense smoke rising from the land, like smoke from a furnace (19:24, 27-28).

According to the Bible, it appears, we have no ultimate rights. Before other human beings, our rights are inalienable. Before the one who created us, however, we have no ultimate rights. He who creates can justly destroy.

But God's holiness is not only displayed through his external judgments; his special people are called to internalize his holiness. So Abraham and his offspring are commanded to remain distinct from the surrounding nations. In particular, God forbids intermarriage with the Canaanites.[5] And sure enough, it seems that Abraham's family just doesn't like those Canaanite women. Abraham and Isaac go to elaborate lengths in order to get non-Canaanite wives for their sons. Some of the passages are almost amusing.

Why was God so opposed to intermarriage? Was he concerned about the mixing of the races? I do not believe we have any grounds for assuming that. As becomes more and more evident as biblical history unfolds, God knew that marriages between the Israelites and foreigners would have one chief problem: the foreigners would lead his people into worshiping foreign gods. That was what he opposed, and that was exactly what happened. As long as the people worshiped other gods, they could not be God's special people. So he strenuously forbade intermarriage.

Additionally, God wanted to restore his holiness and character within his people. He had originally created man not to be sinful (murderous, idolatrous, adulterous) but to be holy (loving, faithful to God, commited to one spouse). So when God began the work of restoration, he underscored certain creation truths: marriage is for a man and a woman, and a man and a woman are to unite around the worship of the one true God. The command against intermarriage was one way of helping his people recover these truths.

You realize, don't you, that to be human does not mean to be sinful? Sometimes people misunderstand depravity and equate humanness and fallenness, as in the phrase, "Well, he's only human." But this is a wrong equation. To be a *fallen* human means to be sinful. At one time, Adam and Eve were human but not sinful. And in heaven we will be human but not sinful. Jesus was also truly human but not sinful. He was holy. He lived the kind of life that God intended for us to live and that we can increasingly live by his Holy Spirit's work. So God calls us to live distinct lives of sexual purity. We are not to sleep with anyone who is not our spouse. And we are not to take anyone as a spouse who is not an evidently sincere believer in Christ. This is part of what God's call to holiness means for us as Christians.

As a church, we want to encourage growth in holiness. We encourage you, as Paul says, to examine yourself before you come to the Lord's Table. If you

---

[5] 24:3; 26:34-35; 27:46; 28:8-9; 34:9; 38:2.

regularly attend, you will have noticed that our church always announces communion a week ahead of time. Do we make this announcement because we are afraid people will forget? No, we have held communion on the first Sunday of the month for years. Rather, we announce it to issue a call to repentance and faith. We realize that as God's special people, the ones called by his name, we must not allow unrepented sin to continue in our lives, whether sexual immorality or anything else. Allowing unrepented sin to abide in our lives lies about the God who has called us, and it deceives the world about what God is like. God is committed to his own holiness and to the holiness of his special people.

God's Mercy

God's commitment to holiness, which we have seen in the second half of Genesis, does not eliminate his mercy. Indeed, if the presentation of his holiness seems to intensify in the second half of this book, so does the presentation of his mercy. For instance, we find more examples of God's merciful "remembering." In the midst of bringing the terrible judgment on Sodom and Gomorrah, the Lord is "merciful" to Lot and his family (19:16), which the author summarizes with the language of remembering: "So when God destroyed the cities of the plain, he remembered Abraham, and he brought Lot out of the catastrophe that overthrew the cities where Lot had lived" (19:29). Later, after Abraham dies, his grandson Jacob's beloved wife Rachel cannot bear children. Yet, we read, "God remembered Rachel; he listened to her and opened her womb. She became pregnant and gave birth to a son. . . . Joseph" (30:22-24).

Throughout the stories in this book, God makes it crystal clear that Abraham and his children will be special only by trusting him. In themselves, they can do nothing. He emphasizes this visibly in chapter 15 by making a covenant with Abram. The Lord and the Lord alone swears to the covenant (15:17-18), thus showing that he and he alone will accomplish its fulfillment. The covenant will not depend on Abram. This asymmetry is brought out even more clearly many years later when God calls Abraham in chapter 22 to sacrifice his long-promised son, Isaac. While approaching the place of sacrifice, Isaac asks his father where the lamb for the burnt offering is. Abraham replies perhaps better than he knows: "God himself will provide the lamb for the burnt offering, my son" (22:8). Then God does provide a lamb, even as he would later provide the Lamb of God, his only Son. God's call to Abraham and God's work among the children of Abraham occur entirely by his own mercy and grace. His people in Genesis deserve nothing.

Indeed, this is the story of God's people throughout the Bible and in his church today. We are redeemed by grace! We in the church do not gather as a moral impovement society to survey our own virtue and condescendingly look down on those outside the church. We gather as those who recognize we are redeemed by God's grace alone. And gratefully, God's grace is redeeming. So when Judah sinfully sleeps with his daughter-in-law in chapter 38—a tawdry story—the Lord graciously redeems the outcome. We learn in Matthew 1:3 that their union was one of several sinful liaisons through which Jesus, the promised seed of Abraham, would come. It is not that Judah's actions were okay. They were not. But God used them to display his amazing mercy and grace. He takes the worst situations in the lives of the ones called by his name and works them for our good.

I hope you can see that being included in God's special people—being saved—is nothing we can do ourselves. If you know yourself well, you realize that only God can save you. If it were left up to you, you would be as immoral as Judah, as deceptive as Abraham, as desperate as Rachel. We can no more save ourselves than Lot could have led himself out of Sodom or Abraham could have called himself away from his homeland. If we are God's people, it is because he has called us out of our own terrible sins and messed-up situations.

And praise God he does! Praise God he does not let his people's sins finally rule them! Praise God he has provided a sacrifice for his people's sins that we could never have provided for ourselves. Even if you died for your own sins, God's justice would not be infinitely satisfied. Your sins have offended an infinitely holy and eternal God, and you deserve more than a death that lasts but a moment. Praise God that he has sacrificed his sinless Son, Jesus Christ. Jesus died on the cross to bear the sins of all those who would turn from their sins and trust in him.

I pray that *you* have known that forgiveness and amazing blessing of God. This is one of the reasons I urge members of our church to come back Sunday evenings to gather a second time on the Lord's Day. Among other things, that is the time during the week when we hear testimonies of God's grace in one another's lives in order to bring glory to God and to encourage ourselves. God is merciful and gracious.

God's Sovereignty

In this second part of Genesis, which emphasizes God's work among his special people, we also see God's sovereignty more clearly. You might wonder, "How can we see God's sovereignty more clearly than we do in the Creation, the Fall, the Flood, and the destruction of Babel?" Well, it may not be more dramatic, but it does become more specific. How else could God work out his saving plan to have a people of his own unless he is sovereign? So through-out these chapters we find God sovereignly working. He chooses Abraham, not his brother Nahor. He chooses Isaac, not his brother Ishmael. He chooses Jacob, not his brother Esau. This sovereign God prohibits King Abimelech from acting out his affections toward Abraham's wife Sarah (20:6). It is this sovereign God who tells Abram, "your descendants will be strangers in a country not their own, and they will be enslaved and mistreated four hundred years. But I will punish the nation they serve as slaves, and afterward they will come out with great possessions" (15:13-14). We learn in the early chapters of Exodus that he was right on every count. From great matters to small, this God reigns.

Most prominently, we witness God's sovereign reign in the story of Joseph, which takes up the final chapters of Genesis. God tells both Pharaoh and Joseph something about the future because he is the one who controls it. And all these final chapters perfectly line up to do exactly what God promises. He plans to let Joseph irritate his brothers so that they will sell him to the Egyptians. He plans to have Joseph sold into Potiphar's house both to give Joseph an opportunity to display his competence and to provide an occasion for Potiphar's wife to falsely accuse him; for God knows what she is like. He plans to let Joseph be imprisoned so that Joseph will be known for interpret-ing dreams; to be known for interpreting dreams so that he will be distin-guished before Pharaoh; to be distinguished before Pharaoh so that he will be given authority; to be given authority so that Egypt will have food; for Egypt to have food so that his brothers will be brought down into Egypt. Do you see how carefully God has it all planned? It is amazing! God has done everything from the tiniest to the grandest in order to achieve and display his glory. How carefully he lines everything up in order to fulfill his promises to Abraham.

Do you think Joseph saw all that? I believe he saw much of this by faith, which we learn in some of the most amazing words in the Bible. By chapter 41, Joseph essentially has absolute authority in Egypt. In chapter 45, the broth-ers who had beat him and sold him into slavery stand before him, entirely within his power. No one can tell Joseph not to do with them as he pleases. He is the law of the land. Now, you may think you have made godly advances in your heart against revenge. But what if you had the people who beat you and sold you into slavery fully within your control? Yet notice what Joseph says to his brothers: "*God* sent me ahead of you to preserve for you a remnant on earth and to save your lives by a great deliverance. So then, it was not you who sent me here, but God. He made me father to Pharaoh, lord of his entire house-hold and ruler of all Egypt" (45:7-8). Several chapters later, their father Jacob dies, and the brothers again fear that Joseph will take revenge on them. Yet once again, as they stand before Joseph, entirely within his power, he says, "You intended to harm me, but God intended it for good to accomplish what is now being done, the saving of many lives" (50:20).

If you are following this study as someone who does not know God, be very careful not to make the mistake of underestimating him. He is sovereign over nature and over nations, over my life and over yours. He is the Creator of this world. And by the resurrection of Jesus Christ, he has shown himself to be sovereign even over death. We may temporarily ignore him, but we can never permanently avoid him. Remember that! If you do not know God by faith in Christ, know that you *can;* and when you do, you will have confidence in this God and courage in his service. You can believe his words and obey his instructions.

Christian friend, of all people, as his special people, we should know this. Our church should be marked not by casually approaching God but by approaching him with the reverence he deserves as Creator and Lord and Judge. And we do not need to approach him with worry, but with confidence; not with sadness, but with joy. We know who he is and what he is like. We have already seen something of his grace in our own lives and in the lives of those with whom we gather. Our God is the Sovereign Lord of the world, the Almighty Creator, and our Redeemer. This life-giving Spirit who, by his word, called forth life from the chaos in Genesis 1 is the same Spirit who, by his word, called forth spiritual life from the chaos that was my soul and was your soul, if you are a Christian. This is the God we serve.

Our Response: Obedience and Faith

How do we have this life? By responding as Abraham did: in obedience and faith. As we have seen, the writer to the Hebrews describes Noah as acting in faith. But nowhere in the whole Old Testament does *justification by faith alone* appear as clearly as it does in the account of Abraham's life—at least that is what the New Testament writers tell us. In Romans 4 and Galatians 3, the New Testament chapters most clearly and carefully devoted to justification by faith alone, Paul points to Abraham and his faith; not Moses, not David, not Malachi. In particular, Paul turns to the statement in Genesis 15:6: "Abram believed the LORD, and he credited it to him as righteousness." If you mark in your Bible, this is a verse you should mark. According to New Testament usage, this is one of the most important verses in the Old Testament. Again and again we find it quoted.[6] Why? Because it is the beginning of our faith.

Throughout his story in chapters 12–25, Abraham hears, believes, and

---

[6] Rom. 4:3, 9, 22, 23; Gal. 3:6; James 2:23.

obeys God's word. He obeys when God calls him to leave his father's home in Haran (12:1, 4). He believes God's promises to give him offspring, to bless those offspring, and to multiply them greatly, even though Abraham was well past childbearing years (12:2; 15:1-6; 17:2, 6; 18:10; 21:2-5). He believes God's promise to give him land (13:15; 15:18-21; 17:8). And he obeys God's command to circumcise himself and his offspring as a confirmation of the covenant (17:10, 23). Yet we observe Abraham's remarkable faith most clearly in chapter 22, when God calls Abraham to sacrifice Isaac, his only son through Sarah. When Abraham tells Isaac that God will provide the sacrifice (22:8), we have no reason to think that Abraham has in mind the ram God eventually provides (22:13). His son asks a simple, nontheological question: "We've got wood; where's the sacrifice?" By all appearances, Abraham thought God *had* provided the sacrifice, and it was Isaac. Abraham planned to give his only son's life to God at God's command. How could he do that? The writer to the Hebrews helps us again:

> By faith Abraham, when God tested him, offered Isaac as a sacrifice. He who had received the promises was about to sacrifice his one and only son, even though God had said to him, "It is through Isaac that your offspring will be reckoned." *Abraham reasoned that God could raise the dead* (Heb. 11:17-19).

That was Abraham's faith. He knew his God so well that if this God called him to slay his own son, he could obey because he knew God would be faithful to raise his son. He knew that the one who created the world and made life could give life to his son again. *That* is knowing God and taking him at his word! *That* is the faith that alone saves! Praise God that he gave Abraham such an intimate knowledge of himself and such a close relationship with him.

Our Creator is holy and perfect, and he made us to be like himself. But we have sinned and separated ourselves from him. We have brought his rightful judgment on ourselves. And regardless of how difficult your life may have been, I assure you that you have not yet experienced God's judgment of your sins as fully as you will, if you remain apart from faith in Christ. You will be utterly lost unless you, like Abraham, and like Noah before him, turn from your sin to righteousness. Turn from yourself and your own wits and begin trusting God and his Word.

God has come in Christ, and God has borne his own righteous wrath against sin by his death on the cross, a death for all of those who will trust him as their substitute. Will you do this? Will you so take Christ? Believe God's promises in Christ, trust him, and so find life! Because we cannot heal ourselves, God has sent us healing in Christ. But we must trust and obey. Be confident in the truth of God's Word! Be careful in obedience to his commands!

CONCLUSION

We mentioned at the start "seeds and weak beginning." And we have seen both beginnings and weak beginnings in this book of Genesis, haven't we? We have seen the self-existent God creating our world and creating humanity. We have seen the beginning of our problems and the beginnings of our faith. The human race, human sinfulness, and Christian faith are each introduced in this book.

In all of this, God does seem to work through "weak beginnings." Did you notice that in this book the wealthy and powerful cities are judged? Think of Sodom and Gomorrah with their rich merchants, or Babel with its clever engineers. God judges them and chooses instead to bless the world through the family of one Middle Eastern nomad. I assure you, you have never heard of a period of Abrahamic music or great Abrahamic architecture. He and his family were nomads! God does not begin his great plan of redemption through the incredible civilizations of China or India or Egypt. He begins it with a migrant family. That is how God chooses to bless the world.

If you have ever read through Genesis, maybe you have also noticed that among all the genealogical tables and records of sons and daughters, only three women are described as "barren." Sarah, the wife of Abraham, was barren (Gen. 11:30). But when she was an old woman, God opened her womb and she bore Isaac. Rebekah, the wife of Isaac, was also barren (25:21). But God opened her womb, and she bore Jacob and Esau. And Rachel, the wife of Jacob, was barren (29:31). But God opened her womb, and she bore Joseph and Benjamin. God promised Abraham that he would father a great nation. And yet, the first two women (Sarah and Rebekah) in the line of the promise that would ultimately yield the Messiah were originally barren!

Do you sense that God was up to something? That he was making a point? God wanted to make it clear that the promises he made to Abraham and his descendants depended on *nothing* in them, but only on him. He wanted the glory. He wanted the children of Israel, standing on the banks of the Promised Land and reading Moses' account of their forefathers, to know and trust that only he could deliver the Promised Land into their hands. If he had promised it to them, he could complete his promises.

Have you realized that God is this trustworthy and should be utterly obeyed? Have you realized that any prosperity and blessing you are given will not come because of your own great strength and power? Genesis was written to teach us this.

William Shakespeare was not the only writer who could be dramatic. Genesis begins with such power, universal scope, and hope of life: "In the beginning, God created . . ." But then notice how the book ends. Its very last words are, "he [Joseph] was placed in a coffin in Egypt" (50:26). Satan looks as if he has won, doesn't he? His rebellion against God's creation appears to have succeeded. Death has touched all of Adam's sons, and the last hero in Genesis, Joseph, fades away. The book that begins with Creation ends with a coffin!

But look at where that coffin is: in Egypt, the mightiest nation on earth. God knew what he was doing. God knew where to plant his seeds for his purposes. He knew exactly where to leave Joseph's coffin. As we will discover in our study of Exodus, the stage was set for God's great drama of redemption and resurrection, where he would show the whole world that no nation on earth, not even the greatest superpower, could stop his plans. And so he leaves Joseph's coffin in Egypt. Genesis, the book of beginnings, ends. But God's business is not finished yet. Not nearly finished!

Do you think you have experienced something that has finished off God's plan in your life? Some circumstance that is too horrible? Some situation that is too messed-up? Some sin that is just too serious? Then you have not carefully considered the Creator of this world . . . or Joseph's coffin. You think the story is over? God was not finished then. And, thank God, he is not yet finished today!

Let us pray:

O God, the dead ends of our lives call us to turn to you in repentance. This account of your creation and your merciful re-creation in Christ calls us to trust in you through Christ, our risen Lord. Amen.

Questions for Reflection

1. List several of the advantages of reading an entire book of the Bible like Genesis in one sitting. Do you have plans to do this anytime soon?

2. When was the last time you meditated on the horror of the Flood? Not to be gruesome, but imagine for a moment what that must have been like for *everyone* except Noah and his family. Does God intend such considerations to teach you something about your future? Your family's future? Your friends' future?

3. Is God unjust in promising to judge all sin? Why or why not?

4. What is the holiness of God? What is the mercy of God? How can God live precisely according to the requirements of his holiness *and* offer mercy to those who deserve punishment?

5. If a church were to attempt emulating both God's holiness and his mercy, what would that church look like? What sort of practices would characterize the lives of its members in their life together?

6. Hopefully you noticed that this sermon cycles through the same attributes of God twice: his holiness, his mercy, and his sovereignty. In the first cycle, these attributes are revealed through his work in creation. In the second cycle, they are revealed through his work among his special people. Where can you see God's holiness, mercy, and sovereignty at work in creation today? Where can you see his holiness, mercy, and sovereignty at work among his special people today?

7. Assuming the Bible's purpose for teaching about the sovereignty of God is *not* to give scholars and seminary students something to argue about, what purpose does the Bible have for teaching us about God's sovereignty? Why is the doctrine of the sovereignty of God something you should teach your children?

8. How should the doctrine of God's sovereignty affect your church's practice of evangelism and missions?

9. You may have noticed, this sermon treats faith and obedience kind of like two sides of one coin. So Noah *believed* God and *built* an ark. Abraham *trusted* God and *went*. But aren't faith and works different things? As Christians, we are justified by faith, not works, right? How then can we say the right response to God is faith *and* obedience? Do faith *and* obedience characterize your life?

10. Have you ever been tempted to think some situation you were stuck in was too complicated for God's rescue? Have you been tempted to believe that some sin you have committed is too heinous to be forgiven? Consider these moments, and then ask yourself what the author of Genesis would say in response. If God really did create the heavens and the earth with the breath of his mouth, and if Abraham and his descendants really were wholly dependent on God's grace for their status as God's children, what words of encouragement might he offer?

THE MESSAGE OF EXODUS: "ALL THE WORLD'S A STAGE"

A GRAND DISPLAY

GOD WORKS SOVEREIGNLY

In Moses

God raises up Moses

God calls Moses

God uses Moses to lead his people

In Pharaoh

God places Pharaoh in his position

God hardens Pharaoh

God defeats Pharaoh

GOD WORKS SOVEREIGNLY TO SAVE A SPECIAL PEOPLE

By Distinguishing His People from the Egyptians

By Distinguishing His People from All the Peoples of the Earth

God grants them his law and a covenant

God teaches and calls them to holy obedience

God grants them his special presence

GOD WORKS SOVEREIGNLY TO SAVE A SPECIAL PEOPLE FOR HIS OWN GLORY

CONCLUSION

2

THE MESSAGE OF EXODUS:
"ALL THE WORLD'S A STAGE"

A GRAND DISPLAY[1]

Some of William Shakespeare's most popular plays were his comedies. And among them, *As You Like It* is one of the most popular. It is the story of two brothers who become alienated when the younger brother usurps the elder's place and has him exiled into a forest. In classic Shakespearian fashion, mistaken identities, romance, and folly all collide to produce a good laugh. The play also includes a plain-speaking fool who gives one of the most famous speeches of any Shakespeare play. The fool summarizes the seven stages of a man's life, from infancy to old age. Yet the most quoted part of the speech is the very first line, in which the fool says, "All the world's a stage, and all the men and women merely players . . ."

That initial phrase, "All the world's a stage," well captures how the Bible presents this world as a divinely made stage for playing out the great story of human history. The Bible is a theatre full of comedy and tragedy, indeed, more than ever entered Mr. Shakespeare's fertile mind. And it is a theatre above all for the display of God's glory.

Really, this is the message of the whole Bible. I could preach an overview not only of Exodus but of the Old and New Testament together as a grand display of God's glory. This is especially the theme of the first five books of the Bible, which are called the Pentateuch or, sometimes, the Law, since they contain the Ten Commandments (and many others!). These five books begin with God's work in creation, the ruinous first sin, and God's great plan for the world—to save a people through Abraham's line. We considered all this in our previous study of Genesis. The other four books tell the story of Abraham's descendants from their time in Egypt until just before they enter the Promised

[1] This sermon was originally preached on January 27, 2002, at Capitol Hill Baptist Church in Washington, D.C.

Land. And the most dramatic episode, perhaps one of the most dramatic episodes in the Bible, is found in the second book, the book of Exodus.

On Sunday mornings at our church, we generally study smaller sections of Scripture than an entire book like Exodus. But some things can only be seen from a great height. So from time to time we divert from spending multiple weeks in one book in order to have what we call "overview sermons." Right now, we are in a series of five such studies on the first five books of the Bible. Here, we look at the second book, the book of Exodus. It takes about two-and-a-half to three hours to read. We won't take time to do that, but I would encourage you to read it on your own. Also, we will not consider just one text in Exodus, but we'll jump around the book, taking in as much as we can. In order to help us, I offer a thesis sentence that has arisen from my own reading of Exodus over this last week and that will give focus to our investigation. This study has three points and, as you'll see, each point will provide a part of our thesis sentence and will state something positively about God's work. We will also find that each point challenges some misconception that people often have about God.

GOD WORKS SOVEREIGNLY

We begin with point one: God works sovereignly. In essence, Exodus challenges the common notion that God is passive. How many times have you heard God presented as a resource or power for improving your life, should you decide to use him? We saw in our previous study that God is not a passive God at all. In Genesis, he creates the world out of nothing. He judges the world through the Flood. He calls Abraham and then fulfils his promise to give Abraham children, despite age and barrenness. And then the amazing story of Joseph occurs. Do you remember Joseph's statement to his brothers? "You intended to harm me, but God intended it for good" (Gen. 50:20).

In Exodus, the great story of God working sovereignly continues. We see this in many ways throughout this book, but perhaps we see it most clearly in the lives of the book's two main human opponents: Moses and Pharaoh.

In Moses

God raises up Moses (chapters 1–2). We see God's sovereign work in Moses' life first in the manner in which God raises him up. Chapter 1 of Exodus covers the span of several centuries. Chapter 2 covers about eighty years. And the rest of the book—chapters 3–40—transpires over a little more than one year. That one event-filled year shows us where the book's emphasis lies. Still, the introductory chapters give us some important information. When the story in

Genesis 50 left off, the sons of Israel were a few score in number and living in privilege, since their brother Joseph was the all-powerful prime minister of Egypt. Then at the very end of Genesis, Joseph died. In the first few paragraphs of Exodus, we learn that the memory of Joseph has faded in subsequent decades and centuries, that the Israelites have grown in number, and that the Egyptians have become alarmed. Nationalism and xenophobia often lead to ugly things, as populations feel threatened or even overwhelmed by a surging minority. In Egypt's case, the king (we don't know exactly which one) decides cleverly to turn this problem into an advantage: he will use this growing population as a large pool of cheap, forced labor to build great public works—all to increase his own reputation, no doubt. So the Israelites, instead of knowing the privilege they had become accustomed to, come to know oppression. In fact, the oppression is severe: servitude is not regarded as sufficient for keeping them down; the king instructs his servants to kill the young male children of the Israelites.

The times are dark, yet in precisely this context, against this dangerous background, we find in chapter 2 God sovereignly working. Like an infant Noah, as it were, the baby Moses is protected from the king's murderous rampage in a little ark of papyrus, coated with tar and pitch. God sovereignly allows Moses to be found and raised by, of all people, the Pharaoh's daughter. Everything we know about the first eighty years of Moses' life is contained in Exodus 2. And we have no reason to suppose he belonged to any kind of nuclear family with Mom and Dad Pharaoh, daughter princess, and two grandson prince heirs apparent, Ramses and Moses, as Dreamworks's animated *Prince of Egypt* suggested several years ago. The second half of the chapter tells what we do know. We know that Moses becomes a murderer. Perhaps you haven't thought of that, but he was. The Bible clearly teaches that the greatest deliverer of God's people in the Old Testament was a murderer. He sees an Egyptian beating a Hebrew worker, and he takes justice into his own hands by killing the Egyptian. As a result, he has to flee, and he ends up in the land of some other descendants of Abraham, the Midianites, east of Egypt in the desert. In Midian, Moses marries, settles down, and probably thinks retirement is upon him as he nears his eightieth birthday, as if God's only plan for Moses involved preserving his life. But then, something even more amazing happens to him.

God calls Moses (chapters 3–4). In chapters 3 and 4, we read that God calls Moses. And as much as Exodus is a story about Moses, when I read it again this week, I found that God is really the main character in this story. God appears to the aging Moses in the burning bush. God reveals his name to Moses—Moses was not out there looking for it. God commissions Moses to speak to Pharaoh and bring God's people out of Egypt. Moses was not sitting around reading the Federalist Papers, determining that the Hebrews needed to take freedom into their own hands. No, Moses is an eighty-year-old shepherd. God is the actor in this story. Even the amazing signs that God tells Moses to perform in front of Pharaoh and his court are conceived, scripted, choreographed, and powered by God! God is not finished with Moses. He chooses him to bring his people out of bondage.

God uses Moses to lead his people (chapters 5–18). God not only sovereignly calls Moses, he sovereignly accomplishes his plans through Moses. We see this throughout the amazing chapters 5–18. Perhaps you know the story, and we don't have time to rehearse it here. But very briefly, Moses returns to Egypt toward the end of chapter 4. He announces the Lord's plans and performs his signs before the Hebrew people, and the people "believed" (4:31). They buy in. "Yes, this sounds like the Lord. We believe this." But things get worse before they get better. Moses demands that Pharaoh release the Lord's people (chapter 5). Pharaoh decides Moses' request means the people lack work and have become lazy. So he makes their work more arduous. But Pharaoh's opposition does not deter the Lord from his plan to deliver his people through Moses. With God-given vigor, no doubt, this octogenarian confronts Pharaoh again and again throughout chapters 7, 8, 9, 10, 11, and 12.

The last straw comes in chapters 11 and 12. Chapter 11 predicts the plague on the firstborn. Chapter 12 explains the Passover feast, which will remind future generations of Israelites about this plague, and then it describes the plague itself:

> At midnight the LORD struck down all the firstborn in Egypt, from the firstborn
> of Pharaoh, who sat on the throne, to the firstborn of the prisoner, who was in
> the dungeon, and the firstborn of all the livestock as well. Pharaoh and all his
> officials and all the Egyptians got up during the night, and there was loud wailing in Egypt, for there was not a house without someone dead (12:29-30).

Then finally, toward the end of chapter 12, Moses leads his people in the Exodus proper: "The Israelites journeyed from Rameses to Succoth. There were about six hundred thousand men on foot, besides women and children. . . . And on that very day the LORD brought the Israelites out of Egypt by their divisions" (12:37, 51).

Chapter 13 and chapter 14 feature the climactic account of God's victory over the Egyptians. Chapter 13 begins with regulations about consecrating the firstborn to the Lord. Then in the latter half of 13 and throughout chapter 14 God victoriously triumphs over the Egyptians as Moses leads the Israelites safely through the parted waters of the Red Sea. The pursuing Egyptians, having reversed their decision to release the Israelites, find themselves trapped:

> The Egyptians pursued them, and all Pharaoh's horses and chariots and horsemen followed them into the sea. During the last watch of the night the LORD looked down from the pillar of fire and cloud at the Egyptian army and threw it into confusion. He made the wheels of their chariots come off so that they had difficulty driving. And the Egyptians said, "Let's get away from the Israelites! The LORD is fighting for them against Egypt."
>
> Then the LORD said to Moses, "Stretch out your hand over the sea so that the waters may flow back over the Egyptians and their chariots and horsemen." Moses stretched out his hand over the sea, and at daybreak the sea went back to its place. The Egyptians were fleeing toward it, and the LORD swept them into the sea. The water flowed back and covered the chariots and horsemen—the entire army of Pharaoh that had followed the Israelites into the sea. Not one of them survived (14:23-28).

This is the God presented in the book of Exodus. He is sovereign even over wheels getting stuck in the mud and coming off! In chapter 15, Moses leads a song of victory to God. Then throughout the rest of chapters 15, 16, 17, and 18, Moses and the people take a three-month journey to Mount Sinai. These chapters include stories of God sovereignly providing both food (water, manna, and quail) and victory for his people when attacked by the Amalekites. Throughout all of these episodes, God sovereignly works through Moses.

In Pharaoh

But God performs his sovereign works not only in Moses' life. Particularly in the early chapters of Exodus, we also see God working sovereignly in and through Pharaoh, king of Egypt. In many ways, Pharaoh is Moses' opposite in this story. Moses has nothing, but gains everything. Pharaoh has everything, but loses it all. And God is sovereign over both.

God places Pharaoh in his position. Just as God raises up Moses to lead the people, he places Pharaoh in his position of power. God purposed to install a pharaoh, as it says in the book's opening verses, "who did not know about Joseph" (1:8). And a little later he explicitly tells Pharaoh, "I have raised you up" (9:16). Surely you realize that God was no less sovereign in raising up Pharaoh than in raising up Moses. What does Paul say in Acts 17? "From one man he made every nation of men, that they should inhabit the whole earth; and he determined the times set for them and the exact places where they should live" (Acts 17:26). We find throughout the Scriptures that the Lord is the one who humbles and exalts—even kings (1 Sam. 2:7).

God hardens Pharaoh. Then comes the part of the story that troubles people the most, but is undeniably crucial to the great escape from Egypt. God works sovereignly in Pharaoh not only in putting him in his position of authority but also in hardening his heart. God warns Moses ahead of time that he will do this (just as he will later warn the prophet Ezekiel that the people to whom he will send him will have hard hearts so that they will not listen). Look back at Exodus 4:21: "When you return to Egypt, see that you perform before Pharaoh all the wonders I have given you the power to do. But I will harden his heart [notice this purpose clause] so that he will not let the people go." If you ever have discussions about God hardening Pharaoh's heart—and all Christians seem to get around to this discussion one time or another—Exodus 4:21 is worth noticing. Sometimes people say, "Okay, God hardened Pharaoh's heart in the sense that he allowed Pharaoh to harden his own heart." I appreciate the attraction of that interpretation; it is not lost on me. Yet I want to point out that this is not what the text says. I don't claim to understand everything about how God hardened Pharaoh's heart, or all of its implications. But the verse certainly says that God had a purpose in hardening Pharaoh's heart. Further, 4:21 appears to be the controlling verse for what follows in the rest of the story. This is the first time the matter is mentioned. And many more statements about Pharaoh's hard heart follow during the plagues in chapters 7–11. Some say that the Lord hardens Pharaoh's heart (7:3-5; 9:12; 10:20, 27; 11:10). Some simply report that his heart became or was hard (7:13-14, 22; 8:19; 9:7). And some state that Pharaoh hardens his own heart (8:15, 32). All three kinds of descriptions are used at the end of chapter 9 and the beginning of chapter 10, and the text is clear: right after the plague of hail and before the plague of locusts, Pharaoh hardens his heart and is described as sinfully culpable; yet God concludes the matter by describing himself as the ultimate cause:

> When Pharaoh saw that the rain and hail and thunder had stopped, *he sinned again: He and his officials hardened their hearts.* So Pharaoh's heart *was hard* and he would not let the Israelites go, just as the LORD had said through Moses.
>
> Then the LORD said to Moses, "Go to Pharaoh, for *I have hardened his heart* and the hearts of his officials" (9:34–10:1a).

God defeats Pharaoh. God's sovereign work through Pharaoh culminates in Pharaoh's final defeat in chapter 14. In the dramatic account of the Israelites crossing the Red Sea, God works sovereignly not only in Pharaoh but in all circumstances: he holds back the waters and he causes the Egyptians' chariots to fall apart and lose their wheels. Most important, he tells Moses, "I will harden

Pharaoh's heart, and he will pursue" the people of Israel (14:4). Several verses later, he broadens his scope: "I will harden the hearts of the Egyptians so that they will go in after them" (14:17). And that is exactly what happens.

According to the Bible, and according to this book of Exodus in particular, God is *not* passive. Circumstances do not determine God's plan; God's plan determines circumstances. Friend, that is the story of the whole Bible. That is why so many unlikely things happen—from promising and then giving a child to a barren hundred-year-old couple, to God putting on flesh and dying on the cross for sin. The Bible rarely deals in the likely. The great story of Scripture, from start to finish, presents God's sovereign purposes amazingly worked out. So God works sovereignly in both Moses' and Pharaoh's life. And that is what we are supposed to witness, so that we will personally hear God's promises to us, believe those promises, and obey him, knowing that he will accomplish everything he has said he will do.

GOD WORKS SOVEREIGNLY TO SAVE A SPECIAL PEOPLE

But that is not all of what we are supposed to observe. We are also supposed to observe that God works sovereignly (now let's add a little bit to the sentence to make our second point) *to save a special people*. That is transparently what God is doing in this story.

Exodus challenges the common notion that God treats all people in the same way, or that God is a committed egalitarian. No, that is not the story in Exodus. God is certainly fair; he is the standard of justice. But God does mysteriously and graciously choose to extend mercy to some. And no one can require mercy from him. It is *his* mercy. From a foundation of utter fairness, God chooses to extend mercy.

By Distinguishing His People from the Egyptians

Throughout the first part of this book, God dramatically and sovereignly distinguishes his people from the Egyptians by calling out the Israelites as his special people. This happens fully and finally, of course, in the Exodus itself. But he explicitly distinguishes his people much earlier. In chapter 8, God promises Pharaoh that he will "make a distinction between my people and your people" (8:23) by sending the plague of flies upon the Egyptians but not upon the Israelites. He does the same thing in the next plague, the plague on the livestock. Through Moses, God states, "But the LORD will make a distinction between the livestock of Israel and that of Egypt, so that no animal belonging to the Israelites will die" (9:4). Then a couple verses later: "And the next day the LORD did it: All the livestock of the Egyptians died, but not one animal belonging to the Israelites died" (9:6). Are God's sovereign purposes clear? It seems like it. He wants to distinguish his people from others. He does it again in the plague of hail: "The only place it did not hail was the land of Goshen, where the Israelites were" (9:26). God is making a point. These plagues are not freaks of nature; he brings a host of them to make that obvious. The sovereign God is purposively acting through these plagues to specially call a people to himself.

We even observe God's distinction-making during the great and final plague on the firstborn. The Lord promises Moses that this terrible grief will not fall upon the Israelites, and then he says, "Then you will know that the LORD makes a distinction between Egypt and Israel" (11:7). He also instructs Moses to memorialize this lesson into the annual Passover ceremony: "when your children ask you, 'What does this ceremony mean to you?' then tell them, 'It is the Passover sacrifice to the LORD, who passed over the houses of the Israelites in Egypt and spared our homes when he struck down the Egyptians'" (12:26-27a). So the message of Exodus is clearly that God distinguishes between his people the Israelites and the Egyptians.

By Distinguishing His People from All the Peoples of the Earth

As the book continues beyond the Exodus (chapters 1–18), we learn that God not only works sovereignly to distinguish his people from the Egyptians; he also works to distinguish them from all the peoples of the earth (chapters 19–40).

God grants them his law and a covenant. To begin with, God uniquely grants the Israelites his laws and makes a covenant with them. This happens around and on Mount Sinai in chapters 19–31. In chapter 19, God is specially present at Mount Sinai and speaks first to Moses and then to the people through Moses. God says to them,

> "You yourselves have seen what I did to Egypt, and how I carried you on eagles' wings and brought you to myself. Now if you obey me fully and keep my covenant, then *out of all nations* you will be my treasured possession. *Although the whole earth is mine, you* will be for me a kingdom of priests and a holy nation" (19:4-6).

The Lord then gives them the Ten Commandments (chapter 20), along with other statutes and ordinances (chapters 20, 21, 22, and 23). Why does God give the people all these laws? To reflect his character? Yes! But he also wants his people to live distinctly from the fallen world around them, where people do not naturally reflect his character. His special people should be distinguished from the nations by the way they live. They must not worship idols. They must treat their servants carefully. They must ensure that justice is done; that responsibility is taken; that property is respected; that compassion is shown; and so on. After all, this is the God who says, "I am compassionate" (22:27). He wants his people to live and look like him.

God knows the life of mercy-giving to which he calls his people will be difficult. So he warns them that such living will not always be popular: "Do not follow the crowd in doing wrong" (23:2), he says. He even instructs them to help people who hate them: "If you see the donkey of someone who hates you fallen down under its load, do not leave it there; be sure you help him with it" (23:5). Do you see that? This is not the normal way people live! Ah, but these are not to be normal people. They are to be God's special people—specially set apart for God in their lives. They even have special weekly Sabbath observances and three annual festivals to remind them of who God is and what he has done for them (chapter 23).

Chapter 24 describes the formal sealing or confirming of the covenant. Moses ascends Mount Sinai at the end of chapter 24 and remains upon it for forty days and nights, receiving the instructions recorded in chapters 25–31. These instructions describe God's plans for the tabernacle, its offerings, the ark, the table, the lampstand, the courtyard, even the oil and the things the priests are to wear, as well as other miscellaneous matters pertaining to the worship of God. All of these practices, and the covenant generally, are part of God's plan to distinguish his people from all other peoples on the earth. So God says to Moses, "Say to the Israelites, 'You must observe my Sabbaths. This will be a sign between me and you for the generations to come, so you may know that I am the LORD, who makes you holy'" (31:13). To be holy means to be set apart for God's purposes. And God makes the people holy by giving them his laws and uniquely covenanting with them.

God teaches and calls them to holy obedience. But God also works sovereignly to make them his special people by teaching and calling them to holy obedience. As far as I can tell, five capital offenses are laid out in Exodus: murder,[2] sorcery (22:18), bestiality (22:19), sacrificing to other gods (22:20), and—the only one mentioned twice—desecrating the Sabbath by working (31:14-15; 35:2). As the sovereign Lord and lawgiver, God intends to make his people visibly holy. As they obey his laws, they will be distinct from all other peoples, a distinction that reflects his holy character. Perhaps this is why the laws seem so sharp to us.

---

[2] Though this can include other killing that one is responsible for (cf. 21:14-17, 23, 29).

Negatively, we observe how important the law is when the people horribly break it in chapter 32. In a story rife with irony upon irony, the people forge a golden calf to worship. Moses has been away, up on the mountain, for forty days and nights receiving instruction from the Lord, when the Lord suddenly sends him back because the people of Israel have made this great idol. Whereas formerly they grumbled for food while journeying toward Sinai (15:24; 16:2; 17:3), now they give way to idolatry. It is so often that way. Lesser sins prepare the way for greater sins. We look at them; we tolerate them; we consider them. Then we give in to them and adopt them as our own. Before we know it, they have adopted us. Beware, my friend, of your own tolerance of grumbling at the Lord, or of impatience at his ways. Aaron forges a golden calf from the gold the people give him, and the people see it and proclaim, "This is your god, O Israel, who brought you up out of Egypt!" Can you imagine! Aaron is the person God has set aside to be his high priest. And at the very time God is giving Moses his plans for the tabernacle, his place to specially dwell with the people, the people are busy worshiping an idol. This is like committing adultery on your honeymoon! What a terrible thing! In the moment God most tenderly and carefully draws Israel to himself and lays out what it means to be his people, they betray him most clearly and sharply. God then demonstrates the seriousness of his people's sin—and simultaneously tests Moses—when he says to him, "Leave me alone so that my anger may burn against them and that I may destroy them. Then I will make you into a great nation" (32:10). What was Moses' response to this tempting offer? What would *yours* have been? Imagine that the Lord said to you, "That church you are involved with is just too sinful. I am going to abolish them, and I will make a new people from you." Well, it seems Moses thinks more about God's name than his own name (which is why the Pentateuch rightly says of Moses later on, "Moses was a very humble man, more humble than anyone else on the face of the earth"—Num. 12:3). Look at what Moses says:

> "Why should the Egyptians say, 'It was with evil intent that he brought them out, to kill them in the mountains and to wipe them off the face of the earth'? Turn from your fierce anger; relent and do not bring disaster on your people. Remember your servants Abraham, Isaac and Israel, to whom you swore by your own self: 'I will make your descendants as numerous as the stars in the sky and I will give your descendants all this land I promised them, and it will be their inheritance forever'" (Ex. 32:12-13).

What do you make of that? Is Moses teaching God? It seems, I think, that Moses is beginning to understand what God is doing with his people.

But then Moses himself descends from the mountain, and when he actually sees what is happening, his "anger burned," as the New International Version puts it, or "waxed hot," as the King James Version has it. And he "threw the tablets [upon which the Lord had written the Ten Commandments] out of his hands, breaking them to pieces at the foot of the mountain" (32:19). Moses then takes steps to punish the people. Three thousand are executed by sword, and the Lord strikes even more with a plague. It seems God will even distinguish between those who really are his people and those who merely appear to be externally. He is intent on having a visible people, a people visibly allied to him. We then read,

> The next day Moses said to the people, "You have committed a great sin. But now I will go up to the LORD; perhaps I can make atonement for your sin."
> So Moses went back to the LORD and said, "Oh, what a great sin these people have committed! They have made themselves gods of gold. But now, please forgive their sin—but if not, then blot me out of the book you have written" (32:30-32).

Again, note Moses' humility. He thinks of others before himself.

In chapter 34, the covenant is renewed. And in chapters 35–40, the tabernacle is built according to the instructions given in chapters 25–31. It should be said that after the covenant is renewed in chapter 34, the people obey and construct the tabernacle precisely according to Moses' instructions. They appear not to miss a beat. When God gives his instructions in the earlier chapters, he tells Moses the tabernacle and its furnishings must be made exactly "according to the pattern shown you on the mountain."[3] According to a summary statement in chapter 39, that is what the people do: "The Israelites had done all the work just as the LORD had commanded Moses. Moses inspected the work and saw that they had done it just as the LORD had commanded. So Moses blessed them" (39:42-43). They would continue to be God's special people, set apart from all the other peoples of the earth.

God grants them his special presence. Of course, the most special thing that distinguishes the people of Israel from all other peoples on earth—the very heart of what it means to be God's people—is his special presence with them. This particularly comes to the fore in the aftermath of the golden calf fiasco. In the beginning of chapter 33, God instructs Moses to take the people on to the Promised Land. He assures Moses that he will send an angel ahead of them to ensure their success; but, he says, "I will not go with you, because you are a stiff-necked people" (33:3). I don't mean any disrespect by this, but I am sure

[3] Cf. 25:9, 40; 26:30; 27:8.

any parent can understand what the Lord is feeling here. He loves his people dearly, but he feels he cannot abide with them because of their disobedience. What is the people's response when they hear this? Note their humility. They are not defiant. They don't become self-centered. They mourn. In other words, they tacitly admit the legitimacy of God's charges, and they mourn. So Moses goes back to the Lord and says,

> "If your Presence does not go with us, do not send us up from here. How will anyone know that you are pleased with me and with your people unless you go with us? What else will *distinguish* me and your people from all the other people on the face of the earth?" (33:15-16).

Do you see that Moses has gotten to the very heart of what it means for the people to be holy and special? It is not certain circumstances or events, or even their obedience. At the heart, their holiness is a reflection of God's special presence with them. This is what it means to be God's people.

Well, the Lord says he will stay with them. Yet since both his holiness and their sinfulness must be accounted for when dwelling together, great care is given to the design of the tabernacle. The tabernacle is a very interesting thing. We cannot linger here long, but think about it for a moment. The tabernacle is a very special place that God gives specific instructions about, including that it should be placed in the middle of the Israelites' camp. On the one hand, the tabernacle itself symbolizes God's special presence with his people. He promises no other nation the blessing of dwelling with them. So the people must be faithful to him alone (thus he warns against intermarriage, knowing that foreign wives will lead their hearts toward foreign gods—34:16). On the other hand, the very design of the tabernacle reminds the Israelites of their sin. It must be carefully constructed and maintained, served by individuals specially set apart. Within the tabernacle, sacrifices are required for the sins of the people. And specific restrictions indicate which people can approach the most sacred parts, namely, the Most Holy Place. All this reminds the Israelites that the God who dwells with them, to whom they belong, is perfectly holy, unlike them. Though he specially dwells with them, he is separate from them in their sins. Yet they too are called to be separate from the peoples around them, and separate from their own sins. All of this is kind of like the Lord's Supper is for us. It reminds us of Christ's presence with us, but it also reminds us of our sin.

God intends us, his people, to be different from the world around us. He does not mean for this to look arbitrary, such as having a special handshake or using odd language. No, of far greater significance, he means for us to reflect his character. It will look like a concern for justice, a willingness to give of ourselves, a love and care for our enemies and those who would hurt us. We should be marked as God's people because we share in God's character. Oh, friend, let me exhort you to live like this. Why wouldn't you? Popularity with man is too trifling a thing to stand in the way of following God in obedience. Will you give up obedience to God simply because he calls you to live differently, in a manner that might not be popular with those around you? Passing popularity with a passing set of friends should never be counted as equal to God's own pleasure that he shares with the people made in his image, regenerated by his Spirit, and living according to his character. His people are called to be holy, special, and distinct. God is a distinguishing God, and he works sovereignly to save a special people.

So do you think you are getting to know the story of Exodus? Let's quickly review:

Chapters 1–4 describe the circumstances of Moses' birth and calling.

Chapters 5–15 chronicle Moses' confrontation with Pharaoh, the plagues, and the Exodus itself.

Chapters 16–18 tell about the three-month journey to Mount Sinai.

Chapters 19–23 detail the initial covenant making at Mount Sinai when the Ten Commandments are given.

Chapters 24–31 are about Moses' forty days on Mount Sinai and the instructions God gives him about the tabernacle.

Chapter 32 describes the horrible golden calf incident.

Chapters 33–34 present the aftermath of that incident and the renewal of the covenant.

And chapters 35–40 conclude with the people's punctilious obedience to God's instructions as they build the tabernacle.

That is Exodus.

Does it feel as if you know the message of the book? God works sovereignly to save a special people. That is what this book says. I hope you see that. But we will not finally understand the message of Exodus unless we see one more crucial point.

GOD WORKS SOVEREIGNLY TO SAVE A SPECIAL PEOPLE FOR HIS OWN GLORY

God works sovereignly to save a special people *for his own glory*. Above all else, throughout Exodus, God aims to display his own glory. But you will learn this only by reading the book itself. Every popular retelling or movie about the Exodus, from Cecil B. DeMille's *The Ten Commandments* to *The Prince of Egypt,* misses this entirely. Usually, the Hebrew people are presented as types of American colonists or African-American slaves. Moses is some combination of Washington and Jefferson, Frederick Douglass and Abraham Lincoln, liberator and lawgiver, concerned above all else for human liberty. But this story is not primarily about human liberty. It may have a few implications that tend in that direction, but that is not the point of this book.

In fact, Exodus directly challenges the idea that God does everything for humanity's sake. Humans *are not* the ultimate purpose of creation. God's own glory is! Let's take one more quick tour through the book to make sure that you get its main point. The whole book, you could say, is about God establishing his own fame! You see it everywhere. If you have never noticed these statements before, I think it will change the way you read Exodus, and perhaps your whole Bible.

Why does God call Moses to bring the Israelites out of Egypt in the first place? "I will take you as my own people, and I will be your God. *Then you will know that I am the* LORD *your God, who brought you out from under the yoke of the Egyptians*" (6:7). God's purpose is for the Israelites to recognize Yahweh as their God.[4]

Why does God harden Pharaoh's heart, causing him to oppose God's own plans?

> "But I will harden Pharaoh's heart, and though I multiply my miraculous signs and wonders in Egypt, he will not listen to you. Then I will lay my hand on Egypt and with mighty acts of judgment I will bring out my divisions, my people the Israelites. *And the Egyptians will know that I am the* LORD when I stretch out my hand against Egypt and bring the Israelites out of it" (7:3-5).

God's purpose is for the Egyptians to recognize Yahweh as God.

Why does Moses, amid the plague of frogs, ask Pharaoh to set the time for when God should remove the frogs from Egypt? Have you noticed this? Pharaoh answers Moses' request, "Tomorrow." Moses then replies, "It will be as you say, *so that you may know there is no one like the* LORD *our God*" (8:10). God's purpose is for Pharaoh to recognize that Yahweh alone is God.

Why does God, amid the plague of hail, tell Pharaoh he is pressing against him so hard? "This time I will send the full force of my plagues against you and against your officials and your people, *so you may know that there is no one like me in all the earth*" (9:14). Keep in mind, he is saying this to a man whose nation had as many gods as we have people in church. The liberation

---

[4] When our newer English Bible translations have "LORD" in small caps, it stands for the Hebrew *YHWH*, usually transliterated as Yahweh, which is God's name for himself.

this book promises is the merciful liberation from the falsehood of idolatry to the truth of worshiping the one true God.

As we continue reading in chapter 9, we find some of the Bible's clearest statements about God's sovereign purposes. At one point, God explicitly tells Pharaoh why he has raised him up:

> "For by now I could have stretched out my hand and struck you and your people with a plague that would have wiped you off the earth. But I have raised you up for this very purpose, that I might show you my power and *that my name might be proclaimed in all the earth*" (9:15-16).[5]

Moses makes the point again when he tells Pharaoh the precise time the plague of hail will stop: "When I have gone out of the city, I will spread out my hands in prayer to the LORD. The thunder will stop and there will be no more hail, *so you may know that the earth is the LORD's*" (9:29).

And why don't the plagues stop here? After all, Pharaoh had sounded repentant several verses earlier: "This time I have sinned" (9:27). Yet his repentance does not last. God has further purposes for him. Look again at the beginning of chapter 10:

> Then the LORD said to Moses, "Go to Pharaoh, for I have hardened his heart and the hearts of his officials so that [God always has a purpose] I may perform these miraculous signs of mine among them *that you may tell your children and grandchildren* how I dealt harshly with the Egyptians and how I performed my signs among them, *and that you may know* that I am the LORD" (10:1-2).

And again in chapter 11, why does Pharaoh keep refusing to listen to the Lord, even though it is bringing disaster on himself and his nation? "The LORD had said to Moses, 'Pharaoh will refuse to listen to you—*so that my wonders may be multiplied* in Egypt'" (11:9).

Such statements come to a climax in chapters 14–15. After Pharaoh has released the Israelites, the Lord causes him to change his mind: "And I will harden Pharaoh's heart, and he will pursue them. But *I will gain glory for myself* through Pharaoh and all his army, and *the Egyptians will know that I am the LORD*" (14:4). The Israelites see the Egyptians approaching, but Moses reassures them, "Do not be afraid. Stand firm and *you will see* the deliverance the LORD will bring you today. The Egyptians you see today you will never see

---

[5] Though Christians sometimes argue about what Paul says in Romans 9:17, Paul is just quoting what the Lord said in Exodus 9!

again" (14:13). The Lord then sends the Egyptians after the Israelites through the Red Sea:

> "I will harden the hearts of the Egyptians so that they will go in after them. *And I will gain glory* through Pharaoh and all his army, through his chariots and his horsemen. *The Egyptians will know that I am the* LORD when I gain glory through Pharaoh, his chariots and his horsemen" (14:17).

Watching Pharaoh's army drown, the Israelites come to the same conclusion: "And when the Israelites saw the great power the LORD displayed against the Egyptians, *the people feared the* LORD and put their trust in him and in Moses his servant" (14:31).

Throughout all these episodes, God gains the reputation he both desires and deserves among creatures made in his image. Moses' celebratory song in chapter 15 exults in this God's unique glory: "*Who among the gods is like you,* O LORD? Who is like you—majestic in holiness, awesome in glory, working wonders?" (15:11). And several verses later:

> "*The nations will hear and tremble*;
>   anguish will grip the people of Philistia.
> The chiefs of Edom will be terrified,
>   the leaders of Moab will be seized with trembling,
> the people of Canaan will melt away;
>   terror and dread will fall upon them.
> By the power of your arm
>   they will be as still as a stone—
> until your people pass by, O LORD,
>   until the people you bought pass by" (15:14-16).

This, of course, is why the Lord sovereignly placed his people in Egypt, which we thought about at the conclusion to our study of Genesis, when Joseph's body was placed in a coffin and buried in Egypt. Why did he leave him there? Because Egypt was a great power. Because Egypt provided the perfect stage on which God could display his glory. If God wants to make his might known and his renown great, what good would it do to triumph over a tribe of nomads or some lesser nation? God led Joseph down into Egypt and placed Israel's children there, because he was preparing Egypt to be the special stage on which he would display his glory for all the world to witness.

And God meant for the deeds recorded in this book to be recounted, so that his fame would continue to be magnified and increased. One of the first times those deeds are recounted occurs in chapter 18, where Moses meets his father-in-law Jethro in the desert. Notice how Jethro responds to hearing what the Lord has done:

> Moses told his father-in-law about everything the LORD had done to Pharaoh and the Egyptians for Israel's sake and about all the hardships they had met along the way and how the LORD had saved them.
>
> Jethro was delighted to hear about all the good things the LORD had done for Israel in rescuing them from the hand of the Egyptians. He said, "Praise be to the LORD, who rescued you from the hand of the Egyptians and of Pharaoh, and who rescued the people from the hand of the Egyptians. *Now I know that the LORD* is greater than all other gods" (18:8-11a).

That is the message of Exodus: the Lord—Yahweh—is greater than all other gods. God worked sovereignly to save a special group of people so that we would behold his greatness. He is not just another projection of human hopes or philosophical ideas. God acted in time and space, so we could see his power and worship his majesty.

God works sovereignly to save a special people for his own glory. He did then, and he still does today. That is what he is doing in the church!

CONCLUSION

Exodus is a marvelous book, isn't it? It is full of richness about God, who he is, and what he is like. Christians have always known that about Exodus, and they have always loved it. Do you want to know how you should live? Come to this book, and memorize the Ten Commandments, as Christians have done for a couple thousand years. Jesus, Paul, and James all turned to these commandments and taught from them. They treated the book as authoritative. Stephen and Paul turned to Exodus to understand why so many of God's people did not accept the Messiah. In Exodus, they found the resources to answer that question. They learned that God's people have always been recalcitrant. The fact that we are God's people says nothing good about our natures or us. We are God's people only by his grace, because our natures are entirely too prone to evil and rebellion. Stephen and Paul found in Exodus that many of God's people may reject him, yet that God has a sovereign purpose behind even this.

Of course, not everything in Exodus is so clear. In chapter 34, at the end of the golden calf debacle, we find something I have called the riddle of the Old Testament:

> Then the LORD came down in the cloud and stood there with [Moses] and proclaimed his name, the LORD. And he passed in front of Moses, proclaiming, "The

LORD, the LORD, the compassionate and gracious God, slow to anger, abounding in love and faithfulness, maintaining love to thousands, and forgiving wickedness, rebellion and sin. Yet he does not leave the guilty unpunished" (34:5-7).

How can this be? How can God both "forgive wickedness, rebellion and sin" and yet "not leave the guilty unpunished"? This really is *the* riddle of the whole Old Testament.

The book of Exodus does not quite answer this question. To find an answer, we have to go outside the bounds of this book. In the Gospel of John's presentation of the passion of Christ, the Jews ask Pilate to break the legs of the bodies on the cross. They did not want bodies hanging during the Sabbath, and broken legs cause asphyxiation, thus accelerating the death process. When the soldiers come to Jesus and find that he is already dead, they do not break his legs. Jesus has already given up his Spirit. And John writes, "These things happened so that the scripture would be fulfilled: 'Not one of his bones will be broken'" (John 19:36). What Scripture does John mean? You have to go back to Exodus 12, where God gives Moses instructions on the Passover meal for commemorating the people's salvation during the plague on the firstborn. Concerning the Passover lamb that is killed in place of the family's firstborn, God tells Moses, "Do not break any of the bones" (Ex. 12:46). That is what the evangelist John has in mind when he writes about Jesus' death.

John and the early Christians knew that Christ is our Passover lamb slain for us. Paul writes, "For Christ, our Passover lamb, has been sacrificed" (1 Cor. 5:7). Our sin calls down God's righteous wrath. Yet if we repent of our sins and trust in Christ's atoning death—if we look to him as our Passover lamb—God's righteous judgment will pass over us and be applied to him. Our sins will be forgiven. The salvation of Israel in Exodus was God's greatest act of salvation in the Old Testament. Yet it merely points to his greatest act of salvation ever: his salvation of his people by the substitution of Christ as the Passover lamb, dying in our place so that we might live to God's glory forever.

And the ultimate end of all of this is the glory of God! God intends for his creation to see him for who he is, that all may acknowledge him, fear him, obey him, praise him, and love him. That is what this Exodus is about. It challenges our ideas of God as a passive, egalitarian servant, doesn't it? According to Exodus, God sovereignly saves a special people for his own glory.

This is why God brought the Israelites through the circumstances in their lives, and that is why he brings you through the circumstances of your life too. You are not dead yet. The story of your life is not over. You could be at the same time in your life that the Israelites were as they toiled away in that last year before Moses came. Do not give up hope! Do not give up faith in the promises God has spoken. I pray that you too learn to fear him alone and to serve and love him alone—not to your glory and fame, but to his. His glory was seen in the Exodus; it is shown even more clearly in Christ; and today it is displayed in the lives of his people. What a responsibility! What a privilege! Why else would we live?

Let us pray:

Dear God, when we contemplate ourselves, we realize there is no other reason you would save us but for your glory. We cannot save ourselves. There is nothing special about us, nothing that separates us from others. And Lord, honestly, having marred your image and sinned against you, we know that you do not need anything from us or depend on us in any way. Your glory does not need augmenting. Yet for you to love and pursue us to the point of your own Son's death, God—that shows us such love that our hearts are won over to trusting your purposes, even when we do not fully understand them. O God, when our minds cannot fully lead the way, we pray that you would cause our hearts to be won by love to you, as we observe your love for us in Christ. Do that in each of our hearts, we pray, for your glory through Jesus Christ our Lord, our Passover Lamb slain for us. Amen.

Questions for Reflection

1. At the beginning of this study, the story line of the whole Bible is likened to Shakespeare's quote, "All the world's a stage, and all the men and women merely players." If that's true, who's writing and directing the play? Can you summarize in a paragraph the story that is played out through all of Scripture? Do you have a role in the drama?

2. Read Genesis 15:13-16 and consider the fact that God spoke these words several hundred years before the Exodus. Then consider Pharaoh's enslavement of the Israelites, and even his slaughter of all the male Hebrew infants. Was God on his throne throughout these horrific acts? Why didn't he do anything to prevent them from happening? What does it mean to say God was "sovereign" amid these events?

3. Now that you have answered question 2, what answer do you give for the tragedies that occur in your own life? Consider some recent tragedy or set of difficult circumstances you experienced. Is it possible that God specifically

planned those particular circumstances for you? If so, why would this be comforting?

4. As we have considered, Moses was a murderer. So was King David. And Saul (later the apostle Paul) was little better, if not a murderer outright. Why do you think God calls such unlikely characters? Do you regard your own calling as likely or unlikely? Does it cost God more to forgive a murderer than it cost him to forgive you? Explain.

5. How do we as Christians take credit for our status as God's children? How does this wrongful attitude get reflected in our churches?

6. As we have seen, Moses often interceded before God for the sake of the sinful people. In whose life are you a Moses?

7. God saves his people from Egypt, he hardens Pharaoh's heart, and he performs the many miraculous signs ultimately for his glory. Does this make God vain? Why or why not?

8. Why is God glorified by our obedience?

9. What qualities characterize a church that is centered on God's glory? What does such a church look like? What qualities characterize a church that is not centered on God's glory?

10. What significance does the Passover Lamb have in the story of the Exodus? What does Paul mean when he refers to Jesus as our Passover Lamb (1 Cor. 5:7)? What significance does this New Testament Passover Lamb have in your life?

11. What is the riddle of the Old Testament, found in Exodus (see Ex. 34:5-7)? How does Christ resolve this riddle?

THE MESSAGE OF LEVITICUS: "THE WORLD IS NOT THY FRIEND NOR THE WORLD'S LAW"

3

THE MESSAGE OF LEVITICUS: "THE WORLD IS NOT THY FRIEND NOR THE WORLD'S LAW"

WHERE WILL YOU FIND THE ANSWERS?[1]

"The world is not thy friend nor the world's law." So says Romeo in the last act of what was perhaps William Shakespeare's most famous play, *Romeo and Juliet*. He says these words to a poor apothecary who is not sure if he should sell Romeo the poison that will end his sorrow and reunite him to Juliet, who he thinks is dead. The laws forbid the sale. Romeo, bending the situation to his own will, takes advantage of the pharmacist's financially impoverished state. Holding out forty gold coins, Romeo chides and sympathizes, urges and commiserates with the poor man to give him the poison he desires:

> Art thou so bare, and full of wretchedness,
> And fearest to die? Famine is in thy cheeks,
> Need and oppression starveth in thine eyes,
> Contempt and beggary hang upon thy back;
> The world is not thy friend nor the world's law,
> The world affords no law to make thee rich;
> Then be not poor, but break it, and take this (V.i.68-74).

The world and its laws are against you, Romeo is saying, so do what you must to care for yourself. The poor apothecary is not the only one who's ever felt the crosscurrents of duty and desire pulling in different directions. How

---

[1] This sermon was originally preached on February 3, 2002, at Capitol Hill Baptist Church in Washington, D.C.

many of us have found ourselves persevering in one direction yet being pulled in another? Does the world feel like your friend today?

If you are confused by the directions in your own heart, I have another story I want to tell you. It involves a deeper tragedy than anything Shakespeare ever wrote, and yet it ends full of joy and triumph. If you have never heard it before, I want to introduce you to the Great Story in the Bible. It is a true story. It is the story of why God made this world, and what he is doing in your life, and what he is calling you to do and be. And it is the story we will consider in this study. This world and its laws will give you no answer to life's greatest questions. For that you must turn to this story of what God is doing in this world.

INTRODUCING LEVITICUS

For the last few studies, we have been looking at what is called "the Pentateuch," or the first five books in the Old Testament (*penta* means five; *teuch* means book). We have already looked at Genesis and Exodus. Today, we come to Leviticus. I do need to tell you that this is not a normal sermon. Normally, I preach from a smaller passage than an entire book. But sometimes it is good for a church to take a whole book of the Bible all at once, because you can see things from a great height that you cannot see when you are close-up. Patterns emerge, and themes become more visible than when you meditate on just a phrase, sentence, or paragraph. That means we will flip around a lot in the book of Leviticus.

I don't know what you think of when you hear "Leviticus." If you have never read it, maybe you are tempted to confuse it with Thomas Hobbes's *Leviathan*. Or maybe you think of Levi's blue jeans. Or maybe you think of nothing; it just sounds obscure. If you have read it, maybe you think of priests or sacrifices or lots of rules, and still it sounds obscure. That is the way Leviticus is. It does have some famous parts. For example, did you know that America's Liberty Bell takes its name from this book? If you have ever seen the bell in Philadelphia, you probably saw the words inscribed on the bell, "Proclaim Liberty Lev. 25:10." That's from this book!

I admit, the book is a formidable one. If you open your Bible, you will find it is the third book in the Old Testament. It takes about three hours to read all at once. Just as I would encourage your family to gather together and read the books of Genesis and Exodus, I might even encourage you to read Leviticus together. It is God's Word, and it is certainly better than watching several hours of television. Just be aware that it is not structured around a story line like

Genesis or Exodus, and your kids may ask a number of unusual questions. But it is always good for the kids to see Mom and Dad say, "I don't know."

As I said, Leviticus does not contain much narrative. Mostly, it contains the instructions God gave Moses when the people of Israel were camped at the bottom of Mount Sinai. You may recall, the people remained at Sinai for about a year after receiving the Ten Commandments. And the first and last verses of Leviticus pretty much tell us what the book contains. At the very beginning, we read, "The LORD called to Moses and spoke to him from the Tent of Meeting" (1:1). If we flip to the last verse, we read, "These are the commands the LORD gave Moses on Mount Sinai for the Israelites" (27:34).

What do we learn from all this divine teaching? Much! Providentially, I received in the mail this week a copy of *Christianity Today*'s publication devoted to pastors and church leaders called *Leadership Journal*. The issue contained an article called "Preaching in Leviticus for a Year." Some pastor planting a church in Michigan spent his first year preaching through the book of Leviticus. As he put it, he "lived in Leviticus" for a year, and apparently his congregation loved it. So you can find a lot in Leviticus that is interesting. In this study, I simply want to point out two of the main things we should take away from the book. First, we see that God's people are distinct; so they should live holy lives. Second, we see that God's people are sinful; so they should offer sacrifices. I pray that you will see what both of these truths mean for your own life.

GOD'S PEOPLE ARE DISTINCT, SO THEY SHOULD LIVE HOLY LIVES

First, we see that God's people are distinct, so they should live holy lives. The book of Leviticus is divided into several major sections. Chapters 1–7 describe the various kinds of sacrifices the people must make. Chapters 8–10 focus on the preparation of Moses' brother Aaron as high priest. Chapters 11–15 outline the purity laws. And chapters 17–27 enumerate various laws about holiness. But I want to begin with a story in the middle section devoted to a special group of people in the nation, a people upon whom special demands are made—the priests.

The Priests Must Be Especially Distinct

As I said, there are not many stories in Leviticus, but the stories it does contain are striking, like this one about the sons of Aaron, Nadab and Abihu. Like their father who was the high priest, Nadab and Abihu were also priests:

Aaron's sons Nadab and Abihu took their censers, put fire in them and added incense; and they offered unauthorized fire before the LORD, contrary to his command. [We don't know what the unauthorized fire is. All we know is that it's unauthorized, which Moses emphasizes by referring to it as "contrary to God's command."] So fire came out from the presence of the LORD and consumed them, and they died before the LORD. Moses then said to Aaron, "This is what the LORD spoke of when he said:

> "'Among those who approach me [the priests]
>   I will show myself holy;
>   in the sight of all the people
>   I will be honored.'"

Aaron remained silent.

Moses summoned Mishael and Elzaphan, sons of Aaron's uncle Uzziel, and said to them, "Come here; carry your cousins outside the camp, away from the front of the sanctuary." So they came and carried them, still in their tunics, outside the camp, as Moses ordered.

Then Moses said to Aaron and his sons Eleazar and Ithamar, "Do not let your hair become unkempt, and do not tear your clothes, or you will die and the LORD will be angry with the whole community. But your relatives, all the house of Israel, may mourn for those the LORD has destroyed by fire" (10:1-6; cf. 16:1).

Now, what sense can we make of this story? What's going on? Well, understanding this story will help us understand Leviticus. Right at the heart of the people God is creating, he places a whole tribe of priests, the Levites. And the Levites are called to be especially distinct. They had to be ceremonially clean. They had to be physically whole (21:5, 16-23). Like Christian elders, their children could not behave in a manner that would bring public shame (21:9). By acting contrary to the commands of God, however, Nadab and Abihu fail to fulfill their very purpose as priests—acting distinctly.

Special duties. To begin with, the priests were called to be especially distinct because they had special duties. First, they performed the sacrifices. An ordinary Israelite citizen would bring an animal to the tabernacle to be sacrificed, and then the citizen himself or herself would slit the animal's throat. Once the animal's blood was drained, the priest would carry the blood to the altar with the special utensils made for the tabernacle. He placed the blood on the altar and the base of the altar, according to the type of sacrifice being made. Then the priest would take the remainder of the animal outside the camp and burn it in order to demonstrate its uncleanness. Other types of sacrifices were also offered, such as grain offerings; yet whatever kind of sacrifice was offered, the priests were responsible for all these special tabernacle duties.

The priests' other main duty is mentioned only once in Leviticus: teaching. It was a duty we rarely think about, but an important one: "You must distinguish between the holy and the common, between the unclean and the clean, and you must teach the Israelites all the decrees the LORD has given them through Moses" (10:10-11). Perhaps we fail to notice the teaching job of the priests because teaching about the sacrifices in Sunday school class is much more dramatic! You can sketch the tabernacle on the white board, and then show the class where the blood is placed on the altar. But if we consider the number of all the people in Israel, most of the priests must have been involved in teaching. The minority of them would have been at the tabernacle—or, later in Jerusalem, at the temple—performing these sacrifices.

Special provisions. The priests also received a special provision for their livelihood. After performing most sacrifices, the priests would then eat the animal used for the sacrifice. Did you realize that? Only some of the sacrifices would be completely consumed in the sacrificial ceremony itself, namely, the "burnt offerings." Most of the sacrifices, however, would be eaten by the citizen bringing the sacrifice and by the priests. This is how God provided for his tribe of priests. The citizens of every other tribe labored for their food. Yet the Levites' labor consisted of teaching God's Word and maintaining the sacrifices in the tabernacle. So God supported them by these sacrifices.

Special judgment. But along with their special recognition, duties, and privileges, the priests also bore a special judgment, which brings us back to Nadab and Abihu. Nadab and Abihu, like every priest, were held out publicly as models. They were to teach and exemplify what it means to obey the Lord. Yet Nadab and Abihu decided to approach the Lord on their own terms. And, friend, we cannot approach the Lord just however we please.

The Lord even warns Aaron, the high priest and the holiest man in the land, that he cannot enter God's presence however and whenever he pleases. God says to Moses, "Tell your brother Aaron not to come whenever he chooses into the Most Holy Place . . . or else he will die" (16:2). It is a serious thing to worship this God. He is not at our beck and call. He is not that kind of God, and we are not that kind of people. These priests were dealing with serious matters, and they would be seriously judged (consider Aaron's fear, in 10:19-20).

I don't know how all this sounds to you so far. If you are not used to reading the Christian Bible, especially the Old Testament, you may be surprised to learn about this elaborate system of priests and sacrifices set up by God. Yet the Bible clearly teaches that God provides for his people in a way we cannot provide for ourselves. If you happen to be wondering about becoming a Christian, one good place to begin is to realize that you do not have everything you need within yourself. Our goal as a church is not to tell you whatever will burnish your self-esteem, so that you will have the confidence to pick yourself up by the bootstraps and deal with every problem life throws at you. In fact, we would like to save you the time and tell you that you can't do that. We are made in God's image, but we are fallen. All the answers you need are not lying inside of you, innate and untapped, just waiting to be elicited by Socratic questions or an epiphany of self-understanding. If you want to find God, you must first come to the end of yourself. You must first realize your own limitations—what you can do and what you cannot do. Only then can you find God. Does that make sense? If it does not, talk to a Christian friend and continue to read through the Scriptures. Read through the Gospel of Mark and consider what Jesus' life and words say about knowing this God.

In one way, these Levite priests are like the teachers and elders in our churches today.[2] In another way, they point to everyone who is a Christian. The New Testament calls the Christian church a "kingdom of priests," who are called to mediate God to the world and to one another.[3] Not only should pastors like me care for other Christians and share the good news of Jesus Christ with our non-Christian neighbors; every one of us is called to care for one another and to evangelize.

Supremely, though, the priests and their activities point not to us but to Christ, who is our great high priest. As the writer to the Hebrews says,

> We do have such a high priest, who sat down at the right hand of the throne of the Majesty in heaven, and who serves in the sanctuary, the true tabernacle set up by the Lord, not by man.
>
> Every high priest is appointed to offer both gifts and sacrifices, and so it was necessary for this one also to have something to offer. If he were on earth, he would not be a priest, for there are already men who offer the gifts prescribed by the law. They serve at a sanctuary that is a copy and shadow of what is in heaven. This is why Moses was warned when he was about to build the tabernacle: "See to it that you make everything according to the pattern shown you on the mountain." But the ministry Jesus has received is as superior to theirs as the covenant of which he is mediator is superior to the old one, and it is founded on better promises (Heb. 8:1b-6).

At the center of God's people today is the one who makes us special: Christ.

---

[2] E.g., James 3:1 or 1 Tim. 3.
[3] 1 Pet. 2:9; Rev. 1:6; cf. Ex. 19:6.

The Whole People Must Be Distinct

But not only were the priests to be specially set apart. We began with the priests because they provide the most obvious picture of what God is trying to do. Yet if we want to understand what Leviticus teaches us, we must see that God intends for his whole people to be distinct. This is why, I think, the priests Nadab and Abihu are not the only ones in Leviticus to receive God's swift judgment. We find one other account of an unnamed man who, as a member of the tribe of Dan and therefore not a Levite priest, receives a similarly swift act of God's judgment. The man, described as "the son of an Israelite mother and an Egyptian father," gets involved in a fight and then "blasphemed the Name [of the LORD] with a curse." The Lord tells Moses the man must be stoned, and so we read "they took the blasphemer outside the camp and stoned him. The Israelites did as the LORD commanded Moses" (24:10, 11, 23). God's people must be distinct. Otherwise, they lie about who God is.

Cleanness and ritual purity. Throughout Leviticus, we also find a great deal of concern with issues of cleanness and ritual purity. So God says to Aaron, as we have seen, "You must distinguish between the holy and the common, between the unclean and the clean."[4] This theme is found throughout the books of the Law (the Pentateuch), but nowhere more so than the book of Leviticus. Over half of the occurrences of the word "unclean" in the Bible are in the book of Leviticus.

To understand this idea of clean versus unclean, it might be helpful to picture a graph: a great big circle called "clean." Almost everything in life would be inside the circle. This was the normal state of most things. Some kinds of food were declared unclean and would have been outside the circle. And through certain actions, clean things could be pushed outside the circle and become "unclean." Yet being unclean was generally not an irredeemable state. Most unclean things could be cleansed and brought back into the circle. And unclean things were not necessarily wrong, or even avoidable. A person who committed immoral actions such as adultery, homosexuality, murder, and many other things listed in this book was certainly unclean. But so too was someone who had a miscarriage or an infectious skin disease. A person could be made unclean by a number of activities that the average Israelite was right to engage in. Say someone had died, and you were preparing a corpse; that would make you unclean. You should do it, but then you would have to tend to certain measures to remedy your ceremonial uncleanness. Sexual intercourse in marriage, menstruation, and childbirth all made you unclean, though none of these things were sin. They were all good and right.

---

[4] 10:10; cf. 11:47; 15:31; 18:3, 24-28, 30; 19:19; 20:23-26.

In addition to the distinction between unclean and clean, Leviticus makes a distinction between "holy" things and "common" things. We might begin by thinking of everything—both the clean and the unclean—as "common." But then, you could push a clean thing into another, smaller circle called "holy." Pushing the clean thing into that smaller circle would be called "sanctifying" it, or making it holy. Pulling the holy thing out of the smaller circle—profaning it—would make it common again. Also, unclean common things could never come into contact with holy things. When they did, the law stipulated consequences that were most grave. For example, God commands that unclean people who touched or ate holy things be "cut off" from God's people (7:20-21; 22:3). Some things should simply never meet. If you have ever jumped a car battery, you know that connecting jumper cables to the wrong pole can cause sparks to fly, because some things were just not meant to touch. And unclean things could never touch holy things. So again and again God instructs the people to take unclean things outside the camp, because in the middle of the camp is the tabernacle of the Lord.[5]

This basic idea that everything is divided between clean and unclean as well as between holy and common runs throughout the law in Leviticus. Why did it work this way? Much could be said, but let me make two observations. First, it shows us that God is indifferent about *nothing*. All of life matters to God. So everything in ancient Israel—absolutely everything—was either holy or common. In this, God taught the Israelites that life involves making distinctions, and that they should never assume that something is morally neutral. What if you viewed your life like that? Would it look different? Would you be more sensitive to what the Lord really values in your life? Would you become more alive to God? I think this is one of the reasons that people enjoy John Bunyan's *Pilgrim's Progress,* C. S. Lewis's *Screwtape Letters,* or even Frank Peretti's novels about spiritual warfare. Each of these books shows us how everyday matters have eternal importance.

Second, God cares tremendously about how he is worshiped, and he refused to allow his people to worship him in the way the surrounding nations worshiped their false gods. In the ancient near east, fertility rites, cult prostitution, and child sacrifice played a prominent role in worship. So as you read through Leviticus, you find that anything having to do with sexuality, birth, or human death makes a person unclean (e.g., 15:16-33; 22:4). And unclean people could not be touched. They had to remain separate. God did not want such abominations as child sacrifice or cult prostitution to ever happen, much less

---

[5] 4:21; 11:24-26; 13:46; 14:3, 8, 40-41, 44-45; 16:27, etc.

be seen as a part of his worship. So he set up these series of laws, not just for the priesthood but for the whole nation.

Through all of these rules, the people began to grasp that God's concern for purity was fundamental to entering and remaining within a relationship with him. The laws taught that every phase of life should be lived in a way pleasing to God. The laws were, in a sense, the protective shell that allowed the seed of purity and holiness to grow amid a hostile environment.

Holiness. God's concern for holiness becomes even more pronounced in the last half of Leviticus—in chapters 17–27. God wants all his people to live as he has commanded them, and so he reinforces the teaching he gave in Exodus by drawing out the ramifications of this earlier teaching. There must be no false worship and idolatry, child sacrifice, or sorcery.[6] In chapter 18, many sexual sins are forbidden. He calls the Israelites to exercise a transparent concern for honest weights,[7] the poor,[8] the blind and the deaf,[9] the elderly,[10] and fairness in law, especially toward the foreigners among them.[11]

There are some wonderful instructions in this section of Leviticus. Consider this verse in chapter 19: "Do not curse the deaf" (19:14a). Isn't that wonderful? The deaf will not know if you curse them. But God knows, and he does not want his people cursing the deaf. Or consider the following verse: "Do not pervert justice; do not show partiality to the poor" (19:15a). We tend to think the Bible shows a special regard for the poor, and in many ways it does. Even Leviticus contains a number of provisions concerning treatment of the poor, yet the poor should not be set beyond the reach of justice.

But neither should the rich. In case you are one who is tempted to feather your nest, look at the rest of the verse: "or [do not show] favoritism to the great, but judge your neighbor fairly" (19:15b). Justice is blind to wealth, position, or status. Or you might consider this verse: "rise in the presence of the aged, show respect for the elderly, and revere your God. I am the LORD" (19:32). Doesn't that present a beautiful picture? I would not mind if we tried to recover this lesson. Indeed, Leviticus contains many things that are worth careful reflection.

In fact, did you know that this book of Leviticus contains Jesus' favorite verse? At least we can say it contains the verse that Jesus quotes the most often from the Old Testament. In chapter 19, we find the famous words, "Love your neighbor as yourself" (19:18). Yes, that's from Leviticus! In the Sermon on the

---

[6] 17:7; 18:21; 19:4, 26, 31; 26:1.
[7] 19:35-36.
[8] 5:7, 11; 19:10, 15, 33-34; 23:22; 25:35-38; 27:8.
[9] 19:14.
[10] 19:32.
[11] 19:15; 24:22.

Mount, Jesus uses this command to clarify other commands in the law.[12] In his conversation with the rich young ruler, he summarizes the law's demands by quoting this command.[13] And he illustrates this command by telling one of his most famous stories—the parable of the good Samaritan. Also, James calls this command the "royal law" (James 2:8), while Paul tells both the Romans and the Galatians that it is a summary of the law (Rom. 13:9; Gal. 5:14).

Have you thought much about the fact that love is the root and summary of the law? If you read through Leviticus and consider its laws, you might want to ask yourself what each command has to do with love. That is how Jesus understood them.

The command to love our neighbors demonstrates that holiness involves not only refraining from committing sins but taking care not to omit obedience. When our church approaches God for forgiveness at the Lord's Table, we often confess with the words, "We have done what we ought not to have done, and we have left undone those things which we ought to have done." We incur guilt for not doing what we should do as much as for doing what we should not do. God's people should be marked not only by the holiness of *don't* but also by the holiness of *do!* Is that your understanding of the Christian life? That being a child of God means doing what God values?

One category of sin in Leviticus that often surprises people but that is important to notice is the category of unintentional sins—sins committed through ignorance, or unwittingly. Now, perhaps certain aspects of your worldview just collapsed when I said that. Many people simply assume that, by definition, there is no such thing as an unintentional sin. After all, sin is about the intentions of the heart, right? Like what Jesus says in the Sermon on the Mount about looking at a woman with lust. Well, it is certainly true that our intentions are crucial, and they can be sinful. You can appear righteous and not be righteous. But sin is more than just that. Chapters 4 and 5 of Leviticus refer to sins of ignorance. For example, "If a person sins and does what is forbidden in any of the LORD's commands, even though he does not know it, he is guilty and will be held responsible."[14]

Have you ever thought of such a category of sin? It is significant because it shows us that sin is not fundamentally subjective. Sin is not, at root, something you do against your own conscience, your own nature, or what you perceive to be right. Sin is fundamentally objective. It is something you do against God's laws. Therefore, ignorance is no excuse. Of course, this has huge implications. Let me point to just three. First, have you ever heard a preacher say,

---

[12] E.g., Matt. 5:43-44.
[13] Matt. 19:19; 22:39; Mark 12:31, 33; Luke 10:27.
[14] 5:17; cf. 4:2, 13-14, 22-23, 27-28; 5:2-4, 15, 17-18.

"There is just one unforgivable sin: not receiving the Lord Jesus Christ"? Well, I understand what he means, but this can be misleading. Aside from the fact that the Bible never really says that, the statement neglects the fact that all of us who are Christians refused the Lord Jesus Christ before we were Christians, perhaps for years. Yet, at some point, we were forgiven for that previous refusal. On the other hand, those people who die never having heard the gospel will not stand before God and be judged because they did not hear the gospel. No, they will be judged, according to Scripture, because of their sins (see Rom. 2:12). Again, ignorance is no excuse.

Second, realizing that we can sin in ignorance provides a great motivation to get knowledge. Oh, friend, if it is true that God is holy and that we will one day give an account to this all-holy, all-knowing God, then we need to know how we have offended him. We cannot lazily rely on a casual inspection of our own heart's motives; instead, we must search God's Word and know his will.

Third, we should feel the urgency of sharing the news of the gospel with other people. The news is vital. The news is good. God has provided a way for people who have sinned against him to be forgiven and reconciled.

We must, as God's people, live distinctly holy lives. The importance of living a holy life is shown by the severity of punishment required for unholiness. Many of the sins enumerated in Leviticus, of course, were unprovable in a human court. God knows witnesses will not be present for every crime. But he will always know the truth, and so he often promises in Leviticus to punish the guilty himself. Among God's people, no one should curse his or her parents. No one should commit adultery or incest. No one should engage in perversions against the created order like homosexuality or bestiality. No one should engage in the false worship of mediums or cult prostitution. No one should blaspheme the Lord. No one should murder. God's people should be marked by the exclusive worship of him, by respect for others, and by faithfulness and purity in their relationships. Through capital punishment, God was teaching the Israelites that the quality of their lives mattered more than the duration. It was more important for his people to be holy than to be old. Have you ever thought about that? I love the line in the hymn "O Sacred Head, Now Wounded" in which we pray, "O make me Thine forever, and should I fainting be, Lord, let me never, never outlive my love to Thee."[15] Do not simply pray, "God, give me a long life"; pray instead, "God, give me a good life; a life that brings glory and honor to you."

The holiness that was supposed to mark the Israelites as individuals was also supposed to mark them as a whole people. God's concern with the nation

---

[15] "O Sacred Head, Now Wounded," ascribed to Bernard of Clairvaux, 1153, trans. James W. Alexander.

is summarized in chapter 26 in a list of blessings for obedience and a longer list of threats against disobedience. It's a very serious chapter, and would repay your careful reading. Among other threats, God says, "I will scatter you" (26:33), in the event they choose the unholiness that characterizes every other nation. If they as a people will not be distinct in *practice,* why should they be distinct in *place?* Disobedience will result in exile. This is the first time God threatens the people with exile—here at the base of Mount Sinai, speaking to the generation that escaped from Egypt. Yet God will make the same threat forty years later in the second reading of the law to the next generation preparing to enter the Promised Land. There, in Deuteronomy 28, God provides a similar list of blessing and promises, and he repeats this threat.

As for us today, I don't know all the spiritual forces and social changes at work in and among the nations. But I do know that if God's people are undisciplined and indistinct from the people around them, it would seem that God has little incentive to grant religious liberty to churches that mislead the world about what it means to be a Christian.

So why should God's people obey him? I can find at least six reasons in this book. First, they should obey him because they want to prosper.[16] Again and again, God promises to grant prosperity to the obedient. And yes, I do mean earthly prosperity. That does not mean God promises financial wealth. But he does promise something of a good life.

Second, they should obey him because he promises to be with them.[17] The primary thing that makes God's people what they are as his people is his presence.

Third, they should obey him because they fear him.[18] Again and again we read in Leviticus, don't do action *x,* but instead fear God. Don't curse the deaf, but fear God (19:14). Don't take advantage of one another, but fear God (25:17). And so on.

Fourth, they should obey God because of his special relationship with them. In chapter 25, the Lord says, "The Israelites belong to me as servants" (25:55). They belong to him. God possesses Israel in the Old Testament even as Christ possesses his church in the New (see Acts 9:4). And how God loves those who are his! If you have read through Leviticus, perhaps you have noticed all the language about covenants. When God speaks of covenants, he is not using the cold language of negotiation or the formal language of law courts; he is using the heated language of committed love.[19] Remember this every time you read about covenants in the Bible. In Exodus 20, God

---

[16] 18:5; 25:18-19; 26:3-12.
[17] 9:4, 23-24; 26:11-12.
[18] 19:14; 25:17, 36, 43.
[19] Cf. 24:8; 26:9, 15, 25, 42, 44-45.

exchanges wedding vows with his people. And in Exodus 34, he renews those vows. He will love his people as his own.

Fifth, they should obey him because they are called to reflect his character. In Leviticus 19 alone, we hear God exhort the people fourteen times to follow this or that command "because I am the LORD"! In other words, the morality of the Bible is objectively based. It is founded on the character of God. So in 19:2 we have what might be called the motto of Leviticus: "Be holy because I, the LORD your God, am holy."[20]

Sixth, they should obey God because God intends for them to be a witness to the nations. What a wonderful and positive basis for obedience. Consider these words in chapter 20:

> "'You must not live according to the customs of the nations I am going to drive out before you. Because they did all these things, I abhorred them. But I said to you, "You will possess their land; I will give it to you as an inheritance, a land flowing with milk and honey." I am the LORD your God, who has set you apart from the nations.
>
> "'You must therefore make a distinction between clean and unclean animals. . . . You are to be holy to me because I, the LORD, am holy, and I have set you apart from the nations to be my own'" (20:23-26).

Friend, I hope that you see in these verses that the God Christians talk about is not simply our intuition. He is not a passing religious feeling. He is not our comfortable traditions or our familiar rituals. This God we speak about is utterly holy. He is unlike us.

If you are a non-Christian, I ask you to think about the Christians you know. One thing you should find in your Christian friend, and among God's people generally, is this elusive and surprising quality we have been talking about—holiness. And I would expect that your Christian friend's holiness would both comfort and unsettle you at the same time. Does it? Be honest in your heart about this.

If you are a Christian, on the other hand, you must understand the importance of holiness among God's people. If you don't, turn loose of the name of Christian! Do not bring added judgment on your head for confusing other people about what it means to be a follower of Christ! We as Christians are to be holy. And we as churches should be holy. Capitol Hill Baptist Church should have a reputation in the community for holiness, a reputation that, again, both comforts and unsettles our neighbors. That is why church membership is important. If you regularly attend a church, consider becoming a member.

---

[20] 11:44-45; 19:2; 20:7-8, 26; 21:8, 15; 22:31-32; cf. 1 Pet. 1:16.

Consider sitting through its membership classes. Commit yourself to faithfully attending the church's gatherings, and integrate yourself into the lives of other members. Let them know that you are committed to the work in that place. God intends a vital aspect of evangelism to be our corporate witness as churches—the witness that we have as a body. This is how the world will know that you are my disciples, Jesus said, by the love you have for one another (see John 13:35). Jesus does not say they will know we are Christians because you, as an individual Christian, are so loving. He says they will know because you, as Christians gathering together, are loving one another. This is the way Jesus set things up. It's his idea, not ours.

Of course, the holiness of God's people in this world will always be partial. The people of the Old Testament looked forward to one who would be completely holy. How much excitement surrounded that day when, as Luke recounts it, the angel announced to the virgin Mary, "The Holy Spirit will come upon you, and the power of the Most High will overshadow you. So the holy one to be born will be called the Son of God" (Luke 1:35)!

He was holy. Perfectly holy. And he has become our holiness, if we belong to him. As Paul later reflected to the Corinthian Christians, "It is because of him that you are in Christ Jesus, who has become for us wisdom from God— that is, our righteousness, holiness and redemption" (1 Cor. 1:30).

GOD'S PEOPLE ARE SINFUL, SO THEY SHOULD OFFER SACRIFICES

There is much more we could say about how we are to be a distinct people, but we need to move on to this other part of Leviticus. In addition to teaching that God's people must live distinctively holy lives, Leviticus teaches that God's people are sinful and therefore they should offer sacrifices.

That's what we observe in chapter 9, as Aaron begins his priestly ministry. In chapter 8, Aaron is consecrated, ordained, and set apart as a priest. Then in chapter 9, he performs his first sacrifices, and they go well. We read,

> Then Aaron lifted his hands toward the people and blessed them. And having sacrificed the sin offering, the burnt offering and the fellowship offering, he stepped down.
>
> Moses and Aaron then went into the Tent of Meeting. When they came out, they blessed the people; and the glory of the LORD appeared to all the people. Fire came out from the presence of the LORD and consumed the burnt offering and the fat portions on the altar. And when all the people saw it, they shouted for joy and fell facedown (Lev. 9:22-24).

Sinful People Need Sacrifices

God's people need sacrifices because they inevitably fail to be holy. Inevitably, they sin.

The first seven chapters of Leviticus provide instruction for offering sacrifices in the tabernacle. God commands the unclean, the sinful, and the grateful to bring their offering into the tabernacle courtyard around the Tent of Meeting. Upon entering the courtyard, presumably, the individuals bringing a sacrifice would tell the priest why they were making a sacrifice. What did they bring to sacrifice? Sometimes they would bring a food item, as in a grain offering. More significantly, however, they would bring the finest animals that they owned, animals "without defect," as the book says over and over.[21] The sacrifices were to be valuable in themselves and costly to the one giving them. The sacrifice was a loss of goods but also a destruction of life. As God says in chapter 17, "For the life of the creature is in the blood, and I have given it to you to make atonement for yourselves on the altar; it is the blood that makes atonement for one's life" (17:11). The sacrifices taught the Israelites that sin brings death, and that only shed blood brings atonement.

Once the sacrifice was brought into the courtyard, the individuals making the sacrifice would lay their hands on the head of the animal.[22] By doing this, they publicly identified themselves with the offering itself, as if to say, "What happens to this animal should happen to me because of my sins." And then they, not the priest, would "slaughter" the animal. After the animal was slaughtered, the priests would take the blood of the sacrificed animal and sprinkle it on the altar and around the base in whatever way was required for the particular sin or occasion. Not even the elders of the community were exempt from this exercise:

> "If the whole Israelite community sins unintentionally and does what is forbidden in any of the LORD's commands, even though the community is unaware of the matter, they are guilty. When they become aware of the sin they committed, the assembly must bring a young bull as a sin offering and present it before the Tent of Meeting. The elders of the community are to lay their hands on the bull's head before the LORD, and the bull shall be slaughtered before the LORD" (4:13-15).

What a clear picture of substitution! The animal is portrayed as dying in the whole community's place.

In addition to the irregular sacrifices offered to make atonement for some particular sin or to give thanks to God for a specific provision, sacrifices were

---

[21] 1:3, 10; 3:1, 6; 4:3, 23, 28, 32; 5:15, 18; 6:6; 9:2-3; 14:10; 22:19-25; 23:12, 18.
[22] E.g., 1:4; 3:2, 8, 13; 8:14, 22.

regularly scheduled events—daily, weekly, monthly, and annually. Now, if sacrifices were made primarily to atone for sins, how could the nation schedule them ahead of time and at regular intervals? Because the Lord knew the people would sin. Behind the whole sacrificial system was the assumption that the people would keep sinning. No immediate end would come to this bloody procession of sin and sacrifice. That's why God tells the priests the fire on the altar must never go out (6:12-13; 24:2-4).

Perhaps this whole process shocks you. But Leviticus and every other book of the Bible clearly teach that we deserve death for our actions. Our righteousness has failed us, and we too need a sacrificial substitute. To find that sacrificial substitute, we turn to the book that could be called the New Testament commentary on Leviticus—the letter to the Hebrews. The author of Hebrews writes,

> The blood of goats and bulls and the ashes of a heifer sprinkled on those who are ceremonially unclean sanctify them so that they are outwardly clean. How much more, then, will the blood of Christ, who through the eternal Spirit offered himself unblemished to God, cleanse our consciences from acts that lead to death, so that we may serve the living God! (Heb. 9:13-14).

We have sinned against God by doing what we want rather than what he wants. So we should mourn for our sins and repent of them. We should turn from our sins and to God, placing our trust in the sacrifice for sins that God has offered us in Jesus Christ.

How can we do that? Regularly gather with the church and learn from God's Word. Establish relationships with others. Read books that discuss the nature of sin and what God requires. Avail ourselves of opportunities to sit under good teaching, whether in Sunday school or elsewhere. All of these avenues will help instruct us on how to put sin to death and live as the Lord calls us to live. If we want to offer ourselves as living sacrifices, surely we need to know what that looks like. And gaining such understanding takes effort and prayer on our part.

Sinful People Need Atonement

What Leviticus makes absolutely clear is that sinful people need atonement. The distinctions the book makes between objects that are clean and unclean, holy and common, tell us that even the things we touch become corrupted by our sins (cf. Jude 23). Something must be done, or our souls will be lost! And that's where atonement comes in. We are never told exactly how sacrifice effects atonement, but it does.

Atonement means "at-one-ment." Atonement is how estranged parties are reconciled. And atonement is necessary because our sin has caused a rupture not merely between others and ourselves, but most important, between God and ourselves. Our sins are a personal affront to him! As the psalmist says, "Against you, you only, have I sinned" (Ps. 51:4). The curses listed in Genesis 3—of pain in childbirth and in toil, and of death—all remind us of our broken relationship with God. Now, if we wish to come to God and be reconciled to him, we can come only in the manner that God himself has appointed; and that is the way of sacrifice and atonement.

The Day of Atonement. Chapter 16 introduces an annual day of fasting prescribed for the nation, called "Yom Kippur" or the Day of Atonement. On that day, a special sin offering was to be offered for the whole nation, and the fact that it was to be offered annually reminded them that no Levitical sacrifice could finally atone for sins. On this day and only on this day the high priest, representing all the people, entered the presence of God in the Most Holy Place. He entered bearing the blood of a bull and the blood of a goat. First, he would offer the blood of the bull to make atonement for himself—he himself must first be clean—and then he would offer the blood of the goat in order to make atonement for the sins of all the people.

It's a strange ceremony, when you think about it. He brings blood—first of a bull, then of a goat—into an always-empty room. Nobody is there; nobody is ever there. He is the only one who is there, and that only once a year. He then pours this blood on the top of the mercy seat, which is atop the ark of the covenant. And who can see this blood? No one. No one but God, against whom the people have sinned.

On this same day, the high priest places his hands on a second goat and confesses the sins of Israel over it. This goat, the scapegoat, is then released into the desert in order to symbolize the total removal of sin by the penalty of alienation and estrangement:

> "When Aaron has finished making atonement for the Most Holy Place, the Tent of Meeting and the altar, he shall bring forward the live goat. He is to lay both hands on the head of the live goat and confess over it all the wickedness and rebellion of the Israelites—all their sins—and put them on the goat's head. He shall send the goat away into the desert in the care of a man appointed for the task. The goat will carry on itself all their sins to a solitary place; and the man shall release it in the desert" (Lev. 16:20-22).

The Day of Atonement, of course, was held not just once but annually and in perpetuity. Other religions have had their sacrifices—sometimes even human sacrifices. But those sacrifices are given only when things are not going well. God gave Israel, on the other hand, a regular calendar of sacrifices. He wanted them to know they lived in a *state* of sin. The people themselves were sinful. And there was no perfect sacrifice. Each year the sacrifice was made, and each year the Israelites continued to be separated from God by their sins.

Christ. The insufficiency of the high priest's atonement should be obvious. It is shown by the way he made atonement for himself first, and then for his people. And it is shown by the fact that it had to be repeated! Again and again. Again and again. And again, the book of Hebrews helps us understand why:

> The law is only a shadow of the good things that are coming—not the realities themselves. For this reason it can never, by the same sacrifices repeated endlessly year after year, make perfect those who draw near to worship. If it could, would they not have stopped being offered? For the worshipers would have been cleansed once for all, and would no longer have felt guilty for their sins. But those sacrifices are an annual reminder of sins, because it is impossible for the blood of bulls and goats to take away sins (Heb. 10:1-4).

And from the previous chapter:

> the law requires that nearly everything be cleansed with blood, and without the shedding of blood there is no forgiveness. . . .
>
> [Christ] has appeared once at the end of the ages to do away with sin by the sacrifice of himself. . . . Christ was sacrificed once to take away the sins of many people (Heb. 9:22, 26, 28).

Our purity and righteousness is found only in the atoning sacrifice of Jesus Christ, the spotless Lamb of God. If you have sinned, he is the atonement that you need. No one else has ever shared your human nature entirely and yet remained without sin. No one else has been able to absorb the full wrath of God and satisfy it entirely. Only in Christ has God, who is deeply offended by your sin and mine, made a provision for salvation. God is the plaintiff who stands in accusation against our sins, and God the Son is the punished one who satisfies the demands of God's own justice. What other god acts as both the plaintiff and the punished?

Do you remember what John the Baptist said when he first beheld Jesus approaching him? "Look, the Lamb of God . . . !" (John 1:29a). After considering Leviticus, does this have a little more meaning to you?

Peter also called Christ "a lamb without blemish or defect" (1 Pet. 1:19). After reading and studying the Old Testament, it is amazing how rich the imagery of the New Testament becomes!

Hebrews might seem more vivid as well: "The high priest carries the blood of animals into the Most Holy Place as a sin offering, but the bodies are burned outside the camp. And so Jesus also suffered outside the city gate to make the people holy through his own blood" (Heb. 13:11-12). Jesus became unclean. The Holy One of God became unclean for us.

And, as Paul wrote to the Corinthians, "Christ, our Passover lamb, has been sacrificed" (1 Cor. 5:7). Trust in Christ's righteousness alone. No one else can atone for your sins. If you want to find mercy, you must find it in Christ or you will not find it at all.

CONCLUSION

That's the book of Leviticus. In this book, we see the impress of God upon his people, both positively by these laws and negatively by these sacrifices. What do we see about God? That he is unwaveringly right, just, pure, and holy. And what do we see about his people? That we should be holy too, but that we are not.

What do we do with all these Old Testament laws today? Apply them word-for-word? No, that won't do. Do we ignore them as worthless? No, that won't do either. As the New Testament says, the law helps us become conscious of sin. If it had not been for the law, we would not have known what sin is (Rom. 3:20; 7:7). So on the one hand, the law exposes our sin. On the other hand, its commands to offer sacrifices of atonement prepare the way for the solution to our sin—Christ! And the effect is glorious. It is almost as if Leviticus and the rest of the Old Testament build a mighty organ for us, an organ upon which the New Testament authors come and play the themes of the gospel itself for us to hear, learn, and eventually sing!

John Bunyan, the author of *Pilgrim's Progress,* recounts in his autobiography his own struggles with guilt over sin. He tells about his search for a sufficient righteousness, so that he could be assured of his salvation. But wherever he searched, he could find no such righteousness, even in the best of his deeds. "But one day" he writes,

> as I was passing in the field, and that too with some dashes on my Conscience, fearing lest yet all was not right, suddenly this sentence fell upon my Soul, *Thy righteousness is in Heaven*; and methought withal, I saw with the eyes of my Soul, Jesus Christ at God's right hand, there, I say, as my Righteousness; so that wherever I was, or whatever I was doing, God could not say of me, *He wants [lacks] my righteousness,* for that was just before him. I also saw moreover, that it was not my good frame of Heart that made my Righteousness better, nor yet my bad frame that made my Righteousness worse: for my

Righteousness was Jesus Christ, himself, the same yesterday, and to-day, and for ever (Heb. 13:8).[23]

I have two final questions for you:
Are you perfectly holy?
If not, what sacrifice will make atonement for your sins?

Let us pray:

O holy Lord, you know our hearts and lives. You know our thoughts and loves. You know our need for you. Reveal to us our poverty and your plenty. Give the gifts of repentance and faith, we pray in the name of the only sufficient sacrifice of Jesus Christ. Amen.

Questions for Reflection

1. What qualities of Christ enabled him to be the perfect high priest? Be sure to praise him for each attribute as you think of them.

2. We have considered the fact that God involves himself in every aspect of our lives. He is indifferent about nothing. That means being a Christian affects everything in your life. Are there any areas of your life where you exclude God?

3. If God cares tremendously about how he is worshiped, what steps do you take to ensure you approach him in worship rightly?

4. What steps should leaders in a church take to ensure that God is worshiped rightly in the church's public gatherings?

5. You have been told that if you call yourself a Christian but don't care very much about holiness, then you should turn loose of the name of Christian. Whatever for? Why such a radical charge?

6. As we have seen, Leviticus lays quite an emphasis on obedience. But do Christians really need to be as concerned about obedience as the Old Testament Israelites? After all, don't we live under a dispensation of grace, not works?

7. The holiness of a Christian's life, we have seen, should be both unsettling and comforting to non-Christians. What does this mean? What would this look like in the office? Among friends? With members of the family who are not

---

[23] John Bunyan, *Grace Abounding to the Chief of Sinners*, paragraph 229.

Christians? Who, more than anyone else in history, had a presence that was both comforting and unsettling to those around him? Can you think of occasions when people responded to this one in both of the ways mentioned above?

8. Given God's desire to save sinners, why did Christ have to die?

9. In recent times, some writers have contested that the Christian gospel does not have so much to do with justification through faith and the forgiveness of sins as it has to do with the proclamation of the kingdom of God to the nations. In other words, the forgiveness of sins and the kingdom of God are pitted against one another. How do these writers fail to recognize the significance of Leviticus?

10. Other writers today decry what they describe as an overemphasis on "truth" and an underemphasis on "experience" among evangelical Christians. How would the author of Leviticus address this claim?

11. Does Leviticus teach the gospel? How?

THE MESSAGE OF NUMBERS: "PAST AND TO COME SEEM BEST, THINGS PRESENT, WORST"

NEVER HAPPY NOW

INTRODUCING NUMBERS

GOD PREPARES THE PEOPLE (AT SINAI, CHAPTERS 1–10)

> By Teaching Them About Purity (Chapters 4–5; 6:1-21)
>
> By Giving Them Priests (1–4, 7–8)
>
> By Giving Them His Presence (6:22-27; 9–10)

BUT THE PEOPLE DO NOT TRUST GOD (AT KADESH, CHAPTERS 11–16)

> By Constantly Complaining (11–12)
>
> > They complain about their hardships
> >
> > They complain about their food
> >
> > Miriam and Aaron (sister and brother of Moses) complain
>
> By Rebelling (13:1–14:10a)
>
> Result: God Punishes the People (14:10b–16:50)

YET GOD PERSEVERES WITH THE PEOPLE (AT MOAB, CHAPTERS 17–36)

> By Providing Instructions for Priests and for Purity
>
> By Remaining Gracious Despite Continued Sin (17; 20:9-12; 21:4-9; 25)
>
> By Giving Them a Second Chance
>
> By Enabling Them to Reach the Promised Land!

CONCLUSION

4

THE MESSAGE OF NUMBERS: "PAST AND TO COME SEEM BEST, THINGS PRESENT, WORST"

NEVER HAPPY NOW[1]

"Past and to come seem best, things present, worst." So says the conspiring archbishop of York, Richard Scroop, to his coconspirators Lord Mowbray and Lord Hastings as they plan together to overthrow the king in William Shakespeare's historical play *The Second Part of Henry IV*. Archbishop Scroop, a real historical character, did in fact help to take down one king and enthrone another. Now, as he attempts in Shakespeare's version to lead a rebellion against the king he helped enthrone, he begins to have second thoughts. He does not like the forces he sees on the king's side, and he is unsure of those on his own. The present situation looking worse, his hopes dim. He becomes uncertain and discontent. Perhaps he wishes he had never set himself up to make and unmake kings. Finally, he laments, "Past and to come seem best, things present, worst."

It is amazing what changes can be wrought in our feelings and judgments as facts slowly assemble themselves, as the future steadily becomes the present, as the distant terrain draws closer. For many people, the present is always a seedbed for discontent. One Puritan writer said this about discontent: "The proud man hath no God, the unpeaceable man hath no neighbour, the distrustful man hath no friend, but the discontented man hath not himself."[2]

---

[1] This sermon was originally preached on February 17, 2001, at Capitol Hill Baptist Church in Washington, D.C.
[2] Charles Herle, cited in James Reid, *Memoirs of the Westminster Divines*, 2 vols. (Paisley, UK: Stephen & Andrew Young, 1815), 2:28.

INTRODUCING NUMBERS

We come in our study through the Pentateuch (the first five books of the Bible) to the culmination of human discontent. As you may recall, Genesis describes the Creation and the Fall, as well as God's promises and blessings to Abraham and his descendants. Genesis contains everything the Bible has to say about human history until the birth of Moses. Exodus picks up with the birth of Moses and the first eighty years of his life in chapters 1 and 2. Beginning with Exodus 3 and proceeding through Leviticus and much of Numbers, the narrative slows way down and covers the span of only one year. Then, in the middle of Numbers, a forty-year period of wandering begins for the Israelite people, followed by another one-year section that closes out Numbers and fills all of Deuteronomy. It is in the book of Numbers that the discontentedness of God's chosen people reaches its highest pitch, even amid God's blessings upon them.

Numbers is an interesting book. It has thirty-six chapters and can be divided into three basic sections based on geographic setting: Chapters 1–10 are set around Mount Sinai. Chapters 11–16, which record the forty-year wanderings, are set around Kadesh. Then chapters 17–36 are set on the plains of Moab across from the Promised Land. In this study, we will look at all three sections of the book.

Let me first mention, these overview sermons are unusual sermons. I don't normally preach through an entire book of the Bible, though the length of my sermons might make it feel that way sometimes. Normally, I take smaller sections of Scripture, like a parable of Jesus or a chapter from a letter by Paul. Yet in this five-part series, we are looking at the first five books of the Bible in order to understand the basic message of each book. That means we will be flipping around the book of Numbers a bit. But I will try to do this largely in order and according to these three sections, each represented by a short sentence.

GOD PREPARES THE PEOPLE (AT SINAI, CHAPTERS 1–10)

In the first ten chapters of Numbers, God prepares the people. That is our first sentence. Specifically, he prepares them for their journey and entrance into Canaan. The book begins at Sinai where, as you might recall, the Israelites have camped since arriving, in Exodus 19. In that time, God has given the Ten Commandments through Moses. The people have rebelled and been forgiven. God has laid out for Moses his designs for the tabernacle, which the people built exactly according to design. God has also taught the people about their sin and his provision for them. Specifically, sacrifices were prescribed and regulations for purity were put in place. And now in the first part of Numbers, still at the base of Mount Sinai, God continues to prepare his people.

By Teaching Them About Purity (Chapters 4–5; 6:1-21)

First, he prepares the people by teaching them about purity. In chapter 5, God teaches them that their camp must be pure, as well as their marriages. Verses 1-21 of chapter 6 present a group of people who choose to live by a higher than normal standard of separation and purity, the Nazirites (not related to the Nazarenes or Nazareth). In part, the Nazirites function as a mobile sign and reminder to the Israelite people about how God has set the whole nation apart. In that sense, they are a walking Lord's Supper, as it were, reminding the people that they are special and set apart for God's work.

By Giving Them Priests (1–4, 7–8)

The first four chapters of Numbers really give the book its name. If you have read it, you know it has a lot of numbers! Chapter 1 provides a tribe-by-tribe census. Chapter 2 presents instructions for where each tribe should camp relative to one another as they migrate toward the Promised Land. These two chapters, though, seem to set up chapters 3 and 4, which are all about one tribe, the Levites. God gives the Israelites the Levites as a priestly tribe for helping to prepare them for being his special people.

Charged with transporting the tabernacle and polishing its utensils, the Levites are placed in the middle of the camp around the tabernacle, where the Israelites offer sacrifices and where Moses meets with God. The Levites' special status, their special function, and their central location within the camp all reflect the fact that the whole tribe centers on the tabernacle. Chapters 7–8 go on to describe the sacrifices and offerings every tribe brings to the tabernacle for its opening dedication, as well as the consecration of the Levites.

By Giving Them His Presence (6:22-27; 9–10)

Most especially, though, God prepares the people by giving them his presence. The tabernacle fundamentally represents God's presence with the people, and the priests' service identifies these people as specially belonging to the Lord. So the blessing that the Lord teaches Moses to teach the priests—what we call the Aaronic blessing—promises God's abiding presence:

"Tell Aaron and his sons, 'This is how you are to bless the Israelites. Say to them:

> """The LORD bless you and keep you;
> the LORD make his face shine upon you
> and be gracious to you;
> the LORD turn his face toward you
> and give you peace.""'

"So they will put my name on the Israelites, and I will bless them" (6:22-27).

Chapters 9–10, in particular, center on God's presence with his people. The first half of chapter 9 recounts the first Passover celebration in the wilderness (9:1-14), a celebration that, supremely, reminds them of God's presence when he remarkably delivered them from Egypt. In the second half of chapter 9, God promises he will provide a cloud to the travelers for leading them and for reminding them of his continual presence:

> On the day the tabernacle, the Tent of the Testimony, was set up, the cloud covered it. From evening till morning the cloud above the tabernacle looked like fire. That is how it continued to be; the cloud covered it, and at night it looked like fire. Whenever the cloud lifted from above the Tent, the Israelites set out; wherever the cloud settled, the Israelites encamped. At the LORD's command the Israelites set out, and at his command they encamped. As long as the cloud stayed over the tabernacle, they remained in camp. When the cloud remained over the tabernacle a long time, the Israelites obeyed the LORD's order and did not set out. Sometimes the cloud was over the tabernacle only a few days; at the LORD's command they would encamp, and then at his command they would set out. Sometimes the cloud stayed only from evening till morning, and when it lifted in the morning, they set out. Whether by day or by night, whenever the cloud lifted, they set out. Whether the cloud stayed over the tabernacle for two days or a month or a year, the Israelites would remain in camp and not set out; but when it lifted, they would set out. At the LORD's command they encamped, and at the LORD's command they set out. They obeyed the LORD's order, in accordance with his command through Moses (9:15-23).

The trumpets at the beginning of chapter 10 are also meant to remind God and the people of one another (10:9-10). And in the following verses, the cloud begins to move for the first time:

> On the twentieth day of the second month of the second year, the cloud lifted from above the tabernacle of the Testimony. Then the Israelites set out from the Desert of Sinai and traveled from place to place until the cloud came to rest in the Desert of Paran. They set out, this first time, at the LORD's command through Moses (10:11-13).

Chapter 10 then concludes with this summary statement:

> So they set out from the mountain of the LORD and traveled for three days. The ark of the covenant of the LORD went before them during those three days to find them a place to rest. The cloud of the LORD was over them by day when they set out from the camp.
>
> Whenever the ark set out, Moses said,
>
> > "Rise up, O LORD!
> > May your enemies be scattered;
> > may your foes flee before you."
>
> Whenever it came to rest, he said,
>
> > "Return, O LORD,
> > to the countless thousands of Israel" (10:33-36).

The first part of Numbers, then, is a summary of how God specially prepares his people by instructing them on purity, by giving them priests, and most of all, by giving them his own special presence.

God prepared his people then, and he prepares his people today too. Have you thought about that? Have you thought about the way God has prepared you? Maybe all of this seems like random religious information to you, but God carefully made you in his image. You have been designed to be able to comprehend words. You have the ability to think and understand. In fact, the Bible teaches that all creation testifies to you and me about God. If the starry heavens above are not enough, God has given you a faculty for discerning the truth about him and about yourself: your conscience. In its fallen state, your conscience is not flawless, but it is telling, and it is made by God to prepare you for knowing him. If you are a Christian, you have been prepared for God most crucially because you heard the good news of Jesus Christ: he died on the cross for your sins and took on himself the wrath of God that you deserved; and you believed! You repented of your sins and followed him. So God made you his own. Do you see what God has already done in your heart to prepare you for himself?

Christian friend, God has brought us to know him. Knowing him involves knowing about him and knowing him in relationship. So we feed our minds by studying his Word, then we walk by faith with his Spirit. Sometimes people wonder what we Christians mean by speaking about "having a relationship with God." We mean both of these things: first, learning about him and his will for our lives through his Word. So he has given us his Word and called individuals to teach his Word. Yet, second, we have his Spirit. God's own Spirit is in us; rather, his Spirit has us! We are indwelt. In one sense, we are more fully indwelt than the camp in Israel ever was! Today, God's Spirit is not specially limited to one particular physical location, ethnic tribe, or political nation. No, God has come in Christ. He is Immanuel! He is God with us, and he is specially present with his people, not by tabernacle or temple, but by his own Spirit. He himself, in his Spirit, is dwelling with us and has made us his own.

So as a church, we are a community of people who individually and (even more) corporately know God's special presence with us. God gifts us with his Word. He gifts us with parents and preachers who teach his Word. And he grants his Spirit who convicts, inspires, enlivens, and changes us. Look at how richly God has blessed us as individuals and as a church family! God did not have to give us as a church anyone who could teach his Word. He did not have to give me the ability to preach. He did not have to give our church the elders we have or any of the members who teach Bible studies or Sunday school or even disciple other members. He did not have to give us any knowledge or understanding of himself. He could have stayed separate from us because of our sin, but look at how richly he has blessed us. He has prepared us for all that we will face, as a church of Jesus Christ. Do you see God's providing, preparing hand in all this? Oh, please do. Don't just see some individual's work or some church's fortune. See the hand of God. See his preparation of his people.

BUT THE PEOPLE DO NOT TRUST GOD (AT KADESH, CHAPTERS 11–16)

God prepared the people at Sinai. That was our first sentence. Our second sentence is this: But the people did not trust God. We see this in every chapter of the Bible, but it particularly stands out in Numbers 11–16 when the people are at Kadesh. This abysmal lack of trust is the tragedy of the book of Numbers. In chapter 10, a beautiful picture is presented of God leading his people as a kind of liturgical procession or royal progress. Tribe after tribe in the divinely prescribed order marches out, following God who leads the people he has redeemed from captivity toward the land he once promised to Abraham. From the call of Moses to the plagues on Egypt to the Exodus with the plunder of the Egyptians to the water and manna in the desert, God has faithfully and miraculously provided for his people. But amazing as it may seem, after all of this, the people did not trust God.

By Constantly Complaining (11–12)

As on the journey from Egypt to Mount Sinai, the people continue to be terrified and anxious as they migrate toward the Promised Land, causing them to grumble against Moses and even accuse God. And remember what we just said about these people: God delivered them from Egypt with miracles so amazing that we know about them to this day. Has any generation witnessed a more spectacular work of God? Maybe those who saw the resurrection of Christ? Or anyone present to witness the Flood? You might have a few contenders. Yet God's public acts against Egypt for all the world to see are unprecedented.

And how do the people of God respond? They complain. They constantly complain. These are the kind of people who would complain about the temperature of water miraculously gushing from a rock in the desert, or about mud on their shoes while walking across the bed of a parted sea.

They complain about their hardships. The Israelites were no longer slaves, building the pharaoh's pyramids. They were in the desert, sustained by God, and headed, by direct route, toward the Promised Land. Still, they complain about "their hardships" (11:1). They had set out from Sinai in chapter 10, as we have seen. And remarkably the very next thing the author tells us is that they complain about their hardships.

They complain about their food. Complaining about the food occupies the rest of chapter 11. "If only we had meat to eat! We remember the fish we ate in Egypt at no cost—also the cucumbers, melons, leeks, onions, and garlic. But now we have lost our appetite; we never see anything but this manna!" (11:4b-6). "Give us meat to eat!" (11:13). "If only we had meat to eat! We were better off in Egypt!" (11:18). "Why did we ever leave Egypt?" (11:20). This is not a preacher embellishing. Those are all direct quotations. Can you still hear their whining across the centuries?

Miriam and Aaron (sister and brother of Moses) complain. Even Miriam and Aaron, the sister and brother of Moses, oppose Moses by complaining: "Miriam and Aaron began to talk against Moses because of his Cushite wife, for he had married a Cushite. 'Has the LORD spoken only through Moses?' they asked. 'Hasn't he also spoken through us?'" (12:1-2a). I don't think the point being made here is that Moses' wife was a Cushite. The chapter doesn't mention this fact again. Rather, the issue seems to be Miriam and Aaron's jealousy of Moses' authority.

Throughout chapters 11–12, God decisively meets all these challenges. He provides quail for the people to eat, and he underscores the authority of Moses. Still, the people do not trust God.

By Rebelling (13:1–14:10a)

In fact, they rebel. Chapters 13–14 bring us to the center of the book of Numbers, and it is a sad center. Chapter 13 begins laden with so much hope. And if you don't know what is ahead, you read through the chapter as untroubled and expectant as a child on Christmas Eve. Oh, the hopes that are so close to being fulfilled! After all the centuries of waiting, after all the amazing miracles, the people stand poised to enter the Promised Land. The spies have gone ahead into the land. They have returned. And now they begin their report of what they have seen: "They gave Moses this account: 'We went into the land to which you sent us, and it does flow with milk and honey! Here is its fruit'" (13:27). This verse is probably the high point of expectation. And, oh, if only they had stopped here! What they said next was anything but helpful. They let all their doubts, worries, and concerns come out. The next verse begins, "But . . ." Whenever you respond to a promise of God with "But," you are heading in a bad direction:

> "But the people who live there are powerful, and the cities are fortified and very large. We even saw descendants of Anak there. The Amalekites live in the Negev; the Hittites, Jebusites and Amorites live in the hill country; and the Canaanites live near the sea and along the Jordan."
>
> Then Caleb silenced the people before Moses and said, "We should go up and take possession of the land, for we can certainly do it."
>
> But the men who had gone up with him said, "We can't attack those people; they are stronger than we are." And they spread among the Israelites a bad report about the land they had explored.

When you can't take 'em on directly, gossip. Just say a little bit here, a concern you have there. Acknowledge all the good things, but then raise those questions you have. To continue . . .

> They said, "The land we explored devours those living in it. All the people we saw there are of great size. We saw the Nephilim there (the descendants of Anak come from the Nephilim). We seemed like grasshoppers in our own eyes, and we looked the same to them" (13:28-33).

Can you imagine a clearer picture of the importance of leadership? At the beginning of chapter 13, the Lord had told Moses, "from each ancestral tribe send one of its leaders" to spy out the land (13:2). These men are the leaders. But where they should put courage in the hearts of the people, they put fear in them. Where they should be examples of trusting God, they doubt and contradict God. And what is the effect of this "leadership"? Absolute devastation. They lead the people, alright; but they lead them into open rebellion against God!

> That night all the people of the community raised their voices and wept aloud. All the Israelites grumbled against Moses and Aaron, and the whole assembly said to them, "If only we had died in Egypt! Or in this desert! Why is the LORD bringing us to this land only to let us fall by the sword? Our wives and children will be taken as plunder. Wouldn't it be better for us to go back to Egypt?" And they said to each other, "We should choose a leader and go back to Egypt" (14:1-4).

Joshua and Caleb then plead with them, "do not rebel against the LORD. And do not be afraid of the people of the land" (14:9). But at this point, the people of Israel have given themselves so wholly over to fear and rebellion that "the whole assembly talked about stoning them" (14:10a). Once they set their hearts on rejecting God's truth, they will not even tolerate hearing it. The people God has so carefully prepared for centuries rebel against him.

Result: God Punishes the People (14:10b–16:50)

In response to their rebellion, God punishes the people. The Lord's verdict directly follows their talk of stoning Joshua and Caleb:

> Then the glory of the LORD appeared at the Tent of Meeting to all the Israelites. The LORD said to Moses, "How long will these people treat me with contempt? How long will they refuse to believe in me, in spite of all the miraculous signs I have performed among them? I will strike them down with a plague and destroy them, but I will make you into a nation greater and stronger than they" (14:10b-12).

As he has so often before, Moses again intercedes for the guilty people even while they grumble against him. What a good leader!

> Moses said to the LORD, "Then the Egyptians will hear about it! By your power you brought these people up from among them. And they will tell the inhabitants of this land about it. They have already heard that you, O LORD, are with these people and that you, O LORD, have been seen face to face, that your cloud stays over them, and that you go before them in a pillar of cloud by day and a pillar of fire by night. If you put these people to death all at one time, the nations who have heard this report about you will say, 'The LORD was not able to bring these people into the land he promised them on oath; so he slaughtered them in the desert.'
>
>   "Now may the Lord's strength be displayed, just as you have declared: 'The LORD is slow to anger, abounding in love and forgiving sin and rebellion. Yet he does not leave the guilty unpunished; he punishes the children for the sin of the

fathers to the third and fourth generation.' In accordance with your great love, forgive the sin of these people, just as you have pardoned them from the time they left Egypt until now" (14:13-19).

The Lord does forgive the people: "The LORD replied, 'I have forgiven them, as you asked'" (14:20). He does not immediately sweep them from the face of time and eternity, as their sins warrant. Even so, they receive the due consequences of their sin, and those consequences are mortal. Disobeying God is always a capital offense. And, in this case, the accuser, the plaintiff, and the star witness are also the judge. The Lord passes judgment upon them and hands down a sentence of death that we see executed over the next three chapters:

> "Nevertheless, as surely as I live and as surely as the glory of the LORD fills the whole earth, not one of the men who saw my glory and the miraculous signs I performed in Egypt and in the desert but who disobeyed me and tested me ten times—not one of them will ever see the land I promised on oath to their forefathers. No one who has treated me with contempt will ever see it" (14:21-23).

These verses tell us how to understand what happens during the Israelites' forty years in the wilderness. The prolonged journey is not some mammoth-sized "time out." Not at all. It is God's death sentence on a whole generation. Not one individual who witnessed the miracles or was delivered from Egypt will see the land—except for the two faithful spies, Caleb and Joshua. They have scorned God's ways and spurned God himself by their insolence, distrust, and disobedience. So God punishes them. The wilderness will not be a bypath but a cemetery.

God hands down a sentence of death on the whole unbelieving generation, but he executes it much more quickly on those who gave the bad report in order to underscore the grievousness of their sin:

> So the men Moses had sent to explore the land, who returned and made the whole community grumble against him by spreading a bad report about it— these men responsible for spreading the bad report about the land were struck down and died of a plague before the LORD (14:36-37).

The presumptuousness of trying to reenter the Promised Land in their own strength (chapter 14) along with the Sabbath-breaking and the opposition to Moses (chapters 15 and 16) all fall under God's sentence of death for rebellion against him.

Does God's punishment sound harsh to you? It is helpful to go back to the beginning and remember that God had warned Adam and Eve about the fearful fruit produced by disobedience. Still, they disobeyed, and death came into the world. Paul would also one day warn the church in Rome that "the wages of sin is death" (Rom. 6:23). Clearly, these episodes in Numbers both confirm what God had said in the past and anticipate what he would say again in the future. Now, the judgment of death upon sin does not mean that we die as soon as we sin. If that were the case, I would not be speaking to you now. I would be dead! And you wouldn't be hearing me, either. However, it does mean that we have forfeited our lives and our relationships with God. God has the right to take them, and he has promised these forfeitures will be the normal course for sinners like you and me. What's worse, physical death is simply a picture of spiritual death, the separation that happens between us and the God who made us in his image. Whatever differences may exist between human beings— age or gender, race or religion, job or place of origin—we all have this in common: we deserve death because of our sins.

This story is also a picture of God's sovereignty, which we have noticed again and again in these early books of the Bible. God picks up whole nations and then puts them down. He lifts up Egypt and then humbles it. He humbles Israel and then calls Israel out. And now, he justly decides to frustrate the hopes of a whole generation because of its disobedience. The rise and fall of nations, the waxing and waning of peoples, are all in the hands of God.

Was this generation the worst ever? We don't have any theological reason to think so. The very first generation ensnared us all in sin; and the generation who crucified Christ committed the darkest deed. Yet every generation has joined together in this vast rebellion. Every child of Adam has been tempted by sin and has succumbed—at least, everyone except one. There was "one who has been tempted in every way, just as we are—yet was without sin" (Heb. 4:15). And our hope must rest in this one.

Oh, friend, consider the seriousness of sin. Think about how much death occurs in the book of Numbers. The punishment should be tailored to the crime, we say. And the suitable result or reward for sin must be death, the most serious of punishments. Rebelling against the author of life kills life; it is dangerous in the extreme. It is spiritually suicidal. Do not underestimate the seriousness of sin or trifle with it, as if you can perceive all its consequences. As Moses says later in Numbers, "you may be sure that your sin will find you out" (Num. 32:23). Read the seriousness of sin in God's just sentence against it. And remember that no one sin is ever content to be alone. Puritan minister Richard Steele once observed, "all possible care must be used to avoid all occasions and incentives of wandering desires from home [he's warning against adultery]; and the rather, because he or she that is not content with one, will not be content with more; for sin is boundless, and nothing but grace and the grave can limit the desires of the heart."[3]

Consider, too, the roots of sin. One piece of wisdom in particular that I have seen while reflecting on Numbers is this: notice the connection between dissatisfaction and sin. Again and again, the people complain, and then they sin. In fact, you could say they sin in complaining. Well, shouldn't we complain against some things? Certainly, some criticisms are just. And we should work to change things that are bad: poor solutions, unjust laws, wicked actions. But we should never complain against God and his ways, and that is what the Israelites are doing. It is these very complaints about the hardships, food, and leaders that God has given them that reveal their spiritual state. It tells us where they are. Reading these stories, you and I can see that God has spectacularly delivered the Israelites from slavery without asking them to fight a battle or cast a vote. You and I can see that God has supernaturally fed them in the desert without asking them to work. You and I can see that God has given them the most humble and faithful leadership imaginable, who again and again choose the good of those under their charge rather than their own good. But the people themselves cannot see any of this. They are blind. They are not satisfied with God and his great gifts to them, so they grumble about the things they don't have. They imagine evils that do not exist, and they ignore the blessings that do. Yet what we can see in their lives, we often fail to recognize in our own. In our lives, too, dissatisfaction is often the root of sin. Such dissatisfaction tells us more about our souls than about our circumstances. It indicates that our souls are feeding at the wrong place, trying to sate themselves on the slop in the trough rather than the feast on God's banquet table. And once we complain about God's provision, sinning against his will is a short step away. Every sin, no matter how unconnected with religion it might seem to be, is really a short, sharp message to God: "I don't like you. I would rather have these things than you. They give me what I want." Friend, consider carefully the roots of sin in your dissatisfactions.

This is why I pray that we as a church family would cultivate a spirit of encouragement toward one another and obedience to God's Word. The two go together. God uses a culture of encouragement to bring godliness and holiness. Thank God not just for great preachers but for great congregations that show this in their life together. In my experience, Covenant Life Church (Gaithersburg, Maryland), Grace Community Church (Sun Valley, California), and Tenth Presbyterian Church (Philadelphia) are remarkable examples of the very spirit of encouragement I am talking about.

---

[3] Richard Steele, "What Are the Duties of Husbands and Wives Towards Each Other?" in *Puritan Sermons 1659–1689,* 6 vols. (Wheaton, Ill.: Richard Owen Roberts, 1981), 2:277.

After all, the opposite is also true. Complaining and disobedience accompany each other, whether in the church or in the home. And their fruits are always bitter: gossip and divisiveness; mistrust and slander; ultimately, spiritual death.

What do you expect to accomplish by complaining? Do you expect you will surprise us by telling us that so-and-so is a sinner? Yes, we know that. We are a church full of sinners! You don't need to get the tastiest morsels and spread them out. We come here because we know that Christ offers forgiveness for our sins. Let's concentrate on that. Yes, avenues for constructive criticism must be present. But we must also know how to recognize and even celebrate God's good provision and his many blessings, including good and godly leadership. I thank God for the leaders he has given this church. And I pray that we as a church will not be like the complaining Israelites. God is worthy of our complete trust and praise, particularly in how he has provided for us in this local church. I don't want you to go another year, another week, another day, without seeing God's goodness to you and for you! Out of his love, concern, and care for you, he has blessed this church. See that and acknowledge it, to the glory of God.

So are you getting the story of Numbers? God prepares the people spectacularly, carefully, and lovingly. But the people do not trust God. This much, I trust, is clear to you. But if you stop there, you miss the point of the story.

YET GOD PERSEVERES WITH THE PEOPLE (AT MOAB, CHAPTERS 17–36)

True, the Israelites do not trust God, and God punishes them, particularly the older generation. But ultimately, God perseveres with the people, just as he persevered with Adam and Eve when they failed to trust him. God would be well within his rights to cut the people loose entirely, but he does not. He forgives and perseveres, just as he promised Moses. Numbers is a book of enduring tragedy, but more than that it is a book of enduring hope.

By Providing Instructions for Priests and for Purity

God perseveres with his people by providing instructions for priests and for purity. Chapter 18 is filled with more instructions from God on the special duties and offerings of the priests, and this is after the nation's rebellious refusal to enter the Promised Land. God continues to teach the nation about purity in chapter 19. He reviews the times for required offerings and festivals in chapters 28–29. And in chapter 30, he continues to teach the leaders what faithfulness means, specifically, how a man should take responsibility for himself, his word, and his household.

At the same time, I don't want you to get the wrong idea about the people. They do not suddenly become docile and obedient after chapter 14, as if their refusal to enter the Promised Land worked like some sort of catharsis for disobedience and, now that they have gotten it out of their system, they can be holy and happy. No! Sin never works like that. Sin is never vanquished through indulging it.

By Remaining Gracious Despite Continued Sin (17; 20:9-12; 21:4-9; 25)

God perseveres with the people by remaining gracious despite the fact that they continue to sin. In chapter 17, the people misrepresent what God has said: "The Israelites said to Moses, 'We will die! We are lost, we are all lost! Anyone who even comes near the tabernacle of the LORD will die. Are we all going to die?'" (17:12-13). Of course, God had never said that. This is just like the serpent in the Garden of Eden: take something God has said, twist it around, and get everyone all worked up!

In chapter 20, Moses proves that even he is not immune to dishonoring the Lord. In a fit of anger, he disobeys the Lord's instructions to get water from a rock by striking it rather than speaking to it (20:8-12). So God promises him that he will share in the sentence handed down to the generation that escaped from Egypt: he will not enter the Promised Land. Does that sound awfully severe? Remember, leaders are judged by a stricter judgment. You can be sure I remember that as a pastor.

Still, Moses is God's man, and the people provoke God's anger by grumbling against him, as they do again in chapter 21. God initially responds by sending venomous snakes. Yet just as quickly he offers a way of salvation, displaying his persevering graciousness (see 21:4-9).

In chapter 25, the Israelite men indulge in immorality and idolatry, which the Lord addresses with a plague. Yet even this seems to be gracious since, by all appearances, it clears out the generation that came out of Egypt and brings the forty years of wandering in the wilderness to an end.

By Giving Them a Second Chance

God also perseveres with his people by giving them a second chance through the next generation. In the midst of miserable sin, deliverance and new life are granted. As we have seen, the book's tragic climax comes in chapter 14 with the Lord's command to "turn back tomorrow and set out toward the desert along the route to the Red Sea" (Num. 14:25). In other words, go back to where you came from! At this point, a number of Israelites belatedly and presumptuously try to enter the Promised Land in their own strength, only to have the Canaanites quickly beat them back. But the story does not end there.

In chapter 20, a new journey commences when the people set out from Kadesh (cf. chapter 33), where they have been moving around in circles for almost forty years. New battles begin, but this time the Israelites win. In chapter 21, the Israelites fight and beat the Canaanites for the first time (21:21-25)—a precursor of more victories to come. In chapters 22–24, the strange story of the Moabite Balak and Balaam is used to show that God even uses Israel's enemies to bless the nation. So sovereign is God that he brings blessings from whom he will. In chapter 26, another census is taken now that the Exodus generation has died out. In chapter 27, Joshua is designated the new leader for this next generation. Chapter 31 then describes a victory over the Midianites.

By Enabling Them to Reach the Promised Land!

By the book's close, we know that God perseveres with his people, finally, by enabling them to successfully reach the Promised Land! In spite of their chronic rebellion, they succeed. In chapter 32, the first tribes settle just east of the Promised Land. In chapter 34, God gives the people instructions for assigning land to the Israelite tribes in Canaan. In chapter 35, he instructs them to set aside special cities for certain purposes. And in chapter 36, special provisions are made for how land will remain within each tribe. Though the book of Numbers does not formally usher the Israelites into the Promised Land, only to its doorstep, God is certain of his plans. He is not thrown by the people's rebellion; he will persevere with his purposes. If you have read through Numbers, maybe you have noticed the two interesting little phrases in chapter 15: "after you enter the land I am giving you as a home" (15:2) and "When you enter the land to which I am taking you . . ." (15:18). One thinks of a divine, "As I was saying . . ." Despite the sinful rebellion of his people, God's plans will not be thwarted.

Does this picture of God surprise you? God as the mighty and holy one who carefully prepares his people? God as the punisher of all heinous rebellion against him? God as the one who perseveres in mercy? I fear that many people do not understand God's mercy because his mercy is all they want to see. But God's mercy is meaningless without his justice. You will not understand the mercy of God if you do not look long and hard at the justice of God. The Bible is filled with teaching on both God's justice and his mercy. This is the God of the Bible, and this is the God who has come to us in Christ.

One of the most poignant pictures in Numbers of this God of justice and mercy occurs back in chapter 14. Interceding for the people, Moses invokes the Lord's own description of himself from Exodus 34: "The LORD is slow to anger, abounding in love and forgiving sin and rebellion. Yet he does not leave the guilty unpunished; he punishes the children for the sin of the fathers to the third and fourth generation" (Num. 14:18; cf. Ex. 34:6-7). In other studies, we have referred to this Exodus 34 passage as the riddle of the Old Testament. How can God forgive sin and rebellion, yet not leave the guilty unpunished? Or, you might ask, how can both God's justice and his mercy be satisfied at the same time? The answer is found, of course, in Christ. Through the work of Christ, God is able to forgive sinners and also punish their sin. When Christ died on the cross, he took upon himself the punishment of everyone who would ever repent and believe, opening a way for us to be reconciled to God for eternity.

So the apostle John writes, "God so loved the world that he gave his one and only Son, that whoever believes in him shall not perish but have eternal life" (John 3:16). Who will believe? Jesus answers, "I tell you the truth, no one can see the kingdom of God unless he is born again" (3:3). Oh, friend, those belonging to the generation God rescued from Egypt were not the only ones who needed a new beginning. Every one of us needs to be born again. And some of us, by God's grace, have been! If we are Christians, we have been given a new birth! We have become new creations! We have been made into forward-looking children of the Promise, defined more by where we are going than by where we are coming from. Our words may still bear the accents of sin, but our eyes are filled with the hope of heaven.

I pray that God will make this changed orientation typical of our church family. Just as individual Christians are no longer defined by past sins, we as a local church are not doomed to endlessly repeating our past mistakes. If you think we are, you have not understood who is at work here: God is at work here! God builds a people for his own glory. The local church is God's idea. He has underwritten it, and he assures its success! How else could we go on? In trying to build a true church, we are as helpless as the children of Israel trying to win the Promised Land if God is not with us. But if God *is* with us, success is assured. Despite any obstacles and despite all our sin, God perseveres with his people.

CONCLUSION

So this is the message of Numbers: God prepares the people, but the people rebel against him. Still, God graciously perseveres with his sinful people.

The story of Numbers comes up at least a couple of times in the New

Testament, once with a non-Christian and another time with Christians. First, in his conversation with the unbelieving Nicodemus, Jesus alludes to the episode in which the people grumble against Moses, provoking God to send venomous snakes. As we have seen, after sending the snakes God publicly offers a way of salvation: "The LORD said to Moses, 'Make a snake and put it up on a pole; anyone who is bitten can look at it and live.' So Moses made a bronze snake and put it up on a pole. Then when anyone was bitten by a snake and looked at the bronze snake, he lived" (21:8-9). Jesus uses this story with Nicodemus to describe how his own death on the cross will publicly proclaim the way of salvation for all who look and believe: "Just as Moses lifted up the snake in the desert, so the Son of Man must be lifted up, that everyone who believes in him may have eternal life" (John 3:14-15). God has provided Christ as a remedy for our sins. Christ was lifted up—crucified—for us, so that all we need to do is look and live. Respond with faith to God's Word of promise. Repent of your sins, and believe in Christ. Trust him.

The great preacher Charles Haddon Spurgeon came to a saving knowledge of Christ when, during a snowstorm, he stumbled into a primitive Methodist chapel and heard a layman expounding on another text about "looking." The regular preacher of the church was absent that day, and Spurgeon recounts in his autobiography this untutored man's words from the pulpit: "Young man, look to Jesus Christ. Look! Look! Look! You have nothin' to do but to look and live."

And then, Spurgeon says,

> I saw at once the way of salvation. I know not what else he said,—I did not take much notice of it,—I was so possessed with that one thought. Like as when the brazen serpent was lifted up, the people only looked and were healed, so it was with me. I had been waiting to do fifty other things, but when I heard that word, "Look!" what a charming word it seemed to me! Oh! I looked until I could have looked my eyes away. There and then the cloud was gone, the darkness had rolled away, and that moment I saw the sun; and I could have risen that instant, and sung with the most enthusiastic of them, of the precious blood of Christ, and the simple faith which looks alone to him. Oh that somebody had told me this before, "Trust Christ, and you shall be saved."[4]

That is the good news. Repent of your sins and believe this good news! "God made him who had no sin," though he was tempted in every way just as we

---

[4] Charles Haddon Spurgeon, *C. H. Spurgeon's Autobiography*, 4 vols. (London: Passmore & Alabaster, 1897), 1:106.

are, "to be sin for us, so that in him we might become the righteousness of God" (2 Cor. 5:21).

Second, Paul recounts the story of Numbers in his letter to the Christians in Corinth. After retelling the story, he warns his readers about temptation and then urges them to be careful. We too have just considered the story of Numbers; so if you are a Christian, consider soberly what Paul says here:

> For I do not want you to be ignorant of the fact, brothers, that our forefathers were all under the cloud and that they all passed through the sea. They were all baptized into Moses in the cloud and in the sea. They all ate the same spiritual food and drank the same spiritual drink; for they drank from the spiritual rock that accompanied them, and that rock was Christ. Nevertheless, God was not pleased with most of them; their bodies were scattered over the desert.
>
> Now these things occurred as examples to keep us from setting our hearts on evil things as they did. Do not be idolaters, as some of them were; as it is written: "The people sat down to eat and drink and got up to indulge in pagan revelry." We should not commit sexual immorality, as some of them did—and in one day twenty-three thousand of them died. We should not test the Lord, as some of them did—and were killed by snakes. And do not grumble, as some of them did—and were killed by the destroying angel.
>
> These things happened to them as examples and were written down as warnings for us, on whom the fulfillment of the ages has come. So, if you think you are standing firm, be careful that you don't fall! No temptation has seized you except what is common to man. And God is faithful; he will not let you be tempted beyond what you can bear. But when you are tempted, he will also provide a way out so that you can stand up under it (1 Cor. 10:1-13).

Christian brother or sister, learn from the negative examples in this book. Do not rebel, but trust God in his plans. Trust him even in his timing. He is always right, and he is always good. When God makes promises, he fulfills them—in his own time and way, even if it seems amazing to us. Back in Numbers 11, God promises to give the complaining people meat, a promise that almost sends Moses over the edge. In what must have been a momentary lack of faith, Moses wonders out loud how God will fulfill this promise. God's answer exposes the ridiculous nature of Moses' doubt: "Is the LORD's arm too short?" (Num. 11:23).

Christian, do you find yourself wondering if God can fulfill his promises in Scripture for your life and for his church? Do you find yourself wondering if God has already given you everything he can? That this is it? That Christianity comes down to what you are experiencing right now? Do you wonder if God is able to use you to build his kingdom? Take a moment to reflect on these questions. Find the seeds of your discontent with God right now. Do you feel that God is unable to do what he has promised? Or that maybe he is not really so good? Does the present seem worst, and the past always better?

If you wonder about any of these things, confess it honestly to God and maybe to a Christian friend. Confess your discontent with God and with his ways. And meditate on the God we encounter in the book of Numbers. Do not go the way of the complaining, unbelieving children of Israel, but believe God's Word. The message of this book is our only hope. If God is not like this—forgiving, persevering, saving—we are all sunk! We don't have a chance. Yes, life can feel like a walk in the wilderness, so as Christians we must remind one another that this world is not our home. Rather, we are on a journey headed home. And this hope of home is no bleary-eyed romanticism; it is a clear-eyed hope for the future. Because we see what God has done with our rebellious past, we believe what he can do with our unseen future. So we trust him today. Through foes, temptations, heartbreaks, storms, and sins, we have Immanuel, God with us, the friend for sinners. So we have hope.

Let us pray:

O God, we have seen in this book of Numbers a mirror of our own souls. We pray that you would help us see our own discontent with you, to identify it clearly, and to confess it, even now. You know what unsettles us or causes us to struggle with trusting you. O Lord, forgive and change us. Grow our love for you and our satisfaction in you. We do exult in your forgiveness of our sins and your persevering with us. We pray that you will help us to know your perseverance individually in our lives and to exemplify your perseverance in our churches and communities. For your glory we ask all this, in the name of our Savior, Jesus Christ. Amen.

Questions for Reflection

1. Which phrase most characterizes you: nostalgic about the past, content in the present, or expectant for the future? In other words, where do you seek joy most?

2. How should churches strive to live purely unto the Lord together? How should churches respond when members willfully and unrepentantly choose lifestyles characterized by impurity?

3. As we have seen, the tabernacle was situated at the center of the Israelite camp. What significance does that have, if any, for Christian gatherings? Does it mean we should place a cross at the center of the room, or something else?

4. If you are a Christian, how did God prepare you for your conversion?

5. What do you complain about? What does your complaining communicate to God about his provision for you? What does it say about your belief in his wisdom and goodness? Or perhaps we can approach the question like this: Suppose a person believed that he was wiser than God; suppose he also thought he was "more good" than God? How would that person act? Now, do you ever act like that person?

6. When was the last time you felt genuinely satisfied? Why were you satisfied?

7. How can complaining lead to worse sins? What steps should we take to fight against our own complaining hearts?

8. What does all the death in the book of Numbers teach us about sin? Do you take sin this seriously? Does your church take sin seriously? How? Since, as Christians, we live under grace, do we really need to take sin this seriously?

9. Does God's decision to forbid the older generation from entering the Promised Land—and make them die in the desert—sound harsh to you? Is this the same God about whom the apostle John said, "For God so loved the world that he gave his one and only Son . . ."? How can God be both loving and wrathful?

10. Following up on question 9, is the God that you worship as wrathful as the God of Numbers? How would your life and worship be changed for the good if you were to see God in this way?

11. Following up on question 10, do you ever praise God for his holiness, his wrath, and his promise of judgment? How would cultivating a heart that praises God for his coming wrath actually enable you to be more loving, patient, and peace-making both among other Christians and among non-Christians?

12. Suppose a non-Christian says to you, "I can never believe in the Bible. After all, God tells Moses to stone to death a man found gathering wood on the Sabbath. That's crazy!" (see Num. 15:32-36). How would you respond?

13. Where have you observed God's perseverance in your life? Be sure to thank him for what you see.

14. As we have seen, Moses lifted up the bronze snake on a pole in order for Israelites who had been bitten by venomous snakes to look and be healed. Jesus then used this incident as an analogy to explain something about his own death on the cross. What does the analogy explain? What implications does this have for preaching and evangelism?

THE MESSAGE OF DEUTERONOMY: "WHAT'S PAST IS PROLOGUE"

PROLOGUE OR PROPHECY?[1]

"What's past is prologue." So the usurping duke of Milan, Antonio, says to Sebastian, the traitorous brother of a king, in one of William Shakespeare's stranger romances, *The Tempest*. Antonio is trying to persuade Sebastian to seize the throne of Naples, a throne not Sebastian's by right. So Antonio urges him not to feel bound by the past but to see it only as a prologue to the future he can make for himself. Really, Antonio's words present a more genteel expression of Henry Ford's definition of history as "bunk." In a similar vein, Leo Tolstoy characterized history as "a collection of fables and useless trifles."

Antonio is a villain, and his advice exposes a sinister disregard for the law that Sebastian is bound to honor. But his disregard for the power the past exerts over one's life raises an interesting topic. Certainly history is important, but is it controlling? We enjoy reading biographies in part because we often perceive in the child the outlines of what becomes the adult. Yet can the future always be discerned in the past? Is history prophecy? Or is it merely a dispensable prologue, as Antonio wants Sebastian to believe?

This is an important question to consider in our own lives. We all possess a history. Both you and I have a trail of actions and attitudes behind us that is as long as our lives. It is our own history. It is the history that we own and that owns us. Our histories have made us what we are even now—and we have made them.

So what do you think: does your past present an argument for why you can expect God's blessing on your future, or does it argue for something less hopeful? We want to have all this in mind as we turn one more time to the Pentateuch.

---

[1] This sermon was originally preached on February 24, 2002, at Capitol Hill Baptist Church in Washington, D.C.

INTRODUCING DEUTERONOMY

The Pentateuch is the name given to the first five books in the Bible. These books begin the Bible's history. They provide its prologue and its foundation. And they have been our special object of study for the last four sermons.

We began by looking at the book of Genesis, which presents the stories of Creation, the Fall, and the beginning of God's plan of redemption through Abraham, his son Isaac, and Isaac's son Jacob, also called Israel. In the later chapters of Genesis, Jacob's son Joseph is taken down to Egypt, eventually to be followed by his brothers and father. Next, we looked at the book of Exodus, whose first chapter summarizes four hundred years in the life and slavery of the children of Israel in Egypt. The first eighty years of Moses' life follow in the second chapter. Then, the story line from Exodus 3 on through Leviticus and up to the middle of Numbers covers the span of only one year. It is a great year in which the Lord calls Moses as an eighty-year-old man to return to Egypt and lead the children of Israel out of slavery. He does so, and he brings them to Mount Sinai with God's amazing help. At Mount Sinai, God gives the people his law, he makes them his own special people, and he instructs them in his ways, even though they sin repeatedly. The book of Leviticus provides more instruction for the Lord's people, particularly on their sin and need for atonement. The book of Numbers begins with yet more instruction, and then describes the people's procession toward the Promised Land. In Numbers 13 and 14, however, the greatest tragedy since the Fall occurs: the people rebel against God's plan for them by turning away from the land he has promised. So he sends them back the way they came, toward the Red Sea. The rest of Numbers tells the story of the people wandering around Kadesh for almost forty years, suffering the fruits of their disobedience. Yet God perseveres with the people. Once the original generation entirely dies out, the people begin moving again in the last part of Numbers toward the Promised Land. And that brings us to the last book in the Pentateuch, the book of Deuteronomy.

Basically, Deuteronomy is a record of the three last speeches Moses gave to the nation of Israel as they stood across the Jordan, preparing to enter the Promised Land. Scholars say that the book was written in the form of a treaty or a covenant: it begins with a historical prologue, it then lays out the stipulations or laws to be kept by the people, and it concludes with a list of blessings and curses that will accrue to the people according to their obedience or disobedience. I thought of structuring this sermon in those three parts—recapitulation, exposition, and exhortation: recapitulation, what's the past; exposition, what's the law; and exhortation, the need to obey it. This does give you a rough sense of how this book is laid out. It is easy to remember. And it makes for a wonderful sermon outline. But I am not going to preach that sermon. I don't think it would teach us everything we need from Deuteronomy. Although that approach is helpful to a point, Deuteronomy is much more textured than these three simple divisions suggest.

A number of people have asked, "Why is this book called Deuteronomy?" The answer to this question is unimportant for our purposes here. But in case you are curious, the name "Deuteronomy" comes from a word in chapter 17 of the Greek translation of the book. Verse 18 of that chapter instructs the king of Israel himself to make a *second* copy of this *law,* or a *deuteronomion*—from *deutero,* meaning second, and *nomos,* meaning law. No photocopiers or printers existed in those days, of course. More important, God wanted the king to know the law well, and handwriting his own second copy would aid that process. So he was to do this, letter by letter.

Deuteronomy is a beautiful book to read. It is no wonder Jesus quotes from it more than from any other Old Testament book. Of course, Deuteronomy does not have much action. After the great dramas of Genesis, Exodus, and Numbers, Deuteronomy may seem a little tame. Yet it does contain some well-known passages: Chapter 5 repeats the Ten Commandments for the generation about to enter the Promised Land. Chapter 6 records what is famously called the *shema:* "Hear, O Israel: The LORD our God, the LORD is one. Love the LORD your God with all your heart and with all your soul and with all your strength" (6:4-5).[2] And maybe you have heard the saying in chapter 29: "The secret things belong to the LORD our God" (29:29). Then there is that passage about newly married men taking a whole year off (24:5)!

As I say every time I preach an overview sermon, this is an unusual sermon. We go through an entire book of the Bible in one study, which is not how I normally preach. Typically, I preach much shorter passages of Scripture, such as a few verses or a chapter or two. But there are some shapes and patterns we can see only from a great distance or height.

I believe we can summarize the message of Deuteronomy with two very simple statements. First, God chooses his people. Second, God's people must choose him. I pray that as we consider this message, we will more and more come to understand who God is and who we are as his people.

GOD CHOOSES HIS PEOPLE

God chooses his people. That seems clear enough. But to really understand this point, let's ask a few clarifying questions.

---

[2] *Shema* is the imperative form of the Hebrew for *hear.*

Who Is This God Who Chooses?

First, who is this God who does the choosing? Well, we could say many things about him. But a couple of overwhelmingly obvious things about God—things often forgotten today—are particularly important in the account here. As you read through Deuteronomy, these two things should strike you.

The one true God. First and quite simply, this God is the one true God. There is no other. The book declares this exclusive word again and again. Toward the end of Moses' first speech, he reminds the people that the great acts God performed in their midst during the Exodus show his uniqueness:

> Ask now about the former days, long before your time, from the day God created man on the earth; ask from one end of the heavens to the other. Has anything so great as this ever happened, or has anything like it ever been heard of? Has any other people heard the voice of God speaking out of fire, as you have, and lived? Has any god ever tried to take for himself one nation out of another nation, by testings, by miraculous signs and wonders, by war, by a mighty hand and an outstretched arm, or by great and awesome deeds, like all the things the LORD your God did for you in Egypt before your very eyes?
>
> You were shown these things so that you might know that the LORD is God; besides him there is no other. From heaven he made you hear his voice to discipline you. On earth he showed you his great fire, and you heard his words from out of the fire. Because he loved your forefathers and chose their descendants after them, he brought you out of Egypt by his Presence and his great strength, to drive out before you nations greater and stronger than you and to bring you into their land to give it to you for your inheritance, as it is today.
>
> Acknowledge and take to heart this day that the LORD is God in heaven above and on the earth below. There is no other (4:32-39).

The book is replete with such references to God's uniqueness: "the LORD your God, who is among you, is a great and awesome God" (7:21). Or later: "There is no god besides me. I put to death and I bring to life, I have wounded and I will heal, and no one can deliver out of my hand" (32:39). In Deuteronomy, God's uniqueness shines out. This book is about the only God who is.

The sovereign God. Second, this choosing God is unique in part because he is the sovereign God. Deuteronomy reveals his sovereignty to be stunningly complete. He establishes and delivers nations as easily as you and I lift a piece of paper or hand someone a book.

As the people prepare to enter the Promised Land and face even more adversaries than they had faced in the wilderness, Moses does not want them to perceive themselves as great military conquerors; he wants to remind them that

God alone saves. In chapters 2 and 3, Moses recalls how God gave them the nations of Heshbon and Bashan (3:2-3). Several chapters later, he tells them to

> "remember well what the LORD your God did to Pharaoh and to all Egypt. You saw with your own eyes the great trials, the miraculous signs and wonders, the mighty hand and outstretched arm, with which the LORD your God brought you out. The LORD your God will do the same to all the peoples you now fear" (7:18b-19; cf. 3:21-22).

Moreover, the people should expect God's sovereignty to be displayed even by the pace at which they defeat their enemies: "The LORD your God will drive out those nations before you, little by little. You will not be allowed to eliminate them all at once, or the wild animals will multiply around you" (7:22; cf. 9:3). God has his purposes in everything, including the timing in which he fulfills his promises.

Moses also points to the task's immensity and Israel's inadequacy for accomplishing the challenges that lie ahead. Why? In order to make God's supremacy clear: "the LORD will drive out all these nations before you, and you will dispossess nations larger and stronger than you."[3] Israel's fate lies squarely in God's hands (28:15). This is the God who hardens the hearts of kings and pharaohs (2:30). He reigns over the lying lips of false prophets (13:3). He gives and takes away understanding from the minds of his people (29:4). This God is sovereign, and remembering this fact will help his people to trust him (31:6, 8).

Friend, turn and consider the long trail of actions and attitudes that you brought with you to this study. As you turn and survey the good things in your past, you may well feel gratitude. Yet if you feel even a trace of pride, you have not really understood what God has done or who you are. As you consider the good things in your life, you must attribute them to God's hand. Every blessing comes from a sovereign God.

Why Did He Choose This People?

But why did God choose this particular people? He clearly considers Israel rebellious and disobedient, and he says it to their face again and again in a way that almost seems strange.[4] He is completely honest: they are stiff-necked and unwilling to obey.[5] Likewise, Moses openly says the people "did not trust the LORD" (1:32). And he warns them not to be self-deceived on just this point:

---

[3] 11:23; cf. 20:1, 4; 21:10; 31:3-8.
[4] 1:26, 43; 9:7, 23, 24; 31:27.
[5] 9:6, 13; 10:16; 31:27.

> After the LORD your God has driven them out before you, do not say to your-
> self, "The LORD has brought me here to take possession of this land because of
> my righteousness." No, it is on account of the wickedness of these nations that
> the LORD is going to drive them out before you. It is not because of your righ-
> teousness or your integrity that you are going in to take possession of their land;
> but on account of the wickedness of these nations, the LORD your God will drive
> them out before you, to accomplish what he swore to your fathers, to Abraham,
> Isaac and Jacob. Understand, then, that it is not because of your righteousness
> that the LORD your God is giving you this good land to possess, for you are a
> stiff-necked people (9:4-6).

Deuteronomy is not a good book for our pride, is it? This is not "God helps
those who help themselves" or "build your self-esteem first." I checked my copy
of *The Positive Bible*,[6] and the editors omitted these verses in chapter 9! God
wants to assure the people that, yes, he will bless them; but, no, it will not be a
result of their own righteousness. He will bless them because he is good.

So now we know what reasons God does *not* give for choosing Israel. But
why does he choose them? The answer is found in a number of places, and the
answer might surprise you, since this is a book of the Law. In chapter 4, we read,

> Because he loved your forefathers and chose their descendants after them, he
> brought you out of Egypt by his Presence and his great strength, to drive out
> before you nations greater and stronger than you and to bring you into their land
> to give it to you for your inheritance (4:37-38).

Because he loves them? Certainly, then, there must be something special
about them, right? Apparently not. Turning to chapter 7, we find this same
amazing idea at a little more length:

> For you are a people holy to the LORD your God. The LORD your God has cho-
> sen you out of all the peoples on the face of the earth to be his people, his trea-
> sured possession.
>   The LORD did not set his affection on you and choose you because you were
> more numerous than other peoples, for you were the fewest of all peoples. But
> it was because the LORD loved you and kept the oath he swore to your forefa-
> thers that he brought you out with a mighty hand and redeemed you from the
> land of slavery, from the power of Pharaoh king of Egypt (7:6-8).

God does not choose this people because of their righteousness. He does
not choose them because of their numerical strength. They are stiff-necked, and

---

[6] Kenneth Winston Caine, compiler, *The Positive Bible: From Genesis to Revelation: Scripture That Inspires,
Nurtures, and Heals* (New York: Avon, 1998).

they are small. He chooses them because he loves them![7] This great and sovereign God chooses to set his love upon this people for no reason inherent to them but simply because he loves them.

What Do His Chosen People Receive (What Does It Mean to Be Chosen)?

There is one more question we want to ask in order to unpack our statement that God chooses his people. He chooses people, okay, but what does that mean? What do his people receive?

The law. Well, in calling the Israelites to be his special people, God gives them a number of gifts. Perhaps the most obvious gift God gives in the book of Deuteronomy is his law. That is what the title of the book means, remember? Second law. Chapters 4 to 6 provide a nice summary of the law, and chapter 5 presents the Ten Commandments for the second time in the Pentateuch. In a sense, this whole book is a re-presentation of the law for the people just before they enter the land. God is reminding *his people* of *his rule* before bringing them into *his place*. So they look together at the playbook one more time before heading into the game. That way everyone is on the same page.

Clearly, God's law should be central among his people. Therefore, the people are commanded to write the law upon easily visible large stones once they cross the Jordan into the Promised Land (27:8). The Lord does not want an image of himself erected; instead he wants his laws publicly displayed. A set of laws depicts God's character far better than any form that a human can fashion. Furthermore, God wants the whole law to be read aloud to the people every seven years (31:10-11).

God calls his people to be specially set apart by living according to his will. So the particular laws work to keep the people pure and to help them maintain their respect for God's truth—for life, for the family, for faithfulness in marriage, and for the law itself. The laws in this book protect private property, and they promote concern for those in need. In some ways, the law begins the work of fulfilling God's promise to Abraham by refining this people he is making his own.

Descendants. In addition to giving them the law, God gives his special people many descendants. Back in Genesis, God said to Abraham, "Look up at the heavens and count the stars—if indeed you can count them. . . . So shall your offspring be" (Gen. 15:5). At the time, the promise sounded fanciful. Abraham and his wife Sarah were both old and had no children. Now, here in

---

[7] Also 10:14-15; 14:2.

Deuteronomy, we read "now the LORD your God has made you as numerous as the stars in the sky" (Deut. 10:22). God has done what he promised.

Land. God has promised land to his people as well. Again, he had said to Abraham, "To your offspring I will give this land" (Gen. 12:7). Now, here in Deuteronomy, they stand on the edge of seeing that promise fulfilled. In fact, God's description of the land sounds so good it could be advertising copy!

> The land you are entering to take over is not like the land of Egypt, from which you have come, where you planted your seed and irrigated it by foot as in a vegetable garden. But the land you are crossing the Jordan to take possession of is a land of mountains and valleys that drinks rain from heaven. It is a land the LORD your God cares for; the eyes of the LORD your God are continually on it from the beginning of the year to its end (11:10-12).

God's own presence. The law, descendants, and the land are all a part of what God gives his chosen people. But beyond all these, and most important, God gives himself to his people.

Throughout Deuteronomy, we read about sacrifices and festivals held "in the presence of the LORD."[8] As you may remember from our previous studies, the Lord is also present with his people through the tabernacle, from the cloudy pillar over it to the ark of the covenant within it. These objects remind the people that God himself is with them in a special way. Even the nations can see it. Moses says to the people,

> See, I have taught you decrees and laws as the LORD my God commanded me, so that you may follow them in the land you are entering to take possession of it. Observe them carefully, for this will show your wisdom and understanding to the nations, who will hear about all these decrees and say, "Surely this great nation is a wise and understanding people." What other nation is so great as to have their gods near them the way the LORD our God is near us whenever we pray to him? And what other nation is so great as to have such righteous decrees and laws as this body of laws I am setting before you today? (4:5-8).

In chapter 31, Moses publicly commissions Joshua to succeed him and says twice—first to the people and then to Joshua—"the LORD your God goes with you; he will never leave you nor forsake you" (31:6, 8). Two chapters later, after blessing each tribe, Moses makes another beautiful promise: "The eternal God is your refuge, and underneath are the everlasting arms" (33:27).

When God chooses a people, above all other things he gives them himself.

---

[8] 12:7, 18; 14:23, 26; 15:20; 27:7.

The children of Israel may be standing on the banks of the Jordan poised to enter the Promised Land, but God's promise to dwell with them in the land is far more important than inheriting the land itself. Have you ever thought about that in terms of your own life? That God's most precious gift to us is himself? Every other gift he gives you, every blessing you have received, is meant to draw your eyes and heart to this first gift—the Giver himself. I am thankful when I hear people thank God for answering their prayer requests for the things they need such as money, a job, health, or even guidance. Those are great things to thank God for. But do you realize that all those things, good in and of themselves, are never meant to be what a believer is ultimately thankful for? They are meant to direct the believer's mind to God as we acknowledge that he is the giver of everything. He is the one we should ultimately love and treasure. God's people are made special because God gives himself to them, as a mother gives herself to her child or a husband gives himself to his wife. Above all else, this is what being chosen means.

Now, many people today do not believe that human beings are very special. But I think you are. I think you as an individual are special. So-called ethicists like Peter Singer at Princeton may tell you that you have no special value that distinguishes you from any other animal. But the Bible clearly teaches that every human being is made in the image of God, whether one is a Christian or not. Since you are made in God's image, you are special.

Yet though you are special, you are not sovereign. You are not the Lord. The "specialness" of humanity in the Bible is clearly subjugated to the uniqueness and sovereignty of God. He is our Creator. He is infinitely different from us. And he alone rules. God is the one who chooses a people for himself and his own pleasure.

Of course, the man whom God chose to father the nation, Israel, showed himself to be unfaithful, as did his children. Ultimately, the true Chosen One who was perfectly faithful is Jesus Christ. And to be a Christian means to be chosen *in* Christ. As Paul wrote to some early Christians,

> Praise be to the God and Father of our Lord Jesus Christ, who has blessed us in the heavenly realms with every spiritual blessing in Christ. For he chose us in him before the creation of the world to be holy and blameless in his sight (Eph. 1:3-4).

How do we become Christians? Aside from whatever we may need to do, it begins here: God chooses us. Meditate on this, Christian. If you are ever tempted to feel proud for having made the right choice, meditate on the fact that God chose you.

When you begin to grasp the great truth of this book—that God chooses his people—you begin to realize that our fundamental posture as Christians should never be anxiety or pride, but gratitude and hope. Anxiety may look more humble than pride, but it's really just pride with no makeup on. More than anything else, a confident knowledge of God and his Word will kill our pride and fuel our hope. It was true for God's people back in Moses' time, and it is true for God's people today. If you want to kill pride and fuel hope, study and learn God's Word. Grow in your confidence in him.

In our churches today, we are as radically dependent on God as the Israelites, who could take possession of the land only through God and his action. We may not be interested in overtaking any real estate; but in those areas where God has called us to faithfulness, our success depends on his gracious power alone. How many times have I heard people say they sensed God was moving in a congregation in an unusually powerful way. That should not cause pride in the leaders or members of the congregation; it should cause humble thankfulness and praise. Whenever the Lord does decide to use a church in a special way, all glory goes to him. You should practice this same gratitude when God works in your own life as well. Do not neglect to thank God for his blessings.

Fundamentally, it is God who chooses his people, who raises them up, and who uses them for his purposes.

GOD'S PEOPLE MUST CHOOSE HIM

Our second summary sentence for the message of Deuteronomy is this: God's people must choose him. If the book were only about God's choices, then it would not contain any imperative verbs. But there are plenty of imperatives in this book; command after command after command is given. And the basic command is, the people must choose God. This is an essential part of being God's special people. As we did with our first statement, let's unpack this second statement by asking several clarifying questions.

What Does Choosing God Look Like?

First, what does choosing God look like? Throughout the three speeches that comprise this final book of the Pentateuch, Moses exhorts the people to keep God's words or commands. The person who chooses God, in other words, is a person who keeps his commands. This insistence resonates throughout Deuteronomy. At the beginning of chapter 4, for instance, we read,

> Hear now, O Israel, the decrees and laws I am about to teach you. Follow them
> so that you may live and may go in and take possession of the land that the

Lord, the God of your fathers, is giving you. Do not add to what I command you and do not subtract from it, but keep the commands of the Lord your God that I give you (Deut 4:1-2).

Did you notice all the imperatives? Hear, follow, do not add or subtract, keep (cf. 12:32).

Many Christians today are puzzled about how to respond to Old Testament imperatives. Some Christians assume that the Old Testament commands provide helpful historical background for understanding the New Testament but that they are generally irrelevant to us today. Other Christians think the Old Testament's laws should be reenacted today, and a few of them mean this quite literally, as if the U.S. Congress should pass a Senate or House Resolution: "HR1: Be it resolved, Exodus to Deuteronomy"!

In fact, I think the choice between these two options is a false one. I cannot answer all the knotty questions about how the Old Testament Law relates to the New Testament gospel, but two simple facts should be clear to us. First, Israel was specially called to prepare a people for the coming Messiah. Therefore, God revealed his laws to the nation in an unusually clear way. Not incidentally, this meant they experienced immediate retribution for violating God's laws in a way that (as far as we know) no other nation ever has. Israel was unique.

Second, every law in the Old Testament tells us something about the character of the God who gave it. I quickly admit, it is harder to figure out what some of the laws reveal about his character than others. But then, that is what you have Sunday afternoons for! We can be confident that God had a reason for every law he gave his people. And the truths these laws reveal about his character are not limited to any one time or nation. This is why people today, like the people then, must study these imperatives and understand them. Choosing to love God and keep his commands is choosing the path of life. So Moses exhorts the people in his final speech, "This day I call heaven and earth as witnesses against you that I have set before you life and death, blessings and curses. Now choose life" (30:19).

Christian friend, that same call still stands before us. We are called to choose life. And choosing life entails action. That's why the New Testament book of James says that faith without works is dead faith. It isn't the real thing. It's a dummy and a counterfeit. Now, I am *not* telling you for a moment that your works will save you. They won't! Rather, I am asking you to examine your works in search of evidence that God has graciously saved you. Do you understand the difference? As the apostle Peter also teaches, the person whom God has saved will increasingly look different. Peter writes,

> For this very reason, make every effort to add to your faith goodness; and to goodness, knowledge; and to knowledge, self-control; and to self-control, perseverance; and to perseverance, godliness; and to godliness, brotherly kindness; and to brotherly kindness, love. For if you possess these qualities in increasing measure, they will keep you from being ineffective and unproductive in your knowledge of our Lord Jesus Christ. But if anyone does not have them, he is nearsighted and blind, and has forgotten that he has been cleansed from his past sins. Therefore, my brothers, be all the more eager to make your calling and election sure (2 Pet. 1:5-10a).

Have you recently stopped to examine your life and make your calling and election sure? Do you find yourself marked by what Peter writes about? Even the great passage on grace in Ephesians 2 clearly teaches that God intends his special people to act specially: "For it is by grace you have been saved, through faith—and this not from yourselves, it is the gift of God—not by works, so that no one can boast" (Eph. 2:8-9). Now notice the next verse: "For we are God's workmanship, created in Christ Jesus to do good works, which God prepared in advance for us to do" (2:10).

If you want to understand the Bible better, let me caution you against two mistakes. First, do not turn down the volume on God's sovereignty. Don't say, "Oh, I don't understand these ideas of predestination, election, or God choosing us." You do not need to understand it to your complete satisfaction. Read it in Scripture and believe.

Second, do not turn down the volume on what we are called to do. Don't say, "Oh, it's all about grace. Don't talk to me about imperatives. That's legalism." The imperatives are here in Scripture. God's people are called to live a certain way, and we *get* to live a certain way. God, by his Holy Spirit, breaks into our lives and changes us so that we can live in a manner that brings glory and praise to him. What a privilege! God chooses his people, yes, but we must choose God. You cannot get around this when you read through the Bible and this book of Deuteronomy.

What Kind of Choice Is It?

What kind of choice, then, does Deuteronomy say we have to make? We have to make a profoundly personal choice, personal for us and personal in its significance toward God. Let's look at both sides of that equation. First, it is incumbent upon us as individuals to make the choice. Throughout its pages, Deuteronomy presents the very stark contrast of a choice between blessing and curse:

See, I set before you today life and prosperity, death and destruction. For I command you today to love the LORD your God, to walk in his ways, and to keep his commands, decrees and laws; then you will live and increase, and the LORD your God will bless you in the land you are entering to possess.

But if your heart turns away and you are not obedient, and if you are drawn away to bow down to other gods and worship them, I declare to you this day that you will certainly be destroyed. You will not live long in the land you are crossing the Jordan to enter and possess.

This day I call heaven and earth as witnesses against you that I have set before you life and death, blessings and curses. Now choose life, so that you and your children may live and that you may love the LORD your God, listen to his voice, and hold fast to him (Deut. 30:15-20a; cf. 11:26-32).

While God's people can choose to do wrong in any number of ways—sin comes in many forms—the choice we face basically boils down to two ways to live: we can bow down to the one true God or we can bow down to other gods, or idols.

This brings us to the other side of the equation. Not only is our decision to choose God personal to us, it is personally significant toward God. He regards our choices and our sins quite personally. Whatever the particulars, when you sin you serve an idol; you serve someone or something other than God. And that is a personal affront to God. Therefore, Deuteronomy, along with the rest of the Bible, sometimes expresses disobedience as "not trusting" God (e.g., 1:32; 9:23). Have you thought of that before? At the root, sin is basically not trusting God. And idols are the focus of this distrust. They are God's rivals, as it were, for the hearts of his people. To make the point even more sharply, the Bible will refer to idolatry as spiritual unfaithfulness and adultery. It is also a spiritual sickness and an infectious sickness. Therefore, God promises to banish the people if they become idolatrous:

if you then become corrupt and make any kind of idol, doing evil in the eyes of the LORD your God and provoking him to anger, I call heaven and earth as witnesses against you this day that you will quickly perish from the land that you are crossing the Jordan to possess. You will not live there long but will certainly be destroyed. The LORD will scatter you among the peoples, and only a few of you will survive among the nations to which the LORD will drive you. There you will worship man-made gods of wood and stone, which cannot see or hear or eat or smell (4:25b-28).

The infectiousness of idolatry is why God opposes intermarriage between Israelites and foreigners. God is not a racist. His opposition has nothing to do with our modern idea of race. It has everything to do with idolatry and whether we will be uniquely and supremely allied to God. God knows foreign wives "will turn your sons away from following me to serve other gods" (7:4). Nature abhors a vacuum. Do not fool yourself with the notion that you are neutral, non-aligned, and self-sufficient. You are not! God reminds his people powerfully of this in chapter 8:

> You may say to yourself, "My power and the strength of my hands have produced this wealth for me." But remember the LORD your God, for it is he who gives you the ability to produce wealth, and so confirms his covenant, which he swore to your forefathers, as it is today. If you ever forget the LORD your God and follow other gods and worship and bow down to them, I testify against you today that you will surely be destroyed. Like the nations the LORD destroyed before you, so you will be destroyed for not obeying the LORD your God (8:17-20).

All of chapter 13 is devoted to dealing with idolatry among God's people. If a prophet comes and says to worship other gods, he should be put to death (13:1-5). If a member of an Israelite's own family says to worship other gods, he or she must be put to death (13:6-9). If the citizens of a town worship other gods, everyone in that town must be put to death (13:12-15). In short, idolatry must be purged from the people (cf. 17:2-7), just as God had done after the people had worshiped the Golden Calf and the Baal of Peor (Exodus 32; Numbers 25). Interestingly, Paul quotes from Deuteronomy 13 when he rebukes the Corinthians about the man who is sleeping with his father's wife (1 Cor. 5:13). Such sin must be purged from God's people.

The Lord is severe on all kinds of idolatry because idolatry is sin in its purest form: it is trusting something other than God. Too easily idolatry transmutes into justifying sexual immorality, burning your sons and daughters to death, or taking the lives of strangers for the sake of religious worship (Deut. 18:9-13). Such practices may constitute religious worship for some, but it is certainly not the worship of the one true God.

Sometimes people read Deuteronomy and are put off by the commands to destroy the Canaanites who live in the land. But if you want to understand this book, much less these commands, you must understand God's concern to be worshiped exclusively. In chapter 20, for instance, he tells the Israelites to destroy the Canaanites completely, and then he provides his reason: "Otherwise, they will teach you to follow all the detestable things they do in worshiping their gods, and you will sin against the LORD your God" (20:18; cf. 29:16-21). In chapter 12, his concern about idolatry extends to those who claim to worship the Lord but do so in ways he has not commanded (e.g., 12:4,

13-14, 31). God intends, in other words, to be worshiped alone and in a manner entirely consistent with his character.

And what if God's people choose not to follow him? Well, consider God's ironic judgment upon the rebellious generation who left Egypt but then refused to enter God's land and justified their actions by crying out, "Our wives and children will be taken as plunder" (Num. 14:3). In Deuteronomy 1, Moses reminds the people of God's response to their pitiful excuses: "the little ones that you said would be taken captive, your children who do not yet know good from bad—they will enter the land. I will give it to them and they will take possession of it" (Deut. 1:39). There is, I dare say, a kind of beauty in God's judgment. The very thing the people use to excuse sin God uses to expose his greatness, power, and might. It's as if God is saying, "Do you think that you know how to protect your children better than I do? You are so proud that I will dispense with you and your rebellious hearts, and I will raise up your children to do what you say I cannot do. They will enter the land by my great power, for you and all of the nations of the world to see."

Disobeying God is opposing him personally. It cannot and will not be tolerated, whether it is an individual, a town, a generation, or even a whole nation that disobeys (see chapter 28). Could God be any clearer?

The people can, however, repent and change their ways. God put sacrifices and offerings in place to teach them the meaning of sin and forgiveness. He also gives them eloquent promises of forgiveness and restoration. Immediately following his threat to disperse them among the nations for worshiping idols, he promises them,

> But if from there you seek the LORD your God, you will find him if you look for him with all your heart and with all your soul. When you are in distress and all these things have happened to you, then in later days you will return to the LORD your God and obey him. For the LORD your God is a merciful God; he will not abandon or destroy you or forget the covenant with your forefathers, which he confirmed to them by oath (4:29-31).

Through all of this, we begin to understand what a personal matter sin is, from the standpoints of both the one who sins and the one against whom we sin. As we said in our study of Numbers, every sin, no matter how unconnected with religion it seems, is really a short, sharp message to God, saying, "I don't like you. I would rather have these things than you. They give me what I want."

Friend, if you can presently hear my words, I pray that you understand that the most important meeting of your life remains before you. You will not miss it. Even if you lose your date book, you will be there on time. On a coming day you will stand before God, who is more loving, holy, righteous, and pure than you or I can imagine. And you, who have been fearfully and wonderfully made in his image, will give an account to this holy one for all that you have said and done or left unsaid and undone. At that meeting, you will find no help from your connections in this life, your money, your good deeds, or your family. That ever-lengthening line of actions and attitudes from your past, which we thought about earlier, will follow you into the meeting—almost like Jacob Marley's chains in *A Christmas Carol*. This line will assemble itself in the presence of Almighty God, and you will have to present an explanation to this One who can plainly see all your secrets and desires, your actions and motives of heart, perfectly and beyond dispute. The day is coming on which you will have this meeting.

If you are not yet convinced that our choice to follow God is personal, if you are still inclined to think, "Oh, this is the Old Testament, and it's all about the cold, impersonal law," then consider one more striking feature of this book: all the language about loving God. There is a lot!

We do not tend to associate love with the law, but Deuteronomy is filled with both. The book is, after all, in some sense a marriage covenant between God and his people. We have seen God's love for his people.[9] But notice that the people are also called to choose to love him! This is explicit in the *shema*: "Hear, O Israel: The LORD our God, the LORD is one. Love the LORD your God with all your heart and with all your soul and with all your strength" (6:4-5). Similarly, we read in chapter 7 that God keeps his covenant of love to "those who love him and keep his commands" (7:9). In chapter 10, Moses says to the people, "what does the LORD your God ask of you but to fear the LORD your God, to walk in all his ways, to love him, to serve the LORD your God with all your heart and with all your soul" (10:12). And again in chapter 11: "Love the LORD your God" (11:1). Deuteronomy contains many more summonses to love the Lord.[10] We even find that God will test the people in order to expose "whether you love him with all your heart and with all your soul" (13:3).

I remember once asking a friend in seminary if he loved the Lord. He looked at me uncomfortably and said, "That's language I don't really use. I don't like it." I remember another time when I attended a gathering of Muslims in Cambridge, England, where the Muslim apologist Ahmed Deedat gave a talk about the glories of Islam. In the talk, he made light of the way Christians speak about "having a relationship with God." After the talk, I said to a couple of Muslims, "I have a relationship with God. I know him and love him, and I

---

[9] E.g., 4:37; 5:10; 7:12-13; 10:15, 18; 23:5; 33:3.
[10] Cf. 11:13, 22; 19:9; 30:16, 20.

know that he loves me." Whether or not they believed me, this is what the book of Deuteronomy and the rest of the Bible teach.

Let me ask you a question: When a temptation to sin confronts you, and you turn to prayer, do you simply ask God for protection from the sin? Protection is a good thing to pray for, and I want you to keep praying for it. But there is more. Pray that God will also act in your heart to cause you to love him more, especially more than the sin tempting you. We should be aware of our own weaknesses, and we should build up defenses against sin. But positively, we want our hearts to grow in loving God more than anything else. In his final speech, Moses says, "The LORD your God will circumcise your hearts and the hearts of your descendants, so that you may love him with all your heart and with all your soul, and live" (30:6). In context, Moses is referring to God's promises to restore the people as they repent and turn back from their sin. Moses knows that God himself will need to act in order for the people to love God. So, pray for that. Pray that God would do that in your own heart. We will love him only because he first loved us.

So Deuteronomy clearly teaches that the choice of whether to follow idolatrous desire or God is your choice to make, and that your decision will be evidenced by your actions. Also, this choice is not a matter of dry religious accounting; it is a deeply personal choice, both to you and to God. God's commands reflect his character. When you disobey God's commands you disobey God himself, not just some impersonal laws.

What Implications Does Your Choice Have Beyond You?

But there is one more thing we must ask about our choices: What implications do our choices have beyond ourselves? God's purposes involve more than just you or me! The decision to follow God is personal, but that decision is not made in isolation. Amid countless personal choices, God does dramatic things in his people as a whole.

In the book of Deuteronomy, the results of the nation's choices are huge. When the people follow the Lord's way, God says, he will put "the terror and fear" of them on the nations. The nations "will hear reports of you and will tremble and be in anguish because of you" (2:25; cf. 11:25; 28:10). He also wants the wisdom he gives to Israel through his law to be perceived by the nations, so that the nations will proclaim, "Surely this great nation is a wise and understanding people" (4:6). In short, God desires Israel to act as a display of his blessings upon an obedient people for the entire world to see.

Yet God also promises to use Israel as a display of his character even if the people forsake obedience and its blessings. One of the most hair-raising chapters in the Bible is Deuteronomy 28, which contains parts I would hesitate to read out loud if I were not actually preaching it. In the chapter, God summarizes the blessings and curses that will fall upon the people according to their decision to follow God or not. If the people choose not to follow God, for instance,

> The LORD will drive you and the king you set over you to a nation unknown to you or your fathers. There you will worship other gods, gods of wood and stone. You will become a thing of horror and an object of scorn and ridicule to all the nations where the LORD will drive you (28:36-37).

And then several verses later:

> Then the LORD will scatter you among all nations, from one end of the earth to the other. There you will worship other gods—gods of wood and stone, which neither you nor your fathers have known. Among those nations you will find no repose, no resting place for the sole of your foot. There the LORD will give you an anxious mind, eyes weary with longing, and a despairing heart. You will live in constant suspense, filled with dread both night and day, never sure of your life. In the morning you will say, "If only it were evening!" and in the evening, "If only it were morning!"—because of the terror that will fill your hearts and the sights that your eyes will see. The LORD will send you back in ships to Egypt on a journey I said you should never make again. There you will offer yourselves for sale to your enemies as male and female slaves, but no one will buy you (28:64-68).

And what will result from theses curses falling upon the nation? "All the nations will ask: 'Why has the LORD done this to this land? Why this fierce, burning anger?'" (29:24). Do you get the point? The results of the nation's choices are huge. They are God's special people, and they will act as a display to the nations one way or the other. Whether through blessing or through judgment, they will display to the entire world the truth about God.

God works in this way so that Israel will know him and so that the nations will know him through Israel. When God first called Abraham and promised to bless him and his descendants, he also promised that "all peoples on earth will be blessed" through Abraham's line (Gen. 12:3). God always planned to make himself known to and through the Israelites to the nations (cf. Deut. 9:28; 32:26-27). Have you noticed that? He never blessed them merely for their own sake, but so that they would be a blessing to all the world.

This is true for us as a church. We have a continuing obligation to submit to God's Word by hearing it, obeying it, and receiving its blessings. And as we do, we must turn and be a blessing to others—all to God's glory. However poorly or imperfectly we do it, our church should be defined by knowing his blessings then turning and blessing others for the sake of his glory.

So what did God's Old Testament people do? They made a public decision for God. They chose him. In chapter 29, Moses officially pronounced this generation to be God's people (29:10-15; cf. 27:9). They accepted the obligation to keep the covenant and obey God. In the same way, the people of God now are called to make the infinitely important choice to follow God personally, both for their own sake and for the sake of God's purposes among the nations.

CONCLUSION

So we come to the conclusion of this series of overview sermons in the Pentateuch. Of course, the great story of the Old Testament does not stop there. I would love to say it did and tell you the people went off and lived happily ever after. That's how Shakespeare concluded *The Tempest*. But I cannot end this story in that way. If you turn to Deuteronomy 31, you will find one of the stranger things in the Bible. The Lord instructs Moses to write a song that testifies to the fact that God knows the people will disobey him: "Now write down for yourselves this song and teach it to the Israelites and have them sing it, so that it may be a witness for me against them" (31:19). You will then find the song recorded in the next chapter, and I cannot imagine the people liked to sing it! It is all about how they will disobey God! Here's just a portion of the song:

> Jeshurun [that's another name for Israel] grew fat and kicked;
> > filled with food, he became heavy and sleek.
> He abandoned the God who made him
> > and rejected the Rock his Savior.
> They made him jealous with their foreign gods
> > and angered him with their detestable idols.
> They sacrificed to demons, which are not God—
> > gods they had not known,
> > gods that recently appeared,
> > gods your fathers did not fear.
> You deserted the Rock, who fathered you;
> > you forgot the God who gave you birth (32:15-18).

Throughout these first five books of the Bible, the Lord knows his people will desert and betray him. Yet he has a purpose even in their disobedience: to make known his justice and—ultimately—his forgiveness.

Through the prophecies of this song, we see something of the rest of

Israel's history. In the coming days and years, the people would take the land God promised to Abraham, and they would flourish. But over the following centuries the people would forsake God. So he would forsake them. He would destroy ten of the tribes of Israel through the armies of Assyria, and the remaining two tribes he would send into exile in Babylon. Eventually, a remnant of the exiles would be restored. Psalm 85 presents the cry for such a restoration:

> Restore us again, O God our Savior,
>   and put away your displeasure toward us.
> Will you be angry with us forever?
>   Will you prolong your anger through all generations?
> Will you not revive us again,
>   that your people may rejoice in you?
> Show us your unfailing love, O LORD,
>   and grant us your salvation.
> I will listen to what God the LORD will say;
>   he promises peace to his people, his saints—
>   but let them not return to folly.
> Surely his salvation is near those who fear him,
>   that his glory may dwell in our land.
> Love and faithfulness meet together;
>   righteousness and peace kiss each other (Ps. 85:4-10).

The dilemma the rebellious Israelites would find themselves encountering again and again, or really, the dilemma God would encounter again and again in the face of this rebellious people, is found in this idea of righteousness and peace kissing. How can righteousness and peace kiss? How can God love his people while acting in accordance with his holiness? An answer is suggested in the last line of this song that God gives Moses to teach the people in chapter 32: the Lord promises he will "make atonement for his land and people" (Deut. 32:43). How? Well, the verse does not say. And notice, Moses is not the one who will provide atonement for the people. He can't. He is a sinner. And we know from elsewhere in Scripture that this atonement must be perfect, without spot, and without sin (Heb. 4:15; 1 John 3:5). God must be the one who provides this atonement. Only then will both his holiness and his love be satisfied.

Moses truly was a great man. These first five books of the Bible are often called the books of Moses, and he has certainly been the central figure in them. What a life he led. Consider all he saw and heard!

It is interesting to reflect, however, that Moses lived to be 120 years old (Deut. 34:7), yet we know almost nothing about 119 of his 120 years. Almost everything we know about Moses happened during the eightieth year of his life, when he was called at the burning bush to lead the people out of Egypt and to the Promised Land. Besides that, we know one story about the circumstances of his birth. We know he grew up in Pharaoh's household, murdered an Egyptian at age 40, and then spent 40 years as a shepherd. We don't know much about the last 40 years of his life in the wilderness leading the people. And we only know this tiny bit about the very end: The people are encamped across from the Promised Land preparing to enter. Moses gives the three speeches that comprise the book of Deuteronomy. At one point, he entreats God to let him enter the Promised Land, but God tells him no, and not to bring it up again (3:24-27; cf. 32:51). (If you have been following this series, you remember that Moses dishonored the Lord at one point in the wilderness, so God promised he would never enter the land.) In chapter 31, the Lord tells Moses the day of his death is near (31:14). Then in chapter 34, we read, "And Moses the servant of the LORD died there in Moab, as the LORD had said. He buried him in Moab, in the valley opposite Beth Peor, but to this day no one knows where his grave is" (34:5-6). And that's it! That's the life of Moses in Scripture.

And yet Moses cuts a unique figure across the history of Israel. Deuteronomy even closes by testifying to this fact:

> Since then, no prophet has risen in Israel like Moses, whom the LORD knew face to face, who did all those miraculous signs and wonders the LORD sent him to do in Egypt—to Pharaoh and to all his officials and to his whole land. For no one has ever shown the mighty power or performed the awesome deeds that Moses did in the sight of all Israel (34:10-12).

But doesn't this assessment of Moses' unique greatness contradict an earlier passage in the book? In chapter 18, the Lord said that he would raise up another prophet like Moses:

> The LORD your God will raise up for you a prophet like me from among your own brothers. You must listen to him. For this is what you asked of the LORD your God at Horeb on the day of the assembly when you said, "Let us not hear the voice of the LORD our God nor see this great fire anymore, or we will die."
>
> The LORD said to me: "What they say is good. I will raise up for them a prophet like you from among their brothers; I will put my words in his mouth, and he will tell them everything I command him. If anyone does not listen to my words that the prophet speaks in my name, I myself will call him to account" (18:15-19).

At the time when the concluding postscript was added at the end of the book, no prophet had yet fulfilled this prediction. Today, we know who that promised prophet is: Jesus Christ. Jesus Christ is the one who speaks God's words perfectly. He is the one sent from God to teach us the way to God.

One traditional objection to the argument that Christ fulfills this prophecy in Deuteronomy 18 is the fact that Christ was killed by crucifixion. Not only did the people of Jesus' day reject him, they rejected him in a way that Deuteronomy itself would testify brought God's curse upon him. A verse in chapter 21 reads, "anyone who is hung on a tree is under God's curse" (21:23). And the logic runs, "Well, if he's under God's curse, he certainly cannot be God's special servant."

Really? The prophet Isaiah says otherwise:

> Surely he took up our infirmities
>   and carried our sorrows,
> yet we considered him stricken by God,
>   smitten by him, and afflicted.
> But he was pierced for our transgressions,
>   he was crushed for our iniquities;
> the punishment that brought us peace was upon him,
>   and by his wounds we are healed.
> We all, like sheep, have gone astray,
>   each of us has turned to his own way;
> and the LORD has laid on him
>   the iniquity of us all (Isa. 53:4-6).

If Jesus was cursed, and if he was sinless and did not deserve that curse, then whose curse was laid upon him? The answer brings us to the good news of Christianity: he received the curse that I deserved for *my* sins and that you deserved for *your* sins, if only you will turn from those sins, choose God, and believe in the promise of forgiveness he offers you—not in Moses, as great as he was—but in Christ. Moses died for his own sin, remember? He could not enter the land because of his sin. But why did Christ die? Writing to the Corinthians about this, Paul says, "God made him who had no sin to be sin for us, so that in him we might become the righteousness of God" (2 Cor. 5:21). My friend, this is the good news that Christians have!

For the Israelites who read Deuteronomy in the first few centuries following Moses' death, the past *was* prophecy. God's predictions of their disobedience proved to be correct. But thank God the Bible did not stop with the Israelites' rebellion. The question for us today is, will the past prove to be prophecy or a dispensable prologue? Our history of sin and rebellion against

God necessarily condemns us. No one who ever hears these words of mine can honestly know his or her past—all of it, unedited!—and feel good about presenting it to the Lord. We can delude ourselves and enjoy an imaginary peace, or we can acknowledge the truth about our lives and so despair. But thank God our past is not the whole story. You *are* hearing my words, and so your story must not yet be over. But the only way to break decisively with the divine curse that your past (not to mention the present and future) warrants is to acknowledge Christ as the sacrifice for sin, the Passover Lamb provided by God and slain on your behalf to bring life now and forever.

This is the great story of Deuteronomy and of the first five books of the Bible; indeed it is the story of the whole Bible. I pray that this is the great and true story of your life as well.

Let us pray:

Dear Lord, you have led us with such clarity and tenderness, with such holiness and love. Lead each one of us now home to you, we pray, through Jesus Christ. Amen.

Questions for Reflection

1. Who or what are some of the gods people believe in today?

2. If you are a Christian, what does Deuteronomy teach about why God chose you for salvation? What effect should this have on how you compare yourself with other people? What effect should it have on why you feel good about yourself and on what you boast about?

3. If God has chosen us for salvation, what cause do we have for anxiety and worry? If you struggle with anxiety, what particular truths and what particular verses in Deuteronomy can you memorize in order to fight that anxiety?

4. We saw that, in lieu of an image of God himself, the people of Israel were commanded to write the law upon easily visible stones once they crossed the Jordan into the Promised Land (27:8). After all, a set of laws, we said, depicts God's character far better than any image that a human can fashion. Let's make what this means really clear: God wants his people to be *word-centered* and not *image-centered* as they seek to know him, his purpose for their lives, and how they should live with one another. Of course one kind of image *is* important: the image of seeing God's people live by God's Word. What does this mean for how we *do* church? What does this mean for evangelism? For

missions? Can you think of any New Testament passages that make these same points?

5. If you are a Christian parent, read Deuteronomy 6:7-9 and 11:18-21. According to these verses, what should you, as a Christian parent, teach your children? How often should you do this? What steps are you presently taking to do this? What steps can you take?

6. What advantages do we gain from a rigorous understanding of human responsibility—the fact that we have to choose to obey God and follow him?

7. What advantages do we gain from a rigorous understanding of divine sovereignty—the fact that God chooses us and plans out all our days?

8. Peter says to make our "calling and election sure." What kind of evidence should you look for in your own life to do that? What kind of evidence should you find in your involvement in your local church?

9. Do non-Christians recognize that their sin is a personal affront against God? What are some ways you can communicate this fact in your evangelistic conversations?

10. John Calvin said that our hearts are idol factories. Are you able to name some of the idols your heart has produced? What are they?

11. Deuteronomy predicted that the people of Israel would be unfaithful to God's Word, which they were—leading God to scatter them among the nations, which he did. What can we expect God to do with local churches that are unfaithful to his Word? What are several ways a church might be unfaithful to God's Word? Will it necessarily mean a church contradicts it?

12. Are you ready to stand before God's throne of judgment? What defense will you make for yourself and your sin? Will anyone plead on your behalf?

PART TWO

THE OTHER

MILLENNIUM

THE MESSAGE OF JOSHUA: CONQUEST

6

THE MESSAGE OF JOSHUA: CONQUEST

IS THERE A REASON?[1]

Do things happen for a reason? Are there reasons why this army wins and that commander is exalted, while the other army loses and their political leaders fall from power? Yes, there are immediate reasons, like this army had more troops or that army had little air support. But are there larger, more grandiose reasons for why things happen? In the grand scheme of things, are there ultimate causes and meanings to the events of history?

The answer to this question exposes a great divide among people today. Many people—most?—do not believe history has a higher, greater, or deeper meaning. History shows, they claim, that such thinking only endangers freedom. In fact, such thinking encourages the very religious fanaticism and terrorist activity that many countries around the globe are now readjusting to defend themselves against.

I leave it to you to sort out whether the latest constellation of political allegiances bears a higher significance. Right now, I want to direct your attention particularly to the nation of Israel. I don't mean the modern state established in 1948, but the nation conceived in a promise of God to Abraham and then born in the Exodus from Egypt more than three thousand years ago. Over the next dozen studies, I want us to consider the stream of history recorded for us in the Old Testament concerning the nation of Israel. If we can understand the meaning of the history recorded here, we will better understand the meaning of life itself—even of our own lives.

---

[1] This sermon was originally preached on May 12, 2002, at Capitol Hill Baptist Church in Washington, D.C., during the same service in which Dr. Michael Lawrence was installed as the associate pastor. Specific exhortations given to Dr. Lawrence on that date have been kept in the following text with the hope that Christian leaders, whether in the church or the home, will find the applications pertinent to their own lives and ministries.

INTRODUCING JOSHUA

To begin, let me suggest that you open your Bible to the table of contents. You may not know that Bibles have tables of contents, but they do! They are hidden at the beginning, and they are very useful, particularly when you are finding your way around the Bible for the first time, or when you are trying to find an unfamiliar part. Never be ashamed to open a Bible to the table of contents.

We have already considered the very first books you see in the Old Testament portion of your table of contents: Genesis, Exodus, Leviticus, Numbers, and Deuteronomy. Together, these five books are called the Torah, or the Law, and we covered one book per study. Here, I want to begin another series, called "The Other Millennium," that will take us through the next twelve historical books of the Old Testament. These books, beginning with Joshua and going through Esther, will allow us to trace the history of God's Old Testament people for roughly one thousand years, from about the fourteenth century B.C. to the fifth century B.C. The twelve books are basically in chronological order, with several minor exceptions, and they are important because they reveal how God deals with a people he has set apart for his own special purposes. We begin this series with the book of Joshua, the first of these historical books.

Let me add, this is an unusual sermon for our church. Normally, we preach sermons on shorter passages of Scripture, but this is what I call an "overview sermon," where we look at an entire book of the Bible in one sermon. Lord willing, I will preach only sixty-six of these types of sermons in my career at Capitol Hill Baptist Church.

I can tell you the outline of the whole book of Joshua very easily. Joshua has twenty-four chapters. The first half, or the first twelve chapters, covers the conquest of Canaan, while most of the second half covers the division of the conquered land between the various tribes of Israel. The last couple of chapters are devoted to Joshua's final words.

Why was this book written? Well, as a Christian, I would answer, "Because God wanted it written!" But more immediately, many things in ancient Israel required an explanation; and as you read through this book, you find that it provides those explanations. It sets the record straight. I have compiled here a list of the questions an Israelite might have asked for which the book of Joshua provides an explicit answer. People may have wondered,

- Why is that pile of stones sitting next to the Jordan? Find the answer in Joshua 4:9.
- Why is this placed called Gilgal? Look at 5:9.

- Why does Rahab (and her descendants) live among us; why wasn't she destroyed with everyone else in Jericho? Look at 6:25.
- Why is there that heap of stones in the valley? Look at 7:26.
- Why is that heap of stones there by the gate? Look at 8:28-29.
- Why are the Gibeonites working and living here? Look at 9:27.
- Why are these stones set up outside this cave? Look at 10:27.
- Why are there still people of Geshur and Maacah east of the Jordan? Look at 13:13.
- Why are the Jebusites in Jerusalem and the Canaanites in Gezer? Look at 15:63 and 16:10.

The book of Joshua was written to answer these and other questions.

But beyond these many smaller, more specific questions, I would like for us to find the answers to the two main questions this book poses, because I expect that when we do, we will have accomplished something that will be helpful in our lives. Specifically, we want to know *what* happened. And then we want to know *why* these things happened.

Before jumping in, I also want to say this is an unusual sermon in another way. I intend to apply the message of this book particularly to Michael Lawrence, as we celebrate and ask God to consecrate his ministry within our congregation as our associate pastor. Aside from wedding sermons, you will not hear me address an individual in a sermon. Please don't think that every Sunday I pick out one individual at random and start publicly applying my sermon to him or her. I don't. I will let you do that, and I will let God do that as his Spirit works with you.

So first, let's look at what happened, and then we will go back and consider why it happened.

WHAT HAPPENS? THE PEOPLE CHOOSE

What happens in the book of Joshua? In one sense, you could say that Joshua is about choices. The first half of Joshua is about Joshua leading the Israelite people through the choice their parents had failed to make—to invade the land of Canaan. In the second half they choose to divide the land the Lord has given them.

To Conquer the Land and Destroy Their Enemies

The first half of this book, chapters 1–12, presents an account of the Israelites conquering the land and destroying their enemies. In the first five chapters, the people send spies into the fortified city of Jericho, cross the Jordan River, consecrate themselves to the Lord, and then prepare themselves for their first military move against Jericho—an important city located at the intersection of the main north-south trade route and the roads heading west through the interior into the heart of Canaan. Chapter 6 describes the amazing story of how, at God's command, the people mark Jericho for destruction by circling it with shouts and trumpet blasts for seven days and then watch its walls topple by God's might. In chapters 7–8, a military thrust is made into the geographic center of the land, and, after a setback, Ai is taken. Chapters 9–10 describe the next military campaign, in which the people defeat key cities in the southern part of Canaan. In chapter 11, their attention turns to the conquest of the northern cities of Canaan; and we read, "Joshua waged war against all these kings for a long time. Except for the Hivites living in Gibeon, not one city made a treaty of peace with the Israelites, who took them all in battle. . . . So Joshua took the entire land" (11:18-19, 23a).

The conquest of Canaan was not a campaign for political control, like most of our wars today. It was a campaign to utterly destroy those living in the land. Chapters 6–10 are full of verses like this: "They devoted the city to the LORD and destroyed with the sword every living thing in it—men and women, young and old, cattle, sheep and donkeys."[2] The people do this to Jericho and Ai in the center of the land (5:13–6:27; 8:1-29). They do this to cities in the south.[3] They do this to the cities in the north.[4] Then, we read, "the land had rest from war."[5]

Honestly, whether you are a Christian or not, Joshua is one of the most difficult books in the Bible to come to grips with. If you are new to the Christian faith, Joshua may not be the place to start. But in God's providence, here you are working through this study, and God may have some crucial ideas for you about himself and about yourself.

To begin with, you need to see that God's people conquered Canaan. Does this sound like an ancient fact removed by too much space and time to be relevant? It isn't. It foreshadows what God is doing today as he calls together his people into his place under his rule. Having led this conquest, Joshua was a type of Jesus Christ, our great captain who has conquered not a passing earthly kingdom but sin and sin's horrible offspring, death. And Christ calls us to follow in his train. All Christians enter into the victory that Christ won for us. And ministers of the Word of God are particularly called to follow our captain as guardians, protectors, and guides of God's people.

Michael, our congregation is convinced that God has called you to this

---

[2] 6:21; cf. 6:24.
[3] 10:20, 29, 31, 33, 34, 36, 38, 42.
[4] 11:7-9, 10, 12-15.
[5] 11:23; 14:15.

work, here in Washington, D.C., alongside me and the other elders God has given us.

To Divide the Land Tribe by Tribe

Most of the second half of the book of Joshua describes the process of dividing up the land tribe by tribe. That's the focus of chapters 13–22. In chapter 13, the people recall that Moses had already allotted the land to the east of the Jordan to two-and-a-half of the tribes. The chapter also recalls that no one tract of Canaan had been assigned to the Levites, since "the LORD, the God of Israel, is [the Levite's] inheritance" (13:33). Certain towns scattered throughout the twelve tribes are given to the Levites so that their ministry of teaching the law can be given to the whole nation. Then in chapter 14 we read, "So the Israelites divided the land" (14:5), referring to land west of the Jordan. An interesting story of Caleb's allotment follows (14:6-15). Chapter 15 describes Judah's allotment in the south, while chapters 16–17 describe the land reserved for the sons of Joseph in the north. The remaining seven tribes are given their land in chapters 18–19, and we then read, "So they finished dividing the land" (19:51). Chapter 20 designates the cities of refuge. Chapter 21 lists the towns reserved for the Levites. And then in chapter 22 Joshua bids farewell and blesses the two-and-a-half tribes that return to their lands on the eastern side of the Jordan.

So the people divide up the land that they have conquered.

To Vow to Fear and Obey God

The Israelites' choice to conquer and divide the land of Canaan fills almost all of Joshua. In that sense, this is *what* the book is about. But preceding all this activity, and continuing through it, you find an important subtext. The people do this *because* they have vowed to fear and obey God.

If you have read Joshua, I wonder if you noticed this, or if you were simply taken up in the remarkable stories of spies and tumbling walls. In chapter 1, they promise to obey Joshua, the Lord's spokesman (1:16-18). In chapter 5, after crossing the Jordan but before moving on Jericho, they begin practicing circumcision and observing the Passover again (5:7-10). God had given these two ordinances to his people forty years earlier at the time of the Exodus, but the ordinances had been neglected since then. By reinstituting these practices, the people are vowing to have the Lord as their God. They are, in a sense, becoming God's people again after a veritable state of suspended animation during the forty years in the wilderness. Then in chapter 8, once Jericho and Ai are defeated, thereby marking the beginning of the conquest, the people stand and listen to Joshua reread the entire Law of Moses (8:34-35). This amazing time of teaching—reenacting God's instruction of the people at Mount Sinai—powerfully symbolizes the fact that they are indeed God's people.

At the end of the book, in his last recorded public act as their leader, Joshua leads the people to renew their covenant with God. In what has to be one of the more unusual interchanges recorded in the Bible, Joshua sounds as though he is urging the people to choose *not* to follow God. That is not the case, of course; he is trying to ensure they understand the seriousness of the choice they are making. He says,

> "Now fear the LORD and serve him with all faithfulness. Throw away the gods your forefathers worshiped beyond the River and in Egypt, and serve the LORD. But if serving the LORD seems undesirable to you, then choose for yourselves this day whom you will serve, whether the gods your forefathers served beyond the River, or the gods of the Amorites, in whose land you are living. But as for me and my household, we will serve the LORD."
>
> Then the people answered, "Far be it from us to forsake the LORD to serve other gods! It was the LORD our God himself who brought us and our fathers up out of Egypt, from that land of slavery, and performed those great signs before our eyes. He protected us on our entire journey and among all the nations through which we traveled. And the LORD drove out before us all the nations, including the Amorites, who lived in the land. We too will serve the LORD, because he is our God."
>
> Joshua said to the people, "You are not able to serve the LORD. He is a holy God; he is a jealous God. He will not forgive your rebellion and your sins. If you forsake the LORD and serve foreign gods, he will turn and bring disaster on you and make an end of you, after he has been good to you."
>
> But the people said to Joshua, "No! We will serve the LORD."
>
> Then Joshua said, "You are witnesses against yourselves that you have chosen to serve the LORD."
>
> "Yes, we are witnesses," they replied.
>
> "Now then," said Joshua, "throw away the foreign gods that are among you and yield your hearts to the LORD, the God of Israel."
>
> And the people said to Joshua, "We will serve the LORD our God and obey him" (24:14-24).

Over the years (or even decades) recounted through the course of this book, this is exactly what the people do. They keep their vows to serve the Lord their God. At the same time, however, they continue to sin.

The people keep their vows. The spies who return from investigating Jericho do not sound like the spies from their parents' generation, whose fearful reports about the people of Canaan exposed their own unbelief. Just the opposite, these younger spies report that "all the people [in Canaan] are melting in fear because of us" (2:24b). And in response to this report, the people believe and obey. The people's faith is demonstrated again in chapter 5 when they practice circumcision and observe the Passover, as well as in chapter 8 when they listen to God's law.

The Israelites clearly have a desire to fear God. This comes out most clearly, perhaps, in the odd but significant account in chapter 22. The eastern tribes have built their own altar, which greatly alarms the western tribes (22:10-12). After all, the nation's one altar must be kept together with the Law and the ark of the covenant, thereby symbolizing that God's worship is regulated by God's Word. But when the western tribes investigate, they find that matters are not as worrisome as they first thought. In fact, the eastern tribes have built this altar to be a replica and a reminder that they worship the Lord only, in case the day ever comes that the western people say, "Hey, you have no part of us." If that were to happen, the replica altar would continue to act as a mute witness saying, "We worship the Lord our God alone" (see 22:21-30).

Such faithfulness, of course, we see supremely not in these people but in Jesus Christ. Christ promised he would do the will of the Father, and he did it as no one else ever has. As Christians, we are called to trust in him and to follow his example. We should publicly profess our faith in Christ. We should take vows, if you will, and live to fulfill them, like the people in this book.

This is one reason our church covenants together as a congregation, and then regularly reads that covenant out loud in our public meetings. Like the people of God of old, we want to publicly profess our allegiance to God, as all Christians do through their baptism and participation in the Lord's Supper.

And so will you, Michael, when you stand before the congregation to receive its confirmation. You will publicly profess your faith and some of your commitments to God and to us. We, as a congregation, will act as a sacred witness before God of those commitments. And we will pray for God to strengthen you to live according to them, even as you spend yourself teaching God's Word and attempting to build his church.

The people also sin. I wish I could stop the story of the people's choices with fearing and obeying God, but I cannot. The people continue to sin, and disastrous consequences follow. As I have looked through the book of Joshua, I have found only one striking sin of commission, where an Israelite does something wrong. I have found many more examples of sins of omission, that is, of *not doing* what they should do.

An Israelite named Achan commits the sin of commission in chapter 7. God had commanded the Israelites to eliminate the inhabitants of Jericho and their possessions, wanting them to be free from the influence of the previous inhabitants' corrupt practices. Yet Achan stole things from Jericho that the Israelites had been told to destroy. And they had been told to destroy these things not because they were needless, but because they were dangerous. Joshua later reminds the people about the incident by asking, "When Achan son of Zerah acted unfaithfully regarding the devoted things, did not wrath come upon the whole community of Israel? He was not the only one who died for his sin" (22:20).

But beyond this, the book of Joshua records a number of significant sins of omission. In chapter 9, for instance, the elders do not pray before making a peace treaty with the Gibeonites. The people of Gibeon, who live nearby, know they will soon be eliminated. So they approach the Israelites, pretending to have traveled from far away, and ask for a treaty. What do the Israelites do? "The men of Israel sampled their provisions but did not inquire of the LORD. Then Joshua made a treaty of peace with them to let them live, and the leaders of the assembly ratified it by oath" (9:14-15). When the truth was discovered, the Israelite people were unhappy with their leaders, but it was too late. They had omitted praying to the Lord, and that sin led to significant problems down the road for Israel.

More often, the sins of omission in the book of Joshua have to do with people not taking parts of the land they are supposed to take. At one point, the Lord says to Joshua, "there are still very large areas of land to be taken over" (13:1). Yet in chapters 15–19, the people cut corners as they divide up the land. Tribes say they are unable to take the land or that they are the victims of inopportune circumstances. Maybe they are just unwilling. Finally, Joshua exclaims, "How long will you wait before you begin to take possession of the land that the LORD, the God of your fathers, has given you?" (18:3). The people ultimately conquer the land, but they sin significantly in the process.

If you are a non-Christian and you want to understand this book, indeed, if you want to understand your own life, you must understand the idea of sin. The Bible teaches that God has made you like him—in his image—but that you have rebelled against his authority in your life. How have you rebelled? Think about the last time you did something you knew was wrong. The guilt you felt at the time was, according to the Bible, not some Freudian superego acting up, but the testimony of your God-given conscience concerning the sin you committed fundamentally against God himself, even if the sin was perpetrated against another or yourself. It is this sin that explains the many problems in our lives and the many problems we cause for others. It is this sin that provides the backdrop for God's dramatic judgments in this book of Joshua. It is this sin for which we desperately and eternally need forgiveness and deliverance.

And it is this sin that Christ, though fully human like us, entirely avoided, so that he might die as the sinless sacrifice and provide the forgiveness and salvation you and I need.

Oh, friend, whoever you are, do examine yourself. Pray that God would give you eyes to see the truth about yourself. Pray that he would help you see and confess your sins of omission—those things that you ought to have done but have not done. And pray that he would help you see and confess your sins of commission—those things that you have done that are wrong. And pray that he would then grant you, as it says in the book of Acts, "repentance unto life" (Acts 11:18).

Michael, I charge you to consider the portrait of sin painted in this book. Even as the people accomplish large and apparent successes, they continue to sin in significant ways. As I have prayed for you and considered your role as a pastor, I have thought particularly about the Israelite leaders who were confident in their analytical abilities to discern the Gibeonites' motives, so they neglected to pray. My bright brother, may God never leave you with only your own wits to serve and guide his church. May he always drive you to inquire of him in prayer, and then to obey him both in what you do and in what you do not do. Pray that he gives you a sensitive heart. Remember that your sins will affect your family and the church. You have a double reason to glorify God through obedience and holiness: it will conduce not only to your own edification but also to ours. The church's health is never improved by any member's sin, but no one's sin hurts a congregation more than the pastor's. When the Corinthian congregation tolerated the sin of a member, Paul merely told them to throw the unrepentant man out. They did, and both the church and the man seem to have benefited. But when the Galatian congregation tolerated the sins of false teaching and false teachers, Paul wrote to defend the gospel itself, and in the most severe terms. You and I have been involved in at least three local congregations that have been seriously hurt by the sins of their pastors. Let's pray and resolve publicly that, by God's grace, we will not follow their wicked examples.

WHY DOES THIS HAPPEN? GOD CHOOSES

If Joshua is a book about choices, most fundamentally it is a book about God's choices. This brings us to the question of why everything happens as it does.

To Fight for the People and Give Them the Land

Remember, we said that the Israelite people conquer the land. Well, they do, but they do because God has chosen them to inherit it. So he fights for them and gives them the land. Notice how Joshua exhorts the people as they prepare to cross the Jordan River: "Consecrate yourselves, for tomorrow the LORD will do amazing things among you" (Josh. 3:5). He does not say, "You're gonna do great tomorrow!" He says, "The LORD will do amazing things among you."

Once they have entered the land, but before the conquest begins, Joshua encounters what appears to be an angel, standing with a drawn sword in his hand. The angel tells Joshua that he has come as the "commander of the army of the LORD" (5:14). Then, in a moment reminiscent of Moses' encounter with God at the burning bush, this commander of the Lord's army tells Joshua, "take off your sandals, for the place where you are standing is holy" (5:15). So the conquest of the land begins. The Lord God himself lets the sword of his justice fall. For the Canaanites, the time for God's mercy has run out.

We are not surprised to then read, several chapters later, "All these kings and their lands Joshua conquered in one campaign, because the LORD, the God of Israel, fought for Israel" (10:42). The text does not say, "Joshua conquered because he was such a skilled military commander." No, he conquers because the Lord fights for Israel. In his farewell address, Joshua gives the Lord credit for all Israel's victories: "You yourselves have seen everything the LORD your God has done to all these nations for your sake; it was the LORD your God who fought for you" (23:3).

All the miracles that occur during Israel's conquest are also evidence of God's involvement. He has brought the army of Israel to Canaan, sustaining it through the desert on manna (cf. 5:12). Now he will fight for them. After all, who makes the flow of the Jordan River stop so the entire nation can walk across? Who makes Jericho's walls fall? Who defeats the Israelites themselves when they sin, and then identifies the primary culprit as Achan? Who restores Israel's fortunes, by raining down hailstones on their enemies and even causing the sun to stand still so that the armies of Israel can complete their victory? As great a leader as Joshua may be, he does none of these things, nor can he. The Lord God himself does all these things! This is what God means when he says he will fight for them. The Lord "gave" the Amorites over to Israel (10:12). And he gives cities and armies to the Israelites again and again![6] We read this summary statement toward the end of the book: "So the LORD gave Israel all the land he had sworn to give their forefathers, and they took possession of it and settled there" (21:43; cf. 1:2-3).

This is one of the main problems people have with understanding the Bible. They do not understand that we have a sovereign God, who can act

---

[6] E.g., 8:7; 10:30; 11:8.

without negating our own actions and responsibility. Now, I cannot answer every question you may have about how that works, but I can say the Bible teaches that both his sovereignty and our responsibility are true, and you will get in trouble if you try to hold only one truth and not the other. If you think that God acts no further than what you do, and you treat this book as a manual for moral instruction, then you do not understand who God is. But if you think that because God is sovereign your decisions do not matter, then you have not understood what Scripture says. Scripture clearly teaches that the Lord was sovereignly active even in the hearts of Israel's enemies. In what may be the most severe verse in this book, we read, "It was the LORD himself who hardened their hearts to wage war against Israel, so that he might destroy them totally, exterminating them without mercy" (11:20). God acted, then Israel acted.

Have you realized how centrally God presents himself in this story? Yes, it is a story about the Israelites conquering the Promised Land. But think back on our study of Exodus. We saw that Exodus is not merely a story about a people being liberated but about the God who liberates them. So here in the "other half of the Exodus"—he brought them out, now he is bringing them in—we find that this story is primarily about the God who conquers.

Joshua knows this. In one of his final speeches, he retells the entire story of Old Testament history up to the present, and he does so with a radically God-centered view. Notice who the primary actor is in Joshua's account:

> Joshua said to all the people, "This is what the LORD, the God of Israel, says: 'Long ago your forefathers, including Terah the father of Abraham and Nahor, lived beyond the River and worshiped other gods. But *I took* your father Abraham from the land beyond the River and led him throughout Canaan and gave him many descendants. *I gave* him Isaac, and to Isaac *I gave* Jacob and Esau. *I assigned* the hill country of Seir to Esau, but Jacob and his sons went down to Egypt.
>
> "'Then *I sent* Moses and Aaron, and *I afflicted* the Egyptians by what *I did* there, and *I brought* you out. When *I brought* your fathers out of Egypt, you came to the sea, and the Egyptians pursued them with chariots and horsemen as far as the Red Sea. But they cried to the LORD for help, and *he put* darkness between you and the Egyptians; *he brought* the sea over them and covered them. You saw with your own eyes what *I did* to the Egyptians. Then you lived in the desert for a long time.
>
> "'*I brought* you to the land of the Amorites who lived east of the Jordan. They fought against you, but *I gave* them into your hands. *I destroyed* them from before you, and you took possession of their land. When Balak son of Zippor, the king of Moab, prepared to fight against Israel, he sent for Balaam son of Beor

to put a curse on you. But *I would not listen* to Balaam, so he blessed you again and again, and *I delivered* you out of his hand.

"'Then you crossed the Jordan and came to Jericho. The citizens of Jericho fought against you, as did also the Amorites, Perizzites, Canaanites, Hittites, Girgashites, Hivites and Jebusites, but *I gave* them into your hands. *I sent* the hornet ahead of you, which drove them out before you—also the two Amorite kings. You did not do it with your own sword and bow. So *I gave* you a land on which you did not toil and cities you did not build; and you live in them and eat from vineyards and olive groves that you did not plant'" (24:2-13).

All the Bible's history, and certainly this book's history, has God at the center. If we want to understand the Bible, or history, or our lives, we must see this fact. God is at the very center of everything! Joshua led the people in conquering the land, but God fought for his people and gave them the land. God sovereignly accomplishes his every purpose.

And just as he was sovereign in Joshua's day, so he is sovereign today over nations and history.

If you are a Christian, you have experienced God's good sovereignty in a most personal and miraculous way. He has given you a new life. He has forgiven your sins. He has given you a new affection for him. None of these things could you give yourself.

Look also at your own obedience: do you not see the hand of God? Surely you do not ascribe your obedience to your own virtue? Did you really obey in this or that instance? Yes, you did! But why did you obey? Oh, be patient and humble enough to consider this carefully. See the sovereign goodness of God even in the smallest obediences. Did you really succeed in this project or in that struggle? Yes you did! But why did you succeed? Behold again the sovereign goodness of God to you. In God's great and sovereign goodness, he has acted to thwart your very plans to sin because he loves you so!

Even in your calamities, can you not see God's overruling hand? And when you cannot see it, can you not still believe it is there? God often moves in ways that are mysterious to us. As we read in Romans 8:28, he makes all things work together for good for those who love God and are called according to his purpose. So he worked for the Israelites' good through the foolish treaty their leaders made with the Gibeonites. In chapter 10, the Gibeonites' peace treaty with Israel lures the mightiest kings of the south to gather together and attack Gibeon. Ultimately, this attack expedites a great victory for the Israelites as they destroy the southern kings in one fell swoop. God uses, turns, and redeems the Israelites' disobedience. Does that mean that what the Gibeonites or the Israelite leaders do is not bad? No, it is bad, but God is so sovereign that he uses their bad actions for good. Now, go back and examine your own life, and then tell me if you cannot see this same sovereign goodness even in your darkest times.

Michael, you must believe in this sovereign goodness of God so that you will be humble in success and encouraged in trials. You must labor to see his sovereignty. Look for it in your life and ministry. All of us must look, if we want to persevere in serving God.

To Lead the People in Dividing the Land

The people conquer the land but it is God who fights for them. Likewise, the people divide the land by tribes but it is God who leads the people to divide it. We read in chapter 14, "the Israelites divided the land, just as the LORD had commanded Moses" (14:5). God also leads Joshua to establish the cities of refuge, so that there might be both justice and mercy throughout the land:

> "Then the LORD said to Joshua: 'Tell the Israelites to designate the cities of refuge, as I instructed you through Moses, so that anyone who kills a person accidentally and unintentionally may flee there and find protection from the avenger of blood'" (20:1-3).

Given God's obvious care to see both justice and mercy exercised among his special people, as with these cities of refuge, many people find it surprising to consider how differently he appears to treat the Canaanites. Without a doubt, God's command to the Israelites to destroy the people of the land is one of the most controversial aspects of this book, if not the whole Old Testament. And it is worth pausing to consider the fact that not only do the Israelites destroy their enemies completely, *God commands* them to do so! You can find his commands in 6:17, in 7:12, in 8:2, and elsewhere.

When you stop and survey the destruction in this book, resulting as it does from the will of God, it becomes clear that the slaughter of the Canaanites is the most pronounced destruction in the Bible between the Flood in Genesis and the end of the world in Revelation. Upon entering Canaan, of course, Israel had already witnessed striking instances of God's judgment, both upon others (like the plagues on Egypt) and upon themselves (as in the death of the entire generation who left Egypt). And like the Flood in Genesis, like the destruction of the Egyptians, like the destruction of the generation who left Egypt, and like every other act of God's judgment in the Bible, the destruction of the Canaanites is but a foreshadowing of the great final judgment at the end of the world in Revelation. All these judgments not only preview the great coming judgment, they echo the fall of man in the Garden, where every one of us, through our representative, Adam, wrongly spurned God and called down his righteous wrath upon us. Since then, every day we have drawn breath and enjoyed health has been a day of God's gracious mercy toward us.

Though we may look respectable and harmless to one another as we sit in our church pews listening to sermons, when God looks at us he sees the truth. He sees our sins crying out for judgment, so that his creation will know that the judge of the earth will do right. Yet he forbears. He is patient with us, even right now—with me as I speak these words and with you as you listen. He is patient. He shows mercy.

But God will not finally endure injustice. He will pour out the wrath we so richly deserve. Amazingly, for all those who repent of their sins and trust in him, God's wrath has been poured out on Christ, our loving substitute who laid down his life at the cross on Calvary. Yet those who do not repent and believe will receive God's wrath upon themselves.

So it was with the Canaanites. In their destruction we see an expiration of God's mercy. Every time they ignored their own consciences and defied the image of the true God within them, they spent his mercy. Every time they hated another, or got drunk, or worshiped the fertility god Baal through cult prostitution, they spent more of this rich mercy. Every time they worshiped their god Molech by putting a knife through the hearts of their own children or casting them into the flames, they spent still more. Indeed, every day the people of Canaan drew breath and failed to repent, they cried out for the end of God's mercy and the beginning of his justice. Finally, God said "Enough!" To use the language of the Bible, the cup of their sins had become full to overflowing.[7] God's mercy expired. And so he commanded Joshua and the Israelites to be partial ministers of the judgment all humankind will one day face, apart from Christ.

Do we need to justify God's actions here? The longer I think about it, the harder time I have justifying our own questions. God commanded the Israelites to accomplish his good and just purposes, even as he commanded them to obey him in other matters.

To Keep His Promises and to Persevere with the People

The people conquer the land because God fights for them. They divide the land because he apportions it. And they vow to fear and obey him because he alone keeps his promises and perseveres with them in spite of their sin.

He keeps his promises. Back in Genesis 17:8, the Lord had said to Abraham, "The whole land of Canaan, where you are now an alien, I will give as an everlasting possession to you and your descendants after you; and I will

---

[7] Gen. 15:16; Isa. 51:17, 22; Jer. 25:15.

be their God." In the book of Joshua, God brings to pass the promises he had made centuries earlier. Toward the close of the book, Joshua testifies to God's faithfulness: "Now I am about to go the way of all the earth. You know with all your heart and soul that not one of all the good promises the LORD your God gave you has failed. Every promise has been fulfilled; not one has failed" (Josh. 23:14). Ever since God made his promises to Abraham, he has shown himself utterly and completely faithful.

Obedience is the only appropriate response to the God who keeps his promises. That's why God charges Joshua at the beginning of the book,

> "Be strong and very courageous. Be careful to obey all the law my servant Moses gave you; do not turn from it to the right or to the left, that you may be successful wherever you go. Do not let this Book of the Law depart from your mouth; meditate on it day and night, so that you may be careful to do everything written in it. Then you will be prosperous and successful" (1:7-8).

God's promise to give Abraham and his descendants the land of Canaan has sometimes been misunderstood. Some have interpreted this promise to mean that the actual physical land of Canaan will eternally remain a place of special concern for God. Yet if that is true, what do we make of the Bible's promise to destroy this present world with fire and to replace it with a new heaven and a new earth? Still others have interpreted this promise to mean that Abraham's physical descendants—the Jewish nation—have an inalienable right to that land. Yet if that is true, why does Jesus put so little stock in physical descent from Abraham, even calling some of them children of the devil; and why does Paul say the true children of Abraham are not children of the flesh but of the promise?[8] We could say more about this, but for now let it suffice to say that no nation-state or ethnic people group today, including the modern nation-state of Israel, possesses a special covenant with God. Old Testament Israel was God's special people only to prepare for the coming of the Messiah. The Messiah has now come, and God's people today are no longer linked to any one nation. They are truly international, in a way only foreshadowed in the book of Joshua by God's mercy on the Jericho native Rahab, and perhaps on the Gibeonites.

What does God promise us today as Christians? He promises us adoption as sons and, ultimately, inheritance of the whole earth. Yet our command as Christians is not to take or defend certain physical territory. There is no "holy land" for us as there was for Joshua and the Israelites. There is no crusade or jihad for the Christian. "The earth is the LORD's and the fullness thereof" (Ps.

---

[8] E.g., Matt. 8:11-12; John 8:44; Rom. 9:8ff; Gal. 4:22-31.

24:1, ESV). We might say there is no *unholy* land! And so we are called to make war against spiritual powers, not against flesh and blood. This is the real conflict we wage today as Christians, and the conflict is waged in lands that are experiencing bloodshed and in lands that are experiencing peace. Spiritual warfare with eternal consequences is raging around the globe. Christ commands his followers to fight our spiritual enemies by loving all people—all of whom are made in God's image—through telling them the good news of Jesus Christ: the promise of forgiveness for our sins and new life offered in him.

My Christian friend, are God's promises and commands the central concerns of your life? Do these things most capture your heart? Or has something or someone else usurped Christ's position and become your real commander, your true captain? Christ's great commandment is to love your neighbor as yourself. Christ's great commission is to go and make disciples of all nations.

Michael, as you take up your duties here, God's promises and commands need to capture your mind. Are there other commandments or commissions that absorb your attention? Dear brother, love the Lord your God with all your heart, mind, soul, and strength, and love your neighbor as yourself. Then teach the congregation to do the same, and you will have honored our Lord's command and commission.

He perseveres with his people. We need to notice one more thing in this book of Joshua. When the people choose to sin, God perseveres with his people. When you read through the book, you will notice quite a few piles of stones.[9] Every single pile of stones is a reminder to the people of a time when God acted in a merciful and gracious way toward them. Every pile is a reminder that forgiveness and redemption are held out to the repentant. In a similar way, God establishes the cities of refuge to be pictures of a greater and deeper mercy he offers.

In our upcoming study in the book of Judges, we will continue to witness God showing mercy again and again when the people sin against him but then turn and flee to him.

Has anything you have heard or considered in this sermon helped you to see your own need for God's mercy? Do you perceive anything of your own spiritual poverty before God? Until you perceive that, you will never be a Christian. That is where we all must begin with God. As the great Congregational minister Edward Payson said, "You cannot make a rich man beg like a poor man; you cannot make a man that is full cry for food like one

---

[9] By the Jordan River (4:6-7); where Achan was stoned (7:26); over the king of Ai's body (8:28-29); at the cave of the five Amorite kings (10:27); at Shechem by the oak tree set up by Joshua as a witness against the people should they sin (24:25-27).

that is hungry: no more will a man who has a good opinion of himself cry for mercy like one who feels that he is poor and needy."[10] Christian churches are not congregations of the righteous, the morally successful, and the completely obedient. Such people do not exist in this world. Christian congregations are founded on a recognition of our own poverty, our own spiritual need, and Christ's fullness. Christ died to procure mercy, and he calls you to turn away from your sins and to trust in him. Oh, friend, leave your sins for Christ!

And Michael, if you would serve us well, carefully cultivate a sense of your own poverty and need. You don't have to pile up stones in your backyard, but you can memorialize times of God's kind perseverance with you. Mention them to your wife. Make note of them on your computer. Labor to make your heart soft before God, to sense your need of him, and to remember when he has shown his mercy to you most clearly. Share with us not only when you have been most merciful to others but when God has been most merciful to you.

Because our God is a persevering God, isn't he!

CONCLUSION

That's the message of Joshua. On one level, the people chose to obey God and conquer the land he had promised them. On another level, God fought for them and gave them the land. When they obeyed, they were only acting in accordance with his promises. And when they sinned, God was merciful to them and persevered with them.

Do you remember those "why" questions at the beginning? Why is that pile of stones sitting next to the Jordan? Why is this place called Gilgal? And so forth. Really, all of these "why" questions point to the one big "why" question that pervades the entire book and encompasses all the smaller "why" questions: why does any of this stuff happen at all?

The answer to that main "why" question is found in chapter 4, where in fact Joshua answers the question about why the stones are piled next to the Jordan River. If you were going to memorize one verse from the book of Joshua, this might be it: "The LORD your God did to the Jordan just what he had done to the Red Sea when he dried it up before us until we had crossed over. He did this *so that* . . ."—here it comes; here is the answer to the book's big "why" question—". . . *so that* all the peoples of the earth might know that the hand of the LORD is powerful and *so that* you might always fear the

---

[10] Cited in Iain H. Murray, *Revival and Revivalism: The Making and Marring of American Evangelicalism 1750–1858* (Carlisle, Pa.: Banner of Truth, 1994), 219.

LORD your God" (4:23b-24). Do you see how Joshua divides the passage? He says "so that" twice. First, he says that God did these things so that all peoples might *know* that the Lord is, as he is called earlier, "the Lord of all the earth" (3:11, 13; cf. 7:9). He is not merely the god of a nomadic tribe, or of the desert, or of the Exodus. He acts as he does in this book so that all peoples might know that God is the Lord of all the earth.

Second, Joshua says God did all these things for you and for himself. He did them, in other words, so that God's own people might fear the Lord. He alone should be feared because he alone deserves all praise and glory.

God even raises Joshua up as the Israelites' leader for the sake of his own glory. The Lord says to Joshua, "Today I will begin to exalt you in the eyes of all Israel . . ." Why? ". . . so they may know that I am with you as I was with Moses" (3:7). And God does this. We read in the next chapter, "the LORD exalted Joshua in the sight of all Israel; and they revered him all the days of his life, just as they had revered Moses" (4:14; cf. 6:27). When Moses first met Joshua, his name was Hoshea, which means "salvation" (Num. 13:16). Moses renamed him "Joshua," meaning "the LORD is salvation." The New Testament equivalent of this name is Jesus. Jesus the Lord is salvation.

Since Joshua was a faithful servant of God, raising him up had the effect of exalting the Lord he served. That has always been God's purpose in raising up special messengers and leaders. So it is today with anyone who ministers God's Word to his people. If God blesses a minister of his Word, if the Lord lifts him up and prospers him, you can be sure that God's ultimate purpose is not the minister's glory but his own, as it shines through the faithful ministry of the one He blesses.

My dear brother Michael, may God make you so transparent that God's glory shines clearly through you, and may you be so blessed that God may be exalted through you.

Let us pray:

Lord, we have considered many things from your Word, but all of it resolves into this: that you do what you do for your own glory, and that you call us as your people to exult in you and your glory. We pray that you would drive that message home in our hearts. Give us hearts that are alive to you, that you would bless us in lifting you up and exalting you. We pray for your glory's sake through our Lord Jesus Christ, the great captain of our salvation. Amen.

Questions for Reflection

1. Do the big events of history (wars, presidencies, economic depressions) all have an eternal purpose in the plan of God? Do the small events of your own life all have an eternal purpose in the plan of God?

2. What does the destruction of people of Canaan foreshadow? Why is their destruction *extremely* relevant to your life and the life of everyone you love?

3. Clearly, God's command to Joshua to destroy the Canaanites demonstrated his wrath. But how does it demonstrate his mercy and love?

4. Like Joshua, Jesus came to conquer. What did Jesus conquer? What will he one day conquer completely? If you are a Christian, can you look back over your life and see the areas where he has already asserted his conquering rule? Praise Christ as conqueror for what you find!

5. What role does a church covenant play in a church's life?

6. What is the difference between a sin of commission and a sin of omission? Can you think of several sins in each category that tempt you?

7. Did the people in Canaan deserve to die? Why or why not? Do you conceive of yourself as deserving anything more than they received? If you are a Christian, what separates you in God's eyes from the Canaanites? Is it *anything* you have done?

8. How should a local church respond to a flagrantly public, unconfessed, and unrepented sin of a member? Why is it so important for a church to deal with such sin? Is taking action against such sin unloving?

9. Colossians 3 says, "Put to death, therefore, whatever belongs to your earthly nature: sexual immorality, impurity, lust, evil desires and greed, which is idolatry. Because of these, the wrath of God is coming" (Col. 3:5-6). You might say that the Christian, kind of like Joshua, is called to make war on the different cities of sin in his or her own heart. Put to death the city of immorality! Put to death the city of greed! Set fire to the factories that manufacture your favorite idols, and level the playgrounds on which your illicit fantasies swing. How then is your battle going? Whose strength are you relying upon to win? What role does your local church play in doing battle with you?

10. As Christians, we must fight the battle against sin, but we must also remember that the most important battle has already been fought and won (see question 4 above). How can you, at the same time, both *do* battle and *rest* in the battle Christ has already won?

11. What's the answer to the biggest "why" questions of all: Why do we exist? Why did God create the universe? Why do bad things happen and why do good things happen? Is the answer an abstract theological statement, or should it be the most practical lesson of all?

THE MESSAGE OF JUDGES: STALEMATE

THE IMPORTANCE OF LEADERSHIP

INTRODUCING JUDGES

THE PEOPLE RESPOND TO GOD'S BLESSING WITH SIN
  God Blesses
  God Warns
  But the People Sin

GOD'S PEOPLE RESPOND TO PUNISHMENT WITH REPENTANCE
  God Punishes
  And the People Repent

GOD TEMPORARILY DELIVERS THE PEOPLE THROUGH IMPERFECT JUDGES
  God Delivers Through Imperfect Judges
  God Delivers Temporarily

THE PEOPLE NEED WHAT GOD WOULD ULTIMATELY GIVE—A PERFECT SAVIOR
  The People Need a Savior
  God Will Give Them a Savior

CONCLUSION

7

THE MESSAGE OF JUDGES: STALEMATE

THE IMPORTANCE OF LEADERSHIP[1]

"What cities need, we have learned the hard way, is not egotistical designers and heavy-handed planners. Cities need chaos, not planning. Order will emerge—not the artificial and deadly order of the planners, but the spontaneous order of real people coordinating their activities around each other."

So said Frank Buckley, professor at George Mason University, in a recent issue of *The American Enterprise* magazine.[2] Order naturally emerges, Buckley believes. It does not need to be imposed from the top. Is he right? These are exactly the kind of debates the Lower Manhattan Development Corporation (LMDC) and the New York Port Authority (NYPA) are engaged in these days, as they examine different plans for what should be done with the former site of the World Trade Center twin towers. Among the countless options, some parties are pushing to avoid large structures, and to instead reopen some of the old streets and re-create the neighborhood of the pre-twin towers days.

The difficulty of deciding what to do with the site is compounded by the fact that the LMDC and the NYPA cannot agree on who is in charge of the decision. In fact, over the past week the two organizations have been debating who has the right to pick the urban design team that will propose six different schemes to present to . . . well, whoever they will present them to.

Authority is crucial, isn't it? And this is just one example. Looking through the newspaper yesterday, I found many more examples that would make the same point. In every area of our lives, we need good leadership. Without clear guidance, the best of plans are stymied, and projects go astray.

---

[1] This sermon was originally preached on May 19, 2002, at Capitol Hill Baptist Church in Washington, D.C.
[2] Frank Buckley, "Modern Architecture's Nasty Authoritarianism," *The American Enterprise*, January/February 2002, 31.

INTRODUCING JUDGES

As much as any other book in the Old Testament, the book of Judges is about leadership. Judges, the second of the Old Testament's twelve historical books, describes twelve leaders God raised up in Israel.

We do not know exactly how many years the story line of Judges covers, because we do not know the exact date of the Exodus from Egypt. But it is somewhere between two and four centuries, and it ends around the time the monarchy was established with Saul in approximately 1050 B.C. The book can be divided into three parts. Chapters 1–2 are introductory. Chapters 3–16 cover the twelve judges. And chapters 17–21 show the moral decline that typified much of the nation.

For our purposes here, I want to summarize the book in four sentences and see what we can learn, especially about what kind of leader we need.

THE PEOPLE RESPOND TO GOD'S BLESSING WITH SIN

First, it is clear from reading this book that the people of Israel respond to God's blessing with sin. This is a sad fact, but it is the true message of Judges.

God Blesses

At the book's beginning, we know that God has blessed these people, as he had richly promised to do. He delivered them from bondage in Egypt. He brought them through the wilderness. He parted the Jordan River. And he led them to victory under Joshua in the whole of Canaan—the north and the south. Speaking to the Israelites in chapter 2, the Lord says, "I brought you up out of Egypt and led you into the land that I swore to give to your forefathers. I said, 'I will never break my covenant with you'" (2:1).

God Warns

Because God promises not to break his covenant, he forbids the people to make other covenants of their own. In the next verse, God says, "and you shall not make a covenant with the people of this land, but you shall break down their altars" (2:2).

Looking back, of course, we know that God had given the people such warnings many times. In the first giving of the law, God commands the people, "You shall have no other gods before me." He also commands them, "You shall not make for yourself an idol" (Ex. 20:3, 4).

In the second giving of the law, as the aged Moses prepares the people to enter the Promised Land, God tells the people through Moses what they will specifically have to do in order to keep these first two commandments:

> "When the LORD your God brings you into the land you are entering to possess and drives out before you many nations—the Hittites, Girgashites, Amorites, Canaanites, Perizzites, Hivites and Jebusites, seven nations larger and stronger than you—and when the LORD your God has delivered them over to you and you have defeated them, then you must destroy them totally. Make no treaty with them, and show them no mercy. Do not intermarry with them. Do not give your daughters to their sons or take their daughters for your sons, for they will turn your sons away from following me to serve other gods, and the LORD's anger will burn against you and will quickly destroy you. This is what you are to do to them: Break down their altars, smash their sacred stones, cut down their Asherah poles and burn their idols in the fire. For you are a people holy to the LORD your God. The LORD your God has chosen you out of all the peoples on the face of the earth to be his people, his treasured possession" (Deut. 7:1-6).

In others words, destroy or be destroyed. In fact, God says exactly this several chapters later: "Completely destroy them. . . . Otherwise, they will teach you to follow all the detestable things they do in worshiping their gods, and you will sin against the LORD your God" (Deut. 20:17a, 18). Many other passages in the Law say something similar.

Joshua even repeats these warnings right before he dies. In some of his last words, Joshua says,

> "Be very strong; be careful to obey all that is written in the Book of the Law of Moses, without turning aside to the right or to the left. Do not associate with these nations that remain among you; do not invoke the names of their gods or swear by them. You must not serve them or bow down to them. But you are to hold fast to the LORD your God, as you have until now.
>
> "The LORD has driven out before you great and powerful nations; to this day no one has been able to withstand you. One of you routs a thousand, because the LORD your God fights for you, just as he promised. So be very careful to love the LORD your God.
>
> "But if you turn away and ally yourselves with the survivors of these nations that remain among you and if you intermarry with them and associate with them, then you may be sure that the LORD your God will no longer drive out these nations before you. Instead, they will become snares and traps for you" (Josh. 23:6-13a).

How do the people respond to God's rich blessing? And what do they make of his warnings?

But the People Sin

All is well in the first eighteen verses of Judges. Israel's conquest of the territory of Canaan continues, as it had during Joshua's life. The first half of the nineteenth verse even summarizes, "The LORD was with the men of Judah. They took possession of the hill country" (Judg. 1:19a).

But a sad word comes halfway through the verse—"but": "but they were unable to drive the people from the plains, because they had iron chariots" (1:19b). In what follows, a long list of the Israelites' failures to take the land God has promised them is presented:

"The Benjamites, however, failed to dislodge the Jebusites" (1:21).

"Manasseh did not drive out the people of Beth Shan or Taanach or Dor or Ibleam or Megiddo and their surrounding settlements, for the Canaanites were determined to live in that land" (1:27).

"Nor did Ephraim drive out the Canaanites living in Gezer" (1:29).

"Neither did Zebulun drive out the Canaanites living in Kitron or Nahalol" (1:30).

"Nor did Asher drive out those living in Acco or Sidon or Ahlab or Aczib or Helbah or Aphek or Rehob" (1:31).

"Neither did Naphtali drive out those living in Beth Shemesh or Beth Anath" (1:33).

The people sin, and they sin in the precise way God has repeatedly warned them about: they partially obey God's commands; they omit a crucial step of obedience; they do not exterminate the Canaanites completely. And, yes, consequences come. Going back to chapter 2, we see that God says, "you have disobeyed me. Why have you done this? Now therefore I tell you that I will not drive them out before you; they will be thorns in your sides and their gods will be a snare to you" (2:2b-3). Following the Israelites' acts of omission, sins of commission follow.[3] Terrible sins of commission follow. They join with the Canaanites and others in idolatry. As chapter 2 continues, the story recaps this descent into sin as one generation gives way to the next:

After Joshua had dismissed the Israelites, they went to take possession of the land, each to his own inheritance. The people served the LORD throughout the

---

[3] A sin of omission is a failure to do what one should do (think "omit"), while a sin of commission is doing something one should not do (think "commit").

lifetime of Joshua and of the elders who outlived him and who had seen all the great things the LORD had done for Israel.

Joshua son of Nun, the servant of the LORD, died at the age of a hundred and ten. And they buried him in the land of his inheritance, at Timnath Heres in the hill country of Ephraim, north of Mount Gaash.

After that whole generation had been gathered to their fathers, another generation grew up, who knew neither the LORD nor what he had done for Israel. Then the Israelites did evil in the eyes of the LORD and served the Baals. They forsook the LORD, the God of their fathers, who had brought them out of Egypt. They followed and worshiped various gods of the peoples around them. They provoked the LORD to anger because they forsook him and served Baal and the Ashtoreths (2:6-13).

God has warned them! Why don't they listen! What begins as slight omissions quickly slides into the gravest violations: a complete forsaking of God. As we think back on these warnings—look at Deuteronomy 7 again—the summary words of Judges 3 bear the saddest irony: "The Israelites lived among the Canaanites, Hittites, Amorites, Perizzites, Hivites and Jebusites. They took their daughters in marriage and gave their own daughters to their sons, and served their gods" (Judg. 3:5-6).

Some sins seem worse than others. They are simply more horrible, more satanic even. In another sense, no sin is worse than any other sin. Every sin is an act of rebellion against a perfect God, and every sin breaks the perfect relationship of love and fellowship for which we were created. And because all sins break this relationship, what might seem like a slight sin of omission can quickly lead to more grievous sins—the kind of sin into which Israel falls.

This is the story of Judges. God had given them rich blessings. He had brought them into existence as a people and made them his own special people called to bear his name. And now they return his creative love by rejecting him and worshiping other gods.

What about you? Do you realize that God made you? That he created you specially in his own image? Christianity teaches that human beings are a strange mixture. On the one hand, we are incredibly special because we are made in God's image, and so we enjoy a wonderful creativity. We beget children; we make music; we start companies; we build buildings; we form and enjoy friendships; we cook and bring order. All these creative things show something of the image of God in us. But the truth is, there is more to the story. We seethe with darker possibilities, and our creativity can be harnessed for wrong ends. Not only can we create good; we can also create evil. And we want to! We have become what the Bible calls sinful. In fact, Christianity's textured understanding of human nature and the human condition is so telling and so obviously true that even those who do not call themselves Christians often find it compelling.

For some reason—our gullibility, I guess—we fall again and again into thinking that we can make this world a paradise. Some think they will build their utopia through government; others through prosperity, medical advances, or something more apocalyptic. This world is not bereft of the knowledge of God, but that does not keep us from thinking we can do it all ourselves. God's gifts to us in creation and in our consciences, as great as they are, do not provide the redemption we need from our sin, our self-deceit, or the promise of his judgment. We require a greater blessing still. We need the blessing that this world—in its typical fashion—has rejected and even crucified. We need Christ.

I hope you see this. Particularly if you are a Christian, I pray that you will be mindful of God's blessings to you. Do not be forgetful like the people described in the book of Judges. Take note of God's blessings, literally if you must: take a pen and a piece of paper and write down everything God has done for you, so that you will not forget. Be obedient to his Word. Be wary of sins of commission. And don't forget those sins of omission. As we have seen, failing to obey God leads to terrible things. Don't take God's rich blessings and throw them back in his face.

As a church, we have certainly known God's blessings. God has been kind to us. How are we responding? With gratitude and praise to God? Or are we sinfully listening to the secular folk around us who say God's prosperity results from the good things we are doing? "Have confidence in yourself." "Rely on yourself." That is what the people "of the land" today say. But let's pray as a church that we would avoid a wrong self-reliance.

GOD'S PEOPLE RESPOND TO PUNISHMENT WITH REPENTANCE

It is true that the people respond to God's blessings with sin. But we go on to find a strange corollary in a second sentence that will help us unpack the meaning of Judges: God's people respond to punishment with repentance. We find this again and again in the book of Judges.

God Punishes

God is not indifferent to his people's sin. He acts against their sin for the sake of his name. The punishment described in chapter 2 summarizes what we see throughout the book:

> In his anger against Israel the LORD handed them over to raiders who plundered them. He sold them to their enemies all around, whom they were no longer able

to resist. Whenever Israel went out to fight, the hand of the LORD was against them to defeat them, just as he had sworn to them. They were in great distress (2:14-15).

God appears to join with his people's enemies in order to bring distress upon them. Yet though he may join the actions of their enemies, his motives could not be more different. Israel's enemies act in sin and hate. But God means to punish and, as we will consider momentarily, to drive his people to repentance.

The book of Judges is really the repeated story of this cycle. God uses the Arameans from Mesopotamia to punish them:

> The Israelites did evil in the eyes of the LORD; they forgot the LORD their God and served the Baals and the Asherahs. The anger of the LORD burned against Israel so that he sold them into the hands of Cushan-Rishathaim king of Aram Naharaim, to whom the Israelites were subject for eight years (3:7-8).

He also uses the Moabites:

> Once again the Israelites did evil in the eyes of the LORD, and because they did this evil the LORD gave Eglon king of Moab power over Israel. Getting the Ammonites and Amalekites to join him, Eglon came and attacked Israel, and they took possession of the City of Palms. The Israelites were subject to Eglon king of Moab for eighteen years (3:12-14).

In chapter 4, he uses the Canaanites:

> After Ehud died, the Israelites once again did evil in the eyes of the LORD. So the LORD sold them into the hands of Jabin, a king of Canaan, who reigned in Hazor. The commander of his army was Sisera, who lived in Harosheth Haggoyim. Because he had nine hundred iron chariots and had cruelly oppressed the Israelites for twenty years . . . (4:1-3a).

In chapter 6, God uses the Midianites in the same way:

> Again the Israelites did evil in the eyes of the LORD, and for seven years he gave them into the hands of the Midianites. Because the power of Midian was so oppressive, the Israelites prepared shelters for themselves in mountain clefts, caves and strongholds. Whenever the Israelites planted their crops, the Midianites, Amalekites and other eastern peoples invaded the country. They camped on the land and ruined the crops all the way to Gaza and did not spare a living thing for Israel, neither sheep nor cattle nor donkeys. They came up with their livestock and their tents like swarms of locusts. It was impossible to count

the men and their camels; they invaded the land to ravage it. Midian so impoverished the Israelites . . . (6:1-6a)

If you look down in chapter 10, you see he also uses the Ammonites:

> Again the Israelites did evil in the eyes of the LORD. They served the Baals and the Ashtoreths, and the gods of Aram, the gods of Sidon, the gods of Moab, the gods of the Ammonites and the gods of the Philistines. And because the Israelites forsook the LORD and no longer served him, he became angry with them. He sold them into the hands of the Philistines and the Ammonites, who that year shattered and crushed them. For eighteen years they oppressed all the Israelites on the east side of the Jordan in Gilead, the land of the Amorites. The Ammonites also crossed the Jordan to fight against Judah, Benjamin and the house of Ephraim; and Israel was in great distress (10:6-9).

Then in chapter 13, God uses the Philistines: "Again the Israelites did evil in the eyes of the LORD, so the LORD delivered them into the hands of the Philistines for forty years" (13:1).

Do you see what is happening here? God employs the actions of Israel's enemies for his own ends. Of course, God acted with motives different from those of his enemies. When the Philistines attack God's people, for instance, they are not thinking to themselves, "Ah, we want to be the tool of God to oppress the Israelites and bring them to repentance." No, they are acting entirely in selfish malice. Basic to the Bible is the idea that God is sovereign. For every real set of human actions, at least two sets of motives are involved: a human set (because we are responsible, freely choosing what we most desire) and a divine set (because God reigns over all things). Though the specifics are incomprehensible to us, God is so sovereign that the purposes of his will employ even the most malicious human actions. Is he not marvelous!

And the People Repent

Consider then what happens when God punishes his people: they repent. After eight years under the Arameans, "they cried out to the LORD" (3:9a).

After eighteen years under the Moabites, "Again the Israelites cried out to the LORD" (3:15a).

After twenty years of Canaanite rule, the Israelites "cried to the LORD for help" (4:3b).

After seven years of rule, "Midian so impoverished the Israelites that they cried out to the LORD for help" (6:6).

And after eighteen years under the Ammonites,

the Israelites cried out to the LORD, "We have sinned against you, forsaking our God and serving the Baals."

The LORD replied, "When the Egyptians, the Amorites, the Ammonites, the Philistines, the Sidonians, the Amalekites and the Maonites oppressed you and you cried to me for help, did I not save you from their hands? But you have forsaken me and served other gods, so I will no longer save you. Go and cry out to the gods you have chosen. Let them save you when you are in trouble!"

But the Israelites said to the LORD, "We have sinned. Do with us whatever you think best, but please rescue us now." Then they got rid of the foreign gods among them and served the LORD (10:10-16a).

The pattern is consistent: God blesses the people. They respond by sinning. He punishes them. Then they repent.

I wonder if you began this study feeling as if you were under a load of trials. Your trials may not be a sword-wielding Ammonite or Philistine, but the trials oppress you nonetheless. Just as he did with the ancient Israelites, God uses trying circumstances to cause us to examine ourselves and our allegiances, and to teach us that we need to change. Every one of us needs—in the Bible's language—to repent. Have you discovered that need in your own life?

The wisest of people have always used times of challenge and calamity to take stock of their lives. One day early in the American Revolution, John Adams and Benjamin Rush were sitting in the Congress, when Rush leaned over and asked Adams in a whisper if he thought America would succeed in their struggle against Britain. "Yes," Adams replied, "if we fear God and repent our sins."[4] Whether or not America's repentance of sins and fear of God played a part in God's decision to give the nation victory in that struggle, surely Christians in every nation should pray that God would chasten their nation through trials. We should pray that our countries would repent both from neglecting to do what God would have us do and from doing what God tells us not to do. Who can object to such prayers for repentance?

People who want a religion that will merely affirm them will find Christianity disappointing. Christianity is about repentance. Now, if you believe you have never sinned, you may believe that you don't need to repent. If you do have sins to repent of, then Christianity is for you. Christianity is the religion for sinners. Every other religion on the planet will explain everything you must do to make yourself right with God. Christianity alone will explain that you have already failed; that, though majestically made in God's image, you have selfishly turned in on yourself and rebelled against him; and that your only hope lies in acknowledging your sin and crying out to God to forgive you

---

[4] In David McCullough, *John Adams* (New York: Simon & Schuster, 2001), 160.

for Christ's sake. Friend, according to the Bible, there has been only one person who had no sin to repent of. There has been only one on whom God's justice had no claim. At the same time, there has been only one who bore the punishment for the sin of whoever would repent and turn to him.

If you have repented of your sins and trusted in Christ, then I hope you realize these accounts in the book of Judges point to how God normally deals with his own children. Notice, for instance, that we are told toward the beginning of chapter 3 why God allows the Canaanites to remain in the Promised Land: "They were left to test the Israelites to see whether they would obey the LORD's commands, which he had given their forefathers through Moses" (3:4). This is a good verse to meditate on. Yes, the Canaanites remained in the land because of Israel's own disobedience. But in God's strange sovereignty, they also remained because of God's design and purpose. When the next trial comes your way, know that God has purposes in it. And more trials will come, whether you inflict them on yourself or someone else does. Either way, you can be sure that God is behind it and that his purposes are good. This is how God deals with his people.

As I read through Judges this week, I kept thinking of Hebrews 12. The previous chapter, Hebrews 11, presents the "great hall of faith"—many examples of faithful people in the Old Testament. Then in chapter 12, the author turns to encouraging struggling Christians with instructions about what to make of hardships in this world:

> Therefore, since we are surrounded by such a great cloud of witnesses, let us throw off everything that hinders and the sin that so easily entangles, and let us run with perseverance the race marked out for us. Let us fix our eyes on Jesus, the author and perfecter of our faith, who for the joy set before him endured the cross, scorning its shame, and sat down at the right hand of the throne of God. Consider him who endured such opposition from sinful men, so that you will not grow weary and lose heart.
>
> In your struggle against sin, you have not yet resisted to the point of shedding your blood. And you have forgotten that word of encouragement that addresses you as sons:
>
> "My son, do not make light of the Lord's discipline,
>   and do not lose heart when he rebukes you,
> because the Lord disciplines those he loves,
>   and he punishes everyone he accepts as a son."
>
> Endure hardship as discipline; God is treating you as sons. For what son is not disciplined by his father? If you are not disciplined (and everyone undergoes

discipline), then you are illegitimate children and not true sons. Moreover, we have all had human fathers who disciplined us and we respected them for it. How much more should we submit to the Father of our spirits and live! Our fathers disciplined us for a little while as they thought best; but God disciplines us for our good, that we may share in his holiness. No discipline seems pleasant at the time, but painful. Later on, however, it produces a harvest of righteousness and peace for those who have been trained by it" (Heb. 12:1-11).

This chapter in Hebrews feels like a little sermon on the book of Judges. And it tells us exactly how we as Christians should perceive trials in our lives. So deal very carefully with your trials. Do not let them drive you away from God. Let them instead draw you closer to him, by trusting him and asking him to help you react appropriately to what he is teaching you.

If you follow Christ, there will be trials in this world! I mean, we are sinners, and we are supposed to believe in forgiveness? We are miserable, and we are supposed to believe in eternal glory? Our bodies are decaying, and we are supposed to believe in eternal life? We know death awaits us, and we are supposed to believe in a resurrection? Given such a foolish gospel, we should not be surprised by the world's opposition to us and our message. Yet we can trust God's guiding hand through the opposition. He will use it to test and refine us for his own good purposes. In that sense, we can look at our trials as valuable allies. They will teach us what we will not learn any other way. So beware of despising them. They remind us of what matters most. We might even say that, in his love, God sometimes frustrates us until we recognize our need for his power; he exhausts all of our "I'll do it my way" solutions. Don't you see his love in that? Nothing you have in this life will last forever, no matter how tightly you hold on to it. God knows what he is doing, and we must trust him.

Our congregation has certainly seen God's faithfulness. Yes, he has allowed us to face hard times. In the last fifty years, we have faced people leaving the area and we have seen declining numbers. We have faced picketers outside the building and racial prejudice inside the building. We have been guilty of wanting entertainment instead of exposition, and decisions instead of discipleship. We have had pastors who deceived and divided us. And we have had members who sinfully rebelled against God's Word. Yet through it all, God faithfully maintained a witness to himself among the people who remained, even while he allowed his witness to be extinguished in so many other churches in the District of Columbia. Is this not a reason to thank God? Even for his discipline? And know that he has not preserved our witness because of any virtue we possess, but because of his love. Clearly, we should pray that he continues to change us by his Word and Spirit. He knows how we need to know him still better, to love him still more, to hope in him more faithfully. These are good things to pray about as we reflect on the book of Judges, because God's people—then and now—respond to God's punishments with repentance. That is how we know we are God's people.

GOD TEMPORARILY DELIVERS THE PEOPLE THROUGH IMPERFECT JUDGES

There is a third matter at the center of Judges. And this may be what confuses people most about the book. God gave the people temporary deliverance through imperfect judges, individuals called to deliver the people from their oppressors and to resolve disputes among the Israelites themselves. Several verses in chapter 2 once again summarize this third point well:

> Then the LORD raised up judges, who saved them out of the hands of these raiders. Yet [the Israelites] would not listen to their judges but prostituted themselves to other gods and worshiped them. Unlike their fathers, they quickly turned from the way in which their fathers had walked, the way of obedience to the LORD's commands. Whenever the LORD raised up a judge for them, he was with the judge and saved them out of the hands of their enemies as long as the judge lived; for the LORD had compassion on them as they groaned under those who oppressed and afflicted them. But when the judge died, the people returned to ways even more corrupt than those of their fathers, following other gods and serving and worshiping them. They refused to give up their evil practices and stubborn ways (2:16-19).

God Delivers Through Imperfect Judges

Really, the book of Judges is structured around these imperfect judges that God raises up. As I have said, the book has 21 chapters. The first two are introductory, chapters 3–16 provide accounts of twelve judges, and the last five chapters present an extended and depressing account of how low the people sink.

If you flip through chapters 3–16 in your Bible and look at the section headings—if your Bible has them—you will see the names of people you may remember from Sunday school stories if you were brought up going to church. These are the judges that give the book its name. There are twelve of them. Deborah, Gideon, Jephthah, and Samson are treated at the greatest length, and it is their stories you may have heard. The story of the only female judge, Deborah of Ephraim, takes up chapters 4–5. The story of Gideon of Manasseh takes up chapters 6–8. The story of Jephthah of Manasseh takes up chapters 10–11. And the account of Samson of Dan takes up chapters 13–16. Interspersed among these four, shorter accounts are provided for the judges Othniel, Ehud, Shamgar, Tola, Jair, Ibzan, Elon, and Abdon. All of these judges come from various tribes, work regionally, and deliver Israel from various enemies. For instance, Deborah is in the north of the land, Gideon is in the middle, Jephthah is across the Jordan in the east, and Samson is in the southwest. No one of them has a central role over the whole nation. There is no central office for judge management. God does this. God raises up deliverers for the people, as they need them.

Some people are surprised when they read these stories. It is strange to observe, say, that Deborah is a judge when she, as a woman, would not be allowed to be a priest. Gideon, the son of idolaters, comes across as presumptuous with God, and the religious object he fashions (an ephod) provokes the people to worship it. His son Abimelech is one of the worst characters in the book. Jephthah, the son of a prostitute, makes a famously terrible vow, which ultimately costs him his daughter. And Samson, well, Samson is an absolute mess, between marrying a foreign woman; being violent, deceptive, and vengeful; and egregiously failing to keep his commitments. One introduction to the Old Testament characterizes five of the more prominent judges as "a reluctant farmer, a prophetess, a left-handed assassin, a bastard bandit, a sex-addicted Nazirite and others."[5] And that is exactly what they are! Those are accurate descriptions.

But this is not the whole story. Despite their faults, these judges believe the word of the Lord and act heroically in faith. God calls them to deliver his people from their oppressors, and they trust and obey. In the next generation, the great prophet Samuel will recall in his own farewell address how God delivered his people through Gideon, Barak (who assisted Deborah), and Jephthah (1 Sam. 12:11). And in the New Testament hall of faith mentioned earlier, the writer refers to Gideon, Barak, Samson, and Jephthah. All their faults notwithstanding, these people act on faith, and God delivers his people through them.

God Delivers Temporarily

However, God uses the judges to deliver the people only partially and temporarily. Each of these judges delivers only a part of the nation—the part experiencing oppression. Some of them even appear to work at the same time in different parts of Israel. If you read the text carefully, it appears that Jephthah is active as a judge in the area east of the Jordan at the same time that Samson

---

[5] Raymond B. Dillard and Tremper Longman III, *An Introduction to the Old Testament* (Grand Rapids, Mich.: Zondervan, 1994), 127.

is fighting against the Philistines in the southwestern area of the country. And each judge can deliver the people only as long as he or she is living. As we have seen, "when the judge died, [the Israelites] returned to ways even more corrupt than those of their fathers, following other gods and serving and worshiping them" (2:19).

So what does this teach us? Well, though faithful and helpful, the judges were not enough in and of themselves. Friend, I hope you realize that all of God's good gifts in your life cannot replace God. If God has caused you to be born in a land of liberty and prosperity, with good health care and education opportunities, then he has certainly blessed you. But none of these things are meant to answer your deepest problems. Do you realize that? All such gifts are only the dimmest reflections of the great good that God intends in Christ for those who repent of their sins and trust in him.

Christian, you should thank God for whatever means he has used to bless you. But you should also realize that every means he uses in this world is imperfect—every single one. We finally rely on God alone, and not upon any of the human instruments he uses. Has this hymn writer or that author, this preacher or that church been particularly helpful to you? Praise God! But never mistake the likes of any preacher like me for the one who actually gives you life through his Spirit and his Word. At best, I am a waiter in the house of God. I'm no chef. I just bring you a meal someone else has made. God alone creates all the good that you and I enjoy, whatever means he may use to bring that good to us.

That is why we as a church must always remember that even the best pastors and elders, the best deacons, and the best role models in the faith, like the best judges in this book, will always have faults and sins. That's the way it is! No congregation is perfect, even though God has used this congregation to be a means of great blessing to others. No church is perfect, and no exception exists to that rule. I hope God will use your own considerations of the imperfections of the leaders in the church to remind you that we are not yet home.

This world is not our ultimate home. Our ultimate home is so much better than this. In that place, God will be with his people forever. No leadership marked by sin will exist. All leadership will be perfect leadership, balancing perfect love and perfect knowledge.

THE PEOPLE NEED WHAT GOD WOULD ULTIMATELY GIVE— A PERFECT SAVIOR

That brings us to our fourth statement: the people need what God would ultimately give—a perfect Savior. These people were desperate. This is evident as you read through the book, and particularly in the final chapters. The situation in the land is evidently bleak.

The People Need a Savior

The people needed a savior. Perhaps some today would say that the Israelites simply needed to be saved from their own hang-ups about other local deities, that they needed to stop being so totalitarian and exclusivistic. But God wanted to liberate them not from intolerance toward other gods but from tolerance to them! The people needed liberation from false worship; their false worship is what caused the nation to degenerate.

Only a first-class, devilish liar could have coined the phrase "religion is a private matter." Religion is a personal matter, true, but by no means is it private. If you want to read an example of what a dramatic, public impact religion makes, read the last five chapters of Judges. The "private" sins of a few people dramatically affect the entire nation, even leading Israel to civil war. Changing your most deeply held beliefs about God and the universe, life and morality—to say nothing of actually changing the nature of your relationship with God—will have the most profound impact imaginable upon your life. I know advertisers try to tell us that other things have a profound impact—you know, the aspirin you use or the car you drive. But none of this is true. We know that. But this *is* true: what you believe about God and your purpose in life will have a tremendous effect on you and everyone around you. When you change the religion of a people, you change the nation.

People become like the god they worship. James Montgomery Boice, late pastor at Tenth Presbyterian Church in Philadelphia, in a sermon on the Psalms, said,

> "No people ever rise higher than their idea of God, and conversely, a loss of the sense of God's high and awesome character always involves a loss of a people's moral values and even what we commonly call humanity. We are startled by the disregard for human life that has overtaken large segments of the western world, but what do we expect when countries like ours openly turn their back upon God? We deplore the breakdown of moral standards, but what do we expect when we have focused our worship services on ourselves and our own often trivial needs rather than on God? Our view of God affects what we are and do . . ."[6]

When the people of Israel stop worshiping the Lord, the one true God, and begin worshiping the Baals and the Ashteroths of the Canaanites, they become

---

[6] James Montgomery Boice, *Psalms, Volume 3: Psalms 107–150* (Grand Rapids, Mich.: Baker, 1998), 912.

like the Canaanites. One commentator even referred to the story of Judges as one long painful account of the Canaanization of Israel. Yes, the people enter the land and take it, but the land ends up taking them. In chapter 9, the Israelites have a bloodthirsty king—Gideon's son Abimelech. In the final chapters, 17–21, they sink to new lows of cowardice, unfaithfulness, idolatry, rape, and murder. Their false religion leads to outrageous immorality, marked by strife, disrespect, and irreverence in the extreme.

If you read through the book, you will find that these final chapters contain no repentance. We have already looked at several verses about Israel repenting and crying out to the Lord. In fact, we looked at every single sentence containing repentance in the book of Judges. As we have seen, the middle chapters—3–16—contain this cycle where the people sin, they repent, God raises up a judge to save them, the judge dies, they sin again, and so forth. But following Samson's death in chapter 16, there is no cycle and there is no account of repentance. The sin just gets worse and worse and worse. At the end of Judges, the story simply trails off, and the state of Israel seems anything but hopeful. The book's last verse concludes by repeating the despairing—and summarizing—refrain: "in those days Israel had no king; everyone did as he saw fit."[7]

In the following books of Samuel, Kings, and Chronicles, Israel will be given a king. Ultimately, the king will not be able to resolve Israel's sin problem. But he will point the way to a king who does—Christ. Do you see where I am going?

When your state is genuinely desperate, it's good to know it. So once Adam and Eve had sinned and earned God's wrath, it was imperative for them to realize this. When God cast them out of the Garden, therefore, he was, in effect, mercifully giving them the opportunity to see that they could not save themselves. And as they saw their offspring die, they began to perceive that their own predicament affected all their descendants.

God then called Abraham to show Abraham and his descendants that he is a promise-making and a promise-keeping God. But could Abraham's own faith save all his descendants? No, all the great patriarchs died.

God then gave the people of Israel his law and his priests. Did he do this in order to save them through the law or the priests? No, but he taught them more about his own holy character and their own sin. And he taught them that neither the law nor merely human priests and animal sacrifices could save them.

God then gave them these judges. Did he do this so that these judges would save them? No, but these judges taught them more about God's power and

---

[7] 21:25; cf. 17:6; 18:1; 19:1.

authority. They also taught the people that a mere human judge could not save them.

After the judges, God would give the people what they would begin clamoring for in 1 Samuel: a king. Would he give them a line of kings so that the kings would save them? No, but the kings would teach the people still more about God by foreshadowing the kind of rule God would ultimately assume with his people. And the kings taught them that a mere human king could never save them.

God would also give the prophets to his people. Would he do this so that the prophets would save them? No, but the prophets would teach still more about God and his words. And they would teach the people that a mere human prophet could not save them.

God would let this sinful people, who were determined not to rely on him, rely on every other possible means, until every other possible means was exhausted. Finally, they would learn that the only one who could save them was God himself, and then they would turn to him. This is what the book of Judges is meant to do for us as well. We are meant to be morally and emotionally tired by the time we finish reading it. And we are meant to despair of trusting in some other judge to save us.

God Will Give Them a Savior

The good news is that not only do the people *need* a Savior, but God will *give* them a Savior. In chapter 2, we are told that God raises up these judges "who saved them out of the hands of these raiders" (2:16). Yet the judges could only save *some* of the people from *some* of the raiders *some* of the time. What they—what we—need is something far more powerful. And that is what God has provided in Christ.

God will provide you not just a new boss, a new guru, a new role model, or a new president; he will give you a whole new identity, a new view, a fresh start with God. You need what only Jesus Christ can give you. Jesus alone is fully man and fully God. He alone is the perfect priest, law-keeper, judge, king, and prophet that we need. He alone lived a perfect life and then died on the cross for the punishment you deserved for your sin, if only you will turn from your sin and trust in him. Do you see that you are as desperate and needy as these ancient Israelites? In order to be a Christian, you must begin by seeing this.

Do not be deceived by how important you think your work is. You will outlast your work. You will outlast the most significant role you ever play, whether it is parent or pastor, professor or president. Whoever you are, you need someone to save you from the wrath of God against you. Because you have sinned, you need forgiveness. And no one else can give you forgiveness except our Lord Jesus Christ. What we need, God has provided in Christ: a perfect Savior.

I hope that, if nothing else, we as a church help each other to clearly see our need and God's full provision for us in Christ.

CONCLUSION

In his powerful book *Flags of Our Fathers,* James Bradley recounts the scarcity of certain goods in the United States during World War II. (My own grandmother once showed me some of her ration tokens for meat and other goods.) In response to this scarcity, Bradley says, the whole nation rallied together:

> The entire nation . . . seemed overnight to have snapped out of its Depression-era lethargy. Everyone scrambled to be of help. Rubber was needed for the war effort, and gasoline, and metal. A women's basketball game at Northwestern University was stopped so that the referee and all ten players could scour the floor for a lost bobby pin. Americans pitched in to support strict rationing programs and their boys turned out as volunteers in various collection "drives." Soon butter and milk were restricted along with canned goods and meat. Shoes became scarce, and paper, and silk. People grew "victory gardens" and drove at the gas-saving "victory speed" of thirty-five miles an hour. "Use it up, wear it out, make it do, or do without" became a popular slogan. Air-raid sirens and blackouts were scrupulously obeyed. America sacrificed.[8]

Why did Americans act like that? Because they realized their need.

I wonder what you think you most need.

According to the book of Judges, it is clear that we are sinful, and that God is merciful. What we need is God's mercy to us in Christ. And that is what our church intends to hold out to you. If you are a non-Christian, accept that mercy by repenting of your sins and believing in Christ.

My Christian brother or sister, trust in him and him alone. Do you realize that he is what you most need? What has been filling your mind with desperate anxiety—or with exhilarated excitement? The Bible tells us that we are as lost as the people in the days of the judges—apart from Christ. In fact, the Bible repeatedly describes us as sheep—and lost sheep—because we have this tendency to stray. And what a lost sheep most needs is a shepherd.

Pastors like me are sent here to tell you things like this. But we are only under-shepherds; the chief shepherd is Christ himself. The prophets in the Old Testament pointed not to more merely human judges or kings. After all, both

---

[8] James Bradley, *Flags of Our Fathers* (New York: Bantam, 2000), 62.

had been tried and both had failed. No, they pointed to the Lord. And so the Lord says in Jeremiah 23,

> "I myself will gather the remnant of my flock out of all the countries where I have driven them and will bring them back to their pasture. . . .
>
> "The days are coming," declares the LORD,
> "when I will raise up to David a righteous Branch,
> a King who will reign wisely
> and do what is just and right in the land" (Jer. 23:3a, 5).

And several chapters later, the Lord says, "I will lead them beside streams of water on a level path where they will not stumble. . . . He who scattered Israel will gather them and will watch over his flock like a shepherd" (Jer. 31:9b, 10b). Centuries earlier, of course, David had written, "The Lord is my shepherd" (Ps. 23:1). And centuries later, Jesus would tell his disciples that he would be the Savior, the leader, the judge they needed:

> "I am the good shepherd; I know my sheep and my sheep know me . . . and I lay down my life for the sheep. . . .
>
> "My sheep listen to my voice; I know them, and they follow me. I give them eternal life, and they shall never perish; no one can snatch them out of my hand" (John 10:14, 15b, 27-28).

Let us pray:

O God, forgive us for the replacements we have set up for you in our lives. They are all inadequate. Be our Leader and Guide, our Savior and Judge, we pray. In Christ's name. Amen.

Questions for Reflection

1. How do people in our culture today tend to view leadership and authority? How do you view leadership and authority?

2. Ralph Waldo Emerson said, "Nothing is at last sacred but the integrity of your own mind." In the same vein, he said elsewhere, "No law can be sacred to me but that of my own nature." What do you think? Is he right?

3. Can you think of a time when another person's authority over you clearly benefited and served your good? What leadership qualities did the person bearing authority have that makes this occasion stand out?

4. How do we ignore God's blessings? When have you responded to God's blessings with sin?

5. What are some practical steps you can take to start becoming more mindful of God's blessings in your life? How can you cultivate a spirit of gratitude?

6. Can you describe the difference between sins of omission and sins of commission? Name several sins in each category that tempt you. Why do we tend not to worry as much about our sins of omission?

7. Is God's punishment against his people a product of his wrath or of his mercy? How so?

8. When has God's punishment brought you to repentance? How can a local church apply the principle at work here in its life together (think about church discipline—both formative and corrective)?

9. As we have seen, God uses trying circumstances in our lives to cause us to stop and examine ourselves. When do you "stop"? Do you? Or does Satan keep you entirely too busy? What regular and uninterrupted times have you built into your schedule for quiet reflection and self-examination?

10. In the sermon, we considered the fact that Christianity is about repentance. If you have sins to repent of, then Christianity is for you. Now, describe what the church that *gets this* looks like. Describe what the church that does not get this looks like.

11. If God used deeply imperfect judges to deliver the people of Israel, we can expect he will use deeply imperfect people in our own lives and in our church's life together to deliver us and accomplish our good, right? How should that assurance affect your ability to forgive, love, and be patient with others? Think of two "imperfect" people in your non-church life and two "imperfect" people in your church life whom God just might be using to accomplish your good. Now, how will you extend greater patience toward those imperfect people? How will you—think practically!—cultivate gratitude for them?

12. What "need" can Christ satisfy?

THE MESSAGE OF RUTH: SURPRISE

THE STUFF OF GOOD STORIES

INTRODUCING RUTH

A DISPLAY OF HUMAN KINDNESS
In Orpah
In Naomi
In Ruth
The Challenge: Are People Kinder Than God?

A DISPLAY OF GOD'S KINDNESS
In Providing Food
In Providing a Husband
In Providing a Child
In Providing a King—David!

CONCLUSION

8

THE MESSAGE OF RUTH: SURPRISE

THE STUFF OF GOOD STORIES[1]

"No fear can stand up to hunger, no patience can wear it out, disgust simply does not exist where hunger is; and as to superstition, beliefs, and what you may call principles, they are less than chaff in a breeze."

That is from Joseph Conrad's great short story of 1902, *Heart of Darkness,*[2] in which he writes about his experience on a river steamboat in the heart of Africa, the Congo. He deliberately traveled to Africa to experience hunger, corruption, and other evils, and to find what he called "darkness" in himself. And that is what he found, he writes, as he never had before.

Many types of trials—as many as there are people—can expose the hearts of darkness within us. There is hunger and poverty, surely, but there is also loneliness, hopelessness, faltering families, and crumbling societies. As Christians, we know the trial of all trials lies in the struggle against our own sin. We say we love and worship God, yet we can still live contrary to his commands.

Ironically, we have to admit that such troubles make for the stuff of good stories. Who wants to read a story about how Sally got up in the morning and had a great day! We just don't! There needs to be a little threat, a little danger, a little moral ambiguity and tension, even if we like to have all that tension resolved by the end. Authors often say it is easier to describe evil than good, to bring to life a bad character than a virtuous one. Evil characters seem more understandable, more explicable, more *real*. They have a depth and texture that is absent in the good characters. After all, every one of us has experienced

---

[1] This sermon was originally preached on May 26, 2002, at Capitol Hill Baptist Church in Washington, D.C.
[2] Joseph Conrad, *Heart of Darkness: An Authoritative Text, Backgrounds and Sources, Criticism,* ed. Robert Kimbrough, 3rd ed. (New York: Norton, 1988), 43.

troubles and trials, difficulties and defeats. Such experiences are the stuff out of which the best stories are made.

INTRODUCING RUTH

The book of Ruth in the Old Testament is a tremendous story. It is brief, lasting four short chapters. It is one of two books in the Bible named after a woman, and the only Old Testament book named after a non-Jew. It is set in dark times. Yet remarkably it has no bad characters—unless, that is, God himself is the bad guy. We will see momentarily that this is the question the book of Ruth poses.

People have suggested many reasons for why Ruth was written. Some treat it as a plea for racial tolerance; Ruth was a Moabite, after all. Others see it as a call for family responsibility. Some suggest that it shows the importance of individual faithfulness in times of widespread immorality, while others maintain that it shows that God rewards wisdom. Some regard the story as demonstrating the influence of godly women, and still others say that Ruth is a beautiful story with no purpose other than itself. It is just a wonderful story to tell! I think that all these proposals contain aspects of what this book is about. There might be other ways to put it, but this story is fundamentally about kindness and mercy.

Look at it with me. As I said, the story is set in very dark times:

> In the days when the judges ruled, there was a famine in the land, and a man from Bethlehem in Judah, together with his wife and two sons, went to live for a while in the country of Moab. The man's name was Elimelech, his wife's name Naomi, and the names of his two sons were Mahlon and Kilion. They were Ephrathites from Bethlehem, Judah. And they went to Moab and lived there.
>
> Now Elimelech, Naomi's husband, died, and she was left with her two sons. They married Moabite women, one named Orpah and the other Ruth. After they had lived there about ten years, both Mahlon and Kilion also died, and Naomi was left without her two sons and her husband (Ruth 1:1-5).

As you see in the opening phase, the story takes place "when the judges ruled." For that reason, some people have treated Ruth as the last installment in the book of Judges. Whether it picks up where Judges leaves off or not, we know from our study of Judges that these were bleak days. And within this bleak setting, the story shows us two things we want to notice: first, the many displays of human kindness; and second, the argument this book makes for God's kindness. Who knows what surprises God has for us as we examine this short and well-known tale!

A DISPLAY OF HUMAN KINDNESS

First, we should notice that this story is a display of human kindness. Amid trying circumstances, the book's primary characters live in a manner characterized, at least in part, by kindness. As we continue reading, you will see this:

> When she [Naomi] heard in Moab that the LORD had come to the aid of his people by providing food for them, Naomi and her daughters-in-law prepared to return home from there. With her two daughters-in-law she left the place where she had been living and set out on the road that would take them back to the land of Judah.
>
> Then Naomi said to her two daughters-in-law, "Go back, each of you, to your mother's home. May the LORD show kindness to you, as you have shown to your dead and to me. May the LORD grant that each of you will find rest in the home of another husband."
>
> Then she kissed them and they wept aloud and said to her, "We will go back with you to your people."
>
> But Naomi said, "Return home, my daughters. Why would you come with me? Am I going to have any more sons, who could become your husbands? Return home, my daughters; I am too old to have another husband. Even if I thought there was still hope for me—even if I had a husband tonight and then gave birth to sons—would you wait until they grew up? Would you remain unmarried for them? No, my daughters. It is more bitter for me than for you, because the LORD's hand has gone out against me!"
>
> At this they wept again (1:6-14a).

In Orpah

Along with Ruth, Orpah weeps for Naomi and offers to return to Naomi's homeland with her. And Naomi describes this support as "kindness." In Naomi's trials, Orpah shows her kindness.

In Naomi

Naomi, too, is kind. She prays for both of her daughters-in-law, asking God to bestow upon them the same kindness they have bestowed upon her. She also prays that both women would find rest in the home of another husband. Eventually, we will learn that God answers this prayer—at least for Ruth—and not in the way Naomi expects!

In Ruth

So Orpah is kind and supportive. And Naomi is kind, looking out for the good of her daughters-in-law. But an even greater kindness is shown by Ruth. Perhaps this is why the book is named after her. Look again:

Then Orpah kissed her mother-in-law good-by, but Ruth clung to her.

"Look," said Naomi, "your sister-in-law is going back to her people and her gods. Go back with her."

But Ruth replied, "Don't urge me to leave you or to turn back from you. Where you go I will go, and where you stay I will stay. Your people will be my people and your God my God. Where you die I will die, and there I will be buried. May the LORD deal with me, be it ever so severely, if anything but death separates you and me." When Naomi realized that Ruth was determined to go with her, she stopped urging her. So the two women went on until they came to Bethlehem (1:14b-19a).

Ruth must first overcome what sounds like Naomi's "anti-evangelism." Did you notice that? Naomi insists that Ruth should go back with Orpah to the Moabites and to "her gods." I don't entirely know what Naomi means by this. Jewish rabbis have said that in these verses Naomi is a model of how to handle proselytes (those who want to convert to Judaism). Naomi's example teaches us, the rabbis say, to rebuff a proselyte three times both to see if he is sincere and to show him that it is hard to be a Jew! Think what you will about the rabbis' suggestion. I myself am not persuaded that Naomi is trying to teach, evangelize, or anti-evangelize Ruth. I think she is trying to be considerate. She is probably fearful about not being able to support herself, let alone Ruth, once back in Judah.

So the two daughters-in-law stand at a crossroads with a choice to make. And Naomi successfully dissuades one from following her, but not the other. Orpah turns back to serve the gods of her fathers; Ruth continues onward with Naomi. Clearly, neither daughter-in-law is forced in her decision. Both freely choose their course of action. The journey to Israel is voluntary. Ruth even makes her choice against some opposition. We might be reminded of the old comment about the two thieves at Calvary: "One was saved, that none might despair; but only one, that none might presume."

Ruth's journey with Naomi from Moab to Judah probably covered a distance of only fifty miles. But the journey is far more important than its short distance suggests. In leaving her own people and going to Bethlehem with Naomi, Ruth shows great kindness to Naomi, just as she will later show to Boaz, who is in all likelihood considerably older than she.

As we will see late in the story, Boaz is also marked by kindness. This book is absolutely full of human kindness.

Our lives are also filled with experiences of kindness. Notwithstanding the terrible things that happen through terrorists and war, unemployment and ill health, cultural decay and personal trial, we would be lying if we did not acknowledge all the kindnesses shown to us: not by everyone always, but often and by many people. As a Christian, I am not surprised by all the kindness we witness and experience. We are all made in the image of God—Christians and non-Christians alike. And regardless of our religion, age, education, or nationality, God's image will occasionally show itself! People will do wonderful things. People will be kind. People will be caring. Human beings are depraved, no doubt, but I still expect that people will act kindly, even people who act horrendously otherwise. We are sinful and fallen, but we are still made in God's image and have a capacity to reflect something of his character.

On the other hand, if you are a non-Christian, I don't know how you deal with this: how can great acts of kindness and great acts of terror come from the same individual?

If you are in public service, I hope you realize that the need for the gospel in no way negates the importance of your work of addressing other human needs—in the workplace, in schools, in the economy, and in government. Promoting good laws and a more civil society will never replace proclaiming the gospel, but it is a worthy activity for people who believe the gospel. We should thank God for everyone who works for the good of society as a whole.

As a church, we should encourage caring for our more vulnerable members, members like Naomi and Ruth would have been. Pray for the ministry of our deacons of member care, as they care for the members of the congregation who are older and need help. Pray for our outreach to the children of prisoners, and get involved in this vital ministry. Pray for relationships that you may have with people who are in need. Pray that we as a church become more obedient in these areas.

Friend, I hope you realize how important kindness is. In the whole array of Christian virtues, do not leave this one out. Kindness is a great virtue, and it is one of the fruits God's Spirit bears in the personalities of his children (Gal. 5:22). As one writer says, "to put on kindness is to clothe ourselves with the very character of God himself."[3]

That brings us to the point at issue in this book.

The Challenge: Are People Kinder Than God?

As I have read and reread this book over the last week, I have found that it basically lays out a challenge: are people kinder than God? Through Orpah and Ruth, Naomi experiences great love and care. But what does she receive

---

[3] Barry Webb, *Five Festal Garments: Christian Reflections on the Song of Songs, Ruth, Lamentations, Ecclesiastes, and Esther*, New Studies in Biblical Theology, D. A. Carson, gen. ed. (Downers Grove, Ill.: InterVarsity Press, 2000), 57.

from God's hand? Let's rejoin the story at the point where Naomi and Ruth arrive back in Bethlehem:

> When they arrived in Bethlehem, the whole town was stirred because of them, and the women exclaimed, "Can this be Naomi?"
>
> "Don't call me Naomi [Naomi means "sweetness"]," she told them. "Call me Mara, because the Almighty has made my life very bitter. I went away full, but the LORD has brought me back empty. Why call me Naomi? The LORD has afflicted me; the Almighty has brought misfortune upon me."
>
> So Naomi returned from Moab accompanied by Ruth the Moabitess, her daughter-in-law, arriving in Bethlehem as the barley harvest was beginning (1:19b-22).

Naomi says the Lord has brought her back home "empty." She has Ruth, of course, and Ruth will be the key to all the blessings that lie in store. But Naomi does not see that yet. Her eyes are fixed on everything she has to complain about. And consider, she has some real reasons for complaining. She and her husband had experienced famine. (Few if any of us have experienced famine. How terrifying it must be to wonder whether you will have enough food for your children or even for yourself.) The famine was so bad that Elimelech took his wife and two sons and left Israel. He exiled himself, as it were, to live with the Moabites, who were not exactly Israel's best friends. How desperate he must have been! Naomi too! What would it have been like to raise two young boys among the Moabites in a foreign land? And then to have the husband who brought her there die? I wonder how vulnerable she felt. Then her sons married local girls. Did she know that marrying foreign wives was against the law of God? If she didn't, pity her ignorance. If she did, lament her sin. Either way, it was not good. Then one son died before he had fathered any children. Then the second son died, also before fathering any children. Naomi has now endured the death of both sons; and with their deaths her husband's name will vanish into oblivion. All her life's labors seem to have been for nothing. She is, in that sense, the very definition of a failure.

These are some of the reasons we know Naomi has for complaining. But praise God! He had already begun to work out blessings of his own, even amid her complaining! Did you notice that? While the narrator lets our ears hear Naomi complain in verse 21, what does he direct our eyes to see in verse 22? Ruth and the beginning of the barley harvest.

Before we continue with the story, you should stop and think for a moment: how do you respond to life's devastating events, whether in your own life or in the lives of others? I have noticed that people seem to have an unstoppable reflex to ask "Why?" in those tragic moments. Even unbelievers do this;

have you noticed that? People who never go to church, who claim no religious faith, who perhaps attest to being atheists, when something devastating happens, will ask, "Why?" It is as if they assume that somewhere behind the terrible event must be a purpose. We should not be surprised by this. Our assumption of purpose is natural. It is part of the image of God in us. If you are a non-Christian, I would encourage you to see our assumption of purpose as testifying to the fact that what Christians say is true.

In every line of his great hymn "God Moves in a Mysterious Way," William Cowper reminds us not to judge God's ways only by what we can see with our eyes:

> God moves in a mysterious way
> his wonders to perform;
> he plants his footsteps in the sea,
> and rides upon the storm.
>
> Deep in unfathomable mines
> of never-failing skill
> he treasures up his bright designs,
> and works his sovereign will.
>
> Ye fearful saints, fresh courage take;
> the clouds ye so much dread
> are big with mercy and shall break
> in blessings on your head.
>
> Judge not the Lord by feeble sense,
> but trust him for his grace;
> behind a frowning providence
> he hides a smiling face.
>
> His purposes will ripen fast,
> unfolding ev'ry hour;
> the bud may have a bitter taste,
> but sweet will be the flow'r.
>
> Blind unbelief is sure to err,
> and scan his work in vain;
> God is his own interpreter,
> and he will make it plain.[4]

---

[4] "God Moves in a Mysterious Way," words by William Cowper, 1774.

God rides upon storms. The dreaded clouds come, yes, but they actually bring mercy for God's people. Behind God's "frowning providence" is "a smiling face." Unbelief cannot see all this. It is blind. But we can expect that God will make his purposes plain in due time, and he will give us all we need to trust in his goodness in the meantime. We know this, in part, because we can read about God's providences in the lives of Naomi and Ruth. God has left us this inspired record where he himself has interpreted events for us, that we might be instructed.

So how are you with difficult and trying times? It's a very practical question. The New Testament author James tells us,

> Consider it pure joy, my brothers, whenever you face trials of many kinds, because you know that the testing of your faith develops perseverance. Perseverance must finish its work so that you may be mature and complete, not lacking anything (James 1:2-4).

Amid the trials you presently face, do you really think God has no plans or purposes for you? Do you really think he has completed everything he means to do in your life? Don't you know that God's work has just begun? He's not finished yet, and the harvest may be about to begin. So don't lash out at other people as though God is finished with you and you're stuck. No, God knows what he is doing.

One of the delights of having walked with the Lord for a number of years is to see, again and again, God's faithfulness proven even after I have worried or gotten upset. How careful our God is to have purpose in all his actions! How he uses all his children's sorrows for good ends! Many times I have observed the truth of the proverb, "Affliction is a good man's shining time." Any of us can look calm when life is prosperous. Ah, but let afflictions come, and then you will see what we really serve. Have we really been serving our good circumstances, or have we been serving our loving, sovereign, faithful, unchanging Lord?

May God teach each one of us such faith, and may we as a church endure in trust no matter what difficulties come.

A DISPLAY OF GOD'S KINDNESS

Indeed, the story of Ruth is more than just an account of human kindnesses. At its root, it is an argument for God's kindness. Yes, it contains many instances of human kindnesses. But even more, the book displays most remarkably the kindness of God. It is a small, dramatic Job; only where Job begins and ends with Job's blessings and reflects on his trials throughout, Ruth begins with trials and then lays out an elegant story of God's blessings. Consider also that, in Job, God's vindication comes only to Job's family, while in Ruth, God's vindication affects us all.

Naomi had left Bethlehem hungry years earlier and went to Moab. The question before her now is, will she, as a widow with no sons to support her, again find herself hungry back in Bethlehem? From the way she talks at the end of chapter 1, you would think so. But then there is Ruth and the barley harvest. Let's read chapter 2:

> Now Naomi had a relative on her husband's side, from the clan of Elimelech, a man of standing, whose name was Boaz.
>
> And Ruth the Moabitess said to Naomi, "Let me go to the fields and pick up the leftover grain behind anyone in whose eyes I find favor."
>
> Naomi said to her, "Go ahead, my daughter." So she went out and began to glean in the fields behind the harvesters. As it turned out, she found herself working in a field belonging to Boaz, who was from the clan of Elimelech.
>
> Just then Boaz arrived from Bethlehem and greeted the harvesters, "The LORD be with you!"
>
> "The LORD bless you!" they called back.
>
> Boaz asked the foreman of his harvesters, "Whose young woman is that?"
>
> The foreman replied, "She is the Moabitess who came back from Moab with Naomi. She said, 'Please let me glean and gather among the sheaves behind the harvesters.' She went into the field and has worked steadily from morning till now, except for a short rest in the shelter."
>
> So Boaz said to Ruth, "My daughter, listen to me. Don't go and glean in another field and don't go away from here. Stay here with my servant girls. Watch the field where the men are harvesting, and follow along after the girls. I have told the men not to touch you. And whenever you are thirsty, go and get a drink from the water jars the men have filled."
>
> At this, she bowed down with her face to the ground. She exclaimed, "Why have I found such favor in your eyes that you notice me—a foreigner?"
>
> Boaz replied, "I've been told all about what you have done for your mother-in-law since the death of your husband—how you left your father and mother and your homeland and came to live with a people you did not know before. May the LORD repay you for what you have done. May you be richly rewarded by the LORD, the God of Israel, under whose wings you have come to take refuge."
>
> "May I continue to find favor in your eyes, my lord," she said. "You have given me comfort and have spoken kindly to your servant—though I do not have the standing of one of your servant girls."
>
> At mealtime Boaz said to her, "Come over here. Have some bread and dip it in the wine vinegar."

When she sat down with the harvesters, he offered her some roasted grain. She ate all she wanted and had some left over. As she got up to glean, Boaz gave orders to his men, "Even if she gathers among the sheaves, don't embarrass her. Rather, pull out some stalks for her from the bundles and leave them for her to pick up, and don't rebuke her."

So Ruth gleaned in the field until evening. Then she threshed the barley she had gathered, and it amounted to about an ephah. She carried it back to town, and her mother-in-law saw how much she had gathered. Ruth also brought out and gave her what she had left over after she had eaten enough.

Her mother-in-law asked her, "Where did you glean today? Where did you work? Blessed be the man who took notice of you!"

Then Ruth told her mother-in-law about the one at whose place she had been working. "The name of the man I worked with today is Boaz," she said.

"The LORD bless him!" Naomi said to her daughter-in-law. "He has not stopped showing his kindness to the living and the dead." She added, "That man is our close relative; he is one of our kinsman-redeemers."

Then Ruth the Moabitess said, "He even said to me, 'Stay with my workers until they finish harvesting all my grain.'"

Naomi said to Ruth her daughter-in-law, "It will be good for you, my daughter, to go with his girls, because in someone else's field you might be harmed."

So Ruth stayed close to the servant girls of Boaz to glean until the barley and wheat harvests were finished. And she lived with her mother-in-law (chapter 2).

In Providing Food

From the very beginning, Boaz shows a kind concern for Ruth. And here God clearly works through Boaz to provide Naomi and Ruth with food. In verse 8, Boaz sees Ruth, immediately speaks to her in a fatherly fashion, and invites her to feed from his harvests. She then gleans in Boaz's fields, "until the barley and wheat harvests were finished" (2:23), and that would have been a couple of months' worth of food—probably from late April into June. We can never perceive what future results will come from our present acts of faithfulness, regardless of how small they may appear.

So Ruth and Naomi are fed! In chapter 1, Naomi laments her emptiness. But in chapter 2, Boaz makes sure her provisions are abundant. In chapter 3, he will even tell Ruth that he does not want her to return to Naomi "empty-handed" (3:17).

Also, Ruth's hard work ensures that Naomi has something to eat. In chapter 2, she gleans till evening. In chapter 3, she brings Naomi Boaz's bountiful provision.

But behind Boaz's generosity and Ruth's hard work, you also see the activity of God. God vindicates himself from Naomi's charge that he does not care for her hunger. For one, God's law is at work. God had stipulated that some of the harvest should be left for the poor to gather, or "glean," after someone else had cut it.[5] The law even commands harvesters not to reap all the way to the edge of a field, so that the fatherless, the foreigners, and the widows will have something to gather. God is also at work in the weather and in the harvest. As we have seen, chapter 1 ends on this note of hope: Naomi and Ruth arrived "in Bethlehem as the barley harvest was beginning" (1:22). God brought Naomi home at just the right time.

Of course, the famine that had occurred a decade earlier had had a spiritual significance. When we read in chapter 1 that Elimelech led his family to Moab to seek food, we can assume that Elimelech was trying to avoid repenting before God. Back in Leviticus and Deuteronomy, God promised that he would send famine on his people if they were disobedient.[6] So Elimelech should have helped lead his family and Bethlehem toward repentance and trust in God to provide. Repentance, not flight, would have been the right response to famine. Instead, Elimelech tried to dodge repentance by addressing only the physical problems.

Now, Naomi has some understanding of this spiritual dimension. Deuteronomy had also promised that God would restore the people and grant them food when they repented.[7] God wants the people to know that, ultimately, he is the giver of food. When Naomi "heard in Moab that the LORD had come to the aid of his people by providing food for them" (1:6), she decides to return to the Lord's land and live among his people under his law. Still, she calls herself "bitterness" and says the Almighty has brought misfortune on her (1:20-21). But when Ruth comes home and tells Naomi she has been gleaning in Boaz's field, Naomi praises God for his kindness, giving evidence that her heart has begun to catch up with her mind's decision to return: "He [the LORD] has not stopped showing kindness to the living and to the dead" (2:20).

Naomi recognizes that God is behind Boaz's decisions. It's a quiet realization, perhaps, but this story is about God's providence for his own. He is good, and he gives his people food! In the book of Ruth, the Lord does not take center stage with miraculous works or great prophets. Nothing like that occurs. Instead, we take our cues from the characters themselves, as they look to God and observe his loving care and faithfulness.

---

[5] Lev. 19:9; 23:22; Deut. 24:19, 22.
[6] Lev. 26:26; Deut. 28:17-18, 22-24.
[7] Deut. 30:1-3, 8-10; 32:24.

In Providing a Husband

Of course, Naomi's trials do not merely concern food. She is also destined to be alone, and therefore ruin and destitution will always threaten to overtake her. That is where finding a husband for Ruth comes in. This is the center of the story, really. We pick up the story line at the beginning of chapter 3:

> One day Naomi her mother-in-law said to her, "My daughter, should I not try to find a home for you, where you will be well provided for? Is not Boaz, with whose servant girls you have been, a kinsman of ours? Tonight he will be winnowing barley on the threshing floor. Wash and perfume yourself, and put on your best clothes. Then go down to the threshing floor, but don't let him know you are there until he has finished eating and drinking. When he lies down, note the place where he is lying. Then go and uncover his feet and lie down. He will tell you what to do."
>
> "I will do whatever you say," Ruth answered. So she went down to the threshing floor and did everything her mother-in-law told her to do.
>
> When Boaz had finished eating and drinking and was in good spirits, he went over to lie down at the far end of the grain pile. Ruth approached quietly, uncovered his feet and lay down. In the middle of the night something startled the man, and he turned and discovered a woman lying at his feet.
>
> "Who are you?" he asked.
>
> "I am your servant Ruth," she said. "Spread the corner of your garment over me, since you are a kinsman-redeemer."
>
> "The LORD bless you, my daughter," he replied. "This kindness is greater than that which you showed earlier: You have not run after the younger men, whether rich or poor. And now, my daughter, don't be afraid. I will do for you all you ask. All my fellow townsmen know that you are a woman of noble character. Although it is true that I am near of kin, there is a kinsman-redeemer nearer than I. Stay here for the night, and in the morning if he wants to redeem, good; let him redeem. But if he is not willing, as surely as the LORD lives I will do it. Lie here until morning."
>
> So she lay at his feet until morning, but got up before anyone could be recognized; and he said, "Don't let it be known that a woman came to the threshing floor."
>
> He also said, "Bring me the shawl you are wearing and hold it out." When she did so, he poured into it six measures of barley and put it on her. Then he went back to town.
>
> When Ruth came to her mother-in-law, Naomi asked, "How did it go, my daughter?"
>
> Then she told her everything Boaz had done for her and added, "He gave me these six measures of barley, saying, 'Don't go back to your mother-in-law empty-handed.'"

Then Naomi said, "Wait, my daughter, until you find out what happens. For the man will not rest until the matter is settled today."

Meanwhile Boaz went up to the town gate and sat there. When the kinsman-redeemer he had mentioned came along, Boaz said, "Come over here, my friend, and sit down." So he went over and sat down.

Boaz took ten of the elders of the town and said, "Sit here," and they did so. Then he said to the kinsman-redeemer, "Naomi, who has come back from Moab, is selling the piece of land that belonged to our brother Elimelech. I thought I should bring the matter to your attention and suggest that you buy it in the presence of these seated here and in the presence of the elders of my people. If you will redeem it, do so. But if you will not, tell me, so I will know. For no one has the right to do it except you, and I am next in line."

"I will redeem it," he said.

Then Boaz said, "On the day you buy the land from Naomi and from Ruth the Moabitess, you acquire the dead man's widow, in order to maintain the name of the dead with his property."

At this, the kinsman-redeemer said, "Then I cannot redeem it because I might endanger my own estate. You redeem it yourself. I cannot do it."

(Now in earlier times in Israel, for the redemption and transfer of property to become final, one party took off his sandal and gave it to the other. This was the method of legalizing transactions in Israel.)

So the kinsman-redeemer said to Boaz, "Buy it yourself." And he removed his sandal.

Then Boaz announced to the elders and all the people, "Today you are witnesses that I have bought from Naomi all the property of Elimelech, Kilion and Mahlon. I have also acquired Ruth the Moabitess, Mahlon's widow, as my wife, in order to maintain the name of the dead with his property, so that his name will not disappear from among his family or from the town records. Today you are witnesses!"

Then the elders and all those at the gate said, "We are witnesses. May the LORD make the woman who is coming into your home like Rachel and Leah, who together built up the house of Israel. May you have standing in Ephrathah and be famous in Bethlehem. Through the offspring the LORD gives you by this young woman, may your family be like that of Perez, whom Tamar bore to Judah."

So Boaz took Ruth and she became his wife (3:1–4:13a).

So that's the story of Ruth. If chapter 1 presents the introduction and the end of chapter 4 provides the conclusion, the rest of the book is about two key days in Ruth's life: the day she is fed (in chapter 2) and the day she is wed (in chapters 3–4).

Now, Naomi certainly has a hand in this wedding. In fact, that's probably an understatement. Some have wondered if she is not a bit too scheming. But

I don't think she is; I think we should defend Naomi. Naomi has a responsibility both to perpetuate her husband's name by raising up an heir for him and to provide for her daughter-in-law. All the "knowing advice" she gives to Ruth aims to fulfill those obligations. So she instructs Ruth on how to act in accordance with the protection afforded by the law of the land. In ancient Israel, that did not mean appealing to a town official, a welfare officer, or a court. It meant going straight to an individual who could help you. That is what Naomi, wisely, advises Ruth to do.

And that is what Ruth does. Ruth, too, has a part in getting a husband. After all, she chooses to come to Bethlehem with her mother-in-law to ensure that Naomi is not left alone. She chooses what field to work in. She conducts herself honorably when she first meets Boaz in chapter 2. Then in chapter 3, she follows her mother-in-law's instructions by approaching Boaz quietly, uncovering his feet, and lying down (3:7). Some people have wondered if the author is being coy here, that Ruth actually seduces Boaz. But the story does not support such speculation. Boaz immediately understands what she is doing: she is acting honorably by appealing to him to be possibly her husband, at the very least her protector. She is a childless widow with no one to protect her. According to the Jewish law given by God to Moses, she has the right to ask him as a near relative to protect her. Advised by her mother-in-law, she does so. So on the one hand, Ruth takes a lot of initiative here in a relationship with a man! There's no question about that. On the other hand, she deals with her unusual and special situation "by the book."

Boaz, too, has a part. He is clearly interested in Ruth from the first moment he sees her. In chapter 3, he agrees to "spread the corner of his garment" over her (3:9ff.), not to hide sexual immorality, as a reader today might suppose, but to accept her request for protection. Interestingly, the word for "garment" here is the same word Boaz uses in chapter 2 that translates as "wing." Boaz says to Ruth, "May you be richly rewarded by the Lord, the God of Israel, under whose wings you have come to take refuge" (2:12). Boaz himself becomes the answer to that prayer. Like a mother hen who spreads her protective wings over her chicks, he spreads his garment, or "wings," over Ruth, symbolizing his commitment to her. In this story, that means an engagement to pursue marriage, which he does the very next day.

The image of protective wings is common in the Old Testament. Psalm 104 describes the oceans as God's garment spread out over the earth, indicating that he protects and takes responsibility for the world (Ps. 104:6). In the book of Ezekiel, the Lord says to his people, "I spread the corner of my garment over you and covered your nakedness. I gave you my solemn oath and entered into a covenant with you, declares the Sovereign LORD, and you became mine" (Ezek. 16:8).

By telling Boaz that he is her kinsman-redeemer, Ruth is pointing toward something like a Levirate marriage, a type of Old Testament marriage that has to do with preserving the family line as well as with providing for the needs of the poor and landless. In Deuteronomy, God tells the Israelites that if a married man dies and his widow is left without children, a brother of the man is responsible for marrying the widow and producing offspring through her, thereby preserving the dead brother's line (Deut. 25:5-6). Ruth's dead husband Mahlon had no surviving brothers for her to marry, but his father, Elimelech, had other relatives in Bethlehem, among whom is Boaz. By marrying Ruth, Boaz is, in a sense, fulfilling this role.

He is also, in a sense, acting as her kinsman-redeemer. When a poor person in ancient Israel had to sell his or her property to make money to live on, the nearest relative, or kinsman, was to come and redeem what the family member sold (Lev. 25:25). This law ensured that nobody became landless and locked in a cycle of poverty. It was an inside-the-clan welfare system, where debts and obligations would be paid by one family member so that the poor family member could be freed, or restored. In a similar way, Boaz offers to be Ruth's redeemer after he is asked, on the threshing floor, to do so.

Of course, this is the kind of redeemer the Lord will be for Israel. One day, he will say through the prophet Isaiah, "you will know that I, the LORD, am your Savior, your Redeemer, the Mighty One of Jacob" (Isa. 60:16).

The next morning in the town square, Boaz acts exactly as Naomi had predicted he would by quickly fulfilling this family obligation. Through some honest yet shrewd moves, Boaz is able to ward off the one kinsman closer in relation to Ruth. Very wisely, he points to the attractive features first: here's a piece of land for sale! The other kinsman shows some interest. Then Boaz points to the negative features: oh, but there is this—you have to marry a Moabitess. The other kinsman decides not to purchase the piece of property, and Boaz is able to publicly announce his intentions to take Ruth as his wife. Then we read, "Boaz took Ruth and she became his wife" (Ruth 4:13).

Even though Boaz, Ruth, and Naomi all act in clever ways in this story, you can see, can't you, that the Lord is behind everything? Naomi can see this. Remember, she prays in chapter 1 for the Lord to give Ruth rest in the home of another husband. And now God has! That does not mean Naomi thinks she should be passive. No, she is very active. But she also knows the results are from God, which is why she prays to him in the first place.

In Providing a Child

Beyond hunger and loneliness, Naomi and Ruth also struggle with hopelessness. Would God also provide children and a future for the family? Let's keep reading:

> Then [Boaz] went to her, and the LORD enabled her to conceive, and she gave birth to a son. The women said to Naomi: "Praise be to the LORD, who this day has not left you without a kinsman-redeemer. May he become famous throughout Israel! He will renew your life and sustain you in your old age. For your daughter-in-law, who loves you and who is better to you than seven sons, has given him birth."
>
> Then Naomi took the child, and laid him in her lap and cared for him. The women living there said, "Naomi has a son." And they named him Obed (4:13b-17a).

For Naomi, this must have been the story's climax: little baby Obed lying in her lap. She has an heir. She has placed her hope in God, and now she can see her hopes in little baby Obed. The women living there recognize this and say, "Naomi has a son."

Once again, it is worth observing that while Naomi had schemed for this child, and while Boaz and Ruth had certainly lent their involvement—God uses human means!—the book of Ruth reveals that even this final provision comes from the Lord. Verse 13 states, "the LORD enabled her to conceive." God, who is good and constant in lovingkindness, not only provides food and a home for Naomi and Ruth, he provides a future family.

Yet are these provisions merely islands of individual blessing in a sea of chaos? Do one marriage, one child, and a couple of full stomachs matter all that much when society is disintegrating and sinking into a morass of immorality, as the book of Judges shows?

In Providing a King—David!

Well, consider who this child is. They name him Obed. And who is Obed? We find out in the book's final lines:

> He was the father of Jesse, the father of David.
> This, then, is the family line of Perez:
>
> > Perez was the father of Hezron,
> > Hezron the father of Ram,
> > Ram the father of Amminadab,
> > Amminadab the father of Nahshon,

Nahshon the father of Salmon,
Salmon the father of Boaz,
Boaz the father of Obed,
Obed the father of Jesse,
and Jesse the father of David (4:17b-22).

Ruth, Naomi, and Boaz may live in the times of the judges, but God will use this little family to prepare the nation for a king, and a king after God's own heart—David!

And do not forget that Ruth, the great-grandmother of this coming king, is a Moabite. Who were the Moabites? The Moabites were a terrible people. They had sent Balaam to prophesy destruction upon Israel when Israel was preparing to enter the Promised Land (Numbers 22–24). They were the first ones to seduce the sons of Israel into worshiping false gods (Num. 25:1-3). Why would God now bless a Moabite in this way? Elimelech's decision to move his family to Moab was questionable at best. But allowing his sons to marry local Moabite women was a clear transgression of God's law.[8] Yet when Boaz marries Ruth in our story, more factors must be considered. Ruth is not just a Moabitess, she is also the widow of an Israelite husband, and God has a special concern for widows. Also, she is a landless alien in Bethlehem, and God's law makes special provision for aliens. So one law says one thing, yet a couple of other laws bring other factors into play. As is always the case with law, one must judiciously weigh a number of variables. Perhaps most important of all, Ruth is a woman who appears to sincerely desire to follow Yahweh, the Lord, and to take refuge in him. Like Rahab the Canaanite before her, she appears to be genuinely converted and incorporated into the people of God. She leaves everything she knows in Moab to follow what looks like a fruitless path. Why? The plain words of the text suggest she does it for love of Naomi and love of Naomi's God! In chapter 1, verse 16, Ruth says that she chooses Israel's God. Shortly thereafter, Boaz recognizes her decision as such (2:12).

Naomi also chooses to return to God's land and God's people. The word for "return," which is also translated as "repent" through the Old Testament, is used over and over in chapter 1 (vv. 6, 11, 12, and 22). Like Ruth, Naomi chooses to turn away from evil and toward God's people, God's laws, God's provision, and, in all this, God himself.

God's plans in the Old Testament center on the Israelites, to be sure, but only in order to prepare the way for the salvation of all the nations—for Moabites like Ruth and Canaanites like Rahab, for Jew and Gentile, for you

---

[8] See Deut. 7:3; 23:3-6.

and me. The story of Ruth clearly teaches that God wills for Gentiles to share in the covenant blessings of Abraham. He takes a young Moabitess and makes her the great-grandmother of King David. Chapter 4, verse 17, which names David as the grandson of the baby born to Boaz and Ruth, has been the climax of the book for readers ever since.

So, are people kinder than God? That is the challenge we said the book generally poses, and that Naomi levels against God upon her return to her native Bethlehem. And the answer is a resounding no! God is not only kind; God is supremely kind. The very eyes of the child that looked up at Naomi as grandmother would one day look down at a grandson named David. And perhaps the ears of this very child, Obed, would one day hear songs about the Lord's kindness sung as they had never been sung before. Perhaps he would hear the songs his grandson would compose about the Lord's *hesed*—his "everlasting love," as the Hebrew word is translated in some places; his "kindness," as it is translated here in Ruth. And maybe David could sing about God's lovingkindness with such certainty, in part, because he knew the story of his Grandpa Obed's birth! In Psalm 36, David sings of the Lord, "How priceless is your unfailing love! Both high and low among men find refuge in the shadow of your wings" (Ps. 36:7). The word translated "unfailing love" here is translated "kindness" in Ruth.[9] The kindness that Naomi praises God for is a love that does not fail. That is God's kind of kindness.

Jesus teaches that God "causes his sun to rise on the evil and the good, and sends rain on the righteous and the unrighteous" (Matt. 5:45). God has given many blessings to all of us, regardless of how we regard him. Are you grateful to God for those blessings? Do you offer him thanks in response? My Christian friend, recognize God's kindness toward you in everything. Realize that "in all things God works for the good of those who love him, who have been called according to His purpose" (Rom. 8:28).

God provides richly for us, doesn't he? He has blessed us as a church in so many ways. One blessing the story of Ruth makes me think about is how many members of our congregation are from other countries. Praise God for the little foretaste of heaven we get in this one little local church, as we get to see Christians from every continent! God's kindness to us is so evident.

Upon careful consideration, God is exonerated from the charges Naomi leveled against him in bitterness. He was always working in faithfulness for the good of his own, even if he was working quietly and invisibly to Naomi's eyes. Remember, even while she was complaining, she had Ruth by her side and the

---

[9] Ruth 1:8; 2:20; 3:10.

barley harvest beginning all around them. And over them both was a God who is both sovereign and kind.

CONCLUSION

There you have the story of Ruth. The book starts very down, and ends very up. We move from death to life, from barrenness to fruitfulness, from emptiness to fullness, from curse to blessing, from bitter to sweet, from living in exile to producing the grandfather of a king!

The very fact that the little story of Ruth takes place in Bethlehem is itself pregnant with meaning. It moves from being a place of famine to being a place of fruitfulness. Bethlehem was the burial place of Jacob's beloved Rachel. Now, it is where Obed, his son Jesse, and his son David would be born. And a few centuries later, the Lord would say through the prophet Micah, "But you, Bethlehem Ephrathah, though you are small among the clans of Judah, out of you will come for me one who will be ruler over Israel, whose origins are from of old, from ancient times" (Mic. 5:2).

Then, hundreds of years later still, when Herod asked where the Messiah would be born, this passage from Micah was quoted (Matt. 2:4-6; cf. John 7:42). When the fullness of time came, God used the offices of the mighty Roman Empire to order a census, so that people would return to their native towns. So Joseph and his betrothed wife Mary, who lived in the north of Israel in Galilee, had to travel south to Bethlehem. And there in Bethlehem, Jesus was born.

The only place in the New Testament where Ruth's name is mentioned is in Matthew 1. In Matthew's genealogy, Ruth, along with the other names found in the last few verses of the book of Ruth, appear in the line of descent that culminates in Christ (Matt. 1:5-6; Ruth 4:18-22). And it is in the Gospel of Matthew that God shows his kindness to the nations. After all, Matthew begins with Jesus' birth as the son of David and son of Abraham, and he concludes with Jesus' charge to make disciples of all nations (Matt. 1:1; 28:19)! Really, that is how the story of Ruth ends—in the ministry of Jesus Christ. God worked through Boaz to redeem not just Ruth and Naomi, but to bring about the great Redeemer Jesus Christ!

Jesus will redeem us not only from earthly worries but from the most serious worry we can have—being lost in our sin. As I said earlier, we are made in the image of God but we are all fallen and have sinned against God. Yet God will not leave us in slavery to sin forever. In his great love, he sent Jesus Christ, who lived a perfect life and, owing no penalty for his sins, died on the cross for whoever will repent of their sins and believe. In spite of any Moabite-like gods we have served, he died for us if we will turn from our sins and trust in him. When we do, he grants forgiveness from sin and new life in Christ. Jesus Christ will be our Redeemer.

If you are a brother or sister in Christ, you have surely seen God's kindness, haven't you? He has been good.

Consider what Paul says to the Ephesians: "God raised us up with Christ and seated us with him in the heavenly realms in Christ Jesus, in order that in the coming ages he might show the incomparable riches of his grace, expressed in his *kindness* to us in Christ Jesus" (Eph. 2:6-7; cf. Titus 3:3-7).

Or hear what he says to the Romans: "What, then, shall we say in response to this? If God is for us, who can be against us? He who did not spare his own Son, but gave him up for us all—how will he not also, along with him, graciously give us all things?" (Rom. 8:31-32).

By nature, we are as obnoxious to God as any Moabite ever was! If you look at our lives and how we live, you know we are undeserving of God's grace. And yet he has been good to us. He has been kind to us. Amid our complaining, he continues to bless us. He gives us a Ruth, and a barley harvest. Our sovereign and loving Lord provides. When you are tempted, like Naomi, to doubt him during bad times, remember that God provides.

God lets us go through trials in order to expose the depths of our need and to show us the fullness of his provision. God digs deep when he plans on building high. We know that from our lives and from the Word.

Do you see the depths of your sin? Do you realize that, left to yourself, you are lost in sin?

Then hear this great good news of the kinsman-redeemer we all need! Peter writes, "you know that it was not with perishable things such as silver or gold that you were redeemed from the empty way of life handed down to you from your forefathers, but with the precious blood of Christ" (1 Pet. 1:18-19). Amen.

Let us pray:

O God, we confess the foolishness of our doubts about your goodness. Our experiences, your Word, even our life today all testify against our doubts and for you. We believe in you. Help us in our struggle with unbelief. For Jesus' sake. Amen.

Questions for Reflection

1. What is your favorite kind of story? Romance? Comedy? History? Tragedy? Have you ever noticed that every good story, whether comedy or

tragedy, includes some type of tension that must be resolved? Have you considered the fact that God might be using the tension in our lives in just the same way?

2. Suppose a non-Christian said to you, "Why should I become a Christian? I know non-Christians who are extremely kind, and Christians who are downright rude!" How would you respond?

3. Think of the names of three people in your life who are in material or social need: First, pray for them. Second, how will you strategize to care for them in God-like fashion?

4. If your five closest friends were asked whether you are kind, what would they say? What about five acquaintances in your life? What about the servers at the last five restaurants at which you ate?

5. What causes one church to be marked by kindness and another one not?

6. After a massive earthquake killed thousands in Lisbon, Portugal in 1755, the Enlightenment philosopher Voltaire wrote a short poem that included the lines,

> "Oh, miserable mortals! Oh wretched earth!
> Oh, dreadful assembly of all mankind!
> Eternal sermon of useless sufferings! / . . . /
> Will you say: 'This is result of eternal laws
> Directing the acts of a free and good God!'
> Will you say, in seeing this mass of victims:
> 'God is revenged, their death is the price for their crimes'? / . . . /
> Did Lisbon, which is no more, have more vices
> Than London and Paris immersed in their pleasures?
> Lisbon is destroyed, and they dance in Paris!"[10]

Now think back on William Cowper's "God Moves in a Mysterious Way." How do the two men's views of humanity differ? Does Cowper sound as if he was just less familiar with suffering? How do the two men's views of God differ?

---

[10] Voltaire, 1755, "Poem on the Lisbon Disaster, or: An Examination of That Axiom 'All Is Well.'"

7. Given Jesus' own response to suffering, what do you think he understood that Voltaire did not? How does Christ's work on the cross give us great hope amid very real suffering?

8. Why does the fact that this story is set during the time of the judges—a time of moral rebellion and chaos in Israel—especially highlight the kindness of God?

9. How are foreigners and people of minority races received in your church? As we have seen in the book of Ruth, God especially blesses a foreigner, Ruth the Moabitess, in order to bring blessing upon both Israel and all the nations. What relevance might this have for how we live our lives together as Christians?

10. Look again at 1 Peter 1:18-19, quoted at the end of the sermon. What do we need to be redeemed from? How does Christ's blood redeem us? In other words, it's easy to see how gold or silver can redeem something: gold is valued by people, and so you give them the gold in exchange for whatever it is you want in return. But blood? How does that work?

11. Do you have a redeemer? Do you perceive yourself as standing in need of one?

THE MESSAGE OF 1 SAMUEL: FAITH IN FAITHLESS TIMES

9

THE MESSAGE OF 1 SAMUEL: FAITH IN FAITHLESS TIMES

HOW TO BE AN EFFECTIVE LEADER[1]

Leadership is a terribly important issue. We are social beings, as Aristotle said. Wherever people gather, leadership matters.

Even in the most unlikely places—such as committees—leaders will rise up. So Joseph Chamberlain, father of the twentieth-century British prime minister Neville Chamberlain, once stated, "On every committee of thirteen persons there are twelve who go to the meetings having given no thought to the subject and ready to receive instructions. One goes with his mind made up to give those instructions. I make it my business to be that one."[2]

What do you think is the essence of good leadership? Do you think that this is an important topic for us to consider in a Christian church?

INTRODUCING 1 SAMUEL

Leadership is certainly addressed in the Bible, and it is addressed in few places more clearly than in the Old Testament book of 1 Samuel. To see that, we will look at portraits of three different kinds of leaders: Samuel, the man of God's Word marked by obedience; Saul, the impressive man marked by self-reliance; and David, the impressed man marked by faith.

We will be flipping around 1 Samuel as we go. It is a long book, with thirty-one chapters. But chapters in the Bible are not long, so it covers only ten or fifteen pages in most Bibles. It took me two-and-a-half hours—and a patient, listening son!—to read the entire book out loud last week. First Samuel also contains some of the most famous stories in the Bible.

---

[1] This sermon was originally preached on July 28, 2002, at Capitol Hill Baptist Church in Washington, D.C.
[2] Cited in A. G. Gardiner, *Pillars of Society* (London: J. M. Dent & Sons, 1916), 48.

So let's look and see what we can learn from the history of God's people about leadership, and about our own lives.

LEADER PORTRAIT #1: SAMUEL, A MAN OF GOD'S WORD MARKED BY OBEDIENCE

The first remarkable leader we encounter in 1 Samuel is the one whose birth begins the book, and after whom the book is named. Samuel provides a picture of a leader who is *a man of God's Word*. Samuel is the last judge of Israel. He is one of the greatest prophets in the Old Testament, and this book contains his life story.

In chapter 1, a barren woman named Hannah asks God for a child. God miraculously enables her to bear Samuel. Hannah then gives him over to the Lord's service, and Samuel is reared in the precincts of the temple (then at Shiloh) where Eli serves as the priest.

In the first half of chapter 2, we find the beautiful prayer of thanksgiving that Hannah gives to God, which we will consider later. In the latter half of chapter 2, we find the sad account of Eli's wicked sons. At the end of the chapter, an anonymous "man of God" prophesies against the house of Eli and tells him that his sons will die shortly.

Immediately after this prophecy, we read the famous story in chapter 3 about the Lord speaking to Samuel as a boy. If you went to Sunday school as a child, you probably know the story:

> Then the LORD called Samuel.
>
> Samuel answered, "Here I am." And he ran to Eli and said, "Here I am; you called me."
>
> But Eli said, "I did not call; go back and lie down." So he went and lay down.
>
> Again the LORD called, "Samuel!" And Samuel got up and went to Eli and said, "Here I am; you called me."
>
> "My son," Eli said, "I did not call; go back and lie down."
>
> Now Samuel did not yet know the LORD: The word of the LORD had not yet been revealed to him.
>
> The LORD called Samuel a third time, and Samuel got up and went to Eli and said, "Here I am; you called me."
>
> Then Eli realized that the LORD was calling the boy. So Eli told Samuel, "Go and lie down, and if he calls you, say, 'Speak, LORD, for your servant is listening.'" So Samuel went and lay down in his place.
>
> The LORD came and stood there, calling as at the other times, "Samuel! Samuel!"
>
> Then Samuel said, "Speak, for your servant is listening" (3:4-10).

This anxiousness to listen typifies Samuel's life. His ministry occurs in very dark days for Israel. If you remember from our study of the book of Judges, the nation of Israel has been descending into moral anarchy. And 1 Samuel more or less picks up where Judges leaves off, right when Israel was about to face its worst disaster—the destruction of the worship of the Lord. In chapter 4, the Philistines capture the ark of the covenant, which symbolizes God's presence and power with the people and which resides at the center of Israelite worship. On the exact same day, Eli and both of his sons die. It is almost as if God is walking out on this corrupt nation!

In chapter 6, the ark returns to Israel.

Chapter 7 shows Samuel leading Israel in national repentance away from idolatry and, at the same time, winning a great victory against the Philistines. This is where Samuel sets up the "Ebenezer" we sing about in the hymn "Come, Thou Fount of Every Blessing." Maybe you remember the second verse that begins, "Here I raise my Ebenezer, hither by thy help I've come."[3] Did you ever wonder what that means? It comes from 1 Samuel 7:12. In Hebrew, Ebenezer means "stone of helping," and Samuel sets up this stone to remind Israel that the Lord helped them at this location against the Philistines.

Ironically, Samuel receives what must have been one of his most trying assignments at this same location in chapter 8: Israel asks for a king. When they do, Samuel immediately turns to the Lord for wisdom, and the Lord tells him, "it is not you they have rejected, but they have rejected me as their king" (8:7). Samuel then warns the people about the dangers of having a king like the nations around them. Yet the people persist in their plea, and then the Lord tells Samuel, "Listen to them and give them a king" (8:22).

Think about that for a minute. Did you ever consider that sometimes God will grant our very requests as part of his punishment of us?

Well, Samuel obeys, and in chapter 9 he finds Saul. Then in chapter 10 he anoints Saul, who is the next leader we will consider.

Concerning this plea for a king, it is interesting to notice how our church polity reflects our doctrine of man.[4] If you have a higher or stronger view of the fallenness of man, you will want to see authority diffused. You will not trust a polity that concentrates authority in the hands of a sinner, regardless of how rich or educated he is or who his parents are. On the other hand, if you have a lower or weaker view of depravity, and you believe that the Fall did not affect humankind so badly or is even a myth, and that people are basically good, then you will tend to feel more comfortable with a polity that concentrates power

---

[3] Robert Robinson, "Come, Thou Fount of Every Blessing," 1758.
[4] A church's "polity" concerns its authority structures and rules for decision-making.

in fewer hands. This applies in politics, and this applies in churches. I will leave you to work that out over lunch. What makes Samuel such a good leader is the fact that he does not trust the goodness of man; he trusts the goodness of God.

Samuel is a leader marked by obedience to God, even when God calls him to do unusual things, like anointing another, less outwardly impressive king, David (16:1-13). Samuel's life epitomizes the words he speaks to Saul in chapter 15: "to obey is better than sacrifice" (15:22). He is given to hearing God's voice and telling it to others. His very name means "God hears," because God had heard his mother's prayer. He is a man of prayer, and he is a man of God's Word. He obeys God and exhorts others to do the same. In some of his last words, Samuel in typical fashion exhorts the people of Israel to obedience:

> "Do not be afraid," Samuel replied. "You have done all this evil; yet do not turn away from the LORD, but serve the LORD with all your heart. Do not turn away after useless idols. They can do you no good, nor can they rescue you, because they are useless. For the sake of his great name the LORD will not reject his people, because the LORD was pleased to make you his own. As for me, far be it from me that I should sin against the LORD by failing to pray for you. And I will teach you the way that is good and right. But be sure to fear the LORD and serve him faithfully with all your heart; consider what great things he has done for you. Yet if you persist in doing evil, both you and your king will be swept away" (12:20-25).

Samuel is the culmination in a series of judges God began with Moses and Joshua and continued through Gideon, Samson, and the others (7:15). And while he is not the main character of 1 and 2 Samuel (the books are named after him because his birth begins them), he characterizes some of the best things about godly leadership. His ministry centers on hearing, speaking, and obeying God's Word.

I wonder if that seems important to you.

If you are not a Christian, you might be saying to yourself, "This has nothing to do with me." But that's not true. Christianity does not teach that we are all obligated to obey the commands of whatever religion we claim, or that we should simply be true to ourselves. No, we understand that God has revealed in his Word that every single person on this planet has been made by God and is obligated to know God's will and obey it. There are no exceptions or exemptions from this obligation! *You,* my friend, regardless of how you define yourself religiously on some poll, *you* are obliged to know God's will and to obey it! And he will call you to account for yourself, your life, your actions, your thoughts. Are you prepared to give that account?

Christian, follow the example of Samuel here. He is a tremendous example for us. Give yourself to studying, praying through, and obeying God's Word. Can there be a more fruitful life? And let me give you some practical suggestions: start by canceling your cable subscription. I don't want to put this to a church vote, but I will say it again: cancel your cable subscription. Set your alarm a little earlier. Read each morning from the passage that will be preached on the coming Sunday in church. Meditate on it. Pray that God would help you understand what he is saying. Read through Psalm 119 about the word of the Lord. Purchase a copy of Don Carson's book *A Call to Spiritual Reformation: Priorities from Paul and His Prayers*,[5] which our church keeps in the church library and in the church bookstore. Read through this study of Paul's prayers in the New Testament and learn how to pray like Paul. Become a person shaped by God's Word. Yes, you say you believe the Bible is God's Word. But how do you live in light of that belief?

One study last year found that Mormons "are more likely to read the Bible during a typical week than are Protestants."[6] My own grandmother was a Christian Scientist who got up every morning around 5 o'clock to read through the Bible and Mary Baker Eddy's *Science and Health with Key to the Scriptures*. She never missed a day! Are these people who do not know Christ more devoted to God's Word than we are? Fathers and mothers, do you ever read the Bible aloud to your children at home? Christians, do we spend any time reading the Bible aloud in our evangelical churches, or do we have to go to a Greek Orthodox or a Roman Catholic church to hear the Bible read?

Our need to hear God's Word is why our own church centers on this Word. The pulpit is at the center of the stage, and the sermon is the center of our main weekly gathering Sunday mornings. The entire service is planned so that, like Samuel, we can hear God's Word. Then we use hymns and prayers to meditate on this Word. (But remember, we give him worship not just when we are moved through music—as good as that is—but when God's Word moves us to live through the week in a way that brings praise to God.) Our need to hear God's Word is also why, during our Sunday evening services, we listen to a portion of God's Word with the same theme but from the opposite Testament we heard in the morning. Then on Wednesday nights, we meet again to inductively study the Bible as a whole congregation, even if that means taking three years to go

---

[5] D. A. Carson, *A Call to Spiritual Reformation: Priorities from Paul and His Prayers* (Grand Rapids, Mich.: Baker, 1992).
[6] *The Barna Update,* July 9, 2001 (online at www.barna.org).

through 1 Thessalonians or three months to go through Matthew's genealogy. We believe in the centrality of God's Word!

As Christians, we learned that we were going to hell, although not as quickly as we deserved. The only thing that arrested a quicker damnation was God speaking his saving Word to us, a Word that first surprised and contradicted us, but then convicted and converted us. And so, like Samuel, we build our lives together to hear God's Word, to pray over it, to obey it, and to tell it to others.

LEADER PORTRAIT #2: SAUL, AN IMPRESSIVE MAN MARKED BY SELF-RELIANCE

But Samuel is not the only leader in 1 Samuel. Really, the book is even more about Saul, the first king to rule over Israel. It was by no means clear that plans were in place for the people to have a king, but they wanted one. So God commanded Samuel to accede to their request by anointing Saul as king. As with Samuel, this book contains the entire life of Saul.

Yet Saul is in good form and looks like a bright prospect for only a couple of chapters—chapters 10 and 11. In chapter 10, he is chosen and anointed as king. In chapter 11, he wins a great victory over the Ammonites, which leads to a national affirmation of Saul and his kingship.

Saul provides a picture of a leader as *the impressive man*. Very naturally, he impresses others. As the narrator says, Saul is "an impressive young man without equal among the Israelites—a head taller than any of the others" (9:2).

Height can be important, you know! The first American president, George Washington, was tall. After first meeting George Washington at a reception in Cambridge Massachusetts, John Adams's wife, Abigail, normally a shrewd judge of character and a withering critic, thought her husband did not say half enough in praise of Washington. Well, like Washington, Saul seems to look the part. He is a head taller then everyone else and is an impressive man to look at. Even Samuel says of him, "Do you see the man the LORD has chosen? There is no one like him among all the people" (10:24). Saul is an impressive person!

After chapter 11's high point, however, Saul's life and career go downhill for the next twenty chapters—or the next forty years. As I have read and reflected on these chapters, it has become clear that Saul is not just impressive to others; that in and of itself is not a problem. He is impressive to himself. And that's a problem. He has a tendency to shape God's words to be what he wants them to be. He hears God's commands through Samuel. He will, in some sense, listen, take in, and acknowledge God's words. But then he will reshape the commands until they become more sensible to him, unlike Samuel, who is just plain obedient.

Saul does this repeatedly. In chapter 13, he disobeys Samuel's commands to wait for Samuel's arrival before offering a sacrifice. Waiting shows trust in the Lord to give protection; going ahead and offering the sacrifice himself shows more trust in his own judgment. Samuel then rebukes him and tells him that God will now choose someone else to establish Israel's throne.

In chapter 14, Saul's son Jonathan attacks the Philistines, and God sends a panic through the Philistine army so that Israel can rout them. Still, Saul's fate remains set. In chapter 15, Saul again disobeys God's clear commands. When Samuel confronts him, Saul basically concedes, and then says, "but please honor me before the elders of my people and before Israel" (15:30). It's clear where Saul's eyes are fixed: *What will the people think of me?* Indeed, right before Samuel confronts Saul, we learn that Saul has set up a monument in his own honor (15:12)!

This episode with Samuel then sets the stage for all the difficulties Saul faces in the second half of the book. Saul becomes tormented by jealousy as his kingship is increasingly eclipsed by the real main character of 1 and 2 Samuel: David. As David grows in fame, Saul grows in resentment and repeatedly tries to kill David. In fact, he becomes so obsessive in his pursuit of David that at one point he orders an Edomite to kill eighty-five Israelite priests of the Lord because one of them had helped David (22:18)! In other words, Saul, the leader of God's people, becomes the opponent of God's will: He leads a foreigner to kill God's priests. Later, he consults a medium, not God (28:7ff.). Finally, he kills himself as the nation is defeated by the Philistines (chapter 31).

In all this, Saul epitomizes the kings of Israel. In the centuries to come, they will on the whole lead the nation not to greater obedience to God but to greater disobedience. They will lead the people not to freedom from the surrounding nations, as God had done through the judges, but to oppression from them. Yet in 1 Samuel, the people want "kings, like the other nations have" (see 8:5, 20); and this desire to be like the other nations, combined with their lack of trust in God, leads to idolatry, atrocity, and self-destruction, even as we see in Saul's life. Following their kings, the people will begin to marry foreign wives, worship foreign gods, and ultimately find themselves ruled by foreign kings. How ironic: the people Joshua led into Canaan to be a witness to the nations become a mere imitation of them!

In the middle of the nineteenth century, a popular philosophy called transcendentalism flourished first in New England and then throughout the United States through the writings of Henry David Thoreau and the ex-Unitarian minister Ralph Waldo Emerson. These writers trumpeted *self-reliance* as the supreme virtue. To march to the beat of your own drummer, regardless of the crowd, is heroic. "Self-command is the main elegance," Emerson wrote. "I call on you to live for yourselves," he wrote elsewhere. Not that self-reliance is anything new. God helps those who help themselves, Aesop taught us (not the Bible!). And "If you want a thing done well, do it yourself," we say.

I wonder if you have realized that many of these oh-so-American sentiments are not completely true. My friend, you are *not* able to do everything yourself, and it is in your best interest eternally to realize this. The Bible teaches that you by nature are lost in your sins and at enmity with God. What's worse, God is at enmity with you! You have sinned against him. And even if you try to change from this day on, the sins you have already committed will always stand as grim witnesses, waiting to give their damning testimony against you on the last day. Our virtues cannot blot out our vices. Our good deeds do not hide our sins from the all-seeing, ever-just eye of God. In this vein, the priest Eli asks a good question early in the book: "If a man sins against the LORD, who will intercede for him?" (2:25). The men of the city Beth Shemesh, observing the death of some of their number when the ark of the covenant is brought into their town, understand this point precisely: "Who can stand in the presence of the LORD, this holy God?" (6:20).

We must confess that we are sinners. That is why our church often includes a time of confession for sin in our services. We want it to be clear that we are people who have sinned against God. We must know this about ourselves and about others, about our spouses and our elected officials, about our bosses and our children. Unlike the transcendentalists and so many people generally, we Christians must rely not on ourselves but on God.

We must also be aware of our sin as a nation, so that we do not rely on our economic, military, and political strength in a wrongful way. Yes, we should be faithful at our jobs. We should support our government and its role in executing and judging our laws. But we Christians, of all people, must know that the times are in God's hands and that human power alone is never a sure safeguard in this world. So we should not act as if it were!

Christian, do you want to know how you can witness to your friends at work? Give evidence of the fact that you understand that our days are in God's hands and that you rely on him—particularly at times when the world would be worried and troubled.

Also, pray that God will help you see how you wrongly rely on yourself as well as on others' perceptions of you. Do not be like Saul, who wrote off a relationship with God but begged Samuel to act in such a way that Saul would *appear* to have such a relationship. Do not be a hypocrite like that. Hypocrisy never hurts anyone so much as the hypocrite, and that is true of hypocrites in boardrooms and in jails, in pulpits and in pews, in earthly prosperity and in an eternal hell.

How can you work to protect yourself against the sort of hypocrisy cultivated by Saul? Well, here is some very practical advice: become a member of a local church. Let a congregation of Christians become central to your Christian life. Let yourself become known to other Christians.[7]

Also, initiate sharing your weaknesses with others—not all of them with everyone—but share several of your weaknesses—and some embarrassing ones—with a couple of people, especially with Christian brothers or sisters that you have felt the urge to impress. Start putting to death your reputation and your love for what others think of you. Beware of those whom you want to impress.

Seek instead service that is humble and hidden. I thank God for our congregation members who are going overseas to do childcare for International Mission Board workers this summer. Their quiet and humble service is great. I am also thankful for those who serve the Southern Baptist Convention not just as employees but as trustees. Since we are the only SBC church in the District of Columbia, we have several SBC trustees in our congregation. They show a humble willingness to give their time and not be the chief leader in the room for a weekend, and they perform a service that must be done. Quiet service is not unimportant.

The community of the congregation is so important! All worldly impressiveness is partial and passing, and the intimacy of membership in a Christian congregation will expose it as such.

LEADER PORTRAIT #3: DAVID, AN IMPRESSED MAN MARKED BY FAITH

Beyond Saul, however, there is a third leader who comes to the fore throughout the books of 1 and 2 Samuel: David. If Saul is an *impressive* man, David is an *impressed* man. He is not taken up with himself or with what others think of him. He is a man marked by, dominated by, his regard for the Lord. He is impressed—*impressed!*—with God. He lives his life in awe of the Lord and in great confidence in him. Some people desire to impress you with themselves, particularly in Washington, D.C. Others leave you impressed with their God.

In 1 Samuel, David cannot get over the Lord! He seems to see everything in terms of God's perspective. He is overwhelmed with a concern for God's

---

[7] For a very practical look at church life, you might want to read my book *Nine Marks of a Healthy Church* (Wheaton, Ill.: Crossway, 2004); or the book I wrote with Paul Alexander, *The Deliberate Church* (Wheaton, Ill.: Crossway, 2005); or *Polity: Biblical Arguments on How to Conduct Church Life* (Washington, D.C.: 9Marks, 2000), a book I edited and to which I contributed.

honor and prerogatives, God's activities and purposes, God's name and glory. As I read the book again and again this week, that is what I kept seeing in David's words: God's activities, God's purposes, God's name, God's glory! And his perception is accurate! It is what the Bible calls "faith": seeing that this creation is all about God, not you and me.

David's faith provides a picture of what is supposed to characterize the nation of Israel. God calls them to be a people who recognize the Lord as God, and who serve him alone. He has commanded them to be confident in his power, trusting in his goodness, and obedient to his will. Then they will enjoy the results of such faith. David is a shining example of this. He is what God's people are supposed to be like.

This comes out nowhere more markedly than in David's confrontation with Goliath. You may know the story, even if you did not grow up in church. It's used as an analogy for all kinds of situations. Let's look there for a moment. David, the youngest of several brothers and a shepherd, has brought food to his brothers who stand with Israel's army before an unconquerable foe, Goliath:

> As [David] was talking with [his brothers], Goliath, the Philistine champion from Gath, stepped out from his lines and shouted his usual defiance, and David heard it. When the Israelites saw the man, they all ran from him in great fear.
>
> Now the Israelites had been saying, "Do you see how this man keeps coming out? He comes out to defy Israel. The king will give great wealth to the man who kills him. He will also give him his daughter in marriage and will exempt his father's family from taxes in Israel."
>
> David asked the men standing near him, "What will be done for the man who kills this Philistine and removes this disgrace from Israel? Who is this uncircumcised Philistine that he should defy the armies of the living God?"
>
> They repeated to him what they had been saying and told him, "This is what will be done for the man who kills him" (17:23-27).

David then tells Saul the king that he will go and fight Goliath, to which Saul replies, "You are not able to go out against this Philistine and fight him; you are only a boy, and he has been a fighting man from his youth" (17:33).

So David recounts why he knows he can fight Goliath:

> "Your servant has killed both the lion and the bear; this uncircumcised Philistine will be like one of them, because he has defied the armies of the living God. The LORD who delivered me from the paw of the lion and the paw of the bear will deliver me from the hand of this Philistine."
>
> Saul said to David, "Go, and the LORD be with you" (17:36-37).

Then several verses later, it happens: David goes out onto the battlefield, which initially prompts Goliath to jeer. Obviously, the Philistine does not know what lies in store:

> "Am I a dog, that you come at me with sticks?" And the Philistine cursed David by his gods. "Come here," he said, "and I'll give your flesh to the birds of the air and the beasts of the field!"
>
> David said to the Philistine, "You come against me with sword and spear and javelin, but I come against you in the name of the LORD Almighty, the God of the armies of Israel, whom you have defied. This day the LORD will hand you over to me, and I'll strike you down and cut off your head. Today I will give the carcasses of the Philistine army to the birds of the air and the beasts of the earth, and the whole world will know that there is a God in Israel. All those gathered here will know that it is not by sword or spear that the LORD saves; for the battle is the LORD's, and he will give all of you into our hands."
>
> As the Philistine moved closer to attack him, David ran quickly toward the battle line to meet him. Reaching into his bag and taking out a stone, he slung it and struck the Philistine on the forehead. The stone sank into his forehead, and he fell facedown on the ground.
>
> So David triumphed over the Philistine with a sling and a stone; without a sword in his hand he struck down the Philistine and killed him (17:43-50).

Did you notice that David is enraged because of the dishonor shown to God? "I come against you in the name of the LORD Almighty . . . whom you have defied," he says. And did you notice that his confidence at slaying Goliath lies not with his own abilities, but with the Lord? "The LORD who delivered me . . . will deliver me." Here we encounter what is good and right about David. The point is not that David is simply true to himself, or courageous. In fact, if you think this is a story merely about David's courage, you are taking precisely the *wrong* message from it! Go back and tell the kids in your Sunday school class, "Actually, kids, it wasn't what I said." It is not David's courage. It is not his virtue or strength that allows him to face this giant. What is good and right about David is that he has faith and confidence in the God he serves! He knows that God is the point, and that God will supply!

The same thing occurs again later in the book. Saul becomes jealous of David's success and tries to kill him, in chapters 18–19. David establishes friendships with Saul's son Jonathan in chapter 20 and with a number of priests in chapters 21–22. (These are the priests that Saul has the Edomite kill in chapter 22.) Saul's pursuit of David continues into chapters 23–24.

But in chapter 24, David is given the opportunity to kill Saul, this man who is trying to kill him. Yet he doesn't. Why not? After all, couldn't he justify killing Saul in terms of self-defense? Or by some application of the just war theory? David's men certainly press him to kill Saul. And Samuel had anointed David as king way back in chapter 16. Nothing stands in the way of killing Saul! Why doesn't he?

In short, David is guided by another consideration: the fear of the Lord. As David himself says, "The LORD forbid that I should do such a thing to my master, the LORD's anointed, or lift my hand against him; for he is the anointed of the LORD" (24:6). And he says it again several verses later: "I will not lift my hand against my master, because he is the LORD's anointed" (24:10). David is not so foolish as to think Saul has done nothing wrong. Still, he lets judgment remain in the hands of the LORD. So he says to Saul,

> "Now understand and recognize that I am not guilty of wrongdoing or rebellion. I have not wronged you, but you are hunting me down to take my life. May the LORD judge between you and me. And may the LORD avenge the wrongs you have done to me, but my hand will not touch you" (24:11-12).

All this happens again in chapter 26: Saul pursues David; David has the opportunity to kill him; he doesn't; but he rebukes Saul instead. Following David's rebuke, Saul supposedly repents, as he did in chapter 24. But he continues to pursue David anyway. So David lives the life of a scavenging nomad.

In the last five chapters of 1 Samuel, David lives among the Philistines. Ironically, the only place he is safe is with Israel's enemies. The book then ends with Jonathan and Saul both dying on the same day in a battle at Gilboa, during which the Philistines win a great victory and occupy more Israelite land. We will learn more about David's story when we come to 2 Samuel.

But let's appreciate the portrait of David given here. He is presented as what a king should be. Indeed, he is the greatest king of Israel. David provides the picture of a man who is not consumed with himself but is consumed with the Lord. David receives his wisdom and strength by understanding and relying on God.

Perhaps you are not used to hearing so much "God-talk" in a sermon. Maybe you are more accustomed to hearing about six steps to being a great dad, or three keys to a prayer life, or even nine marks of a healthy church! But, friend, I don't have to know anything about your circumstances—except that you are human—to tell you that God is your only hope. God has done for you what you could never do for yourself. Many years after David, one was born in David's line who has been called "great David's greater Son."[8] He was Jesus

---

[8] "Hail to the Lord's Anointed," words by James Montgomery, 1821.

of Nazareth. In Jesus, God became a man and lived a perfect life with no wrongs. Yet he died on the cross to take on himself the punishment that I deserve for my sins. He did this not just for me but for everyone who will ever repent of their sins and trust in him. The question you need to ask yourself is, *is this me?* Have you repented of your sins and learned what it means not to trust in yourself but to trust in God and what he has done in Christ?

If you want to know more about this, speak with a Christian friend or with a pastor. Any Christian would be happy to help you understand more of what it means to be a Christian.

David is a powerful model, isn't he? When you learn that the episodes of his life are not just a bunch of Sunday school stories but that he actually personifies what it means to trust in the Lord, he becomes the model of a leader who knows he does not lead for his own sake but for others' sake. Unlike Saul, David knows that *he* is not the point. Saul may be impressive to look at. And at least one of David's older brothers is impressive to behold as well. Yet God's eyes are fixed on something different. We learn this when Samuel follows God's instruction to go and anoint one of Jesse's sons as Saul's replacement. Before he sees David,

> Samuel saw Eliab [one of David's older brothers] and thought, "Surely the LORD's anointed stands here before the LORD."
>
> But the LORD said to Samuel, "Do not consider his appearance or his height, for I have rejected him. The LORD does not look at the things man looks at. Man looks at the outward appearance, but the LORD looks at the heart" (16:6-7).

What is your heart focused on? No one else can answer that for you. What is your heart focused on? Focus on Christ. Pray that God will so impress you—as he impressed David—that your desires will be shaped around him. Pray that you will find more and more satisfaction in him. The Christian life is the satisfying life because God created us to know him. So do not be surprised when, by giving yourself over to him, you find true joy.

And when you have a heart of love for God, you can happily give yourself in service to him, as David did when he went out against Goliath. A heart that is satisfied in God is a heart that is full. Nothing else in this world satisfies it, and it demands nothing else. It gives itself freely! Such a heart is dangerous to the Evil One and all his hellish lies. May you have such a heart, my friend.

This is why our church labors so hard to point away from ourselves and to Christ in all that we do together on the Lord's Day. And so we sing,

> When Satan tempts me to despair and tells me of the guilt within,
> upward I look, and see him there who made an end of all my sin.

Because the sinless Savior died, my sinful soul is counted free;
for God, the Just, is satisfied to look on him and pardon me.[9]

David's perspective is the truth. May we be people of such faith.

CONCLUSION: GOD, OUR NECESSARY LEADER

No mere human king, of course, not even David, could be the earthly blessing God's people needed. Within one generation, the people were mired in idolatry, where they remained with a few exceptions until they were submerged in the exile to Babylon. A special birth was necessary—the birth of one who would bring David's line to a remarkable fruition; the birth of one who *was* and *is* God himself.

Here in the book of 1 Samuel, the story leading to the birth of this special one starts with the faithful mother of Samuel, Hannah. She seems to understand that both her safety and the safety of the nation lie in the hands of no earthly judge or king but in the hands of God alone. Look at her prayer, or song, at the beginning of the book, and consider her understanding of faith:

"My heart rejoices in the LORD;
  in the LORD my horn is lifted high.
My mouth boasts over my enemies,
  for I delight in your deliverance.

There is no one holy like the LORD;
  there is no one besides you;
  there is no Rock like our God.

Do not keep talking so proudly
  or let your mouth speak such arrogance,
for the LORD is a God who knows,
  and by him deeds are weighed.

The bows of the warriors are broken,
  but those who stumbled are armed with strength.
Those who were full hire themselves out for food,
  but those who were hungry hunger no more.
She who was barren has borne seven children,
  but she who has had many sons pines away.

---

[9] "Before the Throne of God Above," words by Charitie Lees Bancroft, 1863.

The LORD brings death and makes alive;
  he brings down to the grave and raises up.
The LORD sends poverty and wealth;
  he humbles and he exalts.
He raises the poor from the dust
  and lifts the needy from the ash heap;
he seats them with princes
  and has them inherit a throne of honor.

For the foundations of the earth are the LORD's;
  upon them he has set the world.
He will guard the feet of his saints,
  but the wicked will be silenced in darkness.

It is not by strength that one prevails;
  those who oppose the LORD will be shattered.
He will thunder against them from heaven;
  the LORD will judge the ends of the earth.

He will give strength to his king
  and exalt the horn of his anointed" (2:1-10).

What a beautiful way to open this book! This is what the whole Bible is about. More particularly, this is what these books of history—Joshua and Judges, the books of Samuel and Kings—are about. God alone is Lord. He is to be trusted, and he alone is to be trusted!

We don't know when 1 and 2 Samuel were written. Perhaps they were written, like 1 and 2 Kings, during the exile in Babylon. Regardless, it appears they were written at least in part to explain why God's people had been driven out of their land. The reason was, they eventually deserted the one who alone was to be their Lord—God himself. God's people deserted God.

However, Hannah knew whom she should trust. She had seen God's mighty hand close-up. First Samuel begins, after all, when God opens this barren woman's womb and she gives birth to Samuel. That is just like the Lord, isn't it? To clearly establish whom we should rely upon. To take a hopeless situation (according to the world's wisdom) and produce glory for himself. To clear out every other player so that he receives all the credit. To make his victory unmistakable. So God begins this section of the great story with a childless woman.

God makes the same point—that he alone can be relied upon—almost humorously when the ark of the covenant is captured by the Philistines and placed on display in the temple of their false god, Dagon. Does the ark's capture mean that the Lord had been defeated by this other god? Hardly! In fact, I think that God allows the defeat to happen and ensures that it is recorded for his people to read in order to make his point. Do you know the story?

> Then they carried the ark into Dagon's temple and set it beside Dagon [an idol]. When the people of Ashdod rose early the next day, there was Dagon, fallen on his face on the ground before the ark of the LORD! They took Dagon and put him back in his place. But the following morning when they rose, there was Dagon, fallen on his face on the ground before the ark of the LORD! His head and hands had been broken off and were lying on the threshold; only his body remained (5:2-4).

So helpless is this false god that the very people who worship him must come and put the one they worship back in his place! In this episode, God teaches that not only can he not be defeated by a mere idol like Dagon, he doesn't need one Israelite soldier to win a striking victory. The Lord alone is God! He is supreme! The defeat of his people indicates no defect in his power. Indeed, it appears that God's purposes are behind the defeat, as he moves in his mysterious ways.

The books of 1 and 2 Samuel and of 1 and 2 Kings tell us the story about the people's urgent request for a king "like the nations around them," and the tragic results that follow from this request. Yet such results were inevitable. The Lord had promised Abraham in Genesis 17 that kings would come from him. And in Deuteronomy, the Lord had made provision for a king (Deut. 17:14-20). If you think about it, how strange it was to set up a nation at that time with no king. They must have been the strangest nation on the earth! Then again, that was the point, wasn't it? They left Egypt, survived in the wilderness, conquered Canaan, maintained their independence from other nations for centuries, all with a unified religion, and they did these things *with no king!* How could that happen? Well, the very absence of the king pointed to the presence of God. That's the point of these books. Why are the books of Samuel and Kings in the Bible? To teach us that God is his people's king. No other king, finally, can promise the complete and entire deliverance God's people need.

In turn, that's why the people's demand for a king is a rejection of God. So the Lord tells Samuel, as we saw earlier, "Listen to all that the people are saying to you; it is not you they have rejected as their king, but me. As they have done from the day I brought them up out of Egypt until this day, forsaking me and serving other gods, so they are doing to you" (1 Sam. 8:7-8). The whole exercise of kingship in Israel was intended to be one long lesson on how no one but God himself can ultimately lead God's people.

In Samuel's farewell speech, he retells the people of Israel their history, so that they can see how *full* their history is with the Lord's faithfulness:

> Then Samuel said to the people, "It is the LORD who appointed Moses and Aaron and brought your forefathers up out of Egypt. Now then, stand here, because I am going to confront you with evidence before the LORD as to all the righteous acts performed by the LORD for you and your fathers.
>
> "After Jacob entered Egypt, they cried to the LORD for help, and the LORD sent Moses and Aaron, who brought your forefathers out of Egypt and settled them in this place.
>
> "But they forgot the LORD their God; so he sold them into the hand of Sisera, the commander of the army of Hazor, and into the hands of the Philistines and the king of Moab, who fought against them. They cried out to the LORD and said, 'We have sinned; we have forsaken the LORD and served the Baals and the Ashtoreths. But now deliver us from the hands of our enemies, and we will serve you.' Then the LORD sent Jerub-Baal, Barak, Jephthah and Samuel, and he delivered you from the hands of your enemies on every side, so that you lived securely.
>
> "But when you saw that Nahash king of the Ammonites was moving against you, you said to me, 'No, we want a king to rule over us'—even though the LORD your God was your king. Now here is the king you have chosen, the one you asked for; see, the LORD has set a king over you. If you fear the LORD and serve and obey him and do not rebel against his commands, and if both you and the king who reigns over you follow the LORD your God—good! But if you do not obey the LORD, and if you rebel against his commands, his hand will be against you, as it was against your fathers" (12:6-15).

Samuel is telling the people, not even your kings can protect and save you. This is also why, I think, the writer tells us in 13:19-22 that Israel has no weapons. God alone will win the Israelites' victories. You realize, don't you, that the Israelites were the hillbillies of the day? They lived up in the hills, and they did not have the technology for forging iron and, perhaps, bronze. The Philistines were the cosmopolitan people of the times—savvy and technically advanced. Yet the Philistines' very strengths made them less suitable vehicles for God's use in teaching the world about himself. Israel's very apparent disadvantages—no king, no weapons—were all signs of their dependence upon God! It made them precisely the ones God wanted to use to display his own power and strength.

So, my friend, reject your rejection of God. It leads to no good and to only the bitterest of fruit. You were made to be led by God; so take him as your

Lord. Focus your life on him. Set your hopes and affections all on him. Give up your lonely rebellion. Repent of your sins, believe in him, and find the life for which you were created.

Take a moment and consider your need for God. Pray that God will help you see that the weight of your sins is heavier than can be borne by any righteousness of your own. Deliverance is the Lord's business. A spider's web can more easily bear a stone than your righteousness or mine can bear our sins.

If we are genuinely Christians, we have nothing to fear. Our leader—the one behind all the leaders in 1 Samuel—will not fail us nor forget us. He has proved his faithfulness to us again and again. Nor do we need to fear the future as a church. We can be confident in God's strength because he has promised that, having begun a good work in us, he will carry it on to completion (Phil. 1:6).

Someday, God will call us to that place of entire reliance on him. If we are God's people, we can look forward to what John Bunyan imaginatively describes through his character Mr. Standfast in *Pilgrim's Progress*. Near the close of Bunyan's classic, Mr. Standfast receives a summons that informs him "he must prepare for a change of life, for his Master was not willing that he should be so far from Him any longer." Faced with death, Mr. Standfast muses, showing the same faith in the face of trials that David exemplified before Goliath and Saul. Wading out into the River of Death, Standfast reflects,

> "This river has been a terror to many; yea, the thoughts of it also have often frighted me. . . . The waters indeed are to the palate bitter, and to the stomach cold: yet the thoughts of what I am going to . . . doth lie as a glowing coal at my heart. I see myself now at the end of my journey; my toilsome days are ended. I am going now to see that head that was crowned with thorns, and that face which was spit upon for me. I have formerly lived by hearsay and faith: but now I go where I shall live by sight, and shall be with Him in whose company I delight myself. I have loved to hear my Lord spoken of. . . . His name has been to me . . . sweeter than all perfumes. His voice has been to me most sweet; and His countenance I have more desired than they that have most desired the light of the sun."

Bunyan continues from the perspective of those observing Mr. Standfast:

> Now while he was thus in discourse his countenance changed. . . . he ceased to be seen of them.
>
> But glorious it was to see how the upper region was filled with horses and chariots, with trumpeters and pipers, with singers and players on stringed instru-

ments, to welcome the pilgrims as they went up, and followed one another in at the beautiful gate of the City.[10]

So this is the message of 1 Samuel: Our lives should be marked not by trust in our own wisdom but by trust in God's. We should be marked not by being impressive but by being impressed with God—absolutely taken with him and trusting him alone. May we have such leaders. May we live such lives.

Let us pray:

O God, investigate our hearts. Insofar as we remain committed to serving ourselves, grant us a gracious liberation. Cause our sins to seem too heavy to bear. Help us to look to Christ. O Lord, teach each of us to forsake those things that we have as substitutes for you. Give us hearts and hopes centered on you and you alone, we pray, in great anticipation of joy in your presence. Amen.

Questions for Reflection

1. What are the attributes of a good leader? What attributes does the leader of a church need that the leader of a business or some other organization may not need?

2. How do individuals discern whether or not God has called them to a position of leadership in the church?

3. Samuel's life was typified by an eagerness to listen. Is yours? How well would your spouse say you listen? Your children? What about your boss? Or the people who work for you? Your pastor? The friends with whom you are in an accountability relationship? Does your life demonstrate the practice of listening to God, and if so, how?

4. Teaching us about the Lord Jesus, the prophet Isaiah writes, "The Sovereign LORD has given me an instructed tongue, to know the word that sustains the weary. He wakens me morning by morning, wakens my ear to listen like one being taught. The Sovereign LORD has opened my ears, and I have not been rebellious; I have not drawn back" (Isa. 50:4-5). And the Gospel writer Luke then tells us about the young Jesus, "The Child continued to grow and become strong, increasing in wisdom; and the grace of God was upon Him" (Luke 2:40; NASB). Can you think of episodes in Jesus' life where he demonstrated a

---

[10] John Bunyan, *The Pilgrim's Progress* (1678; repr., Chicago: John C. Winston, 1930), 329-330.

perfect submission to listening to his heavenly Father? Given who Jesus is, why is this striking? In this regard, what does Jesus teach us about good leadership?

5. Where do you think the Lord Jesus went morning by morning to listen as one being taught? Where should you go?

6. Following up on question 5, is there any value to reading long sections of Scripture (say, a chapter or two) in a church service or during a sermon? How can more Scripture be incorporated into the prayers of a church gathering?

7. As we have seen, Saul was wrongfully self-reliant. Are you? Here are several further questions that might help you get at the answer to that simple yes/no question:

- Are you happy to ask people for help or do you resist it?
- Can someone beneath you (professionally, socially, intellectually) instruct you, or tell you something you don't already know?
- How much do you pray, and do you pray consistently?
- Do you study God's Word consistently?
- Do you have accountability relationships in your life?
- When was the last time you learned something in a sermon?
- When was the last time you learned something from your spouse? From a friend?
- Do you respond to backseat drivers with annoyance or with a "thank you"?

8. As Christians, we do not believe that narcissism is simply a "psychiatric disorder," as many might define it. It's sin. It's pride. Still, the American Psychiatric Association's definition of "Narcissistic Personality Disorder" provides an apt profile of Saul as well as a good checklist for examining our own hearts! A person is "narcissistic," so they say, when he or she has "a pervasive pattern of grandiosity (in fantasy or behavior), need for admiration, and lack of empathy." More specifically, a narcissistic person displays *some* of the following qualities:

- A grandiose sense of self-importance: you tend to exaggerate achievements and talents; you expect to be recognized as superior without commensurate achievements.
- A preoccupation with fantasies of unlimited success, power, brilliance, beauty, or ideal love: really, you feel like you deserve these things.
- An opinion of oneself as "special" or unique: you tend to feel understood by—or prefer associating with—other special or high-status people.
- Desirous of admiration from others.

- A sense of entitlement: you expect people (parents, spouses, employers, restaurant servers, anyone behind a counter) to grant you special treatment, or to automatically comply with your desires and expectations.
- Interpersonally exploitive: you quietly and subtly take advantage of others for your own ends.
- A lack of empathy: you are unwilling to recognize or identify yourself with the feelings and needs of others.
- Feelings of envy: you tend to be envious of others, and you like to think they are envious of you.
- Arrogance: you are often haughty in your behaviors or attitudes.[11]

How would you feel about handing this list to two of your closest friends and asking them to evaluate you?

9. As we have seen, a leader who is *impressed* with God, a leader like David, sees everything in terms of God's perspective: God's honor, God's prerogatives, God's activities and purposes. What leader exemplified this absolutely perfectly in his life? If being impressed with God is the "key" to successful leadership, and if David and this other one are our models, what are some of the things a manual on successful leadership might say?

10. It is true that leaders will be judged more strictly (James 3:1). But it is also true that if you are a Christian, ironically, God looks upon your own imperfect leadership in your home, work, or church—and sees instead the righteousness of Christ! As Christians, our whole lives are covered with Christ's righteousness, including the way we lead. That does not mean we are not responsible. But it does mean we are freed from leading others in order to prove something or gain something (we have all we need in Christ!). We are freed up to genuinely lead for others' good and Christ's glory. All of this leads to one conclusion: at the very heart of good leadership is a deep and deepening understanding of one primary thing. What is it? (Hint: the answer rhymes with "dospel.")

---

[11] See the American Psychiatric Association's *Diagnostic and Statistical Manual of Mental Disorders*, 4th ed. (Washington, D.C.: APA, 2000), 717.

THE MESSAGE OF 2 SAMUEL: REPENTANCE

THE MESSAGE OF 2 SAMUEL: REPENTANCE

POWER: A DELICATE BALANCE[1]

Over the last several months, I have had the opportunity to read several books on the American Revolution. Something these books have stressed over and over is that the Revolution was not significant simply because the colonists successfully rejected British rule by military power. Much more significant, arguably, was their attempt to build a new kind of government in which the government became responsive to many more of the nation's citizens than had ever been the case in history, at least in a country of this size.

On September 11 of this last year, America experienced a tragic loss of life. And many of us will participate in special events to commemorate that day in this coming week. On that day, more than people and buildings fell. So did the country's unfailing certainty that America is invincible; that tomorrow is *ours;* that the future means progress; and that progress means America. Not since the War of 1812 have symbols of our nation been destroyed by a foreign power on our own mainland, and never with such loss of life. This tragic event brought to this country something that has been missing for over one hundred years—a sense of our own national fragility and the understanding that America is not inevitable.

Ironically, such a sense was common among our nation's founders. They referred to the new constitutional government that they devised as an "experiment." And they meant it. Maybe you have blithely assumed that, except for a few wild-eyed terrorists, no one has ever seriously questioned the continuing existence of America. But if you read the letters of the founders who survived into the early 1800s, you find that almost every one of them had become pes-

---

[1] This sermon was originally preached on September 8, 2002, at Capitol Hill Baptist Church in Washington, D.C.

simistic about their experiment's prospects. In fact, they seemed pretty certain that the American government would fall. Benjamin Franklin, the oldest delegate to the Constitutional Convention, was at a banquet to celebrate the convention's conclusion. A leading lady of Philadelphia asked him, "O! Mister Franklin, what have you gentlemen wrought, after so many weeks of secrecy behind those thick doors?" Franklin is said to have adjusted his glasses and then offered his famous reply, "A republic, madam. If you can keep it."[2] Franklin and others understood the difficulty of what they were trying to accomplish, of creating a sufficiently powerful federal government, but powerful exactly so that it could protect states' rights and individual liberties. Granting the government so much power made many people nervous; they had just rebelled against a strong central government. Yet the strength of this new kind of central government was meant to serve liberty, at least for a lot of citizens. The difficulty of striking the right balance between governing authority and freedom has marked much of America's history.

Power has always been recognized as being a dangerous thing. And yet authority is necessary for our lives. This is true at home and at work, in our cities and in our churches. Power—the ability to carry out your will—is necessary. But what about when power is used wrongly? Or used to achieve wrongful ends? Then what? What about when *you* use power wrongly—when you sin?

INTRODUCING 2 SAMUEL

In this sermon, we want to look through the whole book of 2 Samuel, a book filled with one of the most well-known, beloved, and colorful life stories in the Bible: the life of David, a man well-acquainted with power and authority as well as its limitations and temptations.

The story of David provides the centerpiece of 1 and 2 Samuel and 1 and 2 Kings. We don't know when these four books were written, but it probably occurred when Israel was in exile in Babylon. Treated collectively, the thesis of the four books is an ironic one: the nation that Joshua led into Canaan was called to be God's distinct witness to the nations; but that nation rebelled and became an imitation of the nations it had displaced. For the first readers, then, the four books were a call to repentance. They provide the story of God's people rejecting God, and implied in that story is the call to reject their rejection. Turn back to God! Repent!

Though it may surprise you, can you guess who the prime example of

---

[2] In Michael Novak, *On Two Wings: Humble Faith and Common Sense at the American Founding* (San Francisco: Encounter, 2002), 73.

godly repentance is in Israel's history? The answer is David, who was probably the best king Israel ever had. The most enlightened leader. The king most known for justice. And the most intense man of worship. In 2 Samuel, David becomes the clearest picture of what it means to repent of sin.

The zenith of the kingdom of Israel is found in David. The first half of David's life is recounted in 1 Samuel, which we covered in our last study. That first book covers his boyhood and how he initially comes to prominence through the anointing of Samuel and the demise of Saul. The second book of Samuel, our subject of study here, covers the remainder of David's life. I would encourage you to read it this week if you have not. It takes about an hour and a quarter to read. Surely that's better than what you will watch on television. Read it aloud to your family, or a group of friends. It is an amazing story of God's grace in David's life.

Now because this is an overview sermon, we will be flipping around a lot. In this series of sermons, we have been looking at the historical books of the Old Testament, from Joshua to Esther. In Joshua and Judges, we saw how God originally brought his people into the Promised Land, and how they brought several centuries of tumultuous times upon themselves. Then we looked at 1 Samuel and saw how a kingship was established. When we turn next to 1 and 2 Kings, 1 and 2 Chronicles, Ezra, Nehemiah, and Esther in our subsequent studies, we will watch Israel plummet from the heights it experiences with David and his son Solomon down to the depths of exile and then back up somewhat in a restoration. About seven hundred years of time is left to be covered by the books in this series. In 2 Samuel we see the nation of Israel, as I said, at its zenith, when David reigns.

The book's structure is fairly simple: The first ten chapters (1–10) are good things. The next ten chapters (11–20) are bad things. And the last four chapters are a bit miscellaneous. In chapter 21, David sorts out an old sin and its implications from Saul's reign. In chapter 22, David sings a psalm of praise to God (it also appears as Psalm 18). Chapter 23 contains David's last words. And chapter 24 contains one last story about the sin David commits by numbering the troops. Honestly, chapter 24 can feel like, "Oh yeah, and we wanted to include this story from David's reign." There it is—2 Samuel.

In this study, let's look at the story of David in three parts: First, we will examine God's blessing and David's virtue in the first half of the book. Second, we will turn to David's sin in the latter half of the book. Third, we will consider David's repentance.

I hope that looking through this book together will help you better understand what you should do with the power and opportunities God gives you, as well as what you should do when you fail and sin. With that in mind, let's turn to David. Hold his life up to yours, and see what you find.

DAVID RECEIVES GOD'S BLESSING

First, David receives God's blessing. To understand this, let's turn to some of David's last words:

> "The God of Israel spoke,
>   the Rock of Israel said to me:
> 'When one rules over men in righteousness,
>   when he rules in the fear of God,
> he is like the light of morning at sunrise
>   on a cloudless morning,
> like the brightness after rain
>   that brings the grass from the earth'"(2 Sam. 23:3-4).

It is a beautiful image, isn't it? Just a brief cameo. Imagine an old man's voice speaking these words after he had reigned for forty years. This is the last prophecy the prophet-king David receives from the Lord. Toward the end of his reign, he provides an amazing image of ruling—ruling, that is, "in righteousness" and "in the fear of God." How does David characterize such a ruler? With two striking images. Such a ruler is like *the light of morning at sunrise on a cloudless morning.* And such a ruler is like *the brightness after rain that brings the grass from the earth.*

Think about this pair of images. First, such a ruler is like the light of morning at sunrise on a cloudless morning. Can you picture that? Light itself is attractive to us. We are made to be drawn to it. But here, David draws us not to just light but to the light of morning. The warm light of afternoon and the mellow light of a summer's evening are also pleasant. But there is something unique about the light of morning. We all know that. It seems especially clear and straightforward, or so it feels after a refreshing sleep. Somehow it pierces whatever sleepiness remains and then reassures us, offering cheer and hope for another day. After all, this is not simply morning light, but the earliest, freshest morning light—the light at sunrise, and a sunrise on a cloudless morning! Can you picture such a sunrise in your mind? Take a moment and find one in your memory . . .

That is exactly what this king, on his deathbed, says authority well used is like. The thrill, the freshness, the sense of awe you feel in that image will also be felt when we rule in righteousness and in the fear of God.

It is true, isn't it? How *splendid* such leadership is to behold! How God-like!

Friend, have you considered the powerful witness you can have in wielding authority well? If you are a parent, do you understand the opportunity you have to show your children what God is like by the way you use your authority? You can teach them that authority—and God's authority in particular—can actually be trusted, and that he uses it for our good! Husbands in your homes, friends at work, pastors and elders in your churches, those of you in positions of political authority, do you realize the opportunity you have to display a witness to God? When you rule over men in righteousness, when you rule in the fear of God, you are like the light at sunrise on a cloudless morning. My politician friends, God has set you in a place where you can, by your very life and the way you fulfill the responsibilities he has given you, powerfully demonstrate the character of God to all who can see! Praise God for the privilege all of us have when wielding whatever authority we have been entrusted with.

Then David uses that second image: such a ruler is like the brightness after rain that brings the grass from the earth. Do you know what he means? It is another picture of a wonderfully attractive "brightness." We like brightness. So we are speaking positively when we remark that someone "brightens up a room." The brightness is then heightened by a contrast—it's a brightness "after rain," he says. Then he adds this one further description: it is the brightness after rain "that brings the grass from the earth." This last phrase is what really distinguishes this second picture from the first one. The camera turns, as it were, from the sky to the ground. We are no longer looking at the splendor of the thing itself; we are looking at its glow on the little green shoots sprouting up due to the brightness after the rain. In other words, a good ruler produces good in others. He is beneficent. He is fruitful.

So when a man rules over others in righteousness and in the fear of God, he is splendid in himself and he is beneficent, benevolent, a blessing to those he rules.

I remember staying at a hotel outside of St. Petersburg, Russia, and sharing a room with Sasha, our group's tour guide. At one point, we were both quietly reading when he looked over at me, interrupted the silence, and asked, "I have heard that people are given the governments they deserve. Do you think that is true?" Well, a long conversation followed, but here in 2 Samuel, it is pretty clear that Israel received in David a better ruler than they deserved. Throughout this series on the histories of the Old Testament, we have seen that the people of Israel were reluctant, at best, in their obedience to God. Idolatry and injustice were common. God's law and rule were frequently flouted. Yet God gave them a good ruler in David.

Chapters 1 to 10 catalog for us David's military victories and his exercise of impartial justice among his people. And in these chapters we find that David's rule, like his picture of good leadership in chapter 23, was splendid and beneficent in many ways. Even the three thousand years that separate us from him do not entirely obscure from us the greatness of his victories or the striking justice of some of his decisions.

We do not have time to notice everything in the first half of the book, of course, so let me lead you through it quickly. First Samuel, you may remember, ends with Israel's defeat by the Philistines as well as with King Saul's and his son Jonathan's death. Second Samuel begins in chapter 1 with David learning about these events. He is not gleeful over Saul's downfall, as one might expect him to be. After all, Saul had pursued him and stood in his way to the throne. No, David actually executes the Amalekite who killed Saul, and then he leads the Israelite people in lamenting the deaths of Saul and Jonathan.

Chapter 2 tells how one of Saul's sons becomes anointed as king, and then it describes the strife that ensues between the house of Saul and David's followers.

Chapter 3 follows the story of a remarkable defection by a leader in the house of Saul. This leader is then murdered by one of David's men for personal reasons.

Chapter 4 contains the tragic end of the house of Saul, and, by implication, the collapse of its resistance to David's rule.

Chapter 5 records two significant victories for David, first over the Jebusites, which gives him Jerusalem (which is why it is called the City of David); and second over Israel's old enemies the Philistines. David's power is therefore consolidated, and he is able to protect the nation from outside attack.

Chapter 6 shows David bringing the ark of the covenant into Jerusalem.

Chapter 7 presents God's great promise to David to establish his royal line forever.

Chapter 8 appears to be the apex of David's greatness as victory after victory is recounted against the Philistines, the Moabites, the Edomites, and others. All are defeated and become subject to Israel's law.

Chapter 9 describes David's kindness to a grandson of Saul and son of Jonathan—Mephibosheth.

Chapter 10 is the story of David defeating the Arameans and the Ammonites.

In all this, we see David as a great ruler: he "rules over men in righteousness"; he "rules in the fear of God"; and for these reasons "he is like the light of morning at sunrise on a cloudless morning, like the brightness after rain that brings the grass from the earth." We observe his splendor in his victories: over the house of Saul (chapters 2–5), over the Jebusites (5:6-7), over the Philistines (5:20-25), and over the Arameans and Ammonites (chapter 10). And we observe his beneficence as he blesses his people with goodness, kindness, and justice. He brings justice against Saul's killer (chapter 1), even though Saul had tried to kill David. He does the same against the killers of Saul's son, even though he was rivaling David as king of Israel (chapter 4). He initiates public mourning after the death of Saul's military leader, Abner (3:31-37). He blesses the people in the name of the Lord when he brings the ark into Jerusalem (6:17-18). He shows kindness to Mephibosheth, this descendant of Saul, in chapter 9 as well as to the family of a foreign king at the beginning of chapter 10. He even sorts out the consequences of earlier sin from Saul's time in chapter 21. And he regularly inquires of the Lord for guidance, so he can know and do God's will (2:1; 5:19, 23; 21:1). David rules in righteousness and the fear of God. He is a good ruler.

A couple of verses in chapter 8 well summarize this first half of 2 Samuel, giving concise statements of both David's victories and his goodness. About his victories, verse 6 says, "The Lord gave David victory everywhere he went" (cf. v. 14). About his goodness, verse 15 reads, "David reigned over all Israel, doing what was just and right for all his people." David was Israel's greatest king. He led them to more military victories, political control, and intense worship of the Lord than any other ruler had or would. Why was he a good king? Because God blessed him. Because God himself chose this shepherd boy and used him.

From a human standpoint, David was a good king because he realized that he was not the final authority. Based on the biblical record, he was more prayerful than any other king of Israel. He realized that his power was derivative; that it had limits. Again, David ruled in righteousness and in the fear of God.

What does ruling in the fear of God mean? It means that when you rule, you never forget that you will give account to God for how you treat those who are weaker than you or are dependent on you. Therefore, you use whatever authority God has given you to rule or lead in such a way that God would approve. As we have seen, your careful use of authority reflects the very character of God and his authority. So your authority should be nothing short of splendid! Glorious! Brilliant! And a blessing to everyone around you! When you lead well at work, at home, in government, at school, among your friends, or in the church, you bless those who are under your care.

I wonder what blessings you feel you have received from God or from others who are in authority over you. Have you thought about those blessings lately? Amid your deadlines and job uncertainties, your health problems and your family difficulties, have you taken time to stop and consider what good things God has given you? Take a moment and try to think of some particular blessing God has given you in the past few months.

Now, wouldn't these blessings alone be enough reason for you to praise God and give him thanks?

We are in God's hands, and they are good hands to be in! Your talents are gifts, and your gifts are blessings given to you by God. Christian, I pray that God will deliver you from any pride you have in your giftedness. The gifts that God gives to us, he gives for serving others, for caring for our families, for building up the church, for blessing our cities. They should never be regarded as ornaments for drawing attention to ourselves. They are not for show, but for work. Therefore, purpose to bring glory to God in the way you employ your gifts; use yourself for God's good. That means we should pray that God would cultivate in us attitudes of humility and gratitude for every good thing he has entrusted to our care.

Our church has certainly experienced God's goodness. I could give you a list as long as my arm of things that are going well. Are they going well because the congregation is so great? No, that's not the reason. The congregation is filled with sinners. Has the church experienced God's goodness because I'm so great? No, I'm just one more sinner. Our church is doing well because God is so great. It is because he desires to glorify himself in a group of people like you and me. And he knows that if he picks people like you and me, he will get more glory than if he picked some others. Once again, the blessings we have received are not the grounds for pride. They are things we should observe, consider, and thank God for, because they allow us to see his goodness. *Contrary to what we might expect, taking our gifts for granted will encourage pride in us; but pausing and enumerating them will encourage our hearts to be grateful and humble before God.*

The Lord blesses you and he blesses me, and he has blessed this church as surely as he blessed David.

DAVID SINS

Though David was blessed, we see clearly that he was far from a perfect ruler. And that brings us to the second aspect of David's life that we must notice: David sins.

Now if you happen to be an advanced Bible student, you might wonder, if David is far from a perfect man, why does he talk about his own righteousness? After all, in chapter 22 he says, "I have been blameless before him and have kept myself from sin" (22:24; cf. Ps. 18:20-24). And we see this again and again in the Psalms. For instance, Psalm 26 reads, "I lead a blameless life; redeem me and be merciful to me" (Ps. 26:11).

Consider that first line, "I lead a blameless life." Does that mean David thinks he has been without any sin throughout his whole life? I don't think so. David's sin was known to others, and he acknowledges his sin as well. In Psalm 51, David makes one of the most moving confessions of sin in the whole Bible. In fact, right after he says, "I lead a blameless life" in Psalm 26, his very next phrase is "redeem me and be merciful to me." Who needs redemption? Who needs mercy? Not someone who has led a perfect life entirely without sin. David knows he is not like that. What he means, I believe, is not that he is completely innocent of any charge but that he has acted with integrity (as the KJV renders the word), walked in God's ways, and done what is right; and he has done these things particularly in how he has treated Saul and his family, even though Saul had been his implacable opponent. David has been nothing but fair, just, and kind to Saul. David has been correct in light of the present subject, not in terms of everything in his whole life.

David clearly was not righteous in every action in his whole life. He needed redemption and he needed God's mercy, as he confessed.

Counting the Troops

At the end of the book, David orders a census—a counting. He tells his military commander, Joab, "Go throughout the tribes of Israel from Dan to Beersheba and enroll the fighting men, so that I may know how many there are" (24:2). Why does he do this? Apparently, for his own knowledge. Yet Joab understands that this is a horrific order: "why does my lord the king want to do such a thing?" (24:3b). Now, we read David's order and think he just wants a little census work done. Surely there is nothing wrong with that, we say. If there were, some in our church would have to resign their jobs! But no, something is happening that is clearly and obviously wrong to those around David, even if the story does not tell us what. Is it David's pride, as in, "Look at how powerful I am; here's the proof"? Is it self-reliance, like the rich man who continually counts his money to reassure himself of his security? In that sense, could it even have been a declaration of independence from God, as in, "I don't need to inquire of the Lord, I just need to cash out the number of troops I've got and see how far I can extend my power"? We don't know, the story does not say. Whatever it was, it was bad, and it was known to be bad.

Adultery and Murder

But beyond this one episode in chapter 24, chapters 11–20 make it painfully clear that David was far from perfect in his righteousness. This whole, sprawling middle section of this book is one long tragic epic of sin and sin's multiplying consequences.

This central epic ends with two little words: "threw it" (20:22). And it begins ten or fifteen years earlier (we don't know how long exactly) with the two little words back in chapter 11: "he saw" (11:2). The "threw it" refers to the head of someone who had led a rebellion against David. The "he saw" refers to David seeing the lovely and desirable Bathsheba. And in between that look and that pitch is David's sin, the partial self-destruction of his family, and the agony of his nation. How many mothers were made childless, and young wives made widows, because of David's careless glance and his selfish lust on that day! If David could have known all the things that would have followed from that gaze, I believe he would have torn his eyes out before turning, looking, staring, and then acting on such lust. Oh, that we could see the consequences of our own sins before we commit them! How many sins would we be dissuaded from! And yet life is not like that. We are told in Proverbs that you can enter into the house of destruction and ruin through a doorway of pleasure (e.g., Proverbs 7). Our consciences tell us that something is amiss, and we know that sin is a deceiver; but we cannot read our own futures so precisely, so we flagrantly barge ahead. But that is why we have God's Word. You can turn there; you can read and know it; you can hide it in your heart, see what God does, and see how people sin.

Chapter 11 contains this well-known, tragic story of David sinning against the Lord by lusting after the beautiful Bathsheba, pursuing and sleeping with her, and then, after she becomes pregnant, having her husband surreptitiously killed in battle so that he could marry her.

Responding to David's sins, the Lord tells David through the prophet Nathan that David has "despised the word of the LORD" (12:9). In making his sinful decision, David broke God's law. He flouted God's authority. He betrayed God's rule. And when you despise the words that come out of God's mouth, the words that express his character, you despise his person; you despise him. In the very next verse, aside from pointing to the consequences of David's action, God says exactly this: "Now, therefore, the sword will never depart from your house, because you *despised me* and took the wife of Uriah the Hittite to be your own" (12:10). David obviously sinned against Bathsheba and against Uriah. But in doing this, he despised God.

Friend, I want you to notice this last point. You may think the most serious consequence of your sin is how you harm someone else, whether a colleague, a spouse, a child, a friend, a parent, or the person you slandered. Well, this is not quite true. The hurt against another person is real and serious, but that is not the most important hurt that occurs. Or maybe, in our narcissistic age, you think the most important harm you do by sinning is the harm you cause yourself. You lament the fact that sin hinders and stifles your personal development. But no, that is not the worst consequence either. Most significantly, when you sin, you despise the Lord.

Do not mistake the personal nature of sin. Sin is a personal affront to those affected by it, directly and indirectly. And it is most fully and thoroughly a personal affront against God, who made you and has more claim upon you than anyone else, whether parents, spouse, employer, friends, or yourself. He is the one you fundamentally offend when you sin.

The Consequences

Throughout the rest of the book, the sword does not depart from David's family. In chapter 12, the child of David that Bathsheba conceives and gives birth to dies.

In chapter 13, David's eldest son, Amnon, repeats David's sin, but with a twist: the woman Amnon illicitly takes is his own half sister, Tamar. He rapes her. David does nothing, but one of David's other sons, Absalom, who is Tamar's full brother, waits for two years and then acts. Almost certainly seething with frustration over his father's passive injustice, Absalom steps into the gap. He ambushes and kills Amnon, and then he flees Jerusalem. Again, David does nothing—except to express his sorrow.

In chapter 14, after a three-year exile, David is persuaded to bring Absalom out of exile and back to Jerusalem. By then, however, Absalom's despising of his father David has ripened.

In chapter 15, therefore, Absalom uses his new, restored position to rebel against David. He claims the throne, and David, still in passive mode, evacuates Jerusalem!

In chapter 16, David travels east with his followers, while Absalom consolidates his power in Jerusalem.

In chapter 17, Absalom pursues David, but this is where Absalom overreaches. After all, his father is a practiced military man.

In chapter 18, Absalom is captured and killed by Joab and his armorbearers, even though David had said to "be gentle" with Absalom (18:5). David responds with sheer grief: "O my son Absalom! My son, my son Absalom! If only I had died instead of you" (18:33).

In chapter 19, David returns to Jerusalem. Yet even when he returns, strife arises between the men of Judah and the men of Israel (the northern tribes) concerning the king's return.

In chapter 20, then, a man named Sheba leads the northern tribes into rebellion against David. This rebellion ends when Joab's forces lay siege of the town where Sheba had taken refuge, and the town's people, in order to avoid destruction, "cut off the head of Sheba son of Bicri and *threw it* to Joab" (20:22a).

There it is, what appears to be the earthly conclusion to what we know of the consequences of David's sins. The people threw the head of the man who had led the rebellion against David upon his return from exile, an exile caused by a previous rebellion, which itself followed a failure to render justice, which followed a murder, which followed a rape, which followed a first murder, which followed an affair, which followed a simple but lust-filled look. Now, Joab "sounded the trumpet, and his men dispersed from the city, each returning to his home. And Joab went back to the king in Jerusalem" (20:22b). So the curtain drops on the saga of David's sins and their consequences for his own life, his family, and his nation—at least in his own lifetime.

David committed dark sins of omission: those kinds of sins that often miss our observation because they are passive; in David's case, this included indifference, injustice, and self-centeredness.

And David committed brighter sins of commission: the sins more easy to spot because they are actively committed. In David's case, this included pride, adultery, and murder.

Yet all of David's sins were apparent to God. He coveted his neighbor's wife. He stole his neighbor's wife by committing adultery. He deceived his neighbor. And he murdered him, and so brought dishonor on his own house. In all of this, David mocked God and despised God's Word. David, this poet-king after God's own heart, is really among the great sinners in the Bible. Have you thought of that before? David had received all of God's blessings, and then he despised God by rejecting his rule!

If you are a non-Christian, I want you to especially notice a couple of things about David's sin. First, note the very realistic accounts the Bible presents us. Even the characters who are the stars or protagonists in the story, the people you are supposed to root for, are shown as they really were. They are not airbrushed and perfect; they are full of faults and sins. The Bible is true. Its historicity, its veracity, its truth is reflected in its honesty concerning the failings of its greatest characters. Second, David's life is a good example for you to consider. Outward religiosity does not cancel inward sin. You cannot read the Bible long enough to wipe out murder; you cannot give enough money to the church to outweigh adultery or theft; you cannot become so involved in church that your sin will remain hidden from God's view and verdict.

Let me also appeal to you if you have some measure of power: be careful of it. Power corrupts not only in stories of fiction, like holders of the ring in J. R. R. Tolkien's *Lord of the Ring*. Power corrupts today just as it has throughout history. From the absolute monarchs of yesterday to the corrupt governors and mayors of today, power gives the corruption that exists in your soul an opportunity to exercise itself and grow stronger. Be very careful of it. An ancient Greek proverb says that the opposite of a friend is not an enemy but a flatterer (cf. Prov. 27:6). Be careful not to become incorrigible—unable to be corrected. You want to be so adamantine, so fixed, so unchanging only when you are perfected in heaven, and not a moment before. In the meantime, you should crave the ability to be corrected and to humbly receive instruction. Christ alone, of all of Adam's sons, is perfect.

My Christian brother or sister, hear this! Be sure that the virtues you observe in yourself do not give you a sense of license for hidden vices. Do not abuse your authority by indulging either sins of commission (things you do) or sins of omission (failing to do what you should do). Always keep the all-seeing eye of God in mind. One day you will give an account to this one who knows all things, and from his bar of justice there is no appeal.

And pray that we as a church would rely on the teaching of God's Word. Pray that we would grow in developing a culture typified by discipleship. Pray that God would protect us from sin and grow in us an attractive holiness. Pray also for the godliness of my own life as your pastor. Pray for me particularly that God would keep me from sin.

We can learn so much by considering David's sins, but we must go on.

DAVID REPENTS

As all of us have, David received God's blessings. As all of us have, David sinned grievously. And were that the whole story, it would be a sad tale. But David's life included a third component that made all the difference: he repented. In this way, he is *not* like all of us.

We have all been blessed, and we have all sinned. I can say both of those things without fear of contradiction. But I do not think every one of us has repented. If you are a non-Christian or even a fairly new Christian, I want to make sure you understand that the whole question of redemption from sin is much clearer in the New Testament than in the Old. The Old Testament sets up patterns and gives us promises; it narrates God's actions and tells us about him. But the New Testament brings all this to fruition in Jesus Christ.

With that said, the life of David is probably the most fully recorded life in the Bible, apart from the life of Jesus Christ himself. Abraham, Moses, David's son Solomon, and Paul are all major figures. But with David we get all the twists and turns, which is why he is such an immensely sympathetic figure, like Peter in the New Testament. David gives us hope because, by God's grace, his flaws and foibles do not finally destroy him. So we read about him, and we have hope.

Amid this terrible second half of this book, the account of David's sin is punctuated by some of the clearest examples in the Bible of an individual struggling against his sin. We don't get the complete picture with any one incident, but, putting them all together, we do get a composite picture that is fairly full. In the life of David as recorded in 2 Samuel, we find at least five steps for dealing with sin. You may find more in your own reading of the book, but let's note these five together now:

1. Rebuke

First, there is a rebuke. The most famous rebuke David receives is given by Nathan in chapter 12, after David had committed adultery with Bathsheba and had Uriah killed. This is such a moving story, my wife and I named our son after this courageous prophet:

> The LORD sent Nathan to David. When he came to him, he said, "There were two men in a certain town, one rich and the other poor. The rich man had a very large number of sheep and cattle, but the poor man had nothing except one little ewe lamb he had bought. He raised it, and it grew up with him and his children. It shared his food, drank from his cup and even slept in his arms. It was like a daughter to him.
>
> "Now a traveler came to the rich man, but the rich man refrained from taking one of his own sheep or cattle to prepare a meal for the traveler who had come to him. Instead, he took the ewe lamb that belonged to the poor man and prepared it for the one who had come to him."
>
> David burned with anger against the man and said to Nathan, "As surely as the LORD lives, the man who did this deserves to die! He must pay for that lamb four times over, because he did such a thing and had no pity."
>
> Then Nathan said to David, "You are the man! This is what the LORD, the God of Israel, says: 'I anointed you king over Israel, and I delivered you from the hand of Saul. I gave your master's house to you, and your master's wives into your arms. I gave you the house of Israel and Judah. And if all this had been too little, I would have given you even more. Why did you despise the word of the LORD by doing what is evil in his eyes? You struck down Uriah the Hittite with the sword and took his wife to be your own. You killed him with the sword of

the Ammonites. Now, therefore, the sword will never depart from your house, because you despised me and took the wife of Uriah the Hittite to be your own'" (12:1-10).

Nathan spoke clearly, directly, and carefully to his king about the king's sin. That took courage and love. Love for David.

Actually, the individual who rebukes David more than anyone else in 2 Samuel is not Nathan, though Nathan's story is the most famous—it is Joab. Joab confronts David about his sin on three different occasions: concerning David's refusal to forgive and restore Absalom (chapter 14); concerning David's numbering of the troops (24:3); and concerning David's inappropriate mourning for his son Absalom. In fact, this last rebuke is the most direct and rough rebuke we read. Here's the scene: David's army has just risked their lives in suppressing Absalom's revolt. They have won. And they now return to the city and find David their king in mourning for the enemy they have just killed. Joab is absolutely incensed:

> Joab was told, "The king is weeping and mourning for Absalom." And for the whole army the victory that day was turned into mourning, because on that day the troops heard it said, "The king is grieving for his son." The men stole into the city that day as men steal in who are ashamed when they flee from battle. The king covered his face and cried aloud, "O my son Absalom! O Absalom, my son, my son!"
>
> Then Joab went into the house to the king and said, "Today you have humiliated all your men, who have just saved your life and the lives of your sons and daughters and the lives of your wives and concubines. You love those who hate you and hate those who love you. You have made it clear today that the commanders and their men mean nothing to you. I see that you would be pleased if Absalom were alive today and all of us were dead. Now go out and encourage your men. I swear by the LORD that if you don't go out, not a man will be left with you by nightfall. This will be worse for you than all the calamities that have come upon you from your youth till now" (19:1-7).

Now that's a rebuke, particularly when it is given to a king!

Friend, rebukes are often the first step in dealing with sins. The lights have to be turned on. You cannot deal with a sin you cannot see, which is why you need to cultivate good relationships now, even if you don't think you need them. You want friends who will speak to you clearly, as you will most certainly need them to speak.

Now, having the lights come on does not always involve other people. Sometimes, the Lord convicts us directly. He will recall to our minds something we have read in Scripture, or something someone has said in the past. In chapter 24, for example, Joab's rebuke in verse 3 does not change David's decision to number his troops. It is not until the counting is completed that we read in verse 10, "David was conscience-stricken." The Lord is able to reach his children. As Proverbs says, "The LORD disciplines those he loves . . ." (Prov. 3:12).

Do you feel loved by God? He disciplines those he loves. Do not mistake his discipline for punishment. Thank God for his discipline, as David often did.

2. Confession

A second step for dealing with sin shown to us by David's life is confession. When Nathan confronts David for his sin with Bathsheba, does David deny it? Does he ask Nathan for proof, get angry, or have Nathan killed? No, he immediately humbles himself and says, "I have sinned against the LORD" (12:13). And when David feels convicted over numbering the troops, he says, "I have sinned greatly in what I have done" (24:10). Acknowledging your sin and describing your actions in the same way that God does is fundamental to change. No change can occur until you "fess up." A good diagnosis is half the cure. So David takes God's view about his own sins, and he confesses them.

3. Repentance

But more than good words are necessary. David backs up his words with action. And that is called repentance. This is a third—and vital—aspect of dealing with sin. When Joab rebukes David concerning his need to restore Absalom, David simply says, "Very well. I will do it" (14:21). David, confronted and convicted, submits to the one rebuking him. He changes his mind and so changes his direction. He repents. It happens again in chapter 19, when Joab confronts David for his inappropriate mourning over Absalom. Joab speaks to David, and then we read, "so the king got up" (19:8). Again, that is repentance.

Sometimes people mistake sorrow for repentance, but sorrow is the precursor to repentance. If sorrow leads to a change in life, Paul says in 2 Corinthians 7:10, then it is *godly sorrow,* and that is the beginning of repentance. *Worldly sorrow,* however, is mere grief. It is just sullen, sinking regret. It brings no change and no life. By God's grace, David repents of his sins. He grieves *and* he changes!

4. Taking Responsibility for the Consequences of Sin

Another step in dealing with sin that David displays is taking responsibility for the consequences of sins. This fourth step shows the sincerity of the confession and the maturity of the repentance. In chapter 24, when David repents of numbering the troops, he takes responsibility for the consequences of his actions. He prays to God, "Let your hand fall upon me and my family" (24:17; cf. 1 Chron. 21:17; Job 42:1-6). He knows the sin is his alone, and his enlivened heart longs for the punishment to belong to him alone.

5. Forgiveness

Finally, there is forgiveness. In the case of the numbering of the troops, an action that seems particularly aimed at God, David asks God for forgiveness: "David was conscience-stricken after he had counted the fighting men, and he said to the LORD, 'I have sinned greatly in what I have done. Now, O LORD, I beg you, take away the guilt of your servant. I have done a very foolish thing" (24:10). God's prophet then presents David with several punishments from which he can choose, and he chooses the one that leaves out any human intermediaries; he wants the punishment that comes directly from God, because, as he says, "his mercy is great" (24:14). David knows God is not tolerant and slack, but he also knows that God is not unmerciful and unloving. David knows that the one, true God is holy, loving, and full of mercy.

All the Bible's talk of God's holiness sounds foreign to our culture, but never miss the fact that God's holiness only highlights his mercy. God is more merciful than anyone you know. Are you aware of God's mercy and his tender kindness? What do we find in the last verse of 2 Samuel? "David built an altar to the LORD there and sacrificed burnt offerings and fellowship offerings. Then the LORD answered prayer in behalf of the land . . ." (24:25). God forgives David.

David has known and experienced God's forgiveness. He learned it from Nathan. The same prophet who confronted David over his sin with Bathsheba also told David about God's forgiveness: "The LORD has taken away your sin" (12:13b). Of course, God's forgiveness is rooted in God's mercy and not in David's virtue. But then that is the very nature of God's forgiveness. It trades on his character and his promise to be merciful to his own. So, referring to Solomon, God had told David through Nathan back in chapter 7,

> "I will be his father, and he will be my son. When he does wrong, I will punish him with the rod of men, with floggings inflicted by men. But my love will never be taken away from him, as I took it away from Saul, whom I removed from before you. Your house and your kingdom will endure forever before me; your throne will be established forever" (7:14-16).

David rested his request for forgiveness on God's own promises of faithful love.

What are you doing about your own sin today? Doubtless you attend church week after week with some sin on your mind. Probably, because you are such a sinner, you attend with the sins of other people on your mind—maybe sins they have committed against you. Our own sins, of course, are very hard to see. They dart around in the shadows and hide in the corners. Yet you have almost reached the end of this sermon, and perhaps God's Spirit has used the light of God's Word to begin exposing some of the sins that love to hide from your gaze. Not someone else's, but yours. Second Samuel teaches us how to deal with those sins.

Do you have relationships where you allow people to rebuke you? Especially if you are in a position of influence, do you have people around you like Nathan and Joab who can speak the truth to you? Don't ever think you are above such accountability. As somebody said to me just this last week about Washington, D.C., "The cemeteries in this city are full of *indispensable* people." You may feel as if life is permanent, but realize that the time will come when you will give an account to God; and you want to hear what God is going to say *before* he says it on that Day. Be willing to hear the truth about yourself now, so that you can live in light of that truth and prepare for that Day.

When people become members of this church, we often tell them that one of the most important things they can do is let other people get to know them. Then we work together to encourage a culture that cultivates forgiveness and change. That means we must keep God's Word central, we must learn to hear godly criticism with humility, and we must learn to be honest with other people. If you are not a member of a church, let me first implore you, become one!

According to God's Word, we should never sin. But when we do sin, our sin should always be followed—as David's was—by repentance.

CONCLUSION

One of those promises of God that we read a few moments ago in chapter 7 did not seem to come true in the history of Israel. Did you notice it? God said to David, "Your house and your kingdom will endure forever before me; your throne will be established forever" (7:16). We know from 2 Kings that Jerusalem was sacked and destroyed a little over three centuries later, in 587 B.C. The Babylonians carried most of the leaders into captivity. David's descendants continued, but they did not regain the throne, even when the Israelites resettled in Jerusalem in the time of Ezra and Nehemiah. So what happened? The promise that the Lord made to David about his descendants was fulfilled; but it was fulfilled in a way different from how David probably imagined it would be.

Let's go back to David's last words, the words we began with:

> "The God of Israel spoke,
>   the Rock of Israel said to me:
> 'When one rules over men in righteousness,
>   when he rules in the fear of God,
> he is like the light of morning at sunrise
>   on a cloudless morning,
> like the brightness after rain
>   that brings the grass from the earth'" (23:3-4).

Who has ever ruled so righteously? At the end of the day, we have to admit that David ruled like this only in the most approximate way. Finally, the only one whose reign has been so splendid, benevolent, and beneficent is God's. Only God's.

And David knew that. As he sings in his beautiful psalm in chapter 22,

> "As for God, his way is perfect;
>   the word of the LORD is flawless.
> He is a shield
>   for all who take refuge in him.
> For who is God besides the LORD?
>   And who is the Rock except our God?" (22:31-32).

As you study David's reign in this book, it becomes obvious that David's blessings were never to point ultimately to David, but *to God*. They were to make God's name great! When we go back to the blessings promised in chapter 7, we find that God did what he did "to redeem a people for himself, and to make a name for himself" (7:23). As David himself prays, "Do as you promised, so that your name will be great forever. Then men will say, 'The LORD Almighty is God over Israel!'" (7:25-26).

God rules over people in perfect righteousness. His reign is "like the light of morning at sunrise on a cloudless morning," "like the brightness after rain that brings the grass from the earth."

One day, through the mystery of the Incarnation, "the sun of righteousness [would] rise" (Mal. 4:2). David's passing, sinful kingship would be outshone and eclipsed by the glories of "great David's greater Son" and his kingdom—by the eternal rule and perfect reign of the Lord Jesus Christ. In Christ, the promises to David are fulfilled.

God is always faithful to fulfill his Word. We are made to know him as our Lord and king; but we, like David, have sinned against God. This is why God took on flesh and became a man, lived a perfect life, and died as a substitutionary sacrifice for the sins of all those who would ever turn from their sins and trust in him. And this is exactly what he calls us to do today—to repent and trust in Christ. If you want to know more about this, please talk to a Christian friend.

Certainly, our hope cannot be in David himself. There is hope for us only in Christ. Shouldn't our sins be punished? Yes, but if we trust Christ, our punishment falls on him! And just to make this point extremely clear, the Bible uses some of the most terrible sinners to play the roles of its greatest characters. Think about it: Moses, David, and Paul? All of these men were murderers of one sort or another. What a strange group for God to use. It's as if he simply wants to make our insufficiency and his all-sufficiency clear!

Friend, I don't know what sins are on your mind, but I know that Jesus can give you new life. He is the one who can forgive your sins and then lead and guide you perfectly. His rule is splendid and benevolent. I can tell you this from the experience of my own life, and it is the testimony of Scripture.

So did God fulfill his promise to David to have a descendant of his reign forever? Consider the last words of Jesus in that last chapter of the Bible:

> "Behold, I am coming soon! My reward is with me, and I will give to everyone according to what he has done. I am the Alpha and the Omega, the First and the Last, the Beginning and the End. . . .
>
> "I am the Root and the Offspring of David, and the bright Morning Star. . . .
>
> "Yes, I am coming soon" (Rev. 22:12-13, 16b, 20b).

David took responsibility for his own sins by confessing them and repenting of them. But Jesus—well, Jesus, though perfect, took responsibility for the sins of many, as he had said he would.[3]

Trust in him. Our hope is not in the president or in the director of the Department of Homeland Security. Our trust is not in the pastor or our boss. Our hope is in Christ. Only Christ can save us from what the hymn calls "the guilt within."

Surrender your rebellion and acknowledge his wonderful rule.

---

[3] Matt. 20:28; 26:28; Mark 10:45.

Let us pray:

O God, you know the things that consume our thoughts. Lord, you know the sins that cloud our minds and cause us to forget the final accounting we will give to you. O Lord, teach us that our biggest problem is not a potential terrorist act but the far more awesome problem of appearing before you, a righteous God, as sinners. And show us in your great mercy how to be under the rule and reign of our just and loving and merciful God, as you have revealed yourself to us in the Lord Jesus Christ. We pray for his sake. Amen.

Questions for Reflection

1. Why is good leadership like "the light of morning at sunrise on a cloudless morning"? Have you ever known any leaders like this? Why is good leadership like "the brightness after rain that brings the grass from the earth"? Have you known leaders like this?

2. Following up on question 1, would those who are in your care describe you this way in the positions of leadership you hold, whether in the home, at work, or in the community?

3. What does it mean to lead "in righteousness"? What does it mean to lead "in the fear of God"?

4. How can members of a congregation help its elders lead in the fear of God and not in the fear of man?

5. As we have seen, taking our gifts for granted will encourage pride in us; but pausing and enumerating them will encourage our hearts to be grateful and humble before God. Take a few moments to enumerate some of the gifts God has given you. Now enumerate some of the gifts he has given your church. With these gifts in mind, pray that God would give you a heart of gratitude for them and the desire to use them for his purposes and gain. It might also be helpful to spend a few moments meditating on Paul's words to the Corinthian believers: "For who makes you different from anyone else? What do you have that you did not receive? And if you did receive it, why do you boast as though you did not?" (1 Cor. 4:7).

6. We have considered the fact that all sin is fundamentally against God and not against others or ourselves. How should we as Christians employ this fact

in our evangelism among non-Christians? Do you take care to make this clear in your evangelistic conversations?

7. David's sin with Bathsheba, which wreaked havoc in his family and in his nation, began with one lust-filled look—one moment of letting his guard down. If we assume for a moment that not all of us are equally susceptible to the exact same sins, a question each one of us should ask ourselves is, "Where am I particularly susceptible?" What are the sins in your life that might seem small in the beginning but that could snowball?

8. What is "repentance"? Do you have to repent in order to be saved? Suppose a very close friend or family member calls himself a Christian but gives no sign of having repented of his sins. Should you rest in the fact that he calls himself a "Christian" and even distinctly remembers the time when he "first trusted Christ"? What is the most loving thing you could say to this friend or family member?

9. Let's take these steps of repentance one at a time:

- Are you able to receive the *rebukes* of others—even from individuals who don't deserve to give them? Are you willing, for the sake of love, to rebuke a brother or sister who is in sin?
- When was the last time you *confessed* sin to God? To another person? Are you willing to embarrass yourself before those you want to impress with a frank acknowledgment of your sin? (In doing so, of course, you should take care that no weaker or younger Christian is attracted to the sin you are confessing.)
- When you are confronted with your sin, either by another person or by the quick flashes of your conscience, do you take steps to *repent,* that is, to cease and desist? Or do you, honestly, go easy on yourself? Are you quick to point to circumstances? Can you think of a recent occasion where you went easy on yourself?
- Once you have confessed a sin and owned up to your responsibility, do you get angry when the other parties *still* ask you to *take responsibility for the consequences of your sin*? When was the last time you did that?
- How quickly would your spouse (or parent, sibling, friend, or work partner) say you *grant forgiveness*? Or would they say you tend to let bitterness fester? Or consider the question like this: Jesus told us to pray, "Forgive us our debts, as we also have forgiven our debtors" (Matt. 6:12). Would you really want God to answer that prayer?

10. How can a local church promote these five steps of repentance within its discipleship relationships? What are you doing to promote these things within your church?

11. Both what was good and what was bad about David point us to Christ. The fact that he was God's chosen king over God's people (what was good) points us to Christ's reign over God's people. Yet the fact that David sinned horribly (what was bad) also points us to Christ, because Christ alone would be without sin (David is not the one you should put your hope in!). What is wrong, therefore, with teaching a Bible study, a Sunday school lesson, or a sermon from 2 Samuel and referring only to David? How should we, as Christians, teach about David?

THE MESSAGE OF 1 KINGS: DECLINE

11

THE MESSAGE OF 1 KINGS: DECLINE

TINY TRAJECTORY CHANGES CAN BE TRAGIC [1]

A small difference in trajectory can make a big difference in destination. You know what I mean if you have ever crossed the Interstate 395 bridge into Washington, D.C. If you veer left at the Fourteenth Street Bridge fork after crossing the Potomac River, you will be at your D.C. destination in minutes. If you are not paying attention and remember you want that left fork two seconds too late, you will need to cancel that next appointment. A small difference in trajectory can make a big difference in destination.

A few months ago, my son Nathan and I were returning to our Weehauken Hotel in New Jersey from an evening jaunt into Manhattan, and somehow I ended up on the wrong highway just after coming out of the Lincoln Tunnel. I'm still not entirely sure how. I could see the road I wanted to be on, but we couldn't get to it from where we were. After indulging my male proclivity to resist asking directions for about forty-five minutes—and wandering through the close-by New Jersey suburbs—I finally stopped and asked for directions. We were back at our hotel in a matter of minutes. A small difference in trajectory can make a big difference in destination.

Sin often begins with what may feel like a minor concession—maybe an allowance for this shortcoming or a brief indulgence for that desire. But that simple change of trajectory can set you on course to a deadly destination.

People sometimes talk about the "unintended consequences" of an action, referring to an unexpected and unusual set of effects that follow the action. I don't know about you, but *most* of the consequences of my actions are unin-

---

[1] This sermon was originally preached on September 15, 2002, at Capitol Hill Baptist Church in Washington, D.C.

tended. Take almost any action that I carefully thought about beforehand, and you will find results of the action I certainly did not intend.

Maybe you are a non-Christian and are concerned that your life is headed in the wrong direction. Maybe you are concerned that our country is going downhill. Maybe you are a Christian who has noticed that your heart has grown cold. Perhaps you are concerned about the direction of the church.

INTRODUCING 1 KINGS

If you have any of these concerns, the books of 1 and 2 Samuel and 1 and 2 Kings should have more than an antiquarian's interest for you. If you listen carefully, they will speak vitally both to who you are and to your concerns. And that should interest all of us.

In these books, the nation of Israel makes some crucial trajectory changes. Ironically, the nation that Joshua led out of the wilderness into the Promised Land in order to be a witness to the nations makes a number of choices that make them a mere imitation of the nations. Taken together, then, these books constitute a call for repentance, for turning, for change. They tell the story of God's people rejecting God and of God's call to them to reject their rejection.

First and Second Kings contain the second half of this story, beginning with a stable, united kingdom under Solomon and ending with the fall of Jerusalem and mass deportation to Babylon almost four centuries later.

Our particular study here is in the book of 1 Kings, which is divided into four basic sections: Solomon's story (chapters 1–11); the kingdom's division (chapters 12–14); Israel's (the northern kingdom) decline (chapters 15–16); and Elijah and Ahab's story (chapters 17–22). These four divisions also provide a structure for our investigation, as we observe, respectively, the seeds of decline, two pictures of decline, the fruit of decline, and the ends of decline. I pray that through this study you will be warned about spiritual decline and will be armed against it.

THE SEEDS OF DECLINE: SOLOMON'S STORY (CHAPTERS 1–11)

First, we find the seeds of decline in the story of Solomon's reign, chapters 1–11. In particular, we learn that *religious decline can start in surprising places.*

Solomon's Blessings (Chapters 1–10)

The first ten chapters of 1 Kings cover Solomon's abundant blessings and all the hopefulness of his reign. In chapter 1, Solomon prevails in the dispute over who will succeed David. David gives his charge to Solomon in chapter 2, followed by David's death. In chapter 3, Solomon prays for wisdom and God grants it. The Lord's first appearance to Solomon occurs in this context. Solomon then demonstrates the wisdom that God has given him in the famous story of the two women who fight over one baby. Solomon's wisdom becomes even more evident in chapter 4 through his careful administration. In chapter 5, he prepares to build the temple of the Lord, and he builds it in chapter 6. He turns to building his palace in chapter 7, followed by his work to furnish the temple. In chapter 8, the glory of the Lord fills the temple, and Solomon dedicates the temple by prayer and worship of the Lord. The Lord appears to Solomon a second time, in chapter 9, to warn him against idolatry. It's strange to think that Solomon has to be warned about idolatry immediately following his construction of the temple. Some of Solomon's trade is recounted at the end of chapter 9. Then chapter 10 provides a summary of Solomon's wisdom and wealth:

> All King Solomon's goblets were gold, and all the household articles in the Palace of the Forest of Lebanon were pure gold. Nothing was made of silver, because silver was considered of little value in Solomon's days. . . .
>
> King Solomon was greater in riches and wisdom than all the other kings of the earth. The whole world sought audience with Solomon to hear the wisdom God had put in his heart (10:21, 23-24).

In many ways, Solomon sounds like the personification of those beautiful, final words of David we considered in our study of 2 Samuel:

> "The God of Israel spoke,
>   the Rock of Israel said to me:
> 'When one rules over men in righteousness,
>   when he rules in the fear of God,
> he is like the light of morning at sunrise
>   on a cloudless morning,
> like the brightness after rain
>   that brings the grass from the earth'" (2 Sam. 23:3-4).

God blessed Solomon remarkably, and he in turn remarkably blessed the nation.

Solomon was, of course, famous for his wisdom. We see it in his first words (1 Kings 1:52). We see it in his politics, as he shrewdly consolidates power in chapter 2. We see it in his practice of international trade, in chapter 9. And we see his wisdom's effects in the peace and prosperity of the nation under his leadership: "For he ruled over all the kingdoms west of the River, from Tiphsah to Gaza, and had peace on all sides. During Solomon's lifetime Judah and Israel, from Dan to Beersheba, lived in safety, each man under his own vine and fig tree" (4:24-25). Then after the dedication of the temple: "On the following day he sent the people away. They blessed the king and then went home, joyful and glad in heart for all the good things the LORD had done for his servant David and his people Israel" (8:66). The nation prospered with Solomon as king.

At the core of all Solomon's blessings was his relationship with God. In chapter 3, we read about his love for the Lord: "Solomon showed his love for the LORD by walking according to the statutes of his father David" (3:3a). In case you thought that speaking about a loving relationship with God is just a contemporary and casual evangelical-American way of speaking—as Muslim friends of mine have thought—notice that the idea is found not just in the New Testament but in the Old as well. According to the Bible, we can have a relationship with God, an experience with him, such that we can actually speak of loving the Lord, as Solomon does here.

Ultimately, it was because Solomon's heart was correctly disposed toward God that he made the kind of request he does in chapter 3. When the Lord says to Solomon, "Ask for whatever you want me to give you" (3:5), Solomon does not ask for what would just benefit him, he asks for what would bless others through him—wisdom. And he does this, I think, because of his relationship with God. Notice how God responds to this request: "The LORD was pleased that Solomon had asked for this" (3:10).

There is much more that we could say about the splendor and blessings of Solomon's reign.

Solomon's Sin and Idolatry (Chapter 11)

I wish we could just stop at chapter 10. But we must continue to chapter 11. There we find Solomon's sin, his idolatry, and his end. Solomon's non-Israelite wives lead Solomon into the worship of false gods, just as God, through Moses, had warned would happen when Israelites married foreigners who worshiped false gods: "And when you choose some of their daughters as wives for your sons and those daughters prostitute themselves to their gods, they will lead your sons to do the same" (Ex. 34:16). Therefore, we are not surprised in this chapter when adversaries arise and peace departs from the kingdom. Samuel had prophesied this: "If you fear the LORD and serve and obey him and do not rebel against his commands, and if both you and the king who reigns over you follow the LORD your God—good! But if you do not obey the LORD, and if you rebel against his commands, his hand will be against you, as it was against your fathers" (1 Sam. 12:14-15). Solomon's death is also recorded in chapter 11.

So what happened? According to verse 9, Solomon's heart "turned away from the LORD" (11:9). Again, this is not simply the subjective and relational speech of contemporary evangelicals. It's Old Testament speech. Solomon's heart turned away from the Lord! The kind of Christianity we learn from the Bible and experience in our lives together in the church is not just a bunch of head knowledge. It is not simply a set of doctrines that we believe. It involves the affections of our hearts: whom we love, whom we trust, whom we live in relationship with. Sadly, Solomon, with all of his wonderful human wisdom, turned his heart away from the Lord and placed it on other gods (11:8, 10). We are under no illusions that he loved God perfectly earlier in the book (see 3:3b). But the love he did have, he turned away from in order to worship idols.

God had warned Solomon about idolatry (9:6-9). But now, as a result of his idolatry, the Lord promises him, "I will tear it [the kingdom] out of the hand of your son" (11:12). What a terrible legacy to leave your children—disobedience and its many consequences! The amount of money Solomon left his son mattered not. His disobedience was his most significant legacy. This inheritance far outweighed whatever material prosperity Solomon left for him. So the God who brought his people out of Egypt into the Promised Land, the God who gave Solomon his wisdom, promised to tear the kingdom out of the hands of Solomon's descendants because Solomon and his people "have forsaken me and worshiped Ashtoreth the goddess of the Sidonians, Chemosh the god of the Moabites, and Molech the god of the Ammonites, and have not walked in my ways, nor done what is right in my eyes, nor kept my statutes and laws as David, Solomon's father, did" (11:33).

Solomon was greatly blessed, but he also greatly sinned. Great gifts do not excuse great sin! If you are not a Christian, I hope you will consider this. Many people in our nation have good religious upbringings. But all the religious knowledge and religious practice in the world will not make up for having a *heart* turned away from God and his ways. According to the Bible, this is the natural state of everyone's heart. Our hearts are more attached to sin, to created things, and to ourselves than they are to God. In other words, sin starts with the terrible affliction of loving created things more than our Creator. Then all the actions that we call "sins" simply flow out of our wrongly oriented hearts.

So ask yourself this question, and the truth of your answer matters more to you than to anyone else: do you love the Lord? What does it mean when you say you love the Lord?

Now, there is no law that we can pass to remedy the state of sinful hearts. I am very thankful for the work of people in our government, but the government cannot provide what we most need. The human heart is beyond the power of the most searching court, the most powerful military, and the most effective legislature in the world. As Abraham Lincoln said, "With public sentiment, nothing can fail; without it, nothing can succeed. Consequently he who molds public sentiment goes deeper than he who enacts statutes or pronounces decisions. He makes statutes and decisions possible or impossible to be executed."[2]

If we want to see people's hearts change, we must pray. Changing hearts is God's work. God has come to dwell with us more than he ever did in the great temple built by Solomon. And it is through this greater dwelling place of God with man—the Lord Jesus Christ—that the answer to sin is found.

It is our work as Christians, however, to share and to live out the good news. It is also our responsibility to warn people of their sin. This is not the responsibility primarily of the Congress and courts! Our land may be financially sound and yet morally bankrupt, even as Solomon's Israel became. At the height of their foreign trade, the cancer of idolatry was already spreading in the land.

Christian, I hope you realize that in this life you will never experience so much blessing, material or spiritual, that you will be placed beyond sin's grasp or beyond the call to obedience. Do not follow Solomon's example here. Do not repay God's blessings to you with sin. Even the best among us struggle with sins that must be forgiven by Christ and forsaken by God's power.

Pray for your pastors, elders, and other church leaders, that we would be faithful stewards of all the good that God has committed to our hands; that we would not respond to God's great blessings on the church with callous sins. Pray that we would be models of spiritual diligence, even during times of spiritual blessing. Pray that we as a church would not take our blessings for granted, and that our blessings as a church would not lull us into spiritual indifference over the things that still need to change.

Religious decline can start in surprising places.

TWO PICTURES OF DECLINE: THE KINGDOM'S DIVISION (CHAPTERS 12–14)

But we must move on from the seeds of decline planted in Solomon's reign to the two pictures of decline that emerge in chapters 12–14. In these chapters, we read the account of Solomon's son and successor, Rehoboam, and the man who leads a rebellion against him, Jeroboam. As a result of this rebellion, the kingdom divides between the southern tribes of Judah and Benjamin (referred to as Judah) and the ten northern tribes (referred to col-

---

[2] Cited in Philip Van Doren Stern, ed., *The Life and Writings of Abraham Lincoln,* 2000 Modern Library Paperback Edition (New York: Random House, 1940), 472-473.

lectively as Israel). The southern kingdom centers on Jerusalem and maintains descendants of David on the throne, while the northern kingdom of Israel centers on Samaria. In these two pictures, we learn that *religious decline can have different appearances.*

These three chapters can be summarized pretty quickly. In chapter 12, Rehoboam succeeds his late father Solomon. He makes unreasonable demands on the people, attested to by his ridiculous boast, "my little finger is thicker than my father's waist" (12:10). He does not mean that he is physically gigantic. He is simply responding to the people who are complaining about the amount of work—conscripted labor—they had to do under Solomon. "You haven't seen anything yet!" Rehoboam basically responds. "I'm going to require even more." So Jeroboam leads the northern tribes to revolt and then into idolatry. Chapter 13 contains a remarkable sign of God's judgment on Jeroboam's idolatry, involving two prophets. And chapter 14 tells of Jeroboam's end. It also summarizes Rehoboam's reign in Jerusalem.

At first glance, Rehoboam and Jeroboam seem pretty different, apart from their names. Rehoboam, the grandson of King David and son of King Solomon, was groomed and prepared for the throne. But Jeroboam—who was he? He grew up without his father and had nothing like royal blood (see 11:26). Despite his royal upbringing, Rehoboam, evidently, was stupid in how he dealt with his people. He was a man of hubris. Jeroboam, on the other hand, was a savvy manager of people. And Solomon had noticed his talent years earlier: "Now Jeroboam was a man of standing, and when Solomon saw how well the young man did his work, he put him in charge of the whole labor force of the house of Joseph" (11:28).

Yet the Lord would use Jeroboam to chasten the house of David for the sins of Solomon. A prophet of the Lord, Ahijah, comes to Jeroboam and tells him,

> "this is what the LORD, the God of Israel, says: 'See, I am going to tear the kingdom out of Solomon's hand and give you ten tribes. But for the sake of my servant David and the city of Jerusalem, which I have chosen out of all the tribes of Israel, he will have one tribe'" (11:31-32).

Presumably having heard of this prophecy, Solomon (eerily reprising the role Saul had played in the life of Solomon's father, David) tries to kill Jeroboam. He seems to fear that Jeroboam is the Lord's new anointed one. So Jeroboam flees to Egypt and lives there until Solomon dies (11:40). When Solomon dies, Jeroboam is sent for, and many begin looking to him as an important player in the succession. Rehoboam, this one born to the throne, handles the initial parlaying with his own people so poorly that Jeroboam has his opportunity. He leads the ten northern tribes to rebel, and the nation of Israel divides in two.

But for all their differences, Rehoboam and Jeroboam had one great, overriding similarity: they were both idolatrous. Solomon's son received more than the throne and the genes of his father; he received his sins. Under Rehoboam's leadership, the southern kingdom of Judah

> did evil in the eyes of the LORD. By the sins they committed they stirred up his jealous anger more than their fathers had done. They also set up for themselves high places, sacred stones and Asherah poles on every high hill and under every spreading tree. There were even male shrine prostitutes in the land; the people engaged in all the detestable practices of the nations the LORD had driven out before the Israelites (14:22-24).

Again, consider the irony: the nations that Judah replaced, Judah imitated.

Jeroboam, too, with all of his skill and talent, led his people in the northern kingdom into idolatry. We don't know if the northern tribes followed the same unabashed course of Canaanite paganism that flourished under Rehoboam in Judah, but the syncretistic religion that grew up in the north was more personally tied to the king himself. Notice how closely the author associates the king with Israel's idolatry:

> After seeking advice, *the king made* two golden calves. *He said* to the people, "It is too much for you to go up to Jerusalem. Here are your gods, O Israel, who brought you up out of Egypt." One *he set up* in Bethel, and the other in Dan. And this thing became a sin; the people went even as far as Dan to worship the one there.
>
> *Jeroboam built* shrines on high places and *appointed* priests from all sorts of people, even though they were not Levites. *He instituted* a festival on the fifteenth day of the eighth month, like the festival held in Judah, and *offered* sacrifices on the altar. This *he did* in Bethel, *sacrificing* to the calves *he had made*. And at Bethel *he also installed* priests at the high places *he had made*. On the fifteenth day of the eighth month, a month of *his own choosing, he offered* sacrifices on the altar *he had built* at Bethel. So *he instituted* the festival for the Israelites and *went up* to the altar to make offerings (12:28-33).

Do you see how personally Jeroboam is implicated in all this? When Ahijah the prophet promised him the ten northern tribes, he also (speaking for the Lord) promised that Jeroboam would be blessed with a dynasty as enduring as David's "*if* you do whatever I command you and walk in my ways and do what is right in my eyes by keeping my statutes and commands" (11:38). But Jeroboam did not do this. He behaved like the Israelites in the wilderness all over again, making golden calves, of all things! If you decided to head down the road of idolatry in Israel, surely you would choose some image besides the one that had brought such trouble in the wilderness, wouldn't you? Yet Jeroboam made not one but two golden calves, brilliant genius of sin that he was. Then he placed them at both ends of the nation so that idolatry would be convenient for the people. And the author is crystal clear about Jeroboam's responsibility: *he* made, *he* built, *he* instituted, and so forth. This was a man-made religion, not the real, God-made one! But that's the problem with the kind of gifts Jeroboam had— the competence and power; sometimes such people begin to think that they can do anything, even tailor-make their own religion.

In chapter 13, an unnamed man of God cries out against Jeroboam's idolatry and causes Jeroboam's hand to shrivel. The man of God is then killed himself after he disobeys God's Word. What's the point? God will judge idolatry and disobedience to his Word, no matter who commits the transgression. Jeroboam, sadly, does not learn the lesson:

> Even after this, Jeroboam did not change his evil ways, but once more appointed priests for the high places from all sorts of people. Anyone who wanted to become a priest he consecrated for the high places. This was the sin of the house of Jeroboam that led to its downfall and to its destruction from the face of the earth (13:33-34).

In chapter 14, the prophet Ahijah returns to the scene to thunderously denounce Jeroboam in the name of the Lord: "You have done more evil than all who lived before you. You have made for yourself other gods, idols made of metal; you have provoked me to anger and thrust me behind your back" (14:9). Ahijah then promises that Israel will be uprooted and scattered "because of the sins Jeroboam has committed and has caused Israel to commit" (14:16). Leaders bear tremendous responsibility before God!

Jeroboam, Rehoboam, and their nations should have heeded God's Word. Rehoboam may have been inept and Jeroboam may have been savvy, but they were united in iniquity. Together they divided the nation, and separately they led their people into idolatry.

Perhaps you are skeptical by nature. Maybe you think it's all man-made, like the religion of Jeroboam. Someone devises a scheme for giving hope to the masses and getting paid in the process. It's all artificial. As for you, well, you are not particularly religious.

If this is you, I would simply urge you to reconsider your self-assessment. Maybe you, like all of us, *are* deeply religious. It's exposed in what you trust, what you do, how you spend your money and time, what you hope in, and what causes you to despair. All these things expose your real religion. Depending on how you answer such questions, you probably will find—if you reflect carefully—that the question is not *if* you are a worshiper, but *whom* or *what* you worship.

Jeroboam and Rehoboam were both confused about whom they worshiped, and it hurt the countries they led. After all, how a culture responds toward God and his laws is the most important thing about it. False notions of God, the afterlife, judgment, the good, or the purpose of life are a bane to any nation.[3]

No man-made religion, like Jeroboam's, will answer the need we have for the true God. We are creatures made in the image of the only God who exists. And we need the true high priest whom God has appointed—Jesus Christ. As the book of Hebrews says,

> When Christ came as high priest of the good things that are already here, he went through the greater and more perfect tabernacle that is not man-made, that is to say, not a part of this creation. He did not enter by means of the blood of goats and calves; but he entered the Most Holy Place once for all by his own blood, having obtained eternal redemption (Heb. 9:11-12).

The Lord Jesus Christ is our hope. My Christian friend, what are you relying on? What are you trusting in? I hope that you realize your virtues sink in comparison with your sins. The wrong thing, whether done poorly or well, is still the wrong thing. No set of talents or virtues can make up for rebelling against God. They did not for Jeroboam—who personally received the promises of God—and they won't for you. Only Christ will do for you what you need.

As a church, regardless of our other strong or weak points, we must ask ourselves the question, "Are we following God?" Those of us who are leaders in the church must continually refocus ourselves on the question, "Are we leading the church in following God?" Other responsibilities and questions may arise in the course of leadership, and we must be good stewards of these other things. But overriding everything, we must continually refocus our attention on whether we are leading the church to follow God.

Anything less is dangerous—even disastrous—regardless of how good it may look.

Religious decline can have different appearances.

---

[3] If you want to read more about that in the history of the American nation, get Michael Novak's book *On Two Wings: Humble Faith and Common Sense at the American Founding* (San Francisco: Encounter, 2002), where he cites quotations from the founding fathers of America. Though they would not have all signed the same theological statement, they shared some basic religious ideas that they felt were necessary for the American experiment to work.

THE FRUIT OF DECLINE: ISRAEL'S PLUMMET (CHAPTERS 15–16)

So much for the seeds of decline and the two pictures of decline. We turn now to look at the fruit of decline, which we particularly see in chapters 15 and 16. These two chapters cover several decades and describe the northern kingdom of Israel's quick plummet.

Ultimately, we learn that *religious decline can cause other kinds of decline.*

Let me briefly summarize the two chapters for you. In chapter 15, Rehoboam's son Abijah briefly reigns as king over the southern kingdom of Judah. He is then followed by the long reign of Abijah's righteous son Asa.

Meanwhile in Israel, Jeroboam's son Nadab is Jeroboam's only descendant to ever sit on this throne. An Israelite named Baasha kills Nadab and the rest of his family and then assumes the throne. In chapter 16 Baasha is succeeded by his son Elah, who is then killed and succeeded by one of his officials named Zimri. Zimri, in turn, is pursued by the army commander Omri. Eventually, Zimri commits suicide and Omri becomes king. Omri is then succeeded by his son, Ahab, whom we will focus on in the next section. All of this occurs over several decades.

Did you notice how many of these kings of Israel were succeeded by someone who killed them? In the space of several decades, there were effectively three assassinations! That should give you some idea of the character of these kings.

About Nadab we read, "He did evil in the eyes of the LORD, walking in the ways of his father [Jeroboam] and in his sin, which he had caused Israel to commit" (1 Kings 15:26).

About Baasha we read, "He did evil in the eyes of the LORD, walking in the ways of Jeroboam and in his sin, which he had caused Israel to commit" (15:34).

About Baasha and his son Elah, we read of, ". . . all the sins Baasha and his son Elah had committed and had caused Israel to commit, so that they provoked the LORD, the God of Israel, to anger by their worthless idols" (16:13).

About Zimri we read of, ". . . the sins he had committed, doing evil in the eyes of the LORD and walking in the ways of Jeroboam and in the sin he had committed and had caused Israel to commit" (16:19).

About Omri we read, "Omri did evil in the eyes of the LORD and sinned more than all those before him" (16:25). And it was no small, mean group of sinners that preceded him!

About Ahab we read,

> Ahab son of Omri did more evil in the eyes of the LORD than any of those before
> him. He not only considered it trivial to commit the sins of Jeroboam son of
> Nebat, but he also married Jezebel daughter of Ethbaal king of the Sidonians,
> and began to serve Baal and worship him. He set up an altar for Baal in the tem-
> ple of Baal that he built in Samaria. Ahab also made an Asherah pole and did
> more to provoke the LORD, the God of Israel, to anger than did all the kings of
> Israel before him (16:30-33).

It just got worse and worse! The northern kingdom quickly deteriorated, sinking into repeated lawless revolts against the king, which of course mirrored and symbolized their forsaking of God's law. And the premature and violent deaths of their kings were tragic and ironic reminders of what God was preparing for them because of their rebellion against him.

I wonder if you can see any of the signs in your life of your rebellion against God. Maybe you think the question of your rebellion against God is a private matter, best kept between you and God; that it is self-contained like nuclear waste (we hope), sealed up in one place. It cannot get out, you think, and there is no reason to believe that the bad effects of your rebellion against God will seep into other parts of your life.

But really, do you think that flouting God's law will have no consequences? Admittedly, many bad things happen to us that do not directly result from our own rebellion against God. In the book of Job, the most righteous man on earth goes through the most suffering. Having said that, it would be wrong to conclude, for your psychological comfort, that sin will have no dire effects in your life. It does, and if you know your own life and the lives of your friends well, you have seen it again and again. In our study of David in 2 Samuel, we saw the spreading consequences of David's look, his lust, and his actions—a family was divided and a nation went to war with itself!

Ungodliness affects more than just your religion. It affects your whole life, your family, your work, your neighborhood. Maybe even more. What if the 9/11 hijacker Mohammed Atta, who helped fly a passenger airplane into New York City's World Trade Center, had believed that taking human life was wrong? What if he had been trained to appreciate the innocence of noncombatants and to even love his neighbor as himself? Personal morality matters.

"Public" morality also matters. The brief summaries above of the reigns of the kings of Judah and Israel remind us of the importance of our public leaders. As we considered in our study of 2 Samuel, ruling well both brings glory to God and benefits the nation. If you are a public servant, allow me to encourage you: pursuing godliness in your own life and in the prosecution of your duties will do good for the community. You have the opportunity to promote education; to improve the moral tenor of the community; to enhance the prosperity of your city; and to enact laws and pass budgets that protect life, protect property, and preserve order. All of these goods are given to our cities and nation—in substantial part—through your work in public service. Thank you. Do it well for the public good and God's glory.

At the same time, I remember hearing one former president refer to his campaign victory with the words, "you put your hopes in us." And I remember thinking, "Mr. President, I did vote for you, but I certainly never 'put my hopes' in you!" My vote is decided on a limited amount of knowledge, for important but limited reasons, for important but limited goals. But I will never put my hopes in any politician. I will never put my hopes in the congregation or any member of it. And certainly I will never put my hopes in myself. No, I put my hopes only in Christ, the "KING OF KINGS AND LORD OF LORDS" (Rev. 19:16).

Public officials, you have important roles and a wonderful opportunity to display God's character; but, thank God, you have limited roles. Our hope is in God alone.

As for you, Christian, I hope that you are sensitive to how the Lord disciplines you for your sins. Richard Sibbes, the justly celebrated seventeenth-century Puritan, was fond of saying, "you can read the sin in the cross." What he meant was, we can often determine what sins we might have committed based on the affliction, trouble, or trial (what he referred to as a "cross") we find ourselves bearing. For instance, Sibbes was corresponding with one person who had found himself lonely and, therefore, slowing in spiritual growth and becoming coldhearted. In response, Sibbes pointed to the sin that the man had committed by separating himself from God's people when they gathered. This sin of separation had precipitated the loneliness, the slowing in spiritual growth, and the coldheartedness. In short, Sibbes read the sin in the cross. We cannot always do as much, but we often can.

Friend, look at the problems in your life. You can be sure that at least some of them can be traced back to your inattention to some good provision God has given you in Christ. *Religious decline can cause other kinds of decline.*

Whatever straits your sins have brought you into right now, whatever crosses they have brought, repent of those sins and trust God again. We must do this individually and we must do this as a church. If we take our focus off following God, we will lose our purpose for existing as a church and as individual Christians.

THE ENDS OF DECLINE: ELIJAH AND AHAB'S STORY (CHAPTERS 17–22)

Finally, we should observe the ends of decline, which we find in chapters 17–22 in the famous stories of Elijah and King Ahab of Israel. Here we learn that *religious decline ends either in repentance or in the judgment of God.*

This final section of the book begins, really, at 16:29 with the summary of Ahab's reign, including his sin. Chapter 17 then recounts a couple of miracles connected with Elijah, which demonstrate that he is God's spokesman. God supernaturally feeds Elijah through ravens, then uses Elijah to feed a Gentile widow way up in Sidonian Zarephath. In what amounts to a resurrection, God then gives Elijah the power to bring the woman's dead son back to life.

Chapter 18 presents the famous story of Elijah and the prophets of Baal. In a sense, this episode acts as a little recap of Exodus, where God demonstrated his power over the gods of the Egyptians in a spectacular way. Here, the story begins when Elijah accuses Ahab of abandoning the Lord's commands and challenges him to meet him on Mount Carmel with the prophets of Baal (Baal is the god of nature and weather, and the northern kingdom of Israel has been experiencing a drought and a severe famine for some time):

> So Ahab sent word throughout all Israel and assembled the prophets on Mount Carmel. Elijah went before the people and said, "How long will you waver between two opinions? If the LORD is God, follow him; but if Baal is God, follow him."
>
> But the people said nothing.
>
> Then Elijah said to them, "I am the only one of the LORD's prophets left, but Baal has four hundred and fifty prophets. Get two bulls for us. Let them choose one for themselves, and let them cut it into pieces and put it on the wood but not set fire to it. I will prepare the other bull and put it on the wood but not set fire to it. Then you call on the name of your god, and I will call on the name of the LORD. The god who answers by fire—he is God."
>
> Then all the people said, "What you say is good."
>
> Elijah said to the prophets of Baal, "Choose one of the bulls and prepare it first, since there are so many of you. Call on the name of your god, but do not light the fire." So they took the bull given them and prepared it.
>
> Then they called on the name of Baal from morning till noon. "O Baal, answer us!" they shouted. But there was no response; no one answered. And they danced around the altar they had made.
>
> At noon Elijah began to taunt them. "Shout louder!" he said. "Surely he is a god! Perhaps he is deep in thought, or busy, or traveling. Maybe he is sleeping and must be awakened." So they shouted louder and slashed themselves with swords and spears, as was their custom, until their blood flowed. Midday passed,

and they continued their frantic prophesying until the time for the evening sacrifice. But there was no response, no one answered, no one paid attention.

Then Elijah said to all the people, "Come here to me." They came to him, and he repaired the altar of the LORD, which was in ruins. Elijah took twelve stones, one for each of the tribes descended from Jacob, to whom the word of the LORD had come, saying, "Your name shall be Israel." With the stones he built an altar in the name of the LORD, and he dug a trench around it large enough to hold two seahs of seed. He arranged the wood, cut the bull into pieces and laid it on the wood. Then he said to them, "Fill four large jars with water and pour it on the offering and on the wood."

"Do it again," he said, and they did it again.

"Do it a third time," he ordered, and they did it the third time. The water ran down around the altar and even filled the trench.

At the time of sacrifice, the prophet Elijah stepped forward and prayed: "O LORD, God of Abraham, Isaac and Israel, let it be known today that you are God in Israel and that I am your servant and have done all these things at your command. Answer me, O LORD, answer me, so these people will know that you, O LORD, are God, and that you are turning their hearts back again."

Then the fire of the LORD fell and burned up the sacrifice, the wood, the stones and the soil, and also licked up the water in the trench (18:20-38).

After Elijah's spectacular demonstration of the Lord God's power, the people repent and are blessed, as we see in the following verses. This, too, is like a little picture of what God had done for them in the Exodus:

When all the people saw this, they fell prostrate and cried, "The LORD—he is God! The LORD—he is God!"

Then Elijah commanded them, "Seize the prophets of Baal. Don't let anyone get away!" They seized them, and Elijah had them brought down to the Kishon Valley and slaughtered there.

And Elijah said to Ahab, "Go, eat and drink, for there is the sound of a heavy rain." So Ahab went off to eat and drink, but Elijah climbed to the top of Carmel, bent down to the ground and put his face between his knees.

"Go and look toward the sea," he told his servant. And he went up and looked.

"There is nothing there," he said.

Seven times Elijah said, "Go back."

The seventh time the servant reported, "A cloud as small as a man's hand is rising from the sea."

So Elijah said, "Go and tell Ahab, 'Hitch up your chariot and go down before the rain stops you.'"

Meanwhile, the sky grew black with clouds, the wind rose, a heavy rain came on and Ahab rode off to Jezreel (18:39-45).

Chapters 19–22 continue to focus on these two characters, Elijah and Ahab. In chapter 19, Elijah flees to Judah, the Lord speaks to him, and Elijah anoints Elisha as his successor. Chapter 20 presents Ahab's victory over the Arameans and his condemnation by a prophet of the Lord. In chapter 21, Ahab's wife Jezebel helps Ahab connive and kill in order to steal Naboth's vineyard. The Lord sends Elijah to condemn them. Chapter 22 records Ahab's defeat and death, the reign of Jehoshaphat over Judah, and the reign of Ahaziah, Ahab's son, over Israel.

Throughout these final chapters, Israel continues to decline. Yet throughout that decline, God stood astride Israel's path, confronting them as they tried to move away from him. The Lord, not Baal, brought a drought. And then the Lord, not Baal, brought rain.

God also raised up Elijah—that greatest of the prophets before John the Baptist—to call for repentance. Through this prophet who fed the Gentile widow and raised her son to life, God taught the Israelites that life comes from him and that he will use his messengers to bring life again to his people. And remember, the widow was a foreigner. God is the real and true God, not just of Israel, but of the whole world. He alone is the author of life.

Elijah was the Lord's chosen instrument for this work of confronting Israel. His very name means "My God is Yahweh." *El* means "God"; the *i* makes it possessive—"my God"; and *jah* is short for "Yahweh." So, Eli-jah means "my God is Yahweh." His name was his calling card. It let people know what he was all about. Elijah knew the Lord and had been commissioned to reintroduce him to God's own people, and that meant teaching God's Word.

In chapter 19, after Elijah flees to Judah, we read,

> The LORD said, "Go out and stand on the mountain in the presence of the LORD, for the LORD is about to pass by."
>
> Then a great and powerful wind tore the mountains apart and shattered the rocks before the LORD, but the LORD was not in the wind. After the wind there was an earthquake, but the LORD was not in the earthquake. After the earthquake came a fire, but the LORD was not in the fire. And after the fire came a gentle whisper. When Elijah heard it, he pulled his cloak over his face and went out and stood at the mouth of the cave.
>
> Then a voice said to him, "What are you doing here, Elijah?" (19:11-13).

Notice that God determines to reveal himself verbally, rather than through mere acts of power. God's own Word would be at the center of Elijah's ability to know God and to bring God's people back to knowing him. When God calls his people to repent, he will do it by his Word. He reveals himself when he speaks.

God also called Ahab to be the king who would lead his nation to repentance. So God sends his prophets to begin the process by rebuking Ahab. Do you remember how humbly and kindly King David received the prophet Nathan's rebuke for his sin with Bathsheba? Well, that is nothing like how King Ahab received the prophet Elijah's rebuke. When he met Elijah on the road, Ahab caustically asked, "Is that you, you troubler of Israel?" (18:17). This leader was so blind that he could not see who the real troubler of Israel was—himself! He was the one bringing problems on his nation. He led the nation into sin, with its manifold and terrible consequences. The man in front of him, however, brought blessing on the nation. The writer summarizes all this by saying, "There was never a man like Ahab, who sold himself to do evil in the eyes of the LORD, urged on by Jezebel his wife. He behaved in the vilest manner by going after idols, like the Amorites the LORD drove out before Israel" (21:25-26).

King David sinned but repented. In 1 Kings, we have several kings who sinned but never repented. The nation was being given kings who reflected the nation's own character. Israel was hard-hearted toward God and his Word, so God gave them kings who were heard-hearted toward God and his Word.

And yet, we have to say, Ahab repents! Who would have thought! After Ahab has Naboth killed and steals his vineyard, Elijah confronts him and promises that God will destroy him and cut off his descendants:

> When Ahab heard these words, he tore his clothes, put on sackcloth and fasted. He lay in sackcloth and went around meekly.
>
> Then the word of the LORD came to Elijah the Tishbite: "Have you noticed how Ahab has humbled himself before me? Because he has humbled himself, I will not bring this disaster in his day, but I will bring it on his house in the days of his son" (21:27-29).

We don't know what happened to Ahab after this act of repentance. We are not told. I know the whole trajectory of his life was not good; and we see that any repentance by the nation as a whole was limited and temporary. Listen to how the book of 1 Kings ends:

> Ahaziah son of Ahab became king of Israel in Samaria in the seventeenth year of Jehoshaphat king of Judah, and he reigned over Israel two years. He did evil in the eyes of the LORD, because he walked in the ways of his father and mother and in the ways of Jeroboam son of Nebat, who caused Israel to sin. He served and worshiped Baal and provoked the LORD, the God of Israel, to anger, just as his father had done (22:51-53).

Sad to say, that final paragraph seems to summarize the book well, doesn't it? God's Word came through Elijah and led to repentance in Israel for a time. But temporary repentance is not true repentance.

Do you know the difference between temporary repentance and true repentance? To determine if you do, ask yourself whether you have a sense of your own sin and your need to find forgiveness, not so much from someone else or from yourself, but from God. That is why God sent Christ. Christ took on himself the punishment for the sins of all those who would truly repent and trust in him. Will you respond in true repentance and faith in the work of Christ?

Some Christians read the book of 1 Kings and wonder what it has to say to us as a nation. Are we supposed to physically execute everybody who doesn't agree with us? Hardly. Please know that this book does not call us to establish true religion by law. The time of a theocracy—a nation ruled directly by God's revealed law—has passed with the coming of Christ and the establishment of his international church. There will come a future day when King Jesus will visibly reign, and we live in the hope of that day. But we will not accomplish it ourselves.

The political doctrine that says the state is responsible for the work of the Christian church is called Erastianism, and it is a corruption of biblical teaching. The state is not to be responsible for the preaching of the Word, the administration of baptism and the Lord's Supper, and the practice of church discipline. Rather, the state is to be responsible for making sure that churches are left free and unhindered in such work. We are not called to legislate Christianity but rather to legislate freedom for Christianity to be practiced. That does mean working against an aggressive secularism, which, frankly, is antagonistic to freedom. If we want to champion freedom, we must work for freedom for practicing religion. And it is the function of those in public life and government to promote and protect that freedom for the practice of religion.

Immediately after the American Revolution, our very thoughtful Presbyterian friends had to rewrite one portion of their confession of faith because it included an establishmentarian, or Erastian, view of the church and state. Chapter 23 of the original Westminster Confession of Faith said that it is the responsibility of the state to provide for the true religion. John Witherspoon, one of the leading Presbyterian theologians in America and also one of the leading proponents of the American Revolution, knew he needed to biblically rethink this idea. In fact, his work to reformulate the relationship between the church and state before the revolution was one of the factors in causing it. Here is part of the 1787 revision of the Westminster Confession on the role of the government and religion:

As Jesus Christ hath appointed a regular government and discipline in his Church, no law of any commonwealth should interfere with, let or hinder, the due exercise thereof, among the voluntary members of *any* denomination of Christians, according to their own profession and belief. It is the duty of civil magistrates to protect the person and good name of all their people, in such an effectual manner as that no person be suffered, either upon pretence of religion or infidelity, to offer any indignity, violence, abuse or injury to any other person whatsoever: and to take order, that all religious and ecclesiastical assemblies be held without molestation or disturbance (chapter 23, article 3).

As great as Elijah was, it was not finally up to him to establish the kingdom of God. That would be done by the greatest of all the prophets, the one to whom all other prophets pointed, Jesus Christ—the Word become flesh. Neither was it finally given to any of the kings (even the good ones) to establish God's kingdom. Again, these kings merely pointed to the great coming king, Christ. What does this mean for you personally? It means you need to take responsibility for the ways that you have rejected God. You need to stop turning away from him and running from his Word. You need to repent of your sins and look to Christ as the Word of God and as King.

If you are a Christian, it means you must continue to repent through every day of life that God gives you.

May our church be characterized by sincere repentance and the following of God's Word. May we always remember that *religious decline ends either in repentance or in the judgment of God.*

CONCLUSION

At one point in the story, Elijah, fairly down-in-the-mouth, says, "I'm the only one left," thinking that he was the only Israelite who had repented, believed, and known God's forgiveness (1 Kings 19:14). The Lord rebukes him and says "I have seven thousand in Israel who have not bowed their knee to Baal" (see 19:18). In his letter to the Romans, Paul picks this story up, including Elijah's complaint and the Lord's rebuke, and immediately follows it with, "So too, at the present time there is a remnant chosen by grace" (Rom. 11:5).

Why is God so gracious that he chooses us? Because he wants a name for himself. At the dedication of the temple, Solomon prays for God to bless his people, "so that all the peoples of the earth may know that the LORD is God and that there is no other" (1 Kings 8:60).

Again and again, 1 Kings refers to God acting as he does so that the nations will know that he is the Lord. At one point, the Arameans plan an attack on Israel, and God appears set to use the Arameans to punish disobedient Israel.

But the Arameans are both proud and foolish, and the Aramean king's advisors tell him, "[The Israelites'] gods are gods of the hills. . . . if we fight them on the plains, surely we will be stronger than they" (20:23). Well, the Israelites deserve defeat and God's chastisement, but God decides to use the Israelites to destroy the Aramean army to make a point: "because the Arameans think the LORD is a god of the hills and not a god of the valleys, I will deliver this vast army into your hands, and you will know that I am the LORD" (20:28). He is the God of the hills and the plains and—indeed—the whole world.

Do *you* know that he is the Lord of all the earth? Do you know that he has claim as Lord over your own life?

God calls a people to be his own for his own glory. Hearing and accepting that call is the way forward and upward. Refusing that call, however small the refusal begins, leads only to decline. And the end is not good. I pray that your end will be good and that the choices you make even today will be in his direction.

Let us pray:

O Lord, in this book we have pictures from Solomon to Rehoboam, from Jeroboam to Ahab, of people who make bad choices, whose hearts are against you. And examining our own lives, we see that our own hearts are too often committed to serving ourselves first. Lord, we pray that you would bring clarity to the confusion in our minds and hearts, teaching us from your word by your Spirit, so that we would know the truth about ourselves and about you. Cause us to turn from our sins and to trust in you.

God, we know that we cannot live so righteously that we deserve a place in your family. But we also know of your love for us, because you have not only sent prophets like Elijah, you have sent the Lord Jesus Christ to bear our sins. O God, hear our plea for forgiveness and new life through our Lord Jesus Christ. We pray in great confidence, in his name. Amen.

Questions for Reflection

1. It's hard to make a prescription without looking for symptoms and making a diagnosis. So take a few moments to reflect: is there any place in your life where you are heading in the wrong direction? Maybe your trajectory is only a couple of degrees off. Attend to the sin now, before you travel farther.

2. If you are a leader or a teacher of some sort in a local church, are you leading or teaching in the right trajectory? Are there any bad habits in yourself that you have allowed to fester and which could impact others? Are there things

you are not doing that you know you should be doing? How much is your prayer life involved in setting the trajectory of your leadership?

3. As we have seen, the southern kingdom of Judah "engaged in all the detestable practices of the nations the LORD had driven out before the Israelites" (14:22-24). Why is this such a problem? Don't people act like their predecessors all the time? What relevance does this have for the church today?

4. Solomon left a legacy of sin and idolatry for his children. What legacy are you leaving for yours?

5. As we saw, Solomon knew much blessing. But his blessing led to complacency, then to a cold heart toward God, then to idolatry. Where have you experienced God's blessings? What would it look like for complacency to begin setting in, in those areas of your life?

6. Have you ever looked to the government to offer remedies only the church is equipped—with the Spirit and the Word—to offer? When?

7. If a friend at work told you that all religions are man-made, how would you respond?

8. What "false gods" are churches today tempted to follow?

9. You have been exhorted to look at the problems in your life, and then to trace them back—if you can—to your inattention to some good provision God has given you in Christ. Okay, so let's try, and particularly in regard to your involvement in your local church. Name some frustration or problem that you are experiencing with your church. Now, is it possible to trace your frustration back to some sin of neglect, failure of charity, failure to involve yourself more fully in the lives of others, failure to confront, determination to hold on to bitterness, or any other sin?

10. Following up on question 9, name some frustration in your marriage, if you are married. Now, how can you read *your* sin in that cross, to use Sibbes's phrase?

11. What's the difference between temporary repentance and true repentance? What fruit of true repentance can you see in your life?

12. Toward the end of the sermon, you were challenged, as a Christian, to continue to repent through every day of life that God gives you. What does that mean? Don't we just become a Christian once? How do you repent every day?

13. If you were teaching a Bible study or a Sunday school class on 1 Kings, how would you use the lesson to point to Jesus Christ?

THE MESSAGE OF 2 KINGS: FALL

12

THE MESSAGE OF 2 KINGS: FALL

AN INEVITABLE DEFEAT?[1]

"Lord, open the king of England's eyes." This prayer was uttered 466 years ago today, October 6, 1536. William Tyndale cried out these words in public, an unusually bold public prayer in those days. They implied, of course, the king's eyes needed opening. But then, Tyndale had little left to lose. These were his last words. Immediately after he prayed, an executioner strangled him to death and then burned his body.

For more than ten years, Tyndale had been a fugitive on the Continent, laboring to translate the Bible into English so that his countrymen back in Britain could read it. For this reason, he was hunted down, betrayed by a mock friend, imprisoned for a year and a half, and executed. The established church of the day forbade laymen to read the Bible in the vernacular. So translating the Scriptures was a capital crime.

Tyndale's translation lies behind much of the King James Version, and therefore, behind much of all English versions of the Bible.

The aspect of Tyndale's life that is probably most remembered is the end—this dramatic story of betrayal and imprisonment. So good was his witness in that year and a half in prison that some of his captors were converted. Then he was killed.

God's people in this world have often faced trials. That is nothing new for those who call themselves Christians. Some trials are external, brought on by outsiders; others are internal. Whatever the particulars may be, God's people often seem to have been defeated.

---

[1] This sermon was originally preached on October 6, 2002, at Capitol Hill Baptist Church in Washington, D.C.

INTRODUCING 2 KINGS

One of the clearest pictures of this in the Bible—certainly the picture of the most epic proportion—comes in the book that is the subject of our study here, 2 Kings. This study is one in a series on the historical books of the Old Testament, in which we have been looking at the history of God's people from the time Joshua leads the Israelites into the Promised Land until the return of the exiles from Babylon a thousand years later. I have called this series of studies "The Other Millennium."

Second Kings is the final in a series of four books that seem to have been written at the same time—1 and 2 Samuel and 1 and 2 Kings. But 2 Kings is a bit different from the three preceding it. Each of these three contains large, dominating characters. First Samuel tells the stories of Samuel and Saul. Second Samuel is dominated by David. And around half of 1 Kings focuses on Solomon and his great reign. Second Kings, however, is not like that. No one figure dominates, and all the figures that carry the story are more like a montage than a single portrait. Or, you might say, presenting 2 Kings is less like painting the clearly outlined peaks of David or Solomon and more like painting the blur of an avalanche, where clear lines are lost amid the falling stones. In some ways, 2 Kings is like the book of Judges: it covers a similar amount of time—roughly three hundred years—and introduces a lot of characters. In fact, while the book of Judges covers only twelve judges, the book of 2 Kings covers twenty-nine kings between Israel and Judah, not to mention kings from Aram, Moab, Assyria, Babylon, and Egypt, as well as the prophets Elisha and Isaiah! Now, contrary to what you probably expect if you have sat through a number of my sermons, I will not speak about each one of those people. Instead, I'm going to discuss the overall message of the book.

As I have suggested, the movement of the whole book is clear—as clear as an avalanche! It is downward. Second Kings tells the story of the fall of God's people. The northern kingdom of Israel falls in 722 B.C. (in chapter 17), followed over a century later by the southern kingdom of Judah in 587 B.C. (in the last two chapters, 24–25).

When we look at 1 and 2 Samuel and 1 and 2 Kings together, the overall thesis is ironic, but clear: the nation that Joshua led into Canaan to be a witness to the surrounding nations becomes instead an imitation of those nations. Israel does the exact opposite of what it is taught to do; God's people reject God. And because the people have become just another nation, the story ends with Judah in exile and dispersed among the nations. Some Judeans even flee back to Egypt—their original captors. Talk about irony of ironies! Viewed from the end, then, these four books called God's people to repentance.

Therefore, 2 Kings, which explains why the people were destroyed and carried off to exile, was originally a call for the people to reject their rejection and return to faith in God.

The story line in this book jumps back and forth between the kings of Israel (the northern kingdom) and the kings of Judah (the southern kingdom). Remember, the original nation had divided between these two kingdoms following the reign of Solomon (see 1 Kings 12:16-24). If you have been reading through 2 Kings over this past week, you may have found this jumping back and forth a little confusing. But essentially, the narrator will follow one kingdom for a while, generally until a king dies, then he will jump to the other kingdom and trace the story of another king till he dies or is killed, and so on. Sometimes there is interplay between the two countries, and the book generally moves in chronological order.

The pivotal midpoint of the book occurs in chapter 17, when the northern kingdom falls. The nation of Israel is finally defeated and dispersed. I want us to read that account, but we will begin back in chapter 16 just to see what is going on in the southern kingdom of Judah:

> In the seventeenth year of Pekah son of Remaliah, Ahaz son of Jotham king of Judah began to reign. Ahaz was twenty years old when he became king, and he reigned in Jerusalem sixteen years. Unlike David his father, he did not do what was right in the eyes of the LORD his God. He walked in the ways of the kings of Israel and even sacrificed his son in the fire, following the detestable ways of the nations the LORD had driven out before the Israelites. He offered sacrifices and burned incense at the high places, on the hilltops and under every spreading tree (16:1-4).

Under Ahaz's rule, Judah in the south has certainly reached a low point. Yet looking to the north, we find an even worse situation:

> In the twelfth year of Ahaz king of Judah, Hoshea son of Elah became king of Israel in Samaria, and he reigned nine years. He did evil in the eyes of the LORD, but not like the kings of Israel who preceded him.
>
> Shalmaneser king of Assyria came up to attack Hoshea, who had been Shalmaneser's vassal and had paid him tribute. But the king of Assyria discovered that Hoshea was a traitor, for he had sent envoys to So king of Egypt, and he no longer paid tribute to the king of Assyria, as he had done year by year. Therefore Shalmaneser seized him and put him in prison. The king of Assyria invaded the entire land, marched against Samaria and laid siege to it for three years. In the ninth year of Hoshea, the king of Assyria captured Samaria and deported the Israelites to Assyria. He settled them in Halah, in Gozan on the Habor River and in the towns of the Medes.

All this took place because the Israelites had sinned against the LORD their God, who had brought them up out of Egypt from under the power of Pharaoh king of Egypt. They worshiped other gods and followed the practices of the nations the LORD had driven out before them, as well as the practices that the kings of Israel had introduced. The Israelites secretly did things against the LORD their God that were not right. From watchtower to fortified city they built themselves high places in all their towns. They set up sacred stones and Asherah poles on every high hill and under every spreading tree. At every high place they burned incense, as the nations whom the LORD had driven out before them had done. They did wicked things that provoked the LORD to anger. They worshiped idols, though the LORD had said, "You shall not do this." The LORD warned Israel and Judah through all his prophets and seers: "Turn from your evil ways. Observe my commands and decrees, in accordance with the entire Law that I commanded your fathers to obey and that I delivered to you through my servants the prophets."

But they would not listen and were as stiff-necked as their fathers, who did not trust in the LORD their God. They rejected his decrees and the covenant he had made with their fathers and the warnings he had given them. They followed worthless idols and themselves became worthless. They imitated the nations around them although the LORD had ordered them, "Do not do as they do," and they did the things the LORD had forbidden them to do.

They forsook all the commands of the LORD their God (17:1-16a).

At this point, the narrator continues to list the specific sins of the people of the north, but only to further confirm that Israel's story is at an end.

When we then turn back to the south, we find in chapter 18 that the mighty king of Assyria has now trained his sights on Judah. If he has been able to conquer Israel with such facility, what will become of Judah?

In the third year of Hoshea son of Elah king of Israel, Hezekiah son of Ahaz king of Judah began to reign. He was twenty-five years old when he became king, and he reigned in Jerusalem twenty-nine years. His mother's name was Abijah daughter of Zechariah. He did what was right in the eyes of the LORD, just as his father David had done. He removed the high places, smashed the sacred stones and cut down the Asherah poles. He broke into pieces the bronze snake Moses had made, for up to that time the Israelites had been burning incense to it. (It was called Nehushtan.)

Hezekiah trusted in the LORD, the God of Israel. There was no one like him among all the kings of Judah, either before him or after him. He held fast to the LORD and did not cease to follow him; he kept the commands the LORD had given Moses. And the LORD was with him; he was successful in whatever he undertook. He rebelled against the king of Assyria and did not serve him. From watchtower to fortified city, he defeated the Philistines, as far as Gaza and its territory (18:1-8).

The narrator briefly interrupts his account of Hezekiah by turning again to the northern kingdom, then resumes several verses later:

> In the fourteenth year of King Hezekiah's reign, Sennacherib king of Assyria attacked all the fortified cities of Judah and captured them. So Hezekiah king of Judah sent this message to the king of Assyria at Lachish: "I have done wrong. Withdraw from me, and I will pay whatever you demand of me." The king of Assyria exacted from Hezekiah king of Judah three hundred talents of silver and thirty talents of gold. So Hezekiah gave him all the silver that was found in the temple of the LORD and in the treasuries of the royal palace.
>
> At this time Hezekiah king of Judah stripped off the gold with which he had covered the doors and doorposts of the temple of the LORD, and gave it to the king of Assyria (18:13-16).

Why Hezekiah thought he could pay off the king of Assyria with a little bit of gold is not clear. One is tempted to think it only whetted the foreign king's appetite. And sure enough, he then sends his army with force:

> The king of Assyria sent his supreme commander, his chief officer and his field commander with a large army, from Lachish to King Hezekiah at Jerusalem. They came up to Jerusalem and stopped at the aqueduct of the Upper Pool, on the road to the Washerman's Field. They called for the king; and Eliakim son of Hilkiah the palace administrator, Shebna the secretary, and Joah son of Asaph the recorder went out to them.
>
> The field commander said to them, "Tell Hezekiah:
>
>> "'This is what the great king, the king of Assyria, says: On what are you basing this confidence of yours? You say you have strategy and military strength—but you speak only empty words. On whom are you depending, that you rebel against me? Look now, you are depending on Egypt, that splintered reed of a staff, which pierces a man's hand and wounds him if he leans on it! Such is Pharaoh king of Egypt to all who depend on him. And if you say to me, "We are depending on the LORD our God"—isn't he the one whose high places and altars Hezekiah removed, saying to Judah and Jerusalem, "You must worship before this altar in Jerusalem"?'" (18:17-22).

Clearly the king of Assyria and his emissary are confused. Yes, Hezekiah is taking down the high places and idols all over Jerusalem and Judah, as the Assyrians claim; but he is right to do so. These idols and high places were devoted to other, false gods, not the one true God of Israel. Yet the Assyrians do not understand this. So the emissary continues,

> "'Come now, make a bargain with my master, the king of Assyria: I will give you two thousand horses—if you can put riders on them! How can you repulse one officer of the least of my master's officials, even though you are depending on Egypt for chariots and horsemen? Furthermore, have I come to attack and destroy this place without word from the LORD? The LORD himself told me to march against this country and destroy it'" (18:23-25).

Now, I don't know if the Lord had told him any such thing. Maybe the commander is thinking, "Hey, these are superstitious people. I should appeal to their fears." Or maybe God really told the Assyrians, "March against this country and destroy it." I don't know:

> Then Eliakim son of Hilkiah, and Shebna and Joah said to the field commander, "Please speak to your servants in Aramaic, since we understand it. Don't speak to us in Hebrew in the hearing of the people on the wall."
>
> But the commander replied, "Was it only to your master and you that my master sent me to say these things, and not to the men sitting on the wall—who, like you, will have to eat their own filth and drink their own urine?"
>
> Then the commander stood and called out in Hebrew: "Hear the word of the great king, the king of Assyria! This is what the king says: Do not let Hezekiah deceive you. He cannot deliver you from my hand. Do not let Hezekiah persuade you to trust in the LORD when he says, 'The LORD will surely deliver us; this city will not be given into the hand of the king of Assyria'" (18:26-30).

At this point, I almost wonder if God would have let the Assyrians take Judah, since the Judean people had become so sinful; but because this Assyrian blasphemes and ridicules the Lord, he instead guarantees his own defeat. Reading this account, you find yourself thinking, "Oops, he shouldn't have said that! He just crossed the line!" But the Assyrian continues:

> "Do not listen to Hezekiah. This is what the king of Assyria says: Make peace with me and come out to me. Then every one of you will eat from his own vine and fig tree and drink water from his own cistern, until I come and take you to a land like your own, a land of grain and new wine, a land of bread and vineyards, a land of olive trees and honey. Choose life and not death!
>
> "Do not listen to Hezekiah, for he is misleading you when he says, 'The LORD will deliver us.' Has the god of any nation ever delivered his land from the hand of the king of Assyria? Where are the gods of Hamath and Arpad? Where are the gods of Sepharvaim, Hena and Ivvah? Have they rescued Samaria from

my hand? Who of all the gods of these countries has been able to save his land from me? How then can the LORD deliver Jerusalem from my hand?"

But the people remained silent and said nothing in reply, because the king had commanded, "Do not answer him."

Then Eliakim son of Hilkiah the palace administrator, Shebna the secretary and Joah son of Asaph the recorder went to Hezekiah, with their clothes torn, and told him what the field commander had said.

When King Hezekiah heard this, he tore his clothes and put on sackcloth and went into the temple of the LORD. He sent Eliakim the palace administrator, Shebna the secretary and the leading priests, all wearing sackcloth, to the prophet Isaiah son of Amoz. They told him, "This is what Hezekiah says: This day is a day of distress and rebuke and disgrace, as when children come to the point of birth and there is no strength to deliver them. It may be that the LORD your God will hear all the words of the field commander, whom his master, the king of Assyria, has sent to ridicule the living God, and that he will rebuke him for the words the LORD your God has heard. Therefore pray for the remnant that still survives."

When King Hezekiah's officials came to Isaiah, Isaiah said to them, "Tell your master, 'This is what the LORD says: Do not be afraid of what you have heard—those words with which the underlings of the king of Assyria have blasphemed me. Listen! I am going to put such a spirit in him that when he hears a certain report, he will return to his own country, and there I will have him cut down with the sword.'"

When the field commander heard that the king of Assyria had left Lachish, he withdrew and found the king fighting against Libnah.

Now Sennacherib received a report that Tirhakah, the Cushite king of Egypt, was marching out to fight against him. So he again sent messengers to Hezekiah with this word: "Say to Hezekiah king of Judah: Do not let the god you depend on deceive you when he says, 'Jerusalem will not be handed over to the king of Assyria.' Surely you have heard what the kings of Assyria have done to all the countries, destroying them completely. And will you be delivered? Did the gods of the nations that were destroyed by my forefathers deliver them: the gods of Gozan, Haran, Rezeph and the people of Eden who were in Tel Assar? Where is the king of Hamath, the king of Arpad, the king of the city of Sepharvaim, or of Hena or Ivvah?"

Hezekiah received the letter from the messengers and read it. Then he went up to the temple of the LORD and spread it out before the LORD. And Hezekiah prayed to the LORD: "O LORD, God of Israel, enthroned between the cherubim, you alone are God over all the kingdoms of the earth. You have made heaven and earth. Give ear, O LORD, and hear; open your eyes, O LORD, and see; listen to the words Sennacherib has sent to insult the living God.

"It is true, O LORD, that the Assyrian kings have laid waste these nations and their lands. They have thrown their gods into the fire and destroyed them, for they were not gods but only wood and stone, fashioned by men's hands. Now, O LORD our God, deliver us from his hand, so that all kingdoms on earth may know that you alone, O LORD, are God" (18:31–19:19).

Judah is delivered from the hand of Assyria. Yet after Hezekiah, the kingdom resumes its decline, until it too is destroyed by an invading army in the book's last chapter (25)—this time, by the Babylonians.

Well, that is a summary of 2 Kings, with a close-up of the middle chapters that describe Israel's end and Hezekiah's repentance (18–20), which appears to delay Judah's end.

In order for us to come to grips with the overall message of 2 Kings, I want us to notice four aspects of the story: blessings, failure, punishment, and hope.

BLESSINGS: GOD HAS BLESSED HIS PEOPLE

First, notice that God has blessed his people.

The backdrop to all these stories is that God has blessed the people of Israel greatly. He has given them a temple, where he has set his name. He has given them a king, as they wanted. And he has given them the land itself. As you may recall, he brought them up out of Egypt from under the power of Pharaoh, drove out the occupying nations, and gave them this land that had been promised to their forefathers.[2]

Most important, God has specially given them his Word, as well as great prophets, such as Samuel, Elijah, and (in 2 Kings) Elisha and Isaiah, to teach and honor the law of his Word. Through this law, God made the Israelites his special covenant people and promised to give them his presence.

This is where we must begin in our consideration of the people of God in 2 Kings. Yes, it is a story about a fall, and that means we first have to ask, "From what have they fallen?" And the answer is, they have fallen from all these blessings.

So, friend, when you approach the Scriptures and their meaning, you too must begin from this point. Begin by considering the blessings God has given you, whether you are a Christian or not. We are all made in the image of God, and we all have received his blessings. Jesus said that God causes the rain to fall on the righteous and the unrighteous (Matt. 5:45). There is no one who will ever hear these words who has not received many, many blessings from God.

As Christians, of course, we realize that God's greatest blessing to us is Christ himself. So, Christian, thank God for Christ! Give thanks to God for his saving and reconciling love. No matter what questions or trials you are

---

[2] 2 Kings 17:7-8, 11, 36; 21:8.

working through, acknowledging God's indescribable gift to you in Christ must be your starting point.

As a church, our starting point must be acknowledging our great indebtedness to God and our deepest thanks to him. He has given us his Spirit and his Word. He has given us teachers of his Word, and he has given us one another. God blessed his people then, and he blesses us today.

Whether we are Christians or not, everything else in this sermon presupposes God's many blessings on all of us.

FAILURE: THE LEADERS OF GOD'S PEOPLE LEAD THEM INTO SIN

But sadly, this story only begins with God's blessings. What follows these blessings is tremendous failure. Twenty-nine rulers are mentioned in this book (twelve from Israel; nineteen from Judah), and almost all of them are characterized as having done evil. We have already read about one of the worst in chapter 16: Ahaz, king of Judah.

But the worst king of all is another king of Judah, Manasseh. He is described in chapter 21: "He did evil in the eyes of the LORD, following the detestable practices of the nations the LORD had driven out before the Israelites" (21:2). The very reason God brought the people into the land—to be a nation different from the others—is forfeited as Manasseh leads them to follow the practices of the people who had lived in the land before them. The narrator continues:

> He rebuilt the high places his father Hezekiah had destroyed; he also erected altars to Baal and made an Asherah pole, as Ahab king of Israel had done. He bowed down to all the starry hosts and worshiped them. He built altars in the temple of the LORD, of which the LORD had said, "In Jerusalem I will put my Name." In both courts of the temple of the LORD, he built altars to all the starry hosts. He sacrificed his own son in the fire, practiced sorcery and divination, and consulted mediums and spiritists. He did much evil in the eyes of the LORD, provoking him to anger (21:3-6).

And the list continues.

Manasseh, Ahaz, most of the kings of Judah, and all of the kings of Israel lead the people into sin, even the sin of idolatry, which directly denies the Lord himself. Now when I say "denies," I do not mean they entirely suppress the worship of the true God. No, if you had asked one of those kings, he would have probably said he was simply "supplementing" the worship of God with the worship of other gods, not supplanting it. So you will not see them overtly and directly opposing the worship of the true God. No, their opposition is much more subtle than that. Yet we know from Scripture that when you try to worship any other God along with the Lord, you show that you do not really know the one, true God. To know him is to know there is no other.

Therefore, the particular sins of these kings are laid out in black and white. The writer wants no doubt left as to how sinful they are.

When we read about the nation of Israel, we must realize that no nation today is a theocracy. After reading these books, people wonder again and again, "Okay, then, should we go out and tear down the churches of other denominations or temples of other religions?" The answer is no. No nation today is ruled by divine law in the way Israel was. As Christians, we have no interest in trying to use coercive power—whether through the state or the manipulative methods of persuasive individuals—to suppress any worship we deem false. God uniquely used the nation of Israel to prepare for the coming of Christ, and with his coming, that age of using a nation in such a way is over. Christ's church is international and should not be fully identified with any country, certainly not with the United States of America.

Having said that, however, I am not saying the state no longer has a role in bringing justice. Of course, it does. Leaders still have a special responsibility to wield their power with care, and for the good of those they lead. All of us are accountable to God for the good exercise of the power and opportunities with which we are entrusted. (For more on this, see the overview sermon on 2 Samuel, where we thought about the rule of King David and the way God is glorified when we exercise worldly authority well.)

The kings of Israel and Judah failed badly at keeping their charge. They were called to protect the people and to foreshadow the perfect and righteous reign of Jesus Christ. Yet they sinned and led their people into sin! How different from the King of kings, our Lord Jesus Christ, who neither sinned nor leads his people into sin.

We Christians can disagree among ourselves about many things, but none of us can deny our own sin. So as we read these depressingly repetitive accounts of sin, we recognize people not too different from us. As Christians, we know we are not righteous but unrighteous. We realize, like the great King David, that our sin is fundamentally and personally against God. We also realize, unlike these kings, how serious and how idolatrous our sin is.

In certain respects, elders in the church are in a parallel position to these Israelite kings. They are called to take a special responsibility for protecting God's name and blessing God's people. For this very reason, therefore, the New Testament tells church leaders that "we who teach will be judged more strictly"

(James 3:1). We who are elders should be motivated to avoid the pitfalls of bad leaders as much as we are motivated to emulate the virtues of great leaders.

As a congregation, we should therefore require the elders among us to faithfully protect us all through the ministry of God's Word. How will a congregation remain faithful to God over decades? By being fed with God's Word. By learning the truth. The best-instructed congregation will prove to be the most faithfully enduring congregation. The leaders and people together must be regulated by God's Word, so that the leaders do not, as the Israelite kings did, lead God's people into sin. May God preserve us who are leaders in this church from the failures of the kings.

PUNISHMENT: GOD PUNISHES HIS PEOPLE

Following the failures of the kings and the nation, God punishes his people. This is the third thing we want to notice about 2 Kings. As the nation spiritually and morally declines, the peace and prosperity that once characterized it seem to leave the people. In the very first verse, for instance, we learn that Moab rebels against being ruled by Israel (1:1; 3:4ff.). Reading through the chapters, you will find these types of disturbances again and again. At one point, the narrator describes what is happening in theological terms: "In those days the LORD began to reduce the size of Israel" (10:32)!

Then it finally happens. As we read in chapter 17, the northern kingdom reaches the nadir, the trough, the lowest point of their history as all ten northern tribes are swallowed up by the growing Assyrian Empire. The cities fall, and their populations are exiled, deported, and scattered, never to return and lost forever to history.

Why did all of that happen? Chapter 17 tells us explicitly: "All this took place *because* the Israelites had sinned against the LORD their God, who had brought them up out of Egypt from under the power of Pharaoh king of Egypt." So does chapter 18: "This happened *because* they had not obeyed the LORD their God, but had violated his covenant—all that Moses the servant of the LORD commanded. They neither listened to the commands nor carried them out."[3]

After this happens to the northern kingdom, the inevitable question becomes, will Judah receive the same punishment as Israel? They are every bit as deserving. Their sins are no less. In chapter 21, God tells us what he will do with Judah:

---

[3] 17:7a; 18:12; cf. 17:17-23.

> The LORD said through his servants the prophets: "Manasseh king of Judah has committed these detestable sins. He has done more evil than the Amorites who preceded him and has led Judah into sin with his idols. *Therefore* this is what the LORD, the God of Israel, says: I am going to bring such disaster on Jerusalem and Judah that the ears of everyone who hears of it will tingle. I will stretch out over Jerusalem the measuring line used against Samaria and the plumb line used against the house of Ahab. I will wipe out Jerusalem as one wipes a dish, wiping it and turning it upside down. I will forsake the remnant of my inheritance and hand them over to their enemies. They will be looted and plundered by all their foes, because they have done evil in my eyes and have provoked me to anger from the day their forefathers came out of Egypt until this day" (21:10-15).

Now, the picture this passage gives of God is not a view that people today like very much. As sinners, we have a vested interest in believing that God does not punish sin. It is advantageous for our purposes to define God's character in such a way that we are not responsible for our wrongs. Yet God's promise to Judah here in chapter 21 stands in stark contradiction to this desire of ours.

Interestingly, God does not immediately execute this judgment. According to his own purposes, he waits several generations, even allowing a good king, Josiah, Manasseh's grandson, to temporarily ascend the throne and partially restore Judah's worship. Still, judgment has been promised, and in chapter 24 it falls. Just as he used the mighty nation of Assyria to humble Israel, so he uses the Babylonian empire to punish Judah:

> During Jehoiakim's reign, Nebuchadnezzar king of Babylon invaded the land, and Jehoiakim became his vassal for three years. But then he changed his mind and rebelled against Nebuchadnezzar. The LORD sent Babylonian, Aramean, Moabite and Ammonite raiders against him. He sent them to destroy Judah, in accordance with the word of the LORD proclaimed by his servants the prophets. Surely these things happened to Judah according to the LORD's command, in order to remove them from his presence because of the sins of Manasseh and all he had done, including the shedding of innocent blood. For he had filled Jerusalem with innocent blood, and the LORD was not willing to forgive (24:1-4).

Then, several verses later, we read this most horrific of all verdicts: "in the end [God] thrust them from his presence" (24:20).

I am occasionally asked whether God still judges nations today, and surely the answer must be yes. I don't know much about this, and the Scripture does not directly address the question. But we do know that God causes the rise and fall of nations (e.g., Isa. 33:3). And we know through the prophets that God brought judgment upon the nations surrounding Israel and Judah. They are held accountable to God's own universal standard of righteousness. God sends

Jonah to the city of Nineveh, for instance, to warn them that God's wrath will overturn them in forty days (Jonah 3:4). Having noted this, however, we cannot conversely assume that every nation that is prosperous is steadfastly following the Lord. For his own purposes, God sometimes allows unrighteous nations to temporarily prosper—as he clearly allowed both Assyria and Babylon to prosper for a season. Nor can we assume that every nation that falls, falls because of its unrighteousness. The story of righteous Job, indeed, the life of our perfectly righteous Jesus, teach us otherwise. So we should be reminded that in this fallen world, a simple correlation between *earthly* prosperity and God's approval does not always exist.

As individuals, we should observe in God's judgment upon Israel and Judah his hatred for seeing other things—whether idols made of wood or idols made of selfish desire, whether evils large or evils small—take his place. He alone should be revered and worshiped as God. He is the only true God, and he is holy. It is a part of his very nature, therefore, to oppose all that is unholy. Part of that opposition includes holding *you* responsible for any wrong you have done.

Now, I do not know you or all the members of the church equally well. But I do doubt that any of us has ever led entire nations into idolatry. So, in one sense, you may not feel convicted over the sins of these kings, and I would not argue with you. Yet I would challenge you to ask yourself whether you have been a participant in idolatry. Perhaps you have been a willing idolater yourself in how you have made other things chief in your life besides the one true God? Surely, you can find places in your life where you have given your heart's primary affections and allegiance to more than just God? That, my friend, is your idol. From that wrong love comes your sin. And for your sins, you will be judged.

The question we all face is this: when we stand before God's righteous judgment, who will bear the certain punishment for our sins? Someone will! None of the Israelite kings will bear the punishment for *your* sin, neither the worst nor the best of them. It will not be the leader of your nation. It will not be your parents, and it will not be me. You must bear the punishment for your own sins. Unless! Unless you have a substitute who will bear them for you. And the only substitute there is or has ever been is the Lord Jesus. *He* bore the punishment for the sins of his people on the cross. He came and lived a perfect life, requiring no punishment. God's justice did not need to send him to death, yet Christ willingly took God's justice on himself for the sins of all those who would ever turn from their sins and trust God. That is the good news that Christians proclaim. While the kings of ancient Israel led their people into sin,

Jesus, the King of kings, leads his people out of sin by bearing God's just punishment for them and causing them to escape from sin's power.

Christian, do you consider very often the punishment that you deserve? We can read about the immorality recorded in 2 Kings and recoil in horror—the idolatry, the shedding of innocent blood, the sacrifice of sons in the fire—and well we should be horrified! But have you considered how horrible your own sin looks to our holy God? He is our holy Creator. He has given us everything we have. For our sins against him, we deserve more punishment than we could ever receive.

God punished his people then with exile. Yet remarkably, he causes the punishment of his people today to fall on Christ, *if* we repent of our sins and trust in him.

HOPE: GOD'S PEOPLE STILL HAVE HOPE

There is one final thing we must notice. We have considered God's blessings and the people's failure and punishment. Yet we must also not fail to see their hope.

If They Will Repent

For all the sin in this book, there's a lot of repentance, too. A temporary revival occurs in the northern kingdom when King Jehu destroys Baal worship (10:28). At around the same time, the priest Jehoiada destroys Baal worship in the southern kingdom (11:17-18).

In fact, the Lord gives the southern nation of Judah three special kings who lead the nation in repentance at roughly one hundred year intervals: Joash, Hezekiah, and Josiah.

King Joash, who reigns at the end of the ninth century B.C., does what is "right in the eyes of the LORD all the years Jehoiada the priest instructed him" (12:2), including repairing the temple.

King Hezekiah, who reigns at the end of the eighth century, is used by God to revive the southern kingdom after the particularly evil reign of Ahaz. As we read about him in chapter 18, "He did what was right in the eyes of the LORD, just as his father David had done" (18:3).

King Josiah, who rules at the end of the seventh century and just before Judah's final fall, appears to be a sign of God's continuing mercy toward his people. He is characterized much like Hezekiah: "He did what was right in the eyes of the LORD and walked in all the ways of his father David, not turning aside to the right or to the left" (22:2). During Josiah's reign, the long-lost and forgotten book of the Law is recovered, and Josiah leads the nation in national repentance and a covenant renewal with God. Josiah is so thorough in his repentance that he seeks to undo sins his people had been indulging in since the time of Solomon three hundred years earlier (23:13)!

Certainly we live in a fallen world, and unrighteous people and nations often seem to prosper for a time. But surely it is good for leaders to lead their nations, their cities, their companies, their families in rejecting sin and embracing godliness. Surely that will benefit everyone in their care. May God always bless us with leaders who will lead our own nation to repent of its sins. May he so bless other nations.

For you as an individual, particularly if you are a non-Christian, I would encourage you to confess your sin and to turn from it. Have you done certain things that you feel unsure about? Sit down with a Christian friend and talk with him or her. Ask what the Bible says about such things. Are you currently doing things that you know are wrong? Forsake them. Give them up. Sin never brings what it promises; have you ever noticed that? Sin is a liar. It promises good things but it never delivers on its promises. Exchange the paltry, false promises your sins offer with the true promises you have in Christ! These promises are the way of life for you and for those whom God has committed to your care.

When we Christians practice baptism and give that visual confession of our need to be cleansed from sin, we remember how Jesus identified himself with sinners. Jesus himself was perfect. He had no sin to repent of. Yet in his baptism he began to assume the posture of one who had offended God, a posture he would finally and fully assume in his death on the cross, where he identified with us as sinners most completely. That death was for you, if you will repent of your sins and trust in Christ.

Jesus taught that he came to give his life as a ransom for many (Mark 10:45). For whom? For those who would repent. Some have tried to sell a kind of "cheap grace," a watered-down imitation Christianity in which you can have faith but no repentance. When the topic of repentance is addressed, they respond with, "That's works; that's legalism; that's not grace or Christianity." Well, the Bible defines faith as something that includes repentance. Saving faith involves turning away from our sins and turning to God. We do this only by God's power, but do it we must if we want to truly worship God. In some ways, faith without repentance is like the false worship of the kings who claim to worship the one, true God *and* their other gods. It is worshiping God on our terms.

My friend, apart from repentance there is no salvation. Christ's was the only perfect life, true. But that is no excuse for our continuing in sin impenitently. The gospel holds out the hope of ultimate forgiveness, but also of change beginning *now!* We can, by God's Spirit, change and be released from captivity to sin! In its definition of sanctification, the Westminster Shorter Catechism addresses this hope: Sanctification is "the work of God's free grace, whereby we are renewed in the whole man after the image of God, and are enabled more and more to die unto sin, and live unto righteousness" (A35). If you are a Christian, you know something of God's redeeming power. He has forgiven your sins, but he has been changing you even now.

I pray that we will remember this as individuals and as a church. We are not finally captive to any of our current flaws or shortcomings. God promises us great things and gives us great things, if we will repent.

Because of God's Promises

Ultimately, however, our hope does not rest in our repentance. It rests in God's promises. After all, our repentance can never erase or bring justice to our past sins. This is what separates Christianity from any kind of moral improvement society. A moral improvement society may tell you to make up for the past by doing better in the future. But that is misleading. Doing better is always good, but doing better does not make up for having done bad. Christianity is an entirely different thing. Christianity says, you have sinned against God, and your sin is far more serious than you realize. Only the infinite sacrifice of Christ is capable of completely assuaging God's wrath for your sins. So you must trust in his sacrifice.

We can have hope only because of God's promises. Throughout 2 Kings, what finally wins God's heart is not the attractiveness of his people but his own determination to be faithful to his promises and to himself. So we learn that King Ahab does evil, but "for the sake of his servant David, the LORD was not willing to destroy Judah" (8:19). When the king of Aram oppresses Israel, the Lord shows grace to Israel "because of his covenant with Abraham, Isaac and Jacob" (13:23). When Hezekiah finds both himself and the city in dire straits, the LORD promises, "I will deliver you and this city from the hand of the king of Assyria. I will defend this city for my sake and for the sake of my servant David" (20:6).

Hezekiah seems to understand all this. He knows Israel has hope because of God's promises to David, and to Israel, and to Abraham; and behind all this is God's desire to magnify his own name. When the minister from the king of Assyria speaks and defames the Lord's name, Hezekiah pleads to God on this basis:

And Hezekiah prayed to the LORD: "O LORD, God of Israel, enthroned between the cherubim, you alone are God over all the kingdoms of the earth. You have made heaven and earth. Give ear, O LORD, and hear; open your eyes, O LORD, and see; listen to the words Sennacherib has sent to insult the living God.

"It is true, O LORD, that the Assyrian kings have laid waste these nations and their lands. They have thrown their gods into the fire and destroyed them, for they were not gods but only wood and stone, fashioned by men's hands. Now, O LORD our God, deliver us from his hand, so that all kingdoms on earth may know that you alone, O LORD, are God" (19:15-19).

Do you understand this? Behind all of God's promises and everything he does is his desire to glorify himself as God.

Hezekiah's prayer here is what you must pray for your own life. The reason you are alive is, in at least one respect, the same reason God called the people of Israel to himself: to be a stage upon which God displays his glory to creation. That is why you, as a creature made in God's image, are alive. That is why he offers you the opportunity to repent and believe. That is why he calls you to trust in him. God wants the truth about himself to be known. I hope you see this.

My non-Christian friend, I pray that you will learn that the Lord alone is God. Learn his promises. Take him at his word. God's promises are the only hope we Christians have to share with you. His promises are the only hope we hold on to, because they promise us freedom from our sins.

This hope in God's promises is why our church structures our Sunday morning gathering as we do. We center it upon studying God's Word carefully and prayerfully. And we study all of it, from the New Testament to the Old. Our meetings are no disinterested gatherings of gentlemanly scholars. No, we come hungry. We come to find bread for our souls, because we know that apart from God's actions we are lost. And we ransack our resources in the Word, in the church, in each other, in prayer, in relying on God's Spirit to know what we can believe, and then to believe it.

Apart from God's words of promise, we have no hope. We have no reason to be here as a church. With God's promises, regardless of how bleak the circumstances, we have hope.

CONCLUSION: AFTER THE FALL

Within a year of Tyndale's dying prayer, "Lord, open the king of England's eyes," God answered it. The translation of the Bible on which he had labored with John Rogers and Miles Coverdale was legally published in England with the king's imprimatur on it. God has the heart of even sovereign despots in his hands.

From Tyndale's work, how many generations have fed on God's Word?

William Tyndale may not be alive today, but that does not mean he was not a real person. He lived and bled and died. God buries the worker, but his work goes on. God's Old Testament people had to learn that—that God would accomplish his purposes even if he had to do it in spite of them rather than through them.

God's people read the book of 2 Kings—and the three before it—in exile, and it explained to them why they were there. It gave them hope, not because they could look back and see their own righteousness but because they could see that God is faithful to his promises. Even after their great fall, God's promises gave them hope.

"And I come back to you now, at the turn of the tide." So Gandalf says to Aragorn in the film version of the *Two Towers,* the second in J. R. R. Tolkien's *Lord of the Rings* trilogy. Though Tolkien denied it, it seems clear that Gandalf's return is a reflection of Christ's resurrection.

Even more, the story of God's people in the Old Testament prefigures Christ's death and resurrection. Just as the remnant of Israel is exiled and then brought back, so Christ is surrendered to death and then resurrected to life three days later. Christian hope does not end where this world's hope ends. The whole Bible is structured to show us that! Do you wonder what all those Old Testament books that you read and get confused over are about? The basic story is this: God calls a people for his own name. They rebel against him. He judges them in exile. If God were not really alive, you might think the story just ends there. But to show that he is alive and that he means to forgive and to redeem, he brings those people back from exile, prepared for their real hope, the coming of the Lord Jesus, the Messiah. That is the whole story of the Old Testament. It is the story of God giving hope to his people even though they have completely spent, wasted, and discarded any hope they might have had on their own.

What about you? Do you have hope? Do you have *this* hope?

At the moment, you may be facing some very difficult circumstances. Perhaps you are facing unemployment or sickness. Maybe you have a deteriorating situation at home or financial problems that just will not end. All of these issues are important, and God cares about all of them. He says he even knows the number of hairs on your head. He says not one sparrow falls to the ground apart from his notice.

And yet we have an even deeper message from God's Word. It's one thing to endure trying circumstances; it is another to give an answer for your own sin.

If you know yourself to have made someone or something other than God central to your life, if you know you have participated in that kind of idolatry, where you rest your ultimate concerns not in carved idols but in things that are not God, rejecting and even ridiculing his claims on your life, then I tell you that there is hope for you in Christ. Every Christian can give that testimony because God delights in showing mercy; he delights in saving; and he delights in showing his holy and loving character, his justice and grace, his power and his glory.

Whatever the foe or the woe, the grief or the pain, the storms or the darkness, Christ is our only hope. Repent of your sins and trust in him. If you do not, you will fall and you will never get up.

Let us pray:

O Lord God, we pray that we would not be like the northern nation of Israel, that sinned, was scattered forever, and was lost to history. We pray that we would see in the story of Judah a story of hope, as your people are given fresh life even after being punished for their sins. O God, each of us has known separation from you because of our sins. We pray that each of us would know the true faith in you and your work in Christ that brings us into a restored relationship with you. O God, restore us to yourself whatever the circumstances of our lives, for your glory, so that all the world will know that you are the true and living God. We pray in Jesus' name and for his glory. Amen.

Questions for Reflection

1. Can you think of a story in the Bible in which God's people (or God's person) look ready to suffer defeat, but God then brings victory? Why do you think God so often seems to bring his people into this situation?

2. Our study of 2 Kings began with noticing the backdrop of God's many blessings. In the same way, we have been told, we must continually remember the backdrop of God's many blessings in our lives. Why is this important to do? Suppose you have two people, one who is characterized by a grateful attitude toward God and one who is not. What basic beliefs does the first individual probably take for granted as compared to the second individual? (What's going on behind the scenes?) All other things being equal, how do the fruits of their two lives probably differ? (What's happening onstage?) Which of these two individuals are you?

3. Why is it important to remember *daily* what we have been given in the gospel if we are Christians? Have you ever heard Christians talk about "preaching the gospel daily to yourself"? Even if you haven't, what do you think that means? How do you do it?

4. How can citizens of a nation today *wrongly* identify themselves with the people of Old Testament Israel? How can the members of a church today *wrongly* identify themselves with the people of Israel? How should we relate to the people of Israel?

5. If you are the leader of a church or a home, what bad habits, characteristics, and sins of *yours* might the individuals within your care be inclined to emulate when they in turn lead others? Have you ever stopped to ask those whom you lead what sins they perceive themselves as having reduplicated as a result of your being the one who taught them leadership? Have you asked God's Spirit to show you this?

6. Why does the fallibility and sinfulness of leaders present a strong argument for leaving final authority within a church with the congregation? In order for a congregation to *rightly* and *helpfully* catch and curb unbiblical instruction and activity among its elders, what must the congregation have?

7. What are some practical ways a pastor can lead a church in corporate repentance? In individual repentance? He can no longer break down idols and Asherah poles. What will he do? Will you be able to follow him?

8. In this sermon, repentance has been characterized as exchanging the paltry, false promises your sins offer you for the true promises you have in Christ. These promises are the way of life for you and for those whom God has committed to your care. If you are a leader at church, at work, or in the home, what false promises might you be tempted to follow? What true promises does Christ offer in their place?

9. The most important thing that a leader can know is the gospel of Jesus Christ. Only a leader who approaches his leadership with the understanding that he himself has been crucified with Christ will be freed from trying to prove himself or achieve his own ends through his position. Only a leader who approaches his leadership knowing that he has been resurrected with Christ will know that all victory, gain, and success in his leadership will be accomplished only through the power of Christ and for Christ's glory. Unfortunately, not too many books on leadership have much to say about the gospel. How can you begin applying a gospel-centered perspective to your leadership at home, work, or church?

10. Are you resting your hope in anything besides Christ? What?

THE MESSAGE OF 1 CHRONICLES: HEIGHTS

MAN IS THE MEASURE OF ALL THINGS

INTRODUCING 1 CHRONICLES

GOD IS SOVEREIGN

Over Nations

Over Individuals

GOD IS CENTRAL

To His People

To Himself

To You

David

David's descendants

Jesus Christ, the Son of David

CONCLUSION: AN EXAMPLE OF GOD-CENTEREDNESS

13

THE MESSAGE OF 1 CHRONICLES: HEIGHTS

MAN IS THE MEASURE OF ALL THINGS[1]

"How great an artist dies here!"

These were the last words of one of the greatest egoists of all time—the Roman emperor Nero, as he looked out on the funeral pyre that his own servants were preparing for him. Nero had been ejected from Rome in a military coup against his tyrannous reign. And like King Saul on the battlefield against the Philistines, he decided it would be more honorable to take his own life than to fall into the hands of his enemies. So he looked out on the pyre, wept, and said of himself, "How great an artist dies here!"

Yet, honestly, can we say Nero's self-centeredness is unusual? Maybe his words were especially audacious, but was his heart unique? Let me offer a concrete illustration: when someone talks to me at length and I become impatient, when I am sitting in a poorly chaired meeting and I become frustrated, when a family member asks me to do a simple task and I become annoyed—sadly, I could go on and on—then *I* am being self-centered.

Now, the question we are posed with today is, is such self-centeredness good or bad? After all, ours is a very friendly age for selfishness. We cultivate it in the countless choices we have in everything from beverages to Internet sites. And this surfeit of choice reflects something deeper about our society. From our economics to our religion, our history to our psychology, our biology to our art, self-centeredness is treated as the rightful core and foundation for our lives today. Few theses are less disputed than "Look out for number one!" And we all know who "number one" is. Number one is "you"! Intellectual leaders as different as Richard Dawkins and Ayn Rand, Jean-Paul

---

[1] This sermon was originally preached on October 27, 2002, at Capitol Hill Baptist Church in Washington, D.C.

Sartre and Adam Smith, have all argued that selfishness is the essence of virtue. Problems emerge only when other people are not centered on the same self that I am centered on.

This is true not only in our culture at large. Some Christian leaders encourage us to imagine that we control this world—they call it "overcoming faith"! I remember once sharing a hotel room with a good friend of mine, observing what he liked to watch on TV. Have you ever done that? It's fun to guess what someone you are sharing a room with will want to watch while you are flipping through the channels. Will it be the documentary on digging up mummies in Egypt? The wildlife show on sharks? Anyway, we were flipping through the stations and a noted television evangelist came on the screen. I was about to move on, when my friend said, "No, wait, I like him."

"You like him?" I asked.

"Yes, he's pretty good. He's not like all the others," my friend responded.

"What do you mean? He teaches that faith is for getting everything you want."

He said, "Aw, he doesn't teach anything like that." No sooner had those words come out of his mouth than the program broke for one of their own commercials that said, "Get Preacher _____'s new video, *Dominates*. It shows how you as a Christian can use your faith to control the circumstances of your life!"

And it is not just television evangelists who get carried away by bad thinking. If you are a church member, do you think of yourself as the center of the church? Now you are probably thinking, "No, not me. I'm never up on the platform. Of course I don't think I'm the center of the church." Really? How quickly do you assume that how *you* feel about something is how most of the church feels about it—from the temperature of the room, to the length of the sermon, to the selection of music, to the choice of teachers?

When Pastor John Piper recently preached at our church, he unflinchingly asserted that God's chief concern in the entire universe is God himself! Are you at all offended by this idea? Does it sound strange to you to hear that God's chief concern is not you or any human or even all of humanity, but himself? The strange truth is that we are so egocentric that we naturally think of ourselves as central to God! So we say things like, "He *had* to create us, or he would have been lonely!" Or, "He *had* to give us a choice between good and evil, or we would have just been puppets!" Or, "He *has* to save us; after all, he made us!" In short, we think of ourselves as central to God.

And we certainly think of ourselves as central to ourselves. If we don't think about ourselves, what should we think about? Isn't narcissism natural? We are told from every side that it is. And yet the irony is that our very preoccupation today with the self is causing the self to disappear. It becomes more and more mysterious as we stare at it longer and longer. What is the self? No one knows anymore. The ancient Greek philosopher Protagoras said, "Man is the measure of all things." Was he right?

INTRODUCING 1 CHRONICLES

Around the same time that Protagoras spoke these words, a few hundred miles to the east of him in Asia an alternative thesis was proposed that followed an opposite way of thinking. To consider this alternative, we turn to the Old Testament book of 1 Chronicles.

We don't know who wrote 1 Chronicles. Writers tend to refer to the author as "the chronicler." Many think that Ezra is the most likely candidate for having written the books of 1 and 2 Chronicles as well as Ezra and Nehemiah, sometime in the fifth century B.C.

First Chronicles is a great book of Old Testament history, covering more years than any other book in our present series. It starts at Adam and ends with the death of David. It includes dramatic scenes such as the conquest of Canaan and the great sacrifices offered when Solomon ascends the throne of Israel. Let me give you a simple outline of the book in two parts. Chapters 1–9 contain the genealogies of the tribes of Israel (which allude to the people's history). Chapters 10–29 are about the people's hero, David. That's it, really. Chapter 10 is a transition chapter, mentioning Saul's death as a sort of prelude to David. Then chapters 11–29 contain an account of David's reign.

The first nine chapters of genealogy are somewhat infamous. When people want to accuse the Bible of being irrelevant, they take you to these chapters. Maybe they will pretend to open the Bible randomly, yet, sure enough, they turn to these genealogical lists, this veritable Sahara desert of names in which the best intentions of so many readers eager to read the Bible straight through have perished. These lists are full of familiar names, like David, Jesse, Abigail, and Caleb. But many names are less familiar. For example, there is the Ephraimite wall builder named Sheerah (7:24)! And any expecting parents might want to make special note of this verse in chapter 2: "She also gave birth to Shaaph the father of Madmannah and to Sheva the father of Macbenah and Gibea. Caleb's daughter was Acsah" (2:49). Anyway, you will find the sons of David in chapter 3, along with the lists of the kings of Judah, who become central to the stories of 2 Chronicles. In general, chapters 2–7 provide lists of the descendants of the twelve tribes of Israel.

All these lists serve an important purpose in 1 Chronicles, indeed, in the histories generally. They remind us that these books are not just philosophy.

They do not simply recount somebody's way of looking at the world. No, these books present themselves as history, and history is far "pushier" than philosophy. Philosophy says, "Here is one way you could have more coherence when you observe the world around you. You can explain more things." History says, "Look, whether or not that's the case, this happened. This is reality." That is what these books do.

First Chronicles covers roughly the same territory as 2 Samuel, while 2 Chronicles covers roughly the same time period as 1 and 2 Kings. The biggest difference is that 2 Chronicles does not include the account of the northern kingdom. It focuses entirely on Judah. Interestingly, the early Greek translation of the Old Testament titles the books *Paraleipomenon,* which translates into English as "matters omitted" or "things left out." Chronicles leaves out more than just the account of the northern kingdom. In the retelling of the life of King David in 1 Chronicles, for instance, nothing is mentioned about David's personal life, including the episodes with Bathsheba or Absalom. On the other hand, 1 Chronicles does include things not found in the other books, such as the genealogical lists that comprise chapters 1–9.

Still, why this apparent repetition in Scripture? Why does the Bible include a third pair of books that rehearses historical material already covered in the books of Samuel and Kings? You can think up your own ideas during lunch today, but let me give you what I have learned as I have studied and considered this question. The books of Samuel and Kings work like a pocket history for the northern tribes of Israel and the southern tribes of Judah, written shortly after both nations had fallen. They seek to give a more complete record of the past as well as to answer the questions, "What happened?! How did we end up in exile?" First and Second Chronicles also address these questions, but they have a different overall purpose in mind. They appear to have emerged at the very end or shortly after the exile, and were written to be placed into the hands of the exiles either on their way back to Judah or freshly returned. These returning exiles would need a link with their past in order to guide them as they returned to the land. Therefore, 1 and 2 Chronicles do not provide a comprehensive history of Israel. Rather, the chosen material is more selective, aiming to guide them in resettling the land and rebuilding the temple, to encourage them with God's faithfulness to his promises to Abraham and Jacob and David, and to remind them that God's blessings require obedience to his ways.

That said, the history presented by 1 Chronicles is ambitious. Consider the very first verse: "Adam, Seth, Enosh" (1:1). The chronicler starts with the first man! If you then follow along through the lists, the chronicler always zeroes in on the line of promise—Abraham to Isaac to Jacob and so forth. So in chapter 1, verses 5 to 16 focus on the descendants of the two sons of Noah who are *not* predecessors of Abraham. Then, beginning in verse 17, the account shifts to the line of Shem, Noah's son who does lead to Abraham. Then everything else in the lists follows from this one line, while the lines of Noah's first two sons are not continued beyond three generations. After all, the chronicler is not interested in chronicling the whole earth. The line following from Abraham's son Ishmael is traced for only one generation (1:29-31). But Isaac's line continues indefinitely (1:34ff.). It begins with his two sons Esau and Israel (originally named Jacob). Esau's descendants are listed first, like Ishmael. But Israel's descendants are the ones pursued at length, like Isaac's. And this is the chronicler's basic pattern. He mentions all of a man's sons for the sake of being complete and for the sake of mentioning the lines of descent that eventually lead to some of the nation's enemies—like the sons of Esau, who become the Edomites. Yet then he turns to the line of promise and goes into more detail. Clearly, the focus is the line of promise and where it is heading.

In these first few chapters of the book, the record stretches wide to incorporate the whole human race as it descends from Adam and then from Noah. But then it narrows on Abraham and follows along to his descendant Israel and Israel's twelve sons. The record stretches wide again with the descendants of Israel's son Judah, who is prominently placed first even though he is not the oldest of the twelve (2:3ff.). Why is Judah first? Through Judah's line we watch for the coming king David, and beyond David, still far off in the future, another one who would come in this royal line of descent—the Lord Jesus.

So history will end with multitudes of the sons of Adam standing in the Lord's presence, enjoying and glorifying their King—this descendant of Abraham, this descendant of Judah, this descendant of David after the flesh.

But now we have outstretched the chronicler! Before we get to the new heavens and the new earth, we need to see more of what God does here in 1 Chronicles. The points I want to make as we consider 1 Chronicles are two: that God is *sovereign*, and that God is *central*.

GOD IS SOVEREIGN

First, God is *sovereign*. You and I maintain the illusion of control, and we carefully cultivate the illusion. But the illusion is constantly challenged by the circumstances of our lives: through powerlessness and poverty, age and disease, and finally death. Sometimes God uses sharper reminders—like the recent tragedies in Washington, D.C., of terrorism, anthrax, and a sniper—to remind us that our power has limitations. But God always means to use books of the Bible like 1 Chronicles to present the unlimited power of his sovereignty.

God is the one who is sovereign. Why, in these first chapters, is Abraham chosen to lead the line of promise? Why Isaac and not Ishmael? Why Jacob and not Esau? Why Judah and not Reuben? Why David and not Saul? For all of these questions, the answer is God. In these first chapters of lists, we see the author following God's electing love down the corridors of history.

Over Nations

Throughout 1 Chronicles, God is presented as sovereign over nations. Now, this is a humbling admission for a people in exile. Just imagine, your country has been conquered, your oppressors have torn you from your family and your home, and you have been forcibly resettled in a foreign land. And now you are being told that God is sovereign! Yes, that is exactly what this book is saying. Consider these summary words in chapter 5 concerning the northern kingdom of Israel: "they were unfaithful to the God of their fathers and prostituted themselves to the gods of the peoples of the land, whom God had destroyed before them. So the God of Israel stirred up the spirit of Pul king of Assyria . . . who took [them] into exile" (5:25-26). History is not accidental and without purpose. Israel's disobedience led to God's sovereign actions.

Of course, we can speak of history having a purpose only if it has a purposer—a creator, director, and sovereign. And 1 Chronicles clearly speaks of such a purposing ruler, like the rest of these history books we have been considering. That purposing ruler is not you or me; it is the Lord God Almighty, Yahweh, the God of Abraham, Isaac, and Jacob. He is not simply one among many gods; he is the one true God. His plans and purposes *will* be carried out, and he will even use the mighty kings of Assyria or Babylon for his ends. As the chronicler says in chapter 6 regarding the southern kingdom of Judah, "the LORD sent Judah and Jerusalem into exile by the hand of Nebuchadnezzar" (6:15). The *Lord* sent! Both the destruction of the northern kingdom and the defeat, dispersal, and exile of the southern kingdom were actions of God, regardless of the world leader's name who is employed to effect his purposes. As with the northern kingdom, God acts against the southern kingdom not on a whim but because the people had been unfaithful: "The people of Judah were taken captive to Babylon because of their unfaithfulness" (9:1).

God's sovereignty over kings and nations is on display throughout 1 Chronicles. In chapter 10, King Saul's death and David's ascendance to the throne demonstrate God's sovereign dominion over all earthly sovereigns. "Saul died because he was unfaithful to the LORD . . . so the LORD put him to death and turned the kingdom over to David son of Jesse" (10:13-14).

In chapter 11, we are told that King David then prospers in his reign. Why?

"David became more and more powerful, because the LORD Almighty was with him" (11:9).

In chapter 12, God's Holy Spirit tells David that he succeeds in his military campaigns for the same reason. Through one of David's men, the Spirit says to David, "Success to you, and success to those who help you, for your God will help you" (12:18). The Spirit does not tell David success would come to him "because *you* are so powerful" or "because I have trained you so well" or "because you are so clever and well-connected." He says, "success to you, . . . *for* your God will help you"!

In chapter 14, God assures David of success against the Philistines. He even promises he will go out in front of the Israelites to strike the Philistines (14:10, 15). In fact, "the LORD made all the nations fear [David]" (14:17).

In chapter 17, the Lord says to David, "I have been with you wherever you have gone, and I have cut off all your enemies from before you" (17:8).

In chapter 18, twice we read the refrain, "The LORD gave David victory everywhere he went" (18:6, 13).

In chapter 19, Joab rallies the troops and encourages them to fight bravely with the promise, "The LORD will do what is good in his sight" (19:13). Friend, need the Scriptures be clearer for you to believe in God's sovereign rule over nations and events? This is not an idea that Abraham Lincoln devised for his Second Inaugural Address.[2] This is a deeply biblical idea. And is it not comforting to know this in days of uncertainty and war? There is a good God who is sovereign over nations and peoples.

Over Individuals

Yet God's sovereignty is not limited to outward things, like the victory or defeat of an army in battle. No, even the hearts of people are in God's hands. So David prays in the last chapter of this book, "O LORD, God of our fathers Abraham, Isaac and Israel, keep this desire in the hearts of your people forever, and keep their hearts loyal to you. And give my son Solomon the wholehearted devotion to keep your commands" (29:18-19). David knows that even the hearts of humans—the very seat of our motivations and desires—are in God's hands.

Often, when people are confronted with the doctrine of God's sovereignty in the Scriptures, they quickly turn to asking "why," especially as they consider life's tragedies and injustices. If God is sovereign, *why* do murderers and terrorists run loose in the world? *Why* is there so much suffering? *Why* are some people born with many advantages and others with none? Have you noticed

---

[2] In the context of his discussion on whether or not God would allow slavery to continue in the war-torn United States, Abraham Lincoln states, "The Almighty has His own purposes."

this? People seem to reflexively ask the question "why" when something bad happens. Something in our very bones assumes that something or someone must be responsible for such events.

Maybe that reflex is just left over from childhood, as the psychiatrists tell us. But I don't think so. I think it points us to a good God who created us for something far different from what we find in this fallen world. How can we know this God is in fact good in the face of such evil? Our faith is centered on a God who suffered the most horrendous evil of all—the guiltless Son of God himself dying on the cross. In meditating on that event, we Christians find that our trust in God grows. Our *doubts* grow only when we focus on things other than the cross of Christ. Christians do not claim to answer the "why" question to everyone's complete satisfaction; but we do trust that this God who both suffered and conquered suffering, sin, and death in his resurrection will accomplish his purposes, that those purposes are good, and that they will be seen to be good.

If you are a non-Christian, and you would like to talk about such things, I would encourage you to find a Christian friend and ask him or her about what Christians call the gospel. Find a church that preaches this gospel and begin listening carefully to the sermons.

If you are a Christian, let me especially encourage you to get your arms around this idea of God's sovereignty. It is one of the most helpful doctrines a Christian can know. It is not only basic to this book of 1 Chronicles, it is basic to all the Bible. And it is basic to living the Christian life. The God to whom we pray is the God who answers prayer. That's why we pray. The God we know is the God who acts. Nothing can confuse him or stop him. Nothing can sully his character or exceed his understanding. Nothing can change him or resist his will!

We must also have this confidence in God's sovereignty as a church. When I began pastoring at Capitol Hill Baptist, another minister asked me why I had chosen this church. At the time, the church's aging demography and landlocked geography did not bode well for its future. The neighborhood appeared to be decaying, and the previous pastorates had been troubled. What was my vision, he wondered. What was my plan for how I was going to rescue the church and make it grow and thrive? After he asked, I was quiet for a moment and then answered, "Actually, I think that anyone who comes to a church like this needs to know in his bones, first and foremost, that the church of Jesus Christ is victorious! Its survival does not hang in the balance. Christ founded his church and he *will* bring it to fruition. The fate of the church does not rest with any one little congregation. The church of Jesus Christ around the world is victorious and will march from victory to victory until God himself brings it to con-

summation. As for Capitol Hill Baptist, God's sovereign will and good pleasure will decide whether he wants me to shepherd these few saints for the few
years before the Lord calls them home or they move and then close the congregation down, or whether he wants to reignite the witness of this congregation. That's in his hands. For my part, I simply need to remember that the fate
of God's kingdom is not coextensive with the fate of this one congregation. I
simply need to get about the business of faithfully preaching the Word." We
have a sovereign God who is good, and whose plans are not on the line. We
don't have to worry for him. We don't have to defend him at a party so that
he does not lose out. He's going to be fine. Not only that, he invites us into his
victory and what he is doing in history.

GOD IS CENTRAL

The first thing we have to learn from this book of 1 Chronicles is that God is
sovereign. The second thing we learn is that God is *central*.

To His People

God is central to his people. We can see this in the central role played by the
ark of the covenant and the temple in Israel's worship. As you read through
1 Chronicles, you find that much of David's energy is devoted to bringing the
ark of the covenant back to Israel, and then to Jerusalem particularly. He even
asks God for permission to build the temple in order to house the ark of the
covenant.

The ark of the covenant was the mobile container for the two stone tablets
on which the Ten Commandments were written. It was ignored during Saul's
reign (13:3), and to ignore the ark was to ignore God. Notice, it was called "the
ark of God the LORD, who is enthroned between the cherubim—the ark that
is called by the Name" (13:6). (When you see "LORD" in small caps, it means
"Yahweh," God's proper name.)

Essentially, the ark was the visible symbol of God's presence on earth! The
Israelites had to remain at a certain distance from the ark, even when transporting it. Poles were to be placed through rings on the ark, so that it could be
transported reverently, without being touched. The infamous story of Uzzah
and the ark illustrates the point:

> When they came to the threshing floor of Kidon, Uzzah reached out his hand to
> steady the ark, because the oxen stumbled. The LORD's anger burned against
> Uzzah, and he struck him down because he had put his hand on the ark. So he
> died there before God (13:9-10).

In part, this incident highlights David's failure as a leader, because David has oxen pulling the ark instead of men carrying it by poles, as God had instructed in Exodus (25:12-14). As a divinely ordained symbol of his own presence, God intends for the ark to also symbolize his majesty and power, a kind of throne occupied by him alone and touched by him alone.

After the incident with Uzzah, the ark is left at Obed-Edom's house for several months, and notice what happens: "the LORD blessed his household and everything he had" (13:14).

When the ark finally comes to Jerusalem, it is carried with poles, "as Moses had commanded in accordance with the word of the LORD" (15:15). David had learned from his earlier mistakes.

In addition to bringing the ark to Jerusalem, David "takes great pains to provide for the temple of the LORD" in 1 Chronicles (22:14). You may remember from our study of 2 Samuel the sin David committed by numbering the troops, causing a great plague to fall on the people. In 1 Chronicles, we learn that David dedicates the plot of land where God stops the plague for building the temple. He dedicates the very place where God shows mercy to David in spite of David's sin. God then tells David that he will not be the one to build the temple; his son Solomon will (22:8-10). Still, the final eight chapters are spent preparing for the construction of the temple (chapters 22–29).

So let's make sure we understand this. Why is Jerusalem central in the Old Testament and particularly here in 1 Chronicles? Jerusalem is central because the temple is located in Jerusalem. Why is the temple central? The temple is central because the ark is located in the temple. Why is the ark central? The ark is central because it symbolizes the presence of God. And God is at the center of everything. In short, the ark and the temple are central to 1 Chronicles because God is central.

The ark therefore acts as a reminder that God's own holy presence is at the center of Judah's national identity. In that sense, ironically, the people were defined more by their relationship with him than they were by the ark or the temple or their borders. A relationship with God was the heart of the nation! Even when they went into exile in Babylon away from the land and away from the temple, God gave a vision of himself to the prophet Ezekiel. They were in a different place, with no temple, but they were still his people. And now, this book, which recalls so many generations of Israelites and guides them into the future, is placed into their hands. Clearly, the message is, "You are still my people."

From our vantage point today, having both the Old and New Testaments, we can see that 1 and 2 Chronicles were written to encourage the people to rebuild the temple, but we can also see that the true temple was never this earthly building. God did not finally need the Israelites to build an earthly building for him. Finally, he planned to create another temple—in the womb of the virgin Mary.

The earthly temple of Israel simply foreshadowed the fullness of God's presence as it would be given in Jesus Christ. As Jesus said in the Gospel of John, "Destroy this temple, and I will raise it again in three days. . . . But the temple he had spoken of was his body" (John 2:19, 21). So John himself begins his gospel, "The Word became flesh and made his dwelling among us. We have seen his glory, the glory of the One and Only, who came from the Father, full of grace and truth" (John 1:14). Then, in his final vision of the heavenly city, John says he "heard a loud voice from the throne saying, 'Now the dwelling of God is with men, and he will live with them. They will be his people, and God himself will be with them and be their God'" (Rev. 21:3). But when he looks for a temple in this heavenly city, he "did not see a temple in the city, because the Lord God Almighty and the Lamb are its temple" (Rev. 21:22).

Friend, you are alive in order to know this God and to rejoice in him. Are you doing that? That is why you are drawing breath right now. That is why our church exists. Those of us who are truly Christians are Christians, ultimately, because we have come to know God and to rejoice in him as the center of our lives. At the very center of the life of God's people is God.

To Himself

But not only do we see in this book that God is central to his people, we also see that God is central to himself. I want to press this point home, lest you think this is just a novel idea some preacher-theologian like John Piper or Jonathan Edwards came up with!

God calls a people to himself ultimately for his own glory. We see this in the context of 1 Chronicles in three different prayers of David. In chapter 16, we find David's beautiful psalm of thanksgiving (which you will also find partly reproduced in Psalm 96 and Psalm 105):

> Give thanks to *the* LORD, call on his name;
>> make known among the nations what *he* has done.
> Sing to *him,* sing praise to *him;*
>> tell of all *his* wonderful acts.
> Glory in *his holy name;*
>> let the hearts of those who seek the LORD rejoice.
> Look to the LORD and his strength;
>> seek his face always.

Remember the wonders *he* has done,
    his miracles, and the judgments *he* pronounced,
O descendants of Israel his servant,
    O sons of Jacob, his chosen ones.

He is *the* LORD our God;
    his judgments are in all the earth.
He remembers his covenant forever,
    the word *he* commanded, for a thousand generations,
the covenant *he* made with Abraham,
    the oath *he* swore to Isaac.
He confirmed it to Jacob as a decree,
    to Israel as an everlasting covenant:
"To you I will give the land of Canaan
    as the portion you will inherit."

When they were but few in number,
    few indeed, and strangers in it,
they wandered from nation to nation,
    from one kingdom to another.
He allowed no man to oppress them;
    for their sake *he* rebuked kings:
"Do not touch my anointed ones;
    do my prophets no harm."

Sing to *the* LORD, all the earth;
    proclaim *his* salvation day after day.
Declare *his* glory among the nations,
    his marvelous deeds among all peoples.
For great is *the* LORD and most worthy of praise;
    he is to be feared above all gods.
For all the gods of the nations are idols,
    but *the* LORD made the heavens.
Splendor and majesty are before *him;*
    strength and joy in *his* dwelling place.
Ascribe to *the* LORD, O families of nations,
    ascribe to *the* LORD glory and strength,
    ascribe to *the* LORD the glory due *his name.*
Bring an offering and come before *him;*
    worship *the* LORD in the splendor of *his* holiness.
Tremble before *him,* all the earth!
    The world is firmly established; it cannot be moved.
Let the heavens rejoice, let the earth be glad;

let them say among the nations, *The* L<small>ORD</small> reigns!'"
Let the sea resound, and all that is in it;
   let the fields be jubilant, and everything in them!
Then the trees of the forest will sing,
   they will sing for joy before *the* L<small>ORD</small>,
   for *he* comes to judge the earth.

Give thanks to *the* L<small>ORD</small>, for *he* is good;
   his love endures forever.
Cry out, "Save us, *O God* our Savior;
   gather us and deliver us from the nations,
that we may give thanks to *your holy name,*
   that we may glory in *your praise.*
Praise be to *the* L<small>ORD</small>, the God of Israel,
   from everlasting to everlasting.

Then all the people said "Amen" and "Praise *the* L<small>ORD</small>" (16:8-36).

Then in chapter 17, here is what David prays in response to God's promise to bless him:

Then King David went in and sat before the L<small>ORD</small>, and he said:

"Who am I, O L<small>ORD</small> God, and what is my family, that you have brought me this far? And as if this were not enough in your sight, O God, you have spoken about the future of the house of your servant. You have looked on me as though I were the most exalted of men, O L<small>ORD</small> God.

"What more can David say to you for honoring your servant? For you know your servant, O L<small>ORD</small>. For the sake of your servant and *according to your will,* you have done this great thing and made known all these great promises.

"*There is no one like you,* O L<small>ORD</small>, and there is no God but you, as we have heard with our own ears. And who is like your people Israel—the one nation on earth whose God went out to redeem a people *for himself,* and *to make a name for yourself,* and to perform great and awesome wonders by driving out nations from before your people, whom you redeemed from Egypt? You made your people Israel your very own forever, and you, O L<small>ORD</small>, have become their God.

"And now, L<small>ORD</small>, let the promise you have made concerning your servant and his house be established forever. Do as you promised, so that it will be established and *that your name will be great forever.* Then

men will say, 'The LORD Almighty, the God over Israel, is Israel's God!'
And the house of your servant David will be established before you"
(17:16-24).

Finally, let's turn to the last chapter of the book, where we find this beautiful prayer of David:

David praised the LORD in the presence of the whole assembly, saying,

> "Praise be to *you*, O LORD,
>   God of our father Israel,
>   from everlasting to everlasting.
> *Yours*, O LORD, is the greatness and the power
>   and the glory and the majesty and the splendor,
>   for everything in heaven and earth is yours.
> *Yours*, O LORD, is the kingdom;
>   *you* are exalted as head over all.
> Wealth and honor come from *you*;
>   *you* are the ruler of all things.
> In *your* hands are strength and power
>   to exalt and give strength to all.
> Now, our God, we give *you* thanks,
> and praise *your glorious name*" (29:10-13).

Do you see the centrality of God in all this? And we could keep going. This is the picture presented by the whole Bible! But we have lost sight of this picture because our self-centeredness clouds out what God means to display of himself. Too often, we read the Bible selectively. We simply scan for passages that seem to promise what we crave for ourselves.

Yet as Christians we are called to make God's name known among the nations, to tell of his wonderful acts, and to "glory in his name." Can you imagine a better calling to have? What does it mean to *glory in his name*? It means to relish God, to enjoy his character, to savor him.

Why has God done all that he has done, according to 1 Chronicles? For the praise of his glorious name!

How can you have victory over your sins? How can you be liberated from the things that oppress you and keep you in bondage? By coming to see God as central. By coming to know him as more lovely and more desirable than your most seductive sin. Center your affections on *him*. This is really my last point.

To You

God is central to his people. He is central to himself. And he is to be central to *you*. We can see this if we go back one more time and ask why David is so central to 1 Chronicles.

David. David's reign is clearly central to the story line. That's what the book is about! After nine chapters of genealogy and a brief mention of Saul's death in chapter 10—really just the segue to David's coming to the throne—the rest of the book is about David's reign. Chapter 11 describes David's ascendance to the throne, as well as how he defeats the Jebusites and seizes Jerusalem. The latter part of chapter 11 and all of chapter 12 tell of the many warriors who join David. Chapters 13, 15, and 16 narrate how he brings the ark to Jerusalem. Chapter 14 tells us more about David's house, family, and victories. Jumping up to chapter 21, we find the story of how David sinfully counts the fighting men in Israel. Chapter 22 discusses preparations for building the temple. Chapters 23–26 are full of lists of temple personnel. In chapter 28, David describes his plans for the temple. The last chapter, chapter 29, includes accounts of the gifts given by David for building the temple, Solomon's divinely appointed succession to the throne of David, and David's death.

David's descendants. In addition to focusing on David's reign, 1 Chronicles focuses on the reign of his descendants. As I said earlier, 1 and 2 Chronicles were intended to encourage the people to rebuild the temple and to reestablish the throne of David. And the returned exiles would rebuild the temple, perhaps even while this book was being written. Yet once the temple was rebuilt, there was still no king. No descendant of David sat on the throne.

In chapter 17 (echoing 2 Samuel 7), God promises David that a descendant in his line would forever sit on David's throne. It is an ironic promise; at the time, David had it in mind to build a house for the Lord. But what does the Lord say to David? *Actually, David, I'll be building a house for you.* Nathan, inspired as a prophet, goes to David and gives him this word in the Lord's name:

> "I declare to you that the LORD will build a house for you: When your days are over and you go to be with your fathers, I will raise up your offspring to succeed you, one of your own sons, and I will establish his kingdom. He is the one who will build a house for me, and I will establish his throne forever. I will be his father, and he will be my son. I will never take my love away from him, as I took it away from your predecessor. I will set him over my house and my kingdom forever; his throne will be established forever."[3]

---

[3] 17:10b-14; cf. 2 Sam. 7:12-16.

Several chapters later, David prays to God and exhorts his son Solomon on the basis of God's promise:

> "May the LORD give you discretion and understanding when he puts you in command over Israel, so that you may keep the law of the LORD your God. Then you will have success if you are careful to observe the decrees and laws that the LORD gave Moses for Israel. Be strong and courageous. Do not be afraid or discouraged" (22:12-13).

God makes the promise again toward the end of the book, and again David exhorts his son Solomon. God says, "I will establish his kingdom forever if he is unswerving in carrying out my commands and laws" (28:7a). So David exhorts,

> "And you, my son Solomon, acknowledge the God of your father, and serve him with wholehearted devotion and with a willing mind, for the LORD searches every heart and understands every motive behind the thoughts. If you seek him, he will be found by you; but if you forsake him, he will reject you forever" (28:9).

Did Solomon follow his father's counsel? The Lord certainly did bless him greatly, as we read in the final chapter: "The LORD highly exalted Solomon in the sight of all Israel and bestowed on him royal splendor such as no king over Israel ever had before" (29:25). But did Solomon remain unswerving in carrying out God's commands? Also, was God's promise to David then fulfilled in Solomon? Well, no and no, at least not fully. Solomon did not remain fully unswerving, and God's promise was not fully fulfilled in him.

Okay, but were God's promise to David about his descendants *ever* fulfilled?

Jesus Christ, the Son of David. Yes. This promise was fulfilled in Christ. So say the genealogies in Matthew and Luke. So said the praises of children and infants as he entered Jerusalem. So say countless places in the Gospels and epistles of the New Testament. Jesus is the Son of David! God's promises to David are fulfilled in Jesus Christ.

And that is what brings *us* into the picture (after our slight detour). God's promise to David all those centuries ago was a promise that involves us! How?

God has always intended to magnify his own name by making a people for himself. So God raised up and exalted David. Why? As it says in chapter 14, "the LORD had established him as king over Israel and . . . his kingdom had been highly exalted *for the sake of his people Israel*" (14:2). God always meant for the kings of Israel to be a blessing to his people. Yet God never intended to limit his blessings and promises simply to the people of Israel.

When he promised to have a son of David (a descendant of David) forever on David's throne, he did *not* mean the earthly throne of Israel. One of David's sons would be called the King of kings and the Lord of lords. And this King of kings, Jesus Christ, the Son of David, did come for the sake of all God's people—for *our* blessing and benefit, if we are Christians! First Chronicles points to Christ above all else, to God himself coming in glory as Immanuel, as "God with us," to dwell in human form.

We have sinned. We have rebelled against God. But he has come in Christ and lived a perfect life. In his death on the cross, Christ's spirit—inexplicably to us—became separate from the Father; and he took on his own body the sufferings due as punishment for the sins of everyone who would ever turn from their sins and trust in him. And he calls us to do that now: to turn from our sins and to trust in him.

This week is the 485th anniversary of the Protestant Reformation. During the Reformation, the great truth of Romans 4:5 that "God . . . justifies the wicked" was recovered. The Roman Catholic Church had taught—and still officially teaches—that God must make us holy before he can savingly love us. By God's grace, Martin Luther correctly understood that the Scriptures teach no such thing. They teach instead that the holy God has mysteriously, powerfully, and sovereignly decided to reach out in love to save those who are in sin, those who are alienated and estranged from him, those who are in fact dead in their sin. So great is God's love! We come to know God not because of any good in us that causes us to cooperate with the sacraments of the church, but because he alone is good and glorious; and he gives spiritual life. So we repent of our sins and trust in him. It is by faith alone in Christ alone that we are given forgiveness for our sins and a restored relationship with God.

God's promise to David in 2 Samuel 7 and 1 Chronicles 17 to establish an eternal throne for his descendants was never merely about an earthly kingdom, because that kingdom never happened. It has always been about an eternal throne. And it has been about a promise for us—a promise of a restored relationship with God through Jesus Christ, the Son of David; a promise to bless us for his glory.

So God is sovereign over nations and individuals. God is central to his people and to himself. And God is to be central in your life, too.

What are you centering your life upon? You are centering it upon something. Is it your family? Your job? Your financial security? Your sport? The esteem of others? Right now, you are in the process of making everything else in your life fit around that center point. What is it? Friend, God alone must be at the center of your life. He alone must be the center of your heart and affections. You must be taken up with him. Build your life around him.

It will make all the difference if you do. When we build our lives around God, it will show. Pray for me as a pastor, and pray for our church, that we may be so centered on God.

CONCLUSION: AN EXAMPLE OF GOD-CENTEREDNESS

Adoniram Judson had many advantages. He was a white male, and he had all the legal benefits attending that fact in early-nineteenth-century New England. He grew up as the eldest son in a pastor's home. And he was privileged educationally, graduating from Brown University with the highest honors of his class and from Andover Theological Institution.

Yet Judson perceived what was at the center of this Christian faith he had accepted, and so he felt compelled to leave the United States and bring the good news of Jesus Christ to some place that had never heard it. He reorganized his whole life around this desire, though it did not immediately win him favor with many people. Even his Christian friends and family were skeptical of taking the gospel overseas to a people who had expressed no desire to hear it. Judson had no "Macedonian man" calling to him, "Come over here and help us," as the apostle Paul did. But so consumed was Judson by a passion for God's glory among the nations—the same passion that lies at the heart of 1 Chronicles—that he led the first missions movement among American Christians. He sacrificed settled success and social esteem for the God whose Word was precious to him.

Repeatedly, people asked Judson in cynical fashion about his prospects of success. Why throw away this young, promising life? Judson once replied to a friend, "If they ask again, what prospect of ultimate success is there?—tell them as much as there is an Almighty and faithful God who will perform his promises, and no more."[4]

So Adoniram Judson pursued his young fancy. He boarded a ship for England, where he planned to connect and cooperate with another missions-sending society. But *en route,* he was captured by a French vessel and imprisoned in France for a time. After returning to the States, he set out from New England a second time with his wife and survived many months of rough sea crossing, first landing in India but eventually reaching Burma. In Burma he endured seemingly endless commercial, social, and political opposition to his work. And he struggled to find a place where it would be legal for him to speak publicly about Christianity.

After several months, Judson had not seen anyone won to the faith. Nor

---

[4] Cited in Edward B. Pollard and Daniel Gurden Stevens, *Luther Rice: Pioneer in Missions and Education* (Philadelphia: Judson, 1928), 39.

did he see anyone won in the first year or two. How painful it must have been to fill out a report to his supervisors! A third year passed with no conversions. Surely by now the folks back home were saying things like, "Get the man out of there. Let's send him to where people respond to the gospel." Yet Judson stayed. After four years, the visible fruit of his work remained elusive. After five years, nothing had changed. Throughout this time, Judson labored incessantly to learn and translate the Bible into the Burmese language, even though no one was asking for it. Six years passed and still no conversions. Finally, in Judson's seventh year in Burma, he baptized the first Burmese to confess Christ.

Yet the trials never ended. Judson's work was declared illegal. His house was plundered and everything valuable confiscated. He was mistaken for a British spy and imprisoned for nineteen months in terrible conditions. In fact, the conditions were so severe that other prisoners died from them. During one significant stretch of months that included the hot season, Judson was imprisoned in one small room with almost a hundred prisoners. The room was too tightly crowded to lie down, and it had no window for admitting fresh air. While he was in prison, his wife and children had no one to protect and provide for them, and both his wife and a daughter became gravely ill. Judson was sentenced to death, though the sentence was not carried out. Soon thereafter, his wife died. So did the daughter. In the ensuing years, Judson again married and again was made a widower because of the ravages of disease. He also buried a number of children in Burma.

Toward the end of his life, Judson wrote to an individual back in America who had asked him how and why he could persevere in his tasks amid such trials. He wrote,

> Oh, I feel as if I were only just beginning to be prepared for usefulness. It is not because I shrink from death that I wish to live. Neither is it because the ties that bind me here, though some of them are very sweet, bear any comparison with the drawings I at times feel towards heaven, but a few years would not be missed from my eternity of bliss, and I can well afford to spare them, both for your sake and for the sake of the poor Burmans. I am not tired of my work, neither am I tired of the world; yet when Christ calls me home, I shall go with the gladness of a boy bounding away from his school.[5]

Judson's palpable sense of joy in serving and knowing God is the same joy that David displays in this book of 1 Chronicles:

> Sing to the LORD, all the earth;

---

[5] John Allen Moore, *Baptist Mission Portraits* (Macon, Ga.: Smyth & Helwys, 1994), 106.

proclaim his salvation day after day.
Declare his glory among the nations,
  his marvelous deeds among all peoples.
For great is the LORD and most worthy of praise;
  he is to be feared above all gods.
For all the gods of the nations are idols,
  but the LORD made the heavens.
Splendor and majesty are before him;
  strength and joy in his dwelling place.
Ascribe to the LORD, O families of nations,
  ascribe to the LORD glory and strength,
  ascribe to the LORD the glory due his name.
Bring an offering and come before him;
worship the LORD in the splendor of his holiness (16:23-29).

In Jesus, Adoniram Judson found his true king and his true temple—his Savior and his Lord.

Let me ask you several dramatically awkward questions, but ones that I hope will be even more awkward in your soul:

What have you considered Christ more valuable than?
Are you trusting in God's sovereignty?
Are you centering your life on Christ?

You should. That's why you were made. And by God's grace, you can.

Let us pray:

O God, when we get a vision of a sweeping affection for you (like David's, or Judson's), this passion that leaves no area of a life untouched, we confess that we often feel cold and dead. O Lord, inflame our hearts and remind us that our passion does not save us, the passion of our Lord Jesus Christ saves us—his righteousness applied to us by faith. O God, help us to lay aside our excuses and to turn fully to you, for Jesus' sake we ask it, and for the glory of your great name. Amen.

Questions for Reflection

1. If you are a member of a local church, are there ways in which you are tempted to think your feelings about some aspect of the church should immediately be implemented as church policy? Does this say more about you or about the church, and why?

2. If someone were to ask you why 1 and 2 Chronicles repeat many of the same stories as the books of Samuel and Kings, what would you say?

3. What if this person were to ask you why 1 Chronicles has to start out with this long list of boring names—what would you say?

4. As we have seen, you and I maintain the illusion of control, and we carefully cultivate that illusion. But the illusion is constantly challenged by the circumstances of our lives: through powerlessness and poverty, age and disease, and finally death. Does this mean that God might actually use tragedy and even evil in our lives for good purposes?

5. Why is the fact that God is sovereign over nations and peoples comforting in times of war and national upheaval?

6. If God is sovereign over the rise and fall of kings and presidents, should we bother with voting? Why or why not?

7. As we have seen, David prays for his son Solomon, "give my son Solomon the wholehearted devotion to keep your commands" (29:19). What does this imply about God's ability to affect hearts? Do you pray for what God can do in your heart? For what he will do in the hearts of others?

8. Trusting in God's sovereignty over nations and individuals requires trusting that Christ is victorious, even when the world around you doesn't look like it. Of course, that's what the word "trust" suggests, doesn't it? If you are a church leader, how can you build your church on the idea that Christ *is* victorious? If you are a Christian father or mother with children at home, how can you raise your children, whose salvation is yet to be revealed, on the basis of Christ's certain victory?

9. Why is the idea that God is central to the universe, central to the purpose of our lives, central to his own affections, central to everything, so offensive to our sinful hearts?

10. What does a church gathering that makes God central look like compared to a church gathering that does not?

11. Why does the church that is centered upon serving and praising God have something to genuinely offer its neighborhood and community, while, ironi-

cally, the church that exists entirely to serve human wants and needs does not have anything to offer?

12. One man in history was perfectly centered on God, and trusted the sovereignty of God most perfectly. Yet that one, though trusting in the most powerful God, was brutally beaten and killed. Does this show his trust to have been misplaced? Do difficult, even insurmountable circumstances in our lives mean that our trust in God's sovereignty is misplaced? Where will we find the strength to trust God as Jesus did?

13. Following up on question 12, the good news of Christianity is that God looks upon those of us who have repented and believed as if *we* had been the one man, Jesus Christ; as if we had perfectly centered our lives on God and trusted his sovereignty. Christ's righteousness is imputed to us! Now, how will remembering this fact enable us to willingly pursue the sort of gospel-proclaiming work (whether vocationally or not) that could result in more suffering and trials, as in the life of Adoniram Judson? In other words, how will knowing the gospel enable us to persevere amid the trials that beset the Christian who is obedient to the Great Commission?

THE MESSAGE OF 2 CHRONICLES: DEPTHS

HONESTY VERSUS HOPE

INTRODUCING 2 CHRONICLES

GOD'S GLORY: GOD PLANS TO DISPLAY HIS CHARACTER

In His Greatness (Incommunicable Attributes)

He alone is unique

He alone is sovereign

He alone deserves worship

In His Goodness (Communicable Attributes)

God is faithful

God is just

God is kind

OUR SIN: WE RESPOND TO GOD'S PLAN BY REBELLING

With Bad Ruling

With Idolatry

With Loving What Is Not God as if It Were God

GOD'S JUDGMENT: GOD JUDGES US FOR OUR REBELLION

Through War

Through Exile

THE RESOLUTION: GOD'S PEOPLE REPENT, AND GOD DELIVERS THEM

The Pattern of Repentance

Several Examples of Repentance

The Role of the Temple

The Teaching of the Word

A Final Caution: No Idolatrous Wives! No Divided Loves!

CONCLUSION

14

THE MESSAGE OF 2 CHRONICLES: DEPTHS

HONESTY VERSUS HOPE[1]

"The life of Man," said early-twentieth-century philosopher Bertrand Russell, "is a long march through the night, surrounded by invisible foes, tortured by weariness and pain, towards a goal that few can hope to reach, and where none may tarry long."[2] Russell was certainly honest about the meaningless hardship of life. In fact, he insisted in his essay "A Free Man's Worship" that we too must acknowledge the meaninglessness of all life before we will be able to truly *worship*.

Cynicism like Russell's may have been honest, but surely it left little room for hope.

Others view life through much more hopeful lenses. They almost seem to have been born with an optimistic attitude about life. Describing the Revolutionary War era patriot Benjamin Rush, historian Gordon Wood writes, "Even the invention of a water pump for ships sent Benjamin Rush into raptures over the hope it promised 'that the time will come when, comparatively speaking, "evil there shall be none" upon the surface of the globe.'"[3] Such optimists seem to always project increased earnings or endless growth. They are as optimistic as young children. But are such optimists guilty of wishful thinking? Water pumps for ships appear not to have ended evil on the globe, at least not yet. Without a rigorous honesty that ties a hopeful attitude to reality, how much can such hopes be worth?

The question for us is, can we have both? Can we have both honesty and

---

[1] This sermon was originally preached on November 3, 2002, at Capitol Hill Baptist Church in Washington, D.C.
[2] Bertrand Russell, "The Free Man's Worship," in *Contemplation and Action, 1902–14,* edited by Richard A. Rempel, Andrew Brink, and Margaret Moran (London and Boston: Allen & Unwin, 1985), 71.
[3] Gordon Wood, *The Radicalism of the American Revolution* (New York: Vintage, 1991), 191.

hope? And can the two go together in a fallen world? In an atheistic world, we cannot have both honesty and hope. To achieve hope, an atheistic understanding of the world must lighten up on the honesty. It must discount certain facts in order not to eclipse its fragile, self-made hope.

By contrast, the story of God's holy dealing with his sinful people tells us that we *can* have both honesty and hope. We can have full honesty and real hope *because of God*. He is the reason we can.

INTRODUCING 2 CHRONICLES

That is the story of 2 Chronicles, the book we have reached in our series of overview sermons on the historical books of the Old Testament.

Second Chronicles is the longest of the twelve historical books. It is composed of 36 chapters and takes about two-and-a-half hours to read in one sitting. I would love to have a sermon outline that goes neatly along with the structure of the book. But I can't really do that here. I will give you the outline of the book. Chapters 1–9 are an account of Solomon's reign. These chapters center mainly upon Solomon's dedication of the temple. Chapters 10–36 are an account of the rest of Judah's kings for the 350 years before the nation is conquered by Babylon and deported. And there's just no clearer, more helpful outline than that. Twenty kings in all are covered in this book.

The book seems to have been written toward the end of the Jewish exile in Babylon, if not soon after the resettlement of Jerusalem and Judah had started, maybe around 500 B.C. or a little later. And it appears to have been written for two basic reasons: first, to give a reason for why the exile had happened; second, to give the people a guide for how to restart and rebuild. That is why the northern tribes are left out of 2 Chronicles. They had been *permanently* dispersed and were not part of the return from exile. Therefore, this book had no purpose in mind for them. That may also be why the historian, under the influence of the Holy Spirit, selects the material that he does. He does not recite all the sins of all the kings that we read about in 1 and 2 Kings. Those books already served the purpose of making those sins known. Instead, he specifically focuses on the temple and on the sin of idolatry.

Let's read a couple of passages to get our bearings on the book, one from the beginning of the book that occurs during Solomon's reign, and one from the end of the book that occurs four centuries later. In this first passage, we find the Lord's response to Solomon's prayer at the dedication of the temple:

> When Solomon had finished the temple of the LORD and the royal palace, and had succeeded in carrying out all he had in mind to do in the temple of the LORD and in his own palace, the LORD appeared to him at night and said:

"I have heard your prayer and have chosen this place for myself as a temple for sacrifices.

"When I shut up the heavens so that there is no rain, or command locusts to devour the land or send a plague among my people, if my people, who are called by my name, will humble themselves and pray and seek my face and turn from their wicked ways, then will I hear from heaven and will forgive their sin and will heal their land. Now my eyes will be open and my ears attentive to the prayers offered in this place. I have chosen and consecrated this temple so that my Name may be there forever. My eyes and my heart will always be there.

"As for you, if you walk before me as David your father did, and do all I command, and observe my decrees and laws, I will establish your royal throne, as I covenanted with David your father when I said, 'You shall never fail to have a man to rule over Israel.'

"But if you turn away and forsake the decrees and commands I have given you and go off to serve other gods and worship them, then I will uproot Israel from my land, which I have given them, and will reject this temple I have consecrated for my Name. I will make it a byword and an object of ridicule among all peoples. And though this temple is now so imposing, all who pass by will be appalled and say, 'Why has the LORD done such a thing to this land and to this temple?' People will answer, 'Because they have forsaken the LORD, the God of their fathers, who brought them out of Egypt, and have embraced other gods, worshiping and serving them—that is why he brought all this disaster on them'" (2 Chron. 7:11-22).

That's what the Lord tells Solomon. And what happens? Do Solomon and his heirs obey God's command or forsake them? Let's turn to the last chapter of the book, where we find a good summary:

The LORD, the God of their fathers, sent word to them through his messengers again and again, because he had pity on his people and on his dwelling place. But they mocked God's messengers, despised his words and scoffed at his prophets until the wrath of the LORD was aroused against his people and there was no remedy. He brought up against them the king of the Babylonians, who killed their young men with the sword in the sanctuary, and spared neither young man nor young woman, old man or aged. God handed all of them over to Nebuchadnezzar. He carried to Babylon all the articles from the temple of God, both large and small, and the treasures of the LORD's temple and the treasures of the king and his officials. They set fire to God's temple and broke down the wall of Jerusalem; they burned all the palaces and destroyed everything of value there.

He carried into exile to Babylon the remnant, who escaped from the sword, and they became servants to him and his sons (36:15-20a).

This is a profoundly sad passage, isn't it? When you consider all that God does for these people, and then how they respond, you find a stark contrast indeed. It is shocking. And keep in mind this is not a fantasy story. This is history; these are real-life, flesh-and-blood people. Well, I cannot read you the whole book. I hope you will do that this afternoon or evening. There are worse ways you can spend several hours than reading over the portion of God's Word you just heard preached.

We want to note four things about this book, and this will be our sermon outline:

- first, God's glory;
- second, the people's sin;
- third, God's judgment;
- and fourth, the resolution.

This will summarize what happens in the four centuries covered by 2 Chronicles. And I hope these four aspects of the book will help you to consider more of how you, like the people of God in the Old Testament, can live in both honesty and hope.

GOD'S GLORY: GOD PLANS TO DISPLAY HIS CHARACTER

First, we need to notice what the book of 2 Chronicles teaches about God's glory. Some people think that human history is all about humans, and that the old saying remains true: the proper subject of study of man is man. But 2 Chronicles opposes such a human-centered understanding of life on this planet. It would not be a welcome history book in most universities these days. No, every chapter and every page of this book calls us to consider who this God is.

When I was a child growing up in the public schools of Kentucky, our whole class would line up in the classroom and pray for our meal before proceeding down the hall to lunch. The brief prayer always ended with "let us thank him for this food, amen." And it began with the simple statement, "God is great and God is good." As I thought about 2 Chronicles, it occurred to me that this children's prayer actually well summarizes the incommunicable and communicable attributes of God displayed in this book.

Those words "incommunicable" and "communicable" may seem technical and off-putting, but you probably know them from thinking about diseases! If we say a disease is communicable, we mean that it can be transferred from one person to another. In the same way, God's communicable characteristics (or attributes) are characteristics that we humans can share and imitate, such as his mercy. His incommunicable attributes, on the other hand, are the characteristics that are unique to him, such as his omniscience. We can see both types of characteristics are in 2 Chronicles.

In His Greatness (Incommunicable Attributes)

To begin with, God is great in a way that you and I as creatures can never be great. That makes God's greatness an incommunicable attribute. We see his greatness in 2 Chronicles in at least three ways:

He alone is unique. First, God alone is utterly unique. As King Solomon exclaims, "O LORD, God of Israel, there is no God like you in heaven or on earth" (6:14). This is the God for whom Solomon builds a temple—even though he admits no building can hold God!

> "The temple I am going to build will be great, because our God is greater than all other gods. But who is able to build a temple for him, since the heavens, even the highest heavens, cannot contain him? Who then am I to build a temple for him, except as a place to burn sacrifices before him?" (2:5-6).

Once Solomon completes the temple, God's glory fills it. In fact, we read, "the priests could not enter the temple of the LORD because the glory of the LORD filled it" (7:2; cf. 5:13-14). God is unique. He is the only God.

He alone is sovereign. Second, this God is sovereign, as we considered in our study of 1 Chronicles. Who else raises up and deposes kings at will? Who else controls the fates of people and nations? According to 2 Chronicles, Yahweh (marked as "LORD" in most English Bibles) alone does. It was the Lord who "made [Solomon] exceedingly great," as it says in the first sentence of the book (1:1). And it was the Lord who "aroused against Jehoram," an evil king of Israel, "the hostility of the Philistines and of the Arabs" (21:16; cf. 25:20). Statements like this occur again and again in the book, as God exercises his sovereignty over the nations.

One of the most interesting pictures of God's sovereignty in the book—for that matter, in the whole Bible—is the account of how the Lord brings about the death of another evil king of the northern kingdom, King Ahab. You will find the story in chapter 18. In short, the prophet of the Lord prophesies that Ahab will be killed in the coming battle. Ahab tries to thwart God's plan by persuading Jehoshaphat, king of the southern kingdom of Judah, to accept the danger of dressing like a king in the battle that they are fighting together against the Arameans. Jehoshaphat is a good king, you see, but he's not incredibly bright. He fails to make wise choices a number of times, as on this occasion. Well, you can guess what happens: Jehoshaphat, dressed as a king, is pursued, but he escapes with his life. Meanwhile, Ahab slips into battle dressed as an ordinary soldier, and no one pursues him; "but someone drew his bow at random and hit the king of Israel between the sections of his armor" (18:33). Ahab dies, exactly as God had willed.

Again and again in this book, God demonstrates that he alone is the sovereign God. He delivers one nation into the hands of another (e.g., 13:16). As a Levite says to Jehoshaphat, "Do not be afraid or discouraged because of this vast army. For the battle is not yours, but God's."[4]

This aspect of God's character is so basic that it is part of the very definition of God. In 2 Chronicles, not only do the Israelites recognize God's sovereign rule over the world, even foreign monarchs—from the Queen of Sheba to Hiram of Tyre and Cyrus of Persia—understand that their authority comes from God.[5] This was not a surprising idea! When people call themselves Christians but begin to limit the Creator's power for the sake of preserving some notion of the creature's power, I warn you, they are slipping back into paganism, with paganism's imitation gods and pretend powers. That is not the story of 2 Chronicles. The story here and throughout Israel's history is of a sovereign, all-powerful God, who rules over all the creation he has made.

He alone deserves worship. Finally, since God is so great, it is not surprising that 2 Chronicles calls for the same kind of God-centeredness we saw in 1 Chronicles. This God alone deserves worship.

Again and again in this book, the southern tribes attempt to bring the northern tribes, who have descended into idolatry, back to the worship of the Lord. When Jeroboam first leads the northern tribes to separate from the southern tribes and Jerusalem, many Levites leave their northern tribes and rally to Jerusalem (11:13-17). They know that religious loyalty is more basic than political loyalty. When Jeroboam then lines his northern army up against the army from the south, King Abijah from the south pleads with Jeroboam and all the soldiers from the north, "Men of Israel, do not fight against the LORD, the God of your fathers, for you will not succeed" (13:12). Even three centuries later, decades *after* the northern kingdom has been destroyed by the Assyrian empire, southern King Hezekiah sends messengers throughout all the towns of Israel in the north inviting them back to worship the true God: "People of Israel, return to the LORD, the God of Abraham, Isaac and Israel, that he may return to you who are left, who have escaped from the hand of the kings of Assyria" (30:6).

But it is not just the ten northern tribes of Israel that Chronicles calls to

---

[4] 20:15; cf. 20:17; Ex. 14:13-14.
[5] 2:11-12; 9:8; 36:23.

worship this God. All the people of the earth should worship him! So when Solomon dedicates the temple of the Lord, he specifically prays for foreigners:

> "As for the foreigner who does not belong to your people Israel but has come from a distant land because of your great name and your mighty hand and your outstretched arm—when he comes and prays toward this temple, then hear from heaven, your dwelling place, and do whatever the foreigner asks of you, *so that all the peoples of the earth may know your name and fear you,* as do your own people Israel, and may know that this house I have built bears your Name" (6:32-33).

Solomon wants all peoples of the earth to fear the Lord.

Sure enough, one century later, during King Jehoshaphat's reign, God gives another victory to his people; and "The fear of God came upon all the kingdoms of the countries when they heard how the LORD had fought against the enemies of Israel" (20:29). God displayed his power to show that he is the proper focus for the adoration and allegiance of all men, whether from Israel or any nation on earth.

Christian friend, our work of evangelism and missions continues this very ministry—of calling creation back to its Creator; of telling the world why God created us humans; of working to bring all peoples to the knowledge and worship of God!

God is great!

In His Goodness (Communicable Attributes)

In addition to God's incommunicable attributes, 2 Chronicles lays out several of his communicable attributes, which we can place under the umbrella of his goodness. These are the attributes that we are called to imitate, and again let me point out just three:

God is faithful. First, God is faithful. He was faithful to fulfill his promise to Abraham and Jacob by making their descendants as numerous as the dust of the earth.[6] And he demonstrates his faithfulness to fulfill his promise to David in this book by installing one of his descendants over the people of Israel.[7]

Solomon knows that God is faithful, and so he prays on the basis of God's promises. Notice how he concludes one of his prayers in chapter 6: "Remember the great love promised to David your servant" (6:42). Solomon tells God to remember something God already knows! Isn't that interesting? Of course, we do that whenever we pray, because God knows all things. We

---

[6] 1:9; Gen. 13:16; 28:14.
[7] 1:9; 6:4, 10, 15; 21:7; 23:3.

should specifically follow Solomon's pattern in our prayers by citing God's own Word. Why? Because God has demonstrated that he does what he promises! He is not insulted when we quote his promises back to him. Rather, he invites us to "lean into" his faithfulness. As the hymn says, "They who trust him wholly find him wholly true."[8]

This is why we pray. One way we could explore this book would be to slowly work through its wonderful prayers: whether Solomon's prayers in chapter 1 or chapter 6, or Jehoshaphat's prayer of dependence on God in chapter 20, or Hezekiah's prayer for God's mercy in chapter 30. This book presents a God who is faithful and who is known to be faithful. We as God's people can call on him in prayer because our prayers highlight his promises and present occasions for him to display his faithfulness. And his faithfulness moves *us* to faithfulness, so that we will reflect his character. God is faithful. We should be faithful as well.

God is just. Second, we see that God is just. That is evident in many places in this book, including in some of the prayers we just mentioned (e.g., 6:23). But his justice is most explicitly presented in chapter 19, where King Jehoshaphat appoints judges to serve throughout the land:

> He [Jehoshaphat] appointed judges in the land, in each of the fortified cities of Judah. He told them, "Consider carefully what you do, because you are not judging for man but for the LORD, who is with you whenever you give a verdict. Now let the fear of the LORD be upon you. Judge carefully, for with the LORD our God there is no injustice or partiality or bribery" (19:5-7).

How much is packed into these few sentences! I could preach a sermon on these sentences alone! Among other things, we see that God's character has tremendous practical implications. The appointed judges are called to judge carefully *because* the Lord is just. In this we see something of how important judges and the judicial system are in our land today. If you are a lawyer, let me encourage you to give time to reading and considering chapter 19. God is just. He wants justice in his creation. So too should we seek to promote and pray for justice in our nation and world.

God is kind. Third, God is kind. This book is largely an account of sin and decline, but God's kindness is portrayed in so many ways. We can see his kindness in the blessings of wealth, wisdom, and prosperity he gives to Solomon (1:15; 9:20-27). We see his kindness in the great times of worship and celebration he gives to his people that make their hearts glad.[9] We also see his

---

[8] "Like a River Glorious," words by Frances R. Havergal, 1874.

[9] At the dedication of the temple in Solomon's time (7:10); in Hezekiah's time (30:26); in Josiah's time (35:18).

kindness in how patient he is despite the people's sin. He even delays his judgment upon a deserving nation because one man, King Josiah, repents (34:26-28). God is kind. So too should we be kind.

God is good, isn't he? God is great and God is good. The book of 2 Chronicles is an account of God's glory displayed in history. His plan is to display his character in his greatness and in his goodness through the history of Israel.

OUR SIN: WE RESPOND TO GOD'S PLAN BY REBELLING

But if this book is an account of God's glory, it also is a record of our sin. We respond to God's plan by rebelling.

Many people today think that humans are basically good. We tend to excuse sins as "mistakes." We attempt to shift the responsibility for sin by pleading a deprived upbringing or a lack of understanding. Yet 2 Chronicles alone, to say nothing of the rest of the Bible, places a question mark four centuries tall against these conclusions! It provides a picture of a people given over to sin, and it holds all of us unrelentingly responsible for our own sins.

Who is at the forefront of this rebellion in 2 Chronicles? Here is what's shocking when you read this book: it is the rulers! The guys with the power! The ones in charge!

With Bad Ruling

One of the worst sins this book records, which the returning exiles are called to avoid as much as anything, is the sin of bad ruling—using political power for bad ends. King after king was placed on the throne in Israel to be a blessing to God's people. Instead, many of these kings became a snare to the people.

Rehoboam listens to arrogant counselors and oppresses his own people.[10]

Jeroboam weakens his nation by expelling the real priests and creating false ones (11:14-15).

Jehoram kills his brothers (21:4).

Ahaziah listens to his father Jehoram's evil counselors (22:4-5).

Jehoshaphat, largely a good king, hurts his nation by picking bad allies—people he should know not to make a treaty with.[11]

Uzziah and Hezekiah, also generally good kings, become prideful (26:16; 32:25).

Then there is Ahaz, whose sins we'll look at in a moment. Ahaz actually becomes worse amid trials. You might think that trials help to clarify a per-

---

[10] 10:14-15; contra David's last words in 2 Sam. 23:3-4.
[11] 19:2-3; 20:35-37; also observe the background of his marriage in 18:1.

son's allegiances, to show what is real and what is not, to drive an individual to God. But not Ahaz. At one point, he is being defeated by the armies at Damascus, and so he leads his nation into idolatry thinking that might provide a solution. He follows a kind of pragmatic paganism: "Hmm, these gods seem to work for our enemies. Let's see how they work for me" (see 28:23). He never considers the possibility that it is not the other nation's gods, but *his own sins* that are leading to his nation's defeat!

In the Christian church, we realize that teachers will be held to a stricter standard (James 3:1). So, too, in our public life, we must realize why bad rulers are so detrimental: they affect others! Increased influence means increased responsibility. And as we watch David's line degenerate through the centuries in this book, we can understand why God has so rarely allowed one family to wield much power for many generations at any point in history. As Lord Acton famously said, "Power tends to corrupt." This coming Tuesday, some of us will vote for representatives and senators in the U.S. Congress. Others of us will not be afforded that privilege, either because we are citizens of another nation or of the District of Columbia. Still, when we have the opportunity to vote, we should take that responsibility seriously and vote. And we should not vote for leaders who will hurt their nations by leading the people into ungodliness! That is wrong. That is sin.

With Idolatry

Bad ruling is one of the worst sins, as we have seen, because it leads the people being ruled into the worst actions. We see that in 2 Chronicles in the sad sight of idolatry.

As we read earlier in chapter 7, the Lord warned Solomon against abandoning the Lord and serving other gods. But that is exactly what happens. The leaders—the ones who hold their positions because of God's faithfulness to his promise to David—lead the people into the terrible sin of idolatry.

So Jehoram in the middle of the ninth century B.C., Amaziah at the beginning of the eighth century, Ahaz at the end of the eighth century, and Manasseh in the middle of the seventh century all introduce or encourage idolatry among the people entrusted to their care. Jehoram "had caused the people of Jerusalem to prostitute themselves" (21:11). Amaziah "brought back the gods of the people of Seir. He set them up as his own gods, bowed down to them and burned sacrifices to them" (25:14). These are David's descendants! And Ahaz "burned sacrifices in the Valley of Ben Hinnom and sacrificed his sons in the fire, following the detestable ways of the nations the LORD had driven out before the Israelites" (28:3).

Ever since the first book in our present series on the histories of the Old Testament, Joshua, we have heard the same thing again and again. God drove the Canaanites out of Canaan because of their detestable practices, and he put his own people in the land to be different, to be a light, to be a reflection of God's character to the world. Yet his people become just like the nations he has driven out. Clearly, that is the worst condemnation the people can receive, because the entire project becomes futile and vain. The conclusion Ahaz reaches following his defeat in Damascus, which we alluded to earlier, provides just one glaring and tragic example of how God's people began to reflect the nations rather than God: "He offered sacrifices to the gods of Damascus, who had defeated him; for he thought, 'Since the gods of the kings of Aram have helped them, I will sacrifice to them so they will help me'"(28:23a). And sadly, the effects of his sin do not stop with him:

> But they were his downfall and the downfall of all Israel. Ahaz gathered together the furnishings from the temple of God and took them away. He shut the doors of the LORD's temple and set up altars at every street corner in Jerusalem. In every town in Judah he built high places to burn sacrifices to other gods and provoked the LORD, the God of his fathers, to anger (28:23b-25).

Yet it was Manasseh's idolatry that was the worst in Judah's history. He led the people to greater evil than characterized the nations that God had driven from the land. Look with me at chapter 33:

> He did evil in the eyes of the LORD, following the detestable practices of the nations the LORD had driven out before the Israelites. He rebuilt the high places his father Hezekiah had demolished; he also erected altars to the Baals and made Asherah poles. He bowed down to all the starry hosts and worshiped them. He built altars in the temple of the LORD, of which the LORD had said, "My Name will remain in Jerusalem forever." In both courts of the temple of the LORD, he built altars to all the starry hosts. He sacrificed his sons in the fire in the Valley of Ben Hinnom, practiced sorcery, divination and witchcraft, and consulted mediums and spiritists. He did much evil in the eyes of the LORD, provoking him to anger.
>   He took the carved image he had made and put it in God's temple, of which God had said to David and to his son Solomon, "In this temple and in Jerusalem, which I have chosen out of all the tribes of Israel, I will put my Name forever. I will not again make the feet of the Israelites leave the land I assigned to your forefathers, if only they will be careful to do everything I commanded them concerning all the laws, decrees and ordinances given through Moses." But Manasseh led Judah and the people of Jerusalem astray, *so that they did more evil than the nations the LORD had destroyed before the Israelites* (33:2-9).

Throughout this book, we do encounter attacks on idolatry by kings and people.[12] But none of these attacks bring about a lasting change. King after king and movement after movement tried and failed to eradicate the evil of idolatry from the land. Reading through the book last week, I was struck by how many individuals are involved in trying to clean up what a few bad leaders had led people to do! So many hands tried to repair the damage, but the damage could not be fixed.

With Loving What Is Not God as if It Were God

This book teaches something about the nature of sin, particularly, about its extent and its root. The heinous and spectacular nature of the idolatry in 2 Chronicles should not hide from us the universal *extent* of human sinfulness. As Solomon says in one of his prayers, "there is no one who does not sin" (6:36). Friend, I don't know what you think when you read these passages about idolatry. You may not have sacrificed your son in the fire, but you by your sins have sacrificed God's Son on the cross!

We should also observe what 2 Chronicles teaches us is at the *root* of sin— what sin's very nature consists of. And that nature is not as alien as a statue people pray to. There are a couple of places in this book where sin's essence becomes clear. First, during Jehoshaphat's reign, a prophet of the Lord criticizes the king for, as he put it, "help[ing] the wicked and lov[ing] those who hate the LORD" (19:2). Apparently, loving and hating differently than God loves and hates is near the heart of sin. Of course, what or whom should we love supremely? The Lord! And that brings us to the second example: why does the chronicler tell us that Solomon's son Rehoboam did evil? (This would be a good one to memorize.) "He did evil because he had not set his heart on seeking the LORD" (12:14). You can always trace the sins of the hands and feet back to the head and heart. Our bodies sin when our heads and hearts are not set on God.

The core of sin is to love what is not God as if it were God. That was the core of sin then, and that's the core of sin now. Our response to God's plan, like the ancient Israelites', is by nature "No!"

GOD'S JUDGMENT: GOD JUDGES US FOR OUR REBELLION

So then what happens? That brings us to our third point: God judges us for our rebellion. Many people today seem to think that because God made us, he will accept us any way we are, and that our sin has no consequences. But that

---

[12] By Abijah (13:9ff.); by Asa (14:3-5; 15:8); by Jehoshaphat (17:3-6; 19:2-3); by the people (23:17; 30:14; cf. 2 Kings 11:18); by Hezekiah and the people (31:1); by Josiah (34:3-7, 33).

is not the message 2 Chronicles presents. Second Chronicles opposes any idea of God's indifference to our sin.

God punishes sin in many different ways in this book, such as through disease and death. In some ways, his allowing sinners to continue in their sin presents a special kind of punishment. Being given over to worshiping something less than yourself may not be a sufficient punishment for sin, but it is certainly appropriate.

Through War

One of the most frequent ways God disciplines his people for their sins in 2 Chronicles is through war. We do not think about war much today as a punishment for sin, even if people in the past did.

Second Chronicles certainly presents war as a tool of divine chastisement and discipline. God uses other nations to punish his people for their disobedience to him during the time of Rehoboam: "Because they had been unfaithful to the LORD, Shishak king of Egypt attacked Jerusalem in the fifth year of King Rehoboam. . . . The leaders of Israel and the king humbled themselves and said, 'The LORD is just'" (12:2, 6). God does the same thing a century later during the reign of Joash: "Although the Aramean army had come with only a few men, the LORD delivered into their hands a much larger army. Because Judah had forsaken the LORD, the God of their fathers, judgment was executed on Joash."[13] There are many other such examples in the book.

Have you ever thought about war as the judgment of God? That's how our American forebears understood it, both among those who called themselves Christians and those who did not! Just five blocks from our church, facing out onto East Capitol Street, Abraham Lincoln delivered his Second Inaugural Address, in which he stated, "The Almighty has his own purposes." Those words are now engraved on the wall of the Lincoln Memorial. Have you seen them? And that's not all he said in this address:

> If we shall suppose that American slavery is one of those offenses which, in the providence of God, must needs come, but which, having continued through his appointed time, He now wills to remove, and that He gives to both North and South this terrible war, as the woe due to those by whom the offense came, shall we discern therein any departure from those divine attributes which the believers in a living God always ascribe to him? Fondly do we hope—fervently do we pray—that this mighty scourge of war may speedily pass away. Yet, if God wills that it continue until all the wealth piled by the bondsman's two hundred and fifty years of unrequited toil shall be sunk, and until every drop of blood drawn

---

[13] 24:24; cf. during Amaziah's time (25:14-20); during Ahaz's time (28:5-8, 19); on the Assyrians (32:10-21).

by the lash shall be paid by another drawn with the sword, as was said three thousand years ago, so still it must be said, "The judgments of the Lord are true and righteous altogether."

This man was commander-in-chief of America's armed forces, and he was not speaking treasonously! To acknowledge that God sovereignly controls the beginning and end of wars is in no way treasonous. And you will find that statements like Lincoln's are typical in the history of our country. A sovereign God has his own purposes in war and peace.

Of course, God has had purposes for war not only in ancient Israel and modern America. Preaching in London during the early days of World War II, D. Martyn Lloyd-Jones said,

> Then came a crisis in September, 1938. Men and women crowded to places of worship and prayed for peace. Afterwards they assembled to thank God for peace. But was it because they had decided to use peace for the one and only true purpose, namely to "live a quiet and peaceable life in all godliness and honesty"? Was it in order that they might walk "in the fear of the Lord and in the comfort of the Holy Ghost?" The facts speak for themselves. Thus I ask the questions: Had we a right to peace? Do we deserve peace? Were we justified in asking God to preserve peace and to grant peace? What if war has come because we were not fit for peace, because we did not deserve peace; because we by our disobedience and godlessness and sinfulness had so utterly abused the blessings of peace? Have we a right to expect God to preserve a state of peace merely to allow men and women to continue a life that is an insult to His holy Name?[14]

What God may decide about our own day has yet to be revealed. It remains in the future, invisible to us. But what God has done in the past is clear. In the last chapter of 2 Chronicles, we learn that God uses the mightiest empires of the day to punish his people for their sins. He uses the Egyptians to take King Jehoahaz (36:3). And he uses the Babylonians to first take Jehoiakim and then take Jehoiachin (36:5-10). God decided when and how the end would come.

Through Exile

That brings us to the final kind of judgment God uses to punish his people's sins: exile. God's people are taken into captivity in Babylon. One of the closing camera shots of the book places us at the temple, the great temple that Solomon had built four centuries earlier, where the people had experienced so

---

[14] Cited in Iain H. Murray, *David Martyn Lloyd-Jones: The Fight of Faith, 1939–1981* (Carlisle, Pa.: Banner of Truth, 1990), 25.

much ruin and revival, idolatry and cleansing, worship and celebration. We read this passage at the beginning of the message, but look again:

> They set fire to God's temple and broke down the wall of Jerusalem; they burned all the palaces and destroyed everything of value there.
>
> He [Nebuchadnezzar] carried into exile to Babylon the remnant, who escaped from the sword, and they became servants to him and his sons . . . (36:19-20a).

The story (almost) ends, with God's judging his people for their sins.

THE RESOLUTION: GOD'S PEOPLE REPENT, AND GOD DELIVERS THEM

At the beginning of this sermon, we considered the possibility of both honestly addressing our desperate condition and yet maintaining real hope. This tension between honesty and hope, as well as the dilemma posed by God's righteous anger and our sin, can be resolved only when God's people repent of their sins and God delivers them.

A great deal of thinking and writing these days goes into arguing that people cannot change. "I am what I am," we say, and then let the responsibility slip off our shoulders. We say that our person and behavior are the result of our genes, or our upbringing, or our parents, or our divorce. Second Chronicles, on the other hand, presents a more dynamic situation. It teaches that our situations can change, because *we* can change. And we can change because there is a God who speaks and gives life! That is why we can hope.

The Pattern of Repentance

We find this pattern of repentance and deliverance in what is probably the most famous verse in 2 Chronicles. After Solomon dedicates the temple, the Lord answers him, "If my people, who are called by my name, will humble themselves and pray and seek my face and turn from their wicked ways, then will I hear from heaven and will forgive their sin and will heal their land" (7:14).

You will often find this verse reprinted next to an American flag, evidently flapping in the breeze of destiny. But how does this verse apply to us as Americans today? The Lord refers to "my people." Are *we,* the people of the United States, *his* people? Well, we are his by creation, in the same way those of us who are Mexican or Ecuadorian or Guatemalan are. But God's promise here is made in the context of his *special* people. If you read elsewhere in this book or the Old Testament generally, you find that this was how God referred to the nation of Israel. While America has been privileged with liberty and prosperity, we are *not* the chosen people of God, Israel, ruled by David's line, preparing for the Messiah.

Alright, then, perhaps this verse applies to us as a church. Surely the church can rightly be called by God "my people"! Yes, the church members are God's people, but the church has no "land" to be "healed." In 7:13, one verse prior to the verse we just read, the Lord warns of how he will "shut up the heavens so that there is no rain, or command locusts to devour the land or send a plague among my people." When he promises healing in verse 14, then, he means he will bring physical drought, pestilence, or plague to an end. As the church, however, we do not own farms. We are not the nation!

When the Messiah came, God concluded the work of his special people in their own land. Between the Messiah's first and second coming, God's people are *not* identified with a particular physical location, as they were here in 2 Chronicles and throughout the history of Israel. Now, in between the two comings of the Messiah, God's people are truly an international people! You can see that very clearly in the New Testament book of Revelation, where the 144,000 of Israel are revealed to be "from every nation, tribe, people and language" (Rev. 7:9). So while this particular promise no longer applies directly to church or state, the pattern of repentance and blessing is the pattern repeated throughout 2 Chronicles, and indeed throughout Scripture.

Several Examples of Repentance

For example, we read of King Rehoboam that "because Rehoboam humbled himself, the LORD's anger turned from him, and he was not totally destroyed" (2 Chron. 12:12; cf. vv. 7-8). When the good king Hezekiah falls into pride, he must also repent. And he does: "Then Hezekiah repented of the pride of his heart, as did the people of Jerusalem; therefore the LORD's wrath did not come upon them during the days of Hezekiah" (32:26). Second Chronicles even presents the worst king of Judah as an example of God's mercy. Manasseh, whom we read about a few moments ago, repents!

> The LORD spoke to Manasseh and his people, but they paid no attention. So the LORD brought against them the army commanders of the king of Assyria, who took Manasseh prisoner, put a hook in his nose, bound him with bronze shackles and took him to Babylon. In his distress he sought the favor of the LORD his God and humbled himself greatly before the God of his fathers. And when he prayed to him, the LORD was moved by his entreaty and listened to his plea; so he brought him back to Jerusalem and to his kingdom. Then Manasseh knew that the LORD is God. . . .
>
> He got rid of the foreign gods and removed the image from the temple of

the LORD, as well as all the altars he had built on the temple hill and in Jerusalem; and he threw them out of the city. Then he restored the altar of the LORD and sacrificed fellowship offerings and thank offerings on it, and told Judah to serve the LORD, the God of Israel (33:10-13, 15-16).

That's just like the Lord! Among those he brings to repentance, he includes even the worst of sinners, so that we are sure not to mistake repentance for something that springs from our own virtue. In his goodness, God has brought people like Manasseh to repentance—*and people like you and me!*

The Role of the Temple

Second Chronicles was written to encourage the returning exiles toward this response to God: repentance and faith. As they resettled the land of Judah, therefore, they were called to rebuild the temple.

As we said in our study of 1 Chronicles, the temple was central to the Israelite people because God is central. The temple was great, remember, because God is great (2 Chron. 2:5-9). Even the temple's location was to speak of God's mercy since it was where God stayed his judgment on David's sin (3:1; 1 Chron. 22:1). Now, it would be the place where God's verdicts would be rendered (6:14-42).

There was only one temple in order to symbolize the fact that there is only one God, and that he alone should be worshiped and relied upon. This book is full of stories of people relying on the Lord. Kings Asa, Jehoshaphat, Jotham, and Hezekiah all do.[15] The temple was a symbol and a reminder of God's centrality and his call to repentance.

The Teaching of the Word

How are God's people to be called to repentance? The answer brings us to one of the remarkable aspects of this book that is often overlooked: God's people are called to repentance by the teaching of God's Word. God's Word reveals God's self and his call upon our lives. Again looking back to our study of 1 Chronicles, we learned that the temple contained the ark of the covenant. Do you remember what is inside the ark? "There was nothing in the ark except the two tablets that Moses had placed in it at Horeb, where the LORD made a covenant with the Israelites after they came out of Egypt" (5:10; cf. 6:11).

In short, the ark contained God's Word.

When Jehoshaphat wants to lead his people in reformation, what does he

---

[15] 13:18; 14:11; 20:3, 6-13; 27:6; 32:7-8.

do? He sends his officials "to teach in the towns of Judah" (17:7). What happens? Keep reading:

> They taught throughout Judah, taking with them the Book of the Law of the
> LORD; they went around to all the towns of Judah and taught the people.
> The fear of the LORD fell on all the kingdoms of the lands surrounding
> Judah, so that they did not make war with Jehoshaphat (17:9-10; cf. 20:4).

The blessings of God follow after the teaching of his Word. It has always been that way. Put the faithful preaching of God's Word in the middle of someplace and watch life appear! Not because some mechanical property produces life, but because God receives glory when his name is exalted, when his character is lifted up, when his truth is explained and expounded; and so then he gives life.

This is why King Ahab from the north looks so ridiculous when King Jehoshaphat from the south visits him and Jehoshaphat asks for a prophet of the Lord instead of a prophet of Baal, whom Ahab listens to. Ahab replies to Jehoshaphat's request, "There is still one man through whom we can inquire of the LORD, but I hate him because he never prophesies anything good about me, but always bad" (18:7). How stupid to reject something regardless of whether it is true, simply because you don't like it! Can you imagine sending back a low bank balance report, or a high credit card bill, or a medical x-ray, just because you don't like what it says? Well, that is what Ahab does here. The Word of God instructs us. It presents us with reality.

In 2 Chronicles, we can also see the effect the Word's *absence* has. After Jehoiada the priest dies (Jehoiada had renewed Israel's covenant with the Lord and led the people according to the Word), King Joash becomes very wicked (24:17-22). King Uzziah, too, remains righteous only as long as he is instructed (26:4-5, 16). And King Josiah repents when he hears the Word of God and then has the Bible read to all the people (34:19, 30).

For us today, we need to know that reformation and life always come from the Word of God. That's why our church is patient and sits and listens to me for sometimes an hour preaching, explaining, and expounding God's Word. If you are a Christian, you know that God has given life to your own soul through his Word! He has revealed himself to you in his Word! The Spirit then takes up and uses that Word, which is what we desire, what we pray for, and what we long for.

Friend, we need to hear *the gospel*—the message of Christ for our souls. We need to hear that, yes, we are as sinful as 2 Chronicles says, but that God has so loved us that he has taken on flesh, come in Christ, and died on the cross for the sins of all those who would ever turn and trust in him. We need to hear that! We need to hear that so that we will repent of our sins, turn from them, and rely on God and his promises alone. And he calls us to just this now—to turn and trust!

A Final Caution: No Idolatrous Wives! No Divided Loves!

There is a final caution we must observe from 2 Chronicles. Repentance includes not taking an idolatrous wife, because she will divide your heart.

Most scholars contend that Ezra wrote 1 and 2 Chronicles, along with the books of Ezra and Nehemiah. Yet one leading commentator has argued that this book probably was not written by Ezra because the concern about intermarriage that is prominent in the book of Ezra is not present in Chronicles. I could not disagree more.

The chronicler does not spend a lot of time discussing the king's spouse, but when he does, it is significant. Much of the idolatry in Israel came from marrying idolatrous wives. So King Jehoram, one of the evil kings, marries a daughter of Ahab, another evil king, and she apparently plays a role in his evil: "He walked in the ways of the kings of Israel, as the house of Ahab had done, for he married a daughter of Ahab. He did evil in the eyes of the LORD" (21:6). The good King Jehoshaphat—again not so swift—marries himself to one of Ahab's family (18:1). During King Asa's reign, we learn that the king has to depose his grandmother Maacah because she has been leading the people into sin (15:16). Who was Maacah? She was the wife of King Rehoboam, the son of Solomon and the king who reigned when the kingdom divided in half. And Rehoboam himself, the chronicler explicitly tells us, is the son of one of Solomon's Ammonite wives (12:13)! All this goes back to Solomon himself. Marrying someone—hitching your life to someone—who is not fully allied to God will always yield grief and perhaps even great evil.

For those returning to Jerusalem, the clear message was, "Do not intermarry!" Intermarriage played a significant role in ruining Jerusalem in the first place, even though the Lord had warned the Israelites against it before they ever entered the land (Deut. 7:3). They did not listen, and it led to their downfall.

We are not trying to set up a nation in the same way, but we are instructed in 2 Corinthians not to join ourselves with unbelievers (2 Cor. 6:14-18). Why? Well, how attractive can you, who say you are supremely attracted to Christ, find someone who is not! How attractive can that person be? Now, if you came to Christ after you were married, God can wonderfully sustain you in a loving relationship with your spouse even if he or she is not a believer. But if you are single and free, and you are biblically able to marry, then the Bible tells you to seek a spouse who loves the Lord as much as or more than you do. He or she will then help you and influence you as God intends. As Christians, this is what we desire, so that we will have an exclusive allegiance to God and so become a people who show forth God's character.

CONCLUSION

Second Chronicles ends on a surprisingly hopeful note. I have already read to you the grim summary in the last chapter about the temple being destroyed and the people being carried into exile (36:15-20). But look at what follows from where we left off:

> He carried into exile to Babylon the remnant, who escaped from the sword, and they became servants to him and his sons until the kingdom of Persia came to power. The land enjoyed its sabbath rests; all the time of its desolation it rested, until the seventy years were completed in fulfillment of the word of the LORD spoken by Jeremiah.
>
> In the first year of Cyrus king of Persia, in order to fulfill the word of the LORD spoken by Jeremiah, the LORD moved the heart of Cyrus king of Persia to make a proclamation throughout his realm and to put it in writing:
>
> "This is what Cyrus king of Persia says:
>
> "'The LORD, the God of heaven, has given me all the kingdoms of the earth and he has appointed me to build a temple for him at Jerusalem in Judah. Anyone of his people among you—may the LORD his God be with him, and let him go up'" (36:20-23).

Who would have ever thought that the king of Persia would be used to deliver God's people! But then remember, God is sovereign. An order to build the temple had begun the book (2:4). And now an order to rebuild the temple ends the book.

This book of 2 Chronicles, this story of God's people, warns us against the dishonest and shallow hopes that are so popular in our day. God is holy. Do not be deceived. Sin is terrible. And God's judgment is certain.

Yet this book of 2 Chronicles also warns us against the hopelessness that entraps so many in our day. God is good. Christ has borne the terrible punishment for the sins of all those who would ever believe in him. And Christ comes to us today through his Word, offering that same promise to anyone who knows himself or herself to be in exile—far off from God—and who will take God at his word.

Many people before you have taken God at his word, like John Newton, the slave-trader who became a Christian and, among other things, encouraged

William Wilberforce in his fight against slavery. Or like Saul of Tarsus, who worked to persecute Christians before he himself became the great missionary to the Gentiles.

This news is for people who have sinned, and who are lost.

This news is for the Washington sniper, wherever he is incarcerated right now.

And this news is for you.

Let us pray:

Lord God, your ways with your people are mysterious. Yet we see how your Word so clearly vindicates your character—your glory and holiness, your justice and kindness, your mercy. O God, even your mercy displays your character of righteousness. Truly in the Lord Jesus Christ we see justice and mercy meet. We pray that you would take any idolatry in our hearts and, in love, destroy it. Release us from our illusions, from those things in which we place our trust but that are not God. And we pray, God, that you would give great glory to yourself as you bring each one of us back from our exile in sin to you. We pray for Jesus' sake. Amen.

Questions for Reflection

1. At the beginning of this sermon, we considered the fact that some worldviews emphasize brutal *honesty* while others emphasize *hopefulness*. In the day-to-day life of most people, however, we assume we have both: we live according to some *hope*, and we live assuming that we are being *honest* with ourselves. Why do we naturally make these assumptions? When we as Christians share the gospel with non-Christians, why is simply pointing to the *hope* we have in Christ insufficient? (Hint: consider the role of *honesty*.)

2. What was God's plan for Israel's history? What is his plan for all of human history?

3. What is meant by God's "sovereignty"? How should God's sovereignty over the nations affect our view of presidents and prime ministers we do not favor? How can we reconcile God's sovereignty over the nations with evil governments like Hitler's Nazi regime? Does God's sovereignty over the nations mean Christians are free to take themselves out of the political sphere?

4. Where are God's faithfulness, justice, and kindness seen most fully?

5. What is the value of praying through Scriptures? Of, in particular, praying God's promises back to him?

6. Why is it sometimes so hard to believe in God's goodness? What in our lives seems to argue against the goodness of God? Why might it be hard to believe in God's greatness? What in our lives seems to argue against his greatness? Does the Bible seem to be aware of the challenges daily life seems to present to our ability to believe in God's goodness and greatness? In other words, does it present a blissfully naïve portrait of faith? What replies does the Bible offer to these dilemmas?

7. Looking at the example of Israel, why is bad leadership so detrimental to the New Testament church? What does the Bible give the church for protecting it against bad leadership?

8. How would you respond to a non-Christian friend who admits that "everyone makes mistakes," but who also says that the idea of "sin" is just "old-fashioned"?

9. We have considered the fact that failing to love and hate what God loves and hates, respectively, is at the root of sin. What do you fail to hate that God hates? What do you fail to love that God loves?

10. Does God bring punishment into a Christian's life these days, as he did with Old Testament Israel? If so, how should a Christian respond to such punishment? Does God bring punishment upon nations for their sins today, as he did with Old Testament Israel and its neighbors?

11. What will happen in a church where things other than the preaching of the Word are emphasized?

12. Is repenting of a sin the same thing as confessing it? If not, what else is entailed? Is repentance necessary for salvation?

THE MESSAGE OF EZRA: RENEWAL

15

THE MESSAGE OF EZRA: RENEWAL

IS THE CHURCH BECOMING INVISIBLE?[1]

"There was a time when American evangelicals prized and cultivated biblically chaste Christian thought and an incisive analysis of the culture from a perspective apart from it. But the past few decades have seen an erosion of the old distinctions, a gradual descent into the 'self' movement, a psychologizing of the faith, and an adaptation of Christian belief to a therapeutic culture. Distracted by the blandishments of modern culture, we have lost our focus on transcendent biblical truth. We have been beguiled by the efficiency of our culture's technique, the sheer effectiveness of its strategies, and we have begun to play by these rules. We now blithely speak of marketing the gospel like any other commodity, oblivious to the fact that such rhetoric betrays a vast intrusion of worldliness into the church."[2]

So says David Wells, one of my professors from Gordon-Conwell Seminary, writing in his 1994 book *God in the Wasteland*. In this book, Wells suggests that we Christians have surrendered our green cards and taken up full citizenship in the world. We are done with this "just passing through" stuff! Instead, we have settled down, bought homes, opened IRAs, and dug in for the long run. We have, in short, become like the world around us. As our parents or grandparents might say, we have become worldly. That is what has happened to evangelical Christians in America today.

There are countless problems with this situation. For one, let's just admit the world does worldliness better than the church does, no matter how hard we try. If we want to please the world by being like the world, we lose. So as

[1] This sermon was originally preached on November 17, 2002, at Capitol Hill Baptist Church in Washington, D.C.
[2] David Wells, *God in the Wasteland: The Reality of Truth in a World of Fading Dreams* (Grand Rapids, Mich.: Eerdmans, 1994), 58.

the church's distinctive mission fades, membership numbers fall. Why do people keep publishing stories about declining church numbers as if this is a surprise? When I lived in Britain, I remember hearing the archbishop of Canterbury declare the 1990s the "Decade of Evangelism." But between 1989 and 1998, Sunday church attendance in Great Britain fell from 4.7 million to 3.7 million among all Christian denominations combined, a decline of 22 percent in one decade.[3] If that was the decade of evangelism, I hope they stop evangelizing fast, or there won't be any churches left!

On our side of the Atlantic, the situation is not much better among most of the major denominations. Within the same time period—1989 to 1998—our nation's population grew substantially, but the absolute numbers of Lutherans fell by 2 percent, Episcopalians by 5 percent, Methodists by 7 percent, Presbyterians by almost 12 percent, and Congregationalists by almost 15 percent.[4] I am not certain, but I would guess the only thing that kept the Roman Catholic Church in the United States from joining these declining ranks was the massive levels of immigration into the country. Southern Baptists did not decline either, but we are probably statistically shielded by our unattractive combination of really poor record keeping and an increased willingness to baptize at younger and younger ages! Meanwhile the number of Americans who say they have "no religion" almost doubled, from 8 percent of the population to 14 percent.

Our churches seem not to follow the Gospel of Mark so much as the satirical wisdom of Mark Twain, who mockingly advised, "To be good is noble but to show others how to be good is nobler and no trouble." In everything from the amount of money placed in the offering plate to the number of marriages that fail, studies suggest that many churches today bear more resemblance to the world around them than to what God calls his people to be in the Bible.

What can be done? In our own day, there is no doubt that the mission of the church needs to be *renewed*!

INTRODUCING EZRA

Few books are better suited for calling us to the renewal of the church than the Old Testament book of Ezra, the next book in our present series of overview sermons on the historical books of the Old Testament. In an overview sermon, I try to preach the message of a whole book of the Bible in just one sermon.

---

[3] Philip Jenkins, *The Next Christendom: The Coming of Global Christianity* (New York: Oxford University Press, 2002), 95.
[4] If measured as a percentage of population, the decline would be even greater.

Ezra is a comparatively short book. It is only ten chapters long and can be read in less than an hour.

Originally, in the Hebrew canon, Ezra was combined with Nehemiah as one book. They were divided in the Christian Bible around the end of the fourth century A.D. because of the main characters who carry the story line in each. Together, the two books cover about one century of history—from 539 to 433 B.C. The book of Ezra describes a first wave of exiles who return to Judah under King Zerubbabel to rebuild the temple in the years 539–516 B.C.,[5] as well as a second wave who return with Ezra more than fifty years later (around 458). Nehemiah, whom we will look at in our next study, rebuilds the walls a little more than ten years later (445–433 B.C.).[6]

Let's quickly walk through the book of Ezra in order to familiarize ourselves with it. Remember, the people of Judah were exiled in 586 B.C. when the Babylonian empire crushed Jerusalem. The Babylonians literally tore down the walls and carried tens of thousands of Jews away to Babylon. About fifty years then pass, during which time the Babylonian empire actually crumbles, almost from within, and the Persian empire eats it up. Daniel would still be alive at this time, though he appears to have died shortly after the end of the exile. At the opening of Ezra, Cyrus is the great king over Persia, and among his subjects are the captives from Israel. In the first few verses, we read the decree Cyrus issued in 539 B.C. that released the exiles to return to Judah.

Chapters 1–2 go on to describe the first exiles who return and some of the goods they bring back with them for rebuilding the temple.

Chapters 3–6 then describe the rebuilding of the temple. At the beginning of chapter 3, the altar is rebuilt and the people start offering sacrifices again. The foundation of the temple itself is then laid. In verses 1–5 of chapter 4, some opposition to this work arises, and the work ceases. We don't know exactly how long it stopped, but probably for about fifteen years. Then in chapter 5, the two prophets Haggai and Zechariah begin to preach and the people start rebuilding again. This occurs sometime around 520 B.C. Also, Tattenai, the governor over the geographic region that included Judah, sends a letter to the emperor Darius, asking if the Jews had indeed received permission to rebuild their temple. In chapter 6 Darius writes back, confirming that they have his permission. The temple is then completed and celebrations are held. This occurs around 516 B.C.

And that's the first six chapters of Ezra.

---

[5] Zerubbabel is the grandson of Jehoiachin, who was king of Judah in the third and final wave of Babylonian conquest in 586.

[6] Since we are in B.C., the numbers work backwards. The further back in time we go, the higher the numbers are, which can be confusing if you are not used to working with ancient history!

About a fifty-year break follows, which is when we think the events described in the book of Esther took place. Picking up again in chapter 7, the Persian emperor Artaxerxes, who reigned in the middle of the fifth century B.C., issues a decree sending Ezra the priest back to Jerusalem. Chapter 8 lists some of the people who return with Ezra. In chapters 9–10, Ezra discovers that the Jews have already begun to intermarry with the idolatrous people of the land, and he mourns over their sin. He then leads the people in repentance.

The latest event in the book of Ezra, chronologically, appears to be in chapter 4. After talking about the opposition to rebuilding the temple in the first five verses of chapter 4, the author of Ezra decided to insert two letters that would be written many years later, one to and one from Emperor Artaxerxes, regarding the opposition to rebuilding the walls around Jerusalem. Perhaps these later letters were inserted simply to show that the sort of opposition that begins over the temple would continue for years to come.

That's a quick walk through of the book. In this sermon, we will consider the story of the book of Ezra in three stages:

First, the people of God return to the land (chapters 1–6).
Second, the people of God have their sin revealed (chapters 7–9).
Third, the people of God repent of their sin (chapter 10).

Or we can say it like this: God's hand restores, God's Word reveals, and God's people repent. That's the story of Ezra, and I pray that the Lord will meet you with his Word and do business with your soul today.

GOD'S HAND RESTORES (CHAPTERS 1–6)

In the first six chapters of Ezra, we find the story of God's people returning to the land. Indeed, God's hand restores them to their land.

The Return

In the first two chapters is the return itself, as decreed by Emperor Cyrus himself:

In the first year of Cyrus king of Persia, in order to fulfill the word of the LORD spoken by Jeremiah, the LORD moved the heart of Cyrus king of Persia to make a proclamation throughout his realm and to put it in writing:

"This is what Cyrus king of Persia says:

"'The LORD, the God of heaven, has given me all the kingdoms of the earth and he has appointed me to build a temple for him at Jerusalem in Judah. Anyone of his people among you—may his God be with him,

and let him go up to Jerusalem in Judah and build the temple of the
LORD, the God of Israel, the God who is in Jerusalem. And the people
of any place where survivors may now be living are to provide him with
silver and gold, with goods and livestock, and with freewill offerings for
the temple of God in Jerusalem.'"

Then the family heads of Judah and Benjamin, and the priests and Levites—
everyone whose heart God had moved—prepared to go up and build the house
of the LORD in Jerusalem. All their neighbors assisted them with articles of silver and gold, with goods and livestock, and with valuable gifts, in addition to
all the freewill offerings. Moreover, King Cyrus brought out the articles belonging to the temple of the LORD, which Nebuchadnezzar had carried away from
Jerusalem and had placed in the temple of his god (1:1-7).

An inventory of these articles is then provided in the remainder of chapter 1, followed in chapter 2 by a list of the families who returned. Then toward
the conclusion of chapter 2 we read, "When they arrived at the house of the
LORD in Jerusalem, some of the heads of the families gave freewill offerings
toward the rebuilding of the house of God on its site" (2:68).

The Restoration of the Sacrifices

So the decree has gone out. The people have packed up and left. They have
arrived at home. The work has begun. And then, at the beginning of chapter
3, a second great thing happens. They restore the sacrifices:

When the seventh month came and the Israelites had settled in their towns, the
people assembled as one man in Jerusalem. Then Jeshua son of Jozadak and his
fellow priests and Zerubbabel son of Shealtiel and his associates began to build
the altar of the God of Israel to sacrifice burnt offerings on it, in accordance with
what is written in the Law of Moses the man of God. Despite their fear of the
peoples around them, they built the altar on its foundation and sacrificed burnt
offerings on it to the LORD, both the morning and evening sacrifices (3:1-3).

The Rebuilding of the Temple

Having begun the sacrifices, the people were ready to rebuild the temple itself,
which takes up the rest of chapter 3.

Foundation. They begin by laying the foundation:

In the second month of the second year after their arrival at the house of God in
Jerusalem, Zerubbabel son of Shealtiel, Jeshua son of Jozadak and the rest of
their brothers (the priests and the Levites and all who had returned from the cap-

tivity to Jerusalem) began the work, appointing Levites twenty years of age and older to supervise the building of the house of the LORD. Jeshua and his sons and brothers and Kadmiel and his sons (descendants of Hodaviah) and the sons of Henadad and their sons and brothers—all Levites—joined together in supervising those working on the house of God.

When the builders laid the foundation of the temple of the LORD, the priests in their vestments and with trumpets, and the Levites (the sons of Asaph) with cymbals, took their places to praise the LORD, as prescribed by David king of Israel. With praise and thanksgiving they sang to the LORD:

> "He is good;
>   his love to Israel endures forever" (3:8-11a).

If you go back and you look in 1 and 2 Chronicles, you will find that the people sang these same words—"he is good; his love endures forever"—when the ark was first brought to Jerusalem by David and placed in the tabernacle, as well as when the temple was first dedicated by Solomon.[7] But to continue:

> And all the people gave a great shout of praise to the LORD, because the foundation of the house of the LORD was laid. But many of the older priests and Levites and family heads, who had seen the former temple, wept aloud when they saw the foundation of this temple being laid, while many others shouted for joy. No one could distinguish the sound of the shouts of joy from the sound of weeping, because the people made so much noise. And the sound was heard far away (3:11b-13).

Isn't that a great account of how moving the moment must have been—some weeping and some with joy? Certainly, we get a sense of the emotion of the event.

Opposition. But this happy picture is soon spoiled by opposition. At the beginning of chapter 3, we learn that the returned exiles were, in fact, proceeding in their program of building the altar "despite their fear of the peoples around them" (3:3). Why did they fear the surrounding peoples? Because these people, called "enemies" at the beginning of chapter 4, were "interested" in the returning Israelites and even offered to "help" (see 4:1-2). There had been a long history of antagonism between the Jews and the people of the land—even the ones who had half-adopted Jewish practices—and they knew their enemies did not really want to help.[8] They wanted to discourage the Jews and

---

[7] 1 Chron. 16:34; 2 Chron. 5:13; 7:3.
[8] Cf. 2 Kings 17:24-41.

make them afraid. In fact, they even managed to successfully frustrate the Jews' building efforts for a number of years:

> Then the peoples around them set out to discourage the people of Judah and make them afraid to go on building. They hired counselors to work against them and frustrate their plans during the entire reign of Cyrus king of Persia and down to the reign of Darius king of Persia (4:4-5).

That's a time of about fifteen years!

Incidentally, it is right after these verses that the author decides to mention the two later episodes of opposition against the Jews' work which we mentioned earlier, first during the reign of Xerxes (4:6) and second during the reign of Artaxerxes and closer to the time the book of Ezra was written (4:7-23). The opposition mentioned in verses 4-5 above concerns the building of the temple in the final years of Cyrus down to the time of Darius. The opposition mentioned during the reign of Artaxerxes concerns the building of the wall, which occurred in the 440s under the direction of Nehemiah. Again, the author simply seems to be making note of how opposition continued off and on for almost a century. So don't be confused by this digression in verses 6-23.

Verse 24 appears to pick up where verse 5 leaves off, back in the 530s when the building of the temple was frustrated by these counselors. In the second year of Darius, we learn, the work of rebuilding the temple resumes. Notice the word "until" in verse 24: "Thus the work on the house of God in Jerusalem came to a standstill until the second year of the reign of Darius king of Persia" (4:24).

The opposition to the Jews was a serious thing, and it is given prominence in the book of Ezra. Friend, if you are uncertain about the truth of Christianity, please hear this one piece of advice: do not try to determine *what is true* by *what is popular*. Other religions like Islam may equate worldly success with success in God's eyes. But we Christians do not follow conquistadors like Muslims; we follow the Christ who was crucified. We understand that the natural disposition of all people—including you and me—is to oppose God and perversely assume that our best interests are at odds with God's commitment to himself. So we oppose God and hate his truth. So should we determine what's true by what's popular? In a world of God-haters? Now, perhaps "a world of God-haters" sounds like an exaggeration to you. If it does, I would just ask you to consider what we did to the Truth Incarnate when he came and lived among us. We killed him. We rejected him thoroughly. We crucified him! Christian or non-Christian, we must know that votes do not determine what is true and right and good. It will never be that way in a fallen world.

If you are a Christian, let me ask you to consider these people of old who faced persecution and persevered. Take courage. When you find that you have opponents for no reason except that you are a Christian, take their example to heart. After all, we will face persecution. As the apostle Paul told his disciple Timothy, "everyone who wants to live a godly life in Christ Jesus will be persecuted" (2 Tim. 3:12). Where did Paul get this idea? Was he just paranoid because of his own history of persecuting Christians? No, he got the idea from Jesus. Jesus himself had said, "If they persecuted me, they will persecute you also" (John 15:20).

I know these words may sound strange to many of us today, but I promise they don't sound strange to our Christian friends from Africa, especially in Nigeria and Sudan. Nor do they sound unreal to our one church member from Indonesia. Thousands have been killed in Indonesia because of their Christian profession. The persecutions you face may be less violent, like the discouragement faced by the exiles here in Ezra. Yet do not be surprised if you face persecution from your neighbors and coworkers, even your family and friends, for following Christ. Pray that we as a church would be faithful to persevere and not to gauge our success by how popular we become with the community around us. That is not the right way for a Christian church to behave. Don't misunderstand me—we want to be good neighbors in every way possible. But we must not be surprised if some of our neighbors on Capitol Hill view us with suspicion and even hostility because of what we believe about God the Father, Christ the Lord, the Holy Spirit, what God teaches in his Word, or how he calls us to live. If we are God's people, we will face opposition. We have Christ's word on that in John 15.

I hope you take this point to heart. We will face opposition in this life, and I am not talking about the opposition you face because of your own stupidity and sin. Sometimes we feel sorry for ourselves when we think about the terrible situations we find ourselves in because of our own mistakes. But Jesus is referring to the kind of opposition we will face for faithfully following him, just like the Jews in Ezra's day.

Completion. But as we continue through Ezra, we find that the opposition against the Jews was not finally successful. The temple was brought to completion!

> Then, because of the decree King Darius had sent, Tattenai, governor of Trans-Euphrates, and Shethar-Bozenai and their associates carried it out with diligence. So the elders of the Jews continued to build and prosper under the preaching of Haggai the prophet and Zechariah, a descendant of Iddo. They finished building the temple according to the command of the God of Israel and the decrees

of Cyrus, Darius and Artaxerxes, kings of Persia. The temple was completed on the third day of the month Adar, in the sixth year of the reign of King Darius.

Then the people of Israel—the priests, the Levites and the rest of the exiles—celebrated the dedication of the house of God with joy. For the dedication of this house of God they offered a hundred bulls, two hundred rams, four hundred male lambs and, as a sin offering for all Israel, twelve male goats, one for each of the tribes of Israel. And they installed the priests in their divisions and the Levites in their groups for the service of God at Jerusalem, according to what is written in the Book of Moses.

On the fourteenth day of the first month, the exiles celebrated the Passover. The priests and Levites had purified themselves and were all ceremonially clean. The Levites slaughtered the Passover lamb for all the exiles, for their brothers the priests and for themselves. So the Israelites who had returned from the exile ate it, together with all who had separated themselves from the unclean practices of their Gentile neighbors in order to seek the LORD, the God of Israel. For seven days they celebrated with joy the Feast of Unleavened Bread, because the LORD had filled them with joy by changing the attitude of the king of Assyria, so that he assisted them in the work on the house of God, the God of Israel (6:13-22).

So the temple is completed, which may be the most important event in this book. A great celebration ensues, followed by a joyful celebration of the Passover.

God's sovereign hand. Now, if the opposition against the Jews is so serious—the opposition that began with the exile and continued through these events in Ezra—how are they able to successfully rebuild the temple? The short answer is, because God's hand sovereignly moves. Reading through this book, we see clearly that God changes hearts and attitudes. In the very first verse, the Lord acts sovereignly in the life of the Persian king Cyrus: "The LORD moved the heart of Cyrus" (1:1). And God moves not just in Cyrus's heart. He moves in the hearts of all the Jews who return to resettle in Jerusalem—"everyone whose heart God had moved" (1:5). Later in the book, God changes the attitude of the king of Assyria (6:22). And later still, he puts it into the heart of King Artaxerxes to bring honor to the house of Yahweh (7:27-28). Indeed, both Cyrus and Artaxerxes, these foreign kings, explicitly recognize God's sovereignty (1:2; 7:23)! Also, we are told that one campaign of opposition to the Jews was unsuccessful because God's eye watched over the elders and builders (5:5).

Throughout the book of Ezra, we find a reoccurring phrase about God's *gracious hand* being *on* the ones he intends to protect. In chapter 7, God's gracious hand is on Ezra (7:9). In chapter 8, God's gracious hand is on the party preparing to return to Jerusalem (8:18). Ezra also tells King Artaxerxes that "the gracious hand of our God is on everyone who looks to him" (8:22). Then, after Ezra and his entourage safely arrive in Jerusalem after a four-month journey, Ezra writes that "the hand of our God was on us, and he protected us from enemies and bandits along the way" (8:31).

So how do God's people survive all the opposition they face? *God.* They survive because God sovereignly and graciously brings his people back to the land and enables them to rebuild his temple. That is what the story of Ezra is about.

I wonder how this sounds to you. Hopefully you realize that we Christians understand God in absolutely *awesome* terms! The God we worship is not a tribal deity. He is not a construct of our own minds. Rather, he is the one who existed in eternity past and has all power in himself. From him came all things that were created. The God we worship is also completely good. There is no evil in him, and he is entirely righteous and right in all things.

That is what Christ said God is like. When Christ stood before the Roman governor Pilate, he told him, "You would have no power over me if it were not given to you from above" (John 19:11). Consider who really arrested whom! As Jesus had said earlier, "*I* lay down my life—only to take it up again. No one takes it from me, but *I* lay it down of *my own* accord. *I* have authority to lay it down and authority to take it up again" (John 10:17-18).

Our public authorities and armed forces do and should have responsibility for promoting the security of the nation. Yet I would never trust any human instrument ultimately to provide security. Only God can do that. As Paul says in Acts, "From one man *[God] made* every nation of men, that they should inhabit the whole earth; and *he determined* the times set for them and the exact places where they should live" (Acts 17:26).

Prayer. If this is really the God we believe in, my Christian friend, why don't we do more of what Ezra does—fast, humble ourselves, and pray for this great God to work? This is the question that struck me as I reflected on this book and meditated on my own life as a Christian. So let me ask you:

- If you really believe that God is all-powerful and able, why don't you pray more?
- Why don't you have longer prayer times at the beginning of your day?
- Why don't you pray more in your family instead of arguing, fighting, worrying, or planning?
- Why don't you join us more faithfully to pray together as a church?

I have no clever rhetorical flourishes to add to all these questions. I simply put them to your soul as a fellow saved sinner and as a pastor. If God really is the Creator of everything and the all-powerful Lord of the universe, and not just a comforting idea for when you feel low, why don't you more faithfully join us to pray together as a church? If you *really* thought that God was sovereign, wouldn't you?

Belief in a sovereign God shows itself in a commitment to prayer (e.g., 8:21-23).

I thank God for how some of the great figures in Christian history prayed better than their theology should have allowed them to pray. They might have argued over the sovereignty of God, but get them on their knees and something inherent in their Christian hearts knew that the One in heaven reigns! So they prayed with boldness, fervency, and humility!

As a church, we should be unapologetic about stating that God is our only hope for making it through life. Our hope resides in this great and sovereign God alone. And we should be committed to demonstrating our belief in God's sovereignty in our prayers together as a church. Let's be biblical and let's be bold about what we ask of God.

If you are a member of our church who does not regularly join us for our Sunday night prayer meetings, let me ask you to reconsider your practice. You reap the benefits of all your brothers and sisters who make a point to regularly come and pray for you, the church's ministry, and God's glory in this place. You might even faithfully attend the church's members' meetings to vote on the affairs of the church. But could it be that praying regularly with the whole church, modeling your belief in God's sovereignty, and building your family around the life of this congregation as the children grow up is more significant than coming to members' meetings? Consider teaching by example, and join us in the evening to pray. That would be the right thing to teach the younger Christians around you, and that is what I am actively trying to teach the whole congregation. I thank God for the young mothers and the harried students, the older members and the families who live at a distance, the busy and the broken—all of those who teach their families and friends that praying with God's people is a priority. And I thank God for the privilege of pastoring a church where so many members do join us regularly on Sunday evening for prayer. Let us resolve afresh to go to our great God in prayer, because he is able to answer us!

We see here in Ezra that God restored his people. They did not restore themselves through their good planning or their stewardship drives. They did pray, however, and God sovereignly acted to answer their prayers.

GOD'S WORD REVEALS (CHAPTERS 7–9)

We also see in the book of Ezra that God's Word reveals. We learn in chapters 7–9, in particular, that God's Word reveals the sins of his people.

The Word Restored to the People

As we said earlier, a time gap of more than fifty years separates chapters 6 and 7. Beginning in chapter 7, Ezra is sent to restore God's Word to God's people in Judea. That is what chapters 7–8 are about in particular. When the story picks up, Ezra is still in exile with a number of other Jews:

> After these things, during the reign of Artaxerxes king of Persia, Ezra son of Seraiah, the son of Azariah, the son of Hilkiah, the son of Shallum, the son of Zadok, the son of Ahitub, the son of Amariah, the son of Azariah, the son of Meraioth, the son of Zerahiah, the son of Uzzi, the son of Bukki, the son of Abishua, the son of Phinehas, the son of Eleazar, the son of Aaron the chief priest—this Ezra came up from Babylon. He was a teacher well versed in the Law of Moses, which the LORD, the God of Israel, had given. The king had granted him everything he asked, for the hand of the LORD his God was on him. Some of the Israelites, including priests, Levites, singers, gatekeepers and temple servants, also came up to Jerusalem in the seventh year of King Artaxerxes.
>
> Ezra arrived in Jerusalem in the fifth month of the seventh year of the king. He had begun his journey from Babylon on the first day of the first month, and he arrived in Jerusalem on the first day of the fifth month, for the gracious hand of his God was on him. For Ezra had devoted himself to the study and observance of the Law of the LORD, and to teaching its decrees and laws in Israel.
>
> This is a copy of the letter King Artaxerxes had given to Ezra the priest and teacher, a man learned in matters concerning the commands and decrees of the LORD for Israel:
>
> Artaxerxes, king of kings,
>
> To Ezra the priest, a teacher of the Law of the God of heaven:
>
> Greetings.
>
> Now I decree that any of the Israelites in my kingdom, including priests and Levites, who wish to go to Jerusalem with you, may go. You are sent by the king and his seven advisers to inquire about Judah and Jerusalem with regard to the Law of your God, which is in your hand. Moreover, you are to take with you the silver and gold that the king and his advisers have freely given to the God of Israel, whose dwelling is in Jerusalem, together with all the silver and gold you may obtain from the province of Babylon, as well as the freewill offerings of the people and priests for the temple of their God in Jerusalem. With this money be sure to buy bulls, rams and male lambs, together with their grain offerings and drink offerings, and sacrifice them on the altar of the temple of your God in Jerusalem.

You and your brother Jews may then do whatever seems best with the rest of the silver and gold, in accordance with the will of your God. Deliver to the God of Jerusalem all the articles entrusted to you for worship in the temple of your God. And anything else needed for the temple of your God that you may have occasion to supply, you may provide from the royal treasury.

Now I, King Artaxerxes, order all the treasurers of Trans-Euphrates to provide with diligence whatever Ezra the priest, a teacher of the Law of the God of heaven, may ask of you—up to a hundred talents of silver, a hundred cors of wheat, a hundred baths of wine, a hundred baths of olive oil, and salt without limit. Whatever the God of heaven has prescribed, let it be done with diligence for the temple of the God of heaven. Why should there be wrath against the realm of the king and of his sons? You are also to know that you have no authority to impose taxes, tribute or duty on any of the priests, Levites, singers, gatekeepers, temple servants or other workers at this house of God.

And you, Ezra, in accordance with the wisdom of your God, which you possess, appoint magistrates and judges to administer justice to all the people of Trans-Euphrates—all who know the laws of your God. And you are to teach any who do not know them. Whoever does not obey the law of your God and the law of the king must surely be punished by death, banishment, confiscation of property, or imprisonment.

Praise be to the LORD, the God of our fathers, who has put it into the king's heart to bring honor to the house of the LORD in Jerusalem in this way and who has extended his good favor to me before the king and his advisers and all the king's powerful officials. Because the hand of the LORD my God was on me, I took courage and gathered leading men from Israel to go up with me (7:1-28).

At the beginning of chapter 8, a list of these leading men follows, as well as some of the preparatory steps Ezra took to organize their return journey. Particularly striking is how he prepared himself and the returning exiles by casting themselves into the Lord's hands:

There, by the Ahava Canal, I proclaimed a fast, so that we might humble ourselves before our God and ask him for a safe journey for us and our children, with all our possessions. I was ashamed to ask the king for soldiers and horsemen to protect us from enemies on the road, because we had told the king, "The gracious hand of our God is on everyone who looks to him, but his great anger is against all who forsake him." So we fasted and petitioned our God about this, and he answered our prayer (8:21-23).

Then several verses later we read about their arrival in Jerusalem:

On the twelfth day of the first month we set out from the Ahava Canal to go to Jerusalem. The hand of our God was on us, and he protected us from enemies and bandits along the way. So we arrived in Jerusalem, where we rested three days.

On the fourth day, in the house of our God, we weighed out the silver and gold and the sacred articles into the hands of Meremoth son of Uriah, the priest. Eleazar son of Phinehas was with him, and so were the Levites Jozabad son of Jeshua and Noadiah son of Binnui. Everything was accounted for by number and weight, and the entire weight was recorded at that time.

Then the exiles who had returned from captivity sacrificed burnt offerings to the God of Israel: twelve bulls for all Israel, ninety-six rams, seventy-seven male lambs and, as a sin offering, twelve male goats. All this was a burnt offering to the LORD. They also delivered the king's orders to the royal satraps and to the governors of Trans-Euphrates, who then gave assistance to the people and to the house of God (8:31-36).

So, who would bring God's Word to God's people? The man God had clearly prepared to bring it: Ezra. You can see Ezra's résumé in the first verses of chapter 7. His lineage goes back to Aaron (7:5), and he is called "a teacher well versed in the Law of Moses" (7:6). In his letter, King Artaxerxes refers to Ezra as "the priest, a teacher of the Law of the God of heaven" and as one who possesses "wisdom" (7:21, 25).

Lest you misunderstand, notice that "wisdom" in this context does not mean Ezra knew a lot about math, engineering, or history, or that he was quick on his feet in a debate. It means, rather, that he knew the Word of God, and that he was well-studied in the law. After all, "Ezra had devoted himself to the study and observance of the Law of the LORD, and to teaching its decrees and laws in Israel" (7:10). (You might want to mark that verse as a good one to meditate on later!) If you read through the book of Ezra, you find that the people often do what they do "in accordance with . . . the Law of Moses" (3:2), "in accordance with what is written" (3:4), "as prescribed by David king of Israel" (3:10), "according to the command of the God of Israel" (6:14), or "according to what is written in the Book of Moses" (6:18). That's why it was important for Ezra to be "a teacher well versed in the Law of Moses, which the LORD, the God of Israel, had given" (7:6).

In short, Ezra had devoted himself to 1) studying the Word of God, 2) doing the Word of God, and 3) teaching the Word of God.[9] His mission was to go and teach in Judah and Jerusalem "the commands and decrees of the LORD."[10] God sovereignly brought Ezra—through the edict of Artaxerxes—to Jerusalem to teach his Word.

---

[9] Cf. 7:25-26; Matt. 28:19-20.
[10] 7:11; cf. 7:12, 14; 9:10-11.

As a brief side note, you may be surprised to read that Emperor Artaxerxes of Persia promoted Ezra's teaching back in Jerusalem. Artaxerxes was not Jewish. Why did he care what the Jews were taught, and why would he want Ezra to go and teach? Well, that should not surprise us too much. Many of the world's empires whose inhabitants have espoused different religions have instituted policies—wisely—allowing for the tolerance of religious diversity. There is nothing new about this idea. In fact, our own nation is far less religiously diverse than many nations in the world throughout history, especially when compared to empires of Persia's size. Respecting the religious beliefs of others—even the beliefs that you know are wrong—is a necessary part of coexisting and even prospering in a society with people different from us. In Ezra's day, God used such tolerance to accomplish his own purposes for his people. Surely he can use the liberties we enjoy in this country no less.

Notice, then, how powerful God's Word proves to be in the book of Ezra. In chapter 4, for instance, the opposition manages to stymie the rebuilding of the temple. What got it started again? Was it Darius's letter in chapter 6? Well, his letter gave the Jews permission to proceed with building. But what started the whole process was the preaching of God's Word by the prophets Haggai and Zechariah in chapter 5 (5:1-2; 6:14). Their preaching met the opposition, defeated the discouragement of God's people, and restarted everything! In chapter 9, when the sin of God's people is exposed, they respond with grief. A number of the people are described as those who "trembled at the words of the God of Israel" (9:4).

Do not underestimate the power of the Word of God! That is how God brings his life into this fallen world again and again.

Do you wonder how you can know the truth? How you can know whether it is worthwhile to keep on living? Turn to the Word of God. Read it, and hear it preached. Give yourself to praying to the God revealed in the Bible. If you are a non-Christian, I would especially advise you to read the Gospels. The four Gospels are found at the beginning of the New Testament, and they talk about the life of Jesus Christ. More than Ezra ever could, Jesus Christ personifies God's Word. In fact, he *is* the Word of God. John's Gospel opens with these amazing words: "In the beginning was the Word, and the Word was with God, and the Word was God. . . . The Word became flesh and made his dwelling among us" (John 1:1, 14).

For your own life, Christian, resolve to *study the Bible*. Resolve to *obey the Bible*. Resolve to *teach the Bible,* as God gives you opportunity.

As a church, may we continue to keep the Bible at the center of our life together. May we be a church where the love of God's Word, the knowledge of it, and the ability to teach it are regarded as the most important qualification for service among us, and where our times together are marked by careful attention to it.

The Word Exposing the Sins of the People

What was the effect of God's Word when it was clearly taught once again in Jerusalem? It exposed the sin of the people. Let's look at what happens in chapter 9, after Ezra's arrival in Jerusalem:

> After these things had been done, the leaders came to me and said, "The people of Israel, including the priests and the Levites, have not kept themselves separate from the neighboring peoples with their detestable practices, like those of the Canaanites, Hittites, Perizzites, Jebusites, Ammonites, Moabites, Egyptians and Amorites. They have taken some of their daughters as wives for themselves and their sons, and have mingled the holy race with the peoples around them. And the leaders and officials have led the way in this unfaithfulness."
>
> When I heard this, I tore my tunic and cloak, pulled hair from my head and beard and sat down appalled. Then everyone who trembled at the words of the God of Israel gathered around me because of this unfaithfulness of the exiles. And I sat there appalled until the evening sacrifice.
>
> Then, at the evening sacrifice, I rose from my self-abasement, with my tunic and cloak torn, and fell on my knees with my hands spread out to the LORD my God and prayed:
>
> "O my God, I am too ashamed and disgraced to lift up my face to you, my God, because our sins are higher than our heads and our guilt has reached to the heavens. From the days of our forefathers until now, our guilt has been great. Because of our sins, we and our kings and our priests have been subjected to the sword and captivity, to pillage and humiliation at the hand of foreign kings, as it is today.
>
> "But now, for a brief moment, the LORD our God has been gracious in leaving us a remnant and giving us a firm place in his sanctuary, and so our God gives light to our eyes and a little relief in our bondage. Though we are slaves, our God has not deserted us in our bondage. He has shown us kindness in the sight of the kings of Persia: He has granted us new life to rebuild the house of our God and repair its ruins, and he has given us a wall of protection in Judah and Jerusalem.
>
> "But now, O our God, what can we say after this? For we have disregarded the commands you gave through your servants the prophets when you said: 'The land you are entering to possess is a land polluted by the corruption of its peoples. By their detestable practices they have filled it with their impurity from one end to the other. Therefore, do not give your daughters in marriage to their sons or take their daughters for

your sons. Do not seek a treaty of friendship with them at any time, that you may be strong and eat the good things of the land and leave it to your children as an everlasting inheritance.'

"What has happened to us is a result of our evil deeds and our great guilt, and yet, our God, you have punished us less than our sins have deserved and have given us a remnant like this. Shall we again break your commands and intermarry with the peoples who commit such detestable practices? Would you not be angry enough with us to destroy us, leaving us no remnant or survivor? O LORD, God of Israel, you are righteous! We are left this day as a remnant. Here we are before you in our guilt, though because of it not one of us can stand in your presence" (9:1-15).

What we find here in chapter 9 is what we can see throughout Ezra (indeed, throughout all the historical books of the Old Testament we have studied): an example of the sinfulness of these people, and a testimony of why they had been exiled in the first place. Back in chapter 4, two characters in the Persian government, Rehum and Shimshai, sent a letter to Artaxerxes, warning of the danger of letting the Jews rebuild Jerusalem's walls since the city had a history of rebellion and wickedness (4:12). Ironically, they spoke better than they knew; they didn't know the half of it! And in chapter 5, the Jewish elders themselves gave an interesting summary of their people's history: "because our fathers angered the God of heaven, he handed them over to Nebuchadnezzar the Chaldean, king of Babylon, who destroyed this temple and deported the people to Babylon" (5:12).

The testimonies of the Persians and the Jewish elders line up with what we read in Deuteronomy and Joshua, as well as with what the books of Kings and Chronicles say about Israel's fall. All this history is summarized in one sentence toward the beginning of Ezra's prayer in chapter 9. Did you notice it? He prayed, "From the days of our forefathers until now, our guilt has been great. Because of our sins, we and our kings and our priests have been subjected to the sword and captivity, to pillage and humiliation at the hand of foreign kings, as it is today" (9:7).

So what is the great sin exposed by God's Word here in chapter 9? Ezra states the answer explicitly: "we have disregarded the commands you gave" (9:10-11). Which commands? "Do not give your daughters in marriage to their sons or take their daughters for your sons" (9:12). The people of Israel had received this command a number of times. Moses, for instance, had instructed them in Deuteronomy, "Do not give your daughters to their sons or take their daughters for your sons, for they will turn your sons away from following me to serve other gods, and the LORD's anger will burn against you and will quickly destroy you" (Deut. 7:3-4). Yet the people of Israel, once again, had not kept themselves separate. No sooner had they returned to the Promised Land than they began mixing themselves with the non-Israelites who loved, worshiped, and served other gods. And in thus failing to keep themselves separate, they were unfaithful to God.

Some people misunderstand what God was referring to as sin in passages like these. He was in no way calling interracial marriage sin. The focus of concern here was not skin pigment or racial purity. His comments were not xenophobic or racist. Instead, their intent actually takes us to the theological heart of the Old Testament: God has always wanted his people—including his post-exile people—to be preserved from idolatry, from spiritual adultery, from cheating on God, so that they will persevere in faithfulness to God. So he says to them, "Don't marry people who don't worship me!" Now, clear allowances were made in Deuteronomy for those non-Israelites who wished to join Israel, like Ruth who decided to accept the God of Israel as her God. But that is a different matter. A situation like Ruth's does not introduce the problem of having one marriage and two gods.

Yet standing there, freshly returned from exile and beholding the sin around him, Ezra knew what his Bible taught well enough to observe, "You have punished us less than our sins have deserved" (9:13). What an amazing statement, especially when you consider the ruin the Jews had encountered in exile. God had warned his people over and over that if they would not separate from the idolatrous nations around them, then he would disperse them into the nations. After all, what's the purpose of having a non-special special people? A non-separate separate people? If God's people are intent on living just like the world, then they should not be called God's special people! They are a sham. So disperse them; dismiss them back into the world.

It is the function of God's Word to call God's people to separate themselves from sin, and that is why God sent Ezra. It is also why Zerubbabel, in chapter 4, discouraged non-Israelites from helping the Israelites rebuild the temple (4:3). Faithfulness to the Word of God meant keeping separate.

Today, my Christian friend, we are not called to geographically *separate* ourselves from the nations (see what Jesus says about where we should worship, in John 4:21). But we are called to live *distinct* lives for the very same reasons the Jews were called to separate themselves in their land. So study the Bible and you will find that it will have a tremendous effect on your life, as in the book of Ezra. It will show you what a distinct life looks like. Just as God's Word exposed the sin of intermarriage among God's Old Testament people, so I study the Bible every morning because it exposes sin in my heart. That is one of the reasons I go back to it, because it is such a faithful friend in that sense. As I give myself to reading and studying his Word, God kindly and (it can seem) unsparingly uses it by his Spirit. He will use it in your life, too, if you will give time to studying it.

You realize, don't you, that when you attend church you don't fool anyone? We know you are a sinner, whether you have been a member of the church fifty years or you have visited just once. We are well acquainted with the fact that all of us are sinners. So please realize that your appearance misleads no one. We know you have revolted against God, not because we know everything about your life, but because you share the same fallen human nature as us. The only human who was ever without sin was Jesus Christ. Only he, says the writer of the New Testament book Hebrews, "meets our need—one who is holy, blameless, pure, set apart from sinners, exalted above the heavens" (Heb. 7:26).

God uses the Bible to expose our sin. And God uses the Bible to guide us to holiness—to lives that are distinct from the world around us. Has that been your experience as a Christian? If it has been, tell fellow Christians about it. Encourage them to find solace, direction, comfort, and challenge in God's Word. Yes, feel free to recommend other books. But please never regard any other book as highly as the Bible, this book that God's Spirit has specially inspired.

We as a church must always be giving ourselves over to being re-fashioned, re-shaped, and re-formed by the Word of God. We want services that place God's Word at the heart of our time together and preaching that expounds the Bible. We know how badly we need it.

God's Word reveals our sin, and God's Word is how we come to know God and love him with all of our lives.

GOD'S PEOPLE REPENT (CHAPTER 10)

Now we come to the last chapter in Ezra, where we find that God's people repent. Let's look at chapter 10:

> While Ezra was praying and confessing, weeping and throwing himself down before the house of God, a large crowd of Israelites—men, women and children—gathered around him. They too wept bitterly. Then Shecaniah son of Jehiel, one of the descendants of Elam, said to Ezra, "We have been unfaithful to our God by marrying foreign women from the peoples around us. But in spite of this, there is still hope for Israel. Now let us make a covenant before our God to send away all these women and their children, in accordance with the counsel of my lord and of those who fear the commands of our God. Let it be done according to the Law. Rise up; this matter is in your hands. We will support you, so take courage and do it."

So Ezra rose up and put the leading priests and Levites and all Israel under oath to do what had been suggested. And they took the oath. Then Ezra withdrew from before the house of God and went to the room of Jehohanan son of Eliashib. While he was there, he ate no food and drank no water, because he continued to mourn over the unfaithfulness of the exiles.

A proclamation was then issued throughout Judah and Jerusalem for all the exiles to assemble in Jerusalem. Anyone who failed to appear within three days would forfeit all his property, in accordance with the decision of the officials and elders, and would himself be expelled from the assembly of the exiles.

Within the three days, all the men of Judah and Benjamin had gathered in Jerusalem. And on the twentieth day of the ninth month, all the people were sitting in the square before the house of God, greatly distressed by the occasion and because of the rain. Then Ezra the priest stood up and said to them, "You have been unfaithful; you have married foreign women, adding to Israel's guilt. Now make confession to the LORD, the God of your fathers, and do his will. Separate yourselves from the peoples around you and from your foreign wives."

The whole assembly responded with a loud voice: "You are right! We must do as you say. But there are many people here and it is the rainy season; so we cannot stand outside. Besides, this matter cannot be taken care of in a day or two, because we have sinned greatly in this thing. Let our officials act for the whole assembly. Then let everyone in our towns who has married a foreign woman come at a set time, along with the elders and judges of each town, until the fierce anger of our God in this matter is turned away from us." Only Jonathan son of Asahel and Jahzeiah son of Tikvah, supported by Meshullam and Shabbethai the Levite, opposed this.

So the exiles did as was proposed. Ezra the priest selected men who were family heads, one from each family division, and all of them designated by name. On the first day of the tenth month they sat down to investigate the cases, and by the first day of the first month they finished dealing with all the men who had married foreign women (10:1-17).

Following this passage, the final verses of the book are a list of all the descendants of priests who had married foreign wives (10:18-44). But what a vivid passage these first seventeen verses are! The whole assembly responds with a loud voice in the pouring rain. Most significant, though, was their response to the exposure of their sin.

Confession and Sorrow for Sin

When their sin is exposed, they express sorrow for their sin and they confess it.

Back in chapter 9, we saw that Ezra was appalled and astonished. As one scholar has observed, "Our greatest security against sin is to be shocked by it."[11] And the depth of Ezra's shock and sorrow is clear. He abases himself (9:5), and then the sorrow in his heart wells up and compels his lips to prayer: "O my God, I am too ashamed and disgraced to lift up my face to you, my God, because our sins are higher than our heads and our guilt has reached to the heavens" (9:6).

One interesting aside: you may have heard Christians debate the idea of corporate responsibility for sin back in 1995 when the Southern Baptist Convention issued a formal apology for slavery. Other denominations have taken similar actions. But can an individual or a group really take corporate responsibility for sin? I am not entirely sure, but it is worth observing that Ezra prays about "our sins." And he is not simply referring to sin generically; he is referring to the recent sins of intermarriage, even though he himself had not participated in the sin of intermarriage. That's interesting, isn't it? You can think about that more over lunch.

Anyway, Ezra's sorrow for sin spreads in chapter 10. In verse 1, a large crowd gathers around Ezra and joins him in weeping bitterly. In verse 2, one member of the crowd leads in a public confession of sin. Then Ezra calls "all the men of Judah and Benjamin" to "make confession to the LORD" (10:9, 11). And they do! The whole assembly responds with a loud voice, "we have sinned greatly" (10:13). God led Ezra and the people into sorrow for their sin and a confession of it. Again, the light of Scripture exposes sin.

What is sin? It is rejecting God's will. It is following our own desires rather than God's. It is loving other people and other things more than him. All of this, we have done. And all of us must give an account to him. Friend, if you recall your sin with only cool indifference, pray that God would change your heart. Pray that he would sovereignly move in your heart to change your indifference to sorrow. Pray that you would begin to understand how morally bankrupt your sin leaves you.

What hope remains for you? Your only hope is in this One I have mentioned who had no sins of his own to cause him sorrow—the Lord Jesus Christ. The only sorrow for sins he ever knew was sorrow for your sins and mine, and particularly for the sins he bore in his own death on the cross. As Peter wrote, "He himself bore our sins in his body on the tree" (1 Pet. 2:24).

I know we do not think much about sorrow and confession these days. *Modesty* seems outmoded and *humility* seems ancient. *Circumspection* is an unknown word and *shame* is a rarely seen commodity, at least shame for the appropriate things. But let's pray that God would use us to help resurrect these

---

[11] Edward Musgrave Blaiklock, in a sermon titled "Temptation," at the Keswick Convention, 1959. Available online at http://rgwitty.com/kesserout.html.

ideas that are so important for our culture. Can you imagine a culture with no modesty or humility, no sense of shame or responsibility? We may soon reach that point in the West. But let us do our part to resist this movement. At work, exhibit modesty. In speaking about yourself, model humility. In your homes, encourage your spouse and train your children to be careful and circumspect. Ask yourself, would anyone who knows you describe you as humble? You lawyers, find good language to express shame. You Capitol Hill staffers, watch for conceit in your own hearts, and gently oppose it in your friends. You businessmen, are you successful? Realize that even your most diligently pursued prizes come to you by God's grace.

If you want to be concerned for our country today, take care that we as a culture do not become anesthetized to any unpleasant emotion caused by a violated conscience. Let us as Christians conspire to do our best to keep a moral vocabulary alive, for us, for our children, and, ultimately, for the glory of God!

As for your own heart, my Christian friend, cultivate a godly sorrow for your sins. Consider God's grace by meditating on what you *deserve* for your sins and then contrasting that with what God has given you! It is hard to proudly defend your own rights when you realize that God has given you so much better than you deserve, as Ezra said in his prayer.

Practice consistently confessing your sins to God. You won't surprise God when you acknowledge what he knows anyway. But you will instruct yourself, and, by God's grace, you will humble yourself. One way to help you confess your sins to God is to confess them to others. Are you impatient? Confess that to someone with whom you have been impatient. And generally speaking, find someone with whom you would be ashamed to confess your sin, and then confess it to them. You and I must learn to be vulnerable and transparent, because we are not well, wise, or honest enough to tend our souls by ourselves.

Then pray for us as a church, that we would consistently and clearly teach about God's holiness. We do deliberately plan to make his holiness a prominent theme during our gatherings together. Pray also that we would model confession for one another. And pray that we would cultivate discipling relationships and friendships marked by deliberate humility and honesty. All of these things we want to do to help us understand what God thinks about our sins.

Repentance and Change

But all this sorrow and confession should lead beyond themselves to repentance and change. We see that here in chapter 10. Ezra not only says, "Make confession to the LORD," he also says, "and do his will" (10:11). And what was

God's will in their case? Look at the rest of the verse: "Separate yourselves from the peoples around you and from your foreign wives."[12]

This is certainly a radical answer, and I know I cannot answer all the questions you may have about it. I can't even answer all the questions that I have about it, like how did these wives and children support themselves? I do know the Bible can say radical things. For example, Jesus taught, albeit in hyperbole, "If your hand or your foot causes you to sin, cut it off and throw it away"; and "if your eye causes you to sin, gouge it out and throw it away" (Matt. 18:8, 9). The family members of the exiles were not killed. But they were "cut off" from their Jewish spouses.

Does this mean that repentance requires Christians married to non-Christian spouses to divorce them? Not at all. Both the apostles Paul and Peter address the Christian married to a non-Christian, and neither of them tells such an individual to seek a divorce (1 Cor. 7:12-16; 1 Pet. 3:1-2). Since the coming of Christ in the first century, God's people are no longer tied to a particular nation or ethnicity, as they were in Old Testament times.

Israel, on the other hand, was to maintain this separate nation status, marked and specially formed by God's Word in preparation for the coming of God's Messiah. Leading the Israelites out of these marriages to foreign wives was leading them, in a sense, out of exile. The people remained in exile as long as they kept their homes divided. So, these marriages, like the geography, were simply illustrative, pedagogical, and preparatory. Jerusalem existed to remind them of God's faithfulness, of their sin, and of God's mercy. Their repentance was their real restoration.

Would the people really repent? That is the question Ezra asks at the end of his prayer in chapter 9:

> "Shall we again break your commands and intermarry with the peoples who commit such detestable practices? Would you not be angry enough with us to destroy us, leaving us no remnant or survivor? O LORD, God of Israel, you are righteous! We are left this day as a remnant. Here we are before you in our guilt, though because of it not one of us can stand in your presence" (9:14-15).

Now, my non-Christian friend, what will happen to you in the future? Will you keep your sin as your own, or will you give it up and receive the gift of God's forgiveness for your sins and a righteousness credited to you by faith? God has provided for forgiveness through the death of the Lord Jesus on the cross. In his death, Jesus paid the penalty for the sins of all those who would ever repent and trust in him. Are you someone who has repented and trusted?

---

[12] Cf. 10:3-5, 11-12, 16-17, 19.

Oh, you should be. No sin is worth keeping at the cost of losing Christ. Yet that is the decision that sits before you right now. Believe the Bible and what it says about Christ! Believe this good news! Turn loose of your sins, and grab hold of Christ by faith. Believe the Bible when it says about Christ that "God made him who had no sin to be sin for us, that in him we might become the righteousness of God" (2 Cor. 5:21).

Today we can freely meet to talk about these things. But I cannot promise you that we will be able to meet tomorrow. I don't know about the future of our freedoms. I don't know the future of your health or mine. For all I know, this may be the last sermon you hear. I was reading Thomas Watson's arresting little book *Heaven Taken by Storm* this week in my quiet times. At one point, he challenges the reader with this idea:

> It may be the last time that God will ever speak to us in his Word; it may be the last sermon that we shall ever hear; we may go from the place of hearing to the place of judging. If people would think thus when they come into the house of God, "Perhaps this will be the last time that God will counsel us about our souls, the last time that ever we shall see our minister's face," with what devotion would they come![13]

Have you considered that this may be your last time to hear God's Word preached? Do your business with God. When you hear his Word preached, do business with God. Repent of your sins. Believe this good news of Jesus Christ!

Now, my Christian friend, what repentance is God calling you to through this picture of separating from foreign wives, here in the last chapter of Ezra? I have some suggestions. If you are engaged to a non-Christian, break off the engagement. Let me repeat that, lest I be misunderstood: if you are engaged to a non-Christian, break off your engagement. It is not sin, and ultimately it is the most loving thing to do. Better to lose your deposits on receptions and invitations than your soul. "Are you saying that I can lose my salvation by marrying a non-Christian?" No, I am simply saying that your actions reveal what you really love. If you are in a position where you can freely choose, you should not freely choose to step into a life of torn allegiances by pledging to love someone who you know—according to Scripture—hates the One you most love. Surely you should never take this step.

What repentance is God calling you to, Christian? Let me give you another possibility. Break up with your boyfriend or your girlfriend if he or she is not

---

[13] Thomas Watson, *Heaven Taken by Storm: Showing the Holy Violence a Christian Is to Put Forth in the Pursuit After Glory* (Ligonier, Pa.: Soli Deo Gloria, 1992), 17-18.

laboring with you to grow in Christ. You may happily concede that you should not marry a non-Christian, but think that it is okay to date them. But why are you dating them? To excite one another's affections when you say you are resolved not to bring those affections to fruition until marriage? What kind of strange and selfish cruelty is that? Your selfish enjoyment now means you will break their heart more deeply later. My Christian friend, if the person you are dating will not or cannot be a member of the same church as you, you need to stop and consider, is it possible that the issues preventing them from doing so are significant? God has a wonderful plan for us in marriage, and part of it includes finding someone with whom we can establish a peaceful unity, where we reinforce one another, not where we disagree and chafe over the matters that we claim are closest to our hearts.

What repentance is God calling you to, Christian? I've got just one more. Relinquish your passive approach to friendships. Realize that you should actively seek out and cultivate friendships that will bring you closer to God. I do not have to be a prophet to tell you what you will be like one year from now. All I have to know is whom you hang around with; whom you spend your time with; whom you feel affection for; whom you enjoy.

In a fallen world, so many things that come easy are not right; and so many things that are right, don't come easy. So let's pray for one another. Pray for our church, that we will be a community strong enough and loving enough that we can help each other be countercultural in these matters. No, we will not save ourselves *by* being distinct and countercultural. But I will tell you this: in today's world, we will not be saved *without* being distinct and countercultural.

God's people are marked out from others by our repentance; we have turned away from our sins. When you are confronted over your sin, do you hold on to your sin even more tightly and resent the person who confronts you? That is the sign of a person going to hell. The heart won by the grace of Christ has turned loose such defensiveness and pride and has said, "Yes, I'm a sinner. I need help. Step into my life." God's people are marked by that kind of repentance.

CONCLUSION: WILL THE CHURCH BECOME VISIBLE?

We learn in the book of Ezra that the distinct people of God bear testimony to the distinctiveness of God, and therefore they hold out hope to others through the very things that make them distinct.

A lot of people are walking around Washington, D.C., today—you will probably see some of them this afternoon—who are hope*less,* even despairing. Do you know why they are like that? They are like that because they do not know what God is really like! If they knew what God is really like, they would have the hope they need for their lives.

We find in Ezra that God is *good*.[14] We discover that he is *gracious* and *kind* (9:8-9). We learn that he is *merciful* (9:13). We find those blessed words in chapter 10: "But in spite of all this, there is still hope" (10:2).

How will the world today find hope in the truth of who God is? Well, they could read Ezra. That's true. But they will probably not read Ezra. So how will they find out? Most likely, they will find hope by reading *you*. If you are a Christian, you are here as a witness to God in the world. People are supposed to be able to look at you and me in order to find the answer to the question, "What is God like?"

Can they? Well, if we call ourselves Christians, they *are* looking at us. I guess the question is, will they get the right answer by looking at us?

Let us pray:

O God, we pray that you would crucify our selfishness upon the cross of your love. We pray that, in your love, you would humble us. Bring your Word deep into our hearts and heal us, we pray. Do your work in our hearts for Jesus' sake and for your glory through your people. Amen.

Questions for Reflection

1. Why is a *worldly Christian* the worst combination of two things? Why is this the sort of person Jesus promises to spit out of his mouth (Rev. 3:15-17)?

2. Consider your own church for a moment. If a non-Christian friend of yours spent time with the members of your church, in both formal gatherings and informal social settings, would he or she say, "Wow, these people are different from everyone I know at the office" or "at school" or wherever? If yes, what differences would your friend notice? If no, what are *you* doing to change that?

3. We learned in the book of Ezra that the distinct people of God bear testimony to the distinctiveness of God, and therefore they hold out hope to others through the very things that make them distinct. Based on this line of reasoning and what we read in Ezra, what is the most important thing a church can do for its evangelistic outreach?

---

[14] 3:11; cf. 1 Chron. 16:34; 2 Chron. 5:13; 7:3; Ps. 106, 107, 118, 136.

4. God opposed intermarriage with foreigners among his special Old Testament people because he knew that foreigners would lead the hearts of his people astray to other gods, thus destroying their very witness to other nations. When Ezra found that the exiles who had returned before him had married foreign spouses, he *exposed* their sin with the *Word of God*. What does this mean for our churches today? In other words, what should pastors in particular do before anything else if they want to strengthen their church's evangelistic outreach?

5. In this sermon, we have been instructed not to try to determine *what is true* by *what is popular*. In your personal life, where are you tempted to make this mistake? Where are you tempted to determine what is true by what comes easy or what feels good? If you are a pastor or any other sort of church leader, where are you tempted to pattern your ministry after what's popular instead of what's true? If you are a church member, where are you tempted to criticize your church according to your own preferences rather than according to what the Bible teaches?

6. Do people at church know that you are a sinner? Do you tell them? What do you tell them? Whom do you tell? Or would you prefer for them to think your soul is as nicely pressed as your shirt and as polished as your shoes?

7. What is repentance? Are there any sins in your life that you refuse to repent of (turn away from)? Why does the eternal fate of your soul hang on your answer to these two questions?

8. Is there someone in your life whom you love very much, who calls himself or herself a Christian, yet who does not live in repentance of sin? Have you confronted him or her directly, specifically, and gently about his or her lack of repentance? Why do you think you love this person?

9. Do you believe that God is the all-powerful Creator and Lord of the universe? Then why don't you pray more? Are you certain you believe what you say you believe?

10. How does Ezra—both who he was and what he did—point us to Jesus Christ? Think particularly about i) why Artaxerxes sends him back to Judah in chapter 7, ii) the role he plays on behalf of the people in his confession in chapter 9, and iii) his exhortation to the people in chapter 10.

THE MESSAGE OF NEHEMIAH: REBUILDING

16

THE MESSAGE OF NEHEMIAH: REBUILDING

ASSERT YOURSELF[1]

Well, I got it again:

> "Dear Mr. Dever,
>   "Your career isn't just about money, is it?
>   "I didn't think so. It's about something deeper.
>   "Something so central to your core, to what makes you tick, that you can't imagine living without it.
>   "It's about leadership. Having your say. Making things happen. Putting your stamp on the future."

Twice now I have received this letter from the *Harvard Business Review.* I must be scheduled to get it mid-summer every even-numbered year. Aside from the humor of the fact that they have sent me the same form letter twice, the letter itself is actually quite instructive. The most concise and highly researched conclusions about where our society is today can often be found in the advertising campaigns that depend on split-second appeals. These appeals give us a peak into how people think. Surely, the *Harvard Business Review* must offer us an accurate reflection of what people today think about leadership. Apparently, we like to think of ourselves as leaders, and a leader is someone who, as they say here, "has your say," "makes things happens," "puts *your* stamp on the future." Leadership is self-assertiveness. It's self-confidence. Really, it's self-centeredness.

Is that right? Are these things the core of leadership?

[1] This sermon was originally preached on November 24, 2002, at Capitol Hill Baptist Church in Washington, D.C.

INTRODUCING NEHEMIAH

In considering the nature of leadership, few books speak more clearly than the Old Testament book of Nehemiah, which was originally the second half of the book of Ezra (see the sermon on Ezra for more on this). We have reached Nehemiah in our present series of overview sermons on the books of history in the Old Testament. Our series began with the book of Joshua, which is set about one thousand years earlier than Nehemiah. Joshua described for us Israel's conquest and initial settlement of the Promised Land. Judges followed, which recounted three centuries of leaders, some good and some bad. Next was Ruth, a marvelous little cameo of God's providential care for his people in desperate times. After Ruth came 1 and 2 Samuel, 1 and 2 Kings, and 1 and 2 Chronicles, which told and retold the story of God dealing with his people through Samuel, Saul, David, Solomon, and all the kings of Israel and Judah until the northern kingdom was destroyed and the southern kingdom was exiled to Babylon in 586 B.C. Then in Ezra, the Jewish exiles returned from Babylon to Jerusalem and rebuilt the temple, completing the work in 516 B.C., seventy years after the old temple was destroyed. And now in Nehemiah, the place where Old Testament history ends in about 440 B.C., God's people rebuild the walls of Jerusalem.

In Nehemiah, we watch the people of God resettle the land, build Jerusalem's walls, and prepare to fight. They accomplish much, and many of their names are prominently placed in the lists scattered throughout the book. In the foreground of the unfolding story, however, are the leaders: the priests who work in the temple and teach God's law—chief among whom is Ezra— and the governor himself, Nehemiah.

As we look at the portraits presented in the books of Nehemiah and Ezra, we want to ask an always crucial question: What kind of leadership does the Bible present as exemplary? Even more concisely, what is godly leadership? This question will help guide us through the book of Nehemiah, where we will note *eight* aspects of godly leadership.

I pray that through this time, God will give you more understanding of what he calls you to be, as well as how he calls you to use the time, influence, and opportunities that he gives you.

1. A GODLY LEADER PRAYS

First, we see that a godly leader prays. The book begins in Babylon with Nehemiah getting some bad news. Nehemiah recounts the story:

Hanani, one of my brothers, came from Judah with some other men, and I questioned them about the Jewish remnant that survived the exile, and also about Jerusalem.

They said to me, "Those who survived the exile and are back in the province are in great trouble and disgrace. The wall of Jerusalem is broken down, and its gates have been burned with fire."

When I heard these things, I sat down and wept. For some days I mourned and fasted and prayed before the God of heaven (1:2-4).

We do not think much about city walls these days, and so the news Nehemiah hears about the sad state of Jerusalem's walls may not seem like a big deal to you. But actually, a city's walls were arguably more important than its army. Without walls, a city would be at the mercy of whatever band of marauders came through. It could not control its own affairs. Thus the proverb: "Like a city whose walls are broken down is a man who lacks self-control" (Prov. 25:28). Such a man is destroyed by any passing temptation or outside influence.

At the beginning of this book, Jerusalem was in such a state. Nehemiah hears about it, is moved, and immediately turns to prayer. His first act is to go to God, who is sovereign over all the empires that might descend upon Jerusalem. He prays,

"O LORD, God of heaven, the great and awesome God, who keeps his covenant of love with those who love him and obey his commands, let your ear be attentive and your eyes open to hear the prayer your servant is praying before you day and night for your servants, the people of Israel. I confess the sins we Israelites, including myself and my father's house, have committed against you. We have acted very wickedly toward you. We have not obeyed the commands, decrees and laws you gave your servant Moses.

"Remember the instruction you gave your servant Moses, saying, 'If you are unfaithful, I will scatter you among the nations, but if you return to me and obey my commands, then even if your exiled people are at the farthest horizon, I will gather them from there and bring them to the place I have chosen as a dwelling for my Name.'

"They are your servants and your people, whom you redeemed by your great strength and your mighty hand. O Lord, let your ear be attentive to the prayer of this your servant and to the prayer of your servants who delight in revering your name. Give your servant success today by granting him favor in the presence of this man."

I was cupbearer to the king (1:5-11).

It is a beautiful, compact prayer, beginning with praise, moving to confession, then citing God's promises back to God. Nehemiah reminds God of how his name is tied up with his people's name, and then asks God to move the king of Persia's heart. Adoration, confession, scriptural promise, honoring of God, the request itself—this is not a bad model for a prayer! If you are a leader in any capacity and you want to know how to pray, Nehemiah's brief prayer in chapter 1 is a good model.

Not only was Nehemiah moved to prayer in chapter 1, we find him praying throughout the book. In chapter 2, he shoots up an "arrow prayer," as some call it, when King Artaxerxes asks him a question and he wants to answer well: "The king said to me, 'What is it you want?' Then I prayed to the God of heaven, and I answered the king, 'If it pleases the king . . .'" (2:4-5a). You can be sure that Nehemiah did not open his mouth and utter a long pastoral prayer as we do in church on Sunday mornings. I assume he prayed silently and briefly. You don't want the king to think you are not paying attention! These types of prayers seem to typify Nehemiah's life. He utters brief prayers to God over everything that concerns him throughout the book: "Remember me in mercy, O God"; "Frustrate my enemies, O Lord"; and so on.[2]

I wonder how alone *you* feel when you receive bad news, or when you are enduring a time of tragedy. If you do not believe in the God of the Bible, I expect one of the loneliest feelings in the universe must be experienced when you hear about something of great magnitude—good or bad—and you feel an innate desire to talk to him. To say, "Thank you!" or "Why?" I have seen this happen so many times, and I believe you know what I am talking about. Perhaps you just thought you were talking to yourself. But I don't think so. I think you were trying to talk to someone else, someone whom you don't even know.

And you *can* know him! God cares about us in ways no one else does. When God's people were in Jerusalem and no one paid attention to them, they were not ultimately at the disposal of their Persian overlords. By God's providence, news came to Nehemiah in Babylon, and Nehemiah was sent to the people in Jerusalem! God alone is finally sovereign, and he can always be approached in prayer. That is an amazing thought! That this One who is sovereign over the universe is always approachable by us in prayer! Even those of you who meet with the president of the United States with some regularity may not be able to talk with him at will. But those of us who know God through Christ can always speak with the One who holds the president's heart in his hands. That is the privilege that you and I have in Christ—the privilege of prayer.

---

[2] 4:4-5; 5:19; 6:14; 13:14, 22, 29, 31.

My Christian friend, cultivate your prayer life. Cultivate your desire to talk to God. What is your first response to challenges? To bad news? For that matter, what is your first response to good news? What stirs up your heart? When you hear anything of significance, you should respond in prayer. Especially if you would be a leader of God's people!

For those of you who are leaders in the church, I hope you realize that Nehemiah should not encourage us to pray for our nation's armies so much as it should push us to pray that God's people would be distinct from the surrounding world. *That's* ultimately why Nehemiah was concerned about Jerusalem's walls. Today, we don't need to pray that God would erect a physical boundary between his people and others; we need to pray that he would preserve the distinction between the people he has redeemed and the people who remain in darkness and rebellion. That is how the world will see the light—through people like us, as we live new lives. And that is what we should pray for as leaders in the church, if we would be godly leaders.

2. A GODLY LEADER ACTS

If this book is anything, it is a book of action, which brings us to the second characteristic of a godly leader: a godly leader acts.

In large part, the book reads like Nehemiah's own memoirs. By this I don't mean his autobiography, which would be a record of his own internal life. No, they're memoirs because they recount great events and his own part in them. What emerges in these memoirs is a skillful political actor, whose concern for his own people apparently coincides with the desires of his king, Artaxerxes. It is Artaxerxes who commissions Nehemiah to go to Jerusalem:

> In the month of Nisan in the twentieth year of King Artaxerxes, when wine was brought for him, I took the wine and gave it to the king. I had not been sad in his presence before; so the king asked me, "Why does your face look so sad when you are not ill? This can be nothing but sadness of heart."
>
> I was very much afraid, but I said to the king, "May the king live forever! Why should my face not look sad when the city where my fathers are buried lies in ruins, and its gates have been destroyed by fire?"
>
> The king said to me, "What is it you want?"
>
> Then I prayed to the God of heaven, and I answered the king, "If it pleases the king and if your servant has found favor in his sight, let him send me to the city in Judah where my fathers are buried so that I can rebuild it."
>
> Then the king, with the queen sitting beside him, asked me, "How long will your journey take, and when will you get back?" It pleased the king to send me; so I set a time (2:1-6).

What an interesting account! Nehemiah is "very much afraid" of this absolute monarch's power to deal with him simply for looking sad in his presence, yet he continues with his plea despite his fear. He prays, as we mentioned before, and he acts! He speaks to the king about his troubles! Nehemiah is a man of action. "And because the gracious hand of my God was upon me," he says, "the king granted my requests" (2:8; cf. 2:18). Before you know it—the next verse, in fact (2:9)—Nehemiah is off with permission letters from the king in hand.

Upon arriving in Jerusalem, Nehemiah again takes the initiative by setting out on a fact-finding mission:

> I set out during the night with a few men. I had not told anyone what my God had put in my heart to do for Jerusalem. There were no mounts with me except the one I was riding on.
>
> By night I went out through the Valley Gate toward the Jackal Well and the Dung Gate, examining the walls of Jerusalem, which had been broken down, and its gates, which had been destroyed by fire (2:12-13).

Now, Nehemiah does not wrap up his work after collecting facts. He takes on the challenge of caring for Jerusalem and, in chapter 3, leading the people to rebuild the wall.

And he does it skillfully! He divides up the work between various groups of people, giving many of them responsibility for the parts of the wall near their own homes, so that they would have an obvious interest in it (3:23, 28-30; cf. 7:3). Throughout chapter 3, we find the people zealously repairing the wall.

By the end of chapter 6, the wall is completed, but Nehemiah continues to be a man of action throughout the book. In chapter 7, he deals with the problems created by a city population that was too small. In chapter 12, he orchestrates the celebrations for dedicating the completed walls. By God's providence, no significant part of Jerusalem's rehabilitation was accomplished apart from the activity of this one leader, Nehemiah! It is a striking story.

Today, Christian, you and I do not need to act by physically separating ourselves from others. God does not call Christians to live in separate gated communities, or to build high walls around their churches. That is *not* how we apply Nehemiah's efforts to ourselves. Rather, for as long as we live in this world, we want to be identified as those who are ransomed by the death of Christ. Christ has granted us a newness of life, and we want this change to mark us out. After all, it is our newness of life, more than any wall, that points the world to him!

Therefore, repentance and trust must be our chief actions. As we continually repent of our sins and trust in Christ, the wonderful fruit of our newness becomes more and more evident. So we must encourage one another toward continual repentance of the sins that make us look as if we still belong to this world.

If that is how godly leaders must act, then pray that God would give the elders of his church wisdom to act in ways that bless this church, preserve the witness of the church, and protect God's people from being dissolved into the world around.

A godly leader acts.

3. A GODLY LEADER FACES OPPOSITION

Third, a godly leader will face opposition. The first stirrings of opposition emerge in chapter 2 when Nehemiah announces his plans to return to Jerusalem (2:10, 19). But the opposition really begins to dominate the story in chapter 4, after Nehemiah has led the people to begin rebuilding the walls:

> When Sanballat heard that we were rebuilding the wall, he became angry and was greatly incensed. He ridiculed the Jews, and in the presence of his associates and the army of Samaria, he said, "What are those feeble Jews doing? Will they restore their wall? Will they offer sacrifices? Will they finish in a day? Can they bring the stones back to life from those heaps of rubble—burned as they are?"
>
> Tobiah the Ammonite, who was at his side, said, "What they are building— if even a fox climbed up on it, he would break down their wall of stones!" (4:1-3).

The rebuilding continues amid mockery and opposition. But then the stakes rise:

> But when Sanballat, Tobiah, the Arabs, the Ammonites and the men of Ashdod heard that the repairs to Jerusalem's walls had gone ahead and that the gaps were being closed, they were very angry. They all plotted together to come and fight against Jerusalem and stir up trouble against it. But we prayed to our God and posted a guard day and night to meet this threat.
>
> Meanwhile, the people in Judah said, "The strength of the laborers is giving out, and there is so much rubble that we cannot rebuild the wall."
>
> Also our enemies said, "Before they know it or see us, we will be right there among them and will kill them and put an end to the work."
>
> Then the Jews who lived near them came and told us ten times over, "Wherever you turn, they will attack us."
>
> Therefore I stationed some of the people behind the lowest points of the wall at the exposed places, posting them by families, with their swords, spears and bows. After I looked things over, I stood up and said to the nobles, the offi-

cials and the rest of the people, "Don't be afraid of them. Remember the Lord, who is great and awesome, and fight for your brothers, your sons and your daughters, your wives and your homes."

When our enemies heard that we were aware of their plot and that God had frustrated it, we all returned to the wall, each to his own work.

From that day on, half of my men did the work, while the other half were equipped with spears, shields, bows and armor. The officers posted themselves behind all the people of Judah who were building the wall. Those who carried materials did their work with one hand and held a weapon in the other, and each of the builders wore his sword at his side as he worked (4:7-18a).

When the opposition increases, Nehemiah prays and posts a guard. He both invokes God's aid and acts. I hope you realize there is nothing inconsistent about doing these two things together. When his fellow citizens become discouraged, likewise, Nehemiah exhorts them not to fear these people, to trust in the Lord, and, if need be, to fight them.

The opposition continues into chapter 6, yet here the Jews' opponents begin to focus on slandering and intimidating Nehemiah himself. Nehemiah turns to God in prayer, and God gives him the wisdom he needs to respond to this opposition (6:9-13).

Let me add, facing opposition well is usually more complicated than people imagine. But this is what a leader does! Like Nehemiah, we must not let opposition drive us *from* God, but *to* him. There is nothing surprising about the fact that Nehemiah's opponents try to intimidate him personally. The adversary of God's people will always go for the leaders. Discredit and manipulate the leaders, and the flock will be disorganized, confused, and ineffectual (see Zech. 13:7).

The wall is completed in fifty-two days despite the opposition (6:15)! Still, Nehemiah's adversaries do not rest. He writes,

Also, in those days the nobles of Judah were sending many letters to Tobiah, and replies from Tobiah kept coming to them. For many in Judah were under oath to him, since he was son-in-law to Shecaniah son of Arah, and his son Jehohanan had married the daughter of Meshullam son of Berekiah. Moreover, they kept reporting to me his good deeds and then telling him what I said. And Tobiah sent letters to intimidate me (6:17-19).

Tobiah continues insidiously to infiltrate the ranks of Nehemiah's helpers and to sow opposition against him and his policies. Thank God that he gave his people a leader as fearless as Nehemiah! How easy it would have been for Nehemiah to be deflected into doing whatever he could to stop all the ill reports. But that is never an option for those who aspire to leadership. Leaders will face opposition.

I wonder if you think of yourself as fearless? Perhaps you laugh at that question and say, "No, of course not!" Or maybe you do think of yourself as fearless. Let me ask, when you are having a conversation with yourself, how important do you find other people's thoughts of you to be? How much do you care what others think about you? The only liberation we will ever find from a debilitating fear of man is a real, true, and correct fear of God. He is the One whose respect we should desire. He is the One whose opinion we should cherish. Everyone from our best friends to our most determined opponents can misunderstand us. But God knows the truth. If you fear him alone, you will not have to fear any opposition he may call you to endure. He is the one we are supposed to ultimately fear. And his opposition is truly fearful. The one being in the universe we do *not* want to oppose us is God!

Jesus Christ faced opposition, and so will we if we follow him. Remember Jesus' words, "If they persecuted me, they will persecute you also" (John 15:20). Peter, who was present when Jesus uttered these words, later wrote to a group of Christians,

> To this you were called, because Christ suffered for you, leaving you an example, that you should follow in his steps.
>
> "He committed no sin,
>   and no deceit was found in his mouth."
>
> When they hurled their insults at him, he did not retaliate; when he suffered, he made no threats. Instead, he entrusted himself to him who judges justly. He himself bore our sins in his body on the tree, so that we might die to sins and live for righteousness (1 Pet. 2:21-24).

My Christian brother or sister, examine yourself. Remind yourself of whom you really serve, so that when you are put to the test, you, like the people of God of old, can face opposition. And pray that we who are leaders in the church will rightly respond when our leadership is opposed.

Godly leaders will face opposition.

4. A GODLY LEADER CARES

Fourth, a godly leader cares. This comes to the forefront of the story in chapter 5.

When Nehemiah returns to Jerusalem, broken walls are not the only problem he finds. A number of the weaker people in the community are being abused. Wealthier citizens are taking economic advantage of the poor, so that the poor are becoming poorer and the rich are becoming richer:

> Now the men and their wives raised a great outcry against their Jewish brothers. Some were saying, "We and our sons and daughters are numerous; in order for us to eat and stay alive, we must get grain."
>
> Others were saying, "We are mortgaging our fields, our vineyards and our homes to get grain during the famine."
>
> Still others were saying, "We have had to borrow money to pay the king's tax on our fields and vineyards. Although we are of the same flesh and blood as our countrymen and though our sons are as good as theirs, yet we have to subject our sons and daughters to slavery. Some of our daughters have already been enslaved, but we are powerless, because our fields and our vineyards belong to others" (5:1-5).

Once again, Nehemiah acts, and this time to stop the usury. He exhorts the wealthier citizens to fear the Lord and stop extorting money from the poor, to which they respond, "We will give it back. . . . And we will not demand anything more from them. We will do as you say" (5:12). Nehemiah then uses a very interesting image to warn the wealthy about the consequences of not keeping their word:

> I also shook out the folds of my robe and said, "In this way may God shake out of his house and possessions every man who does not keep this promise. So may such a man be shaken out and emptied!"
>
> At this the whole assembly said, "Amen," and praised the LORD. And the people did as they had promised (5:13).

This robe Nehemiah shakes would have had little pockets where personal things could be kept, and he wants these wealthier citizens to know that if they do not keep their pledges, God will shake *them* out of *his* pockets. If they continue to treat God's weaker ones in this fashion, they can expect to no longer be God's special possession.

In short, Nehemiah cares. He is a godly leader who cares enough to act against abuse. More than that, he turns down some of the privileges he could have exercised as governor for the sake of feeding the people. He perceives their needs and he pours himself out for them (5:14-15).

I wonder if your heart goes out to people you know are in need. Or do you find yourself cold toward them? At least be honest with yourself in answering this question: Do you find your heart toward others is cold? Do the needs of others have any voice amid the crowd of desires in your head all clamoring for attention? They did have such a voice with Nehemiah, because Nehemiah cared. In that sense, he points us to Christ, who *cares* for his church: "Christ loved the church and gave himself up for her" (Eph. 5:25).

We cannot take the Old Testament as a blueprint for our nation today and use Israel's laws for our laws. But we can see what God values and consider how we might incarnate those values in our country. Clearly, he values caring for the poor. So how do we encourage that concern within our weekly lives? Do we? Or have we mailed in that concern along with our tax payments to the government?

We must cultivate a genuine concern for others that leads us to action. For instance:

Do you know any older members in the church who have difficulty getting out of their house for church or shopping or who have other needs? What could you do to establish a relationship with an older member to encourage and serve him or her?

What about our ministry to the children of prisoners? Have you thought about purchasing a gift for one of these children? Many of them ask for basics, like jeans or school shirts.

Also, our congregation has a benevolence fund for helping members in need as well as elderly non-members in the area who cannot afford medicine and other basics. You can quietly act in benevolence with the money you give to the benevolence fund.

So many things can be quietly done. But my concern is for you. Do you have a way in which you live out God's concern for others, particularly for those who are poor?

Pray that the leaders of our church—and the church as a whole—will be marked by a concern for the needy among and around us. Pray that God will make those of us who are leaders especially self-sacrificial in our love.

Godly leaders care.

5. A GODLY LEADER TURNS PEOPLE TO GOD'S WORD

Fifth, a godly leader turns people to God's Word. We see this particularly in chapter 8, where Ezra the priest reads the Law of God:

> When the seventh month came and the Israelites had settled in their towns, all the people assembled as one man in the square before the Water Gate. They told Ezra the scribe to bring out the Book of the Law of Moses, which the LORD had commanded for Israel.
>
> So on the first day of the seventh month Ezra the priest brought the Law

before the assembly, which was made up of men and women and all who were able to understand. He read it aloud from daybreak till noon as he faced the square before the Water Gate in the presence of the men, women and others who could understand. And all the people listened attentively to the Book of the Law.

Ezra the scribe stood on a high wooden platform built for the occasion . . .

Ezra opened the book. All the people could see him because he was standing above them; and as he opened it, the people all stood up. Ezra praised the LORD, the great God; and all the people lifted their hands and responded, "Amen! Amen!" Then they bowed down and worshiped the LORD with their faces to the ground.

The Levites—Jeshua, Bani, Sherebiah, Jamin, Akkub, Shabbethai, Hodiah, Maaseiah, Kelita, Azariah, Jozabad, Hanan and Pelaiah—instructed the people in the Law while the people were standing there. They read from the Book of the Law of God, making it clear and giving the meaning so that the people could understand what was being read (7:73b–8:4a, 5-8).

The people are gathered at the Water Gate, the gate through which the townspeople would exit the city to get to their nearest source of water. They have come to hear Ezra read the Law from daybreak till noon. It's a dramatic scene: Ezra stands on the platform with an open book; the people respond by standing and lifting their hands, then bowing down; and the Levites instruct the people so that they "could understand what was being read."

Notice how Nehemiah leads the people to respond to God's Word. He says,

"Do not mourn or weep." For all the people had been weeping as they listened to the words of the Law.

Nehemiah said, "Go and enjoy choice food and sweet drinks, and send some to those who have nothing prepared. This day is sacred to our Lord. Do not grieve, for the joy of the LORD is your strength" (8:9-10; cf. Isa. 30:15).

Undoubtedly, the people are convicted of their sins, as we saw in Ezra 10. But here, interestingly, Nehemiah forbids them from responding with weeping, because "the joy of the LORD is your strength." So, quite simply, they depart in order "to eat and drink, to send portions of food and to celebrate with great joy" (8:12). In fact, "From the days of Joshua son of Nun until that day, the Israelites had not celebrated [the Feast of Tabernacles] like this. And their joy was very great" (8:17). Why all the joy? "[B]ecause they now understood the words that had been made known to them" (8:12)!

Ezra then proceeds to read God's law to God's people for seven straight days (8:18)! A godly leader turns people to God's Word.

If you are a non-Christian, hopefully I can help you understand at least this one thing: We Christians do not believe that ultimate truth is something human beings can figure out through the hard work of the intellect. Nor is the truth something that humans create through cultural discourse or long-agreed-upon political conventions. Instead, we believe that God has taken the initiative of revealing himself to us in the Bible, which means the Bible is ultimate truth. God has spoken, and so we will call the Bible God's Word. But not only that: God went a step further and sent his Word in the flesh! Jesus is the Word of God (John 1:1, 14).

If you are a Christian, consider whether you make God's Word central to your own life. When you hear God's Word read or preached, how do you respond? Does your heart leap? The hearts of the Jews in this passage clearly do. Or does your response to the Word depend on the skill of the one preaching it? On how well the sermon is delivered? If you are bored by God's Word, then whose words excite you? The words of your friends or family members, your teacher or coach? What would need to change in order for God's Word to stir your heart in the same way the words of other people can?

The most important thing we do at church is teach God's Word, because God's Word alone generates life. As the apostle Paul said to the Romans, "faith comes from hearing the message" (Rom. 10:17). People who hear God's Word and believe it have their lives changed.

That is certainly the testimony of our church. I and the other elders serve the congregation best by making sure God's Word is accurately and forcefully presented in everything from the Sunday morning gathering to the Sunday evening devotion; from the music we sing to the prayers we publicly pray; from the church's Wednesday night Bible study to the small groups meeting in homes; from discipling relationships to evangelistic outreaches; from the books on the bookstall to the sermons mailed out to seminarians and shut-ins. God's Word is the seed that gives birth to God's people.

This is how God has always done it. He created the world by his word. He created Abraham by calling him out. And he created his people at Mount Sinai by giving them his commands. In Ezekiel's great vision of the valley of dry bones, God speaks and the bones are clothed with flesh and brought to life. Then, of course, there is the Word of God himself, the Lord Jesus, who came, took on flesh, and died for the sins of all who would ever repent of their sins and believe these words about who he is and what he has done. As we said, "Faith comes from hearing the message" (Rom. 10:17).

A godly leader turns people to God's Word because God's Word brings life!

6. A GODLY LEADER CONFESSES SINS

Sixth, a godly leader confesses sins. As we saw, the people celebrated the reading of God's Word. Two days after the people finished feasting, the leaders turned their attention to the sins of the people and led them in confession. The text does not tell us if the following prayer was prayed by Nehemiah, Ezra, or the Levites. But everyone stood, listened, and—we assume—agreed with this leader's prayer:

"Stand up and praise the LORD your God, who is from everlasting to everlasting.

"Blessed be your glorious name, and may it be exalted above all blessing and praise. *You* alone are the LORD. *You* made the heavens, even the highest heavens, and all their starry host, the earth and all that is on it, the seas and all that is in them. *You* give life to everything, and the multitudes of heaven worship you.

"*You* are the LORD God, who chose Abram and brought him out of Ur of the Chaldeans and named him Abraham. *You* found his heart faithful to you, and *you* made a covenant with him to give to his descendants the land of the Canaanites, Hittites, Amorites, Perizzites, Jebusites and Girgashites. *You* have kept your promise because you are righteous.

"*You* saw the suffering of our forefathers in Egypt; *you* heard their cry at the Red Sea. *You* sent miraculous signs and wonders against Pharaoh, against all his officials and all the people of his land, for *you* knew how arrogantly the Egyptians treated them. *You* made a name for yourself, which remains to this day. *You* divided the sea before them, so that they passed through it on dry ground, but *you* hurled their pursuers into the depths, like a stone into mighty waters. By day *you* led them with a pillar of cloud, and by night with a pillar of fire to give them light on the way they were to take.

"*You* came down on Mount Sinai; *you* spoke to them from heaven. *You* gave them regulations and laws that are just and right, and decrees and commands that are good. *You* made known to them your holy Sabbath and gave them commands, decrees and laws through your servant Moses. In their hunger *you* gave them bread from heaven and in their thirst *you* brought them water from the rock; *you* told them to go in and take possession of the land you had sworn with uplifted hand to give them.

"But *they,* our forefathers, became arrogant and stiff-necked, and did not obey your commands. *They* refused to listen and failed to remember the miracles you performed among them. *They* became stiff-necked and in their rebellion appointed a leader in order to return to their slavery. But *you* are a forgiving God, gracious and compassionate, slow to anger and abounding in love. Therefore *you* did not desert them, even when they cast for themselves an image of a calf and said, 'This is your god, who brought you up out of Egypt,' or when they committed awful blasphemies.

"Because of your great compassion *you* did not abandon them in the desert. By day the pillar of cloud did not cease to guide them on their path, nor the pillar of fire by night to shine on the way they were to take. You gave your good Spirit to instruct them. *You* did not withhold your manna from their mouths, and *you* gave them water for their thirst. For forty years *you* sustained them in the desert; they lacked nothing, their clothes did not wear out nor did their feet become swollen.

"*You* gave them kingdoms and nations, allotting to them even the remotest frontiers. They took over the country of Sihon king of Heshbon and the country of Og king of Bashan. You made their sons as numerous as the stars in the sky, and *you* brought them into the land that you told their fathers to enter and possess. Their sons went in and took possession of the land. *You* subdued before them the Canaanites, who lived in the land; you handed the Canaanites over to them, along with their kings and the peoples of the land, to deal with them as they pleased. They captured fortified cities and fertile land; they took possession of houses filled with all kinds of good things, wells already dug, vineyards, olive groves and fruit trees in abundance. They ate to the full and were well-nourished; they reveled in your great goodness.

"But *they* were disobedient and rebelled against you; *they* put your law behind their backs. *They* killed your prophets, who had admonished them in order to turn them back to you; *they* committed awful blasphemies. So *you* handed them over to their enemies, who oppressed them. But when they were oppressed *they* cried out to you. From heaven *you* heard them, and in your great compassion *you* gave them deliverers, who rescued them from the hand of their enemies.

"But as soon as they were at rest, *they* again did what was evil in your sight. Then *you* abandoned them to the hand of their enemies so that they ruled over them. And when *they* cried out to you again, *you* heard from heaven, and in your compassion *you* delivered them time after time.

"*You* warned them to return to your law, but *they* became arrogant and disobeyed your commands. *They* sinned against your ordinances, by which a man will live if he obeys them. Stubbornly *they* turned their backs on you, became stiff-necked and refused to listen. For many years *you* were patient with them. By your Spirit *you* admonished them through your prophets. Yet *they* paid no attention, so *you* handed them over to the neighboring peoples. But in your great mercy *you* did not put an end to them or abandon them, for you are a gracious and merciful God.

"Now therefore, O our God, the great, mighty and awesome God, who keeps his covenant of love, do not let all this hardship seem trifling in your eyes—the hardship that has come upon us, upon our kings and leaders, upon our priests and prophets, upon our fathers and all your people, from the days of the kings of Assyria until today. In all that has happened to us, you have been just; you have acted faithfully, while we did wrong. Our kings, our leaders, our priests and our fathers did not follow your law; they did not pay attention to your commands or the warnings you gave them. Even while they were in their kingdom, enjoying your great goodness to them in the spacious and fertile land you gave them, they did not serve you or turn from their evil ways.

"But see, we are slaves today, slaves in the land you gave our forefathers so they could eat its fruit and the other good things it produces. Because of our sins, its abundant harvest goes to the kings you have placed over us. They rule over our bodies and our cattle as they please. We are in great distress" (9:5b-37).

So there they stood, confessing their own sins and the sins of their fathers. But notice, this prayer of confession begins with praising God: "Blessed be your glorious name" (9:5). Really, the whole prayer is cast in the form of praise to God: *you* saw, *you* came, *you* are, *you* sent, and so forth. At the same time, the prayer is both a confession and a summary of Old Testament history. It is awful to observe, isn't it, that a nation's history is well-summarized as a confession of sin? But so it was (cf. Ezra 9).

And consider this admission: "In all that has happened to us, you have been just; you have acted faithfully, while we did wrong" (9:33). Just imagine some individual or group stating that publicly today! "In everything that has happened, O Sovereign God, you have acted faithfully. We got what we asked for. Our sins deserved it." Surely such an admission demonstrates an amazing understanding of who God is and of who we are. It assumes that God is sovereign and that God is good. And surely such faith is difficult to sustain when life is not going well. Yet that is what the people said: all of this happened "because of our sins" (9:37). They did not shift the responsibility at all.

What a day it was! They spent one-quarter of the day reading God's Word and one-quarter confessing their sins and worshiping (9:3). Do you see the pattern? By reading God's Word and perceiving his holy character, they became more and more aware of their sins and the *need* to confess them. Yet by reading God's Word and perceiving his patient love, they became more and aware of their *ability* to confess these sins. Scripture reminded them that God is from everlasting to everlasting, and that they could rely on his ancient promises of love.

Oh, friend, if we will only hear it, Scripture will stir our hearts, too, and move us to confession and worship of this magnificent God. He is perfect. He is holy. He is just. He is loving. He is merciful. He will not let us saunter into his presence, unaware of our sin. But nor will he let our sin keep us from him—if we will only look to his Son—because he is a God of persistent love.

We, too, are guilty of sinning against this good God. The Jews' confession of sin is no mere historical record, unrelated to your experience or mine! Just think for a second: what sins of yours have weighed on your conscience this week? Now consider, if they weigh on your conscience at the moment, as filthy, corrupted, and deadened as your conscience has become through repeated compromise with sin, becoming accustomed to and learning to even accommodate that sin, can you imagine how your sins will appear when they are brought out of the stygian darkness of our present state and into the bright and piercing radiance of God's purity?

And yet (!) we can still come with those darkened consciences into his presence to be forgiven of our blackest sins. If you are separated from God by your sins, the most important business you can conduct is to find out how your sins will be forgiven. The Puritan William Gurnall was right when he said plainly, "Better die in a prison, die in a ditch, than die in [your] sins."[3]

How can you be forgiven of your sins? You must look to Jesus Christ. In Christ, God became a man, lived a perfect life, and died on the cross, taking the penalty deserved by all of us who would ever repent of our sins and turn to him in faith. Christ is the answer to our sins. He himself was without sin, but he was made sin for us (Heb. 4:15; 2 Cor. 5:21).

If you are a Christian, you are not surprised at this connection between reading God's Word, worshiping him, and confessing your sins. Yet some Christians have been taught that we confess our sins only once—when we become a Christian—and never again. But in Scripture, from Psalm 32 to James 5:16, we watch as believers confess their sins again and again. They repeatedly go to God and find their forgiveness in him. My basic rule of thumb is this: as soon as you stop sinning against God, you can stop confessing your sins to him.

A godly leader confesses his sins and leads his people to confess their sins.

---

[3] William Gurnall, *The Christian in Complete Armour* (Carlisle, Pa.: Banner of Truth, 1964; Glasgow: Blackie & Son, 1864; first published 1662), 169.

7. A GODLY LEADER LEADS PEOPLE IN SPECIFIC COMMITMENTS

Seventh, a godly leader leads people in making specific commitments.

Right after chapter 9's Scripture reading and prayer of confession, the people take an oath to keep God's law: "In view of all this, we are making a binding agreement, putting it in writing, and our leaders, our Levites and our priests are affixing their seals to it" (9:38). The content of this pledge is then found in chapter 10:

> "The rest of the people—priests, Levites, gatekeepers, singers, temple servants and all who separated themselves from the neighboring peoples for the sake of the Law of God, together with their wives and all their sons and daughters who are able to understand—all these now join their brothers the nobles, and bind themselves with a curse and an oath to follow the Law of God given through Moses the servant of God and to obey carefully all the commands, regulations and decrees of the LORD our Lord.
>
> "We promise not to give our daughters in marriage to the peoples around us or take their daughters for our sons.
>
> "When the neighboring peoples bring merchandise or grain to sell on the Sabbath, we will not buy from them on the Sabbath or on any holy day. Every seventh year we will forgo working the land and will cancel all debts" (10:28-31).

And the pledges continue through the end of the chapter, all of them promising, basically, to follow the laws God gave to Moses (10:32-39). These pledges do not negate the authority of God's Word but they helpfully summarize God's law. Really, their pledges act like a church covenant. Church covenants should not be used to supplant Scripture, but they can helpfully summarize the things that Scripture requires of our churches. Nehemiah leads the people in making these public promises to God.

Have you ever made any promises to God? Have you ever resolved to repent of your sins, and to believe in Christ? If you have not, that is the most important commitment you can make today. As Jesus himself said, "The time has come. The kingdom of God is near. Repent and believe the good news!" (Mark 1:15).

For you, Christian, take note of how these people make specific resolutions to God and to one another. Are you reluctant to make such specific promises? Is there something in you that wants to avoid committing to a particular group of God's people with whom you say "we"? If so, you deprive *them* of something God intends for them through you, and you deprive *yourself* of what God intends for you through them. But you are thinking more highly of your own abilities than you should; you deceive yourself. So commit yourself to a particular local church where the gospel of Jesus Christ is preached. Embrace its covenant. And engage with the work of God in that local place.

A good local church will help you not to be a person who picks and chooses which of God's commands to obey. This is one of the reasons that our church uses a covenant. It is a useful summary of our Christian obligations to God and to each other. Yes, it takes humility to submit to one another—and to leaders.

Which raises the flip side of the coin. Should church elders commit themselves to giving the time, trouble, and effort to *leading* well when the other members do not commit themselves to giving the time, trouble, and trust to *following* well? There's as much art in the one as the other. The late historian Stephen Ambrose said several years ago,

> I used to tell my students that President Harry Truman was wrong to use the atomic bombs against the Japanese. I believed the Japanese were already ready, even eager, to surrender, as long as they could keep their emperor. I was wrong. New documents reveal that the Japanese intended to fight to the death. I realized that Truman was exactly right and that his decision saved uncounted American and Japanese lives.[4]

Regardless of your assessment of Truman's decision, hopefully you can see what Ambrose was saying. Truman, as the president, had a number of facts at his disposal that others (even professional historians) did not have, and so he made the decision he did. As someone who has been in leadership, I can simply tell you how often leadership works this way. There are often considerations and information that only the leadership has, and that may not be widely understood or known. So in our churches, we should follow God by following those whom God has placed in leadership. Do not follow them into sin and error—that is where congregational responsibility kicks in (as in 2 Tim. 4:3; Gal. 1:6-9). But follow them as they lead according to Scripture.

A godly leader leads God's people into making specific commitments.

8. A GODLY LEADER KEEPS LEADING

Finally, a godly leader keeps leading.

What do I mean by that? Well, let's remember a couple of things about our place in the story line. First, we are at the end of Old Testament history. This series on the historical books of the Old Testament will conclude in the next study, on Esther, but only because Esther appears last canonically. The story of

---

[4] Stephen Ambrose, "Old Soldiers Never Die," in *Forbes ASAP,* October 2, 2000, 110.

Esther actually takes place a little earlier in time. Chronologically, Nehemiah and the rebuilding of the walls in Jerusalem is the last bit of Old Testament history we have, which brings us to a second thing worth remembering.

Throughout this entire series, we have seen God underscore the fact that his people are to be distinct from the nations around them. This has been the main theme of all of these histories, from Joshua to Nehemiah. God pulled a nation out of Egypt to be a distinct people and to display his character to the nations. How appropriate then for the histories to conclude with the rebuilding of the walls that are supposed to set the people apart.

Now consider: Nehemiah leaves Jerusalem for a time—probably not months, but years. We read in chapter 13, "I was not in Jerusalem, for in the thirty-second year of Artaxerxes king of Babylon I had returned to the king. Some time later I asked his permission and came back to Jerusalem" (13:6-7). Then he returns to this place into which he has poured so much of his life, and what does he find? The temple is being used for nonreligious purposes (13:7-9). The singers, priests, and other temple servants have gone back to farming because they were not being paid (13:10-11). The Sabbath is being forgotten and desecrated (13:15-22). What's worse, look at verses 23 and following. Here is the last chapter of Nehemiah. Here is the end of Old Testament history:

> Moreover, in those days I saw men of Judah who had married women from Ashdod, Ammon and Moab. Half of their children spoke the language of Ashdod or the language of one of the other peoples, and did not know how to speak the language of Judah. I rebuked them and called curses down on them. I beat some of the men and pulled out their hair. I made them take an oath in God's name and said: "You are not to give your daughters in marriage to their sons, nor are you to take their daughters in marriage for your sons or for yourselves. Was it not because of marriages like these that Solomon king of Israel sinned? Among the many nations there was no king like him. He was loved by his God, and God made him king over all Israel, but even he was led into sin by foreign women. Must we hear now that you too are doing all this terrible wickedness and are being unfaithful to our God by marrying foreign women?" (13:23-27).

Oh, friend, when you read this, do you not want to scream! You have *one thousand years of God's faithfulness,* and look at what happens! Nehemiah has been gone for maybe a few years; he comes back, and what are they doing? The same thing that Solomon did, which eventually led the people into worshiping other gods! You read this and think to yourself, what's the point of all this history! What else can be done! These people are hopeless! Quite contrary to the many utopian visions of the world, the Old Testament paints a picture of mankind that, on one level, is profoundly pessimistic and—we must admit—

realistic. The sins they struggled with in Joshua's day were the same sins they struggled with in Nehemiah's day—one thousand years later.

What would God do with such a constantly misled and misleading people?

In fact, God had told them what he would do decades earlier. While the people were still in exile, the Word of the Lord came to the prophet Ezekiel, who was in Babylon at the time. Through Ezekiel, God criticized the leaders of Israel—whom he refers to as "shepherds"—for the way most of them (unlike Ezra and Nehemiah) misled God's people. And here is what God promised he would do:

> "Son of man, prophesy against the shepherds of Israel; prophesy and say to them: 'This is what the Sovereign LORD says: Woe to the shepherds of Israel who only take care of themselves! Should not shepherds take care of the flock? You eat the curds, clothe yourselves with the wool and slaughter the choice animals, but you do not take care of the flock. You have not strengthened the weak or healed the sick or bound up the injured. You have not brought back the strays or searched for the lost. You have ruled them harshly and brutally. So they were scattered because there was no shepherd, and when they were scattered they became food for all the wild animals. My sheep wandered over all the mountains and on every high hill. They were scattered over the whole earth, and no one searched or looked for them.
>
> "'Therefore, you shepherds, hear the word of the LORD: As surely as I live, declares the Sovereign LORD, because my flock lacks a shepherd and so has been plundered and has become food for all the wild animals, and because my shepherds did not search for my flock but cared for themselves rather than for my flock, therefore, O shepherds, hear the word of the LORD: This is what the Sovereign LORD says: I am against the shepherds and will hold them accountable for my flock. I will remove them from tending the flock so that the shepherds can no longer feed themselves. I will rescue my flock from their mouths, and it will no longer be food for them.
>
> "'For this is what the Sovereign LORD says: I myself will search for my sheep and look after them. As a shepherd looks after his scattered flock when he is with them, so will I look after my sheep'" (Ezek. 34:2-12a).

God himself would come as the good shepherd. And he would come in the fullness of divinity and humanity together in the Lord Jesus Christ. This was necessary because no prophet from Samuel to Malachi and no ruler from Saul to Zedekiah—not even Ezra or Nehemiah—was able to lead God's people in such a way that the people's hearts actually changed. This could only be done when God's Word himself, Jesus Christ, went to work within them.

So the Word would come. And he would come to convict God's people of sin and give them new life through the preaching of his good news. Yes, he would have people who would be ruled well, and who would rule well. For we finally see, in the book of Revelation, the completion of the story, when the great figures surrounding God's throne praise the Lamb upon the throne, saying, "with your blood you purchased men for God from every tribe and language and people and nation. You have made them to be a kingdom and priests to serve our God, and they will reign on the earth" (Rev. 5:9b-10). Then Jerusalem, the new Jerusalem, will come down out of heaven and God himself will reign. And this new Jerusalem will not need a temple because the Lord God Almighty and the Lamb are its temple. And this new Jerusalem will not need the sun because the glory of God gives its light, and the Lamb is its lamp (Rev. 21:22-23). That is the hope the Bible holds out for us. That is the hope that the Old Testament points to as its history ends. And that is how a leader must continue to lead—by pointing to this hope!

Christian, what implications does this have for how we live? Simply, you must be prepared to continue to battle against sin throughout this life. The warfare that we are called to wage against sin in our lives is short in view of eternity, even if it sometimes feels very long in this world.

For those who are elders in the church, take note of Nehemiah's experience here: the work of leading a church never ends. This church is not *reformed,* in the sense that its work is now done. Rather, it must continually *be reformed* by the Word of God! As elders, our work is never done. Neither we nor the church as a whole has arrived. We have not learned everything God has to tell us. We still draw breath. We still read the Bible. God's Spirit still works in our hearts. And God's Word still refashions us.

For those of you who are not elders in the church, I plead with you to realize that God has given those who lead the church a great task, and it is our joy to accept that task. Don't ever think that you should not bother the elders. Serving the church is the greatest privilege that God has given us in this life! And please forgive us if we ever appear to forget that privilege. As the apostle Paul wrote to the Thessalonians,

> Now we ask you, brothers, to respect those who work hard among you, who are over you in the Lord and who admonish you. Hold them in the highest regard in love because of their work. Live in peace with each other. And we urge you, brothers, warn those who are idle, encourage the timid, help the weak, be patient with everyone (1 Thess. 5:12-14).

As Paul wrote to Timothy, "Preach the Word; be prepared in season and out of season; correct, rebuke and encourage—with great patience and careful instruction" (2 Tim. 4:2). A godly leader keeps leading.

CONCLUSION

So is godly leadership about putting your stamp on the future? Is it about self-confidence and self-assertion? Not according to Nehemiah.

In this book, you get a very different picture of leadership. In chapter 1, Nehemiah asks God to hear "[those] who delight in revering your name" (1:11). In chapter 5, Nehemiah says that he has not taken advantage of the poor—he has not fleeced the sheep!—"out of reverence for God" (5:15). And in chapter 7, Nehemiah appoints one person to a position of leadership "because he was a man of integrity and feared God more than most men do" (7:2). Here we get to the core of godly leadership in the Bible. Leadership is about fearing God more than others do. Leadership is about revering God's name. Leadership is about taking pleasure in who God is and what he is like. Leadership is about making the chief end of your life helping, instructing, and challenging others to revere and delight in God's name as well.

Do you delight in doing that? Does that give you more joy than any combination of irritations that comes with leadership? Do you take pleasure in seeing others revere and honor God? Then you have the basic components of being a good influence in the lives of others. You will lead well.

Your life isn't just about money, is it? I hope it's about something deeper. Something so central to your core, to what makes you tick, that you can't imagine living without it. I hope it's about leadership. About learning and proclaiming *God's* Word. About praying to *God*. About delighting in seeing *God's* name revered.

Let us pray:

Lord God, we pray that you make us godly leaders and followers as we see depicted in the book of Nehemiah. And give us such persevering love and grace. We pray that we would be like those in the book of Isaiah, who themselves pray, "Yes, LORD, walking in the way of your laws, we wait for you; your name and renown are the desire of our hearts" (Isa. 26:8). O God, we pray that you would make the desire of our hearts the lifting up of your name. Bring glory to yourself though our lives, our church, and all our opportunities for exercising leadership for you. We pray all this so that people will revere your name through our Lord, Jesus Christ. Amen.

Questions for Reflection

1. Do the qualities people prize in their leaders change from culture to culture, or age to age? What are some of the qualities our culture has come to value in its leadership? Can you think of any places where the Bible's characterization of good leadership strikingly diverges from our culture's conceptions?

2. Why is prayer so important for good leadership? What does the presence of an active prayer life reveal about a leader? What does the lack of a prayer life reveal?

3. When you pray for your Christian friends and family members, do you pray that their lives would be marked by a distinctive newness of life? Is this how you pray for other members of your church? Are there many prayers we can pray for other Christians that are more important than this?

4. What is "repentance"? Is it a one-time event, a lifestyle, or both? Explain. Can a person be saved without repenting?

5. What is "the fear of man"? What are some places where "the fear of man" can manifest itself in a Christian's life? Where does it manifest itself in your life? How do we combat the fear of man?

6. As we have seen, a godly leader takes people to God's Word. How do you do this? How do you fail to do this? Assuming there would be some overlap, is there any difference between the advice you give people when dealing with life's difficult issues and the advice an extremely moral, conscientious, and loving non-Christian might give them?

7. As we have seen, Nehemiah ends on a tragic note. The people resume practicing the sins that have—more often than not—characterized them for more than a thousand years. Thinking about the Bible as a whole, why would we as Christians say that this sad ending to Old Testament history is, in fact, both unsurprising and appropriate? What implications does this have for how we teach the Old Testament? Another way of asking this last question might be, how should a Christian teach the Old Testament differently from how a Jewish rabbi would teach it?

8. Following up on question 7, we see that Nehemiah is not finally about how to be a good leader. What is Nehemiah finally about? How would you sum-

marize its message? In answering this question, consider where Nehemiah occurs in the course of *redemption history* (redemption history = Creation, Fall, God's call to Abraham, the giving of the law, the giving of a king, rebellion, exile, return from exile, the coming of Christ, building of the church, Christ's second coming, etc.).

9. Why were Ezra and Nehemiah, finally, completely inadequate leaders for God's people?

10. Based on this sermon and the book of Nehemiah, what would you say the heart of good leadership is? Where in your life has God given you the opportunity to lead? How will you apply the lessons of Nehemiah to your own place of leadership?

THE MESSAGE OF ESTHER: SURPRISE

17

THE MESSAGE OF ESTHER: SURPRISE

WHO WILL DELIVER US?[1]

Our news is full of people in trouble. Indeed, that's what makes the news news. From the firing of the local school principal, to disputes between unions and management, to suffering in Afghanistan, our news mostly consists of the bad stuff, not the good.

Indeed, trouble seems to be the common lot of humanity. One actress who was already having a hard year found out in one day that she was losing her television show and that her husband was leaving her. She responded, "I know the Lord won't send me more trouble than I have the strength to bear, but I do wish He didn't have quite such a good opinion of me."[2]

I'm sure you know the feeling.

Yet some people deny that life has difficulties and maintain that the essence of the Christian faith is denying that such problems exist. "You can't have a negative confession," we are told by some teachers. But this is false, whether it comes from the Christian Scientist Mary Baker Eddy or the charismatic "word-faith" teacher. We like their optimism, but don't think they are realistic.

Other people are quite aware of life's problems but say that there is no answer; there is no deliverance from our trials in this life. This is what the gloomy materialists and depressing existentialists think. Their despair, too, is false. We like their willingness to acknowledge the world's difficulties, but we don't think they are being realistic either. We Christians know that life's problems *do* have solutions.

---

[1] This sermon was originally preached on December 1, 2002, at Capitol Hill Baptist Church in Washington, D.C.
[2] Joey Adams, *The God Bit* (New York: Mason & Lipscomb, 1974), 65.

So what shall we do in times of trouble? Who will deliver us from our trials?

INTRODUCING ESTHER

One of the most perilous times for God's people in the Old Testament is found in the book of Esther, our final study in the histories of the Old Testament.

The book of Esther might be called the Cinderella story of an orphaned Jewish girl who rises to become the queen of Persia at a crucial time. It is also an etiological story, meaning that it was written, in part, to explain how something began, in this case the Jewish feast of Purim.

The story of Esther does not take place in Jerusalem, as most of Ezra and Nehemiah do, but in Susa, the capital of the Persian Empire. It takes place during the reign of King Xerxes (486–465 B.C.), which fell in between the first wave of exiles who returned to Jerusalem and rebuilt the temple (Ezra 1–6) and subsequent waves of exiles who returned, including Ezra and Nehemiah (Ezra 7–10; Nehemiah).

In the book of Esther, the Jews receive what amounts to a sentence of death on the entire people. Around 480 B.C., both the Jews who had already returned to Jerusalem as well as those who remained in exile came under the dark shadow of an imperial edict calling for the extermination of all Jews in the Persian Empire and the seizure of their property on one particular day. The verdict is pronounced in chapter 3:

> Then on the thirteenth day of the first month the royal secretaries were summoned. They wrote out in the script of each province and in the language of each people all Haman's orders to the king's satraps, the governors of the various provinces and the nobles of the various peoples. These were written in the name of King Xerxes himself and sealed with his own ring. Dispatches were sent by couriers to all the king's provinces with the order to destroy, kill and annihilate all the Jews—young and old, women and little children—on a single day, the thirteenth day of the twelfth month, the month of Adar, and to plunder their goods. A copy of the text of the edict was to be issued as law in every province and made known to the people of every nationality so they would be ready for that day.
>
> Spurred on by the king's command, the couriers went out, and the edict was issued in the citadel of Susa. The king and Haman sat down to drink, but the city of Susa was bewildered (3:12-15).

How did this happen? And what can we learn from it? To answer those questions, we look first at the *plot*, then at the *characters*, and finally at the *lessons* of this amazing story of Esther.

THE PLOT

We will begin with the plot, looking at how God's people found themselves in this situation.

In the first chapter of Esther, Vashti, the queen of King Xerxes, refuses to come when the king calls her to join him during a public feast. The book does not say why she refuses. Perhaps she thought he was acting drunk or not treating her with proper respect. For whatever reason, she refuses to come. And so Xerxes, like a good Mesopotamian despot, exercises his right to divorce her and depose her as queen. He then looks for another queen, and in chapter 2 Esther, the woman after whom this book is named, is chosen.

Sometime thereafter, Mordecai, Esther's guardian and adopted father, discovers some interesting information:

> When the virgins were assembled the second time, Mordecai was sitting at the King's gate. But Esther had kept secret her family background and nationality just as Mordecai had told her to do, for she continued to follow Mordecai's instructions as she had done when he was bringing her up.
>
> During the time Mordecai was sitting at the king's gate, Bigthana and Teresh, two of the king's officers who guarded the doorway, became angry and conspired to assassinate King Xerxes. But Mordecai found out about the plot and told Queen Esther, who in turn reported it to the king, giving credit to Mordecai. And when the report was investigated and found to be true, the two officials were hanged on a gallows. All this was recorded in the book of the annals in the presence of the king (2:19-23).

Well, it looks like the king made a good choice in Esther. The family connections of his new and loyal queen help to save his life. He is already being repaid!

Let's keep going with the story in chapter 3:

> After these events, King Xerxes honored Haman son of Hammedatha, the Agagite, elevating him and giving him a seat of honor higher than that of all the other nobles. All the royal officials at the king's gate knelt down and paid honor to Haman, for the king had commanded this concerning him. But Mordecai would not kneel down or pay him honor.
>
> Then the royal officials at the king's gate asked Mordecai, "Why do you disobey the king's command?" Day after day they spoke to him but he refused to comply. Therefore they told Haman about it to see whether Mordecai's behavior would be tolerated, for he had told them he was a Jew.
>
> When Haman saw that Mordecai would not kneel down or pay him honor, he was enraged. Yet having learned who Mordecai's people were, he scorned the

idea of killing only Mordecai. Instead Haman looked for a way to destroy all Mordecai's people, the Jews, throughout the whole kingdom of Xerxes.

In the twelfth year of King Xerxes, in the first month, the month of Nisan, they cast the pur (that is, the lot) in the presence of Haman to select a day and month. And the lot fell on the twelfth month, the month of Adar.

Then Haman said to King Xerxes, "There is a certain people dispersed and scattered among the peoples in all the provinces of your kingdom whose customs are different from those of all other people and who do not obey the king's laws; it is not in the king's best interest to tolerate them. If it pleases the king, let a decree be issued to destroy them, and I will put ten thousand talents of silver into the royal treasury for the men who carry out this business."

So the king took his signet ring from his finger and gave it to Haman son of Hammedatha, the Agagite, the enemy of the Jews. "Keep the money," the king said to Haman, "and do with the people as you please."

Then on the thirteenth day of the first month the royal secretaries were summoned. They wrote out in the script of each province and in the language of each people all Haman's orders to the king's satraps, the governors of the various provinces and the nobles of the various peoples. These were written in the name of King Xerxes himself and sealed with his own ring. Dispatches were sent by couriers to all the king's provinces with the order to destroy, kill and annihilate all the Jews—young and old, women and little children—on a single day, the thirteenth day of the twelfth month, the month of Adar, and to plunder their goods. A copy of the text of the edict was to be issued as law in every province and made known to the people of every nationality so they would be ready for that day.

Spurred on by the king's command, the couriers went out, and the edict was issued in the citadel of Susa. The king and Haman sat down to drink, but the city of Susa was bewildered (chapter 3).

Here we come to the people's plight. Behind it, of course, is Haman's malice. It's hard to say, but it seems that Haman's suspicion and hatred of the Jews, scattered as they are throughout the empire, extends beyond Mordecai's refusal to bow; his plan is so extreme!

We cannot let Xerxes off the hook either. Xerxes' complicity is also to blame for this horrible edict. He gives Haman the signet ring, which actually allows Haman the power to make the edict.

Then we should notice Mordecai's intransigence. The king commands the people to honor Haman. And Mordecai refuses, which is how the Jewish people got into this mess.

So who will save them? As we will read a little later in the story, "no document written in the king's name and sealed with his ring can be revoked"

(8:8). Such a document is out, and the Jews' situation seems hopeless. What's going to happen? Let's look at the next chapter:

> When Mordecai learned of all that had been done, he tore his clothes, put on sackcloth and ashes, and went out into the city, wailing loudly and bitterly. But he went only as far as the king's gate, because no one clothed in sackcloth was allowed to enter it. In every province to which the edict and order of the king came, there was great mourning among the Jews, with fasting, weeping and wailing. Many lay in sackcloth and ashes.
>
> When Esther's maids and eunuchs came and told her about Mordecai, she was in great distress. She sent clothes for him to put on instead of his sackcloth, but he would not accept them. Then Esther summoned Hathach, one of the king's eunuchs assigned to attend her, and ordered him to find out what was troubling Mordecai and why.
>
> So Hathach went out to Mordecai in the open square of the city in front of the king's gate. Mordecai told him everything that had happened to him, including the exact amount of money Haman had promised to pay into the royal treasury for the destruction of the Jews. He also gave him a copy of the text of the edict for their annihilation, which had been published in Susa, to show to Esther and explain it to her, and he told him to urge her to go into the king's presence to beg for mercy and plead with him for her people.
>
> Hathach went back and reported to Esther what Mordecai had said. Then she instructed him to say to Mordecai, "All the king's officials and the people of the royal provinces know that for any man or woman who approaches the king in the inner court without being summoned the king has but one law: that he be put to death. The only exception to this is for the king to extend the gold scepter to him and spare his life. But thirty days have passed since I was called to go to the king."
>
> When Esther's words were reported to Mordecai, he sent back this answer: "Do not think that because you are in the king's house you alone of all the Jews will escape. For if you remain silent at this time, relief and deliverance for the Jews will arise from another place, but you and your father's family will perish. And who knows but that you have come to royal position for such a time as this?"
>
> Then Esther sent this reply to Mordecai: "Go, gather together all the Jews who are in Susa, and fast for me. Do not eat or drink for three days, night or day. I and my maids will fast as you do. When this is done, I will go to the king, even though it is against the law. And if I perish, I perish."
>
> So Mordecai went away and carried out all of Esther's instructions (chapter 4).

When Mordecai hears about the decree, he reacts as naturally as you would expect him to react—by grieving.

But Mordecai also has faith. He does not know where deliverance will come from; but he believes in God and knows deliverance will come.

Notice Esther's faith as well. What does she ask Mordecai? She specifically asks Mordecai to fast—which would include prayer—and to get all the Jews in Susa to do the same. The king does not allow people into his presence unless he first summons them, and she knows her success depends entirely on God's gracious intervention.

Then notice her courage to enter the king's presence unsummoned. The story continues in chapter 5:

> On the third day Esther put on her royal robes and stood in the inner court of the palace, in front of the king's hall. The king was sitting on his royal throne in the hall, facing the entrance. When he saw Queen Esther standing in the court, he was pleased with her and held out to her the gold scepter that was in his hand. So Esther approached and touched the tip of the scepter.
>
> Then the king asked, "What is it, Queen Esther? What is your request? Even up to half the kingdom, it will be given you."
>
> "If it pleases the king," replied Esther, "let the king, together with Haman, come today to a banquet I have prepared for him."
>
> "Bring Haman at once," the king said, "so that we may do what Esther asks."
>
> So the king and Haman went to the banquet Esther had prepared. As they were drinking wine, the king again asked Esther, "Now what is your petition? It will be given you. And what is your request? Even up to half the kingdom, it will be granted."
>
> Esther replied, "My petition and my request is this: If the king regards me with favor and if it pleases the king to grant my petition and fulfill my request, let the king and Haman come tomorrow to the banquet I will prepare for them. Then I will answer the king's question."
>
> Haman went out that day happy and in high spirits. But when he saw Mordecai at the king's gate and observed that he neither rose nor showed fear in his presence, he was filled with rage against Mordecai. Nevertheless, Haman restrained himself and went home.
>
> Calling together his friends and Zeresh, his wife, Haman boasted to them about his vast wealth, his many sons, and all the ways the king had honored him and how he had elevated him above the other nobles and officials. "And that's not all," Haman added. "I'm the only person Queen Esther invited to accompany the king to the banquet she gave. And she has invited me along with the king tomorrow. But all this gives me no satisfaction as long as I see that Jew Mordecai sitting at the king's gate."
>
> His wife Zeresh and all his friends said to him, "Have a gallows built, seventy-five feet high, and ask the king in the morning to have Mordecai hanged on

it. Then go with the king to the dinner and be happy." This suggestion delighted Haman, and he had the gallows built (chapter 5).

Well, it just gets thicker and thicker, doesn't it? Notice here Esther's obedience. I am not sure why she does not make her request of the king the first time. Maybe she is being cunning. Maybe she is getting a little scared. I don't know. The text does not say.

Notice too that Mordecai continues in his intransigence. He simply is not willing to honor this person that the king has ordered to be honored.

And, you can't fail to notice Haman's anger, hatred, and pride.

Now, if you have never read the story, you think things are looking pretty good for Haman. Xerxes has honored him. The edict ordering the execution of the Jews and bearing the king's seal remains in force. And Mordecai continues to dishonor Haman, ensuring that destruction will fall upon Mordecai's head all the more quickly. So here at the end of chapter 5, over halfway through the short book, the situation does not look good at all!

Ah, but what a difference a day makes! Look at chapter 6:

That night the king could not sleep; so he ordered the book of the chronicles, the record of his reign, to be brought in and read to him. It was found recorded there that Mordecai had exposed Bigthana and Teresh, two of the king's officers who guarded the doorway, who had conspired to assassinate King Xerxes.

"What honor and recognition has Mordecai received for this?" the king asked.

"Nothing has been done for him," his attendants answered.

The king said, "Who is in the court?" Now Haman had just entered the outer court of the palace to speak to the king about hanging Mordecai on the gallows he had erected for him.

His attendants answered, "Haman is standing in the court."

"Bring him in," the king ordered.

When Haman entered, the king asked him, "What should be done for the man the king delights to honor?"

Now Haman thought to himself [consider here what a confusing thing pride is], "Who is there that the king would rather honor than me?" So he answered the king, "For the man the king delights to honor, have them bring a royal robe the king has worn and a horse the king has ridden, one with a royal crest placed on its head. Then let the robe and horse be entrusted to one of the king's most noble princes. Let them robe the man the king delights to honor, and lead him on the horse through the city streets, proclaiming before him, 'This is what is done for the man the king delights to honor!'"

"Go at once," the king commanded Haman. "Get the robe and the horse and do just as you have suggested for Mordecai the Jew, who sits at the king's gate. Do not neglect anything you have recommended."

So Haman got the robe and the horse. He robed Mordecai, and led him on horseback through the city streets, proclaiming before him, "This is what is done for the man the king delights to honor!"

Afterward Mordecai returned to the king's gate. But Haman rushed home, with his head covered in grief, and told Zeresh his wife and all his friends everything that had happened to him.

His advisers and his wife Zeresh said to him, "Since Mordecai, before whom your downfall has started, is of Jewish origin, you cannot stand against him—you will surely come to ruin!" While they were still talking with him, the king's eunuchs arrived and hurried Haman away to the banquet Esther had prepared (chapter 6).

Let's just stop for a moment and consider: Xerxes acts with appropriate self-interest here. What he does is not surprising; he wants to honor someone who helped save his life.

Mordecai is rewarded and honored, which makes sense given the service he has provided.

Haman is humiliated, but at this point he is only privately humiliated. The king knows nothing of Haman's hatred for Mordecai. And Haman still has another banquet with the king and queen planned. Yes, he may have to eat some crow with his friends, but perhaps his situation will not turn out as badly as his wife suggests.

And Esther is quietly preparing for the second banquet, perhaps knowing nothing about the king's sleeplessness, nor of his desire to honor Mordecai.

Now comes the second part of God's plans to frustrate the schemes of his enemy:

So the king and Haman went to dine with Queen Esther, and as they were drinking wine on that second day, the king again asked, "Queen Esther, what is your petition? It will be given you. What is your request? Even up to half the kingdom, it will be granted."

Then Queen Esther answered, "If I have found favor with you, O king, and if it pleases your majesty, grant me my life—this is my petition. And spare my people—this is my request. For I and my people have been sold for destruction and slaughter and annihilation. If we had merely been sold as male and female slaves, I would have kept quiet, because no such distress would justify disturbing the king."

King Xerxes asked Queen Esther, "Who is he? Where is the man who has dared to do such a thing?"

Esther said, "The adversary and enemy is this vile Haman."

Then Haman was terrified before the king and queen. The king got up in a rage, left his wine and went out into the palace garden. But Haman, realizing that the king had already decided his fate, stayed behind to beg Queen Esther for his life.

Just as the king returned from the palace garden to the banquet hall, Haman was falling on the couch where Esther was reclining.

The king exclaimed, "Will he even molest the queen while she is with me in the house?"

As soon as the word left the king's mouth, they covered Haman's face. Then Harbona, one of the eunuchs attending the king, said, "A gallows seventy-five feet high stands by Haman's house. He had it made for Mordecai, who spoke up to help the king."

The king said, "Hang him on it!" So they hanged Haman on the gallows he had prepared for Mordecai. Then the king's fury subsided (chapter 7).

Well, what can we say here? Xerxes acts like the absolute despot he is. Esther acts with cunning, bravery, and surprise. To make the request is risky, but I guess she thinks this is her best chance. Haman is surprised, and then desperate and careless. He should have left the room immediately when the king left the room. Finally, he is killed.

But the work was still not done! The edict ordering the execution of the Jews had gone out to 127 provinces! They remained in grave danger. So we turn to chapter 8:

That same day King Xerxes gave Queen Esther the estate of Haman, the enemy of the Jews. And Mordecai came into the presence of the king, for Esther had told how he was related to her. The king took off his signet ring, which he had reclaimed from Haman, and presented it to Mordecai. And Esther appointed him over Haman's estate.

Esther again pleaded with the king, falling at his feet and weeping. She begged him to put an end to the evil plan of Haman the Agagite, which he had devised against the Jews. Then the king extended the gold scepter to Esther and she arose and stood before him.

"If it pleases the king," she said, "and if he regards me with favor and thinks it the right thing to do, and if he is pleased with me, let an order be written overruling the dispatches that Haman son of Hammedatha, the Agagite, devised and wrote to destroy the Jews in all the king's provinces. For how can I bear to see disaster fall on my people? How can I bear to see the destruction of my family?"

King Xerxes replied to Queen Esther and to Mordecai the Jew, "Because Haman attacked the Jews, I have given his estate to Esther, and they have hanged him on the gallows. Now write another decree in the king's name in behalf of the Jews as seems best to you, and seal it with the king's signet ring—for no document written in the king's name and sealed with his ring can be revoked."

At once the royal secretaries were summoned—on the twenty-third day of the third month, the month of Sivan. They wrote out all Mordecai's orders to the Jews, and to the satraps, governors and nobles of the 127 provinces stretching from India to Cush. These orders were written in the script of each province and the language of each people and also to the Jews in their own script and language. Mordecai wrote in the name of King Xerxes, sealed the dispatches with the king's signet ring, and sent them by mounted couriers, who rode fast horses especially bred for the king.

The king's edict granted the Jews in every city the right to assemble and protect themselves; to destroy, kill and annihilate any armed force of any nationality or province that might attack them and their women and children; and to plunder the property of their enemies. The day appointed for the Jews to do this in all the provinces of King Xerxes was the thirteenth day of the twelfth month, the month of Adar. A copy of the text of the edict was to be issued as law in every province and made known to the people of every nationality so that the Jews would be ready on that day to avenge themselves on their enemies.

The couriers, riding the royal horses, raced out, spurred on by the king's command. And the edict was also issued in the citadel of Susa.

Mordecai left the king's presence wearing royal garments of blue and white, a large crown of gold and a purple robe of fine linen. And the city of Susa held a joyous celebration. For the Jews it was a time of happiness and joy, gladness and honor. In every province and in every city, wherever the edict of the king went, there was joy and gladness among the Jews, with feasting and celebrating. And many people of other nationalities became Jews because fear of the Jews had seized them (chapter 8).

Well, I guess the laws of the Medes and Persians are kind of like the U.S. Constitution. Americans cannot take out a pencil and eraser and start erasing the Constitution's clauses and amendments. All we can do is tack on another amendment that cancels out or circumscribes the part we want to change. That is what Xerxes does here. In so doing, Xerxes acts with fairness.

Esther is again courageous. The king has already given her much, yet she asks for still more.

Mordecai wisely handles the whole situation.

And the Jewish people now have hope—not that the story is done. So far, they simply have legal permission to defend themselves. They must still wait for the day nine months hence, set by the fateful casting of the die from the hand of the late Haman. Let's look at what happens at the beginning of chapter 9:

On the thirteenth day of the twelfth month, the month of Adar, the edict commanded by the king was to be carried out. On this day the enemies of the Jews had hoped to overpower them, but now the tables were turned and the Jews got the upper hand over those who hated them. The Jews assembled in their cities in all the provinces of King Xerxes to attack those seeking their destruction. No one could stand against them, because the people of all the other nationalities were afraid of them. And all the nobles of the provinces, the satraps, the governors and the king's administrators helped the Jews, because fear of Mordecai had seized them. Mordecai was prominent in the palace; his reputation spread throughout the provinces, and he became more and more powerful.

The Jews struck down all their enemies with the sword, killing and destroying them, and they did what they pleased to those who hated them. In the citadel of Susa, the Jews killed and destroyed five hundred men. They also killed Parshandatha, Dalphon, Aspatha, Poratha, Adalia, Aridatha, Parmashta, Arisai, Aridai and Vaizatha, the ten sons of Haman son of Hammedatha, the enemy of the Jews. But they did not lay their hands on the plunder.

The number of those slain in the citadel of Susa was reported to the king that same day. The king said to Queen Esther, "The Jews have killed and destroyed five hundred men and the ten sons of Haman in the citadel of Susa. What have they done in the rest of the king's provinces? Now what is your petition? It will be given you. What is your request? It will also be granted."

"If it pleases the king," Esther answered, "give the Jews in Susa permission to carry out this day's edict tomorrow also, and let Haman's ten sons be hanged on gallows."

So the king commanded that this be done. An edict was issued in Susa, and they hanged the ten sons of Haman. The Jews in Susa came together on the fourteenth day of the month of Adar, and they put to death in Susa three hundred men, but they did not lay their hands on the plunder.

Meanwhile, the remainder of the Jews who were in the king's provinces also assembled to protect themselves and get relief from their enemies. They killed seventy-five thousand of them but did not lay their hands on the plunder. This happened on the thirteenth day of the month of Adar, and on the fourteenth they rested and made it a day of feasting and joy (9:1-17).

The people are now safe! They have been delivered from their immediate problem. The rest of chapter 9 describes the history of the Jewish feast of Purim—which means "Lots"—thus named because of evil Haman's casting of the lot (9:18-32). The Jewish year begins in the spring with Passover, which commemorates Israel's deliverance from Egypt. Yom Kippur—the "Day of Atonement"—follows in the fall. Then Purim, the last festival and occurring in March, reminds the people that God will preserve them.

The book of Esther ends with a very short chapter (only three verses) that summarizes the good outcome for Mordecai and all the Jews:

> King Xerxes imposed tribute throughout the empire, to its distant shores. And all his acts of power and might, together with a full account of the greatness of Mordecai to which the king had raised him, are they not written in the book of the annals of the kings of Media and Persia? Mordecai the Jew was second in rank to King Xerxes, preeminent among the Jews, and held in high esteem by his many fellow Jews, because he worked for the good of his people and spoke up for the welfare of all the Jews (chapter 10).

THE CHARACTERS

So much for the plot. Let's turn for a few moments to the main characters of the book.

Haman

Haman was the enemy of God's people. His hidden pride, hatred, and vanity affected his public judgments. He may have been prime minister of the empire, but he was also the first to use the state for his own ends. And his ends were evil. We don't need to say anything more about this enemy of God's people.

Xerxes

Xerxes was a more interesting figure. In one sense, Xerxes was the deliverer of God's people. This great Persian king is especially known in history for his invasion of Greece in 480 B.C., which the ancient historian Herodotus (484 B.C–c.425 B.C.) recounts. Xerxes reigned for twenty-five years and then was assassinated in 465 B.C., about nine years after the events recorded in Esther. Apparently the type of assassination plot uncovered by Mordecai happened more than once during his reign. His son Artaxerxes I, whom we know from the books of Ezra and Nehemiah, then became king.

Of course, Xerxes delivered the people from a trial he played a part in initiating. It was Xerxes who gave his authority to Haman and then used that terrible phrase "do with the people as you please" (3:11). In order for this course of events to be reversed, someone else had to intervene and bring about deliverance. On his own, Xerxes would not have done this.

Mordecai

That's where Mordecai comes in. In a more profound sense, Mordecai was the deliverer of God's people in this story. Mordecai was a low-level official, who through kindness to his family members unwittingly became a person of influence over the queen herself. He had taken her as his own daughter when her mother and father died (2:7). He was a faithful subject of Xerxes, informing Esther when the king's bodyguards were plotting against his life. His public mourning over Haman's edict drew the attention of Esther's maids so that Esther learned of it. He became the queen's informer and motivated her to action. He rallied the Jews in Susa for fasting (and probably prayer) following Esther's request. His faithful service to the king attracted the king's attention at the crucial moment. Only afterward did Esther reveal to the king her family connection with Mordecai. And Mordecai authored the royal edict that countered Haman's earlier edict. No wonder that the king raised him to high position and the Jews esteemed him (10:2-3).

Mordecai was certainly a canny operator. He forbade Esther to reveal her Jewish identity, and no doubt he had a reason for doing so. But perhaps if her Jewish identity had been known, the king would never have agreed to Haman's request. And if Haman had known Esther was Jewish, he may have never asked for the decree in the first place!

Mordecai could also be quite angular. It's difficult to say why he would not kneel down or honor Haman even though the king ordered everyone to do so. The situation was not comparable to the refusal of the three young Jewish men to worship an idol in the book of Daniel. Xerxes was not commanding religious worship. He was only calling for court honor. Yet for whatever reason Mordecai would not do it. Was it because Mordecai knew Haman harbored sinister plans for the Jews? Did Mordecai feel it was wrong to honor Haman because he was an Amalekite, one of the ancient enemies of God's people? We can't say.

By himself, Mordecai could not have delivered the Jews. His public mourning would have accomplished nothing if no one in the royal court cared about his mourning. But someone did.

Esther

That brings us to Esther. In another very real sense, Esther was the deliverer of God's people.

Esther's circumstances were certainly favorable to her. She was beautiful, and God used that beauty. Yes, she had been orphaned, but God even used this to bring her near to power. She was taken to the king, and the king became taken with her. Esther proved her faithfulness to Xerxes by passing him information about his bodyguards' assassination plot. She sought out what troubled Mordecai, and so discovered the plot against her people. She asked for prayer and committed herself to act, even at the risk of her own life. And act she did. She went, stood, and asked. She prepared banquets and asked the king and Haman to come—twice! She was willing to play for high stakes. She revealed her ethnic identity, and then risked the possibility—by naming Haman—that the king might value Haman above her. That took courage indeed! Even after Haman was dead, Esther knew that she needed to ask still more of the king. After all, his edict threatening her people had been promulgated throughout the empire.

In all this, you could say that she was the deliverer of her people.

But she, like Mordecai, was canny. She did not at first reveal her Jewish identity. One might again wonder whether the king would have disallowed Haman's request from the very beginning had he known she was Jewish. Also, did she willingly join a pagan king's harem? This does not seem to be a model of godly virtue. Finally, many commentators have suggested that she was overzealous in her prosecution of justice. Did her zeal move over into vengeance?

In short, questions about the methods and morality of Mordecai and Esther surround them more than they surround other Jewish advisers to pagan kings in the Old Testament, like Joseph in Egypt or Daniel in Babylon.

God

Ultimately, God is the real deliverer of his people in this book. Any uncertainty we may feel about how upright this or that character may have been only highlights the fact that the real deliverer of God's people was none of these individuals, as heroic as a couple of them may have been. The real deliverer of God's people in this book is the gracious, sovereign, providing God. He holds center stage, *even though he is never named.*

Did you notice that as we read through the chapters above? It's true. Except for Song of Songs, Esther is the only book of the Bible that never explicitly mentions God. Yet, as Matthew Henry said, "though the name of God be not in it, the finger of God is, directing many minute events for the bringing about of his people's deliverance."[3] God's ability to accomplish his purposes, despite his hiddenness, only heightens our sense of his power. He may not be named, but this book is one of the longest sustained meditations on the sovereignty and providence of God in the whole Bible. It is really just one long narrative illustration of Romans 8:28: "We know that in all things God works for the good of those who love him, who have been called according to his purposes."

---

[3] Matthew Henry, *Matthew Henry's Commentary on the Whole Bible,* 6 vols. (McLean, Va.: MacDonald, n.d.), 2:1121.

Accordingly, many of the passive verbs throughout the book imply God's action. Consider this sentence, for example: ". . . the time when the Jews *got relief* from their enemies, and as the month when their sorrow *was turned* into joy and their mourning into a day of celebration" (9:22). Who gives the Jews relief and turns their sorrow into joy? God does.

You may have missed God's dramatic role in this book because he does not act in the same spectacular fashion that he does at other points in the Old Testament, such as calling Abraham or delivering the children of Israel from Egypt. Such interventions fall under the heading of *miraculous.* But here he works *providentially*—through the normal actions of people in the normal order of life, as he worked with Joseph and Ruth. God works sovereignly with no apparent miracles, just a lot of "happenings" and just the right "circumstances." Did you notice *that* as we read through the book?

You may have heard the proverb, "large doors swing on small hinges." The course of history is often determined by the smallest particulars. This story of Esther is filled with crucial happenings that might have looked like chance to anyone observing the events at the time, and perhaps they looked that way to you. After all, the book explains the Feast of Purim, which comes from the plural Hebrew word for "lots" or "dice." And the roll of the dice gives us a random outcome, right? If you think so, then to you this book will be nothing more than a really remarkable story of how all this stuff just seemed to happen. What stuff?

- Esther just *happens* to be Jewish, and she just *happens* to be beautiful.
- Esther just *happens* to be favored by the king.
- Mordecai just *happens* to overhear the plot against the king's life.
- A report of this just *happens* to be written in the king's chronicles.
- Haman just *happens* to notice that Mordecai does not kneel down before him and he just *happens* to find out that Mordecai is a Jew.
- When Haman plots his revenge, the dice just *happen* to indicate that the date for exacting revenge is put off for almost a year! (What does Proverbs 16:33 say? "The lot is cast into the lap, but its every decision is from the LORD.")
- Esther *happens* to get the king's approval to speak, but then she *happens* to put off her request for another day.
- Her deferral just *happens* to send Haman out by Mordecai one more time, which just *happens* to cause him to recount it to his friends.
- They, in turn, just *happen* to encourage him to build a scaffold immediately!
- So Haman just *happens* to be excited to approach the king early the next morning.

- It just so *happens* that the previous night, the mighty king could not command a moment's sleep, and he just *happened* to have had a book brought to him that recounted Mordecai's deed.
- He then *happened* to ask whether Mordecai had been rewarded, to which his attendants *happened* to know the answer. Simply consider for a moment the fact that Mordecai *happened* not to have been rewarded for having saved the king's life. How unusual this must have been! Someone who saved the king's life never rewarded? I wonder if Mordecai ever chafed under that: "Doesn't he realize what I did for him?" Well, it all just happened.
- Anyhow, Haman *happens* to approach the king just when the king is wondering how Mordecai should be honored.
- Later on, the king *happens* to return to the queen just when Haman *happens* to be pleading with Esther in a way that can be misconstrued.
- The gallows Haman built for Mordecai just *happens* to be ready when King Xerxes wants to hang Haman.

I could keep going. Is that how you read the story of Esther—as so many happenstances and lucky coincidences? Apart from believing that God actively and sovereignly rules over our world, the book of Esther becomes a mere celebration of Mordecai's wisdom, Esther's courage, and, most of all, simple chance and luck.

But, friend, if you are a Christian, this is not how you should read this book. I assure you, this is not why it was written. This book was written to show that God himself acts to achieve the total defeat of his foes *and* the safety of his people.

Haman described how the man the king delights to honor should be honored, thinking the king meant him; but the king meant Mordecai. Haman also built the scaffold for Mordecai, but it was used for him. In short, Haman meant honor for himself and the scaffold for Mordecai, but God meant the scaffold for Haman and honor for Mordecai. God's will is always accomplished, yet men are perfectly free agents. Wonders can be wrought without miracles, can't they?

I asked my daughter, Anne, last night, what she got out of the book of Esther. "It's amazing the way the Lord works," she said.

"But it never mentions the Lord," I responded.

She replied, "The Lord doesn't have to be mentioned for us to recognize his work."

Very true.

God can deliver his people in whatever way he wants. He can deliver people with the miracles of Exodus. And he can deliver people with sovereignly assisted circumstances, as we see in the book of Esther. God, the unnamed one, is the chief actor in the book of Esther. He is the deliverer of his people.

THE LESSONS

So what are the lessons we learn from this little book?

Well, we could say many things about avoiding the vices and attaining the virtues of each character, and all of these would be true. Be faithful with any position God gives you, just as Mordecai and Esther were. Avoid the pride of Haman. Cultivate prudence and wisdom. Develop a just doctrine of self-defense. Risk yourself for a greater good, as the heroic Esther did. Leaders are important, and we should pray for them. Seek the prosperity of the city in which you are an exile (Jer. 29:4-7).

And, as I said, all of these lessons are true and good to learn.

But if this is an overview of the whole book of Esther, in which we try to understand the weight, the thrust, the point of the book itself, we must see that this book most fundamentally teaches us two truths about God.

God Always Punishes His Enemies

First, God always punishes his enemies. Some people have objected to the bloodthirstiness of this book. The Jews' triumph in chapter 9 is a bloody one, leaving tens of thousands dead. But if that is your reaction to the story, you may want to consider a couple of matters. First, the Jews were given permission to defend themselves only in the event of an attack against them (8:11). All this blood was shed in self-defense. Second, it is right for God to bring retribution against his enemies. In fact, justice demands it! Furthermore, God punishes the enemies of his people, because to be an enemy of God's people *is* to be an enemy of God. That is the clear and unanimous testimony of Scripture.

Perhaps you are wondering, "How relevant today is this idea of God punishing the enemies of his people? Who has enemies now?" If you are a Christian, you have enemies! "Me? Enemies?" Yes, people will oppose you in your faith. Remember what Jesus prayed to the Father, "I have given [my disciples] your word and the world has hated them, for they are not of the world any more than I am of the world" (John 17:14). The world hates God's people, because the world hates the God we represent, the God who made humankind and who would guide and direct all men. Ever since the Fall, every man has hated God. Perversely and wrongly, he seeks his freedom in bondage and his bondage in freedom. So when we, as freed slaves, bring the good news of Jesus Christ to the people who remain in the bondage that they believe to be freedom, ironically, we are hated.

What will happen to those who persevere in wickedness? They will, by God's own hand, come to an ill end. In that sense, this little book of Esther previews the book of Revelation, where we read about a song sung in heaven over the city that has fallen under God's judgment: "Rejoice over her, O heaven! Rejoice, saints and apostles and prophets! God has judged her for the way she treated you" (Rev. 18:20).

If God always punishes his enemies—the enemies of his people—what does this mean for you?

Consider your state carefully. First, it means that you should consider your current state carefully. Many people rush through life feeling healthy and prosperous, and one day they will wake up and find that they have thoughtlessly tumbled into the very presence of God, and that his righteous, complete, unerring and unrepealable judgment awaits them. Resolve today that you will not so thoughtlessly tumble into his presence. While you have your senses and while you have time, stop and consider how you stand before God. Do you believe in him? Have you submitted to him? Do you love him? Have you sought his forgiveness for your sins?

Repent immediately. God's judgment on his enemies also means that you should *repent immediately,* while there is time. God has taken on flesh in the Lord Jesus Christ. Jesus came as our real deliverer to live a perfect life and to die on the cross for the sins of all who would repent and believe in him. He calls you now to repent of your sins and to turn and trust him. If you do, he will grant forgiveness for your sins and a new life in him. What other way do you have for dealing with your sins? You cannot deny them. They are yours, and will cling to you more closely than your skin itself! You will stand before God and give him an account. Every single one of us will; that is unavoidable. What will you say to him about your sins?

Let me exhort you again: Repent! And believe in the Lord Jesus Christ. Receive the forgiveness for sins and the new life he offers! Because God always punishes his enemies.

God Will Certainly Deliver His People

But there is a second lesson we are to take from this book: God will certainly deliver his people. Do you believe that? That's what the book of Esther would teach you.

Now maybe you are wondering, "What about the Chinese believer who I read was imprisoned and tortured for her faith? What of the Christians killed in Nigeria, or the missionaries killed in Lebanon? What about those Christians being killed perhaps right now in Sudan, in Pakistan, in Indonesia? What do you mean 'God will certainly deliver his people'?"

In this fallen world, the Bible does not promise us escape from physical death or even martyrdom, but Esther does tell us this: God will preserve his people for his own purposes and for his own glory. It is just as the Lord told his people centuries earlier through the prophet Isaiah: "'no weapon forged against you will prevail, and you will refute every tongue that accuses you. This is the heritage of the servants of the LORD, and this is their vindication from me,' declares the LORD" (Isa. 54:17). God *will* vindicate all his servants!

Consider then how safe the church of God is. No, not from earthly violence and physical death, but from final ruin before God! What did Jesus say? "I tell you, my friends, do not be afraid of those who kill the body and after that can do no more. But I will show you whom you should fear: Fear him who, after the killing of the body, has power to throw you into hell. Yes, I tell you, fear him" (Luke 12:4-5). God is the one and the only one we should finally fear. And if we are in Christ, we do not need to be anxious about his love. Each child of God has a guardian near God's throne.

Christ is finally the deliverer of God's people. Insofar as God used Esther to deliver his people, she pointed to Christ. Her name is related to the Hebrew word for "star," and she, like the star of Bethlehem, pointed to this deliverer who was to come. God would be with his people, and he would deliver them. The book of Esther reminds us of the certain truth that, as Jesus said, he will build his "church, and the gates of Hades will not overcome it" (Matt. 16:18). Christ's church will not finally be killed! As Christians, we need to rejoice in this.

God's sovereignty is a sweet doctrine for Christians. Throughout these studies in the historical books of the Old Testament, we have seen it on display. Ever since this series began in Joshua, we have watched God use all the circumstances of his people for his own glory. So great is his sovereignty that he brings blessing to his people from the unlikeliest sources. He has even used to glorious end one of the great sins of his Old Testament people—the marrying of non-Jews. God had told the Israelites not to marry people from other nations, not because he opposed interethnic or interracial marriages but because he opposed the interreligious marriages that would draw his people's hearts away from him. And he wanted his people to remain distinct in their worship of him. Still, he used Ruth, the Moabitess who married an Israelite man (but who also adopted Israel's God), to preserve his people. This union gave birth, several generations on, to great King David, and many generations beyond that, to "great David's greater Son"—the Lord Jesus. He also used Esther's marriage to a foreign king, not as an occasion to exterminate his people, letting them intermarry to the point of indistinctness from the peoples they lived among, but as an occasion to keep his distinct people from extermination. God will keep a distinct people for himself! So he ensured that they survived until the coming of the Messiah. And in his sovereign irony, he even used a Moabite wife and a Persian husband to do it! That is how sovereign our God is. That is how certain he is of accomplishing his purposes.

The book of Esther is a display of God's sovereignty!

This fact also points us to Jesus. Jesus, by God's will, relived the history of God's wayward Old Testament people. Yet Jesus relived this history correctly and so reversed the fatal effects of the Fall. Where the Israelites crossed the Red Sea and then spent forty years sinning in the wilderness, Jesus was baptized and then spent forty days resisting temptation in the wilderness. Where Adam chose his will over God's will in the Garden, Jesus chose God's will over his own will in another garden. And where Adam willfully went to a tree demanding life but found death, Jesus submissively went to a second tree accepting death so that he could give life.

So too does the book of Esther fit with God's long pattern of turning the tables on his enemies and providing for his wayward elect.

The point of Esther today does not have to do with Jewishness—that God means to preserve the Jewish people still. Centuries before Esther, the Lord had promised to bless Abraham and his seed, and echoes of that promise do resound in Esther as God's people enjoy his blessing and protection. But the *fullness* of God's promise to Abraham is fulfilled in Jesus Christ and in those who believe in him (Gal. 3:22). As Paul says in Galatians, "There is neither Jew nor Greek, slave nor free, male nor female, for you are all one in Christ Jesus. If you belong to Christ, *then you are Abraham's seed,* and heirs according to the promise" (Gal. 3:28-29). This is the great story in which the book of Esther is a wonderful chapter.

My Christian friend, if God will certainly deliver his people, what does this mean for you?

Be comforted in trials. First, it means that we can be comforted in our trials, because God will not abandon his people. Christian, can you not see this in your life? The Puritan minister John Flavel said that "He who observes providence will never be long without a providence to observe." You know what he means: if you look for God's working in your life, if you thoughtfully trace it out and reflect on it, you will be surprised by how much you begin to see.

In my own life, I can think of countless particulars: going to Duke and meeting my wife; Professor Kerr speaking to me after a lecture about a Puritan named Richard Sibbes; Carl Henry writing me about his church's need for a pastor. Event after event in my life, at the time it occurred, seemed like just another small happenstance, or just another letter in the mail, or just another comment from a friend.

What about your life? How many "ifs" and "coincidences" can you look back on that turned out to be significant, even from our finite vantage point?

Do none of those speak of God's care for you? Can you see how he worked when you were asleep and spiritually unready? Even in such moments, God persevered in showing kindness to you, down to the minutest details of your life. Trust him! Trust that God puts the right people in the right place at the right time. Trust that he restrains his enemies in just the right way. Trust that he tries his people for their good. We must not think that an event is not providential simply because it is hard or even tragic. God's wisdom arranges the smallest events to the greatest tragedies in order to produce great results for his people.

Charles Haddon Spurgeon said,

> We frequently hear persons say of a pleasant or a great event, "What a providence!" while they are silent as to anything which appears less important, or has an unpleasant savour. But, my brethren, the place of the gorse upon the heath is as fixed as the station of a king and the dust which is raised by a chariot-wheel is as surely steered by providence as the planet in its orbit. There is as much providence in the creeping of an aphid upon a rose leaf as in the marching of an army to ravage a continent. Everything, the most minute as well as the most magnificent, is ordered by the Lord who has prepared his throne in the heavens, whose kingdom ruleth over all.[4]

Elsewhere, he said,

> It seems a very small matter whether you or I shall sleep to-night or toss restlessly on our beds, but God will be in our rest or in our wakefulness; we know not what his purpose may be, but his hand will be in it, neither doth any man sleep or wake but according to the decree of the Lord.[5]

When you find yourself in dangerous circumstances or trying days, when you feel as if you have fallen under Haman's edict, read the book of Esther, consider God's overruling care, and be comforted.

Be courageous in obedience. Second, God's certain deliverance of his people means that you can be courageous in obedience. In his providence, God calls his servants to be active. Mordecai knew for certain that help would arise from some quarter (4:14). He knew his God. Yet this certainty did not make Mordecai inactive, or cause him to counsel Esther toward complacency. Instead, it nerved both of them to action. "If God is in this, our plans will succeed!"

That is the assurance we have as Christ's church. The church is not a collection of entrepreneurs trying inventive things with youthful ingenuity and

---

[4] Charles Haddon Spurgeon, *The Metropolitan Tabernacle Pulpit,* 63 vols. (London: Passmore & Alabaster, 1885), 20:619.
[5] Ibid., 621.

hoping that we may hit on something that works. No! We are disciples of Jesus Christ, following him together with his people in ways that are sometimes hard, sometimes trying, and sometimes even dangerous. Yet the knowledge that God will certainly deliver his people steels us to follow and obey him, come what may. My Christian friend, let this knowledge give you not complacency but courage in your obedience!

Be confident with joyful hope in your waiting. If God will certainly deliver his people, then, third, be confident with joyful hope in all your waiting. God brought you to your present station. Again, Spurgeon said, "Every child of God is where God has placed him for some purpose."[6] Now, knowing that God brought you to where you are this very moment, do you not have a reason for confident joy, even if you find yourself in a season of adversity? A confident joy in his work to humble your pride? A confident joy in purposing to lift you up to him through lowly service? He will save you if you simply pray to him. He will bless you if you simply trust in him. Is this not reason for joyful confidence?

God will deliver his people. Knowing this, we can be comforted, courageous, and confident!

CONCLUSION

And so we leave both the book of Esther and this series of studies in the historical books of the Old Testament with God's people experiencing *shalom*— rest, prosperity, and peace in God's presence and under his rule, even though they are outside the land. Who would have thought these twelve histories we have called "the Other Millennium" would close on such a marvelous note! How could little orphan Esther end up as queen, Mordecai as prime minister, and the exiled Jewish people in prosperity, popularity, and safety! Through all of these unlikely circumstances, God's providence proceeded. As with the slavery of Joseph, the curse of Balaam, and the cross of Christ, what man intended for ill, God used for good.

I wonder how all this sounds to you. Like so much wishful thinking? It isn't. We Christians realize there are serious problems in life. But the Christian realism you will find in the Bible points not only to real problems but to real solutions. And real deliverance! We Christians have both realism and hope.

Some people have thought that the conclusion of Esther, as neatly tied up as it is, makes the book more like a novel or a romance—something best placed in the fiction aisle. But then such critics forget that history has a meaning, because God writes history as an author writes a story.

---

[6] Ibid., 616.

The author of Hebrews encourages us, therefore, "let us hold unswervingly to the hope we profess, for he who promised is faithful" (Heb. 10:23). He will finish writing the story he has begun upon the pages of history, even upon the pages of your life. God's people still wait, but we wait in confidence of the God who delivers!

What are you waiting to be delivered from today?

Whatever you are waiting to be delivered from will determine whom you regard as your deliverer. Be careful. Many of the Jews missed the Deliverer that God sent, which says they were not waiting for God at all but for something else.

In the midst of your troubles this morning, what are you waiting for?

Let us pray:

O God, we recognize you as the author of every day of history, and of each day of our own lives. Dear God, help us to wait for you in trust and reliance. Give us confidence for each day of waiting that you call us to. Deliver us from the Evil One and his plans against us, ultimately against you. Grow our trust in you, we pray. Train our hearts on you, now and forever. In Christ's name we ask it. Amen.

Questions for Reflection

1. Who delivered the Jews? Esther, Mordecai, and Xerxes, or God? How would you explain this?

2. Were Esther and Mordecai perfectly upstanding throughout the story? When discussing the Bible both with Christians and non-Christians, why should we *not* feel the need to defend all the behavior even of the "good guys"? In fact, why should we be willing to point out their faults?

3. Let's take our conclusions to question 2 and apply them to ourselves. Why should we be willing to point out our personal flaws, even serious ones, to both Christians and non-Christians (while keeping other considerations of prudence, e.g., don't cause a brother to stumble)?

4. We have considered the fact that the book of Esther works as one long narrative illustration of the apostle Paul's reassuring words in Romans 8:28: "And we know that in all things God works for the good of those who love him, who have been called according to his purpose." First, let's consider, does God work in this fashion for everyone? Does this include non-Christians? Whom does he work for? Second, let's ask, what does Paul mean by "all things"? List two or

three "things" that you often fail to remember God is using for good purposes in your life (for example: someone's death, your struggle with a particular sin, a loved one's refusal to consider Christianity, etc.). What would placing these two or three struggles into the "all things" category mean for your life? How will you do this?

5. No matter what your circumstances are, God has specifically placed you where you are right now. Why is this comforting? Why should this fact not lead us to complacency but to action?

6. What is *significant* about the fact that the book of Esther never names God? What is *wonderful* about the fact, from the standpoint of living by faith in the world today, that the book of Esther never names God?

7. Hopefully, you noticed this sermon's very stern and very loving warning: Many people rush through life feeling healthy and prosperous, and one day they will wake up and find that they have thoughtlessly tumbled into the very presence of God, and that his righteous, complete, unerring and unrepealable judgment awaits them. Resolve today that you will not so thoughtlessly tumble into his presence. Have you made preparations for your certain appearance before God? What responsibility do you have to issue this warning to others, especially those you love?

8. Does God have any enemies who should not be a Christian's enemies? Should a Christian have any enemies who are not God's enemies? Do you? Who? What?

9. What specifically is meant by the promise, "God will certainly deliver his people"? Sometimes Christians claim that the doctrine of God's sovereignty will kill evangelism. But how does a certainty in God's sovereignty, combined with a certainty in the fact that he will deliver his people, actually stimulate missions and evangelism? By the same token, why is it that people who believe in God's sovereignty and certain deliverance so often travel to "closed" countries to share the gospel where Christian evangelism is a punishable offense?

10. What are you waiting to be delivered from? Really, more than anything else in the world, what do you long to be delivered from? Does this help you to see what you most value?

PART THREE
ANCIENT WISDOM

THE MESSAGE OF JOB: WISDOM FOR LOSERS

18

THE MESSAGE OF JOB: WISDOM FOR LOSERS

DO ONLY LOSERS FACE TRIALS?[1]

Sometimes, the misfortunes of life can seem embarrassing. Have you ever felt that way? Everyone else can look so squeaky clean. They look free from deep troubles, or so it appears when we glance around the church on Sunday morning. I am not suggesting that we all need to attend church on Sunday weeping, wailing, and looking disheveled. No, I appreciate the effort you make to clean yourselves up, clear your schedules, and prepare yourselves for worship. I am just observing how embarrassing it can be to feel, in any sense, like *a loser*. In our culture particularly, believing that others perceive you as a loser is embarrassing in the extreme.

Often, it is the trials of life that make us feel like losers. Part of the difficulty, if we are honest, is that we do not always understand why suffering has to afflict *us* personally. I don't know how many times I have sat with a person struggling over a bad report from the doctor, a rough time at work, or some other intense personal difficulty and heard the question asked, "Why me?" Everyone else walking around seems to be wealthy enough and healthy enough. Every cheery greeting and every pleasantly chirping bird can feel specially devised to torment us, since they underscore our pain. Even when we do finally admit our troubles, we can still feel mystified, stupefied, and perhaps terrified at our inability to explain them.

And, if I may continue on this inward journey a bit further, we suffer especially when a trial looks too big to handle. When it seems like just too much. Our troubles are so painful and so difficult to understand that we wonder and worry about the possibility (and maybe we even secretly relish the possibility)

---

[1] This message was originally preached on June 29, 1997, at Capitol Hill Baptist Church in Washington, D.C.

of losing faith in God himself, because surely God could not have had any part in this!

If these types of concerns do not describe you right now, they will almost certainly describe you sometime; and right now they probably do describe someone you know and love.

So we need the wisdom of the book of Job.

INTRODUCING JOB

The book of Job is one of five books in the Old Testament that we call the "Wisdom books." Open your Bible to the table of contents, and right there in the middle of the Old Testament you will see Job, Psalms, Proverbs, Ecclesiastes, and Song of Songs. No great events occur in these five Wisdom books. They are not like the books of history that appear above them in your table of contents and that are concerned with the history of the nation of Israel. Neither are they like the books of prophecy that appear beneath them and that are also concerned with the history of Israel, particularly the end of the nation's history. These books do not even present any new laws as the first five books of the Bible do. Rather, these books could be called the heart of the Old Testament, not only in their position but in their attitude. They are not so much about the whole nation of Israel, like the histories or the prophets, but about individuals and our individual highs and lows. This is why Christians often find them to be their favorite part of the Old Testament; these books seem more accessible. They don't require you to know a lot about the history of Israel and God's work with his people to understand them. They are written to individuals in their individual experiences, which is what we intend to study in this overview series of these five books.

Job, Psalms, Proverbs, Ecclesiastes, and Song of Songs are full of beautiful and expressive poetry. Trees clap their hands. Hills sing for joy. God's enemies melt like wax. And God himself rides upon the clouds. The Psalms are filled with the love and liveliness of an individual relationship with God, while Song of Songs celebrates these things between husband and wife. Proverbs guides us with its practical advice. And Ecclesiastes draws us into humility and awe as it considers some of life's most difficult mysteries.

As does Job.

Job is widely acknowledged to be a literary masterpiece. Even unbelievers admit this. Yet when some people first turn to the Bible for guidance and read the title of this book, they may well think the book is about employment or issues at work. It is, sort of, but not directly. It is about trials and difficulties and God letting things happen that are hard to understand. So it's kind of about work. But the title is pronounced *jōb*, not *jahb*.

Job has important wisdom that we need. Wisdom for people who struggle with loss. Wisdom for people who feel like losers. Wisdom for people who know themselves to be losers.

Job's wisdom is for us and for our times, because it speaks realistically of suffering. It explores the limits of our understanding. And it illustrates compellingly our need to trust God. It is these three simple ideas that summarize Job's message to us, and which we will use to look at the book together. Specifically, we will see that

> we often suffer;
> we sometimes understand;
> we can always trust.

I would prefer for you to read the book of Job instead of memorizing these three sentences, but hopefully they will be of some help to you.

WE OFTEN SUFFER

The first statement that summarizes Job's message to us is, we often suffer.

When we are first introduced to Job in the first five verses of the book, we see that he was a righteous man: "In the land of Uz there lived a man whose name was Job. This man was blameless and upright; he feared God and shunned evil" (1:1).

Not only was Job righteous, he was wealthy: "He had seven sons and three daughters, and he owned seven thousand sheep, three thousand camels, five hundred yoke of oxen and five hundred donkeys, and had a large number of servants" (1:2-3a).

And not only was he wealthy, he was wise:

> When a period of feasting had run its course, Job would send and have [his children] purified. Early in the morning he would sacrifice a burnt offering for each of them, thinking, "Perhaps my children have sinned and cursed God in their hearts." This was Job's regular custom (1:5).

Indeed, Job was a great man. Summarizing all this we read, "he was the greatest man among all the people of the East" (1:3b).[2]

What is most well-known about Job, that for which he is legendary, are his trials. But did you know that all of Job's legendary trials are told in eight short verses? That's it! Seven verses record Job's loss of wealth, and one verse records Job's loss of health. First, he loses his worldly wealth:

---

[2] See also Ezek. 14:14, 20; James 5:11.

One day when Job's sons and daughters were feasting and drinking wine at the oldest brother's house, a messenger came to Job and said, "The oxen were plowing and the donkeys were grazing nearby, and the Sabeans attacked and carried them off. They put the servants to the sword, and I am the only one who has escaped to tell you!"

While he was still speaking, another messenger came and said, "The fire of God fell from the sky and burned up the sheep and the servants, and I am the only one who has escaped to tell you!"

While he was still speaking, another messenger came and said, "The Chaldeans formed three raiding parties and swept down on your camels and carried them off. They put the servants to the sword, and I am the only one who has escaped to tell you!"

While he was still speaking, yet another messenger came and said, "Your sons and daughters were feasting and drinking wine at the oldest brother's house, when suddenly a mighty wind swept in from the desert and struck the four corners of the house. It collapsed on them and they are dead, and I am the only one who has escaped to tell you!" (1:13-19).

Then he loses his health: "So Satan went out from the presence of the LORD and afflicted Job with painful sores from the soles of his feet to the top of his head" (2:7).

Interestingly, Job's trials first afflict his wealth—the outward splendor of the man. Job was known as a great man, and he was known as great because of the things that people can see with their eyes. His flocks and herds took up much land. He had many servants. He had a great reputation. Later in the book, he reminisces about the honor given to him whenever he would go to the city and enter the public square by the city gates (29:7ff.). Yet all of these things were taken from him in a moment.

Not only did he lose his family and possessions; that which was left to him—his health—was then taken. Now, on how many commercials have we been told, "All you really have is your health"? Of course, this is what you hear whenever someone is trying to sell you something supposedly good for your health. Still, if it is true that all we have is our health, then we will all surely lose the one thing that we really have—our health.

Perhaps Job suffered more *suddenly* than any of us have suffered. But in the end, he did not suffer more *comprehensively* than we will suffer. As Sir Walter Scott said of all our lives, "Come he slow or come he fast, it is but death that comes at last."[3]

Indeed, suffering is universal. Yet sometimes we Christians avoid admit-

---

[3] Sir Walter Scott, "Marmion," lines 567-568.

ting the doubt, fear, failure, anger, or conflict that sufferings can bring. We like our church services to be like motivational pep rallies. This is what we want on Sunday mornings. "We have to face a tough week, Preacher. We don't need stuff like this on Sunday mornings."

But if we want to have a realistic understanding about what it means to be a follower of the Crucified One, if we want to live lives in the real world, we should recognize that, although we may be able to psyche ourselves up for a little while with a rose-colored version of Christianity, we won't be able to convince many people around us. And we won't be dealing honestly with ourselves either. By looking at the book of Job, we can see that trouble and strife belong not only to Job but to us as well. We do no one any good by denying it. People around us know it, and there's nothing wrong with admitting it ourselves. Job is a good example for us of someone who suffers, and deals honestly with his sufferings.

So, we often suffer.

WE SOMETIMES UNDERSTAND

The second statement that summarizes Job's message to us is, we sometimes understand. This is really what most of the book of Job is about.

Let me give you a brief overview of the whole book. The first two chapters set out the basic story. They tell us who Job is and what trials he encounters. Then, at the end of chapter 2, three of Job's friends come to comfort him, and they sit with him silently for a week. Finally, in chapter 3, someone speaks, and it is Job. Job pours out his complaint.

Then chapters 4–41—all but the last chapter—are a series of dialogues. Clearly, most of the book is taken up with these dialogues.

Chapter 4–31 contain three cycles of dialogues between Job, Eliphaz, Bildad, and Zophar. Chapters 4–14 are the first cycle, chapters 15–21 are the second, and then chapters 22–31 are the third. In cycles one and two, Eliphaz speaks and Job responds. Then Bildad speaks and Job responds. Then Zophar speaks and Job responds. Really, each of the speakers keeps making the same points. The same thing happens in the third cycle, except the last guy, Zophar, doesn't talk anymore, because the debate is over. Job's human counselors have finished. They have flushed out everything they want to say. Instead, Job makes his final protest and almost demands that God show up so that he can talk to God himself about his suffering.

Instead of God, we hear from a young man named Elihu, who appears in chapter 32 and speaks all the way to 37. Elihu says he has been listening for some time but has not said anything because he is younger and does not want to be disrespectful to his elders. Yet in these chapters, Elihu speaks his mind. He says that Job's charges should be answered, and then he talks about God's greatness and how God's justice cannot be impugned.

Finally, in chapter 38, God himself enters the discussion and criticizes those who have spoken "words without knowledge" (38:2). In one of the most remarkable descriptions in the Bible of God's work in creation, God paints a picture for Job and the others of his unique and sovereign power. As he says at one point, "Who endowed the heart with wisdom or gave understanding to the mind?" (38:36). If you are a zoologist, you should love chapters 38–39. God looks at the natural world and considers the many things he has made, from seas to stars, from ostriches to oxen.

Then in chapter 40, God asks Job directly, "Will the one who contends with the Almighty correct him? Let the one who accuses God answer him!" (40:2).

To which Job's response is simple: "I am unworthy—how can I reply to you? I put my hand over my mouth. I spoke once, but I have no answer—twice, but I will say no more" (40:4-5).

God replies,

> "Would you discredit my justice?
>   Would you condemn me to justify yourself?
> Do you have an arm like God's,
>   and can your voice thunder like his?
> Then adorn yourself with glory and splendor,
>   and clothe yourself in honor and majesty.
> Unleash the fury of your wrath" (40:8-11a).

In the remainder of chapters 40 and 41, God continues to instruct Job and the others about who he is: "Who then is able to stand against me? Who has a claim against me that I must pay? Everything under heaven belongs to me" (41:10b-11).

In chapter 42, the last chapter, Job makes his final confession:

> "Surely I spoke of things I did not understand,
>   things too wonderful for me to know.
> "You said, 'Listen now, and I will speak;
>   I will question you, and you shall answer me.'
> My ears had heard of you
>   but now my eyes have seen you.
> Therefore I despise myself
>   and repent in dust and ashes" (42:3b-6).

The story ends here in chapter 42 with God telling Eliphaz, Bildad, and Zophar that they have been wrong. Then he blesses Job. There are some interesting things that God does not say, but we will come to that in a moment.

That's the summary of the book of Job.

If we turn back and look at the three long cycles of dialogue, we can summarize all the arguments of Eliphaz, Bildad, and Zophar pretty easily: "Job, what has happened to you is really bad. You must have sinned most extraordinarily, because God is just and punishes sin. And though you deny having sinned, we know you must have. There can be no other explanation." And every time, Job basically responds, "Oh no, I didn't." By that, Job does not mean he has never sinned; indeed, he confesses his sinfulness along the way. Rather, he is saying that no great, hidden sin has marked his life that would have called for such calamity.

Yet again and again, Job's friends respond with the proverbial wisdom, "You get what you deserve." Really, their response is like the response of Jesus' disciples when the disciples meet the blind man and ask, "Rabbi, who sinned, this man or his parents, that he was born blind?" (John 9:2). Job's friends, it turns out, were every bit as "right" as the disciples.

Honestly, I understand their situation. They knew Job. He was their friend. They respected him and regarded him highly. So they were struggling to understand why something so horrible had happened to him. They could not bring themselves to deny the reality of the material world like some sort of Christian Scientist or like a Buddhist who says, "This suffering isn't real." Neither could they abandon their orthodoxy by rejecting either God's justice or God's sovereignty.

They could only conclude that their previous perception of Job's virtuousness was mistaken. You can't judge a book by its cover, you know. They had known him all these years, yes, but apparently they didn't know what oppression, greed, lust, even murder had been lurking behind his outwardly pious appearance. Besides, rich and powerful men know how to put on a good show. So who can really say who Job is, after all?

We, too, try to understand our suffering, thinking that we can somehow alleviate the pain by comprehending it.

Some people have tried to make sense of their suffering by saying that God cannot do anything about it.[4] He would like to; he has very good intentions; but he cannot do better than he already has. At a recent seminar on cloning that I attended at the U. S. Capitol, one of the speakers stood up and said,

---

[4] Like Rabbi Harold Kushner, author of *When Bad Things Happen to Good People* (Boston: G. K. Hall, 1981); and in another way, like Clark Pinnock and others who advocate the "limited god" or "open theist" view of how God relates to his creation.

"Honestly, let's just admit that God hasn't done a very good job with this world. He has failed with this world." Well, that is not how the book of Job replies to Job's calamities. The book of Job clearly presents a sovereign God. Job and his counselors all agree about this much. God rules his creation.

Other people have observed the same disconnect between actions and consequences (the righteous man is cursed; the wicked man is blessed) and suggested, "Okay, it's clear that God is by definition God, and that he exists. But if that is so, then we must conclude that he is not really good and just." God may be all-powerful, but he is not righteous. He does not clearly punish evil and reward good. But again, the book of Job speaks clearly to this. Job and all his counselors agree: God is good and God is holy. He does punish evil and he does reward good.

Still other people simply despair of the possibility that life and suffering have any meaning at all.

In all of these suggestions, notice that we are requiring an explanation that meets our limited horizons and personal interests. Yet demanding that suffering have a reason and meaning that fits within the narrow scope of our human understanding prejudices the explanation that can be given. As humans, we must see that, given our limited understanding, there are only a few types of solutions that are available to us. When we fail to recognize our limitations, it's like deciding that because our car radio is not picking up any radio broadcasts, then there must be no radio stations sending out a broadcast anywhere. But why assume that? Is that the only possible explanation? And why assume that we must understand what God intends through suffering?

We all have this tendency. We think to ourselves, "God made us. Surely he must intend for us to understand everything all the time." But how do we know that's what he intends, and why would we condemn him if he does not? These are the questions the book of Job poses for us.

Above all, perhaps, the book of Job teaches us that we do not possess all the facts. In a few moments, we will consider the interchange between God and Satan that sets the stage for all of Job's sufferings. In short, Satan asks God for permission to afflict Job in order to prove something, and God grants Satan permission to do so (1:6-12; 2:1-7). Now, how much did Job know about this dialogue between God and Satan? Job's comforters don't appear to know anything about it. They never mention it. Job says nothing about it in his own musings. And God never references the discussion with Job: "Oh, Job, I am sorry about these troubles you've been having, friend. Let me tell you, it was like this. I was up in heaven and Satan comes along, and I'm trying to teach him some things. So I said to him . . . and then he said to me . . . so I said to him . . ."

Job never hears this! Nowhere in the whole book do we read that Job has access to this knowledge!

Within the context of this story, God displayed his glory through his creation in ways that the characters did not see and could not understand. Neither could we understand, had not God *revealed the truth* to us through this book.

God's revelation of himself in his Word is essential for making sense of our lives. Ultimately, philosophy is a vain endeavor, and I say that realizing that you may study or teach philosophy. But if God has not spoken from outside of this world and given us a sure and certain word by which we will be evaluated, there is finally no grammar for making sense of this life. God says what is right. God says what is wrong.

God has revealed himself to us as both powerful and good. Sometimes we are helped by remembering that God is in control and that nothing is beyond his grasp. At other times we are helped by remembering that God is good and loving, and that he is committed to the good of all his children. This is enough to satisfy us and enable us to continue in our course. And yet, at still other times, like Job, we can be certain of God's power and certain of his goodness even while remaining mystified by what he has allowed to happen in our lives. It is at times like these that we need something even beyond understanding.

We should not be surprised when this is the case. If we are limited creatures, then we must assume that some things will be beyond the scope of our comprehension. God will have purposes that remain hidden to us, either by virtue of our sinful and distorted way of understanding or by virtue of our mere limitedness.

So, we often suffer. We sometimes understand.

WE CAN ALWAYS TRUST

Given our occasional suffering and limited understanding, we must be willing to learn a third thing that the book of Job would teach us: we can always trust.

In his letter to the Philippians, Paul talks about a peace that "transcends all understanding" (Phil. 4:7). In context, he appears to be talking about a state of being reconciled with God such that we are more satisfied in him than in any understanding we may have of our passing circumstances. That's quite a claim, but Paul says it clearly; and if you are a Christian you have experienced it.

You see, friend, we need to trust because of our lack of understanding.

As someone who used to be a skeptic, that can seem burdensome to me. But it is certainly true. If we insist on living only according to our own understanding and completely apart from trust, then we cannot be a Christian. We need to know how to trust.

The good news is, we have a basis for that trust: God's power! In some of the most beautiful poetry you will ever read, the book of Job displays the power of God, this one whom we are called to trust. We see his creation of all things. We consider his power and his competency. We observe his Providence in caring for everything he has created, particularly his care for us. And we know he is the one who can be trusted.

As you read through the dialogues, you find that Job is very dismissive about the state of man's life. In several hauntingly beautiful passages, Job speaks of man's days being a fleeting shadow, flying by faster than the weaver's shuttle, certain to return to the dust, and so forth.[5] Yet is it not amazing that, though Job speaks so dismissively of man, God and all his heavenly court are arranged around the affairs of these sons and daughters of dust? God cares for us!

As I said, however, this basis for trust was never afforded Job. Job was never told about this heavenly court scene that we are allowed to peek into in the first chapters of the book. All the evidence he has for trusting God in these trials is the fact of God himself, and *Job trusted that God.*

Now, in that heavenly court scene, Satan was wrong, you know. Satan accuses Job of serving God for his own selfish ends (1:9-11). He says that Job serves God because he is wealthy. God knows that Satan is wrong, but he allows Satan to take away Job's wealth. And guess what? With all his wealth gone, Job continues to worship God. Satan was as wrong as Dr. Seuss's Grinch was wrong about the Whos down in Who-ville at Christmas time, thinking that if he stole all the toys and treats, surely they would not keep singing and celebrating. But what happens? They keep singing. And so does Job. In spite of his tragedy, Job continues to worship God. Job was very wealthy, but he did not worship God merely because he was wealthy. Satan was wrong.

But Satan has never been one to be put off just because he was wrong. Satan is Satan, and he will try to accuse and find fault with us even amid our obedience to God! It is his nature.

His first effort having failed, Satan then accuses Job of serving God only because his health remains. "Oh surely," Satan says, "you can take everything a man has, but if you touch his body, then you'll find out what he really cares about. Then he will curse you to your face" (see 2:4-5). Again, God knows that Satan is wrong, but, for his own reasons, he allows Satan to take away Job's health, requiring him only not to kill Job. And guess what? Satan is again

---

proven wrong. Even as Job's body wastes away, as his skin erupts into boils all over, as his former ease is replaced by an ever-present pain, Job still worships God.

Job's changing circumstances revealed that, as wealthy as he was, Job was not worshiping God because of his wealth. And Job's changing circumstances revealed that, as healthy as he was, Job was not worshiping God because of his health. The true worship of God does not depend on our circumstances. We can certainly give him thanks for good circumstances, but true worship occurs within us through the grace that God gives, regardless of the circumstances that he sovereignly allows us to endure.

In fact, that brings us to one of the central ironies of this book. I hope you noticed it. Most of the book consists of Job's friends saying to him, "Hey, Job, I know you look virtuous, but there must be some sin here. Otherwise you would not be experiencing such severe punishment." But so far were Job's friends from being right, that, ironically, someone could have said to them, "Eliphaz, Zophar, Bildad, this suffering might have come on you had you been *more* virtuous!" We the readers know that God did not allow Job to face these trials because of Job's vices—but because of his virtue! God looked over the world, wanting to brag on part of his creation to Satan. And he chose to brag about Job!

God said, "Satan, I understand that you are nothing but confused maliciousness, but have you considered my servant Job? He is blameless and upright" (see 1:8; 2:3). No, this is not a Pelagian man-can-choose-what-is-right theology. Job is God's own workmanship. God had caused Job to trust him, and God knew that he did. So he says, "Consider my servant Job, Satan." God wanted to brag on Job.

What does this mean for us, friend? It means that we do not trust God because we are clever or holy but because his character is trustworthy.

Not so many days ago, I sat securely on a plane as we taxied for takeoff from the Dallas–Fort Worth International Airport. Texans have a reputation for priding themselves on the great size of their undertakings, and this airport certainly would seem to validate that perception. With terminals, parking garages, runways, and support roads, DFW Airport covers roughly the same area as Manhattan Island. Thousands of airplanes take off and land every day. Knowing the great mass of air traffic surrounding that airport, as we taxied out and prepared for takeoff, I suppose I could have stood up and said, "Stop the plane!" I could have walked down to the cockpit and demanded that the captain give me copies of the taxiing route, a map of the runways, and a timetable for the other flights taking off and landing around the same time. I could have done this in order to satisfy myself that we would, in fact, be safe.

Regardless of the response I would have probably received, I *could* have done this and tried to satisfy my own understanding of the situation. Or, I could do what I did (more out of habit than virtue): trust the controllers. I recognized the care and order with which this seemingly chaotic and potentially disastrous operation was run. So I sat back as we accelerated and lifted off the ground.

How many times do we want to stop the plane in order to demand that the pilot give us an understanding of all the variables before we go? How much, then, *should* we, *can* we, *must* we trust the True Controller, who makes no errors, who never sleeps nor slumbers, and in whom is not the slightest touch of evil!

That was the only basis for trust that Job was ever given. He had not read the first part of the book. He was only shown the character of God himself.

At times, God does graciously allow us to see how he has used a difficult situation for our good. And surely we should thank him for the consolation such moments of understanding afford. But there is danger in assuming that he *must* give us such understanding. What will follow is a counterfeit trust, a trust in our own abilities to figure out all of God's purposes within any particular trial, rather than a trust in God and in his character as he has finally revealed it in Jesus Christ on the cross. A counterfeit trust in God might work for some things, but it will not finally work. The only one who is worthy of our trust is not ourselves; nor is it our own clever ability to figure out life's knotty questions; it is God himself. Finally, we can trust God because, as Job himself said, "I know that my Redeemer lives, and that in the end he will stand upon the earth" (19:25). How would Job's Redeemer redeem? By living more righteously and perfectly than Job ever could, and by taking upon himself more suffering than Job ever knew. Job's patience amid suffering, you see, was finally meant to point to the genuinely perfect righteousness and wholly undeserved suffering of Jesus Christ on the cross. Through his death on the cross and his resurrection on the third day, Christ would defeat the powers of sin and death. God then promises to forgive everyone who repents of their sins and trusts in Christ. And they, too, along with Job, will stand with their Redeemer in the end.

I mentioned earlier the story of the disciples asking Jesus, regarding a blind man, "Who sinned, this man or his parents, that he was born blind?" Apparently, they were asking the wrong question: "'Neither this man nor his parents sinned,' said Jesus, 'but this happened so that the work of God might be displayed in his life'" (John 9:3).

God intends to display his glory in your life and in the lives of everyone around you. You can be certain of this. Now, how he specifically intends to do this would take us into other books of the Bible. But within the context of Job, we can see very clearly that he intends to display his glory in the lives of his children as they continue to serve him amid life's trials. And if you are a child of his, reconciled to him through Christ, realize that your very suffering can exquisitely display the glory of God as you serve and worship him in a way that simply defies the world's comprehension and abilities. If you, Christian, are presently enduring a season of suffering, it may be that God is sitting in the heavenlies right now and saying to the heavenly host about him, "Have you considered my servant?" and then pointing to you. Could it be that one day you will watch as God shows to all creation the presently unrevealed glories of what he has done by making you in his image and then remaking you as his child!

We often suffer. We sometimes understand. And by God's grace, we can always trust.

CONCLUSION

The book of Job speaks realistically of our suffering. It explores the limits of our understanding. And it illustrates compellingly our need to trust God himself.

As Job says, "'[God] said to man, "The fear of the LORD—that is wisdom"'" (28:28). This is the Bible's wisdom for losers. Regard God in your trials. Focus on him, because he can be trusted. This is the message of Job.

Let us pray:

Lord, words alone seem thin and shallow compared with the depth and texture of our lives and with the mighty power of your Spirit's working. We pray that the Holy Spirit would be poured out on us. We pray that you, by your grace, would overcome our native lack of trust in you as we struggle with suffering. May your Holy Spirit lay siege to the unbelieving bastion of our hearts and gain a great victory for your glory. We confess that in much of life, we do not consider the role that you play. In some things we can be easily thankful. But in other things we are challenged to understand who you are and what you are like. God, we pray that through your work on the cross of Jesus Christ, though the world calls it foolish, you would remind us that you are truly wise and trustworthy. Oh, Lord, we look forward to the time when that trust is made evident, when the source of our hope comes, when our faith will no longer be needed because we can see you. Lord, that is our desire. We pray that you would, by your Spirit, help us to persevere until that time, in Jesus' name. Amen.

Questions for Reflection

1. Who caused Job to suffer?

    a. the Sabeans, Chaldeans, and a mighty wind

    b. Satan

    c. God

    d. all of the above

    Explain.

2. What answer does Job give to question 1, and what does the narrator think of Job's answer (see 1:21-22 and 2:10)?

3. Does God ever tell Job why he suffered? What answer does God give Job? Would you be content with this answer? Why or why not?

4. In order to tempt Eve to eat the forbidden fruit in the Garden of Eden, Satan says to her, "For God knows that when you eat of it your eyes will be opened, and you will be like God, knowing good and evil" (Gen. 3:5). She believes him, and then takes a bite of the fruit. How do we humans fall prey to this exact same lie when we attempt to explain evil and suffering? What are some of the different explanations we can give for suffering in this world that indicate we have believed this lie?

5. Why is Job's response in 42:1-6 indicative of a righteous man (see Prov. 1:7)?

6. In this sermon, the very strong claim is made that, if we insist on living only according to our own understanding and completely apart from trust, then we cannot be a Christian. Why is this true? What does this have to do with suffering?

7. In your mind, which is better? Living according to your own understanding, or living according to a belief in God's power? In times of trial, which do you do?

8. All things being equal, which scenario, arguably, gives God *more* glory?

    a Christian football player kneeling down and thanking God for his touchdown in the end zone a Christian football player kneeling down and thanking God for his provision and mercy in the losing team's locker room

Non–football playing Christian, what does this question have to do with you?

9. How does the man Job point us to Jesus Christ?

10. At the beginning of this sermon, we considered the fact that Christians are often embarrassed to admit they are suffering, feeling down, or experiencing difficulty. Why does such hesitancy potentially *hurt* our gospel witness? What sort of culture and relationships should we cultivate in our churches that would address this issue?

19

THE MESSAGE OF PSALMS: WISDOM FOR SPIRITUAL PEOPLE

SPIRITUALITY AND THE PSALMS[1]

Abraham Lincoln, confiding to a friend, said of the Psalms, "They are the best. I find something in them for *every day of the year.*"

Martin Luther called it, "The Bible in miniature."

If you were a book publisher, publishing the Psalms, you could find comment after comment that would make excellent blurbs for the dust jacket.

It is the Bible's longest book.

It contains more chapters than any other book of the Bible, as well as both the longest and the shortest chapters in the Bible.

It is more quoted in the New Testament than any other book.

It is arguably the most popular book in the Old Testament, if not in the whole Bible.

And it is in this book that these words are found:

"The LORD is my shepherd; I shall not want.
He maketh me to lie down in green pastures: he leadeth me beside the still waters.
He restoreth my soul: he leadeth me in the paths of righteousness
   for his name's sake.
Yea, though I walk through the valley of the shadow of death,
   I will fear no evil: for thou *art* with me; thy rod and thy staff they comfort me.
Thou preparest a table before me in the presence of mine enemies:
   thou anointest my head with oil; my cup runneth over.
Surely goodness and mercy shall follow me all the days of my life: and I will
   dwell in the house of the LORD for ever" (Psalm 23, KJV, emphasis original).

---

[1] This sermon was originally preached on July 6, 1997, at Capitol Hill Baptist Church in Washington, D.C.

The book of Psalms is one of five books in the Old Testament that we call the Writings, or the "Wisdom books." If you look at the table of contents in your Bible, you will find all five right in the middle of the Old Testament: Job, Psalms, Proverbs, Ecclesiastes, and Song of Songs. There are no great events in the Writings, as in the books of History or Prophecy. There are no new laws, as in the first five books of the Bible, which we call the Pentateuch. These books, rather than being about the nation of Israel as a whole, are about individuals and the highs and lows of individual experience. The Writings form the heart of the Old Testament, not only by their position within the Old Testament itself but by what they express. They are interested in how God's law applies to each person, and they reflect on the great issues that we face in our daily lives.

Christians often regard the Writings as their favorite part of the Old Testament. And it is no wonder! In many ways, these books are the easiest to understand. We more immediately grasp and are grasped by an individual's experience of sorrow or joy than we are by the description of an animal sacrifice or an account of a battle. These books are full of beautiful, expressive poetry, with trees clapping their hands, hills singing for joy, God's enemies melting like wax, and God himself riding upon the clouds. They are full of the love and liveliness of Song of Songs, the practical advice of Proverbs, the mysteries of Ecclesiastes and Job. And this very real and rounded spirituality is the object of our study here: the book of Psalms.

The structure of this long and diverse book of Psalms typically goes unnoticed by the casual reader. The psalms are not grouped thematically. You will not find all the psalms of joy or psalms of sorrow lumped altogether. They are not presented in any chronological order. They don't start with the earliest psalm and go through the latest psalm. Rather, the Psalms are divided into five books, and you can see those groupings marked in most translations. On the first page of your own translation of the Psalms, you can probably see something like "Book 1," and Psalms 1–41 comprise Book 1. Psalms 42–72 are Book 2. Psalms 73–89 are Book 3. Psalms 90–106 are Book 4. And Psalms 107–150 are Book 5. Each of these five books ends with a doxology—a call to praise the great God described in all the preceding psalms. Individual psalms often end this way as well, with a single verse giving praise to God. We don't know exactly why there are these five divisions. Some have suggested that the Psalms are structured like this in order to mirror the Pentateuch—the five books of the Law. But we don't really know. We can see that the Psalms as a whole reach a grand climax in the "great doxology," where not just one verse or one psalm but the last five psalms present ecstatic praise to God. Psalms

146–150 are this great doxology that bring the symphony of praise to God to a climax.

The fact that there are one hundred and fifty psalms means, of course, that you can easily read through the Psalms each month, if you read five a day. Or, you could take the day of the month, multiply it by five, and then read that Psalm and the preceding four. If today is the third day of the month, read Psalms 11–15. You can always have the chapters of the book of Psalms ready to read when you can't think of what to read in your quiet time. Spend your whole life getting familiar with the Psalms. And allow a little extra time for Psalm 119!

For centuries and even millennia, people have found some of the clearest examples of what it means to be a spiritual person in the book of Psalms. Now maybe you wonder about such a claim, this being an Old Testament book and all. But have you ever wondered what Old Testament believers were like? How their experience compared with ours as children of the new covenant? How their faith was different? Well, look with me through the Psalms, and let's consider together the picture it gives us of a spiritual life.

Spirituality is, after all, quite popular today. Hollowness and superficiality are not the most esteemed personal attributes in our culture, at least not in sentiment. And so there is a great concern, for reasons good and bad, to find out what it means to be a spiritual person. Probably more people than not would like to be regarded as "spiritual." It sounds vaguely like a good thing to be. Maybe it lends more weight, more gravitas, a kind of air of seriousness, to an individual. And many people crave such respect for their character, their interests, and who they are. Ironically, this very craving bears testimony to the hollowness and superficiality of many lives.

I am not a huge fan of the unqualified adjective "spiritual" or the unqualified noun "spirituality." Both words can be coupled with too many things that entirely change their meanings. There are good spiritual things and bad spiritual things.

How can people tell what is genuinely good spirituality? What does that look like? One person came to see me recently for what he called a "spiritual reality check." This person is not a member of the church, nor does he regularly attend church. But he thought he could see me as he might see a doctor in order to determine whether he is in good spiritual health.

How can we tell what is spiritually good? What should be the guide that I use with such a person?

Since he first published his best-selling book in 1989, Stephen Covey has been telling all of us about *The Seven Habits of Highly Effective People*. I don't believe I will damage his sales too badly if I share them with you: 1) be proactive; 2) begin with the end in mind; 3) put first things first; 4) think win/win; 5) seek first to understand, then to be understood; 6) synergize; and 7) sharpen the saw, that is, take care of yourself.

Well, in this study I want to talk from a book that's been on the best-seller list even longer, which tells us about the *seven characteristics of biblically spiritual people*. It is only when we turn to what the Bible teaches about our fallen state and Christ's work in restoring us to God that we can begin to understand true spirituality. So get out those pens and pencils! I only have time to mention them briefly. You will have to "add water" later by considering, discussing, and praying about them.

BIBLICAL SPIRITUALITY CHARACTERISTIC #1: PRAISE-GIVING

First, a truly spiritual life is characterized by *giving praise*.

The basic flavor of the Psalms, as well as the basic theme God intended to run through all creation, is praise. In the original Hebrew, the Psalms are entitled "Songs of Praise." And we can see why! The Psalms are full of joyful praise to God as he has revealed himself. So we read in Psalm 145:

> I will exalt you, my God the King;
>   I will praise your name for ever and ever.
> Every day I will praise you
>   and extol your name for ever and ever.
>
> Great is the LORD and most worthy of praise;
>   his greatness no one can fathom.
> One generation will commend your works to another;
>   they will tell of your mighty acts.
> They will speak of the glorious splendor of your majesty,
>   and I will meditate on your wonderful works.
> They will tell of the power of your awesome works,
>   and I will proclaim your great deeds.
> They will celebrate your abundant goodness
>   and joyfully sing of your righteousness.
>
> The LORD is gracious and compassionate,
>   slow to anger and rich in love.
> The LORD is good to all;
>   he has compassion on all he has made.
> All you have made will praise you, O LORD;
>   your saints will extol you.
> They will tell of the glory of your kingdom

and speak of your might,
 so that all men may know of your mighty acts
  and the glorious splendor of your kingdom.
Your kingdom is an everlasting kingdom,
 and your dominion endures through all generations (Ps. 145:1-13a).

Here the psalmist praises God as the Creator and Ruler of his world and as the Redeemer of his people. God is praised for what he has *done*—his "mighty acts" of creation and redemption.

Yet the Psalms praise God not only for what he has done, they praise him simply because he *is*. Psalms 148 and 149 reveal the psalmist's joy both in what God has done and in the fact that these things reveal that he alone is God:

Praise the LORD.

Praise the LORD from the heavens,
 praise him in the heights above.
Praise him, all his angels,
 praise him, all his heavenly hosts.
Praise him, sun and moon,
 praise him, all you shining stars.
Praise him, you highest heavens
 and you waters above the skies.
Let them praise the name of the LORD,
 for he commanded and they were created.
He set them in place for ever and ever;
 he gave a decree that will never pass away.

Praise the LORD from the earth,
 you great sea creatures and all ocean depths,
lightning and hail, snow and clouds,
 stormy winds that do his bidding,
you mountains and all hills,
 fruit trees and all cedars,
wild animals and all cattle,
 small creatures and flying birds,
kings of the earth and all nations,
 you princes and all rulers on earth,
young men and maidens,
 old men and children.

Let them praise the name of the LORD,
 for his name alone is exalted;

> his splendor is above the earth and the heavens.
> He has raised up for his people a horn,
>> the praise of all his saints,
>> of Israel, the people close to his heart.

> Praise the LORD (Psalm 148).

And the praise continues in Psalm 149:

> Praise the LORD.

> Sing to the LORD a new song,
>> his praise in the assembly of the saints.

> Let Israel rejoice in their Maker;
>> let the people of Zion be glad in their King.
> Let them praise his name with dancing
>> and make music to him with tambourine and harp.
> For the LORD takes delight in his people;
>> he crowns the humble with salvation.
> Let the saints rejoice in this honor
>> and sing for joy on their beds.

> May the praise of God be in their mouths
>> and a double-edged sword in their hands,
> to inflict vengeance on the nations
>> and punishment on the peoples,
> to bind their kings with fetters,
>> their nobles with shackles of iron,
> to carry out the sentence written against them.
>> This is the glory of all his saints.

> Praise the LORD (Psalm 149).

Fundamental to any biblical spirituality is a real joy in God and in who he has revealed himself to be. Biblical spirituality is never centered on people and the help that God can give us to achieve our ends. Rather, biblical spirituality is always focused on God. It's centered on God. It's transfixed with God. It's enraptured with God. And it is at this very starting point that there is a great gulf fixed between true spirituality and true religion as revealed in the Bible and the countless nostrums that are hawked on all the corners of our culture today. Biblical spirituality is centered on God and rejoices in him.

Steve Turner captures the essence of our culture's approach to spirituality in his poem, "I Wish I Could Believe":

"I'd love a faith like yours," you say,
Although that's not strictly true.
Your faith is like mine, in a way,
But it all folds back on you.[2]

A self-absorbed, praise-less spirituality is a false spirituality. After all, to know the God of the Bible is to learn to praise him and to love him. We fail to praise and love him only by being deaf to his Word and blind to his splendor.

When we turn to the New Testament, we can't help but notice twelve-year-old Jesus worshiping God in the temple courts. And it becomes clear who alone ever sang with a perfectly genuine heart, "How lovely is your dwelling place, O LORD Almighty! My soul yearns, even faints, for the courts of the LORD" (Ps. 84:1-2; cf. Luke 2:49).

A truly spiritual person, according to the Psalms, knows the joy of praise.

BIBLICAL SPIRITUALITY CHARACTERISTIC #2: HONESTY

At the same time, the truly spiritual person in the book of Psalms does not view the world through rose-colored glasses. There is also this second characteristic of biblical spirituality: *honesty*. We see this honesty especially in what are called the psalms of lament.

The psalms of lament are full of sorrow, disorientation, pain, distress, anger, and feelings of abandonment, both among the community and within the individual. Sometimes, these psalms even contain the most blood-curdling curses and the bitterest invective uttered in the Bible.

Amazingly, there are more psalms of lament than any other kind of psalm. Of the one hundred and fifty psalms, sixty-two are complaints or laments. One-fourth of those are communal laments, while three-fourths are individual laments.

Psalm 74 begins with a good example of a communal lament: "Why have you rejected us forever, O God? Why does your anger smolder against the sheep of your pasture? Remember the people you purchased of old, the tribe of your inheritance, whom you redeemed—Mount Zion where you dwelt" (74:1-2). Notice, this psalm raises up its cry on behalf of "us."

---

[2] In Steve Turner, *King of Twist* (London: Hodder & Stoughton, 1992), 81.

Yet the Psalms can get even more pointed in talking about personal pain. Consider Psalm 10:

> Why, O LORD, do you stand far off?
>   Why do you hide yourself in times of trouble?
>
> In his arrogance the wicked man hunts down the weak,
>   who are caught in the schemes he devises.
> He boasts of the cravings of his heart;
>   he blesses the greedy and reviles the LORD.
> In his pride the wicked does not seek him;
>   in all his thoughts there is no room for God.
> His ways are always prosperous;
>   he is haughty and your laws are far from him;
>   he sneers at all his enemies.
> He says to himself, "Nothing will shake me;
>   I'll always be happy and never have trouble."
> His mouth is full of curses and lies and threats;
>   trouble and evil are under his tongue (Ps. 10:1-7).

Then down to verse 12: "Arise, LORD! Lift up your hand, O God! Do not forget the helpless. Why does the wicked man revile God? Why does he say to himself, 'He won't call me to account'?"

What does this mean for us? Christians should honestly express suffering and distress in their individual and church lives.

Sometimes we think it is more spiritual not to feel pain, and if we do, not to acknowledge it. I remember reading an amusing article about the biblical character Job meeting the "spiritual answer man"—a health-and-wealth preacher. This traveling teacher comes up to Job and says something like, "Hallelujah, Job! You have a problem Job? Just name your problem and claim your solution, and it'll be over. Just confess it, and it will be so!" Sometimes, this sounds like the more spiritual way to be. If we can just sail above life's problems by naming and claiming God's promises, we can start living like the king's kid.

But according to the Psalms, the truly spiritual person knows suffering, difficulties, distress, and even something next door to despair. Indeed, one of the main reasons the book of Psalms has been so helpful and is so loved is that it's so empathetic and so realistic, not only in the heights of joy but also in the depths of distress.

And such empathy, of course, is the empathy of God himself. When we turn again to the New Testament, we find the same Jesus who worshiped God in the temple courts later being raised to the cross with the words of the psalmist on his lips: "My God, my God, why have you forsaken me"; "I thirst"; and "into your hands I commit my spirit."[3] Yet it is this lament-inducing work of Christ that is our only hope for salvation!

A truly spiritual person, according to the psalms, knows the real joy of praising God and the real anguish of crying out to him.

BIBLICAL SPIRITUALITY CHARACTERISTIC #3: REMEMBERING

On the whole, the section of the Old Testament we call the Writings is about the individual's experiences with God, as I have said. Yet the Old Testament is contextual, and so a number of the psalms reflect a concern with Israel as a whole. Therefore, you will better understand the psalms that are more corporate in nature if you know something about the history of Israel. All that to say, a third characteristic of biblical spirituality is *remembering*.

It is these psalms that probably feel the most distant from us as individuals today. They can seem disconnected from us and unrelated to our lives. After all, they are concerned with the special agreement, or covenant, that existed between God and this ancient people that he had taken to himself. The psalms in this category will be concerned with renewing this special covenant, or with the king of Israel's enthronement, or with other matters particular to the worship of the Lord in the temple in Jerusalem.

Sometimes the corporate and historical nature of such psalms can be subtle—simply one flavor in an otherwise ordinary hymn of praise—as in Psalm 47:

> Clap your hands, all you nations;
>   shout to God with cries of joy.
> How awesome is the LORD Most High,
>   the great King over all the earth!
> He subdued nations under us,
>   peoples under our feet.
> He chose our inheritance for us,
>   the pride of Jacob, whom he loved.
>
> God has ascended amid shouts of joy,
>   the LORD amid the sounding of trumpets.
> Sing praises to God, sing praises;
>   sing praises to our King, sing praises.
>
> For God is the King of all the earth;
>   sing to him a psalm of praise.

---

[3] Matt. 27:46 (see Ps. 22:1); John 19:28, ESV (see Ps. 69:21); Luke 23:46 (see Ps. 31:5).

God reigns over the nations;
   God is seated on his holy throne.
The nobles of the nations assemble
   as the people of the God of Abraham,
for the kings of the earth belong to God;
   he is greatly exalted (Psalm 47).

In this psalm, the references to the "pride of Jacob" and the "people of the God of Abraham" are hardly obtrusive, but they are present.

In other psalms, the bulk of the psalm will focus on God's work in the nation. Psalm 136 may be familiar to you because of its recurrent phrase, "his love endures forever." Yet in between that phrase, the very specific history of the nation of Israel is recounted. Here is just a sample:

To him who struck down the firstborn of Egypt
                 His love endures forever.
and brought Israel out from among them
                 His love endures forever.
with a mighty hand and outstretched arm;
                 His love endures forever.
to him who divided the Red Sea asunder
                 His love endures forever.
and brought Israel through the midst of it,
                 His love endures forever.
but swept Pharaoh and his army into the Red Sea;
                 His love endures forever.
to him who led his people through the desert,
                 His love endures forever (Ps. 136:10-16).

Throughout most of the psalm, the psalmist continues to specifically recount what God had done in the history of Israel. If you don't know that history, the Psalm may seem a bit removed.

Many Americans love to hear those strains of the country's national anthem, "O say, can you see by the dawn's early light, what so proudly we hailed at the twilight's last gleaming?" These words can be filled with emotion and sentiment. Many things are evoked in our minds and hearts as they are sung: maybe memories from childhood or some Fourth of July celebration; perhaps something we treasure about the nation. Yet no living American experienced the specific events that are narrated by the anthem; most Americans have never heard of them. The young John L. Dagg, however, was present for these most remarkable events. Here is what he recorded in his autobiography:

In August, 1814 . . . the news reached us, that British vessels were ascending the Potomac. When we returned home, we found that a call had been made on the militia of our county en masse. . . . With hasty preparation I joined the march; and, the first night, lodged in a hay loft. . . . From this point we saw the light of the burning capitol, which the British had fired the day before. The day following we crossed the Potomac, and descended, on the Maryland side. . . . On the way, we met some fugitives from the battle of Bladensburg, who seemed to believe that the enemy were close behind them. In a day or two, we received orders to proceed to Baltimore, against which place the British were making their preparation. On arriving, we were posted in the rear of Fort McHenry. From this position, we had a clear view of the British ships, when they landed their forces . . . and soon after, we saw distinctly, across the water, the smoke of the battle. . . . Orders were now received that we should march to meet the enemy. On our way, we met the wounded returning from the battle; and, passing the entrenchments, we halted for the night, between the city and the enemy. Early next morning the bombardment of the Fort commenced. The next day . . . we were several times in expectation of an immediate approach and attack of the enemy; but, as if by mutual consent, the two armies never met. The following night, however, we lay so near them, that their encampment which was visible from the top of the hill, appeared only a half mile distant. That was a fearful night.

The roar of cannon and bombs, which had continued through the day, became fiercer and more tremendous. We lay on our arms; and three times we were alarmed by the signal of our sentinels, and put in order for battle. Just before day the firing ceased. All was still: and now the very silence rendered us uneasy. A question arose, in which our personal safety was deeply involved, whether the Fort had surrendered. If it had, we might expect a bloody conflict with the land forces, next morning; if it had not, they would perhaps retire without giving us battle. At the first dawn, every eye was directed towards the Fort, to see whether the American banner still waved there; and when the morning mists had sufficiently dispersed, we were filled with exultation at beholding the stars and stripes still floating in the breeze.[4]

Imagine then how a person who had experienced these things could sing anthem-writer Francis Scott Key's words celebrating that happy sight: "O say, can you see by the dawn's early light . . . ?" How he would cherish these words! Even we, knowing the situation that gave rise to the song, can sing with more meaning and attention.

In this same way, we can read a psalm about God's salvation of his Israelite nation and, initially, find it distant, old, and foreign. Yet as we learn about the

---

[4] John L. Dagg, *Autobiography* (Harrisonburg, Va.: Gano, 1982), 15-16.

history behind the psalm, we begin to understand the importance of God's salvation and the joy it should bring.

And what event do the different writers of the Psalms primarily have in mind when they write about God's salvation of his people? What's the big event for any ancient Hebrew? The Exodus!

The people of Israel were called to remember God's goodness in bringing them out of Egypt, in giving them his law, in sustaining them through the wilderness, and in ushering them into the land he had promised! And this memory written of God's goodness assured them that he would continue in his goodness to them as individuals and as a people—both in the present and into the future.

If we want to follow the model of spirituality given to us in the Psalms, we, too, need to be a people of memory. God's promises will bring us hope of future goodness, especially when watered by the memories of past goodnesses.

The Puritans littered their calendars with reminders of specific dates when God had been obviously good to them as individuals, as families, as churches, or as a city. When they experienced a particular deliverance from God, they would mark down the day on their calendar and then give thanks to God on that date for the rest of their life.

Like the Puritans, we should take care not to little regard or quickly squander God's goodnesses given to us in so many forms, whether a recovery from illness, the health of a child, the provision of a job, the making of a friendship, the meeting of a financial need, and, most of all, God's provision of Jesus Christ as the sacrifice for the sins of all those who would ever repent of their sins and believe in him. Indeed, the psalmists' call for the Israelites to remember God's provision of salvation in the Exodus, as remarkable as the Exodus was, is merely a pointing to a shadow. The true exodus to which the shadowy Exodus from Egypt points is the Exodus from sin that we can find only through Jesus Christ.

A truly spiritual person, according to the Psalms, praises God and speaks honestly of his or her difficulties. But he or she also remembers.

BIBLICAL SPIRITUALITY CHARACTERISTIC #4: MORALITY

The Psalms begins with the moral choice that has been set before every human being—the choice between righteousness and wickedness. Indeed, biblical spirituality depends on a right *morality*. Psalm 1 describes the spiritual man who delights in God's law and its wisdom and righteousness, rather than in the folly and wickedness of ignoring God's law. This Psalm sets the stage for everything that follows:

Blessed is the man
> who does not walk in the counsel of the wicked
or stand in the way of sinners
> or sit in the seat of mockers.
But his delight is in the law of the LORD,
> and on his law he meditates day and night.
He is like a tree planted by streams of water,
> which yields its fruit in season
and whose leaf does not wither.
> Whatever he does prospers.

Not so the wicked!
> They are like chaff
> that the wind blows away.
Therefore the wicked will not stand in the judgment,
> nor sinners in the assembly of the righteous.
For the LORD watches over the way of the righteous,
> but the way of the wicked will perish (Psalm 1).

God makes his law known to us and shows us the way of truth and righteousness. The psalmist rejoices in the knowledge of God's law because he realizes that in the knowledge of God's law is the knowledge of his will and his character. (Look at Psalms 19 and 119 as great examples of celebrating the wisdom that God gives to us in his law.)

Such knowledge of truth, righteousness, and wisdom should inform the choices of our lives as Christians. If God's wisdom does not inform our decision making, if we feel that we can simply inform ourselves, then we are forgetful and wrong. Consider the words of Psalm 78:

O my people, hear my teaching;
> listen to the words of my mouth.
I will open my mouth in parables,
> I will utter hidden things, things from of old—
what we have heard and known,
> what our fathers have told us.
We will not hide them from their children;
> we will tell the next generation
the praiseworthy deeds of the LORD,
> his power, and the wonders he has done.
He decreed statutes for Jacob
> and established the law in Israel,
which he commanded our forefathers

to teach their children,
so the next generation would know them,
even the children yet to be born,
and they in turn would tell their children.
Then they would put their trust in God
and would not forget his deeds
but would keep his commands (Ps. 78:1-7).

Right belief or words without right behavior has a simple name in the Bible: hypocrisy. Anyone who presents himself as a spiritual or good person and yet lives contrary to God's revealed Word is deluded and deluding. He endangers himself and others as he pretends to live the life that he imagines is acceptable to God. Ironically, we find that in one sense God's law can never be broken by us; it is rather we who break ourselves against it.

The Psalms clearly teach that an acceptable spirituality cannot finally be simple self-expression that is careless of God's revelation. The government of the United States may legitimately be "of the people, by the people, for the people," to use Abraham Lincoln's eloquent formulation. But biblical religion is not fundamentally *of* the people; its origin is of God. It is not fundamentally *by* the people; it works by God's grace. And it is not fundamentally *for* the people; it is for the glory of God. So while I am very thankful that Lincoln's memorable phrase characterizes the governing philosophy of the United States, we must be careful to realize that it should not characterize our faith in Christ. Christian lives are different.

Who, after all, was the wise man, who did "not say anything to them without using a parable" and so "fulfilled what was spoken through the prophet: 'I will open my mouth in parables, I will utter things hidden since the creation of the world'" (Matt. 13:34-35; cf. Ps. 78:1)? And who was the perfectly righteous man who delighted in God's law, meditating on it day and night (Ps. 1:2; cf. Matt. 4:4)?

Truly spiritual people must heed God's words, by God's power, for God's purposes. This, then, is another aspect of biblical spirituality according to the Psalms: not only is there praise, honesty, and memory; there is morality.

BIBLICAL SPIRITUALITY CHARACTERISTIC #5: CHANGING

And then there is the fifth characteristic of biblical spirituality: *change*. We can hear the psalmist's plea for change particularly in the "psalms of penitence."

In our study of Job, we considered the fact that the circumstances of our lives can become extraordinarily difficult for mysterious reasons beyond our comprehension. Many times, however, we are not in Job-like situations. A sit-

uation will turn sour because of our own wrongdoing. Such wrongdoing alien-
ates us from God and from others. When we become aware of our wrong, we
need to observe the psalmist's practice of changing. To use more religious
words, we need to repent or become penitent.

There are seven so-called penitential psalms, or psalms of repentance and
change: 6, 32, 38, 51, 102, 130, and 143. These are good psalms to read and
use in your own life to aid repentance and change.

The early church theologian Augustine had to change much about his life
following his conversion, and his favorite psalm in the entire Psalter became
Psalm 32. It helped him to know how to approach God about the changes he
knew were needed:

> Blessed is he
> > whose transgressions are forgiven,
> > whose sins are covered.
> Blessed is the man
> > whose sin the LORD does not count against him
> > and in whose spirit is no deceit.
>
> When I kept silent,
> > my bones wasted away
> > through my groaning all day long.
> For day and night
> > your hand was heavy upon me;
> my strength was sapped
> > as in the heat of summer.
> Then I acknowledged my sin to you
> > and did not cover up my iniquity.
> I said, "I will confess my transgressions to the LORD"—
> and you forgave
> > the guilt of my sin.
>
> Therefore let everyone who is godly pray to you
> > while you may be found;
> surely when the mighty waters rise,
> > they will not reach him.
> You are my hiding place;
> > you will protect me from trouble
> > and surround me with songs of deliverance.
>
> I will instruct you and teach you in the way you should go;
> > I will counsel you and watch over you.

Do not be like the horse or the mule,
    which have no understanding
but must be controlled by bit and bridle
    or they will not come to you.
Many are the woes of the wicked,
    but the LORD's unfailing love surrounds the man who trusts in him.

Rejoice in the LORD and be glad, you righteous;
    sing, all you who are upright in heart! (Psalm 32).

According to the Bible, this kind of repentance and change *must* be a part of a Christian life. Dwight L. Moody said,

> There are a good many men . . . now who have got . . . a religion, and will tell you that they would not give it up for all the world: but when a man tells you that he would not give up his religion, you may know that he has not much religion to give up. When a man begins to stand up for "my religion," as you very often hear, you may know there is something wrong. That is not what we want. We want them to change their lives, and a religion that does not save men from sin is not worth going across the street after.[5]

A Christian faith that does not bring change is a false faith, even if it is surrounded by much emotion. Non-Christians, after all, can feel bad about their sins. There is, said the apostle Paul, a "worldly sorrow [that] brings death." Only a "godly sorrow brings repentance that leads to salvation and leaves no regret" (2 Cor. 7:10).

When we turn to the New Testament, remarkably, we find that the sinless Jesus Christ never needed to change yet he still suffered the fate described in the psalms of penitence. Because of the sins of men, God's hand was heavy upon him (Ps. 32:4). Because of the sins of men, he was bowed down, he was brought low, and his back was filled with searing pain (Ps. 38:6-7). Only because Christ took upon his own body the curses described in the penitential psalms is salvation available for us. He alone earned the forgiveness for which these psalms plead. And if we are his, we will follow him into righteousness.

So the fifth aspect of true spirituality that we see along with praise, honesty, memory, and morality, is change.

---

[5] D. L. Moody, *Bible Characters* (Chicago: Moody, n.d.), 100.

BIBLICAL SPIRITUALITY CHARACTERISTIC #6: TRUSTING

Along with penitence, there must be *trust,* our sixth characteristic of biblical spirituality. We see this in Psalm 62:

> My soul finds rest in God alone;
> my salvation comes from him.
> He alone is my rock and my salvation;
> he is my fortress, I will never be shaken.
>
> How long will you assault a man?
> Would all of you throw him down—
> this leaning wall, this tottering fence?
> They fully intend to topple him
> from his lofty place;
> they take delight in lies.
> With their mouths they bless,
> but in their hearts they curse.
>
> Find rest, O my soul, in God alone;
> my hope comes from him.
> He alone is my rock and my salvation;
> he is my fortress, I will not be shaken.
> My salvation and my honor depend on God;
> he is my mighty rock, my refuge.
> Trust in him at all times, O people;
> pour out your hearts to him,
> for God is our refuge (Ps. 62:1-8).

The psalmist calls us to release everything else in which we might place our trust and to trust in God alone. Nothing else will hold us! In order to release one set of expectations, we must, like Tarzan swinging from vine to vine, be able to trust that the next set of expectations will hold our weight. We must be able to reach toward it with some kind of rational trust. After all, we must not entrust ourselves to anyone or anything lightly or arbitrarily. In Scripture, God shows us that he alone can hold our weight. He alone can be trusted. (Unlike Tarzan holding the vine, however, God holds us more than we hold him!)

At the end of the day, living the Christian life requires us to deeply and profoundly give up on ourselves and trust God and his Word. We cannot do it any other way. The truly spiritual life is marked by relying on one greater than ourselves. Such trust is not an added option for a truly spiritual life. You cannot say, "Well, I like characteristics 1 through 5. I'll major on those. But characteristic 6 I'm going to skip." No, trust is absolutely basic to being a Christian. In the New Testament, the name for trust is "faith."

Baptist preacher Charles Haddon Spurgeon once warned,

> Beware, I pray thee, of presuming that thou art saved. If with thy heart thou dost trust in Jesus, then art thou saved; but if thou merely sayest, "I trust in Jesus," it doth not save thee. If thy heart be renewed, if thou shalt hate the things that thou didst once love, and love the things that thou didst once hate; if thou hast really repented; if there be a thorough change of mind in thee; if thou be born again, then hast thou reason to rejoice: but if there be no vital change, no inward godliness; if there be no love to God, no prayer, no work of the Holy Spirit, then thy saying, "I am saved," is but thine own assertion, and it may delude, but it will not deliver thee.[6]

Our hearts must genuinely proclaim, as David's did in Psalm 131,

> My heart is not proud, O LORD,
>   my eyes are not haughty;
> I do not concern myself with great matters
>   or things too wonderful for me.
> But I have stilled and quieted my soul;
>   like a weaned child with its mother,
>   like a weaned child is my soul within me.
>
> O Israel, put your hope in the LORD
>   both now and forevermore (Psalm 131).

Gratefully, there was one who, even more than David, entrusted himself to the heavenly Father. And for this he was mocked: "He trusted in God; let God deliver him now," they said, while he was hanging on the cross (Matt. 27:43, KJV; cf. Ps. 22:8). Shall we not ourselves trust this one who learned to perfectly trust God by what he suffered (Heb. 5:8)? Will he not teach us to do the same?

For true spirituality consists not only of praise, honesty, memory, morality, and change, but also trust!

BIBLICAL SPIRITUALITY CHARACTERISTIC #7: THANKSGIVING

Finally, one of the most prominent characteristics of a biblical spirituality is *thanksgiving*. Psalms of thanksgiving comprise one of the three basic kinds of psalms, along with hymns of praise and laments. There are about nineteen such

---

[6] Charles Haddon Spurgeon, from a sermon titled, "The Prayer of Jabez," *The Metropolitan Tabernacle Pulpit*, 63 vols. (London: Passmore & Alabaster, 1885), 17:320.

psalms. About one-third of those offer communal thanks, while about two-thirds offer individual thanks.

Now, perhaps you are wondering, "Wait a minute, aren't psalms of praise the same thing as psalms of thanksgiving?" Well, not quite. We specifically give thanks for something that this praiseworthy God has given. We *praise* the generous Father; we *thank* him for his gifts.

A good example of a communal song of thanks is Psalm 124:

If the LORD had not been on our side—
    let Israel say—
if the LORD had not been on our side
    when men attacked us,
when their anger flared against us,
    they would have swallowed us alive;
the flood would have engulfed us,
    the torrent would have swept over us,
the raging waters
    would have swept us away.

Praise be to the LORD,
    who has not let us be torn by their teeth.
We have escaped like a bird
    out of the fowler's snare;
the snare has been broken,
    and we have escaped.
Our help is in the name of the LORD,
    the Maker of heaven and earth (Psalm 124).

A good example of an individual psalm of thanks, on the other hand, can be found in Psalm 34:

I will extol the LORD at all times;
    his praise will always be on my lips.
My soul will boast in the LORD;
    let the afflicted hear and rejoice.
Glorify the LORD with me;
    let us exalt his name together.
I sought the LORD, and he answered me;
    he delivered me from all my fears (Ps. 34:1-4).

When we read these Psalms, we should be challenged by how quickly God hears us, and by how quickly we forget. Consider, for example, how much time you have spent in the last twelve months worrying. Get a picture in your mind of something you were worried about twelve months ago. Got it? Okay, that month finished out, followed by the next, and the next. That season of the year passed, and so did three more. And now the year has wound around to the present, and here you are, one year later! After all the worry and perhaps all that praying! Friend, have you thanked God—for either solving the problem or at least preserving you to the present?

Let's agree that we cannot out-give God! Let's even agree that we are not able to thank him for every individual gift that he gives us. But can we at least thank him more than we do, both as individuals and as a church? How many things has he given you? Have you thanked him for everything you asked for and received? Everything you worried about?

Every time Jesus broke bread, he "gave thanks," whether before feeding the five thousand, with the disciples on the road to Emmaus, or even before his own crucifixion.[7] Yet isn't Jesus the same one who, as God, owns the cattle on a thousand hills and every animal in the forest (Ps. 50:10)? Did he really come in the flesh and make himself entirely dependent on God's provision for all his needs, and then thank God when God provided?

The truly spiritual person is a person of deep gratitude to God. As David says in Psalm 108, "Great is your love, higher than the heavens; your faithfulness reaches to the skies" (Ps. 108:4).

CONCLUSION

The book of Psalms ends, as we have already noted, in a magnificent chorus of five psalms of praise—Psalms 146 to 150. I think that arrangement was deliberate, and Psalm 150 brings the crescendo to its peak:

Praise the LORD.

Praise God in his sanctuary;
    praise him in his mighty heavens.
Praise him for his acts of power;
    praise him for his surpassing greatness.
Praise him with the sounding of the trumpet,
    praise him with the harp and lyre,
praise him with tambourine and dancing,
    praise him with the strings and flute,
praise him with the clash of cymbals,
    praise him with resounding cymbals.

---

[7] E.g., Matt. 14:19; Luke 22:17-19; 24:30.

Let everything that has breath praise the LORD.

Praise the LORD (Psalm 150).

These seven characteristics, taken together, present the Psalms' picture of true spirituality. The genuinely spiritual person is marked by praise-giving, honesty, remembering, morality, change, trust, and thanksgiving, all with both oneself and the community in view.

On the one hand, therefore, this book does not leave room for the hypocritical member of the community who says, "As long as I'm a member of the community, I'm okay. I don't have to worry about what I do." No, this book is full of heartfelt, individual praise to God, as well as individual distress and lament, sorrow and thanks.

On the other hand, the Psalms are not just for the individual. Many prayers here are for God's people gathered together. And none of them are meant to promote a Lone-Rangerism. The Psalms are written *by* and *for* those who belong to a community of people who know, love, and serve God together.

Now I ask you, if a spiritual sketch artist were to make a drawing based on these seven characteristics, would the drawing bear any resemblance to you? Do these seven things, put together, describe you?

If you remain uncertain of what such a truly spiritual person would look like, I think I can help. I can't point to myself or another member of the church. But I can point to one who fulfilled all seven characteristics perfectly. His picture is described in the pages of the New Testament.

In the life of Jesus, you will find the picture of a man who spent his life praising God even though he himself was worthy of all praise (e.g., Matt 21:16).

In the death of Jesus, you will find an honest picture of a man who suffered, whose body was broken and whose blood was shed.

In the work of Jesus, you will find a deliverance offered greater than any war or any nation can offer.

In the righteousness and wisdom of Jesus, you will find a picture of the righteousness and wisdom of God displayed before us. He knew no sin. And though the world has called his death on the cross utter foolishness, the apostles called it the wisdom of God (1 Cor. 1:18ff.).

In the preaching of Jesus, you will hear a call to repent and believe. And this pledge of holiness will characterize everyone for whom he has won forgiveness by what he suffered.

In the submission of Jesus, you will witness the one who trusted the Father perfectly and who promises us that he himself is perfectly trustworthy.

And at the Last Supper, you will encounter *Jesus* giving thanks for that which *you* most need and cannot provide yourself—the offer of salvation! Is there anything in all the world that more deserves our gratitude?

Do you want to see the truly spiritual life of the Psalms lived out *in the flesh*? Read the words of Jesus Christ and observe his life. Come and see his life poured out for us!

Let us pray:

Lord, we pray that in your goodness this picture of a truly spiritual life from the book of Psalms would drive us to despair, but only as much despair as it takes to drive us into the arms of Christ. Lord, we rejoice as your children in the ways we can see your Spirit working these characteristics into our lives. But, Lord, we know the insufficiency of our own transformation. Though we may be born again, we see how squawking, demanding, and self-centered we remain. And so, Lord, we praise you for your gracious gift of Christ. Thank you for the true spirituality you show in his life and death. We pray, Lord, that you would make us more and more into his image, so that you will be lifted up and glorified. We pray in Christ's name. Amen.

Questions for Reflection

1. What do you think the typical person on the street conceives a "spiritual" person to be?

2. As we have seen, a real joy in God is fundamental to biblical spirituality. On the other hand, false spirituality is self-absorbed. Assuming that a person realizes he or she is self-absorbed rather than God-absorbed, how can he or she use the Psalms to begin changing that?

3. We have been told that Christians should be honest with their laments—certainly to God and sometimes to others. Christ, of course, is our example of one who poured out his laments to God. What could the cost be for the Christian and the church who fail to practice authentic admission of their sins and weaknesses? What could the cost be for the Christian who impatiently refuses to hear the laments of others? Do you take time to listen to the laments of others in the same way you want God to give ear to your laments?

4. If you reread Psalm 1, you will find that it offers two ways to live: the way of the righteous man who delights in God's law, and the way of the wicked who scoff at God's law. The consequences of each path are plain: one will inherit

life; the other will be destroyed. But as Christians, don't we believe in justification by faith? How do we understand the instruction and warnings of this Psalm in light of our Christian faith? Do these two paths and their consequences not apply to us?

5. What differences might you perceive between a church where trusting God is cultivated and one where it is not? In its evangelism? In its missions budget? In its budget generally? In its weekly gatherings? In its practices of hospitality? In its sermons?

6. Is your life characterized by gratitude? Would your family members agree? What fruit could they point to?

7. Why is a Christian's hope found in the fact that Jesus was the only man who could ever pray the Psalms perfectly (confessions of sin aside)? In other words, what do the perfect righteousness and sacrifice of Christ have to do with our salvation?

THE MESSAGE OF PROVERBS: WISDOM FOR THE AMBITIOUS

20

THE MESSAGE OF PROVERBS: WISDOM FOR THE AMBITIOUS

ARE YOU AMBITIOUS?[1]

I wonder what you imagine paradise is like. What is the good life to you? Maybe you are still trying to figure that out. My guess is that for all the people that question confuses, many more know only too well what they regard as the good life—particularly among young people.

Whoever you are, I would surmise that you have at least some goals, some desired set of circumstances. And let's not be more direct or indelicate than that. Let's not say "covet" or "crave," "hunger for" or "lust after." Let's not talk about you "not being able to contemplate yourself having any contentment or satisfaction without them." Let's just get these "desirable circumstances" clearly in mind and then find a better name for them. Let's call them your . . . *ambitions*. That sounds nice and positive.

Who does not organize his life around himself and his ambitions? What GS-11 U.S. civil servant does not want to be a GS-12? What associate does not want to be a partner? What employee does not want to be an employer? (After all, by working faithfully eight hours a day, you may eventually get to be a boss and work twelve hours a day!) What renter does not want to be an owner? What dieter does not want to be thinner, or high schooler more recognized, or retired person more financially secure? Indeed, what minister does not want to see his church grow? It all seems so natural to us. So if I say, "Look out for Number One," I don't need to tell you whom I am talking about!

"Natural" is what people say ambition is. The seventeenth-century philosopher Benedict de Spinoza said that "Desire is the very essence of man." Modern-day British scientist Richard Dawkins, in his celebrated book *The*

---

[1] This sermon was originally preached on August 17, 1997, at Capitol Hill Baptist Church in Washington, D.C.

Selfish Gene, said that this orientation to self is not only entirely natural, it is laudable because it is necessary. Without it, his argument goes, we would not have survived as a species. Other people say that ambition is what makes a capitalist economy work.

And sure enough, we literally *spend our lives* to achieve our ambitions.

INTRODUCING PROVERBS

In many ways, this is what the book of Proverbs is all about. It is a book of wisdom for those who want to fulfill their ambitions.

If you have been following along in this series, you know we have been studying what are called the Wisdom books of the Old Testament. There are five of these books; and if you open up your Bible to the Old Testament's table of contents, you will see them right in the middle: Job, Psalms, Proverbs, Ecclesiastes, and Song of Songs. There are no great events in these five books (as in the books of History or Prophecy) and no new laws (as in the first five books of the Bible). And rather than being about the nation of Israel, these books are about individuals. Together, they form what we could call the heart of the Old Testament. They apply God's laws not so much to the corporate people of God, as the prophets do, but to individuals and to the great issues we face in our lives. Many Christians consider the Wisdom books their favorite part of the Old Testament.

Proverbs itself is basically divided into two parts. The first nine chapters work like a preface that attempts to convince you to read the book, in this case by explaining why wisdom is so valuable. The rest of the book—chapters 10 through 31—are collections of various wise sayings called "proverbs."

The book as a whole is a book of wisdom. It is, in fact, the most extensive straight ethical section in the Bible. It presents much of what the Bible teaches about how we should live our everyday lives.

Christians have always recognized the treasury of practical wisdom found in the Proverbs. When Paul wanted to talk about humility and unity, where did he turn? To the Proverbs.[2] When Peter wanted to write to young churches about conceit, dissensions, folly, and judgment, where did he turn? To the Proverbs.[3] When James wanted to talk about pride and presumption, where did he turn? To the Proverbs.[4] When the writer to the Hebrews wanted to encourage Christians who were enduring suffering, where did he turn? To the Proverbs.[5] Even Jesus himself wove a parable in Luke 14 out of one of these proverbs.[6]

---

[2] Rom. 12:16, cf. Prov. 3:7; Rom. 12:20, cf. Prov. 25:21-22.
[3] 1 Pet. 5:5, cf. Prov. 3:34; 1 Pet. 4:8, cf. Prov. 10:12; 1 Pet. 4:18, cf. Prov. 11:31; 2 Pet. 2:22, cf. Prov. 26:11.
[4] James 4:6, cf. Prov. 3:34; James 4:13-14, cf. Prov. 27:1.
[5] Heb. 12:5-6, cf. Prov. 3:11-12.
[6] Luke 14:8-10, cf. Prov. 25:6-7.

We see the same thing in the history of the church. The fourth-century theologian Jerome told his friends to use Proverbs for instructing children. The seventeenth-century preacher and commentator Matthew Henry was brought up with the words of Proverbs always on his mother's lips (which is appropriate, given Proverbs 1:4 and 4:1). And the twentieth-century evangelist Billy Graham has said that he reads a chapter a day (and, conveniently, there are as many chapters in Proverbs as there are days in the month!).

You could adopt Graham's practice right now for the rest of your life. Whatever the date is, simply read that chapter in Proverbs to familiarize yourself with its wisdom. It's a great book! The other night, my family sat around the dinner table and read Proverbs, and I gave each person a chance to figure out what one proverb meant. Sometimes it is easier; other times it is more challenging; but it can always create good discussion. The wisdom in the book of Proverbs is well worth getting.

How to Read Proverbs

That being said, parts of Proverbs puzzle people. The book is unusual. The rest of the Bible contains poetry, laws, histories, prophecies, and songs, and each of these different styles of writing will take up large sections of verses, chapters, and whole books. In the Proverbs, however, we find short, pithy statements, usually within the confines of a single sentence. Each statement is like a small, bite-sized bit of truth. Because of this, they are not always clear to people. They are the opposite of something like a legal contract, which will be carefully hedged with restrictions and qualifications. These short, crisp statements can just hang there, as it were, with no real explanation or qualification in the immediately preceding or succeeding verses.

Hence, this book—like almost anything else that is good for you—can be misunderstood and misused. It can be perplexing and even dangerous if read the wrong way. In fact, you might liken it to the experience you may have had if you are married, and you said to your spouse (or he or she said to you), "That may be what I said, but that's *not* what I meant." When reading Proverbs, as when communicating in marriage, we must sometimes work to understand the words being spoken.

Here are seven clues to help you in reading Proverbs' proverbs, especially the more difficult or obscure ones. These clues will help you get ahold of the wonderful wisdom this book has for you.

Clue #1: *Common sense* is required. One of the first tools we have to employ for understanding the Proverbs is an important tool for understanding any part of the Bible: common sense. For instance, we sometimes say, "Look before you leap." Well, what if you do leap once without looking, and you don't get hurt? Does that mean that proverb is false? Not at all. We recognize that the saying is useful for indicating what is generally true. Not only that, we recognize that this proverb is applicable to more than the topic of jumping. Well, it's the same way with the individual proverbs in the Bible. The mere fact that you are opening the Bible does not mean that you have to throw common sense out the window. You can look at 16:3, 5, 18, 20, and 22 for proverbs that common sense tells us are generally true.

Clue #2: Individual proverbs are always *ultimately* true. Second, we must realize that individual proverbs will not always appear to be immediately true, but they will always be ultimately true. For instance, one proverb in chapter 16 reads, "When a man's ways are pleasing to the LORD, he makes even his enemies live at peace with him" (16:7). But what about the life of Jesus? His enemies were hardly at peace with him. Still, we know that, ultimately, God will cause Jesus' enemies to live at peace with him. Every knee will bow.

Clue #3: Individual proverbs are *normally* true now. The purpose of a proverb is not to exhaust a topic but to teach a lesson in a way that is memorable. We say, "Look before you leap," again, not to exhaust the topic of jumping, but to teach something about jumping in such a way as to put truth in your mind, so that you can carry it away with you. And the point being made is normally true.

Clue #4: Individual proverbs employ poetic *imagery*. Fourth, remember that the proverbs often employ poetic imagery. For instance, another verse in chapter 16 reads, "The highway of the upright avoids evil; he who guards his way guards his life" (16:17). Now, that does not mean all the righteous people in Israel built a four-lane highway so that they wouldn't have to use the highway all the wicked people traveled on. No, it refers to how the righteous live their lives.

Clue #5: Individual proverbs are *partial* in themselves. Fifth, most proverbs are only partial. For example, one proverb in chapter 17 reads, "A bribe is a charm to the one who gives it; wherever he turns, he succeeds" (17:8). Perhaps that makes you think that bribes are a good thing. But no, if you keep reading, you will find that bribes are condemned: "A wicked man accepts a bribe in secret to pervert the course of justice" (17:23). The first verse is simply making a sardonic observation about real life. Too often, people imagine they can clip individual proverbs out like spiritual coupons to apply however they please. Having read one, they don't read the others. Yet proverbs alone are typically partial. Each one typically attempts to capture one basic idea.

Clue #6: Individual proverbs are sometimes *obscure*. Sixth, you will run into some Proverbs that will seem obscure because you do not have the cultural background to understand everything that was written three thousand years ago. When you encounter such a passage, you can call the pastor or you can consult a commentary. A good example of this can be found again in chapter 16: "He who winks with his eye is plotting perversity; he who purses his lips is bent on evil" (16:30). Does this mean that all winking is bad? No. But in the culture of the day, winking would have been associated with evil scheming. That's what the author is getting at.

Clue #7: As a whole, the proverbs are *religious*. Finally, Proverbs is a profoundly religious book. By that I do not mean that it contains a lot about formal corporate worship, sacrifices, or prayer; but I do mean that it is not simply a book of secular proverbs, like "Early to bed, early to rise, makes a man healthy, wealthy, and wise." It is a book about our lives *before God.* Indeed, it tells us that the good life can be found only in wisdom about God and about ourselves.

In this study, we will look at six areas in which Proverbs instructs us toward godly success and a well-rounded life. First, we will look at a couple of negative examples—the fool and the sluggard. Then we will turn to wisdom about family and friends. And finally we will consider what Proverbs says about words and about the paths of life and death.

THE FOOL

Proverbs teaches us how to be wise people, and part of learning what wisdom looks like is learning to recognize wisdom's opposite. Probably foremost among the cast of contrasting characters is the fool. When many people read the word "fool," they think it refers to someone who is not very intelligent. But that is not what Proverbs is talking about. No, there are things other than lack of intelligence that typify the fool.

According to the book of Proverbs, you can tell someone is a fool *by what he thinks about discipline.* Does a person welcome correction, or does he avoid it? The fool has a hardy disregard for discipline. And this disregard for discipline only points to his disregard for wisdom. In some ways, you could say that the overriding characteristic of the fool is that he has no self-control (17:24).

You can also tell someone is a fool *by what he says.* His words give testimony to the fact that he has no self-control. He talks like a fool. Abraham Lincoln said, "Better to be thought a fool, than to open your mouth and remove all doubt." But a fool's words always expose his folly. Incredibly, he even seems to flaunt it (13:16; 14:29). The fool can travel incognito only if he's silent (17:28). The moment he opens his mouth, all doubt is gone (15:2).

Proverbs also teaches that you can tell a fool *by the people around him.*

Fools like to keep the company of other fools. So a number of the proverbs are addressed not simply to the fool but to those who have to live with them. What should you do if you must live or work with a fool? Part of wisdom, it seems, is knowing how to answer that question, and that is a difficult thing to do. The fool makes for dangerous company; so dangerous, in fact, it is "better to meet a bear robbed of her cubs than a fool in his folly" (17:12). That's pretty dangerous!

You also can tell a fool *by what ultimately happens to him*. What happens? According to Proverbs, his own rejection of correction from the outside and his lack of discipline on the inside ultimately lead to his death (5:23; 9:13). His hatred of wisdom finally turns out to be indistinguishable from a love of death.

Of course, Proverbs is not the only book of the Bible where we can find fools. David observed, "The fool says in his heart, 'There is no God'" (Ps. 14:1; 53:1). Essentially, fools are atheists. They have determined in their hearts to live as if there were no God. Jeremiah described those who worship idols as "foolish" (Jer. 10:8).

God's people, it seems, can also be foolish. Moses warned the disobedient people of Israel that they were behaving foolishly (Deut. 32:6). Israel responded to the prophet Hosea as if *he* were a fool, thereby showing that *they* were the fools (Hos. 4:6; 8:12; 9:7). Through Jeremiah, the Lord said, "my people are fools; they do not know me. . . . They are skilled in doing evil; they know not how to do good" (Jer. 4:22). And through Zechariah, God condemned Israel's leaders for acting like fools—like shepherds who wouldn't care for the lost, or seek the young, or heal the injured, or feed the healthy, but would instead devour their own flock (Zech. 11:15-16).

Yet we do not find fools only in the Bible. We can all make fools of ourselves by our choices. So Proverbs sets a stark alternative before us: the way of folly or the way of wisdom. And the difference between the two, finally, is the difference between trusting in oneself and trusting in God. The fool is one who finally trusts in himself rather than in God (28:26). If we want to know what a successful godly life looks like, we must begin by having an ambition for wisdom.

Proverbs exhorts us to be ambitious for wisdom.

THE SLUGGARD

The godly, wise person is also contrasted with the sluggard in the book of Proverbs. Now, these days, a lot of people talk about the prevalence of workaholics. Isn't that the problem in many homes? But if we look at this character of the sluggard for a moment, we will see something useful for ourselves.

The sluggard is pretty easy to recognize. You can recognize him, first, *by his failure to take advantage of his present opportunities*. He lets opportunities slip by and makes excuses for himself along the way.[7] Commentator Derek Kidner has written that the sluggard "does not commit himself to a refusal, but deceives himself by the smallness of his surrenders. So, by inches and minutes, his opportunity slips away."[8]

More than anything else, I guess, you can recognize the sluggard *by his inordinate love for sleep*. Twice, this proverb is given: "A little sleep, a little slumber, a little folding of the hands to rest—and poverty will come on you like a bandit and scarcity like an armed man."[9] Yet whereas the sluggard would fold his hands and at least get some rest, today we more often fold our hands in front of the television and don't even get the rest! And maybe you are familiar with this famous proverb: "As a door turns on its hinges, so a sluggard turns on his bed" (26:14). You can almost imagine this as a humorous riddle: "What moves without going anywhere? A door on its hinges. What else? A sluggard on his bed." Carefree, lethargic inaction is typical of him. It's disgraceful! Worse, it's as if he's practicing for the grave.

You also can recognize a sluggard *by his failure to ever finish what he starts*: "The sluggard buries his hand in the dish; he is too lazy to bring it back to his mouth" (26:15; cf. 19:24). Obviously, this is an exaggerated image, but it is given in order to make a point. Even when the sluggard has gotten up the energy to start something as basic as eating, he does not finish it! He is the person who begins a hundred projects and finishes none. Distracted rather than diligent, he wastes opportunity after opportunity. He disappoints those around him. He prefers laziness to labor. He wants an easy life rather than one spent in doing good. And he is always making excuses ("The sluggard says, 'There is a lion outside!'"—Prov. 22:13a).

What we are to learn from this, of course, is that work is an appointed part of a godly life. Instead of presenting something like Aristotle's view of work—"the end of labor is to gain leisure"—the Bible presents work in a more positive light. The goodness of work is shown preeminently in the fact that God himself has displayed his wisdom by his work: "By wisdom the Lord laid the earth's foundations, by understanding he set the heavens in place; by his knowledge the deeps were divided, and the clouds let drop the dew" (3:19-20; cf. 8:22-31).

Therefore, we reflect the character of God in caring for others, in producing things, in being purposeful in our actions. Work is not a result of God's

---

[7] 6:6-8; 19:24; 20:4; 22:13; 26:13, 15.

[8] Derek Kidner, *Proverbs: An Introduction and Commentary*, Tyndale Old Testament Commentaries, D. J. Wiseman, gen. ed. (Downers Grove, Ill.: InterVarsity Press, 1964), 42.

[9] 6:9-11; 24:33-34; cf. 10:5; 19:15; 26:14.

curse after the Fall, as some have suggested. In fact, it might even be seen as a gift of God's grace for mitigating the consequences of the Fall. God, in his grace and great love, allows us to continue with purposefulness, thereby diminishing the severity of the Fall and its penalties on us. He gives us work in which we can accomplish goals, in which we can actually see something get done, in which we can continue to imitate our Creator in small ways. As Christians, we must not adopt the culture's attitude of despising our work and worshiping our leisure. Purposeful work, however repetitive or difficult or risky, is a good gift from God. This is what Proverbs teaches us through the sluggard.

In short, Proverbs tells us to have a godly ambition to work.

THE FAMILY

But Proverbs does not only point out wisdom's contrasts. More prominently, it teaches us how to live wisely. The wise and godly life, according to Proverbs, pays particular heed to the family.

Really, the whole book is taken up with the family. It is, after all, cast largely as a father teaching his son (cf. 31:1-2). From the warnings about adultery in chapter 1's prologue to the famous image of the noble wife in the final chapter, the book of Proverbs has much wisdom for our lives as families.

The Married Couple

The family clearly begins with the married couple, and this relationship should be marked by mutual respect and a concern for the practicalities of life. But it should also be marked by a certain specialness. Or call it romance! Chapter 5 tells us to find our emotional and sexual joy in our spouse (5:15-19). Chapter 6 presents the husband's jealousy of his wife as quite natural (6:34). Then there is that little cluster of things that, the writer says, "the earth cannot bear": "a servant who becomes king, a fool who is full of food," and, notice what's next, "an unloved woman who is married" (30:21-23). Never let it be said that in the concern for the wisdom of mutual respect and practicalities, Proverbs forgets love.

At the root of a loving marriage is faithfulness. Nothing should undermine the importance of faithfulness. Therefore, Proverbs impresses upon our minds and hearts with the searing heat of a branding iron the lesson that we must never underestimate the danger of adultery.[10] The adulteress is characterized at great length in five passages early in the book. You might want to note these down and look at them later. Meditating on these passages might even do more

---

[10] 2:16; 6:24, 29; 7:5; 22:14; 23:27; 30:20.

for you than reading any of the popular books on marriage: 2:16-19; 5:1-23; 6:20-35; all of chapter 7; and 9:13-18.

Throughout the Old Testament, the language of marriage is used to describe God's relationship with his people. So breaking our marital covenants with our spouses, as terrible as that is, points to the even greater transgression of unfaithfulness in our relationship with God. For the sake of our relationship with God, therefore, we are exhorted to have homes that are not marked by adultery and other forms of wickedness but that are marked by righteousness and faithfulness.[11]

The Children

The presentation in Proverbs of the godly family has a "Part Two": parenthood. As someone has said, "The value of marriage is not that adults produce children, but that children produce adults." Proverbs has plenty to say about that parent/child relationship.

As in the husband/wife relationship, the parent/child relationship must begin with mutual respect. Children should not shame and disgrace their parents but be a source of joy to them; and parents should be the pride of their children.[12] Parents must also care for their children's practical needs.

Without a doubt, however, Proverbs is preoccupied not with the parents' provision of the children's practical needs but their provision of the children's spiritual needs. The main thing parents must do for children is to *teach* them. Now, if you are a parent, I wonder if you ever thought of that. Or have you consigned the role of teacher to your child's school or the church's Sunday school? Training children is the responsibility of parents.

Again and again, Proverbs warns that if a child goes undisciplined, he will become impervious to discipline:

> "The rod of correction imparts wisdom, but a child left to himself disgraces his mother" (29:15).

> "Discipline your son, for in that there is hope; do not be a willing party to his death" (19:18).

> "Folly is bound up in the heart of a child, but the rod of discipline will drive it far from him" (22:15).

---

[11] 3:33; 12:17; 14:11; 17:13; 21:12.
[12] 17:6; 19:26; 20:20; 27:10; 30:11, 17.

"Do not withhold discipline from a child; if you punish him with the rod, he will not die. Punish him with the rod and save his soul from death" (23:13-14).

"What about child abuse?" you might ask.

Child abuse is a real problem, and we must not belittle it. And Proverbs is deeply concerned about the child abuse that occurs when the child is ignored, and when parents assume that their children possess a natural responsibility and discretion that they do not possess. Children will not learn such responsibility and discretion apart from their parents' instruction. You might as well give the car keys to your five-year-old and turn him loose on the streets.

In the book of Proverbs, the father instructs his son while he is still young. He gives commands and teaches proverbs to the son. He disciplines and corrects the son he delights in.[13] Proverbs leaves us no doubt about a father's active role in these areas. But I wonder how many of the fathers in our church never speak to their children about moral and spiritual matters. If you are a father, what do you think your role with your children is? Are you involved in teaching them? How? It bears thinking about, because Proverbs is clear about children's need to be taught! And it is not fundamentally the responsibility of churches. Sunday school emerged in the nineteenth century A.D. Proverbs was written in the first millennium B.C. Parents have the fundamental responsibility to teach their children. Sunday school can only assist.

Working for marital faithfulness and attending to the spiritual instruction of your children are godly ambitions.

FRIENDSHIP

According to Proverbs, the wise and godly person also pays heed to who his or her friends are. The book is full of talk about friendship, and we find that friends fall into one of two camps: good or bad.

Bad Friends

For starters, you can have bad friends. Perhaps you know that from painful experience. The trouble is, we hear the word "friend" and think it must be a good thing. The word almost deceives us. But we know that a friend can be a snare as well as a blessing. Sometimes people love you only because of your money, or what they can get out of you. Proverbs warns us about this.

Given the time we spend with friends, it isn't surprising that they influence us. For example, we can know that a short temper and lethargy are sinful. But when you choose friends marked by these sins, you will begin to imitate them,

---

[13] 1:8; 3:12; 4:1, 3; 6:20; 13:1; 15:5.

as if by osmosis. So Proverbs specifically warns us not to be the companion of gluttons (28:7) or prostitutes (29:3). More generally, the writer exhorts us, don't desire the company of evil people (see 24:1).

Parents realize the importance of friends. So they tell their young children going off to school to find good friends. And they warn their teenagers against falling into the wrong crowd. Yet sometimes parents are more careless about themselves, as if they were beyond the age of being influenced. Perhaps this sounds as if I am encouraging you not to include non-Christians in your life. Not at all. We have to hold both of these truths: befriend non-Christians and share the gospel; but remember that the people you spend time with will influence you.

Good Friends

We can also have good friends. Good friends last; they don't forsake you (27:10a). Gratefully, Proverbs has helpful instructions for how we can be this kind of real friend. Good friendship is not always natural and effortless. It takes work.

Real friends are sensible. In our friendships, therefore, we should not offer to do what we cannot do. Instead, we should always consider the implications of anything before we make an offer (6:1-5; 17:18).

Real friends are selfless. We should not use other people for our pleasure; rather, we should find pleasure in how we can be used for other people (3:29; 14:21; 25:17).

Real friends forgive, even when our friends wrong us. As Proverbs says, "love covers over all wrongs" (10:12b).

Real friends also tell the truth to one another. Certainly we should not lie to our friends (24:28). But beyond that, the ancient Greeks said that the opposite of a friend is not an enemy but one who flatters. Proverbs agrees: "Wounds from a friend can be trusted, but an enemy multiplies kisses" (27:6). Clearly, most of us could learn to hold our tongues better. But sometimes it is *not* the loving thing to keep silent: "Better is open rebuke than hidden love" (27:5). So-called "love" that never shows itself but always remains invisible does no one any good. Yet when we speak words of correction, our object should not simply be our own self-expression ("I just need to get this off my chest"). No, the goal must be our friends' benefit. Before confronting them, ask yourself, "Will this serve them and build them up?"

You see, just as the Bible uses the marital relationship to point to our relationship with God, so real friendship in the book of Proverbs is based on the model of our friendship with God. Again and again, the reader is exhorted to "trust the Lord," that is, enter into his confidence—as we would with a friend!

It would not be too surprising if real friendship eludes people who elude God, because real friendship begins in our relationship with God. It is as if we get the emotional venture capital in our relationship with God that is necessary for investing trust in other relationships.

After all, only God is the friend we can really trust. Only he is the real friend who really lasts. Jesus said, "Greater love has no one than this, that he lay down his life for his friends. You are my friends if you do what I command. I no longer call you servants. . . . Instead, I have called you friends" (John 15:13-15).

Proverbs encourages us to have the godly ambition to be a good friend like this.

WORDS

Another aspect of the godly life considered in the book of Proverbs is the role of words. Like our friends, our words come in one of two varieties: bad or good; false or true.

What You Say

Interestingly, do you know what most often defeats us in what we say, according to Proverbs? Haste! If you think back over your words from this past week, can you think of any you would like to take back? Proverbs would suggest that a good number of those words were probably spoken in haste.

What's the answer to our hasty words? What shall we do? We can find a clue in chapter 8, where Wisdom is personified as singing a beautiful song:

> "The LORD brought me forth as the first of his works,
>> before his deeds of old;
> I was appointed from eternity,
>> from the beginning, before the world began.
> When there were no oceans, I was given birth,
>> when there were no springs abounding with water;
> before the mountains were settled in place,
>> before the hills, I was given birth,
> before he made the earth or its fields
>> or any of the dust of the world.
> I was there when he set the heavens in place,
>> when he marked out the horizon on the face of the deep,
> when he established the clouds above

and fixed securely the fountains of the deep,
when he gave the sea its boundary
    so the waters would not overstep his command,
and when he marked out the foundations of the earth.
    Then I was the craftsman at his side.
I was filled with delight day after day,
    rejoicing always in his presence,
rejoicing in his whole world
    and delighting in mankind" (8:22-31).

What's the point of this passage? To point out the beauty of creation? To allude to the preexistence of the Word? I think it's the simple fact that God possessed wisdom *before* he did anything. That is to say, his actions were wise. And God is the great model for us. We too should possess wisdom, and wisdom should precede our every action, including the action of speaking. As Proverbs 14 says, "The wisdom of the prudent is to give thought to their ways."[14] Before we do anything, particularly before we speak, we should seek wisdom.

Some time ago, I read the biography of a famous nineteenth-century British naval hero, Sir Edward Pellew, Viscount Exmouth. Exmouth's heroic and noble acts were legendary in the British navy in the nineteenth century. The man himself was also known as decisive, insightful, and self-controlled, as seen particularly in his commands. One officer who served with him recalled, "His first order was always his last." When I read that, I was intrigued. I imagined a man giving a command and every man within his hearing knowing that the command could be trusted. They need not expect it to be countermanded; they knew the first command would stand.

Now, whether Exmouth's words carried such authority or not, the officer's testimony caused me to reflect on my words. How well would my words stand up if, at any given point in time, my mouth was stopped and my last words were allowed to echo through eternity? Proverbs teaches that a fundamental part of wisdom is thinking about what you say before you say it. As you are thinking about which words to use, ask yourself, "Am I happy for these words to echo through eternity?"

What You Hear

It may surprise you, but as you read through Proverbs you will find that the most important thing about words is how we *hear* them! Wisdom is not found

---

[14] 14:8; cf. 14:15; 21:29.

through speaking words, as the fool believes. It is found through listening to the words of others. Listening should be given priority over speaking. Further, the idea of "hearing" in the Bible does not only mean listening, it means listening and following up with right action.[15] "He who has ears to hear, let him hear."[16]

The book of Proverbs exhorts us to have a godly ambition to use words correctly—with our mouths and with our ears.

LIFE AND DEATH

Finally, I want us to notice the wisdom that Proverbs provides for the two great spheres that together comprehend all of our individual lives: the great sphere of life and the great sphere of death.

To use the language of Proverbs, each one of us is either on the way of life or on the way of death. We may try to avoid death, but Proverbs tells us there is actually a whole *way* of death that we travel upon long before reaching the grave itself.

When my wife and I first moved to New England, we lived on Ipswich Road in the town of Topsfield. In addition to being the name of the road we lived on, Ipswich is also the name of the town next door to Topsfield. Initially, I was struck by the fact that as soon as our road, Ipswich Road, gets to the town boundary of Ipswich, it becomes Topsfield Road. Why is this? The roads in this area were not originally named to celebrate their own community, like calling a street Washington Street because it is located in Washington, D.C. They were named to tell you where the road will take you. So it would be silly to have a road in Topsfield named Topsfield Road. You are already in Topsfield! Call the road Ipswich Road, because it will take you to Ipswich.

In Proverbs, there is a way of death! No, you are not dead while you are on the way. The way is taking you to death. And that way is made up of sinful choices. What this book teaches is that sin, by nature, is deadly. Our attraction to it is a fatal attraction.

But there is another way: a way of life. The way of life takes you to life, and Proverbs describes this way with three different phrases: we are called to "know wisdom"; we are called to "do righteousness"; and we are called to "fear the Lord." Together, these present the one way to life. To follow one is to follow the others. There is no true fear of the Lord that does not include wisdom, and there is no true righteousness that is not informed by wisdom and motivated by the fear of the Lord.

---

[15] 10:8; 13:13; 19:16.
[16] Mark 4:9; cf. 4:23; 8:18: Luke 8:8; 14:35.

So these are the two ways: the way of life and the way of death. Each one of us will live on one path or the other.

At the end of our journey, we will all give account to God. He is the certain judge, not we. And this universal accountability is graphically portrayed in the universal experience of death.

In 1534, Sir Thomas More, Lord Chancellor of England, refused to take an oath that King Henry VIII required of his subjects. At one point, the Duke of Norfolk, a friend of More's, became exasperated with More and said, "By the mass, master More, it is perilous to strive with princes; therefore I would wish you as a friend to incline to the king's pleasure; for the anger of a prince brings death."

Yet More answered, "Is that all, my lord? Why then there is no more difference between your grace and me, but that I shall die to-day, and you to-morrow."[17]

More understood that death cannot be avoided by political compromise. Neither can it be avoided by physical fitness, advancing medical technologies, health insurance, or anything else. More also understood that we will all be held accountable to God. And death will come to all of us. God will summon each of us to this final accounting. As the hymn says, "Time, like an ever-rolling stream, bears all its sons away."[18]

What shall we do in preparation for this accounting? Shall we work really hard in order to prove ourselves righteous and wise before God? Sometimes people think that all this practical wisdom in Proverbs means it's a book of morality and that it teaches us to save ourselves by following its requirements. But it doesn't. Proverbs knows we need more than instruction. It knows that we are all accountable to God for our wrong choices, and that our sin hinders our prayers and sacrifices (15:8; 21:27; 28:9). God is offended by our wrong actions, and he will judge us for them. He will repay every person according to what he has done (24:12). Indeed, all of us are debtors: "Who can say, 'I have kept my heart pure; I am clean and without sin'?" (20:9).

So what shall we do?! Proverbs teaches that we must confess our sins and plead for mercy: "He who conceals his sins does not prosper, but whoever confesses and renounces them finds mercy" (28:13). Does he who confesses find a reward? No, he finds mercy! But if God promises to repay every person according to what he has done (24:12), how can anyone find mercy? Well, Proverbs does not provide as full an answer to that question as the New Testament does, but it does provide the general outline of an answer: "Through

---

[17] "Sir Thomas More," in *Lives of Englishmen in Past Days,* four series in one volume (London: Joseph Masters, n.d.), 4th series, 32.
[18] "O God, Our Help in Ages Past," words by Isaac Watts, 1719.

love and faithfulness sin is atoned for" (16:6). Atonement is not tied so much to the ceremonial cleanness of an animal; it is tied to the moral purity of a human heart.

We should have a godly ambition to find atonement for our sins.

CONCLUSION: CHRIST THE WISDOM OF GOD

The question of our final destination may seem somewhat removed for many of us. "What does it have to do with where I am right now?" you may be thinking.

Proverbs promises that this question has everything to do with where you are right now. You are on either one road or another, traveling toward either life or death. We need to recognize the choice before us: to stay on our present path, or change paths. And then we need to choose rightly. In one sense, this whole book is about that choice. It is structured as the father instructing a son who will be called to make this choice. In verse after verse after verse he presents the son with many dichotomies, many pairs of contrasting options, many stark opposites.

But it will not always be this way. At some point, the ability to choose will stop. We are—*right now*—heading toward a time and a place in which we will no longer have this opportunity before us, and the choice for either life or death that we have been making over the years will be ratified.

In that sense, I think, ambition perishes in the afterlife. In the afterlife, we will finally receive that for which all of our ambitions have aimed. Death will present the final ratification of all the choices we have made.

And, friend, that final ratification may come more suddenly than you imagine. Maybe that sounds like a grim note to strike, but Proverbs clearly teaches that God will judge people—people who have gone on careless to his will, hardened to sin in their lives—with suddenness. Remember the warning, "A man who remains stiff-necked after many rebukes will suddenly be destroyed—without remedy" (29:1). If you make yourself deaf to such warnings, don't be surprised when you fall.

All this heightens the importance of *now* and the choices we make *today*. However composed you may look when you attend church in your Sunday clothes, or however disinterested you may feel in church service after church service, God warns that he will deal with us and that he will deal with us quickly.

Not too long ago, I was reading about the seemingly insignificant series of events that led Europe so quickly into World War I, and the writer described the war's suddenness with this arresting sentence: "It is as though with a careless remark about the weather we stumble upon the Day of Judgment." Proverbs assures us that each one of us will stumble upon that Day when we reach the end of our way. And so it urges us, "Choose the way of life now!"

"The path of the righteous is like the first gleam of dawn, shining ever brighter till the full light of day. But the way of the wicked is like deep darkness; they do not know what makes them stumble" (4:18-19).

And wisdom says, "Whoever finds me finds life and receives favor from the LORD. But whoever fails to find me harms himself; all who hate me love death" (8:35-36).

Of course, as good as Proverbs is, it does not provide the final word that we have on the wisdom of God. For that we must turn to the New Testament:

For the message of the cross is foolishness to those who are perishing, but to us who are being saved it is the power of God. For it is written:

"I will destroy the wisdom of the wise;
    the intelligence of the intelligent I will frustrate."

Where is the wise man? Where is the scholar? Where is the philosopher of this age? Has not God made foolish the wisdom of the world? For since in the wisdom of God the world through its wisdom did not know him, God was pleased through the foolishness of what was preached to save those who believe. Jews demand miraculous signs and Greeks look for wisdom, but we preach Christ crucified: a stumbling block to Jews and foolishness to Gentiles, but to those whom God has called, both Jews and Greeks, Christ the power of God and the wisdom of God (1 Cor. 1:18-24).

Christ is the perfect and full wisdom of God! He is the *way* of life (John 14:6). In his final letter, Paul writes, it is "our Savior, Christ Jesus, who has destroyed *death* and has brought *life* and *immortality* to light through the gospel" (2 Tim. 1:10). The truth that Proverbs hints toward is displayed in floods of light through Jesus Christ. In him we find wisdom and atonement, true friendship and true love.

In the last analysis, the Christian learns from Jesus the message found in this book of Proverbs: there is a way of life which is not life, and there is a death which is not death. As Jesus said, "I came that they might have life, and have it to the full" (John 10:10). He calls us, therefore, to repent of our folly and hard-heartedness and for all the times we have chosen the path of death. "Turn to the way of life," Jesus says. "Choose me as the only wise Savior and Lord." Do not choose the worldly wisdom of intellectual improvement. Do not look for the moral or spiritual resources inside of yourself. Choose instead what the world calls God's foolish decision to sacrifice his Son on the cross in order to pay for the sins of all those who would ever repent and believe in him. Choose reconciliation with God through the mouth-stopping wisdom of the Son of God on the cross.

A godly ambition is to live this life to the full by preparing for the next.

Let us pray:

O Lord, we are too often foolish, so we need your wisdom. We are sluggish, so we need your power. We are too often unfaithful, so we need your faithfulness. In our lives. In our families. With our friends. And, most of all, with you. We pray, Lord, for your own glory, show us our need of you. Frustrate us whenever we would stray from you. Compel us in your loving mercy to turn and trust in you. Teach us the truth of your gospel and the depth of your love. In Jesus' name we pray. Amen.

Questions for Reflection

1. Complete these three sentences:

a. "Our culture teaches us we will be happy when _____."

b. "The book of Proverbs teaches we will be happy when _____."

c. "I spent last week living as though I would be happy when _____."

2. How can people misread Proverbs?

3. What does Paul mean when he refers to Christ as our "wisdom" (1 Cor. 1:24)? If we are Christians, and if Christ is our wisdom, why do we need the wisdom of Proverbs?

4. Why does the world call the cross of Christ "foolish"?

5. Are you the wise person or the fool?

6. As we have seen, the fool hates discipline and self-control. Does this describe you? How do you respond to the rebuke of your boss, your parents, your spouse, or your friends? If you are a Christian, do you battle against your sins, or do you quickly take refuge in the fact that "God forgives"? How do you battle?

7. Does Proverbs teach that we are saved through moral instruction? How will we be saved?

8. If you are a parent, what difference will this sermon make in how you raise your children?

9. Do you view work as a blessing or as a curse? What steps can you take to view it as a blessing?

10. Is everyone who attends church on the path of life? Does becoming a member of a church place you on the path of life? Is church membership wise? Explain.

THE MESSAGE OF ECCLESIASTES: WISDOM FOR THE SUCCESSFUL

21

THE MESSAGE OF ECCLESIASTES: WISDOM FOR THE SUCCESSFUL

HOW DO YOU MEASURE SUCCESS?[1]

Is life worth living? These days, some say that it depends on life's *quality*. If a life falls below a certain standard of "quality," however that standard happens to be defined, then that life may be terminated. "Mercifully allow it to end," they say.

In order to answer this haunting question—Is life worth living?—some measure of success is needed. Now, I know that, to a certain degree, success is in the eye of the beholder. The ancient Egyptians counted increased irrigation from the Nile as a success. Business entrepreneurs today count securing financial backing as a success. Economists call job creation a success. Shareholders call rising profits a success. And workers count pay raises as a success. For you, success may be an honest friend, a new job, a different place to live, or a few pounds lost before the Thanksgiving-to-Christmas feast sets in!

INTRODUCING ECCLESIASTES

Success is a topic addressed often in the Bible, particularly in those books in the middle of the Old Testament called the Wisdom books. These five books— Job, Psalms, Proverbs, Ecclesiastes, and Song of Songs—form what we have called the heart of the Old Testament. Rather than being about the nation of Israel, they are about individuals, expressing the highs and lows of an individual's life. They apply God's laws not so much to the corporate people of God, as the prophets do, but to individuals and the great issues that we face in our lives.

Many Christians would consider this their favorite part of the Old

---

[1] This sermon was originally preached on August 24, 1997, at Capitol Hill Baptist Church in Washington, D.C.

Testament. And no wonder! We more immediately grasp and are grasped by an individual's experience of sorrow or joy than by the description of a sacrifice or an account of an ancient battle. These books are full of beautiful and expressive poetry, with trees clapping their hands, hills singing for joy, God's enemies melting like wax, and God riding upon the clouds.

In Ecclesiastes, however, we find more somber material. If the book of Proverbs is about wisdom for people who *want* success, the book of Ecclesiastes offers wisdom for people who *have* success. Particularly, it is for individuals who have gotten what they wanted out of life, or at least what they *thought* they had wanted, and then have found it wanting.

The serious tone of Ecclesiastes has brought encomiums from many. Herman Melville called it "the truest of all books."[2] Thomas Wolfe described it as "the highest flower of poetry, eloquence and truth" and "the greatest single piece of writing I have known."

Nearer to how many of us might read this book, however, is another writer's description of Ecclesiastes as possibly the "strangest" book in the Bible.[3] Many statements in this book are puzzling. Others even seem to be false!

Have you ever seen one of those plastic loaves of bread called "Promise Loaves"? They come with a stack of cards that have verses of the Bible printed on them. Among those cards, you can probably pick out a verse from Ecclesiastes that is quite lovely. But if some of the verses in this book were placed on those little Promise Loaf cards, you would have some very interesting breakfast table conversations in evangelical households!

The puzzling nature of this book has caused people to read it in various ways. Some have tried to understand Ecclesiastes as teaching pious truth sentence by sentence. Others, more recently, have come up with a variation on this idea: the author (who calls himself "the Teacher" [NIV] or "the Preacher" [KJV]) is a "preacher of joy" in the "eat, drink, and be merry, but remember God while you do it" school. If you are a student of Ecclesiastes, you might be taken with reading the book in one of those ways. When I read it, though, I get no such easy application. Its passages are altogether too dark and foreboding, and the book shows too keenly the hollowness of what looks like the fullest life.

Indeed, the book's skepticism is shocking to many. It can feel cynical, even nihilistic, more at home in a play by Camus or an essay by Nietzsche than on the pages of sacred Scripture.

---

[2] Herman Melville, *Moby Dick* (New York: Norton, 1967), 355.
[3] James L. Crenshaw, *Ecclesiastes: A Commentary* (Philadelphia: Westminster, 1987), 23.

So what is the message of this book? And what can we learn about success? To answer these questions, we must turn to the book itself.

Ecclesiastes consists of twelve chapters. A short prologue begins the book, and an even shorter epilogue ends it (1:1-11; 12:9-14). Everything in between is one long monologue by someone simply called *Qoheleth,* which, as we have seen, means "the Teacher." We don't know who this Teacher was. He's never named in the book. Many have said that it was Solomon because of his fame for wisdom, and because the opening lines of the book call him "son of David and king in Jerusalem." Yet a Hebrew writer could have used this word "son" to refer to any direct male descendant of David, no matter how many generations later. Further, the setting described by the book does not sound like the time of Solomon. So this "Teacher" is unknown apart from this book, and he ends up having the timeless presence among us that Job does.

But what does he say?

WHAT IS MEANINGLESS?

The Teacher's basic message is about meaninglessness. He begins in the second verse of the book, "'Meaningless! Meaningless!' says the Teacher. 'Utterly meaningless! Everything is meaningless'" (1:2). I don't know what you think, but to me, that statement is as clear as it is confusing! He says something similar a few verses later: "I have seen all the things that are done under the sun; all of them are meaningless, a chasing after the wind" (1:14; cf. 12:8). As one person said, this book starts out low and gets worse!

The word *hebel,* translated "meaninglessness" in the NIV or "vanity" in the KJV, occurs thirty-five times in this short book. It refers to something insubstantial and ephemeral, and therefore temporary and passing. Whatever the "meaningless" object is, it can be easily, quickly, and permanently whisked away, like smoke, a cloud, or a desert mirage, leaving behind no remainder.

And what exactly does the Teacher say qualifies as meaningless? "Everything," he says. "Everything" falls under his charge.

What does he mean by "everything"? If we look through the book, we see that he does seem to mean *everything!*

Obvious Things

Clearly, he makes this charge against all the *obvious things* that we, too, would quickly recognize as meaningless. "Much dreaming and many words," he says, "are meaningless" (5:7). The "roving of the appetite" is "meaningless, a chasing after the wind" (6:9). The "laughter of fools" is also meaningless, as long-lasting as "the crackling of thorns under the pot" (7:6). Indeed, some things are obviously vain, without substance or significance, without point or profit.

Among the obvious things named by the Teacher as vain are the bad things. The Teacher is not afraid to stare right into the face of life's most difficult realities. So the injustices of life he calls meaningless: "I saw the wicked buried—those who used to come and go from the holy place and receive praise in the city where they did this. This too is meaningless" (8:10). This wise teacher's keen sense of justice was evidently unnerved by the praise in life and honor in death received by the wicked. As he generalizes several verses later, "righteous men . . . get what the wicked deserve, and wicked men . . . get what the righteous deserve" (8:14). At other points in the book, the Teacher affirms that a sovereign and just judge rules over creation, but this judge's justice is at least sorely hidden in many situations. The fact that people get the opposite of what they deserve even seems to mock before all the world any claim that there is justice in life. The Teacher's objection sounds much like Job's:

> "Why do the wicked live on,
>   growing old and increasing in power?
> They see their children established around them,
>   their offspring before their eyes.
> Their homes are safe and free from fear;
>   the rod of God is not upon them.
> Their bulls never fail to breed;
>   their cows calve and do not miscarry.
> They send forth their children as a flock;
>   their little ones dance about. . . .
> They spend their years in prosperity
>   and go down to the grave in peace" (Job 21:7-11, 13).

All such injustice, says the Teacher, is meaninglessness.

Questionable Things

More interestingly, though, the Teacher turns his critical gaze upon things that might seem less obviously empty or wrong to us. These *questionable,* borderline, or neutral things, which we might be slower to categorically condemn, he also denounces as utterly vain!

Pleasure is the first such borderline thing to come under his critical gaze. He begins one of his reports by saying, "I thought in my heart, 'Come now, I will test you with pleasure to find out what is good.' But that also proved to be meaningless" (Eccles. 2:1). In the verses that follow, he then explores the emptiness and worthlessness of pleasure (2:2-11).

At least initially, we would be a lot slower to say what he says here. Pleasure, surely, can be put to self-serving ends.[4] One friend of mine who works at an advertising agency recently told me that the advertising industry recognizes that most people have come to think of themselves more as consumers than as citizens. More than in any other age, we today are openly and fully motivated by our desires, as if they were infallible revelations of truth. When, before our time, have pleasure and ease been so publicly acceptable as the justification for action or inaction?

But a wholesale condemnation of pleasure does seem to go too far, doesn't it? After all, the Westminster Shorter Catechism's famous statement on the purpose of life is not only stirring, it appears to be helpful and accurate: "The purpose of life is to glorify God and *enjoy* him forever" (emphasis added). God does intend for us to *enjoy* him—to take pleasure in him.

Now, I will say, we Christians these days do fall all over ourselves trying to live down the idea that we are prudish kill-joys. We want to be known as the happiest, funniest people around. And so we "courageously" oppose the legalism that would prohibit us from indulging in any of the pleasures of this world, saying that such restrictions are rooted in a flesh-denying Gnosticism. "They are theologically suspect, spiritually dangerous, and socially awkward," we quickly say. We do have difficulty denouncing pleasure, don't we? Well, the Teacher has no such difficulty: "I refused my heart no pleasure," he admits. But he finds all of it "meaningless, a chasing after the wind" (2:10, 11).

Popularity, or public approval, is a second borderline matter the Teacher quickly dismisses as meaningless:

> Better a poor but wise youth than an old but foolish king who no longer knows how to take warning. The youth may have come from prison to the kingship, or he may have been born in poverty within his kingdom. I saw that all who lived and walked under the sun followed the youth, the king's successor. There was no end to all the people who were before them. But those who came later were not pleased with the successor. This too is meaningless, a chasing after the wind (4:13-16).

We don't know what particular historical episodes the Teacher had in mind, as he spoke of kings replacing kings replacing kings—public opinion rising and falling all the while. Perhaps he was thinking about the discontent the people of Israel began to feel with the line of David and the ensuing rebellion that divided the nation into the northern and southern kingdoms. That would

---

[4] The idea represented by the Greek word for "happiness" or "pleasure," from which we get our word "hedonism," is condemned repeatedly in the New Testament (Luke 8:14; Titus 3:3; James 4:1, 3; 2 Pet. 2:13).

fit this passage. After all, the people loved David over Saul. But then David's line fell out of favor with most of the tribes, and they rebelled. Whatever incidents the Teacher had in mind, his point for us is clear: the public is fickle, and their affection should not be overvalued or pursued. It is finally meaningless.

If you happen to make your livelihood by cultivating public approval, as many do in the city of Washington, D.C., take heed. Whether through disaffection or simply mortality, popularity is a passing thing. The public will change its mind, or you will die. And even while you think you have the public in your grip, you might be surprised to discover who is really in whose grasp!

In his essay "Shooting an Elephant," George Orwell describes an incident that happened to him when posted in Burma with the British army. One day a rogue elephant got loose, damaged much property, and even killed a cow; and it fell to Orwell to recapture it. By the time he caught up with the elephant, it had finished its fit and calmed down. No more damage would be done; the elephant could be easily led back to its confinement; and killing the elephant, Orwell knew, was unnecessary, though he had brought a rifle along for self-protection. In fact, he opposed the idea of killing this valuable creature. Yet two thousand Burmese had followed him out into the field where the elephant stood, excited to watch the spectacle of the large beast being shot. As he stood facing the elephant, the crowd said nothing, but he felt two thousand wills boring in on him, expecting, anticipating, delighting in an imminent death. Orwell was there to govern these people, but he found himself needing their approval. In a funny way, he became their tool, and inclined toward doing what they expected and wanted. I won't tell you what happens (I commend the essay to you), but Orwell clearly uses the story to suggest that the crowd that appeared so subservient was actually deeply controlling. Public approval can be as demanding as it is passing.

Popularity is not the ultimate reality, says the Teacher. If you doubt this now, a day will come when you won't.

So, meaninglessness afflicts not only the obvious things, but the less obvious things like pleasure and popularity. The Teacher's skepticism revealingly questions and relentlessly exposes wrongly accepted nostrums like "If it feels good, do it" and "If everyone says so, it must be best." Both statements are false.

Good Things

What is still more amazing, however, is how the Teacher's charge extends even to the things we would call *good*. Surely you have noticed this if you have read the book of Ecclesiastes. These are the passages that most disturb us.

For example, the Teacher declares that "youth and vigor are meaningless" (11:10). Now this is news! We take youth and vigor as self-evidently good. No, they are not good for everything, but they are certainly coveted and desired, and most of us would hardly refer to them as "meaningless"! But the Teacher does.

Not only that, he denounces as meaningless the very thing that most of the original readers would have given—and most readers today give—their lives for: work, as well as the wealth and achievements work brings. All this the Teacher unmasks as meaningless. "What does man gain from all his labor at which he toils under the sun?" he asks in chapter 1 (v. 3). The answer comes in chapter 2:

> I undertook great projects: I built houses for myself and planted vineyards. I made gardens and parks and planted all kinds of fruit trees in them. I made reservoirs to water groves of flourishing trees. I bought male and female slaves and had other slaves who were born in my house. I also owned more herds and flocks than anyone in Jerusalem before me. I amassed silver and gold for myself, and the treasure of kings and provinces. I acquired men and women singers, and a harem as well—the delights of the heart of man. I became greater by far than anyone in Jerusalem before me. In all this my wisdom stayed with me.

> I denied myself nothing my eyes desired;
>   I refused my heart no pleasure.
> My heart took delight in all my work,
>   and this was the reward for all my labor.
> Yet when I surveyed all that my hands had done
>   and what I had toiled to achieve,
> everything was meaningless, a chasing after the wind;
>   nothing was gained under the sun (2:4-11).

All that the hands can do, all that toil can accomplish, is meaningless. The achievements of labor are as passing as the flickering picture on a television screen. It comes and goes, with no trace left behind.

How does the Teacher respond to this discovery? "So I hated life, because the work that is done under the sun was grievous to me. All of it is meaningless, a chasing after the wind" (2:17). Think about this image for a moment: chasing after the wind. What a picture of pointlessness. It makes a dog chasing his tail look purposeful and intelligent! And that is what all our work and labor finally is: a chasing after the wind. After all, labor and achievement all spring from the envy of others (4:4), and whatever is amassed must be given away and enjoyed by others:

I hated all the things I had toiled for under the sun, because I must leave them to the one who comes after me. And who knows whether he will be a wise man or a fool? Yet he will have control over all the work into which I have poured my effort and skill under the sun. This too is meaningless. So my heart began to despair over all my toilsome labor under the sun. For a man may do his work with wisdom, knowledge and skill, and then he must leave all he owns to someone who has not worked for it. This too is meaningless and a great misfortune. What does a man get for all the toil and anxious striving with which he labors under the sun? All his days his work is pain and grief; even at night his mind does not rest. This too is meaningless (2:18-23).

The love of money is also meaningless: "Whoever loves money never has money enough; whoever loves wealth is never satisfied with his income. This too is meaningless" (5:10). In general, the realities of this world mean that creating wealth will never be fulfilling, either because you will not have the family to leave it to, or you will run out of time to enjoy it yourself (4:8; 6:1-9).

War and Peace author Leo Tolstoy wrote a short story called "How Much Land Does a Man Need?" In the story, a peasant spends his life trying to fulfill an insatiable appetite for something that he neither attains nor enjoys because he kills himself in the process of getting it. Again, I won't spoil the story for you, but I will say that the peasant ends up needing far less of that something than he had tried to possess.

Well, we have covered the pursuits of Monday through Friday and maybe even Saturday. But most shocking of all is what the Teacher asserts about what we Christians pursue on our Sundays: wisdom is meaningless. "Then I applied myself to the understanding of wisdom, and also of madness and folly, but I learned that this, too, is a chasing after the wind" (1:17). Perhaps you thought that I was just trying to say that your secular jobs throughout the week are a waste of time, and that you should spend all your time reading the Holy Book alone. Well, the Teacher seems to look at even this and call it meaningless. "Then I thought in my heart, 'The fate of the fool will overtake me also. What then do I gain by being wise?' I said in my heart, 'This too is meaningless'" (2:15).

Indeed, reaching the bottom of his despair, the Teacher refers to his own life as "meaningless" (7:15).

Even that last refuge of hope—the future—he decries as meaningless: "Light is sweet, and it pleases the eyes to see the sun. However many years a man may live, let him enjoy them all. But let him remember the days of darkness, for they will be many. *Everything to come* is meaningless" (11:7-8).

I think we have answered the question we asked at the beginning—what does he mean by "everything"? By "everything" he seems to mean everything. His twelve-chapters-long monologue concludes with the words he began with: "'Meaningless! Meaningless!' says the Teacher. 'Everything is meaningless!'" (12:8).

Ecclesiastes can sound strangely contemporary to us. We may think that despair has merely come of age in our own day, now that we have grown out of our benighted state of imagining light where there is none, and into an enlightened state of seeing the darkness that is. But this book—over two thousand years old, perhaps even three—belies any notion that skepticism is modern. Truly, there is nothing new under the sun, not even skepticism.

I wonder if *you* identify with what the Teacher is saying? Maybe you think that this is one of those sermons for other people. As a minister, I accept that this is sometimes the case. But perhaps you do have a keen sense of what the book is saying. Robert Gordis has written, "Whoever has dreamed great dreams in his youth and seen the vision flee, or has loved and lost or has beaten barehanded at the fortress of injustice and come back bleeding and broken, has passed [the Teacher's] door, and tarried a while beneath the shadow of his roof."[5]

God's ways are often mysterious to us, yet I do believe I have been able to hear at least the echo of the Teacher's words in my life, if not the actual words themselves. Having lived in Durham, in Boston, in Cambridge, and now in Washington, I have watched people with privilege and power show both the strange blindness that can overcome people when they feel completely satisfied and the strange perceptiveness they simultaneously gain of the emptiness of what everyone else around them would die to have. As an undergraduate, I watched as students became jealous of one another over the opportunity to lead small groups in the Christian fellowship or to sit on the executive committees of student organizations, even though my own participation on such committees simply meant enduring multiple phone calls of people complaining and all the hassles of securing a meeting room. Somehow, it looked different to those who were not yet there. As a graduate student, I observed people who had spent their whole lives getting into prestigious academic institutions then build their worlds around the strangest and most obscure ideas. They, remarkably and triumphantly, became the world-acclaimed masters of their field—fields, of course, with only five other people in them who, incidentally, were also world-acclaimed masters. Meanwhile, every other area of their lives was a wreck. And how many times have I met people who have had enough money not to worry about anything. Escaping the demands that weigh most people down, they are bloated with a perverted selfishness. No gravity is left to pull them into a normal shape or form. No one ever tells them no, at least no one right now.

This is how the Teacher teaches us a lesson different from what Job does. Job learned about the vanity of this world by *losing* it all; the Teacher saw it by *having* it all. If you happen to have everything you could possibly ask for in any particular area of life, you know what I am talking about, whether it's friendships, work, wealth, or health. However wonderful these things may be, an ample supply of any of them never leaves you entirely satisfied. Something is always missing.

Picture again that image of chasing the wind. You are standing outside. You feel strong gusts of air on your face and hands. And you begin to chase those gusts. Will you ever catch them? Would this not be completely pointless? You might as well chase after meaning in this world, says the Teacher of Ecclesiastes. So he pursues us, relentlessly pointing toward and exposing the meaninglessness of any life so wrongly spent.

Yet two questions for us remain. First, why does he say that everything is meaningless? Second, how should we respond?

WHY IS EVERYTHING MEANINGLESS?

First, then, why does the Teacher say that everything is meaningless? A clue is given early on: "There is no remembrance of men of old, and even those who are yet to come will not be remembered by those who follow" (1:11). Okay, so the meaningless of everything has something to do with our inability to remember anything. Regardless of the wealth, splendor, or accomplishments of a man, he will be forgotten. Take the great Egyptian king Ramses II, for instance, and consider how memorable his greatness was, as captured by Percy Bysshe Shelly's poem "Ozymandias":

> I met a traveler from an antique land
> Who said: Two vast and trunkless legs of stone
> Stand in the desert. Near them, on the sand,
> Half sunk, a shattered visage lies, whose frown,
> And wrinkled lip, and sneer of cold command,
> Tell that its sculptor well those passions read
> Which yet survive, stamped on these lifeless things,
> The hand that mocked them, and the heart that fed.
> And on the pedestal these words appear:
> "My name is Ozymandias, king of kings:
> Look on my works, ye Mighty, and despair!"

Nothing beside remains. Round the decay
Of that colossal wreck, boundless and bare
The lone and level sands stretch far away.

Even in our best actions, the prospect of not being remembered can discourage us. If you are a longtime member of a church, have you ever looked around the halls and remembered whole groups of people who are now gone? Do you ever remember events into which you poured days and weeks, that you see no more? Have you not found yourself missing the companions with whom you can reminisce about such days? Has no parent of a long-gone child ever looked into a bedroom and considered all the weeks, months, and years of labor poured into that son or daughter? Work that no one noticed in the past, let alone will remember in the future?

Yet not only are the men of old forgotten, says the Teacher, there will be no remembrance of those yet to come! Can we not allow our innocent and optimistic hopes to at least hold on to the future? Even the most morbid among us will grant a deferential silence to the days yet to come. But not the Teacher. He looks out upon generations still unborn, envisions their lives and deaths, and then contemplates the forgetfulness of still later generations. In the same way the physical vastness of the universe can make people feel displaced, insignificant, and finally meaningless, so the Teacher perceives the vastness of time swallowing up any meaning that could be found in the miniscule spans of our lives. After all, the same fate overtakes all people:

I saw that wisdom is better than folly,
    just as light is better than darkness.
The wise man has eyes in his head,
    while the fool walks in the darkness;
but I came to realize
    that the same fate overtakes them both.

Then I thought in my heart,

"The fate of the fool will overtake me also.
    What then do I gain by being wise?"
I said in my heart,
    "This too is meaningless."
For the wise man, like the fool, will not be long remembered;
    in days to come both will be forgotten.
Like the fool, the wise man too must die! (2:13-16).

Here we come to the real culprit behind meaninglessness. No person will be remembered, finally, because everyone dies. It isn't that the Teacher sees nothing good in wisdom. Wisdom is better than folly, he says. But he is frustrated by the fact that both the fool and the wise man come to the same end. They will both be forgotten because both will die.

Indeed, man shares the fate of animals! You would expect some sort of qualitative difference, but no:

> I also thought, "As for men, God tests them so that they may see that they are like the animals. Man's fate is like that of the animals; the same fate awaits them both: As one dies, so dies the other. All have the same breath; man has no advantage over the animal. Everything is meaningless. All go to the same place; all come from dust, and to dust all return" (3:18-20).

We come to the same end as our pets! You see his point, don't you?

I had the opportunity to hear Billy Graham speak last year in the rotunda of the U.S. Capitol building as he received an award. If you have ever been inside the U.S. Capitol, you know that it is filled with myriad statues of great Americans. During his acceptance speech, Graham spoke of walking down the halls of the building, observing its many statues, and asking himself what all the individuals represented had in common. His answer: they are all dead. And then he assured us that both he and we would soon share this fate as well.

Whether we are celebrities like Jimmy Stewart, Supreme Court justices like William J. Brennan, or fashion magnates like Gianni Versace, we will all die.[6] It is the Teacher's loud ringing of this grim note that makes this book's important contribution. It is this note that we need to hear, lest we rest our hope in the wrong place. Perhaps more than anywhere else in Scripture—except the cross of Christ—Ecclesiastes presents the real effects of sin in our world.

This book is a realistic book.

You know, of course, that everything has a basic plot. If you have ever seen one episode of the old television show *Gilligan's Island*, you have seen them all. Every episode begins with some sort of crisis. Onto the island stumbles a well-meaning but hapless individual who has somehow managed to find this island on which Gilligan and his friends are stranded—which no competent rescuer has been able to find! Some mayhem or mix-up follows, with either a romance or a scam. An escape for Gilligan looks possible. But then, just as mysteriously as the outsider appeared, he disappears. There must have been more than 740 people who got off that island while that series ran. But none of them were Gilligan!

Did you know that the Bible, too, has a basic pattern? The basic biblical

---

[6] All three individuals died in 1997, the year when this sermon was originally preached.

pattern can be summarized with the simple chain of creation, fall, and re-creation. God creates something good. Man sins and ruins what God has created. But hope remains because of God's grace called re-creation. It is important that we recognize this pattern because a slight imbalance here can have a large effect. Some people will overemphasize the Fall to the neglect of re-creation, and this leads to a grim despair—though admittedly this is not as common in our desire-and-satisfaction-driven culture.

Other people will overlook the darker tones of parts of the Bible such as Ecclesiastes and heavily emphasize the goodness of creation itself. This tendency is more common today, perhaps, because of the optimistic humanism so prevalent in our culture. Such individuals see the goodness in life, yet they are not sensitive to the ways in which the world has been misshapen or ruined.

Still other people overemphasize re-creation alone in a way that feels shallow, overly pious, and superspiritual. These (mostly Christian) types tend to be surprised by Ecclesiastes' accurate and honestly negative presentation of reality. They are not used to such strong statements.

But the biblical story line does not hesitate to acknowledge fully the goodness of God's creation, the tragic effects of the Fall, and the tremendous hope we have in God—all at the same time!

The book of Ecclesiastes in particular, I would suggest, plays a special role in explicating and expounding the devastating effects of the Fall, which is helpful for a day like ours that idolizes the creation rather than the Creator, this life rather than the Author of this life. The Teacher points to the meaninglessness that death imposes on everything in this life. Indeed, it is death that evacuates meaning from our world, frustrating our hopes and foiling our plans.

HOW SHOULD WE RESPOND?

The second and final question must then be, how should we respond?

Certainly, the grim psychological reality of this book gives it credibility. The author is not whistling in the dark, as we say, but living with his eyes open. As one writer has said, "[A]s in all great literature, the writer earns the right to affirm by doing justice to the negative side of life."[7]

In your own life, I am sure you have noticed how much easier it is to trust someone who has been through what you have been through; who has struggled with your struggles; who can accurately voice your difficulties because he or she has "been there." When such a person commends faith, we don't respond, "He hasn't experienced the depths of evil that I have experienced. If only he had seen what I have seen, he couldn't come up with such clap-trap."

---

[7] Leland Ryken, *Words of Delight: A Literary Introduction to the Bible* (Grand Rapids, Mich.: Baker, 1987), 326.

No, we trust him. And Ecclesiastes, with its realistic appraisal of death and the futility of life, leaves the most skeptical among us feeling that it's reliable.

In an unexpected way, the real-life priest upon whom G. K. Chesterton based his fictional detective Father Brown had a remarkable firsthand understanding of evil. During a discussion with Father O'Connor about crime, Chesterton was astonished, he once wrote, "to find that this quiet and pleasant celibate had plumbed those abysses far deeper than I. I had not imagined that the world could hold such horrors."[8] Two Cambridge undergraduates whom Chesterton and O'Connor encountered on the same day as their discussion about crime, however, failed to perceive O'Connor's deep understanding. The priest impressed both of the younger men with his knowledge of music and architecture, but when he departed from the foursome, one of the undergraduates remarked,

> "All the same, I don't believe his sort of life is the right one. It's all very well to like religious music and so on, when you're all shut up in a sort of cloister and don't know anything about the real evil in the world. But I don't believe that's the right ideal. I believe in a fellow coming out into the world, and facing the evil that's in it, and knowing something about the dangers and all that. It's a very beautiful thing to be innocent and ignorant; but I think it's a much finer thing not to be afraid of knowledge."

Chesterton did not record what he said in response to this young man, but he does tell us what he thought:

> To me, still almost shivering with the appallingly practical facts of which the priest had warned me, this comment came with such a colossal and crushing irony, that I nearly burst into a loud harsh laugh in the drawing-room. For I knew perfectly well that, as regards all the solid Satanism which the priest knew and warred against with all his life, these two Cambridge gentlemen (luckily for them) knew about as much of real evil as two babies in the same perambulator.[9]

Chesterton discovered that an accurate measure of evil within the context of this fallen world is part of godly wisdom. Indeed, much of Ecclesiastes' power does not come from direct commendations of the truth or celebrations of God but from showing how bleak an outlook wrongly limited to what's "under the sun" is.

In fact, some have wondered how the Teacher could be so thorough in this

---

[8] G. K. Chesterton, cited in Martin Gardner, ed., *The Annotated Innocence of Father Brown* (Oxford: Oxford University Press, 1988), 7.
[9] Ibid.

appraisal of life's bleaker themes. I believe he can be so thorough only because of his certainty concerning the larger context. The Teacher knows that death and cynicism are not everything. If this book were merely sullen skepticism, or resigned despair, it would not move people as it does. Yet the picture the Teacher presents is profound not because it is *all* the truth but because it is an extremely important *part* of the truth. It's as if he insists that we listen long and hard to the bad news before he will allow us to consider the good. Chesterton understood something of this dynamic. Describing the change that happened to him at his conversion, he said,

> The Christian optimism is based on the fact that we do *not* fit in to the world. I had tried to be happy by telling myself that man is an animal, like any other that sought its meat from God. But now I was really happy, for I had learnt that man is a monstrosity. I had been right in feeling all things odd, for I myself was at once worse and better than all things. The pleasure was prosaic, for it dwelt on the naturalness of everything; the Christian pleasure was poetic, for it dwelt on the unnaturalness of everything in the light of the supernatural. The modern philosopher had told me again and again that I was in the right place, and I had still felt depressed even in acquiescence. But I had heard that I was in the *wrong* place, and my soul sang for joy, like a bird in spring.[10]

Without an honest look at the curse of death and futility, we miss a key piece of the puzzle that no amount of feel-good optimism can adequately replace. Ecclesiastes is powerful exactly because it presents the tension and struggle between the Teacher's sense of futility and his very real faith in the God who is true, between the way things are and the way they ought to be.

At one point in his life, apparently, the Teacher tried to reconcile these two things. But he learned better: "I have seen all the things that are done under the sun; all of them are meaningless, a chasing after the wind" (1:14). And here we come to the key to understanding Ecclesiastes: the phrase "under the sun." It occurs twenty-eight times in this short book, and it refers to life as viewed entirely from the perspective of this earth, a life considered apart from God. Such a truncated and circumscribed life, of course, is meaningless. "All come from dust, and to dust all return" (3:20).

Friend, can you see how the Teacher's honesty about sin, the Fall, and its consequences helps us understand why the world is like it is, and how we should respond to it? Hear him! This world is a bad place for your final investment! It was not made for that! As long as you keep trying to cobble together meaning from the scraps of this world, the Teacher of Ecclesiastes will pursue

---

[10] G. K. Chesterton, *Orthodoxy* (Wheaton, Ill.: Harold Shaw, 1994), 82-83.

you and point out the paltry and passing, flimsy and fleeting nature of your materials. There is more to life than what we find under the sun, and God has not made us to be satisfied with this world alone. As the Teacher says, God has "set eternity" in our hearts (3:11). Yes, our lives are lived out under the sun, but our hearts' desires stretch infinitely beyond the horizon. Eternity goes beyond the sphere of what is under this sun.

Throughout the book we read of him who dwells in the heavens, above and beyond the sun. The book is not as faithless as it is sometimes made out to be. In the last few verses, we read, "Now all has been heard; here is the conclusion of the matter: Fear God and keep his commandments, for this is the whole duty of man. For God will bring every deed into judgment, including every hidden thing, whether it is good or evil" (12:13-14).

Some people feel that these last verses of the book spoil it. The real message is stark, but it's honest, brave, and commendable, perhaps even necessary to survive in the world. Maybe these last verses were just tacked on, they've thought.

But I don't think so. These verses bring us to the ultimate message of this book: only with God do we have a clear and true perspective that gives meaning to life. *That is the perspective we must have.*

For life to have meaning, we need what lies beyond it. We need judgment (cf. 8:10-13; 12:14); and we need hope. It is because God the Author will finally evaluate what we do that life has meaning. In the same way that a book cannot read itself, you and I cannot give meaning to our own lives. We were created by someone bigger than us, for *his* purposes and for *his* ends. Only from him can we learn meaning and truth.

When we view our lives from his perspective, what do we see? What do we see when we turn away from our self-centered, beneath-the-sun perspectives and adopt the Teacher's own God-centered perspective? We see, first, our rebellion against God. This becomes evident as soon as we stop measuring "success," "fair," "good," and "valuable" from our own vantage point and begin using God's standards. Second, we see the promise of judgment that our rebellion requires. But third, we learn in the Scriptures, marvelously, that God is not only holy, he's loving; and he has given his Son to die on the cross and take upon himself God's judgment for the rebellion of all those who will ever repent of their sins and believe in him!

CONCLUSION

So is futility final? No. Ecclesiastes was never meant to be a substitute for the whole Bible. As we have seen, some of these cynical sayings, taken by themselves, can be confusing and even appear false. To know the truth of God, we need the full revelation of God himself that he gives us in the whole Bible.

So, I ask again, is futility final? Outside of the answer that is found in Christ, there is no final answer to the futility of life. Only God's revelation of himself in Jesus Christ assures us that there is something beyond the sun and beyond the grave. In that sense, the good news that we as Christians have to share is the key to getting "beyond the sun." Christ came to live, die, and rise again in order to bring us forgiveness of sins and a restored relationship with God. This good news is the key to getting beyond and over the sun and to gaining the life full of the meaning and purpose that God intended for us. The afterlife is not an old Christian dogma that we can simply push aside. The afterlife, says the book of Ecclesiastes, is essential to this life and to understanding the truth of who God made us to be. And only through Jesus Christ do we see the death of death and the birth of a new life that will endure forever.

"Therefore if anyone is in Christ, he is a new creation; the old has gone, the new has come!" (2 Cor. 5:17).

"Always give yourselves fully to the work of the Lord, because you know that your labor in the Lord is *not in vain*" (1 Cor. 15:58b).

We will find meaning only when meaning extends beyond this life and world. Only eternity with God makes a life "successful" and "worth living." And we will find such meaning only in Christ!

Let us pray:

Lord, we pray now that your Holy Spirit would powerfully and clearly show us the walls and boundaries that we have put up in our lives. Show us the boxes that we tend to think within. And then, Father, show us your truth beyond them. If we have been calculating only for the day or month or year or even this life, we pray that you would rattle us with reality as Ecclesiastes presents it. Grow in us a deep discontent with this life, so that we would perceive that we were made for more than just this world. Lord, grant the gifts of repentance and faith in Christ, so that we would turn from our sins and trust in you. That is what you tell us to do in your Word. And we know from this book that that is the only way we will find the meaning and joy that you intend to give us in this life. We thank you for it, and we pray that you would continue your work in us for your glory. In Jesus' name. Amen.

Questions for Reflection

1. Are you successful? If not, when will you be successful?

2. Why is Ecclesiastes an excellent book to read with a non-Christian? How would you explain to him or her why this book clearly and rightly belongs in the same Bible as the books of the New Testament?

3. What does the author of Ecclesiastes say death imposes on all of life? In what sense is death, though universal, "unnatural"? Why should we never take any death for granted?

4. As we have seen, God has "set eternity" in our hearts (3:11). What evidence for this do you see in your heart and in the hearts of others?

5. Have you ever worked very hard for something, achieved it, and then discovered that your "success" left you unsatisfied? If so, why do you continue to work for worldly success? What should you do?

6. How can you begin an explanation of the gospel with this sentence? "There's a massive canyon between the way things are and the way they ought to be." Why *must* an explanation of the gospel begin with this sentence or some other sentence that means the same thing?

7. Why is *your* work *meaningful?*

8. How might a deep understanding of life's futility help us in sharing the gospel with others?

9. Did Christ experience the futility and meaninglessness of this world? How? How did he escape it? How do we escape it?

THE MESSAGE OF SONG OF SONGS: WISDOM FOR THE MARRIED

22

THE MESSAGE OF SONG OF SONGS: WISDOM FOR THE MARRIED

RESPONDING TO THE SEXUAL REVOLUTION[1]

If the world lasts long enough for the history books to be written, the most important revolution of the twentieth century, I think, will not be considered to have been a revolution that was won with tanks and torpedoes, bullets and bombs. Almost certainly, it will be the sexual revolution. Begun in the West, this revolution spread rapidly by travel and the media into many of the world's cities and beyond.

In this revolution, simple changes instigated profound effects. Contraception replaced conception, and the "price" of sexual activity seemingly dropped dramatically. Pleasure was separated from responsibility. Contraceptive devices and abortion clinics replaced schools and orphanages. It was as if a license was given out, legitimizing the bending of every part of our lives around serving ourselves.

Since that time, divorce, remarriage, abortion, pre- and extramarital sex, and even homosexuality have been accepted by increasing percentages of the public. The boundaries that once seemed fixed now appear less secure. Sadomasochism, polygamy, pederasty, and bestiality are all represented by groups working to promote their acceptance in our society.

Pornography has also become big business. How many hard-core pornographic videos do you think Americans rented in 1986? Seventy-five million. Yet in 1996, Americans rented 665 million, generating over $3 billion in business. In fact, the whole pornography industry is now estimated to be a $10 billion a year business, and it is reported to be enriching the coffers of corporate giants like AT&T and Time Warner. As one pornography publisher observed

---

[1] This sermon was originally preached on August 31, 1997, at Capitol Hill Baptist Church in Washington, D.C.

in an interview, "The great advantage of capitalism is that greed overrides morality and puritanism."

Now, I am not suggesting that the sexual revolution is a done deal. In fact, it isn't over by a long shot. Over the last several years, mainline churches like the Episcopalians and the Presbyterians have wrestled over their own institutional positions on matters of sexuality. On the more conservative side, the Presbyterian Church in America and the Southern Baptist Convention (SBC) have been forced to consider and reconsider how best to respond to the companies, institutions, and larger cultural forces that push—sometimes explicitly, sometimes subtly—for sexual license and the undermining of biblical mores.

Of course, this revolution has affected not only the public sphere; sins of the flesh ultimately nestle themselves down in the private, personal sphere. Lechery may be publicly celebrated, but it is typically practiced in private. Pornography may be publicly traded, but it is consumed behind closed doors. I wonder how many people today will commit cyber-sins. Cyber-envy. Cyber-lust. Cyber-adultery. And who knows what the effects will be of so-called "virtual sex."

Some people think of the world religions as Christianity's main competitors. Yet I think it can be fairly said that the main competitor that Christianity faces today in the West is not Islam or Judaism. It is not atheism or Hinduism. It is *eroticism*—the increasingly uninhibited search for fulfilling our sexual passions in whatever form we please.

More than anything else in the last half-century, sex and our attitude toward it have reshaped our culture to the point that it must be almost unrecognizable to the oldest among us. In a recent magazine article, one person laments what she calls "the slow and steady sexualizing of the culture." Everything "from the frankness of network news to the graphicness of music videos to the smuttiness of talk shows," she says, "has inevitably led to our inurement." We become deadened to life itself. Even "nakedness is losing its transformative power."

And lest we hear this litany of social ills and feel sanctimoniously removed within the moral safe haven of the church, we had best remember that we are not untouched. This is not just a problem with society *out there*. Many churches have found their members plagued by failed marriages and illicit affairs, by so-called "private" sins that turn into public disgraces, some of which are known, some of which are not yet known. A study by our own SBC finds that the divorce rate among members of Southern Baptist churches is no better—and may even be worse—than among the population at large.

Pornographic images increasingly steal into the view of even the most careful Christian. You need not enter seedy, roadside shops to find them. You can simply glance at the side of a city bus, the racks in a supermarket checkout line, the advertisements in a newspaper, the back cover of a magazine, or the commercials on your television in order to find illustrations in which complex moral and spiritual creatures made in God's image for knowing and enjoying him forever are portrayed as nothing more than fleshly instruments for your own momentary pleasure and satisfaction.

As Christians, how should we respond to the sexual revolution? How do we engage with this assault on our society, our churches, and us as individuals, which is bringing us all to the verge of utter disintegration and final ruin? Some say that we should simply follow our culture and surrender to our desires; that we should be hedonists; that we should not be so uptight; that we should discover the good that comes with freedom and end our self-repression. Others, following more of a stoical impulse, suggest that we should deny these desires altogether; that we should subdue the flesh; that we are not merely animals. Yet neither of these two responses really fits with what God built us to be as humans, and, therefore, neither response is appropriate for us as Christians.

INTRODUCING SONG OF SONGS

We need God's wisdom to deal with such assaults, and so we turn to Song of Songs, the last of our studies in the five books of Wisdom from the Old Testament. No part of the Bible speaks more clearly to the topic of erotic love and the divided impulses we Christians feel to surrender unquestioningly to our urges and our culture on the one hand or to completely deny those urges on the other hand. Yet neither path is right for a Christian; so God, in his wisdom, placed a book in the Bible to particularly address this dilemma and to mark out the true way.

The NIV entitles the book Song of Songs, which is the Hebrew way to construct a superlative. This is the greatest of all songs, just like the King of kings is the greatest of all kings, and the Lord of lords is the greatest of all lords. Sometimes, the book is known as the Song of Solomon since, as you can see in verse 1, this is "Solomon's Song of Songs." We don't know if Solomon really wrote the book. When you read the book, it can sometimes feel as if it's *about* him rather than by him. At the very least, it does seem that either he collected these songs or they were presented to him.

Let's begin by reading some selections from the book:

> Let him kiss me with the kisses of his mouth—
>   for your love is more delightful than wine.
> Pleasing is the fragrance of your perfumes;
>   your name is like perfume poured out.
> No wonder the maidens love you!

Take me away with you—let us hurry!
  Let the king bring me into his chambers.

We rejoice and delight in you;
  we will praise your love more than wine.

How right they are to adore you! (Song 1:2-4).

Tell me, you whom I love, where you graze your flock
  and where you rest your sheep at midday.
Why should I be like a veiled woman
  beside the flocks of your friends?

If you do not know, most beautiful of women,
  follow the tracks of the sheep
and graze your young goats
  by the tents of the shepherds (1:7-8).

I am a rose of Sharon,
  a lily of the valleys.

Like a lily among thorns is my darling among the maidens.

Like an apple tree among the trees of the forest
  is my lover among the young men.
I delight to sit in his shade,
  and his fruit is sweet to my taste.
He has taken me to the banquet hall,
  and his banner over me is love.
Strengthen me with raisins,
  refresh me with apples,
  for I am faint with love.
His left arm is under my head,
  and his right arm embraces me.
Daughters of Jerusalem, I charge you
  by the gazelles and by the does of the field:
Do not arouse or awaken love until it so desires.

Listen! My lover!
  Look! Here he comes,
leaping across the mountains,
  bounding over the hills.
My lover is like a gazelle or a young stag.

Look! There he stands behind our wall,
gazing through the windows,
   peering through the lattice.
My lover spoke and said to me,
   "Arise, my darling,
     my beautiful one, and come with me.
See! The winter is past;
   the rains are over and gone.
Flowers appear on the earth;
   the season of singing has come,
the cooing of doves
   is heard in our land.
The fig tree forms its early fruit;
   the blossoming vines spread their fragrance.
Arise, come, my darling;
   my beautiful one, come with me" (2:1-13).

Come with me from Lebanon, my bride,
   come with me from Lebanon.
Descend from the crest of Amana,
   from the top of Senir, the summit of Hermon,
from the lions' dens
   and the mountain haunts of the leopards.
You have stolen my heart, my sister, my bride;
   you have stolen my heart
with one glance of your eyes,
   with one jewel of your necklace.
How delightful is your love, my sister, my bride!
   How much more pleasing is your love than wine,
   and the fragrance of your perfume than any spice!
Your lips drop sweetness as the honeycomb, my bride;
   milk and honey are under your tongue.
   The fragrance of your garments is like that of Lebanon.
You are a garden locked up, my sister, my bride;
   you are a spring enclosed, a sealed fountain.
Your plants are an orchard of pomegranates
   with choice fruits,
   with henna and nard,
   nard and saffron,
   calamus and cinnamon,
   with every kind of incense tree,
   with myrrh and aloes
   and all the finest spices (4:8-14).

Your stature is like that of the palm,
and your breasts like clusters of fruit.
I said, "I will climb the palm tree;
I will take hold of its fruit."
May your breasts be like the clusters of the vine,
the fragrance of your breath like apples,
and your mouth like the best wine.

May the wine go straight to my lover,
flowing gently over lips and teeth.
I belong to my lover,
and his desire is for me (7:7-10).

Who is this coming up from the desert
leaning on her lover?

Under the apple tree I roused you;
there your mother conceived you,
there she who was in labor gave you birth.
Place me like a seal over your heart,
like a seal on your arm;
for love is as strong as death,
its jealousy unyielding as the grave.
It burns like blazing fire,
like a mighty flame.
Many waters cannot quench love;
rivers cannot wash it away.
If one were to give all the wealth of his house for love,
it would be utterly scorned.

We have a young sister,
and her breasts are not yet grown.
What shall we do for our sister
for the day she is spoken for?
If she is a wall,
we will build towers of silver on her.
If she is a door,
we will enclose her with panels of cedar.

I am a wall, and my breasts are like towers.
Thus I have become in his eyes
like one bringing contentment (8:5-10).

Now this is not the kind of Scripture we normally read in a sermon! These days, few of us would be shocked to encounter this kind of language in a magazine or even a newspaper. But to read something like this in the Bible? That's a little different for us!

We are not the only ones to sense some discomfort with the explicit nature of this book. It was traditional among the ancient Israelites not to allow young men to read the book until age thirty.

I had one friend in eighth grade who took to highlighting his Bible. After reading this book, he highlighted the whole thing! Not in the normal yellow, cool blue, or even exotic green but in hot pink!

No doubt this very discomfort with the plain meaning of the words is what has led Christians in the past to devise so many different ways of reading this book. A first group has taken an *allegorical* approach to understanding Song of Songs. They deny that the lover and the beloved represent two humans. The metaphor of the lovers is just a literary device for displaying some other meaning, usually the love of God for his people.

A second group, not wishing to be so dismissive of the book's historicity, has adopted the *typological* approach. They accept the historicity of the lovers as two real people but, like the allegorical approach, they shift the emphasis to what the couple represents. So the figures are real, but we should pay greater heed to the greater reality they point toward.

A third group has suggested that Song of Songs is to be understood as a *drama* or *story*, complete with well-developed characters and the movement of a structured plot through the stages of an introduction, the onset of a crisis, a climax, and a resolution. Many different suggestions have been made for who the characters are and what the plot is. Yet that points to the very difficulty of this approach: so many suggestions have been made about what the story line is, one cannot help but wonder why it isn't plain enough for everyone to see. Clearly the book has an introduction, but are the stages of a plot really that clear, as we would expect in a story?

It seems to me that it is best to understand Song of Songs as a *song* or *collection of songs* that are, well, basically human love poems. This seems like the natural and literal meaning of the text, doesn't it? Whereas other ways of reading this book turn it into something like an occult puzzle, with the true meaning hidden until someone gives us the key, much of the difficulty clears up when we simply read it as love poems.

In this way, lovers are lovers and desire is desire. It doesn't stand for something else. As the old fast-food chicken restaurant advertisement said, "Parts is parts"! We might be embarrassed—at least in a sermon—by all the talk about breasts and kisses and embracing arms, but we understand it. Those things are clear enough. We know what they mean. And that is how I think we should read this book. Yes, there may still be imagery we have to interpret, but it's simply the imagery of any love poetry we might read.

I have called this sermon "Wisdom for the Married," and Song of Songs certainly is an important book about marital love. But just as certainly it is not an exhaustive book on love or marriage. We should not make more of this song or collection of songs than God means us to. It does not tell us how to respond to our spouse's aging, to a job loss that threatens family security, or to the discovery of an affair. It does not say exactly how to increase our spouse's interest in us. In short, it does not teach us everything we need to know about marriage.

Yet the book depicts several important aspects of longing and loving, and of how God has given us gifts in marriage that meet the very desires he made us to have. As a part of wisdom, then, we need to study this book.

Specifically, God has designed marriage to meet four different types of longings: for enjoying physical intimacy, for building relational intimacy, for establishing identity, and for finding meaning.

ENJOYING PHYSICAL INTIMACY

First, God meets our needs and longing for physical intimacy.

Our Longing

The only references to physical intimacy most of us are accustomed to hearing in sermons are critical ones, as preachers warn against the sin of extramarital sex and the corrupting dangers of lust. Indeed, we have already spoken here about the dangers of our pornographic society, our addiction to eroticism, and the cheapened value of men and women that follows. Such critical discussions are essential. Today's culture constantly bombards us with gender-bending images that blur the objects of our desires while heightening our experience of them. In the name of advertising and entertainment, human bodies become commodities and people become products. Ironically, true romance and intimacy vanish in an age when everything becomes sensual.

Yet setting the distortions and perversions aside, we do see in the Scriptures that the longing for physical intimacy is God-given and good. There is a good longing for physical intimacy. God made us as physical creatures with bodies. We know that. Certainly, an appropriate type of physical intimacy can be shared between members of the same sex: handshakes, hugs, and high-fives! And there are appropriate types of physical gestures among family members.

In Song of Songs, however, the author has an even more specific physical affection in view: the sexual relationship between a husband and wife.

Of course, Song of Songs simply takes this message from the book of Genesis itself. In the story of Creation in Genesis, God told Adam that it was not good for man to be alone, and so God made the woman. God said that his creation was good. Adam and Eve were then joined together. They "knew" each other. And that knowledge was physical, intimate, and good.

The Song of Songs does know that desire can be dangerous. Three times we read in this little book, "Do not arouse or awaken love until it so desires" (2:7; 3:5; 8:4). There are times when such love is appropriately expressed, and times when it is not.

Yet we must understand that Christianity is *not* a religion that says the physical is bad and the spiritual is good. We are not Gnostics. We do not assume that everything having to do with our flesh is evil, and that good can be found only in the immaterial and invisible. Christians should be careful, therefore, not to give the impression that our main message about human sexual desires and longings is negative. We have a positive message! That's why it is good to read Song of Songs in church every once in a while. It helps us to remember that we have a positive message about sex.

Though I have worked with college students for many years, I am always amazed that so many of them continue to be so deceived by the same misunderstandings about what sexuality is for. Again and again, I see young people trade away a very special, privileged gift from God for something that might look like that gift at first but ends up being infinitely less. Yet in part, this might be the result of our failure as Christians to teach the positive message that God created us as male and female, that he actually calls us to have intimate relations with our spouses, and that such intimacy is good!

In many ways, this must be the main message of Song of Songs. We Christians are tempted to downplay or even ignore this important topic. But God has put this book in the Bible to make it more difficult for us to do that!

The Bible's Celebration

The Song of Songs *is* primarily an unabashed celebration of the pleasure of physical intimacy. God intends that our longings for physical intimacy be met! Several times in this book, sexual invitations are given. Notice how the book closes with an invitation and acceptance of sexual union: "You who dwell in the gardens with friends in attendance, let me hear your voice! Come away, my lover, and be like a gazelle or like a young stag on the spice-laden mountains" (8:13-14).

Perhaps these days we are tempted to think that no testimony to the pleasures of physical love is needed. But God has given us this book to constantly remind us that what our culture has abused God still calls good. We are reminded that physical love is *delightful*:

Let him kiss me with the kisses of his mouth—
　for your love is more delightful than wine (1:2).

How delightful is your love, my sister, my bride!
　How much more pleasing is your love than wine,
　and the fragrance of your perfume than any spice! (4:10).

We observe the appreciation, by both the male lover and the female beloved, of *physical beauty:*

How beautiful you are, my darling!
　Oh, how beautiful!
　Your eyes are doves.

How handsome you are, my lover!
　Oh, how charming!
　And our bed is verdant (1:15-16).

We read that physical love is *satisfying:*

Your lips drop sweetness as the honeycomb, my bride;
　milk and honey are under your tongue.
　The fragrance of your garments is like that of Lebanon (4:11).

We may be modest about the love of physical intimacy—and we should be—but we need not be ashamed. So throughout this book, the writer portrays and celebrates the erotic affection two married lovers have toward each other:

Who is this coming up from the desert
　like a column of smoke,
perfumed with myrrh and incense
　made from all of the spices of the merchant? (3:6).

Who is this that appears like the dawn,
　fair as the moon, bright as the sun,
　majestic as the stars in procession? (6:10).

Who is this coming up from the desert
   leaning on her lover? (8:5).

The Song of Songs celebrates the pleasures of physical love God has given us in marriage!

BUILDING RELATIONAL INTIMACY

Our Longing

Having said that, there are more longings in this book worth observing. So the Song of Song's lovers share a clear longing to build relational intimacy. This may be more subtle, but it is nonetheless real.

These days, sadly, we have many ways to speak negatively of relationships, because we know they can be destructive. So we use words like "addictive," "codependent," or "enabling." And surely, as complex and central to the human personality as relationships are, they are dangerous things. This longing for relational intimacy can beget all kinds of troubles.

Still, the Bible does not present the lone hermit as the model for human existence. God did not create us to be alone, as he told Adam in the Garden. That does not mean it is never good for people to be alone, but that is the general rule. We were made to know and to be known. And in Song of Songs, we should not see merely physical attraction. Behind the unembarrassed, even rapturous descriptions of physical attraction, each partner clearly desires a real and full interpersonal relationship. They possess not only the physical desire to have and be had, but the personal desire to know and be known. And once again, this book reminds us that such knowledge is good. We do not need to maintain any false, superspiritual ideas about "going it alone" with Jesus, and we must not regard the need for personal relationships as wrong or as a sign of weakness. This need is natural, healthy, and good. It is part of being human.

The Bible's Celebration

The Song of Songs celebrates the full relationship that physical love consummates.

One writer, observing that the most intimate act of "knowing" another human being occurs with "skin on skin," points to what he calls one of the provocative ironies about human life:

This is piquant irony: here we are with all of our high notions of ourselves as intellectual and spiritual beings, and the most profound form of knowledge for us is the plain business of skin on skin. It is humiliating. When two members of this god-like cerebral species approach the heights of communion between themselves what do they do? Think? Speculate? Meditate? No, they take off their clothes. Do they want to get their *brains* together? No, it is the most appalling of ironies. Their search for union takes them quite literally in the direction away from where their brains are.[2]

While I appreciate this author's frank espousal of the reality of our physical bodies, I cannot fully agree with him. What he misses is the fact that physical love is not context-less. It is not simply the "exchange of bodily fluids," as college students will callously and dismissively say.

And Song of Songs is not simply a book about physical intercourse between two animals. After all, it's a book of words! There's speech! There's poetry! There are people communicating with each other. Verbalizing their desires, longings, needs, hopes, and even fears is a crucial aspect of the relationship between the lover and the beloved.

We long for human relationships. That is how God made us. Notice, then, how this book propels us forward as readers with call and response: the lover calls and the beloved responds; the beloved speaks and the lover answers. There is a two-way relationship. There is a mutuality to their love, because God intends that our physical desires be met within the context of our communal, social, interpersonal desires. Good physical intimacy can occur only within the context of a good relationship, which, not incidentally, is why sex must be reserved for marriage. To have sex without being married is like moving into a house you have not purchased. There is a tentative, insecure quality to it—like trespassing—that does not match what God intends for sex: a deeply satisfying experience of physical and relational love.

Again going back to the first pages of the Bible, we learn that God meant for the physical union between a husband and his wife to provide part of the very foundation for their relationship: "a man will leave his father and mother and be united to his wife, and they will become one flesh" (Gen. 2:24). Then Jesus himself affirms the lesson of this verse: "So they are no longer two, but one. Therefore what God has joined together, let man not separate" (Mark 10:8b-9). Do you see what this means? Physical intimacy between a man and a woman represents and indicates something more—a relational intimacy, a joining of not just bodies but personalities.

God intends for two married lovers to enjoy both the physical pleasure and

---

[2] Thomas Howard, cited in G. Lloyd Carr, *The Song of Solomon: An Introduction and Commentary,* Tyndale Old Testament Commentaries, D. J. Wiseman, gen. ed. (Downers Grove, Ill.: InterVarsity Press, 1984), 35n2. Originally in Thomas Howard, *Hallowed Be This House* (Wheaton, Ill.: Harold Shaw, 1979), 115f., emphasis his.

the relational pleasure of their love. And through the physical love in marriage God gives us a deepened relationship.

ESTABLISHING IDENTITY

Our Longing

There is another longing we can infer from the pages of Song of Songs. Part of our longing for physical and relational intimacy is a desire for establishing our identities. The desire to *know,* in other words, is matched by the desire to *be known*—to define and understand ourselves.

One of the dangers of our world, fraught as it is with discussions of insecurity, is becoming too "plastic." Politicians re-create themselves into the image projected by their polling data. Marketers help devise the products their research shows people will buy. And most of us are tempted to copy in chameleon-like fashion the people we spend time with.

And yet the desire to understand ourselves in relation to other people is a natural and healthy desire. I am sure you know something of what I am saying. If you have ever lost a loved one either to death or a permanently broken relationship, you probably know how—surprisingly and confusingly at first— you lose something of who *you* are. When that person goes, something significant in you goes with them. Your very painful grief is not just for them and your loss of them, it is also for the loss of yourself. This happens because we all know ourselves in our relationships with other people, particularly those we love.

The Bible's Celebration

The Song of Songs celebrates the person that physical love helps us to be, and the identity that physical love helps us to find.

Much of who the lover and the beloved are as individuals is tied up in their relationship. They know and define themselves according to their relationship with each other—as the lover and the beloved. "I am my lover's and my lover is mine" (6:3). And, "I belong to my lover, and his desire is for me" (7:10).

Clearly, this is why personal relationships can be so dangerous. If you enter one wrongly, outside the structures the Bible has put in place, you are playing with the deepest things about yourself and the other person. On the other hand, when you enter one correctly, inside the structures the Bible has put in place, you will find great personal fulfillment.

Remarkably, then, tremendous personal fulfillment is available through the exclusive, monogamous marital love described in this book!

Of course, that is not what people today think when you mention exclusive matrimonial monogamy. Not too long ago, I saw an advertisement for a movie in which one character said to the other, tauntingly, "Remember, I can sleep with whoever I want to. I'm not the one who's married. You are!" What a terrible perspective! Marriage may look like "bondage" from the perspective of those who want to "liberate" sexual love from its confines. Yet, once it is liberated, sexual love becomes like water that has been "liberated" from a glass—spilled on the ground, running in every direction, collecting nowhere, eventually dissipating and vanishing. "Freed" sexual love loses all the meaning it's supposed to have.

Not so in Song of Songs. This book is not about just any relationship. It's about exclusive married love. So the beloved promises she has "stored up" herself for her lover (7:13). And the book as a whole paints a picture not of lust and fantasy but of monogamous, satisfying love.

Remarkably, a strange completeness comes about through the monogamous marriage God has designed. Your role as a woman or a man may be unclear to you in other parts of your life, but not here. Two things are worth noticing about this. First, marriage brings about a type of completeness when it is guarded from other lovers. God created us to couple up. Therefore, you should expect to find the most satisfaction and contentment with *one* other person. When the Song of Songs lovers deliberate about what to do with a sister who is young and not yet ready for love, they determine to protect and guard her with chastity. Then the sister herself responds, "I am a wall, and my breasts are like towers. Thus I have become in his eyes like one bringing contentment" (8:10). The sister's saving herself for her husband appears to be part of what will bring contentment to that future relationship. In fact, the word "contentment" here is the Hebrew word *shalom*, which more broadly speaks of the holistic, harmonious peace of completion. The exclusive and pure commitment she will bring to her husband and that he will bring to her, then, will provide a larger sense of harmony and completeness both to the relationship and to themselves as individuals.

Second, notice that marriage provides this sense of completeness even, it appears, in the absence of children. The book never mentions children, which is particularly striking given the book's ancient Near Eastern context.[3]

Through physical love in marriage, God gives us a greater knowledge of ourselves.

---

[3] See Carr, *Song of Solomon*, 53.

FINDING MEANING

Our Longing

There is one final longing we should observe in Song of Songs. As humans, we long to find meaning. All people, whether they have ever thought it or said it, long to know their reason for living.

I was once speaking to a student who was struggling with whether or not to believe in Christianity. As he talked in circles and repeated himself continually, I finally interrupted him and asked, "Do you *want* Christianity to be true?" He said he did. I asked him why. He replied, "Because I want meaning and purpose in life. I want to understand why I am alive."

Now, it's easy to find bad purposes for our lives. We can easily invest ourselves in false gods and other bad things, such as crime. We can easily turn good things—like our health, wealth, or popularity—into bad things by caring about them too much. Even a loving interpersonal relationship can mislead us and turn out to be destructive if we put too much importance or weight on it.

Still, a truly balanced, intimate, and honest personal relationship is one of the best pictures we can have of what the ultimate purpose of our lives is: having a relationship with God.

Though I have argued that this book is not, in the first instance, either an allegory or a typology, it remains true that any picture of goodness, and particularly any picture of true love, illustrates God's goodness and love toward us. So the apostle Paul uses the picture of a marriage to illustrate the love between Christ and his people (Eph. 5:22-33). In that sense, the beauty and power of our longing for one another's love points to the relationship we are called to have with God, a relationship that signifies our completion, our contentedness, our place of true and eternal *shalom*.

How can you know the love of God and have eternal peace with him? Repent of your sins and trust in Christ wholly for forgiveness. Do you need an illustration to understand what this looks like? Look to the man and the woman of Song of Songs, who forsake all other lovers and commit to one another exclusively. Look to how the man is called to lay down his life for his wife, and how she is called to serve her husband. It's this very concrete picture that Song of Songs gives us. Like the lovers, we too must forsake our sin, our other lovers, our false gods, and look to Christ alone. He alone has laid down his life before the wrath of God for sin and has paid the penalty that we deserve, if only we will look to him as Savior and Lord.

The Bible's Celebration

As we consider how Song of Songs celebrates human love, we get a scent of God's love for us and the love we are to have for him, because the very act of physical love within marriage should draw us toward that far greater love!

God has given us sexuality to enjoy, yes, but he also has given us the gift of sexual union in order to illustrate another more ravishing and fulfilling union of love that awaits! I don't say this to make our human physical love seem any less, but to say that the love that awaits is even more. Christian, is this fulfilling love what you expect and wait for in the appearing of Christ?

In that sense, physical love in the context of marriage helps us to understand and to accept God's love. We learn as Christians to grow in our trust and acceptance of God's love, in part, through our experience with our spouse. Perhaps you have a hard time trusting your friends, or your spouse, or even God because of experiences in the past when you felt betrayed. In the same way, a positive experience with a spouse who is committed in love can begin to teach even the most damaged among us about God's love for us and the love we can have for him. How? Through our relationships with our spouses, we learn to relate to and deeply trust someone who is different than we are. And as we do that, we learn to trust God, who, in his holiness and beauty, is more different from us than our spouses are. So when you hear that imagery in Revelation 3:20 about Jesus standing at the door knocking, think of that same image in Song of Songs of the lover knocking at the door and waiting (Song 5:2).

Consider everything that God gives us through physical love in marriage: physical pleasure, relational intimacy, a greater knowledge of ourselves, and a greater trust in him. Ultimately, he helps us know more of who he is and what it means to be in a trusting, loving relationship with him.

CONCLUSION

Sex should not be taken casually, denigrated, or denied in marriage. Nor should it be worshiped and made out to be the point of life.

Sadly, young people fall for the same cheap trick again and again. In our present erotic age, we must not be beguiled into compromising or scared into surrendering God's very good gifts, and this is a crucial part of our discipleship to Jesus. As churches, therefore, we must warn about the serious dangers of misusing physical love.

This also requires us to teach what the Bible says positively about sexual love as an important part of who God made us to be. In married love, God intends for us to enjoy pleasure, build relationships, establish our identities, and even find meaning in God's love. This is the message that we need to get out!

In the final chapter of Song of Songs, we read about the passionate strength of love: "For love is as strong as death, its jealousy unyielding as the grave. It burns like blazing fire, like a mighty flame. Many waters cannot quench love; rivers cannot wash it away" (8:6-7). Love is a force that's irresistible and immovable. Even as you cannot refuse death's call, neither can you refuse love's call. Elsewhere in Scripture we read,

> In all these things we are more than conquerors through him who loved us. For I am convinced that neither death nor life, neither angels nor demons, neither the present nor the future, nor any powers, neither height nor depth, nor anything else in all creation, will be able to separate us from the love of God that is in Christ Jesus our Lord (Rom. 8:37-39).

Again, Christian, do you recognize that the most zealous commitment shared by the world's most committed lovers is merely a dim picture of Christ's commitment to love us? Though God does offer some fulfillment in this life, complete fulfillment comes later. None of our longings will be perfectly satisfied now, including our longings for love. But they will be.

One of the last verses in the Bible reminds us of this promise: "I saw the Holy City, the new Jerusalem, coming down out of heaven from God, prepared as a bride beautifully dressed for her husband" (Rev. 21:2).

Let us pray:

Lord, forgive us for the ways that we wrongly indulge in physical intimacy or deny ourselves of it. Lord, you know the truth of how you made us. And we pray that in your great love you would teach us those truths and fill us with your Spirit, so that we can live as the people you mean us to be. Lord, we need your help in our relationships. You know all the broken relationships either in our own lives or in the lives of those we love. We pray that your Holy Spirit would come and change us. Teach us more about ourselves, about you, and about your love for us. We praise you as the completely lovely and loving God. We thank you for revealing yourself as our bridegroom in Jesus Christ. And in his name we pray. Amen.

Questions for Reflection

1. In terms of the cultural products we consume (watching movies, listening to music, buying magazines, etc.) and the lives we live (male/female friendships, dating, etc.), how should the church defy the sexual revolution? How should

the church look different from the world in its approach to sexuality? What's the positive message the church should proclaim in this process?

2. What's the best way to read Song of Songs? As an allegory, a typology, a story, or a collection of love poems? What difference does this make?

3. If you are married, let's be creative for a moment: how can you incorporate Song of Songs into your marriage?

4. Who has a more pleasure-promising and appetite-fulfilling view of sex: the Bible, or the culture at large? Defend your answer.

5. How can the church subtly deny, repress, or forget about the message of Song of Songs?

6. What are the main lessons Song of Songs teaches about sex for the married couple?

7. In what sense do marriage and physical intimacy bring *shalom* to a man or a woman? If you are married, how can you pray, work, and strategize toward making this more of a reality in your relationship with your spouse?

8. Does a married couple's sexual life contribute to their emotional and spiritual lives together, or do their emotional and spiritual lives contribute to the sexual life together? How so?

9. What does Song of Songs teach us about Christ's love for the church? How should it encourage us to better love Christ?

PART FOUR
BIG HOPES

THE MESSAGE OF ISAIAH: MESSIAH

23

THE MESSAGE OF ISAIAH: MESSIAH

SHOULDN'T WE KNOW BETTER THAN TO TRUST ANYONE?[1]

I wonder what disappointments you carry with you right now.

Some of life's most serious disappointments have to do with other people. On the one hand, we think of miscarriages of trust that occur on an epic scale. After Germany's defeat in World War I, for instance, its economy was in complete ruins. Inflation rose at runaway rates, and people literally had to wheelbarrow currency to the store to buy bread. Then the nation put its trust in someone who promised hope. The people democratically elected the leader of the Nationalist Social Party, Adolf Hitler. And Hitler betrayed that national trust most tragically.

On the other hand, and much more commonly, we think of miscarriages of trust that occur on a personal level. These are not the things that show up on the cover of news magazines or in the history books. And yet they impact our lives and who we are deeply. We have all experienced it: someone in whom we have put our trust disappoints that trust. They hurt that trust. They betray it.

The book of Proverbs tells us that "hope deferred makes the heart sick" (Prov. 13:12). Have you ever had that kind of heart-sickness? You waited for someone, but they did not come. You planned the event, but they didn't show up. You invested in the relationship, but they were not faithful. They said they would never do it again, but they did. Perhaps you even gave extra hope and extra trust. And even that they betrayed.

That person once seemed so promising, but now the sum and substance of them is only a disappointment.

Why are we so focused on people? What gets our hopes in others so high,

---

[1] This sermon was originally preached on April 6, 1997, at Capitol Hill Baptist Church in Washington, D.C.

particularly when we are aware of our own foibles? Shouldn't we know better? Sometimes, it seems that we just can't avoid trusting and hoping in people. We are hurtling into an unknown future, and so it's natural to place our hope in some of our fellow pilgrims. We don't know what's going to happen, but at least we know these people around us. Maybe they are worthy of our trust, our hope, our faith. But then disappointment comes.

We could simply reject trusting and hoping in others entirely and consign ourselves to skepticism. The playwright Anton Chekhov, referring to how dark some literature can be, said, "When all is said and done, no literature can outdo the cynicism of real life; you won't intoxicate with one glass someone who has already drunk up a whole barrel." Or, as H. L. Mencken put it, "A cynic is a man who, when he smells flowers, looks around for a coffin."

Have we developed that kind of cynicism toward people? How can we trust anyone in the face of so much disappointment? Indeed, that precarious balance between realistic trust and glum cynicism is razor thin.

INTRODUCING ISAIAH

For a Christian, the themes of trust and hope are difficult to get away from. They're always coming up! We look at them again in this new series through the Old Testament's Major Prophets titled "Big Hopes." The books of Isaiah, Jeremiah, Ezekiel, and Daniel are called the Major Prophets not because of a particular rank the prophets held in the Israeli military, nor because they were more important than other prophets in the Old Testament, but because their books are longer. That's it! (Lamentations, a short song of sorrow written by Jeremiah, is also included in this group.) These books provide four powerful pictures of hope. Each one contrasts our true hope with other things that can look similar and be alluring but that finally disappoint.

Here, we will look at that masterpiece of the Old Testament, the book of Isaiah.

Let me give you a basic outline of Isaiah. It has sixty-six chapters. And with the exception of four chapters in the middle, the entire book is made up of poetry, oracles, and prophecy. Chapters 1–35 consist of prophecy and poetry about God and his expression toward his people. Then in chapters 36–39, this middle section, the poetry stops and a dramatic historical event is recorded: the siege of Jerusalem by the Assyrians. In chapters 40–66, the prophecy and poetry return. On a broad scale, we can say that the first half of Isaiah (1–35) contains more doom and gloom, while the second half (40–66) offers more reason for hope. Yet in all of it, the people of Judah are enticed to trust in things they should not trust in.

The book does not occur in *strict* chronological order. Sometimes people, particularly young Christians, turn to the Old Testament and assume that it flows in chronological order, and that whatever they read about in chapter 4 must have occurred after what they read about in chapter 2. But that's not the case in a book like Isaiah. Having said that, we will see that it does follow a *general* historical order.

The book was written during the second half of the eighth century B.C. (approximately 750–700 B.C.). During that time, five different kings reigned in the southern kingdom of Judah, the kingdom built around Jerusalem.

Isaiah's ministry began at the end of King Uzziah's reign, and we think it ended during King Manasseh's reign. Uzziah had reigned for fifty-two years. He was a great king who, in many ways, brought the splendor of Solomon back to the nation (Solomon had been gone for two centuries). During Uzziah's reign, Judah's historically mighty neighbor to the southwest, Egypt, had been faltering; while its up-and-coming mighty neighbor to the northeast, Assyria, was preoccupied with other matters. So Uzziah took advantage of the situation by regaining territory and political prestige for the nation of Judah. His death, around 745 B.C., then left something of a power vacuum. Isaiah describes the beginning of his own ministry in chapter 6 with these famous words: "In the year that king Uzziah died, I saw the Lord seated on the throne, high and exalted, and the train of his robe filled the temple" (6:1).

King Jotham, Uzziah's son, followed; he reigned for sixteen years and continued his father's programs.

King Ahaz, Jotham's son, succeeded him and also reigned sixteen years. By this point, the Assyrian empire had grown in strength and imperial ambition. It gobbled up the northern kingdom and eventually pushed its borders to within eight miles of the walls of Jerusalem. Ahaz then made a bad decision. He decided to put his trust in the Assyrian emperor. So he made a treaty with him, paid tribute to him, and even sent Israelites to Assyria to study their styles of worship to bring back to Jerusalem! In short, he made Judah a vassal of Assyria and Assyria's gods. Ahaz died around 715 B.C.

Ahaz's son Hezekiah followed him, and King Hezekiah reigned twenty-nine years as one of Judah's best kings. It was during his reign that the main historical crisis of the book of Isaiah occurred: the siege of Jerusalem by the Assyrians (chapters 36–37). In a sense, Hezekiah provoked the siege of Jerusalem exactly because he was a godly king. He would not abide the false worship or false gods of his father's reign any longer. Instead, he led the nation in putting their hope once more in the Lord by refusing to pay tribute to the foreign king. In response, almost two hundred thousand Assyrian troops descended upon the land of Palestine. They wiped out fortified city after fortified city until Jerusalem was fairly well alone and surrounded. We will come back to this story later.

Hezekiah's evil son Manasseh followed him, and he reigned fifty-five years. Tradition has it that early in King Manasseh's reign, he captured and imprisoned Isaiah because he hated Isaiah's prophecies against the false worship that Manasseh encouraged. Tradition also says that the king had Isaiah sawn in two, which may be what the author of Hebrews refers to when he speaks of great individuals of the faith being sawn in two (Heb. 11:37).

But this book is not finally about the geopolitical situation of Isaiah's day. That is simply the stage on which the drama of Isaiah unfolds. The prophet is very clear as to what his vision is about. The book begins, "The vision concerning Judah and Jerusalem that Isaiah son of Amoz saw during the reigns of Uzziah, Jotham, Ahaz and Hezekiah, kings of Judah" (1:1). It's a vision about Judah and Jerusalem. Specifically, it's about Judah and Jerusalem's rebellion: "See how the faithful city has become a harlot! She once was full of justice; righteousness used to dwell in her—but now murderers!" (1:21).

God uses Isaiah to pronounce these types of condemnations on his people throughout the book. In chapter 5, they are called a vineyard which, though planted by God, yields only bad fruit (5:4). God "looked for justice, but saw bloodshed; for righteousness, but heard cries of distress" (5:7).

In chapter 48, the Lord says to them, "Well do I know how treacherous you are; you were called a rebel from birth" (48:8).

In chapter 59, Isaiah tells the people, "But your iniquities have separated you from your God; your sins have hidden his face from you, so that he will not hear" (59:2). Then several verses later, he says about them,

> Their feet rush into sin;
>   they are swift to shed innocent blood.
> Their thoughts are evil thoughts;
>   ruin and destruction mark their ways.
> The way of peace they do not know;
>   there is no justice in their paths.
> They have turned them into crooked roads;
>   no one who walks in them will know peace (59:7-8; cf. Rom. 3:15-17).

And in chapter 64, Isaiah laments,

> All of us have become like one who is unclean,
>   and all our righteous acts are like filthy rags;
> we all shrivel up like a leaf,
>   and like the wind our sins sweep us away.

No one calls on your name
    or strives to lay hold of you;
for you have hidden your face from us
    and made us waste away because of our sins (64:6-7).

That was the situation in which God called Isaiah to be a prophet. Concerning the people of Isaiah's day, we want to know what both the problem and solution were. Concerning us, we want to know, in whom shall we place our trust and hope? This is what we want to learn from Isaiah.

THE PROBLEM: TRUSTING THE WRONG THINGS

So how did the people of God specifically rebel? In short, God's people trusted in the wrong things. We see that back at the very beginning of the book:

Hear, O heavens! Listen, O earth!
    For the LORD has spoken:
"I reared children and brought them up,
    but they have rebelled against me.
The ox knows his master,
    the donkey his owner's manger,
but Israel does not know,
    my people do not understand."

Ah, sinful nation,
    a people loaded with guilt,
a brood of evildoers,
    children given to corruption!
They have forsaken the LORD;
    they have spurned the Holy One of Israel
    and turned their backs on him (1:2-4).

Trusting Other Kings

When the people of Judah turned their backs on God, to whom did they turn? They turned to foreign kings. As the Assyrian threat became more and more real, they wanted to trust the king of Egypt. He had chariots and horsemen. He could help. Right? Wrong! Isaiah warns, "Woe to those who go down to Egypt for help, who rely on horses, who trust in the multitude of their chariots and in the great strength of their horsemen, but do not look to the Holy One of Israel, or seek help from the LORD" (31:1). Then two verses later: "But the Egyptians are men and not God; their horses are flesh and not spirit. When the LORD stretches out his hand, he who helps will stumble, he who is helped will fall; both will perish together" (31:3).

Then they trusted in the king of Assyria. Ahaz made a treaty with Assyria to be Judah's overlord and protector—to keep them safe.

Then, when that whole Assyria thing didn't work out, they trusted in Babylon. In the first half of the book (1–39), Assyria is the region's prevailing superpower. But by the middle of the book, soon after the siege of Jerusalem is lifted, Assyria begins to crumble and Babylon begins to emerge. In the second half of the book, then, Babylon is more prominent. Two Babylonian ambassadors visit Hezekiah in Judah in chapter 39, perhaps to get him to join into a treaty against Assyria. It's around this time, or shortly thereafter, that the Jewish nation begins trusting in Babylon to help them.

Trusting Other Gods

But not only did the Jews trust in other kings, they trusted in other gods. So throughout the book, Isaiah attacks the people's idolatry. The people are "full of superstitions" (2:6). "Their land is full of idols; they bow down to the work of their hands, to what their fingers have made" (2:8). Clearly, Isaiah wants them to see the stupidity of what they are doing: "You are worshiping what your hands have made!" Yet that is exactly what happens when you or I worship something our hands produce, whether money, jobs, or even our children: the "creator" worships something he has "created."

The Jews also consulted spiritists: "When men tell you to consult mediums and spiritists, who whisper and mutter, should not a people inquire of their God? Why consult the dead on behalf of the living?" (8:19).

The land was filled with altar stones, Asherah poles, and incense altars (27:9).

The people even tried to make an agreement with death!

> Therefore hear the word of the LORD, you scoffers
>   who rule this people in Jerusalem.
> You boast, "We have entered into a covenant with death,
>   with the grave we have made an agreement.
> When an overwhelming scourge sweeps by,
>   it cannot touch us,
> for we have made a lie our refuge
>   and falsehood our hiding place" (28:14-15).

And we could keep going. Chapters 41, 44, 57, and 65 all have long sections about idolatry, where the people worshiped and gave themselves over to things that were not God.[2]

Trusting Themselves

Of course, the people and their leaders did not simply trust foreign kings and foreign gods, they trusted themselves. In chapter 22, Isaiah observes that as the people prepared to defend themselves (a good thing), they did not simultaneously trust in God to be their defender (a very bad thing!):

And you looked in that day
    to the weapons in the Palace of the Forest;
you saw that the City of David
    had many breaches in its defenses;
you stored up water
    in the Lower Pool.
You counted the buildings in Jerusalem
    and tore down houses to strengthen the wall.
You built a reservoir between the two walls
    for the water of the Old Pool,
but you did not look to the One who made it,
    or have regard for the One who planned it long ago (22:8-11).

He again warns the people against self-reliance in chapter 29. God gives them a scroll filled with his words, but they devise every excuse they can to avoid reading it:

The LORD has brought over you a deep sleep:
He has sealed your eyes (the prophets);
he has covered your heads (the seers).

For you this whole vision is nothing but words sealed in a scroll. And if you give the scroll to someone who can read, and say to him, "Read this, please," he will answer, "I can't; it is sealed." Or if you give the scroll to someone who cannot read, and say, "Read this, please," he will answer, "I don't know how to read."

The Lord says:

"These people come near to me with their mouth
    and honor me with their lips,
    but their hearts are far from me.

---

[2] 41:22-24; 44:9-20; 57:6-9; 65:2-5.

Their worship of me
> is made up only of rules taught by men.
Therefore once more I will astound these people
> with wonder upon wonder;
the wisdom of the wise will perish,
> the intelligence of the intelligent will vanish."
Woe to those who go to great depths
> to hide their plans from the LORD,
who do their work in darkness and think,
> "Who sees us? Who will know?"
You turn things upside down,
> as if the potter were thought to be like the clay!
Shall what is formed say to him who formed it,
> "He did not make me"?
Can the pot say of the potter, "He knows nothing"? (29:10-16).

Trusting Their Own Unfaithful Leaders

The people even trusted, in the wrong way, the good gifts that God gave them—their own leaders, for instance. When the leaders' plans differed from God's plans, the people should have demonstrated whom they truly trusted by refusing to follow their leaders into disobedience (see 3:1-3, 14). But they didn't; they followed their leaders.

Admittedly, such opportunities to prove where our ultimate allegiance lies come subtly and surprisingly. Yet these occasions do help us discern whether we are rightly trusting or wrongly trusting the leader God has provided. Whenever God's appointed leader takes the people of God *away* from God's ways, we must not follow him. Our primary allegiance must remain with God.

Ahaz was one king in a line of kings installed by God. Yet he forsook God. And the people followed him. How could they have known better? They *should* have known better by hearing the Word of God. Had their hearts and hopes been trained on what God had revealed about himself in his Word, had they trusted in God and hoped in him as their protection, they would not have been led astray.

Whom Shall We Trust?

As Christians, we are not exactly the Old Testament people of Judah, but we are similar. We are God's special people, and we are often tempted, individually and corporately, to put our trust in the wrong things.

In your own life, what motivates you? What are your real goals, your real ambitions, your real purposes? And what do you trust in to accomplish those ends? Is what you are hoping in enough to focus your whole being? And is what you are trusting in enough to carry you throughout your life? Maybe it seems so for a while. Perhaps the king of Egypt or Assyria seemed helpful for a time. But time would tell. What will time reveal in *your* life about what *you* are trusting in?

What about the church? Many churches hope in many things other than God. Is it music? Is it growth? In our culture, growing numbers—written figures—can be idols much more easily than carved figures. Do we assume that as long as the number of people walking through the door on Sunday mornings increases we must be doing the right thing? What is the church tempted to trust in?

I recently spoke with a friend who was preparing to publish an article in a journal focused on foreign missions on the uniqueness and exclusivity of the Christian gospel. He was planning on titling the article "Tell Me the Old, Old Story" (based on the old hymn by that name) because it emphasized the gospel's unchanging nature. Well, that's a great thesis, I told him, but I was concerned that the title itself traded pretty heavily on *sentimentalism* as the ally and proof of the gospel. Those words—"Tell me the old, old story"—ask us to believe in the credibility of Christ's exclusive claims based on the fact that we have warm memories of long ago or childhood days. But, friend, we must be careful before we trust in sentiment. Sentiments are not always good. Not everything our grandmother told us was true.

As Christians, we must trust the gospel of Jesus Christ alone. There's finally no pastor you can have, no building renovations you can undergo, no certain programs that you can adopt, that will be worthy of your trust. God alone is worthy of your trust. And that's exactly what Isaiah goes on to say.

THE SOLUTION: TRUSTING GOD

God alone was the right focus of his people's hope, and therefore he alone was the right object of their trust.

In chapter 40, Isaiah sets the idols side by side with God in order to demonstrate the absolute futility and folly of trusting anything other than the everlasting God, the Creator of the ends of the earth:

> To whom, then, will you compare God?
>   What image will you compare him to?
> As for an idol, a craftsman casts it,
>   and a goldsmith overlays it with gold
>   and fashions silver chains for it.

A man too poor to present such an offering
> selects wood that will not rot.
He looks for a skilled craftsman
> to set up an idol that will not topple.

Do you not know?
> Have you not heard?
Has it not been told you from the beginning?
> Have you not understood since the earth was founded?
He sits enthroned above the circle of the earth,
> and its people are like grasshoppers.
He stretches out the heavens like a canopy,
> and spreads them out like a tent to live in.
He brings princes to naught
> and reduces the rulers of this world to nothing.
No sooner are they planted,
> no sooner are they sown,
> no sooner do they take root in the ground,
than he blows on them and they wither,
> and a whirlwind sweeps them away like chaff.

"To whom will you compare me?
> Or who is my equal?" says the Holy One. . . .

Do you not know?
> Have you not heard?
The LORD is the everlasting God,
> the Creator of the ends of the earth.
He will not grow tired or weary,
> and his understanding no one can fathom (40:18-25, 28).

The idols they had been trusting in were nothing compared to the real God![3]

It was no accident that Isaiah had his great vision of God when he did. When the king whom the people had trusted died, Isaiah was allowed to see the *real* king, seated high and lifted up:

In the year that King Uzziah died, I saw the Lord seated on a throne, high and exalted, and the train of his robe filled the temple. Above him were seraphs, each with six wings: With two wings they covered their faces, with two they covered their feet, and with two they were flying. And they were calling to one another:

---

[3] See 43:10, 15; 44:6-21; 45:5-7, 18, 20-21; 46:1-9; 48:5-15; 51:12-13.

> "Holy, holy, holy is the LORD Almighty;
>   the whole earth is full of his glory."

At the sound of their voices the doorposts and thresholds shook and the temple was filled with smoke (6:1-4).

This is the One whom God's people should have always trusted in. It was never to be a great political leader like Uzziah, as godly as he may have been. After all, he died! That's not an insignificant fact. God called them to trust himself alone, and he used Isaiah to show that he alone was uniquely worthy of their trust.

Trusting God's Coming Judgment

So he said he would come in judgment, both upon his own people and upon the nations. Much of this book is filled with oracles promising the judgment of God. "The LORD has a day of vengeance," Isaiah says (34:8).

In chapters 13–24, Isaiah promises God's judgment upon nation after nation. The thunder of God's wrath begins to roll in Babylon in chapter 13. It rolls on through Assyria, Moab, Damascus, Cush, Egypt, Babylon again, Edom, and Arabia in the following chapters. In chapter 22, Jerusalem hears the rumble of God's judgment. Tyre hears it in chapter 23. And then this vision of the storm of God's judgment reaches its cataclysmic finale in chapter 24:

> See, the LORD is going to lay waste the earth
>   and devastate it;
> he will ruin its face
>   and scatter its inhabitants—
> it will be the same
>   for priest as for people,
>   for master as for servant,
>   for mistress as for maid,
>   for seller as for buyer,
>   for borrower as for lender,
>   for debtor as for creditor.
> The earth will be completely laid waste
>   and totally plundered.
>   The LORD has spoken this word (24:1-3).

Trusting God's Coming Deliverance and Salvation

God alone should be trusted not only because he is the one who will bring judgment: he is also the one who will bring deliverance and salvation.

Immediately before the thunder of God's judgment sounds in chapter 13, Isaiah lets us hear a song that will be sung on a future day of deliverance: "Surely God is my salvation; I will trust and not be afraid. The LORD, the LORD, is my strength and my song; he has become my salvation."[4]

We hear something similar in chapter 33: "The LORD is our judge, the LORD is our lawgiver, the LORD is our king; it is he who will save us" (33:22).

It is this very lesson that God teaches in dramatic historical fashion at the center of the book. He promises to save, and then he keeps his promise. As we saw earlier, the Assyrian troops had surrounded Jerusalem. And now, picking the story up, we find that the Assyrian commander proceeds to threaten the city's inhabitants, speaking in Hebrew. Several Israelite leaders ask the commander to speak in Aramaic, in order not to disturb the masses of listening Israelites, most of whom could not understand Aramaic; but he continues in Hebrew, wanting all the people to hear. He shouts,

> "Do not let Hezekiah mislead you when he says, 'The LORD will deliver us.' Has the god of any nation ever delivered his land from the hand of the king of Assyria? Where are the gods of Hamath and Arpad? Where are the gods of Sepharvaim? Have they rescued Samaria from my hand? Who of all the gods of these countries has been able to save his land from me? How then can the LORD deliver Jerusalem from my hand?" (36:18-20).

He really should not have said that! Clearly, Assyria was a very strong power, but when we hear him put Assyria's army beyond the Lord's ability to deliver, we know he has gone one step too far.

Sure enough, in the very next chapter the Lord tells Isaiah to tell King Hezekiah to tell the king of Assyria what God thinks of Assyria's threat:

> Then Isaiah son of Amoz sent a message to Hezekiah: "This is what the LORD, the God of Israel, says: Because you have prayed to me concerning Sennacherib king of Assyria, this is the word the LORD has spoken against him:
>
> > "The Virgin Daughter of Zion
> >   despises and mocks you.
> > The Daughter of Jerusalem
> >   tosses her head as you flee . . ." (37:21-22).

Now remember, this is being said to a king who has surrounded Jerusalem with a hundred and eighty-five thousand troops!

---

[4] 12:2; see also 25:8-9; 26.

"Who is it you have insulted and blasphemed?
  Against whom have you raised your voice
and lifted your eyes in pride?
  Against the Holy One of Israel!
By your messengers
  you have heaped insults on the Lord.
And you have said,
  'With my many chariots
I have ascended the heights of the mountains,
  the utmost heights of Lebanon.
I have cut down its tallest cedars,
  the choicest of its pines.
I have reached its remotest heights,
  the finest of its forests.
I have dug wells in foreign lands
  and drunk the water there.
With the soles of my feet
  I have dried up all the streams of Egypt.'

"Have you not heard?
  Long ago I ordained it.
In days of old I planned it;
  now I have brought it to pass,
that you have turned fortified cities
  into piles of stone.
Their people, drained of power,
  are dismayed and put to shame.
They are like plants in the field,
  like tender green shoots,
like grass sprouting on the roof,
  scorched before it grows up.

"But I know where you stay
  and when you come and go
  and how you rage against me.
Because you rage against me
  and because your insolence has reached my ears,
I will put my hook in your nose
  and my bit in your mouth,
and I will make you return
  by the way you came" (37:23-29).

And this is exactly what happens. God delivers Jerusalem from a hundred and eighty-five thousand Assyrian troops:

> Then the angel of the LORD went out and put to death a hundred and eighty-five thousand men in the Assyrian camp. When the people got up the next morning— there were all the dead bodies! So Sennacherib king of Assyria broke camp and withdrew. He returned to Nineveh and stayed there.
>
> One day, while he was worshiping in the temple of his god Nisroch, his sons Adrammelech and Sharezer cut him down with the sword, and they escaped to the land of Ararat. And Esarhaddon his son succeeded him as king (37:36-38).

When Jerusalem had no other hope, God came as their helper.

Whom Shall We Trust?

As we read through the book of Isaiah, we see that God is utterly unique. There is no one like him. No one else has the moral purity of God. No one else is as righteous as God. And yet no one else is as loving as God. Indeed, one of the most striking things about the book of Isaiah is the tenacity of God's love for his unfaithful people. Again and again they turn from him and spurn him. They trust in other things. And again and again God tenaciously pursues them.

Try thinking of some people in your own life who always seem to be right. Chances are, they are somewhat irritating to you. Their rightness may be a bit too angular. They are right at some of the wrong times. Sometimes you may think that their perception of their rightness is not so right after all.

On the other hand, try thinking of some people in your life who are always loving. People who you know love you without question. They are unfailing in it. Now, I wonder if you ever feel that such people can actually be a bit too indulgent. Maybe they have not challenged you when they should have. They always want you to be certain that they love you, so they have let you get away with things they should not have.

In the book of Isaiah, we see a picture of God that shows us why he is so worthy of his people's trust. He's not like those other kings. He's certainly not like those false idols. He's not even like our best friends who are most right or most loving. He is perfectly right and perfectly loving all the time! It's hard to conceive of, because we don't experience it with anyone around us—ever! But that's the picture Isaiah presents: the God who is perfectly holy and perfectly loving.

Just a few days ago, I attended a wedding in Louisville, Kentucky, and it was a beautiful affair. It was held in a lovely church building and, like most weddings, everything was finely tuned. There was beautiful music. Everybody knew exactly where to stand. The readings were thoughtfully selected and chosen. The food afterward was carefully planned and presented. And yet all of this care for the whole event really focused on the couple themselves. They stood in the middle. We looked at them. We listened for what they would say.

In a sense, Isaiah is doing that. We watch the elaborate work and planning of God throughout the book; but in the end, it's as if he wants us to focus on something even more particularly. God is the solution to the people's trust problem, yes, but he sharpens the focus more than that. The solution isn't just to say "God." The actual fulcrum of the hope for his people seems to come in a person, a Messiah.

THE SOLUTION SHARPENED: HOPING AND TRUSTING IN CHRIST

As you read through the book of Isaiah, it gradually becomes clear that God's great plan for his people and for the world narrows in on one person. "See, I lay a stone in Zion, a tested stone, a precious cornerstone for a sure foundation; the one who trusts will never be dismayed" (28:16).

A stone? A tested stone? A precious cornerstone?

The people had an innate sense for how God's whole plan would turn on an individual, whether one of their own kings or a foreign king. Of course, that innate sense was not unique to them. All of our hearts appear to have this built-in desire to hope and trust in some individual whom we can know and who will know and care for us. We place these hopes on everyone from presidential candidates to sports stars.

Hoping in a Coming Messiah-King

In the first half of Isaiah, the prophet instructs the people to look to a messiah figure. Now, in the Old Testament, every king of Israel and Judah was a "messiah." Messiah simply means "anointed one." But this was *the* Messiah. This was the King of kings that God revealed to Isaiah. "A king will reign in righteousness and rulers will rule with justice" (32:1).

But this coming one would be far more than just a good king:

> For to us a child is born,
>   to us a son is given,
>   and the government will be on his shoulders.
> And he will be called
>   Wonderful Counselor, Mighty God,
>   Everlasting Father, Prince of Peace.
> Of the increase of his government and peace
>   there will be no end.

He will reign on David's throne
   and over his kingdom,
establishing and upholding it
   with justice and righteousness
   from that time on and forever (9:6-7).

Indeed, this one called "Wonderful Counselor" and "Mighty God" would have the Spirit of God upon him in a special way: "The Spirit of the LORD will rest on him—the Spirit of wisdom and of understanding, the Spirit of counsel and of power, the Spirit of knowledge and of the fear of the LORD" (11:2; cf. 11:1-5).

Hoping in a Coming Servant

God promised his people this coming kingly figure; but as we continue reading into the second half of Isaiah, we find that another figure emerges, one that God calls "my servant." This servant would also have God's Spirit upon him, and he too would bring justice to the nations (see 42:1-4). He would also save both Jews and Gentiles, bringing salvation to the ends of the earth (see 49:1-7).

But not all things would be bright for this servant. He would listen to *God,* but not everyone would listen to *him:*

The Sovereign LORD has given me an instructed tongue,
   to know the word that sustains the weary.
He wakens me morning by morning,
   wakens my ear to listen like one being taught.
The Sovereign LORD has opened my ears,
   and I have not been rebellious;
   I have not drawn back.
I offered my back to those who beat me,
   my cheeks to those who pulled out my beard;
I did not hide my face from mocking and spitting.
Because the Sovereign LORD helps me,
   I will not be disgraced.
Therefore have I set my face like flint,
   and I know I will not be put to shame.
He who vindicates me is near.
   Who then will bring charges against me?
   Let us face each other!
Who is my accuser?
   Let him confront me!
It is the Sovereign LORD who helps me.
   Who is he that will condemn me?

They will all wear out like a garment;
>   the moths will eat them up.

Who among you fears the LORD
>   and obeys the word of his servant? (50:4-10a).

The question that cries out throughout the book of Isaiah is this: how would a holy God forgive and restore the very people he charges with rebellion? They would even beat, mock, and spit upon this servant!

Well, the answer comes through this same servant, particularly in the remarkable passage we often read in church—Isaiah 52:13–53:12. Right now, let's look at just the end: "After the suffering of his soul, he will see the light of life and be satisfied; by his knowledge my righteous servant will justify many, and he will bear their iniquities" (53:11). That very beating, mocking, and spitting, it turns out, would serve an unexpected end.

In Isaiah, God's solution is not simply an abstract, unfocused picture of himself as a deliverer; it is a focused picture of a person, a servant. This servant listens perfectly to God and yet he suffers and is rejected in order to bear the sins of God's people.

Hoping in the Messiah-King and Servant as One!

What's most remarkable, this *king* on whom the Spirit rests and this *servant* on whom the Spirit rests are really the same person! What a marvelous union! It points us toward the apostle John's vision in Revelation 5, where a heavenly elder tells John that the Lion of the tribe of Judah has triumphed. John looks to see the lion, but what does he see instead? A lamb that was slain. The lamb is the lion (see Rev. 5:6-7). In the same way, a reader of the first half of Isaiah might ask, where is this great King? Look to the second half, and see this suffering Servant who bears the iniquity of the people. He is the King!

Indeed, we even see that he is "Immanuel" (7:14). He is "God with us." He is, as we saw earlier, the "Mighty God" (9:6). This is the one who will bring salvation to the ends of the earth and will deliver all of us! That's the message of the book of Isaiah.

Hoping in Jesus as This One

And who is this one? In chapter 61, we are given a tremendous clue:

>   The Spirit of the Sovereign LORD is on me,
>   because the LORD has anointed me
>   to preach good news to the poor.

> He has sent me to bind up the brokenhearted,
>   to proclaim freedom for the captives
>   and release from darkness for the prisoners,
> to proclaim the year of the LORD's favor
>   and the day of vengeance of our God,
> to comfort all who mourn (61:1-2).

Then, hundreds of years after Isaiah wrote these words, Luke recorded this account in the life of Jesus of Nazareth. After describing the episode in which Jesus resists Satan's temptation in the wilderness, Luke proceeds to tell us about the beginning of Jesus' public ministry:

> Jesus returned to Galilee in the power of the Spirit, and news about him spread through the whole countryside. He taught in their synagogues, and everyone praised him.
>
> He went to Nazareth, where he had been brought up, and on the Sabbath day he went into the synagogue, as was his custom. And he stood up to read. The scroll of the prophet Isaiah was handed to him. Unrolling it, he found the place where it is written:
>
> > "The Spirit of the Lord is on me,
> >   because he has anointed me
> >   to preach good news to the poor.
> > He has sent me to proclaim freedom for the prisoners
> >   and recovery of sight for the blind,
> > to release the oppressed,
> >   to proclaim the year of the Lord's favor."
>
> Then he rolled up the scroll, gave it back to the attendant and sat down. The eyes of everyone in the synagogue were fastened on him, and he began by saying to them, "Today this scripture is fulfilled in your hearing" (Luke 4:14-21).

Isaiah 61 was fulfilled in Jesus! Jesus is the King. Jesus is the Servant. He came for us, his people.

In Whom Shall We Hope?

Christianity is not an abstract set of ideas; Isaiah shows us that God is a tenacious, personal lover. He made us. He knows our hurts, our pains, our loves. He knows everything about us, including our sin.

Yet he is also holy, and so he had to devise a way to love unholy us while also maintaining his own justice and righteousness. How did he do it? In Christ, God became man, lived a perfect life, and died on the cross, taking on himself the sins of all those who would ever repent and believe in him. In the cross of Christ, the requirements of God's holiness and God's love were both satisfied, so that sinners can be forgiven. Do you want the forgiveness of God? Jesus said that he came for the sick, not the healthy; for sinners, not the righteous. Are you sick and sinful? Then repent of your sins and trust in Christ. Look to this Servant who will bear your sins and who will one day come again to reign victoriously as the King of kings and Lord of lords.

Christianity is centered on Jesus as the Messiah-King and Servant who personally reintroduces us to God, which is why Christianity itself is so well modeled in a collection of people, like a church. It is more than an individual working through the four points of a gospel outline—God, man, Christ, response—or making some decision, as important as those things are. Christianity is best seen in our ongoing interaction with one another, interactions that show the world something about the King and Servant himself, how he has loved us, and what it means to know him.

CONCLUSION

As I read Isaiah this week, I was struck, first, by how much it refers to the rebellion of God's people against him. But second, I was struck by how much more emphasis is given to both God's judgment *against* and love *for* his people. This book is far more about God's tenacious concern in judgment and love for his people than about his people's love for him. Surprisingly, for all the poetry in this book, you will find hardly any praise. There are only two or three psalms of praise in the whole book. Instead, the book is filled with God speaking to his people, telling them about himself and his love for them, whether that love is expressed through his judgment upon their evil or through his promises of future deliverance. This book is all about God's love for his people; it isn't about his people's love for him. Likening his people to a vineyard, God says, "I, the LORD, watch over it; I water it continually. I guard it day and night so that no one may harm it" (Isa. 27:3).

If we want to have any hope, we must ground it not in ourselves but in him. Sadly, so much of what passes for Christianity does the opposite. Have you ever noticed how many Christian songs are about our love for God? They profess to God how delighted we are to be in his presence, how much we love him, how much we like to talk with him, how much we like to walk with him, how much we like to *whatever* with him. None of these things are bad in and of themselves. But as with God's Old Testament people, our only hope is in God's tenacious, pursuing love for us, which we see displayed most remarkably in Christ. We did not go and pull Jesus down from heaven. The Servant came. The Servant took on flesh. The Servant went to the cross and died, bearing the iniquity of his people. And in three days, the Servant, who is really the King, arose, and he will come again to gather his people and establish his rule with power!

So who are the people that God loves? Who are the focus of his concern in this book? It is those who repent of their sins: "'The Redeemer will come to Zion, to those in Jacob who repent of their sins,' declares the LORD" (59:20).

But notice, these "repenters" include more than the people of Israel:

The Sovereign LORD declares—
    he who gathers the exiles of Israel:
"I will gather still others to them
    besides those already gathered" (56:8).

But you are our Father,
    though Abraham does not know us
    or Israel acknowledge us;
you, O LORD, are our Father,
    our Redeemer from of old is your name (63:16).

These "repenters" are the ones who are humble and contrite:

"This is the one I esteem:
    he who is humble and contrite in spirit,
    and trembles at my word" (66:2b).

These "repenters" respond to the Messiah's invitation, and they seek him:

"Come, all you who are thirsty,
    come to the waters;
and you who have no money,
    come, buy and eat!
Come, buy wine and milk
    without money and without cost.
Why spend money on what is not bread,
    and your labor on what does not satisfy?
Listen, listen to me, and eat what is good,
    and your soul will delight in the richest of fare.
Give ear and come to me;
    hear me, that your soul may live.
I will make an everlasting covenant with you,
    my faithful love promised to David. . . ."

Seek the LORD while he may be found;
  call on him while he is near.
Let the wicked forsake his way
  and the evil man his thoughts.
Let him turn to the LORD, and he will have mercy on him,
  and to our God, for he will freely pardon.

"For my thoughts are not your thoughts,
  neither are your ways my ways,"
                                  declares the LORD.
"As the heavens are higher than the earth,
  so are my ways higher than your ways
  and my thoughts than your thoughts.
As the rain and the snow
  come down from heaven,
and do not return to it
  without watering the earth
and making it bud and flourish,
  so that it yields seed for the sower and bread for the eater,
so is my word that goes out from my mouth:
  It will not return to me empty,
but will accomplish what I desire
  and achieve the purpose for which I sent it" (55:1-3, 6-11).

What are you trusting in right now? What are you hoping in? What are you trying to drink to the dregs to fill your soul? "Come," he says to you who are thirsty. Nothing else will fill and satisfy you. And nothing else will bear the weight of your life like God himself, as he has shown us in Jesus.

God loves those who put their trust in him, who hope in him, who are guided by him. That is the message of the Lord through his servant Isaiah for us.

Let us pray:

Lord, help us to see ourselves so we can see how different we are from you. We pray, Lord, that those other things that are eclipsing you in our hearts, those things to which we are too deeply attached, which would obscure you, Father—we pray that in your love you would relocate them. Lord, we pray that you would make yourself the exclusive object of our ultimate devotion. Teach us of your holiness and of your sinfulness and of your love in sending the Servant to bear our iniquities in his body on the tree. Lord, we pray that your Spirit would fill us and would win our hearts to you. We pray, Lord, that we would live showing that we trust in you as individuals and as a church. We pray for Jesus' sake. Amen.

Questions for Reflection

1. As we saw at the beginning, we exercise trust in people both individually and corporately. Do the objects of trust that we share collectively—whether as a nation, a church, or some other group to which we belong—affect the objects of trust we have as individuals? In other words, is there a relationship between our collective trust and our more private trust? Are you tempted to trust what those around you trust? *If so, how will you be able to discern between what is a right object of your trust, and what is not?*

2. What does a wrongful trust in a nation's political leaders look like? What does a right trust in a nation's political leaders look like?

3. These days, Westerners are not trusting in the gods of Assyria or Babylon, or even the gods of other nations, per se. What gods do most people trust in?

4. Is the claim made in this sermon true, that we have a built-in desire to trust some individual? Where can we see evidence for this claim? Where can you see it in your own life?

5. Is self-reliance good?

6. As we have seen, among evangelical churches today, "written figures" (that is, increasing attendance numbers) can be idols much more easily than carved figures. It's easy to assume, in other words, that a church must be doing the right thing as long as the number of people walking through the door on Sunday mornings increases. What's wrong with this way of thinking? What unhelpful paths can it lead down? How can a church avoid turning numerical figures into idols?

7. What's the relationship between hope and trust? Are they the same thing?

8. We have considered the fact that we should trust God because he is the one who will bring judgment. But why exactly should we *trust* the one who will bring *judgment*? What does his judging have to do with our trusting?

9. In this sermon, we have considered the fact that Christ is both King and suffering Servant. How does the dual nature of his work enable him to save condemned sinners like us?

10. Take a few moments to read Isaiah 52:13–53:12. What is this passage talking about? Why is this the very heart of the good news that Christians have to tell the world?

11. If you are a Christian, do you spend more time in your prayers and songs telling God how much you love him, or thanking and praising him for how much he loves you? What's the best way to learn about God's love for us?

12. What do you hope in? Whom do you trust?

THE MESSAGE OF JEREMIAH: JUSTICE

24

THE MESSAGE OF JEREMIAH: JUSTICE

REAL JUSTICE[1]

Injustice is in the eye of the beholder. At least that's how it is regarded in our litigious land these days. The belief that everybody has a right to believe whatever they want to believe has been subtly replaced with the idea that everybody is right. And in a land where everyone "does what is right in their own eyes," to use a biblical phrase, well, doing justice becomes more difficult, if not impossible. After all, how can we say that anything is *wrong?*

Yet some things still *seem* innately wrong to us. Consider the news stories you may have seen on television or read in a newspaper in the last few weeks. I imagine that you read at least one story in which you found yourself feeling deep down inside that "this is wrong" and "it should not be this way." Something of this voice remains in all of us, I believe, calling certain things not just personally offensive but morally evil.

I wonder if you know what a "quisling" is? Vidkun Quisling was a member of the Norwegian army who founded the National Socialist party in Norway in 1933. Six years later he met with Adolf Hitler and urged Hitler to invade and occupy Quisling's own homeland, Norway. Four months later, in April 1940, Hitler did just that. The Germans invaded Norway, thus giving Germany strategic sea and air bases for their operations against the United Kingdom. The invasion was quick, but it was not bloodless. The little nation of Norway suffered a great cost, and many Norwegians would lay Norway's suffering at the feet of Quisling. He served in the puppet government that Germany installed. From that position he became responsible for many atrocities, among them sending hundreds of Jews to concentration camps. When

---

[1] This sermon was originally preached on April 13, 1997, at Capitol Hill Baptist Church in Washington, D.C.

Norway was freed from German rule in May of 1945, Quisling was immediately arrested, tried, found guilty of treason, and executed. You might have heard of him because his name has since passed into infamy in more than one language. "Quisling" can now be found in the English dictionary. It means "traitor," particularly one who collaborates with an enemy to destroy one's own nation—like "Benedict Arnold" in American English.

It is a sad tale, but then Quisling got justice, right? For a time, it looked as if he wouldn't. The might of the German nation supported him and his position in government. But in the end, we can all see, he got justice.

At least, it seems he did.

There *were* all the people who died in prison camps. And there *were* all the people who lost their lives in the invasion. You begin to wonder if one man's execution can really pay for so much suffering and misery. You might even being to wonder, what hope is there for real justice?

That's a good question. What hope is there for justice—real justice!—in a world of slashings and robberies, burnings and bombings, as well as unseen cruelties that are not a crime in any human court. Isn't such justice unattainable and unrealistic?

INTRODUCING JEREMIAH

In our last study, we looked at the prophecy of Isaiah and saw how God provided hope for his people through the promise of a single person. We also saw that this person has come in our Lord Jesus Christ, who revealed God most fully. In this study, we will consider the overwhelming picture of God's justice found in the book of Jeremiah. Jeremiah has fewer chapters than Isaiah, but the text is longer. In fact, it is one of the longest books in the Bible, and I intend to preach on all of it right now!

I should tell you, the books by these prophets are not really books as we think of them today. As you look at Jeremiah, you will not find an introduction, a body, and a conclusion, per se. Perhaps it is better to regard Jeremiah as a collection of speeches, interspersed with several historical episodes in the prophet's life. These speeches, or prophecies, have been compiled and are chronological only in the roughest sense. Chapter 1 presents Jeremiah's original call to prophesy, and chapter 44 records his last prophecy down in Egypt. But at the same time you cannot assume that something you read in chapter 17 happened after something in chapter 13. So, as I say, it is better as we read through this book that we see it as more like a collection of speeches, arranged thematically.

Jeremiah is basically God's message to his people of coming justice.

Whenever we are tempted to feel cynical or jaded about the world we live in, Jeremiah might be good for what ails us. Its message about coming judgment is important for those who long for justice. And it may be even more important for those who have *not* longed for justice, because Jeremiah tells us that justice is coming.

JUSTICE FOR GOD'S PEOPLE (CHAPTERS 1–45, 52)

The first forty-five chapters of Jeremiah clearly focus on God's coming justice against his people.

A little historical background may be helpful here. Jeremiah lived about one hundred years after the prophet Isaiah, who prophesied in the southern kingdom of Judah at the same time the northern kingdom of Israel fell to Assyria, which occurred in 722 B.C. The Assyrians continued to harass the southern kingdom of Judah and Jerusalem through the end of the eighth and much of the seventh century. Yet Assyria gradually declined in power until it was toppled by the Babylonians in 612 B.C. In the midst of Assyria's decline and before Babylon's full maturity, however, Judah took advantage of the situation to regain strength. Josiah became king in 640 B.C., and, as a godly king, he used this power vacuum to help the nation of Judah reform its religious life. He also ended the practice of paying tribute to the emperor of Assyria, because Assyria no longer had the power to back up its demand for tribute.

Yet even if Assyria would fall, Babylon would quickly prove to be an even greater foe. For a time, Egypt seemed to experience a renaissance of its own, and many in Judah began looking to Egypt for protection from Babylon. Yet at the end of the seventh century even Egypt would suffer an embarrassing defeat at the hands of the Babylonians. And Babylon would eventually sack Jerusalem itself.

It was amid these tumultuous times that God brought Jeremiah along.

As I read through this book and thought about the other prophets, it occurred to me that God's great prophets often came amid decay among and around God's people. Whenever the world began to show its passing nature, whenever the supposedly permanent things of life began to fray and crack, that's when God in his mercy would typically provide a glimpse at the things that are lasting. Whenever a nation or government or organization is new, we want to believe that its prospects are bright. But when something slowly plods along and then begins to slope downward toward its final demise, we often find our minds turning to God. So it was when God began speaking through Jeremiah.

The people had enjoyed a great king about a hundred years earlier in Hezekiah, during the days in which Isaiah prophesied. But Hezekiah had been followed by several horrendous kings. Then they had a great king again in Josiah, but Josiah was never able completely to reform the nation. And after his death, the nation quickly lurched back into sin, even terrible sin!

In many ways, the first forty-five of the book's fifty-two chapters read like one long suit for a divorce. God is passionately angry with his people. He promises at one point, "I am beginning to bring disaster on the city that bears my Name" (25:29). Do you see the tragedy here? God decides to bring justice on the very people who bear his name!

The Cause of Judgment

What were the charges? Well, the book lays them out at great length. As I said, the book is not arranged chronologically, yet this theme runs through most of its chapters. It is even enunciated in Jeremiah's original call to prophesy. In the very first chapter, the Lord says, "I will pronounce my judgments on my people because of their wickedness in forsaking me, in burning incense to other gods and in worshiping what their hands have made" (1:16). Jeremiah is called to prophesy precisely because God's people have broken their covenant with the Lord. They have forsaken him. They have worshiped idols. That is God's suit against them. Or, to use his ironic words here, they have worshiped "what their hands have made." What a self-evidently ridiculous thing to do! I mean, have you ever prepared something for the church potluck, like a casserole, and, after taking it out of the oven, fallen to your knees and begun praying to the casserole? No, that's stupid! It's stupid to worship something your own hands have made! Yet this is exactly the charge the all-knowing God brings against his people. Can you imagine?

Actually, if you think about it, you probably *can* imagine such insanity. Not all of our idolatry is as silly as praying to a casserole. There are probably other things that your hands or someone else's hands have made that you found your heart drawn toward.

Well, this self-evidently stupid thing is exactly what God's people were doing. Israel had exchanged the true God for idols. "What fault did your fathers find in me, that they strayed so far from me?" the Lord asks. "They followed worthless idols and became worthless themselves" (Jer. 2:5).

The Lord then breaks this accusation down into two specific charges: "My people have committed two sins: They have forsaken me, the spring of living water, and have dug their own cisterns, broken cisterns that cannot hold water" (2:13). They have, first, forsaken him and, second, dug their own useless wells of life.

Several verses later, God describes what all this means with another shocking image: they are like prostitutes! "On every high hill and under every spreading tree you lay down as a prostitute" (2:20). Clearly, God's words here are stinging. But he continues making his case:

> "How can you say, 'I am not defiled;
>   I have not run after the Baals'?
> See how you behaved in the valley;
>   consider what you have done.
> You are a swift she-camel
>   running here and there,
> a wild donkey accustomed to the desert,
>   sniffing the wind in her craving—
>   in her heat who can restrain her?
> Any males that pursue her need not tire themselves;
>   at mating time they will find her.
> Do not run until your feet are bare
>   and your throat is dry.
> But you said, 'It's no use!
>   I love foreign gods,
>   and I must go after them.'
>
> "As a thief is disgraced when he is caught,
>   so the house of Israel is disgraced—
> they, their kings and their officials,
>   their priests and their prophets.
> They say to wood, 'You are my father,'
>   and to stone, 'You gave me birth.'
> They have turned their backs to me
>   and not their faces;
> yet when they are in trouble, they say,
>   'Come and save us!'
> Where then are the gods you made for yourselves?
>   Let them come if they can save you
>   when you are in trouble!
> For you have as many gods
>   as you have towns, O Judah" (2:23-28).

The indictment continues in chapter 3:

> "If a man divorces his wife
>   and she leaves him and marries another man,
> should he return to her again?
>   Would not the land be completely defiled?

But you have lived as a prostitute with many lovers—
    would you now return to me?"
                            declares the LORD.
"Look up to the barren heights and see.
    Is there any place where you have not been ravished?
By the roadside you sat waiting for lovers,
    sat like a nomad in the desert.
You have defiled the land
    with your prostitution and wickedness.
Therefore the showers have been withheld,
    and no spring rains have fallen.
Yet you have the brazen look of a prostitute;
    you refuse to blush with shame.
Have you not just called to me:
    'My Father, my friend from my youth,
will you always be angry?
    Will your wrath continue forever?'
This is how you talk,
    but you do all the evil you can" (3:1-5).

The book of Jeremiah goes on like this for forty-five chapters! God is clear with his people: They have become brazen in their sin. They have no shame. They have become so accustomed to prostituting themselves to other gods that they don't even know how to blush.[2] And when they claim to be devoted to the Lord, they lie. More than once he tells them, "You have as many gods as you have towns!"[3]

God even asks them quite frankly,

"Why should I forgive you?
    Your children have forsaken me
    and sworn by gods that are not gods.
I supplied all their needs,
    yet they committed adultery
    and thronged to the houses of prostitutes.
They are well-fed, lusty stallions,
    each neighing for another man's wife.
Should I not punish them for this?"
    declares the LORD.
"Should I not avenge myself
    on such a nation as this?" (5:7-9).

[2] 3:3; 6:15; 7:19; 8:12; 12:13; 13:26.
[3] 2:28; 11:13.

This last question rings throughout the book: "Why shouldn't I avenge myself on you? Why should I not punish you?" When God's people call for God's justice, they call his judgment down not only on those evil people *out there,* but on themselves. "Forget about the other guys," the Lord says, "why should I forgive *you?*"

The charges simply add up, and God expresses more and more resolve to punish them:

> "The people of Israel and Judah have done nothing but evil in my sight from their youth; indeed, the people of Israel have done nothing but provoke me with what their hands have made, declares the LORD. From the day it was built until now, this city has so aroused my anger and wrath that I must remove it from my sight. The people of Israel and Judah have provoked me by all the evil they have done—they, their kings and officials, their priests and prophets, the men of Judah and the people of Jerusalem. They turned their backs to me and not their faces; though I taught them again and again, they would not listen or respond to discipline. They set up their abominable idols in the house that bears my Name and defiled it" (32:30-34).

The whole nation had sinned against God. Even their religious devotion was wrong. In what is known as Jeremiah's temple sermon, God mockingly repeats the people's claims to feel safe because the temple of Yahweh is in their presence. Surely, nothing could happen to them in the temple, right? All the while, Babylon draws closer with its army. The Lord scolds them through Jeremiah:

> "Will you steal and murder, commit adultery and perjury, burn incense to Baal and follow other gods you have not known, and then come and stand before me in this house, which bears my Name, and say, 'We are safe'—safe to do all these detestable things? Has this house, which bears my Name, become a den of robbers to you? But I have been watching! declares the LORD" (7:9-11).

They were even burning their sons and daughters in the fire in worship of Molech, offering up human sacrifices of their own family members in their false and detestable religion![4]

They had reached a terrible impasse in which God did not care about their hollow religious worship. They entered the house of Yahweh and sometimes did the right thing, but he knew everything else they were doing. He knew they

---

[4] See 7:31; 32:35.

did not care about his Word (6:19-20). In fact, his Word had become "offensive" to them (6:10).

What happens when God's Word becomes offensive to God's people? They pick teachers and prophets who will teach them something else. God observes, "A horrible and shocking thing has happened in the land: The prophets prophesy lies, the priests rule by their own authority, and my people love it this way" (5:30-31a). Prophets, the spokesmen for God, prophesying lies? Priests, the mediators for Yahweh, living immoral lives? And God's people loving it this way?

Again, we ask, where is the justice in this? Should God not avenge himself on such a nation as this?

The Promise of Judgment

God sent Jeremiah to bear the message of coming justice, even against those people who bore God's name. Indeed, the promises of justice were especially against God's people *because* they bore his name: "They are called rejected . . . because the LORD has rejected them" (6:30).

How exactly would God judge his people? Part of the answer included things like false prophets and famine. But primarily, God would answer his people's disobedience with an army: he would destroy the nation. The Lord symbolizes this destruction with a clay pot he instructs Jeremiah to purchase and then smash in front of a crowd while saying, "This is what the LORD Almighty says: I will smash this nation and this city just as this potter's jar is smashed" (19:11).

A number of so-called prophets may have been running around saying, "Peace, peace," but there was no peace (6:14; 8:11). Instead, God would give his people over to the ones they really trusted. He would exile them to Babylon for seventy years. In the final chapter of Jeremiah (chapter 52), we read the historical account taken directly from the book of 2 Kings (24:18–25:21), describing Jerusalem's fall, King Zedekiah's capture, the destruction of the temple and the city walls, and finally the exile of the people: "So Judah went into captivity, away from her land."[5]

Throughout Jeremiah's prophecies, God passionately responds to his people and their unfaithfulness. He can even sound like a jilted lover or an aggrieved spouse. Over and over God interweaves the images of idolatry and adultery in order to show his people that he has taken them as his special bride, he has wed himself to them, he has committed himself to them, he has even put his reputation on the line by sharing his name with them, but they have

---

[5] 52:27b; see also all of chapter 52.

been unfaithful. They have prostituted themselves to other gods. They have brought disgrace to his name by living and worshiping as they have.

Surely you understand God's concern for his own name. This is not a difficult concept for us. Are you indifferent to the reputation of any of the organizations in which you are heavily involved? Are you entirely unconcerned with how your group, your company, your firm, your agency represents itself or how outsiders represent it? Do you not care what image it likes to cultivate?

What parent is there who does not know the pride or shame that a child bearing the parent's own name can bring on both of their heads?

So would God feel any less about his people whom he made, brought to know himself, and placed his name upon? No! He loves them faithfully and fearfully and tenaciously. It may seem like a strange love after we have read through forty-five chapters of gloom, but it is clearly love. After all, what kind of "love" is it that knows no criticism? What kind of "love" is it that admits no possibility of correction?

When we think of judgment, we often think of what God does toward those who are not his people. Toward the "bad people." Well, friend, I have news for you: if you are not one of the "bad people," you have no need for this or any other sermon. Neither do you have need for a church. The church is specifically for the "bad people." If you read our church's statement of faith, you will see that. The church is for people who know that they need God to love them in such a way that he changes them.

Some people like to present God as a formless ocean of love, engulfing our every part. But the Bible nowhere presents God's love so amorphously. God has revealed himself in the book of Jeremiah and elsewhere as a personal God who is holy and who cares. We cannot demand that such a holy and loving God be so uncritical of people like us. In his love, he will not leave us as the broken, wounded, wrongheaded, self-defeating, and fallen people that we were when he found us. He will love us *effectively* in Christ and make us better than we are. In fact, he will ultimately make us perfect, just like Christ!

The Priority of Judgment

Suppose for a moment, however, that the story ended here. Suppose that God used Babylon to chasten his people in love, and then the story stopped. What would be wrong with that picture?

The question that at least Jeremiah would ask is, what about Babylon itself? Would Babylon escape judgment? If you stopped reading at chapter 45, you might think so. And that doesn't seem fair! Jeremiah raises this topic with the Lord back in chapter 12. Most of the book, you might notice, consists of the Lord speaking through Jeremiah. But here is one place where Jeremiah gets a word in edgewise: "You are always righteous, O LORD, when I bring a case before you. Yet I would speak with you about your justice: Why does the way of the wicked prosper? Why do all the faithless live at ease?" (12:1). This inspired prophet of God asks God quite honestly why the wicked prosper. It does not seem just, but they do!

Will they always so prosper? The answer is: not forever. God *will* ultimately bring judgment on all the wicked. And we'll get to that in a moment.

But as much as both we and Jeremiah may want to rush ahead and hear God make this point, God doesn't want us to jump ahead too quickly. God wants to make sure his people understand the priority he places upon their (*our*—if we are Christians) judgment. Only then will he move to those who are not his people. First things first. The apostle Peter understood this dynamic perfectly. In his first letter, he observes, "For it is time for judgment to begin with the family of God." Then he continues, "And if it begins with us, what will the outcome be for those who do not obey the gospel of God?" (1 Pet. 4:17). Those who are not God's will be judged. But God's people must stop and recognize that judgment begins with the family of God, both corporately and individually.

There is a powerful picture here for us. If Jeremiah spends forty-five chapters focusing on the faults of God's own people, should we spend most of our spiritual lives focusing on the faults of all those around us? On the faults of non-Christians or society at large? On the faults of other members of our own family? No, we should begin as individuals by observing our own hearts and lives, just as God begins with his own people. We should also begin as a church by seeking to be open to the Lord's correction, and not by focusing on how everyone else is wrong and we are right. I trust we are right about our understanding of the gospel of Jesus Christ. But there are many ways in which we will never be right, this side of heaven; if we are truly God's people, we will humbly acknowledge our continuing need for his loving discipline.

The Herald of Judgment

One of the things that struck me most about this book was Jeremiah himself. He appears to understand perfectly well that the message he is called to give is not his own. Consider his situation. He is in the capital city of a nation besieged by a foreign power. And what does he say? He tells them all to surrender! Speaking for the Lord during the reign of Zedekiah, Jeremiah proclaims, "Whoever stays in this city will die by the sword, famine or plague. But whoever goes out and surrenders to the Babylonians who are besieging you will live; he will escape with his life."[6]

These types of messages, however, had caused Jeremiah to build up a number of enemies over the years. More than once, there was an attempt on Jeremiah's life, as happened years earlier in the following account from the reign of Jehoiakim. Still, he knew his message came from God:

> [A]s soon as Jeremiah finished telling all the people everything the LORD had commanded him to say, the priests, the prophets and all the people seized him and said, "You must die! Why do you prophesy in the LORD's name that this house will be like Shiloh and this city will be desolate and deserted?" And all the people crowded around Jeremiah in the house of the LORD.
>
> When the officials of Judah heard about these things, they went up from the royal palace to the house of the LORD and took their places at the entrance of the New Gate of the LORD's house. Then the priests and the prophets said to the officials and all the people, "This man should be sentenced to death because he has prophesied against this city. You have heard it with your own ears!"
>
> Then Jeremiah said to all the officials and all the people: "The LORD sent me to prophesy against this house and this city all the things you have heard. Now reform your ways and your actions and obey the LORD your God. Then the LORD will relent and not bring the disaster he has pronounced against you. As for me, I am in your hands; do with me whatever you think is good and right. Be assured, however, that if you put me to death, you will bring the guilt of innocent blood on yourselves and on this city and on those who live in it, for in truth the LORD has sent me to you to speak all these words in your hearing" (Jer. 26:8-15).

Jeremiah's words remind one of the story of the army officer who finds that he and the few men with him have been cut off from their division, their battalion, and their company, and that the enemy surrounds them on every side, and says something like, "They can't run now. They're surrounded!"

And now, years later, as he stands alone in the temple while all the officials accuse him of treason and threaten him with death, again Jeremiah simply declares that he is speaking for God, and that God will bring disasters upon them. This Jeremiah is no man-pleaser. He has God's message, and he has come to give it to God's people.

At one point, Jeremiah would even tell King Zedekiah that he would be handed over to the enemy: "But when [Jeremiah] reached the Benjamin Gate, the captain of the guard, whose name was Irijah . . . arrested him and said, 'You

---

[6] 21:9; see also 38:17-18.

are deserting to the Babylonians!'" (37:13). Irijah's charge makes sense. Jeremiah had been prophesying that the city should surrender to the Babylonians:

> "That's not true!" Jeremiah said. "I am not deserting to the Babylonians." But Irijah would not listen to him; instead, he arrested Jeremiah and brought him to the officials. They were angry with Jeremiah and had him beaten and imprisoned in the house of Jonathan the secretary, which they had made into a prison.
>
> Jeremiah was put into a vaulted cell in a dungeon, where he remained a long time. Then King Zedekiah sent for him and had him brought to the palace, where he asked him privately, "Is there any word from the LORD?"
>
> "Yes," Jeremiah replied, "you will be handed over to the king of Babylon."
>
> Then Jeremiah said to King Zedekiah, "What crime have I committed against you or your officials or this people, that you have put me in prison? Where are your prophets who prophesied to you, 'The king of Babylon will not attack you or this land'? But now, my lord the king, please listen. Let me bring my petition before you: Do not send me back to the house of Jonathan the secretary, or I will die there" (37:14-20).

Can you imagine Jeremiah's unmitigated gall? He's been arrested, beaten, and imprisoned. And still he tells the king he would be handed over to an invading force! Then he asks the king why he is offended! Later, Jeremiah would even explicitly tell Zedekiah to surrender (38:17-18). Jeremiah could say these things only because he knew he had heard a word from the Lord. These ideas were not his, as if he were trying to publish in *The Jerusalem Post* some sort of op-ed that he had written. When King Zedekiah asked him whether he had any word from God, Jeremiah could answer point-blank, "Yes, you will be handed over to the king of Babylon," and then immediately turn to asking whether he could be released, as if he had nothing to do with what he had just said. Others would accuse him of undermining morale by his statements that seemed to support Babylon (38:4), but he knew he was just a messenger, handing off the note the Lord had handed him.

Jeremiah gave the messages, but he did not invent or generate them. Still, his job did cause him no small amount of consternation and strife. At one point he laments,

> I am ridiculed all day long;
>> everyone mocks me.
> Whenever I speak, I cry out
>> proclaiming violence and destruction.
> So the Word of the LORD has brought me
>> insult and reproach all day long.

But if I say, "I will not mention him
    or speak any more in his name,"
his word is in my heart like a fire,
    a fire shut up in my bones.
I am weary of holding it in;
    indeed, I cannot.
I hear many whispering,
    "Terror on every side!
    Report him! Let's report him!" (20:7-10).

Jeremiah felt divinely compelled to pronounce these terrible threats against his own people. Therefore, many would see him as a traitor. Just think of it: the armies of Babylon surrounding the city, and Jeremiah standing inside saying, "Surrender! Surrender!"

When Jerusalem was finally taken, King Nebuchadnezzar of Babylon himself gave instructions for Jeremiah to be given special care (39:11-12). Can you imagine what that felt like for Jeremiah? The conquering dictator's special care for him would confirm everybody's charges that he was a traitor!

Jeremiah had a difficult message to give. He had to tell God's own people that God was taking their opponent's side in judgment! He had to tell them that their large, powerful, pagan attacker would win, so they had better give up. Does that mean that Jeremiah was a quisling? A traitor?

JUSTICE FOR BABYLON AND THE NATIONS (CHAPTERS 46–51)

Thus far, we have been looking only at God's judgment of his own people, in the first 45 chapters of Jeremiah. In chapters 46–49, it's as if God says, "Don't think I have forgotten the rest of the world." Then in chapters 50–51, God turns his eyes onto Babylon itself.

If you start in chapter 46 and then glance through the headings of the next few chapters, you will see that Jeremiah begins with the promises of judgment upon Egypt and then sweeps eastward, speaking out judgment on nation after nation. Apparently, no one will be left out: Egypt, the Philistines, Moab, Ammon, Edom, Damascus, Kedar, Hazor, and Elam. Then, most extraordinarily, he takes the most space, in chapters 50–51, to make a final, ultimate, climactic declaration of impending judgment. And who is the recipient of this promised condemnation? Babylon, the very nation that Jeremiah's contemporaries thought he was collaborating with.

In these two chapters, God clearly makes the point that the Babylonians were only a tool in God's hand. The nation that once looked so magnificent and majestic and mighty turned out to be a pawn in God's plan to humble his own people. Everything the Babylonians accomplished was accomplished at God's behest, at his pleasure, for his purposes. Apart from him, they could do nothing.

At the beginning of chapter 50, the Lord says through Jeremiah, "Announce and proclaim among the nations, lift up a banner and proclaim it; keep nothing back, but say, 'Babylon will be captured; Bel will be put to shame, Marduk filled with terror. Her images will be put to shame and her idols filled with terror'" (50:2). If you have read straight through the whole book, you will get to this verse and find it amazing! Up until this point, Babylon is just winning, winning, winning. Now, God promises Babylon that it will go the way of the last great empire before it, the way of Assyria: "Therefore this is what the LORD Almighty, the God of Israel, says: 'I will punish the king of Babylon and his land as I punished the king of Assyria'" (50:18). And the promises of judgment simply add up one after the other:

> "Therefore, her young men will fall in the streets;
>   all her soldiers will be silenced in that day,"
>   declares the LORD.
> "See, I am against you, O arrogant one,"
>   declares the Lord, the LORD Almighty,
> "for your day has come,
>   the time for you to be punished" (50:30-31).

> "Babylon was a gold cup in the LORD's hand;
>   she made the whole earth drunk.
> The nations drank her wine;
>   therefore they have now gone mad.
> Babylon will suddenly fall and be broken" (51:7-8a).

> "You are my war club,
>   my weapon for battle—
> with you I shatter nations,
>   with you I destroy kingdoms,
> with you I shatter horse and rider,
>   with you I shatter chariot and driver,
> with you I shatter man and woman,
>   with you I shatter old man and youth,
>   with you I shatter young man and maiden,
> with you I shatter shepherd and flock,
>   with you I shatter farmer and oxen,
>   with you I shatter governors and officials. . . .

"I am against you, O destroying mountain,
   you who destroy the whole earth,"
                                        declares the LORD.
"I will stretch out my hand against you,
   roll you off the cliffs,
   and make you a burned-out mountain. . . .

"The land trembles and writhes,
   for the LORD's purposes against Babylon stand—
to lay waste the land of Babylon
   so that no one will live there" (51:20-23, 25, 29).

"One courier follows another
   and messenger follows messenger
to announce to the king of Babylon
   that his entire city is captured" (51:31).

"Babylon will be a heap of ruins,
   a haunt of jackals,
an object of horror and scorn,
   a place where no one lives.
Her people all roar like young lions,
   they growl like lion cubs.
But while they are aroused,
   I will set out a feast for them
   and make them drunk,
so that they shout with laughter—
   then sleep forever and not awake,"
                                        declares the LORD (51:37-39).

This is what the LORD Almighty says:

   "Babylon's thick wall will be leveled
      and her high gates set on fire;
   the peoples exhaust themselves for nothing,
      the nations' labor is only fuel for the flames" (51:58).

Those are strong words, coming from one little prophet in a failing country against the superpower of the day—which is about to conquer his nation! But then again, maybe Jeremiah said all this to curry favor with the Jews. After all, he had lashed out at them with enough prophecy to fill forty-five chapters. Maybe now he is trying to get on their good side by giving Babylon one good kick.

Well, that's unlikely. I suspect not very many of Jeremiah's Jewish contemporaries would have ever heard this prophecy. Look at how he gave it:

> This is the message Jeremiah gave to the staff officer Seraiah son of Neriah, the son of Mahseiah, when he went to Babylon with Zedekiah king of Judah in the fourth year of his reign. Jeremiah had written on a scroll about all the disasters that would come upon Babylon—all that had been recorded concerning Babylon. He said to Seraiah, "When you get to Babylon, see that you read all these words aloud. Then say, 'O LORD, you have said you will destroy this place, so that neither man nor animal will live in it; it will be desolate forever.' When you finish reading this scroll, tie a stone to it and throw it into the Euphrates. Then say, 'So will Babylon sink to rise no more because of the disaster I will bring upon her. And her people will fall.'"

> The words of Jeremiah end here (51:59-64).

How dramatic! At the very time when Jeremiah was being accused of being a traitor to his own nation, he was sending these words of God's judgment to Babylon.

Jeremiah was the employee of no person or state. He was not the mouthpiece of any political party. And he was not part of some cynical operation to undermine his country. Instead, he was God's spokesman who spoke God's truth in judgment and love to God's creation. He was a prophet of God.

As Christians, we do not tell the good news of Christianity because it initially pleases everyone. There are parts of our message that people often do not like. We tell it, rather, because it is the true message of God. It is the message of the Lord that has come to us and that we give to others, not in pride but in humility. Jeremiah showed such humility when he stood and told his king that he would go into captivity. He showed such humility when he stood and told the Babylonians that they too would perish in God's judgment. In neither case did Jeremiah assume any of this would be done by his might, or that these things would happen through any insight of his own. He simply said what God told him to say.

Friend, this is our position as Christians. We have been given a message that is not our own. We did not make it. We cannot tailor it. God has given it to us to tell the world. What's that message? We have all rebelled against God and deserve his eternal condemnation. We deserve to go to hell. Yet God in his kindness and mercy sent his Son Jesus to live a perfect life and die on the cross for the sins of all who would ever repent and believe in him. In Christ alone can we find forgiveness for our sins and reconciliation with God. The Bible now calls us to repent of our sins and trust in Christ.

CONCLUSION

God brought justice against his people in order to discipline them. And he brought justice against the very nations that he had used to discipline his people.

Yet here is a final question: If everyone receives justice, what then is the difference between God's people and other people?

The difference is mercy. Christians understand that getting what's fair means getting hell. We know that if we demand that God give us what we deserve, we will not receive all things sweet and light, because we deserve holy indignation and fury of the sort found in the prophecies of Jeremiah. We deserve the punishment of hell.

But there is more than justice in this book. There is mercy.

God's people may receive a share of God's condemnation in this world. But God ultimately acts in love toward his people, particularly by "disciplining his people through his justice" (see 30:11; 46:28). Such words are used a couple of times in this book. Though God's methods can be hard, his purposes are good. It is always that way with God. Though God's methods are hard, his purposes are good.

The book of Jeremiah is not entirely a book of gloom. If you are looking for a little sunshine, read through chapters 30–33. They provide a ray of bright sunshine in between the book's many dark thunderclouds and drenching rains. In these chapters, God promises that he will once again gather his scattered people and will make a new covenant:

> "I will surely gather them from all the lands where I banish them in my furious anger and great wrath; I will bring them back to this place and let them live in safety. They will be my people, and I will be their God. I will give them singleness of heart and action, so that they will always fear me for their own good and the good of their children after them. I will make an everlasting covenant with them: I will never stop doing good to them, and I will inspire them to fear me, so that they will never turn away from me" (32:37-40).

To make this hope more concrete, God instructs Jeremiah to buy a piece of land even though the collapse of the domestic economy appears imminent (32:7-9). It's as if God is saying to Jeremiah, "Show the people that you are willing to put your money where your mouth is. Show them that you are serious when you say that my word has come to you and that I will restore my people."

God promises judgment, but he also promises hope.

It is also interesting to note that God saves one person, Ebed-Melech, out of this condemned city of Jerusalem, "because," God says to Ebed-Melech, "you trusted me" (39:18). A whole city stood under judgment, but there was mercy for this one who trusted God!

Though justice is what we want, though justice is what we often demand, consider Portia's words to Shylock in Shakespeare's *Merchant of Venice:*

> "Though Justice be thy plea, consider this,
>   That in the course of justice none of us
>   Should see salvation: we do pray for mercy" (IV.i.182).

Jeremiah puts his hope in God's mercy and compassion. Beholding his besieged and blockaded city, Jeremiah utters this lament:

> He has broken my teeth with gravel;
>   he has trampled me in the dust.
> I have been deprived of peace;
>   I have forgotten what prosperity is.
> So I say, "My splendor is gone
>   and all that I had hoped from the LORD."
>
> I remember my affliction and my wandering,
>   the bitterness and the gall.
> I well remember them,
>   and my soul is downcast within me.
> Yet this I call to mind
>   and therefore I have hope:
>
> Because of the LORD's great love we are not consumed,
>   for his compassions never fail.
> They are new every morning;
>   great is your faithfulness.
> I say to myself, "The LORD is my portion;
>   therefore I will wait for him" (Lam. 3:16-24).

Jeremiah's words were not composed on a sunny, summery day, kicking back amid luxury and abundance. They were spoken by a man who had been arrested, imprisoned, called a traitor by the fellow citizens he loved, and then forced to watch as his besieged home fell into cannibalism because food became so scarce. It was at these very moments that Jeremiah said he had hope because of the Lord's compassion and love!

God's mercies came to his people even amid his judgments.

The same is true for us in our sin and in our lives as God's children. The only reason any of us know God is that God mercifully came to us even when we were rebelling against him. "But God demonstrates his own love for us in this: While we were still sinners, Christ died for us" (Rom. 5:8). His mercy comes amid his judgment.

Our only hope for justice is God. Our only hope for mercy is God.

Let us pray:

Lord, you know the ways that we who are your people have been unfaithful to you. We pray that you would grant us the gift of repentance, and that you would show us mercy. And we ask this, Lord, not for our name's sake, but for your name's sake. We know, as Christians, that you have set your name upon us, and we know that you desire to glorify your name with the truth of who you are in your goodness and glorious holiness alike. So, Lord, we pray that you would persevere with us, and that you would continue to show yourself faithful in all the corners of our lives. Be faithful to us in your judgments and love. We pray for Jesus' sake. Amen.

Questions for Reflection

1. Do people have a natural sense of justice? What evidence do you see? What biblical support can be given for this idea?

2. Does the punishment one human being will receive for a crime that he or she commits against another human being bring complete justice to that situation? If not, what will?

3. Why, amid a world of evil, rebellion, and moral decay, is the message of God necessarily an offensive message that will turn people off?

4. Where does our society "worship what our hands have made" today? Where do we do this in the church?

5. Why is adultery and/or prostitution such an apt metaphor for our idolatry against God?

6. Following up on question 5, does the charge of adulterous idolatry apply primarily to non-Christians or to Christians? Where can churches fall into this kind of idolatry? (As you answer this question, don't begin by looking at other churches or even other people; begin with yourself and what you might want in a church. Let judgment begin with *you*.)

7. Do you ever find God's Word offensive? What parts? When that is the case, are you ever tempted to assume that "maybe it's a mistake in the Bible" or "maybe we are all just interpreting it in the wrong way"? Or do you perhaps offer some such explanation that allows you to ignore the issue? If so, why would you assume that something is wrong with the Bible and not assume that something is wrong with your understanding and your desires? In other words, why would you give yourself the benefit of the doubt and not God's Word? You may wish to ask yourself quite honestly, "Am I willing to shape my understanding and desires after God's Word rather than trying to shape his Word after my desires?"

8. What does the book of Jeremiah, with all its talk of God's judgment, teach us about God's love?

9. Should Christians, who have been the recipients of God's mercy and grace, desire for God to bring his judgment upon his enemies? How can this longing coexist with a right understanding of God's grace?

10. Jeremiah was the recipient of much opposition and persecution because he had to deliver an offensive message—a message of judgment. What can churches learn from Jeremiah's example here? Should we be concerned about a church that is unwilling to offend either members or outsiders with its message (as opposed to offending them with their personality, their culture, their sin, or their traditions—which, hopefully, everyone agrees a church should try to avoid)?

11. Following up on question 10, Christian, let's consider your own practices of evangelism: how willing are you to say things (with gentleness, respect, and love) that people will take offense at? If you are not willing, what is preventing you from doing so?

THE MESSAGE OF LAMENTATIONS: JUSTICE UP CLOSE

25

THE MESSAGE OF LAMENTATIONS: JUSTICE UP CLOSE

HOW TO DEAL WITH SUFFERING[1]

Food is rationed. Then the rations are reduced. And reduced again. And reduced again. Old people begin to starve to death. Children waste away. Eventually, corpses rot in the streets. The stench spreads through the whole city. Pestilence is everywhere. People are scared to leave their homes to look for food lest they be robbed, or even . . . well, it does not bear talking about.

What am I referring to? Some apocalyptic scenario of the end times? No, I am referring to something that has already happened. In September A.D. 408, the Goth king Alaric seized control of the port of Ostia, thus cutting the city of Rome's supply line. Then he besieged Rome itself. For the first time in almost a thousand years, enemy troops stood at the gates of Rome. The siege wore on for months. Finally, after the suffering I have just described, two Roman officials were chosen to exit the city, approach Alaric, and open negotiations. Initially, they tried to threaten him, telling him that if he and his army would not depart, the Romans would be forced to come out of the city and destroy them. Alaric just laughed. So the Roman negotiators next tried asking Alaric what his price was. How much did he want to lift the siege? He answered, "Deliver to me all the gold that your city contains. All the silver, all the moveable property that I may find there, and all your slaves of barbarian origin."

The Roman ambassadors were shocked. "If you take all these things," said one, "what do you leave to our citizens?"

"Your souls," said Alaric.

After two more years and three more sieges, each one of which was negotiated to a peaceful conclusion, Alaric, on the night of August 24, 410, finally

---

[1] This sermon was originally preached on October 28, 1998, at Capitol Hill Baptist Church in Washington, D.C.

led his troops to the task even he had been reluctant to pursue—the sacking and burning of Rome. The Goth army broke through the Salurian gate and poured into the city. Once inside, the one-hundred-thousand-strong army turned into a large ravenous animal, feeding upon the city's civilian population. After half a week of violence, they departed.

The Western world was shocked by the fall of the Eternal City. Jerome, hundreds of miles away in retirement near Jerusalem, was working on his commentary on Ezekiel at the time. When he heard the news, he was shaken and wrote to a friend, "What is safe, if Rome perishes?" Such was the effect that Augustine wrote his great book *The City of God*, a huge volume in which he tried to help his readers understand how God could mysteriously be at work in the world even through such catastrophic things. Augustine wanted his readers to comprehend the nature of God's strange working in history. Even today, historians often regard the fall of Rome as the dividing line between the ancient world and the middle ages.

Moments of suffering and loss often mark the great turning points in history generally, and in our lives particularly.

None of us likes suffering. It goes against our nature. We like prospering. Prospering means getting and gaining. Prospering means having our way. It means acquiring new skills and talents and goods. It means achievements. Suffering usually means losing some of these things, or even losing the community that we love through relocation, through unemployment, or even through the death of important people in our lives.

In Granger Westberg's little book *Good Grief,* Westberg suggests that grieving is an almost daily experience in all of our lives, not simply what we do when a loved one dies. It happens every day through what he calls "little griefs." His book deals with both the little griefs, like a last-minute change of plans or getting a new boss, as well as the large griefs, like losing a job or even a spouse. In one form or another, grief typically occurs in ten stages, he says: 1) we are in a state of shock; 2) we express emotion; 3) we feel depressed and very lonely; 4) we may experience some physical symptoms of distress; 5) we may become panicky; 6) we feel a sense of guilt about the loss; 7) we are filled with anger and resentment; 8) we resist returning to our jobs and responsibilities; 9) gradually, hope emerges; 10) we struggle to affirm reality.[2]

Well, whether it be smaller griefs or larger ones, how do you deal with your suffering? How do you respond to life's difficult circumstances and losses?

---

[2] See Granger Westberg, *Good Grief* (Philadelphia: Fortress, 1971).

INTRODUCING LAMENTATIONS

When the Babylonian army besieged the city of Jerusalem for a year and a half in 588–587 B.C., terrible calamities befell Jerusalem's inhabitants, similar to what befell the citizens of Rome when surrounded by Alaric's army. When the Babylonians finally broke through, they destroyed the temple, the palace, the walls, and Jerusalem itself.

Naturally, the people of Jerusalem lamented their sufferings, and the survivors struggled to deal with the reality—as Westberg would put it—of such an enormous loss. Written in response to this event, the Old Testament book of Lamentations presents five poems of lament, one poem per chapter. The book is called "Lamentations" because it expresses the people's laments over the capture and destruction of Jerusalem.

Chapters 1, 2, and 4 of Lamentations appear in the form of a Hebrew funeral dirge. They were also written as acrostics, where each verse begins with a successive letter of the Hebrew alphabet. That is why chapters 1, 2, and 4 have twenty-two verses apiece. Chapter 5 is not an acrostic, but it contains twenty-two verses as well. Chapter 3, the center of the book, has three times as many verses—sixty-six. And it is a triple acrostic, meaning the first *three* verses begin with the first letter of the Hebrew alphabet (*aleph*), the next three verses begin with the next letter of the Hebrew alphabet (*bet*), and so forth. Chapter 3 gets triple the number of verses in order to emphasize that it is the center of the book.

While we can't be certain who wrote the book, we think it was the prophet Jeremiah. Though the book never claims to have been written by Jeremiah, in 2 Chronicles 35:25 we read, "Jeremiah composed laments for Josiah, and to this day all the men and women singers commemorate Josiah in the laments. These became a tradition in Israel and are written in the Laments." And several significant ancient translations of the Hebrew Bible, like the Greek Septuagint and the Latin Vulgate, refer to this book as written by Jeremiah. Whoever wrote it, the people of God owned it. By the time the New Testament was being written, Lamentations was regularly read in the synagogues as Holy Scripture.

Even today, this book of Lamentations is read publicly in synagogues on the ninth day of the Jewish month of Ab, the day on which the second temple was destroyed by the Romans in A.D. 70. Yet as Jews remember the work of destruction wrought upon Jerusalem by Emperor Titus of Rome, they also remember the even older work of destruction wrought not by the Romans but by the Babylonian emperor Nebuchadnezzar.

That first destruction of Jerusalem was absolutely cataclysmic for the

Jewish people. When the city finally fell to the Babylonians after the prolonged siege, the Israelites lost not only a city but their chief city, and not only their chief city but their capital. Jerusalem was their most defensible point. Losing Jerusalem meant losing all that outwardly represented the nation of Israel: the ruling line of David, the priests, the sacrifices and the temple, and even the Promised Land itself were all lost! We cannot even begin to imagine how devastating this final loss was, because losing the land meant losing God's promise, and losing God's promise meant losing their special relationship with God.

In our study of the book of Jeremiah, we considered the theme of justice. Jeremiah promised in his prophecies that Babylon would come and bring God's judgment upon Jerusalem and Judah. In this study, we observe the effects of God's justice not as a grand, overarching theological theme in history, but up close and personal, in the grotesque suffering of people and the perplexing questions that follow.

Lamentations was written, you see, not simply to express grief over loss, as one might think from its title, "Lamentations." It was also written to help God's people—including the author himself—cope with loss and the temptation to despair by reminding them of God's presence and God's rule. Like Job, Lamentations is a "theodicy." That is, it helps people to see God's goodness and power amid suffering.

Suffering is a significant time in any person's life, as you can probably testify in one way or another. Suffering acts as a check on our hopes; it refines them; maybe it changes them. Suffering will either harden us or make us more pliable in God's hands.

How do you carry on through suffering?

Through the unnamed author of Lamentations, God led his people to do more than just mourn and lament. He led them to do five things, which we might learn from as well.

WHEN SUFFERING COMES, CONFESS YOUR SINS

First, when these calamities came, God led the Israelites to confess their sins.

Their Situation Was Desperate

When you look through Lamentations 1, you see that the people's situation was desperate. The author of this first lament clearly lived through the Babylonian siege of Jerusalem in 588–587 B.C. Such is his description of the tremendous desolation. "How deserted lies the city, once so full of people" (1:1a). You can almost see the newspapers blowing along in the wind. "She who was queen," he says symbolically of the nation, "has become a slave"

(1:1b). "Bitterly she weeps" and "all her friends have betrayed her" (1:2). As we continue through the chapter, we see the affliction and exile. The mourning. The abandoned religious practices. The desolate city. Her princes are fleeing from their pursuers. This queen who was once honored is now despised. The desolation is well captured in this image of a dazed and despondent female figure: "Her filthiness clung to her skirts; she did not consider her future. Her fall was astounding; there was none to comfort her" (1:9). Jerusalem is shocked by her fall. Her treasures have been looted. Her temple has been violated. Her people groan for food, and they sell whatever they have left for bread. Her army has been defeated, and her people's future is in the hands of their enemies. The priests and elders all perished in their own search for food. The Babylonians killed whoever traveled outside Jerusalem's walls; hunger killed whoever remained within.

They Were Called to Confess

Given these grim circumstances, what were the people of God to do? They were called to confess their sins.

In the first half of chapter 1, we are told that this personified female figure who represents Jerusalem has sinned: "The LORD has brought her grief because of her many sins" (1:5). Her sins are the cause of her suffering. "All the splendor has departed from the daughter of Zion" (1:6). In case the reader has somehow missed the point of whom this woman represents, the author repeats, "Jerusalem has sinned greatly and so has become unclean" (1:8).

If the first half of chapter describes Israel's suffering and the causes of this suffering as belonging to this personified female figure, the second half of the chapter has the woman speak. She speaks to confess her sin and rebellion: "The LORD is righteous, yet I rebelled against his command" (1:18). She knows she has been rebellious: "See, O LORD, how distressed I am! I am in torment within, and in my heart I am disturbed, for I have been most rebellious. Outside, the sword bereaves; inside, there is only death" (1:20). Concerning her enemies, she says, "Let all their wickedness come before you; deal with them as you have dealt with me because of all my sins. My groans are many and my heart is faint" (1:22). Those who remained in Jerusalem (at least those represented by the poet) responded to their terrible circumstances by confessing their sins.

So Must We

What about us? How should we begin to deal with our suffering? We should be patient. We should be humble. And we should confess our sins.

If you are anything like me, humility and confession are not your first reactions when suffering hits. My first reaction is to stiffen up and hit back. But God clearly uses suffering in the book of Lamentations to instruct his people. They should patiently wait and learn.

In his last years, the London Puritan pastor William Gouge's health gradually became worse. He used his sufferings as opportunities to calm his soul by reflecting on the Lord's grace. Even amid his most violent fevers or fits, Gouge would respond, "Well, yet in all these there is nothing of hell, or of God's wrath." Gouge's biographer recounts,

> His sufferings were never so deep but he could see the bottom of them, and say, "Soul, be silent: soul, be patient. It is thy God and Father who thus ordereth thy condition. Thou art his clay, and he may tread and trample on thee as He pleaseth. Thou hast deserved much more. It is enough that thou art kept out of hell. Though thy pain be grievous, yet it is tolerable. Thy God affords some intermissions. He will turn it to thy good, and at length put an end to all: None of which things can be expected in hell."

His biographer concluded, "His afflictions greatly contributed to the exercise of his grace."[3]

Friend, in your suffering and loss do not become hardened and bitter. Use your sufferings as opportunities to see your sin and to be humbled by God's Word. Remember, we will be humbled, and the only alternative to being humbled by God's Word is being humbled by his wrath, whether in this life or in the next. I urge you be humbled by God's Word.

Let us labor to be humble.

Let us also labor, therefore, to use occasions of suffering to confess our own sins, not the sins of others. It would have been easy for the Israelites to have used this lament to confess the sins of the cruel Babylonians. But no, they confessed their own sins. That does not mean they exonerated the Babylonians or said that what the Babylonians did was "just fine." No, God clearly promised elsewhere that the Babylonians would be judged (Jeremiah 50–51). But the Israelites realized that they, too, would be judged for their sins. They realized that, finally, God was more worthy of fear than the Babylonians.

Your sufferings are a message to you. Do not despise them or waste them. Take them as a refining and chastening opportunity, and begin by confessing your sins to God.

[3] Cited by James Reid, *Memoirs of the Westminster Divines,* 2 vols. (Paisley, UK: Stephen & Andrew Young, 1815), 1:358.

WHEN SUFFERING COMES, RECOGNIZE YOUR DIVINE JUDGE

When these calamities came, God also led the Israelites to recognize their divine judge.

They Remained Under God's Rule

As we turn to chapter 2, we find further testimony to how desperate the Israelites' situation was. Yet we also see that Jerusalem remained in a special position, even amid God's wrath. Jerusalem still specially displayed God's name and his righteousness. Even in judgment, God was working through them. They were never beyond his rule.

Chapter 2's vivid descriptions also bear evidence of having been written by an eyewitness of Jerusalem's siege and fall. Beginning in verses 8 and following, the writer tells us the ramparts, walls, gates, and bars are destroyed. The leaders are exiled, and self-government has ceased in Jerusalem for the time. Hunger has caused children to faint and die in their mothers' arms. Mothers have eaten their children. (Cannibalism always seems to come during the last stages of a siege, when the remaining population is crazed with hunger.) Young and old alike lie dead in the streets. Young men and maidens have been slaughtered by the sword. Priests and prophets have been killed in the temple. At the same time, worthless prophets continue to spout false visions of peace and security because many want to be soothed (2:14). They have paid prophets to soothe them!

Like chapter 1, much of chapter 2 is obviously filled with descriptions of Jerusalem's devastation. But that description comes with an interesting twist. The writer specifically recognizes that the destructive work is God's! In verses 1-8, he presents God as the actor! God was behind this destruction wrought by the Babylonians:

> How *the Lord has covered* the Daughter of Zion
> with the cloud of his anger!
> *He has hurled* down the splendor of Israel
> from heaven to earth;
> he has not remembered his footstool
> in the day of his anger.

> Without pity *the Lord has swallowed* up
> all the dwellings of Jacob;
> in his wrath *he has torn down*
> the strongholds of the Daughter of Judah.
> *He has brought* her kingdom and its princes
> down to the ground in dishonor.

In fierce anger *he has cut off*
　　every horn of Israel.
He has withdrawn his right hand
　　at the approach of the enemy.
He has burned in Jacob like a flaming fire
　　that consumes everything around it.

Like an enemy *he has strung* his bow;
　　his right hand is ready.
Like a foe *he has slain*
　　all who were pleasing to the eye;
he has poured out his wrath like fire
　　on the tent of the Daughter of Zion.

The Lord is *like an enemy;*
　　he has swallowed up Israel.
He has swallowed up all her palaces
　　and destroyed her strongholds.
He has multiplied mourning and lamentation
　　for the Daughter of Judah.

He has laid waste his dwelling like a garden;
　　he has destroyed his place of meeting.
The LORD has made Zion forget
　　her appointed feasts and her Sabbaths;
in his fierce anger *he has spurned*
　　both king and priest.

The Lord has rejected his altar
　　and abandoned his sanctuary.
He has handed over to the enemy
　　the walls of her palaces;
they have raised a shout in the house of the LORD
　　as on the day of an appointed feast.

The LORD determined to tear down
　　the wall around the Daughter of Zion.
He stretched out a measuring line
　　and did not withhold his hand from destroying.
He made ramparts and walls lament;
　　together they wasted away (2:1-8).

They Were Called to Recognize God as Judge

Amid all the calamity, in other words, the people were called to recognize God as ruler and judge, which they did: "The LORD has done what he planned; he has fulfilled his word, which he decreed long ago. He has overthrown you without pity, he has let the enemy gloat over you" (2:17).

This is amazing when you realize, as we have already mentioned, how easy it would have been to blame others. Amid Jerusalem's suffering, how easy it would have been to say, "It's the fault of the Israelite soldiers who fled and failed! They couldn't keep the wall!" Or, "It's the fault of the stupid engineers and builders who did a poor job of building the wall!" Or, "It's the king's fault. He did something to upset Babylon and bring their wrath upon us!" Or, "It's the fault of these cruel Babylonian soldiers and the tyrannical King Nebuchadnezzar!" They could have gone on and on ascribing guilt and blame for the terrible things that Jerusalem had suffered and endured. There was no shortage of people among whom they could have divvied up the blame. Yet the poet did not lead them that way, as true as any of those ascriptions might have been. Instead, he said, "The LORD has done what he planned. *He* has overthrown you."

So Must We

We too must recognize the fact that we are not beyond God's reach and that he remains our judge and ruler, even in our calamities. Some people struggle with ascribing calamity to God. "Doesn't it seem wrong," they argue, "to suggest that God could do such things and be so angry?" Lactantius, a Christian back in the third century, considered this objection and argued that anger, as with any other passion or emotion, was bad only if it was not controlled and directed toward good ends. Under control and properly directed, emotions, even anger, are good. In fact, he argued that for someone to be in the presence of evil and *not* be angry would be wrong. To truly love the good, one has to hate evil; and not hating evil is tantamount to not loving good.

Well, friend, if this is so, then God not only can be but should be angry at sin. He is right to act in judgment of wrong.

It is easy for us to pass over God's role by quickly blaming others for what goes wrong. We immediately complain about the coworker, the negligent doctor, the ignorant boss, the hurtful spouse, the overprotective parent, the greedy businessman, the lawless thief. And all of these figures may deserve blame. But as Christians, we must beware of behaving like practical atheists and stopping here.

Even if you affirm that you believe in God, what do you think he actually does? Does he sit idly in a watchtower somewhere far off beyond our galaxy? Omnisciently knowing every detail of our lives but never actively controlling those details? I know we can get into great difficulties by talking about God's active control in our lives, but let me warn you against going the other way. If you abandon the view that God is actively in charge of his world, and you adopt instead the view that God is a distant, uninvolved deity who you think is somehow more "loving," you will lose the God and Father of our Lord Jesus Christ, who knows when the sparrow falls, who knows the number of hairs on your head, and who works all things for the good of those who love him and are called according to his purpose (see Rom. 8:28).

If you want more help in understanding how God uses instruments of evil to accomplish his good purposes, the best thing to read about in the Bible is the death of Jesus.

In the Garden of Gethsemane, Jesus was clearly reluctant to move forward to the cross. He knew it would involve pain. Yet he also knew it was the Father's will, so he submitted to the Father. Weeks later, after his resurrection and ascension, the apostles prayed, "Herod and Pontius Pilate met together with the Gentiles and the people of Israel in this city to conspire against your holy servant Jesus, whom you anointed. They did what your power and will had decided beforehand should happen" (Acts 4:27-28). We can then follow the theme all the way to Hebrews, where we learn that Jesus endured the cross in order to attain the joy set before him (Heb. 12:2). In other words, God the Father and God the Son simultaneously acted together with wicked Herod and Pontius Pilate. Truly, God's purposes resound even in the worst sins and through the most exquisite pains.

If you do believe that God actively governs the universe and works through all things, then I have one caution for you. Beware of trying to read divine messages into all of life's particulars. Christians who accept the idea that God is actively involved in our lives can begin to treat every happenstance of their life as a massive riddle that they must figure out. "The taxi was late, and I missed my appointment. What is God saying to me in this?" Well, you can ask that sort of question, and maybe sometimes you will find a good answer. But rather than speculating about what God is saying, I would encourage you to keep reading your Bible. Scripture is plenty clear about what God values and what he wants you to pursue. Don't worry: he will be as loud and clear with you as he needs to be. He won't have trouble getting through to you when he needs to.

When we suffer, we must recognize that God has a good plan and that he is in charge.

WHEN SUFFERING COMES, GIVE SPECIAL ATTENTION TO GOD'S LEADERS

God led the Israelites to do a third thing amid their calamity, and perhaps this was the most unusual thing he asked them to do. He wanted them to realize the responsibility their leaders had for the situation they were in. I think this is the main lesson of chapter 4.

The Priests Had Become Untouchable

Once again tremendous suffering is described in chapter 4, both during and after the siege. In the first ten verses, we learn that fortunes were lost and predatory scavenging took over. Bread and water became scarce, and both parents and children died as a result. The ravages of scarcity made money worthless, so the rich became as destitute as the poor. The law of the jungle took over; and the grim reaper reigned. Those who were once great, like princes, became walking skeletons. Rather than starve within the walls, some preferred to risk the Babylonian sword. Verse 10 is one of the most disturbing verses of all: "With their own hands compassionate women have cooked their own children, who became their food when my people were destroyed" (4:10). Notice that the writer stresses the fact that these are compassionate mothers, not cruel mothers. Compassionate mothers cooked their own children and ate them, so great was their hunger. What a bizarre picture of tragedy, as God destroyed his own people.

Indeed, throughout this chapter, everything is out of kilter. Notice all the strange inversions: "How the gold has lost its luster, the fine gold become dull! The sacred gems are scattered at the head of every street. How the precious sons of Zion, once worth their weight in gold, are now considered as pots of clay, the work of a potter's hands!" (4:1-2). The height of the strangeness comes when the Lord destroys the very city that he had built: "The LORD has given full vent to his wrath, he has poured out his fierce anger, he kindled a fire in Zion that consumed her foundations" (4:11).

But the explanation given in chapter 4 for all these inversions lies with the leaders. Their sin was responsible:

> But it happened because of the sins of her prophets
>   and the iniquities of her priests,
> who shed within her
>   the blood of the righteous.
>
> Now they grope through the streets
>   like men who are blind.

They are so defiled with blood
    that no one dares to touch their garments.

"Go away! You are unclean!" men cry to them.
    "Away! Away! Don't touch us!"
When they flee and wander about,
    people among the nations say,
    "They can stay here no longer" (4:13-15).

Talk about inversions! The very ones who were to teach the people about ceremonial cleanness themselves became untouchable!

They Were Called to Recognize the Responsibility of Their Leaders

God called the people to recognize the responsibility of their leaders. He wanted them to know that leaders will be severely judged. "The LORD himself has scattered them; he no longer watches over them. The priests are shown no honor, the elders no favor" (4:16). As it says, the Lord himself will do this.

So Must We

We learn something from this about the importance of leaders, particularly leaders in our churches. Clearly, it is vital for leaders to be honestly devoted to God. The leaders here and in the book of Jeremiah were not condemned for inexperience, inefficiency, or even ineptitude. They were condemned because their hearts went after the wrong gods, and then heinous sins followed. They were condemned because their hearts had turned bad, and they led the people in a bad way.

If judgment falls on America, presidents and politicians may receive some of the judgment, but I fear that a special portion of it will fall on the prophets and priests of our land: the preachers and pastors. Too often and for too long we have compromised the gospel and cared for ourselves more than for our flocks, our retirement packages more than our sermons, our own peace and quiet rather than the church's good. God's judgment will fall mightily upon the pastors who preach falsehoods and coddle sin, who are more caught up in visions of their own greatness than the greatness of God, who are more interested in the approval of people than the approval of God himself. May God forgive *me* for any ways in which I have been guilty of these things, and may he deliver us all from such debilitating and deadly unfaithfulness among our leaders.

When we suffer, we should give special attention to our leaders, and to those who claim to teach us God's words and God's ways.

WHEN SUFFERING COMES, PRAY FOR THE FUTURE

Amid these calamities, God taught the Israelites a fourth thing. He called them to pray for the future.

The People's Desperation Continues

Chapter 5 continues to describe the people amid their desperate situation. Their land had been occupied by foreigners. The most basic necessities of life had been taken from them and could be purchased only at a dear price. The women had been raped. The men had been slain. All had experienced severe hunger. The more fortunate leaders were ignored. The less fortunate were strung up. The city's culture, civic life, and government had entirely disappeared.

They Were Called to Pray

So what does God call them to do? The whole of chapter 5 is a prayer to God, in which the prophet leads the people. He begins the chapter, "Remember, O LORD, what has happened to us; look, and see our disgrace" (5:1). Then he prays primarily for restoration and renewal. And his prayer ends, "Restore us to yourself, O LORD, that we may return; renew our days as of old unless you have utterly rejected us and are angry with us beyond measure" (5:21-22).

So Must We

So what should you do when you suffer? When you experience some great change or loss? You should pray. What more can you do than pray to God?

Ask God for help to endure your trials and temptations. Ask him to shed the light of understanding that you need to get through your ordeal. You may think God has *heard* enough from you; but at least ask him. You may think God has *had* enough of you; but at least ask him. Even if you are approaching him for the fiftieth time, do not think that he has finally become impatient with you. As long as you have life and breath, you have it for a reason, and therefore you have hope. At least ask God. Go to him in prayer.

How many of us became Christians because something happened that dashed our plans or that exposed the shallowness of our hopes; so we turned to God in sincere and humble prayer in order to know his will!

When we suffer, we should pray.

WHEN SUFFERING COMES, HOPE IN GOD

But if the people of Israel were being punished for their sins, how could they expect God to listen to their prayers? For that, we turn back to chapter 3 and our last point. When these calamities came, God led the Israelites to hope in him.

As we alluded to earlier, Hebrew poetry often reached its climax in the middle, not at the end as in most English poetry. And that is the case with the book of Lamentations. The middle chapter—chapter 3—is the longest, and it carries the heart of the message of the book.

Their Situation Remained Abysmal

The siege had taken a terrible physical toll. The Israelites were trapped by the Babylonians, and they were ignored by God. Their peace and plenty had been replaced by war and want.

They Were Called to Hope in God

What were they to do? We find the answer in the center section of this chapter, which, then, is the very center of the book:

> Yet this I call to mind
>   and therefore I have hope:
>
> Because of the LORD's great love we are not consumed,
>   for his compassions never fail.
> They are new every morning;
>   great is your faithfulness.
> I say to myself, "The LORD is my portion;
>   therefore I will wait for him."
>
> The LORD is good to those whose hope is in him,
>   to the one who seeks him;
> it is good to wait quietly
>   for the salvation of the LORD.
> It is good for a man to bear the yoke
>   while he is young.
>
> Let him sit alone in silence,
>   for the LORD has laid it on him.
> Let him bury his face in the dust—
>   there may yet be hope.
> Let him offer his cheek to one who would strike him,
>   and let him be filled with disgrace.

For men are not cast off
    by the Lord forever.
Though he brings grief, he will show compassion,
    so great is his unfailing love.
For he does not willingly bring affliction
    or grief to the children of men.

To crush underfoot
    all prisoners in the land,
to deny a man his rights
    before the Most High,
to deprive a man of justice—
    would not the Lord see such things?

Who can speak and have it happen
    if the Lord has not decreed it?
Is it not from the mouth of the Most High
    that both calamities and good things come?
Why should any living man complain
    when punished for his sins?

Let us examine our ways and test them,
    and let us return to the LORD.
Let us lift up our hearts and our hands
    to God in heaven, and say:
"We have sinned and rebelled
    and you have not forgiven" (3:21-42).

Here we find the hope that they had, and this hope was based on the character of God (3:21-33), a defense of God's actions (3:34-39), and a call to confession and repentance (3:40-42).

Remarkably, the poet said these words while he was still weeping. He knew that God is a good God! "Because of the LORD's great love we are not consumed, for his compassions never fail." Notice that the word "compassions" here is in the plural. God's compassions are numerous! In the Hebrew, the word for "love" is also in the plural—because of the Lord's great *loves* we are not consumed!

Then we read, "great is your faithfulness." God's compassions and God's loves stand parallel with God's faithfulness!

The poet could look back on the history of Israel and his own life and see that God's record of dealing with his people justified their hope even in the darkest times. Therefore, he could look at their present sufferings and know that the real injustices they had endured at the hands of the Babylonians were also real acts of justice from God: "to deprive a man of justice—would not the Lord see such things? Who can speak and have it happen if the Lord has not decreed it?" Friend, God's just and righteous character is behind everything that happens to you and me.

How can that be? How can God use the injustices of men to accomplish his just purposes in the salvation of his people? Lamentations points us toward the answer, as we consider the one man who stands in for the nation and bears their suffering:

> Streams of tears flow from my eyes
>   because my people are destroyed.
>
> My eyes will flow unceasingly,
>   without relief (3:48-49).
>
> They tried to end my life in a pit
>   and threw stones at me;
> the waters closed over my head,
>   and I thought I was about to be cut off.
>
> I called on your name, O Lord,
>   from the depths of the pit (3:53-55).
>
> You have seen the depth of their vengeance,
>   all their plots against me.
>
> O Lord, you have heard their insults,
>   all their plots against me—
> what my enemies whisper and mutter
>   against me all day long (3:60-62).

Yet,

> O Lord, you took up my case;
>   you redeemed my life.
> You have seen, O Lord, the wrong done to me.
>   Uphold my cause! (3:58-59).

The hope of the people, finally, rested in the one who would come and bear upon himself the sins of the people. Their own injustices, the injustices of the Babylonians, and even the injustices of Herod and Pontius Pilate, as we have seen, would finally be used to crucify Jesus Christ. And once Christ had suffered, bled, and died upon a Roman cross for the sins of all his people, God would redeem his life from the grave and grant that same new life to all those who would ever repent of their sins and trust in him for salvation. How could they pray while being punished? And how can God use the injustices of men to accomplish his just ends? Because Christ would pay for those injustices completely, more than a besieged city ever could. And now, you can know that Christ has paid for your sins entirely, and will grant you reconciliation with God wholly, if only you will repent of your sins and believe.

The survivors of the fall of Jerusalem found hope in God, though it led them down a new path. The fall of Jerusalem in 587 B.C. marked a great turning point in the history of God's people. It began their transition from being a nation state to being a people, from being Israelites to being Jews. After all, the nation was no more. They also learned that God was not limited to a particular building, a particular geographic location, or any particular plan of theirs, but that he was the God of the whole earth.

So Must We

When all of your circumstances begin to look down, where do you look for hope? Clearly not in your circumstances. They are looking down! Will you wait for a change of circumstances? Certainly, any new circumstances will eventually look down as well! No, you must look to God's character of compassion, love, and faithfulness. And you can see those things most clearly through what he has accomplished in Christ, who suffered according to God's purposes more than any of us ever will—all for love's sake. If you are a Christian, I can tell you that God has promised that not only will he dash your hopes, he will give you better ones! And those better ones he will most certainly fulfill.

Knowing this will make a difference amid your sufferings. And I mean *knowing* it. You will be able to endure trials and to experience God's *compassions* and *loves* when you know and trust God as he has revealed himself in Lamentations. If you are convinced that you must understand a particular trial perfectly well before you are willing to trust in God, I will tell you now that you will fail. At some point, if you haven't already, you *will* experience a trial that exceeds your ability to find an explanation. Complete explanations, finally, are God's business. But if you know him for who he is and what he is like, then you will be able to trust his character and all of his promises in Christ even in the trials you cannot understand. You will have a different life, in both the good times and the bad.

When we suffer for God, we should realize that our only lasting hope is in his unchanging character and what he has done in Christ.

CONCLUSION

In his great book *Future Grace,* John Piper tells the story of Evelyn Brand. Brand

> grew up in a well-to-do English family. She studied at the London Conservatory of Art and dressed in the finest silks. But she went with her husband to minister as missionaries in the Kolli Malai range of India. After about 10 years her husband died at age 44 and she came home "a broken woman, beaten down by pain and grief." But after a year's recuperation, and against all advice, she returned to India. Her soul was restored and she poured her life into the hill people, "nursing the sick, teaching farming, lecturing about guinea worms, doing whatever it was that came to hand that needed doing, rearing orphans, clearing jungle land, pulling teeth, establishing schools, preaching the gospel." She lived in a portable hut, eight feet square, that could be taken down, moved and erected again.
>
> At age 67 she fell and broke her hip. Her son, Paul, had just come to India as a surgeon. He encouraged her to retire. She had already suffered a broken arm, several cracked vertebrae and recurrent malaria. Paul mounted as many arguments as he could think of to persuade her that sixty-seven years was a good investment in ministry, and now it was time to retire. Her response? "Paul, you know these mountains. If I leave, who will help the village people? Who will treat their wounds and pull their teeth and teach them about Jesus? When someone comes to take my place, then and only then will I retire. In any case, why preserve this old body if it's not going to be used where God needs me?" That was her final answer. So she worked on.
>
> At the age of 95 she died. Following her instructions, villagers buried her in a simple cotton sheet so that her body would return to the soil and nourish new life. "Her spirit, too, lives on, in a church, a clinic, several schools, and in the faces of thousands of villagers across five mountain ranges of South India." Her son commented that "with wrinkles as deep and extensive as any I have ever seen on a human face . . . she was a beautiful woman." But it was not the beauty of the silk and heirlooms of London high society. For the last twenty years of her life she refused to have a mirror in her house! She was consumed with ministry, not mirrors. A coworker once remarked that Granny Brand was more alive than any person he had ever met. "By giving away life, she found it."[4]

Strangely enough, we don't lose our lives, we gain our lives when we ven-

---

[4] John Piper, *The Purifying Power of Living by Faith in Future Grace* (Sisters, Ore.: Multnomah, 1995), 288-289. The quoted portions are from Paul Brand with Philip Yancey, "And God Created Pain," *Christianity Today,* January 10, 1994, 22-23.

ture out upon the faithfulness of God by trusting him with life's disappointments, whether the death of a husband at age 44, a broken hip at age 67, or discouragement from our own son. We gain our lives when we trust him through suffering, repentance, and obedience all the way to joy. And we can do it because God's grace enables us to discern his gracious character and to love him more than whatever we might lose, even life itself.

Friend, the question for you is, what do you value more than God himself?

Let me offer one last practical illustration, though it is not as eloquent as Evelyn Brand's life story. Just last Sunday morning, as I stood in the church pulpit, I was in great pain. I had not slept one minute the night before, because I had had an abscess in a tooth. On Monday, I went for a root canal. As I lay back on the dentist's chair, the dentist approached me with that little whirring sound we all know—the sound of a drill. Nobody likes that sound. But why did I lie there and allow him to bring both that terrible sound and, what's more, that terrible feeling into my mouth? Because I knew he had a good purpose. On the other hand, if you were to come up to me after a church service with a portable drill in your hand, and you asked, "Hey, Mark, mind if I poke around a bit?" I would say "No way!" If suffering or pain must come, there had better be a reason for it. There had better be meaning in it. There had better be something that Evelyn Brand gave her life for, or else it was a ridiculous and tragic waste!

As a drill in the hands of a good dentist, so are our sufferings in the hands of God. Actually, when God operates on our lives, we can trust that his hands are more skilled than the hands of the most skilled dentist. He knows what he is doing. And we can trust that his purposes are always good, even when we don't always know what those purposes are.

When we get right down to it, there are two responses to suffering: you either *deny* God's hand in it (and become self-righteous and bitter), or you *discern* God's hand in it (and trust that he is making you more like himself).

Is there sin to confess? Can you pray? Can you hope in God?

Suffering will make you *bitter*, or suffering can be part of God's plan to refine you and make you *better*. Choose the latter way. Confess. Pray. Trust and hope.

Let us pray:

The Lord Jesus tells us in his Word, "Do not store up for yourselves treasures on earth, where moth and rust destroy, and where thieves break in and steal, but store up for yourselves treasures in heaven, where moth and rust do not destroy, and where thieves do not break in and steal. For where your treasure is, there your heart will be also." Lord, you know the pain that we feel, because our hearts have been hurt. They have been touched too many times and in too many ways for us to remember it all. But, Lord, we confess that we come with certain memories seared in our minds; and we pray that your Holy Spirit would help us to look again at our sufferings and discern your love for us within those very pains. Father, for whatever we cannot make out in our own wisdom, we pray that you would give us a heavenly wisdom—if not fully to understand your ways, at least to trust your character. The character of the same one who came and died on the cross for us. Lord, teach us to trust and to live as people who know that our final hope cannot be in any earthly Jerusalem or in any earthly circumstances or relationships, but only in you. Lord, we know our own hearts, that we cannot make this happen! And so we pray that you would do it, for your glory's sake. In Jesus' name. Amen.

Questions for Reflection

1. What massive acts of devastation—whether the result of nature or of human decision—have occurred in your lifetime?

2. According to the book of Lamentations, did God have control over those events? Even the events caused by sinful human decisions? If yes, is God guilty of sin? Why or why not?

3. What comfort exists in knowing that God is sovereign over all things?

4. If you were to choose one of the massive acts of devastation you listed in question 1, why would you be irreverently treading in the Almighty's territory by asserting a confident explanation for what God's purposes must have been? What would God prefer for you to do as you consider his governance over such events?

5. Can you name an occasion of suffering in your life where your continued obstinacy and blaming of others only made your difficulties worse? How would the situation have turned out had you begun by cultivating humility and confessing your own sins?

6. How do you live like a "practical atheist"?

7. Does Lamentations' message of God's sovereignty over suffering and his faithfulness amid suffering have any practical applications for our churches?

8. When was the last time you sat down with the members of your immediate family and spent an hour recounting all the instances of God's faithfulness in your lives together over the previous several months? When is the next time you will do this?

9. If you are a leader in your home, church, or office, what difference will the message of Lamentations make in your life?

10. Where do we see God's faithfulness displayed most perfectly?

11. Sadly, people often point to suffering as an excuse not to believe in God. Suppose, then, you asked a non-Christian friend to read Lamentations with you. How could you use the message of Lamentations to point to the gospel of Jesus Christ, a gospel message that has suffering at its very core?

THE MESSAGE OF EZEKIEL: PARADISE

26

THE MESSAGE OF EZEKIEL: PARADISE

HOPING FOR UTOPIA[1]

Almost five hundred years ago, a little volume was published with these words on the title page: "A fruitful, pleasant and witty work, of the best state of a public weal, and of the new isle, called Utopia," a book "written by the right worthy and famous Sir Thomas More, Knight." In *Utopia,* More depicts an imaginary island through the eyes of a traveler, and the society of people living on this island is perfect!

When the book was first released, More's friends could see the humor of the piece. They knew exactly what he was doing: subtly criticizing the imperfections of the real island kingdom of which he was a prominent servant—England under the rule of King Henry the Eighth. Like most nations, the nation of England had good parts and bad. Yet under King Henry, writing about the bad—at least directly—could be dangerous. Through his witty fiction, More had found a vehicle to comment on his times in an entertaining and ostensibly unthreatening fashion to those who would read it.

Even the name he gave to his fictitious island was artfully chosen—*Utopia*. We use that word in English today to refer to a land of ideal perfection. Well, it was coined by More, and it was a pun in Greek. *Topia* means place. And the *U* can either mean "good" (as in eulogy), giving *Utopia* the meaning "good place"; or it can refer to a negation or "no," giving *Utopia* the meaning "no place." Really, the name says it all: such a "good place" is "no place." Not in this world, anyway.

Is that right? Is no place finally the good place we all dream about? Is it

---

[1] This sermon was originally preached on April 20, 1997, at Capitol Hill Baptist Church in Washington, D.C.

only an ancient myth, an old fairy-tale, a child's dream, or the projection of our inner desires? Does paradise really exist?

INTRODUCING EZEKIEL

I don't know how you would answer that question. But if you feel that another, better place must exist, and that for some reason it has not yet been revealed, then the Old Testament book of Ezekiel is well-suited for you.

In our present series in the Major Prophets called "Big Hopes," we turn to this hope for paradise in the book of Ezekiel, where, in some unusual ways, God teaches his people some very important things about himself and about this hope. Our text is the entire book of Ezekiel. We won't read the entire text here, but maybe you can through the coming week.

Three studies ago, we heard the prophet Isaiah warn Judah's King Hezekiah about the Assyrian army, while assuring him of God's care. Two studies ago, we heard the prophet Jeremiah, who lived one century after Isaiah, urge Judah and Jerusalem to follow the Lord's direction by surrendering to the Babylonian army. In the last study, we considered the lamentations of one individual—perhaps Jeremiah—who was in Jerusalem during its siege and fall. In our present study, we encounter the prophet Ezekiel, who lived at the same time as Jeremiah but whose ministry actually took place in exile in Babylon. The Babylonians carted Israelites off to exile in Babylon in several waves, and Ezekiel was among one of the earlier waves. He probably traveled to Babylon in 597 B.C., along with the royal family and other leading citizens of Jerusalem. Remember, Jerusalem was not entirely destroyed until a decade later, in 587 B.C. Ezekiel had been trained as a priest in Jerusalem, and he knew the religious life of his people well. Perhaps he had even heard Jeremiah preach in Jerusalem before he was taken away, though neither prophet ever referred to the other. But once Ezekiel was an exile away from the temple, it may have looked as if this priest had no future serving God's people. After all, a priest's work was tied up with the temple. Similarly, many Jews initially worried that God would be inaccessible once they were away from the Promised Land. But that was not the case—for Ezekiel or the people. God had prepared this young priest to be his special mouthpiece to the Jews in exile.

Anyone who has read the book of Ezekiel knows that the man himself was far from an ordinary individual. W. F. Albright describes Ezekiel as "one of the greatest spiritual figures of all time, in spite of his tendency to psychic abnormality."[2] Ezekiel's behavior has been called many things: "pathological," "psychic," "schizophrenic," "epileptic," "catatonic," "psychotic," and "para-

---

[2] W. F. Albright, *From the Stone Age to Christianity* (Baltimore: Johns Hopkins, 1940), 248.

noid." About fifty years ago, E. C. Broome presented a Freudian analysis of Ezekiel (which is difficult to do in person, let alone with someone who's been dead for almost three thousand years!). He labeled Ezekiel as "a true psychotic characterized by a narcissistic-masochistic conflict, with attendant fantasies of castration and unconscious sexual regression . . . schizophrenic withdrawal . . . and delusions of persecution and grandeur."[3]

Perhaps what makes Ezekiel appear so strange are the bizarre things the Lord called him to do in order to communicate with his people. Quite simply, he called Ezekiel to communicate weird and fantastic visions by performing strange and symbolic actions. During the first period of Ezekiel's ministry (593–586 B.C.), God called him to be a virtual recluse, afflicted with periodic fits, paralysis, and dumbness. For example, we observe episodes of aphasia, where Ezekiel lies motionless on his side for months, even years (4:4ff.). He is bound up in his house with ropes so that he cannot go out among the people (3:25). His tongue is glued to the roof of his mouth so that he cannot speak (3:26). He is ordered not to mourn the death of his wife (24:16-17). He is transported in visions (e.g., 8:7, passim). He is told to make a model of the besieged Jerusalem and hold a sword up against it (4:1-2; 5:1-2). He packs his belongings and digs through the city wall to symbolize the coming exile. I could go on and on.

This book has been regarded as so strange that Jewish rabbis would often not allow young men to read Ezekiel until they were thirty years old, lest they become discouraged at the difficulty of understanding the Scriptures and so despise them.

But it is not really that hard to understand. Let me give you a quick overview before we dive in. Ezekiel's structure is even clearer than Isaiah's or Jeremiah's. It falls into two halves. In chapters 1–24, the Lord tells his people of his judgment on them. The Babylonians and Nebuchadnezzar will destroy Jerusalem, he says. The climax occurs in chapter 24 when word comes to Ezekiel that the siege has begun. Chapters 25–48 then contain more hope. The second half begins with condemnations of the surrounding nations, specifically Ammon, Moab, Edom, Philistia, Tyre, Sidon, and Egypt. Word then arrives in 33:21 that Jerusalem has, in fact, fallen; and from that point Ezekiel begins to prophesy about hope and restoration for God's people. The book largely occurs in chronological order, and Ezekiel's prophecies stretch over a two-decade-plus period—from around 593 to 571 B.C.

Beyond this, there are three basic sequences of visions that God gives

---

[3] E. C. Broome, "Ezekiel's Abnormal Personality," in *Journal of Biblical Literature* 65 (1946): 277-292, at 291-292.

Ezekiel, and if you understand these, you will know the book. The first sequence occurs in chapters 1–3, where Ezekiel, now in Babylon, first sees God coming to him in a vision. The second sequence occurs in chapters 8–11. It is a flashback, as it were, in which God shows Ezekiel how his presence departed from Jerusalem because of the idolatrous worship being practiced in the temple. The book then concludes with a long vision sequence in chapters 40–48 in which God again comes to his people in a rebuilt temple.

That's really the summary of the book of Ezekiel. I want us to follow the three sequences of visions which the Lord gave to Ezekiel in order to learn a bit more about the book and whether or not there really is a utopia, a paradise.

A VISION OF GOD THE KING

Ezekiel's first vision is a vision of God the king. As in other great books in the Bible,[4] this book begins with God in his heavenly court. The scene is also reminiscent of God's appearances to Moses at Mount Sinai and to Isaiah when he calls Isaiah to be a prophet.

God appears to Ezekiel in an extraordinary opening vision, which begins with the words, "In the thirtieth year, in the fourth month on the fifth day, while I was among the exiles by the Kebar River, the heavens were opened and I saw visions of God" (1:1). Ezekiel then describes this vision in the first few chapters.

Having read Jeremiah, I find it both amazing and very significant that Ezekiel had this vision. Jeremiah, who was back in Jerusalem, was telling the people of Judah, "Surrender to Babylon. If you try to stay here, the Lord promises he will not remain with you or bless you. You must go with them, and you will be blessed." The simple fact that God then revealed himself to Ezekiel (Daniel, too) in Babylon confirmed Jeremiah's words. Jeremiah had foreseen this in a vision of two baskets of figs, in which one basket fared well while the other did not (Jeremiah 24). The Lord pledged to continue to bless those who were separated from Solomon's temple, David's throne, and Abraham's land.

Have you ever seen a child do something wrong and then receive a "time out" in their bedroom or the chair in the corner for punishment? The exile was like a big time out for God's people. He gave them a time out from the land, the throne, and the temple, all of which they had begun to misunderstand and even idolize. The Promised Land, the Davidic line of the kings, and the temple, which symbolized God's presence, were all good gifts from him. But the people had misused them. The gifts became too important. So God took them

---

[4] Genesis, Job, John, Ephesians, and Revelation.

away by calling his people out to Babylon. He set them aside for seventy years so that they could refocus on what was important and why. Still, he faithfully went with them into exile, and that's how Ezekiel's vision begins, with God coming to his people apart from the temple, the line of David, or the land of Israel.

The vision itself begins with a mighty wind:

> I looked, and I saw a windstorm coming out of the north—an immense cloud with flashing lightning and surrounded by brilliant light. The center of the fire looked like glowing metal, and in the fire was what looked like four living creatures. In appearance their form was that of a man, but each of them had four faces and four wings (1:4-6).

As the vision continues, we see some very bizarre creatures surrounding God's throne:

> As I looked at the living creatures, I saw a wheel on the ground beside each creature with its four faces. This was the appearance and structure of the wheels: They sparkled like chrysolite, and all four looked alike. Each appeared to be made like a wheel intersecting a wheel. As they moved, they would go in any one of the four directions the creatures faced; the wheels did not turn about as the creatures went. Their rims were high and awesome, and all four rims were full of eyes all around. When the living creatures moved, the wheels beside them moved; and when the living creatures rose from the ground, the wheels also rose (1:15-19).

After further description of these creatures, a voice sounds out overhead. And then the throne itself appears:

> Then there came a voice from above the expanse over their heads as they stood with lowered wings. Above the expanse over their heads was what looked like a throne of sapphire, and high above on the throne was a figure like that of a man. I saw that from what appeared to be his waist up he looked like glowing metal, as if full of fire, and that from there down he looked like fire; and brilliant light surrounded him. Like the appearance of a rainbow in the clouds on a rainy day, so was the radiance around him. This was the appearance of the likeness of the glory of the LORD. When I saw it, I fell facedown, and I heard the voice of one speaking (1:25-28).

God Is Not Like Us

Many people have tried to draw—literally illustrate—what this vision must have looked like to Ezekiel. But that's probably an impossible task. What

Ezekiel could *see* in this vision was that God is not like us. He is strange, other, and different than we are. Often, we assume God is just like us. But Ezekiel's vision lets us *see* how God is an entirely different being than we are. We cannot simply make him over in our own image. He is unusual.

Ezekiel did not hesitate to describe everything he did see, but notice how often he used the words "like" and "as if." It was "like a throne of sapphire," and the figure on it looked "as if" he were "full of fire."

The Bible calls God "holy." And it isn't that he just possesses holiness; he *is* holy. Therefore, we must show reverence to God. Ezekiel himself fell face-down, even after all his theological training! His new knowledge of God did not make him feel more casual about God at all. He was awed by this vision of God, as Job was awed when he had a vision of God.

God is not simply the old man upstairs. He is no mere kind grandfather in the sky with a long white beard. He is not a friendly neighbor, a pal, or chum. The casual happiness we often regard as the height of spiritual intimacy with God is never pictured in the Bible. Every vision of God in the Bible is awesome and inspires reverence.

God Is All-Powerful and All-Wise

We see here, too, that God is all-powerful and all-wise. Perhaps you noticed that the rims of the wheels are covered with eyes (1:18). And the four faces look in every direction (1:6, 10, 17). These things show God's omniscience—he sees everywhere. There is nothing he does not perceive. He is all-knowing. And the fact that God can be on this chariot that moves in all directions shows that he is all-powerful. He can be in any place. Ezekiel could trust this all-powerful and all-wise God!

God Is Not Limited by Circumstances

But the real point for Ezekiel was that he was seeing God at all. After all, he was not in Jerusalem or in the temple. He was in exile when he had a vision of God Almighty! God is not limited to Jerusalem. The vision assured Ezekiel that God would be with his people wherever they were scattered. Indeed, God is not limited to any one place. He has a concern for the whole world, as the rainbow in 1:28, recalling God's covenant with Noah for the whole world, reminds us.

Friend, God is not limited to where you think you last spotted him! Maybe there was a time when you felt especially close to God. Perhaps he had blessed you through a particular author or preacher, a particular church or "worship style," a good friendship or even a job. But now you are troubled, uncertain, afraid you have lost the ability to be near him because the circumstances have changed.

Well, just as God showed Ezekiel and his Old Testament people, he shows us that he is not limited by circumstances. It is wonderful to know God's blessings through any of these avenues, but remember that God can work in many ways. He is not limited to particular circumstances. He is the God of the universe.

God Takes the Initiative

Notice also that God takes the initiative. He is the one who comes to us. Look again at verse 1: "the heavens were opened." He chose to come down. Ezekiel didn't open the heavens and go to *God*. Then verse 3: "the word of the LORD came." And verse 4: "I saw a windstorm coming out of the north." Then in verse 25: "there came a voice." And finally verse 28: "I heard the voice of one speaking."

Like Moses and the burning bush. Like Isaiah in the temple. Like Paul on the road to Damascus. So with Ezekiel. None of these men were out looking for God or trying to initiate contact with him. This God takes the initiative. He comes to us.

God Communicates

This God also communicates. Did you notice that Ezekiel's vision climaxes in a voice? In words? If we were choreographing this vision, we would not do it this way. These days, we would want a spectacle—a show for the eyes. But here, God's vision climaxes not with something for the eyes but with a word to the ears—"I heard the voice of one speaking" (1:28).

God does not merely want to be adored from a distance. He wants a personal relationship. He does not want us merely to encounter him in order to enjoy some visual sensation; he wants covenant love. Do not be satisfied with mere sensation. This kind of verbal communication with God is the foundation of this book, and it is the foundation of any relationship we will ever have with God. Verbal communication is what makes relationships.

Now, you may object by saying that you have a relationship with your dog, and that your dog doesn't talk. But imagine this: what if you got home today and your dog *did* talk to you! I suggest that that would materially change your relationship with your dog. Our relationships are shaped by our verbal communication with each other. And God has graciously communicated with his people.

This is why God's Word is central in our church's gatherings. We take time to hear from God's Word because he speaks to us through his Word. God is committed to speaking to his people, to knowing them, and to having them know him. And so with Ezekiel.

A VISION OF GOD'S DEPARTURE

The second great vision in this book is a flashback. It's a vision of God's departure from the temple in Jerusalem.

As a minister, I have been asked about heaven many times. I am always amazed at all the questions people can ask about heaven! Often, I simply tell people that there are many things I don't know about heaven. But two things I am certain of: there is a heaven, and this world is not it!

I don't know if you are ever tempted to mistake this world for paradise. My guess is that most of us are well aware that it is not. Now, it may be that you feel that you are having a really good life. Your job, your health, your friendships are all going pretty well right now. Still, a vision like Ezekiel's flashback reminds us of how far away we are from paradise.

Certainly, Ezekiel's fellow exiles in Babylon knew this. But what Ezekiel's vision taught them was that not only was Babylon not paradise, neither was Jerusalem! They had gone to great lengths to protect Jerusalem, thinking that holding on to Jerusalem was holding on to God. But that was wrong. So Ezekiel was given another vision, or series of visions, in which he saw the sin of Israel and God's consequent departure. God turned his people over to the care of the gods whom they really loved.

Chapters 6–24 are largely composed of prophecies against Israel because of its sin. God wants the people to know exactly why he has deserted them. The prophecies against Israel begin in chapters 6–7, and the Lord promises, "I will turn my face away from [my people]" (7:22), just as he had promised through Jeremiah ("I will show them my back and not my face"—Jer. 18:17). But the core of God's complaint against his people is shown to Ezekiel in chapters 8–11. Beginning in chapters 8–9, God gives him a very specific vision of the idolatry being practiced in the temple itself. In chapters 10–11, the vision continues, but now Ezekiel sees God departing from the temple and its grounds, just as the people had departed from the worship of God. The vision ends in chapter 11 as the Lord departs the city itself. Here's a sample of this vision:

> . . . the hand of the Sovereign LORD came upon me there. I looked, and I saw a figure like that of a man. From what appeared to be his waist down he was like fire, and from there up his appearance was as bright as glowing metal. He stretched out what looked like a hand and took me by the hair of my head. The Spirit lifted me up between earth and heaven and in visions of God he took me to Jerusalem, to the entrance to the north gate of the inner court, where the idol that provokes to jealousy stood (8:1-3).

And he said to me, "Go in and see the wicked and detestable things they are doing here." So I went in and looked, and I saw portrayed all over the walls all kinds of crawling things and detestable animals and all the idols of the house of Israel (8:9-10).

Then the glory of the LORD rose from above the cherubim and moved to the threshold of the temple (10:4).

Then the glory of the LORD departed from over the threshold of the temple and stopped above the cherubim (10:18).

Then the cherubim, with the wheels beside them, spread their wings, and the glory of the God of Israel was above them. The glory of the LORD went up from within the city and stopped above the mountain east of it. The Spirit lifted me up and brought me to the exiles in Babylonia in the vision given by the Spirit of God. Then the vision I had seen went up from me, and I told the exiles everything the LORD had shown me (11:22-25).

If you don't read any other chapters this week, read chapters 8–11 of Ezekiel. They have a strange *cinema verité*—or "You were there" quality—as if Ezekiel, standing in Babylon, is being given a divine broadcast of pagan services occurring in Jerusalem's temple. God goes through the temple—his house—from the inside out, as if taking one last look. Then he departs the temple and its grounds, leaving it to be destroyed.

The people had caused this unnatural separation, this divorce, between them and God by pursuing other gods. In chapters 16, 20, and 23, the Lord uses the most graphic of language to charge Jerusalem with heinous unfaithfulness. He says to them,

"But you trusted in your beauty and used your fame to become a prostitute. You lavished your favors on anyone who passed by and your beauty became his. You took some of your garments to make gaudy high places, where you carried on your prostitution. Such things should not happen, nor should they ever occur. You also took the fine jewelry I gave you, the jewelry made of my gold and silver, and you made for yourself male idols and engaged in prostitution with them. And you took your embroidered clothes to put on them, and you offered my oil and incense before them. Also the food I provided for you—the fine flour, olive oil and honey I gave you to eat—you offered as fragrant incense before them. That is what happened, declares the Sovereign LORD" (16:15-19).

"Yet the people of Israel rebelled against me in the desert. They did not follow my decrees but rejected my laws—although the man who obeys them will live by them—and they utterly desecrated my Sabbaths. So I said I would pour out my wrath on them and destroy them in the desert" (20:13).

"Also with uplifted hand I swore to them in the desert that I would not bring them into the land I had given them—a land flowing with milk and honey, most beautiful of all lands—because they rejected my laws and did not follow my decrees and desecrated my Sabbaths. For their hearts were devoted to their idols" (20:15-16).

"But she carried her prostitution still further. She saw men portrayed on a wall, figures of Chaldeans portrayed in red, with belts around their waists and flowing turbans on their heads; all of them looked like Babylonian chariot officers, natives of Chaldea. As soon as she saw them, she lusted after them and sent messengers to them in Chaldea. Then the Babylonians came to her, to the bed of love, and in their lust they defiled her. After she had been defiled by them, she turned away from them in disgust. When she carried on her prostitution openly and exposed her nakedness, I turned away from her in disgust, just as I had turned away from her sister. Yet she became more and more promiscuous as she recalled the days of her youth, when she was a prostitute in Egypt. There she lusted after her lovers, whose genitals were like those of donkeys and whose emission was like that of horses. So you longed for the lewdness of your youth, when in Egypt your bosom was caressed and your young breasts fondled" (23:14-21).

If you think these are inappropriate words for a sermon, let me remind you that God told Ezekiel to speak them in public. Clearly, God was upset about how his people had devoted their hearts to idols and false gods. "This is deeply, deeply wrong!" he was saying.

Many years before Ezekiel's day, God had warned his people through Moses that he would send them into exile if they were unfaithful to him. In one of Moses' final speeches to the people of Israel before they entered the Promised Land, he prophesied, "Just as it pleased the LORD to make you prosper and increase in number, so it will please him to ruin and destroy you. You will be uprooted from the land you are entering to possess. Then the LORD will scatter you among all nations" (Deut. 28:63-64).

God's people, as I said, caused this unnatural separation, this divorce. And now they would pay the price. After all of the stinging indictments against Israel's unfaithfulness that we have read, we read at the beginning of chapter 24, "The word of the LORD came to me: 'Son of man, record this date, because the king of Babylon has laid siege to Jerusalem this very day." In the siege, Jerusalem began to bear the punishment of God's desertion.

At the same time, God called Ezekiel to the most painful—and most powerful—symbolic act he was ever asked to endure:

The word of the LORD came to me: "Son of man, with one blow I am about to take away from you the delight of your eyes. Yet do not lament or weep or shed any tears. Groan quietly; do not mourn for the dead. Keep your turban fastened and your sandals on your feet; do not cover the lower part of your face or eat the customary food of mourners."

So I spoke to the people in the morning, and in the evening my wife died. The next morning I did as I had been commanded.

Then the people asked me, "Won't you tell us what these things have to do with us?"

So I said to them, "The word of the LORD came to me: Say to the house of Israel, 'This is what the Sovereign LORD says: I am about to desecrate my sanctuary—the stronghold in which you take pride, the delight of your eyes, the object of your affection. The sons and daughters you left behind will fall by the sword. And you will do as I have done. You will not cover the lower part of your face or eat the customary food of mourners. You will keep your turbans on your heads and your sandals on your feet. You will not mourn or weep but will waste away because of your sins and groan among yourselves. Ezekiel will be a sign to you; you will do just as he has done. When this happens, you will know that I am the Sovereign LORD.'

"And you, son of man, on the day I take away their stronghold, their joy and glory, the delight of their eyes, their heart's desire, and their sons and daughters as well—on that day a fugitive will come to tell you the news. At that time your mouth will be opened; you will speak with him and will no longer be silent. So you will be a sign to them, and they will know that I am the LORD" (24:15-27).

To adequately communicate his feelings for his people, God could not summon language more deep, more intimate, more loving, and more involved than the language of a relationship between a man and his wife. As Ezekiel lost his wife ("the delight of your eyes"), so the people would lose Jerusalem ("the delight of their eyes"). Both of these losses were a dim shadow of God's loss of his people Israel, whom he had called and made, whom he had cared for and delighted in, and whom he, in his holy and jealous love, would now judge.

In chapters 25–32 and 35, Ezekiel's attention shifts away from the Israelites and onto the nations. As we learned from the final chapters of Jeremiah in our previous study, we learn here that God's justice is not confined to his people. The nations that looked victorious, both to themselves and to the exiled Israelites, were in trouble with God. God would judge them as well. God's people could be certain that God alone was sovereign over all nations.

Then in chapters 33–34, God takes his own people to task once more for two reasons. First, he says, the leaders are corrupt and "only take care of themselves" (34:2). Second, the people themselves have ignored his Word:

"As for you, son of man, your countrymen are talking together about you by the walls and at the doors of the houses, saying to each other, 'Come and hear the message that has come from the LORD.' My people come to you, as they usually do, and sit before you to listen to your words, but they do not put them into practice. With their mouths they express devotion, but their hearts are greedy for unjust gain. Indeed, to them you are nothing more than one who sings love songs with a beautiful voice and plays an instrument well, for they hear your words but do not put them into practice" (33:30-32).

The people would simultaneously sit, hear, and enjoy God's Word and then ignore it! They would go through all the motions of worshiping God, but their hearts were devoted to idols.

In short, the people of Israel were tempted to trust the wealth of their land, the political stability of the Davidic line, and even the temple itself, all the while ignoring God's Word. So none of these things would save God's people.

What kind of caution should that be to us!

None of these things will work as objects of our trust today either. Not wealth. Not political stability. Not religiousness. Not even sitting and enjoying the preaching of God's Word. None of these things will save us, the Lord teaches us through Ezekiel. We do not just need "religion"; we need a real and exclusive devotion to the one true God. We should not be like the Israelites, who learned to "enjoy listening" to God's Word even while they ignored its call to obedience.

Revival has become a popular topic among Christians today. Yet revivals have never happened simply because people talked about them. Social commentators may say we need revival for various reasons. Christian leaders may call on us to pray for revival, as though it were a thing in itself. But true revivals have happened only when people have gained a right idea of God and his majesty and his holiness. Revivals have happened when people grew in their sense of accountability before this God. In their sense of their own sin. In their understanding of Christ's work on the cross. In their understanding of the call to trust Christ alone. These are the times when God visits his church with revival by pouring out his spirit on the land.

A VISION OF GOD'S COMING AND THE PROMISE OF PARADISE

The last section of Ezekiel's prophecy contains several more famous visions of hope. In chapter 36, for instance, we read about God's remarkable promise to gather his people from the nations, cleanse them from their impurities and idols, replace their hearts of stone with hearts of flesh, and grant them his Spirit who will move them to follow his ways and keep his commands (36:24-28).

In chapter 37, we watch how this will be done in Ezekiel's remarkable vision of the valley of dry bones. Ezekiel preaches God's Word, and the bones come to life!

The last great series of visions in the book occur in chapters 40–48, where God shows Ezekiel a new temple. The first temple had been destroyed in the Babylonian invasion after God's departure.

Now, some people may regard this final vision of a new temple as a boring addition that clutters our Bibles and confuses our minds, sort of like parts of Hebrews and Revelation in the New Testament. One might even be tempted to think of the description of this temple as nothing more than architectural/theological doodling by an unemployed priest in Babylon with nothing better to do!

But that's not the case at all. This is no personal fixation of Ezekiel's. Instead, God says to Ezekiel, "'Son of man, look with your eyes and hear with your ears and pay attention to everything I am going to show you, for that is why you have been brought here. Tell the house of Israel everything you see'" (40:4). Really, this is the climax of the whole book. Most likely, Ezekiel's listeners would have been enthralled by this vision and its promise of complete cleansing and renewal. Most of all, God's pledge to be with his people would have kept his audience in rapt attention.

This is what the vision of God returning to a rebuilt temple in chapter 43 is all about. Even as Ezekiel had seen the glory of the Lord depart from the temple and the city in chapters 10–11, now he watches God return to his temple:

> Then the man brought me to the gate facing east, and I saw the glory of the God of Israel coming from the east. His voice was like the roar of rushing waters, and the land was radiant with his glory. The vision I saw was like the vision I had seen when he came to destroy the city and like the visions I had seen by the Kebar River, and I fell facedown. The glory of the LORD entered the temple through the gate facing east. Then the Spirit lifted me up and brought me into the inner court, and the glory of the LORD filled the temple (43:1-5).

Ezekiel prophesied that the exiles would return to the land, and here he promised that the destroyed temple would be rebuilt and filled with the presence of God. God would once again be with his people. From God's renewed presence and rule, unnumbered blessings would flow, even as a river would flow out of the new temple (chapter 47).

Some have wondered if Ezekiel intended for the plans described in these chapters to comprise an actual blueprint for rebuilding the temple once the land was resettled. That hardly seems to be the case. Aside from the fact that the exiles who returned and rebuilt the temple did not use Ezekiel's prophecy in this fashion, the idealized numbers in Ezekiel's description, the perfect symmetry, and the central location of the temple all suggest that this vision was intended to symbolize the central and exalted position of God in the life of the people.

The purpose of this temple vision was to highlight a restored relationship of God with his people. So the final verse of the book is a fitting ascription: "And the name of the city from that time on will be: THE LORD IS THERE" (48:35b). The book leaves us with the picture of God forever with his people. Ezekiel is, in a sense, the Old Testament equivalent to the book of Revelation, especially given Revelation's closing visions of God, God's judgment, and the heavenly city.

In the book of Ezra, we learn that the exiles did return to the Promised Land and rebuild the temple, yet we have no record of the glory of the Lord filling the temple as it did at Solomon's inauguration of the first temple. But centuries later, Immanuel himself would enter the precincts of the temple in Jerusalem. And in that final vision of the heavenly city in the book of Revelation, the communion with God would become even more intimate as God's people would celebrate not only in his presence, as wonderful as that is, but in full view of him, dwelling with him forever!

Like Revelation, Ezekiel closes with the glorious hope of paradise. Each tribe is promised a portion of a renewed land, a land that seems to point beyond what Ezra and Nehemiah returned to find. A land we still look forward to.

For our purposes here, two questions still need to be answered. First, *why* would God offer this renewed hope for his unfaithful people? Above all else, God promises to change his people and restore them to himself for his own name's sake:

> "It is not for your sake, O house of Israel, that I am going to do these things, *but for the sake of my holy name,* which you have profaned among the nations where you have gone. I will show the holiness of *my great name,* which has been profaned among the nations, the name you have profaned among them. Then the nations will know *that I am the LORD,* declares the Sovereign LORD, when I *show myself* holy through you before their eyes" (36:22-23).

Second, *how* will God restore sinners to himself? After all, he is holy. How can he disregard heinous sin and bring sinners into his presence? Well, Ezekiel only shines a light dimly on the answer to this question; but we do see that God will not simply disregard this sin, he will deal with it. Again and again, God calls Ezekiel the "son of man," and this son of man symbolizes the bearing of sin on his body when he lies on his side (4:4, 5, 6). And in chapter 16, God promises a time "when I make atonement" for faithless Israel (16:63).

God also promises that a day will come when he will judge the people's useless shepherds and "place over them one shepherd, my servant David, and he will tend them; he will tend them and be their shepherd. I the LORD will be their God, and my servant David will be prince among them" (34:23-24). On that day, he will also grant his people a "covenant of peace" (34:25). Who would this coming shepherd be? None other than Jesus Christ, who did come and lay down his life for his sheep (John 10:15). By laying down his life on the cross, Jesus paid for the sins of all those who would ever repent and believe in him. He brought peace for the rebels ready to lay down their arms. He brought forgiveness for the sinners who wanted to be done with sin and knew they could do nothing to forgive themselves. Only through Christ can we be reconciled to the Father. Will you look to him?

If you will, then this vision of God's people living in a restored relationship with him, this promise of paradise, is a promise for you.

CONCLUSION

The purpose of the book of Ezekiel was to reintroduce God's people to him. Again and again, God tells Ezekiel to give these prophecies "that you may know that I am the LORD." All judgment executed and all hope promised in this book had that purpose. He reveals himself to Ezekiel. He deserts the temple filled with idolatry. He comes again. All so that his people would know him.

You may remember the story of the prophet Hosea, who was called to love his own unfaithful wife, Gomer. At one point, Gomer sells herself back into prostitution, and God calls Hosea even then to go and pay her ransom fee, take her back, and restore her to himself. So gracious is God with his people in Ezekiel. He is the divine Hosea. He is just, but he is also merciful beyond belief.

Admittedly, we fear to hope for such love, such paradise. What if there is no such place! Few things are more dangerous than a wrong utopianism. Just think of everything from the Heaven's Gate cult to Marxist communism. We have seen the coercive and monumentally tragic dangers of a wrong utopianism.

Israel learned those dangers, too. Israel thought that the Promised Land was paradise; and that the Davidic monarchy was paradise; and that the temple was paradise; and that Jerusalem was paradise. But strangely, they found the real paradise while in exile in Babylon. No, it wasn't Babylon. It was the Lord, the Lord coming to be with his people.

Paradise is not just a place, it is a relationship with God. That is the only way we will ever find a real paradise.

What have you taken to be paradise?

Let us pray:

Lord, when we come before you we know our hearts and our lives are fully open to your view. We know the idols that we secretly worship and that are hidden to others are fully displayed before you. You see the truth about us, and so we pray that, in your mercy, you would destroy these idols in our lives. O Lord, come after us, even as Hosea did with his wife and as you did with your people here in the book of Ezekiel. Do not allow us to love anything so much as we love you. Give us this desire, Lord. We pray for Jesus' sake. Amen.

Questions for Reflection

1. Why can the belief in a utopia prove dangerous? Do you believe in a utopia or a paradise?

2. In Ezekiel's initial vision of God in chapter 1, he learned that God is not like us. How do people today remake God in their own image?

3. Are you ever overly casual with God? How?

4. As we saw in chapters 16 and 23, God can use some very graphic imagery to depict his people's unfaithfulness to him, namely, harlotry. How can local churches today corporately fall into this same sin?

5. How have you observed God take the initiative in your relationship with him?

6. The people of Ezekiel's day simultaneously sat and enjoyed God's Word and ignored it. What would that look like in a church today?

7. If revivals depend on a renewed understanding of God's majesty and a deepened conviction of our own sin, what is the best way to promote revival in the land?

8. How is a holy God able to restore a sinful and offensive people to himself?

9. How is a relationship with God "paradise"?

THE MESSAGE OF DANIEL: SURVIVAL

27

THE MESSAGE OF DANIEL: SURVIVAL

SURVIVING THROUGH CHANGE[1]

The one constant in our lives is change. We know it in every sphere of our experience.

We know it in our families. "It seems like just the other day we were dropping our little girl off at school on the way to work; now she's dropping us off at work on her way to school."

We know it in our jobs. "The firm wants me to work more hours, but they'll pay more," or "They have decided to restructure the department," or "The company wants to outsource my position."

We even know it in our churches. "What happened to all the hymns? All we sing are songs that sound like what they play on the radio," or "Nobody dresses up for church anymore."

And to be honest, some of these changes at home, at church, and at work make us nervous. We look around and see society changing, and we don't know how we will fit in. More than one person has suggested that the coming decade will see the largest displacement of labor since the Industrial Revolution, as people's jobs become redundant—unneeded—and as laborers are unable to conceptualize the world or the workplace so transformed by computerization and the Information Revolution.

For example, did you hear about the recent traffic jam that started in Virginia and tied up traffic around the entire nation? I'm not kidding. It was a jam on the Internet, caused by extra signals from one computer processor in Virginia. It tied up businesses and research institutions for hours. It may have affected you. It's a new world, friend, and it is getting newer all the time.

---

[1] This sermon was originally preached on April 27, 1997, at Capitol Hill Baptist Church in Washington, D.C.

There are other changes in our culture as well. Sixty years ago today the first Social Security checks were distributed in the United States. Maybe you remember the event. How much has changed in our social fabric since then, and what we expect of government! In the last couple of decades, the pace of change has only accelerated. Divorce and abortion, once scandalous, almost seem old hat these days. And arguments are in print and on the floor of legislatures from Honolulu to the U.S. Capitol for "equal marriage rights" for all Americans, regardless of the genders involved in the marriage.

I could go on and on, but you get the point: change is everywhere, and change is difficult. Sir Hugh Casson, a prominent British architect, noted some years ago that the British "love permanence more than they love beauty." Yet change is hard on more than just the British. Over twenty years ago, writer and futurist Alvin Toffler summed up our reaction to increasingly rapid changes when he wrote, "Man has a limited biological capacity for change. When this capacity is overwhelmed, the capacity is in future shock."

Still, such change is unavoidable. As the Greek philosopher Heraclitus said, "There is nothing permanent except change." And we must admit, change is not always good; it is sometimes dangerous.

So how do we survive constantly changing circumstances, particularly adverse changes? In such a world, what hope do we have for survival?

INTRODUCING DANIEL

To answer this, we come to the last of our studies on "Big Hopes," which have taken us through the Major Prophets of the Old Testament, one prophet per sermon. And here we turn to the book of Daniel.

I want to give you a quick summary of the book of Daniel. It is much shorter than the other three Major Prophets, containing only twelve chapters. The first six chapters of the book consist of six stories (one per chapter) written in the third person and mainly in Aramaic. The first four chapters occur during the reign of Babylonian king Nebuchadnezzar, chapter 5 transpires during the reign of Belshazzar, and chapter 6 happens during the reign of Darius the Mede. The latter six chapters—chapters 7–12—consist mostly of visions Daniel has about the future. They are written in the first person and largely in Hebrew. So Daniel says "I" in those chapters. Both the stories in the first half and the visions in the second half are well-known to many people, and both halves largely proceed in chronological order.

Chapter 1 contains the famous story about the four young Hebrew boys who refuse to eat the king's food set before them since it is defiled, according to the standards of Jewish food laws. Though their stance is risky, Daniel and his three friends receive an exemption, and they end up prospering as a result.

In chapter 2, King Nebuchadnezzar has a dream he wants interpreted, yet he insists that his wise men must interpret the dream without being told what has happened in the dream. That way Nebuchadnezzar will know they are not lying. None of the Babylonian wise men can give him either the dream or the interpretation, but Daniel can. God gives him both.

Chapter 3 recounts the famous story of Daniel's three Hebrew friends who refuse to bow when Nebuchadnezzar puts up his great idol. So the king throws them into a fiery furnace, but they survive.

In chapter 4, Nebuchadnezzar writes a letter to his whole empire confessing his own ignorance and arrogance. He acknowledges that he had presumed to be the one who rebuilt Babylon. Yet God had humbled him through an illness, and he had come to see that all authority and power belong to God alone.

Chapter 5 tells about the riotous feast for pagan gods held by King Belshazzar. Belshazzar and his party are drinking wine from goblets taken from the Lord's temple in Jerusalem when handwriting appears on the wall. Daniel is brought into the party to interpret the handwriting, and he tells the king that he has been weighed in the balance and found wanting. That night Belshazzar is slain.

Chapter 6 contains what may be the most famous story of all, and it takes place toward the end of Daniel's life, during the reign of Darius the Mede when Daniel is probably in his eighties. Daniel is thrown into a den of lions, where he remains overnight. Yet God closes the mouths of the lions and delivers Daniel.

The last six chapters consist mainly of Daniel's visions. Chapters 7 and 8 contain visions Daniel has during Belshazzar's reign about the rise and fall of earthly kingdoms. Chapter 9 records a long prayer Daniel utters during Darius's reign. Knowing that the seventy years of exile for the children of Israel are almost over, he prays for God's deliverance. Chapters 10, 11, and 12 present another vision of Daniel's about the end of time.

That's a summary of Daniel. In order for us to reflect further on this book, I want us to notice three things: first, the changing kings; second, the unchanging God; and finally, Daniel the survivor. And let's see what we can learn about our own survival amid change.

CHANGING KINGS

First, the kings. The story of Daniel is set against the backdrop of the splendor of a Babylonian renaissance under Nebuchadnezzar in the sixth century B.C. Nebuchadnezzar is not famous just because of the mention of him in the Bible.

He is famous in Near Eastern culture and history. He was one of the most important figures in revitalizing the thousand-year-old Babylonian empire that had been in decline for centuries. His renaissance was marked by power and magnificence, as country after country in the ancient Near East fell to Babylonian military might.

We know from extrabiblical sources that Nebuchadnezzar laid siege to the nation of Tyre for thirteen years, so adamant was he about not allowing any nation to stand outside his rule. He even invaded the distant, decaying, but still powerful Egyptian empire. Under Nebuchadnezzar the Babylonian empire reached the largest size it would ever attain.

Yet Nebuchadnezzar was not interested merely in military superiority. He was interested in cultural renewal as well. He cared about the Babylonian heartland. He wanted to rebuild the great cities in Mesopotamia and particularly Babylon itself. So he would take the materials gained through his conquests and bring them back to finance his rebuilding projects.

We get a taste of Nebuchadnezzar's pride over his rebuilding of Babylon in chapter 4. As the king walks on the roof of his royal palace and beholds the city before him, he boasts, "Is not this the great Babylon I have built as the royal residence, by my mighty power and for the glory of my majesty?" (4:30). Archaeologists have shown us that Nebuchadnezzar was not simply full of hot air. He had indeed transformed Babylon into the greatest city of the ancient world. Even today, its ruins spread over two thousand acres to form the largest archeological site from ancient Mesopotamia. The Greek historian Herodotus asserted, "In addition to its enormous size, it surpasses in splendor any city of the known world." The city had magnificent walls with eight great gates. The entrances were bedecked in vivid colors—bright red, white, and blue. Great avenues sixty-five feet wide led up to these gates. Nebuchadnezzar built tall temples, perhaps as many as fifty, and some of them were probably three hundred feet high! He also built a magnificent new palace, which included a museum for antiquities (this is in the sixth century B.C.!) and the famous hanging gardens of Babylon. All these things were Nebuchadnezzar's work.

As part of their push toward general cultural renaissance, the Babylonian kings pushed to reinvigorate their religion as well. Whenever the Babylonians conquered another nation, they assumed that their gods were superior to the gods of the conquered nation. They would then bring implements of worship from the conquered land back and place them in their own temples in order to indicate subjection, just as a king might place articles from a conquered king's palace in his own palace. We see at the very beginning of Daniel's book that the Babylonians had done this with the Israelites: "And the Lord delivered Jehoiakim king of Judah into [Nebuchadnezzar's] hand, along with some of the articles from the temple of God. These he carried off to the temple of his god in Babylonia and put in the treasure house of his god" (1:2).

We could continue to cite evidence of the splendor of Nebuchadnezzar and the Babylonian kings, but what struck me when reading Daniel this week is that these powerful men, these men who built for the ages, who endowed great building schemes and institutional reforms that shaped their society, even these great men came and went. This great Nebuchadnezzar, after a spectacular forty-three-year reign, died in 562 B.C. Nebuchadnezzar was then succeeded by other rulers, some of whom are named in this book: Belshazzar, Darius the Mede, Cyrus the Persian. These rulers changed, and other unnamed rulers came and went in the years covered through the course of this book. "Time, like an ever-rolling stream, bears all its sons away."[2]

In fact, in chapter 2, Nebuchadnezzar himself dreams about the passing nature of leaders. In his dream, he sees a large and dazzling statue of a man built with different materials, which then crumbles when struck by a rock. The dream troubles him greatly, but he cannot understand it. Neither can any of his wise men. Daniel alone can explain the dream to him: Nebuchadnezzar's kingdom will be succeeded by another one, and another one, and another one, and still another one—with each of the statue's materials representing a different empire. Finally, all these worldly kingdoms will come to naught because of God's hand and the establishing of his everlasting kingdom.

The vision of great beasts in chapter 7 and the vision of a ram and a goat in chapter 8, all of which represent kingdoms, reinforce this same theme. Kingdoms will rise and dominate the world stage; and then just as surely as they have risen, they will decline. The visions in chapters 10, 11, and 12 all reinforce this same truth.

Kingdom after kingdom in the book of Daniel, including the most powerful kingdoms with the most powerful kings, seem to bear signs over them that say, "This too shall pass."

In the event that you are someone who exercises considerable power—in this country, in your firm, in your church, in whatever sphere—do not be deceived. Read and understand the book of Daniel. The power you exercise did not come from you. It is not something you can keep. You will keep it only as much as these supposedly almighty kings kept their power. In spite of how much power you presently have, you will be judged, even as the mighty Nebuchadnezzar, Belshazzar, Darius the Mede, and Cyrus the Persian were judged.

Christian, you must not be entranced by your own achievements and authority. It is God who lifts up and who puts down. Do not forget that. If you

---

[2] "O God, Our Help in Ages Past," words by Isaac Watts, 1719.

are a follower of Christ in a position of power and authority, do not let yourself be fooled by that power and authority. It did not come from you, you will not keep it, and you will be held accountable for how you use it. The city of Washington, D.C., is a place full of people impressed by their own resumes. But the Lord is not impressed by anyone's résumé. Any power and authority we have now, in whatever sphere, will surely pass.

In the event you are ambitious for power, remember both the passing nature of power and the judgment that falls upon everyone who seeks power. Maybe you are anxious to inherit the power of the person over you; remember that you will inherit their liability to judgment as well. And then remember that you too will be replaced. Before you become consumed with climbing up the power ladder, consider the book of Daniel as a warning shot across your bow: everyone who seeks power for his or her own sake will fall.

Be careful, Christian. Are you seeking great things for yourself? Know that what you *want* indicates more of who you are than what you *have*. Let me say that again: what you *want* indicates more of who you are than what you *have*. As with Joseph in Egypt, so with Daniel in Babylon: power, authority, and responsibility seemed to seek Daniel; he did not spend his life seeking them. Be careful with the authority and power of this world.

One thing this book teaches us about survival is that earthly power will not remain. Kings come. And kings go. As surely as their reigns commence, they will conclude. They don't finally survive, at least not with their robes of office on.

But as you read through the book of Daniel, someone else stands in striking contrast to the shifting sovereigns of this world. Do you know who?

GOD UNCHANGING

The second thing I want us to notice is the Unchanging Sovereign—God.

After God reveals Nebuchadnezzar's dream and its meaning to Daniel in chapter 2, Daniel prays,

> "Praise be to the name of God for ever and ever;
>   wisdom and power are his.
> He changes times and seasons;
>   he sets up kings and deposes them.
> He gives wisdom to the wise
>   and knowledge to the discerning.
> He reveals deep and hidden things;
>   he knows what lies in darkness,
>   and light dwells with him.

> I thank and praise you, O God of my fathers:
>> You have given me wisdom and power,
>> you have made known to me what we asked of you,
>> you have made known to us the dream of the king" (2:20-23).

Notice that Daniel begins this prayer by expressly praising God for his sovereignty over kings. After all, the dream God had revealed and interpreted for Daniel not only exposed the passing nature of every king's greatness; it also showed that every kingdom will end "not by human hands," Daniel said twice, but by the hand of God (2:34, 45)! "[T]he God of heaven will set up a kingdom that will never be destroyed, nor will it be left to another people. It will crush all those kingdoms and bring them to an end, but it will itself endure forever" (2:44).

Daniel then returns to Nebuchadnezzar to announce the meaning of the dream. "You, O king, are the king of kings," he begins. And, of course, Nebuchadnezzar was. As emperor of Babylon, he had many sovereigns and kings under him. Daniel continues, "The God of heaven has given you dominion and power and might and glory; in your hands he has placed mankind and the beasts of the field and the birds of the air. Wherever they live, he has made you ruler over them all" (2:37-38). Daniel's flattery of the sovereign is quite artful! He celebrates the king's sovereignty, but he celebrates it all as a gift of an even greater sovereign. Daniel well understands the dream he is interpreting for Nebuchadnezzar.

After Daniel tells Nebuchadnezzar his dream and then interprets it for him, we read, "Then King Nebuchadnezzar fell prostrate before Daniel and . . . said to Daniel, 'Surely your God is the God of gods and the Lord of kings and a revealer of mysteries, for you were able to reveal this mystery'" (2:46a, 47). What a remarkable picture this is! Nebuchadnezzar, the mightiest of kings, falls down before a man his troops had captured and led into exile, and then he acknowledges the God of this man to be in authority over him and his gods! What a picture the bowing Nebuchadnezzar makes for where true authority lies!

In chapter 3, after the three Hebrew men are preserved amid the fiery furnace, Nebuchadnezzar again confesses, "no other god can save in this way" (3:29).

In chapter 4, Nebuchadnezzar himself writes a letter to "the peoples, nations and men of every language, who live in all the world," confessing his own ignorance and recounting a dream he had had, along with its interpretation and the story of its fulfillment (4:1-2). He recounts the whole story, so that his readers will see "How great are [the Lord's] signs, how mighty his wonders! His kingdom is an eternal kingdom; his dominion endures from generation to generation" (4:3). In his dream, says Nebuchadnezzar in his letter, he had seen a mighty tree that grew tall and was then felled. A heavenly messenger told him that the tree had been felled "so that the living may know that the Most High is sovereign over the kingdoms of men and gives them to anyone he wishes and sets over them the lowliest of men" (4:17). Nebuchadnezzar goes on in his letter to recount how Daniel then interpreted this dream for him, telling him that he would be brought down from his high place. Moreover, Daniel had said that he would not be restored until "you acknowledge that Heaven rules" (4:26). Sure enough, twelve months later Nebuchadnezzar went mad and was driven away from his throne for a time, during which time he lived like an animal. Finally, says Nebuchadnezzar's letter, God restored his sanity and his throne, prompting him finally to acknowledge God:

> I praised the Most High; I honored and glorified him who lives forever. His dominion is an eternal dominion; his kingdom endures from generation to generation. All the peoples of the earth are regarded as nothing. He does as he pleases with the powers of heaven and the peoples of the earth (4:34b-35a).

In chapter 5, God once again demonstrates that all kings will pass, as compared to the one true and eternal Sovereign, God. One of Nebuchadnezzar's successors, Belshazzar, holds a banquet for a thousand of his nobles. In the midst of their feast, Belshazzar gives orders to bring in the gold and silver goblets taken from the temple in Jerusalem. Drinking wine from these goblets, Belshazzar and his guests praise "the gods of gold and silver, of bronze, iron, wood and stone" (5:4). Suddenly, a hand appears and writes words on the wall that no one can read or interpret. Daniel is brought in to interpret the writing, and Belshazzar offers to reward Daniel, perhaps thinking he can placate him and his God. Daniel answers the king,

> "You may keep your gifts for yourself and give your rewards to someone else. Nevertheless, I will read the writing for the king and tell him what it means.
>
> "O king, the Most High God gave your father Nebuchadnezzar sovereignty and greatness and glory and splendor. Because of the high position he gave him, all the peoples and nations and men of every language dreaded and feared him. Those the king wanted to put to death, he put to death; those he wanted to spare, he spared; those he wanted to promote, he promoted; and those he wanted to humble, he humbled. But when his heart became arrogant and hardened with pride, he was deposed from his royal throne and stripped of his glory. He was driven away from people and given the mind of an animal; he lived with the wild donkeys and ate grass like cattle; and his body was drenched with the dew of heaven, until he acknowledged that the Most High God is sovereign over the kingdoms of men and sets over them anyone he wishes" (5:17-21).

Daniel proceeds to tell Belshazzar that he has not humbled himself like his father, that he has "set himself up against the Lord of heaven" (5:23), that he has been weighed in God's scales, that he has been found wanting, and that his kingdom will be given away. That very night, Belshazzar is killed and someone else assumes "sovereign control" of Babylon.

King Darius, too, would eventually confess the eternal, unchanging nature of God's sovereignty. The story, in chapter 6, is familiar enough: jealous members of Darius's government set a legal trap for Daniel, by persuading the king to implement a law that no one could pray to anyone but him, the king. When Daniel violates this rule by continuing to pray to the real God, these administrators manage to have him thrown into a den of lions. Yet when Daniel is drawn unharmed out of the lions' den the next day, Darius, like Nebuchadnezzar before him, confesses, "I issue a decree that in every part of my kingdom people must fear and reverence the God of Daniel. For he is the living God and he endures forever; his kingdom will not be destroyed, his dominion will never end" (6:26).

Do you see what is happening through this kaleidoscope of changing kings? Every king originally believes that he is all-powerful and that his kingdom will endure. Yet God in his gracious and powerful sovereignty helps each king slowly to recognize that this is not the case, but that God's own kingdom alone will endure. God is the mighty king who has no equal and who judges all.

In chapter 7, Daniel is given a vision of the true Throne Room:

"As I looked,

"thrones were set in place,
    and the Ancient of Days took his seat.
His clothing was as white as snow;
    the hair of his head was white like wool.
His throne was flaming with fire,
    and its wheels were all ablaze.
A river of fire was flowing,
    coming out from before him.
Thousands upon thousands attended him;
    ten thousand times ten thousand stood before him.
The court was seated,
    and the books were opened" (7:9-10).

Still, some sovereigns never learn. In chapter 11, Daniel sees a future king who "will do as he pleases. He will exalt and magnify himself above every god and will say unheard-of things against the God of gods" (11:36). Indeed, this appears to provoke the true God to finally show himself and usher in the end of history. God will teach this final and worst sovereign the limits of his power (11:45–12:1ff.).

The second half of the book of Daniel is often described by scholars as "apocalyptic," like the book of Revelation in the New Testament. Apocalyptic books, through their use of dramatic imagery and emphasis on ultimate outcomes, would be written to provide a clear look at God's overarching sovereignty in the world. Typically they would be written in times when God's rule and power looked most invisible. It would have been invisible to the apostle John exiled on the island of Patmos before his vision, and it would have been invisible to the Israelites languishing in captivity. How sovereign could their God look from captivity? But what God showed Daniel, as he would one day show John, was that these kings came and went. God alone remained the true king. In fact, in the book of Daniel, God brings the kings themselves to confess his eternal dominion. Changing kings, and God unchanging. That could be a summary of the whole book of Daniel. Changing kings, and God unchanging.

DANIEL THE SURVIVOR

But we must not forget the title character of the book: Daniel. We have said very little about him. Daniel was probably taken into captivity in 605 B.C. as part of the first wave of exiles to Babylon, ten years before Ezekiel went and almost twenty before Jerusalem finally fell. By the time we get to his prayer in chapter 9, almost seventy years have passed since the events of chapter 1. Daniel was an old man by the book's end.

Throughout these changing times—from Israel to Babylon, from one king to the next—the threats faced by Daniel and others were great. He and several fellow Hebrews were placed in the king's circles at the book's beginning, and that was a dangerous place to be. Perhaps you have heard the phrase, "You play with the big boys and you'll get hurt." Well, that was one of the "occupational hazards" of Daniel's job. He was playing with some of the biggest boys around—Nebuchadnezzar and his court. The odds of survival for young exiles were never good. And showing allegiance toward some other sovereign, like God, only made those odds worse, exposing the captives to everything from embarrassment to death.

It is in chapter 1 that we first learn that Nebuchadnezzar decides to bring some young, able Israelites into his court to serve the kingdom. The court officials set the diet for these men, but Daniel and his friends ask permission not to defile themselves with the king's food. Surely they risked at least embarrassment and lost opportunity by taking this stand. Surely they were tempted by the thought, "If I just eat a little food, I will be in a more influential position and will have more opportunities to serve God!" How many sins have been committed in Washington, D.C., in the name of not wanting to lose an opportunity! How many individuals have been willing to pay an "incidental" moral price so that they would not lose a great opportunity! Faithfulness to God for Daniel and his friends could have required tremendous earthly loss. And in the stories that follow in chapters 2–6, the threats only became worse. Usually, it was their lives that were on the line.

Now, if *you* were an adviser to Daniel and his friends, how would you have counseled them? "Oh, Daniel, you're being a bit rigid over this food matter. You're just a young exile. It's a great privilege, you know, that you've been brought into the court. Think of the people you'll meet. Think of the influence you'll have." Or maybe: "Daniel, it's just a little food. It's being offered to gods that you know aren't real anyway. Go ahead, you can take your stand once you've gotten inside and earned a little trust." Or maybe, "Daniel, you need to be realistic here. A little more *realpolitik* and a little less Wilsonian idealism, please. You know, you can't make an omelet without breaking eggs." So you would whisper in Daniel's ear, and he would eat the food.

Or, how would you have advised him in chapters 2 or 4, when the God-given interpretation of the king's dreams exalted God's kingdom and put down Nebuchadnezzar's? "Oh, Daniel, Daniel, you don't need to explain the dream to the king quite *that* way. He has not had a good morning. You won't accomplish anything with that tone. Just state it a bit more vaguely. Give him some good general counsel. You don't have to lie. Packaging, Daniel. Spin is everything here."

Or, what would you have said to him when chapter 6's edict came that he could no longer pray to his own God, but only to Darius? "Daniel, you can still pray in your heart to the Lord. God doesn't care about your bodily posture. He knows the truth of your heart, Daniel. Look, you don't want to lose your position. Consider all the decades of building this great influence. Look how respected you are! Don't throw it all away for some little religious thing. You can do more good if you would just be quiet and play by the rules right now."

And finally, I can just hear some false counselor speaking to the young men as they stood before the idol of Nebuchadnezzar in chapter 3: "Oh, come on, just bow down. You don't have to bow down in your heart. It's just your body. You won't really be worshiping this idol."

Now, I am not talking about legislative compromise. Our church has more than one person who works on Capitol Hill. I realize that in a representative democracy like ours, different opinions must be represented, at least until we are all clones of one person—and even then, knowing some of us, there may still be differences of opinion! Legislative compromises are essential for our type of government.

I am talking about moral compromise, the abandoning of principles, the breaking of God's law. There is no such compromise here in the book of Daniel.

Some critics don't like this about Daniel—either the man or his book. They read the book, and Daniel leaves them cold. They say he looks like a cardboard character. "There's no depth of development," they say. "No sin, you know. With Joseph, you've got his ego. With Jacob, deception. With Moses, even murder! But with Daniel, nothing. He just does the right thing all the time. It makes him seem unreal." But the point of the book is not Daniel's *sinfulness* (which he clearly confesses in his prayer in 9:20), but his *steadfastness*. God has called him to put starch into the backs of the exiles when they are being tempted to compromise.

Consider the response of the three young men who refuse to bow to the statue of Nebuchadnezzar. They are surrounded by hundreds, perhaps thousands, of people bowing down on the ground. Some of those on the ground who know and love these three young men are shaking with terror as they look up and see them standing upright and staring the sovereign of all the Babylonian empire in the face in defiance of his decree to bow to this idol. And then what do these three say? "O Nebuchadnezzar, we do not need to defend ourselves before you in this matter." Really? You don't? "If we are thrown into the blazing furnace, the God we serve is able to save us from it, and he will rescue us from your hand, O king. But even if he does not, we want you to know, O king, that we will not serve your gods or worship the image of gold you have set up" (3:16-17). Now that is backbone!

These three young men knew that the almighty pagan king had nothing they finally needed. Nothing! So they remained *unbendingly* faithful to the true Sovereign. Surely, these are some of the best verses to read when you feel tempted to compromise.

In this book, Daniel survives the deportation to Babylon, the reigns of Nebuchadnezzar, Belshazzar, Darius the Mede, and Cyrus the Persian (6:28). He survives everything from the crisis of whether to eat the king's food in chapter 1 to the crisis of being thrown to the lions in chapter 6. He even survives the end of the Babylonian empire itself as the Persians enter it. And I am sure there were more crises of which we have no record.

Perseverance. Endurance. Daniel is an example of survival.

Daniel would die, of course, like all other mortals. Yet the last verse of the book expressed Daniel's final hope. God says to Daniel through a messenger, "As for you, go your way till the end. You will rest, and then at the end of the days you will rise to receive your allotted inheritance" (12:13).

Ultimately, this book is not just about Daniel's survival. It's about the survival of all God's people. They will be victorious. This same divine messenger says to Daniel, "But at that time your people—everyone whose name is found written in the book—will be delivered" (12:1).

Looking at the book as a whole, we can see that the first six chapters contain great stories of individual deliverance in the present, while the last six chapters promise corporate deliverance in the future. I think the small deliverances Daniel experienced in his life were meant to give him hope and confidence of a final deliverance that would come.

So it is for you and for me. The small deliverances God has given us in our lives should give us hope. They are a preview and a down payment on the final great deliverance that will come for all God's people. Remember, that which appears permanent is not. Only God is. If we are allied with him, we will share in his final victory.

Friend, hear this story and beware. Do not fully hitch your wagon to what will inevitably be a falling star. Serve the powerful people you work for well, but remember that they are not ultimate, even if they act as if they were. No amount of money, influence, or knowledge in this world can make someone ultimate or sovereign. No matter how they perceive themselves. Do not hitch your whole life to someone who God promises will fall.

Christian, be personally uncompromising about obedience to God, even if it brings you into conflict with your ruler or your boss. It is dangerous, but it is a good witness. It shows the world and your boss what God is like. You may be delivered, as Daniel was in this book. You may be rewarded for your principles, as Daniel was in this book. And you may even help your boss not to continue suffering under his or her illusions.

All of us will face God's judgment. God will judge unfaithful rulers and bosses and parents, yes, but he will also judge everyone who has been unfaithful to him. In the book of Daniel, not only do rulers fall, whole cities and nations tumble.

At the same time, hope is available. For the children of God, God's future victory is certain. It does not hang in the balance of any election or battle or merchandising war or technological breakthrough or academic finding. God's victory among his people is assured.

The question then becomes, are you a child of God or are you a child of the kingdoms of this world? Listen again to what Daniel says to Belshazzar after describing how Nebuchadnezzar had acknowledged that God alone is king: "But you his son, O Belshazzar, have not humbled yourself, though you knew all this. Instead, you have set yourself up against the Lord of heaven" (5:22-23).

And now *you*, like Belshazzar, have heard this. Will you humble yourself, confess your sin of being ruled by the tyrannical appetites of this world, turn away from them, and trust God alone in Christ for your salvation? Will you make Christ your king?

Daniel was told that all of God's kingly power would one day be concentrated in the hands of one who was "like a son of man." Earlier, we saw the Ancient of Days sitting upon his throne. But Daniel's vision did not stop there:

> "In my vision at night I looked, and there before me was one like a son of man, coming with the clouds of heaven. He approached the Ancient of Days and was led into his presence. He was given authority, glory and sovereign power; all peoples, nations and men of every language worshiped him. His dominion is an everlasting dominion that will not pass away, and his kingdom is one that will never be destroyed" (7:13-14).

Jesus Christ, born to the virgin Mary, is this Son of Man. In Christ, God put on human flesh and came to declare the beginning of his new kingdom within the hearts of his people. This otherworldly kingdom then accomplished its most shocking and greatest victory through the very death of this king on the cross, because in that death he paid the penalty for the sins of all those who would ever repent of their sins and believe in him. Then, the penalty of sin being paid, the Father raised this king from the dead, thereby conquering the power of death over all those who would be God's children. Again I ask, will you forsake the passing power this world offers, repent of your own lust for it, trust in the forgiveness of the Son of Man alone, and follow his rule alone?

By God's grace, that is how Daniel survived, and how you too can be a survivor.

CONCLUSION

In Washington, D.C., most people think of survivors a little differently. Survivors are the ones who know how to compromise. In Daniel, a survivor is one who does not compromise the principles of God and faith in his rule. Daniel squarely places his survival in the hands of this sovereign, unchanging God. He fully entrusts himself to this God.

Recently, our church has been praying for Christian brothers and sisters in Egypt who are being persecuted. Egypt is one of the largest recipients of United States foreign aid, yet it is also the scene of much persecution of Christians. The Egyptian government has no policy that promotes the persecution of Christians, though certainly governmental decisions, or, really, the lack of governmental decisions, do play a role. Either way, the amount of persecution has been increasing for decades.

So what hope do our Christian brothers and sisters in Egypt have? What hope do they have if they cannot see any way to effect change? Their ultimate hope, like ours, is in God, and in no place else.

It has been wonderful to look at the four Major Prophets together in these last four sermons. We heard the great brooding theme of judgment in Isaiah, as well as his glorious chimes of future hope. Then in Jeremiah we heard the dark and tragic crescendo of God judging his nation by sending them into exile. The crescendo continued in Ezekiel; but then hope returned for God's people when they learned that God's object of love was never a place, but a people. Now here in Daniel, the trumpet choruses of God's promised victory are sounded in chapter after chapter as God displays his sovereign rule over all the mighty rulers of false empires, all of them confessing that he is the true Sovereign.

If we are Christians, God will sustain us. The unchanging God has revealed his plan, and his plan is to sustain and to preserve his people in him. Isn't that amazing? Why would he do that? Daniel knew. His prayer in chapter 9 gives it away. He prays, "O Lord, listen! O Lord, forgive! O Lord, hear and act! For your sake, O my God, do not delay, because your city and your people bear your Name" (9:19). Daniel knew, in other words, that God is merciful and forgiving, and that all his powers would be used to bring compassion and mercy to his people. In Christ's sacrificial work of atonement on the cross, that power and mercy are made most clear.

In the end, that is our only hope for survival.

Let us pray:

Lord, many other hopes clutter our minds. We know that in this last week we have put hope in many other things. But we know that circumstances will change and overturn all those other things we put our hopes in. Lord, we know that you alone are our only true hope. We desire to be people who bear your name and who are known by your name. So we pray that you would make us like yourself—holy and uncompromising in your justice and your goodness, in your love and your perfection. We pray, for Jesus' sake. Amen.

Questions for Reflection

1. Why does God allow so much change to come into our lives? After you answer this question, consider the different areas of your life in which you tend

to resist and detest change. Now, what might God want to teach you in these areas, based on your answer to this first question?

2. How can our greatest victories, triumphs, and accomplishments be the very things that deceive us most? If you are unsure of the answer, you may wish to consider the example of Nebuchadnezzar.

3. Where do you aspire to have more power, control, or prominence in your life? In answering this question, you may wish to consider some of life's different domains: your work, your home, your social life, your church, your reputation, your finances, and so forth. What does the book of Daniel teach about these aspirations? What does Christ's journey to the cross teach about these aspirations?

4. How can we as Christians learn to strike the right balance between trusting and honoring other people with power over us and remembering that they are only human and that God alone must be feared?

5. Do you presently hold any positions of authority? Do you exercise authority in those domains with a continual awareness that you will be judged by God for your use of that authority? If you did so, what would change?

6. In which of your relationships do you care more about what the other person thinks than what God thinks? What steps can you take to begin making God the king in that relationship, so that you fear him and desire his approval more than the other person's?

7. In what areas of your life are you most tempted to compromise? What are some of the arguments that the voice of temptation successfully uses with you?

8. What lessons did Jesus' death on the cross teach us about how God often demonstrates his power in this world?

9. If Jesus is the king toward whom Daniel pointed in Daniel 7:13-14, why did Jesus have to die?

10. If most of your life has been spent making moral compromises, what hope do you have for God's deliverance?

PART FIVE

ETERNAL QUESTIONS

THE MESSAGE OF HOSEA: WHAT IS LOVE?

28

THE MESSAGE OF HOSEA: WHAT IS LOVE?

LOVE IS . . . [1]

"Love is blind, and marriage is an eye-opener." So goes the old saying.

But what is love? To many, the word itself is exciting. Love is pure positive emotion. Love is a force to be experienced. Love is uncontrollable, thrilling, bliss!

Others, particularly those in university settings, would say that such bright ideas are naïve. After all, power is what motivates all of our decisions. Selfishness, then, is a better approximation of what love is. Love is an expression of power. It is an exercise in self-interest.

Still others would say that simply equating love with power is too deliberate, especially since love is such an evocative topic. We don't simply go about acquiring everything we desire; rather, desires sometimes "come over us." We might even say that desires acquire us. We begin to feel that we must *have* or *do* or *be* something. And then we say that we "love" that thing. We "need" it. Surely our consumerist culture has turned the Beatles' song around. They sang, "All we need is love"; but we know that all we love is need. If we love something, then we need it. We must have it. And so, love becomes something far different from exciting. In fact, love can become habit, something that we have become accustomed to and that we regularly require. Ultimately, love becomes something that we in fact take for granted.

The more elevated souls among us, though, say that love is not nearly as self-interested as all this. Love, they insist, is actually concern for others. Morrie Schwartz, whose struggle with Lou Gehrig's disease is chronicled in Mitch Albom's best-selling *Tuesdays with Morrie*, said that "Love is when you are as concerned about someone else's situation as you are about your own."[2]

---

[1] This sermon was originally preached on May 25, 2003, at Capitol Hill Baptist Church in Washington, D.C.
[2] Cited in Mitch Albom, *Tuesdays with Morrie: An Old Man, a Young Man, and Life's Greatest Lesson* (New York: Doubleday, 1997), 178.

The more cynical souls hear this and respond that such "love" is simply dependence, that when you investigate the claims people have made to "love" each other, what you find is some service that two individuals provide one another, whether that is esteem, laundry, money, compassion, or companionship.

Then there are some who look at their experience of love and cannot recognize it in these cynical terms. Love, they say, is admiration and delight. It is not so much depending on someone else as it is losing yourself in someone you care about—forgetting about yourself for their sake and their good. It is the farthest thing in the world from being selfish.

Whatever else love may be, it is certainly treated these days as the supreme value in our culture. We effectively reverse what the Bible says about "God is love" by talking as if "love is God." Call something "love" and you have justified it beyond all questioning. No defense is needed. No explanation is required. "It's love, can't you see!" People speak of wars fought in the name of religion. Surely, no fewer wars have been fought in the name of "love."

So what, finally, is love?

INTRODUCING THE MINOR PROPHETS

This is the first of twelve "Eternal Questions" that we will address from an often neglected part of God's Word—the Minor Prophets of the Old Testament. These prophets, as you can already see, have at least two strikes against them. First of all, they are in the "Old" Testament. The Old's not as good as the New, right? And second, these guys are not even in the same league as the "major" prophets. If you are going to go to the trouble of reading the Bible, why give time to the "minor" prophets? Isn't that like watching a minor league baseball game when you could be watching a major league game?

First of all, the Old Testament is God's Word. In fact, it is most of God's Word. Just open your Bible to the beginning of Matthew's Gospel, the first book of the New Testament, and place your finger there. You will see that most of the Bible, more than three-fourths of it, in fact, is to the left of your finger, in the Old Testament. Now, I'm not saying that the Old Testament is better because it is longer. But I am saying that the New Testament was never meant to eliminate the Old. In the Old Testament Law, Histories, Prophets, and Writings are accounts of centuries of God's dealings with his people. The Old Testament lays out the human situation that the New Testament—covering only thirty to forty years of history—addresses so decisively. The Old Testament presents the riddle to which Jesus Christ is the answer, and you won't understand the answer nearly as well without understanding the riddle.

So what about this name "Minor Prophets"? Clearly, names are important. I was a medieval history major in college, and all sixteen of us medieval history majors were always on a crusade to make sure that people stopped calling it the "dark ages"! We didn't like that. After all, scholars know a lot about what happened in the Middle Ages. The situation is similar with these Minor Prophets—people misunderstand the name. "Minor" does not mean "unimportant"; it means "short." The Major Prophets are simply the longer books of Isaiah, Jeremiah, Ezekiel, and Daniel (Daniel is shorter than a couple of the Minor Prophets, but it is rooted in the same event that Jeremiah and Ezekiel are centered on—the destruction of Jerusalem). On the whole, the Minor Prophets are simply shorter, ranging from fourteen chapters to just one. The prophets themselves may have been every bit as influential in their own times as the so-called major prophets.

So, they are not the two-bit players of the Old Testament. And in their day they were not the Johnny-come-latelies, the add-ins, the Oh-just-one-more-things. They were written by the inspiration of God's Spirit for serious purposes and serious uses.

The prophets and their writings represent the last four centuries of Old Testament history, from the eighth to the fifth century B.C. And we are pretty sure that these twelve prophets were placed together in one scroll as early as the third century B.C. In other words, they have been recognized as Holy Scripture for a long time.

INTRODUCING HOSEA

The Minor Prophet that we are studying here and that comes first in your Old Testament, Hosea, is unusual among the Minor Prophets for several reasons. First, it is longer than most of them. Hosea has fourteen chapters. Zechariah is the only other Minor Prophet that is this long.

Second, Hosea was one of the earliest Minor Prophets. We don't know the exact dates of these twelve books, but they do appear to fall into four groups of three, about one group per century. Haggai, Zechariah, and Malachi were the last three books written in the Old Testament—in the *fifth* century. Moving back in time, Joel, Obadiah, and maybe Jonah were written in the *sixth* century, after the fall of Jerusalem in 587 (remember, we are in B.C.). Nahum, Habakkuk, and Zephaniah were probably written around the same time Jeremiah began his ministry, in the late *seventh* century, before the fall of Jerusalem. Hosea, Amos, and Micah, then, are the oldest three, having been written in the *eighth* century. They are the three "old men" of the minor prophets, prophesying before the northern kingdom of "Israel" fell to the Assyrians in 722.

That brings us to a third unusual thing about Hosea. Not only is it one of the longest and oldest books of the Minor Prophets, it focuses on the northern kingdom of Israel rather than on the southern kingdom of Judah. Most of the minor prophets focus on the southern kingdom of Judah because only Judah existed when they were prophesying. And one of the three "old men," Micah, focused on Judah before Israel fell. But the other two, Hosea and Amos, prophesied about the northern kingdom—the ten tribes who had followed Jeroboam in rebelling against Solomon's son a couple of hundred years earlier.

In your Bible, the northern kingdom is sometimes called Samaria because that was its capital city. It is sometimes called Ephraim because Ephraim was its most prominent tribe (like Judah in the south). But generally it is called Israel.

The northern kingdom of Israel was beset with troubles from the very beginning. The decades before Jeroboam II, who reigned when Hosea prophesied, were tumultuous. The nation had gone through king after king after king; and by the time of Jeroboam II and Hosea in the second half of the eighth century, the country appeared to be in terminal decline.

The empire of Assyria, located just north of Israel, was the great power of the day, and it continually nibbled away at Israel's borders, often threatening to strike its very heart. While Isaiah and Micah prophesied down south in Jerusalem, God called Amos and Hosea to prophesy in the waning days of the northern kingdom.

Hosea does not have a very clear outline. But very broadly we can say that chapters 1–3 contain everything we know about Hosea's personal history as well as some prophecy. Then chapters 4–14 are a collection of prophecies that warn of God's coming judgment as well as several promises of hope.

It is amid all these particulars that we learn a lot about real love. In fact, I am so confident that we can learn about love from Hosea that for years I have had couples read Hosea as part of their last counseling assignment before I marry them.

LOVE'S STRANGE STORY: HOSEA AND GOMER

So what does God say to his people in Israel's waning days? We can find out by zeroing in on just one word. It's right there in the third verse of the first chapter. It's the word "married." On a human level, that is what this book of Hosea is about—a man married a woman.

The man is Hosea. Who is Hosea? Well, verse 1 tells us his father's name as well as the era in which he lived. But the most important thing about him, clearly, is that God spoke to him and told him to marry this woman.

Who is the woman? Her name is Gomer. That may not be a fetching name for women in our day and culture. But we have no reason to think that it was unusual in their day. Verse 3 also tells us that her father's name was Diblaim, but it is her character that most draws our attention. Let's read Hosea's own words:

> The word of the LORD that came to Hosea son of Beeri during the reigns of Uzziah, Jotham, Ahaz and Hezekiah, kings of Judah, and during the reign of Jeroboam son of Jehoash king of Israel:
>
> When the LORD began to speak through Hosea, the LORD said to him, "Go, take to yourself an adulterous wife and children of unfaithfulness, because the land is guilty of the vilest adultery in departing from the LORD." So he married Gomer daughter of Diblaim, and she conceived and bore him a son.
>
> Then the LORD said to Hosea, "Call him Jezreel, because I will soon punish the house of Jehu for the massacre at Jezreel, and I will put an end to the kingdom of Israel. In that day I will break Israel's bow in the Valley of Jezreel."
>
> Gomer conceived again and gave birth to a daughter. Then the LORD said to Hosea, "Call her Lo-Ruhamah, for I will no longer show love to the house of Israel, that I should at all forgive them. Yet I will show love to the house of Judah; and I will save them—not by bow, sword or battle, or by horses and horsemen, but by the LORD their God."
>
> After she had weaned Lo-Ruhamah, Gomer had another son. Then the LORD said, "Call him Lo-Ammi, for you are not my people, and I am not your God" (1:1-9).

Notice that we are told immediately what this book is: "The word of the LORD that came to Hosea" (1:1). Then we have this historical account of God's instruction to Hosea, Hosea's obedience, and the children he has with Gomer.

After chapter 1, the book fades into a prophecy, as the Lord speaks to Israel through Hosea as if Israel was the mother of the people while the Lord was her husband and their father. The only other time Hosea the man is clearly discussed occurs in the brief chapter 3:

> The LORD said to me, "Go, show your love to your wife again, though she is loved by another and is an adulteress. Love her as the LORD loves the Israelites, though they turn to other gods and love the sacred raisin cakes."
>
> So I bought her for fifteen shekels of silver and about a homer and a lethek of barley. Then I told her, "You are to live with me many days; you must not be a prostitute or be intimate with any man, and I will live with you" (3:1-3).

Apparently, Hosea's wife had been unfaithful to him. Perhaps she had even sold herself into some kind of temple prostitution. Whatever the exact situation was, God told Hosea to go and buy her back and to continue to love her.

Hosea never talks about himself again in his prophecies. We have just read everything the Bible tells us about him. What, then, is the significance of the man Hosea and his wife? Throughout this book, Hosea and Gomer—real characters in history—stand for God and Israel. In much of the prophetic portions of the book, God and Israel are directly personified as husband and wife, as in chapter 2. Then, at other times, all the images are dropped, and God talks directly to Israel about himself and about them, as revealingly as in any other book in the Bible.

On the whole, Hosea's prophecy is menacing. It foretells a coming judgment. Over one hundred times in this fairly brief book you can find the little word "will," as God warns of the punishment he *will* inflict on Israel. Look again at these verses in chapter 1:

> Then the LORD said to Hosea, "Call him Jezreel, because I *will* soon punish the house of Jehu for the massacre at Jezreel, and I *will* put an end to the kingdom of Israel. In that day I *will* break Israel's bow in the Valley of Jezreel."
>
> Gomer conceived again and gave birth to a daughter. Then the LORD said to Hosea, "Call her Lo-Ruhamah, for I *will* no longer show love to the house of Israel, that I should at all forgive them" (1:4-6).

In the first thirteen verses of chapter 2, the Lord more explicitly describes Israel as his wayward wife, and he promises that he will inflict punishment upon her.

Then in chapters 4–14, God thunders his promises to punish, to ignore, to destroy, to sweep away, to bring shame, to withdraw himself, to discipline, to devour, to lay waste, to pour out his wrath like a flood, to tear like a lion and carry off, to catch like a fowler, to ensure their fall and ridicule, to pursue, to send back into slavery, to burn their cities and consume their fortresses, to exile, to afflict with curses, to bereave of their children, to reject, to disgrace, to deprive of kings and city gates and plans, to leave, and to repay.

Why did God become the attacker of his own people? And, again, what does this have to do with love? Therein hangs a tale, a tale involving sin, repentance, restoration, and *you*.

LOVE'S CHALLENGE: SIN

We must begin with the challenge to love: sin. Israel's sin occasioned Hosea's prophecy. What exactly was the spiritual state of Israel at the time? Well, the book was written almost three millennia ago, so we cannot say exactly. But it wasn't good. The Lord says, "they have sunk deep into corruption" (9:9). And not only were they corrupt, they were stubborn about their corruption: "The Israelites are stubborn" (4:16), and they "refuse to repent" (11:5).

They had "rejected what is good" (8:3). They had "rejected knowledge" and "ignored the law of [their] God" (4:6). They had "rebelled against" God's law (8:1). They regarded it "as something alien" (8:12). And in rebelling against God's law, of course, they had "rebelled against . . . God" himself (13:16). "They had not obeyed him" (9:17). The Lord himself summarizes, "my people are determined to turn from me" (11:7).

Wow! What determination! Did you ever think of sin as something so personal, something so directly involving God? That's how God describes it. Rejecting God's law is turning away from him! Sin, God goes on to say, is "contempt" (12:14). Contempt for whom? Contempt for him, of course. Breaking the law was not merely the breaking of some impersonal principle. It was the betrayal of a personal covenant, like a marriage covenant. God says, "like Adam, they have broken the covenant" (6:7). And clearly these Israelites were children of Adam. They had followed Adam's example and sinned: "the people have broken my covenant and rebelled against my law" (8:1).

The Acts of Sin

These are all sweeping characterizations of the people. But what were the specific sins that Hosea found in Israel? There were too many to mention all of them, but here are some. To begin with, their rulers were not righteous (which you might know from our study of 2 Kings[3]): these rulers "dearly love shameful ways" (Hos. 4:18), and "all their leaders are rebellious" (9:15). How were they rebellious? They turned to Assyria and Egypt for help instead of to the Lord, even though the Lord had made Israel a separate nation and a special people (5:13; 7:11; 12:1).

And sin was hardly limited to the ruling classes. The nation was characterized by drunkenness, mocking, insolent words, and cursing (4:2, 11; 7:5, 16). Over and over they lied and practiced deceit. The people "make many promises, take false oaths and make agreements; therefore lawsuits spring up like poisonous weeds in a plowed field."[4]

They also stole. In fact, it sounds as if they stole at every opportunity they got—breaking into homes, robbing in the streets, even defrauding in the stores (4:2; 7:1; 12:7). "The merchant uses dishonest scales; he loves to defraud" (12:7).

As long as they were breaking the eighth and ninth commandments prohibiting stealing and lying, the people decided to go ahead and break the sixth commandment against murder as well. So they murdered, shed blood, multiplied violence, left footprints stained with blood, even massacred (1:4; 4:2; 6:8; 12:1). Hosea uses all these images.

---

[3] Cf. Hos. 8:4; 1 Sam. 8:7.
[4] 10:4; see also 4:2; 7:1, 3; 10:13; 11:12; 12:1.

Then they disobeyed the seventh commandment, which forbids adultery. Hosea, of course, was personally acquainted with how that commandment was defied. Illegitimacy and prostitution were rife (4:2, 10, 13; 5:7; 7:4).

Hearing all this, you may well wonder, "How did it all get so bad and disordered? After all, these were God's special people. Had he not gone out of his way to deliver them, lead them, prosper them, give them his law and his prophets, and make them his own?"

The Core of Sin

If you read through Hosea, I believe that you will find the core of the Israelites' corruption is pretty clear: their *religion* was all wrong! Consider these particularly grotesque verses in chapter 4: "The more the priests increased, the more they sinned against me; they exchanged their Glory for something disgraceful. They feed on the sins of my people and relish their wickedness" (4:7-8). The religious leaders were feeding on the sins of the people and relishing the people's wickedness! They were cheerleaders for sin because they personally profited from it! Can it get any worse? While these charlatans in shepherds' clothing filled the religious posts in the land, the real religious leaders, like Hosea, perhaps, were treated far differently: "the prophet is considered a fool, the inspired man a maniac" (9:7). Whatever religion the people may have had was false and insincere. The Lord himself laments, "they do not cry out to me from their hearts" (7:14; cf. 8:2).

Idolatry was the Israelites' biggest problem. In fact, you could say the whole book is about their idolatry. In Hosea's day, Israel was dotted with sites of cultic worship of assorted gods—Baal, Yahweh, and others—and they would all be mixed together (cf. 9:10, 15). At one point, the Lord says, "Israel has forgotten his Maker" (8:14). And earlier, "There is no faithfulness, no love, no acknowledgment of God in the land" (4:1). The word translated "acknowledgment" can also be translated as knowledge, referring particularly to the intimate relational knowledge shared in marriage. And that fits with the context, doesn't it? God is saying that his people no longer *love, know,* or *are exclusively faithful to* him, as one should be with a spouse. They have forsaken him. That's why the book itself opens with the charge, "the land is guilty of the vilest adultery in departing from the LORD" (1:2). Throughout Hosea's prophecies, the Lord uses the images of adultery and unfaithfulness to depict his people's turning from him and serving other gods.[5] Adultery and idolatry very much go together in the Bible, because *idolatry is a spiritual adultery.* And God's own people, through their idolatry, commit such spiritual adultery.

---

[5] Cf. 2:2, 5; 4:15; 5:7; 6:7; 7:13, 15.

The Appearance of Sin

What did the Israelites' adulterous idolatry actually look like? It looked like a number of things. It included sacrifices: "They sacrifice on the mountaintops and burn offerings on the hills, under oak, poplar and terebinth, where the shade is pleasant" (4:13). It included altars with sacred stones and pillars in the high places of wickedness (cf. 8:11; 10:1-2, 8). It included "idolatrous priests" (10:5), a whole class of people who made their living by servicing this false religion.

Full-fledged idolatry, of course, must also include idols, of which the Israelites had plenty. "They consult a wooden idol and are answered by a stick of wood" (4:12). The people were "joined to idols" (4:17). They were "intent on pursuing idols" (5:11). They made idols for themselves:

> "They set up kings without my consent;
> > they choose princes without my approval.
> With their silver and gold they make idols for themselves
> > to their own destruction.
> Throw out your calf-idol, O Samaria!
> > My anger burns against them.
> How long will they be incapable of purity?
> > They are from Israel!
> This calf—a craftsman has made it;
> > it is not God.
> It will be broken in pieces,
> > that calf of Samaria" (8:4-6; cf. 10:5).

Hosea speaks about these calf-idols again later. Evidently, the people were quite taken with them: "they make idols for themselves from their silver, cleverly fashioned images, all of them the work of craftsmen. It is said of these people, 'They offer human sacrifice and kiss the calf-idols'" (13:2). Think about that for a moment. They kill people, but they kiss idols!

This is where false worship leads. This is what false religion does. It turns people upside down. It inverts them. What they should love they hate; what they should hate they love. And when a people are saying "our gods!" to what their hands have made, you can be sure all sorts of other perversions follow (cf. 14:3, 8). For their part, the Israelites consorted with harlots and sacrificed with temple prostitutes (4:14, 18; 5:3). Hosea says at one point, "I have seen a horrible thing in the house of Israel. There Ephraim is given to prostitution and Israel is defiled" (6:10).

The people had also given themselves over to worship of the fertility god,

Baal (cf. 2:17; 13:1). They had not become irreligious; they had simply switched the object of their worship (cf. 2:8). So they had ascribed their blessings, like the blessings of harvest, to Baal (2:12-13). They burned incense, ate sacred raisin cakes, had New Moon celebrations, and performed all the rituals they thought would give them full harvests of grain and grapes. And in front of these images they had made, they prostituted themselves and offered sacrifices, even human sacrifices.[6] You can see why the Lord says that "Ephraim has sold herself to lovers" and "sold themselves among the nations" (8:9-10). She was no different than they were.

The Root of Sin

What was at the root of such sin? Based on my reading of Hosea, I believe it was the Israelites' arrogance (5:5; 7:10). The Lord tells them, "you have depended on your own strength and on your many warriors" (10:13). Elsewhere he says of them, "When I fed them, they were satisfied; when they were satisfied, they became proud; then they forgot me" (13:6).

But God is not someone you can easily ignore. You have to expend energy to ignore the One in whose image you are made. You have to consciously work to put him out of the center of your thoughts, which is why he can charge the people, "you are against me" (13:9). He can even say, in some of the sharpest words in the book, that "they consecrated themselves to that shameful idol and became as vile as the thing they loved" (9:10).

God's special people, chosen and precious, delivered and blessed, had descended to this. They squandered his blessings; they lost his grace: "now she is among the nations like a worthless thing" (8:8). These words have the ring of an annulment, a fate, a doom. And his final pronouncement upon them is most tragic: "they will be wanderers among the nations" (9:17). God's people were to obey all his laws, especially his first two commandments: to worship only him, and to not make any idols. But they had been thoroughly disobedient. So the Lord spoke this word of judgment through Hosea: those whom he had made his special people were no longer his people; they were simply among the nations.

Our day is not too dissimilar from Hosea's. Private vices abound. And as private vices abound, society becomes more vicious. Private vices become public, because the root of public vice lies in our private lives.

My friend, if you are a non-Christian, I wonder if you have considered how personally God takes your sins. When you, as someone made in God's image, do something wrong, such as dishonor your parents or covet, you are

---

[6] 2:13; 3:1; 4:10; 5:3-4, 7; 7:14; 9:1; 11:2; 13:2.

acting against God. Maybe you have thought of yourself as a nice, moral, but religiously neutral person. Examine your own heart. See if you can discern what an illusion religious neutrality is. What was it Jesus said in Matthew? "He who is not with me is against me" (Matt. 12:30).

In light of the people's sin of offering human sacrifices in the high places outside of Jerusalem, it is all too ironic how God finally dealt with the sin of his people. In Christ, God took on human flesh, lived as one of the people of Israel, and became involved in a human sacrifice on a high place outside of Jerusalem—except he was the sacrifice! God himself, in Christ, bore the wrath of God against the sins of all those who would ever repent and believe in him.

What does all of this mean for us? As we read through Hosea and encounter these unfaithful, wrong-loving, prostituting people, we must realize that Hosea's condemnation does not apply so much to all the non-Christians "out there." No, what he says applies to us—God's people in the church! We do not want to be a self-righteous, conservative evangelical church that tut-tuts over the problems of our country as the country "goes down the tubes." That would be a good tune for us to whistle on our way to hell, unconcerned about our own sins. No, Hosea means for God's people to examine themselves and their own sin.

Staring into the picture Hosea paints of the Israelites, can you not see the lines of your own double-facedness and the wandering paths of your own heart?

Outwardly associating ourselves with God's people does not deliver us from sin. It is almost certain that in a gathering of people as large as our church, there are some who believe they are worshiping God but are not. They worship what the pastor, or their spouse, or their friends think of them. They worship the blessings of God, the fellowship of his people, or the encouragement they feel when the church sings.

So ask yourself this: should your present circumstances change, while God remains the same, would you continue to worship him? Or is it simply the alignment of circumstances that you enjoy, that evokes what you think is the worship of God? My friend, examine your heart. What kind of heart do you have for God? That's the question Hosea places before us, because the desires of our hearts are the root cause of all our actions and all our worship. Everything else is a symptom. This is why John Piper's books are incredibly insightful and helpful. Piper is exactly right when he says that God should be at the center of our heart's desires. Insofar as we delight in God himself, the joy we experience in what he gives us will merely draw us back to our joy in him. God himself must be the true object of delight in a Christian's heart. All the things he gives us will change, but he himself will never change.

Also, reading through Hosea helps us to see one of the great differences between God's people under the Old Covenant and God's people under the New. A person entered the Old Covenant community by being born. Not so for God's New Covenant community (which I say with much love for my paedo-baptist friends). A person enters the New Covenant by being *born again* by God's Spirit. Therefore, if idolatry was inappropriate for the Old Testament people of God, how much more inappropriate is idolatry among the New Covenant people of God! The very fact that we have become members of the church is the result of the work of God's Spirit. From a human standpoint, then, what unifies us is not ethnicity, as in the Old Testament; it is our heart's moral and affectional commitment to God.

In our congregation, may we always bear witness to God's wonderful grace in giving us new life in Christ!

If you know yourself to have been born again, know that God has given you new life so that you would have a heart for him. Therefore, continually take an axe to the root of the sin that separates you from God and his love. If you are one who regularly attends but has not become a member of a church, let me exhort you to do so, whether ours or someone else's. You will find that God will use his people to help you fight for holiness and for the ability continually to delight in God.

LOVE'S RECOVERY: REPENTANCE

Clearly, sin presents the challenge to love, and, specifically, it challenges God's love toward us, because God is holy. How then can love be recovered? Love can be recovered through repentance. Throughout the dark night of Hosea, God calls his people to repentance.

In chapter 2, he calls Israel to remove the adulterous look from its face and unfaithfulness from its chest (2:2).

In chapter 6, Hosea sounds the first fully explicit call to repentance:

> "Come, let us return to the LORD.
> He has torn us to pieces
>   but he will heal us;
> he has injured us
>   but he will bind up our wounds.
> After two days he will revive us;
>   on the third day he will restore us,
>   that we may live in his presence.
> Let us acknowledge the LORD;
>   let us press on to acknowledge him" (6:1-3).

In chapter 8, Hosea decries the Israelites' false repentance (see 8:2-3) but then calls them to "throw out your calf-idol" (8:5)—a very concrete call.

In chapter 10, Hosea proclaims, "Sow for yourselves righteousness, reap the fruit of unfailing love [what a beautiful phrase! You may want to underline that in your Bible] and break up your unplowed ground; for it is time to seek the LORD" (10:12a).

In chapter 12, he instructs them, "you must return to your God; maintain love and justice, and wait for your God always" (12:6).

Along with the verses we just read from chapter 6, the call to repentance in chapter 14 is one of the two clearest calls in the book: "Return, O Israel, to the LORD your God. Your sins have been your downfall! Take words with you and return to the LORD. Say to him: 'Forgive all our sins and receive us graciously, that we may offer the fruit of our lips'" (14:1-2).

Finally, the book itself concludes with what is essentially a call to repentance, righteousness, understanding, discernment, and wisdom. The very last verse reads, "Who is wise? He will realize these things. Who is discerning? He will understand them. The ways of the LORD are right; the righteous walk in them, but the rebellious stumble in them" (14:9).

The empire of Assyria did eventually destroy the kingdom of Israel, as Hosea prophesied (9:3; 10:6; 11:5). They did so within a few short years of Hosea's writing. God's threat of punishment could not be avoided, because Israel had ignored God too much. They had sinned too grievously. Still, God would use Hosea to graciously call his people to repentance. No sin is so grievous that God will not forgive the repenting sinner.

My friend, I pray that you would realize how serious God is about sin, and that this seriousness should motivate us to repentance. I cannot imagine that you have actually found the sin that is worth giving your life for. Turn from your sins! It is not worth it! See the truth about them. Be revolted by the degrading, self-centered, and self-destructive nature of all sin. Pray that God would show you the connection between all of your sin and your attitude toward him.

I promise you this: your sin will not look more beautiful when you consider it in the light. Sin looks good only in the dark. It looks best when it is barely considered, quickly indulged, and never reflected upon. So bring it into the light of thought, reflection, prayer, and especially of God's Word. You were made in God's image to know him. You were made to reflect his character and his love.

Take special note of how God's love is *never* divorced from his holiness. God's love does not mean that he accepts us just as we are and then leaves us in our sins. That is not the biblical picture of God's love. Rather, God's love calls us to join him in his holy hatred of sin. Indeed, it is his holy character that gives form and shape to his love. His love is never a love of moral indifference and unconcern. Rather, his love is the searching love of the father, the husband, the true friend who wants the best for the beloved. That's the kind of love that God has for us!

So, confess your sins and repent of them. Do not be duped into believing that sin is your master. It isn't! Sometimes evangelicals think that praying a prayer once is all there is to being a Christian. But they have missed what the Bible says about the Christian's ongoing fight against sin. That is why our church regularly includes a prayer of confession in its services. That is why we announce the Lord's Supper to the congregation a week ahead of time, so that members of the congregation have the opportunity to examine themselves. The New Testament teaches us to examine our hearts for sin not just once, but continually—not because we're uncertain of God's grace; no, we are certain about that! God's justifying grace *is* given at one moment in the Christian's life. It is our own hearts we are uncertain about! Our hearts and the fruit they yield need continual examination.

Listen to God's Word here in Hosea, and repent of your sin! Identify it, consider it, confess it, and repent of it.

LOVE'S HOPE: RESTORATION

Sin challenges love. Repentance offers the way of recovery. And then the restoration of love becomes our hope. This is the third thing we need to learn from this book. Hosea is filled not only with warnings of judgment and calls to repentance; somehow, piercing all these divine forebodings of doom, we find prophecies of hope!

In the very first chapter, the Lord promises,

> "Yet the Israelites will be like the sand on the seashore, which cannot be measured or counted. In the place where it was said to them, 'You are not my people,' they will be called 'sons of the living God.' The people of Judah and the people of Israel will be reunited, and they will appoint one leader and will come up out of the land, for great will be the day of Jezreel" (1:10-11).

Allow me to make a brief side note here. Mormon missionaries sometimes flummox ignorant Southern Baptists who say they believe the Bible but have never, in fact, read it. The Mormons will pull verse 11 out of context and ask, "Now, has your preacher ever talked to you about this verse?" And, honestly, most Southern Baptist preachers have probably never preached on Hosea, much less this verse. Then our Mormon friends will say that the appointed leader here is Joseph Smith. Given every other verse in the Bible, however, it is better to understand this one leader as Jesus Christ. As Jesus himself tells us in the Gospels, he is the leader of his people and he will bring them together (e.g., John 10:16). Hosea is not prophesying about a restoration that will come through some cult leader, but the restoration we find only in the Messiah and Savior, Jesus Christ.

In chapter 2, after God clearly pronounces a coming judgment upon Israel because of her unfaithfulness, he also promises her restoration! The Lord says,

"Therefore I am now going to allure her;
   I will lead her into the desert
   and speak tenderly to her.
There I will give her back her vineyards,
   and will make the Valley of Achor a door of hope.
There she will sing as in the days of her youth,
   as in the day she came up out of Egypt.

"In that day," declares the LORD,
   "you will call me 'my husband';
   you will no longer call me 'my master.'
I will remove the names of the Baals from her lips;
   no longer will their names be invoked.
In that day I will make a covenant for them
   with the beasts of the field and the birds of the air
   and the creatures that move along the ground.
Bow and sword and battle
   I will abolish from the land,
   so that all may lie down in safety.
I will betroth you to me forever;
   I will betroth you in righteousness and justice,
   in love and compassion.
I will betroth you in faithfulness,
   and you will acknowledge the LORD.

"In that day I will respond,"
   declares the LORD—
"I will respond to the skies,
   and they will respond to the earth;
and the earth will respond to the grain,
   the new wine and oil,
   and they will respond to Jezreel.
I will plant her for myself in the land;
   I will show my love to the one I called 'Not my loved one.'
I will say to those called 'Not my people,' 'You are my people';
   and they will say, 'You are my God'" (2:14-23).

Notice, God promises to lead his people out into the desert, almost like a second exodus through which he will once again deliver them: "Okay, we are going to take this again from the top. Once again you are among the nations, so once again I am going to bring you out of the nations." He tenderly allures her. He takes her to himself. She calls him "my God."

In chapter 3, as we have seen, God calls the prophet Hosea not only to speak these words of restoring love but also to exemplify them. So he instructs Hosea concerning Gomer, "Love her as the LORD loves the Israelites, though they turn to other gods" (3:1). In the same way that Gomer will return, God's people will return: "Afterward the Israelites will return and seek the LORD their God and David their king. They will come trembling to the LORD and to his blessings in the last days" (3:5).

In the verses we have already looked at in chapter 6, God promises restoration if the people repent: "let us return to the LORD. . . . After two days he will revive us; on the third day he will restore us, that we may live in his presence" (6:1, 2).

In chapter 7, God wonderfully reveals his heart to us. Have you ever noticed the little phrase that God inserts right in the middle of a list of his people's sins? "I long to redeem them," he says (7:13). That is God's will, his wish, his desire, his heart!

In chapter 8, he promises, "Although they have sold themselves among the nations, I will now gather them together" (8:10).

And then there is chapter 11. Chapter 11 should have a whole sermon to itself, or several. But we must leave that for another day. This magnificent picture of restoration must be one of the best chapters in the Bible:

"When Israel was a child, I loved him,
    and out of Egypt I called my son.
But the more I called Israel,
    the further they went from me.
They sacrificed to the Baals
    and they burned incense to images.
It was I who taught Ephraim to walk,
    taking them by the arms;
but they did not realize
    it was I who healed them.
I led them with cords of human kindness,
    with ties of love;
I lifted the yoke from their neck
    and bent down to feed them.

"Will they not return to Egypt
   and will not Assyria rule over them
   because they refuse to repent?
Swords will flash in their cities,
   will destroy the bars of their gates
   and put an end to their plans.
My people are determined to turn from me.
   Even if they call to the Most High,
   he will by no means exalt them.

"How can I give you up, Ephraim?
   How can I hand you over, Israel?
How can I treat you like Admah?
   How can I make you like Zeboiim?
My heart is changed within me;
   all my compassion is aroused.
I will not carry out my fierce anger,
   nor will I turn and devastate Ephraim.
For I am God, and not man—
   the Holy One among you.
   I will not come in wrath.
They will follow the LORD;
   he will roar like a lion.
When he roars,
   his children will come trembling from the west.
They will come trembling like birds from Egypt,
   like doves from Assyria.
I will settle them in their homes,"
   declares the LORD (11:1-11).

Then in chapter 13, the Lord promises, "I will ransom them from the power of the grave; I will redeem them from death. Where, O death, are your plagues? Where, O grave, is your destruction?" (13:14).

Finally, in chapter 14, God assures those who are listening,

"I will heal their waywardness
   and love them freely,
   for my anger has turned away from them.
I will be like the dew to Israel;
   he will blossom like a lily.
Like a cedar of Lebanon
   he will send down his roots;
   his young shoots will grow.

His splendor will be like an olive tree,
    his fragrance like a cedar of Lebanon.
Men will dwell again in his shade.
    He will flourish like the grain.
He will blossom like a vine,
    and his fame will be like the wine from Lebanon" (14:4-7).

Do you see what all these promises of restoration are based on? They are based entirely on God's own love, and the fact that his compassion has been aroused (11:8). They are not based on what the people deserve.

Now, how could God make such promises? There was no nationwide revival of prayer and fasting that prompted his blessing. In fact, the Assyrians came and destroyed Israel.

Well, the Old Covenant kingdom of Israel was destroyed, but God's true people were not. In Romans 9, Paul quotes from Hosea's passages of restoration twice (Rom. 9:25, 26). Paul understood that Hosea's prophecy would not be fulfilled in some Middle Eastern nation-state to come, but in the church.

Friend, God offers restoration for you too! If you will turn to God and see the truth about him and the great hope he holds out to you, you can take that hope as your own. What is that great hope? It is Christ, who paid sin's penalty for all those who would ever repent and believe in him. "God made him who had no sin to be sin for us, so that in him we might become the righteousness of God" (2 Cor. 5:21). If you will only repent of your sins and trust in the one whom God made sin for us, you can know this new life. Repent of your sins and trust in Christ.

If you are a pastor or are studying to be a pastor, observe what a remarkable model Hosea is for us. Hosea's life was consumed by the ministry that God wanted him to have for his people. Even the most personal and intimate areas of Hosea's life were devoted to instructing others. Take note of that, pastor. Our lives as ministers must be lived for the instruction of others. So pray and prepare.

What do these promises of restoration mean for the rest of us? They mean hope for the backslider (that's you, if you had thought you were a Christian but now realize that you are lost in sin like the Israelites). These promises also mean rest for the weary and confidence for the timid. Praise God for his persevering love!

CONCLUSION: THIS IS LOVE

Which brings us to our conclusion. Have you learned anything about what love is by considering Hosea's love for Gomer and God's love for his people? A. W. Pink said,

All religion is in effect love. Faith is thankful acceptance, and thankfulness is an expression of love. Repentance is love mourning. Yearning for holiness is love seeking. Obedience is love pleasing. Self-denial is the mortification of self-love. Sobriety is the curtailing of carnal love. . . . The affections of man cannot be idle; if they do not go out to God, they leak out to worldly things. When our love for God decreases, the love of the world grows in our soul.[7]

Surely Pink was right. Hosea's prophecy points both backward to the deep wells of God's love in calling Israel out of Egypt the first time, and forward to an eventual fulfillment. As we read earlier, God reminded the people, "When Israel was a child, I loved him, and out of Egypt I called my son." He did indeed call Israel out; but as he goes on to say in the rest of chapter 11, Israel ultimately failed as a son. He deserted the Lord. He worshiped false gods, and he refused to repent. Behind Hosea's prophecy is Moses' warning to the people before they entered the Promised Land that God would drive them out of the land if, in their prosperity, they forgot God and turned to idols (Deut. 28:15ff.). God had even given Moses a song to teach the people that told them they *would* be disobedient. Gratefully, that song concluded with another promise: "Rejoice, O nations, with his people, for he will avenge the blood of his servants; he will take vengeance on his enemies and make atonement for his land and people" (Deut. 32:43). Did you notice that? God promised he would "make atonement" because of their sins in the land. And so he would.

As we turn from looking backward to Moses and look forward in search of a fulfillment, we discover that another Son came up "out of Egypt" *who did not fail!* The Gospel of Matthew quotes Hosea 11:1 to describe the young Jesus' return from Egypt after the death of Herod, who had been hoping to kill infant Jesus (Matt. 2:15). The disobedient, adopted son Israel sinned. But the obedient, eternal Son, Jesus, made the atonement through his perfect life and sinless death on the cross.

Once he made atonement for God's people by dying, God raised him on the third day "in fulfillment of Scripture," Paul says (1 Cor. 15:4), perhaps alluding to Hosea 6:2. It is only because of Christ's payment and restoration that you and I can be restored. If you are in Christ, then you have forgiveness for your sins. You have new life.

Consider God's remarkable promise in Hosea 13: "I will ransom them from the power of the grave; I will redeem them from death. Where, O death, are your plagues? Where, O grave, is your destruction?" (13:14). Did God simply mean he would reconstitute the physical nation of Israel? That he would metaphorically bring her back from the dead? Well, Paul's citation of this verse

---

[7] Cited in Iain H. Murray, *The Life of Arthur W. Pink* (Carlisle, Pa.: Banner of Truth, 2004), 255-256.

in 1 Corinthians 15:55 shows that he regards it as pointing to the victory that Christians—God's new Israel—have been given over sin and death through Jesus Christ! Jesus is the fulfillment of Hosea's love. And that is great news for you and me.

I wonder whom you have identified yourself with while we looked through this little book. Hosea, perhaps? Have you sympathized with him? After all, God called him to love an adulterous wife by taking her back. And we all know how hard it can be to love sinners.

But you realize who you really are, don't you? I am here to tell you, you are Gomer.

You are Gomer.

Regardless of all the ways you may compare your righteousness with someone else's, when you compare yourself with God and what he has called you to be, it should be clear that you are Gomer. You and I are the unfaithful objects of God's ever-faithful love. Only when we understand this do we begin to understand what love is.

Consider how strongly God in his holiness desires justice and so desires to punish our sin. Consider then how great his love must have been in order to devise and execute his plan of redemption through the cross. This is love!

May God give us cross-centered lives of grace and love![8]

I have been asked more than once by visitors to our church where the cross is. They look around and are surprised when they don't see one. Depending on who they are, I will offer various explanations. But I will say the cross is here in the Bible. And it is in our hearts. If you are truly a Christian, you know what it means that God has loved you.

Listen to these words of the apostle John in the New Testament:

> I am not writing you a new command but one we have had from the beginning. I ask that we love one another. And *this is love:* that we walk in obedience to his commands. As you have heard from the beginning, his command is that you walk in love (2 John 5-6).

> This is how we know that we love the children of God: by loving God and carrying out his commands. *This is love* for God: to obey his commands. And his commands are not burdensome (1 John 5:2-3).

> This is how God showed his love among us: He sent his one and only Son into the world that we might live through him. *This is love:* not that we loved

---

[8] If you want to know how you can practically live with the cross at the center of your life, I would encourage you to get a copy of C. J. Mahaney's little book *The Cross Centered Life* (Sisters, Ore.: Multnomah, 2002).

God, but that he loved us and sent his Son as an atoning sacrifice for our sins (1 John 4:9-10).

Gomer's only hope was in a love that she never deserved. And this is your only hope as well. That's the message of Hosea.

Let us pray:

O God, you know how our self-righteous hearts seek out the sins of others like radars so that we can compare ourselves to others and then feel that we deserve your love, or even require you to love us. So we give you praise for this breath-taking picture in Hosea of how your love wells up from deep inside of you, not from a consideration of any goodness, desert, or merit in us. It is your own nature alone that causes you to love. O God, we give you praise for this love. We praise you for the costly way that you have been faithful to us who are unfaithful. We praise you for the love and work of our Lord Jesus Christ.

Lord, we pray that you would humble us. That you would encourage us. That you would give us hope and the ability to graciously deal with others as you have so graciously dealt with us. O God, teach us the message of this book. For our souls' sake and for your glory, we ask it, through our Redeemer, Jesus Christ. Amen.

Questions for Reflection

1. Based on what you have observed, how would you say our culture today misunderstands love? How would you define love?

2. Why does God take sin so personally? When you sin, do you typically perceive yourself as personally attacking God? How would growing in your understanding of the personal nature of sin affect your desire to fight sin?

3. It's easy to say you love someone. It's even easy to think you really do love someone when you don't. How then can we know whether we really love someone as we think and say we do? What's the standard or measurement? As Christians, how can we determine whether God is truly uppermost in our affections as we say he is?

4. Why does the Bible so closely relate adultery and idolatry?

5. Given the close connection between adultery and idolatry in the Bible, why is a church's best strategy for fighting against adultery in the lives of its mem-

bers to preach about God, his attributes, his work in salvation, and his glory in our lives?

6. Consider for a moment your own sins of adultery, whether they are physical or mental. Can you discern how idolatry led you to these sins?

7. What idols do evangelical churches worship today?

8. Where is God's love for us most clearly displayed? Why does this act of love seem foolish to the world? What does that teach us about the world's understanding of love?

9. If it's so easy to worship and love our circumstances more than God himself, why should we be grateful to God for life's trials and tragedies?

10. Can you think of any sin in your life right now that would look good if it were brought into the light (i.e., held up for God and everyone you know to look at)?

11. Why should a Christian continually examine his or her heart?

12. Do most people perceive themselves as Gomer? Do you? Why or why not? What hope exists for a Gomer? Does hope exist for anyone who does not perceive himself or herself as a Gomer?

THE MESSAGE OF JOEL: WHOM WILL GOD SAVE?

THE MESSAGE OF JOEL: WHOM WILL GOD SAVE?

WHOM WILL GOD SAVE?[1]

Frederick the Great, the Prussian ruler of the late eighteenth century, once famously said, "All religions must be tolerated . . . for . . . every man must get to heaven his own way." Given the religious wars that had wracked Europe for a century after the Reformation, you can understand why Frederick felt this way. He wanted a more enlightened, less violent path. Around the same time, Edward Gibbon, one of the period's preeminent historians, was busy presenting the Roman Empire as a model of exactly this sort of tolerance. In his famous *Decline and Fall of the Roman Empire,* Gibbon wrote, "The various modes of worship, which prevailed in the Roman world, were all considered by the people as equally true; by the philosopher, as equally false; and by the magistrate, as equally useful."[2]

Yet not all eighteenth-century advocates of religious freedom were so cynical. Here in America, through the good offices of our representatives, a constitution and a bill of rights were fashioned which guaranteed not just religious toleration, as in European countries, but religious *liberty.* The American Founding Fathers' belief in an absolute God who made moral creatures in his image demanded that such liberty be extended to persons of all faiths.

Now, more than two centuries later, many have forgotten the Christian roots of such thinking and have wrongly (and dangerously) assumed that religious liberty can be protected only by *in*difference to the differences between religions. Studying those differences can make for polite work in sociology, but when such differences are treated as serious, significant, related to reality, and

---

[1] This sermon was originally preached on June 1, 2003, at Capitol Hill Baptist Church in Washington, D.C.
[2] Edward Gibbon, *The History of the Decline and Fall of the Roman Empire* (New York: Heritage, 1946; first published 1776–1788), 22.

even determinative of eternal destinies, then "enlightened" minds begin to worry. Editorials are written and forums are held equating Christian evangelism with terrorism! (Of course, true Christian conversion is never the result of coercion. By its very nature, Christian conversion cannot happen by coercion.)

Ironically, as the nation continues to discuss both the events in Iraq and radical Islam, many secular Americans, I think, have begun to discover how Christian some of their thoughts and values are. Running into thoroughly non-Western ways of thinking has exposed many of their Christian presuppositions.

Turning from the important social and political aspects of how people of different faiths cooperate in one society, surely a more pressing matter is the question of salvation, and whether any one of these different religions is right. What if what *this* religion says is true, and *that* religion is wrong? Is there really a Creator who made us? Is this Creator just? What demands does he place on our lives? Does he care if we are good? If he does, what will he do if we are not good? Is he committed to justice, and what bearing does that have on our lives today? These questions—largely dismissed in polite company—are the questions that we Christians insist are most important. Questions of political policy and procedure, of social rights and responsibilities, must be asked and answered. But nowhere are our personal interests more involved than when we turn to the question of salvation, particularly our own salvation. Whom will God save? Will he save me?

INTRODUCING JOEL

This brings us to the next "Eternal Question" we are considering in our series of studies through the Old Testament's Minor Prophets. The prophet Joel will help us answer this most important question, whom will God save?

As you may have noticed, I called Joel a "minor" prophet. Did I mean that as an insult? No, everyone calls Joel a minor prophet, not because he was unimportant, but because his book is brief when compared to the longer books of the "major prophets," like Isaiah, Jeremiah, and Ezekiel.

Interestingly, Joel's book is unusually devoid of the specifics of historical setting. In the book of Hosea, which we looked at in our previous study, Hosea included in the very first verse a detailed list of kings who reigned when he prophesied. Joel includes nothing like that. No mention of kings. Nothing about the Babylonians or Assyrians. No reference to the temple. We really don't know when Joel prophesied. Some people have suggested that Joel deliberately omitted such specifics in order to make the book's message easily transferable from his own day to the ages that would follow.

Whatever the situation, let's turn now to the "word of the LORD" that came to Joel and look for what we can learn about salvation.

SAVED FROM WHAT?

The first question we should consider when talking about salvation is, "Saved from what?"

God's Judgment on the Nations

I formerly worked at a church where an elderly minister once told the story about a stranger approaching him on the street and asking him the question, "Have you been saved?" to which this Christian minister replied, "Saved from what?" My colleague's tone in recounting his reply to the evangelist, sadly, was caustic and dismissive. Perhaps if his life had been a little less prosperous and his conscience a little more active he would have known what he needed to be saved from.

According to the book of Joel, there is much we need to be saved from, for there is much that we have done wrong. According to the Bible, God made the world. Therefore, he is the world's rightful judge. The Bible also teaches that God made human beings in his image, which means that he designed us to reflect his good and holy character. But we have not done that. We are fallen, and we have sinned against God. We do things that we should not do, and thereby hangs the problem addressed in Joel and in every other book of the Bible.

The first two chapters of Joel focus on the nation of Judah. Judah, you may remember, was comprised of the two tribes in the south around the city of Jerusalem. The ten northern tribes, called Israel after the nation divided in half, were wiped out by an Assyrian invasion in 722 B.C.

At the beginning of chapter 3, the Lord speaks against the nations, and this is where we will begin our study:

> "In those days and at that time,
>   when I restore the fortunes of Judah and Jerusalem,
> I will gather all nations
>   and bring them down to the Valley of Jehoshaphat.
> There I will enter into judgment against them
>   concerning my inheritance, my people Israel,
> for they scattered my people among the nations
>   and divided up my land.
> They cast lots for my people
>   and traded boys for prostitutes;

they sold girls for wine
    that they might drink.

"Now what have you against me, O Tyre and Sidon and all you regions of Philistia? Are you repaying me for something I have done? If you are paying me back, I will swiftly and speedily return on your own heads what you have done. For you took my silver and my gold and carried off my finest treasures to your temples. You sold the people of Judah and Jerusalem to the Greeks, that you might send them far from their homeland.

"See, I am going to rouse them out of the places to which you sold them, and I will return on your own heads what you have done. I will sell your sons and daughters to the people of Judah, and they will sell them to the Sabeans, a nation far away." The LORD has spoken.

Proclaim this among the nations:
    Prepare for war!
Rouse the warriors!
    Let all the fighting men draw near and attack.
Beat your plowshares into swords
    and your pruning hooks into spears.
Let the weakling say,
    "I am strong!"
Come quickly, all you nations from every side,
    and assemble there.

Bring down your warriors, O LORD!

"Let the nations be roused;
    let them advance into the Valley of Jehoshaphat,
for there I will sit
    to judge all the nations on every side.
Swing the sickle,
    for the harvest is ripe.
Come, trample the grapes,
    for the winepress is full
    and the vats overflow—
so great is their wickedness!"

Multitudes, multitudes
    in the valley of decision!
For the day of the LORD is near
    in the valley of decision.
The sun and moon will be darkened,

and the stars no longer shine.
The LORD will roar from Zion
    and thunder from Jerusalem;
    the earth and the sky will tremble (3:1-16a).

God describes the nations as a crop that is "ripe" with wickedness and crying out for the harvest of judgment (3:13). Joel does not present a complete inventory of the sins of the nations, but he picks out several that typified Israel's nearby neighbors Tyre, Sidon, and Philistia—like theft, slavery, and bloodshed (3:3, 5, 6). These were not merely the charges of one angry prophet over injustices done to his people. They were words of condemnation leveled by a Creator against his creatures. God as judge was calling the nations to account.

So God tells the nations to "Prepare for war!" (3:9). And then he reverses his famous promise in the book of Isaiah about beating swords into plowshares and spears into pruning hooks: "Beat your plowshares into swords and your pruning hooks into spears" (3:10; cf. Isa. 2:4; Mic. 4:3). The nations should prepare to defend themselves!

How could they defend themselves against God? What would all the swords and spears in the world accomplish against him! Well, nothing, and rhetorically that is the point. We have no defense against God when he charges us with sin.

What initially sounds like a challenge to assemble for a contest (3:9-11; e.g., "Let all the fighting men draw near and attack," 3:9) is really a call to assemble for judgment, as we learn in verses 12-16. This contest will be so one-sided that the prophet Joel has to change the image from military action to agricultural action. The days ahead won't look like the clashing of two mighty armies; it will look more like the farmer swinging a sickle through the grain or a vinedresser trampling on his grapes! "Swing the sickle, for the harvest is ripe. Come, trample the grapes, for the winepress is full and the vats overflow—so great is their wickedness!" (3:13). Their wicked deeds are greater and more serious than anyone first realized—the "vats overflow."

What's happening here? God is calling the nations to judgment: "Let the nations be roused; let them advance into the Valley of Jehoshaphat, for there I will sit to judge all the nations on every side" (3:12). "Jehoshaphat" literally translated means "Yahweh judges." When God summons the nations, he does not politely extend an invitation to which they can casually RSVP "accept" or "decline." No, he gives an inexorable summons.

This summons will be given to all nations: "Multitudes, multitudes in the valley of decision! For the day of the LORD is near in the valley of decision" (3:14). Joel says "multitudes, multitudes" as if he is even surprised and terrified—though he is an Israelite—for the sake of the veritable sea of humanity before him in this vision, awaiting God's judgment. Clearly, the "valley of decision," or the "valley of Jehoshaphat," is the valley in which God would bring justice. Had the nations sold the Israelites into slavery? Yes, they had invaded, captured, and sold many Israelites. "Therefore," the Lord basically says, "I will do the same to you" (see 3:8).

You might be interested to know that God did deliver on his promise. In 343 B.C. Artaxerxes conquered and enslaved Sidon. A few years later, in 322 B.C., Alexander the Great took Tyre. Surviving records indicate that more than thirteen thousand inhabitants of Tyre were sold into slavery.

Preachers have sometimes taken these verses and misread the phrase "valley of decision" as if the valley represented a swelling throng of people at a mass evangelistic crusade waiting to make a decision for Christ. But no, these swelling masses have gathered to hear God's terrible judgment on them. It is not a place where *they* must make a decision; it is where they will hear *God's* decision—God's final verdict. The valley of Yahweh's judgment is the valley of his *verdict*. The court is in session. The judge has weighed all the evidence, including the evidence which could never be known or admitted in a human court of law. The defendants stand to hear the judge read his verdict and pronounce his judgment. And once he does, they can make no appeal, because his judgments are always without error!

All creation seems to hide "before the coming of the great and dreadful day of the LORD" (2:31; cf. 2:10). So here in chapter 3, the Lord promises, "The sun and moon will be darkened, and the stars no longer shine. The LORD will roar from Zion" (3:15-16a). The very voice that called worlds into existence at the beginning of time will roar like a lion preparing to tear apart its prey. And this roar will echo as loudly as thunder: "The LORD will roar from Zion and thunder from Jerusalem; the earth and the sky will tremble" (3:16). It's no wonder the earth and sky will tremble. Can you imagine if the loud and rolling sound of thunder took on the vocal qualities of a roar?

One day, friend, you too will find yourself in a time and place where all the guessing and doubting and wondering and sneaking and lying and cheating and harming and engorging and murdering finally stops, and God says, "No!" It is the time and place where the world's *might* meets *right*, and *right* proves most *mighty*. One day, we will all come to the valley of God's verdict on human action.

God's Judgment on His People

Not only will God bring his judgment on the nations; he will bring it upon his own people as well. In fact, that is what prompts Joel's prophecy in the first place. As we turn back to chapter 1, we see that God's people have found themselves both in present trouble and faced with the prospect of future trouble.

Trouble now—invading locusts. In the opening verses of Joel, we immediately encounter the people's present trouble:

The word of the LORD that came to Joel son of Pethuel.

Hear this, you elders;
    listen, all who live in the land.
Has anything like this ever happened in your days
    or in the days of your forefathers?
Tell it to your children,
    and let your children tell it to their children,
    and their children to the next generation.
What the locust swarm has left
    the great locusts have eaten;
what the great locusts have left
    the young locusts have eaten;
what the young locusts have left
    other locusts have eaten.

Wake up, you drunkards, and weep!
    Wail, all you drinkers of wine;
wail because of the new wine,
    for it has been snatched from your lips.
A nation has invaded my land,
    powerful and without number;
it has the teeth of a lion,
    the fangs of a lioness.
It has laid waste my vines
    and ruined my fig trees.
It has stripped off their bark
    and thrown it away,
    leaving their branches white.

Mourn like a virgin in sackcloth
    grieving for the husband of her youth.
Grain offerings and drink offerings
    are cut off from the house of the LORD.

The priests are in mourning,
　　those who minister before the LORD.
The fields are ruined,
　　the ground is dried up;
the grain is destroyed,
　　the new wine is dried up,
　　the oil fails.
Despair, you farmers,
　　wail, you vine growers;
grieve for the wheat and the barley,
　　because the harvest of the field is destroyed.
The vine is dried up
　　and the fig tree is withered;
the pomegranate, the palm and the apple tree—
　　all the trees of the field—are dried up.
Surely the joy of mankind
　　is withered away (1:1-12).

If you are reading a modern translation of the Bible like the NIV, you can see the editor's subheading above verse 2 in chapter 1, "An Invasion of Locusts." Joel does say "locusts" in the following verses, but he also uses language of an army. Really, chapter 1 reads as if Joel is trying to convey two ideas at once.

Judah was experiencing a horrible infestation of locusts, and the first half of chapter 1 describes the destruction wrought by these invaders. Evidently, the invasion was absolutely terrible because Joel challenges the elders to remember a time when it had been worse (1:2). Vines and fig trees, symbols of security and peace in the ancient Near East, were "laid waste" (1:7). Everyone, from priest to drunkard, was ruined! The drunkards could not drink and the priests could not offer sacrifices, because nothing remained to drink or sacrifice (1:5, 9-10)! That's how complete this devastation was.

While we have every reason to believe that this disastrous infestation of locusts was a real event historically, it foreshadowed another event: the day of the Lord. Joel first alludes to this day in the latter half of chapter 1:

Alas for that day!
　　For the day of the LORD is near;
　　it will come like destruction from the Almighty.

Has not the food been cut off
　　before our very eyes—
joy and gladness

from the house of our God?
The seeds are shriveled
  beneath the clods.
The storehouses are in ruins,
  the granaries have been broken down,
  for the grain has dried up.
How the cattle moan!
  The herds mill about
because they have no pasture;
  even the flocks of sheep are suffering.

To you, O LORD, I call,
  for fire has devoured the open pastures
  and flames have burned up all the trees of the field.
Even the wild animals pant for you;
  the streams of water have dried up
  and fire has devoured the open pastures (1:15-20).

In the face of such comprehensive devastation, Joel was prompted to think about God's ultimate purposes and the end of the world. In theological language, we would say the devastation prompted him to think "apocalyptically." You might say his response was similar to how many people in Washington and around the world responded to the destruction of New York's World Trade Center on September 11, 2001. In the days following September 11, almost everyone thought a little more seriously about ultimate matters. Witnessing disaster helps us realize that the things we too often build our lives upon are not as certain as we think. As the prophet contemplated the ruin wrought by the locust swarms, he could see an even greater devastation beyond it, a devastation so complete that it almost looked like an *un*-creation—the Creator himself undoing his own work for the sake of judgment.

Trouble ahead—the day of the Lord. What begins as an allusion in verse 15 of chapter 1 is declared with a full-blown trumpet blast at the beginning of chapter 2:

Blow the trumpet in Zion;
  sound the alarm on my holy hill.
Let all who live in the land tremble,
  for the day of the LORD is coming.
It is close at hand—
  a day of darkness and gloom,
  a day of clouds and blackness.
Like dawn spreading across the mountains

a large and mighty army comes,
such as never was of old
nor ever will be in ages to come.

Before them fire devours,
behind them a flame blazes.
Before them the land is like the Garden of Eden,
behind them, a desert waste—
nothing escapes them.
They have the appearance of horses;
they gallop along like cavalry.
With a noise like that of chariots
they leap over the mountaintops,
like a crackling fire consuming stubble,
like a mighty army drawn up for battle.

At the sight of them, nations are in anguish;
every face turns pale.
They charge like warriors;
they scale walls like soldiers.
They all march in line,
not swerving from their course.
They do not jostle each other;
each marches straight ahead.
They plunge through defenses
without breaking ranks.
They rush upon the city;
they run along the wall.
They climb into the houses;
like thieves they enter through the windows.

Before them the earth shakes,
the sky trembles,
the sun and moon are darkened,
and the stars no longer shine.
The LORD thunders
at the head of his army;
his forces are beyond number,
and mighty are those who obey his command.
The day of the LORD is great;
it is dreadful.
Who can endure it? (2:1-11).

Chapter 2 then ends with the same declaration: "The sun will be turned to darkness and the moon to blood before the coming of the great and dreadful day of the LORD" (2:31).

If chapter 1 provides a description of invading locusts, chapter 2 turns to describing the more terrible and destructive event that the locusts merely anticipate: the coming day of the Lord. The trouble here is all-encompassing, "spreading across the mountains" (2:2). It is like an invincible army or a consuming fire—"nothing escapes them" (2:3-11). The shift from chapter 1 to chapter 2 almost feels like the Lord saying, "You haven't seen anything yet!"

After all, notice who is behind all the destruction: the Lord! "The LORD thunders at the head of his army; his forces are beyond number, and mighty are those who obey his command. The day of the LORD is great" (2:11).

Our world today has little or no comprehension of a God who would do such things. To most, God is whatever they conceive of as nice and sweet. Lump all these nice and sweet things together like Play-Doh and call *that* "God." Anything else that is not immediately appetizing, well, whatever it is, it isn't God.

Scripture, on the other hand, provides a far more nuanced understanding of who God is. Certainly God is good; this much should be obvious. But what is good and what is not good is not always obvious to us. Therefore, we need to recalibrate our understandings of "good" according to what God reveals in Scripture. Here we see the Lord thundering at the head of his army, and we trust that he must be up to something good.

When God's people prepared to enter the Promised Land, Moses taught them how to invoke God's curses for disobedience to God's laws.[3] Yet in the following centuries, the nation of Israel basically became creative, you could say, in how they disobeyed God's laws. Disobedience was the one thing they were good at! So God kept his word and brought judgment upon them. "That's what these locusts are!" Joel says. "But know this," the prophet continues, "these present judgments are just a foretaste, or a preview, of the main event— God's ultimate and final judgment on sin. That day is still ahead."

Joel, like all of the prophets in the Old Testament, is not a good book to read if you simply want reassurance that the world is all good and contains nothing bad. Christian Science, Buddhism, and many other worldviews try to imagine life all positively. If that's you, you will find the Christian Bible challenging. It is a good book for you to read; you will find it helpful and realistic. But it will not affirm such erroneous ways of thinking. This world is not an illusion; and our troubles do not dwell merely in our imaginations. The human

---

[3] Deut. 27:15-26; cf. Deuteronomy 28 and 32.

landscape presents one vast picture of death and destruction, of ruin and misery. Yes, it is certainly pierced with rays of good, but it is tragically strewn with trials and troubles, with sin and selfishness, with crimes against our neighbors and rebellion against God. Simple optimism in the face of such sin is nothing more than ignorance. The Bible is clear—and our lives amply demonstrate— that we have all sinned and fallen short of the glory of God!

We cannot begin to understand salvation until we understand what we must be saved *from*. It is not, fundamentally, all the difficult circumstances of this life. We must be saved from our sin and its consequences—the judgment of God. In a very real sense, then, we need to be saved from God himself and his righteous anger.

That means we need to be far less concerned about what has happened to us and far more concerned about what we have done against God. We have offended him! That is how the Bible diagnoses our problem. I once told a friend that he would begin going to church when he became less concerned about what others thought of him and what he thought of others, and more concerned about what God thought of him.

Why do you think Christians share the Lord's Supper so often? Because we want regularly to remember the death of Christ, which the Lord's Supper depicts. Why did Christ die? He died to bear God's wrath against sin.

Sin is real, and, outside of Christ, God will judge us for it. God's just condemnation of our sins is what we need to be saved from.

WHAT IS SALVATION?

Given our predicament as convicted sinners, Joel points toward hope by answering a second question: What is salvation?

We learn in this little book that God is not only committed to justice, he is committed to mercy. He will not only judge his people, he will save them. What does that salvation look like?

God's Rescue from Enemies

First, we see that God rescues his people from their enemies. In chapter 2, God promises, "I will drive the northern army far from you, pushing it into a parched and barren land, with its front columns going into the eastern sea and those in the rear into the western sea. And its stench will go up; its smell will rise" (2:20). The nations may pursue Judah, but the Lord will rescue his people by bringing the nations to judgment. We saw that in chapter 3. Remember? God promises explicitly, toward the end of chapter 3, "But the LORD will be a refuge for his people, a stronghold for the people of Israel. 'Then you will know

that I, the LORD your God, dwell in Zion, my holy hill. Jerusalem will be holy;
never again will foreigners invade her'" (3:16b-17).

God's Restoration of Prosperity

Most of Joel's prophecies about salvation, however, describe God's promise to
restore his people to prosperity. That's the picture of salvation Joel spends the
most time describing:

> Then the LORD will be jealous for his land
> and take pity on his people.
>
> The LORD will reply to them:
>
> "I am sending you grain, new wine and oil,
> enough to satisfy you fully;
> never again will I make you
> an object of scorn to the nations.
>
> "I will drive the northern army far from you,
> pushing it into a parched and barren land,
> with its front columns going into the eastern sea
> and those in the rear into the western sea.
> And its stench will go up;
> its smell will rise."
>
> Surely he has done great things.
> Be not afraid, O land;
> be glad and rejoice.
> Surely the LORD has done great things.
> Be not afraid, O wild animals,
> for the open pastures are becoming green.
> The trees are bearing their fruit;
> the fig tree and the vine yield their riches.
> Be glad, O people of Zion,
> rejoice in the LORD your God,
> for he has given you
> the autumn rains in righteousness.
> He sends you abundant showers,
> both autumn and spring rains, as before.
> The threshing floors will be filled with grain;
> the vats will overflow with new wine and oil.

"I will repay you for the years the locusts have eaten—
  the great locust and the young locust,
  the other locusts and the locust swarm—
my great army that I sent among you.
You will have plenty to eat, until you are full,
  and you will praise the name of the LORD your God,
  who has worked wonders for you;
never again will my people be shamed.
Then you will know that I am in Israel,
  that I am the LORD your God,
  and that there is no other;
never again will my people be shamed" (2:18-27).

Notice in this passage how Joel refers to their promised prosperity in both the present and the past tense: "the open pastures *are becoming* green" and the "trees *are bearing* their fruit" and "he *has given* you the autumn rains" (2:22, 23). He does not say this because Judah had already begun to experience prosperity but because God's promise of restoration was as certain as if it already had been fulfilled. (Paul does the same thing when he refers to a Christian's glorification in the past tense. God's promises warrant that much confidence! See Romans 8:30.)

Land, animals, and people had all been affected by the crisis of locusts, so now Joel declared that all would be blessed as the Lord drove them away. Wild animals, trees, and vines would prosper when the Lord sent rain: ". . . abundant showers, both autumn and spring rains, as before. The threshing floors will be filled with grain; the vats will overflow with new wine and oil" (2:23-24). The further we move away from an agricultural economy, the less we understand how beautiful these images are. In ancient Palestine, the people were deeply dependent on the rain. They understood that life literally and physically came from the rain. Only a little rain would typically fall in the summer. But autumn rains were necessary for softening the ground to receive the seeds. Winter rains might then be light and soft. But heavier spring rains were essential for strengthening the crops for their final growth and ripening before harvest. If rain did not fall in either fall or spring, crops would be decimated. During their crisis of locusts, Judah lacked both. But now God promised both; and so his blessings would once again flow from rain, to land, to plants, to animals, and then to people. The people would be restored to prosperity.

Joel provides another picture like this at the end of the book:

"In that day the mountains will drip new wine,
  and the hills will flow with milk;

all the ravines of Judah will run with water.
A fountain will flow out of the LORD's house
    and will water the valley of acacias.
But Egypt will be desolate,
    Edom a desert waste,
because of violence done to the people of Judah,
    in whose land they shed innocent blood.
Judah will be inhabited forever
    and Jerusalem through all generations.
Their bloodguilt, which I have not pardoned,
    I will pardon."

The LORD dwells in Zion! (3:18-21).

Wine-dripping mountains. Milk-flowing hills. Water-filled ravines. All of these are dramatic signs of prosperity stretched to an unimaginable degree. It's a picture of total prosperity and full salvation!

The fountain flowing out of the Lord's house is reminiscent of the prophet Ezekiel's vision, where he saw "water coming out from under the threshold of the temple" and watering the city and the land of Jerusalem (Ezek. 47:1). The apostle John, too, saw in his great apocalyptic vision "the river of the water of life, as clear as crystal, flowing from the throne of God and of the Lamb down the middle of the great street of the city" (Rev. 22:1-2).

After everything Judah had endured—the invasions of locust armies, human armies, or both—God would still preserve and bless them. The effects of the recent devastation would be completely and permanently reversed. The land that was parched would drip with wine, flow with milk, and run with water. More than that, these dramatic symbols would point to the inner spiritual reality of the people's reconciled relationship with God: "Their bloodguilt, which I have not pardoned, I will pardon" (Joel 3:21).

God's Residing with His People

This brings us to the core of Joel's salvation prophecies. Not only will God restore his people to prosperity, he will reside with his people himself:

"And afterward,
    I will pour out my Spirit on all people.
Your sons and daughters will prophesy,
    your old men will dream dreams,
    your young men will see visions.
Even on my servants, both men and women,

> I will pour out my Spirit in those days.
> I will show wonders in the heavens
>   and on the earth,
>   blood and fire and billows of smoke.
> The sun will be turned to darkness
>   and the moon to blood
>   before the coming of the great and dreadful day of the LORD.
> And everyone who calls
>   on the name of the LORD will be saved;
> for on Mount Zion and in Jerusalem
>   there will be deliverance,
>   as the LORD has said,
> among the survivors
>   whom the LORD calls" (2:28-32).

In these verses of promise and prophecy, the Lord again presents fearful aspects of his coming. The valley of decision, or the Day of Judgment, lies ahead. But there is more. Superimposed upon this prophecy is another prophecy for what we have come to know as Pentecost. In other words, Joel describes one thing that has since been fulfilled at Christ's first coming, and another thing that has yet to be fulfilled at Christ's second coming. Prophecy in the Bible often works like this. Two things will be described together and no mention will be made of the time interval in between them, even though one exists. It's like looking at a mountain range from a great distance, where all the mountains appear to stand next to one another. But drive into the mountains and you find that great distances separate them. So it is here.

In the very first Christian sermon after the ascension of Jesus, Peter quotes this passage from Joel about the Spirit's outpouring and its effects. Peter knows that what the people of Jerusalem are witnessing in his day is the fulfillment of this aspect of Joel's prophecy (see Acts 2:16-18).

At the very core of God's promised salvation, then, is closeness with God himself. Salvation means experiencing the presence of God: "I will pour out my Spirit in those days."

A thousand years before Joel's day, after God led his people out of Egypt and into the wilderness, the people built a golden calf and provoked God to anger. So he told them that he would not continue with them: "I will not go with you, because you are a stiff-necked people and I might destroy you on the way" (Ex. 33:3). Having learned from God something about God's purposes, Moses offered the perfect reply:

"If your Presence does not go with us, do not send us up from here. How will anyone know that you are pleased with me and with your people unless you go with us? What else will distinguish me and your people from all the other people on the face of the earth?" (Ex. 33:15-16).

Moses knew that only God's presence, finally, distinguishes the people who bear his name from all other people.

Compared to the presence of God himself, mountains dripping with wine and hills dripping with milk don't amount to much. *What good is the Promised Land if God is not there?* God's chief blessing to his people is himself! Here in Joel, God promises, as we have read, "the LORD will be a refuge for his people, a stronghold for the people of Israel. 'Then you will know that I, the LORD your God, dwell in Zion, my holy hill'" (Joel 3:16b-17a). The Lord does not intend finally to protect his people with some cave or weapons system. He will protect them himself. He himself will dwell with them.

Friend, the entire Bible, not just Joel, presents salvation most fundamentally as God restoring his people to himself and his own presence. That's the heart of salvation. The preachers on television and the writers of self-help books who present God as a way to achieve all our own ends just don't get it. They are not simply presenting a different variety of Christianity, they are presenting something *other* than Christianity. We cannot expect to use God for our own ends. He is not simply one way to practice positive thinking, or one way to reason toward what we want. No! Such prosperity teachers miss, first of all, what a dangerous predicament our sins put us in, given God's holiness. If we really are sinful and he really is holy, we have a serious problem, whether we realize it or not. Second, such false teachers do not appear to value God himself. They only value all the things that God gives them. He almost becomes an impersonal principle by which they say we can get the health, the child, the home, the job, the promotion, the car, the prosperity, the respect, and the worldly future that we want. Such a foolish fascination with the gift above the Giver indicates a complete failure to recognize both what our Savior has saved us *from*—God's just wrath—and whom the Savior has saved us *to*. God made the world and everything in it. He made you and me. And now he invites sinful people like us into a holy fellowship with him through Jesus Christ, even though he should judge us. That is extraordinary! But that is salvation. God is the one who has come in Christ to save us from our own sins and to bring us back to himself.

If you are a non-Christian and you do not understand what I am saying, I encourage you to talk with a Christian friend or the pastor of the church you attend. This message of God's salvation is the most important thing you can ever understand, and it is what every truly Christian church—whatever the denomination—preaches on Sunday mornings. This is why the church gathers, and it's the heart of our hope.

Sadly, this central Christian message is widely misunderstood. One survey a few years back reported,

> 84 percent of those who claim the evangelical label embrace the notion that in salvation God helps those who help themselves, 77 percent believe that human beings are basically good and that good people go to heaven regardless of their relationship with Christ, while more than half of those surveyed affirmed self-fulfillment as their first priority.[4]

Salvation is about God's reestablishing his relationship with us, the relationship that was severed at the Fall. The craving for approval that you experience, which you try to fill with appearance, success, self-congratulation, or flattering remarks from your boss, parents, or friends, will never be met by any of these things! That craving was made by God to draw you to him. He made you to crave his approval. As the psalmist says, "You have made known to me the path of life; you will fill me with joy in your presence" (Ps. 16:11a).

If you are happy to go to heaven whether or not Jesus is there, you have not yet understood what Christians mean when they talk about the hope of heaven. The perfectly restored relationship with God promised in heaven is the climax; it is the core of what we understand salvation to be. God with us. Us with God:

> The Word became flesh and made his dwelling among us. We have seen his glory, the glory of the One and Only, who came from the Father, full of grace and truth (John 1:14).

> And I heard a loud voice from the throne saying, "Now the dwelling of God is with men, and he will live with them. They will be his people, and God himself will be with them and be their God" (Rev. 21:3).

Do *you* have a restored relationship with your Maker? When a friend asked John Newton his opinion on a particularly hopeless mutual acquaintance, Newton replied, "I have never despaired for any man since God saved me."

Joel also places a restored relationship with God at the very heart of salvation:

---

[4] Cited by Gary Johnson, "Does Theology Still Matter?" in John H. Armstrong, ed., *The Coming Evangelical Crisis: Current Challenges to the Authority of Scripture and the Gospel* (Chicago: Moody, 1996), 61.

The LORD will be a refuge for his people (Joel 3:16).

"Even on my servants, both men and women, I will pour out my Spirit in those days" (2:29).

WHY WILL GOD'S PEOPLE BE SAVED?

Joel answers yet another question for us about this salvation: why will God's people be saved? Many people today seem to think God will save us because we deserve it. "Sure, we do some bad things, but then we do some good things to make up for it." This is *not* a Christian idea. We are not saved because of any moral or religious actions of our own. Salvation depends entirely on God, not on us.

Probably the most famous verse in the book of Joel is the last verse in chapter 2: "Everyone who calls on the name of the LORD will be saved; for on Mount Zion and in Jerusalem there will be deliverance, as the LORD has said, among the survivors whom the LORD calls" (2:32). Many people are familiar with the first part of this verse—"Everyone who calls on the name of the LORD will be saved"—because Paul quotes it in Romans 10:13 (cf. Acts 2:21). It is used in many Christian tracts, and people quote it when sharing the gospel. And that's fine. But few people have read the rest of the verse. The last phrase tells us *who* will call on the name of the Lord: those "whom the LORD calls." God calls those who call on him! He has his own purposes in salvation:

> "You will have plenty to eat, until you are full,
>   and you will praise the name of the LORD your God,
>   who has worked wonders for you;
> never again will my people be shamed.
> Then you will know that I am in Israel,
>   that I am the LORD your God,
>   and that there is no other" (2:26-27).

God saves his people in order to make himself known, to display his own character, and to display his glory. He says this again later: The Lord is his people's refuge and stronghold so that "you will know that I, the LORD your God, dwell in Zion" (3:17).

God's salvation of his people displays his character. In fact, it is the supreme revelation of what God is like. One way you can know what God is like is to read the Bible, and I would strongly encourage you to do that. But you can also know what he is like by watching his people. In one sense, you can watch anyone in the world because everyone is made in the image of God.

But you should particularly be able to watch those who have been regenerated and filled by God's Spirit. Watch his people as they live together, and you will understand something more about him. God's salvation of his people displays his character.

Joel calls God's people to return to him because of the Lord's character: "for he is gracious and compassionate, slow to anger and abounding in love" (2:13). In other words, Joel motivates his readers to action with theology. He expects that teaching them what God is like will have an effect on their daily lives.

William Cowper said, "Man may dismiss compassion from his heart, but God never will."

The Lord's name has always been associated with grace and compassion. Joel simply adopted what the Lord said of himself to Moses: "The LORD, the LORD, the compassionate and gracious God, slow to anger, abounding in love and faithfulness, maintaining love to thousands, and forgiving wickedness, rebellion and sin. Yet he does not leave the guilty unpunished" (Ex. 34:6-7a).

In the book of Joel, God shows his grace and compassion by intervening with swarms of locusts and saying no to sin and unrighteousness. It is hardly gracious to allow the sinful to continue sinning with impunity, with no change of heart or life. What kind of grace is that?

Grace has been defined as God's unmerited favor to us. It is more than forgiving a wrong and granting mercy; it is the extending of favor which goes above and beyond forgiving the wrong. We would call it "mercy" if someone broke into your house to rob you and you captured him but did not harm or punish him. We would call it "grace" if you proceeded to offer this intruder a warm meal. Grace is not merely doing something good when the good is unmerited. It is doing something good when demerits argue to the contrary![5]

Friend, you and I are the robbers and God is the householder. When we look to Christ in repentance and faith, he will treat us not merely with mercy but with grace.

In Joel's prophecy, God's grace was not fundamentally God's response to his people's cries. God graciously took the initiative. He gave Joel this prophecy. He told Joel to proclaim these words to the people. He stirred them up! Someone who is really your enemy won't tell you he is about to destroy you. He will just wipe you out. But God warned his people, telling them they could respond in one of two ways—either in repentance and faith or in rejection and more sin. The warnings of this book are more like a doctor's warning, a teacher's admonishment, or a mother's loving rebuke.

---

[5] See J. I. Packer, "The Grace of God," in *Knowing God* (Downers Grove, Ill.: InterVarsity Press, 1973).

Why would God care so much about his people? I don't know! But for some reason he has chosen to tie up his reputation with the welfare of his people:

> Let the priests, who minister before the LORD,
>   weep between the temple porch and the altar.
> Let them say, "Spare your people, O LORD.
>   Do not make your inheritance an object of scorn,
>   a byword among the nations.
> Why should they say among the peoples,
>   'Where is their God?'" (Joel 2:17).

Joel, like Moses before him, pleaded with God on the basis of God's own stated commitment to his people. God was a God of pity, mercy, and compassion, and he would be known to be such a God. As Paul wrote to the Ephesians, "his intent was that now, through the church [God's people] the manifold wisdom of God should be made known to the rulers and authorities in the heavenly realms, according to his eternal purpose which he accomplished in Christ Jesus our Lord" (Eph. 3:10-11). For some reason, God has decided to win glory for himself through us, his people.

Ultimately, God saves his people for his own name's sake. Some people do not like the sound of that; but what should God value more highly than himself? What has more worth than God? For you or me to regard ourselves as the center of the world would be egotistical to the point of being delusional, not to mention rebellious against God. But for God to regard himself supremely is no more wrong than for the sun to be at the center of the solar system. Our own planet could never occupy the sun's role at the center of the solar system. It does not have the gravity for that. God is the Creator of all! He must be supreme to us and to himself. Apart from the exercise of his sovereign rule in creating and judging—in holiness and love, in righteousness and compassion—the world becomes a cruelly hollow place. Joel's prophecy clearly teaches that God saves for his own purposes—for himself.

CONCLUSION: WHO WILL SAVE YOU?

So what do you think *you* need to be saved from?

Christians believe that every one of us needs to be saved from our sins, like the people of Joel's day. That's one reason why our church includes a prayer of confession in our Sunday morning gatherings. That's also why our church affirms our belief "in the forgiveness of sins" as recited in the Apostles' Creed. And we don't just mean the forgiveness of sins for people "out there"; *we* need to be forgiven!

But whose sins will be forgiven? Who will be saved? What about people who remain more committed to their sins than to God, and who do not believe in Christ? As we have seen, the first section of chapter 2 promises a coming destruction, and that section ends, "The LORD thunders at the head of his army; his forces are beyond number, and mighty are those who obey his command. The day of the LORD is great; it is dreadful. Who can endure it?" (2:11). That is our question. Who can endure the day of the Lord? Who will be able to withstand God's just judgment for sin? We all have a vested interest in the answer to that question, whether we realize it or not.

Joel knows that not everyone will be saved. After all, God will judge his enemies (3:19). Yet he will also be a refuge for "his people" (3:16).

It is God's people who will be saved.

Who are God's people, and how can we be among them? In the book of Joel, God's people, the saved, are those who respond to God's Word. The fact that God is sovereign does not rule out our responsibility to respond to the gospel. First, we must respond to his Word by repenting of our sins. That means acknowledging our sins as wrong and offensive to God, regretting them, and turning from them. Joel exhorts the priests,

> Put on sackcloth, O priests, and mourn;
>   wail, you who minister before the altar.
> Come, spend the night in sackcloth,
>   you who minister before my God;
> for the grain offerings and drink offerings
>   are withheld from the house of your God.
> Declare a holy fast;
>   call a sacred assembly.
> Summon the elders
>   and all who live in the land
> to the house of the LORD your God,
>   and cry out to the LORD (1:13-14).

We have sinned against the Lord, so we must cry out to him. Joel repeats this air-raid-siren call to repentance in chapter 2: "'Even now,' declares the LORD, 'return to me with all your heart, with fasting and weeping and mourning.' Rend your heart and not your garments . . ." The custom at the time was, for some particularly grievous matter, to literally tear one's clothing as an outward sign of inner distress and utter desolation. "Return to the LORD your God, for he is gracious and compassionate, slow to anger and abounding in love, and he relents from sending calamity. Who knows? He may turn and have pity and leave behind a blessing—grain offerings and drink offerings for the

LORD your God. Blow the trumpet in Zion, declare a holy fast, call a sacred assembly. Gather the people, consecrate the assembly; bring together the elders, gather the children, those nursing at the breast. Let the bridegroom leave his room and the bride her chamber" (2:12-16).

God enjoins a repentance that involves all the formal actions of repentance—fasting, weeping, and mourning—but also a true change of mind, heart, and will: "Rend your heart." Our hearts have to break because they have been attached to the wrong things, and they must turn back to the Lord. Repentance is turning away from all the things we so tightly clutch—our loves, our fears, our joys, and our sorrows—and turning to God. It isn't just feeling bad; it is changing. Apart from change, our feelings of regret can be deceiving. True repentance, Ambrose said, "is to cease from sinning." Fundamentally, it is changing from being insensitive to God, to being responsive to him. How can we do that? By giving attention to his word. By heeding his warning. By recognizing and confessing our sins.

We must genuinely recognize and confess our sins. John Chrysostom knew something of the sham confessions that we are tempted to make. He said, "If we speak evil of ourselves a thousand times, and yet are affronted when another says anything of the kind, this is not humility; this is not a confession of sin, but only pretense and vanity. . . . we assume the appearance of humility that we may be admired and praised." True repentance confesses sin and turns from it.

Second, we must respond to God's Word by believing it: "Everyone who calls on the name of the LORD will be saved" (2:32). What does it mean to call on the name of the Lord? When Paul quotes this verse in his letter to the Romans, he uses "call" synonymously with "believe" and "trust":

> If you confess with your mouth, "Jesus is Lord," and believe in your heart that God raised him from the dead, you will be saved. For it is with your heart that you believe and are justified, and it is with your mouth that you confess and are saved. As the Scripture says, "Anyone who trusts in him will never be put to shame." For there is no difference between Jew and Gentile—the same Lord is Lord of all and richly blesses all who call on him, for "Everyone who calls on the name of the Lord will be saved" (Rom. 10:9-13).

To call on God is to trust in him. It is to pray to him, to own him as your Lord, and to have him own you.

It has been said that God intended to have two thieves on either side of Christ at Calvary, so that "One was saved, that none might despair; but only one, that none might presume."

Whom will God save? Those who have repented of their sins and called on the Lord. Those who trust him and no other. Do you?

Let us pray:

O Lord, you know what it means for us to turn from the sins to which we are attached and to turn to you. We pray that your Holy Spirit would be active in our own hearts, O Lord, for your glory and our good. Show yourself to us as our all-sufficient Savior, we pray for the glory of the name of Christ. Amen.

Questions for Reflection

1. Do you believe hell exists? How much time do you spend thinking about hell? Who will go to hell? Is it unloving to teach people about hell? Why or why not?

2. Do most people live anticipating the judgment of God? Do you?

3. How can the leaders and the members of a local church more effectively encourage one another to live in light of the Lord's coming judgment?

4. In the book of Joel, the invasion of the locusts was a small act of God's judgment that pointed toward another, greater judgment that will come to all. Does God bring smaller acts of judgment into the lives of people today in order to point toward the greater judgment to come?

5. In the book of Joel, God was behind the destruction wrought on the land of Judah through the locusts. Is the Lord in control of natural disasters that happen today and the effects of those disasters? All of them? Does this make God cruel? Why or why not?

6. Why do we naturally assume that our understanding of "good" and "bad," "fair" and "unfair," is correct? Are we typically right to assume this? What is the only thing we can do to ensure that our evaluations of things are increasingly correct?

7. True or False: "As much as anything else, sinners need to be saved from God himself." Explain your answer.

8. True or False: "More than anything else, a sinner's only hope is in this same God." Explain your answer.

9. When you share the gospel with your friends, how can your explanation include elements from both statements in the previous two questions?

10. What instances in the last month can you think of in which you were more concerned about what others said or did to you than about what you said or did against God?

11. Does God promise earthly prosperity for Christians? Explain.

12. According to this sermon, what is the very heart of salvation? Is that the salvation that your church points sinners toward? Is that the salvation that you most long for? How do you know?

THE MESSAGE OF AMOS: DOES GOD CARE?

30

THE MESSAGE OF AMOS: DOES GOD CARE?

DOES GOD CARE?[1]

Several years ago, *Forbes ASAP* magazine interviewed Steven Weinberg, best-selling author, Nobel Prize winner in physics, and a professor of physics and astronomy at the University of Texas in Austin. At one point in the conversation, the interviewer observed,

> "The scientific view of humanity is a minority view. The majority view, in religion particularly, is that humans are special—that we're somehow apart from nature. To younger people presented with these two claims for absolute truth, one based on religious faith and the other on science, what in your view commends them to the scientific approach?"

Professor Weinberg replied:

> "The fact that it's true. There isn't anything in the laws of nature that bestows any special role on human beings. We did evolve from other animals, and we are not immortal. We each face the dissolution of our own personalities at death, and we just have to get used to that. It may not be as great as thinking that we play a starring role in a cosmic drama, but there is a certain satisfaction in being able to confront our position as just part of an impersonal universe, in realizing that what gives our lives meaning, which is not given to it by the stars, is what we give it ourselves. W. H. Auden has a lovely poem called 'The More Loving One,' about someone confronting the fact that nature doesn't seem to care that we care—that we're not part of an all-embracing, loving universe. He asks the question:

---

[1] This sermon was originally preached on June 8, 2003, at Capitol Hill Baptist Church in Washington, D.C.

"'How should we like it were stars to burn
With a passion for us we could not return?
If equal affection cannot be,
Let the more loving one be me. . . .
Were all stars to disappear or die,
I should learn to look at an empty sky
And feel its total dark sublime,
Though this might take me a little time.'

"There's a certain satisfaction in being able to confront this situation, and still go on—to find a meaning in our lives that comes, not from outside, but from inside."[2]

Is the only meaning in life the meaning that we create ourselves, as Professor Weinberg suggests?

Of course, most people do not agree with the professor's atheism, as the interviewer stated. The overwhelming majority of people in every demographic slice of the world population believe in God. Still, many people might agree with Professor Weinberg in his belief that *whoever* or *whatever* is ultimate in the universe is not concerned with you and me. Even if a Creator does exist, he seems to be as impersonal and disengaged as Auden's stars. This is the question we are unsure about: *does God care?* Does God care about evil and suffering in the world? Or about the poverty and malnourishment that so many people are experiencing at this very moment? Or about the people who died in the Pentagon attack several years ago or in the recent Algerian earthquake? Does God care about Saddam Hussein or George Bush or Martha Stewart or Sammy Sosa and the justice or injustice of their actions?

Does God care specifically about your life and mine? What if our lives do not affect the lives of countless others, as in the case of the people I just mentioned—does the great Creator of this unimaginably vast universe really care about what you and I do in our free time, in our work, in our thoughts? Or whether you eat meat or not? Or about your relationships? Or what you call him? Or whether you prayed this morning? Does God even care that you are here?

People ask that question with regard to issues ranging from the most philosophical (Does God care about the human situation?) to the most personal (Does God really care about me?).

What do you think?

Does God care when someone takes advantage of you sexually? Or when

---

[2] Steven Weinberg, interview by Timothy Ferris, "Many Questions, Some Answers," *Forbes ASAP*, October 2, 2000, 270.

you suffer the effects of someone else's pride? Or when someone else's self-indulgence leaves you neglected and ignored? Or when others do not care about you? Does he care when religious leaders lead you astray?

Then again, I wonder if you really want God to care. In all of the examples I just gave, the question pertains to whether God cares, as it were, in your favor. But do you really want God to care if *you* obstruct justice? Or if you take advantage of another person? Or when you ignore or abuse the poor? Do you want him to care if you cheat in business, or on your taxes, or in your marriage? Does he care about such situations? Does he care when you continually do what you know is wrong and contrary to the teaching of the Bible and the instruction of your own conscience?

What does it mean if he does care?

INTRODUCING AMOS

"Does God care?" is the next "Eternal Question" for us to consider in our present series on the twelve Minor Prophets of the Old Testament. In this series we are considering the messages of whole books of the Bible—one sermon per book. And in this study we will look particularly at the book of Amos.

Amos is considered a minor prophet not because his prophecy is unimportant but because his book is shorter than the books of Isaiah, Jeremiah, and Ezekiel, whom we call the major prophets. In fact, Amos was an important prophet, and one of the very first "writing prophets," the prophets of the Old Testament who wrote down their prophecies so that we now possess books by their names (unlike the "historical prophets"—Elijah, Elisha, and so forth). Based on the information Amos gives us in the first verse of his book, we know that he prophesied somewhere around 760–750 B.C., about the same time the Greeks were settling Spain. Amos was a contemporary of Hosea, Isaiah, and probably Jonah.

We don't know much about any of the minor prophets, such as where they were from or what they did besides prophesy. They simply were not that interested in talking about themselves. Yet Amos does give us a little information about himself. His book begins, "The words of Amos, one of the shepherds of Tekoa—what he saw concerning Israel two years before the earthquake, when Uzziah was king of Judah and Jeroboam son of Jehoash was king of Israel" (1:1). In other words, we know that he was from Tekoa, which was located in the south, below Jerusalem and toward the Dead Sea. We know that he was a sheep and fruit farmer (see also 7:14). We know that he was neither the son of a prophet nor a professional prophet himself (7:14). Whether he was rich and prosperous or poor and struggling we cannot say. But for a brief time, God called him to serve as a prophet in the northern kingdom of Israel. Since he was from Judah, he would have been a foreigner in Israel. To his prophetic calling, then, he brought a sharp businessman's eye and an outsider's honesty. I think you will find this as we read through parts of his book.

That being said, Amos would not have been the personnel committee's choice for his role. He was not from Israel, but Judah. He was not a professional prophet (and there were plenty of those around); he was simply what we might call a church layman. Despite all this, God chose him for the task.

God often calls surprising people to serve him in surprising ways, doesn't he? Just think back through the stories in the Old Testament. The pagan Abraham became the father of the faithful. The eighty-year-old and stuttering Moses became the great lawgiver and liberator of Israel. The young shepherd boy David became Israel's greatest king. On and on we could go. And Amos, a church layman and a farmer, was called by God to be a prophet to a nation that appeared to be prosperous and successful. Who would have planned such things?

I recall Paul's words to the Corinthians:

> Brothers, think of what you were when you were called. Not many of you were wise by human standards; not many were influential; not many were of noble birth. But God chose the foolish things of the world to shame the wise; God chose the weak things of the world to shame the strong. He chose the lowly things of this world and the despised things—and the things that are not—to nullify the things that are, so that no one may boast before him (1 Cor. 1:26-29).

So Amos the farmer was given a thunderous word from God "two years before the earthquake," the very first verse tells us. We don't know much about this earthquake, but we do know that a great land rift runs from Africa, through Palestine near the Dead Sea, and up into Asia, and that that part of the world can have horrific earthquakes. The ancient Jewish historian Josephus reports that an earthquake occurred in 31 B.C. in which thirty thousand people died. Evidently, the earthquake Amos mentioned was significant enough that it was remembered long afterward. The prophet Zechariah referred to it hundreds of years later, even mentioning King Uzziah by name (Zech. 14:5). We may well surmise that God used this earthquake to drive home to Israel Amos's message of their dependence upon God as well as their need to turn to him in repentance.

Amos gave his prophecy during one of the most prosperous periods in Israel's history since Solomon's day.[3] So Amos's sharply critical prophecy

---

[3] See 2 Kings 14:23-29.

would have had both the unexpected suddenness of an earthquake and the sobering ferocity of a lion's roar.

As we turn now to the book of Amos, we find that God cares. God cares a lot! And he let the Israelites (and us) know that beyond a shadow of a doubt. To see that, we will consider first *the Judge and the judged* in 1:1–3:8. Second, we will consider *the focus of God's judgment* in 3:9–6:14. And third, we will consider *the character and cause of God's judgment* in chapters 7–9. I hope that in this study you will see something of how much God cares about you and then how you should respond.

THE JUDGE AND THE JUDGED

Let's begin where Amos begins, with the Judge and the judged. In the first few chapters, we learn that God will speak judgment against the nations and against his people.

The Judge (1:1-2; 3:3-8)

Understanding the book of Amos requires knowing who its main character is, and it isn't Amos. It's the Lord God: "The LORD roars from Zion and thunders from Jerusalem; the pastures of the shepherds dry up, and the top of Carmel withers" (1:2). Amos may be the prophet, but he is only the prophet. The primary actor here is the Lord himself. And consider how the Lord presents himself in this preface to the book: as one who roars! This judge has more than a mere passing interest in human affairs. He roars about them!

Now what do we normally think of as *roaring?* A mighty waterfall. Ocean waves. A great storm. The tumult of a battle. A great crowd.

Yet the image of roaring in the opening lines of Amos is more directed. It's a menacing roar. It's the roar of a pursuing lion. The word "roar" describes both the manner in which God's Word came—abruptly and ferociously—and its sobering content. In chapter 3, the image of a roaring lion is used in parallel with the sovereign Lord:

> The lion has roared—
>   who will not fear?
> The Sovereign LORD has spoken—
>   who can but prophesy? (3:8; cf. 3:4, 12; 5:19).

The image of a roaring lion may or may not be evocative today for people living in cities like Washington, D.C. Maybe you have heard a lion roar within the safe confines of the zoo. But I remember hearing roaring lions in the wild when I was in South Africa several years ago; it's a mind-concentrating sound! Once you have seen a lion's speed, power, and prowess, and then you recall that a roar often signifies a lion's hunger, you pay attention to their bellows. In Amos's day, lions roamed about Judah and Israel. It was a ferocious image for a prophet to use.

Notice also, Amos presents the Lord as roaring "from Zion" and "Jerusalem" (1:2). That would have grabbed the attention of his Israelite readers! Jerusalem was the religious center that the northern kingdom's founding rebel—King Jeroboam I—had rejected. Jeroboam had built his own imitation "Jerusalems" in Bethel and other places, so that the northern Israelites could avoid traveling south to Jerusalem. Yet surely the northern people would have learned the great stories of the past involving Jerusalem, such as when King David brought the ark of the covenant to rest in the city. So when Amos comes from Judah and says he is bringing the word of the Lord from Jerusalem, or rather, that the Lord is *roaring* from Zion, the effect would be tremendous. Memories would be provoked. People would sit up and pay attention. "The Old One stirs!"

The Judge speaks. Yes, and God would do more than stir. He would speak.

Amos lists a string of rhetorical questions at the beginning of chapter 3, all of which serve to accentuate the necessary connection between a cause and an effect: "Do two walk together unless they have agreed to do so? Does a lion roar in the thicket when he has no prey?" (3:3-4). Two people walk together *because* they have an agreement. A lion roars *because* he has prey. And so forth. The list culminates with the question, "When disaster comes to a city, has not the LORD caused it?" (3:6b). The implied answer is, "Yes, disaster comes *because* the Lord causes it!"

Then this interesting verse follows: "Surely the Sovereign LORD does nothing without revealing his plan to his servants the prophets" (3:7). And the verse we have already read comes next: "The lion has roared—who will not fear? The Sovereign LORD has spoken—who can but prophesy?" (3:8). God is sovereign; he even causes disasters.[4] And this sovereign God speaks! He is a God of words.

Some people are impatient with words. They want action, not talk. But action alone is never enough. An action without an explanation leaves us to guess at our own interpretations of events. But God is not like that. The true God of the Bible incessantly talks. He explains. He teaches us the truth about himself and about us. He is not a powerful but mute God. He comes bringing words! "Surely the Sovereign LORD does *nothing* without revealing his plan" (3:7).

Amos felt compelled to prophesy. We should feel compelled to listen. So

---

[4] See also Deut. 32:39; 1 Sam. 2:6-7; Isa. 45:7.

it is with all of Scripture. Our churches should be shaped by the preaching of God's words. Our individual lives as Christians should be spent learning God's words. And if you are a non-Christian, the only hope that we Christians can offer you is found in God's Word. It tells us about Christ and the hope of forgiveness of sins and newness of life that we have in him.

The Judge speaks in judgment. We—churches, Christians, non-Christians—should also notice exactly what God speaks about through his prophet Amos: he speaks about judgment. Back in one of Amos's opening verses, we read, "I will not turn back my wrath" (1:3b). Amos comes bearing a message of judgment—never a popular message, but always an important one. We don't always need to be told when our actions are right and good; but it is crucial to know when they are not. Our Creator cares. And he will act as our Judge.

The Judged (1:3–3:2)

If God is the Judge, who are the judged?

The nations. First, we see that the Lord judges the nations. The pagan nations may not have realized that the Lord was their God, but their ignorance did not diminish their accountability. No one is excluded from God's judgment. All of us will give account to him.

Amos begins by casting his prophecies of judgment against Israel's neighbors: Damascus (the Arameans) to their northeast, Gaza (the Philistines) to the southwest, Tyre (the Phoenicians) to the northwest, Edom to the southeast, and Ammon and Moab to the east. The nations all around them are indicted: "For three sins of Damascus, even for four, I will not turn back my wrath" (1:3). That phrase—"For three sins . . . even for four"—is repeated for different nations throughout the chapter.[5] The point is not that God will judge each nation once a certain number of sins are reached—perhaps three, perhaps four—but that he will judge each nation for its multiple sins. And Amos does not so much cite the idolatry of these nations; rather, he condemns their cruelty against fellow humans: "Because she took captive whole communities and sold them to Edom," or "Because he ripped open the pregnant women of Gilead in order to extend his borders."[6]

If the northern Israelites were put off by Amos's southern accent, you can be sure they liked what he said about their enemies. "This is a preacher we can listen to! He tells us what's wrong with everybody else!" I can imagine a crowd gathering around Amos and enjoying what they were hearing: the sins of their

---

[5] 1:6, 9, 11, 13; 2:1.
[6] 1:6, 13; cf. 1:3, 9, 11; 2:1.

neighbors exposed. Incidentally, one of the fastest ways to build a friendship with someone is to complain together about the same people.

What do Amos's condemnations against the nations teach us? They show us that the whole world is accountable to the one true God. People do not need God's special revelation in order to know right from wrong and how their Creator intends them to order their lives, their families, and their societies. In fact, people do not need God's special revelation in order to be finally accountable to him as their Judge. Here in Amos, God promises the nations that had never received the Ten Commandments that he would judge them (see also Romans 1–3). Every man and woman in these nations had a conscience that knew enough to hold him or her accountable before God.

Notice, too, the Lord's concern for cruelty against human beings. It is not so much the political possession of this or that territory that concerns him, but the cruelty with which people are treated by whoever the governing authority is.

God cares.

So, as we said, the crowd was probably enjoying what Amos was saying at this point. But then he turned to what people call "meddlin'."

God's people. Amos promised that God would not only judge the nations, he would also judge his own people. Perhaps the Israelites thought they were exempt from God's judgment because they were his special people. But such thinking could not have been more mistaken.

Amos does not begin by launching into an attack on Israel's sins, but Judah's: "This is what the LORD says: 'For three sins of Judah, even for four, I will not turn back my wrath'" (2:4a). Notice, God's condemnation of Judah makes her sound like just another nation! Yet that condemnation is explicitly religious: "they have rejected the law of the LORD and have not kept his decrees . . . they have been led astray by false gods" (2:4b).

More than a few breaths must have been drawn when Amos began enumerating the sins of Israel's southern neighbors. You can imagine the crowd becoming strangely quiet! True, it wasn't they that Amos was condemning. But it was their "other half"—the people who shared their heritage and history. Probably they felt a mixture of sympathy and unease at Amos's charges. His words demonstrated that God's own people were not above criticism.

Then, finally, Amos turned to them and announced their sins and the judgment that was about to befall them. The indictment was sweeping. They had committed sins of economic and religious oppression. The righteous, the needy, and the poor had been abused. Despite God's grace to them in the Exodus, they had rejected his commands. Their idolatrous worship had taken a grotesquely immoral form: "Father and son use the same girl and so profane my holy name. They lie down beside every altar on garments taken in pledge" (2:7b-8).

In response to Israel's gross immoralities, God's promise was most severe: "I will crush you" (2:13).

The Israelites thought their background meant they were immune from God's judgment. They did not realize that great privilege meant great accountability: "You only have I chosen of all the families of the earth; therefore I will punish you for all your sins" (3:2).

In case you are ever tempted to think that attending church removes the threat of God's judgment, allow me to suggest that a church is a lousy place to hide from God. He will find you wherever you are. He will certainly find you in his church. Everyone is under God's just condemnation. The nations are, and so too are God's special people. The Bible is clear about this. The God who made us is holy and perfect, and he made us in his image so that we might imitate him, whatever nation we belong to. Yet each one of us, like these Israelites, has fallen. We have sinned against God, and we have separated ourselves from him by our sins. And God *will* speak judgment against all sinners—no matter what tribe, language, or background we come from.

THE FOCUS OF GOD'S JUDGMENT (3:9–6:14)

More specifically, Amos taught that God judgment's focuses in on his people, particularly their leaders, and especially their religion.

His People (3:9-15; 6:8-14)

First, in the middle chapters of the book Amos continued to develop the idea that God would judge his people. God, frankly, seems angry in these chapters. He demands to be heard. He becomes his own people's foe. And he summons witnesses—surprising witnesses—to indict his own people:

> Proclaim to the fortresses of Ashdod
>   and to the fortresses of Egypt:
> "Assemble yourselves on the mountains of Samaria;
>   see the great unrest within her
>   and the oppression among her people."
>
> "They do not know how to do right," declares the LORD,
>   "who hoard plunder and loot in their fortresses" (3:9-10).

Ashdod? Egypt? These were the enemies of Israel! Yet God was calling *them* to assemble and be witnesses against the wrongs of his own people. God then tells these enemies to testify to what God will do to his people:

"Hear this and testify against the house of Jacob," declares the Lord, the LORD God Almighty.

> "On the day I punish Israel for her sins,
>   I will destroy the altars of Bethel;
> the horns of the altar will be cut off
>   and fall to the ground.
> I will tear down the winter house
>   along with the summer house;
> the houses adorned with ivory will be destroyed
>   and the mansions will be demolished,"
>
> declares the LORD (3:13-15).

God would destroy Israel's sinful altars and tear down its mansions. His judgment would be thorough. The "altars of Bethel" probably refers to altars dedicated to the Lord but built in unauthorized places (not in Jerusalem). We know from 1 Kings that Jeroboam, two centuries earlier, had placed one golden calf in Bethel and one in Dan (see 1 Kings 12:25-33).

So their altars were false. Their opulent homes testified to their self-indulgence. Indeed, there are many indications throughout Amos's little book that the people were characterized by indulging themselves. They seemed to think they deserved everything. They had become proud. "Did we not take Karnaim by our own strength?" (6:13). When people cultivate this way of thinking, it's hardly surprising when they give themselves over to gross immorality.

How bizarre Amos's words must have sounded on the streets of what looked like a secure nation! The Egyptian and Assyrian Empires had been in decline for several decades. Israel was at the zenith of its power and prosperity. Then along came Amos charging Israel with abusing the privileges of their special covenant with God. How odd! Everything was going so well.

Regardless of how prosperous the nation may have seemed at the time, the Lord promised to bring doom because he abhorred their pride and unrighteousness: "The Sovereign LORD has sworn by himself—the LORD God Almighty declares: 'I abhor the pride of Jacob and detest his fortresses; I will deliver up the city and everything in it'" (6:8)! Too often, present blessings consumed selfishly give way to future trials.

Pride feeds so many sins, doesn't it? It has terrible offspring. It indulges our self-centered delusions and leaves us defenseless against temptations. Satan knows that his efforts to tempt us with illicit pleasures will meet with the greatest success when those temptations are accompanied by flattery. Maybe we could resist the pleasures if they were offered by themselves. But our souls are ever-hungry for the approval of others, and so what pleasure cannot do by itself, flattery can.

Israel had become proud. So God would humble his people. He would prevent them from being awed at themselves and cause them to be awed by him. So he would decimate them, and devastate them: "I will stir up a nation against you, O house of Israel," the Lord promises, forecasting the invasion of Assyria several decades later (6:14). God would judge his people.

Their Leaders (4:1-3; 6:1-7)

God promised particularly to judge the leaders of Israel. And he did not only mean male leaders:

> Hear this word, you cows of Bashan on Mount Samaria,
>> you women who oppress the poor and crush the needy
> and say to your husbands,
>> "Bring us some drinks!"
> The Sovereign LORD has sworn by his holiness:
>> "The time will surely come
> when you will be taken away with hooks,
>> the last of you with fishhooks" (4:1-2).

Amos called the leading women of Samaria (another name for Israel) "cows" not to comment on their appearance, but because of their lazy, luxurious, self-indulgent lives. These women had sinned against the poor and needy, and God cared about the people toward whom these women were mindless. In his holiness, therefore, God would judge them. No one else had effectively turned these women (or the whole nation) back to God, so God would turn them back—like fish caught by fishhooks.

Israel's notable men also received God's condemnation because they had been using the people for their own ends. They too were wrongly complacent, or as the old translations put it, "at ease in Zion." So the Lord blasted them:

> Woe to you who are complacent in Zion,
>> and to you who feel secure on Mount Samaria,
> you notable men of the foremost nation,
>> to whom the people of Israel come!
> Go to Calneh and look at it;
>> go from there to great Hamath,
>> and then go down to Gath in Philistia.

> Are they better off than your two kingdoms?
>> Is their land larger than yours?
> You put off the evil day
>> and bring near a reign of terror.
> You lie on beds inlaid with ivory
>> and lounge on your couches.
> You dine on choice lambs
>> and fattened calves.
> You strum away on your harps like David
>> and improvise on musical instruments.
> You drink wine by the bowlful
>> and use the finest lotions,
>> but you do not grieve over the ruin of Joseph.
> Therefore you will be among the first to go into exile;
>> your feasting and lounging will end (6:1-7).

These leaders of Israel were at ease because of their money, which shows how blind they were to the truth. Money has never bought one moment of lasting security. Notice also how Amos denounces them for being compassionless: "you do not grieve over the ruin of Joseph" (6:6), that is, over the ruin of God's people. They were lounging! They didn't care what happened to others! Of course, such a coldhearted lack of compassion is one more bitter fruit of pride. People should be honored, treasured, and protected, not exploited. Leaders should especially exemplify such care. But these leaders did not. So the Lord promised them they would be the first to go into exile—"You want to be leaders? Okay, you'll lead, right into Assyria!"

Good leadership is a gift of God for the blessing of his people. By God's grace, what a leader does and who a leader is blesses others. If you aspire to leadership, you should ask yourself, do you give yourself for building others up, or do you simply use people so that others will think of you as a leader? Also, is God blessing your leadership?

"To whom much has been given, from him shall much be required." Israel's leaders were bad, so God called them to account.

Their Religion (4:4–5:27)

So Amos taught that God's judgment focused in on his own people, particularly their leaders. Yet he also taught that God's judgment focused especially on the nation's religion.

Israel's brand of religion allowed them to sin and to maintain a sense of God's favor at the same time. They loved their sin and they loved their religion. So they constructed a religion that let them have both. They made idols for themselves that could not speak, and in the silence of these idols, they heard consent.

Clearly, Israel's religion was a sham. Yet how many people today follow the same path! Church congregations that welcome sin are congregations that banish Christ. There is no such thing as a saving faith that does not produce works.

God warned the Israelites by famine and plague, but they would not listen:

> "I gave you empty stomachs in every city
>   and lack of bread in every town,
>   yet you have not returned to me,"
>   declares the LORD.

> "I also withheld rain from you
>   when the harvest was still three months away.
> I sent rain on one town,
>   but withheld it from another.
> One field had rain; another had none and dried up.
> People staggered from town to town for water
>   but did not get enough to drink,
>   yet you have not returned to me,"
>   declares the LORD.

> "Many times I struck your gardens and vineyards,
>   I struck them with blight and mildew.
> Locusts devoured your fig and olive trees,
>   yet you have not returned to me,"
>   declares the LORD.

> "I sent plagues among you as I did to Egypt.
>   I killed your young men with the sword,
>   along with your captured horses.
> I filled your nostrils with the stench of your camps,
>   yet you have not returned to me,"
>   declares the LORD.

> "I overthrew some of you
>   as I overthrew Sodom and Gomorrah.
> You were like a burning stick snatched from the fire,
>   yet you have not returned to me,"
>   declares the LORD (4:6-11).

The Israelites were characterized by a deliberate unrepentance. Fueled by a wrongful pride, they ignored God's warnings. They didn't think they needed to pay any attention to them.

Trials are meant to turn the faces of rebellious people toward God. In stupidity and selfishness we refuse to learn. In mercy he sends more trials.

So God summoned Israel to appear before him: "Therefore this is what I will do to you, Israel, and because I will do this to you, prepare to meet your God, O Israel" (4:12). Then he reminded them who it was that summoned them: "He who forms the mountains, creates the wind, and reveals his thoughts to man, he who turns dawn to darkness, and treads the high places of the earth—the LORD God Almighty is his name" (4:13). Terrible judgment awaited them, but they could still repent:

> This is what the LORD says to the house of Israel:
>
> > "Seek me and live;
> > > do not seek Bethel,
> > do not go to Gilgal,
> > > do not journey to Beersheba.
> > For Gilgal will surely go into exile,
> > > and Bethel will be reduced to nothing."
> > Seek the LORD and live,
> > > or he will sweep through the house of Joseph like a fire (5:4-6).

Israel's homemade gods—bull statues in Dan and Bethel—would not save them, especially from God's wrath at their blatant, grievous sins:

> you hate the one who reproves in court
> > and despise him who tells the truth.
>
> You trample on the poor
> > and force him to give you grain.
> Therefore, though you have built stone mansions,
> > you will not live in them;
> though you have planted lush vineyards,
> > you will not drink their wine.
> For I know how many are your offenses
> > and how great your sins.
>
> You oppress the righteous and take bribes
> > and you deprive the poor of justice in the courts.
> Therefore the prudent man keeps quiet in such times,
> > for the times are evil (5:10-13).

One of the most obvious ways we can see that these days of prosperity in Israel were marked by sinfulness was in how the people abused the poor. The poor were valued less than silver, less even than a pair of sandals (2:6; 8:6). Their heads were trampled on (2:7). They were oppressed and crushed. They were forced to give what little money they had to make the rich fatter! The poor were treated merely as difficulties to be overcome or, at least, ignored.

While abusing the poor, the Israelites also denied justice. In fact, they actively worked to obstruct it. A few more dollars in the pocket was worth more to them than justice. Righteousness did not matter so much as money. No wonder Amos says, "the times are evil" (5:13). What a tragic summary of days supposedly filled with peace and prosperity! But so it was, from God's perspective.

The evaluations of Wall Street and the evaluations of heaven are not always the same.

A failure to show concern for the poor shows a misunderstanding of our own fragile situation—our own pressing need for God's merciful attention to us in our sin. A religion that allows its adherents to take advantage of the poor, oppress the righteous, obstruct justice, and ignore God's warnings is a false religion.

So Amos again exhorts Israel, "Seek good, not evil, that you may live. Then the LORD God Almighty will be with you, just as you say he is. Hate evil, love good; maintain justice in the courts. Perhaps the LORD God Almighty will have mercy on the remnant of Joseph" (5:14-15).

If any Israelites thought their false religion would help them, they were about to find out otherwise. The real God was about to show up, not the false god they had constructed in their minds and who always approved of them:

> Woe to you who long
>   for the day of the LORD!
> Why do you long for the day of the LORD?
>   That day will be darkness, not light.
> It will be as though a man fled from a lion
>   only to meet a bear,
> as though he entered his house
>   and rested his hand on the wall
>   only to have a snake bite him.
> Will not the day of the LORD be darkness, not light—
>   pitch-dark, without a ray of brightness?
>
> "I hate, I despise your religious feasts;
>   I cannot stand your assemblies.

Even though you bring me burnt offerings and grain offerings,
  I will not accept them.
Though you bring choice fellowship offerings,
  I will have no regard for them.
Away with the noise of your songs!
  I will not listen to the music of your harps.
But let justice roll on like a river,
  righteousness like a never-failing stream! . . .

"Therefore I will send you into exile beyond Damascus,"
  says the LORD, whose name is God Almighty (5:18-24, 27).

Israel's false religion would not save them from the Assyrian army. They had acted like the nations, so God would treat them like the nations, disbursing them among their neighbors.

God would judge his people, particularly their leaders, and especially because of the nation's sin-tolerant religion.

THE CHARACTER AND CAUSE OF GOD'S JUDGMENT

Finally, we should observe in Amos the character and cause of God's judgment. In the last three chapters of Amos's prophecy, we learn that God will judge sin with mercy, with justice, and with certainty.

The Character of God's Judgment (Chapters 7 and 9)

With mercy. Being notified of God's coming judgment is alarming, yet God's warning came accompanied with assurances of and opportunities for mercy. At the beginning of chapter 7, the Lord gives Amos visions of judgment by locusts and fire, but then God twice promises, "this will not happen" (7:3, 6). Why then did God give Amos these visions? The visions taught the Israelites what their sins truly deserved. God was instructing them. They had lived in such a way that their land should be devoured by locusts and consumed by fire.

In the same verses, Amos tells us that "the LORD relented" (7:3, 6). What does it mean for God to relent? Didn't the prophet Samuel once say, "He who is the Glory of Israel does not lie or change his mind; for he is not a man, that he should change his mind"?[7] Yet we know from several places in Scripture—not just Amos—that the Lord will relent. In the book of Exodus, for instance,

---

[7] 1 Sam. 15:29; cf. Num. 23:19; Ps. 110:4.

the Lord tells Moses he will bring disaster on the people because of their obstinacy; but Moses pleads with the Lord and the Lord relents (Ex. 32:9-14). Did
Moses really persuade God to change his plans? No, what changed was the
clarity of Moses' perception. God is a personal God; he leads us and teaches
us by interacting with us. Just as he taught Abraham by asking him to offer
Isaac as a sacrifice, so he warned Moses of an impending destruction on Israel
in order to elicit a reaction from Moses and thereby teach Moses. Likewise,
God threatened his people through Amos so that his people might learn to
repent and then experience God's mercy.

God's mercy becomes even clearer in the last few verses of the book, where
God promises that the long night of his judgment will end:

> "In that day I will restore
>   David's fallen tent.
> I will repair its broken places,
>   restore its ruins,
>   and build it as it used to be,
> so that they may possess the remnant of Edom
>   and all the nations that bear my name,"
>   declares the LORD, who will do these things.
>
> "The days are coming," declares the LORD,
>
> "when the reaper will be overtaken by the plowman
>   and the planter by the one treading grapes.
> New wine will drip from the mountains
>   and flow from all the hills.
> I will bring back my exiled people Israel;
>   they will rebuild the ruined cities and live in them.
> They will plant vineyards and drink their wine;
>   they will make gardens and eat their fruit.
> I will plant Israel in their own land,
>   never again to be uprooted
>   from the land I have given them,"
>   says the LORD your God (9:11-15).

Prosperity will return with God's mercy. Indeed, it never comes otherwise
in this fallen world.

That's why I love answering the everyday question "How are you doing?"
with the words "Better than I deserve." It's one quick way to remind myself of
the gospel. All that you and I have is by God's mercy.

With justice. God's judgment will come accompanied by mercy, but it will also be characterized by justice. He will measure out his justice with precision:

> The Lord was standing by a wall that had been built true to plumb, with a plumb line in his hand. And the LORD asked me, "What do you see, Amos?"
> "A plumb line," I replied.
> Then the Lord said, "Look, I am setting a plumb line among my people Israel; I will spare them no longer.
>
>> "The high places of Isaac will be destroyed
>>   and the sanctuaries of Israel will be ruined;
>> with my sword I will rise against the house of Jeroboam" (7:7-9).

God's judgment is entirely just. That which should be destroyed will be destroyed. We can also trust that his justice is perfectly discerning: "'Surely the eyes of the Sovereign LORD are on the sinful kingdom. I will destroy it from the face of the earth—yet I will not totally destroy the house of Jacob,' declares the LORD" (9:8).

When God judges all the people of the earth, he will be shown as perfectly just in all his judgments.

With certainty. God will also judge his people with certainty. We learn this in the book's one autobiographical interlude:

> Then Amaziah the priest of Bethel sent a message to Jeroboam king of Israel: "Amos is raising a conspiracy against you in the very heart of Israel. The land cannot bear all his words. For this is what Amos is saying:
>
>> "Jeroboam will die by the sword,
>>   and Israel will surely go into exile,
>>   away from their native land."
>
> Then Amaziah said to Amos, "Get out, you seer! Go back to the land of Judah. Earn your bread there and do your prophesying there. Don't prophesy anymore at Bethel, because this is the king's sanctuary and the temple of the kingdom."
> Amos answered Amaziah, "I was neither a prophet nor a prophet's son, but I was a shepherd, and I also took care of sycamore-fig trees. But the LORD took me from tending the flock and said to me, 'Go, prophesy to my people Israel.' Now then, hear the word of the LORD. You say,
>
>> "'Do not prophesy against Israel,
>>   and stop preaching against the house of Isaac.'

"Therefore this is what the LORD says:

> "'Your wife will become a prostitute in the city,
>> and your sons and daughters will fall by the sword.
> Your land will be measured and divided up,
>> and you yourself will die in a pagan country.
> And Israel will certainly go into exile,
>> away from their native land'" (7:10-17).

It seems that Amos had begun preaching at Bethel, the northern kingdom's most important shrine. Amaziah, a priest at the royal shrine and a high official, forbade Amos from prophesying and sent a message to the king misrepresenting Amos's words (our critics are rarely the most accurate sources for what we say). Yet Amaziah could not stop God or his word by banishing Amos back to Judah. We don't know much about this interaction, but Amaziah's words are ironic: "Go back to the land of Judah. Earn your bread there and do your prophesying there" (7:12). Amaziah, this priest-for-hire, assumed that he was talking to another priest-for-hire just like him; but for perhaps the first time in his life, he was speaking to the real thing: a prophet sent by God who didn't care a whit about the money.

Amaziah typified the direct opposition to God that marked Israel in his day. Rooted together with their pride and false worship was opposition to God, which is why the people refused to repent even after God warned them. They may have borne the *name* of God, but their *lives* demonstrated that they were his opponents. That's why those who were truly righteous were oppressed. These people were not neutral; they were committed to rebelling against their Creator and Lord and everyone who represented him.

Of course, Amos rejected Amaziah's attempt to banish him, and simply recounted his own humble obedience to the LORD's will—"I didn't ask for this job. I was a shepherd. God just picked me out and told me to do this." Amaziah could have tried to avoid God's judgment, but he could not avert it from himself or his land. God's judgment was coming:

I saw the Lord standing by the altar, and he said:

> "Strike the tops of the pillars
>> so that the thresholds shake.
> Bring them down on the heads of all the people;
>> those who are left I will kill with the sword.
> Not one will get away,
>> none will escape.

Though they dig down to the depths of the grave,
  from there my hand will take them.
Though they climb up to the heavens,
  from there I will bring them down.
Though they hide themselves on the top of Carmel,
  there I will hunt them down and seize them.
Though they hide from me at the bottom of the sea,
  there I will command the serpent to bite them.
Though they are driven into exile by their enemies,
  there I will command the sword to slay them.
I will fix my eyes upon them
  for evil and not for good."

The Lord, the LORD Almighty,
  he who touches the earth and it melts,
  and all who live in it mourn—
the whole land rises like the Nile,
  then sinks like the river of Egypt—
he who builds his lofty palace in the heavens
  and sets its foundation on the earth,
who calls for the waters of the sea
  and pours them out over the face of the land—
  the LORD is his name (9:1-6).

God's judgment would come with mercy, yes, and with justice, of course; but come it certainly would!

The Cause of God's Judgment (Chapter 8)

Chapter 8 provides the final reminder of the cause of God's judgment: God would judge because of sin. The chapter should also remind us of how much God cares about people.

The Lord presents Israel's sin as a basket of summer fruit—ripe for the harvest. The picture is perhaps the grimmest picture in this grim book:

This is what the Sovereign LORD showed me: a basket of ripe fruit. "What do you see, Amos?" he asked.

"A basket of ripe fruit," I answered.

Then the LORD said to me, "The time is ripe for my people Israel; I will spare them no longer.

"In that day," declares the Sovereign LORD, "the songs in the temple will turn to wailing. Many, many bodies—flung everywhere! Silence!"

Hear this, you who trample the needy
   and do away with the poor of the land,

saying,

"When will the New Moon be over
   that we may sell grain,
and the Sabbath be ended
   that we may market wheat?"—
skimping the measure,
   boosting the price
   and cheating with dishonest scales,
buying the poor with silver
   and the needy for a pair of sandals,
   selling even the sweepings with the wheat.

The LORD has sworn by the Pride of Jacob: "I will never forget anything they have done.

"Will not the land tremble for this,
   and all who live in it mourn?
The whole land will rise like the Nile;
   it will be stirred up and then sink
   like the river of Egypt.

"In that day," declares the Sovereign LORD,

"I will make the sun go down at noon
   and darken the earth in broad daylight.
I will turn your religious feasts into mourning
   and all your singing into weeping.
I will make all of you wear sackcloth
   and shave your heads.
I will make that time like mourning for an only son
   and the end of it like a bitter day" (8:1-10).

The people's greed was fed by their self-centeredness and self-indulgence. They took bribes instead of giving justice. Centered on themselves and having little compassion for others, they cheated others out of what they would never realize they had lost. And all this came easy to them! They were, you might say, infernally gifted.

Since they ignored God's Word, God would take his Word from them. In some of the most chilling words in the book, we read,

"The days are coming," declares the Sovereign LORD,
  "when I will send a famine through the land—
not a famine of food or a thirst for water,
  but a famine of hearing the words of the LORD.
Men will stagger from sea to sea
  and wander from north to east,
searching for the word of the LORD,
  but they will not find it" (8:11-12).

In Israel's history, this prophecy would come true as prophets like Amos and Hosea died or at least ceased to prophesy and God sent none to replace them. Instead of hearing the cries of God's prophets, the people of Israel would, several decades later, hear the battle cry of Assyrian invaders.

My non-Christian friend, it is difficult to express to you what a great gift we have in hearing God's Word. I said earlier that church is a lousy place to hide from God; but it is a great place to be found by him! In the church you will hear God's Word set out and explained. Listen for God to come for you through his Word!

In North Africa and Asia, God sent a famine of his Word. For centuries the Bible was preached freely in all the lands from Algeria to Afghanistan. Yet a darkness came. A famine came. Is that what God is doing now in Western Europe, sending a famine of his Word? And will we live to see a famine of his Word in North America, not because it is illegal but because there are no faithful preachers? Or because there are no faithful people who want to hear his Word?

I once taught an all-day seminar on Puritanism in London. I guess the attendees had nothing better to do on Saturday than to sit through a six-hour history lesson in a church basement. At one point I asked whether any of them had ever observed the iron ring beside a pulpit. A few of them nodded, but nobody seemed to know what they were. I told them that such rings would have been the gifts from church congregations to preachers in the late sixteenth and early seventeenth centuries, and that the rings held hourglasses. Preachers would have one or two turns of the hourglass allotted to them for preaching.

When I said this, one woman audibly gasped, and then asked, "What time did that leave for worship?"

At that moment I could feel the whole Reformation crashing down around me. I let a couple moments of silence pass in order to compose myself, and then I said to her, "Please understand that when these gifts were given, some of the people in the churches would have been old enough to remember the smell of the burning flesh of people who had died trying to translate God's Word into the common language. These churches were hungry for God's Word. They realized that their greatest blessing in life was hearing, embracing, and living out God's Word."

Do you recognize the blessing we have in hearing God's Word? Losing it would be the worst judgment imaginable. Treasure every opportunity you have to hear God's Word.

CONCLUSION

So, does God care? The witness of the book of Amos is that he does. In fact, he cares so much, he promises to judge the nations and his people. He will judge his people, particularly their leaders, and especially the people's sin-tolerant religion. He will judge us for our sin with mercy, with justice, and with certainty.

You can be certain about that!

If God's judgment is certain, can we escape it? After all, isn't God also merciful? God's justice and mercy have been reconciled in one place only: the cross of Jesus Christ. In Jesus Christ, a holy God came and took on flesh. He lived a perfect life in order to offer himself as a sinless sacrifice. On the cross of his crucifixion, he then took on himself the punishment of God for the sins of all of those who would turn and trust in him. Then God raised him in victory over death; and now he invites us to repent of our sins and believe in him.

When God's judgment roars—and it will—how will it find you? When the heavens disappear, the final angel shouts, and we appear before the throne of God,[8] will you be a part of that other roar we read about in Revelation 19?

After this I heard what sounded like the roar of a great multitude in heaven shouting:

"Hallelujah!
Salvation and glory and power belong to our God,
for true and just are his judgments" . . .

Then I heard what sounded like a great multitude, like the roar of rushing waters and like loud peals of thunder, shouting:

"Hallelujah!
For our Lord God Almighty reigns.
Let us rejoice and be glad
and give him glory!" (Rev. 19:1-2a, 6-7a).

---

[8] 2 Pet. 3:10; Rev. 10:3; 14:1-4.

Oh, friend, God certainly cares. The question is, do you?

Let us pray:

O Lord, you know the nooks and crannies of our hearts. You know those areas in which we disobey and ignore you. You know us better than we know our- selves. We pray that your Spirit would faithfully and mercifully reveal those things to us, so that we would be able to see them clearly and honestly. And we pray that you would give us a taste for you, so that we would choose you above all other things. O Lord, do that for your own glory and for our good. We pray in the name of our Redeemer and Savior, the Lord Jesus. Amen.

Questions for Reflection

1. Do you believe God cares about you? Where are you tempted not to believe in his care?

2. Does God care about your neighbors and your colleagues at work as much as he cares about you? How does your answer to that question affect your rela- tionship with them?

3. Why does the fact that God judges sin indicate the fact that he cares about humanity?

4. Do you believe in a God who roars? How does whether or not you believe in a God who roars affect how you live? How does this affect what you expect from your church?

5. Do most non-Christians believe they will judged by God? Will they? Do most evangelical churches regularly teach that God will bring judgment? Should they? Why or why not?

6. Why is the man or woman on the island who has never heard the Word of God preached still accountable to God for his or her sin?

7. Do you treat any of your sins as if God is comfortable with them, or at least happy to overlook them?

8. If a prophet of God accused the evangelical church in the West today of being self-indulgent and lazy, what role could he accuse *you* of playing in these sins?

9. Why are the trials of our lives signs of God's mercy?

10. Should Christians or the church care for the poor? Explain.

11. If you moved to a country in which no Bibles existed (and you could not bring one with you), how much would your Bible reading schedule change? Why is the absence of God's Word one of the greatest judgments that can fall upon an individual or a land?

12. When God roars in judgment, how will you respond? How do you know you won't be destroyed?

THE MESSAGE OF OBADIAH: DOES GOD HAVE ENEMIES?

31

THE MESSAGE OF OBADIAH: DOES GOD HAVE ENEMIES?

DOES GOD HAVE ENEMIES?[1]

Does God have enemies? How would you answer this question?

If you are one kind of Muslim, you might answer that question, "Yes, God's enemies are the Americans and Israelis!"

If you are a Hindu nationalist, you might say, "Yes, it's the Muslims and the Christians!"

If you are like most Americans, you probably find the whole question strange, maybe to the point of being absurd: "God? Have enemies?" Perhaps the last time most Americans would have said yes to this question would have been in the 1950s, when God's enemies were "those godless communists"! But these days, the whole idea of God having enemies seems to go against the whole definition of God. Having "enemies" is not something God does, right? People have enemies, sure, but not God!

Well, it is true that people do have enemies. Our lives confirm it daily. Everything from the personal trials we face to the terrible actions of September 11, 2001, reminds us that humans simply make enemies of one another. Faced with the "ubiquity of conflict" in this world, Samuel Huntingdon has observed, "It is human to hate."[2] Most of us can agree with this much.

But the idea of *God* hating? That sounds more alien. Another observer of international affairs, Bernard Lewis, reflecting on the phrase "enemies of God" in the context of the Iranian government, said that such phrases "seem very strange to the modern outsider, whether religious or secular. The idea that God

---

[1] This sermon was originally preached on September 21, 2003, at Capitol Hill Baptist Church in Washington, D.C.
[2] Samuel Huntington, *The Clash of Civilizations and the Remaking of World Order* (New York: Touchstone, 1997), 130.

has enemies, and needs human help in order to identify and dispose of them, is a little difficult to assimilate."[3]

So, does God have enemies? I am not asking whether there are political or religious organizations that use such language emotionally to intimidate and bully people; we know that there are. I am asking whether the God who exists actually has enemies. If he does, surely we want to know who they are. We know how implacable some humans become once they turn against us; we can scarcely imagine what having the Almighty himself as an enemy would be like!

INTRODUCING OBADIAH

"Does God have enemies?" is one of the eternal questions raised by the series of books we are presently surveying in the Old Testament called the "Minor Prophets." The Minor Prophets are the shorter books at the end of the Old Testament. "Minor" does not mean "unimportant"; it just means "short" as compared to the generally longer "Major Prophets." In this study, we will look particularly at the shortest book in the Old Testament—the book of Obadiah.

As I have reflected on the book of Obadiah, it has occurred to me that this book, perhaps uniquely among the prophets of the Old Testament, speaks more directly to a time like our own. Most of the other prophets speak to Old Testament believers—and to Christians in churches. But Obadiah proclaimed a vision from the sovereign God to a people who knew no theology and who had no place for the knowledge of God in their lives. Unlike the audience of the other prophets, Obadiah's audience made no pretence of acknowledging God. In other words, he spoke to a society much like our own.

In this little book, God teaches us about who he is, who his friends are, and who his enemies are. Let's begin by reading, in its entirety, this brief prophecy of Obadiah, as he prophesies God's judgment on the people of Edom, the people who lived just southeast of Judah:

The vision of Obadiah.

This is what the Sovereign Lord says about Edom—

We have heard a message from the Lord:
An envoy was sent to the nations to say,
"Rise, and let us go against her for battle"—

"See, I will make you small among the nations;
you will be utterly despised.

[3] Bernard Lewis, "The Roots of Muslim Rage," *Atlantic Monthly,* September 1990, 47-60.

The pride of your heart has deceived you,
    you who live in the clefts of the rocks
    and make your home on the heights,
you who say to yourself,
    'Who can bring me down to the ground?'
Though you soar like the eagle
    and make your nest among the stars,
    from there I will bring you down,"
                      declares the LORD.

"If thieves came to you,
    if robbers in the night—
Oh, what a disaster awaits you—
    would they not steal only as much as they wanted?
If grape pickers came to you,
    would they not leave a few grapes?
But how Esau will be ransacked,
    his hidden treasures pillaged!
All your allies will force you to the border;
    your friends will deceive and overpower you;
those who eat your bread will set a trap for you,
    but you will not detect it.

"In that day," declares the LORD,
    "will I not destroy the wise men of Edom,
    men of understanding in the mountains of Esau?
Your warriors, O Teman, will be terrified,
    and everyone in Esau's mountains
    will be cut down in the slaughter.
Because of the violence against your brother Jacob,
    you will be covered with shame;
    you will be destroyed forever.
On the day you stood aloof
    while strangers carried off his wealth
and foreigners entered his gates
    and cast lots for Jerusalem,
    you were like one of them.
You should not look down on your brother
    in the day of his misfortune,
nor rejoice over the people of Judah
    in the day of their destruction,
nor boast so much
    in the day of their trouble.

You should not march through the gates of my people
    in the day of their disaster,
nor look down on them in their calamity
    in the day of their disaster,
nor seize their wealth
    in the day of their disaster.
You should not wait at the crossroads
    to cut down their fugitives,
nor hand over their survivors
    in the day of their trouble.

"The day of the LORD is near
    for all nations.
As you have done, it will be done to you;
    your deeds will return upon your own head.
Just as you drank on my holy hill,
    so all the nations will drink continually;
they will drink and drink
    and be as if they had never been.
But on Mount Zion will be deliverance;
    it will be holy,
and the house of Jacob
    will possess its inheritance.
The house of Jacob will be a fire
    and the house of Joseph a flame;
the house of Esau will be stubble,
    and they will set it on fire and consume it.
There will be no survivors
    from the house of Esau."
                    The LORD has spoken.

People from the Negev will occupy
    the mountain of Esau,
and the people from the foothills will possess
    the land of the Philistines.
They will occupy the fields of Ephraim and Samaria,
    and Benjamin will possess Gilead.
This company of Israelite exiles who are in Canaan
    will possess the land as far as Zarephath;
the exiles from Jerusalem who are in Sepharad
    will possess the towns of the Negev.
Deliverers will go up on Mount Zion
    to govern the mountains of Esau.
    And the kingdom will be the LORD's.

Again, as we look at Obadiah, we will consider,

> Who are God's enemies?
> Who are God's friends?
> And who is God?

I pray that our study will help you to better answer the question, "Does God have enemies?" and to understand why the right answer to this question is so important in your own life.

WHO ARE GOD'S ENEMIES? (VERSES 1–16)

First, then, who are God's enemies?

The Proud

In the first few verses of the book, we immediately observe one answer to that question: the proud.

Historically, Obadiah appears to have been written sometime after the fall of Jerusalem to Babylon in 587 B.C. Amid this terrible plight among God's people, their next-door neighbors to the southeast, the Edomites, did nothing to help (to put it mildly!). The Edomites were the descendants of Jacob's brother Esau (see Genesis 36).

But this little book is not merely the condemnation of an outraged Israelite. In fact, we don't even know that Obadiah was an Israelite; we don't know anything about him, really. Twelve different people in the Old Testament bear his name. And it may not have actually been the author's name. "Obadiah" means "servant of Yahweh," so perhaps the name was simply a descriptive title for this messenger who wrote it. Obadiah brought not his own message but the Word of God: "This is what the Sovereign LORD says about Edom—We have heard a message from the LORD. An envoy was sent to the nations to say, 'Rise, and let us go against her for battle'" (Obad. 1).

It's possible that there were rumblings of war about the time this book was written, and the Edomites may have been slightly fearful that Babylon would invade them. Obadiah's language of wartime was not mere scaremongering. He was genuinely warning them. Disaster was coming, and it was coming from God! The envoy calling to the nations to do battle was calling, it seems, to the nations of the Babylonian empire to wage battle on Edom.

At the same time, nothing in the book suggests that Edom was in a particularly low state when Obadiah delivered his message. In fact, God's promise to make Edom "small among the nations" (v. 2) suggests that they regarded themselves somewhat highly among the nations. They were proud. Obadiah's message would probably have come as a surprise to them. Yes, a few rumors of war may have been circulating, but the people certainly were not aware of any looming "judgment." Besides, they lived in a naturally impregnable position, atop mountains in cities that could be reached only by narrow, winding passages. Judah had just fallen, and, to be honest, its fall had enriched Edom. More north/south trade was now passing through Edom's side of the Jordan. In short, times were good.

But then that's how pride always works. If you are a non-Christian, please recognize the futility of making anything your final security other than God himself. God made us in his image so that we might know him, and one day he will call us to account. There is nothing else in this world that is so certain. It does not matter how strong or prosperous or successful you feel. God made you to give account to him, and you will. He is your only security.

That is what Obadiah told the nation of Edom, who felt so strong and self-sufficient. The Lord said to Edom, "The pride of your heart has deceived you, you who live in the clefts of the rocks and make your home on the heights, you who say to yourself, 'Who can bring me down to the ground?'" (v. 3). Edom was a small nation, but it was situated, like Switzerland, in an apparently impenetrable region of rocky heights and passes. And their hearts were well symbolized by their geography—high and hard, certain and proud.

But that's where they made a fatal error. They thought they could see and survey all the surrounding country because of their position. But they could not see themselves. Their pride deluded them. "'Though you soar like the eagle and make your nest among the stars, from there I will bring you down,' declares the LORD" (v. 4). God was not as impressed with their natural strategic defenses as they were. Even if they were in the most impregnable place on earth, God recognized no earthly power or material advantage that could withstand the course of his justice. Once he decided to bring down a proud and boasting people, he would. But the Edomites were mindless of all this. Remember, their pride had deceived them. That's the nature of pride, isn't it?

It is amazing to see what people proudly put their trust in. You may remember learning about the famous Maginot Line between France and Germany. From 1929 to 1938, the French built a line of defensive fortifications along their border with Germany under the direction of French war minister André Maginot. Heavy guns, thick concrete, air-conditioned living areas, areas for recreation, and even underground railways all assured the French that they would be safe against German aggression. When the German military began to build itself back up under Adolf Hitler, the French smugly thought they could ignore the matter. They had the Maginot Line! Of course, when the Germans finally invaded, they came through Belgium, outflanking the Maginot

Line and rendering it utterly useless. It took ten years to build. It took the Germans a few weeks to march around it.

Friend, that is a just a small picture of what it means to trust anything apart from God. Spend as much time as you want building something; imagine all the things it can protect you from; it still won't protect you.

Yet we want our own Maginot Lines, and then we put our trust in them. So we give obsessive attention to our appearance, our bodies, our possessions, our accomplishments, our jobs, or our friendships. We trust in *them* to bring peace and security. All of these things, of course, are extensions of our own power, reflections of our own ability, declarations of our own proud independence from God. But what if none of these things last as long as you do? Consider for a moment, what is it that you expect will last as long as you do? Then ask yourself, what will you do if it doesn't? What if your employer, your wealth, your parents or children, your house, your health, your ministry, a particular relationship, *even your physical life* does not last as long as you do? That's what the Bible teaches will happen. Listen again: "'Though you soar like the eagle and make your nest among the stars, from there I will bring you down,' declares the LORD" (v. 4).

When God decides to judge a proud nation, no economic stimulus package or Department of Homeland Security can save it. The nation that puts its trust in its own strength is the nation that will soon encounter the limits of its strength and eventually the loss of it, just as God promises Edom in Obadiah.

The grandest of this world's powers have always declined. It has been fashionable ever since America's war with Vietnam to write about American decline. Since September 11, 2001, the world's sole remaining superpower, a so-called imperial power, has almost always been written about in terms of its limitations and attendant problems. British decline has been an accepted fact of life in Britain for most of the past century. The U.S.S.R. fell, as did the short-lived empires of proud power built by Hitler and Mussolini and Hirohito and Kaiser Wilhelm and Franz Joseph and on and on. For the rise of every great power in world history, a decline follows. Having power is one of the most trying experiences that humans—individually or collectively—can ever know. It will not last. Christians need to be the ones who understand the reality of power's passing nature and address it—honestly, humbly, and lovingly.

Edom was not a superpower; it was a small nation. But it was a proud nation. And such pride is never appropriate for creatures like us.

Humility is the way of God himself. In humility, God put on human flesh in Jesus Christ. In humility, Christ came and washed the feet of his disciples, pointing to an even greater cleansing. In humility, Christ went to his death on the cross, offering this greater cleansing from sin for all those who would ever repent and believe in him. Humility is the way of Christ.

So must it be for all Christians. God hates the proud (cf. Prov. 6:16-17). Therefore, we must humble ourselves before God.

If you are a Christian, let me remind you that humility is the fruit of God's Spirit in you. It is the typical result of God's typical work. Be encouraged when you observe yourself fighting against pride. That is God's Holy Spirit working! In the same way, be concerned when you regard your pride with complacent indulgence. John Stott has wisely written, "At every stage of our Christian development, and in every sphere of our Christian discipleship, pride is our greatest enemy and humility our greatest friend."[4]

If you are offended by the idea that pride is your greatest enemy, consider what other things offend you. If you were more humble, you would find fewer things that offend you. If you knew what you deserve because of your sins, and how merciful God has been to you in Christ, then there would be less cause to take offense when someone treats you far better than your sins deserve. That's true for us as individuals, and for us as a church. May our churches never forget that we are utterly dependent on God. The danger of the blessings God gives our churches is that we begin to trust in the blessings rather than in the God who gives them. May God preserve us from such pride, the pride that makes him our enemy. He will judge us for it.

The Opponents of God's People

But what exactly had Edom done? How had their pride shown itself? Those are the questions that verses 5–16 answer. Here we find that God opposes not just the proud, but those who oppose his people.

In verse 5, God shows that Edom's pride has led it into heinous sin against Judah, which he compares with the actions of robbers and grape pickers: "If thieves came to you, if robbers in the night . . . would they not steal only as much as they wanted? If grape pickers came to you, would they not leave a few grapes?" In other words, neither robbers nor grape pickers will take *everything*. They take only what they need. But Edom had been merciless in its treatment of Judah. If you have ever been the victim of a robbery, you have probably felt the strange thoughts of vulnerability, anger, and violation often experienced by such victims. But that feeling of injustice that victims of robbery can feel, God is saying to Edom, does not adequately portray the injustice that the Edomites had committed against the Israelites.

---

[4] John Stott, "Pride, Humility, and God," in J. I. Packer and Loren Wilkinson, eds., *Alive to God* (Downers Grove, Ill.: InterVarsity Press, 1992), 119.

Also, the picture of what a robber does was inadequate for portraying the loss God would bring upon Edom: "Oh, what a disaster awaits you," God says in the middle of verse 5. Their ruination would not be partial; the nations would enter their strongholds and leave their towns and houses bare. "How Esau will be ransacked, his hidden treasures pillaged!" (v. 6). No investments were secure and no dwellings were safe. All protections and precautions would be useless, because God would use the Babylonians to conquer and plunder. With God's protection, there is safety amid unnumbered dangers; without God's protection, all other protections are finally worthless.

And who better to bring God's judgment than the very ones Edom had trusted and relied upon in place of God. "Your allies will force you to the very border; your friends will deceive and overpower you" (v. 7a). If you like suspense films, you know that skillful directors often employ the gullible, inordinate trust one character will place in another individual who appears to be a friend or ally but is really a mortal enemy. The Edomites placed such an inordinate trust in the Babylonians, and now their protectors would become their devourers: "those who eat your bread [meal-sharing companions] will set a trap for you, but you will not detect it" (v. 7b). The Edomites thought they were wise, but they were deceived. They detected nothing.

God promises that the proud will be humbled. And he abhors the nation who treats other people as if those other people belonged to the nation rather than to God.

Especially when those others are God's own special people!

God makes this point throughout the Bible. Do you remember what the risen Christ said to the Christian-persecuting Saul when he appeared to him on the road to Damascus? "Saul, Saul, why do you persecute *me?*" (Acts 9:4). Christ identifies so closely with his people that he refers to them as himself. God demonstrates a similar kind of identification with his people in the book of Obadiah. Actions against God's people are actions against God.

If you have acted against God's people, you have sinned against God. In fact, the Bible teaches that all of us have sinned, not just Edom—"all have sinned and fall short of the glory of God" (Rom. 3:23). All of us have alienated God by our actions.

In verse 8, God restates his promise to destroy Edom, but in much more explicit terms: "'In that day,' declares the LORD, 'will I not destroy the wise men of Edom, men of understanding in the mountains of Esau?'" Whatever cleverness or wit had been previously demonstrated in arranging Edom's political affairs was shallow and short-sighted. Their wise men could not save them now.

Neither could their strong men: "Your warriors, O Teman, will be terrified, and everyone in Esau's mountains will be cut down in the slaughter" (v. 9). Why would this happen? "Because of the violence against your brother Jacob . . ." (v. 10a). The Lord refers to Edom's "brother Jacob" because Edom, or Esau, was the brother of Jacob (also called "Israel"). God is referring to them according to the individual ancestors to whom they trace their identity— Esau for the Edomites and Jacob for the Israelites. The larger point being made, of course, is to demonstrate how outrageous it was for Edom not to offer hospitality to fleeing Israelites, but violence instead. Their violence was not violence against strangers, but against *brothers*. Because of this outrage, says God, "you will be covered with shame; you will be destroyed forever" (v. 10b). Notice, God would not temporarily destroy them, as he temporarily sent the Israelites into exile. He would destroy them forever. God cares how his people are treated.

That's why I will use my Sunday morning pastoral prayers to ask God to give Christians around the world just governments that will not oppose the spread of God's gospel. Every nation and government around the world should realize that it is not in the best interest of the nation to abuse its citizens. God has made all people in his image to worship him freely, and he has called his people to worship him particularly. As we have already said, opposing God's people is opposing him, as Edom did.

In verses 11–14, Obadiah explains more fully the nature of Edom's violence against Israel. Part of their violence was simply to comply with the violence of others: "On the day you stood aloof while strangers carried off his wealth and foreigners entered his gates and cast lots for Jerusalem—you were like one of them" (v. 11).

Any nation should have known better; but given their relationship to Judah, Edom especially should have known better. So God reproaches them: "You should not look down on your brother in the day of his misfortune, nor rejoice over the people of Judah in the day of their destruction, nor boast so much in the day of their trouble" (v. 12). By "look down," God is not referring to a passive stare; he means an active condemnation and gloating. What's more, the Edomites joined in with their brother's destroyers. "You should not march through the gates of my people in the day of their disaster, nor look down on them in their calamity in the day of their disaster, nor seize their wealth in the day of their disaster" (v. 13). Edom took advantage of the situation and exploited Judah's weakness. Like looters after a hurricane, they plundered the family's store. Edom became an accessory to the destruction and murder of his own brother.

In all this, the book of Obadiah foreshadows the figure of Herod, who we know from extrabiblical literature was a descendant of the Edomites. He too attacked the infants in Bethlehem, attempting to kill God's chosen one.

This chosen one faced throughout his life the kind of opposition described in Obadiah. He was opposed and rejected by men. And like the Edomites in Obadiah's book, those who oppose God and God's people will one day face "the wrath of the Lamb" (Rev. 6:16).

The Edomites had been ruthless in their sin. "You should not wait at the crossroads to cut down their fugitives, nor hand over their survivors in the day of their trouble" (v. 14). If robbers take only what they need, robbers are more considerate than the Edomites! Edom waited at the crossroads for those who fled. When they found survivors, they handed them over to their killers. The invaders would not have known the local roads, but the Edomites did. And they guided the invaders right to the miserable people who were fleeing.

Keep in mind, this is not some grim fairy tale, this really happened. This is history. There were a real attack, a real siege, and a real fall. Real people ran from Jerusalem screaming. And it was in the very roads of Edom, reached after an exhausting flight, roads leading to the Israelites' only hope for survival, that their cousins the Edomites waited in ambush and then pounced, hoping to ingratiate themselves with the Babylonian superpower.

Some people have thought that the book's indignant tone suggests that Obadiah's relatives must have been cut down by the Edomites. We don't know. We do know that the Lord was indignant with the Edomites, whether or not Obadiah's relatives were present. The Edomites could hardly complain that God was being too severe on them.

God would bring justice: "The day of the LORD is near for all nations. As you have done, it will be done to you; your deeds will return upon your own head" (v. 15).

There are many implications of God's justice that we could consider, but let me point to just one. The promise of divine justice should encourage us as Christians. It should encourage us when we personally face unjust suffering, and it should encourage us when we hear of our Christian brothers and sisters around the world facing unjust suffering. It will not always be so!

Furthermore, we can expect that the world will hate and oppose us, even as they hated and opposed the one we follow—Christ. If you complain about the trials that you have experienced for following Christ, I wonder who it is you thought you were following. After all, what was Christ's life like? How can we complain when lesser things happen to us? Suffering and persecution was the way of Christ (cf. 1 Peter 2).

We know from other prophets that we have studied in this series that Judah was punished by God because of their idolatry. Through God's sovereign rule, he used the Babylonian army to invade, conquer, and exile his people. Likewise, we trust that Edom's sinful compliance was also ordained by God as part of God's punishment of his own people. How God worked all this out is beyond us. But this much is clear: even though *God* employed the Edomites to participate in bringing his judgment on Judah, the *Edomites* had no intention of serving as God's minister of justice. Where God sought what was holy and right, the Edomites sought what was carnal and wrong, just like the marauding hordes who destroyed Job's family according to their own malicious desires, all the while being used by God to accomplish his good and perfect ends. God uses his enemies as skillfully as a surgeon uses a scalpel to cut, but that does not mean God's enemies are exempt from responsibility or punishment. They earn his judgment for their malice. "As you have done, it will be done to you; your deeds will return upon your own head" (v. 15b). Or as Jesus would later say, "in the same way you judge others, you will be judged, and with the measure you use, it will be measured to you" (Matt. 7:2).

Oh, Christian friend, we who belong to the church must never be unwitting coconspirators with those who persecute God's people; we are part of God's people who are persecuted! We must therefore remember the importance of membership in the church, which assists us in clearly and publicly identifying ourselves with God's people. Church membership helps us to remember that we cannot rely on the culture of the world to define virtue and good.

Sadly, the American church has become diluted for a number of decades by its embrace of American culture. The United States as a whole experienced great reforms in the nineteenth century, and many Christians laid down their guard and began to assume that God would use the culture-at-large as his primary instrument for reforming and caring for his people. But that is not so! We see the effects of this mistake today in everything from marriage to modesty, from morality to murder itself, in which the church has been shaped by the culture. Christians must recognize that God teaches us to live according to his laws, regardless of what the state or the culture says is vice or virtue.

For those of you who work in the government, the law, or are responsible for shaping public opinion in any number of ways, you have your own responsibilities for building public arguments that promote God's justice. But we Christians must never limit our understanding of what is good and right to the evaluations of the culture at large. No, we build a culture in the church, and our church culture must be given to helping, not hurting, God's people.

Also, we must not limit our helping other Christians to those in our own congregations. Instead, we must actively work to help other churches, even as Paul did again and again with the churches in the New Testament. He both exemplified and taught churches the practice of tenderheartedness toward other congregations through prayer, sending teachers, and taking up collections. Therefore, our own congregation holds "Weekenders," in which we invite pastors and seminarians to join us for a series of seminars and services on three weekends a year. Our guests neither pay us nor benefit us in a direct way, other than the encouragement of their fellowship; but we hope to bless them and the churches they labor in. We pray publicly on Sunday mornings for other churches in our city, our nation, and around the world. We send out literature and interviews to other churches and church leaders. We began a pastoral internship program. We began 9Marks to accomplish a number of these goals. We support seminarians. We give money to the Southern Baptist Cooperative Program. The church allows me to travel and preach in other pulpits. Does that directly help our congregation? Perhaps it exposes me to other churches, which in turn benefits our congregation. But mostly it is an export of love, care, and concern. Likewise, when one of the elders goes to central Asia, or when one of the deacons travels to Romania, or when members of the congregation head into their many places of ministry, our whole church family prays and attempts together to export this love, care, and concern for other Christians. About one quarter of the money our church takes in we give to purposes outside the walls of this church, and we attempt to increase the missions percentage of our church budget each year. In short, we attempt, by God's grace and kindness, to do the opposite of what the Edomites did to God's people. God calls all Christians and all churches to do the same.

Christian churches should be marked by that kind of generosity as we labor to specially love those whom God specially loves. In the book of Obadiah, God is a fierce personal enemy to the proud and to the opposers of his people, because he fiercely loves his people.

WHO ARE GOD'S FRIENDS? (VERSES 17–21A)

It is God's fierce, personal love that brings us to our second question: Who are God's friends?

In verse 13 of Obadiah, we saw that God called the Israelites "my people." Yet maybe you are wondering if all people are not in fact God's people. After all, he made all people, and he made them in his image. In that sense, yes, all people are God's people. But throughout the Old and New Testaments, God also displays a special concern for a smaller circle of people whom he refers to as "my people," like the Israelites here. This smaller circle consists of those to whom God has spoken, and who have repented of their sins and accepted God at his word. God also promises to judge those in the "larger circle," if you will, for persecuting or rejecting those in the smaller circle. Remember what Jesus said about the cities who would not receive his disciples:

> "If anyone will not welcome you or listen to your words, shake the dust off your feet when you leave that home or town. I tell you the truth, it will be more bearable for Sodom and Gomorrah on the day of judgment than for that town" (Matt. 10:14-15; cf. 2 Thess. 1:6-8).

In other words, Obadiah teaches not only that God is the Judge of all who are proud and who oppose his people, he teaches that God is the Friend of his people. He cares for his people.

If you are a non-Christian, have you thought about becoming one of God's people? Maybe you have assumed that you were one of God's people by birth. But the only way you can truly be one of God's people—one who belongs to him—is by hearing the promises of God's Word, believing those promises, and then responding to them. Apart from a belief in God's promises, you can only expect God's correct judgment for your sin. Yet if you will receive God's promises in Jesus Christ, you can become God's friend, now and forever. That is why God took on flesh, became a man, lived a perfect life among us, died on the cross, and bore the right punishment for the sins of all of those people who would ever turn from their sins and trust in Christ and his promises.

Here in Obadiah, the nation of Israel had fallen under God's judgment, but God was not finished with them yet. Though they too suffered, their fate would ultimately be different than Edom's.

In a reversal of fortunes for Israel and Edom, the Lord speaks:

> "But on Mount Zion will be deliverance;
>   it will be holy,
> and the house of Jacob
>   will possess its inheritance.
> The house of Jacob will be a fire
>   and the house of Joseph a flame;
> the house of Esau will be stubble,
>   and they will set it on fire and consume it.
> There will be no survivors
>   from the house of Esau."
>   The LORD has spoken (vv. 17-18).

Amid God's words of judgment against Edom, God also speaks words of hope for his people. Not only would the wicked receive justice, God's people would be restored.

Undeniably, our experiences of suffering and pain as God's children cause us to explore the depth and breadth of God's love more fully, as we have to depend on him more completely. Our trials teach us to despair of those other things we wrongly trust in; they teach us to despair of ourselves; they teach us to trust in Christ, God's Son, who makes us God's friends. As Jesus said to his followers, "You are my friends if you do what I command. I no longer call you servants, because a servant does not know his master's business. Instead, I have called you friends" (John 15:14-15).

So here in Obadiah, God's people are given hope amid despair, as if God were promising to bring them back to life from the dead. Indeed, in these final verses, God promises his people that they will return from exile and regain their lost lands:

> People from the Negev will occupy
>   the mountain of Esau,
> and the people from the foothills will possess
>   the land of the Philistines.
> They will occupy the fields of Ephraim and Samaria,
>   and Benjamin will possess Gilead.
> This company of Israelite exiles who are in Canaan
>   will possess the land as far as Zarephath;
> the exiles from Jerusalem who are in Sepharad
>   will possess the towns of the Negev.
> Deliverers will go up on Mount Zion
>   to govern the mountains of Esau (vv. 19-21a).

God will make Mount Zion holy again; he will again dwell with his people.

In one sense, these promises were fulfilled within a few decades, when a number of the Israelites returned from the exile in Babylon to the land of Judah. But the author also seems to perceive dimly that this resurrected kingdom will include *all* of God's people. Thus he includes a reference to the "house of Joseph." The house of Joseph was a part of the northern kingdom that had been dispersed among the nations 150 years earlier. The fulfillment to which Obadiah alludes was not ultimately experienced by Ezra or Nehemiah, two of the returning exiles. Rather, God's words through Obadiah will be ultimately fulfilled when God's people are in God's place under God's rule through the Lord Jesus Christ. What blessings we have in Christ! Deliverance. The promise of an inheritance in him. Justice. God's Word. God's undeserved love. As God's people in his church, we have already begun to experience these blessings from

God. God's friends are his own special people, set apart in Christ to enjoy the blessings that we enjoy!

WHO IS GOD? (VERSE 21B)

Finally, we must look at the last phrase in Obadiah: "And the kingdom will be the LORD's" (v. 21b). This sentence points us to all kinds of things that people today do not understand at all. But we must understand these things if we want to understand Obadiah, the Old Testament, and even the Bible. The kingdom will be the Lord's. In other words, the Lord is king over all nations, and he showed that by the way he treated both Edom and Judah. God's kingship is the real message of this little book. God used Obadiah to show both Edom and Judah that he is the king. He used it to show Babylon that he is the king.

Now, is the fact that God proclaims himself king encouraging or alarming to you? Certainly it was encouraging to God's Old Testament people. Yet remember that this vision was primarily addressed to unbelievers—the Edomites. In fact, Obadiah appears to be the only book in the Bible written primarily to unbelievers. Why prophesy to unbelievers? To people God would judge? Who were proud, unjust, and hardened? Who were God's enemies? Who didn't believe? Because God will declare the truth about himself and what rebellion brings *even to his enemies.*

For many people, the language of God having "enemies" simply sounds scary. These days, in fact, we associate it with acts of terror and escalating violence in certain regions of the world. The idea that God has a purpose in everything, and that we must align ourselves with that purpose, sounds, well, so absolute! Skeptics will certainly object, "Isn't the idea that history is going somewhere an illusion, invented to give our brief lives meaning? Hitler watered the fields of Europe with the blood of millions in order to build his dream of a thousand-year Reich. Karl Marx's vision of giving meaning to people's lives by placing them into the inevitable march of history spawned revolutions and tyrannies that led to countless deaths as well. Are not visions of ultimate purpose and meaning like these not only false but terribly dangerous?" If you attended a secular university like me, this is what you were taught.

The political philosopher Karl Popper adopted this line of skepticism in his magnum opus, *The Open Society and Its Enemies,* where he charges Plato, Hegel, Marx and others with imposing meaning on history at the expense of freedom. Surely there is much that Christians can agree with in Popper's charges. We, too, do not want the state to coercively and violently impose some philosopher's concept of meaning on the nation's public and private institutions. But we find Popper's solution to tyranny troubling as well. He said that states and individuals must remain perpetually open to every possibility of meaning and truth, except for all the possibilities that have been falsified (proven false). By that Popper did not mean we should remain "open" until we find the right answer to life's ultimate questions. He meant we should remain *perpetually open*—forever, by principle. Open to what? Don't ask. After all, we cannot prove anything is true, Popper says; we can only prove something is not true. One wonders what truths *he* discovered that allowed him to "close" upon this solution! No, the answer to untruth and dangerous untruth is not to put the very concept of truth off limits, as Popper does. That itself is a self-contradictory untruth. Instead, we Christians believe that the answer to tyranny is to remember the *truth* that all human authority in government, business, home, and church is only partial, temporary, and subordinate to God's authority. Those for whom we are responsible do not belong to us. They belong only to God. We are only stewards of his authority in this world; we are never owners.

In case you are skeptical about the idea of history having meaning, much less the idea that God has friends and enemies, I would simply like to ask you this question: Why does it seem as though everyone throughout history has sought meaning in their lives? Why do they want it? Lots of different proposals have been offered for what the meaning of life is, surely, but what interests me is the fact that everybody wants to know. Maybe that's because, as Freud suggested, the lack of meaning leaves all of us wanting to manufacture meaning. But why is there this instinct to manufacture meaning? Perhaps you remember that great theological classic *Raiders of the Lost Ark*. At the end of the movie, the U.S. government, now in possession of the ancient Israelites' ark of the covenant, hides the real ark in an ordinary looking crate in the middle of a warehouse with hundreds of thousands of similar looking crates. Very often, counterfeits prove *not* that there is nothing but counterfeits but that there *is* an original.

The day will come when all the philosophical debates about the meaning of life will end, and you and I will stand before God, the very one who made us and will judge us. If you are a non-Christian, I must warn you, a meeting will occur that you can neither avoid nor delay. And on that day, whatever you have trusted in throughout your life will be exposed, whether you have trusted in your obedience to the Ten Commandments, the fact that you were baptized, the fact that you were a citizen in what you thought was a "Christian" country, the fact that you never abused your spouse, or the fact that you were pretty good, at least some of the time. I am here to tell you that *nothing* that you will have trusted in up until that meeting with God will save you. God will and should judge you for your sins, because he is a righteous God. Your only hope lies in the One who has given himself to take the penalty for sinners. The only hope for you and me is to turn and trust in Christ. If you believe and rely upon Christ's work on the cross, there is great hope in Obadiah's promise that "the kingdom will be the LORD's."

If you are one of God's people, meditate on this last sentence in Obadiah. It reveals God's purpose for history. Then consider the completeness of God's rule over all of life, and the certainty of his rule. He will triumph, and his triumph will be complete. This is what we need to know for our own lives.

This is also what our churches need to know for the times in which they experience decline, for the times in which they experience growth, and for the times in which they encounter legal hostility, as they probably will if pastors continue to faithfully preach the Bible. Whatever the circumstances, we must remember that God is the great King, the Creator and Judge of the universe, and the Lord of History. He is the One who will bring retribution upon his enemies (cf. Jeremiah 51); and he is the one who will bring friendship to sinners, if only they will draw near to him in Christ.

CONCLUSION: WHO ARE YOU?

The people who first heard Obadiah's brief prophecy would have been struck by God's commitment to avenge his people's loss. God's commitment is clear and uncompromising.

So was Edom destroyed? Yes, Edom was first invaded in the next century by Arabs. Then it suffered wave after wave of invasion until the nation finally dissolved. It was never reconstituted.

Were the Israelites restored? Yes, partially. But the fuller restoration Obadiah prophesied about began when Jesus Christ came and declared that the kingdom of God had begun, and then ushered many Jews and non-Jews into God's reign over their lives. When Christ took on flesh and lived among us, he showed us truth and gave our lives the possibility of meaning. As Jesus said to his disciples, "Anyone who has seen me has seen the Father" (John 14:9). Jews and Gentiles came together in their new life in Christ's church, and God's rule became visible.

That is something of who God is, who God's friends are, and who his enemies are.

My question for you is, who are you? Are you an enemy or a friend of God? The Bible teaches that every one of us is God's enemy by nature. That is the language of the Bible, not some group of fundamentalist Christians who are mean-spirited and narrow-minded. The apostle Paul taught that "Jews and Gentiles alike are all under sin" (Rom. 3:9). He also taught that we are all "by nature objects of [God's] wrath" (Eph. 2:3). And Jesus taught that all of our sinful actions and thoughts reveal that we have sinful hearts (Mark 7:20-23).

But "enemies"? Does God really have "enemies"? Here is how the author of Hebrews put it: "If we deliberately keep on sinning after we have received the knowledge of the truth, no sacrifice for sins is left, but only a fearful expectation of judgment and of raging fire that will consume the enemies of God" (Heb. 10:26-27). God's enemies are those who continually and willfully sin. Or as James put it, "don't you know that friendship with the world is hatred toward God? Anyone who chooses to be a friend of the world becomes an enemy of God" (James 4:4).

Friend, I ask you, are you one of God's enemies? If so, hear Paul's words to an earlier generation of God's enemies: "We implore you on Christ's behalf: Be reconciled to God. God made him who had no sin to be sin for us, so that in him we might become the righteousness of God" (2 Cor. 5:20-21; cf. Rom. 5:10).

According to the Bible, we have all been God's enemies. The question is whether you have been reconciled to God through Christ.

Let us pray:

O God, we see in your Word your right opposition to us in our rebellion against you. And we see in our own hearts our wrong opposition to you in your loving authority. Forgive us and change us; for Christ's sake we ask it. Amen.

Questions for Reflection

1. Does God have enemies? Who are they? Where does the Bible describe God as hating someone? Whom does it say he hates?

2. How does pride lead to placing our trust in something other than God?

3. What is your Maginot Line? In other words, what have you worked hard to build over the last several years of your life that you think will provide peace and security?

4. History amply demonstrates that every great power passes. How then should Christians identify themselves with their faith and their churches compared to how they identify themselves as citizens? What will be the peculiar challenges for Christian citizens of a nation with a large role on the world stage? What will be the peculiar challenges for Christian citizens of a nation with a minor or no role on the world stage?

5. As we have seen, John Stott has written, "At every stage of our Christian development, and in every sphere of our Christian discipleship, pride is our greatest enemy and humility our greatest friend." Accepting that our knowledge of ourselves is far from perfect, what "stage" of Christian development are you presently at? How does pride sneak up on people at your particular stage? What steps are you taking to fight pride with humility? What stage of development follows your present stage? How does pride sneak up on people at that stage?

6. God promised to judge the Edomites, in part, because God so closely identifies himself with his own people, and the Edomites had abused his people. Where has God identified himself with us most perfectly? What does his identification with us mean for the trouble we as Christians will endure in this world?

7. Why is the doctrine of God's justice encouraging? What are churches robbing their members of when they fail to teach about God's justice?

8. Why should the trouble we receive for being Christians not surprise us? How should we respond to those who cause us trouble?

9. How do Christians unwittingly conspire with the world in persecuting and abusing fellow Christians? Why is membership in a local church one of the best defenses against this sort of in-house abuse?

10. How can you encourage your church to do a better job of caring for other churches in your own city?

11. Why is the idea that God is the king who gives meaning to history a scary proposition for people? In what ways can we as Christians legitimately sympathize with their fears? Why is the solution offered by the contemporary skeptic—throw the concept of "truth" out the window—an insufficient and dangerous solution?

12. Can you think of an example where the presence of counterfeits indicates that the real thing exists? What relevance does this analogy have for the surfeit of different religions in the world?

13. Are you a friend or an enemy of God? How do you know? Are you certain? What if you are wrong?

THE MESSAGE OF JONAH: CAN YOU RUN FROM GOD?

THE MESSAGE OF JONAH: CAN YOU RUN FROM GOD?

LOVING AND LIVING LIKE GOD[1]

In a recent lecture at our church, John Piper described heaven as the place where God himself supremely resides. Even if we arrived in heaven and received everything else that we wanted—friends, family, health, riches—we would be uninterested in being there if God himself was not present. He is the center of it all.

In that sense, the people who are preparing for heaven are the people who are increasingly centered on God and God's presence already.

As I meditated on this idea, it occurred to me that the opposite is true as well. Hell is the place where God and his presence are absent (his pleasing presence, anyway; God is present in hell only to judge). And the individuals whom Scripture promises will go to hell are individuals whose lives are already marked by indifference to God, by coldness to God, by opposition to God. These individuals follow laws different than God's laws, and they pursue loves different than God's loves.

Does that sound like the life you live, a life characterized by loving what God does not love and by ignoring what he does love?

INTRODUCING JONAH

One of the stranger places to find a man running away from God's laws and God's loves is in the Bible's account of one of God's own prophets—the account of Jonah. The book of Jonah is the next in our series of studies through the Minor Prophets of the Old Testament. These prophets are not called "minor"

---

[1] This sermon was originally preached on September 28, 2003, at Capitol Hill Baptist Church in Washington, D.C.

because they are unimportant but because their books are shorter. They comprise the last twelve books of the Old Testament.

The most well-known minor prophet these days must be Jonah. Jonah's book is composed of four short chapters, and each chapter reflects a different setting. The first chapter is set mostly at sea. The second chapter is set in the belly of a great fish. The third is set in the city of Nineveh, then the capital of the Assyrian Empire. And the fourth is set just outside of Nineveh.

Jonah's book is unique among the prophets because it is a story and contains very little "prophecy." Some people have suggested that we should read this story as a fable, a myth, or, at best, a parable. In support of their interpretation, these commentators cite the miraculous storm, the description of the fish, the vast size of Nineveh, the speed at which the people of Nineveh repent, the quickly growing vine, and so forth.

Yet arguing against this view is how *unlike* a parable this story is: It's too long. It's too detailed. Its characters are too life-like. It's set in real cities with real names. And it appears to be set in a specific time of history—the eighth century B.C. More important than our analysis of Jonah is the fact that Jesus treated the story of Jonah as historical.[2] What does it suggest about us—and about our opinion of Jesus—if we do otherwise?

When we turn to investigate the history of the eighth century B.C. from sources outside the Bible, we find several items that corroborate Jonah's account. Did the Ninevites listen and immediately repent when Jonah preached to them (as we'll see in chapter 3)? Based on what we have found at the site of ancient Nineveh, we know that prophecies were regularly brought to this great city; so many, in fact, that a number of officials were employed full-time to sift through all the messages. Nineveh was filled with polytheists, after all, and they believed that the gods spoke to them and about them. Also, we know from ancient Assyrian records that a complete solar eclipse occurred on June 15, 763 B.C. Soon after the eclipse, floods and a famine followed. If Jonah traveled to the city about the time that we think he did—based on information from 2 Kings 14:25, the only other place in the Old Testament that Jonah, son of Amittai, is mentioned—he would have arrived in Nineveh in the months or years after the eclipse, flood, and famine. Given the traumatic nature of their recent disasters, the Ninevites may have been fully inclined to believe their city was about to be "overturned," as Jonah tells them in 3:4. It's also worth considering the fact that the city's greatest century and a half followed what would have been this special period of repentance.

In our study here, we want to think about Jonah, his story, and the book's

---

[2] Matt. 12:40-41; Luke 11:30, 32.

basic themes. Thinking back for a moment, we saw in our study of Hosea that God loves his people. In our study of Amos, we observed God's promise of judgment on his people, but also his offer of hope. In our study of Obadiah, we saw that God promised to judge the foreign nation of Edom as an enemy; and after that study you may well have wondered whether God loves the nations as he loves Israel, because the same promise of rescue and deliverance is not explicitly extended to them. Is God concerned about anyone other than Israel? Well, the story of Jonah answers this question. But it also raises questions for us today—questions like, are *you* running from God's will? And are *you* running from God's love? Let's consider these two questions now, as we look through the story of Jonah.

ARE YOU RUNNING FROM GOD'S WILL? (CHAPTERS 1–2)

First, are you running from God's will? That is the first question that naturally confronts us when we read the first couple of chapters in this powerful book. Will we do what God calls us to do?

God Calls Jonah to Preach

In Jonah's first couple of verses, we see that God calls Jonah to preach: "The word of the LORD came to Jonah son of Amittai: 'Go to the great city of Nineveh and preach against it, because its wickedness has come up before me'" (1:1-2).

Where was Nineveh? Today, you can find the ruins of this once great city on the edge of Mosul, Iraq, on the east side of the Tigris River, about forty miles east of Syria. Jonah's association with that area remains well-known. There is an old Muslim mosque and cemetery in that site called Nebi Yunus ("the tomb of Jonah"). In Jonah's day, it was a grand city and the last capital of the Assyrian empire. Nineveh was the city to whom Israel paid tribute in Israel's declining years (2 Kings 15:19-20; Isa. 8:4).

The city of Nineveh, covering some 1,850 acres, contained famous hanging gardens, water dams, parks, a fifty-mile aqueduct to bring water from the mountains, great roads, a double wall protecting the city, administrative buildings, and a large library. King Sennacherib's magnificent palace was also in Nineveh. The palace boasted almost two square miles of carved stone reliefs, including the famous scenes of Sennacherib's siege of Lachish (2 Kings 18:14-17; 2 Chron. 32:9).[3] All of this we know from excavations. Truly, it was a great city in size, influence, and splendor.

---

[3] The stone reliefs of Sennacherib's siege of Lachish can be seen in the British Museum in London.

It was also a wicked city, says the Lord in these opening verses. In his mercy, however, the Lord sometimes decides not to immediately judge such places of wickedness but to first send warning of impending judgments, as he did with Sodom and Gomorrah and so often with Jerusalem.[4] So here, with the wickedness of Nineveh in view, God summons Jonah to cry out against the city within its own walls—a daring thing for Jonah to do!

God's charge is a striking way to open this little book. Yet it reminds us right from the beginning that God is holy. You and I might become accustomed to lying and cheating, adultery and idolatry, hatred and murder, as commonplace as these sins are. But God has always been revolted by these things. Sin provokes God's anger, and in the book of Jonah God declares that the time has come for the judgment of Nineveh. His concern for righteousness was not limited to his own people in Israel. He has always been concerned about every creature made in his image throughout the whole world. The book of Jonah underscores this point, as he calls Jonah to go and bear God's testimony of judgment to the people of Nineveh.

If you are a Christian, this book should remind you that your salvation did not begin with you. Sometimes we get into the Christian life and gradually begin to think and act as if we have saved ourselves. But we didn't. Or maybe you think you were saved because this or that person shared the gospel with you. Well, God surely used such a person. Yet that was not the beginning of your story either. According to his sovereign plan, God quickened that person's heart—perhaps in a manner that was insensible to him or her—to share the gospel with you. Maybe God used your Sunday school teacher. Maybe he used your parents or your friends. But whoever it was, God was behind it. He was working all along. Just as God sent Jonah to Nineveh, God sent someone to you to tell you about God's holiness, your sin, and the remedy offered only in Christ. Your salvation began with God himself.

God had created Israel by his word. And now he would save Nineveh by his word.

As churches today, we can thank God for the blessings he has given us through the preaching of his Word. We can thank God for the faithful gospel-living and gospel-teaching of the countless members of our own churches who came before us and prepared the way. We can thank God for the Christians who started our own congregations as well as for the churches from which those individuals came. But behind it all, whichever way you trace it, is Christ, who founded his church. So we give praise to him.

God calls his own people together by his own Word.

---

[4] Genesis 18; Jeremiah 18; 36; Joel 2; etc.

Jonah Flees from God

If you have not read the book of Jonah, you might expect a straightforward story line to follow verses 1–2: Jonah hears God, travels to a hostile land, and obediently preaches, sort of like Obadiah or even Jesus did. But verse 3 throws us a curveball:

> "But [never a good word to see after God issues a command] Jonah ran away from the LORD and headed for Tarshish. He went down to Joppa, where he found a ship bound for that port. After paying the fare, he went aboard and sailed for Tarshish to flee from the LORD" (Jonah 1:3).

Jonah responds to God's call by disobediently fleeing! Traveling to Nineveh from Galilee (in northern Israel) would have required him to head eastward over land. Instead, he headed south and west to the coastal town of Joppa. There, he paid a fare, boarded a boat (something an ancient Hebrew would do only out of desperation), and sailed for Tarshish, a Phoenician trading port in Spain at the other end of the Mediterranean Sea. That would have been at the opposite end of the known world! Jonah could not have conspired to travel farther from where God had called him to go. Clearly, he ran in sheer disobedience to God. He ran from God's will. Did he think he could physically take himself beyond the reach of God, like moving out of cell phone range? What a ridiculous idea!

To be fair to Jonah, we must admit that he was not the only prophet who initially objected to God's call. Moses first responded to God's call in his life by making excuses and listing all the reasons why he was inadequate for the job.[5] Jeremiah claimed he did not know how to speak, as if God had made some kind of mistake (Jer. 1:6). And Elijah, a bit later in his ministry, became afraid and ran for his life (1 Kings 19:3).

If you are a non-Christian, let me point out that Jonah's disobedience is only one of many accounts in the Bible that describe the reality that faces all of us: we all sin and stand under God's judgment. Do you know what sin is? Sin is disobeying God. Sin is not doing what God calls us to do. Sin is fleeing from God and his rule as Jonah fled. The Bible teaches that everyone—from the wicked Ninevites, to Jonah the running prophet, to you and me—sins, for which God will call us to account. I will give an account, and you will give an account. More on that in a moment.

We need to notice another thing about Jonah's flight: it was entirely legal. Sometimes, Christians can be tempted to equate "illegal" with "immoral" and

---

[5] Ex. 3:11, 13; 4:1, 10, 13.

"legal" with "moral." Yet Jonah booked passage on a ship and paid for it. He was not a stowaway. He acted legally. But what he did was still a sin. I hope you understand that we can disobey God in ways that are legal as well as in ways that are illegal. Like Jesus Christ, Jonah was a Galilean called to preach to the lost. Unlike Jesus Christ, he sinned and ran away. He ran away from God.

Friend, we should obey God. If you are a Christian and you are trying to run away from God in some area of your life, realize that you will never succeed. You can never outrun God. Do not try. It is a waste of time, and it will only bring sorrow. Do you really think he won't know about you? Or notice what happened? Or won't come looking for you, as he did with Adam or Jonah or so many others in Scripture? Do you really think you can avoid giving an account to him?

Our churches must also realize that being tough on unrepented sin is actually a display of kindness. Barring someone from church membership because of his or her unrepented sin is much better than letting him or her stroll unwarned toward being barred from the Kingdom of God. It is a vain, empty, and foolish thing to run from God; if our congregations don't say that clearly, no one else will.

Disobeying God gets us nowhere good.

God Catches Up with Jonah

Well, now that we see Jonah fleeing, we might be tempted to think this is one of those Bible stories where decline is only followed by more decline, as with Dathan, Solomon, or Demetrius, all tragic Bible figures who hear God's call, run the other way, and never seem to come back. But not here in Jonah. God is not done with him. Beginning in chapter 1, verse 4, we watch as God catches up with Jonah:

> Then the LORD sent a great wind on the sea, and such a violent storm arose that the ship threatened to break up. All the sailors were afraid and each cried out to his own god. And they threw the cargo into the sea to lighten the ship.
>
> But Jonah had gone below deck, where he lay down and fell into a deep sleep. The captain went to him and said, "How can you sleep? Get up and call on your god! Maybe he will take notice of us, and we will not perish."
>
> Then the sailors said to each other, "Come, let us cast lots to find out who is responsible for this calamity." They cast lots and the lot fell on Jonah.
>
> So they asked him, "Tell us, who is responsible for making all this trouble for us? What do you do? Where do you come from? What is your country? From what people are you?"

He answered, "I am a Hebrew and I worship the LORD, the God of heaven, who made the sea and the land."

This terrified them and they asked, "What have you done?" (They knew he was running away from the LORD, because he had already told them so.)

The sea was getting rougher and rougher. So they asked him, "What should we do to you to make the sea calm down for us?"

"Pick me up and throw me into the sea," he replied, "and it will become calm. I know that it is my fault that this great storm has come upon you."

Instead, the men did their best to row back to land. But they could not, for the sea grew even wilder than before. Then they cried to the LORD, "O LORD, please do not let us die for taking this man's life. Do not hold us accountable for killing an innocent man, for you, O LORD, have done as you pleased." Then they took Jonah and threw him overboard, and the raging sea grew calm. At this the men greatly feared the LORD, and they offered a sacrifice to the LORD and made vows to him (Jonah 1:4-16).

Well, this book is clearly full of surprising twists! God actually sends a storm after this runaway prophet. When Jonah then tells the polytheistic Phoenician sailors that his God had made the sea, we expect them to kill Jonah then and there to appease this God. But—another surprise—they don't! These Gentiles have mercy on Jonah and try to spare him. They heroically try to row back to shore, and it looks as if that will be the end of the story. But God doesn't allow it. He has another point to make. So the storm grows worse and worse—"the sea wrought and was tempestuous," as the King James Version puts it (1:11). Finally, the sailors have no choice: They throw Jonah overboard. Immediately the seas become calm, and the Gentiles fear God and worship him with sacrifice and obedience. In a sense, they repent and believe.

Even the wind and the waves obey this God, just as one day they would obey his Son.

God can save us in the most amazing situations. If you worry that you have run for too long or too far from God to be saved, be assured by this account from Jonah that you have not. God is able to reach you wherever you are. If you can hear my words at this moment, there is hope. Let the storms in your own life cause you to take stock of your situation. What are you putting your hope and trust in? Why are you running from God's ways?

God is tenacious with his people. May we always exalt God's saving power!

Jonah Responds to God with Praise

The story might have ended with Jonah cast into the sea—the fleeing prophet "dealt with" by a just God. But not only does God catch up with Jonah, he delivers Jonah, to which Jonah responds with praise:

> But the LORD provided a great fish to swallow Jonah, and Jonah was inside the fish three days and three nights.
>
> From inside the fish Jonah prayed to the LORD his God. He said:
>
> "In my distress I called to the LORD,
>> and he answered me.
>
> From the depths of the grave I called for help,
>> and you listened to my cry.
>
> You hurled me into the deep,
>> into the very heart of the seas,
>> and the currents swirled about me;
>
> all your waves and breakers swept over me.
>
> I said, 'I have been banished
>> from your sight;
>
> yet I will look again
>> toward your holy temple.'
>
> The engulfing waters threatened me,
>> the deep surrounded me;
>> seaweed was wrapped around my head.
>
> To the roots of the mountains I sank down;
>> the earth beneath barred me in forever.
>
> But you brought my life up from the pit,
>> O LORD my God.
>
> "When my life was ebbing away,
>> I remembered you, LORD,
>
> and my prayer rose to you,
>> to your holy temple.
>
> "Those who cling to worthless idols
>> forfeit the grace that could be theirs.
>
> But I, with a song of thanksgiving,
>> will sacrifice to you.
>
> What I have vowed I will make good.
>> Salvation comes from the LORD."

And the L0RD commanded the fish, and it vomited Jonah onto dry land (1:17–2:10).

Was the animal that swallowed Jonah a whale? I don't know. Whether a whale or a fish did the swallowing, the event was miraculous. The entire affair was the work of God. This man-holding fish swims under the boat at just the right time, it swallows just the right large object, it keeps Jonah inside for three day (a significant number of days, as we'll see), and then it spits him back onto the shore. No matter how you attempt naturally to explain this episode, God was clearly sovereign over these events. He used a storm and a fish to bring Jonah back to the place where he wanted him to be. Storms can destroy the most powerful navies and wreak havoc on the most powerful nations. Great sea creatures can kill the strongest of men. But God uses them all for his purposes.

My Christian brother or sister, as you read about Jonah, consider the great deliverance God has worked in your life. Perhaps God saved you in the last few months or years, and in the process he delivered you from difficulties and trials, sinful addictions and degrading passions. Your experience has been like walking from the dark, stormy night into the broad, cloudless sunshine of morning. Or perhaps you came to Christ as a child, years ago. Either way, all of us as Christians share in Christ's deliverance from God's just punishment of our sins—a punishment far worse than anything a raging ocean can deal out. So praise God for the way he saved you! When you sing spiritual songs and hymns about the great salvation that God has wrought in your life, sing with your whole heart! Realize that you were heading in the wrong direction, just like Jonah. Realize that you were as helpless as a man among raging waves. Yet God saved you! Give praise to God for this, because there is no greater news that you can hear.

ARE YOU RUNNING FROM GOD'S LOVE? (CHAPTERS 3–4)

The first two chapters of Jonah bring to our minds the question of us running from God's will and ways, his law and command. Chapters 3 and 4, however, bring another, perhaps sharper question to the fore: are you running from God's love? Another way of asking that might be, will you love those whom God loves?

God Again Calls Jonah to Preach

Once more, we might have thought that the whole story would end after the fish vomited Jonah back onto the dry land. He was alive and he sounded sorry.

But more surprises follow, as we pick up the story in chapter 3. "Then the word of the LORD came to Jonah a second time: 'Go to the great city of Nineveh and proclaim to it the message I give you'" (3:1-2). God calls Jonah to preach again! If you have not read this book before, you are probably beginning to realize what an amazing story it is. You think it is all over for Jonah, and then God effectively says, "Take two." Then he puts Jonah back into the same position he was in before the storm and the fish. Yes, it would have been easier if Jonah had obeyed the first time God called him. But at least he is getting a second chance. God isn't done with Jonah.

If you are not a Christian, you might be surprised to find out how much this holy God who will judge every sin is also characterized by second chances. There is no Christian you will ever meet who does not know this. The God whom we praise in worship and song is a God of extraordinary mercy.

That does not mean we can *presume* upon his grace and mercy in any particular situation. Jonah didn't flee from God knowing that God was going to do remarkable things; but Jonah may not have been terribly surprised either when God did deliver him. He knew that God was merciful and compassionate.

During his ministry, Jesus described this same God of second chances to the religious leader Nicodemus when he told Nicodemus that he needed a whole new life. Nicodemus needed to be "born again," as Jesus put it (John 3:3). Of course, Jesus *is* this God of second chances through whom we can even be *born* again, if we would only repent of our sins and believe in him.

Christian, has God given you a particular responsibility, situation, relationship, talent, or opportunity that you have taken and messed up? And about which you feel terrible? Remember that our God is the God who gave hope to Adam after the Fall. Whatever you have done, you have *not* plunged the whole human race into eternal misery as Adam did! This same God used the malice of Joseph's brothers to deliver his people from a devastating famine. This same God forgave King David and Mary Magdalene. This same God died for whatever responsibility, situation, or relationship you have messed up. His righteousness has been accounted to you, and you will be treated as Christ deserved. This same God caused you to be born again through his own Spirit to make you a new creation. Christian, this is the God you believe in. And in Jonah's second chance we see a picture of the second chances God gives you again and again.

I do pray that our church learns to exercise care both in taking people into membership and in putting them out of membership whenever unrepented sin warrants a person's removal. But I also pray that our church will be known as a place where broken sinners get a second chance and where we show mercy to others because we have known God's mercy to us in Christ. What good is all our theological understanding of mercy if we cannot *feel* and *sense* both the mercy we have been given from God and the mercy that we then share with one another! May God make us famous for our persistence in love, to the praise of his glorious, gracious, and patient name.

God called Jonah *again!*

Jonah Obeys God and Goes

Well, the next question surely must be, how will Jonah respond? Last time, he ran as far as he could in the opposite direction. Picking up the story in chapter 3, we read, "Jonah obeyed the word of the LORD and went to Nineveh. Now Nineveh was a very important city—a visit required three days. On the first day, Jonah started into the city. He proclaimed: 'Forty more days and Nineveh will be overturned'" (3:3-4). This time, Jonah obeys, goes to Nineveh, and preaches.

People have sometimes wondered why a visit to Nineveh "required three days" (3:3). The phrase probably means that because Nineveh was a large and important city, it took time to walk into it and see the appropriate officials. As I said earlier, we know from excavations that a number of court officials were employed full-time to meet with foreign visitors, including prophets. This was no country village. This was a great city. It is also interesting to note that Jonah spent the same amount of time in Nineveh that he did in the fish—three days. By saving a city in the same amount of time that Jonah spent in the belly of a fish, was God teaching Jonah how many opportunities are wasted when his people flee from him? And was he subtly reminding Jonah of his own grace to him?

As you mentally imagine Jonah's trip to Nineveh to preach God's word, consider carefully how you have responded to the opportunities God has given you to hear his warnings. Particularly if you are not a Christian, how many more opportunities do you think he will give you to hear and rightly respond? Surely God is gracious in Christ; we know that. But you must not presume upon his grace. How dare we ever think we can safely ignore him, assuming that any necessary "adjustments" can be made tomorrow! When we think this way, we deceive ourselves. As James says in the New Testament, "Why, you do not even know what will happen tomorrow. What is your life? You are a mist that appears for a little while and then vanishes" (James 4:14).

We should also observe how much Nineveh benefited by granting Jonah the freedom to preach his message of impending judgment on the city. Can you imagine entering a city ruled by an absolute monarch, asking to preach a message of judgment, and being allowed to do so? Talk about the importance of freedom of speech, freedom of religion, and freedom of association! Try entering Cairo or Riyadh or Beijing today and preaching this message! Jesus himself was persecuted and killed when he preached in Jerusalem.

Christian, resolve this day to obey God, especially in any areas in which you have been disobedient. Given how we have failed him in the past, God has been nothing but gracious in giving us fresh opportunities to serve him. Pray that God would increasingly cause you to pattern your motives after his motives. Pray that he would cause your loves to reflect his loves.

Pray also that God would use individual congregations to facilitate his call to particular individuals to preach. Throughout Scripture, God does great good in the lives of countless people through his preachers and teachers. And just as he called them to preach, he calls some today to preach the gospel of Jesus Christ. Let us pray, on the one hand, that God would raise up elders in our own congregation to teach God's Word. Let us also pray, on the other hand, for those in the congregation who are wrestling with whether God is calling them to leave us and preach his Word full-time. Finally, let us pray for those who have already gone out from us to preach his Word.

Encourage people as they respond to God's call in their lives, and pray for them.

God Delivers Nineveh

So Jonah goes to Nineveh and preaches, "Forty more days and Nineveh will be overturned." What happens next? The people of Nineveh repent, and God spares them! He spares the city from the judgment he is about to pour out on them!

> The Ninevites believed God. They declared a fast, and all of them, from the greatest to the least, put on sackcloth.
>
> When the news reached the king of Nineveh, he rose from his throne, took off his royal robes, covered himself with sackcloth and sat down in the dust. Then he issued a proclamation in Nineveh:
>
> "By the decree of the king and his nobles:
>
> Do not let any man or beast, herd or flock, taste anything; do not let them eat or drink. But let man and beast be covered with sackcloth. Let everyone call urgently on God. Let them give up their evil ways and their violence. Who knows? God may yet relent and with compassion turn from his fierce anger so that we will not perish."

When God saw what they did and how they turned from their evil ways, he had compassion and did not bring upon them the destruction he had threatened (3:7-10).

The Ninevites believed Jonah's warnings of judgment and repented of their sins. And then God showed them mercy.

This is always the aim of faithful preaching. A faithful preacher of God's Word never revels simply in God's judgment. He tells you about your sin so that you will turn to Jesus Christ, because Christ is the one who did not sin, who lived a perfect life deserving no punishment, and who went to the cross and took upon himself the punishment for the sins of everyone who would ever repent of their sins and trust in him. God then raised Christ from the dead to show us that his sacrifice was effective in assuaging God's wrath for our sins. You, like the Ninevites, can have God's right judgment on you averted, if you will only turn from your sins and trust in Christ.

Christian brother or sister, let me encourage you to continue this pattern of repenting and believing throughout your life. If you are truly a Christian, you will not repent and believe only once; you will continue to do so throughout your life. A normal part of Christian discipleship consists of regularly confessing your sins to God (that means saying what God says about your sins) and turning away from those sins and back to God. Repeating these actions does not save you over and over; that happens once. But this is how you live out the relationship you have with our holy God. It is how you freshly lean on his mercy day by day and grow more and more in his likeness.

God graciously delivered Nineveh; the Ninevites repented and believed.

Jonah Resents the Ninevites

Now, this is where we really think the book of Jonah should end (maybe like you are thinking about this sermon!). And the book would be a lot easier to understand if it did end here. But it doesn't. In fact, we have not yet reached the main point of the book. Let's pick up the story line in chapter 4:

> But Jonah was greatly displeased and became angry. He prayed to the LORD, "O LORD, is this not what I said when I was still at home? That is why I was so quick to flee to Tarshish. I knew that you are a gracious and compassionate God, slow to anger and abounding in love, a God who relents from sending calamity. Now, O LORD, take away my life, for it is better for me to die than to live."
>
> But the LORD replied, "Have you any right to be angry?"
>
> Jonah went out and sat down at a place east of the city. There he made himself a shelter, sat in its shade and waited to see what would happen to the city. Then the LORD God provided a vine and made it grow up over Jonah to give

shade for his head to ease his discomfort, and Jonah was very happy about the vine. But at dawn the next day God provided a worm, which chewed the vine so that it withered. When the sun rose, God provided a scorching east wind, and the sun blazed on Jonah's head so that he grew faint. He wanted to die, and said, "It would be better for me to die than to live."

But God said to Jonah, "Do you have a right to be angry about the vine?"

"I do," he said. "I am angry enough to die."

But the LORD said, "You have been concerned about this vine, though you did not tend it or make it grow. It sprang up overnight and died overnight. But Nineveh has more than a hundred and twenty thousand people who cannot tell their right hand from their left, and many cattle as well. Should I not be concerned about that great city?" (4:1-11).

God is compassionate, isn't he? The king of Nineveh may wonder if God is compassionate, but Jonah knows that he is (3:9; 4:2). Throughout Scripture, God consistently reveals himself as compassionate. He says so through Moses: "The LORD, the LORD, the compassionate and gracious God, slow to anger, abounding in love and faithfulness, maintaining love to thousands, and forgiving wickedness, rebellion and sin" (Ex. 34:6-7a). He says so through the prophet Joel: "Return to the LORD your God, for he is gracious and compassionate, slow to anger and abounding in love, and he relents from sending calamity. Who knows? He may turn and have pity and leave behind a blessing" (Joel 2:13-14).

Still, the Lord has to defend his compassion to Jonah: "Should I not be concerned about that great city?" (4:11).

Hopefully by now you can see that the true "star" of this book is not Jonah, but God. G. Campbell Morgan once observed, "Men have been looking so hard at the great fish that they have failed to see the great God."[6] God is the one presented on the pages of this book as great in compassion and power. In chapter 1, he provides the fish. In chapter 4, he provides the vine, the worm, and the wind. The verb translated "provided" (*manah*) is the same word, when turned into a noun, that translates as "manna" in Exodus 16, referring to the bread that God provided for the Israelites to eat when they traveled in the wilderness.[7] Just as God provided for his people in the wilderness, so he provided for Jonah again and again, even when Jonah did not know what he needed. Salvation truly is, as Jonah says, from the Lord (2:9).

God provides for our comforts (like the vine). He provides our losses (as caused by the worm). He even provides our trials (as through the wind).

---

[6] G. Campbell Morgan, *The Minor Prophets: The Men and Their Messages* (Westwood, N.J.: Revell, 1960), 69.

[7] Jonah 1:17; 4:6, 7, 8; cf. Ex. 16:31, 33, 35.

If God is the star, what do we learn from Jonah in chapter 4? Frankly, it is hard to characterize Jonah's response to the deliverance of the Ninevites as anything other than resentful. He does not run from God's will this time, but he does run from God's love. That is, he chooses not to love what God loves.

So God confronts Jonah concerning his resentment toward God's grace. Specifically, God prepares a vine or gourd (some kind of broad-leafed plant) for Jonah's comfort. But then Jonah's heart becomes entwined around the comfort this vine gives. So God uses Jonah's concern about the vine to teach Jonah about something else: "Jonah, if you're concerned about the vine, why are you not concerned about all these people?" Jonah's concern about the vine was not necessarily wrong in itself. Yet it provided a suitable parable for Jonah—if concern for this, why not concern for all these?

The last words in this book—"Should I not be concerned about that great city?"—provide the book's climax, almost like a Great Commission for the Old Testament. Millennia earlier, God had promised to Abram that his descendants would be a blessing to all people (Gen. 12:1-3). Now in Jonah, we find God displaying that exact same concern for all people, while one of Abram's descendants is reluctant to share his concern.

Even God's true messengers are not as loving as God, are they—are *we?* God's love extends to all humanity, since he made all people in his image. To illustrate the breadth of God's love, Jesus taught that God "causes his sun to rise on the evil and the good, and sends rain on the righteous and the unrighteous" (Matt. 5:45). Jesus also called us to love our enemies and pray for them (Matt. 5:44). Our example for loving enemies, the apostle Paul said, is Jesus himself: "when we were God's enemies, we were reconciled to him through the death of his Son" (Rom. 5:10).

Whereas Christ died for his enemies, Jonah responded with resentment. Why? This question has puzzled many people who have read this book. Some have suggested that Jonah grew resentful because he was profoundly embarrassed. After all, Jonah promised them destruction, then God gave them mercy. Not one hair of their tens of thousands of heads was injured. Only Jonah's reputation was injured. At best, God made Jonah look like the bad guy. At worst, God made him look like a false prophet! Surely Jonah's prophetic career back in Israel would be imperiled.

Or maybe, to go a little easier on Jonah, he was worried about *God's* own name and honor—again, because God didn't do what he said he would do.

Or maybe Jonah was simply resentful of God's mercy to people who were *Jonah's* enemies? Jonah loved his own countrymen. He knew that Assyria was a threat to Israel. Perhaps he even knew, as a prophet, that God would use Assyria to judge and destroy Israel, as he did several decades later. So Jonah, a prophet of God, was grace-less even though he had just experienced God's grace so powerfully in his own life through the storm and the great fish. In that sense, Jonah was a real-life example of the ungrateful steward Jesus described in a parable—who had been forgiven much but who would not forgive (Matt. 18:23-35). Jonah celebrated God's grace to himself (chapter 2), but he resented God's grace to his enemies (chapter 4).

Still, look at what God accomplishes even through a resentful heart like Jonah's: the conversion of an entire city! God is amazing, isn't he? He sovereignly uses not only storms and fish for his purposes; he uses resentful humans to cause people to praise his name.

Oh, friend, pray that God would make your heart bigger and bigger like his. And pray that your church would be a good picture of our big-hearted God. May Christ's churches become marked by love across the lines of human division.

CONCLUSION: GOD'S EXPANSIVE LOVE

Look again at the final verse of the book of Jonah: God says to Jonah, "But Nineveh has more than a hundred and twenty thousand people who cannot tell their right hand from their left, and many cattle as well. Should I not be concerned about that great city?" (4:11).

The book ends here with this question left unanswered. We don't know how Jonah would have answered it. Neither do we know anything about Jonah's own fate. Many Christians have suggested that Jonah wrote this book because he was humbled and wanted to represent himself in a harsh light as a part of his repentance. I hope that is the case. But nothing in the Bible says that this is what happened.

We do know that Jonah presents a powerful picture of a man who ran from God's will and from God's love.

Yet remarkably, Jonah also pointed to Jesus Christ. At one point in Jesus' ministry, when the Jews asked for a sign (a miracle-on-demand to prove that what he was saying was true), Jesus said that no sign would be given "except the sign of the prophet Jonah," meaning the resurrection (Matt. 12:39; Luke 11:29). God delivered Jonah from the sea through the fish after three days. God delivered the city of Nineveh from destruction after Jonah's visit of three days. And God will deliver all those who repent of their sins and believe in Christ's death and resurrection, which also occurred after three days (Matt. 12:38-42; 16:4). Jonah, like Jesus, was a preacher from Galilee who brought, to God's enemies, God's news of a possible salvation from coming judgment. But the similarities end there.

Where Jonah was reluctant, Jesus was willing

Where Jonah complained, Jesus went meekly.

Where Jonah was merely uncomfortable, Jesus was scourged.

Where Jonah merely preached, Jesus died.

I wonder how Jonah looks to you right now. Do you feel confident that you can understand his problems? That you can understand and diagnose them?

I wonder if you can see anything of Jonah in yourself. You would never resent anyone's salvation, would you? Consider this story in Luke:

> To some who were confident of their own righteousness and looked down on everybody else, Jesus told this parable: "Two men went up to the temple to pray, one a Pharisee and the other a tax collector. The Pharisee stood up and prayed about himself: 'God, I thank you that I am not like other men—robbers, evil-doers, adulterers—or even like this tax collector. I fast twice a week and give a tenth of all I get.'
>
> "But the tax collector stood at a distance. He would not even look up to heaven, but beat his breast and said, 'God, have mercy on me, a sinner.'
>
> "I tell you that this man, rather than the other, went home justified before God" (Luke 18:9-14a).

As you read along in the book of Jonah through the course of this sermon, did your attitude reflect this Pharisee's? "O God, I thank you that I am not like this Jonah here." As I studied this book in preparation for this sermon, I confess that I had such thoughts. Then I had to pray and ask God to help me see my own sin, the sin that he sternly questions and gently condemns in the final chapter of Jonah.

Can you see your sin? Maybe you do not resent the thought of your enemies being saved (or maybe you do). Yet maybe you are strikingly unconcerned about their fate and the fate of so many of God's creatures. Have you considered that your lack of concern for hundreds of thousands, even hundreds of millions, of people made in God's image is a matter of great grief to God?

Throughout the Bible, God shows us something of how wide his concern is for all nations. When Hagar and Ishmael are sent away because they are not in the chosen line of God's special people, God provides for them (Gen. 21:8-21). When Naaman, the commander of the Aramean army, contracts leprosy, God uses his prophet Elisha to cure him (2 Kings 5). And through the prophet Isaiah, we hear God's great promise, "The LORD Almighty will bless them, saying, 'Blessed be Egypt my people, Assyria my handiwork, and Israel my inheritance'" (Isa. 19:25). And God has allowed much time to elapse between Christ's first and second coming so that people might repent of their sins and turn to him: "The Lord is not slow in keeping his promise, as some understand slowness. He is patient with you, not wanting anyone to perish, but everyone to come to repentance" (2 Pet. 3:9).

God has always been more committed to reaching the world than his own people have been.

It is not difficult to convince people today that God loves everyone—even Ninevites. You might even say that the idea is culturally popular. This is a difference between our day and Jonah's. Indeed, Jonah's assumption that God is specially concerned for his own people—an assumption implicit in his reaction to God's grace to the Ninevites—is what's strange to us these days.

Nonetheless, the point here is God's universal concern. As Christians, the Great Commission should ring in our ears:

> Then Jesus came to them and said, "All authority in heaven and on earth has been given to me. Therefore go and make disciples of all nations, baptizing them in the name of the Father and of the Son and of the Holy Spirit, and teaching them to obey everything I have commanded you" (Matt. 28:18-20a).

If the book of Jonah ended at chapter 3, we could say that the point of the book would be, "God brings his enemies to himself." And that is certainly a true statement and one of the main points of this book. But the message of Jonah goes further. Chapter 4 teaches us that this book really is about Jonah, Jonah's heart, and the hearts of all those who know themselves to be God's people. The point of this book is *us* and *our hearts!* That's why chapter 4 is included. God wants our hearts to be more conformed to his heart. Though Jonah is historical, it also functions as a parable. We are not supposed to read Jonah and then think to ourselves, "How ungrateful that Jonah is! I would never be so unloving to others as he is." Rather, we are supposed to think, "If the heart of a prophet of God can become so wrongly hardened to God's priorities, God's love, and God's mercy, how much more do I need to watch over my own heart!" We need to ask ourselves, "Is there any coldness in my heart toward the things for which God's heart is warm—the things for which he shows love, mercy, and compassion?"

Now, as I have said, the idea of God's universal concern is no longer strange to us. What is strange to us, perhaps, is seeing lives committed to living out God's concern for others. By that I don't simply mean kindness shown to people in one's immediate circles. I mean the kindness that would cause you to move thousands of miles away to a people of a different language and culture, perhaps even a people who are hostile to outsiders, because you care for these fellow creatures made in the image of God, and you want to warn them of God's coming judgment and tell them of his mercy held out to us in Christ!

When God first called Jonah to the Ninevites, he fled to the coastal city of Joppa. Do you know when Joppa is next mentioned in the Bible? At the end of Acts 9, the apostle Peter raises a woman from the dead in Joppa. Then immediately following that episode, we read the story of the first Gentile convert. God gives a Gentile named Cornelius a vision in which he tells Cornelius to send for Peter in Joppa, so that Peter might share the good news of the gospel with him (Acts 10:5). While Cornelius's messenger is still making his way to Peter, God gives Peter a vision teaching him that God will have his gospel go to all nations, and he will involve his people in that great task and privilege. So Jonah set out from Joppa. So Peter set out from Joppa. No coincidences here.

Practically speaking, what should we do? Let me offer several suggestions:

First, learn about the "Ninevehs" around you. Learn what the non-Christians at your work or in your neighborhood care about and enjoy. It is difficult to care about people when you know nothing about them. So give them a chance by learning about them. Also, begin learning about foreign countries, the state of the church in those countries, and the prayer needs of those places. Many resources can help you to do this, but one of the best must be Patrick Johnstone's *Operation World.*[8] Buy a copy and begin praying through its daily calendar.

Second, show hospitality to all the "Jonahs" who travel through your city and circles. When you encounter people committed to moving to places like Nineveh to share the good news of Jesus Christ, welcome them, greet them, and help them on their way.

Third, give support to Jonah and his work. We have done that in our church by making foreign missions one of the line-items on our budget. We also do that in special ways like providing free housing for mission families on furlough. This housing allows missionaries to return to the United States for four, five, even six months to resuscitate and renovate without having to worry about housing. We could not do this if the church did not make the funds available.

Fourth, pray for the Jonahs who go. Pray for the Ninevites they are going to minister to. Pray regularly. Do not pray just about your own self and your own life. Let your prayers increasingly reflect the wideness of God's love!

Fifth, reach out to Ninevites in your city. Many people in the United States come from countries where Christ cannot be freely proclaimed and where the gospel is not known. Yet while these guests are in the United States, you have

---

[8] Patrick Johnstone, *Operation World* (Exeter, UK: Paternoster, 2001).

the opportunity to freely share the gospel with them. As Christians, we should take advantage of this situation. When I consider how multiethnic many cities in the West have become, I sometimes wonder if God has not brought the world to us because we Western Christians have become too lazy and self-satisfied to go to the world.

Sixth, build a church to support all this work. None of these suggestions can be accomplished apart from local churches. If you have been attending a church regularly but have not become a member, I plead with you to go to a church that you will commit yourself to, and build up the body of Christ by carrying on his mission work through them.

Seventh, go to Nineveh yourself. Maybe you are Jonah! Maybe you are the one called to go to a foreign people. Remember what Paul says in Romans: "'Everyone who calls on the name of the Lord will be saved.' How, then, can they call on the one they have not believed in? And how can they believe in the one of whom they have not heard? And how can they hear without someone preaching to them? And how can they preach unless they are sent?" (Rom. 10:13-15).

Are there groups of people that you don't particularly care for or like? Perhaps you have experienced injustice at the hands of rich people, white people, women, Germans, Japanese, Muslims, Americans, tall people, Midwesterners, members of Al-Qaeda—pick your group. And maybe you *have* experienced real injustice from them! Still, whatever that group is for you, know that God's heart is larger than your own, and he wants his gospel to go to that group.

We read in Revelation 15, "Who will not fear you, O Lord, and bring glory to your name? For you alone are holy. All nations will come and worship before you" (Rev. 15:4). God will accomplish his purposes. Praise God! How will you be a part of it? Are you running *from* God or *for* God?

Let us pray:

> From prayer that asks that I may be
> Sheltered from winds that beat on Thee,
> From fearing when I should aspire,
> From faltering when I should climb higher,
> From silken self, O Captain, free
>   Thy soldier who would follow Thee.
>
> From subtle love of softening things,
> From easy choices, weakenings,
> (Not thus are spirits fortified,

> *Not this way went the Crucified,)*
> *From all that dims Thy Calvary,*
>   *O Lamb of God, deliver me.*
>
> *Give me the love that leads the way,*
> *The faith that nothing can dismay,*
> *The hope no disappointments tire,*
> *The passion that will burn like fire,*
> *Let me not sink to be a clod:*
>   *Make me Thy fuel, Flame of God.*[9]

Amen.

Questions for Reflection

1. Based on the first three paragraphs in the introduction to this sermon, why is heaven a suitable place for God-lovers? Why is hell a suitable place for God-haters? Are you a God-lover or a God-hater? Given how high the stakes are for this question, how sure are you of your answer?

2. What is the most important reason why we should treat the book of Jonah as historical? What principle can we learn here for reading and interpreting the Old Testament generally?

3. Are you ever tempted to feel that some sin that you committed in the past (or continue to struggle with) puts you beyond the reach of God's grace? What encouraging news does the book of Jonah have for you? How can you encourage others who struggle with the same temptation?

4. The book of Jonah accomplishes at least two grand tasks at once: it demonstrates God's love for the nations, and it exposes the hypocrisy in the hearts of God's own people, much like Jesus' diatribes against the Pharisees. Let's consider each of these purposes in turn.

   a. First, can you name any other god who loves the nations as much as the God of the Bible? Who is the most loving person that you know? Describe, if you can, what that person would be like if he or she were many times more loving than he or she already is. Now, what do you think God must be like?

---

[9] Amy Carmichael, "Flame of God," cited in Elisabeth Elliot, *A Chance to Die: The Legacy of Amy Carmichael* (Old Tappan, N.J.: Revell, 1987), 221.

Toward you? Toward your non-Christian friends? Toward your enemies? Toward the enemies of your nation?

b. Second, how does the book of Jonah expose you as a hypocrite? When and where have you responded to Jesus' Great Commission (Matt. 28:18-20) as Jonah did by fleeing to Tarshish? What names could you give to "Tarshish" in your life—that is, where do you go to flee from God (a city, home, comfort, food, video games, alcohol, the telephone, a vacation spot, fantasies of success, etc.)?

5. Does God's universal love for people preclude his willingness to judge and condemn? Whom will he judge and condemn?

6. Christian, are you surprised by your conversion, or does it feel like "a given"? No matter one's age at the time of conversion, why should every Christian be *surprised* by his or her conversion? In other words, why is *every* conversion as remarkable as Jonah's deliverance through a great fish?

7. Christian, is there some relationship, job, or opportunity in your life of late that you have "messed up"? What encouragement might you take from the God of second-chances in the book of Jonah for your particular situation?

8. Is it possible for a church to be known *both* for excommunicating unrepentant sinners *and* for being a church that gives second chances? Is this a desirable goal? How can a church work toward this?

9. How can you strive to have a bigger and bigger heart that looks more like God's? Specifically, how can you learn to love more broadly and deeply?

THE MESSAGE OF MICAH: WHAT DOES GOD WANT?

33

THE MESSAGE OF MICAH:
WHAT DOES GOD WANT?

WHAT DO YOU WANT OUT OF RELIGION?[1]

The religions that are championed these days are religions of mystery, tolerance, and change. The rising generation has been taught to give the benefit of the doubt to the unknown, so mystery is in style. Since truth is personal—my truth may not be your truth—tolerance is the least we can offer to people with different values than ours. And in this sort of environment, the ability to make changes is essential. Changes in your moral standards? Yes. Change in your religious practices? Of course.

One study a few years ago concluded that church-shopping has become a way of life among Christians in America. One in seven adults changes churches each year; one in six regularly rotates among different congregations. The so-called process theologians even go so far as to suggest that God changes. He, too, develops and grows along with everything else in the universe, they say.

Surely the ultimate being is mysterious. Many people today prefer the idea of a god who is so removed and different from us that he is more like a force than a father. I once asked a Christian clergyman with whom I regularly met whether he thought God was personal. He paused for a moment, said he'd never been asked that question before, stared thoughtfully into the fire by which we sat, and then concluded that, no, he didn't think that God was personal.

Tolerant, changing, accommodating, tantalizingly mysterious and indefinable—does this describe what you understand Christianity to be? Is that what you look for in your own spiritual renewal and religion?

---

[1] This sermon was originally preached on October 19, 2003, at Capitol Hill Baptist Church in Washington, D.C.

INTRODUCING MICAH

If so, you might be interested in the next minor prophet we come to in our series of "Eternal Questions"—the prophet Micah. Let me remind you, these prophets are "minor" not because they are unimportant but because their books are short. Several centuries before the birth of Christ, these books were collected together in one scroll and became known as "the twelve," although the twelve prophets represented prophesied over five different centuries!

Micah wrote in a day not too unlike our own. Prophesying around the same time as Isaiah prophesied (in the eighth century B.C.), Micah found the nation of Israel in deep trouble with God, as God's people had fallen to terrible moral depths. Society was dissolving and misery was ensuing. In this passage, Micah speaks as the personification of the people of Judah:

> What misery is mine!
> I am like one who gathers summer fruit
>   at the gleaning of the vineyard;
> there is no cluster of grapes to eat,
>   none of the early figs that I crave.
> The godly have been swept from the land;
>   not one upright man remains.
> All men lie in wait to shed blood;
>   each hunts his brother with a net.
> Both hands are skilled in doing evil;
>   the ruler demands gifts,
> the judge accepts bribes,
>   the powerful dictate what they desire—
>   they all conspire together.
> The best of them is like a brier,
>   the most upright worse than a thorn hedge.
> The day of your watchmen has come,
>   the day God visits you.
>   Now is the time of their confusion.
> Do not trust a neighbor;
>   put no confidence in a friend.
> Even with her who lies in your embrace
>   be careful of your words.
> For a son dishonors his father,
>   a daughter rises up against her mother,
> a daughter-in-law against her mother-in-law—
>   a man's enemies are the members of his own household (Mic. 7:1-6).

Misery abounds. There are no grapes or figs. Cravings go unfulfilled. These people are supposedly God's people, but the godly are not to be found: they are swept from the land. Instead, murder is widespread. Rulers are corrupt. Justice is perverted through bribery. It's a rich man's world!

The rot of this land has gotten so bad that people cannot trust each other, not even spouses. The family has disintegrated.

I once shared dinner with a friend from China who described for me the denunciations that occurred during Chairman Mao's Cultural Revolution in the 1960s. With evident shame and distress from memories then over thirty years old, he recounted the party meetings in which one person after another would stand up and denounce someone else in a frantic attempt to appear loyal and remove themselves from any suspicion. Even family members would denounce one another to their own advantage. The deeply destructive and bitter effect was felt at every level of society.

From Chinese Communist Party meetings, to crowds gathered around a guillotine in Revolutionary Paris, to the streets of ancient Israel, we humans have mastered the art of caring about ourselves more than we care about others as well as about God. Yet learning to cultivate our selfish desires by getting drunk, lying, sleeping with someone who is not our spouse, stealing, or murdering both embitters life and belittles our experience of it.

Truly, the human situation, like the situation in Micah's Israel, is grim. Yet Micah was not hopeless. He says in the verse following the passage above, "But as for me, I watch in hope for the LORD, I wait for God my Savior; my God will hear me" (7:7). Micah's hope in this terribly difficult situation was based on something more than himself or even God's people. It was based on God! Notice the first word of verse 7: "but." You could sum these verses up by saying, "Yes, the situation is grievous, *but* God will hear me." Micah separates himself from the sin that he has described; then he watches and waits for God to see, hear, and respond. So he calls God "my Savior."

If this is the situation in which Micah finds the southern kingdom of Judah in the years just before and after the fall of the northern kingdom of Israel—a situation full of sin and evil abhorred by the Lord—what is it that Micah says the Lord wants? Is God basically tolerant, changing, and mysterious? What does God desire?

As we look through the book of Micah, we will observe three things that God says he wants.

GOD WANTS WRONGS TO BE REBUKED

What does God want? Most clearly, Micah teaches that God wants wrongs to be rebuked, especially among his own people. This theme predominates throughout Micah, except for a couple of the more hope-filled chapters (e.g., chapters 4 and 7). The book appears to fall into three series of prophecies—chapters 1–2, 3–5, and 6–7—and the sins of God's people are condemned in each one of these series.

After providing an introduction and a summons to listen in the opening verses of his book, Micah promises that God is coming to confront Judah for its sins:

> The word of the LORD that came to Micah of Moresheth during the reigns of Jotham, Ahaz and Hezekiah, kings of Judah—the vision he saw concerning Samaria and Jerusalem.
>
> > Hear, O peoples, all of you,
> >   listen, O earth and all who are in it,
> > that the Sovereign LORD may witness against you,
> >   the Lord from his holy temple.
> >
> > Look! The LORD is coming from his dwelling place;
> >   he comes down and treads the high places of the earth.
> > The mountains melt beneath him
> >   and the valleys split apart,
> > like wax before the fire,
> >   like water rushing down a slope.
> > All this is because of Jacob's transgression,
> >   because of the sins of the house of Israel.
> > What is Jacob's transgression?
> >   Is it not Samaria?
> > What is Judah's high place?
> >   Is it not Jerusalem?
> >
> > "Therefore I will make Samaria a heap of rubble,
> >   a place for planting vineyards.
> > I will pour her stones into the valley
> >   and lay bare her foundations.
> > All her idols will be broken to pieces;
> >   all her temple gifts will be burned with fire;
> >   I will destroy all her images.
> > Since she gathered her gifts from the wages of prostitutes,
> >   as the wages of prostitutes they will again be used" (1:1-7).

God's promise of destruction continues at the beginning of chapter 2:

> Woe to those who plan iniquity,

> to those who plot evil on their beds!
> At morning's light they carry it out
> because it is in their power to do it.
> They covet fields and seize them,
> and houses, and take them.
> They defraud a man of his home,
> a fellowman of his inheritance.

Therefore, the LORD says:

> "I am planning disaster against this people,
> from which you cannot save yourselves.
> You will no longer walk proudly,
> for it will be a time of calamity" (2:1-3).

As chapter 2 continues, we learn that the people of Judah had even sunk to loving false prophets and their false prophecies! Not content with lying with their own mouths, they wanted to put lies in God's mouth: "'Do not prophesy,' their prophets say. 'Do not prophesy about these things; disgrace will not overtake us'" (2:6). You can understand why God then describes them by saying, "If a liar and deceiver comes and says, 'I will prophesy for you plenty of wine and beer,' he would be just the prophet for this people" (2:11). The point here is not so much their interest in "wine and beer" as it is in their willingness to sacrifice truth for the sake of wine and beer—and plenty of it! They wanted prophets who would tell them nothing more than that the land was going to be full of good things for them. Those are the prophets they would listen to. You could say that they picked their prophets as people might pick their psychics, but not as people pick their bankers or their doctors. Can you imagine picking your doctor based on how cheery and optimistic his diagnoses are! This is what Judah was doing.

So God would judge them for their sin. Both Samaria and Jerusalem—the northern and the southern kingdoms—would be judged.

Notice how severe this judgment would be: "The LORD is coming from his dwelling place; he comes down and treads the high places of the earth" (1:3). And when God "treads," he does not lightly skip from stepping stone to stepping stone. No, he crushes! All the weight of his divine righteousness bears down on the treasonous creatures who are more committed to their sins than they are to him. Some commentators, like C. H. Dodd, have tried to redefine and depersonalize God's wrath as "the inevitable process of cause and effect in a moral universe."[2] But the picture of judgment in Micah is much more per-

---

[2] C. H. Dodd, *Romans* (New York: Harper & Brothers, 1932), 23.

sonal than that—God wanted wrong rebuked and he would ensure that judgment came. He would use foreign military powers. He would use a decaying culture. He would do it himself.

We know from history that the Assyrians destroyed Samaria (another name for the northern kingdom of Israel) several years after Micah gave his prophecy. The northern ten tribes of Israel disappeared from the pages of history forever. One hundred and fifty years later, Jerusalem and the southern kingdom of Judah were defeated and carried off into exile.

The second series of prophecies, comprising chapters 3–5, also focuses on the sin that required rebuke. Micah states his own commission in terms of rebuking sin: "But as for me, I am filled with power, with the Spirit of the LORD, and with justice and might, to declare to Jacob his transgression, to Israel his sin" (3:8).

More of the sins among God's people are cataloged throughout these middle three chapters. Primary among those sins were the sins of the leaders, who abused the people for their own ends. The graphic language in the opening verses of chapter 3 reflects the horror of the nation's life under these leaders as well as the terrible perversion that the abuse of authority is (see 3:1-3). The leaders are also guilty of not respecting the sanctity of human life, with despising justice and distorting rights, and even with bribing judges. "Her leaders judge for a price" (3:11).

At its root, of course, sin is a matter of the heart: "you . . . hate good and love evil" (3:2). It is disaffection for God, and greater affection for the things he has made. As Jesus said, "For out of the heart come evil thoughts, murder, adultery, sexual immorality, theft, false testimony, slander" (Matt. 15:19). When a heart is twisted, no one should be surprised when it does evil.

In response to the sins of the leaders (and the people too, we'll see), God says that he will punish the nation by abandoning it to its invaders: "Then they will cry out to the LORD, but he will not answer them. At that time he will hide his face from them because of the evil they have done" (3:4). He will ensure they are besieged and destroyed. He will wipe out their leaders. Those who remain will be taken into exile in Babylon. Other nations will gloat at their fall, as God deserts his people and returns them to the nations from whence they came.

Sin has consequences, and the most fundamental consequence of sin is the alienation it causes between humans and God. It separates us from him. The leaders of Israel may seek God in prayer—how much more religious can you get!—but God "will not answer them," we read, "because of the evil they have done." God will treat the corrupt leaders as they have treated their people: by not hearing them when they come for help.

God also promises the false prophets that he will not hear them. These for-profit prophets are giving out false information. They are not leading people to God but away from him. So God promises not to answer them:

> "Therefore night will come over you, without visions,
>   and darkness, without divination.
> The sun will set for the prophets,
>   and the day will go dark for them.
> The seers will be ashamed
>   and the diviners disgraced.
> They will all cover their faces
>   because there is no answer from God" (3:6-7).

This is the heart of God's punishment upon his people: cutting off his communication with them. He will not take their calls. He will not speak to them. He wants a separation because of their sins.

Indeed, the sin of Israel was not limited to its leaders and prophets. The whole nation was guilty of false worship and false trust. So in chapter 5 God promises to destroy the objects of both their political and their religious security:

> "In that day," declares the LORD,

> "I will destroy your horses from among you
>   and demolish your chariots.
> I will destroy the cities of your land
>   and tear down all your strongholds.
> I will destroy your witchcraft
>   and you will no longer cast spells.
> I will destroy your carved images
>   and your sacred stones from among you;
> you will no longer bow down
>   to the work of your hands" (Mic. 5:10-13).

Remember, these were the people to whom God had revealed himself. These were the people whom God specially loved. But they had begun to trust horses and walls. They sought out divinity by observing clouds and reading chicken entrails! They loved sacred stones. They dotted the land with carved images that essentially told God to get lost—"these are our gods that we will rely on." It was as if they plastered labels all over themselves that said they belonged to someone else. Their cities were full of people who bowed down to the work of their own hands (5:13). Did God rescue them from slavery in Egypt for this! No, so God promised that "Israel will be abandoned" by him (5:3). They had chosen their sins, rather than him, so he would ratify their choice by giving them what they asked for.

If you are a non-Christian, I expect that the book of Micah might seem severe to you. But then, the reality of sin is severe. Separating ourselves from God is severe. Every sin that we commit, according to the Bible, is a personal affront to God, a rebellion against his authority, a refusal of his wisdom, and a rejection of his love.

Consider how stupid sin really is! Consider what havoc it wreaks in your life! What has been the harvest of your selfishness and pride? Of your anger? Of that bribe that you offered or took? Of your physical involvement with that person who is not your spouse? Of your love of what God hates? Of your indifference to what God loves? Of your ignoring God and his Word day after day? What has come of this way of life? Are you sick of it yet? Friend, I promise you, sin produces nothing good.

Even if you are a Christian, I wonder if this picture looks severe to you. It should be obvious that, considering the times we live in, we worship a God that no Christian publisher would invent—a God who not only has a capacity for wrath but is committed to responding to our sin in wrath. If you continue to puzzle over God's wrath and the idea of hell, Christian, let me encourage you to look at the cross. How much does God hate sin? You will find the answer at the cross, where you can witness the extent to which God was willing to go in order to deal with sin.

God wants to rebuke wrong, especially the wrongs among his own people.

GOD WANTS HIS PEOPLE TO BE RESTORED

What else does Micah tells us that God wants? God wants his people to be restored. In every section of his prophecy in which we read about the severity of God's judgment, we also read about the sweet hope of his salvation.

After Micah's initial denunciations in chapter 2, surprising words of light burst out of the darkness: "I will surely gather all of you, O Jacob; I will surely bring together the remnant of Israel. I will bring them together like sheep in a pen, like a flock in its pasture; the place will throng with people" (2:12). Notice the trilogy of saving promises: "I surely will gather . . ."; "I will surely bring together . . ."; "I will bring them together . . ." God would save his remnant.

That does not mean he would not judge. He would judge by sending Judah into exile. But he would rescue Judah as well:

As for you, O watchtower of the flock,
O stronghold of the Daughter of Zion,

the former dominion will be restored to you;
    kingship will come to the Daughter of Jerusalem. . . .

Writhe in agony, O Daughter of Zion,
    like a woman in labor,
for now you must leave the city
    to camp in the open field.
You will go to Babylon;
    there you will be rescued.
There the LORD will redeem you
    out of the hand of your enemies (4:8, 10).

God would fulfill these promises by sending a first group of people from Judah and Jerusalem into exile about 150 years later, around 605 B.C. The rest of the city would eventually follow. God would then fulfill his promise to restore his people seventy years after this first deportation, when the first group of Jews returned from exile to Jerusalem. Eventually, Ezra and Nehemiah would also return to the land to lead the people in recovering God's Word and rebuilding Jerusalem's walls. God would restore his people, as he promised through Micah.

In chapter 7, the prophet Micah personifies the restored Jerusalem:

Do not gloat over me, my enemy!
    Though I have fallen, I will rise.
Though I sit in darkness,
    the LORD will be my light.
Because I have sinned against him,
    I will bear the LORD's wrath,
until he pleads my case
    and establishes my right.
He will bring me out into the light;
    I will see his righteousness (7:8-9).

Jerusalem was beleaguered not fundamentally because of Judah's weakness or Assyria's strength but because of God's justice. God's justice would continue until God brought his people to victory and restoration. That means, Assyria's sin against Israel would be dealt with in God's time and in God's way.

So the ferocious language of God's judgment against his people in the book of Micah should not leave us with the idea that God said nothing more to his people. He did say more! He spoke words of restoration to these rebuked, chastened people. A remnant would inherit the promises of Israel as a whole (2:12). After all the trials and troubles, God would reestablish his people in righteousness and justice. God's Word to his people was stern and ominous, yes, but it was not finally hopeless or despairing. Everyone who loved God more than God's blessings would see their way through the initial chastening. They—or their children after them—would be restored. God's people would again be lifted up.

If you are not a Christian, I hope that you, more than anything, would want to become one of the people whom God will save. Surely you know something of your own sins. You may well believe that there is a God. And you may have some sense of the fact that you will give an account to him. So, what will you do?

I was recently speaking with a Muslim who agreed with me that all people sin, but he had a more optimistic imagination than I do about his ability to defend himself before God. He thought that if he lived a life that was "good enough," God would forgive him. He had the idea that if his sins were not *so bad* or *so many,* then he could act virtuously enough that his sins would be outweighed or even erased. But that is not the picture presented in the Bible. You cannot simply "erase" past sins. The damage has been done. If you could erase them, there would be no justice in the universe.

You cannot save yourself from the guilt of your sin, but you do need to be saved. How can you be saved? You must begin by acknowledging that your sins require God's justice, and that he must exact that justice either from you or from some substitute who will pay on your behalf. The bad new is, if you try to pay the penalty, you will spend an eternity in hell doing it. Your only hope is to look to Christ and see what he has done by living a perfect life and dying on the cross to pay the penalty for the sins of all those who would ever repent and trust in him. By repenting and trusting in Christ, you will be counted among God's people.

While there is time, hope remains. Repent of your sins. Believe in Christ.

What do God's promises of restoration through Micah mean for us as citizens? War and diplomacy are hugely important, but neither statesmanship nor military victory will have the final say in this world, not even in Washington, D.C. Democracies and dictators will come and go on the stage of history. Assyria rose up, invaded other nations, and fell. So did Babylon. So did Greece. So did Rome. So did the Ottoman Empire. And we could go on. Through it all, God is working out his sovereign purposes. They will not be thwarted, and they will not revolve around any human government, whether America's or someone else's. God will exalt his people, a people belonging to every nation, tribe, and language.

God will exalt sinners only through Christ, because God's justice is satisfied only when Christ's righteousness is accounted to the sinner and when the sinner's unrighteousness is accounted to Christ. Only through Christ can we be received by God. Christ is the center of our hope!

If you are a Christian, you must also realize that the salvation of God's people was not only God's desire, it was his decision. He decided to *effect,* to *accomplish,* to *make certain* the salvation and restoration of his people. How else could we have a part in the heavenly city? We could not work our way *out* of our sin and *into* God's holy presence in a thousand years. But God has decreed it. It will happen. This is the foundation of our hope!

As individual congregations, our so-called fortunes may wax and wane. Our own church has seen good times and bad times in its 126-year history. We have experienced decades of growth and decades of decline. But no congregation's hope is finally tied to a building, a meeting, a pastor, or even other members of the congregation. A congregation's hope must be reserved for the God who saves. At any point, God may decide to scatter and disperse this or that congregation. He may allow the religious freedoms we presently enjoy in the West to erode so that we can no longer expound Scripture openly. Public meetings may become difficult. On the other hand, he may decide to grant this or that congregation so much growth that it has difficulty gathering in the same old building. But none of these matters—great or small—are determinative of our final restoration. Christ's work and God's will alone are determinative. Our hope, our certainty, our confidence as a church must rest in God, because God *will* gather and exalt his people.

In the book of Micah, we learn that God wants wrongs rebuked and his people restored.

GOD WANTS HIS CHARACTER TO BE KNOWN

God also wants his character to be known. If the basic message of Micah is that wrongs will be rebuked and that God's people will be restored, behind and above these two basic points is God's commitment to make himself known both through his judgment and through his mercy. This commitment is the foundation of all else that he does. Yet not only is the display of God's character the *foundation* of what he does, it is also the *crown jewel* that glistens most brightly.

Through the Acknowledgment of His Supremacy

First, God wants his character to be known through the acknowledgment of his supremacy:

In the last days

the mountain of the LORD's temple will be established
as chief among the mountains;

> it will be raised above the hills,
>   and peoples will stream to it.

Many nations will come and say,

> "Come, let us go up to the mountain of the LORD,
>   to the house of the God of Jacob.
> He will teach us his ways,
>   so that we may walk in his paths."
> The law will go out from Zion,
>   the word of the LORD from Jerusalem.
> He will judge between many peoples
>   and will settle disputes for strong nations far and wide.
> They will beat their swords into plowshares
>   and their spears into pruning hooks.
> Nation will not take up sword against nation,
>   nor will they train for war anymore.
> Every man will sit under his own vine
>   and under his own fig tree,
> and no one will make them afraid,
>   for the LORD Almighty has spoken.
> All the nations may walk
>   in the name of their gods;
> we will walk in the name of the LORD
>   our God for ever and ever.

"In that day," declares the LORD,

> "I will gather the lame;
>   I will assemble the exiles
>   and those I have brought to grief.
> I will make the lame a remnant,
>   those driven away a strong nation.
> The LORD will rule over them in Mount Zion
>   from that day and forever" (4:1-7).

God did not intend for the nation to be reassembled simply for the good of his own people but ultimately so that his supremacy would be acknowledged. He wanted his sovereign rule over the nations to be understood. He had delivered his people from Egypt in the Exodus, thus showing his supremacy over Egypt's gods; now he would deliver his people from Babylon, showing his supremacy over Babylon's gods. The famous picture of peace in these verses—nations beating their swords into plowshares (4:3)—will not come through a

League of Nations, a United Nations, or a Pax Americana. It will be established through God's own reign. On that day, there will be no more covetousness, robbery, war, or injustice of any kind; there will be no more fear. Justice and peace—separated ever since sin came into the world—will reign together.

If we return to chapter 3 for a moment, we recall the severity of God's promises of judgment. Chapter 3's last verse, in fact, reads, "Zion will be plowed like a field, Jerusalem will become a heap of rubble, the temple hill a mound overgrown with thickets" (3:12). Yet the beautiful imagery of chapter 4's opening words indicates a 180-degree turn: "In the last days the mountain of the LORD's temple will be established as chief among the mountains; it will be raised above the hills, and peoples will stream to it" (4:1). God ultimately plans to exalt this place as a reflection of his own greatness.

Why will the peoples stream to this place? Look at the next verse: "Many nations will come and say, 'Come, let us go up to the mountain of the LORD, to the house of the God of Jacob. He will teach us his ways, so that we may walk in his paths" (4:2a). People of all nations will turn to God. And, as a result, "The law will go out from Zion, the word of the LORD from Jerusalem" (4:2b). The Word of God, which had become scarce among God's people in Micah's day, would, in this day of redemption, become like a river of life going out from God's people to all of God's world! What a glorious vision and great hope: God reconciling the world to himself, and God ruling supreme over his world (cf. 7:16)!

God exalts his people as a means of exalting himself. We are not the ultimate end of his plans. Even the bride of Christ in the book of Revelation is glorious only insofar as she reflects the glory of the Son, the bridegroom. God's people are restored and exalted ultimately for the glory of God. With wrongs rebuked and his people restored, God assumes his obvious rule and reign.

Through the Remembrance of His Righteousness

Second, God wants his character to be known through the remembrance of his righteousness:

> Listen to what the LORD says:
>
>> "Stand up, plead your case before the mountains;
>>   let the hills hear what you have to say.
>> Hear, O mountains, the LORD's accusation;
>>   listen, you everlasting foundations of the earth.
>> For the LORD has a case against his people;
>>   he is lodging a charge against Israel.

"My people, what have I done to you?
　How have I burdened you? Answer me.
I brought you up out of Egypt
　and redeemed you from the land of slavery.
I sent Moses to lead you,
　also Aaron and Miriam.
My people, remember
　what Balak king of Moab counseled
　and what Balaam son of Beor answered.
Remember your journey from Shittim to Gilgal,
　that you may know the righteous acts of the LORD" (6:1-5).

In these verses, God recalls his blessings to Israel. He reminds them of his miraculous delivery from Pharaoh's power, his preservation of them through the wilderness, and his giving of the Promised Land.

God had acted righteously toward them, and he wanted them to remember his righteousness. By chastening and delivering his people, God called to their minds not only *their unrighteousness,* he demonstrated *his* utter and complete righteousness in his dealings with them. In fact, their wickedness made God's own *right*-ness stand out all the more, lest they be tempted to charge God with unrighteousness in a time of judgment. In no way could they say he had dealt harshly with them.

God is supreme; he wanted that to be known. And God is righteous; he wanted that to be known as well.

Through the Demonstration of His Mercy

But third, God is also merciful, and he wants that to be known. This is how the book of Micah concludes:

Who is a God like you,
　who pardons sin and forgives the transgression
　of the remnant of his inheritance?
You do not stay angry forever
　but delight to show mercy.
You will again have compassion on us;
　you will tread our sins underfoot
　and hurl all our iniquities into the depths of the sea.
You will be true to Jacob,
　and show mercy to Abraham,
　as you pledged on oath to our fathers
　in days long ago (7:18-20).

There is pardon for sins and forgiveness for transgressions! God's compassion will liberate us from the tyranny of our sins! In all of this, of course, God means to display his mercy, so that Micah can sing, "Who is a God like you." This is the Lord's final word through Micah to his people!

Notice also whose transgressions are forgiven: God "forgives the transgressions of the remnant of his inheritance." Not everyone is forgiven. Some people think that it is God's business to forgive. Forgiveness is God's job, they say. Not so, according to the Bible. Not even all Israel, God's visible "inheritance," will be forgiven. Only "the remnant of his inheritance" will be. The remnant consists of those who truly fear the Lord, who humble themselves before God alone, who repent of their sins, and who put their hope in God.

In fact, I wonder if you have ever considered the question of why God would forgive at all. In some ways, this is the most puzzling question we can ask. People sometimes puzzle over the "the problem of evil" and over why God allows sin. In my estimation, the more pressing question, once you have begun to understand more of God's goodness and justice, is why God would not immediately and ultimately punish all of us for our sins. Given that God hates sin as he does, why would God ever forgive?

To get to the answer to that question, we need to observe that Micah's prophecy of judgment ends with a consideration of what God is like: "Who is a God like you?" God ultimately forgives because of who God is. It is only because of his character—what he is really like, in and of himself—that we have any hope at all! In fact, Micah's name means "Who is like our God?"

So in verse 18, Micah poses the question, "Who is a God like you, who pardons sin and forgives the transgression of the remnant of his inheritance?" The implied answer to this rhetorical question, of course, is "no one!" If God does not forgive sins, then Micah is wasting his time. Why turn up and prophesy at all? For that matter, I am wasting my time, and so are you! Why sit here listening to all this stuff if you do not believe that you have sinned and that God just might forgive your sins? If God does not forgive the sins of his people, we're sunk! We've traveled beyond the region of hope.

But this is not the case. Verse 18 continues: "You do not stay angry forever." Micah knew that God would punish sin, but he also knew that God, out of love for his people, would pardon and forgive. Why? In no small part, he forgives because of what we learn about God at the conclusion of verse 18: God delights to show mercy! What a wonderful thing to know about God. He delights to show mercy!

Sometimes we are tempted to think of a holy God with his head turned away, his nose upturned, begrudgingly loving us, almost as if the atoning Son had outwitted the judgmental Father—you know, God *had* to accept us. But that is not the picture of God presented by the Bible, either in the New Testament or the Old. Our God is a God whose desire and joy is to show mercy.

What great news that is for us, friend, because you and I need mercy! God speaks honestly to us of our sins; he prophesies restoration so that he will be exalted; and he fulfills his prophecy by showing mercy to us.

Micah knew that God would answer his people's prayers for mercy: "You will again have compassion on us; you will tread our sins underfoot and hurl all our iniquities into the depths of the sea" (7:19). He knew God would deliver his people from bondage to sin as surely as he delivered the Israelites from their bondage to the Egyptians. "You will be true to Jacob, and show mercy to Abraham, as you pledged on oath to our fathers in days long ago" (7:20). God will be true to his word and merciful to his people.

God wants his character to be known. He wants his supreme, righteous, and merciful person to be recognized and adored.

CONCLUSION

So that's what God wants.

What do you want?

God wants wrong to be rebuked. Do you? Or are you more committed to holding onto your sin? Really, this describes all of us until we are saved.

God wants his people to be restored. Do you? Maybe this sounds a little better to you. You might be on board with the morality of the Bible. Morality is a good thing; you have always known that. But perhaps you have never thought much about God's people, and God's special concern for his people.

God wants his character to be known. Do you? Here's the real bull's-eye in this book. God acts so that his supreme sovereignty, his righteousness, and his mercy will be known. He acts to reveal himself. Honestly, do you care that much about God? Perhaps you think of religion more as guilt-induced fire insurance. Your conscience bothers you, and this is one way of playing it safe. Or maybe religion is a social thing. You like some of the people at church and some of the meetings. Or maybe religion provides your moral encouragement—helps keep you and the kids walking straight. But consider, does your religion have much to do with God? Is knowing him the center of your religion? Is learning to know him better the center of your life and ambition? If you are a Christian, it is:

> With what shall I come before the LORD
>   and bow down before the exalted God?
> Shall I come before him with burnt offerings,
>   with calves a year old?

Will the LORD be pleased with thousands of rams,
  with ten thousand rivers of oil?
Shall I offer my firstborn for my transgression,
  the fruit of my body for the sin of my soul?
He has showed you, O man, what is good.
  And what does the LORD require of you?
To act justly and to love mercy
  and to walk humbly with your God (6:6-8).

God does not want us to give sacrifices. Rather, he wants us to humble ourselves before him and submit to his authority. He also wants us to act justly and love mercy. By doing so, we will reflect to the world around us the God that we worship. Loving justice and mercy reflects God's own character. Choosing humility acknowledges and displays his supremacy.

If you have failed to do this, then you need to be forgiven by God. How can you be forgiven? Only through the Messiah (see 5:1-5a). We hear something about the Messiah in this famous prophecy of Micah's: "But you, Bethlehem Ephrathah, though you are small among the clans of Judah, out of you will come for me one who will be ruler over Israel, whose origins are from of old, from ancient times" (5:2). The deliverance of God's people would come from the least expected place. The word translated here as "small" is perhaps better translated as "trifling." The hope for God's people would not come from mighty Jerusalem but from trifling Bethlehem, a town of absolutely no national (let alone international) consequence except for the small detail that King David came from Bethlehem. Then again, God has always delighted in choosing what is obscure and unexpected in order to underscore *who* is making everything happen.

So who was this ruler of Israel coming from Bethlehem, "whose origins," we are additionally told, "are from of old, from ancient times"? Whatever else that phrase means, it is certainly never used about an individual person. The phrase is used to refer to our lot in life (Job 20:4). God has been his people's Redeemer from of old (Isa. 63:19; cf. v. 16). God's people have failed to listen to God from of old (Isa. 48:8). God's attributes of mercy, love, sovereignty, and truth are from of old (Ps. 25:6; 74:12; 78:2). But nowhere is an individual described as having "origins . . . from of old." Has Micah gone off his rocker? He just said the person is from Bethlehem, but he also said his origins are "from of old." What could that mean? It could only be referring to Jesus Christ, who *is* the eternal Son of God and who *was* born of the virgin Mary in Bethlehem.

This coming ruler will have a glorious ministry: "He will stand and shepherd his flock in the strength of the LORD, in the majesty of the name of the LORD his God. And they will live securely, for then his greatness will reach to the ends of the earth" (5:4). God intends for justice to be done in this world. Who alone can perfectly represent God and promise justice so lavishly? Jesus Christ alone will judge the world. His greatness will extend to the ends of the earth. He embodies both the sovereignty and the righteousness of God.

More than this, this one ruler "will *be* their peace" (5:5). In him the people's peace will be embodied. In him the people's peace will be accomplished. In him the people's peace will be secured. God's mercy is embodied in Jesus Christ. This one whose origin is from of old actually died on the cross as a sacrifice, taking God's wrath for the sins of all of us who turn from our sins and turn to God through Christ.

God's love for his people is amazing because of our faithless response to his perfect faithfulness to us. That is why it is beneficial to begin a meditation on God and what he wants by considering God's judgment of sin. A deeper understanding of God's judgment leads to a deeper understanding of his love and faithfulness. We could pick Micah apart and study only the encouraging-sounding promises. But if we did, we would never appreciate those promises for what they really are, and we might be tempted to take them for granted: "Well, of course God forgives. He's loving. He does good things. That's him." But place the promises of Micah in their right context—God's hatred of sin, and our saturation with it—and God's love is far less likely to seem a tired and assumed sentiment and far more likely to become an astounding basis for wonder. I don't care how many times you have heard about Jesus' death on the cross in church growing up. There is nothing to take for granted in his death and what it accomplished. If you are aware of your sin and what you deserve because of it, then you will be astounded by the love God has shown us by Christ's death on the cross. His death was a stunning display of the height, the depth, the length, and the breadth of God's love for those who have rejected him. How much God's love cost him makes its freeness to us all the more amazing!

You see what God is like. He will have wrong rebuked, his people restored, and his sovereign, righteous, merciful character displayed. The question for you is, then, do you love this God? Has this God captured your heart, soul, and spirit?

If you do love God, you are one of his people. You belong to the remnant. If you do not love God, you can love him, if only you will ask him to forgive your sins for Christ's sake, and then turn from your sins. Pray that he would give you a heart of love for him, so that you, too, will be one of his people, walking in justice, mercy, and humility. Pray that you would forgive others even while he forgives you. Pray that you would be willing to suffer his discipline in this world, while waiting—like Micah—in hope for the next. That is what God wants, for your good and for his glory.

Is that what you want?

Let us pray:

O God, our desires too often are fickle, turned regularly toward only ourselves, our own pleasures and comforts, our own conveniences. O God, in your mercy, we pray that you would distract us from ourselves and attract us to you by your own love and mercy. Teach us of your love for us through the Lord Jesus Christ. O Lord, deliver us from our sins. Seek us out in your love, we pray. In Jesus' name. Amen.

Questions for Reflection

1. What do you want out of religion? What's the most important thing religion offers?

2. From the standpoint of a sinful, self-ruling heart, what's the advantage of having an impersonal God rather than a personal God?

3. Why are the sins of a church's leaders so damaging?

4. This sermon argues that the heart of God's punishment upon his people—at least in this life—is cutting off communication with them. Why is this such an awful punishment? Why do we underestimate its severity? Would God punish a local congregation in this way? What would this look like?

5. Does the picture of judgment in Micah strike you as severe? Is it appropriate? Why or why not?

6. If God's judgment does seem severe, why does remembering what Christ did on the cross help us to understand that severity?

7. Why can God not simply "erase" or "overlook" our sins and remain holy and just?

8. According to this sermon, why (at the most foundational level) does God judge and give mercy? What is his reason for doing everything? Why is the answer to these questions good news for us?

9. Why is Christ's work on the cross the best display we have in all of Scripture of God's justice and mercy?

10. Is God at the center of your religion? Your church's religion?

THE MESSAGE OF NAHUM: WHO'S IN CHARGE?

34

THE MESSAGE OF NAHUM:
WHO'S IN CHARGE?

WHO'S IN CHARGE?[1]

Authority, it has been said, is like soap: the more you use it, the less you have of it. Holman Jenkins, writing in the *Wall Street Journal* a few years ago, observed,

> It's safe to say that many CEO's see what they do as little more than a variation on inglorious widget making. They enjoy the opportunity to be in charge, but most don't kid themselves about the exalting nature of the work. At the pinnacles of American business, they're treated literally like [donkeys], nose to the ground following a bunch of carrots laid out in a row, tied to the stock price. How many senior executives would give it all up for a bucket of warm spit? Probably more than you think.[2]

I am not a CEO, so I cannot speak to the accuracy of Jenkins' statement. Yet I do know the vicissitudes of life eventually lead all of us to recognize the illusion of our own control.

As I've mentioned before, a few years ago I was honored to attend the ceremony in the U.S. Capitol rotunda in which Billy Graham was presented with a congressional medal. In his remarks, Graham observed that all the people honored with statues in the rotunda and hallways had one thing in common: they were all dead.

Graham's point is a powerful one. The cemeteries in Washington, D.C., are filled with "indispensable people."

---

[1] This sermon was originally preached on November 9, 2003, at Capitol Hill Baptist Church in Washington, D.C.
[2] Holman W. Jenkins, Jr., "Optioning Out of the CEO Life—and Into Veephood," *The Wall Street Journal*, August 23, 2000, A23.

I wonder what circumstances of life remind you of how little you are in charge. Certainly it could be thoughts of your own mortality. But it could be other things too: haunting sins from your past, whose repercussions continue to outstretch your original expectations; uncertainty about the future; fear of other people; things you don't like about yourself; desires you cannot seem to control; the toll the years have taken on you; the uncertainty of how you will continue caring for that person as you should. So many circumstances; so little control.

INTRODUCING NAHUM

That was exactly the situation in which God's people found themselves in the middle of the seventh century B.C., when the prophet Nahum wrote his book. Nahum is one of the minor prophets, whose books comprise the last twelve books in the Old Testament. They are called "minor" not because they are unimportant, but because their books are short. We do not know anything about Nahum the man, except that he was an Elkoshite. Of course, we don't know where Elkosh was. Nahum is unusual among the prophets for writing a book: "An oracle concerning Nineveh. The book of the vision of Nahum the Elkoshite" (Nah. 1:1). Usually, the prophecies were verbally given and then written down. But Nahum seems to have been composed as a book.

To give you a quick overview, chapter 1 of Nahum begins with an introductory psalm on the character of God (1:2-8). In the rest of chapter 1 and the beginning of chapter 2 (1:9–2:2), Nahum moves back and forth between addressing God's people, Judah, and addressing the city of Nineveh, the capital of Assyria. Several verses into chapter 2, the prophet begins to speak to Nineveh at length (2:3–3:19), and it becomes clear what this vision is about: God's promise to destroy the Ninevites utterly as judgment for their sins.

As we look through the book of Nahum, we will look for the answer to the question, *who is in charge?*

ARE GOD'S PEOPLE IN CHARGE?

I guess the self-confident answer to the question of who is in charge would be, "We are! We as God's people are in charge." But is this what Nahum says? Let's begin by looking at the latter part of the first chapter and the beginning of the second chapter, where God addresses both Judah and Nineveh:

> The LORD is good,
>   a refuge in times of trouble.
> He cares for those who trust in him,
>   but with an overwhelming flood

he will make an end of [Nineveh];
   he will pursue his foes into darkness.

Whatever they plot against the LORD
   he will bring to an end;
     trouble will not come a second time.
They will be entangled among thorns
   and drunk from their wine;
     they will be consumed like dry stubble.
From you, [O Nineveh,] has one come forth
   who plots evil against the LORD
   and counsels wickedness.

This is what the LORD says:

"Although they have allies and are numerous,
   they will be cut off and pass away.
Although I have afflicted you, [O Judah,]
   I will afflict you no more.
Now I will break their yoke from your neck
   and tear your shackles away."

The LORD has given a command concerning you, [Nineveh]:
"You will have no descendants to bear your name.
I will destroy the carved images and cast idols
   that are in the temple of your gods.
I will prepare your grave,
   for you are vile."

Look, there on the mountains,
   the feet of one who brings good news,
   who proclaims peace!
Celebrate your festivals, O Judah,
   and fulfill your vows.
No more will the wicked invade you;
   they will be completely destroyed.

An attacker advances against you, [Nineveh].
   Guard the fortress,
   watch the road,
   brace yourselves,
   marshal all your strength!

> The LORD will restore the splendor of Jacob
>   like the splendor of Israel,
> though destroyers have laid them waste
>   and have ruined their vines (1:7–2:2).

According to this passage, the Old Testament people of God (and by implication, we, if we are Christians) clearly did not have control. No, they needed a refuge (1:7). They had been afflicted, their necks had been weighed down with yokes, and their arms and legs had been bound with shackles (1:12-13). Now, whether Nahum was literally referring to enslavement or metaphorically referring to the fact that Judah had to pay a crippling tribute to the king of Assyria, we cannot say. Many people in the northern kingdom of Israel *had* been carried into captivity—perhaps some in actual shackles—by the Assyrians decades earlier, before Nahum prophesied.

Assyria was the great power in that region of the world in the eighth and most of the seventh century B.C. The capital city of Nineveh—located on the east side of the Tigris in an area bordering what is today the city of Mosul, Iraq—was one of the grandest and most powerful cities on earth. Its size, power, and wealth inspired fables. Its walls were a good picture of this magnificence. At least two series of walls surrounded the whole city, running on for miles and miles. The inner wall, the higher of the two, was about one hundred feet high and broad enough for three chariots to race abreast. On the outside of the two sets of walls was a moat 150 feet wide and 60 feet deep. The Tigris and other smaller rivers surrounding Nineveh made the city appear impregnable. It was a gigantic city!

Jonah had preached in Nineveh perhaps a century earlier, leading the polytheistic Ninevites to repent. But that was the middle of the eighth century; it was now the middle of the seventh, and their repentance was a thing of the past. They destroyed the northern ten tribes of Israel and their capital, Samaria, in 722 B.C., probably just a few decades after their repentance in Jonah's day. Under Ashurbanipal, they pushed their conquests hundreds of miles into Egypt by 663, even reaching the city of Thebes (3:8), and Egypt fell to them.

Throughout these conquests all around them, Judah sat there in the mountains, watching. You realize, don't you, that the people of Judah were the "hillbillies" of their day? The waterfront folk—whether on coastlines or great inland waterways—are always the cosmopolitan and sophisticated ones. Think of the Phoenicians, the Greeks, the Assyrians, or the Babylonians, with their fertile valleys and coastlines. The people of Judah, on the other hand, lived up in the hills—Jerusalem is over 2,500 feet above sea level and without major rivers flowing into the sea. And they were regarded as backward. If they had showed up in a big cosmopolitan city like Washington, D.C., they would have looked awkward and culturally clumsy. Yet there they sat for years and decades, watching the tide of the Assyrian empire rise up and wash around them, threatening their cities as its power grew higher and higher.

In fact, much of Judah experienced more than Assyria's threats. We know from surviving Assyrian records that the Assyrians destroyed almost fifty cities of Judah, including Lachish, a southern city that guarded Jerusalem from the coastal plain along the Mediterranean.[3] Graphic pictures of Lachish's destruction survive to this day on Assyrian bas-reliefs, showing impaled men and dismembered bodies, victims of the Assyrian push into Judah's hills.

It was during this time, a time when the greatest power in the world was cutting Judah's limbs, torturously approaching its heart in Jerusalem, that Nahum prophesied. And it is right here that we find the book's enduring relevance for today: God's people could not have had *less* control of their dire circumstances than they did; but God continued to call them through his prophet and his Word to trust him as *much* as ever.

I don't know exactly how your life is going right now. Maybe things are going really well for you, and you are in one of the "fat and happy" periods of your life. If that describes you, you should stop and check yourself. Do you really think that you are in charge of your world? I would agree that you are in charge of every world that you *create!* You know what world I'm talking about: the one in your mind where you always say the right words, have the right things, know the right people, have the right health and appearance, and so on. If you are playing with any such delusions right now, allow me to be the one to inform you of some unwelcome news: that world that you are in charge of *does not exist*. It never has and it never will. Maybe you have been reading too much Tony Robbins. Maybe you have been experiencing a lot of "Personal Power" these days. Maybe you have been reading any of Robbins's numerous religious copycats, the ones who use Jesus Christ as one more way to teach positive thinking. But, friend, it is a lie. And if you are honest with yourself, you know that.

The book of Nahum presumes that people—especially God's people—will have a hard time of it in this world. If you are a Christian, perhaps you want to protest, "But I'm a King's kid!" Yes, you are a King's kid, living in a world that hates your Father and is in rebellion against his rule. If you really are his kid, hard times will come. Be assured of that.

Christian, realize that you claim to follow the One who allowed himself to be humiliated in this world. Who allowed himself to be born in a way that

---

[3] Cf. 2 Kings 18:13-17; 2 Chron. 32:9; Isa. 36:1-2.

might have led all the neighbors to think his birth was illegitimate. Who grew up in a poor family in the backward part of a backward nation. Who had no fixed address as an adult. Who endured the scorn of the nation's leaders. Who, after some briefly exciting but unstable popularity, experienced betrayal by his friends and then by the crowds. Who then allowed himself to be hounded, arrested, falsely accused, tried, whipped, beaten, stripped, and finally crucified to death, all to bear the sins of people like you and me—people who know ourselves to be in need. This is the One that we say we follow.

As Christians, we must realize that God is good and that he is our only hope. We cannot depend on ourselves, and we cannot depend on our circumstances. Sometimes we forget this and begin to put our hope in circumstances, other people, or ourselves because life is going well. God does bless us in many ways. Yet our hope must not finally be placed in any of these blessings but only in the sovereign God who gives them. He is our restorer and the Lord of the future. As Nahum says, "The LORD is good, a refuge in times of trouble. He cares for those who trust in him" (1:7).

I wonder what it means for you to trust God today. Nobody else can answer or figure that out for you fully. Reflect on this for just a moment. Today, have you yet considered that you are completely dependent on God? That your lungs have not drawn one breath nor your heart pounded out one beat apart from him? When you woke up this morning and put your feet on the ground, what did you do to acknowledge that you need God? Did you think to acknowledge him, or the fact that you would not have had last night's rest and this morning's life apart from his decision? Did you remind yourself of these things, or did a million other facts rush in on your mind? Have you meditated on your own neediness and God's faithfulness to you? Perhaps you could stop right now and reflect on some ways that you could teach yourself about your dependence on God.

In our churches, our corporate gatherings should be times where we regularly rehearse, through song and prayer, our dependence on God's love and Christ's righteousness. We *need* him to forgive our sins. We *need* him to lead us. We *need* him to provide for our needs. We *need* him to reveal more of himself to us so that we might know him better. So let the church's prayers and songs say as much. Our regular gatherings on the Lord's Day should remind us as individuals and as a people that we depend completely on him, and that he is the one who should be celebrated, thanked, and praised.

Who's in charge? So far, we know this much: it isn't us!

ARE THEIR ENEMIES IN CHARGE?

If self-confidence does not provide the right answer to the question of who is in charge, perhaps a more despairing outlook would help us find the answer. Are the enemies of God and of God's people in charge?

Most of Nahum's book is taken up with the enemies of God's people—and for good reason. These harassers were powerful and cruel. We know from extrabiblical sources that the mighty Assyrian king Ashurbanipal (ruled 668–629 B.C.) wanted no question left about whether *he* was in charge. On one occasion, he boastfully wrote down (or caused to be written down) how he dealt with plotters against his throne who had been discovered:

> "As for those common men who had spoken derogatory things against my god Asher and had plotted against me, the prince who reveres him, I tore out their tongues and abased them. As a posthumous offering I smashed the rest of the people alive by the very figures of protective deities between which they had smashed Sennacherib my grandfather. Their cut-up flesh, I fed to the dogs, swine, jackals, birds, vultures, to the birds of the sky, and to the fishes of the deep pools."[4]

I remember looking at bas-reliefs in the British Museum in London that clearly depict the brutality with which the Assyrians treated their opponents in battle. There were no internment camps. There were no Geneva Conventions of War with the Assyrians. No, these reliefs depict men impaled by spikes, piles of heads, and otherwise mutilated bodies. The Assyrians *were* what Joseph Stalin only aspired to be. When they conquered a city, they would completely depopulate it and then resettle it with people from various other places so that no trouble would ever come from that place again. That's what the Assyrians were famous for.

Yet God is not intimidated by any nation. No king has any power except for the power that God gives. And he deposes kings and kingdoms as quickly as he raises them up. Nahum's remarkable book, written in the face of such an awful and awesome earthly power, reminds these enemies of God who is and who is not in charge.

You may have noticed earlier, when we were looking at chapter 1, that the editors of the NIV translation have placed "Judah" (1:12) and "Nineveh" (1:8, 11, 14) in small brackets [which I have represented in this book with full-size brackets] whenever the words do not actually appear in the Hebrew text. They did this because it can be a little difficult to know whom the biblical author is

---

[4] Cited in Mike Butterworth, "Nahum," in D. A. Carson et al., consulting eds., *New Bible Commentary*, 4th ed. (Downers Grove, Ill.: Intervarsity Press, 1994), 834.

addressing when he just keeps saying "you," especially since Nahum switches back and forth in the first chapter. Nahum refers to Judah by name for the first time in 1:15, which is why you do not see the word in brackets there; and so with Nineveh in 2:8. Surely, the editors added these names for clarity's sake. Yet when you read the text knowing that those names were not originally present, you get a slightly better sense of the power its original readers would have felt. The text becomes a little confusing, but perhaps deliberately so. You see that someone is going to be blessed and someone is going to be cursed, but you are not entirely sure who receives what. You may have suspicions at this point, but surely the anticipation is building. It becomes clear when Nineveh is mentioned explicitly in chapter 2, verse 8. The suspense helps to make the prophecy more absorbing and, finally, powerful, but it comes to an end when we learn whom God has leveled his sights on and what awful destruction awaits them:

> The shields of his soldiers are red;
>> the warriors are clad in scarlet.
> The metal on the chariots flashes
>> on the day they are made ready;
>> the spears of pine are brandished.
> The chariots storm through the streets,
>> rushing back and forth through the squares.
> They look like flaming torches;
>> they dart about like lightning.
>
> He summons his picked troops,
>> yet they stumble on their way.
> They dash to the city wall;
>> the protective shield is put in place.
> The river gates are thrown open
>> and the palace collapses.
> It is decreed that [the city]
>> be exiled and carried away.
> Its slave girls moan like doves
>> and beat upon their breasts.
> Nineveh is like a pool,
>> and its water is draining away.
> "Stop! Stop!" they cry,
>> but no one turns back.
> Plunder the silver!
>> Plunder the gold!
> The supply is endless,
>> the wealth from all its treasures!

She is pillaged, plundered, stripped!
   Hearts melt, knees give way,
      bodies tremble, every face grows pale.

Where now is the lions' den,
   the place where they fed their young,
where the lion and lioness went,
   and the cubs, with nothing to fear?
The lion killed enough for his cubs
   and strangled the prey for his mate,
filling his lairs with the kill
   and his dens with the prey.

"I am against you,"
   declares the LORD Almighty.
"I will burn up your chariots in smoke,
   and the sword will devour your young lions.
   I will leave you no prey on the earth.
The voices of your messengers
   will no longer be heard" (2:3-13).

And then chapter 3:

Woe to the city of blood,
   full of lies,
full of plunder,
   never without victims!
The crack of whips,
   the clatter of wheels,
galloping horses
   and jolting chariots!
Charging cavalry,
   flashing swords
   and glittering spears!
Many casualties,
   piles of dead,
bodies without number,
   people stumbling over the corpses—
all because of the wanton lust of a harlot,
   alluring, the mistress of sorceries,
who enslaved nations by her prostitution
   and peoples by her witchcraft.

"I am against you," declares the LORD Almighty.
  "I will lift your skirts over your face.
I will show the nations your nakedness
  and the kingdoms your shame.
I will pelt you with filth,
  I will treat you with contempt
  and make you a spectacle.
All who see you will flee from you and say,
  'Nineveh is in ruins—who will mourn for her?'
  Where can I find anyone to comfort you?"

Are you better than Thebes,
  situated on the Nile,
  with water around her?
The river was her defense,
  the waters her wall.
Cush and Egypt were her boundless strength;
  Put and Libya were among her allies.
Yet she was taken captive
  and went into exile.
Her infants were dashed to pieces
  at the head of every street.
Lots were cast for her nobles,
  and all her great men were put in chains.
You too will become drunk;
  you will go into hiding
  and seek refuge from the enemy.

All your fortresses are like fig trees
  with their first ripe fruit;
when they are shaken,
  the figs fall into the mouth of the eater.
Look at your troops—
  they are all women!
The gates of your land
  are wide open to your enemies;
  fire has consumed their bars.

Draw water for the siege,
  strengthen your defenses!
Work the clay,
  tread the mortar,
  repair the brickwork!

There the fire will devour you;
    the sword will cut you down
    and, like grasshoppers, consume you.
Multiply like grasshoppers,
    multiply like locusts!
You have increased the number of your merchants
    till they are more than the stars of the sky,
but like locusts they strip the land
    and then fly away.
Your guards are like locusts,
    your officials like swarms of locusts
    that settle in the walls on a cold day—
but when the sun appears they fly away,
    and no one knows where.

O king of Assyria, your shepherds slumber;
    your nobles lie down to rest.
Your people are scattered on the mountains
    with no one to gather them.
Nothing can heal your wound;
    your injury is fatal.
Everyone who hears the news about you
    claps his hands at your fall,
for who has not felt
    your endless cruelty?

The point of the whole book of Nahum is made most explicit in the last verse of the second chapter, where the Almighty God says to the mighty Assyria, "I am against you" (2:13; also 3:5). More serious words cannot be imagined. God is not just saying that he will desert Assyria or separate from Assyria. He is promising to actively oppose them: *"I am against you!"*

Oh, friend, meditate on this phrase. Imagine what it would be like to have the Almighty God look at you and say, "I am against you."

In the book of Nahum, God notifies Assyria that its time has run out. His patience with its sinful ways has ended, and the self-imagined invincible empire will be defeated. So complete will be its defeat, the Lord says, that "you will have no descendants to bear your name. I will destroy the carved images and cast idols that are in the temple of your gods. I will prepare your grave, for you are vile" (1:14). The king (who represents the nation) and his descendants will be cut off; his line will not endure. Even the so-called gods Assyria worshiped will be destroyed. The king and his kingdom will be utterly destroyed. The king will be killed and laid in his grave.

Nahum uses different images to express the defeat that God will hand the Ninevites. Nineveh is like a powerful lion that once killed at its pleasure but will now be completely lost (2:11-12). Nineveh is like a harlot, an immoral seducer of the nations who allured and enslaved peoples (3:4) but who will now be exposed in her lewdness and made a spectacle (3:5-6). Nahum also reminds Assyria of its own victory over once-proud Thebes, the capital of the southern part of Egypt about four hundred miles south of modern Cairo (3:8-10). Ashurbanipal had destroyed Thebes in 663 B.C. Now, what they did in Thebes will be done to them. Whether the image is of a lion, a prostitute, or another great city, the Lord is clear that Nineveh will be exposed and destroyed.

Keep in mind, Nahum's prophecy would have been written in the fifty-year stretch between Thebes's fall in 663 and Nineveh's fall in 612. He wrote, in other words, when, from Judah's standpoint, Assyria was at the height of its power and the empire was intact. What could Nahum have been thinking! He was a prophet from a tiny nation speaking to the greatest empire in the world. How could something as large, powerful, and old as Nineveh simply be removed?

Several times in chapter 2, Nahum describes the Ninevites attempting to fight off an attack, but failing (for example, "He summons his picked troops, yet they stumble on their way," 2:5). Nahum does not provide a chronological account here so much as "a series of little cameos that conjure up the picture of Nineveh in its last days."[5] Notice his spare descriptions, almost like an impressionist's painting—"She is pillaged, plundered, stripped!" (2:10).

And this is exactly what happened. Nineveh's end was absolutely traumatic. The Medes, in an alliance with the Babylonians and the Scythians, laid siege to the city in 612 B.C. and then found themselves aided by rain and rising rivers. These rivers that had aided in the city's protection flooded up against the city's walls until great sections of the walls fell away, just as Nahum had predicted (2:6). The attackers then poured into the city and sacked it. Before the invaders could grab him, Assyria's king gathered himself and his household together in an immense funeral pyre and burned himself, his wives, and his concubines to ashes. The invaders, running rampant in the city, plundered Nineveh dry. When the site of ancient Nineveh was finally discovered and excavated in the nineteenth century, archeologists found no stores of silver and gold objects, as they were hoping they would. It was absolutely empty. Everything was taken—"stripped" bare (2:10). After pillaging the city, the invaders then

---

[5] Ibid., 837.

burned and razed it to the ground. Indeed, these first archeologists found unusually deep strata of ashes.

When Nineveh fell, it fell hard. A small group of Assyrian exiles tried to keep "Assyria" going for several years, but their attempt quickly failed. Nineveh passed with unusual speed from the very center of history to being entirely forgotten. Its location became lost to human memory and became a matter for speculation for over two thousand years. People knew the name "Nineveh" from the Bible and from Babylonian records, but they could not figure out where it was located. It was not until 1842 that archaeologists rediscovered it.

You may be enjoying some measure of power or success now (probably not as much as the Assyrians did!), but I hope you realize how fast and how far you can fall. The God of the book of Nahum is not only the God over his people; he executes justice against everyone who has sinned against him. In fact, the second verse of the book repeats three times that the Lord will take such vengeance: "The LORD *is a jealous and avenging* God; the LORD *takes vengeance* and is filled with wrath. The LORD *takes vengeance* on his foes and maintains his wrath against his enemies" (1:2). This is a warning for all of God's enemies to beware his judgment.

Now, if you happen to consider yourself an enemy of God, I must tell you on the basis of the book of Nahum, "Beware!" You cannot oppose God with impunity. You will never win. The collected power of the Assyrian nation and every other great power throughout the history of the world—throw in the United States, if you like—will not allow you to sin with impunity. Certainly your *own* power will not allow you to sin like that. God is committed to what is just, right, and good. That is his character. Therefore, he will judge every nation in history, and every individual in eternity. I thank God for the many ways our nation is different from the tyrannical empire of Assyria, but I shudder to consider any similarities that may exist. God will not be mocked. Might does not make right. No amount of military force or explosive power will ever make false ideas true or wrong actions right. Either we are right without our might, or we are not right at all. The United States and every other nation in the world needs to hear this repeatedly. *You* need to hear this repeatedly: *success does not hide sin from God's gaze.*

God's people would not finally be left in the power of God's enemies. Indeed, Jesus Christ deliberately put himself in the power of God's enemies so that his people would not be. Over six hundred years later, the apostle John recorded this account of Jesus' encounter with the Roman governor, Pontius Pilate. Pilate asked Jesus,

"What is it you have done?"

Jesus said, "My kingdom is not of this world. If it were, my servants would fight to prevent my arrest by the Jews. But now my kingdom is from another place."

"You are a king, then!" said Pilate.

Jesus answered, "You are right in saying I am a king. In fact, for this reason I was born, and for this I came into the world, to testify to the truth. Everyone on the side of truth listens to me."

"What is truth?" Pilate asked. With this he went out again to the Jews and said, "I find no basis for a charge against him. But it is your custom for me to release to you one prisoner at the time of the Passover. Do you want me to release 'the king of the Jews'?"

They shouted back, "No, not him! Give us Barabbas!" Now Barabbas had taken part in a rebellion.

Then Pilate took Jesus and had him flogged. The soldiers twisted together a crown of thorns and put it on his head. They clothed him in a purple robe and went up to him again and again, saying, "Hail, king of the Jews!" And they struck him in the face.

Once more Pilate came out and said to the Jews, "Look, I am bringing him out to you to let you know that I find no basis for a charge against him." When Jesus came out wearing the crown of thorns and the purple robe, Pilate said to them, "Here is the man!"

As soon as the chief priests and their officials saw him, they shouted, "Crucify! Crucify!"

But Pilate answered, "You take him and crucify him. As for me, I find no basis for a charge against him."

The Jews insisted, "We have a law, and according to that law he must die, because he claimed to be the Son of God."

When Pilate heard this, he was even more afraid, and he went back inside the palace. "Where do you come from?" he asked Jesus, but Jesus gave him no answer. "Do you refuse to speak to me?" Pilate said. "Don't you realize I have power either to free you or to crucify you?"

Jesus answered, "You would have no power over me if it were not given to you from above" (John 18:35b–19:11a).

God would not ultimately abandon or forget his people. Instead, Christ himself chose to submit to the power of his enemies in order to bear God's wrath for our sins, if we will only repent of those sins and trust in him.

My Christian friend, this is our hope! This is why, for as dark and chilling as Nahum's straightforward depictions of God's justice are, his book comforts and gives hope to God's people! Indeed, Nahum's very name means "comfort" or "consolation." Can you see why? God does not promise consolation for his enemies; God's promises are for God's people! The Lord will make an end of all those foes who wrongly and maliciously oppose us. In that sense, the book of Nahum functions in the Old Testament as the book of Revelation does in the New. When John wrote the book of Revelation, God's people were only a small remnant, feeling the weight of the greatest empire in the world, Rome. Yet John's vision assured the small group of struggling Christians that this great empire did not stand a chance against God. So too did Nahum encourage the people of Judah as they felt the encroaching weight of Assyria.

God's people should be encouraged. These empires don't stand a chance, because they are against God—and God is against them!

Thank God we can know that our trials will not last forever! You and I, Christian, will never meet one trial that will last longer than we will last. By God's grace we can face every difficulty that comes into our lives—we will out-last them!

Consider what this means for us as individuals and as churches. As long as this world endures, trials and difficulties will beset us individually and cor-porately. Trials from within and from without. But the church's hope will endure that long as well, and longer. Christ calls us to be of good cheer because he has overcome the world (John 16:33). As we engage in building a church, we engage in Christ's own work; and he will not let it fail. Remember, Jesus said that he has founded his church, and he *will* build it (Matt. 16:18). So, yes, trials will continue to face us while we are in this world, but *only* so long as we are in this world. If we are his, our hope will outlast our trials. It's true for us as individuals and as churches.

We never need to fear that God's enemies are finally in charge.

IS GOD IN CHARGE?

Okay, if we are not in charge, and if God's enemies are not in charge—even the ones who appear to be most powerful—then who is? Is God in charge?

Of course, that is the answer given by the book of Nahum and every other book in the Bible—God is in charge. Let's look now at Nahum's opening stanza:

> The LORD is a jealous and avenging God;
>> the LORD takes vengeance and is filled with wrath.
> The LORD takes vengeance on his foes
>> and maintains his wrath against his enemies.
> The LORD is slow to anger and great in power;
>> the LORD will not leave the guilty unpunished.
> His way is in the whirlwind and the storm,

and clouds are the dust of his feet.
He rebukes the sea and dries it up;
    he makes all the rivers run dry.
Bashan and Carmel wither
    and the blossoms of Lebanon fade.
The mountains quake before him
    and the hills melt away.
The earth trembles at his presence,
    the world and all who live in it.
Who can withstand his indignation?
    Who can endure his fierce anger?
His wrath is poured out like fire;
    the rocks are shattered before him.

The LORD is good,
    a refuge in times of trouble.
He cares for those who trust in him,
    but with an overwhelming flood
he will make an end of [Nineveh];
    he will pursue his foes into darkness (Nah. 1:2-8).

The implied answer to those two questions in verse 6—"Who can withstand his indignation? Who can endure his fierce anger?"—is "no one!" God is most powerful.

Aside from his power, we also learn something about his character: He is jealous. He does not want false gods to be worshiped, because he is the one and only true God. He is also patient. He is not quick to anger, Nahum tells us (1:3). This is how God has always revealed himself to his people, as he did to Moses on Mount Sinai (Ex. 34:6).

Yet God's patient and long-suffering nature should never be taken to indicate that he is indifferent, as if the fact that he has not yet punished someone means he never will. The one does not follow from the other! There is a world of difference between God's patience and supposed divine indifference. This all-powerful, jealous God has committed himself to the truth and to avenging himself. He will not leave the guilty unpunished (1:3). So Nahum let it be known that God would punish Nineveh. And so he did.

If you are a non-Christian, ask yourself, what would change in your life if you acknowledged, as the Bible teaches, that there is a God and that he is in charge? What would change in your life if you acknowledged, as the Bible teaches, that he is both completely good and morally pure and that you are not? If you acknowledged, as the Bible teaches, that you are in rebellion against him, no matter how "polite" your rebellion may look? Any doubt that you may still have concerning God's sovereignty, God's holiness, and your own sinfulness will one day be removed. I am certain about that.

As Samuel Johnson said to his biographer James Boswell, "Depend upon it, sir, when a man knows he is to be hanged in a fortnight it concentrates his mind wonderfully."[6]

Our end is coming, and we will give an account to God for our lives and our sins. This is an astounding prospect. I wonder if you can say "halt!" for a moment to the rush of thoughts in your head about what is going to happen in the next hour, the next day, or the next week and turn your thoughts to your state for all eternity. You will stand before God and give an account. No excuses will work, even if you make them. Not one excuse will be entertained. The judge before whom you will stand is omniscient, completely holy, determined, and always correct. And there will be no possibility either of appeal or, if convicted, of parole.

God will call the kings and the inhabitants of all nations—Assyria and Judah, Iraq and the United States—to account. And here is what's remarkable: *you* will outlast every nation! All nations will pass, but the Bible teaches that *you* will not end with *your death*. You stand eternally accountable to God. Now I ask, who can stand up under such searching scrutiny? Can you?

Christ perfectly submitted to his Father's will. Have you? Certainly not. Then what will you do about it? The answer is not simply "obey more." No, your current virtues will never hide your old vices. Your sins against God will forever stand because he is an eternal God. Your only answer must be to repent of your sins and trust in Christ, who died on the cross to pay for the sins of people like you and like me.

If you are a Christian, let me encourage you to work to better know and understand the jealousy of God. Given our own human experiences with jealousy, it is difficult to conceive of it apart from sin. But God is right to jealously require our exclusive worship of him, because he is the only true God. Can you imagine what it would say of God if he were indifferent to whether or not we worshiped lies? He is committed to himself, and desires us to be most committed to him, *for our good*. Our sympathies and affections should ultimately rest with God and with none who oppose him, even if you are the one opposing him.

In your own life, what rivals your allegiances to God? Who vies with God for your mind and heart's affections? He will brook no enemies. Consider care-

---

[6] James Boswell, *The Life of Johnson*, in R. W. Chapman, ed., *Oxford World Classics* (New York: Oxford University Press, 1998 ed.), 831.

fully who or what those rivals are, and pray about them. God will help you. He delights to save.

For you as a Christian, Nahum is a wonderful and encouraging book that should strengthen your confidence in God. He acts to protect his name and his people, even if it means taking on the most powerful nation on earth.

The Washington Post recently ran a story about the controversy among evangelicals over the limited-God view, the view that proposes that God does not know the future.[7] John Sanders, one of the biggest proponents of the limited-God view, is reported in the article as saying that he was motivated to adopt that view because of a personal tragedy in his life. Sanders reasoned that God must not know the future because, surely, God would never let something like *that* happen. Well, as a pastor, I have both known and witnessed tragedy. And I understand the impulse to react like Sanders when something terrible happens. But I must ask, is there really consolation in thinking that God is not in charge? Our church recently prayed for the Hmong people in Vietnam, whose government oppresses them terribly. Would the Hmong be consoled if you showed up and began preaching, "God is not in control!"

The great consolation the Bible gives us from beginning to end comes from the fact that there is a good and righteous God who is sovereign! And we get this not from a few proof texts that we pull out of their context. God is sovereign, and he is Lord of time and of history. That's what Nahum called the fearful inhabitants of Jerusalem to believe, while the mighty Assyrian empire brushed by, attacked, and wounded them. Nahum did *not* call Israel to believe that God always does what seems fair to humans; nor did he say that God lets life take its natural course, unable to promise us anything. No, Nahum assured the people of God that even when God allows fifty cities to be attacked and destroyed and the people to be tortured, he remains sovereign and will ultimately do what is most just, as mysterious and difficult as that may be to comprehend. That is our hope.

May we be people who trust in this God! May we never be the enemies of this sovereign God by siding with his enemies! May we not be people to whom God would ever look and say, "I am against you." What a fearful thing that would be!

But how can we avoid this? After all, we all sin, and all sin is opposition to God. Yes, but we can be forgiven of our sins through Christ by repenting of them and trusting in him. Once we belong to Christ, God treats us as he treats

---

[7] Bill Broadway, "Redefining Omniscience: Theologians Who Contend That God Doesn't Know the Future Face Fervent Criticism—and Expulsion from Evangelical Group," *The Washington Post,* November 8, 2003, B9, final edition.

his son. He is for us! As the apostle Paul said to the Christians in Rome, "If God is for us, who can be against us?" (Rom. 8:31). God no longer looks at us and says, "I am against you"; he says, "I am for you; who can be against you?" Our situation has changed entirely! This is what brings glory to God: undermining our rebellion and giving us new hearts marked by repentance and faith.

As our church continues to grow, I pray that we may remember that God is in charge. What have you thought causes churches to grow? The congregation's patience? Good leaders? Well-planned services? Culturally sensitive, age-appropriate evangelism? Paul had a different idea. As he said to the Christians in Corinth, "I planted the seed, Apollos watered it, but God made it grow. So neither he who plants nor he who waters is anything, but only God, who makes things grow" (1 Cor. 3:6-7). God makes things grow! You can take the same methodology and use it in two different churches, and God will sovereignly bless one and not the other. That's up to God! In that sense, my words to you as a preacher are more important than I am. It is the truth of the gospel that God uses.

How then should we look to the future as a church? With fear or foreboding? No, we look to the future with confidence, knowing that our sovereign and jealous God is good and will do what is right. In Christ, he has dealt with our past, and so he will assure our future.

Nahum asks toward the beginning of the book, "Who can withstand his indignation? Who can endure his fierce anger?" (1:6). Of course, the implied answer is "no one," because God alone is sovereign. God alone is in charge.

CONCLUSION

Only two of the minor prophets end their book with a question. In the book of Jonah, God concludes the book by remonstrating Jonah for his callousness toward the people of (of all places) Nineveh: "Should I not be concerned about that great city?" God asks (Jonah 4:11).

Now in the book of Nahum, Nahum concludes by telling the king of Assyria, "Everyone who hears the news about you claps his hands at your fall, for who has not felt your endless cruelty?" By concluding his book with a question, it is almost as if the prophet wants to draw the reader's mind back to Jonah's prophecy from a century earlier and the mercies that God had shown the people of Nineveh. Eventually, Nineveh decided to spurn God's mercies and choose violent materialism, gross selfishness, idolatry, and witchcraft. They had repented of their repentance.

So Nineveh, once the object of God's mercy, became the object of God's wrath. In the final chapter, Nahum promises that Nineveh would be drunk (Nah. 3:11). By that he meant that the city would be required to drink the cup of God's wrath to the bitter dregs (cf. Isa. 51:17, 22; Jer. 25:15). And sure enough, the city fell.

Christ drank that same cup of God's wrath for us, his people. When he prayed in the Garden of Gethsemane, "May this cup be taken from me. Yet not as I will, but as you will" (Matt. 26:39), this is the cup he meant—the cup of suffering God's wrath for our sins. Christ had committed no sins for which to drink of the cup. Yet he drank it for your sins and mine, if we would repent and turn to him!

In the New Testament, God's judgment fell most sharply not on any city, but on Jesus Christ. But when God's judgment fell on the Son, the Son defeated his enemies and ours. Through his death on the cross, Christ "canceled the written code, with its regulations, that was against us and that stood opposed to us; he took it away, nailing it to the cross. And having disarmed the powers and authorities, he made a public spectacle of them, triumphing over them by the cross" (Col. 2:14-15).

The final battle will not consist of the fall of any mere city; it will consist of the ultimate judgment of God's enemies and the establishment of God's reign over God's own people. And we can be confident that this will happen. Why? Because God is in charge.

Let us pray:

O God, we admit that our hearts and minds are full of false imaginings. We imagine that we are in charge, and we imagine that you are wrong. Forgive us for our sins—of believing lies, of trusting ourselves, of not trusting you. Give us the gifts of repentance and faith in Christ for your glory. Amen.

Questions for Reflection

1. Do most people think they have control over their lives? Why is that an illusion?

2. If you are a Christian, how much control over your life do you exercise now versus when you were unsaved? Where does the illusion of control most afflict you today?

3. How is the book of Nahum, which promised Judah that God would judge their powerful enemies, relevant for today?

4. Why should Christians expect to experience trouble and hardship in this life? Is this what you expect over the next decade of your life? How can you prepare for it?

5. Where in your life are you most tempted to think that God's enemies are in charge (work, school, government, home, etc.)? How then does Nahum's promise—"God is in charge!"—translate into your experience? In other words, were you to take this message to heart, how would God's promise to judge his enemies cause you to bear yourself differently toward those in your life who oppose God?

6. What would it *feel like* to stand before the throne of Almighty God and hear him say, "I am against you"?

7. Which will last longest? i) your nation; ii) your place of work; iii) the Christians in your church? How does your life reflect or fail to reflect your answer to this question?

8. Why could Jesus so calmly reply to Pontius Pilate's questions?

9. As we have seen, the book of Nahum promises a dark and chilling judgment for the enemies of God, which in turn acts as a deep consolation for the people of God, who will be persecuted in this world. What does a church rob its people of, and what does a father rob his home of, when they fail to teach about the judgment of God?

10. Why is God's jealousy both righteous *and* life-giving for humans?

11. Do most people regard themselves as enemies of God? Do most enemies of God regard themselves as enemies of God? Are you an enemy of God? What is the only hope an enemy of God has for escaping God's judgment?

THE MESSAGE OF HABAKKUK: HOW CAN I BE HAPPY?

How Can I Be Happy?

Introducing Habakkuk

How Can I Be Happy When It Seems That God Doesn't Care?

For the Non-Christian
For the Christian
For the Church

How Can I Be Happy When God's Care Is So Strange?

For the Non-Christian
For the Nation
For the Christian
For the Church

How Can I Be Happy Under Any Circumstances?

For the Non-Christian
For the Church
For the Christian

35

THE MESSAGE OF HABAKKUK: HOW CAN I BE HAPPY?

HOW CAN I BE HAPPY?[1]

Someone has keenly asked, "If ignorance is bliss, why aren't more people happy?"

All people want to be happy. "Happiness . . . is the motive of every action of every man, even those who hang themselves," Blaise Pascal said.[2]

Clearly we look for happiness in different ways, as Pascal's comment also suggests. Some people try to find happiness by losing themselves in serving others. Others try to find happiness by losing weight. Others lose themselves in introspection and psychotherapy, believing that a new pattern of thinking will put them on the road to happiness.

The publisher's blurb on the back cover of one book on happiness raves about the book, "With a truly holistic approach that synthesizes the best of the many schools of thought" this author "offers new hope—and new life."[3] That's quite a claim. New life? And for only $11.20 on Amazon.com?

The back cover of another book on happiness that has been out for years promises to teach you how to "Learn to change the emotional bad habits that make you unhappy." More specifically, you will learn to

- Recognize Your Own Emotional Bad Habits (and start to break them)
- Throw Off Your Security Blanket (and accept that you can have happiness)
- Talk Tenderly to Yourself (and increase self-esteem) . . .

---

[1] This sermon was originally preached on November 16, 2003, at Capitol Hill Baptist Church in Washington, D.C.
[2] Blaise Pascal, *Pensées,* trans. W. F. Trotter (New York: E. P. Dutton, 1958), 113.
[3] See Richard O'Connor, *Undoing Depression: What Therapy Doesn't Teach You and Medication Can't Give You* (New York: Berkley, 1999).

- Get Rid of the Imposter Phenomenon (and stop devaluing yourself)
- Accept Praise (and cease being your own worst critic).[4]

Of course, most people today do not reach for a book when they want to increase their happiness. Maybe they reach for the prescription, or the remote, or the credit card, or a new job, or a new bottle, or a new relationship. Several years ago in an interview, Laura Huxley, widow of author Aldous Huxley, observed, "Mail-order shopping is exactly like the Hindu hell—samsara— where there is only proliferating desire and sorrow. We are hypnotized into believing that two TV sets will make us twice as happy as one TV set."[5]

But no amount of new television sets, different friends, or better habits will finally deliver happiness to us. These things may mute our concerns, distract us from our emptiness, or even give us a temporary substitute. But they will not provide the kind of permanent, basic, abiding, lasting joy that we *crave*— that we were *made for.*

INTRODUCING HABAKKUK

How can I be happy? That is the eternal question that we turn to in our study of Habakkuk, the next Minor Prophet in this present series. The Minor Prophets are not called "minor" because they are unimportant, but because they are brief. We know even less about Habakkuk than we know about Nahum, whom we considered in our last study. At least we knew the name of the town Nahum was from, even though we don't know where that town was. With Habakkuk, we don't even know that much. Habakkuk's name appears in the book (1:1), but otherwise the man is unknown to us. His book is composed of three brief chapters.

As we consider this book together, we want to pursue the question of happiness, about which Habakkuk speaks with unusual clarity. Specifically, we will follow him through three questions.

HOW CAN I BE HAPPY WHEN IT SEEMS THAT GOD DOESN'T CARE?

At the beginning of his oracle, Habakkuk writes,

The oracle that Habakkuk the prophet received.

How long, O LORD, must I call for help,
but you do not listen?

---

[4] See Penelope Russianoff, *When Am I Going to Be Happy: How to Break the Emotional Bad Habits That Make You Miserable* (New York: Bantam, 1988).
[5] Laura Huxley, interview by Ian Thompson, *The Independent Magazine* (London), April 30, 1994, 36.

Or cry out to you, "Violence!"
  but you do not save?
Why do you make me look at injustice?
  Why do you tolerate wrong?
Destruction and violence are before me;
  there is strife, and conflict abounds.
Therefore the law is paralyzed,
  and justice never prevails.
The wicked hem in the righteous,
  so that justice is perverted (Hab. 1:1-4).

God then replies to Habakkuk's plea:

"Look at the nations and watch—
  and be utterly amazed.
For I am going to do something in your days
  that you would not believe,
  even if you were told.
I am raising up the Babylonians,
  that ruthless and impetuous people,
who sweep across the whole earth
  to seize dwelling places not their own.
They are a feared and dreaded people;
  they are a law to themselves
  and promote their own honor.
Their horses are swifter than leopards,
  fiercer than wolves at dusk.
Their cavalry gallops headlong;
  their horsemen come from afar.
They fly like a vulture swooping to devour;
  they all come bent on violence.
Their hordes advance like a desert wind
  and gather prisoners like sand.
They deride kings
  and scoff at rulers.
They laugh at all fortified cities;
  they build earthen ramps and capture them.
Then they sweep past like the wind and go on—
  guilty men, whose own strength is their god" (1:5-11).

In this passage, Habakkuk essentially asks God, "How can I be happy when it seems that you don't care?" That's the gist of the first four verses where

Habakkuk wonders—complains, really—why God would tolerate so much injustice among his own people. "Why do you tolerate wrong?" (1:3).

Habakkuk had taken a few correct facts and drawn some faulty conclusions from those facts. We often do the same.

God answered Habakkuk by telling him that he does not, in fact, tolerate wrong; he would execute justice against the wrongdoing in the nation of Judah. Yet a surprise came attached with God's reply: God would punish Judah through the Chaldeans (or "Babylonians," as the NIV synonymously has it). And the Lord knew that his words would be big news for Habakkuk: "be utterly amazed. For I am going to do something in your days that you would not believe" (1:5). (The apostle Paul used this verse against the Jews in a synagogue for ignoring God's Word through unbelief while the Gentiles listen to it—Acts 13:41.) And Habakkuk *was* amazed, as we will see momentarily. After all, he probably prophesied in the late seventh century B.C., perhaps between 620 and 610, right around the time Babylon would have eclipsed Assyria as one of the world's greatest powers. And the Babylonians were hardly models of moral virtue and justice. Yet God would use them as his ministers of justice, however surprising that might sound. Babylon would be employed to punish the wrongs of God's own people. Habakkuk did not need to be baffled any longer about why God had left the injustices of his own people unpunished. Punishment would come.

Which is exactly what happened. A decade or so later, Babylon conquered Judah and carried many of its people into exile.

For the Non-Christian

We will consider Habakkuk's response to this surprising news in a moment, but let's first consider what God's promise to judge means for us. If you are not a Christian and are not used to reading the Bible, I wonder if you feel any sympathy for why this ancient prophet was dissatisfied in the first place and why he asked God why he had allowed so much injustice to exist in the land. Habakkuk does not simply say, "Oh well, that's the way the world is." There is no worldly-wise or world-weary cynicism. No, he expects something better! He expects something different!

But what about you? Do you adopt a cynical attitude when things don't go well? Have the difficulties and travails of this world and your own life caused you to conclude, "If there is a God, I'm sure he doesn't care." If so, learn from this ancient oracle that God does care, and he will judge sin. God will look at the wrongful threats, the violent acts, the unjust ambitions, and all destruction and strife, even the destruction that has escaped legal remedy, and he will punish. He will punish all the wrongs that others have done against you, all the wrongs that you have witnessed or heard about, all the wrongs that you have committed. The Bible says that God is perfectly holy and righteous, and he will punish every sin. In that sense, every correct temporal punishment of sin enacted among humans reflects the justice of God himself. Humans can reflect it, but we cannot exhaust it.

Those of us who are Christians know the answer to Habakkuk's charge against God, "Why do you tolerate wrong?" God does not tolerate wrong! He never has. Instead, he waited for the appointed time to send his Son, Jesus Christ. God came himself in Christ and showed his commitment to justice and holiness in ways far more profound than this prophet's vexed soul yet understood. Christ suffered and died on the cross because God was adamant about *not* tolerating wrong, adamant that justice would *not* be perverted, and adamant that the wicked would *not* finally prevail over the righteous (see Rom. 3:21-26). God finally did not even tolerate sin and death's hold on Christ.

For the Christian

Do you see what this should mean for you as a Christian? There is so much rich material for meditation here that I barely know where to start. We have a lot to learn from what the NIV editors subtitled "Habakkuk's Complaint" (1:2-4). Yet Habakkuk was doing more than complaining; he was honestly praying to God over these complex and grief-causing matters, which makes him a good model for us. We often don't pray. And for as brief and pointed as Habakkuk's prayers were, they demonstrate great faith in God's sovereignty. Habakkuk not only assumed that God could do something about the injustice in Judah; he assumed that it was occurring only because God allowed it. Habakkuk also assumed that Judah's injustice and wrongs were inconsistent with God's character, because God's character is good, right, and constructive, not destructive.

In short, Habakkuk is puzzled exactly because he knows and believes that God is both powerful and good. His prayer is not merely an example of cosmic whining that somehow made it into the Bible; it is an enquiring prayer of a believer in anguish who knows he can approach this good and sovereign God with honesty. Surely, Habakkuk's fully informed, heart-engaging prayer puts to shame many of our small and self-focused "bless my toe" or "help my report to go well" prayers. I'm not saying we shouldn't pray about toes and reports, I'm simply noticing that Habakkuk's prayers were taken up with much more. He looked out at what was happening to other people, and then he prayed with heart.

I am also struck by how Habakkuk was able to assume what he did about

God. Somehow, Habakkuk knew a lot about God and God's law. Maybe he was in Jerusalem at the same time as Jeremiah and had heard Jeremiah's preaching. Perhaps he had read the prophecies of Jonah, Micah, or Isaiah. Maybe he had had a chance to take a look at Nahum's book. Certainly he would have known the first five books of the Bible—the Law. He would have known David's psalms, having heard them at the temple. In all of these different parts of God's Word, Habakkuk would have learned about who God is and what God is like.

Friend, how do you and I hope to grow as Christians if we do not study God's Word in order to learn the same?

These opening verses of Habakkuk also challenge us to trust God. When Habakkuk prayed, God answered him and answered him well. The fact that God answered assured Habakkuk that God was not ignoring him. The fact that God answered as he did assured Habakkuk that God did not approve of wrong. God was not finally going to allow his law to be thwarted and his justice to be subverted. The God of all the earth would do right (see Gen. 18:25) and could be trusted. We too can see that God should be trusted.

If you are anything like me, you are probably accustomed to God working in your life in certain ways, and as long as he continues to work in those ways you find it relatively easy to trust him. But the moment the normal operating procedures change (maybe answering your prayers differently; maybe allowing you to go through a surprising set of circumstances), you find yourself getting a little nervous or even upset. Maybe you start complaining. Yet you and I must learn from Habakkuk's experience, from Job's trials, from Paul's thorn in the flesh, that God often uses various means to accomplish his purposes so that you and I do not mistake the means for God himself. He does not want us to ever mistake the good that we know for the one who gives the good.

Many of us will have bad thoughts about God, but then we do not go to the trouble of seriously reflecting on those thoughts and why we had them. Instead, we allow them to dominate our opinion about God as they pass through our heads unhindered. Such thoughts might even escape our mouths, when what we should do is capture them, examine them, and ask whether they hold up in a biblical light: "My heart is saying *this* about God. Why do I think that? Is it true? What does the Bible say?" Submit your thoughts about God to Scripture, pray about them, and perhaps seek counsel from Christians you trust. The mid-twentieth-century pastor Martyn Lloyd-Jones put this question to the Christian: "Have you realized that most of your unhappiness in life is due to the fact that you are listening to yourself instead of talking to yourself?"[6] We must not sim-

---

[6] Martyn Lloyd-Jones, *Spiritual Depression* (1965; repr., Grand Rapids, Mich.: Eerdmans, 2000), 20.

ply take every passing impulse for granted as true, we must instead learn to "talk Bible" to ourselves—in particular, what the Bible says about God. Then we will discover far more of the happiness and joy for which we were made.

For the Church

This opening interchange between Habakkuk and God is also relevant for our lives together in congregations. Our churches should be communities that display trust in God. They should be living pictures of people who know what it's like to pray Habakkuk's prayer *and* to receive God's answer—that he does care and that he will act. And our lives together should indicate our belief in God's answer. If the world is characterized by disbelief in God and his promises, we should be characterized and marked off by our believing God and actually taking him at his word. This is what it means to be God's people.

When this kind of trust in God is displayed not just in isolated instances of this or that "virtuous" person but by a whole community of people, then we see things emerge that we could never see otherwise. God is glorified when you or I learn to give our money to him; but when we do that together, the church is able to employ people to do the work of ministry full-time for the good of the congregation. More money can also be given for doing good outside of the church's own walls! This is possible because a community of faithful people is united together in its vision and in its understanding of God and his will.

A congregation also displays its trust in God by the way the members trust, love, forgive, and serve one another. Community forms as people begin to understand that others will care for them, will pray for them, will not gossip, will work for their best, will bring meals when needed, and will help in any number of ways—not so much because of long friendships but because all acknowledge the lordship of Christ. An agreement, a growing history of experience, and a lengthening list of loving services come to characterize the church and produce a happy community that loves God and one another for his glory. We can do so much more to display God's character in the church than we can ever do alone.

God will not tolerate wrong, and so he taught Habakkuk that he could be trusted. God is faithful. We can rely upon him.

HOW CAN I BE HAPPY WHEN GOD'S CARE IS SO STRANGE?

But we need to return to the shock that Habakkuk felt when God told him *how* he would address Judah's unfaithfulness. The methods God said he would use to answer Judah's sin were so unexpected and difficult to conceive of that God's answer left Habakkuk almost more troubled than when he began the prayer.

So if the first question was, "How can I be happy when God doesn't seem to care?" the answer provokes Habakkuk to ask a follow-up question, sort of like a not-quite-satisfied soldier who says to his commanding officer, "Permission to speak freely, sir." Essentially, Habakkuk then asks, "How can I be happy when God's care is so strange?" After all, God says he will sort out injustice; but then he chooses the most unjust people—the Babylonians—to do it! How does this make sense? Or, in Habakkuk's own words,

> O LORD, are you not from everlasting?
>   My God, my Holy One, we will not die.
> O LORD, you have appointed them to execute judgment;
>   O Rock, you have ordained them to punish.
> Your eyes are too pure to look on evil;
>   you cannot tolerate wrong.
> Why then do you tolerate the treacherous?
>   Why are you silent while the wicked
>   swallow up those more righteous than themselves?
> You have made men like fish in the sea,
>   like sea creatures that have no ruler.
> The wicked foe pulls all of them up with hooks,
>   he catches them in his net,
> he gathers them up in his dragnet;
>   and so he rejoices and is glad.
> Therefore he sacrifices to his net
>   and burns incense to his dragnet,
> for by his net he lives in luxury
>   and enjoys the choicest food.
> Is he to keep on emptying his net,
>   destroying nations without mercy?
>
> I will stand at my watch
>   and station myself on the ramparts;
> I will look to see what he will say to me,
>   and what answer I am to give to this complaint (1:12–2:1).

Really, Habakkuk's reply to God's words in chapter 1 can be boiled down to this: "The Babylonians?! The Babylonians?!"

Once again, God shows himself to be gracious by responding to Habakkuk:

Then the LORD replied:

"Write down the revelation
    and make it plain on tablets
    so that a herald may run with it.
For the revelation awaits an appointed time;
    it speaks of the end
    and will not prove false.
Though it linger, wait for it;
    it will certainly come and will not delay.

"See, he is puffed up;
    his desires are not upright—
    but the righteous will live by his faith—
indeed, wine betrays him;
    he is arrogant and never at rest.
Because he is as greedy as the grave
    and like death is never satisfied,
he gathers to himself all the nations
    and takes captive all the peoples.

"Will not all of them taunt him with ridicule and scorn, saying,

"'Woe to him who piles up stolen goods
    and makes himself wealthy by extortion!
    How long must this go on?'
Will not your debtors suddenly arise?
    Will they not wake up and make you tremble?
    Then you will become their victim.
Because you have plundered many nations,
    the peoples who are left will plunder you.
For you have shed man's blood;
    you have destroyed lands and cities and everyone in them.

"Woe to him who builds his realm by unjust gain
    to set his nest on high,
    to escape the clutches of ruin!
You have plotted the ruin of many peoples,
    shaming your own house and forfeiting your life.
The stones of the wall will cry out,
    and the beams of the woodwork will echo it.

"Woe to him who builds a city with bloodshed
    and establishes a town by crime!

Has not the LORD Almighty determined
   that the people's labor is only fuel for the fire,
   that the nations exhaust themselves for nothing?
For the earth will be filled with the knowledge of the glory of the LORD,
   as the waters cover the sea.

"Woe to him who gives drink to his neighbors,
   pouring it from the wineskin till they are drunk,
   so that he can gaze on their naked bodies.
You will be filled with shame instead of glory.
   Now it is your turn! Drink and be exposed!
The cup from the LORD's right hand is coming around to you,
   and disgrace will cover your glory.
The violence you have done to Lebanon will overwhelm you,
   and your destruction of animals will terrify you.
For you have shed man's blood;
   you have destroyed lands and cities and everyone in them.

"Of what value is an idol, since a man has carved it?
   Or an image that teaches lies?
For he who makes it trusts in his own creation;
   he makes idols that cannot speak.
Woe to him who says to wood, 'Come to life!'
   Or to lifeless stone, 'Wake up!'
Can it give guidance?
   It is covered with gold and silver;
   there is no breath in it.
But the LORD is in his holy temple;
   let all the earth be silent before him" (2:2-20).

If we were to summarize the entire conversation so far, it would sound something like this: Habakkuk begins the book by saying, "God, why don't you care about all the wrong your people are doing? Why won't you do something about it?"

As we have seen, God responds, "I do care, and I will do something! I'm going to send the Babylonians."

To which Habakkuk replies, "The Babylonians? They live more wickedly than your people!" It is during this reply that Habakkuk makes his famous assertion about God's holiness: "Your eyes are too pure to look on evil; you cannot tolerate wrong" (1:13). Why would God, who is holy, use such vicious instruments as the Babylonians if he can scarcely look at them?

God's final response, which we just read, is essentially this: "I know what the Babylonians are like. And after I have used them to judge my people, I will judge them too."

Yet God also told Habakkuk that his judgment would come on his own timetable, not Habakkuk's or anyone else's (2:3). Through turbulent times, the righteous would live by their faith (2:4). God's people would hear God's promise and, as with all of God's promises, believe it and live accordingly. This was the verse that Paul famously used in his letters to the Romans and the Galatians to argue that people are made right with God not through meritorious works but by believing God's promises, just like Abram in Genesis 15 (Gen. 15:6; Rom 1:17; Gal. 3:11). The author of Hebrews also used this verse—"the righteous will live by his faith" (Hab. 2:4; cf. Heb. 10:38)—to demonstrate that a justified person lives by faith.

God then described Babylon in sad but all too common terms: they were drunken, arrogant, restless, greedy, and dissatisfied. In other words, God's judgment of Babylon had already begun in that he had given the nation over to its sin. So it is with all unbelievers. We can see the first traces of their coming judgment in the sins to which they have already been given over.

Once God had used Babylon to judge his people, Babylon itself would fall. The plunderer would be plundered (2:8). The stones of the walls built through thievery would cry out against them (2:11). The Babylonians would discover that their violence ultimately accomplished nothing (2:12-13).

In contrast to the passing fruit of Babylon's criminal labors would be the eternal fruits of God's labors. Perhaps you noticed that midway through the chapter God pulled Habakkuk back and pointed him to what ultimately lies ahead: "For the earth will be filled with the knowledge of the glory of the LORD, as the waters cover the sea" (2:14). What a glorious hope this is amid all the talk of judgment! How reassuring for God's people! The brief, almost parenthetical remark put their struggles back in perspective and provokes the question for *us:* what worries do we presently struggle with? If you are a Christian, you can be assured that within a few decades or even a few years all your worries will have been proven demonstrably unfounded, either because Christ will have returned or because God will have otherwise resolved whatever is causing you to worry. God *will* show himself to be perfectly good and sovereign beyond dispute.

Following this parenthetical moment of assurance, God continued to discuss Babylon's destruction. He said that the destroyer would be destroyed (2:17), and the idol-makers would find themselves without God or wisdom (2:18-19). And what a contrast that is to all who know the Lord: "But the LORD is in his holy temple; let all the earth be silent before him" (2:20). The glory of Babylon's idols was man-made, fruitless, and false. But the glory of the Lord is his own, and it is real. It induces a silence among his people. The silence commanded here is, I think, more than mere silence, even if those of us in quieter churches like to use this verse with people who attend louder churches! Really, God is pointing to something more like reverence, and the silence is a silence of expectancy. The God of Israel is not like the mute idols in the preceding verses; Israel's God speaks! He is for real. So close your mouth and open your ears, because the real God will speak through his Word.

For the Non-Christian

If you are not used to reading or studying the Bible, let me simply ask you, what are you spending your life doing? You're spending it on something. Does your life sound a bit like the Babylonians? A little theft here? Some unjust gain there? Perhaps a touch of violence or debauchery? The occasional using of people for your own ends? Trusting the work of your own hands rather than God's? You can be certain that God sovereignly uses everyone, like these Babylonians. But in the end, you do not want to be among those who oppose Christ and his Church, but among those who become part of it.

For the Nation

I pray that our nation realizes that there is a sovereign God, greater than our military or any terrorist network, who will rule his world for his own ends. And just as the Babylonians would be foolish to feel pride in response to their victory over Judah, so our nation should never feel a boastful pride in response to any military victory. Power should always be used with great humility. God had his eye on the Babylonians' injustices. So does he on every nation.

For the Christian

As Christians, we learn from the latter half of chapter 1 and chapter 2 that God uses surprising means to accomplish his ends. Who would have guessed that he would use the Babylonians to judge and deliver his own people from injustice? What would you say to a human being who devised such a strategy? But then again, what would you say to a person who told you that God would establish his kingdom through a crucified and risen Messiah who was God himself? Our God certainly moves in mysterious ways. We must be silent before him and listen in order to learn what he tells us about himself—because, chances are, you and I are not going to guess it otherwise. That's what God is like.

God's use of the Babylonians also warns us against becoming complacent amid life's successes. God may, for a time, grant an individual, a group, or a nation a degree of worldly success for his own purpose, but then he may judge the very one to whom he grants success. God can use anyone, from Balaam the for-hire prophet, to Balaam's donkey, to hypocritical preachers (cf. Phil. 1:15f.). He has used such preachers in my life; and if you have spent very many years in churches, my guess is that he has used them in your life as well. Now, does that lessen the seriousness of the hypocrite's sin? No, God will judge his sin. Yet God is so sovereign that he can use the wrath of men to bring himself praise (see Ps. 76:10, ESV). In the case of hypocritical preaching, he takes what was offered with wrong motives and still uses it to edify the saints and build up the church, not to the praise of the sinful human instrument but to the praise of the Sovereign God. Friend, God may use you—even greatly—but that by itself does not mean that you trust in him for your salvation. Our only hope for salvation is to live by faith (Hab. 2:4).

Consider for a moment the nature of such saving faith. Sometimes people pray a prayer and mentally assent to the idea that Jesus is their Savior, thinking that this is what the Bible means when it talks about faith. Yet the faith described in Habakkuk is more than that. Yes, we mentally assent to the proposition that we have all sinned and that we can never justify ourselves before God by our own righteousness. We also mentally assent to the proposition that God is perfectly holy—"too pure to look on evil" (1:13)—and that our only hope for standing before God is to have the righteousness of Christ applied to our accounts. But we must do more than mentally assent to these propositions. We must *trust* them. We must *turn away* from our previous way of life that was ruled by sin and we must *follow* Christ.

In other words, true faith shows itself in trusting God and in living by this faith. Notice again that Habakkuk says "the righteous *will live* by his faith" (2:4). True Christian faith will show itself in our lives, which will be marked by repentance for sin. This point cannot be stressed enough, particularly among evangelicals who enjoy proclaiming God's grace (as we should). It is easy to convince ourselves that we have embraced God's grace simply because we have mentally assented to a set of propositions. Yet many who think they believe the truth have not really been subjects of God's saving grace.

One way to know whether you have experienced God's saving grace is to look at your own life. Do you see a track record of conviction for sin and repentance? Repentance, you know, involves more than feeling bad. It means turning away from the sin about which you feel bad. William Arnot insightfully put it like this: "The difference between an unconverted and a converted man is not that the one has sins and the other has none; but that the one takes part with his cherished sins against a dreaded God, and the other takes part with a reconciled God against his hated sins."[7] Do you see the difference? The non-Christian might feel bad about a sin, but ultimately he takes his sin's side against God and continues in it. The Christian, on the other hand, feels bad and then takes God's side against his own sin by waging war against it.

So what do you struggle with today? Have you been struggling with immorality, with sex outside of marriage, with behaving in an ungodly manner toward your family, with impatience at work, with being eaten up by worldly ambitions? What, then, is the difference between you and a child of the world? If you are a Christian, *by faith* you are living. That is, your faith (your trust, your hope) is prompting you to take action against your sin. You experience the Spirit's work of conviction in your life and you respond to that conviction by working against your sin. And when your spouse, your parent, or your friend assists in that work of sanctification by admonishing you, you are not resentful; indeed, you are thankful, because you want to be more like Christ. You want to know Christ's presence and pleasure in your life.

Do not believe the world's lies about sin being the way to happiness. It is not! Preaching on the topic of marriage from Genesis 1 and 2 in our church several years ago, Albert Mohler observed, "We act as if happiness produces fidelity, faithfulness, when it is really the fidelity that produces the happiness."[8] Your task, then, is to identify the ways in which you have believed the world's lies about the path to happiness, and then oppose those lies with all your might. God really does care about the way you live. It seems unlikely he would have sent his Son to die on the cross if he didn't. In your struggle, let other people help you. Or do you care more about your pride than your holiness?

For the Church

For our churches, this passage should encourage us to be marked by characteristics opposite to those that marked the Babylonians. They were marked by theft; our churches should be marked by generosity and giving. They were marked by selfishness and injustice; our churches should be marked by honesty, straight-dealing, and a concern for righteousness. They were marked by violence and crime; our churches should be marked by mutual care. They were marked by debauchery and exploitation, using others for their own pleasure; our churches should be marked by mutual encouragement and the building up

---

[7] William Arnot, *Laws from Heaven for Life on Earth* (London: T. Nelson & Sons, 1884), 311.

[8] Albert Mohler, "Naked and Not Ashamed: The Mystery of Marriage" (sermon, Capitol Hill Baptist Church, Washington, D.C., November 11, 2001).

of one another. They were marked by idolatry; our churches should be marked by worship of the one true God as taught by his Word.

The need for the church to be different from the world is why the context in which Habakkuk 2:20 has been placed is so interesting. In the midst of promising the destruction of Babylon, God says, "But the LORD is in his holy temple; let all the earth be silent before him." As a child, I probably memorized this verse before I ever memorized John 3:16. I grew up as a Southern Baptist in rural Kentucky, and this verse was engraved above every entrance to the main hall at our church: "Let all the earth be silent before him." That's a challenging verse for a six-year-old! In its context, as I have said, the Lord is contrasting an expectant silence that should mark his people with a pointless gaze at speechless idols who have no wisdom to give. They're not alive! The point for our churches, then, is not to have very, very quiet services, but to gather together expecting to hear from God and his Word. The Spirit of the living God will take his Word, speak truth into our lives, change us, and build us up individually and as a congregation for our own good and his glory. To that end, our services should be structured around the exposition of God's Word.

Can you imagine a whole community of people living in expectation of God's Word and God's faithfulness to his promises? Consider the implications for our congregations' lives. Our churches would increasingly become communities marked by confidence, hope, optimism, and joy, because we know that God is committed to turning even our most "Babylonian" circumstances to good! As congregations, what can shake our confidence? As congregations, what can disappoint us? As congregations, what should discourage us and steal our joy? Nothing! We will never face any circumstances that will successfully oppose God from building his church—no antireligious laws, no staff difficulties, no ornery members, no external controversies will ever derail God's good plans for his children. As Paul said to the Romans,

> If God is for us, who can be against us? He who did not spare his own Son, but gave him up for us all—how will he not also, along with him, graciously give us all things? Who will bring any charge against those whom God has chosen? It is God who justifies. Who is he that condemns? Christ Jesus, who died—more than that, who was raised to life—is at the right hand of God and is also interceding for us. Who shall separate us from the love of Christ? Shall trouble or hardship or persecution or famine or nakedness or danger or sword? . . . No, in all these things we are more than conquerors through him who loved us. For I am convinced that neither death nor life, neither angels nor demons, neither the present nor the future, nor any powers, neither height nor depth, nor anything

else in all creation, will be able to separate us from the love of God that is in Christ Jesus our Lord (Rom. 8:31b-35, 37-39).

Such trust, such expectancy, should dominate our minds and hopes as we gather together as God's people.

Every once in a while, I have opportunity to share the words of Richard Sibbes, the Puritan pastor I spent four years studying when I lived in England. Sibbes grasped as well as anyone the kind of comfort, strength, and hope that we should have in Christ: "Oh, the sweet life of a Christian that hath made his peace with God! He is fit for all conditions: for life, for death, for everything."

Therefore, Sibbes said, "what is the reason that there is not anything in the world but it is comfortable to a Christian?" Sibbes answered that because "We are not hurt till our souls be hurt" . . . "Nothing can be very ill with us, when all is well within."

Continuing from Sibbes: "God will have it so, for the comfort of Christians, that every day they live they may think . . . my best is to come, that every day they rise, they may think, I am nearer heaven one day than I was before, I am nearer death, and therefore nearer to Christ. What a solace is this to a gracious heart! A Christian is a happy man in his life, but happier in his death, because then he goes to Christ; but happiest of all in heaven, for then he is with Christ. How contrary to a carnal man, that lives according to the sway of his own base lusts! He is miserable in his life, more miserable in his death, but most miserable of all after death."

"What is the reason that there is not anything in the world but it is comfortable to a Christian? When he thinks of God, he thinks of him as a Father of comfort; when he thinks of the Holy Ghost, he thinks of him as a Spirit of comfort; when he thinks of angels, he thinks of them as his attendants; when he thinks of heaven, he thinks of it as of his inheritance; he thinks of saints as a communion whereof he is partaker. Whence is all this? By Christ, who hath made God our Father, the Holy Ghost our comforter, who hath made angels ours, saints ours, heaven ours, earth ours, devils ours, death ours, all ours, in issue. . . . What can terrify a soul? not death itself, when it sees itself in Christ triumphing. . . . A Christian that sees himself sitting at the right hand of God with Christ, triumphing with him, he is discouraged at nothing; for faith makes things to come present, it sees him conquering already. Let us be exhorted to joy. 'Rejoice, and again I say rejoice.'"

"Comfort is nothing else but reasons stronger than the evil which doth afflict us; when the reasons are more forcible to ease the mind than the grievance is to trouble it."

"No trouble can be very troublesome."

"What can be grievous in this world to him that hath heaven in his eye?"[9]

I could keep going and going. The hope that we have in Christ is incredible. As a Christian, you have no reason to be finally discouraged. You will outlast every trouble that you ever face. You can be confident of that! My Christian brother or sister, you and I are members of the new society that God is building, and we are to be a moving picture that displays the truth of what we preach. We are a people who have found happiness in God and in trusting him.

HOW CAN I BE HAPPY UNDER ANY CIRCUMSTANCES?

After his dialogue with God in chapters 1–2, Habakkuk turns in chapter 3 to help us answer one more question: How can I be happy under any circumstances?

And his answer is simple: only in God.

Chapter 3 is Habakkuk's prayer to God, and it basically breaks into three parts: Verses 1-2 recount Habakkuk's prayer to God for mercy. Verses 3-15, the largest part of the chapter, describe Habakkuk's vision of God. Then verses 16-19 present Habakkuk's wonderful proclamation of his joy in God.

The chapter begins, "A prayer of Habakkuk the prophet. . . . LORD, I have heard of your fame; I stand in awe of your deeds, O LORD. Renew them in our day, in our time make them known; in wrath remember mercy" (3:1-2).

Habakkuk has come a long way since his initial complaint-prayer in chapter 1. Habakkuk now knows for certain that God cares about injustice and will address it, so much so that he prays, "in wrath remember mercy" (3:2).

Then, in the vision that occupies the bulk of this chapter, Habakkuk describes God doing exactly what Habakkuk had prayed for him to do—coming! And when he comes, all of creation reacts in humble submission:

God came from Teman,
the Holy One from Mount Paran.
His glory covered the heavens
and his praise filled the earth.
His splendor was like the sunrise;
rays flashed from his hand,
where his power was hidden.
Plague went before him;
pestilence followed his steps.
He stood, and shook the earth;
he looked, and made the nations tremble.

---

[9] The quotes are from various writings of Richard Sibbes. For more on comfort in Sibbes's writings, see his well-known books *The Bruised Reed and the Smoking Flax* and *The Soul's Conflict With Itself*, both of which can be found in volume 1 of *The Works of Richard Sibbes*, Alexander Grosart, ed. (Carlisle, Pa.: Banner of Truth, 1982). *Bruised Reed* has also been published separately by Banner of Truth (1998).

The ancient mountains crumbled
  and the age-old hills collapsed.
  His ways are eternal.
I saw the tents of Cushan in distress,
  the dwellings of Midian in anguish.

Were you angry with the rivers, O LORD?
  Was your wrath against the streams?
Did you rage against the sea
  when you rode with your horses
  and your victorious chariots?
You uncovered your bow,
  you called for many arrows.

You split the earth with rivers;
  the mountains saw you and writhed.
Torrents of water swept by;
  the deep roared
  and lifted its waves on high.

Sun and moon stood still in the heavens
  at the glint of your flying arrows,
  at the lightning of your flashing spear.
In wrath you strode through the earth
  and in anger you threshed the nations.
You came out to deliver your people,
  to save your anointed one.
You crushed the leader of the land of wickedness,
  you stripped him from head to foot.
With his own spear you pierced his head
  when his warriors stormed out to scatter us,
gloating as though about to devour
  the wretched who were in hiding.
You trampled the sea with your horses,
  churning the great waters (3:3-15).

How does Habakkuk respond to God's coming? The book concludes with these marvelous verses as Habakkuk confesses that his joy is in God alone:

I heard and my heart pounded,
  my lips quivered at the sound;
decay crept into my bones,
  and my legs trembled.

Yet I will wait patiently for the day of calamity
    to come on the nation invading us.
Though the fig tree does not bud
    and there are no grapes on the vines,
though the olive crop fails
    and the fields produce no food,
though there are no sheep in the pen
    and no cattle in the stalls,
yet I will rejoice in the LORD,
    I will be joyful in God my Savior.

The Sovereign LORD is my strength;
    he makes my feet like the feet of a deer,
    he enables me to go on the heights (3:16-19a).

For the Non-Christian

If you are not a Christian, ask yourself this question: "Can I be happy under any circumstances, or is there some set of circumstances that is so important in my life that I cannot be happy without them?" Friend, once you have answered that question, you will have found your god.

Jonathan Edwards, a famous minister in the 1700s, was fired by his congregation because of a theological disagreement. When the church council announced to Edwards that he had lost his job, one person watching Edwards described him by saying, "That faithful witness received the shock, unshaken. I never saw the least symptoms of displeasure in his countenance the whole week but he appeared like a man of God, whose happiness was out of the reach of his enemies."[10]

Where is your happiness? Is it held hostage by certain circumstances? I promise, you will never find the joy and happiness evidenced by Edwards apart from trusting in Christ. You were made to know God. That's why you are alive. Yet you have rebelled against God. Every time you have done something wrong, you have said to God, "I want to run my life my way, rather than your way." That's what sin is. God could rightly condemn us all for our sin. Instead, he came in Jesus Christ, lived a perfect life, and died on the cross as a substitute, bearing God's just wrath for the sins of all of those who would ever turn from their sins and trust in him. Christ was then raised from the dead, show-

---

[10] Recorded in the journal of David Hall, a member of the council. Cited in Iain H. Murray, *Jonathan Edwards: A New Biography* (Carlisle, Pa.: Banner of Truth, 1987), 327.

ing that God accepted his sacrifice. Once he has forgiven us, God leads us into the new life that he promises.

God calls all of us now to repent of our sins and to trust in Christ.

What would it look like for you to make this radical change in your life? What would it require of you to decide that Christ is worth more than the sins that you have been coddling? I have to say quite honestly, it would require you to turn your back on some of the "happiness" you presently enjoy. In one of his parables, Jesus describes people who are spiritually choked by life's worries, riches, and pleasures (Luke 8:14). In other words, there are some pleasures that will choke you. Did you know that? Did you know that some pleasures will choke you? Did you know that having sex outside of marriage is a sin? Or that getting drunk is a sin? So are stealing at the office and lying. I mention these particular sins because they must be some of the most common sins in the city of Washington, D.C., and maybe in most cities. Like all sin, they might be pleasurable for a season, but spiritually, Jesus says, they will choke you. They will cut off your life. I wonder if you have been choking on some of your pleasures, wondering what's been going wrong.

Not only can you be choked by a pleasure, you can be enslaved by a pleasure. The apostle Paul said to Titus, "at one time, we too were foolish, disobedient, deceived and enslaved by all kinds of passions and pleasures" (Titus 3:3). The world will never tell you that pleasures can be enslaving. It isn't in the world's interest to let this get out. But it is true. There are "happinesses" that take away the liberty to know and love God and others and to enjoy an even greater happiness. James warned his readers about such selfish desires and pleasures (James 4:1-3). So did Peter (2 Pet. 2:13-14).

Christ can free you from the pleasures that are confusing in this life and confounding in the next; the pleasures that are passing and wrong. He can lead you to pleasures everlasting—the pleasure of knowing him, for which you were made. And he can lead you to joy as the natural fruit of his Spirit living in you (see Gal. 5:22). If that is the happiness you are looking for, find your sins and be merciless with them by repenting of them and trusting in Christ's death on the cross.

For the Church

We should also think about what chapter 3 means for our churches. For one thing, it means that to find happiness and joy, we must not go down false paths marked by carnally exciting styles of worship, self-focused services, and busy program-packed church schedules. For the sake of the members' joy, churches should lead their members carefully, thoughtfully, and reflectively into God's presence in corporate worship. For the sake of the members' joy, churches should provide serious, God-centered teaching, because only God-centered teaching is weighty enough to deal with the seriousness of life and the situations that Christians find themselves in. For the sake of the members' joy, churches should keep their schedules bare enough for the members to worship God throughout the week in their family lives and in building relationships with non-Christian neighbors, friends, and colleagues.

A congregation must give itself to cultivating a community that presents God as great, and that cultivates in us the same things that Habakkuk exemplifies: an eager anticipation combined with patience (Hab. 3:16)—what an unusual combination!—as well as a growing knowledge of God that yields satisfaction and joy in him (3:17-19).

How can we cultivate a community that finds its joy in God? First, churches must make the exposition of God's Word central in their times together. Knowledge *of* God is what fed Habakkuk's longing *for* God. God is so lovely that the more we know him, the more we will want to know him. Second, we Christians should practice sharing, in our personal conversations with one another, testimonies of how God has been faithful to us. How much do you use your conversation at church to edify others? Finally, churches should encourage their members to read good books, especially biographies of Christians who gave their all and found God faithful—people like Amy Carmichael, William Carey, George Whitefield, Jim Elliot, Adoniram Judson, and so many others. May God make our churches increasingly happy communities as we observe and model for one another and the world how satisfying God is!

For the Christian

What does Habakkuk 3 teach us as individual Christians? Again, several things. To begin with, we should ask ourselves whether perhaps we are disciples only because our life circumstances have been nice so far. What would we do if Christ asked us to take up our cross by repenting of a certain sin or by following him down a difficult path? Would you follow him then? Would you be willing to forgo a job opportunity? Would you forgo some particular pleasure because it's sinful and because you know that more joy can be found in Christ? That is the question Habakkuk poses to you and me.

Many of the sins that tempt Christians (and others) are sins that bear a dim echo of where real joy is found. For example, pornography portrays a crude shadow of the intimacy of relating to another person. Premarital sex provides a projection of the joy found in a marriage relationship, but that joy is thin and ripped out of context. It only tears down, and uses the other person selfishly, without commitment. These sins and others point to the fact that real joy is found in real relationships, but relationships as God meant them to be, and ultimately in a relationship with God himself. He made us personal, spiritual beings with a good craving for relationships, but a craving that will be fulfilled finally and especially in our relationship with him.

It's interesting that Habakkuk expresses his great contentment in God at the end of chapter 3, after he has been considering God, praying to God, meditating on God, and then observing this vision of God's coming. You and I should also learn more of God if we want to be happy and content. Just consider his promises for us in Christ! Our God is honest. Our God is just. Our God is faithful to the covenant he has made. This is the God we are called to love.

Habakkuk, through his honest questioning, learned that what he most wanted was this God. As Augustine said at the beginning of his autobiography, *Confessions,* "You move us to delight in praising You; for You have formed us for Yourself, and our hearts are restless till they find their rest in You" (*Confessions,* I.i.).

I love the New England hymn that presents Jesus Christ as the fruitful apple tree:

> The tree of life my soul hath seen,
> Laden with fruit, and always green;
> The trees of nature fruitless be
> Compared with Christ the apple tree.
>
> His beauty doth all things excel;
> By faith I know, but ne'er can tell
> The glory which I now can see
> In Jesus Christ the apple tree.
>
> For happiness I long have sought,
> And pleasure dearly I have bought;
> I missed of all; but now I see
> 'Tis found in Christ the apple tree.
>
> I'm weary with my former toil,
> Here I will sit and rest awhile;
> Under the shadow I will be,
> Of Jesus Christ the apple tree.
>
> This fruit doth make my soul to thrive.
> It keeps my dying faith alive;

Which makes my soul in haste to be
With Jesus Christ the apple tree.[11]

Have you been seeking happiness long and buying pleasure dearly—expensively to yourself and others? Start staking your life on God by obeying him, and watch your heart grow in affection for him as he shows himself to be faithful. So the three Hebrew exiles, Shadrach, Meshach, and Abednego, had their hearts so taken by God that they would not give up their faith in God even for physical survival (Daniel 3). So the Christians in the New Testament prayed for Christ's return with joyful anticipation and longing, as typified by Paul's life: "If only for this life we have hope in Christ, we are to be pitied more than all men" (1 Cor. 15:19). If your version of Christianity makes sense even if there is nothing after the grave, then you have gotten hold of a false product. The Christianity of the Scriptures does not necessarily lead to a better life on this side of the grave. Yet we believe in eternal realities and we live for them for Christ.

So it is that we Christians are happy under any circumstances in this world! Even with all our resources entirely spent, says Habakkuk, we have God, and he is our strength and our hope.

Let us pray:

O God, we confess that our hearts are distracted and divided. Concentrate our hearts' love on you. Build our hope. Invigorate our lives with trust in you. For your name's sake, we ask it through Jesus. Amen.

Questions for Reflection

1. What would you say is the key to happiness? Explain.

2. Is Habakkuk honest with God regarding his grievances? Does his honesty cause him to become irreverent? How can we be both honest and reverent in our prayers? How do you do this?

3. Does God use the evil purposes of others to accomplish good ends? Does this cause him to become tainted with evil?

4. As we have seen, Habakkuk did not submit to cynicism but approached God in prayer. Are there areas in your life in which you have submitted to cynicism

---

[11] From *Divine Hymns or Spiritual Songs*, compiled by Joshua Smith, 1784.

and failed to submit yourself to the promises of God and the hope that you can have? Why would we choose cynicism over hope in God?

5. Do you give serious reflection to your thoughts about God, or do you simply go with your first impulses? How do you monitor, measure, and correct those first impulses?

6. How do earthly blessing and success lead to spiritual complacency? Should earthly blessing be regarded as a sign of God's favor? Explain.

7. In your own words, can you characterize the nature of biblical faith? How is it different from mere mental assent? How can we distinguish one from the other in a person's life? In our own life?

8. Do Christians sin? If your answer is "yes," what distinguishes a Christian from a non-Christian?

9. *Why* and *how* can churches do more than individual Christians to display the glory of God and God's character?

10. What circumstances do you require in order to be happy?

11. What pleasures that you presently "enjoy" are actually enslaving you? Choking you? How can you break free of their grip? (Hint: the answer is *not* simply an assertion of your own will and personal discipline.)

12. What might a church that cultivates its joy in worldly things look like? What might a church that cultivates its joy in God look like?

13. In this sermon, the statement was made, "If your version of Christianity makes sense even if there is nothing after the grave, then you have gotten hold of a false product." Do you agree? Explain.

THE MESSAGE OF ZEPHANIAH: WHAT'S THERE TO BE THANKFUL FOR?

36

THE MESSAGE OF ZEPHANIAH: WHAT'S THERE TO BE THANKFUL FOR?

WHAT'S THERE TO BE THANKFUL FOR?[1]

The history of Thanksgiving in the United States is an interesting one. Its roots trace back to the common Christian custom of having special days set aside to praise God for his great blessings. In New England, this Christian custom meshed with the English custom of a harvest day celebration. After the European settlers arrived in Plymouth Colony (now Massachusetts) in 1621 and enjoyed their first harvest following many difficulties, they gave a special feast of thanks. They also invited the local Americans, the Wampanoags. Over the next 150 years, the colonies frequently held such thanksgiving days after the harvest had come in.

In 1782, the Continental Congress decreed,

> It being the indispensable duty of all nations, not only to offer up their supplications to Almighty God, the giver of all good, for his gracious assistance in a time of distress, but also in a solemn and public manner to give him praise for his goodness in general, and especially for great and signal interpositions of his Providence in their behalf: therefore the United States in Congress assembled . . . do hereby recommend . . . the observation of . . . a day of solemn thanksgiving to God for all his mercies; and they do further recommend to all ranks, to testify to their gratitude to God for his goodness, by a cheerful obedience to his laws, and by protecting, each in his station, and by his influence, the practice of true and undefiled religion, which is the great foundation of public prosperity and national happiness.

[1] This sermon was originally preached on November 23, 2003, at Capitol Hill Baptist Church in Washington, D.C.

The first national observance of Thanksgiving by presidential proclamation—still our practice today—occurred in November 1789 at the recommendation of President Washington and the U.S. Congress. No regular national celebration of the day occurred in the early 1800s, though increasing numbers of states set such a day in the fall.

As tension in the nation over slavery grew and the country moved toward civil war, the poet and editor Sarah Hale began lobbying tirelessly for a nationally recognized Thanksgiving holiday. But it was not until the height of the Civil War in 1863 that President Lincoln proclaimed the last Thursday in November a national day of Thanksgiving. Presidential proclamations from the 1870s until the 1930s did the same.

In 1939, President Roosevelt, trying to help the economy by lengthening the Christmas shopping season, proclaimed the third Thursday in November as a national holiday for Thanksgiving. He did this again in 1940 and 1941 against a good amount of popular controversy over when the country should thank God. Congress then took up the matter and passed a joint resolution in 1941 calling for a compromise. They decreed that Thanksgiving should fall not on the third, nor necessarily the last, but the fourth Thursday of November. Ever since, every president has proclaimed Thanksgiving on the fourth Thursday of November.

Amid current events, many Americans may wonder what the nation should be thankful for. The ongoing attacks by insurgents in Iraq upon U.S. troops and Iraqi citizens themselves bring distressing news each day. The Islamic terrorist organization Al-Qaeda continues to conduct bombings in many countries, and no doubt many Americans will approach their Thanksgiving tables feeling less safe than we have on Thanksgivings past.

In addition to these kinds of worries, some will approach the meal of Thanksgiving with more personal worries. Some have worries about money. Others have troubles in their family. And some—maybe you—have questions about God.

"Is God really in control? Would the world be like it is if he were?"

"Why doesn't he help me?"

"Is he fair?"

"Will God ever forgive me?"

"Does he really care about what's going on in the world?"

Some Christians may come to Thanksgiving wondering if their best days are behind them, or if God has anything good left for them for which they will be able to give thanks next Thanksgiving. Or maybe the Thanksgiving after that.

INTRODUCING ZEPHANIAH

To help us figure out what we have to be thankful for, we turn to the next book in our series on the Minor Prophets of the Old Testament, the book of Zephaniah. Zephaniah is not called a "minor" prophet because he was unimportant, but because his book is short compared to the "major" prophets. We know more about the man Zephaniah than we do about most of the minor prophets, particularly from the first verse: "The word of the LORD that came to Zephaniah son of Cushi, the son of Gedaliah, the son of Amariah, the son of Hezekiah, during the reign of Josiah son of Amon king of Judah" (1:1). Zephaniah's father, grandfather, great-grandfather, and even great-great-grandfather are listed. Why would they all be listed? Well, to show who his great-great-grandfather was—the great king Hezekiah from the previous century. If your great-great grandfather was Thomas Jefferson, you would probably mention that fact if you were called on to address the entire American nation. Zephaniah did not descend through the royal line of Manasseh, Hezekiah's evil son, but through one of Hezekiah's younger sons. There's no way anyone could accuse Zephaniah of not being loyal, of not being a Hebrew of Hebrews, even as he said the difficult things that he would say in this book.

We also know from the first verse that Zephaniah prophesied during the reign of King Josiah, who reigned from 639 to 609 B.C. We have a couple of further reasons to believe that he prophesied early in Josiah's reign, maybe around 630 B.C.—just after Nahum's prophecy against Nineveh and just before Habakkuk's prophecy against Judah. First, Zephaniah prophesied against the still powerful Nineveh (2:13-15), and Nineveh fell to the Babylonians in 612. Second, Zephaniah's severe condemnation of Judah suggests that the great religious awakening for which Josiah was known had not yet occurred.

Whatever the precise date, Zephaniah helps us to learn at least five things about God. And as we learn about God, perhaps we will discover that for which we should be most thankful.

GOD ALONE IS GOD

First, Zephaniah teaches us that God alone is God. We can be thankful for this awesome God who alone deserves our reverence and awe.

Right from the beginning of his book, Zephaniah points to God's judgment to show that God alone is God. After the introductory verse 1, we read,

> "I will sweep away everything
> from the face of the earth,"
>   declares the LORD.

"I will sweep away both men and animals;
    I will sweep away the birds of the air
    and the fish of the sea.
The wicked will have only heaps of rubble
    when I cut off man from the face of the earth,"
                           declares the LORD.

"I will stretch out my hand against Judah
    and against all who live in Jerusalem.
I will cut off from this place every remnant of Baal,
    the names of the pagan and the idolatrous priests—
those who bow down on the roofs
    to worship the starry host,
those who bow down and swear by the LORD
    and who also swear by Molech,
those who turn back from following the LORD
    and neither seek the LORD nor inquire of him.
Be silent before the Sovereign LORD,
    for the day of the LORD is near.
The LORD has prepared a sacrifice;
    he has consecrated those he has invited.
On the day of the LORD's sacrifice
    I will punish the princes and the king's sons
and all those clad
    in foreign clothes.
On that day I will punish
    all who avoid stepping on the threshold,
who fill the temple of their gods
    with violence and deceit" (1:2-9).

Avoiding "stepping on the threshold" refers to some aspect of worshiping other gods, yet scholars are not exactly sure of what was entailed. Still, the point is clear: Zephaniah was confronting the wickedness of God's own people in Jerusalem, and God would punish them.

These opening verses must be some of the most dramatic opening verses of any prophecy in the Bible: "I will sweep away everything from the face of the earth," the Lord says through Zephaniah. Three times he promises to "sweep away" (1:2, 3)! Twice he says they will be "cut off" (1:3, 4). Once he says he will "stretch out his hand against" them (1:4). And twice he promises to "punish" them (1:8, 9). The verbs say it all! God would be severe with his people.

And God delivered on his promise. One generation after Zephaniah's prophecy, Jerusalem fell to the Babylonians. First, they invaded the city and carried away many exiles. Then, they came back and destroyed the city, its walls, and the great temple of the Lord. Zephaniah might have even lived to witness this destruction.

I wonder what the religious situation described by Zephaniah sounds like to you. We have just read about religious pluralism and the many different gods that were being worshiped in Jerusalem (1:4, 5, 6, 8, 9). And certainly we are familiar with the same kind of religious variety in our nation today. You personally may worship the Lord. Or you may worship someone else. By God's grace, we are free to worship whom we please in our country.

Whom do *you* worship?

In Zephaniah's prophecy, of course, the Lord was addressing the people of Jerusalem, all of whom were supposed to be his true worshipers. Had we asked them, some of them might have said they were simply worshiping both the Lord *and* other gods—being inclusive; being respectful; getting the best from all the different traditions; doing a little hedging of the irreligious bets, just in case there was some truth here or some power there. But the true God has no co-regents. Worshiping the true God and some other god is not worshiping the true God at all.

Sometimes, people hear us Christians profess our belief in only one God who alone should be worshiped and then assume that we also think the worship of other gods should be illegal. As someone who regularly preaches about the existence of only one God and the exclusivity of salvation through Jesus Christ alone, let me be absolutely clear: we do not teach or propagate this idea at all! True worship cannot be coerced by law. In fact, Christians have a long tradition of advocating legal protections for the free exercise of religion, even of those religions that claim *they* alone are the only true way to God.

At the same time, we Christians are adamant about proclaiming what the Bible says: there is one God and one path of salvation. Such exclusive claims are not part of a recent rightward lunge by religious folk in reaction to growing cultural diversity. No, they are stamped on almost every page of the Old Testament. Certainly we see it here in Zephaniah. The Lord will tolerate no rivals! Jesus taught this as well. He said that he was the only *way* to the one true God (e.g., John 14:6). What's more, he said that he *was* the one true God! And he had come in human flesh to seek and save us through the sacrifice of his own body.

Pray that our churches would be clear on this hard truth in our inclusive age. Pray that the other churches in your city and country would faithfully teach that salvation comes through Christ alone. We must be clear and unashamed and not back down from this precious truth. Also, within our own church bodies, we must be clear that we can live with no other Lord. We cannot allow unrepented sin to characterize our lives. Our witness to the gospel must not be compromised by tolerating, among those who call themselves believers, lifestyles that are opposed to God's will. As individual congregations, therefore, we must commit ourselves to clear preaching and to a clear practice of church discipline.

Christian, do you see what this should mean for you particularly? It means that your loyalties should not be divided. You should not look around for ways to hedge your religious bets. You should not follow the bad example of God's Old Testament people in Jerusalem as they mixed their worship of God with the worship of other so-called deities. God calls his people to be silent before the Lord (1:7), not before these other purported gods. His people were called to uniquely acknowledge him in worship.

Notice also that God's command to "be silent" assumes that a connection exists between awe and reverence and a hushed quiet. In our entertainment-driven culture today, it's easy to understand the idea of going crazy with applause. But some things—perhaps the greatest things—still cause us to go silent, speechless, hushed. Consider the grandness of nature, an amazing act of kindness, or even the truth of the gospel. Our silence can echo and express our humble reverence of this great God.

This silence enjoined on God's people also points to our need for submission and obedience to him. Whether we truly worship God as we claim will be reflected in our actions. Being silent before the Lord means giving yourself to more carefully studying his Word—as carefully as you study the newspaper or a bank statement, your legal books or the television schedule. Think of how you give yourself to receiving information during the week. Do you give yourself to receiving the information of God's Word in the same way? His sovereignty and lordship in our lives is experienced as his Spirit picks up his Word that we read and hear and then wields it in our hearts and lives. What has God instructed you in Scripture to do today? Do it. That is part of how you worship him. It is part of how you uniquely recognize his authority in your life.

We should praise and thank our God for who he is as the sovereign God, and for who he has made us to be as his people. And remember that "Thankfulness is a soil in which pride does not easily grow."[2] You and I have no reason to be proud before this God.

God alone is God.

---

[2] Michael Ramsey, *The Christian Priest Today* (London: SPCK, 1972), 79-81.

GOD IS ACTIVE

Zephaniah teaches a second thing about God for which we can be thankful: God is active. If you have been living in an unjust manner, but have counted on God's apathy or indifference, says Zephaniah, "wail!"

> "On that day," declares the LORD,
>   "a cry will go up from the Fish Gate,
>   wailing from the New Quarter,
>   and a loud crash from the hills.
> Wail, you who live in the market district;
>   all your merchants will be wiped out,
>   all who trade with silver will be ruined.
> At that time I will search Jerusalem with lamps
>   and punish those who are complacent,
>   who are like wine left on its dregs,
> who think, 'The LORD will do nothing,
>   either good or bad.'
> Their wealth will be plundered,
>   their houses demolished.
> They will build houses
>   but not live in them;
> they will plant vineyards
>   but not drink the wine" (1:10-13).

In these verses, Zephaniah becomes even more specific about Jerusalem's coming destruction. The Lord's command changes from "be silent" before him (that is, worship him alone) to "wail!" The people of Jerusalem are told to shout out their distress.

All of Jerusalem will wail (1:10-11)! Zephaniah mentions the merchants and traders with their houses and vineyards, but he does not condemn them for their trade, per se. Rather, like a legal form folded in thirds, he begins by pointing to those who "are complacent"—those who are self-satisfied and pleased with themselves and their lot; those who have a habit of pardoning their own faults. Who are these people? Zephaniah unfolds the second third of this legal form, which gives a further explanation: these are the ones "who are like wine left on its dregs." The prophet is referring to the stuff that coagulates at the bottom of a flask of wine during fermentation and makes the wine undrinkable. The people in Jerusalem may be God's people, but they are spiritually apathetic and unaffected by God, like such wine. Of course, people who are unaffected by God implicitly tell the world that God himself is unaffecting and apathetic. Their complacency lies about him. Hence, we read in the third fold, these people think, "The LORD will do nothing, either good or bad." As is so often the case, those who are the most ignorant of true religion are also the most certain of it—certain that God is just like them!

Friend, is it possible that you are a member of a church who has signed that church's statement of faith *honestly* but, as it turns out, *emptily?* That is, you say you believe in God, but you are, as the Puritans called it, a "practical atheist"—someone who lives as if there were no God? In your day-to-day life, you rely entirely on yourself and your own wisdom, even if your lips can form the words, "I believe in God"? Let me promise you, wealth and apparent success will never hide a person, a city, or a nation from God's searching judgment of where that person's trust really resides.

Consider carefully the complacent man's presumption that "The LORD will do nothing, either good or bad." How ironic that such a statement is often uttered by people who claim to know God! Is God really a do-nothing God? Consider the love of God in Christ for us: He came to us when we ran from him. He loved us when we hated him. He died for us when we wanted only to kill him. He saved us when we were ever too ready to condemn him. This is the God of the Bible, the God of our Lord Jesus Christ, the God of Israel, the God some in Jerusalem were quietly accusing of "doing nothing"!

Do you see what this means for us? The Lord sharply says, "Wail" (1:11); and he says this to those who claim to be God's people but who live like hypocrites. You, then, if you have been baptized and call yourself a Christian yet are not living according to God's desires and Word, God's exhortation to you is simple: you should wail! If you do not change, the destruction promised by Zephaniah will come upon you. And on that day no silence will contain your misery, nor quietness your pain. You will encounter the displeasure of God himself when he unmasks your fake faith and your false religion. Beware of cultivating the appearance of godliness instead of godliness itself. Give up the attempt to be *thought of* as godly; strive to *be* godly. God's regard—not the regard of others—will finally matter.

And certainly, do not give your heart over to silver and gold. I enjoy some of the things that God gives us in this world, but I know that every-thing that I enjoy will turn into no-thing. My watch will turn into no-thing. My copy of the Bible will turn into no-thing. Every-thing will turn into no-thing! But people are not like that. God has made people in his own image, and people will endure. When the sun has been burned out for ten thousand ages, then all the people you have seen today will still be enduring. That's what the Christian Bible teaches. So do not let your heart be captivated by small and vanishing things like silver and gold. It will not serve you well.

Be thankful that the God we have is *not* the God that some in Jerusalem in Zephaniah's day supposed he was—indifferent and inactive. The God we worship cares and will act. That's the second matter we learn about God in Zephaniah's prophecy.

GOD IS JUST AND MERCIFUL

A third matter for us to consider is that God is both just and merciful! How grateful we can be for each of these aspects of his character! Let's turn again to Zephaniah's prophecy:

"The great day of the LORD is near—
   near and coming quickly.
Listen! The cry on the day of the LORD will be bitter,
   the shouting of the warrior there.
That day will be a day of wrath,
   a day of distress and anguish,
a day of trouble and ruin,
   a day of darkness and gloom,
   a day of clouds and blackness,
a day of trumpet and battle cry
   against the fortified cities
   and against the corner towers.
I will bring distress on the people
   and they will walk like blind men,
   because they have sinned against the LORD.
Their blood will be poured out like dust
   and their entrails like filth.
Neither their silver nor their gold
   will be able to save them
   on the day of the LORD's wrath.
In the fire of his jealousy
   the whole world will be consumed,
for he will make a sudden end
of all who live in the earth."

Gather together, gather together,
O shameful nation,
before the appointed time arrives
   and that day sweeps on like chaff,
before the fierce anger of the LORD comes upon you,
   before the day of the LORD's wrath comes upon you.
Seek the LORD, all you humble of the land,
   you who do what he commands.

Seek righteousness, seek humility;
   perhaps you will be sheltered
   on the day of the LORD's anger (1:14–2:3).

Zephaniah describes this coming day of God's justice with power and pungency. In the Bible's prophetic literature, we often find a prophecy about the near future mixed together with more distant and final apocalyptic elements. Here, as Zephaniah looks forward in the Spirit, he sees both the fall of Jerusalem that occurred several decades later and a preview of God's final judgment of the world. The prophecy is sobering. You can almost *hear* the desperate shouts and cries, and *see* the looks of anguish and the darkness, and *smell* the dust and the destruction, and *feel* the heat of the fire of God's jealousy, and *taste* the bitterness of the day. This day would be "the day of the LORD's anger" (2:3). Yet God gives this warning to his people because he wants them to hear it, heed it, and not fall under his judgment. He wants them to turn and seek him!

Now, given that we are nearing the Thanksgiving holiday, I assume that you might be surprised to hear a message about God's anger like this. But this is the message of this book of the Bible. And Zephaniah is only repeating what we have heard from the other prophets (Amos, Isaiah, and so forth) and what God's people would hear again from Jesus Christ himself. In fact, when you read the New Testament Gospels, you discover that the most ferocious prophet of God's judgment is the Lord Jesus Christ.[3]

Consider Zephaniah's words again:

"I will bring distress on the people
   and they will walk like blind men,
    because they have sinned against the LORD.
Their blood will be poured out like dust
   and their entrails like filth.
Neither their silver nor their gold
   will be able to save them
   on the day of the LORD's wrath.
In the fire of his jealousy
   the whole world will be consumed,
for he will make a sudden end
   of all who live in the earth" (1:17-18).

Everyone is going to be judged. Everyone! That's what Zephaniah is saying. And we will not be judged for how our resumes look or how high we

---

[3] E.g., Matt. 8:12; 10:34-36; 13:41-42; 25:41f.

climbed on this or that ladder. No, we will be judged because we have "sinned against the LORD" (1:17).

Have you stopped to consider this? Friend, you must! This is why God will judge you. What are sins against God? You have an interest in being able to answer this question. And your conscience has already alerted you to some of those sins, perhaps many of them. The Bible will tell you what the rest of them are. So study the Bible. Learn it. Figure out why God has made you, how he calls you to live, and what he calls you to do. Silver and gold cannot save you. The whole world, Zephaniah says, will be judged.

So what should you do if you have concluded that you have sinned against the Lord? "Seek the LORD, all you humble of the land, you who do what he commands. Seek righteousness, seek humility; perhaps you will be sheltered on the day of the LORD's anger" (2:3). Zephaniah tells us to seek God. Why would we seek the very one who is going to judge us? Doesn't that sound a bit like the mouse looking for the cat? We seek him because he is the One against whom we have sinned, and so he is the One who must forgive us. He is our only hope. If you do seek him with humility, acknowledging your need, perhaps you will be sheltered on the day of his anger.

My non-Christian friend, seek the Lord. Pray to God. You do not have to be in a church to pray. You can pray at home. There's no magic formula of words that "work." The honesty of your own heart is what's necessary. After you pray, read God's book. Meet with God's people. Join them in hearing his Word taught, explained, and lived out. It is in your best interest to do this.

Can you see that silver and gold are neither sufficient answers for sin nor sufficient motivations for living? In the medieval play "Everyman," Everyman has been told he is about to die and stand before God. So he goes around to all of his friends and family and asks them, "Will you go with me to help make my account on this great day of accounting?" Everyone tells him he must take that journey by himself. His spouse. His children. His friends at work or the pub. The goods he has amassed. All say the same thing. Everyman's goods are represented by a chest in the corner of the room (a person's voice speaks from behind or under the chest, of course), and "Goods," too, responds negatively to Everyman's plea for help in giving an account to God, disappointing Everyman gravely: "Alas, I have thee loved, and had great pleasure all my life-days on good and treasure. . . .

> *Goods*: That is to thy damnation, without leasing,
>   for my love is contrary to the love everlasting;
>   But if thou had me loved moderately during,
>   As to the poor to give part of me,

> Then shouldst thou not in this dolour be,
> Nor in this great sorrow and care.
>
> *Everyman*: Lo, now was I deceived ere I was ware,
> And all I may wite my spending of time.
>
> *Goods*: What, thoughtest thou that I am thine?
>
> *Everyman*: I had thought so.
>
> *Goods*: Nay, Everyman, I say no.
> As for a while I was lent thee;
> A season thou hast had me in prosperity.
> My condition is man's soul to kill;
> If I save one, a thousand I do spill.
> Thoughtest thou that I will follow thee?
> Nay, not from this world, verily.
>
> *Everyman*: I had thought otherwise.
>
> *Goods*: Therefore to thy soul Goods is a thief;
> For when thou art dead, this is my guise—
> Another to deceive in this same wise
> As I have done thee, and all to his soul's reprief.[4]

Do not be so deceived by the objects and goods that all too soon will belong to someone else. Do not allow your possessions to possess you. No good will come of it.

As Christians, we know that the most amazing display of God's judgment occurred when he poured out his wrath on Christ on the cross. We also know that the most astounding display of God's mercy occurred when Christ, hanging on the cross, took upon himself God's wrath for our sins. If you trust in Christ, the themes of both God's judgment and his mercy in Zephaniah's prophecy build toward and meet at the cross of Christ.

If you do not accept the righteousness of Christ offered to you by faith, and you choose instead to hold your own righteousness up before God on that last day, then you, like Everyman, will meet your end in fear. Thank God that he has provided such an amazing and costly shelter for us in Christ!

If you are a Christian, listen to God's warnings in his Word! Repent of your sins. You, too, should seek the Lord. Seek his righteousness. Seek shelter from his judgment in his mercy in Christ. And be thankful this week for the shelter God offers you by faith. Pray for your church as well, that it would be honest about God's judgment and active in spreading the good news of his love in Christ. These days, both parts of this message are regarded as unloving!

But the truth is, God is just and God is merciful.

---

[4] A. C. Cawley, ed, *Everyman and Medieval Miracle Plays* (London: J. M. Dent & Sons, 1974), 218-220.

GOD IS JUDGE OF ALL THE WORLD

Zephaniah teaches us a fourth thing about God about which we can be thankful: God is Judge of the entire world. We can be thankful because we know that he will do what is just and right, even if we have to wait for it.

So far, Zephaniah's prophecy has largely been directed to God's own people. But beginning in 2:4, he broadens his scope and makes it clear that all nations are in God's sight. First, he addresses the people on the coast of Canaan, the Philistines:

> Gaza will be abandoned
>   and Ashkelon left in ruins.
> At midday Ashdod will be emptied
>   and Ekron uprooted.
> Woe to you who live by the sea,
>   O Kerethite people;
> the word of the LORD is against you,
>   O Canaan, land of the Philistines.
>
> "I will destroy you,
>   and none will be left."
>
> The land by the sea, where the Kerethites dwell,
>   will be a place for shepherds and sheep pens.
> It will belong to the remnant of the house of Judah;
>   there they will find pasture.
> In the evening they will lie down
>   in the houses of Ashkelon.
> The LORD their God will care for them;
>   he will restore their fortunes (2:4-7).

Next, he addresses the Moabites and the Ammonites:

> "I have heard the insults of Moab
>   and the taunts of the Ammonites,
> who insulted my people
>   and made threats against their land.
> Therefore, as surely as I live,"
>   declares the LORD Almighty, the God of Israel,
> "surely Moab will become like Sodom,
>   the Ammonites like Gomorrah—
> a place of weeds and salt pits,
>   a wasteland forever.

The remnant of my people will plunder them;
  the survivors of my nation will inherit their land."

This is what they will get in return for their pride,
  for insulting and mocking the people of the LORD Almighty.
The LORD will be awesome to them
  when he destroys all the gods of the land.
The nations on every shore will worship him,
  every one in its own land (2:8-11).

The Cushites, who lived in Ethiopia, then hear a dire word: "You too, O Cushites, will be slain by my sword" (2:12).

Even the mighty power of Assyria will fall under God's judgment:

He will stretch out his hand against the north
  and destroy Assyria,
leaving Nineveh utterly desolate
  and dry as the desert.
Flocks and herds will lie down there,
  creatures of every kind.
The desert owl and the screech owl
  will roost on her columns.
Their calls will echo through the windows,
  rubble will be in the doorways,
  the beams of cedar will be exposed.
This is the carefree city
  that lived in safety.
She said to herself,
  "I am, and there is none besides me."
What a ruin she has become,
  a lair for wild beasts!
All who pass by her scoff
  and shake their fists (2:13-15).

Finally, Jerusalem is again addressed. Since she acts like the nations, God will treat her like the nations:

Woe to the city of oppressors,
  rebellious and defiled!
She obeys no one,
  she accepts no correction.
She does not trust in the LORD,
  she does not draw near to her God.

Her officials are roaring lions,
    her rulers are evening wolves,
    who leave nothing for the morning.
Her prophets are arrogant;
    they are treacherous men.
Her priests profane the sanctuary
    and do violence to the law.
The LORD within her is righteous;
    he does no wrong.
Morning by morning he dispenses his justice,
    and every new day he does not fail,
    yet the unrighteous know no shame.

"I have cut off nations;
    their strongholds are demolished.
I have left their streets deserted,
    with no one passing through.
Their cities are destroyed;
    no one will be left—no one at all.
I said to the city,
    'Surely you will fear me
    and accept correction!'
Then her dwelling would not be cut off,
    nor all my punishments come upon her.
But they were still eager
    to act corruptly in all they did" (3:1-7).

As we hear the nations called off one by one, we begin to realize where the prophet is going—God will judge the whole earth:

"Therefore wait for me," declares the LORD,
    "for the day I will stand up to testify.
I have decided to assemble the nations,
    to gather the kingdoms
and to pour out my wrath on them—
    all my fierce anger.
The whole world will be consumed
    by the fire of my jealous anger" (3:8).

God would judge everyone for their sinfulness. No one would escape—from Ethiopia to the coast of Canaan to Assyria. He would judge the nations for callously rejecting his own people, as with Moab and Ammon. He would judge the nations for proudly rejecting him, as with Assyria. And he would judge those who knew themselves to be God's people—at least externally—as with the city of Jerusalem. God pointed to all the nations around Judah and then pointed to Judah itself to teach that he was the Judge of all the world— he makes no distinctions!

One of the great myths that has infiltrated our churches today is that if you have been baptized and become a member of a church externally, then you are safe spiritually. I hope you do not construe what I am about to say as having ill intent, but it must be said: those churches are lying to you. It isn't true. That is a false gospel. There is no such thing as a church that you can join—whether it's called Eastern Orthodox or Roman Catholic or Lutheran or Baptist—and, because you accept its baptism, automatically become safe spiritually. Some churches teach such a message, and they are terribly wrong. Zephaniah was addressing people who were *in* the city of Jerusalem. They had the signs of the covenant. Yet they would be judged by God and would be lost.

If you are not a Christian, I encourage you to carefully consider the Bible's claim that God will judge everybody, including you. You realize, don't you, that Zephaniah's prophecy ultimately reaches out and points to you? God will judge you. We see the universal scope of God's concern when he says that he will "destroy" the gods of the other nations (2:11) and when he promises "The whole world will be consumed by the fire of my jealous anger" (3:8). You and I are certainly part of the whole world. We are no exception. Our only choice, therefore, is to follow the instructions he offers to ancient Jerusalem: fear the Lord and accept his corrections (3:7).

Maybe you are someone who respects God. Maybe you want to know more about who he is. Then consider carefully how he would oppose you or any of your actions. And we are not talking about *his* opinion against *your* opinion; we are talking about the truth against a lie. Right against wrong. Life against death. Oh, my friend, choose life! Examine your conscience in order to see if you cannot find something about which you feel convicted. He has placed that sense of conviction in you for a reason. Then talk with a Christian friend and ask whether God might be using your conscience to begin dealing with you and your soul.

Identify your sins and repent of them. Turn away from them, and turn to God.

As I have already mentioned, the Bible teaches that Jesus Christ will be this world's ultimate Judge. Preaching in Athens, the apostle Paul said, "For [God] has set a day when he will judge the world with justice by the man he has appointed. He has given proof of this to all men by raising him from the dead" (Acts 17:31). Jesus will be the ultimate Judge of all nations.

In the meantime, we who are God's people must wait: "Therefore wait for me," God says (3:8). Perhaps those in Jerusalem who truly belonged to God were tempted to believe their cynical and complacent neighbors who reasoned that because God had not yet "fixed" the injustice of the land, he never would; that he didn't care. Please do not fall to this same temptation. We do not have all the facts, but you may be certain that life will not always remain the way it presently looks. Our knowledge is pathetically finite. So we must wait, persevering in trust and hope. And our trust and hope are not blind; we have not been asked to trust someone whom we don't know or have no track record with. Our trust and hope are in God.

Difficulties in life will come one after another; and opportunities to sin will be offered again and again. Yet we must deny ourselves sinful pleasure. Pleasure is only a guise that sin assumes in order to lure us in. The immediate pleasure placed in front of us—whether sex, deception, laziness, lust, ambition, resentfulness, and so on—is as deceptive as a mousetrap is to a mouse: it promises life but delivers only death. So we Christians must wait, and thank God for his commitment to the good and the right. Do not set your heart on what is small and vanishing.

This is why our churches must be committed to having someone preach all of the Bible to us—even the Minor Prophets during Thanksgiving season! As members of churches, we do not simply need to hear about our own individual spirituality, with neat tips on life and purpose. We need God's Word in its fullness, including the truths about God's holiness and his righteous judgment on our sin. We must know and relish God's promises to us in Christ. Scripture's promises of heaven should be sweet to us, and the prospect of fellowship with God in Christ should be held up as our chief joy and desire. In order to bear the heavy weights that fall upon us in this world, we Christians need an even grander counterweight to keep us moving through this life, to keep us waiting through every day, week, month, year, and decade that God gives us on this difficult journey. Therefore, we want churches where the congregation's identity is not built around smaller or lesser hopes—joy in this or that circumstance—but around the long-lasting and durable hopes that will even endure both our physical demise and God's final judgment.

We need such hope because God is the judge of all the world.

GOD IS THE SAVIOR OF HIS PEOPLE

A fifth and final thing Zephaniah teaches us about God is this: God is the Savior of his people. Truly, it is not difficult to see what should provoke gratitude in us here, as God follows up his promises of judgment with promises of restoration:

"Then will I purify the lips of the peoples,
> that all of them may call on the name of the LORD
> and serve him shoulder to shoulder.
From beyond the rivers of Cush
> my worshipers, my scattered people,
> will bring me offerings.
On that day you will not be put to shame
> for all the wrongs you have done to me,
because I will remove from this city
> those who rejoice in their pride.
Never again will you be haughty
> on my holy hill.
But I will leave within you
> the meek and humble,
> who trust in the name of the LORD.
The remnant of Israel will do no wrong;
> they will speak no lies,
> nor will deceit be found in their mouths.
They will eat and lie down
> and no one will make them afraid" (3:9-13).

Hearing these promises, the prophet calls God's people to sing:

Sing, O Daughter of Zion;
> shout aloud, O Israel!
Be glad and rejoice with all your heart,
> O Daughter of Jerusalem!
The LORD has taken away your punishment,
> he has turned back your enemy.
The LORD, the King of Israel, is with you;
> never again will you fear any harm.
On that day they will say to Jerusalem,
> "Do not fear, O Zion;
> do not let your hands hang limp.
The LORD your God is with you,
> he is mighty to save.
He will take great delight in you,
> he will quiet you with his love,
> he will rejoice over you with singing" (3:14-17).

The book of Zephaniah then closes with God repeating his promises of restoration:

"The sorrows for the appointed feasts
  I will remove from you;
    they are a burden and a reproach to you.
At that time I will deal
  with all who oppressed you;
I will rescue the lame
  and gather those who have been scattered.
I will give them praise and honor
  in every land where they were put to shame.
At that time I will gather you;
  at that time I will bring you home.
I will give you honor and praise
  among all the peoples of the earth
when I restore your fortunes
  before your very eyes,"

says the LORD (3:18-20).

The great news of Zephaniah is that God will save all his people. He will *vindicate* and *change* and *gather* and *exult in* his people! That is his plan and our great hope. In that sense, these last verses provide an Old Testament equivalent to the last chapters of the New Testament book of Revelation, where God lovingly gives his people who are about to endure a great trial a clearer view of their final end, so that they might be strengthened, encouraged, and prepared to follow him down a difficult path to a worthwhile destination.

Do you want to be one of God's restored, praised, and honored people? Has your own journey thus far, whether difficult or not, lacked such a worthwhile goal? You need to settle up with God.

The day is coming when God will stop judging governments in history, and will more directly rule his creation. That is the day for which you must prepare, and why you must be one of God's saved people. God made you to know him, but you have sinned against him. Now, you have an accounting to give, but you cannot give it. And God will justly judge all of us for our sins, not because he is hard but because he is right. Yet in his amazing love, God came in the flesh and lived among us. He lived a perfect life and died on the cross as a sacrifice—a substitute—for the sins of all of us who would ever turn and trust in him. This God-man, Jesus, was then raised to new life, showing God's acceptance of his sacrifice and vindicating his ministry and his claims. Jesus calls us now to repent of our sins and to trust in him. When we do, his own perfect righteousness is accounted as our own. That is the great good news that we have as Christians.

In our churches, we should have cultures marked by such faith, hope, certainty, and confidence. Church members should continually be encouraged to meditate on our great hope. The joy that follows will testify to the work of God's Spirit. Humility will also follow, as we see that we deserve nothing more and that we could not even begin to ask for all the good that God has already lavished on us in Christ. Church members should also get involved in one another's lives, so that when discouragement comes, we can remind each other of these things.

For Christians, there is no doubt that the point of this book is to worship God: "Sing, O Daughter of Zion; shout aloud, O Israel! Be glad and rejoice with all your heart, O Daughter of Jerusalem!" (3:14). How can we rejoice like this if we do not consider the salvation that has been promised to us!

> On that day they will say to Jerusalem,
>   "Do not fear, O Zion;
>   do not let your hands hang limp.
> The LORD your God is with you,
>   he is mighty to save.
> He will take great delight in you,
>   he will quiet you with his love,
>   he will rejoice over you with singing" (3:16-17).

This is the God who will rightly judge, but who has also promised his own people that "you will not be put to shame for all the wrongs you have done to me" (3:11).

How can all these blessings come to us? Only in Christ, who has borne our sins. Christ will bring us to the day when we will experience no more harm, when chapter 1's silence of awe will be changed into the quietness of utter contentment and satisfaction. Notice the wonderful phrases of verse 17:

> "The LORD your God . . .
> will take great delight in you . . .
> will quiet you with his love . . .
> will rejoice over you with singing."

Do you see in these words the same God we see in Jesus' parable about the woman who searches for the lost coin? Or the shepherd who goes out to gather the lost sheep? Or the father who runs out to embrace the prodigal son? In these last verses of Zephaniah's prophecy, the judge has become the father; the warrior has become the lover.

I don't know about you, but I have a lot to be thankful for.

Let us pray:

O God, we thank you for all the blessings you have given and continue to give. Most of all, we thank you for yourself, given to us despite our sins. Teach our hearts to give ourselves to you, through Jesus Christ we ask it. Amen.

Questions for Reflection

1. What presently prevents you from being more thankful to God for all that he has given you, even if your circumstances are difficult?

2. Religious pluralism is the idea that there are many right ways to worship "God" because "God" comes in many different forms. Why does religious pluralism appeal to our sinful nature?

3. In our day, the exclusive claims of Christianity are becoming more and more unpopular. What will churches have to do in order to remain faithful to the biblical message? What are some of the subtle ways churches can begin to compromise that message?

4. What would "hedging your religious bets" look like in your own life?

5. Does the gospel cause you a sense of awe? Why or why not?

6. Based on your personal practices of evangelism, would a non-Christian assume that God is active or that he is apathetic?

7. What is your favorite possession? Will you outlast that possession? What possession would you like to have more than anything else? Will you outlast that?

8. Will God judge you? How can you prepare for his judgment?

9. Will God restore all people to himself? If not, just whom *will* he restore?

THE MESSAGE OF HAGGAI: ARE YOUR INVESTMENTS SOUND?

37

THE MESSAGE OF HAGGAI: ARE YOUR INVESTMENTS SOUND?

ARE YOUR INVESTMENTS SOUND?[1]

I spent some time in the business and personal finance sections of a bookstore this week. Maybe you haven't noticed, but the money-related sections are some of the largest sections in bookstores these days. They include every kind of book on investing, from Benjamin Graham's 1949 classic *The Intelligent Investor,* just revised and released in its fourth edition, to the brand-new book by William O'Neil, *The Successful Investor,* where he advocates a plan known by its acronym, CAN SLIM. I am not sure that is an acronym you really want for your investments. There is even an *Investing for Dummies* volume—which is a kind idea, isn't it!

Moving over to the magazine section, I observed that the recent issue of *Smart Money* had its list of the thirty most influential people in investing over the last twelve months, led by Warren Buffett and Alan Greenspan. *Forbes* had its annual richest people list, topped by Bill Gates, Warren Buffett, and Paul Allen. The current issue of *Money* magazine had the inviting cover headline, "The Path to Wealth: How to Succeed in 2004, Earn More, Save Smarter, Invest Better." Inside the *Money* issue were all kinds of interesting things about investing I had never heard. For instance, if you save just $100 a month at a 4 percent interest rate, you will have a million dollars—in eighty-nine years!

Yesterday on the phone, I asked the only CEO that I know how to think through investing $10,000. First, he said to avoid speculative gains. People are mesmerized by stories of windfall profits, but such things rarely happen, and people lose money that way. Second, he said to invest in mutual funds through companies with good reputations. Third, he said to have a long-term perspec-

---

[1] This sermon was originally preached on November 30, 2003, at Capitol Hill Baptist Church in Washington, D.C.

tive. Investing is not a good place for an instant return. Instead, a 7 or 8 percent annual growth is very good.

Well, after this little excursion out of my normal sections of the bookstore, I concluded that America today is money-mad. Of course, America was money-mad yesterday, and it will be money-mad tomorrow, if we are still here. American historians have said that one of the key transitions in the early New England colonies was the transition from being settlements based on Christianity to being settlements based on commerce. We moved from Puritan to Yankee, as one author famously described this transition.

Greed must be one of the most reliable of all desires, right up there with lust and envy, and it might even have greater endurance than these two. Certainly, it's more respectable. Greed can easily appear as "thrift," or appear not at all. People today seem more willing to talk openly about sex or religion than they are about their salaries, their spending, or their savings.

What about you? Are you content with the soundness of your investments?

INTRODUCING HAGGAI

The book we come to now in our study through the Minor Prophets may challenge your confidence in your investments. It is the second-shortest book in the Old Testament, the book of Haggai.

Let me first tell you a little bit about Haggai. His preaching is mentioned in Ezra 5 and 6 in connection with the rebuilding of the temple. Yet nowhere else is his name mentioned outside this little book. His name comes from the Hebrew word *hagh,* which means "festival" or "pilgrim to a festival," not unlike the Arabic word *hajj* ("to go on a pilgrimage"). This prophet is "haggai"—one who has been on the pilgrimage.

As for the historical background, we need to trace briefly back to the days of the prophets Jeremiah and Ezekiel, when Jerusalem was first invaded by the Babylonians (606 B.C.). At that time, many people were taken away as exiles, including Daniel. A second invasion occurred in 597, during which Ezekiel was taken away. The city was then besieged again in 587. In 586, Jerusalem fell and was burned. The temple was destroyed. And there was another great deportation of Jews to Babylon. The Jews stayed in Babylon for decades. In 538, the Babylonians themselves were overrun by Cyrus of the Medo-Persian Empire. Cyrus, a couple of years into his reign, issued a decree allowing the Jews to return to Jerusalem and even promising to help finance the rebuilding of the temple of the Lord.

So in 536 B.C., a large number of Jews (maybe 50,000) made the nine-hundred-mile journey from Babylon back to Jerusalem. Many more Jews remained in Babylon, where they had settled and flourished. Those who returned laid the foundation stone to rebuild the temple that had been destroyed, but then they were effectively stopped by the nearby Samaritans. A number of years passed. The Persian Empire went through a couple of rulers. Then in 522 Darius came to the throne, and it was during the period that Darius reigned over Persia that Haggai preached. From late August to mid-December 520 B.C., Haggai gave four prophecies—four little God-inspired sermons—that comprise the two chapters of his book. After Haggai started preaching, Zechariah began preaching as well. But more on that in our next study.

In brief, Haggai called the returned exiles to prioritize the rebuilding of the Lord's temple in Jerusalem. And the people listened to him. Though Haggai's prophecies stop in December of 520 B.C., we know from the book of Ezra that the temple was rebuilt, completed, and dedicated scarcely more than three years later, by March 516. Chronologically, then, Haggai stands in between the exiled Ezekiel's vision of the rebuilt temple (Ezekiel 40–48) and the reforms of Ezra and Nehemiah in the books by their names.

In this overview study of Haggai, we learn three things: First, poor investments show themselves (1:1-11). Second, bad investment strategies must be corrected (1:12-15). Third, sound investments prove themselves in their returns (chapter 2). As we look through this little book, I hope you will be moved to review what you are investing your substance in, and whether your investments are wise.

POOR INVESTMENTS SHOW THEMSELVES (1:1-11)

We learn in the first eleven verses of Haggai that poor investments show themselves:

> In the second year of King Darius, on the first day of the sixth month, the word of the LORD came through the prophet Haggai to Zerubbabel son of Shealtiel, governor of Judah, and to Joshua son of Jehozadak, the high priest:
> This is what the LORD Almighty says: "These people say, 'The time has not yet come for the LORD's house to be built.'"
> Then the word of the LORD came through the prophet Haggai: "Is it a time for you yourselves to be living in your paneled houses, while this house remains a ruin?"
> Now this is what the LORD Almighty says: "Give careful thought to your ways. You have planted much, but have harvested little. You eat, but never have enough. You drink, but never have your fill. You put on clothes, but are not warm. You earn wages, only to put them in a purse with holes in it."
> This is what the LORD Almighty says: "Give careful thought to your ways. Go up into the mountains and bring down timber and build the house, so that

I may take pleasure in it and be honored," says the LORD. "You expected much, but see, it turned out to be little. What you brought home, I blew away. Why?" declares the LORD Almighty. "Because of my house, which remains a ruin, while each of you is busy with his own house. Therefore, because of you the heavens have withheld their dew and the earth its crops. I called for a drought on the fields and the mountains, on the grain, the new wine, the oil and whatever the ground produces, on men and cattle, and on the labor of your hands" (1:1-11).

In these verses, God acts to convict the spiritual and secular officials of Israel and the nation at large of their godlessly selfish priorities. The Israelites had been living back in the land for more than sixteen years at this point. They had spent several months rebuilding the temple at the beginning of those sixteen years. But then they had become indifferent to the rebuilding effort, and foreign opposition gave them all the more reason to spend their money elsewhere. In fact, they were taking the meager amount of money they did have and were spending it on their own homes. So the Lord used Haggai to rebuke them and tell them that this was not right.

It is amazing, isn't it, when we don't like work, how easy it is for us to find excuses? We will use any opposition we can to delay our work.

Some Israelites, it appears, actively opposed rebuilding the temple. Maybe they thought the nation should wait for the Messiah to begin rebuilding. Maybe they thought the nation was too poor to undertake the rebuilding of such a magnificent building at that time. Whatever their reason, they found a way instead to care for and to remodel their own houses. They found a way to spend money on the comforts that they wanted. They were living in nice, paneled houses and managed to keep busy with those houses (1:4, 9). They might have claimed, "We don't have money"; but the unfinished walls of the temple and the paneled walls of their homes stood as visible testimonies to their indifference.

Indeed, it does sound as if the economy was in a wreck. Haggai portrayed their distress in bold strokes: "You have planted much, but have harvested little. You eat, but never have enough. You drink, but never have your fill. You put on clothes, but are not warm. You earn wages, only to put them in a purse with holes in it" (1:6). Harvests had been poor. Inflation was rampant. As one writer put it, "Prices were high and wages low, it seemed as if their money just dropped through holes in their pockets."[2]

Yet it was in this context that God inspired Haggai to preach these messages telling the people to rebuild the temple of the Lord. Why? It would please him and honor him, the Lord says. It would be an acceptable offering to him.

[2] J. E. McFadyen, "Haggai," in *The Abingdon Bible Commentary,* Frederick Carl Eiselen, Edwin Lewis, and David G. Downey, eds. (New York: Abingdon-Cokesbury, 1929), 816.

Why do you think that the rebuilding of the temple would be an acceptable offering to God? It was just a building. Honestly, when David first brought it up with God, God did not seem all that excited about it (2 Sam. 7:2-7). So why would God care so much now? From the people's standpoint, the rebuilt temple would be a clear and public statement that they still wanted and valued God. It would indicate that he was a higher priority than everything else clamoring for attention in their lives. It would be a mark of their faith in God and their recognition of his priority in their own national identity.

From the nations' standpoint, it would be a sign that the God of Israel had not gone out of business when Jerusalem fell. It would publicly vindicate God before the world.

From God's standpoint, the temple was a visible sign of the covenant that bound him and his people together, and it represented his continuing favor to them and his continuing design to fulfill his promises, such as his promises to David (e.g., 2 Sam. 7:11, 16; Jer. 33:17-22). The Lord had told David that his son, Solomon, would build the temple for the Lord's name (1 Kings 5:5). And so Solomon had. The temple was then a symbol of God's living among the Israelites and not abandoning them (1 Kings 6:13; cf. Ps. 132:13-14). The Lord then predicted through the prophet Isaiah that the temple would be destroyed and rebuilt (Isa. 44:28). Several other prophets before Haggai had also mentioned God's promise of a future temple.[3] When the Babylonians took Jerusalem, they set fire to the temple and took the people away into captivity (2 Kings 25:9-21). And these two events would have been associated in the minds of the Israelites: when the temple was destroyed, the people were scattered. Now, God had sovereignly regathered his people. What should happen next? The returned exiles should have immediately rebuilt the temple as a symbol, a visible sign, of God's presence with them. They should have made this a priority in their lives.

But they didn't. So God used a drought and this preacher/prophet Haggai to draw their attention to their sin of self-indulgence and of God-neglect.

What about *you*? How are your investments going? Are they sound? Think about this for a moment. You are investing in something—right now, in fact. And all this month, you invested in something. You have been placing your life on the line, giving it away, hour after hour, day after day, month after month, even year after year. My question to you is, *what* are you investing your life in? Also, what will your return be on this life investment of yours?

We learn in the Scriptures that God has made us in his image, to know him. But we have sinned by rebelling against God and separating ourselves from

---

[3] See Isa. 2:2-4; Mic. 4:1-4; Ezek. 37:26; Mal. 3:1.

him. Now, we desire to be away from him and, in our rebellion, to invest in a different and self-centered way. Yet the Bible explicitly teaches what the wages of our sin are: the wages, or return, of our sin is death (Rom. 6:23). You may not be guilty of neglecting to rebuild an ancient Middle Eastern temple, but you are every bit as guilty of neglecting the God who made you. God sent Jesus Christ to die for sinners like you; but if you neglect Christ, God will one day judge you. This neglect is abominable to him! I pray, for your soul's sake, that you begin to understand this. Oh, my friend, is Christ being neglected by you?

If you claim to be one of God's people—a Christian—have you neglected God's church, God's household, God's congregation, as the ancient Israelites neglected the temple? Why do you think you are any less guilty than they were?

Christian, there is so much we can learn from contemplating this little prophecy. Are you investing your all in Christ? How? What has kept you back from investing your all in him? Perhaps you think you lack adequate resources. Perhaps you are in a relationship in which you are not trusting God as you know you should. Perhaps some decision that you need to make looms before you. God promises us much in Christ. But he also calls us to a commitment that is whole and entire!

Notice how in Haggai's day God carefully matched the discipline to the sin. They had neglected God, and so what happened? They found the very sources of their life failing. Sure, calamities will befall us that are unrelated to our specific sins. We learn that in the Old Testament and the New, as in the examples of Job, Paul's thorn, and supremely, Jesus himself. But if we are careful students of God's providences in our lives, we must also admit that sometimes there is a ministry of exposing our sin in the trials and difficulties that God's sovereignty allows to befall us.

In the situation addressed by Haggai, the people were stingy with God, and, ironically, that stinginess kept them poor. Charles Haddon Spurgeon said, "If men are selfish and keep their wealth to themselves, and rob God of his portion, they shall not prosper, or if they do, no blessing shall come with it."[4]

As God exhorts his people here, "give careful thought to your ways" (1:7). Consider if your lack of giving is leading to your financial difficulties. No, you have not turned to a TV preacher. You have turned to the book of Haggai. Consider your life and consider how you give, Haggai says. Why should God entrust his wealth to you? What do you do with it? What if he created the wealth he has given you specifically to do good things in his creation, but instead of being a highway of blessing, you have become the dead end for the

---

[4] Charles Haddon Spurgeon, *Spurgeon's Devotional Bible* (Grand Rapids, Mich.: Baker, 1964), 460.

wealth he gave? Why would he give you any more? Pray for the grace of God to lead you and to teach you from his Word what to do with your money.

Give careful thought to your ways! Where does your "discretionary money" go? And have you reduced the amount of discretionary money you have to spend because of your financial pre-commitments to homes, cars, hobbies, subscriptions, financial investments, cell phones, frequent vacations, new clothes, and on and on?

Again, give careful thought to your ways! Where does the majority of your "discretionary time" go? You have to sleep. You have to eat. You have to go to work. And there are a number of other commitments about which you may *feel* you have no choice. But do you? What have you committed your schedule to? Pray for the grace of God's Spirit to convict you and give you wisdom, because the Evil One does not want us to think clearly about these things, particularly in a prosperous society. How many of us have reduced the amount of discretionary time we have by the jobs we have chosen and the projects we have undertaken. For any given decision, ask yourself, is this God's will? It may be, but it may *not* be, even if it is best for your career. We have been called to offer ourselves entirely to God. Surely it is right for us to ask such questions and pray that God's Spirit will help us to answer them honestly.

Consider this: what would your life look like if you got what you really wanted? Do you have a picture of that in your mind? Now ask yourself, would God be there? Is he at the center of your desires, or is he repeatedly neglected by the true center of your heart's desires?

Consider also what the local congregation's commitment to God's work should be. A congregation's trials of difficulty and of prosperity should cause the members of a congregation to examine themselves and the Scriptures. What is our congregation holding back? What is God's will for his household, the church, the temple in which his Spirit lives? What if doing God's work means leaving the church where you are comfortable and participating in a church plant?

When so many churches today, in the name of reaching the lost, have given themselves to being remade by the wisdom of advertising and marketing, how can individual churches resist this trend and stay faithful to the convicting edge of the Word of God, which confronts us in our sin, as Haggai's message did here? Pray that our churches would cultivate a congregational life in which we regularly know the conviction of sin and in which we regularly confess our sins and struggles to one another. After all, conviction and confession lead to liberation! The only way to be free of our sins is to recognize them. Sins don't just fall off by themselves. We have to work at that. The Evil One wants us to think of conviction and confession as negative and bad, because, admittedly, they initially taste bitter; and who likes bitter! But through conviction and confession, God lovingly refines us, removing from our lives first this, then that. The only way we can learn the most positive news of all—the gospel—is through the most negative confession of all—how we deserve God's wrath for our sins.

How can we help each other gain victory over our sin if we do not work to know one another in the church, and if we do not make sure that others know the truth about our own lives? When we do the work of discipling, of encouraging, of listening, of praying and instructing, we do the work of building the Lord's house. Do not read Haggai and think primarily of a building program for a church meeting house! The only time I ever heard the book of Haggai preached in my own life, the preacher wanted to begin a building program. I agree that the book might have some third-order implications about church buildings. But please understand that church buildings today should *not* be equated with the Old Testament temple. Christ is the temple! And according to 1 Corinthians 3 and 6, *we* who have been incorporated into Christ and have been called his body are now the temple in which Christ's Spirit lives! This is the temple we want to see built up. If you are a true follower of Christ, you want to see the people who sit all around you Sunday after Sunday built up in Christ. Building his temple today does not have to do with the fabric or furnishings of a meeting-house. The true church will be built as God's truth is courageously preached, as we give ourselves to listen to it, and as we are convicted by it. This is what our congregations must not neglect!

To neglect the work of the ears—of listening to God's Word—will undermine the church. To instead tickle them, and to invest the substance of our lives and devotion to godless ends is a poor investment strategy, and it will show itself one day more ruinously than any bubble that has ever burst on Wall Street.

Poor investments show themselves.

BAD INVESTMENT STRATEGIES MUST BE CORRECTED (1:12-15)

Second, the Lord told them that bad investment strategies must be corrected.

And the people of Israel did correct them! We pick up the story line of chapter 1 in verse 12:

> Then Zerubbabel son of Shealtiel, Joshua son of Jehozadak, the high priest, and the whole remnant of the people obeyed the voice of the LORD their God and the message of the prophet Haggai, because the LORD their God had sent him. And the people feared the LORD.
>
> Then Haggai, the LORD's messenger, gave this message of the LORD to the people: "I am with you," declares the LORD. So the LORD stirred up the spirit of Zerubbabel son of Shealtiel, governor of Judah, and the spirit of Joshua son of

Jehozadak, the high priest, and the spirit of the whole remnant of the people. They came and began to work on the house of the LORD Almighty, their God, on the twenty-fourth day of the sixth month in the second year of King Darius (1:12-15).

Here is a picture of what the Bible calls repentance. The people actually changed their selfish priorities! They feared the Lord and obeyed him, as he stirred up their spirits to renew their work on the temple in Jerusalem.

Observe for a moment the several aspects of repentance. There is the *action* of repentance: the people "obeyed" the Lord after having disobeyed him (1:12). There is the *motivation* of repentance: the people "feared the LORD" (1:12). That is, they began to consider who he is and how they should regard his words. Finally, there is the *cause* of repentance: the Lord "stirred up" the spirits of the people (1:14). The Lord was active in all of this.

Repentance is not a merely human work. It never has been. Article 8 of the Capitol Hill Baptist Church statement of faith (taken from the 1833 New Hampshire Confession), which is entitled "Of Repentance and Faith," reads as follows:

> We believe that Repentance and Faith are sacred duties . . .

Okay, we *do* it; repenting and believing is our duty:

> . . . and also inseparable graces, wrought [worked] in our souls by the regenerating Spirit of God; whereby being deeply convinced of our guilt, danger and helplessness, and of the way of salvation by Christ, we turn to God with unfeigned contrition, confession, and supplication for mercy; at the same time heartily receiving the Lord Jesus Christ as our Prophet, Priest and King, and relying on him alone as the only and all sufficient Saviour.

The Lord works repentance in our souls. He stirs us up. And so our repentance redounds to his praise and glory. That is what happens when God's presence enters the sinner.

So God tells the Israelites through Haggai, "I am with you" (1:13). He stirs up their spirits (1:14). As a result, "They came and began to work on the house of the LORD Almighty, their God" (1:14).

This seems to have been the point of Haggai's prophecy for these first readers. Twenty-three days after the first prophecy, the people obeyed (see 1:1, 15). They found a more sound and long-lasting investment than remodeling their houses.

If you are a non-Christian, how have you answered these questions so far concerning what you are investing your life in? Perhaps you feel fine about your "investments." But then, perhaps, you are less sanguine and more disturbed about the choices you have made or about where you have put your time, money, and heart. As Jesus said, "For where your treasure is, there your heart will be also" (Matt. 6:21).

If you have come to realize that you have sinned against God, then know that God has come in Christ for people just like you: people who recognize their sin, who confess those sins, who will look to Christ and his sacrifice on the cross, and know that he died for them as they repent of their sins and follow Christ.

Oh, friend, *this* is the time to repent! Soon enough this whole world will slip away. The very fabric of what we regard as permanent will be revealed as passing. And you do not know when that day will be. Now is the time for you to repent, like the people of Israel in Haggai's day. Turn from your godless life to a life filled with and focused on God! The day called "tomorrow" is not promised to you, nor is this evening. Repent, and put God first in your life!

Christian, as you review in your own life the three aspects of repentance listed above, which ones do you need to address? First, are you obeying God, as you have been called to do in his Word? Can you think of an outstanding issue of obedience in your life that you are not addressing? What hinders you from obeying God in that area?

Second, what are you doing to cultivate the fear of the Lord? Whether or not we fear God is at the root of our ability to obey. Obedience naturally flows out of a proper reverence for who God is. And this fear, we know from Scripture, is the beginning of wisdom. Have you begun to be wise? Do you fear the Lord?

Third, have you been stirred up by the Lord, as the ancient Israelites were stirred up to action? The whole person—not simply the affections—should be engaged in repentance and obedience. A true fear of the Lord will not lead to a petrified inaction but to a vital, moving obedience. When you are stirred up, action will follow as you begin to work in obedience to God's commands, not just in church but in all the areas of your life in which God calls you to live and work.

Now, none of the fruit of repentance will ever appear if you are hardened against correction and conviction. And frankly, all of us need correction *most* in the areas of our lives where we will listen *least*. That is the nature of our sin, and that is why we must constantly be washing ourselves in the Word and in Christian fellowship. If you are truly a Christian, be encouraged by the good fruit that words of rebuke (from yourself or others) against you can bear! When these words are accurate and well-placed, God will use them to grow wonderful fruit.

So, how do you respond to conviction? Do you defend your own sin? Or do you thank God for his tender tenacity, his enduring and penetrating care for you? The writer of Hebrews said,

> Our fathers disciplined us for a little while as they thought best; but God disciplines us for our good, that we may share in his holiness. No discipline seems pleasant at the time, but painful. Later on, however, it produces a harvest of righteousness and peace for those who have been trained by it (Heb. 12:10-11).

Christian, our commitment to Christ is a commitment to revere him, to love him, to obey him, and to give our lives for him. That is the Christian's stance in true repentance.

How then can we cultivate lives of repentance? Let me suggest four simple aids that will help us cultivate lives of repentance:

(i) Study the Word of God. The Bible is the central way God corrects us. That is how the people in Haggai's day were corrected. God's Word came to them.

(ii) Consider God's nature, particularly in contrast with your own nature. I assure you, this will prove significant and humbling. As you consider more of who he is, you will find yourself more ready to submit to him and to trust him obediently and confidently.

(iii) Pray for God to stir your affections for him. Pray also that he would make you disaffected toward your sin. May we Christians not be a people who are stoically obedient but a people who are stirred up!

(iv) Seek out the wisdom and leadership of godly individuals around you.

Through Bible study, God-ward meditation, prayer, and counsel, conviction should flourish in your life; and as true conviction flourishes, so will your soul. *That* is a sound investment!

I recently finished reading a biography of John Wesley, truly a man who had cultivated such a life of repentance. The biographer recounts a story that took place at one of the regular meetings of ministers in London that Wesley attended in order to share breakfast and serious discussion. During such a meeting, one of the youngest men present corrected an older minister, which in turn prompted one of Wesley's friends, a Scottish minister, to rebuke the younger man for the impertinence of rebuking his elder. Wesley then interrupted his good friend and remonstrated, "I will thank the youngest man among you to tell me of any fault you see in me; in doing so, I shall consider him as my best friend."[5]

If your own life is not moving toward such humility, I don't even know if

---

[5] Cited in Luke Tyerman, *The Life and Times of the Rev. John Wesley, Founder of the Methodists,* 3 vols. (London: Hodder & Stoughton, 1876), 3:567.

you are a Christian. You may have been striving for others to think of you as godly. But what virtue dwells in the approval of others if the bubble simply pops when you die? If you are really a Christian, if you really know God, you are not surprised when I call you a sinner—you knew that already. You publicly admitted it in the baptismal pool. You admitted that you need to be changed. There is a humility that comes with truly being a Christian.

What does it mean for our churches to cultivate a culture of conviction? It means that they must commit themselves to having God's Word preached in a way that is faithful not flattering, courageous not cowardly, central in our times together and not peripheral!

We must also approach our weekly gatherings with an openness and readiness to hear God's Word. After a Sunday morning service not too long ago, I asked a visitor at the door how he had found the sermon. He said that it was long, that his mind wandered toward the end, and that he had gotten lost. At the time, I made my typical self-deprecating comment. But later, I thought further about how I should have responded. Do you do that? I do that all the time. I should have said, "I work hard at preaching and I do preach long sermons; it's true. But I do it because I think it's so important. Our congregation works hard at listening, because they think it's so important! It is hard work, but it is fruitful work. We give ourselves to the Word of God because we see its fruit in our lives. We see the glory that this gives to God. And we believe that this is God's normal way of granting grace to our lives. So we give ourselves to the Word."

Consider here in Haggai how important the task of bringing God's Word to God's people is. Haggai is called "the Lord's messenger" (1:13). What would have happened if Haggai had not been faithful as the Lord's messenger in delivering an unpopular message? After all, he did not bring them a feel-good message. What if Haggai had wanted to say something more popular and easier to listen to? What if he had tried to speak in a way that would ensure that more people would come back and listen again? They never would have heard God's truth and never would have been given the opportunity to repent.

The message God gave Haggai contradicted the people. In fact, the nature of the message and the audience made for a difficult, even dangerous, combination. The message was critical, confronting their sin very specifically; and for his audience, Haggai singled out the powerful governor and chief priests. If you are going to deliver a critical sermon, at least preach it to those who can't harm you! But that was not what God called Haggai to do. He was given a specific message for a specific people. Faithful preaching is always what God's people need, and it is always a source of great blessing!

It must be said that faithful preaching does not always receive such a positive response. Jeremiah and Ezekiel were roundly rejected by their listeners.

Still, when God intends to move his people, he sends them faithful preachers to do it. That is his way in the Old Testament and the New, and his way throughout the history of the church.

Therefore, a good church will be God-centered in its preaching and in its whole life together. God is the great fact that moves us from our small worlds of self-absorption to the larger world in which he and his concerns dominate. Brothers and sisters in Christ, may our congregation have the faith and courage to obey him. So work to remember what God has done in your life, and share it with others in order to encourage them. It should be normal in our congregations to testify to one another about God and his work in our lives.

May we be a people who have changed our bad investment strategies, who have repented of our sins, who invite loving correction, and who respond to correction in humble repentance!

SOUND INVESTMENTS PROVE THEMSELVES IN THEIR RETURNS (CHAPTER 2)

Finally, a third matter: sound investments prove themselves in their returns, which we learn in chapter 2. God will grant his blessings to those who truly fear and obey him—blessings physical and spiritual. Ultimately, he would bless the returned exiles through the coming of the Messiah.

Physical Blessings

Let's look first at the physical blessings that God promised:

> On the twenty-fourth day of the ninth month, in the second year of Darius, the word of the LORD came to the prophet Haggai: "This is what the LORD Almighty says: 'Ask the priests what the law says: If a person carries consecrated meat in the fold of his garment, and that fold touches some bread or stew, some wine, oil or other food, does it become consecrated?'"
>
> The priests answered, "No."
>
> Then Haggai said, "If a person defiled by contact with a dead body touches one of these things, does it become defiled?"
>
> "Yes," the priests replied, "it becomes defiled."
>
> Then Haggai said, "'So it is with this people and this nation in my sight,' declares the LORD. 'Whatever they do and whatever they offer there is defiled.
>
> "'Now give careful thought to this from this day on—consider how things were before one stone was laid on another in the LORD's temple. When anyone came to a heap of twenty measures, there were only ten. When anyone went to a wine vat to draw fifty measures, there were only twenty. I struck all the work of your hands with blight, mildew and hail, yet you did not turn to me,' declares

the LORD. 'From this day on, from this twenty-fourth day of the ninth month, give careful thought to the day when the foundation of the LORD's temple was laid. Give careful thought: Is there yet any seed left in the barn? Until now, the vine and the fig tree, the pomegranate and the olive tree have not borne fruit.

"'From this day on I will bless you'" (2:10-19).

The editors of the NIV have set this passage off, calling it "Blessings for a Defiled People." Spiritual realities do not consist of wood or stone. You could not make something consecrated simply by bringing it into contact with something else that was consecrated (2:12). Building a temple does not consecrate, or sanctify, someone. Defilement, however, could be passed on by touching, and Haggai warned the people that defilement was spreading, which he knew from the law (2:13; cf. Num 19:22). Perhaps God was referring to their godless selfishness denounced in chapter 1. Perhaps they were defiling themselves in other ways—marrying foreign wives, idolatry, the types of things addressed in the next century by Ezra. Clearly, the chief sin in this book was their lack of enthusiasm for rebuilding the temple and restoring worship there.

Even our most "religious" actions are not necessarily acceptable.

Still, as the people began to repent, God promised an end would come to the scarcity they had known (2:15-17). When the Lord asks, "Is there yet any seed left in the barn?" he basically means, "I hope you planted all those seeds, because I'm going to make them grow!" Unlike their recent past, that year's harvest would be good. "From this day on I will bless you!" (2:19). Once again, God was renewing his covenant with them in the land.

Spiritual Blessings

But the main blessings Haggai points to are spiritual blessings, which God promises in the first half of chapter 2:

On the twenty-first day of the seventh month, the word of the LORD came through the prophet Haggai: "Speak to Zerubbabel son of Shealtiel, governor of Judah, to Joshua son of Jehozadak, the high priest, and to the remnant of the people. Ask them, 'Who of you is left who saw this house in its former glory? How does it look to you now? Does it not seem to you like nothing? But now be strong, O Zerubbabel,' declares the LORD. 'Be strong, O Joshua son of Jehozadak, the high priest. Be strong, all you people of the land,' declares the LORD, 'and work. For I am with you,' declares the LORD Almighty. 'This is what I covenanted with you when you came out of Egypt. And my Spirit remains among you. Do not fear.'

"This is what the LORD Almighty says: 'In a little while I will once more shake the heavens and the earth, the sea and the dry land. I will shake all nations, and the desired of all nations will come, and I will fill this house with glory,' says the LORD Almighty. 'The silver is mine and the gold is mine,' declares the LORD Almighty. 'The glory of this present house will be greater than the glory of the former house,' says the LORD Almighty. 'And in this place I will grant peace,' declares the LORD Almighty" (2:1-9).

God promised that his Spirit would remain among them (2:5), referring back to God's ancient promises to always remain with his people. Perhaps they had been worried that God had left them, because Babylon had taken them into captivity, or because they had disobediently failed to rebuild the temple now that they were back from exile. But God assured them that he would continue with them.

God also promised them his blessing of peace—*shalom*. "And in this place I will grant peace" (2:9). What did this peace include? All the returns you could ever want on your investments. Working on their houses got them nicer houses, but it did not improve the lives that were lived inside those houses. As they turned from their will to God's will, God would bless them with a peace that would include not just prosperity but, more important, forgiveness of sins and peace with God. God's approval, and the profound peace and happiness that would flow from it, would be granted in the precincts of this new temple.

God had promised the people such peace, such shalom, back in Leviticus when they were preparing to enter the Promised Land the first time, if only they would be obedient:

> "Do not make idols or set up an image or a sacred stone for yourselves, and do not place a carved stone in your land to bow down before it. I am the LORD your God.
>
> "Observe my Sabbaths and have reverence for my sanctuary. I am the LORD.
>
> "If you follow my decrees and are careful to obey my commands, I will send you rain in its season, and the ground will yield its crops and the trees of the field their fruit. Your threshing will continue until grape harvest and the grape harvest will continue until planting, and you will eat all the food you want and live in safety in your land.
>
> "I will grant peace in the land, and you will lie down and no one will make you afraid" (Lev. 26:1-6a).

Of course, they were not obedient, and their land experienced little peace. But now, God was once again predicting and providing this peace.

God also promised that his glory would come to his people: "I will fill this house with glory" (2:7; also v. 9). When would his glory come? We get a clue from the prior verse, in which the Lord says, "I will once more shake the heavens and the earth, the sea and the dry land" (2:6). Perhaps the shaking referred to the instability the kingdom of Persia was then experiencing. But fundamentally, we know from the author of Hebrews that Haggai was prophesying about something Haggai himself could only remotely grasp—the second coming of Christ (see Heb. 12:26). The particular blessings promised by the Old Testament prophets often seem to merge into the final eschatological blessing that we experience in Christ, and that we will experience in the new heavens and the new earth.

Messianic Blessings

Indeed, chief among God's promised blessings through Haggai was the promise of a Messiah, which becomes most explicit in the final verses of the book:

> The word of the LORD came to Haggai a second time on the twenty-fourth day of the month: "Tell Zerubbabel governor of Judah that I will shake the heavens and the earth. I will overturn royal thrones and shatter the power of the foreign kingdoms. I will overthrow chariots and their drivers; horses and their riders will fall, each by the sword of his brother.
> "'On that day,' declares the LORD Almighty, 'I will take you, my servant Zerubbabel son of Shealtiel,' declares the LORD, 'and I will make you like my signet ring, for I have chosen you,' declares the LORD Almighty" (2:20-23).

In these last few verses of the book, the Lord addresses the governor of Judah, Zerubbabel. Once again, God uses an image of the final judgment and promises to bring to an end all the world's empires and to rule directly over his creation. But God also makes a strange promise to take Zerubbabel, his chosen one—to make him like his signet ring.

Some people are confused by this language about Zerubbabel. Nobody really knows what God used Zerubbabel to do. He vanishes from the historical record at this point. Some think that King Darius of Persia saw Zerubbabel as a potential rival in Judah and so knocked him off, which would explain why we do not hear anything more about him. But we just don't know.

Still, the Lord does say he made Zerubbabel his signet ring, which is quite an honor. A king would give his signet to an important minister to show the king's confidence in the man and to grant him his own authority. Almost a century earlier, God had pronounced through the prophet Jeremiah a curse on Zerubbabel's grandfather, Jehoiachin, and in the process declared that "even if you, Jehoiachin son of Jehoiakim king of Judah, were a signet ring on my right hand, I would still pull you off" (Jer. 22:24). And God did pull him off!

Jehoiachin was one of the last kings of Judah before the people were sent into exile. But now, God was picking up the royal Davidic line through Zerubbabel, and saying, "I will put you back on." Turning to the first chapter of Matthew's Gospel, sure enough, we find that Zerubbabel is listed in the line of kings leading to Jesus Christ (Matt. 1:12-13).

In other words, God's promises in the last verses of Haggai are messianic. They were not made to Zerubbabel the man so much as they were made to Zerubbabel the heir to David's throne and predecessor to Christ. He was a chosen guardian of the chosen people, the rebuilder of God's house, the restorer of dignity to the line of David. In all these ways Zerubbabel is a type of Christ who points to Christ.[6] All of God's promises through Haggai would ultimately be fulfilled in Christ.

For instance, who is "the desired of all nations" who "will come" (Hag. 2:7)? The word for "desired" could also be translated "treasures," which goes well with the following verse's reference to gold and silver that belongs to the Lord (2:8). In its immediate context, this treasure, this gold and silver, would refer to the treasure of other nations that was used to rebuild the temple. Indeed, King Darius provided some of the funds for rebuilding it. So at least there was Persian treasure in the temple! In the larger context of redemptive history, however, God was promising his Messiah—*he* is the desired of all nations! You might even know a Christmas hymn or two that uses this language, like "Angels from the Realms of Glory."

Another example of messianic fulfillment can be seen in the next verse, where God promises, "The glory of this present house will be greater than the glory of the former house" (2:9). How will the glory of this present house be greater than the glory of the former house, Solomon's temple? After all, Solomon's temple had glories that the second temple did not have. All the surfaces of its interior were overlaid with gold. It contained the ark of the covenant, the Urim and Thummim, the visible Shekinah glory. None of these items are ever mentioned in the biblical text in connection with the second temple. So how would its glory be greater?

The answer must be in the greatest glory it could have—God's bodily presence in Christ. This second temple was desecrated at one point in the second century B.C., but it hung on until Herod the Great, who rebuilt and extended it. This was the temple that was standing in Jerusalem when Jesus came and entered its precincts. Of course, God's setting apart the temple in Jerusalem was only the faintest indication of the glory of God physically with his people in Jesus, Immanuel—God with us. So we read in the first chapter of John's

---

[6] See Ezek. 34:23-24; 37:24; 39:19-23; Dan. 2:44.

Gospel, "The Word became flesh and made his dwelling among us. We have seen his glory, the glory of the One and Only, who came from the Father, full of grace and truth" (John 1:14). And then the author of Hebrews points us directly to the glory that would surpass the glory of the first temple: "The Son is the radiance of God's glory and the exact representation of his being, sustaining all things by his powerful word" (Heb. 1:3).

So those were some of the blessings that were given to the repentant people of Haggai's day. What about you? What blessings will you have? Will you be one of the repentant people? Will you trust in God's physical and spiritual blessings for your life in time and eternity?

Certainly God normally blesses obedience to him, whether offered by an individual, a city, or a nation. Of course, the greatest blessing indicated here comes not because of our obedience but despite our lack of it; and that's the blessing of the Messiah. The greatest benefit we gain is from no investment we have made, but one that God has made for us. In the book of Acts, Luke says that God bought the church with his own blood (Acts 20:28).

In a secondary sense, obedience is a place of blessing. It is where we want to dwell as Christians. We have heard Haggai's rebuke of our self-absorption and our God-neglect. Now we can repent of those things and be blessed! We will not always experience physical blessing through faith in Christ, but we may sometimes (see James 5:13-16).

We Christians have been given the gift of God's indwelling Spirit. And we have been given peace with God through the work of Christ. Repenting Christians are given all of this!

My Christian friend, work in your own life to magnify the cross of Christ so that everyone can see some of what Christ's work on the cross accomplished in your life! Trials and hard times will come, as will conviction for sin; and occasionally you will be tempted to condemn God. Yet when you stop to look at the cross and the ways God has blessed you through the cross, it becomes difficult to condemn him. At the cross, you see how he has loved you. You see the care and trouble he has taken for you.

You know your own heart. You know those things—whether a hymn, a book, a passage of Scripture, a memory—that magnify Christ's cross to your own soul. Find those things and use them in your own life. Find books and hymns that magnify the cross by speaking of Christ's atonement, and feed your soul on the magnificent love of God for sinners like you and like me.

May our churches also know God's blessings in our lives together! Of course, attending church will not save you, nor will becoming a member of a church. Certainly giving to a church's building program will not save you. None of these things are what the message of Haggai is for us. Still, we should give evidence for our salvation in our churches. Our churches should not be marked by a godless selfishness! That is the most immediate implication of the book of Haggai for us today. Rather, generosity should be the fruit of God's work among us. Surely, that fruit can be seen at Capitol Hill Baptist Church (and every other gospel preaching church). The congregation gives generously so that this particular local missionary movement in Washington, D.C., will flourish. That's what a gospel-proclaiming church staff is, you know—a team of missionaries. Christians in Nigeria or France could send their money to employ another missionary at our church, if they wanted to! Another part of our own church's giving is set aside for the pastoral internship program, where we help to train pastors for other congregations. And still another portion of the church's budget goes to 9Marks, through which we try to help other local churches. And then we set apart hundreds of thousands of dollars each year for Christian work around the world. I hope our church is typical among evangelical churches in this respect!

As individual Christians in the church, then, Haggai calls us not to be self-absorbed in our finances but to give generously to God's work. Our generosity is measured not in how much we give but in how much we keep. We learn that from Jesus himself:

> Jesus sat down opposite the place where the offerings were put and watched the crowd putting their money into the temple treasury. Many rich people threw in large amounts. But a poor widow came and put in two very small copper coins, worth only a fraction of a penny.
>
> Calling his disciples to him, Jesus said, "I tell you the truth, this poor widow has put more into the treasury than all the others. They all gave out of their wealth; but she, out of her poverty, put in everything—all she had to live on" (Mark 12:41-44).

Again, our generosity is measured not in how much we give, but in how much we keep and what we are keeping it for. This will surely become clear to all of us one day. As John Piper has observed, "There are no U-Hauls behind hearses."[7]

CONCLUSION

As I was reading the John Wesley biography mentioned above, I noticed that in his closing years Wesley was greatly concerned about what he perceived as the growing worldliness of Methodists. Wesley lamented what seemed to be the insoluble problem of people's conversions leading to higher levels of indus-

---

[7] John Piper, *The Dangerous Duty of Delight* (Sisters, Ore.: Multnomah, 2001), 69.

try and frugality, leading in turn to higher levels of wealth, which then led to pride, anger, and love of the world. The only answer Wesley could resolve upon was "Give all you can!" Give that money away. Sign your checks as a declaration of independence from the power of the world over your life.

Of course, we are far more at home with wealth today. We sanguinely think that we have tamed it and can keep it as a domestic pet, using it without danger. But let me ask, when was the last time you increased the percentage of your income that you give to the church? When was the last time you even considered it, or had a conversation with your spouse about it? I don't say this because I want you to give more to our church, per se. You can give your money someplace else. Rather, I am saying this for your own soul's sake, to help you compare your bank balance with where your heart is. Haggai says we should give ourselves for the Lord's work. In what sense is the Lord's work your life-dominating aim, goal, or perspective?

At age 84, Wesley wrote,

> If you have a family, seriously consider, before God, how much each member of it needs, in order to have what is needful for life and godliness. And, in general, do not allow them less, nor much more than you allow yourself. This being done, fix your purpose, to gain no more. I charge you, in the name of God, do not increase your substance! As it comes daily or yearly, so let it go: otherwise you lay up treasures upon earth; and this our Lord as flatly forbids, as murder and adultery. By doing it, therefore, you would treasure up to yourselves wrath against the day of wrath, and revelation of the righteous judgment of God. But suppose it were not forbidden, how can you, on principles of reason, spend your money in a way, which God may possibly forgive, instead of spending it in a manner which He will certainly reward? You will have no reward in heaven, for what you lay up: you will, for what you lay out. Every pound you put into the earthly bank is sunk; it brings no interest above. But every pound you give . . . is put into the bank of heaven; and it will bring glorious interest; yea, and such as will be accumulating to all eternity.[8]

Interest accumulating for all eternity? That is a lot longer than eighty-nine years, and it's a lot more than a million dollars. *That's* a sound investment!

Invest your life, all of it, from your money to your minutes, in Christ and in his work. Or do you have a better investment idea?

Let us pray:

O Lord, *we see that practical and radical call that you gave to your people through Haggai. We pray that your Spirit would so lovingly and pointedly, so*

---

[8] Cited in Tyerman, *Life and Times of the Rev. John Wesley*, 3:519.

tenderly and mercifully, work in our own lives to free us from our false lords and to give you praise and glory with all of our substance, each day that we live. We pray, for Jesus' sake. Amen.

Questions for Reflection

1. If an objective observer looked at your bank statements from the last three months, what would he say your priorities are? If you are a Christian, would he say that your priorities are any different than those of someone who is not a Christian? Explain.

2. When was the last time you increased your percentage of giving to the church? When was the last time you thought about it? Strategized for it?

3. What financial commitments keep you from giving more to your church? To missions? To the poor in your city?

4. What time commitments keep you from serving the people of God in your local church?

5. In what area of your life are you holding the most back from Christ? Do you really think this is in your best interest?

6. How important is your material comfort to you? Would you be willing to give it up for the sake of the gospel? Are you doing so? If you have made an idol of material comfort, how would you know?

7. What does it mean to repent? Is repentance necessary for salvation?

8. What do you do to cultivate the fear of the Lord? How can a church encourage its members to cultivate the fear of the Lord?

9. Christians today are not to invest their money or time in a temple. Rather, they are called to build up the church. Keeping in mind the fact that the "church" is the gathering of the people, not the building, how can Christians today build up the church?

10. What role does the Word of God play in building up the church?

THE MESSAGE OF ZECHARIAH: DOES GOD GIVE SECOND CHANCES?

38

THE MESSAGE OF ZECHARIAH: DOES GOD GIVE SECOND CHANCES?

THE NEED FOR SECOND CHANCES[1]

I don't know about you, but I am deeply interested in second chances. I say this for myself, because I have made stupid and wrong decisions in my own life; and I find myself wanting some way to make up for those decisions or even to undo them entirely. But I also say this for people I love dearly, who have also made stupid and harmful decisions. I hope—I pray—that there is some way that God can be good, holy, just, moral, perfect, and righteous *and* still give us the opportunity to try over, to start again, to have a new beginning and a second chance.

Some of our most beloved stories are about people being given second chances—from the conversion of Christian in John Bunyan's *Pilgrim's Progress* to the reformation of Ebenezer Scrooge in Charles Dickens's *A Christmas Carol*. One is about a man who has played out his hand in the City of Destruction. The other is about a rich, miserly recluse. But even people like them need another chance.

What about you?

Are there situations at work or home, at school or church, that you have simply blown? Have you failed in your friendships or family? Has a precious opportunity passed you by? Have you spoken destructive words that appear to be irrevocable, forever closing off this possibility or that hope?

Let me take it a step further: I wonder if that is how you feel in your relationship with God. I wonder if you attend church on Sundays and join in by singing praise songs and hymns, but you simultaneously feel that you have blown it with the one you are singing about. You know that you have so

---

[1] This sermon was originally preached on December 7, 2003, at Capitol Hill Baptist Church in Washington, D.C.

abused, ignored, and mistreated him that you have no claim left on his attention, let alone on his affections. On Sunday mornings, we often try not to look as if we are as desperate as we feel. But are you discouraged with where your relationship with God is—or isn't?

INTRODUCING ZECHARIAH

If so, then you are right to turn to the Scriptures; and you have come to the right book in the Bible in our study through the Minor Prophets—the book of Zechariah. Zechariah is the longest Minor Prophet. It takes about thirty-five minutes to read the whole book out loud. Yet he is also the most obscure minor prophet. Old Testament professor Douglas Stuart has said that most people find it "an especially difficult read, even for a prophetic book." Having worked on it for a week, I can certainly agree with that statement. Also, I have never before preached on Zechariah!

Zechariah began prophesying at the same time as Haggai—in 520 B.C. Like Haggai, he exhorted the Jews who had returned from exile in Babylon to Jerusalem to get on with rebuilding the temple of the Lord. Through a series of eight visions, two sermons, and two oracles, God used Zechariah to tell God's people that they would have a second chance! We will look at the book in these three natural sections:

Chapters 1–6, which are taken up by eight visions, describe the second chance God would provide through *his rule*.

Chapters 7–8, comprised of two sermons, describe the second chance God would give through *his Word*.

Chapters 9–14, made up of two oracles, describe the second chance God would offer through *his Son*.

I pray that as we study this book, you will discover what second chance God may have in store for you.

GOD WILL GIVE A SECOND CHANCE THROUGH HIS RULE

First, we find that God gave his people a second chance through his rule.

As we saw in our study of Haggai, life for the Jews in the last part of the sixth century B.C. felt disjointed and uncertain, especially in their relationship with God. They were back in the land of Palestine, but it was easy to wonder whether God would re-own them as his own people. After all, he had exiled them so dramatically to Babylon. Would he give them a second chance? From the book's opening words, it sounds as if he would:

In the eighth month of the second year of Darius, the word of the LORD came to the prophet Zechariah son of Berekiah, the son of Iddo:

"The LORD was very angry with your forefathers. Therefore tell the people: This is what the LORD Almighty says: 'Return to me,' declares the LORD Almighty, 'and I will return to you,' says the LORD Almighty. Do not be like your forefathers, to whom the earlier prophets proclaimed: This is what the LORD Almighty says: 'Turn from your evil ways and your evil practices.' But they would not listen or pay attention to me, declares the LORD. Where are your forefathers now? And the prophets, do they live forever? But did not my words and my decrees, which I commanded my servants the prophets, overtake your forefathers?

"Then they repented and said, 'The LORD Almighty has done to us what our ways and practices deserve, just as he determined to do'" (1:1-6).

The basic imperative for this book is there in verse 3: "return to me." That seems to imply a second chance!

The first six chapters of this book are presented as a series of eight visions. I readily confess that by themselves the visions are difficult to understand, and even quite strange. For instance, what does the prophet mean when he says, "When the powerful horses went out, they were straining to go throughout the earth. And he said, 'Go throughout the earth!' So they went throughout the earth" (6:7)? Is this a story about a Bible-times Pony Express with a global reach? No, not quite.

This section is a series of visions—eight visions from chapter 1 to chapter 6—that the Lord gave the prophet Zechariah to make a point. If you have an NIV Bible, you can see the subheadings that the editors have given to each of these visions:

- "The Man Among the Myrtle Trees" (1:8-17)
- "Four Horns and Four Craftsmen" (1:18-21)
- "A Man With a Measuring Line" (chapter 2)
- "Clean Garments for the High Priest" (chapter 3)
- "The Gold Lampstand and the Two Olive Trees" (chapter 4)
- "The Flying Scroll" (5:1-4)
- "The Woman in a Basket" (5:5-11)
- "Four Chariots" (6:1-8)

Already, you can probably guess that there will be more "Bible introduction" material in this sermon than we have had in the other Minor Prophet overview sermons. I hope this will help you, but I wanted to tell you that up front. As we begin each of these three sections, I will briefly try to explain it *to* you before I then preach it *at* you.

What helped me to understand these eight visions were the patterns I began to notice while studying them. In the Hebrew Scriptures, a story's climax often comes at the end, as it does in English literature. But Hebrew literature can also be structured so that the climax occurs in the middle—at the top of a symmetrical pinnacle, as it were. Sure enough, I realized that the middle two visions—visions four and five, in chapters 3 and 4—both point to the Messiah. Vision four is about the high priest Joshua, who is symbolically covered with the filth of the people and must be cleansed. Vision five is about God's everlasting presence being restored to his people through the temple rebuilt by Zerubbabel, the governor of the land who represents the renewed line of David (4:9). Then, at the end of the fifth vision, an angel promises that two individuals would be anointed to serve the "Lord of all the earth" (4:11-14). Who are these two individuals? Presumably, they are the priest who represents the cleansing of God's people in vision 4, together with the king who accomplishes God's purposes in vision 5. The anointed one that God would send would be both priest and king.

Once I noticed that the center of these visions is occupied with these two individuals, I noticed another pattern: the first and last vision both present four horses that go throughout the earth and then return to report peace (1:8-17; 6:1-15). In the first vision, they report the peace that exists before the Lord judges the nations. It is the peace of self-righteous nations who believe that they can win their own security and rest. In the last vision, the horses report the peace that follows the coming of the Messiah (especially 6:13). This peace extends to even "the land of the north," the direction in the Old Testament usually associated with the enemies of God's people. This is the peace that will be established when God's enemies are vanquished and God reigns over all. It will be a complete and all-incorporating peace.

With the patterns of visions one, four, five, and eight settled, I then noticed something about visions two and three together with visions six and seven. The second and third visions show God winning victories over his people's enemies, while protecting his people who lived among them (1:18-21; 2:1-13). The sixth and seventh visions show God purging his own people of their sin (5:1-8; 5:9-11). All together, then, these four visions picture the defeat of *all* opposition to God's rule—both external and internal opposition.

In short, the eight visions present a picture of the whole world at peace under the rule of God's anointed priest and king.

Which is who Christ is! Jesus Christ, the anointed one, would be the great high priest and king whose kingdom would not be of this world. His rule was the great hope that the Lord held out to his beleaguered and uncertain people through these eight visions given to Zechariah.

Now, most of us are not accustomed to meditating on the meaning of Old

Testament visions. Yet notice how powerfully God presents himself: as Lord, or ruler. In fact, the Bible says that God created us to acknowledge his rule, which is why you and I have a conscience. And God promises to judge us for how we have responded to his rule. When you and I die, or when the world ends, our Maker will become our Judge. No opposition to him can prevent this Day of Judgment.

One day the whole world will be ruled by God. The God of Zechariah is no mere tribal deity. He is "the Lord of the whole world" (6:5). The entire world is his concern!

So what does this mean for us as Christians? Mainly, it means that we have hope! It means that we will never encounter circumstances too great for this God to handle. When we can see no more reason to hope, our faith in Christ shows us a new basis and cause for hope.

That's why, throughout these visions, the Lord does not often tell Zechariah to *do* this or that. I'm a preacher, so I looked for the imperative verbs, where God tells the people what to do. But God does not tell Zechariah to do much of anything except to *know* this or *see* that. Beyond that, God tells all mankind to "be still" before the Lord (2:13), and he tells the leaders to listen to him (3:8). So important was it for Zechariah to pay attention to these visions that the angel continually asked Zechariah if he understood, almost like a teacher who tries to make sure his pupil is understanding (e.g., 4:2, 5, 13; 5:2, 5). And repeatedly, the angel commands the prophet to "see," directing our attention to the particular image he wants the prophet (and us) to consider (e.g., 3:4, 9).

In short, we are not lectured about a bunch of stuff that we are supposed to do. Rather, we are shown what God is going to do! He will rule his world. He will judge his people's enemies. He will dwell with his people and protect them. He will send his Messiah and cleanse the guilt of his people. He will purge and purify his people, separating them from their own evils. So comprehensive is God's Lordship!

Christian, in case your circumstances have not already taught you the lesson, know that the basis of your hope is not in yourself. Our hope is in who God is, what he has done, and what he promises to do.

What great news! This is why we must give ourselves to studying God's Word, even if these visions are more difficult to understand than other parts of Scripture: they are all true and they are all centered on God. They point us to this great One who made us and everything in the world. And if we want to have hope in what appear to be hopeless circumstances, we must turn to *this* God who is the only source for hope.

My friend, do you study the truth about God in the Scriptures? Do you give yourself to it? Do you carefully observe God's ways with you in your own life?

Do you study the book of your own heart? If you don't, who will? Your parents, your children, your spouse, your friends, and fellow church members can all be helpful in reading your heart. But no one can read your heart as you can.

As you read God's Word, do you carefully do those things that God tells us to do, and avoid those things that he, in his love, forbids us from doing? This kind of studiousness should mark us as God's people.

Sometimes our congregation is accused of being a studious lot! Why is that? We as a church are committed to cultivating a studiousness about God's Word because we know our own flesh. We know our own ignorance about God. And we know that such cultivation will bear fruit as our hearts are appropriately humbled. So we give ourselves without apology to study—to studying God, to studying his Word, and to studying our own hearts.

This studiousness is evident in many ways in our church's life. But consider just one of them: this sermon. Our church gives an unusually long amount of time in our public weekly gathering to studying God's Word, and the sermon is given a prominent role in our weekly congregational life. That's intentional! Here are eight ways we encourage the congregation to make the sermon central to our life together:

(i) The sermon text and title are printed ahead of time on bookmark-sized note cards for church members to use in their quiet times and to pass out when inviting non-Christian friends to church.

(ii) The preacher gives himself to seriously and prayerfully preparing this weekly meal, while the congregation commits to allowing the preacher to take this time.

(iii) The whole service (prayers, Scripture readings, and music) is structured around the themes found in the day's Bible text.

(iv) Approximately one hour (sometimes more) is devoted to the sermon every week.

(v) The very last sixty seconds of the weekly gathering is devoted to quiet, personal meditation. In other words, before we all stand up and quickly start chatting about the afternoon's events and where to eat lunch, we want to give people the chance to quietly reflect on what God's Spirit has taught them as individuals. We want them to take hold of these things and to prepare themselves to edify and encourage others.

(vi) If you have ever walked by me at the door after a sermon and said something like, "Nice sermon, Pastor," you will have heard me reply something like, "Well, I hope Zechariah was helpful to you this morning." In other words, I will try to direct your attention away from grading me about how well I preached and back to letting the biblical text grade your own spirit and heart. You will never stand before God and provide a review of my sermons. Instead, you will stand before him and give a review of your own life. God does not bring people into our church so that I have a bigger audience or to pay my salary. He brings them to hear his Word. That's why I stand in the pulpit week after week—to give God's Word to God's people.

(vii) The text of the Sunday evening sermon will be on the same (or related) theme, but it is always taken from the opposite Testament of Scripture. This encourages us to know all of God's Word, and it helps us to see its unity.

(viii) I often encourage small group leaders to make the portion of Scripture that was preached on Sunday to be the subject of their small group fellowship. That allows individuals to spend more time searching together for how the week's Scripture passage applies to their lives.

Now, all this studiousness should *not* encourage pride in us. Rather, it should help develop humility in us. The study of who God is and who we are in the Scriptures should only expose the dramatic differences between us and God, to which humility is the only right response. Pride cannot long coexist with a true knowledge of God's Word and of ourselves. That's why our church takes the time to confess our sins in each weekly gathering. And that's why we announce the Lord's Supper a week before we have it, giving the congregation time to examine themselves. The knowledge you learn at school may grow pride; the knowledge you learn at church should grow humility.

In addition to humility, such studiousness should also lead to a confident hope in God, because we know more and more of what he is like. It's no wonder that so few people are satisfied in God—we know so little of him! We don't take the time to consider who he is, what he is like, what he has done for us, what he has promised us, and how faithful he has been throughout our lives. We seldom stop to reflect on these things as we should. Yet the desire and attention of our congregation's life together should help all of us refocus our lives and hearts on God and his amazing provision for us in Christ. So we praise God by prayer; we sing his praises; we speak to each other of Christ and of what he has done for and in us.

You cannot praise God when you don't know him. So give yourself to studying God's Word and to knowing better the rich provision he has made for you. Since God is infinitely praiseworthy, we can be certain that the more time we spend learning about him, the more reason we will have to praise him.

So as we study and meditate on these difficult visions of Zechariah, we clearly find God's sovereignty and goodness, his promises and his perfections, calling for our praise. And our churches must be committed to God's praise by knowing him and making him known.

This is the God who would give us a second chance through his gracious rule in our lives.

GOD WILL GIVE A SECOND CHANCE THROUGH HIS WORD

Second, God will give a second chance through his Word. This is what we learn in the two sermons in chapters 7 and 8, both of which begin with the phrase, "the word of the LORD came" (7:1; 8:1).

Today's date, December 7, is an auspicious one. Most Americans think of December 7 as the day when Japan bombed the U.S. Naval facilities at Pearl Harbor. More than twenty American ships were sunk or severely damaged. More than 150 aircraft were destroyed. And more than 2,000 lives were lost in one morning of two quick bombing raids.

But did you know something else that happened on today's date? Based on information in their books, we can actually decipher the exact days on which God revealed his words to the prophets Haggai and Zechariah. And the content of Zechariah 7 was given to Zechariah on December 7, 518 B.C. Today is the 2,521st anniversary of the day that God gave this word to the prophet Zechariah!

Let's hear this message again:

> In the fourth year of King Darius, the word of the LORD came to Zechariah on the fourth day of the ninth month, the month of Kislev. The people of Bethel had sent Sharezer and Regem-Melech, together with their men, to entreat the LORD by asking the priests of the house of the LORD Almighty and the prophets, "Should I mourn and fast in the fifth month, as I have done for so many years?"
>
> Then the word of the LORD Almighty came to me: "Ask all the people of the land and the priests, 'When you fasted and mourned in the fifth and seventh months for the past seventy years, was it really for me that you fasted? And when you were eating and drinking, were you not just feasting for yourselves? Are these not the words the LORD proclaimed through the earlier prophets when Jerusalem and its surrounding towns were at rest and prosperous, and the Negev and the western foothills were settled?'"
>
> And the word of the LORD came again to Zechariah: "This is what the LORD Almighty says: 'Administer true justice; show mercy and compassion to one another. Do not oppress the widow or the fatherless, the alien or the poor. In your hearts do not think evil of each other.'
>
> "But they refused to pay attention; stubbornly they turned their backs and stopped up their ears. They made their hearts as hard as flint and would not listen to the law or to the words that the LORD Almighty had sent by his Spirit through the earlier prophets. So the LORD Almighty was very angry.
>
> "'When I called, they did not listen; so when they called, I would not listen,' says the LORD Almighty. 'I scattered them with a whirlwind among all the nations, where they were strangers. The land was left so desolate behind them that no one could come or go. This is how they made the pleasant land desolate'" (7:1-14).

This is the first of two messages that came to Zechariah, probably two years after the eight visions of chapters 1–6. And these two messages are quite different. The first message, which we have just read, looks back and explains why God sent the people of Judah into exile. It theologically interprets their history and points to their disobedience to God's demands.

In a deliberate contrast, the second sermon—comprising chapter 8— looks forward and describes what God will do for his people according to his grace. If the first sermon explains how terrible consequences had overtaken them because they had ignored God's Word, the second sermon explains how God will reestablish his people according to his grace. In short, he will give them a new beginning—a fresh start. The chapter begins,

> Again the word of the LORD Almighty came to me. This is what the LORD Almighty says: "I am very jealous for Zion; I am burning with jealousy for her."
>
> This is what the LORD says: "I will return to Zion and dwell in Jerusalem. Then Jerusalem will be called the City of Truth, and the mountain of the LORD Almighty will be called the Holy Mountain."
>
> This is what the LORD Almighty says: "Once again men and women of ripe old age will sit in the streets of Jerusalem, each with cane in hand because of his age. The city streets will be filled with boys and girls playing there."
>
> This is what the LORD Almighty says: "It may seem marvelous to the remnant of this people at that time, but will it seem marvelous to me?" declares the LORD Almighty.
>
> This is what the LORD Almighty says: "I will save my people from the countries of the east and the west. I will bring them back to live in Jerusalem; they will be my people, and I will be faithful and righteous to them as their God" (8:1-8).

Chapter 8 adds more to the picture of a people at peace presented in the visions of the first six chapters (1:11; 2:4). We learn that God will be the one who gives this prosperity to his people according to his promises. This future will be marked by truth and love. Jerusalem will be called "the City of Truth" (8:3), and the people are instructed to "Speak the truth to each other, and render true and sound judgment in your courts; do not plot evil against your neighbor, and do not love to swear falsely" (8:16-17). They are also enjoined to "love truth and peace" (8:19).

My friend, if you are not a Christian, let me assure you that God does not lie. What he speaks is truth. Therefore, you should desire to hear God's Word and obey it! All of your sin—from your favorite sins to the ones you detest— must be given up, deserted, left off, quit! Those sins are lying to you by telling you they will do you good. They will not. You must turn from your sins, and to God. He will give you a far better future than any of your lying sins could ever give you, regardless of what promises they might make.

Christ is not only our priest and king, he is our prophet: his word is truth. He is the Word made flesh. He is the Word who brings hope. And he is the One that we are to obey because we know that what he says is true.

As God's people, we certainly should obey him, even as we hope for and wait for the future reign of Christ, which will provide mercy and justice, goodness and right. We should live under his rule even now. That is what chapter 7 is all about—through a negative example. This inspired interpretation of Israel's history let them know they were exiled because they did not heed God's Word: "they refused to pay attention; stubbornly they turned their backs and stopped up their ears. They made their hearts as hard as flint and would not listen to the law or to the words that the LORD Almighty had sent by his Spirit" (7:11-12).

My Christian brother or sister, what have you been refusing to hear in God's Word?

Some of us will be able to answer that question easily. Most of us are at least aware of some of our faults. But even for those of us who find it challenging to specifically identify areas where our heart is hard toward the Lord, we must give ourselves to the effort. This is how God searches us. "Was it really for me that you fasted?" he asks the Israelites (7:5). Through questions like this, God helped his people of old to see something of the perversity of their hearts. You, too, can use God's Word to help find something in your own life to confess and repent of. We must listen to God's Word, because this is how he begins to break us loose from our wrong affections. We all like to hear things we agree with already, and we like to hear flattering remarks. But you will gain little from such remarks. If you will stand and listen to correction, particularly correction from God in his Word, you begin to know the benefit of God's Word in your life.

As I have already suggested, Zechariah's prophecy is largely devoid of instructions for telling us what we should *do*. The two exceptions occur in the middle of chapters 7 and 8, where God instructed his people to live in a way that would honor him by their love and truth. First, in chapter 7, he told them, "Administer true justice; show mercy and compassion to one another. Do not oppress the widow or the fatherless, the alien or the poor. In your hearts do not think evil of each other" (7:9-10). Yet Israel refused to follow these commands, which is why they were exiled. Still, these commands revealed something of God's heart. So they would be repeated in chapter 8 as the Lord speaks about the future society of his people: "Speak truth to each other, and render true and sound judgment in your courts; do not plot evil against your neighbor, and do not love to swear falsely. I hate all this" (8:16-17). God would deliver his people in the future from the sins that they had succumbed to in the past. Still, he enjoined them to forsake those sins immediately. Turn loose of your sins and let the future begin now!

Hearing God's Word, in other words, requires us to depend completely upon God. After all, why will these blessings come? Why can we have hope? "Again the word of the LORD Almighty came to me. This is what the LORD Almighty says: 'I am very jealous for Zion; I am burning with jealousy for her'" (8:1-2). "I will save my people" (8:7). "I will save you" (8:13). In other words, all of these blessings are given not because God's people are so deserving but because God is so loving and tenaciously committed to them! Christian, you and I owe all of our joy and happiness, our blessings and hope, to God and God alone. Apart from him, we would be left to our disobedience and sin. We would be left in chapter 7, experiencing the bitter fruits of our sin. Yet because of God, we have been given new life and a second chance.

May our churches be so marked by truth and love. These middle chapters of Zechariah clearly teach that God values both. How can our churches cultivate such love and truth-telling? Here are a few ideas:

(i) We can commit to being actively honest with one another by confessing our sins, shortcomings, and struggles. Too many people in our churches are infected by a sad and lonely, sin-coddling, encouragement-starving individualism that produces lean, mean, and isolated souls. And keep in mind, our Western culture will not encourage us to think any differently! So I exhort you to work to break out of that. Make the joys of others in your church *your* joys. And reach out to accept the pain of others as *your* pain. Begin to live more largely than just yourself.

(ii) We can read biographies of heroic individuals who showed courage and bravery in how they loved and told the truth. A church library and bookstore should be well-stocked with such volumes. Other people's lives can challenge us to live more as God would have us live.

(iii) We should also learn to pray for other members of the church. Someone's personal victory over this or that sin should not help just the individual but everyone in relationship with him. Prayer helps to stir up a godly concern and love for one another.

In short, the kind of frankness that we want to encourage in our churches is far more than an individual virtue. Learning to communicate in a loving and truthful fashion requires a community to be worked out, to be rounded off, to show its multiplying splendor. We will have to forbear with one another as mistakes are made and as we sin against one another. And we will have to encourage one another for sincere attempts and intents. In order for God's Word to encounter and shape hearts, we must be correctable. And correctability does not come naturally to any of us.

One small way in which I try to cultivate correctability in myself and the church pastoral staff is through the time we set aside to review together the Sunday morning and evening services. On Sunday night, after the evening service, the pastoral staff and interns review every element of the day and speak truthfully and honestly with each other. We do this in order to practice and model what giving and receiving godly criticism looks like, as well as what giving and receiving godly encouragement looks like (which can require every bit as much vulnerability). Giving and receiving criticism and encouragement can initially be difficult due to our natural self-protectiveness. But learning these practices will bear good fruit. The church should continually be reformed according to the Word of God, and such conversations of godly criticism and encouragement play one role in this kind of reformation.

Are there ways you can practice modeling criticism and encouragement according to God's Word in your family, in your small group, or among your friends?

Through God's Word, we get a new beginning in life.

GOD WILL GIVE A SECOND CHANCE THROUGH HIS SON

Third, God will give a second chance through his Son.

The last six chapters of Zechariah are divided into two oracles. Chapters 9–11 comprise the first, while chapters 12–14 comprise the second. Both oracles begin with the promise of judgment on Israel's enemies (9:1-8; 12:1-9). Next, both oracles point to One who would come. In the first oracle he is called Israel's "king," the "LORD," and a shepherd (9:9, 14-16; 11:4-9). In the second oracle he is called "the one they have pierced" and a "shepherd" (12:10; 13:7).

Thus far, the two oracles match one another: a promise of judgment on the nations, followed by the provision of the good shepherd.

At this point, however, their paths diverge. The first oracle ends with the divine shepherd-king being detested by the flock: they reject him (11:8). This figure is also rejected in the second oracle. In fact, the description is far worse: he is pierced and struck (12:10; 13:7), implying that he dies. Yet this second oracle does not end with the divine shepherd-king's rejection. In chapter 14, the prophet describes a celebration of the day of the Lord and the consummation of the kingdom. As in the first two sections of Zechariah's book that we have already examined, this third section ends with the Lord reigning.

I don't know how complicated all this sounds to you, but once I scratched it out on a piece of paper, it became pretty clear, interesting, and compelling.

Of course, the question that has to be answered is, why do these last two oracles include that interesting plot twist, in which the divine shepherd-king is rejected. Zechariah does not answer that question as clearly as a New Testament book like Romans, but it does point to the answer. Consider the first verse of chapter 13: "On that day a fountain will be opened to the house of David and the inhabitants of Jerusalem, to cleanse them from sin and impurity." Throughout Zechariah is a clear awareness of sin and of our need to be cleansed of sin before we can have fellowship with a holy God.

God has sent someone who will cleanse us from our sin. This someone is God himself, who came in human flesh as Jesus of Nazareth. He was then struck down and pierced. Yet his death was the death that you and I should have died for our sins. Christ died as a substitute for all who will ever repent of their sins and turn to him. Therefore, the most important thing that you can do today is not to detest him and reject him as your Savior and Substitute, but to love him, accept him, and take him as your own. Take his death for your death, and his life for your life. Trust in Christ's claims to have answered God's wrath for all those who would repent and believe the good news.

There is so much in this little book of Zechariah about Christ. It is quoted more than any other book of the Old Testament in the Gospels' accounts of the crucifixion. Christ is the Good Shepherd! Christ is the rejected one! Christ is the One who was pierced and stricken! One of the most amazing and commented upon verses in the whole Old Testament occurs in chapter 12. The Lord says,

> "And I will pour out on the house of David and the inhabitants of Jerusalem a spirit of grace and supplication. They will look on me, the one they have pierced, and they will mourn for him as one mourns for an only child, and grieve bitterly for him as one grieves for a firstborn son" (12:10).

What an extraordinary verse! What on earth would a Jewish prophet who has been taught monotheism in the sixth century B.C. be doing, putting these words into the mouth of God and speaking it to priests? *They will look on me, the one they have pierced!*

In his gospel, the apostle John recounts the crucifixion and includes the story of the soldier who pierced Jesus' side with a spear. And he quotes this passage from Zechariah and declares it fulfilled.

Yet consider further what the Lord is saying in this verse: they *will* look on me (future tense), the one they *have pierced* (a form of past tense). Questions quickly crowd into the head. Who is this? It's the Lord. How could they pierce Yahweh? Only if he had flesh. Okay, but how could they look in the future on this one they have pierced and killed in the past? Only if he comes to life again. Only if he returns!

Oh, my Christian brothers and sisters, we should praise this great Messiah Jesus and honor him! We should do this, as Zechariah exhorts us to do, by rejoicing over him (9:9). We should sing about him. And so we do. Our weekly church bulletin is deliberately filled with music that centers on who Jesus is as the Messiah and on what he has done for us. Here are several of this week's selections:

Lamb of God[2]

Your only Son, no sin to hide;
But You have sent him from Your side
To walk upon this guilty sod
And to become the Lamb of God.

O Lamb of God, sweet Lamb of God,
I love the holy Lamb of God.
O wash me in Your precious blood,
My Jesus Christ the Lamb of God.

Your gift of love they crucified,
They laughed and scorned Him as He died.
The humble King they named a fraud
And sacrificed the Lamb of God.

I was so lost I should have died;
But You have brought me to Your side
To be led by Your staff and rod
And to be called a lamb of God.

How Deep the Father's Love[3]

How deep the Father's love for us, how vast beyond all measure,
That he should give his only Son to make a wretch his treasure.
How great the pain of searing loss: the Father turns his face away,
As wounds which mar the chosen one bring many sons to glory.

Behold the man upon a cross, my sin upon his shoulders;
Ashamed I hear my mocking voice call out among the scoffers.

---

[2] "Lamb of God," words by Twila Paris, ©1985 Mountain Spring Music/Straightway Music. All rights reserved. Used by permission.
[3] "How Deep the Father's Love," words by Stuart Townend, copyright © 1995 Thankyou Music. All rights reserved. Used by permission.

It was my sin that held him there until it was accomplished;
his dying breath has brought me life—I know that it is finished.

I will not boast in anything, no gifts, no power, no wisdom;
But I will boast in Jesus Christ, his death and resurrection.
Why should I gain from his reward? I cannot give an answer,
But this I know with all my heart, his wounds have paid my ransom.

The Servant King (From Heaven You Came)[4]

From heav'n you came, helpless babe,
Entered our world, Your glory veiled,
Not to be served, but to serve,
And give your life that we might live.

This is our God, the Servant King,
He calls us now to follow him;
To bring our lives as a daily offering
Of worship to the Servant King.

There in the garden of tears,
My heavy load he chose to bear,
His heart with sorrow was torn
Yet "Not my will, but Yours" he said.

Come see his hands and his feet,
The scars that speak of sacrifice,
Hands that flung stars into space
To cruel nails surrendered.

So let us learn now to serve
And in our hearts enthrone him,
Each other's needs to prefer,
For it is Christ we're serving.

Lo, He Comes with Clouds Descending[5]

Lo, he comes with clouds descending,
Once for favored sinners slain;

---

[4] "The Servant King (From Heaven You Came)," words by Graham Kendrick, © Thankyou Music. All rights reserved. Used by permission.
[5] "Lo, He Comes with Clouds Descending," words by John Cennick, 1752; Charles Wesley, 1758; and Martin Madan, 1760.

thousand thousand saints attending
swell the triumph of his train.
Hallelujah! Hallelujah! Hallelujah!
God appears on earth to reign.

Every eye shall now behold him,
robed in dreadful majesty;
those who set at naught and sold him,
pierced, and nailed him to the tree,
deeply wailing, deeply wailing, deeply wailing,
shall the true Messiah see.

The dear tokens of his passion
still his dazzling body bears;
cause of endless exultation
to his ransomed worshipers;
with what rapture, with what rapture, with what rapture,
gaze we on those glorious scars!

Yea, Amen! Let all adore thee,
high on thine eternal throne;
Savior, take the power and glory,
claim the kingdom for thine own.
Hallelujah! Hallelujah! Hallelujah!
Everlasting God, come down!

The services of our church are filled with this message from the book of
Zechariah. In Zechariah, God himself comes as our Messiah Deliverer. He
judges the nations and protects his people. He purges his people and blesses
them. He makes the difference! His jealous love impels him to return to his
unresponsive people. God has determined that "the LORD will be king over the
whole earth. On that day there will be one LORD, and his name the only name"
(14:9). And God has determined that all the lying substitutes, the false
prophets, and the idols they serve will be put out of business. My Christian
friend, take no pride in the fact that you "believe." It is God who must save
you and me, for we can certainly never save ourselves!

If you have reached this point in the sermon, and you are wondering, "But
if this is true, why don't more people believe it?" let me point you to the last
two verses in chapter 13:

"In the whole land," declares the LORD,
"two-thirds will be struck down and perish;

yet one-third will be left in it.
This third I will bring into the fire;
    I will refine them like silver
    and test them like gold.
They will call on my name
    and I will answer them;
I will say, 'They are my people,'
    and they will say, 'The LORD is our God'" (13:8-9).

God always seems to work with a minority. Polling the crowds is a rotten way to determine truth. Yet God is determined to preserve his own people. The faithfulness of God is the basis of our hope.

If you are a Christian who struggles hard with some particular sin, let me encourage you, in light of God's blessings, return to the Lord. Forsake your disobedience! Repent of that sin you have been harboring. Your sin will do you no good. The earlier you get rid of your sin, the more heartache you will save yourself!

As for our churches, may we always be clear that Christianity is *not* a self-help religion. It is a religion that acknowledges that we have heinously rejected God and yet that God has tenaciously pursued us in love in order to save us. This is why we should sing hymns like the ones we just read. This is why our church repeats the gospel in our prayers and in our readings. Because Christ has died for us!

Our churches should be committed to having only one leg to stand on, and it should not be our leg, but God's!

God will give us new life through his Son.

CONCLUSION

So does God give second chances? He certainly did for his people of old. Only it is not really a second "chance" that God gives, because nothing is uncertain when God is involved. Through the promise of his reign, his Word, and his Son, God claims his people for himself, even when they throw themselves away. The appeal that God made to his people through Zechariah is summed up in the third verse of the book: "tell the people: This is what the LORD Almighty says: 'Return to me,' declares the LORD Almighty, and I will return to you,' says the LORD Almighty" (1:3). Their return would be both an acknowledgment and a working out of God's rightful sovereignty.

We mentioned that today is the anniversary of the attack on Pearl Harbor, as well as of God speaking to Zechariah. It is also the anniversary of another event, one certainly no less memorable in the annals of heaven. In 1932, John

Stam from New Jersey traveled to China with the China Inland Mission. He did his language study, and then in 1933 he married Betty Scott. In September of 1934, John and Betty had a baby girl. Several months later after the birth of their daughter, on December 6, 1934, John and Betty Stam were arrested by communist soldiers amid the great political turmoil in southern China. The next day, on December 7, 1934—sixty-nine years ago today—the Communist soldiers took them to the house of a wealthy man who had fled the area, where they were kept overnight. The next morning, they were tied tightly and led through the town and out to a little hill. They were questioned and then, in quick succession, beheaded. First John, then Betty. At the time, both of them were 27 years old. They had gone to China to tell people that God would give them another life through his mercy in Christ, since everyone's first life had been spent by sin. John and Betty knew their work would be dangerous. But they had an important message to give. Their faithfulness to proclaim and then even die for this message led many others, including the famous missionary Jim Elliot, to then go and tell the good news—this message of Zechariah. "Return to me," says the Lord Almighty.

I hope you can see the importance and power of this message of forgiveness of sins and new life in Christ. People will even give their lives for it!

I know that I needed the message of new life in Christ. People very close to me need that news. And now I have staked my life on bringing that message to others.

What about you? Do you need a new opportunity with God? Do you need a new life?

Let us pray:

Dear God, you know the foolishness of our lives. You know how much we oppose you. We pray that you will act in sovereign mercy to undercut our hatred with your love, our independence with your care for us. Move by your Spirit and give new life by convicting us of sin and turning us to the Savior, we pray for Jesus' sake. Amen.

Questions for Reflection

1. Is there any area of your life in which you feel that you have blown it with God? Some area where he would never give you a second chance? Where?

2. Would the people in your life who know you and *depend* on you (spouse, children, employees, friends) say that you are someone who gives second

chances? How does giving second chances to those who depend on us commend the gospel?

3. If so many kinds of knowledge can "puff up" our egos, why does a true knowledge of God humble us?

4. Does God rule over the nations today? When Christ comes again, how will his rule over the nations change?

5. What keeps you from studying God's Word more carefully?

6. In terms of how you would rate a church, where does "careful teaching of God's Word" fall on the list of priorities?

7. Why should *who God is* be our greatest source of hope? How do you cultivate this hope?

8. Would your friends and family members describe you as correctable? How do you cultivate teachability? Why is the attribute of "teachability" intimately connected to being a "believer in the gospel"?

9. What, more than anything else, shows us that God is a God of second chances?

39

THE MESSAGE OF MALACHI: DOES IT MATTER HOW I WORSHIP GOD?

ISN'T SINCERITY IN OUR WORSHIP ALL THAT COUNTS?[1]

Sometime back, *Psychology Today* interviewed CNN talk-show host Larry King and asked him why he was so good at his job of interviewing people. King replied, "I'm sincere. I'm really curious. I care what people think. I listen to answers and leave my ego at the door. I don't use the word 'I.'"[2]

I found it amusing that King identified his skill at interviewing as based on his lack of using the word "I," and yet used it six times in the three lines answering the question!

I don't mean to criticize King. He is, without doubt, one of the best interviewers on television. He actually gives his guests time to answer his questions, and that alone sets him apart from many others. But it is striking that King—without any intended irony—focused on himself as not being the center.

Really, I think we are all like that. It isn't just King. All of us find our natural center in ourselves. We simply assume that what Polonius in Shakespeare's *Hamlet* said is true: "This above all: to thine own self be true, And it must follow, as the night the day, Thou canst not then be false to any man" (I.iii.78-80).

Certainly, self-knowledge is important. Sometimes we need to be brutally honest with ourselves. But in our day, we are regularly told that the self must not only be known, it must be regarded, expressed, actualized, and obeyed!

---

[1] This sermon was originally preached on December 14, 2003, at Capitol Hill Baptist Church in Washington, D.C.
[2] Larry King, interview by Manuello Paganelli, "The Every Man Who Would Be King," *Psychology Today* (May/June 1996).

Everything from our economics to our family life, from our health to our politics, must conform to the requirements of the self. Life, liberty, and the pursuit of happiness are not endowments of a Creator; they are the inherent rights of the self. Descartes may have said, "I think, therefore I am." Yet our motto today is "I want, therefore I am."

It's no surprise, then, that *sincerity* has come to be regarded as chief of the virtues. King listed his own sincerity as the first reason why he was a good interviewer. Sincerity appears to be a virtue with no downside. When we say that someone is "sincere," we are suggesting that the person possesses an integrity and an authenticity that are, without question, good. Sincerity has a plain, simple honesty about it—a kind of "what you see is what you get" quality that is fresh, even noble. Longfellow said that sincerity is "Just what I think, and nothing more nor less." Who can object to that?

Surely the alternative is incalculably dangerous: to be insincere is to deceive and to hide from others, from ourselves, and ultimately from God. Insincerity and falseness are certainly bad, we say, and sincerity is certainly good.

But is sincerity as good as we think? I assume there are people who have *sincerely* killed their neighbor, *sincerely* hated their parents, or *sincerely* blasphemed God. By itself, sincerity does not make us right. I can be sincere *and* wrong at the same time. Sincerity is necessary, but it is not sufficient.

Our culture's overemphasis on the sincere self has also affected how we think about religion. Sincere self-expression has come to rule not only in the fields of art, psychology, child-rearing, and education, but in religion. If yesterday's buzz words were "official" and "professional," the buzz words today are "authentic" and "real." Popular religious faith today places a premium on being private, centered on the self, and ambiguous about God.

I wonder if this is the kind of religion that you look for: private, self-centered, vague about the God to whom you sing and pray, but very sincere!

INTRODUCING MALACHI

If so, then you have come to the right book in the Bible—and the last book in the Old Testament—Malachi. We began this series in the Minor Prophets in Hosea in the early eighth century B.C. Now we come to the fifth century B.C. and a prophet about whom we know less than any of the others. We know who wrote it from the first verse of his book: "An oracle: The word of the LORD to Israel through Malachi" (1:1). Malachi's book is quoted by Paul, Luke, Mark, and even Jesus.[3] Yet Malachi himself is never mentioned anywhere else in the

---

[3] Matt. 11:10; Mark 1:2; Luke 1:17; 7:27; Rom. 9:13.

Bible, and his name simply means "my messenger." Still, his little book was important for his own day, and it has an important message for ours as well.

Malachi wrote to the Jewish people who had been restored to their land after exile in Babylon. The temple had been rebuilt, thanks to the faithful preaching of Haggai and Zechariah. Worship at the temple *may* have recommenced (depending on when exactly Malachi wrote), thanks to Ezra's teaching. And Jerusalem's walls may have been rebuilt, thanks to Nehemiah's effective leadership. The Jewish nation's external circumstances looked good. Still, true worship had not been restored. So God inspired Malachi to write this short book.

Before we dive into Malachi, I want to observe that reading and rereading Malachi last week impressed on me how appropriate it was for the Old Testament to end with this book. Now, unlike the Greek Old Testament (the Septuagint) and the English Old Testament, the original Hebrew Bible places the books of the Old Testament in a different order. The prophets appear earlier in its canon. But all three versions understand that Malachi represents the last prophetic book of the Bible. In that sense, Malachi really ends the Old Testament, no matter how the particular Bible you are studying orders the books. And it's such a revealing ending, given the Bible's beginning! After God's marvelous act of creation, Genesis kicks off with the selfish sin of Adam and Eve. Their selfishness plants firm roots, so that by the time we get to Malachi thousands of years later, after God has specially worked with his people again and again, after he has restored them from exile, after the walls and temple have been rebuilt, human selfishness is still flowering in full bloom. No external circumstances will change the hearts of human beings. Selfishness ruled as sovereignly in the temple grounds of post-exile Jerusalem as it did when Adam and Eve listened to the serpent. Times were hard when Malachi wrote. People were selfish. And, as long as good people suffered and bad people prospered, some individuals wondered if God cared at all.

But certainly God cares. And in this little book, God raises six disputes with his people. In a single sermon, we will not be able to deal with all the topics God addresses, but we can see the basic structure:

The first dispute is in 1:2-5;
the second is 1:6–2:9;
the third is 2:10-16;
the fourth is 2:17–3:5;
the fifth is 3:6-12;
and the sixth is 3:13–4:3.

The central disputes—disputes 3 and 4—focus on how the people of Israel were treating one another. Disputes 2 and 5 focus on how the people of Israel were dealing with their own lives. And disputes 1 and 6 focus on how the people regarded God. This is the order we will follow in our study; and I pray that as we proceed, you will discover that it matters very much *how* you worship God.

WORSHIP OF GOD INVOLVES HOW WE TREAT OTHER PEOPLE

First, we learn in the very middle of Malachi's book that worship of God involves how we treat others.

Many people regard religion as a deeply private matter, something that involves how they *think* or *feel about* basic spiritual matters. Furthermore, religion is whatever gives them peace, composure, or a quiet sense of joy. Yet these conceptions could not be further from the picture that Malachi presents of the true religion that is acceptable to God.

Forming and Keeping Our Families

To begin with, God told the people of Israel that true worship of him involved how they treated their families:

> Have we not all one Father? Did not one God create us? Why do we profane the covenant of our fathers by breaking faith with one another?
>
> Judah has broken faith. A detestable thing has been committed in Israel and in Jerusalem: Judah has desecrated the sanctuary the LORD loves, by marrying the daughter of a foreign god. As for the man who does this, whoever he may be, may the LORD cut him off from the tents of Jacob—even though he brings offerings to the LORD Almighty.
>
> Another thing you do: You flood the LORD's altar with tears. You weep and wail because he no longer pays attention to your offerings or accepts them with pleasure from your hands. You ask, "Why?" It is because the LORD is acting as the witness between you and the wife of your youth, because you have broken faith with her, though she is your partner, the wife of your marriage covenant.
>
> Has not *the LORD made them one? In flesh and spirit they are his. And why one? Because he was seeking godly offspring. So guard yourself in your spirit, and do not break faith with the wife of your youth.*
>
> "I hate divorce," says the LORD God of Israel, "and I hate a man's covering himself with violence as well as with his garment," says the LORD Almighty.
>
> So guard yourself in your spirit, and do not break faith (Mal. 2:10-16).

Here in the third vision, God disputed with the people of Israel for their unfaithfulness to him as expressed by their unfaithfulness to one another. They had broken their covenant with God by breaking their covenants of marriage, and they were doing so in two ways: first, they were marrying those who did not worship the Lord: "Judah has desecrated the sanctuary the LORD loves, by marrying the daughter of a foreign god" (2:11b). In this verse, "sanctuary" refers to the people of Israel as a whole.

Throughout Old Testament times, God forbade the Israelites from marrying foreigners, not because he wanted to keep his people racially pure but because he wanted them to be religiously pure—worshipers of one God. The Lord knew that foreign wives and husbands would lead the hearts of his people astray. Yet again and again the Israelites disobeyed the Lord by marrying foreigners, and sure enough, their hearts were led astray. Now, God has brought them back into the land after exile in Babylon, and they are beginning to sin against God in the ways their fathers before them had sinned (2:10, 11, 14, 15, 16).

Second, the Israelites mistreated their families through wrongful divorce. The people had begun to divorce their spouses simply because they disliked them. In recent years, a number of people and one prominent translation have translated the famous "I hate divorce" passage more literally as, "For the man who hates and divorces, says the LORD, the God of Israel, covers his garment with violence, says the LORD of hosts. So guard yourselves in your spirit, and do not be faithless" (2:16, ESV).[4] I believe this translation fits better with the fact that Scripture elsewhere makes allowances for divorce under particular circumstances.[5] It also brings out the fact that God is interested in condemning a particular kind of divorce—one based on feelings of hate. Of course, our own Western culture has wrongly, unwisely, and destructively accepted the idea of a "no-fault" divorce based merely on such feelings of disaffection.

So God told his people that their worship of him included faithful marriages to one another. They were not simply to live self-serving lives, marrying and divorcing whomever they wished. Rather, God was their Father and Creator (2:10), and they expressed faithful submission to him, first, by marrying only other God-worshipers and, second, by not divorcing their spouses "for hate." In choosing their spouses, they demonstrated what God they chose. In remaining faithful to their spouses, they demonstrated faithfulness to this God.

If you are a non-Christian, I hope you are beginning to see how invasive Christianity is. It spreads into every area of your life. Should you become a Christian, God will require you to be allied to him above your spouse. God will share his throne with no one, not even a spouse. Should you become a Christian while you are single, God teaches that his Lordship extends even to where you set your heart's affections. If you decide to love God, you cannot marry someone who is opposed to him or even indifferent to him. Indifference

---

[4] See also Gordon P. Hugenberger's translation in "Malachi," in D. A. Carson et al., consulting eds., *New Bible Commentary*, 4th ed. (Downers Grove, Ill.: InterVarsity Press, 1994), 887.

[5] E.g., Deut. 24:1-4; Matt. 1:19; 5:32; 19:8-9; 1 Cor. 7:15.

to God *is* opposition to God. Friend, God wants to come into your life and convict you of the selfishness you have practiced even in the relationships closest to your heart. How you stand toward them is affected by how you stand toward God.

Society certainly benefits from recognizing the truth of marriage—the union between two people that may lead to more people! Everyone gains when two parents care for each other and their children. Therefore, Christian voters, policymakers, writers, and lawyers need to think through the ramifications of how different policies will affect the state of marriage in a nation. But as Christians, we must not think for a moment that we depend on the state in order to practice marriage and divorce as prescribed by the Scriptures, no matter what the government decides to do with marriage. In our churches and our families, Christ remains our ever-faithful head and we must follow him, regardless of what this or that legislature may decide.

So, Christian, observe that Malachi speaks directly to the idea of marrying an unbeliever, and he says that it is both disobedient and religiously suicidal. The New Testament says the same (e.g., 2 Cor. 6:14). Now, if someone is already married and then he or she comes to Christ, the Christian should continue to honor that marriage. But the Bible clearly teaches us not to set our heart on someone who is not allied to God in the first place. If God is your chief love, how can you?

Also, know that Malachi's condemnation of ending marriages for anything other than biblical reasons applies not just to ancient Israelites but to Christians today. God's laws do not change, no matter what the state decides. In the Bible, divorce is allowed in very particular circumstances, such as adultery and, perhaps, desertion.[6] Yet divorce is certainly never required. The book of Hosea shows the power of love to overcome even the greatest wrongs.

In short, we are called to be careful about whom we marry, and we are called to be faithful in those marriages.

What does this mean for our churches? Let me first say that, as a pastor, I have had the opportunity and privilege of dealing with all sorts of awful and terrible situations in the lives of the congregation. That is part of what God has called me to do. And no issue is more complicated, difficult, and painful than divorce.

Yet for the church as a whole, it is important to remember that how we enter and maintain our marriages is a matter of worship. Paul tells us that we are to offer our bodies as living sacrifices, holy and pleasing to God—which is our spiritual worship (Rom. 12:1). I pray that our churches would be com-

---

[6] Ibid.

munities where worship is cultivated not merely on Sundays, but every day. The Old Testament Israelites selfishly formed and unformed their marriages, and it brought destruction on them again and again. If Christians are able to marry non-Christians or divorce their spouses while the church says and does nothing, that same destruction will come upon us. How many of us have parents who divorced their spouses only to have their churches say nothing? How many of us have friends or even children who, though claiming to be Christians, freely date non-Christians, while the church says nothing. According to the Bible, the manner in which we form and keep our families plays a large role in our worship.

We have taken more time on this disputation than we will on the other five, because it seems to have been one of the Lord's primary concerns in Malachi. But there are a number of other issues that we should examine as well.

Acting Justly Toward Our Neighbors

One of them we see in the next disputation, where God tells us that true worship also involves how we treat our neighbors:

> You have wearied the LORD with your words.
>
> "How have we wearied him?" you ask.
>
> By saying, "All who do evil are good in the eyes of the LORD, and he is pleased with them" or "Where is the God of justice?"
>
> "See, I will send my messenger, who will prepare the way before me. Then suddenly the Lord you are seeking will come to his temple; the messenger of the covenant, whom you desire, will come," says the LORD Almighty.
>
> But who can endure the day of his coming? Who can stand when he appears? For he will be like a refiner's fire or a launderer's soap. He will sit as a refiner and purifier of silver; he will purify the Levites and refine them like gold and silver. Then the LORD will have men who will bring offerings in righteousness, and the offerings of Judah and Jerusalem will be acceptable to the LORD, as in days gone by, as in former years.
>
> "So I will come near to you for judgment. I will be quick to testify against sorcerers, adulterers and perjurers, against those who defraud laborers of their wages, who oppress the widows and the fatherless, and deprive aliens of justice, but do not fear me," says the LORD Almighty (2:17–3:5).

God has always been concerned about justice among his people. The religion he has revealed is not merely private. It has to do with our families. It also has to do with how we treat our neighbors.

In this passage, God's dispute with the people of Israel was over matters of justice. The Israelites, because they did not see wrongs immediately redressed, concluded that God did not care: "Where is the God of justice?"[7]

The Lord answered with words the Gospel writer Mark would take and use to introduce John the Baptist, who in turn introduced Jesus: "'See, I will send my messenger, who will prepare the way before me. Then suddenly the Lord you are seeking will come to his temple; the messenger of the covenant, whom you desire, will come,' says the LORD Almighty" (3:1; see Mark 1:2).

Where is the God of justice? He is coming! This one "whom you desire—the desire of nations," as the prophet Haggai called him (Hag. 2:7), is coming. He would come and he would die on the cross, enduring "the wrath of God . . . revealed from heaven against all the godlessness and wickedness of men" (Rom. 1:18). God would satisfy the requirements of justice more than any of the disputants represented by Malachi could ever imagine.

The Lord gave several brief examples of injustice:

> "So I will come near to you for judgment. I will be quick to testify against sorcerers, adulterers and perjurers, against those who defraud laborers of their wages, who oppress the widows and the fatherless, and deprive aliens of justice, but do not fear me" (Mal. 3:5).

God-worshipers must not practice sorcery or adultery. They must not lie or cheat their employees out of their wages. They must not oppress the defenseless. God cares about how his people treat others. A person who is indifferent to injustice should not pretend to be a God-worshiper.

Do you know what the difference between *indifference to justice* and *injustice* itself is? Not much. If you heart is cold to the topic of injustice, it's cold to something that God cares about. God's character is revealed in justice. That's true in our cities; that's true in our land; that's true around the world.

God wanted his people to know that he is a God of justice (2:17). And he told his people that they should fear and worship him with all their lives.

Have you attended church for a while and, at the same time, accused God of being indifferent to what happens in the world because of pain you have seen or felt? "How could God let *this* happen if he really cared about me?" Oh, friend, you must pull back and take a larger view. The problem that you feel is testimony to this larger situation *you* may have ignored, but God hasn't.

London's National Theatre recently staged a two-part drama called "His Dark Materials," featuring witches, angels, demons, and child-catchers called Gobblers. The play focuses on the theme of injustice in the world and what

---

[7] 2:17; cf. Ps. 73; Jer. 12; 2 Pet. 3.

that means about God. The climax occurs when God is destroyed. He dies, one reviewer said, in the form of "a withered old man." When asked about the production, National Theatre artistic director Nicholas Hytner said the play discusses some of the great questions of the age, including "'If (there is a God), why is He indifferent to our welfare?'"[8]

That's exactly what the people in Malachi's day were asking, and perhaps what your heart has asked from time to time.

Maybe you have assumed that since you have not witnessed God judging wrong, he never will. Or maybe you have assumed he doesn't care. I assure you, neither supposition is right. God, who was never required to care, cared so deeply that he sent his only Son to take on flesh and to die on a cross for the sins of people like you and me. Sins that he never committed. Sins that deserve his just wrath against us. Sins that he, in his amazing love, took upon himself. God calls us now to repent of those sins and to turn to him so that he might grant us forgiveness and new life in him. God's action in Jesus Christ was the greatest display of love and justice that could be imagined!

If you are a Christian, learn from Malachi that your worship of God involves the way you treat others. Adultery is a sin against either your spouse or your future spouse. Perjury is a sin against the person that you lie *about* and the person that you lie *to*. Defrauding the people who work for you of their rightful wages is not just a legal matter, it is a spiritual matter. Oppressing the vulnerable who have no power to protect themselves is also a sin. If you think you worship God because you attend church and sing hymns, while your life is characterized by an unrepentant participation in such sins, you are fooling yourself. You are not worshiping God. It doesn't matter how sincere you are. Sincerity alone is not the point. As the apostle John said, "If anyone says, 'I love God,' yet hates his brother, he is a liar. For anyone who does not love his brother, whom he has seen, cannot love God, whom he has not seen" (1 John 4:20). Our horizontal relationships with one another testify either for or against the reality of our vertical relationship with God.

In our churches, we should work to hold one another accountable, to encourage, to instruct and rebuke one another, so that our faith becomes real and visible in the way we live. The love of God must show itself in the way we regard and care for one another. If we are so self-righteous that we don't allow other Christians to speak into our lives and correct our injustices, we cannot be in church together. You are a sinner, I am a sinner, and every pastor you will ever have is a sinner. We should take ownership of this fact and, in humility,

---

[8] Cited at http://www.darkmaterials.org/article214.html.

admit our own sin before God and approach one another in brokenness. This is the kind of worship that is acceptable to God.

Worship is not just ethereal or private. It necessarily involves how we treat both our families and our neighbors.

WORSHIP OF GOD INVOLVES WHAT WE DO WITH OURSELVES

A second matter that the Lord teaches us through Malachi is that worship of him involves what we do with ourselves, which brings us to the second and fifth disputes.

Here, again, we might think that our own sincerity inoculates us from any criticism, but that is not the case. God cares not only about *what* we do, he cares about *how* we do it.

Giving Our Best

In Malachi's day, temple worship had restarted. Once again, people brought their sacrifices and their tithes to the temple. Yet all was not right. God did not simply want whatever they could spare; he wanted their best. Consider the second dispute:

> "A son honors his father, and a servant his master. If I am a father, where is the honor due me? If I am a master, where is the respect due me?" says the LORD Almighty. "It is you, O priests, who show contempt for my name.
>
> "But you ask, 'How have we shown contempt for your name?'
>
> "You place defiled food on my altar.
>
> "But you ask, 'How have we defiled you?'
>
> "By saying that the LORD's table is contemptible. When you bring blind animals for sacrifice, is that not wrong? When you sacrifice crippled or diseased animals, is that not wrong? Try offering them to your governor! Would he be pleased with you? Would he accept you?" says the LORD Almighty.
>
> "Now implore God to be gracious to us. With such offerings from your hands, will he accept you?"—says the LORD Almighty.
>
> "Oh, that one of you would shut the temple doors, so that you would not light useless fires on my altar! I am not pleased with you," says the LORD Almighty, "and I will accept no offering from your hands. My name will be great among the nations, from the rising to the setting of the sun. In every place incense and pure offerings will be brought to my name, because my name will be great among the nations," says the LORD Almighty.
>
> "But you profane it by saying of the Lord's table, 'It is defiled,' and of its food, 'It is contemptible.' And you say, 'What a burden!' and you sniff at it contemptuously," says the LORD Almighty.
>
> "When you bring injured, crippled or diseased animals and offer them as

sacrifices, should I accept them from your hands?" says the LORD. "Cursed is the cheat who has an acceptable male in his flock and vows to give it, but then sacrifices a blemished animal to the Lord. For I am a great king," says the LORD Almighty, "and my name is to be feared among the nations.

"And now this admonition is for you, O priests. If you do not listen, and if you do not set your heart to honor my name," says the LORD Almighty, "I will send a curse upon you, and I will curse your blessings. Yes, I have already cursed them, because you have not set your heart to honor me.

"Because of you I will rebuke your descendants; I will spread on your faces the offal from your festival sacrifices, and you will be carried off with it. And you will know that I have sent you this admonition so that my covenant with Levi may continue," says the LORD Almighty. "My covenant was with him, a covenant of life and peace, and I gave them to him; this called for reverence and he revered me and stood in awe of my name. True instruction was in his mouth and nothing false was found on his lips. He walked with me in peace and uprightness, and turned many from sin.

"For the lips of a priest ought to preserve knowledge, and from his mouth men should seek instruction—because he is the messenger of the LORD Almighty. But you have turned from the way and by your teaching have caused many to stumble; you have violated the covenant with Levi," says the LORD Almighty. "So I have caused you to be despised and humiliated before all the people, because you have not followed my ways but have shown partiality in matters of the law" (Mal. 1:6–2:9).

The idea that some worship is correct while other worship is incorrect may seem strange to many people today. But think about the news reports that appeared after the capture of former Iraqi dictator Saddam Hussein. One of the first things his captors did was to make sure that it was the real Saddam. It looked like him. Witnesses testified that it was him. They checked his scars. Yet even then his captors persisted in taking measures to confirm his identity and ensure that it was not a mistake. So they did DNA tests.

Their persistence makes sense to us because we are talking about the realm of objective reality, right? But what about worship? Can we test our worship to ensure that it is real and true worship? In the Bible, God shows a great concern for *how* he is approached. He is real—and so are his holiness and our sin. Again, it isn't enough to be sincere, because people can be sincerely wrong. Saddam's captors could have sincerely apprehended the wrong man in Iraq. Likewise, we can sincerely misunderstand this God we claim to worship and what he requires of us. Suppose you sincerely approach God, but you do so at your convenience, or as the eighth most important thing on your list, or without bothering to repent of known sin. Under none of these circumstances will your worship be acceptable to God.

In fact, God is so adamant about how he is worshiped that, in the Old Testament, he set aside a whole tribe of people—the Levites—to teach the people of Israel how to offer correct, God-honoring, God-glorifying worship. The Levitical priests were to guard the sanctuary from unclean offerings.

In this section, therefore, the Lord directly addressed the priests (see 1:6; 2:1)—these ones whom God refers to as "the messenger of the LORD Almighty" (2:7). When the people brought blemished sacrifices (1:14), the priests should have corrected them. Instead, they became complicit: "'When you bring injured, crippled or diseased animals and offer them as sacrifices, should I accept them from your hands?' says the LORD" (1:13). Apparently, they thought, "Who's going to see? Who's going to care?" They should have considered the fact that God specifically forbade such sacrifices in the book of Leviticus (Lev. 22:17-25).

It is never our prerogative to ask God why he does what he does. It isn't really our business. But perhaps we can reverently ask why God cared so much about whether the sacrifices brought to him were unblemished or not. What's going on here? In part, God was interested in the priorities of the Israelites' lives. He wanted to know whether they were willing to bring God their best. I expect we can understand this much. Yet God was also interested in teaching the people that a sacrifice for their sins must be perfect. Above all else, the Levitical sacrifices were meant to point to the sacrifice for sin that was still to come—Jesus Christ, the truly unblemished one, the perfect lamb of God.

The people of Jerusalem in Malachi's day may have questioned whether God really loved them, but the Lord aggressively responded by saying that the real question was not God's love for Israel, but Israel's love for God. God promised that his name would be great among the nations (1:11). But his own people profaned it. They treated it cheaply. One day the nations would be obedient in ways his own people were not obedient now (1:12; cf. Gen. 12:2-3).

We must worship God according to what he has said about how he should be worshiped. He asks us for our best, and so we should give our best.

If you have believed that you can worship God and remain your own Lord, keeping your best to yourself, you are wrong. Truly worshiping God includes taking him as your heavenly Father and almighty master. And he deserves your best.

Giving Our All

God also deserves our all. Consider the fifth disputation:

> "I the LORD do not change. So you, O descendants of Jacob, are not destroyed.
> Ever since the time of your forefathers you have turned away from my decrees

and have not kept them. Return to me, and I will return to you," says the LORD Almighty.

"But you ask, 'How are we to return?'

"Will a man rob God? Yet you rob me.

"But you ask, 'How do we rob you?'

"In tithes and offerings. You are under a curse—the whole nation of you—because you are robbing me. Bring the whole tithe into the storehouse, that there may be food in my house. Test me in this," says the LORD Almighty, "and see if I will not throw open the floodgates of heaven and pour out so much blessing that you will not have room enough for it. I will prevent pests from devouring your crops, and the vines in your fields will not cast their fruit," says the LORD Almighty. "Then all the nations will call you blessed, for yours will be a delightful land," says the LORD Almighty (3:6-12).

Here, the Lord continued his discussion with his people over the way they are worshiping him. They were not only not giving him their best, they were not giving him their all. All what? God required that his people repent and change their ways entirely.

God began this exchange by reminding the Israelites that he does not change (3:6), and the constancy of his gracious character was their only hope amid their widespread disobedience. So he told them, "Return to me, and I will return to you" (3:7), as he had done in Zechariah (Zech. 1:3).

In this passage, the Lord specifically called his people to repent of their failure to tithe (Mal. 3:8-10). The problem was not just with the priests, it was with the whole nation. The children of Israel had been taught—from the example of Abraham with Melchizedek, from the example of Jacob, from the explicit teaching of Deuteronomy[9]—to give annually one-tenth of their property or produce to support the Levites and priests who administered God's worship in the temple at Jerusalem. Here in Malachi, the Lord promised the people that if they would be obedient in this matter, he would bless them with "so much blessing that you will not have room enough for it" (3:10), or, more literally, "until there is no more need" (ESV). The entire world belonged to God, and his people were supposed to acknowledge his ownership through their giving and their trust in his continual provision. Their sacrifices and tithes, then, were what God used to teach them to worship him with their whole selves.

Worship required more than singing songs or memorizing a Psalm on the way to the temple; it required *everything*.

So it is for us today. Christianity is not for people who want to select certain areas of their lives to "subcontract" or "outsource" to God, while they

---

[9] Gen. 14:20; 28:22; Deut. 14:22; 26:12.

hold on to the overall direction of their life's business. God does not operate like that. That's not who he is. Either he is Lord of all or he is not Lord at all. He is God. The Lord had protected his people and brought them back into the land, yet they continued to try protecting themselves by maintaining autonomous control of their wallets and bank accounts. Do you see how this reeks of mistrust? The eternal Creator God asks his followers to bring a tithe of our income to him. This is part of our worship.

Sometimes people today say that any concept of tithing is too legalistic. After all, doesn't Galatians 5 tell us that we are free from the constraints of the law? Yes, but Jesus also told one man to sell everything he had and give it to the poor (Matt. 19:21). In other words, Christians are still called to give their best—and their all! Often, we can see a Christian's willingness to give everything through the spirit of gladness with which they give the percentage they do give. In our church, we encourage members to begin by giving ten percent of their income, and then to pray about giving more.

Our nation is rich by the world's standards. We should try to manage our resources in order to maximize what we give and minimize what we keep for ourselves.

Are you tempted to give God less than your best? Are you tempted to keep back part of what you know is his? If you are from Texas, you have certainly heard about the colorful soldier and politician Sam Houston. What you may not know is that Sam Houston came to Christ—yes, to everyone's amazement! After his baptism, Houston said he wanted to pay half the local minister's salary. When someone asked him why, he responded simply, "My pocketbook was baptized, too."[10] If you want to consider further how to address issues of money and stewardship, get a copy of Randy Alcorn's *Money, Possessions, and Eternity*.[11]

I pray that our churches would grow in faithfulness every year through the committing of our resources to the Lord and his work. As we do, I have no doubt that God will provide, perhaps even entrusting us with more. I praise God for how we have seen that in our church.

Worship of God involves what we do with ourselves. Do we give our best? Do we give our all?

WORSHIP OF GOD INVOLVES HOW WE APPROACH GOD

Finally, worship of God involves how we approach God. We learn this from the beginning and the end of Malachi.

---

[10] Cited in Randy Alcorn, *The Treasure Principle* (Portland: Multnomah, 2001), 59.
[11] Randy Alcorn, *Money, Possessions, and Eternity* (Wheaton, Ill.: Tyndale, 1989).

Fifty years ago, William Miller wrote that "One might say that President Eisenhower, like many Americans, is a very fervent believer in a very vague religion."[12] Whether or not that accurately described President Eisenhower, it certainly describes many Americans today. People today pick and choose among an eclectic mix of various religions and philosophies according to their own tastes and perceived needs. Sociologist Robert Bellah has referred to this worldview as "Sheilaism," based on "Sheila," the name he gave a woman he interviewed who said she believed in the "religion of me." Of course, that's no true religion! Malachi would say to Sheila—and to us—that such vague notions of God and such a low regard for him prevents worship. We cannot worship what we misunderstand, discount, and disregard. You may have a great emotional weekend. You may launch out on a voyage of self-discovery. You may get in touch with your inner child. But you will not get in touch with God without approaching him as he has revealed himself.

Understanding God

This is the point Malachi makes right at the beginning of his book. Part of worshiping God is understanding God:

> "I have loved you," says the LORD.
>
> "But you ask, 'How have you loved us?'
>
> "Was not Esau Jacob's brother?" the LORD says. "Yet I have loved Jacob, but Esau I have hated, and I have turned his mountains into a wasteland and left his inheritance to the desert jackals."
>
> Edom may say, "Though we have been crushed, we will rebuild the ruins."
>
> But this is what the LORD Almighty says: "They may build, but I will demolish. They will be called the Wicked Land, a people always under the wrath of the LORD. You will see it with your own eyes and say, 'Great is the LORD—even beyond the borders of Israel!'" (1:2–5).

God wanted his people to know the truth about him—that he was great and sovereign, even beyond the borders of Israel. The Lord is no village god or tribal spirit. By his own choice, he made Israel his own. And by his own choice, he rejected, even hated, Israel's next-door neighbor, Edom (descendants of Esau). Paul used this passage in his famously controversial Romans 9 to argue that God has sovereignty over all things and all people. (God's sovereignty is not proclaimed only in the Old Testament!)

This was the first dispute the Lord raised with his people because he wanted to ensure that they understood him. He alone was sovereign over Israel

---

[12] William Lee Miller, *Reporter*, July 7, 1953, 15.

and beyond. "Great is the LORD—even beyond the borders of Israel!" (1:5; cf. 1:11; 3:12).

I don't know if this is the God that you attend church to worship, but you cannot be indifferent to what God is like and, at the same time, honestly worship him. If you are indifferent to what he is like, the only god you can worship is a self-constructed, homemade, do-it-yourself god and not the real thing.

In addition to learning in this disputation that God is sovereign, we learn that God loves his people (1:2). God's blessings and faithfulness to his people were not the result of their faithfulness, they were the product of his love. And God wants the truth about his universal greatness and unending love for his people to be known so that we will approach him rightly. Speaking and understanding the truth about God is part of our worship of him. A Christian must *want* to know the truth about God.

In a short biographical account of pastor George Buttrick, Thomas Long writes,

> "George Buttrick . . . was [from 1927 to 1954] pastor of the Madison Avenue Presbyterian Church in New York. One week he had been off on a speaking engagement and was flying back to New York City. On the plane he had a pad and a pencil and he was making some notes for next Sunday's sermon. The man seated next to him was eyeing him with curiosity. Finally, the curiosity got the best of him, and so he said to Buttrick, 'I hate to disturb you—you're obviously working hard on something—but what in the world are you working on?'
>
> "'Oh, I'm a Presbyterian minister,' said Buttrick. 'I'm working on my sermon for Sunday.'
>
> "'Oh, religion,' said the man. 'I don't like to get all caught up in the in's and out's and complexities of religion. I like to keep it simple. "Do unto others as you would have them do unto you." The Golden Rule, that's my religion.'
>
> "'I see,' said Buttrick. 'And what do you do?'
>
> "'I'm an astronomer. I teach at the university.'
>
> "'Oh, yes,' said Buttrick. 'Astronomy—I don't like to get all caught up in the in's and out's and complexities of astronomy. Twinkle, twinkle little star, that's my astronomy.'"[13]

Now, we might be amused by that story because we know that astronomy is enormously complex, and reducing it to a child's song is absurd. Friend, God is there to be known, even more than the stars. And he has revealed the truth about himself to us. Knowing and understanding this truth is part of our worship of him.

---

[13] Cited in Bill Turpie, ed., *Ten Great Preachers* (Grand Rapids, Mich.: Baker, 2000), 87-88.

Fearing God

Yet we are not only supposed to understand God, we are to fear him. That's what we learn in the last dispute between God and the people:

> "You have said harsh things against me," says the LORD.
>
> "Yet you ask, 'What have we said against you?'
>
> "You have said, 'It is futile to serve God. What did we gain by carrying out his requirements and going about like mourners before the LORD Almighty? But now we call the arrogant blessed. Certainly the evildoers prosper, and even those who challenge God escape.'"
>
> Then those who feared the LORD talked with each other, and the LORD listened and heard. A scroll of remembrance was written in his presence concerning those who feared the LORD and honored his name.
>
> "They will be mine," says the LORD Almighty, "in the day when I make up my treasured possession. I will spare them, just as in compassion a man spares his son who serves him. And you will again see the distinction between the righteous and the wicked, between those who serve God and those who do not.
>
> "Surely the day is coming; it will burn like a furnace. All the arrogant and every evildoer will be stubble, and that day that is coming will set them on fire," says the LORD Almighty. "Not a root or a branch will be left to them. But for you who revere my name, the sun of righteousness will rise with healing in its wings. And you will go out and leap like calves released from the stall. Then you will trample down the wicked; they will be ashes under the soles of your feet on the day when I do these things," says the LORD Almighty (3:13–4:3).

In this final dispute in Malachi, God rebuked the harsh words his people had used against him. In response, some of the people feared God (3:16), as they should have.

Throughout the Bible—from Genesis to Revelation (Gen. 22:12; Rev. 14:7)—we are instructed to fear the Lord. Fearing the Lord means having an ultimate regard for him. It means keeping our eye on him and giving our allegiance to him, because a day will come when the Lord will divide all humanity according to whether or not they have "revered" the Lord (Mal. 4:2).

This true reverence is an indispensable part of our worship of God, showing itself in our lives in many ways. To begin with, such fear shows itself through our repentance from sin. It also shows itself as other fears are short-circuited—fears that have ruled us in the past, like the fear of bad news, the fear of ill-regard from others, the fear of pain, even the fear of death. If we are Christians, we fear God. He is our Lord and Father, our Husband and Master. So we worship him with fear, not with disrespect, distrust, or arrogance. God will always speak the truth, because he is truth itself. Being sinners, then, we fear him and we keep the eyes of our hearts fixed on him and his promises.

Hoping in God

Which brings us to the last few verses of Malachi. In order to treat God rightly—in order to worship him rightly—we must not only understand and fear him, we must put our hope in him:

> "Remember the law of my servant Moses, the decrees and laws I gave him at Horeb for all Israel.
>
> "See, I will send you the prophet Elijah before that great and dreadful day of the LORD comes. He will turn the hearts of the fathers to their children, and the hearts of the children to their fathers; or else I will come and strike the land with a curse" (4:4-6).

What an interesting way for the Old Testament to end! In this concluding word, the Lord instructed his people both to look back and to look forward. They were to look back to the Law of Moses, as God has repeatedly done throughout this little prophecy. But they were also to look forward to his coming, and the preparatory work of Elijah. God employed his last prophet before John the Baptist to remind God's people of the Law and the Prophets—Moses and Elijah, the same two who would stand with Jesus on the Mount of Transfiguration pointing to Jesus!

And Elijah did come. His name was John, and he came to baptize, to preach repentance, and to prepare God's people for the coming of the Messiah. Jesus then declared that Malachi's prophecy was fulfilled through this John the Baptist.[14] After reading Malachi, we should not be surprised that the first spoken word of inspired prophecy after several centuries of silence was John the Baptist's call to "Repent!" (Matt. 3:2). Malachi had ended the Old Testament with the word "curse," which can also be translated as "destruction." This is the same Old Testament that began with God and his perfect creation.

Through both John the Baptist and Malachi, then, the Lord called his people to repent of their indifference and lackadaisical disregard for him, and to remember God's commands by living them out. To put their hopes in him and his Word. To put faith in his promises. To live leaning forward into the promises of God! To put their weight into the truth of what God said. That's how you and I can really worship God: by living as if we believe him, by run-

---

[14] See John 1:21; then Matt. 11:14; 17:12-13 (cf. Mark 9:13).

ning with joyous abandon toward him, and by trusting that he will receive us as his own through Christ. This is the sincerity that we need!

I wonder if you noticed that the last phrase in the book begins with the words, "or else" (4:6). The Old Testament began with a deadly choice in the Garden. Now it ends by holding out another choice: will we turn from that fatal choice made by the first Adam, which has been ratified ten thousand times ten thousand times in our own hearts? More specifically, will *you* turn to Jesus? That's the question that Malachi, the Old Testament, and the Bible leave you with today.

Let us pray:

O God, we give you praise for the wonderful provision that you have made for us and our sins in Christ. We give you praise that the punishment we deserved for our self-regard and for all the messes that we have made in our relationship with you and with others has fallen upon Christ, if only we would repent of our sins and turn to you. O God, cause the truth of your good news to weigh upon our hearts. We pray that the hope that we can have in you would be heavy, and would pull us toward you and away from the smaller things that entrap us. We give you praise for the great news that you have given us through your messenger Malachi. We pray in Jesus' name. Amen.

Questions for Reflection

1. Why do we tend to regard a person's sincerity as giving moral legitimacy to what that person says or thinks?

2. How can sincerity be helpful in religion? How can sincerity be unhelpful?

3. Why does God care so much about whom we marry?

4. Practically speaking, what are some of the steps churches should take in response to a member who plans on getting a divorce for biblical reasons? For unbiblical reasons? What are some of the steps a church can take in response to a member who plans on marrying a non-Christian?

5. How does your life reflect a concern for justice, particularly for the downtrodden and oppressed?

6. What does it mean to give "your best" to God? What is your best? What gets in the way of your giving your best to God?

7. Is there some area of your life that you are holding back from God? What is Malachi's message for you?

8. Why must a true understanding of God precede our worship of him? When people believe they are worshiping God, but they have no true knowledge of him, what are they worshiping?

9. If a true understanding of God must precede our worship of him, how will a church best encourage its people to worship well and rightly?

10. Can you worship someone you fear? Can you worship someone you don't fear? Explain.

11. Is Malachi a *Christian* book? In what sense?

PERSON INDEX

Acton, John, 372
Adams, Abigail, 252
Adams, Joey, 441
Adams, John, 209
Aesop, 254
Alaric, 613-614
Albom, Mitch, 671
Albright, W. F., 636
Alcorn, Randy, 938
Ambrose, 23, 717
Ambrose, Stephen, 433
Aristotle, 247, 513
Armstrong, John H., 24, 712
Arnot, William, 847-848
Atta, Mohammed, 304
Auden, W. H., 721-722
Augustine, 497, 614, 856

Bellah, Robert, 939
Boice, James Montgomery, 215
Bolingbroke, Hal (later Henry V), 65
Boswell, James, 829
Bradley, James, 218
Brand, Evelyn, 630-631
Broadway, Bill, 830
Broome, E. C., 637
Buckley, Frank, 201
Bunyan, John, 116, 127-128, 264-265, 905

Buttrick, George, 940

Calvin, John, 176
Camus, Albert, 528
Carmichael, Amy, 788-789, 855
Carson, D. A., 227, 251, 819, 929
Casson, Hugh, 654
Chamberlain, Joseph, 247
Chekhov, Anton, 568
Chesterton, G. K., 540-541
Chrysostom, John, 717
Conrad, Joseph, 223
Coverdale, Miles, 333
Covey, Stephen, 485-486
Cowper, William, 229, 243, 714

Dagg, John L., 492-493
Dawkins, Richard, 339, 507-508
Deedat, Ahmed, 168
DeMille, Cecil B., 99
Descartes, René, 926
Dillard, Raymond B., 213
Dodd, C. H., 797
Douglass, Frederick, 100

Eddy, Mary Baker, 251, 441
Edwards, Jonathan, 349, 853
Eisenhower, Dwight D., 939
Elliot, Jim, 855, 922

SCRIPTURE INDEX

God intends to display the glory of His beauty, perfection, and love through the church.

Imagine what this would look like in our local congregations:

- God's name exalted in song and sermon.
- Relationships tied together by love and service.
- Marriages and families built for endurance.
- Christ's sacrifice pictured in the lives of sinful but repenting people!

At 9Marks, we believe that there is no better **evangelistic tool, missions strategy,** or **counseling program** than the image of God displayed through His gathering of imperfect but transforming people. As we learn more about Him, we look more and more like Him.

Neighborhoods and nations will look with wonder. As will the heavenly host!

Church leaders do not need another innovative method or engaging metaphor for growing their churches. They need to (get to!) embrace the biblical theology and priorities that God Himself designed for cultivating health and holiness in the local congregation. Scripture actually teaches church leaders how to build churches that display God's glory.

At 9Marks, we seek to answer the "how-to" question and develop a biblical vision for your congregation.

- Media: downloadable web resources, audio interviews, e-newsletters, educational curriculum.
- Study: training weekends, conferences, internships, think tanks.
- Publishing: books, pamphlets, papers.
- Outreach: On-site visits, phone conversations.

To learn more, visit www.9marks.org.